Lecture Notes in Computer Science 11735

More information about this series at http://www.springer.com/series/7410

Kazue Sako · Steve Schneider ·
Peter Y. A. Ryan (Eds.)

Computer Security – ESORICS 2019

24th European Symposium
on Research in Computer Security
Luxembourg, September 23–27, 2019
Proceedings, Part I

 Springer

Editors
Kazue Sako
NEC Corporation
Kawasaki, Japan

Steve Schneider 🄳
University of Surrey
Guildford, UK

Peter Y. A. Ryan 🄳
University of Luxembourg
Esch-sur-Alzette, Luxembourg

ISSN 0302-9743 ISSN 1611-3349 (electronic)
Lecture Notes in Computer Science
ISBN 978-3-030-29958-3 ISBN 978-3-030-29959-0 (eBook)
https://doi.org/10.1007/978-3-030-29959-0

LNCS Sublibrary: SL4 – Security and Cryptology

This Springer imprint is published by the registered company Springer Nature Switzerland AG
The registered company address is: Gewerbestrasse 11, 6330 Cham, Switzerland

Preface

This book contains the papers that were selected for presentation and publication at the 24th European Symposium on Research in Computer Security (ESORICS 2019) which was held together with affiliated workshops in Luxembourg, September 23–27, 2019. The aim of ESORICS is to further the progress of research in computer, information, and cyber security, as well as in privacy, by establishing a European forum for bringing together researchers in these areas, by promoting the exchange of ideas with system developers, and by encouraging links with researchers in related fields.

In response to the call for papers, 344 papers were submitted to the conference. These papers were evaluated on the basis of their significance, novelty, and technical quality. Each paper was reviewed by at least three members of the Program Committee and external reviewers, and papers authored by Program Committee members had four reviewers. The reviewing process was single-blind. The Program Committee had intensive discussions which were held via EasyChair. Finally, 67 papers were selected for presentation at the conference, giving an acceptance rate of 19.5%. We were also delighted to welcome keynote talks from Adi Shamir, Véronique Cortier, and Bart Preneel.

Following the reviews, two papers were selected for joint Best Paper Award, to share the 1,000 EUR prize generously provided by Springer: "A Frame-work for Evaluating Security in the Presence of Signal Injection Attacks," by Ilias Giechaskiel, Youqian Zhang, and Kasper Rasmussen; and "Breakdown Resilience of Key Exchange Protocols: NewHope, TLS 1.3, and Hybrids," by Jacqueline Brendel, Marc Fischlin, and Felix Günther.

The Program Committee consisted of 95 members across 24 countries. There were submissions from a total of 1,071 authors across 46 countries, with 23 countries represented among the accepted papers.

ESORICS 2019 would not have been possible without the contributions of the many volunteers who freely gave their time and expertise. We would like to thank the members of the Program Committee and the external reviewers for their substantial work in evaluating the papers. We would also like to thank the organization chair, Peter B. Roenne, the workshop chair, Joaquin Garcia-Alfaro, and all workshop co-chairs, the posters chair, Alfredo Rial, the publicity chair, Cristina Alcaraz, and the ESORICS Steering Committee and its chair, Sokratis Katsikas.

Finally, we would like to express our thanks to the authors who submitted papers to ESORICS. They, more than anyone else, are what makes this conference possible.

We hope that you found the program to be stimulating and a source of inspiration for future research.

July 2019

Kazue Sako
Steve Schneider
Peter Y. A. Ryan

Organization

ESORICS Steering Committee

Sokratis Katsikas (Chair)   NTNU, Norway
Michael Backes   Saarland University, Germany
Joachim Biskup   TU Dortmund, Germany
Frederic Cuppens   IMT Atlantique, France
Sabrina De Capitani   Università degli Studi di Milano, Italy
  di Vimercati
Dieter Gollmann   Hamburg University of Technology, Germany
Mirek Kutylowski   Wroclaw University of Technology, Poland
Javier Lopez   University of Malaga, Spain
Jean-Jacques Quisquater   University of Louvain, Belgium
Peter Y. A. Ryan   University of Luxembourg, Luxembourg
Pierangela Samarati   Università degli Studi di Milano, Italy
Einar Snekkenes   NTNU, Norway
Michael Waidner   Fraunhofer, Germany

Program Committee

Mitsuaki Akiyama   NTT, Japan
Cristina Alcaraz   University of Malaga, Spain
Elli Androulaki   IBM Research - Zurich, Switzerland
Frederik Armknecht   Universität Mannheim, Germany
Vijay Atluri   Rutgers University, USA
Marina Blanton   University at Buffalo, USA
Carlo Blundo   Università degli Studi di Salerno, Italy
Christian Cachin   University of Bern, Switzerland
Alvaro Cardenas   The University of Texas at Dallas, USA
Aldar C-F. Chan   University of Hong Kong, Hong Kong, China
Yan Chen   Northwestern University, USA
Sherman S. M. Chow   The Chinese University of Hong Kong, Hong Kong,
                                China
Mauro Conti   University of Padua, Italy
Jorge Cuellar   Siemens AG, Germany
Frédéric Cuppens   Telecom Bretagne, France
Nora Cuppens-Boulahia   IMT Atlantique, France
Marc Dacier   EURECOM, France
Sabrina De Capitani   Università degli Studi di Milano, Italy
  di Vimercati
Hervé Debar   Telecom SudParis, France
Stéphanie Delaune   CNRS, France

Olivier Pereira	UCLouvain, Belgium
Günther Pernul	Universität Regensburg, Germany
Joachim Posegga	University of Passau, Germany
Bart Preneel	Katholieke Universiteit Leuven, Belgium
Christina Pöpper	New York University, USA
Indrajit Ray	Colorado State University, USA
Giovanni Russello	The University of Auckland, New Zealand
Mark Ryan	University of Birmingham, UK
Reyhaneh Safavi-Naini	University of Calgary, Canada
Kazue Sako	NEC, Japan
Pierangela Samarati	Università degli Studi di Milano, Italy
Damien Sauveron	XLIM – University of Limoges, UMR CNRS 7252, France
Steve Schneider	University of Surrey, UK
Einar Snekkenes	NTNU, Norway
Willy Susilo	University of Wollongong, Australia
Pawel Szalachowski	SUTD, Singapore
Qiang Tang	Luxembourg Institute of Science and Technology, Luxembourg
Qiang Tang	New Jersey Institute of Technology, USA
Juan Tapiador	Universidad Carlos III de Madrid, Spain
Nils Ole Tippenhauer	CISPA, Germany
Helen Treharne	University of Surrey, UK
Aggeliki Tsohou	Ionian University, Greece
Jaideep Vaidya	Rutgers University, USA
Luca Viganò	King's College London, UK
Michael Waidner	Fraunhofer, Germany
Cong Wang	City University of Hong Kong, Hong Kong, China
Lingyu Wang	Concordia University, Canada
Edgar Weippl	SBA Research, Austria
Christos Xenakis	University of Piraeus, Greece
Zhe Xia	Wuhan University of Technology, China
Kehuan Zhang	The Chinese University of Hong Kong, Hong Kong, China
Sencun Zhu	The Pennsylvania State University, USA

Additional Reviewers

Abidin, Aysajan	Al-Mallah, Ranwa	Bamiloshin, Michael
Abusalah, Hamza	Andriotis, Panagiotis	Bampatsikos, Michail
Aggelogianni, Anna	Anglès-Tafalla, Carles	Batra, Gunjan
Ahmed, Chuadhry Mujeeb	Anikeev, Maxim	Belgacem, Boutheyna
Akand, Mamunur	Asif, Hafiz	Belles, Marta
Al Maqbali Fatma	Avizheh, Sepideh	Berger, Christian

Bezawada, Bruhadeshwar
Bkakria, Anis
Blanco-Justicia, Alberto
Blazy, Olivier
Bolgouras, Vaios
Bountakas, Panagiotis
Boureanu, Ioana
Brandt, Markus
Böhm, Fabian
Cao, Chen
Catuogno, Luigi
Cetinkaya, Orhan
Chadha, Rohit
Chan, Mun Choon
Chawla, Gagandeep
Chen, Haixia
Chen, Jianjun
Chen, Liqun
Chen, Long
Chen, Xihui
Chen, Yueqi
Chothia, Tom
Ciampi, Michele
Cook, Andrew
Cortier, Véronique
Costa, Nüria
Cui, Shujie
Dang, Hung
Dargahi, Tooska
Dashevskyi, Stanislav
de Miceli, Jean-Yves
De Salve, Andrea
Debant, Alexandre
Deo, Amit
Diamantopoulou, Vasiliki
Dietz, Marietheres
Divakaran, Dinil Mon
Dominguez Trujillo,
   Antonio
Dryja, Tadge
Du, Minxin
Du, Xuechao
Dufour Sans, Edouard
Duman, Onur
Duong, Dung
Elkhiyaoui, Kaoutar

Englbrecht, Ludwig
Espes, David
Fan, Xiong
Farao, Aristeidis
Farhang, Sadegh
Fdhila, Walid
Fenghao, Xu
Ferreira Torres, Christof
Gangwal, Ankit
Ge, Chunpeng
Geneiatakis, Dimitris
Georgiopoulou,
   Zafeiroula
Giorgi, Giacomo
Groll, Sebastian
Gupta, Maanak
Gusenbauer, Matthias
Han, Jinguang
Hassan, Fadi
Hermans, Jens
Hicks, Christopher
Hirschi, Lucca
Hlavacek, Tomas
Homoliak, Ivan
Horne, Ross
Hu, Kexin
Iliou, Christos
Jacomme, Charlie
Jeitner, Philipp
Jiongyi, Chen
Jonker, Hugo
Judmayer, Aljosha
Kalloniatis, Christos
Kambourakis, Georgios
Karamchandani, Neeraj
Kasinathan, Prabhakaran
Kavousi, Mohammad
Kern, Sascha
Khan, Muhammad Hassan
Kim, Jongkil
Klaedtke, Felix
Kohls, Katharina
Kostoulas, Theodoros
Koutroumpouxos,
   Nikolaos
Kuchta, Veronika

Köstler, Johannes
La Marra, Antonio
Labani, Hasan
Lakshmanan, Sudershan
Lal, Chhagan
Lazzeretti, Riccardo
Lee, Jehyun
Leng, Xue
León, Olga
Li, Li
Li, Shujun
Li, Wanpeng
Li, Wenjuan
Li, Xing
Li, Xusheng
Li, Yanan
Li, Zengpeng
Li, Zhenyuan
Libert, Benoît
Lin, Chengjun
Lin, Yan
Liu, Ximing
Lobe Kome, Ivan Marco
Losiouk, Eleonora
Loukas, George
Lu, Yang
Lu, Yuan
Lyvas, Christos
Ma, Haoyu
Ma, Jack P. K.
Maene, Pieter
Majumdar, Suryadipta
Malliaros, Stefanos
Mardziel, Piotr
Marin, Eduard
Marson, Giorgia
Martinez, Sergio
Matyunin, Nikolay
Menges, Florian
Menghan, Sun
Michailidou, Christina
Milani, Simone
Minaud, Brice
Minematsu, Kazuhiko
Mizera, Andrzej
Moch, Alexander

Moessner, Klaus
Mohamady, Meisam
Mohammadi, Farnaz
Moisan, Frederic
Moreau, Solène
Moreira, Josè
Murayama, Yuko
Murmann, Patrick
Muñoz, Jose L.
Mykoniati, Maria
Ng, Lucien K. L.
Ngamboe, Mikaela
Nguyen, Quoc Phong
Ning, Jianting
Niu, Liang
Nomikos, Nikolaos
Ntantogian, Christoforos
Oqaily, Alaa
Oqaily, Momen
Ouattara, Jean-Yves
Oya, Simon
Panaousis, Manos
Papaioannou, Thanos
Parra Rodriguez, Juan D.
Parra-Arnau, Javier
Pasa, Luca
Paspatis, Ioannis
Peeters, Roel
Pelosi, Gerardo
Petrovic, Slobodan
Pfeffer, Katharina
Pitropakis, Nikolaos
Poh, Geong Sen
Polian, Ilia
Prestwich, Steve
Puchta, Alexander
Putz, Benedikt
Pöhls, Henrich C.
Qiu, Tian
Ramírez-Cruz, Yunior
Ray, Indrani
Reuben, Jenni

Rezk, Tamara
Rios, Ruben
Rizos, Athanasios
Román-García, Fernando
Rozic, Vladimir
Rupprecht, David
Sakuma, Jun
Saracino, Andrea
Schindler, Philipp
Schmidt, Carsten
Schnitzler, Theodor
Schumi, Richard
Sempreboni, Diego
Sengupta, Binanda
Sentanoe, Stewart
Sepideh Avizheh,
  Shuai Li
Shikfa, Abdullatif
Shioji, Eitaro
Shirani, Paria
Shrishak, Kris
Shuaike, Dong
Simo, Hervais
Singelée, Dave
Siniscalchi, Luisa
Situ, Lingyun
Smith, Zach
Smyth, Ben
Song, Yongcheng
Soriente, Claudio
Soumelidou, Aikaterini
Stifter, Nicholas
Sun, Yuanyi
Sundararajan, Vaishnavi
Tabiban, Azadeh
Tajan, Louis
Taubmann, Benjamin
Thomasset, Corentin
Tian, Yangguang
Tripathi, Nikhil
Tueno, Anselme
Ullrich, Johanna

Vanhoef, Mathy
Venugopalan, Sarad
Veroni, Eleni
Vielberth, Manfred
Viet Xuan Phuong, Tran
Walzer, Stefan
Wang, Daibin
Wang, Hongbing
Wang, Jiafan
Wang, Tielei
Wang, Xiaolei
Wang, Xiuhua
Wang, Zhi
Wattiau, Gaetan
Wesemeyer, Stephan
Wong, Harry W. H.
Wu, Daoyuan
Wu, Huangting
Xu, Jia
Xu, Jiayun
Xu, Ke
Xu, Shengmin
Xu, Yanhong
Yang, Kang
Yang, Shaojun
Yang, Wenjie
Yautsiukhin, Artsiom
Yuan, Chen
Zalonis, Jasmin
Zamyatin, Alexei
Zavatteri, Matteo
Zhang, Chao
Zhang, Liang Feng
Zhang, Yuexin
Zhao, Guannan
Zhao, Yongjun
Zheng, Yu
Zhou, Dehua
Zhou, Wei
Zhu, Tiantian
Zou, Qingtian
Zuo, Cong

Abstracts of Keynote Talks

The Insecurity of Machine Learning: Problems and Solutions

Adi Shamir

Computer Science Department, The Weizmann Institute of Science, Israel

Abstract. The development of deep neural networks in the last decade had revolutionized machine learning and led to major improvements in the precision with which we can perform many computational tasks. However, the discovery five years ago of adversarial examples in which tiny changes in the input can fool well trained neural networks makes it difficult to trust such results when the input can be manipulated by an adversary. This problem has many applications and implications in object recognition, autonomous driving, cyber security, etc, but it is still far from being understood. In particular, there had been no convincing explanations why such adversarial examples exist, and which parameters determine the number of input coordinates one has to change in order to mislead the network. In this talk I will describe a simple mathematical framework which enables us to think about this problem from a fresh perspective, turning the existence of adversarial examples in deep neural networks from a baffling phenomenon into an unavoidable consequence of the geometry of R^n under the Hamming distance, which can be quantitatively analyzed.

Electronic Voting: A Journey to Verifiability and Vote Privacy

Véronique Cortier

CNRS, LORIA, UMR 7503, 54506, Vandoeuvre-lès-Nancy, France

Abstract. Electronic voting aims to achieve the same properties as traditional paper based voting. Even when voters vote from their home, they should be given the same guarantees, without having to trust the election authorities, the voting infrastructure, and/or the Internet network. The two main security goals are vote privacy: no one should know how I voted; and verifiability: a voter should be able to check that the votes have been properly counted. In this talk, we will explore the subtle relationships between these properties and we will see how they can be realized and proved.

First, verifiability and privacy are often seen as antagonistic and some national agencies even impose a hierarchy between them: first privacy, and then verifiability as an additional feature. Verifiability typically includes individual verifiability (a voter can check that her ballot is counted); universal verifiability (anyone can check that the result corresponds to the published ballots); and eligibility verifiability (only legitimate voters may vote). Actually, we will see that privacy implies individual verifiability. In other words, systems without individual verifiability cannot achieve privacy (under the same trust assumptions).

Moreover, it has been recently realised that all existing definitions of vote privacy in a computational setting implicitly assume an honest voting server: an adversary cannot tamper with the bulletin board. As a consequence, voting schemes are proved secure only against an honest voting server while they are designed and claimed to resist a dishonest voting server. Not only are the security guarantees too weak, but attacks are missed. We propose a novel notion of ballot privacy against a malicious bulletin board. The notion is flexible in that it captures various capabilities of the attacker to tamper with the ballots, yielding different flavours of security.

Finally, once the security definitions are set, we need to carefully establish when a scheme satisfies verifiability and vote privacy. We have developed a framework in EasyCrypt for proving both verifiability and privacy, yielding machine-checked security proof. We have applied our framework to two existing schemes, namely Helios and Belenios, and many of their variants.

Cryptocurrencies and Distributed Consensus: Hype and Science

Bart Preneel

COSIC, an imec lab at KU Leuven, Belgium

Abstract. This talk will offer a perspective on the fast rise of cryptocurrencies based on proof of work, with Bitcoin as most prominent example. In about a decade, a white paper of nine pages has resulted in massive capital investments, a global ecosystem with a market capitalization of several hundreds of billions of dollars and the redefinition of the term crypto (which now means cryptocurrencies). We will briefly describe the history of electronic currencies and clarify the main principles behind Nakamoto Consensus. Next, we explain how several variants attempt to improve the complex tradeoffs between public verifiability, robustness, privacy and performance. We describe how Markov Decision processes can be used to compare in an objective way the proposed improvements in terms of chain quality, censorship resistance and robustness against selfish mining and double spending attacks. We conclude with a discussion of open problems.

Contents – Part I

Side Channels

Formal Modelling and Verification

Attacks

Secure Protocols

Useful Tools

Blockchain and Smart Contracts

Contents – Part II

Security Models

Searchable Encryption

Privacy

Key Exchange Protocols

Web Security

Machine Learning

Privacy-Enhanced Machine Learning with Functional Encryption

Tilen Marc[1,2], Miha Stopar[1], Jan Hartman[1], Manca Bizjak[1(✉)], and Jolanda Modic[1]

[1] XLAB d.o.o., Ljubljana, Slovenia
{tilen.marc, miha.stopar, jan.hartman, manca.bizjak, jolanda.modic}@xlab.si
[2] Faculty of Mathematics and Physics, University of Ljubljana, Ljubljana, Slovenia

Abstract. Functional encryption is a generalization of public-key encryption in which possessing a secret functional key allows one to learn a function of what the ciphertext is encrypting. This paper introduces the first fully-fledged open source cryptographic libraries for functional encryption. It also presents how functional encryption can be used to build efficient privacy-enhanced machine learning models and it provides an implementation of three prediction services that can be applied on the encrypted data. Finally, the paper discusses the advantages and disadvantages of the alternative approach for building privacy-enhanced machine learning models by using homomorphic encryption.

Keywords: Functional encryption · Cryptographic library · Machine learning · Homomorphic encryption · Privacy

1 Introduction

Today, almost every part of our lives is digitalized: products, services, business operations. With the constant increase in connectivity and digitalization, huge amounts of personal data are often collected without any real justification or need. On the other hand, there is a growing concern over who is in possession of this data and how it is being used. With increasingly more privacy-aware individuals and with ever stricter data protection requirements (GDPR, ePrivacy CCPA), organizations are seeking a compromise that will enable them to collect and analyse their users' data, to innovate, optimize, and grow their businesses, while at the same time comply with legal frameworks and keep trust and confidence of their users.

When individuals themselves use technologies like end-to-end encryption to protect their data, this can greatly improve their privacy online because the service providers never see raw data. But when a service provider does not have

---

T. Marc and M. Stopar—Contributed equally to this work.

© Springer Nature Switzerland AG 2019
K. Sako et al. (Eds.): ESORICS 2019, LNCS 11735, pp. 3–21, 2019.
https://doi.org/10.1007/978-3-030-29959-0_1

access to raw data, it cannot analyse the data and it thus cannot offer functionalities like search or data classification. Indeed, almost all rich functionality to which users are accustomed today is out of the question when encryption is used. However, there are encryption techniques which do not impose a drastic reduction of data utility and consequently functionality. The probably most known such technique is Homomorphic Encryption (HE). HE enables additions and multiplications over the encrypted data, which consequently enables higher-level functionality such as machine learning on the encrypted data. However, HE is computationally expensive and significantly reduces service performance. Another technique, perhaps lesser known, is Functional Encryption (FE). Similarly as HE, it allows computation on encrypted data. More precisely, the owner of a decryption key can learn a function of the encrypted data. This gives a possibility to use the encrypted data for various analysis or machine learning models by controlling the information one can get from it. In this paper we present first two fully-fledged FE libraries, we outline how they can be used to build machine learning services on encrypted data, and we discuss strengths and limitations of FE compared to the HE approach.

While there exist schemes for general FE (see [15, 28, 29, 44]), they rely on non-standard, ill-understood assumptions and are in many cases extremely time-consuming. On the contrary, we focused on the implementation of efficient schemes of restricted functionality but still of practical interest. Our aim was a flexible and modular implementation that can be applied to various applications and does not predetermine usage. We offer our work as open-source; all the code with guidelines is available online on the FENTEC GitHub account [23].

Contributions. This paper addresses the lack of implementations of practical FE schemes that enable computation on the encrypted data through the following contributions:

1. *Implementation of FE libraries.* We present two fully-fledged FE cryptographic libraries, named GoFE and CiFEr. We overview the different underlying primitives (modular arithmetic, pairings, lattices) which can be chosen by the user of the library when instantiating an FE scheme. This is presented in Sects. 2 and 3.
2. *Performance evaluation of FE libraries.* In Sect. 4, we compare the efficiency of various FE schemes and underlying primitives.
3. *Design and implementation of privacy-enhanced machine learning services.* In Sects. 5, 6, 7, we present the implementation and performance of three privacy-enhanced analysis services based on FE.
4. *Comparison of FE and HE approaches.* Furthermore, in Sects. 5, 6, 7, we discuss the advantages and disadvantages of FE compared to the HE approach.

2   Functional Encryption Libraries

FE is a cryptographic procedure which allows to delegate the computation of certain functions of the encrypted data to third parties. This can be achieved by generating specific secret keys for these functions. An FE scheme consists of a set of five algorithms. The *setup* algorithm takes a security parameter as input and generates a mathematical group where operations take place. The *master key generation* creates a public key together with a master secret key. The *functional key derivation* algorithm takes as input the master secret key and a particular function f to generate a key depending on f. To encrypt a message x, the *encryption* algorithm has to be run on input x and using the public key (some schemes are private-key and require also a secret key) to obtain a ciphertext. Then, given the encryption of a message x, the holder of the key corresponding to the function f is able to compute the value of $f(x)$ using the *decryption* algorithm but nothing else about the encrypted data is revealed.

Many recent papers [3,4,6,16,22] developed various FE encryption schemes with an aim to make such schemes practical. Nevertheless, most of them remain theoretical, since they do not provide implementation or practical evaluation of the schemes. We fill this gap by presenting two FE libraries: GoFE [27] and CiFEr [26]. GoFE is implemented in the programming language Go and is simpler to use, while CiFEr is implemented in C and aims at a lower level, possibly IoT related applications. Both provide the same FE schemes via a similar API, any differences are due only to the different paradigms of the two programming languages.

2.1 Implemented Schemes

Due to the computational complexity and impracticality of general purpose FE schemes, different schemes were designed for evaluation of various functions of lesser complexity. We separated them into three categories: inner-product schemes, quadratic schemes, and attribute-based encryption (ABE) schemes.

Schemes in GoFE and CiFEr use cryptographic primitives based on either modular arithmetic, pairings, or lattices. Most schemes can be instantiated from different primitives – the user can choose the primitive based on the performance requirements. In the following sections, we list the schemes and the security assumptions they are based on. The following assumptions are used: Decisional Diffie-Hellman (DDH), Decisional Composite Residuosity (DCR) (both modular arithmetic), Generic Group Model (GGM), Symmetric eXternal Diffie-Hellman (SXDH), Decisional Bilinear Diffie-Hellman (BDH), Decisional Linear (DLIN) (all pairings), Learning With Errors (LWE), and Ring Learning With Errors (ring-LWE) (both lattices).

Inner-Product Schemes. Inner-product FE schemes allow encryption of a vector $x \in \mathbb{Z}^n$ and independently generation of a key sk_y depending on a vector $y \in \mathbb{Z}^n$, such that given the encryption of x together with sk_y one can perform a computation on the encrypted x to obtain the value $x \cdot y$ (inner-product of x and y). This simple function proves itself very useful: simple statistics of encrypted data, linear or logistic regression, and more functions can be seen as computing certain inner-product of the data. We discuss two possible applications based on the inner-product in Sects. 5 and 6.

The libraries currently provide inner-product schemes based on the following papers:

- **Simple Functional Encryption Schemes for Inner Products** [3]. The first efficient schemes for inner-products, based on the DDH or LWE assumptions.
- **Fully Secure Functional Encryption for Inner Products, from Standard Assumptions** [6]. Inner-product encryption schemes with a higher level of (adaptive) security. In addition to DDH- and LWE-based schemes, a more efficient DCR-based scheme is introduced.
- **Multi-Input Functional Encryption for Inner Products: Function-Hiding Realizations and Constructions without Pairings** [4]. Multi-input FE scheme for inner-products is a scheme supporting encryption of elements of vector distributed among different clients. The scheme can be instantiated on DDH, LWE, and DCR assumptions.
- **Decentralized Multi-client Functional Encryption for Inner Product** [16]. This scheme allows various users to generate ciphertexts supporting inner-product evaluation without the presence of a central authority and with functional decryption keys that can also be generated in a decentralized way. Based on SXDH assumption.
- **Decentralizing Inner-Product Functional Encryption** [2]. A general procedure that decentralizes multi-client inner-product schemes. The scheme can be instantiated on DDH, LWE, and DCR assumptions.

Additionally, we implemented a prototype ring-LWE based inner-product scheme for which a security proof will be provided in a future work.

Quadratic Schemes. To provide an FE scheme able to evaluate an arbitrary function on encrypted data, one needs to build an FE system computing polynomials of arbitrary order. Currently, no practical FE schemes for polynomials of order higher than 2 exist. Nevertheless, many complex functions can be realized as evaluations of quadratic polynomials. A quadratic FE scheme, implemented in CiFEr and GoFE, allows encryption of vectors $x_1, x_2 \in \mathbb{Z}^n$ and independently generation of a key sk_H depending on a matrix $H \in \mathbb{Z}^{n \times n}$, such that given the encryption of x_1, x_2 together with sk_H one can obtain the value $x_1^T H x_2$ (quadratic-product of x_1, x_2 and H). In particular, if $x_1 = x_2$, this is a quadratic polynomial of values of x_1. Such functions are sufficient for performing many machine learning tasks on encrypted data. We demonstrate its use in Sect. 7 on a task of classifying encrypted images with a 2-layer neural network.

GoFE and CiFEr provide the implementation of the currently most efficient quadratic FE scheme:

- **Reading in the Dark: Classifying Encrypted Digits with Functional Encryption** [22]. A scheme for quadratic multi-variate polynomials enabling efficient computation of quadratic polynomials on encrypted vectors. It can be instantiated on GGM assumption.

ABE Schemes. Attribute-based encryption is not strictly classified as FE, but it allows secure access control over data and constructions of certain functionalities on encrypted data [45]. For the latter reason, we included two such schemes in the libraries. The basic idea of ABE is that users are given keys depending on their attributes and are able to decrypt given data only if their attributes are sufficient.

- **Attribute-Based Encryption for Fine-Grained Access Control of Encrypted Data** [32]. The first scheme which enables fine-grained sharing of encrypted data with distribution process that enables decryption only for users in possession of specified attributes. Based on BDH assumption.
- **FAME: Fast Attribute-based Message Encryption** [5]. A scheme that enables attribute based limitation of the access to encrypted data specified through the encryption process. Based on DLIN assumption.

3   Implementation of Cryptographic Primitives

GoFE and CiFEr aim at providing a flexible implementation of FE schemes. We do not use specially chosen groups and parameters which enable better performance (this can still be done by the user). Instead, we provide flexibility in terms of choosing the mathematical groups where operations take place and security parameters which determine the key lengths.

Practical FE schemes are based either on modular arithmetic, pairings, or lattices. Implementation of FE schemes based on modular arithmetic is relatively straight-forward. Our implementation is based on the representation of arbitrarily large numbers using the GMP library [43] in C and the standard library package Big in Go. On the other hand, the implementation of schemes based on pairings and lattices requires lower-level math artillery.

Quite surprisingly, we found only one pairings library which provides all required functionality. Furthermore, there is no fully-fledged library for lattice-based cryptography that could be easily reused. In what follows we present cryptographic primitives needed in FE schemes and address the issues of (lack of) their implementations.

3.1   Pairing Schemes

Numerous libraries for pairings are available, but most lack at least some essential functionality or performance optimization. The latter is crucial since the pairing operation presents a bottleneck in many schemes. Considering existing open source implementations such as PBC [36], RELIC [24], Apache Milagro Cryptographic Library (AMCL) [10], the latter was chosen as an underlying pairing library for CiFEr because it is portable, small, and optimized to fit into the smallest possible embedded footprint. Choosing a Go pairing library to be used in GoFE was more challenging. Barreto-Naehrig [11] bilinear pairings are frequently used as they allow a high security and efficiency level. Two well-known

Barreto-Naehrig pairing libraries exist for the Go programming language: bn256 [34] is a part of the official Go crypto library while Cloudflare bn256 [17] is an optimized version of the former. Neither of them provide hashing operations for pairing groups. We forked [17] and provided hashing operations for both groups. For G_1, we implemented the try-and-increment algorithm [12], while for G_2, we implemented the technique from [25]. Further algorithms and optimizations will be considered in the future.

3.2   Lattice Schemes

The resistance of cryptographic protocols to post-quantum attacks is becoming ever more important as we get closer to the realization of quantum computers. Lattice-based cryptography is believed to be secure against quantum computers. Its cryptographic constructions are based on the presumed hardness of lattice problems (e.g., for example, the shortest vector problem). Currently, the most used constructions are based on the Learning With Errors (LWE) problem [41] or its algebraic ring variation (ring-LWE) [37]. At this time, FE schemes are built only on the LWE assumption; however, there are two main bottlenecks in all such schemes. These are sampling random values distributed according to the discrete Gaussian distribution and matrix multiplications.

Discrete Gaussian Sampling. Discrete Gaussian sampling is a problem of sampling values distributed according to Gaussian distribution but limited only to discrete values. Many algorithms and software implementations have tackled this issue, see [20,21,31,33]. Practical implementation of (ring-)LWE schemes available as open source libraries mostly solve this problem in two ways. Either they avoid Gaussian sampling by replacing it with a uniform or binomial distribution or implement a fast sampler optimized by precomputations for chosen parameters. Neither of the two solutions is applicable in FE schemes. On the one hand, proofs of the security of (ring-)LWE FE schemes depend on the distribution being Gaussian and can easily be broken for uniform distribution. Moreover, precomputations are not just in conflict with the flexibility of GoFE and CiFEr, but are not feasible due to higher variance needed in FE schemes.

For this reason, we implemented a discrete Gaussian sampler based on the algorithm from [21]. It is based on sampling discrete Gaussian values with small variance from pre-computed tables together with uniform sampling. Such sampling is efficient but still presents a bottleneck of the schemes.

Matrix Multiplications. The second bottleneck of FE schemes based on the LWE problem is due to matrix-vector and matrix-matrix multiplications. The reason for this is that the matrices generated in the existing FE scheme have much higher dimensions and inputs. This cannot be fixed implementation-wise; thus the construction of efficient LWE based FE schemes remains an open problem. One way of avoiding costly operations and spacious public keys is by replacing LWE schemes with ring-LWE schemes [37].

3.3 ABE Schemes

ABE schemes provide functionality where clients can be allowed (or disallowed) to access the decryption of a ciphertext based on a set of attributes that they possess. Most ABE schemes use pairings as an underlying cryptographic primitive, but there is another, ABE specific, primitive needed: Linear Secret Sharing Scheme (LSSS) matrices.

A part of every ABE scheme is a policy that defines which entity can decrypt the ciphertext based on the attributes. A Monotone Span Program (MSP) is defined as a policy that accepts a subset of attributes as sufficient if a certain subset of chosen vectors spans a vector of ones. Hence, to create an MSP policy, one must carefully choose a set of vectors representing attributes in a way that they describe the desired rules of decryption. This set of vectors is also known as an LSSS matrix. On the other hand, expressing rules of decryption as a boolean expression is preferred for practical usage and interpretability. Therefore, we have implemented an algorithm that transforms a boolean expression into an MSP structure. We have chosen the Lewko-Waters algorithm [35] for this task due to its simplicity and efficiency. The algorithm can transform an arbitrary boolean expression that does not include a "NOT" operation ($\neg$) into a set of vectors (a matrix) whose dimensions only depend on the number of "AND" operators ($\wedge$) and the number of variables in the expression.

4 Benchmarks

In the following section, we focus on a practical evaluation of implemented schemes, comparing the benefits and downsides, and discussing their practicality for the possible uses. As noted in Sect. 3, the schemes are implemented with the goal of flexibility and having an easy-to-use API. Thus, the schemes can be initialized with an arbitrary level of security and other metaparameters. Since there is no universal benchmark to compare all the schemes, we evaluate them on various sets of parameters, exposing many properties of the schemes. Due to space limitations, we do not present the benchmarks of all the implemented schemes here but rather focus on the demonstrative results. All of the benchmarks were performed on an Intel(R) Core(TM) i7-6700 CPU @ 3.40 GHz.

4.1 Inner-Product Schemes

Recall that an inner-product FE scheme is such that it allows encrypting a vector $x \in \mathbb{Z}^\ell$ and independently generating a key sk_y depending on a vector $y \in \mathbb{Z}^\ell$, so that one can perform computations on the encrypted x and use sk_y to decrypt the inner-product $x \cdot y$ and nothing more.

As noted in Sect. 2, the schemes are based on different security assumptions. GoFE and CiFEr include implementation of five inner-product schemes (excluding decentralized and multi-client ones), where two of them are based on the DDH assumption, two of them are based on the LWE assumption, and one on

Table 1. Performance of key generation (in seconds) in inner product schemes w.r.t. vector length l

l	Paillier[Go]	Paillier[C]	LWE[Go]	LWE[C]	DDH[Go]	DDH[C]
1	0.1549	0.0657	12.9523	7.3909	0.0080	0.0041
5	0.5612	0.2938	62.1945	46.2466	0.0402	0.0204
10	1.0600	0.5756	122.7627	74.8795	0.0840	0.0411
20	2.0551	1.1384	266.5059	196.6151	0.1584	0.0849
50	5.0520	2.8410	878.3684	559.6070	0.3954	0.2055
100	10.0916	5.7032	N/A	N/A	0.7829	0.4149
200	20.0883	11.3700	N/A	N/A	1.5710	0.8190

the DCR assumption. Since both of the DDH-based and both of the LWE-based schemes have similar performance, we only compare the DDH-based scheme from [6], the LWE-based scheme from [3], and the DCR-based scheme from [6] which is also known as Paillier-based FE scheme.

The DDH schemes assume the difficulty of computing a discrete logarithm in a quadratic residues subgroup of $\mathbb{Z}_p^*$, where the security of such assumption depends on the bit size of the prime number p. To achieve resistance to all known attacks with complexity less than $O(2^{128})$, it is common practice to pick p to be a safe prime with 3072 bits. The DCR assumption relies on the difficulty of distinguishing the so-called n-residues in $\mathbb{Z}_{n^2}^*$ group, which further relies on the difficulty of factoring a large number n. We choose n to be a 3072-bit number and a product of two safe primes as it is considered safe for attacks with complexity in $O(2^{128})$.

The security level of the LWE assumption is harder to access due to its novelty. The papers developing the LWE-based FE schemes argue its security based on the original work of Regev [41] while it has become a common practice in the recent proposals of (ring-)LWE-based schemes [7,8,13] to evaluate this security through evaluation of attacks on the assumption. For this reason, we implemented a setup procedure that generates the parameters for each instantiation of the scheme that are secure for the so-called primal and dual attack on LWE. This was necessary since the originally proposed parameters are estimated to possess significantly less security than claimed. For additional information on the attacks, we direct the reader to the above references.

Each inner-product scheme comprises five parts: setup, generation of master keys, encryption, derivation of an inner-product key, and decryption. In the following tables, we evaluate the performance for key generation, encryption, and decryption. The complexity of the functional key derivation process is negligible in all the schemes compared to the other steps, while the setup procedure is quite time-consuming but can be avoided for practical applications since generating a new group for every deployment does not bring additional security.

Table 2. Performance of encryption (in seconds) in inner product schemes w.r.t. vector length ℓ

1	Paillier[Go]	Paillier[C]	LWE[Go]	LWE[C]	DDH[Go]	DDH[C]
1	0.0796	0.0461	4.4148	6.5212	0.0120	0.0062
5	0.2389	0.1389	5.5039	6.8358	0.0276	0.0145
10	0.4367	0.2528	6.3218	7.6660	0.0473	0.0246
20	0.8357	0.4840	7.2797	8.9215	0.0864	0.0464
50	2.0245	1.1751	7.8941	12.6611	0.2048	0.1078
100	4.0087	2.3266	N/A	N/A	0.4027	0.2103
200	7.8847	4.6275	N/A	N/A	0.7984	0.4141

We demonstrate the efficiency of the schemes depending on parameters ℓ, defining the dimensionality of the encrypted vectors, and b, being the upper bound for the coordinates of the inner product vectors. All the results are averages of many runs on different random inputs.

In Table 1 we compare the key generation procedure across different schemes with fixed $b = 1000$ and increasing ℓ. The values show that for practical parameters the generation of keys in inner-product schemes is linearly dependent on conventionality ℓ. This is in contrast with the dependency on b (not shown in the table), increasing which only mildly increases the generation if at all, assuming it is not extremely large. The table shows that LWE-based schemes are practical only for small parameters. Note a slightly slower performance of the Paillier scheme compared to the DDH-based scheme which is attributed to the need of Gaussian sampling, described in Sect. 3. In Table 2 similar observations can be done for the encryption process.

The biggest difference between the schemes is demonstrated in Fig. 1, measuring the decryption times of the schemes depending on the bound b of the inputs. While the Paillier scheme has only a slight linear increase in computation times when b is increased, DDH-based schemes prove themselves practical only for vectors with a small bound b. The latter is owed to finding a discrete logarithm in its decryption procedure, the performance of which is directly connected to the size of the decrypted value. Interestingly, LWE-based schemes have the fastest decryption. Figure 1 shows the dependency for bounded random vectors.

4.2   Decentralized Inner-Product Scheme

Multi-client schemes allow encryption of vectors by many independent clients. Decentralized schemes eliminate the need for the central trusted authority for key generation and derivation. See Sect. 6 for an application of a decentralized scheme.

The implemented decentralized inner-product schemes are either based on a decentralizing procedure from [2] applied to schemes from [4] or as described

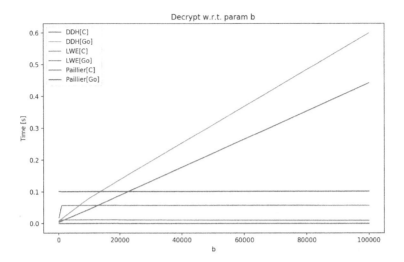

Fig. 1. Performance graph of decryption in inner product schemes w.r.t. bound b

in [16]. Here, we benchmark the latter, which is based on pairings (SXDH assumption). The results are presented in Table 3. Note that the generation of keys and the encryption process have better performance than basic inner-product schemes since both are distributed among users and counted only per user. The communication overhead is not included in the measurements. The decryption process involves computing a discrete logarithm as well as performing a pairing operation.

Table 3. Performance of the decentralized (D) and quadratic (Q) schemes in GoFE (in seconds)

params	KeyGen[D]	KeyGen[Q]	Encrypt[D]	Encrypt[Q]	Decrypt[D]	Decrypt[Q]
b = 1000, l = 1	0.0009	0.0001	0.0001	0.0026	0.0211	0.2903
b = 1000, l = 5	0.0009	0.0001	0.0001	0.0117	0.0401	0.9039
b = 1000, l = 10	0.0009	0.0001	0.0001	0.0224	0.0540	1.6454
b = 1000, l = 20	0.0009	0.0002	0.0001	0.0437	0.0731	2.4223
b = 5000, l = 1	0.0009	0.0001	0.0001	0.0025	0.0827	1.8973
b = 10000, l = 1	0.0009	0.0001	0.0001	0.0027	0.1614	3.1074
b = 5000, l = 10	0.0009	0.0001	0.0001	0.0228	0.2376	14.2446

4.3 Quadratic Scheme

Quadratic schemes are a powerful·tool for evaluating more complex functions on encrypted data. Table 3 evaluates the performance of the quadratic scheme from [22]. The decryption process turns out to be time-consuming as it requires computing a discrete logarithm and pairing operation. Note that the input value for a discrete logarithm is bigger compared to the inner-product schemes due to the quadratic operations applied on the input vector x. We demonstrate in Sect. 7 that the scheme's performance is still sufficient for the real-world use cases.

5   Privacy-Friendly Prediction of Cardiovascular Diseases

In this section, we demonstrate how FE can enable privacy-enhanced analyses. We show how the risk of general cardiovascular disease (CVD) can be evaluated using only encrypted data.

The demonstrator comprises the following components: Key Server is a central authority component generating keys, Analyses Service is a component to which the user sends encrypted data and obtains the risk evaluation of CVD, and Client component which obtains the public key from the Key Server, encrypts user's data with the public key and sends it to the Service, see Fig. 2.

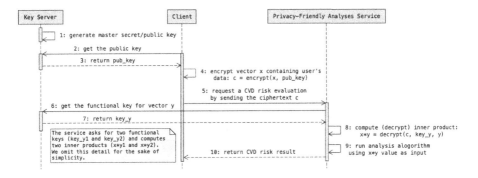

Fig. 2. Interactions between CVD demonstrator components

The Framingham heart study [19] followed patients from Framingham, Massachusetts, for many decades starting in 1948. Many multivariable risk algorithms used to assess the risk of specific atherosclerotic cardiovascular disease events have been developed based on the original Framingham study. Algorithms most often estimate the 10-year or 30-year CVD risk of an individual.

The input parameters for algorithms are sex, age, total and high-density lipoprotein cholesterol, systolic blood pressure, treatment for hypertension, smoking, and diabetes status. The demonstrator shows how the risk score can be computed using only the encrypted values of the input parameters. The user specifies the parameters in the Client program; these are encrypted and sent to the Analyses Service component. The service computes the 30-year risk [39] and returns it to the user.

The source code for all three components is available on FENTEC GitHub account [40]. We use the inner-product FE scheme based on Paillier cryptosystem

[6] due to its fast decryption operation. The Client component prepares a vector x which contains the eight input parameters, which in GoFE looks like:

```
x := data.NewVector([]*big.Int{sex, age, systolicBloodPressure,
totalCholest, hdlCholest, smoker, treatedBloodPressure, diabetic})
```

Framingham risk score algorithms are based on Cox proportional hazards model [18]. Part of it is multiplication of the input parameters by regression factors which are real numbers. In the 30-year algorithm, the vector x is multiplied by two vectors (inner-product):

y_1 = (0.34362, 2.63588, 1.8803, 1.12673, -0.90941, 0.59397, 0.5232, 0.68602)
y_2 = (0.48123, 3.39222, 1.39862, -0.00439, 0.16081, 0.99858, 0.19035, 0.49756)

Regression factors need to be converted into integers because cryptographic schemes operate with integers. This is straight-forward in FE schemes: we multiply factors by the power of 10 to obtain whole numbers. The Client encrypts vector x using public key obtained from the Key Server:

```
ciphertext, err := paillier.Encrypt(x, masterPubKey)
```

The Client then sends ciphertext to the Service. Service beforehand obtained two functional encryption keys from the Key Server: a key to compute the inner-product of x and y_1, and a key to compute the inner-product of x and y_2. Now it can compute the inner-products:

```
xy_1, err := paillier.Decrypt(ciphertext, key_1, y_1)
xy_2, err := paillier.Decrypt(ciphertext, key_2, y_2)
```

To obtain the risk score the algorithm computes $e^{xy_1 - 21.29326612}$, $e^{xy_2 - 20.12840698}$ followed by $1340 \cdot 1340$ power functions, $1340 \cdot 3$ multiplications, and 1340 additions on the obtained values. For details, see [39] or the source code [40]. These operations are executed by the Service and returned to the Client component.

A user thus does not need to know anything about the algorithm to obtain the personal CVD risk score, and at the same time the Service does not know anything about the user's parameters (except the inner-products of x with vectors y_1 and y_2).

However, it has to be noted that the Service does know the risk score. This is one of the main differences with HE. HE computes the encryption of the risk score, which is then decrypted by the user (and thus known only by the user).

Paper [14] reports on the implementation of the 10-year CVD risk score using HE. While this approach has a clear advantage of prediction service not knowing the risk score, it is also far less efficient than the approach with FE. In a setup which enables the evaluation of higher degree polynomials (such as 7), one multiplication of ciphertexts requires around 5 s on a modern laptop (Intel Core i7-3520M at 2.9 GHz). Note that higher degree polynomials are needed to approximate the exponential function by a Taylor series. While in the 10-year CVD risk algorithm, there is only one evaluation of the exponential function, the 30-year algorithm uses two evaluations. An evaluation of the exponential function in [14] requires more than 30 s since computing the Taylor series of the degree 7 takes more than 30 s (the powers of x already require six multiplications at 5 s each). On the contrary, our FE approach returns the result in a matter of milliseconds.

Furthermore, there is a significant communication overhead in HE approach as the ciphertext can grow to roughly one megabyte (16384 coefficients of 512-bit). Communication messages in FE are much smaller – a few kilobytes.

HE approach could be sped up with computing the encryption of only the inner-products (as it is in FE). However, as the prediction service would know only the encryption of the inner-product, the rest of the risk score algorithm would need to be computed at the user's side and would require to move significant parts of the prediction logic to the Client component. In many scenarios, this might not be desirable, especially if the prediction logic is computationally expensive. As a matter of fact, for all services where the prediction logic is computationally expensive, the FE approach is far more performant, but at the expense that the prediction service knows the predicted value.

6   London Underground Anonymous Heatmap

In this section, we demonstrate how a traffic heatmap can be generated based on encrypted data. Given the encrypted information about users of the London Underground, our service can measure the traffic density at each particular station. Thus, congestions and potential increases in traffic density can be detected while the user data is encrypted and remains private.

DMCFE scheme [16] is used for the demonstration [9]. The scheme allows each user to encrypt the location data in a way that neither the central service nor the other users can know it. The only information that the central service can obtain is the information about all the users, preserving the privacy of each individual. Furthermore, the functional keys needed by the central service are derived in a decentralized manner, without a centralized authority for generating keys. Indeed, functional key parts are provided by the users and then combined by the central service.

Each user locally encrypts the vector specifying the path that was traveled. The length of the vector is the same as the number of the stations. It consists of 0s and 1s: 1 for stations which the user visited (see Fig. 3a for a visual representation). In GoFE the code looks like:

```
// pathVec[i] is the value of i-th station, label its name,
// c[i] is its encryption
label = station[i]
c[i], _ := client.Encrypt(pathVec[i], label)
```

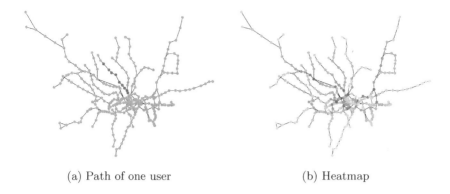

(a) Path of one user   (b) Heatmap

Fig. 3. Information of one user vs. information the central service obtains.

While we use randomly generated user data for this demonstration, one can easily imagine a smartphone app which tracks the user's path, generates a vector, encrypts it (all operations performed locally), and finally sends it to the central service.

In the decentralized scheme [16], the FE keys are generated by the users (no trusted authority is needed). The users thus provide a functional key to a central service component. In our case, a functional key for an inner-product vector y of 1s is provided (the vector length is the number of users). This is because the central authority decrypts the sum of all the users that traveled through that station, i.e. a value that can be represented as an inner-product of y and a vector x of 0s and 1s indicating which users traveled through that station. Each user provides a key share:

```
// create a vector of 1s:
vecOfOnes := data.NewConstantVector(numClients, big.NewInt(1))
// keyShares is a vector of all the key shares
keyShares[k], _ := clients[k].GenerateKeyShare(vecOfOnes)
}
```

The central service component collects all the key shares and can now compute (decrypt) the density for each station. The code for this looks like:

```
for i := 0; i < numStations; i++ {
    label := stations[i]
    dec = fullysec.NewDMCFEDecryptor(vecOfOnes, label, ciphers[i],
    keyShares, numClients)
    heatmap[i], _ = dec.Decrypt()
}
```

Using a described approach, a variety of other analysis services can be built on the encrypted data, for example, the power consumption of a group of houses in a neighborhood, measurements from IoT devices, etc. In the former case, the power consumption could be encrypted for each hour and sent to the central component.

The central component could then compute (decrypt) the overall consumption (across all houses) for each particular hour. Based on such privacy-enhanced computations, various prediction services can be built using only encrypted data. Note that all such applications cannot be built with HE since the derivation of a functional decryption key is needed for the central service to decrypt the results.

7 Neural Networks on Encrypted MNIST Dataset

In the previous two sections, we saw how to implement privacy-friendly predictive services by using efficient FE for inner-products. Using linear functions (inner-products), many efficient machine learning models can be built based on linear or logistic regression.

However, in many cases linear models do not suffice. One of such tasks is image classification where linear classifiers mostly achieve significantly lower accuracy compared to the higher-degree classifiers – for example, classifiers for the well-known MNIST dataset where handwritten digits need to be recognized. A linear classifier on MNIST dataset is reported to have 92% accuracy (TensorFlow's tutorial [42]), while more complex classifiers achieve over 99% accuracy.

GoFE and CiFEr include a scheme [22] for quadratic multi-variate polynomials which enable computation of quadratic polynomials on encrypted vectors. This allows richer machine learning models and even basic versions of neural networks. We provide a machine learning project [38] to demonstrate how an accurate neural network classifier can be built on the MNIST dataset and how FE can be used to apply a classifier on the encrypted dataset. This means that an entity holding an FE key for a classifier can classify encrypted images, i.e., can classify each image depending on the digit in the encrypted image, but cannot see anything else within the image (for example, some characteristics of the handwriting).

The demonstration uses the GoFE library and the widely-used machine learning library TensorFlow [1]. The MNIST dataset consists of 60 000 images of handwritten digits. Each image is a 28×28 pixel array, where each pixel is represented by its gray level. The model we used is a 2-layer neural network with quadratic function as a non-linear activation function. Training of the model needs to be done on unencrypted data, while prediction is done on encrypted images. The images have been presented as 785-coordinate vectors ($28 \cdot 28 + 1$ for bias). We achieved the accuracy of 97%, a result that is reported also in [22]. The decryption of one image (applying the trained model on the encrypted image) takes approximately a second.

Similarly, CryptoNets [30], an HE approach for applying neural networks to encrypted data, needs an already trained model. The model they use is significantly more complex than ours (the trained network has nine layers) and provides an accuracy of 99%. Note that as currently no efficient FE schemes exist for polynomials of degree greater than 2, no such complex models are possible with FE. On the other hand, the execution when using HE approach is significantly slower. Applying the network on encrypted data using CryptoNets takes $570\,\mathrm{s}$

on a PC with a single Intel Xeon E5-1620 CPU running at 3.5 GHz. But note that applying the network allows executing many predictions simultaneously if this is needed.

Thus, compared to the FE approach, HE can provide more complex machine learning models and consequently ones with higher accuracy. Nevertheless, HE has a limitation which is particularly important in the present application. HE can only serve as privacy-friendly outsourcing of computation, while the result of this computation can be decrypted only by the owner of the secret key. FE allows the third party to decrypt the result, in our case the digit in the image, without exposing the image itself. One can easily imagine a more complex FE alert system on encrypted video, where the system detects the danger without violating the privacy of the subjects in the video when there is none. Currently, only primitive versions of such a system are possible as more efficient schemes (in terms of performance and polynomial degree) are needed.

8   Conclusions and Future Work

In this paper, we presented the first two fully-fledged functional encryption libraries. The two libraries are implemented in Go and C programming languages and offer an easy-to-use API to various FE schemes. We focused on creating a flexible and efficient implementation to support various use cases and have demonstrated the practicality by presenting three possible applications of the libraries: an online privacy-friendly predictor of cardiovascular diseases, an anonymous traffic heatmap service, and image classification on encrypted data. We compared the FE with the HE approach on the latter examples, showing how FE can provide new applications or improve performance by revealing some information. The libraries are filling the gap between academic research of FE schemes and their applications to real-life scenarios. As such, they offer a platform for the developers to prototype their products as well as a test place for academic research on FE.

In our future work, we plan to implement further FE schemes, in particular, recent multi-client and multi-input schemes which enable a wide range of applications like running queries on encrypted databases, computation over encrypted data streams, and multi-client delegation of computation. Furthermore, we plan to implement and evaluate function-hiding schemes which enable privacy-preserving queries to the prediction services. Also, further optimizations will be applied.

Acknowledgements. The research was supported, in part, by grant H2020-DS-2017-780108 (FENTEC).

References

1. Abadi, M., et al.: Tensorflow: a system for large-scale machine learning. In: 12th USENIX Symposium on Operating Systems Design and Implementation (OSDI 16), pp. 265–283 (2016)

2. Abdalla, M., Benhamouda, F., Kohlweiss, M., Waldner, H.: Decentralizing inner-product functional encryption. In: Lin, D., Sako, K. (eds.) PKC 2019. LNCS, vol. 11443, pp. 128–157. Springer, Cham (2019). https://doi.org/10.1007/978-3-030-17259-6_5

3. Abdalla, M., Bourse, F., De Caro, A., Pointcheval, D.: Simple functional encryption schemes for inner products. In: Katz, J. (ed.) PKC 2015. LNCS, vol. 9020, pp. 733–751. Springer, Heidelberg (2015). https://doi.org/10.1007/978-3-662-46447-2_33

4. Abdalla, M., Catalano, D., Fiore, D., Gay, R., Ursu, B.: Multi-input functional encryption for inner products: function-hiding realizations and constructions without pairings. In: Shacham, H., Boldyreva, A. (eds.) CRYPTO 2018. LNCS, vol. 10991, pp. 597–627. Springer, Cham (2018). https://doi.org/10.1007/978-3-319-96884-1_20

5. Agrawal, S., Chase, M.: FAME: fast attribute-based message encryption. In: Proceedings of the 2017 ACM SIGSAC Conference on Computer and Communications Security, pp. 665–682. ACM (2017)

6. Agrawal, S., Libert, B., Stehlé, D.: Fully secure functional encryption for inner products, from standard assumptions. In: Robshaw, M., Katz, J. (eds.) CRYPTO 2016. LNCS, vol. 9816, pp. 333–362. Springer, Heidelberg (2016). https://doi.org/10.1007/978-3-662-53015-3_12

7. Albrecht, M.R., Player, R., Scott, S.: On the concrete hardness of learning with errors. J. Math. Cryptol. **9**(3), 169–203 (2015)

8. Alkim, E., Ducas, L., Pöppelmann, T., Schwabe, P.: Post-quantum key exchange – a new hope. In: 25th USENIX Security Symposium (USENIX Security 2016), pp. 327–343 (2016)

9. Anonymous heatmap: https://github.com/fentec-project/anonymous-heatmap

10. Apache Milagro Crypto Library: https://github.com/milagro-crypto/amcl

11. Barreto, P.S.L.M., Naehrig, M.: Pairing-friendly elliptic curves of prime order. In: Preneel, B., Tavares, S. (eds.) SAC 2005. LNCS, vol. 3897, pp. 319–331. Springer, Heidelberg (2006). https://doi.org/10.1007/11693383_22

12. Boneh, D., Lynn, B., Shacham, H.: Short signatures from the weil pairing. In: Boyd, C. (ed.) ASIACRYPT 2001. LNCS, vol. 2248, pp. 514–532. Springer, Heidelberg (2001). https://doi.org/10.1007/3-540-45682-1_30

13. Bos, J., et al.: Frodo: take off the ring! practical, quantum-secure key exchange from LWE. In: Proceedings of the 2016 ACM SIGSAC Conference on Computer and Communications Security, pp. 1006–1018. ACM (2016)

14. Bos, J.W., Lauter, K., Naehrig, M.: Private predictive analysis on encrypted medical data. J. Biomed. Inform. **50**, 234–243 (2014)

15. Boyle, E., Chung, K.-M., Pass, R.: On extractability obfuscation. In: Lindell, Y. (ed.) TCC 2014. LNCS, vol. 8349, pp. 52–73. Springer, Heidelberg (2014). https://doi.org/10.1007/978-3-642-54242-8_3

16. Chotard, J., Dufour Sans, E., Gay, R., Phan, D.H., Pointcheval, D.: Decentralized multi-client functional encryption for inner product. In: Peyrin, T., Galbraith, S. (eds.) ASIACRYPT 2018. LNCS, vol. 11273, pp. 703–732. Springer, Cham (2018). https://doi.org/10.1007/978-3-030-03329-3_24

17. Cloudflare implementation of Barreto-Naehrig bilinear pairings: https://github.com/cloudflare/bn256

18. Cox, D.R.: Regression models and life-tables. J. R. Stat. Soc. Ser. B (Methodol.) **34**(2), 187–202 (1972)

19. D'agostino, R.B., et al.: General cardiovascular risk profile for use in primary care. Circulation **117**(6), 743–753 (2008)

20. De Clercq, R., Roy, S.S., Vercauteren, F., Verbauwhede, I.: Efficient software implementation of ring-LWE encryption. In: Proceedings of the 2015 Design, Automation & Test in Europe Conference & Exhibition, pp. 339–344. EDA Consortium (2015)
21. Ducas, L., Durmus, A., Lepoint, T., Lyubashevsky, V.: Lattice signatures and bimodal Gaussians. In: Canetti, R., Garay, J.A. (eds.) CRYPTO 2013. LNCS, vol. 8042, pp. 40–56. Springer, Heidelberg (2013). https://doi.org/10.1007/978-3-642-40041-4_3
22. Dufour Sans, E., Gay, R., Pointcheval, D.: Reading in the dark: classifying encrypted digits with functional encryption. IACR Cryptol. ePrint Archive **2018**, 206 (2018)
23. FENTEC project Github accunt: https://github.com/fentec-project
24. de Freitas Aranha, D., Gouvea, C.P.L., Markmann, T.: RELIC. https://github.com/dis2/bls12
25. Fuentes-Castaneda, L., Knapp, E., Rodríguez-Henríquez, F.: Faster hashing to G2. In: International Workshop on Selected Areas in Cryptography, pp. 412–430. Springer (2011)
26. Functional encryption library in C: https://github.com/fentec-project/CiFEr
27. Functional encryption library in Go: https://github.com/fentec-project/gofe
28. Garg, S., Gentry, C., Halevi, S., Raykova, M., Sahai, A., Waters, B.: Candidate indistinguishability obfuscation and functional encryption for all circuits. SIAM J. Comput. **45**(3), 882–929 (2016)
29. Garg, S., Gentry, C., Halevi, S., Zhandry, M.: Fully secure attribute based encryption from multilinear maps. IACR Cryptol. ePrint Archive **2014**, 622 (2014)
30. Gilad-Bachrach, R., Dowlin, N., Laine, K., Lauter, K., Naehrig, M., Wernsing, J.: CryptoNets: applying neural networks to encrypted data with high throughput and accuracy. In: International Conference on Machine Learning, pp. 201–210 (2016)
31. Göttert, N., Feller, T., Schneider, M., Buchmann, J., Huss, S.: On the design of hardware building blocks for modern lattice-based encryption schemes. In: Prouff, E., Schaumont, P. (eds.) CHES 2012. LNCS, vol. 7428, pp. 512–529. Springer, Heidelberg (2012). https://doi.org/10.1007/978-3-642-33027-8_30
32. Goyal, V., Pandey, O., Sahai, A., Waters, B.: Attribute-based encryption for fine-grained access control of encrypted data. In: Proceedings of the 13th ACM Conference on Computer and Communications Security, pp. 89–98. ACM (2006)
33. Knuth, D., Yao, A.: Algorithms and complexity: new directions and recent results, chapter the complexity of nonuniform random number generation (1976)
34. Langley, A., Burke, K., Valsorda, F., Symonds, D.: Package bn256 (2012). https://godoc.org/golang.org/x/crypto/bn256
35. Lewko, A., Waters, B.: Decentralizing attribute-based encryption. In: Paterson, K.G. (ed.) EUROCRYPT 2011. LNCS, vol. 6632, pp. 568–588. Springer, Heidelberg (2011). https://doi.org/10.1007/978-3-642-20465-4_31
36. Lynn, B.: The Pairing Based Cryptography library. https://crypto.stanford.edu/pbc/
37. Lyubashevsky, V., Peikert, C., Regev, O.: On ideal lattices and learning with errors over rings. In: Gilbert, H. (ed.) EUROCRYPT 2010. LNCS, vol. 6110, pp. 1–23. Springer, Heidelberg (2010). https://doi.org/10.1007/978-3-642-13190-5_1
38. Neural network on encrypted data: https://github.com/fentec-project/neural-network-on-encrypted-data
39. Pencina, M.J., D'Agostino Sr., R.B., Larson, M.G., Massaro, J.M., Vasan, R.S.: Predicting the thirty-year risk of cardiovascular disease: the framingham heart study. Circulation **119**(24), 3078 (2009)

40. Private prediction analyses: https://github.com/fentec-project/privacy-friendly-analyses
41. Regev, O.: On lattices, learning with errors, random linear codes, and cryptography. J. ACM (JACM) **56**(6), 34 (2009)
42. Tensorflow tutorial: https://www.tensorflow.org/tutorials#evaluating_our_model
43. The GNU Multiple Precision Arithmetic Library: https://gmplib.org
44. Waters, B.: A punctured programming approach to adaptively secure functional encryption. In: Gennaro, R., Robshaw, M. (eds.) CRYPTO 2015. LNCS, vol. 9216, pp. 678–697. Springer, Heidelberg (2015). https://doi.org/10.1007/978-3-662-48000-7_33
45. Zheng, Q., Xu, S., Ateniese, G.: VABKS: verifiable attribute-based keyword search over outsourced encrypted data. In: IEEE INFOCOM 2014-IEEE Conference on Computer Communications, pp. 522–530. IEEE (2014)

Towards Secure and Efficient Outsourcing of Machine Learning Classification

Yifeng Zheng[1,2], Huayi Duan[1,2], and Cong Wang[1,2(✉)]

[1] City University of Hong Kong, Hong Kong, China
{yifeng.zheng,hduan2-c}@my.cityu.edu.hk, congwang@cityu.edu.hk
[2] City University of Hong Kong Shenzhen Research Institute, Shenzhen, China

Abstract. Machine learning classification has been successfully applied in numerous applications, such as healthcare, finance, and more. Outsourcing classification services to the cloud has become an intriguing practice as this brings many prominent benefits like ease of management and scalability. Such outsourcing, however, raises critical privacy concerns to both the machine learning model provider and the client interested in using the classification service. In this paper, we focus on classification outsourcing with decision trees, one of the most popular classifiers. We propose for the first time a secure framework allowing decision tree based classification outsourcing while maintaining the confidentiality of the provider's model (parameters) and the client's input feature vector. Our framework requires no interaction from the provider and the client—they can go offline after the initial submission of their respective encrypted inputs to the cloud. This is a distinct advantage over prior art for practical deployment, as they all work under the client-provider setting where synchronous online interactions between the provider and client is required. Leveraging the lightweight additive secret sharing technique, we build our protocol from the ground up to enable secure and efficient outsourcing of decision tree evaluation, tailored to address the challenges posed by secure in-the-cloud dealing with versatile components including input feature selection, decision node evaluation, path evaluation, and classification generation. Through evaluation we show the practical performance of our design, and the substantial client-side savings over prior art, say up to four orders of magnitude in computation and 163× in communication.

Keywords: Cloud security · Machine learning · Secure outsourcing

1 Introduction

Machine learning classification has gained widespread use in many applications such as healthcare [1,13], finance [15], and more. A well-trained machine learning model can be used to automatically predict the accurate classification label of a unseen/new input. As an example, a model trained by a medical institution or a hospital over a dataset of medical profiles may be used to make a prediction

ⓒ Springer Nature Switzerland AG 2019
K. Sako et al. (Eds.): ESORICS 2019, LNCS 11735, pp. 22–40, 2019.
https://doi.org/10.1007/978-3-030-29959-0_2

about a new patient's health [1]. For practical deployment, outsourcing such classification services to the cloud is intriguing as this brings the machine learning model provider and the client many well-known benefits like ease of management, scalability, and ubiquitous access.

Despite the prominent benefits, such outsourcing also entails critical privacy challenges to both the provider and the client. On the provider side, the trained model could be proprietary as the provider might have invested a significant amount of resources in gathering the training datasets and training the model. Besides, the model may also constitute a competitive commercial advantage. So, the provider might not be willing to expose the plaintext model to the cloud. On the client side, the model input data are personal and could also be sensitive (like medical data or financial data). So, while interested in the classification service, the client may be reluctant to supply the input in cleartext. Therefore, it is important that security must be embedded in the classification outsourcing design from the very beginning so that we can safeguard the privacy of both the provider and client.

In this paper, we focus on secure and efficient classification outsourcing based on decision trees, one of the most popular classifiers due to its effectiveness and ease of use. Decision trees have a wide range of practical applications, such as medical diagnosis [1] and credit-risk assessment [26]. Briefly speaking, a decision tree consists of internal nodes called decision nodes and leaf nodes. Each decision node is used for comparing an attribute in the input feature vector with a specific constant, and each leaf node indicates a classification result. Given a feature vector as input, decision tree evaluation is done via tree traversal until a leaf node is reached.

Contributions. The challenging problem we aim to tackle is how to enable secure and efficient decision tree evaluation outsourcing, which has not been studied before. To this end, we present a secure framework allowing a decision tree model provider to deploy decision tree based classification services in the cloud for the client, while preserving the privacy of both the provider and client. The high-level service workflow in our framework is as follows. Initially, the provider deploys a properly encrypted decision tree model in the cloud. Later, a client can supply an encrypted feature vector to the cloud to get a classification. Throughout the procedure, the decision tree and feature vector are kept private.

To securely and efficiently instantiate the above service, our main insight is to leverage lightweight cryptography and craft a protocol design tailored for decision tree classification outsourcing. This immediately precludes the consideration on using heavy cryptographic techniques such as (fully) homomorphic encryption [5] and generic secure multi-party computation (such as garbled circuits [25] and GMW protocol [9]). Specifically, in our solution, we turn to the lightweight cryptographic technique called additive secret sharing to completely build our decision tree classification outsourcing design. At a high level, with such technique, the encryption of the decision tree and the feature vector can be fast performed via properly splitting the data into secret shares. Secure decision tree evaluation is then conducted over the secret shares of the decision tree model and feature vector in the cloud.

To be compatible with the working paradigm of additive secret sharing and also make the provider and the client free of active online participation in the service, our framework leverages the two-server model and explores the full support for secure decision tree evaluation at the cloud side. In particular, we consider that the power of the cloud is split into two cloud servers maintained by independent cloud providers. Such a two-server model has also gained increasing use in previous security designs tailored for different applications, including privacy-preserving machine learning (over other kinds of models) (e.g., [16,18,23]). We consider our adoption of such model to be among the trend and it is, for the first time, customized for secure and efficient decision tree evaluation outsourcing.

Based on the lightweight additive secret sharing technique, we build our outsourcing protocol from the ground up, and delicately tackle the following challenges. Firstly, how to properly encrypt the decision tree model in the very beginning so that it can later function well at the cloud side for classification? Note that a decision tree model not only contains data values (parameters) that demand protection, but also carry structure-specific information like the mapping for input selection from the feature vector, which should be protected as well. To tackle this challenge, we properly represent the mapping as an input selection matrix so that the encryption of the mapping can be done via encryption of the matrix. As a result, we manage to effectively transform secure input selection into the problem of secure matrix-vector multiplication.

Secondly, at the two cloud servers, how to accomplish secure and efficient comparison at each decision node and produce encrypted comparison results with usability for encrypted tree traversal? We note that for secure comparison at decision nodes, most prior works in the *non-outsourcing* setting (i.e., a client-provider setting, see Sect. 2 for more discussion) rely on protocols that require bitwise (homomorphic) encryption of the inputs from the very beginning. Such highly inefficient restriction on input encryption, together with the incompatibility of prior works with our new outsourcing setting, makes it necessary for us to craft a new design for secure and efficient decision node evaluation from the ground up. Our idea is to transform the problem of secure decision node evaluation into a simpler secure bit-extraction problem so that there is no need for the provider and client to supply inputs in bitwise encrypted form, and the bit-level secure processing is shifted to the cloud. We also further consider how to correctly transform the encrypted comparison results into appropriate secret sharing domain so that they preserve usability for encrypted tree traversal.

Thirdly, at the two cloud servers, how to securely and efficiently evaluate the path to each leaf node so that the leaf node carrying the classification result can be correctly identified by the client? To answer this challenge, we leverage our observation on the latest path cost mechanism [20] and newly bridge it with additive secret sharing technique to support secure and efficient path evaluation for leaf nodes, and correctly produce encrypted classification result ultimately.

We make an implementation of our design and conduct experiments for performance evaluation, over various realistic problem sizes of decision tree classification. The results demonstrate the practicality of our design. To our best knowledge, this paper presents the first framework for secure and efficient machine learning classification outsourcing based on decision trees. The rest of this paper is organized as follows. Section 2 discusses the related work. Section 3 presents the problem statement. Section 4 gives our detailed security design. Section 5 shows the experimental results. Section 6 concludes the whole paper.

2   Related Work

Secure Evaluation of Decision Trees. There have been some previous research efforts on secure decision tree evaluation [4, 7, 10, 20, 21, 24]. These works mostly rely on the use of heavy cryptographic techniques like fully/additively homomorphic encryption, garbled circuits, and ORAM, for the online secure classification service. More notably, all prior works target a client-provider setting, where the provider holding the plaintext decision tree model and the client holding the plaintext feature vector directly engage in a synchronous and interactive protocol. Our work departs definitively from the previous works by, for the first time, targeting secure and efficient outsourcing of decision tree classification to the cloud and designing our tailored protocol from the ground up to enable such outsourcing. With our design, the provider (e.g., a medical institution) and the client (e.g., a patient) are endowed with the opportunity to enjoy the benefits of cloud computing without compromising privacy. They can also both stay *offline* after supplying their respective inputs to the cloud, which is a highly desirable property for practical service deployment. In addition, as will be shown by our evaluation (Sect. 5), our new outsourcing design also brings substantial performance improvement for the client. For example, compared with one state-of-the-art design [20] (ESORICS'17), our design brings the client at least four orders of magnitude improvement in computation and 163× improvement in communication. We emphasize that prior designs are *specialized* for the conceptually different client-provider setting and do not imply simple extensions to work under an outsourcing setting, due to the special structure of decision trees and the complex computation in decision tree classification.

Secure Evaluation of Other Models. Our research is also related to a line of works on secure evaluation of other machine learning models (e.g., [4, 11, 14, 16], to just list a few) such as hyperplane decision [4], Naïve Bayes [4], neural networks [11, 14, 16]. Most previous works operate under the client-provider setting. As different kinds of classifiers require different specific computation, the common blueprint in these works is to build security protocols tailored for different models, using different kinds of cryptographic techniques. For example, Liu *et al.* [14] leverage secret sharing and garbled circuits for secure neural network evaluation; Juvekar *et al.* [11] uniquely combine homomorphic encryption and garbled circuits for low latency secure neural network inference. In addition to the above works, a recent system called SecureML [16] also supports secure evaluation of some machine learning models. The SecureML system also operates under the two-server model, and provides protocols specialized for linear regression, logistic regression, and neural networks [16]. Our design works under the

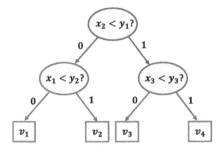

Fig. 1. Illustration of a decision tree.

similar two-server model and newly explore secure and efficient decision tree classification outsourcing.

3   Problem Statement

3.1   Background on Decision Trees

Decision trees is one of the most popular machine learning models used in practice for data classification. As illustrated in Fig. 1, a decision tree consists of internal nodes, called *decision nodes*, and leaf nodes. Each decision node is associated with a specific constant called *threshold*, and each leaf node is associated with a classification value indicating the classification result. So, a decision tree has a threshold vector, and we represent it as $\mathbf{y} = \{y_1, \cdots, y_m\}$, where m denotes the number of decision nodes. With an n-dimensional feature vector $\mathbf{x} = \{x_1, \cdots, x_n\}$ as input, decision tree classification proceeds as follows. Firstly, for each decision node j, a feature $x_{\sigma(j)}$ is *selected* from $\mathbf{x}$ for comparison with the corresponding threshold y_j, according to a mapping $\sigma : j \in \{1, 2, \cdots, m\} \to i \in \{1, 2, \cdots, n\}$ for input selection. Then, starting from the root node, for the current decision node j, the feature $x_{\sigma(j)}$ and threshold y_j is compared. The comparison result b_j ($b_j = \mathbf{1}\{x_{\sigma(j)} < y_j\}$) decides which branch (either left w.r.t. $b_j = 0$ or right w.r.t. $b_j = 1$) to be taken next. This procedure is repeated until a leaf node k with classification value v_k is reached. The length of the longest path between the root node and a leaf node decides the tree depth d. Without loss of generality and as in prior works [7,20,21,24], we assume complete binary decision trees in our security design. This is because the evaluation of non-complete trees might cause leakage of the tree structure [21,24]. Note that a complete binary tree with depth d would have $m = 2^d - 1$ decision nodes and 2^d (i.e., $m + 1$) leaf nodes. And non-complete decision trees can be made complete by introducing dummy decision nodes and setting all the leaf nodes in the subtree of a dummy decision node to the same classification value [24].

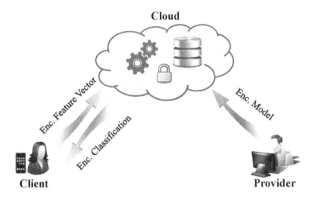

Fig. 2. Our high-level system architecture.

3.2   System Architecture

Our research targets secure and efficient machine learning classification outsourcing based on decision trees. Figure 2 illustrates our system architecture. A provider (e.g., a medical center or a hospital) holds a trained machine learning model, in particular a decision tree in our scenario, and offers classification services via the cloud to the client. The provider chooses to outsource the classification service to the cloud so as to enjoy the benefits of cloud computing such as scalability and ease of management. As the decision tree model is proprietary, the provider would not be willing to place the decision tree in cleartext at the cloud. Therefore, protection for the decision tree model is demanded.

The client holds a feature vector which may encode private information of sensitive attributes (e.g., weight, height, heart rate, and blood pressure) and wants to leverage the cloud-empowered decision tree based classification service to obtain a classification. Due to privacy concerns, the client is not willing to supply the feature vector in cleartext in the service so a ciphertext will be supplied instead. In addition, for practicality, it would not be realistic for the client to promise always staying online to actively participate in the service. For example, the client may be in mobile environments, facing challenges such as resource constraints, network dynamics, and connectivity. So, our system should allow the client to stay offline after providing the ciphertext of the feature vector to the cloud, and later just retrieve the encrypted classification result.

In our system, we consider that the power of the cloud is supplied by two cloud servers $\mathcal{C}_0$ and $\mathcal{C}_1$ which are hosted by independent cloud service providers. The two cloud servers will collaboratively perform secure decision tree evaluation. We are aware that such a two-server model has gained increasing popularity in recent years for facilitating security designs for specific applications [16–18,23]. Our adoption also follows this trend. To our best knowledge, secure and efficient decision tree based classification outsourcing under the two-server model has not been explored before, and requires *specialized* treatment due to the special structure of decision trees and complex computation in decision tree classification.

In our system, for the sake of assuring both privacy and efficiency, we will employ the lightweight cryptographic technique — additive secret sharing, to encrypt the client's feature vector and the provider's decision tree. That is, the client splits the feature vector into two secret shares, each of which will be given to a cloud server. The provider's decision tree is also *specially* encrypted via additive secret sharing and deployed at the cloud in advance for use. Upon receiving the secret shares of the client's feature vector, the two cloud servers will run a tailored secure protocol and produce the encrypted classification result, which can be sent to the client for decryption on demand.

3.3   Threat Model

We consider that the threats are primarily from the engagement of the cloud in the service. Similar to most of prior works under the two-server model (e.g., [6,8,16,27,28], to just list a few), we assume a semi-honest and non-colluding adversary model in our security design. That is, the two cloud servers will faithfully follow our protocol, yet are interested in inferring private information about the client's feature vector and the provider's decision tree and will do so independently. Such a threat assumption is based on the practical intuition that cloud service providers are typically from well-established companies like Amazon and Google, so they have little incentives to put the reputation at risk. Other rationale may include the existence of audits and the fear of legal/financial repercussion. We also remark that although weaker than a malicious adversary model, a semi-honest model allows for much more efficient protocols in practice [2].

Consistent with prior works [12,20,24], we consider that the client wishes to keep private the values $\{x_i\}_{i=1}^n$ in her feature vector $\mathbf{x}$ as well as the classification result (i.e., the classification value v_k corresponding to $\mathbf{x}$). On the provider side, we consider that the provider wishes to keep private against the cloud the proprietary threshold values $\mathbf{y}$ of the decision nodes, the mapping σ for input selection, and the classification value associated with each leaf node throughout the protocol execution. Meanwhile, the provider may also require that per classification query the client should learn no additional private information about the decision tree other than the classification value corresponding to her feature vector. As in prior works [20,24], we do not aim to protect the following generic meta-parameters about the decision tree: the depth d of the decision tree, the dimension n of the feature vector, and the number l of bits needed to represent each element in the feature vector and the threshold vector. These parameters are assumed public in our system. Meanwhile, similar to existing works on private machine learning classification, we deem dealing with attacks on machine learning models via exploiting classification results out of the scope of this paper.

4 Design of Secure and Efficient Outsourcing of Decision Tree Based Classification

4.1 Design Overview

At a high level, our custom protocol consists of the following phases: secure input preparation, secure input selection, secure decision node evaluation, secure path evaluation, and secure classification generation. In the secure input preparation phase, the provider sends a *properly* encrypted decision tree to the cloud and the client supplies the encrypted feature vector. In the secure input selection phase, for each decision node, a feature from the encrypted feature vector will be obliviously selected, according to the (encrypted) mapping for input selection. In the secure decision node evaluation phase, a secure comparison is made for each decision node, between the corresponding encrypted threshold and feature. In the secure path evaluation phase, the path to each leaf node is obliviously evaluated, leveraging the encrypted comparison results from the previous phase. In the secure classification generation phase, the encrypted classification result corresponding to the client's feature vector is generated. All the above phases in our design will be instantiated under the lightweight cryptographic technique— additive secret sharing, in a secure and efficient manner. Our tailored protocol is built from the ground up, through careful examination of the decision tree evaluation procedure and unique combination of the additive secret sharing technique with structure-specific computation of decision tree evaluation. In what follows, we describe in detail each phase of our protocol.

4.2 Protocol

Secure Input Preparation. We adopt additive secret sharing for fast encryption of the client's feature vector and the provider's decision tree. In particular, given the feature vector $\mathbf{x} = \{x_i\}_{i=1}^n$, the client first generates a vector $\mathbf{r}$ of random values, which has the same size as $\mathbf{x}$. Here, each value in $\mathbf{r}$ is random in the ring $\mathbb{Z}_{2^l}$, where l is a parameter that determines the size of $\mathbb{Z}_{2^l}$. Then, the client produces the ciphertext of the feature vector as $[\mathbf{x}]_0 = \{(x_i - r_i) \bmod 2^l\}_{i=1}^n$ and $[\mathbf{x}]_1 = \{r_i \bmod 2^l\}_{i=1}^n$. Here, $[\mathbf{x}]_\alpha$ represents the share to be sent to the cloud server $\mathcal{C}_\alpha$ ($\alpha \in \{0, 1\}$). Note that in an element-wise manner we have $\mathbf{x} = ([\mathbf{x}]_0 + [\mathbf{x}]_1) \bmod 2^l$. Similarly, the provider generates the ciphertexts $[\mathbf{y}]_0$ and $[\mathbf{y}]_1$ for the threshold vector $\mathbf{y}$. As for the classification values $\mathbf{v}$ associated with the leaf nodes, the provider generates ciphertexts $[\![\mathbf{v}]\!]_0$ and $[\![\mathbf{v}]\!]_1$ over $\mathbb{Z}_p$ (p is a prime), which will be used in secure classification generation shown later. In addition, recall that the provider also has a mapping $\sigma : j \in \{1, 2, \cdots, m\} \rightarrow i \in \{1, 2, \cdots, n\}$ for input selection for the decision tree, which demands protection as well.

The challenge here is how to encrypt the mapping σ so that it can be hidden from the cloud servers while still functioning well in the subsequent secure input selection phase. To tackle this challenge, the key idea is to represent the mapping σ as an input selection matrix $\mathbf{M}$, and then encrypt this matrix via additive secret sharing. Here, the input selection matrix $\mathbf{M}$ has a size $m \times n$. Each row vector $\mathbf{w}_j$ of $\mathbf{M}$ is a binary vector with n elements where all are 0 except for the element at the position $\sigma(j)$ set to 1. It is easy to see that $x_{\sigma(j)} = \mathbf{w}_j \mathbf{x}$. With $\mathbf{M}$, the provider generates the secret shares $[\mathbf{M}]_0$ and $[\mathbf{M}]_1$. Finally, the secret shares of $\mathbf{y}$, $\mathbf{v}$, and $\mathbf{M}$ are sent to each cloud server accordingly.

Input: Shares $[\mathbf{M}]$ and $[\mathbf{x}]$.
Output: Shares $[\mathbf{x}_\sigma] = [\mathbf{M} \cdot \mathbf{x}]$.

1: $\mathcal{C}_\alpha$ computes $[\mathbf{E}]_\alpha = [\mathbf{M}]_\alpha - [\mathbf{U}]_\alpha$ and $[\mathbf{f}]_\alpha = [\mathbf{x}]_\alpha - [\mathbf{g}]_\alpha$.
2: $\mathcal{C}_0$ and $\mathcal{C}_1$ jointly reconstruct $\mathbf{E}$ and $\mathbf{f}$.
3: $\mathcal{C}_\alpha$ computes $[\mathbf{M} \cdot \mathbf{x}]_\alpha = \alpha \cdot \mathbf{E} \cdot \mathbf{f} + \mathbf{E} \cdot [\mathbf{g}]_\alpha + \cdot [\mathbf{U}]_\alpha \cdot \mathbf{f} + [\mathbf{z}]_\alpha$.

Fig. 3. Secure input selection.

Secure Input Selection. Given the secret shares of the client's feature vector and the provider's decision tree, we now describe how to perform secure input selection. In this phase, the result is that each cloud server obtains a secret share of the feature corresponding to each decision node, while being oblivious to which feature is selected from the feature vector. Hereafter, all arithmetic operations related with secret shares take place in $\mathbb{Z}_{2^l}$, unless otherwise stated. So, for ease of presentation, we will omit the modulo operation in our design.

Below we first introduce in detail how to support atomic operations (i.e., addition/subtraction and multiplication) under additive secret sharing. Suppose that each cloud server holds a secret share of the values a_1 and a_2. Then, the secret sharing $[a_1 + a_2]$ (resp. $[a_1 - a_2]$) of the addition $a_1 + a_2$ (resp. subtraction $a_1 - a_2$) can be computed by each cloud server locally, i.e., $[a_1 + a_2]_\alpha = [a_1]_\alpha + [a_2]_\alpha$ (resp. $[a_1 - a_2]_\alpha = [a_1]_\alpha - [a_2]_\alpha$). For multiplication by a constant c on the value a_1, each cloud server $\mathcal{C}_\alpha$ can simply compute $[a_1 \cdot c]_\alpha = c \cdot [a_1]_\alpha$.

As for multiplication of secret-shared inputs, we note that the Beaver's multiplication triple trick [3] can be adopted. Suppose that there is a multiplication triple (u, g, z) satisfying $z = u \cdot g$ and is secret-shared between the two cloud servers. To obtain the secret sharing $[a_1 \cdot a_2]$, each cloud server $\mathcal{C}_\alpha$ first locally computes $[e]_\alpha = [a_1]_\alpha - [u]_\alpha$ and $[f]_\alpha = [a_2]_\alpha - [g]_\alpha$. Then, each cloud server broadcasts $[e]_\alpha$ and $[f]_\alpha$, and subsequently reconstructs e and f. With e and f, each cloud server $\mathcal{C}_\alpha$ now produces a secret share $[a_1 \cdot a_2]_\alpha$ via computing $[a_1 \cdot a_2]_\alpha = \alpha \cdot e \cdot f + e \cdot [g]_\alpha + f \cdot [u]_\alpha + [z]_\alpha$. For correctness proof, we refer the readers to [3] for details. The security of the Beaver's trick ensures that each cloud server learns nothing about the underlying plaintext values a_1 and a_2 from the protocol execution. Note that the multiplication triples are data independent, so they can be efficiently made available to the two cloud servers in an *offline* phase, e.g., via an additional semi-honest third party [19]. So, throughout this paper, we assume that the multiplication triples are available at the cloud side for use and focus on the online secure decision tree evaluation procedure.

With the above secure atomic operations, we now describe how to perform secure input selection. Recall that according to our construction for the input selection matrix in the previous phase, we have $\mathbf{x}_\sigma = \mathbf{M} \cdot \mathbf{x}$. So, given that each cloud server $\mathcal{C}_\alpha$ holds a secret share of the feature vector $\mathbf{x}$ and the input selection matrix $\mathbf{M}$, what we need here is secure multiplication which takes as input the secret sharing $[\mathbf{x}]$ and $[\mathbf{M}]$, and produces the secret sharing $[\mathbf{M} \cdot \mathbf{x}]$.

Here, for better efficiency, we adapt the Beaver's trick and work under a vectorized setting, inspired by some recent works [14,16]. In particular, the multiplication triple is now in a vectorized form, say $(\mathbf{U}, \mathbf{g}, \mathbf{z})$, which satisfies $\mathbf{z} = \mathbf{U} \cdot \mathbf{g}$ and is secret-shared between the two cloud servers. Then, as shown in Fig. 3, we can compute the secret sharing $[\mathbf{M} \cdot \mathbf{x}]$ as follows. Firstly, each cloud server $\mathcal{C}_\alpha$ computes $[\mathbf{E}]_\alpha = [\mathbf{M}]_\alpha - [\mathbf{U}]_\alpha$ and $[\mathbf{f}]_\alpha = [\mathbf{x}]_\alpha - [\mathbf{g}]_\alpha$. Then, each cloud server broadcasts $[\mathbf{E}]_\alpha$ and $[\mathbf{f}]_\alpha$, and subsequently reconstructs $\mathbf{E}$ and $\mathbf{f}$. With the reconstructed $\mathbf{E}$ and $\mathbf{f}$, each cloud server $\mathcal{C}_\alpha$ now produces a secret share $[\mathbf{M} \cdot \mathbf{x}]_\alpha$ via computing $[\mathbf{M} \cdot \mathbf{x}]_\alpha = \alpha \cdot \mathbf{E} \cdot \mathbf{f} + \mathbf{E} \cdot [\mathbf{g}]_\alpha + [\mathbf{U}]_\alpha \cdot \mathbf{f} + [\mathbf{z}]_\alpha$. Note that working under a vectorized setting does not affect the security of the Beaver's trick. That is, the plaintext values in $\mathbf{M}$ and $\mathbf{x}$ are still kept confidential.

Input: Shares $[y_j]$ and $[x_{\sigma(j)}]$.
Output: Shares $[\![b_j]\!]$ over $\mathbb{Z}_p$.

1: $\mathcal{C}_\alpha$ computes $[a]_\alpha = [y_j]_\alpha - [x_{\sigma(j)}]_\alpha$.
   // Bit extraction ($\langle \cdot \rangle$ denotes sharing over $\mathbb{Z}_2$)
2: Let p denote $\mathcal{C}_0$'s share $[a]_0$, with the bit string being $p_l, \cdots, p_1$.
   Let q denote $\mathcal{C}_1$'s share $[a]_1$, with the bit string being $q_l, \cdots, q_1$.
   Define the secret sharing $\langle w_k \rangle$ over $\mathbb{Z}_2$ as $\{\langle w_k \rangle_0 = p_k, \langle w_k \rangle_1 = q_k\}$. Also, define $\langle p_k \rangle$ as $(\langle p_k \rangle_0 = p_k, \langle p_k \rangle_1 = 0)$ and $\langle q_k \rangle$ as $\{\langle q_k \rangle_0 = 0, \langle q_k \rangle_1 = q_k\}$.
3: $\mathcal{C}_0$ and $\mathcal{C}_1$ compute $\langle c_1 \rangle = \langle p_1 \rangle \cdot \langle q_1 \rangle$.
4: For $k \in [2, \cdots, l-1]$,
   (a) $\mathcal{C}_0$ and $\mathcal{C}_1$ compute $\langle d_k \rangle = \langle p_k \rangle \cdot \langle q_k \rangle + 1$.
   (b) $\mathcal{C}_0$ and $\mathcal{C}_1$ compute $\langle e_k \rangle = \langle w_k \rangle \cdot \langle c_{k-1} \rangle + 1$.
   (c) $\mathcal{C}_0$ and $\mathcal{C}_1$ compute $\langle c_k \rangle = \langle e_k \rangle \cdot \langle d_k \rangle + 1$.
5: $\mathcal{C}_0$ and $\mathcal{C}_1$ compute $\langle a_l \rangle = \langle w_l \rangle + \langle c_{l-1} \rangle$, with $\langle a_l \rangle$ defined as $\{\langle a_l \rangle_0 = t_1, \langle a_l \rangle_1 = t_2\}$.
   // Conversion from $\mathbb{Z}_2$ to $\mathbb{Z}_p$
6: Let $[\![t_1]\!]$ over $\mathbb{Z}_p$ be defined as $\{[\![t_1]\!]_0 = t_1, [\![t_1]\!]_1 = 0\}$ and $[\![t_2]\!]$ as $\{[\![t_2]\!]_0 = 0, [\![t_2]\!]_1 = t_2\}$.
7: $\mathcal{C}_0$ and $\mathcal{C}_1$ compute $[\![a_l]\!] = [\![t_1]\!] + [\![t_2]\!] - 2 \cdot [\![t_1]\!] \cdot [\![t_2]\!]$.
8: Output $[\![b_j]\!] = [\![a_l]\!]$.

Fig. 4. Secure decision node evaluation (for each decision node j).

Secure Decision Node Evaluation. For each decision node j, given the secret shares of the threshold y_j and the corresponding feature $x_{\sigma(j)}$, a secure comparison needs to be conducted. The result from this phase is that for each decision node j, the two cloud servers obtain the secret sharing of the comparison result b_j. So, here we need to consider how to directly perform efficient and secure comparison over the secret-shared threshold and feature. As mentioned before, prior art requires bitwise encryption of inputs for secure decision node evaluation from the very beginning, so they cannot be extended to work in our scenario and we need to design from the ground up.

We propose to transform the in-the-cloud secure decision node evaluation problem into a simpler bit extraction problem. Our observation is that as long as a large l is used (say typically $l = 64$ [29]), the non-negative values and negative values can be distinctly separate in the lower half ($[0, 2^{l-1} - 1]$) and upper half ($[2^{l-1}, 2^l - 1]$) of the values in the ring $\mathbb{Z}_{2^l}$. So, the most significant bit (MSB) of non-negative values over $\mathbb{Z}_{2^l}$ will be 0 and be 1 of negative values. Based on this important observation, we can first compute the subtraction $a = y_j - x_{\sigma(j)}$ (over $\mathbb{Z}_{2^l}$) and then extract the MSB a_l of a, as the comparison result b_j.

To instantiate this idea in the secret sharing domain, we first need to get the secret sharing $[a] = [y_j - x_{\sigma(j)}]$, which can be easily computed by the two cloud servers locally, given $[y_j]$ and $[x_{\sigma(j)}]$. Then, to obtain the secret sharing of the comparison result b_j, our idea is to employ a bit extraction protocol which can extract the secret sharing of the MSB of a. Our starting point is the protocol in [7], which can take as input the secret sharing $[y_j - x_{\sigma j}]$ and produces a certain secret sharing of the MSB a_l (i.e., b_j).

However, simply adopting this protocol does not facilitate subsequent computation in our design, as the produced secret sharing for a_l is over $\mathbb{Z}_2$, denoted as $\langle a_l \rangle$. Therefore, we need to consider how to convert the secret sharing $\langle a_l \rangle$ over $\mathbb{Z}_2$ to $[\![a_l]\!]$ over $\mathbb{Z}_p$, where p is a sufficiently large prime. Here, the reason that we convert to $\mathbb{Z}_p$ is that we need to perform multiplicative masking later in the secure classification phase, so we need to work over a field [22]. More details will be given later on. Let $\langle a_l \rangle : \{\langle a_l \rangle_0 = t_1, \langle a_l \rangle_1 = t_2\}$ be a valid additive sharing over $\mathbb{Z}_2$. We observe that the value a_l (0 or 1) over $\mathbb{Z}_p$ can be expressed through $a_l = t_1 + t_2 - 2 * t_1 * t_2$ of which the computation is over $\mathbb{Z}_p$. So, if we can compute the secret sharing $[\![t_1 + t_2 - 2 * t_1 * t_2]\!]$ over $\mathbb{Z}_p$, we will get the secret sharing $[\![a_l]\!]$ over $\mathbb{Z}_p$. Let $[\![t_1]\!]$ be defined as $\{[\![t_1]\!]_0 = t_1, [\![t_1]\!]_1 = 0\}$ and $[\![t_2]\!]$ as $\{[\![t_2]\!]_0 = 0, [\![t_2]\!]_1 = t_2\}$. Then, given $[\![t_1]\!]$ and $[\![t_2]\!]$, it is easy to compute the secret sharing $[\![b_j]\!] = [\![a_l]\!] = [\![t_1 + t_2 - 2 * t_1 * t_2]\!]$, just through secure addition/subtraction and multiplication. The details of secure decision node evaluation are given in Fig. 4.

Secure Path Evaluation. In this phase, the path to each leaf node is obliviously evaluated based on the encrypted comparison result at each decision node from the previous phase. Recall that we have managed to obtain the secret sharing $[\![b_j]\!]$ of the comparison result at each decision node j. To utilize the encrypted comparison results for path evaluation, we leverage the state-of-the-art path cost mechanism [20], which deals with linear functions and only needs secure addition. In comparison with [20] which relies on homomorphic encryption, we newly realize the path cost mechanism in the additive secret sharing to enable secure path evaluation in our outsourcing design.

At a high level, this mechanism first computes a path cost for each leaf node, which has a unique path in the decision tree, based on the comparison results at decision nodes. The path cost of a leaf node can then be used to determine whether that leaf node carries the classification result. Specifically, the path cost mechanism is as follows. Firstly, it is noted that each decision node is associated with two outgoing edges. According to [20], for each decision node, we can assign a cost to the left edge as $ec_{j,0} = b_j$, and a cost to the right edge as $ec_{j,1} = 1 - b_j$, respectively. In this way, all the edges in the decision tree has a cost value. Then, the path cost pc_k for each leaf node k is defined by the sum of all the edge costs along that path. A classification value v_k is the classification result if and only if its associated path cost pc_k is 0. For more details about the concept and correctness of path cost, we refer the readers to [20].

Input: Shares $[\![b_j]\!]$ for each decision node j.
Output: Shares $[\![pc_k]\!]$ for each leaf node k.

1: For each decision node j,
  (a) $\mathcal{C}_\alpha$ sets $[\![ec_{j,0}]\!]_\alpha = [\![b_j]\!]_\alpha$ as the secret-shared left edge cost.
  (b) $\mathcal{C}_0$ sets $[\![ec_{j,1}]\!]_0 = 1 - [\![b_j]\!]_0$ and $\mathcal{C}_1$ sets $[\![ec_{j,1}]\!]_1 = [\![b_j]\!]_1$, where $[\![ec_{j,1}]\!]$ is the secret-shared right edge cost.
2: For each leaf node k, the secret-shared path cost $[\![pc_k]\!]$ is computed by summing up each edge cost $[\![ec]\!]$ along that path.

Fig. 5. Secure path evaluation.

With the path mechanism, as shown in Fig. 5, the secure path evaluation in our design works as follows. Firstly, the secret sharings of the left edge cost and right edge cost are computed. For each decision node j, the two cloud servers set the secret sharing $[\![ec_{j,0}]\!]$ of the left edge cost $ec_{j,0}$ to $[\![b_j]\!]$. For the secret sharing $[\![ec_{j,1}]\!]$ of the right edge cost $ec_{j,1}$, the cloud server $\mathcal{C}_0$ sets $[\![ec_{j,1}]\!]_0 = 1 - [\![b_j]\!]_0$ and $\mathcal{C}_1$ sets $[\![ec_{j,1}]\!]_1 = [\![b_j]\!]_1$. After that, for each leaf node k, the secret sharing $[\![pc_k]\!]$ of the path cost is computed by summing up each secret-shared edge cost $[\![ec]\!]$ along that path, which can be easily done by each cloud server locally.

Secure Classification Generation. From the previous phase, we have obtained the secret sharing of the path cost for each leaf node. We now describe how to leverage the secret-shared path costs to generate ciphertexts from which the client is able to derive the classification result.

At a high level, we first apply random masking at the cloud side to the path cost and the classification values in the secret sharing domain, with $[\![r_k \cdot pc_k]\!]$

and $[\![r'_k \cdot pc_k + v_k]\!]$ produced for each leaf node, where r_k and r'_k are random values from $\mathbb{Z}_p^*$. Later, the client reconstructs the randomized path costs and classification values, and extracts the correct classification result by checking which received path cost is equal to zero. The classification value associated with the 0 path cost is then the correct classification result. Otherwise, the client only sees random values. Note that the multiplicative masking applied on the path costs is to randomize the exact values of those non-zero path costs from the client. For this to effectively work, it is crucial that we work over a field such as $\mathbb{Z}_p$ [22]. This accounts for why we convert the encrypted comparison result to $\mathbb{Z}_p$ in the above secure decision node evaluation phase, as we need to leverage them to compute secret-shared path costs over $\mathbb{Z}_p$ for use in secure classification generation.

In more detail, as shown in Fig. 6, the secure classification generation phase works as follows. For each leaf node k, the cloud server $\mathcal{C}_0$ generates two random values r_k and r'_k from $\mathbb{Z}_p^*$. Then, $\mathcal{C}_0$ computes $[\![pc_k^*]\!]_0 = [\![r_k \cdot pc_k]\!]_0 = r_k \cdot [\![pc_k]\!]_0$ and $[\![v_k^*]\!]_0 = [\![r'_k \cdot pc_k + v_k]\!]_0 = r'_k \cdot [\![pc_k]\!]_0 + [\![v_k]\!]_0$. Next, $\mathcal{C}_0$ applies a random permutation π over $\{1, \cdots, K\}$ to $\{[\![pc_k^*]\!]_0\}_{k=1}^K$ and $\{[\![v_k^*]\!]_0\}_{k=1}^K$, and obtains $\{[\![pc_{\pi(k)}^*]\!]_0\}_{k=1}^K$ and $\{[\![v_{\pi(k)}^*]\!]_0\}_{k=1}^K$. Here, K is the number of leaf nodes. The random masks r_k and r'_k and the permutation π are shared with the cloud server $\mathcal{C}_1$. Then, the cloud server $\mathcal{C}_1$ first computes $[\![pc_k^*]\!]_1 = [\![r_k \cdot pc_k]\!]_1 = r_k \cdot [\![pc_k]\!]_1$ and $[\![v_k^*]\!]_1 = [\![r'_k \cdot pc_k + v_k]\!]_1 = r'_k \cdot [\![pc_k]\!]_1 + [\![v_k]\!]_1$. The same random permutation is applied to the resulting shares. So, the cloud server $\mathcal{C}_1$ produces $\{[\![pc_{\pi(k)}^*]\!]_1\}_{k=1}^K$

Input: Shares $[\![pc_k]\!]$ and $[\![v_k]\!]$ for each leaf node k.
Output: Classification result.

1: $\mathcal{C}_0$ computes $[\![pc_k^*]\!]_0 = [\![r_k \cdot pc_k]\!]_0 = r_k \cdot [\![pc_k]\!]_0$ and $[\![v_k^*]\!]_0 = [\![r'_k \cdot pc_k + v_k]\!]_0 = r'_k \cdot [\![pc_k]\!]_0 + [\![v_k]\!]_0$.
2: $\mathcal{C}_0$ applies a random permutation π to the above shares, and obtains $\{[\![pc_{\pi(k)}^*]\!]_0\}_{k=1}^K$ and $\{[\![v_{\pi(k)}^*]\!]_0\}_{k=1}^K$.
3: $\mathcal{C}_1$ computes $[\![pc_k^*]\!]_1 = [\![r_k \cdot pc_k]\!]_1 = r_k \cdot [\![pc_k]\!]_1$ and $[\![v_k^*]\!]_1 = [\![r'_k \cdot pc_k + v_k]\!]_1 = r'_k \cdot [\![pc_k]\!]_1 + [\![v_k]\!]_1$.
4: $\mathcal{C}_1$ applies the same random permutation and produces $\{[\![pc_{\pi(k)}^*]\!]_1\}_{k=1}^K$ and $\{[\![v_{\pi(k)}^*]\!]_1\}_{k=1}^K$.
5: Client receives the secret sharings $\{[\![pc_{\pi(k)}^*]\!]\}_{k=1}^K$ and $\{[\![v_{\pi(k)}^*]\!]\}_{k=1}^K$, and reconstructs $\{pc_{\pi(k)}^*\}_{k=1}^K$ and $\{v_{\pi(k)}^*\}_{k=1}^K$.
6: Checking that a $pc_{\pi(k)}^*$ is 0, client outputs $v_{\pi(k)}^*$ as the classification result.

Fig. 6. Secure classification generation.

and $\{[\![v^*_{\pi(k)}]\!]_1\}^K_{k=1}$. Upon receiving the request for the classification result, each cloud server $\mathcal{C}_\alpha$ sends the shares $\{[\![pc^*_{\pi(k)}]\!]_\alpha\}^K_{k=1}$ and $\{[\![v^*_{\pi(k)}]\!]_\alpha\}^K_{k=1}$ to the client. The client combines the shares to reconstruct the randomized path costs $\{pc^*_{\pi(k)}\}^K_{k=1}$ and randomized classification values $\{v^*_{\pi(k)}\}^K_{k=1}$. The client checks that a particular $pc^*_{\pi(k)}$ is 0 and outputs $v^*_{\pi(k)}$ is the classification result.

4.3 Security Guarantees

Theorem 1. *Our design guarantees that each cloud server learns no private information about the client's feature vector and the provider's decision tree, given the security of additive secret sharing, Beaver's triple trick, and multiplicative masking, and the semi-honest non-colluding assumption. Besides, our design ensures that the client learns no additional private information about the decision tree other than the classification result.*

Proof. We give some sketches here. Firstly, we analyze the security against the cloud servers. In the beginning, the two cloud servers receive respective secret shares of the client's feature vector and the provider's decision tree. The security of additive secret sharing ensures that each cloud server learns nothing about the plaintext values underlying its shares. During protocol execution, the two cloud servers operate over their respective secret shares locally and have some interactions when necessary. The interactions, always with secret-shared values produced, are either for secure multiplication under the Beaver's triple trick (in the secure input selection phase and secure decision node evaluation phase), or for sharing the random masks and random permutation (in the secure classification generation phase). In a nutshell, each cloud server's view of the protocol execution is just random values, so the privacy of the provider's decision tree and the client's feature vector follows.

Table 1. Computation performance of the provider (in ms).

Provider Operation	d = 3, n = 13	d = 4, n = 15	d = 8, n = 9	d = 13, n = 13	d = 17, n = 57
Node Encryption	0.0013	0.002	0.03	0.8791	14.129
Selection Matrix Encryption	0.0131	0.0254	0.2686	13.9693	871.658
Total	0.0144	0.0274	0.2986	14.8484	885.787

As for the security against the client, the client's view of the protocol execution consists of random non-zero numbers, and one zero path cost associated with one classification value. Recall that according to the computation correctness of path costs, there is only one 0 path cost, which corresponds to the classification result. All other path costs are non-zero numbers. Therefore, after the random masking, only the path cost corresponding to the classification result will remain as 0, and the other non-zero path costs are random (non-zero) numbers. Similarly, all randomized classification values except the one associated with the 0 path cost are random numbers. As the masked path costs and classification values are randomly shuffled, the true position of the classification result in the decision tree is also concealed. So, from received randomized path costs and classification values, the client only learns the classification result corresponding to his feature vector.

5   Experiments

5.1   Setup

We implement and empirically evaluate our protocol to demonstrate the practicality. The implementation is in C++, with GNU GMP library used for big number manipulation and Eigen library for matrix operations. We compiled the code with Clang 10.0 and optimization level O3. All experiments are run on a Macbook Pro with 2.6 GHz i7 CPU and 32 GB memory. In our experiments, we use synthetic decision trees with realistic problem sizes that could arise in practice, following prior works [20,24]. In particular, the depth d of a decision tree ranges from 3 to 17, and the number n of features ranges from 9 to 57.

Table 2. Computation performance of the client (in ms).

Client Operation	$d = 3$, $n = 13$	$d = 4$, $n = 15$	$d = 8$, $n = 9$	$d = 13$, $n = 13$	$d = 17$, $n = 57$
Feature Vector Encryption	0.0018	0.0021	0.0017	0.0018	0.0065
Sec. Classification Generation	0.0018	0.0034	0.0504	1.567	25.3779
Total	0.0036	0.0055	0.0521	1.5688	25.3844

5.2   Evaluation

We first examine the computation cost at the provider, the client, and the cloud, respectively. Recall that the provider only needs to have *one-off* encryption of the decision model in the very beginning, which includes the encryption of the values at decision nodes and leaf nodes, as well as the encryption of the input selection matrix. Table 1 shows the computation performance of the provider with varying realistic combinations of the decision tree depth d and the number of features n, as in prior work. As seen, the one-off computation cost of the provider is quite small. Even for our largest tested decision tree ($d = 17$ and $n = 57$), the one-off computation cost of the provider is less than 1 s.

The client's computation cost is due to the encryption of the feature vector, and the extraction of the classification result from the randomized path costs and classification values. Table 2 reports the computation performance of the client. It can be seen that the computation cost is dominated by the component of secure classification generation. In most cases ($d \leq 13$), the cost is below 2 ms; whereas even for the largest decision tree setting ($d = 17$ and thus 131071 decision nodes), it is below 26 ms, which is highly efficient. We emphasize that our design has the distinct advantage that the client can be offline after supplying the encrypted feature vector, which is a highly desirable property for realistic service deployment, especially in mobile environments. Besides, compared with state-of-the-art designs under the client-provider setting, our secure outsourcing design brings substantial computational saving for the client. For example, the design in [20] already takes about 10 s at the client even for the much smaller problem size of 2000 decision nodes; and the design in [21] requires roughly 3 s for a decision tree with $d = 14$. So, with $d = 17$ (131071 decision nodes) in our test, our design outperforms the design [20] by at least four orders of magnitude, and the design [21] by at least 118×.

Lastly, we evaluate the computation cost at the cloud side. Table 3 gives the computation cost at the cloud side (the sum of two cloud servers' computation costs), including the costs of secure input selection, secure decision node evaluation, secure path evaluation, and secure classification generation. Overall, the computation for secure decision tree evaluation at the cloud side is quite efficient, ranging from 0.3034 ms to 14.6396 s.

We now examine the communication performance. Table 4 shows the communication cost of the provider. The provider's communication cost is due to the secret shares of the decision model, which includes the secret shares of the threshold values at decision nodes, classification values at leaf nodes, and the input selection matrix. According to Table 4, the communication cost is dominated by the shares of the selection matrix. For most cases ($d \leq 13$), the communication cost is less than 2 MB. For the largest decision tree in our test, the *one-off* communication cost is about 118 MB.

Table 3. Computation performance at the cloud side (in ms).

Cloud Operation	$d = 3$, $n = 13$	$d = 4$, $n = 15$	$d = 8$, $n = 9$	$d = 13$, $n = 13$	$d = 17$, $n = 57$
Sec. Input Selection	0.2172	0.5141	4.9688	200.836	13054.443
Sec. Decision Node Evaluation	0.0794	0.1726	2.9603	98.6439	1482.1668
Sec. Path Evaluation	0.0022	0.0062	0.1093	3.4813	59.5199
Sec. Classification Generation	0.0046	0.007	0.0672	2.2878	43.4859
Total	0.3034	0.6999	8.1056	305.249	14639.6156

Table 4. Communication performance of the provider (in KB).

Component	$d = 3$, $n = 13$	$d = 4$, $n = 15$	$d = 8$, $n = 9$	$d = 13$, $n = 13$	$d = 17$, $n = 57$
Node Shares	0.23	0.48	7.98	255.98	4095.98
Selection Matrix Shares	1.42	3.52	35.86	1663.8	116735.11
Total	1.65	4	43.84	1919.78	120831.09

The client's communication cost, as shown in Table 5, is from the upload of the secret shares of the feature vector in the beginning, and the download of the secret shares of the randomized path costs and classification values in secure classification generation. The communication cost is dominated by the download of shares. As seen from Table 5, the communication cost of the client in our outsourcing design is fully practical, ranging from 0.45 KB with $d = 3$ to 4 MB with $d = 17$ (131071 decision nodes). In comparison, we note that the state-of-the-art design [20] working under the client-provider setting already requires more than 10 MB for just 2000 decision nodes (thus roughly 655 MB would be required for 131071 decision nodes and thus 163× less efficient), and the design [21] requires about 2 MB for a decision tree with $d = 14$ (4× less efficient compared to about 512 KB for $d = 14$ in our design).

We also report the communication cost at the cloud side, i.e., the amount of data exchanged between the two cloud servers for secure decision tree classification. The communication cost at the cloud side is mainly due to the call of secure multiplication of secret-shared values in secure input selection and secure decision node evaluation, and the sharing of the random masks and random permutation in secure classification generation. Table 6 summarizes the cloud side communication cost in different phases of secure decision tree evaluation. In most cases, the communication cost is less than 3 MB. Even for the largest decision tree, it only requires 132.6249 MB, which is practically affordable at the resource-rich cloud.

Table 5. Communication performance of the client (in KB).

Component	$d = 3$, $n = 13$	$d = 4$, $n = 15$	$d = 8$, $n = 9$	$d = 13$, $n = 13$	$d = 17$, $n = 57$
Feature Vector Shares	0.2	0.23	0.14	0.2	0.89
Classification Result Shares	0.25	0.5	8	256	4096
Total	0.45	0.73	8.14	256.2	4096.89

Table 6. Communication performance at the cloud side (in MB).

Operation	$d = 3$, $n = 13$	$d = 4$, $n = 15$	$d = 8$, $n = 9$	$d = 13$, $n = 13$	$d = 17$, $n = 57$
Sec. Input Selection	0.0016	0.0037	0.0352	1.625	114
Sec. Decision Node Evaluation	0.0008	0.0018	0.0304	0.9764	15.6249
Sec. Classification Generation	0.0002	0.0004	0.0059	0.1875	3
Total	0.0026	0.0058	0.0715	2.7889	132.6249

6   Conclusion

In this paper, we proposed the first framework for secure and efficient machine learning classification outsourcing based on decision trees. Our design allows a provider to leverage the power of the cloud to deliver secure and efficient decision tree based classification service to the client. As we manage to delicately shift the processing to the cloud side, neither the provider nor the client needs to stay online for active participation in the service. Our design operates under the increasingly popular two-server model and provides the first solution for secure and efficient classification outsourcing based on decision trees. We crafted our design from the ground up, leveraging the lightweight additive secret sharing technique and the problem specifics of decision tree based classification. Our evaluation shows the practical performance of our design, as well as the substantial performance advantage for the client over prior art.

Acknowledgement. This work was supported in part by the Research Grants Council of Hong Kong under Grants CityU 11276816, CityU 11212717, and CityU C1008-16G, by the Innovation and Technology Commission of Hong Kong under ITF Project ITS/168/17, and by the National Natural Science Foundation of China under Grant 61572412.

References

1. Azar, A.T., El-Metwally, S.M.: Decision tree classifiers for automated medical diagnosis. Neural Comput. Appl. **23**(7–8), 2387–2403 (2013)
2. Baldimtsi, F., Papadopoulos, D., Papadopoulos, S., Scafuro, A., Triandopoulos, N.: Server-aided secure computation with off-line parties. In: Foley, S.N., Gollmann, D., Snekkenes, E. (eds.) ESORICS 2017. LNCS, vol. 10492, pp. 103–123. Springer, Cham (2017). https://doi.org/10.1007/978-3-319-66402-6_8
3. Beaver, D.: Efficient multiparty protocols using circuit randomization. In: Feigenbaum, J. (ed.) CRYPTO 1991. LNCS, vol. 576, pp. 420–432. Springer, Heidelberg (1992). https://doi.org/10.1007/3-540-46766-1_34
4. Bost, R., Popa, R.A., Tu, S., Goldwasser, S.: Machine learning classification over encrypted data. In: Proceedings of NDSS (2015)
5. Brakerski, Z., Gentry, C., Vaikuntanathan, V.: (Leveled) fully homomorphic encryption without bootstrapping. In: Proceediongs of ITCS (2012)
6. Cai, C., Zheng, Y., Wang, C.: Leveraging crowdsensed data streams to discover and sell knowledge: a secure and efficient realization. In: Proceedings of IEEE ICDCS (2018)
7. Cock, M.D., et al.: Efficient and private scoring of decision trees, support vector machines and logistic regression models based on pre-computation. IEEE Trans. Dependable Secure Comput. **16**(2), 217–230 (2017). 101109/TDSC20172679189
8. Erkin, Z., Veugen, T., Toft, T., Lagendijk, R.L.: Generating private recommendations efficiently using homomorphic encryption and data packing. IEEE Trans. Inf. Forensics Secur. **7**(3), 1053–1066 (2012)
9. Goldreich, O., Micali, S., Wigderson, A.: How to play any mental game or A completeness theorem for protocols with honest majority. In: Proceedings of ACM STOC (1987)

10. Joye, M., Salehi, F.: Private yet efficient decision tree evaluation. In: Kerschbaum, F., Paraboschi, S. (eds.) DBSec 2018. LNCS, vol. 10980, pp. 243–259. Springer, Cham (2018). https://doi.org/10.1007/978-3-319-95729-6_16
11. Juvekar, C., Vaikuntanathan, V., Chandrakasan, A.: GAZELLE: A low latency framework for secure neural network inference. In: Proceedings of USENIX Security Symposium (2018)
12. Kiss, Á., Naderpour, M., Liu, J., Asokan, N., Schneider, T.: Sok: modular and efficient private decision tree evaluation. PoPETs **2019**(2), 187–208 (2019)
13. Libbrecht, M.W., Noble, W.S.: Machine learning applications in genetics and genomics. Nat. Rev. Genet. **16**(6), 321–332 (2015)
14. Liu, J., Juuti, M., Lu, Y., Asokan, N.: Oblivious neural network predictions via minionn transformations. In: Proceedings of ACM CCS (2017)
15. Min, J.H., Lee, Y.: Bankruptcy prediction using support vector machine with optimal choice of kernel function parameters. Expert Syst. Appl. **28**(4), 603–614 (2005)
16. Mohassel, P., Zhang, Y.: Secureml: a system for scalable privacy-preserving machine learning. In: Proceedings of IEEE S&P (2017)
17. Nikolaenko, V., Ioannidis, S., Weinsberg, U., Joye, M., Taft, N., Boneh, D.: Privacy-preserving matrix factorization. In: Proceedings of ACM CCS (2013)
18. Nikolaenko, V., Weinsberg, U., Ioannidis, S., Joye, M., Boneh, D., Taft, N.: Privacy-preserving ridge regression on hundreds of millions of records. In: Proceedings of IEEE SP (2013)
19. Riazi, M.S., Weinert, C., Tkachenko, O., Songhori, E.M., Schneider, T., Koushanfar, F.: Chameleon: a hybrid secure computation framework for machine learning applications. In: Proceedings of AsiaCCS (2018)
20. Tai, R.K.H., Ma, J.P.K., Zhao, Y., Chow, S.S.M.: Privacy-preserving decision trees evaluation via linear functions. In: Proceedins of ESORICS (2017)
21. Tueno, A., Kerschbaum, F., Katzenbeisser, S.: Private evaluation of decision trees using sublinear cost. PoPETs **2019**(1), 266–286 (2019)
22. Wagh, S., Gupta, D., Chandran, N.: Securenn: efficient and private neural network training. PoPETs **2019**(3), 26–49 (2019)
23. Wang, Q., Wang, J., Hu, S., Zou, Q., Ren, K.: Sechog: privacy-preserving outsourcing computation of histogram of oriented gradients in the cloud. In: Proceedings of ACM AsiaCCS (2016)
24. Wu, D.J., Feng, T., Naehrig, M., Lauter, K.E.: Privately evaluating decision trees and random forests. PoPETs **2016**(4), 335–355 (2016)
25. Yao, A.C.: How to generate and exchange secrets. In: Proceedings of FOCS (1986)
26. Yap, B.W., Ong, S., Husain, N.H.M.: Using data mining to improve assessment of credit worthiness via credit scoring models. Expert Syst. Appl. **38**(10), 13274–13283 (2011)
27. Zheng, Y., Cui, H., Wang, C., Zhou, J.: Privacy-preserving image denoising from external cloud databases. IEEE Trans. Inf. Forensics Secur. **12**(6), 1285–1298 (2017)
28. Zheng, Y., Duan, H., Wang, C.: Learning the truth privately and confidently: encrypted confidence-aware truth discovery in mobile crowdsensing. IEEE Trans. Inf. Forensics Secur. **13**(10), 2475–2489 (2018)
29. Ziegeldorf, J.H., Metzke, J., Rüth, J., Henze, M., Wehrle, K.: Privacy-preserving HMM forward computation. In: Proceedings of CODASPY (2017)

Confidential Boosting with Random Linear Classifiers for Outsourced User-Generated Data

Sagar Sharma[✉] and Keke Chen

Data Intensive Analysis and Computing (DIAC) Lab, Kno.e.sis Center,
Wright State University, Dayton, OH 45435, USA
{sharma.74,keke.chen}@wright.edu

Abstract. User-generated data is crucial to predictive modeling in many applications. With a web/mobile/wearable interface, a data owner can continuously record data generated by distributed users and build various predictive models from the data to improve its operations, services, and revenue. Due to the large size and evolving nature of users data, a data owner may rely on public cloud service providers (Cloud) for storage and computation scalability. Exposing sensitive user-generated data and advanced analytic models to Cloud raises privacy concerns. We present a confidential learning framework, SecureBoost, for data owners that want to learn predictive models from aggregated user-generated data but offload the storage and computational burden to Cloud without having to worry about protecting the sensitive data. SecureBoost allows users to submit encrypted or randomly masked data to designated Cloud directly. Our framework utilizes random linear classifiers (RLCs) as the base classifiers in the boosting framework to dramatically simplify the design of the proposed confidential protocols, yet still preserve the model quality. A Cryptographic Service Provider (CSP) is used to assist the Cloud's processing, reducing the complexity of the protocol constructions. We present two constructions of SecureBoost: HE+GC and SecSh+GC, using combinations of homomorphic encryption, garbled circuits, and random masking to achieve both security and efficiency. For a boosted model, Cloud learns only the RLCs and the CSP learns only the weights of the RLCs. Finally, the data owner collects the two parts to get the complete model. We conduct extensive experiments to understand the quality of the RLC-based boosting and the cost distribution of the constructions. Our results show that SecureBoost can efficiently learn high-quality boosting models from protected user-generated data.

1 Introduction

It is a common scenario in which a data owner delivers services such as search engines, movie recommendations, healthcare informatics, and social networking to its subscribing or affiliated users (henceforth referred as users) via web/mobile/wearable applications. By collecting users' activities such as click-throughs, tweets, reviews, and other information, the data owner accumulates

© Springer Nature Switzerland AG 2019
K. Sako et al. (Eds.): ESORICS 2019, LNCS 11735, pp. 41–65, 2019.
https://doi.org/10.1007/978-3-030-29959-0_3

a large amount of user-related data, which are used to build analytic models aimed at improving the quality of related services and operations, and increase revenues. However, due to the ever-growing size of data and associated computation complexities, data owners often rely on easily available public cloud services (Cloud) to outsource storage and computations.

The reliance on Cloud for the massive collection of user data along with building powerful big data analytic models raise great concerns of user privacy and intellectual property protection. First, the Cloud's infrastructures, if poorly secured, can be compromised by external hackers which damages the data owner's reputation and users' privacy. Recent data breach incidents involved Target, Ashley Madison, and Equifax [28,34]. Second, the potential threat of unauthorized retrieval, sharing, or misuse of sensitive data by insiders [7,11] are difficult to detect and prevent. The data owners have a great responsibility for protecting the confidentiality of the sensitive data collection and analytics in Cloud. Thus, confidential data mining frameworks for outsourced data are highly desirable to data owners. Note that differential privacy does not fully address the problem, as it does not protect intellectual property and cannot prevent model-inversion attacks [14,33] as models are exposed to the adversaries.

Naive applications of the well-known cryptographic primitives such as the fully homomorphic encryption (FHE) scheme [18], garbled circuits (GC) [35], and secret sharing [10] in building confidential computing frameworks prove too expensive to be practical [27,30]. A few recent studies [10,29–31] started blending multiple cryptographic primitives and adapted to certain privacy architectures to work around the performance bottlenecks. These "hybrid" constructions mix different cryptographic primitives to implement the key algorithmic components of a protocol with reasonable overheads.

While the hybrid approach is promising, it does not fundamentally address the basic complexity of building a confidential version of a learning algorithm. We believe it is more critical to modify the original algorithm or adopt a "crypto-friendly" alternative algorithm to significantly reduce the associated complexity. However, the current solutions are mostly focusing on translating the original algorithms to confidential ones, from simple linear algorithms with weak prediction power, such as linear classifiers and linear regressions [19,29,31], to powerful yet enormously expensive models, such as shallow neural networks [29].

1.1   Scope of Work and Contributions

While deep learning methods [26] have dominated the image and sequence-based learning tasks, boosting is among the most powerful methods such as SVM and Random Forest [5] for other prediction tasks. For example, it has also been a popular method (e.g., XGBoost [9]) in learning to rank [6] and a top choice of many Kaggle competition winners. Surprisingly, no work has sufficiently explored the power of boosting in confidential learning.

The core idea of our SecureBoost approach is to fully utilize the powerful boosting theory [15] that requires *only* weak classifiers (e.g., each classifier's accuracy is only slightly exceeding 50% for two-class problems) to derive a powerful prediction model. This flexibility allows us to revise the original boosting algorithm (i.e., AdaBoost [15]) that uses non-crypto-friendly decision stumps to adopt crypto-friendly *random linear classifiers* as the base classifiers. We consider our work as the first step towards developing confidential versions for other boosting algorithms such as gradient-boosting [16].

In the popular AdaBoost framework for classification [15], decision stumps (DS) have been used as the weak classifiers for their simplicity and fast convergence of boosting. Although the training algorithm for a decision stump is quite simple, it is expensive to implement its confidential version due to the associated complexity of secure comparisons. Our core design of confidential boosting is to use random linear classifiers (RLCs) as the weak classifiers. For a linear classifier $f(x) = w^T x$, where x is the feature vector and w is the parameter vector to learn, an RLC sets w to be random using a specific generation method independent of training data. This random generation of classifier dramatically simplifies the training step and it only requires to determine whether the random classifier is a valid weak classifier (e.g., accuracy $>50\%$). In experiments, we found that our random RLC generation method works satisfactorily - for every 1–2 random tries we can find a valid weak classifier. The resulting boosting models are comparable to those generated by using decision stumps as base classifiers, although it converges slightly slower. The use of RLC also allows us to conveniently protect feature vectors and labels and to greatly reduce the costs of other related steps.

We have designed two secure constructions to implement the RLC-based boosting framework to understand the effect of different cryptographic primitives on the associated complexities and expenses. The constructions are based on the non-colluding honest-but-curious Cloud-CSP setting that has been used by recent related work [29–31]. CSP is a cryptographic service provider that will be responsible to manage encryption keys and assist Cloud with the intermediate steps of the boosting framework. Cloud takes over the major computation and storage burden but is not interested in protecting user privacy. Both of our protocols result in models with distributed parameters between the Cloud and the CSP: the Cloud holding the RLCs' parameters and the CSP holding the base classifier's weights of the boosted models. An alternate setting (i.e., our SecSh setting) is that two servers take an equal share of computation and storage. For simplicity, we unify the two settings to Cloud-CSP.

We carefully analyze the security of the constructions based on the universally composable (UC) security paradigm [3,4] and show that no additional information is leaked except for CSP knowing a leakage function. Both the constructions of SecureBoost expose a leakage function to CSP - the correctness of RLC's prediction on training examples. We analyze the leaked information of the function and show that it is safe to use under our security assumption.

We summarize the unique contributions as follows:

- We propose to use random linear classifiers as a crypto-friendly building block to simplify the implementation of confidential boosting.
- We develop two hybrid constructions: HE+GC and SecSh+GC, with the combination of GC, SHE, Secret Sharing, AHE, and random masking to show that the RLC-based boosting can be elegantly implemented.
- Our framework provably preserves the confidentiality of users' submitted data, including both feature vectors and their associated labels, and the generated boosting models from both curious Cloud and CSP.
- We conduct an extensive experimental evaluation of the two constructions with both synthetic and real datasets to fully understand the costs and associated tradeoffs.

2   Preliminary

We use lowercase letters for vectors or scalars; capital letters for matrices and large integers; and single indexed lowercase or capital case letters for vectors.

Boosting. Boosting is an ensemble strategy [21] that generates a high-quality classifier with a linear combination of τ weak base classifiers (whose prediction power is slightly better than random guessing). Specifically, given training examples $\{(x_i, y_i), i = 1 \ldots n\}$, where x_i are feature vectors and y_i are labels, it learns a model $H(x) = \sum_{t=1}^{\tau} \alpha_t h_t(x)$, where h_t is a weak classifier that outputs the prediction $\hat{y}$ for the actual label y and α_t is the learned weight for h_t. Algorithm 2 in Appendix A.1 outlines the boosting algorithm for the two-class problem. The most popular weak classifier has been the decision stump [15], which is merely based on conditions like *if $X_j < v_j$, output 1; otherwise, -1*, where X_j is a certain feature and $X_j < v_j$ is some optimal split that gives the best prediction accuracy among all possible single-feature splits for the training dataset.

Additive Homomorphic Encryption. For any two integers α and β, an AHE scheme allows the additive homomorphic operation: $E(\alpha + \beta) = f(E(\alpha), E(\beta))$ where the function f works on encrypted values without decryption. For example, Paillier encryption [32] is one of the most efficient AHE implementations. Conceptually[1], with one operand, either α or β, unencrypted, we can derive the *pseudo-homomorphic* multiplication, e.g., $E(\alpha\beta) = E(\sum_{i=1}^{\beta} \alpha)$. Similarly, we can derive pseudo-homomorphic vector dot-product, matrix-vector multiplication, and matrix-matrix multiplication, as long as one of the operands is in plaintext.

RLWE Homomorphic Encryption. The RLWE scheme is based on the intractability of the learning-with-error (LWE) problem in certain polynomial rings [2]. It allows both homomorphic addition and multiplication. RLWE allows multiple levels of multiplication with a rising cost. For details, please refer to

---

[1] Paillier encryption allows more efficient multiplication.

Brakerski et al. [2]. *Message packing* [2] was invented to pack multiple cipher-texts into one polynomial, greatly reducing the ciphertext size - e.g., we can pack about 600 encrypted values (slots) into one degree-12,000 polynomial. With message packing, vector dot-products and matrix-vector multiplication can be carried out efficiently as shown by [20].

Randomized Secret Sharing. The randomized secret sharing method [10] protects data by splitting it into two (or multiple) random shares, the sum of which recovers the original data, and distributing them to two (or multiple) parties. Several protocols have been developed to enable fundamental operations such as addition and multiplication based on distributed random shares, producing results that are also random shares, such as the multiplicative triplet generation method [10,29].

Garbled Circuits. Garbled Circuits (GC) [35] allow two parties, each holding an input to a function, to securely evaluate a function without revealing any information about the input data. The function is implemented with a circuit using a number of basic gates such as AND and XOR gates. The truth table of each gate is encrypted so that no information is leaked during the evaluation. One party creates the circuit and the other one evaluates it. All inputs are securely encoded as labels and passed to the evaluator via the 1-out-of-2 Oblivious Transfer (OT) [1] protocol. During the recent years, a number of optimization techniques have been developed to minimize the cost of GC, such as free XOR gates [24], half AND gates [36], and OT extension [1].

3   Framework

Figure 1 shows the SecureBoost framework and the involved parties: the data owner, the cloud service provider (Cloud), the users who contribute their personal data for model training, and the Cryptographic Service Provider (CSP). The learning protocol consists of multiple rounds of Cloud-CSP interactions, which builds a boosted model on the global pool of user-contributed training data. Ultimately, Cloud learns the parameter of each base classifier but no additional knowledge about the protected user data; and CSP learns the weights of the base classifiers and a certain type of leakage information that does not help breach the confidentiality of protected user data. The learned models can be either downloaded and reconstructed by the data owner for local applications or used by data owner by submitting encrypted new records to Cloud and undergoing Cloud-CSP evaluation.

Data owner designates a cloud provider to collect user-generated data in encrypted form and undertake the major storage cost and the major computation-intensive components of the confidential learning protocol. CSP is a party with limited resources. It mainly assists Cloud in intermediate steps, e.g. encrypting or decrypting intermediate results and constructing garbled circuits. CSP is allowed to learn some leakage function but remains oblivious to users' data or the learned models. The concept of CSP has been used and justified by other related works [30,31] as a practical semi-honest setting to release

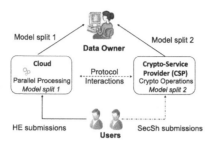

Fig. 1. SecureBoost Framework.

data owner from complex interactions. If using randomized secret sharing, the users upload shares of their submissions to both Cloud and CSP as depicted by the dotted lines in Fig. 1.

3.1   SecureBoost Learning Protocol

In this section, we describe the rationale and benefits of using RLCs as the base classifiers, the major components of the SecureBoost protocol, and the security goals.

RLCs as Base Classifiers. The original boosting framework has used decision stumps as the base classifiers. RLCs are overly ignored due to its slower convergence rate. However, it is expensive to implement decision stumps on encrypted data due to the $O(kn \log n)$ comparisons in the optimal implementation, where n is the number of records and k is the dimensionality. It is known that comparison on encrypted data is expensive for both homomorphically encrypted data [27] or garbled circuits [25]. To reduce the cost involving comparisons, we use randomly generated linear classifiers (RLC) instead. An RLC generates a classification plane in the form of $h(x) = w^T x + b$ with randomly selected w and b, which can be done by one party, i.e., Cloud. Thus, no comparison is needed in base-classifier generation.

However, blindly selecting w and b is not efficient. As Fig. 2 shows, the generated plane needs to shatter the training data space into two partitions of significant sizes. For this purpose, we require the submitted data to be normalized so that the training vectors are distributed around the origin. In practice, with the standardization procedure, i.e., each dimension X_i is normalized with $(X_i - \mu_i)/\sigma_i$, where μ_i is the mean and σ_i is the standard deviation of the dimension X_i, most dimensional values should be in the range $[-2, 2]$. Thus, we can choose b, the intercept, in the range $[-2, 2]$, while each element of w is chosen uniformly from $[-1, 1]$. Note that μ_i and σ_i can be roughly estimated by the data owner with low-cost sampling and aggregation of users' submissions and shared with the users. For clarity, we ignore the details of such simple protocols. With this setting, we find in our experiments that a valid random linear classifier can be found in about 1–2 tries. We have also verified with our experiments that boosting with RLCs can generate high-quality models comparable to those with decision stumps.

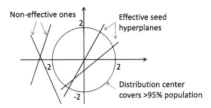

Fig. 2. Effective Random Linear Classifier Generation

RLCs have extra advantages. First, they allow learning with both the feature vectors and labels protected. We can transform the training data as $x \leftarrow (x, 1)$ and $w \leftarrow (w, b)$, with which the hypothesis function simply changes to $h(x) = w^T x$. For a two-class problem with labels $y \in \{-1, 1\}$, if the result $h(x)$ gives a correct prediction, i.e., the same sign as the label y, we always get $h(x)y = w^T xy > 0$; otherwise $w^T xy \leq 0$. Note that xy stays together in the evaluation, and thus users can submit the encrypted version of xy, $E(xy)$, protecting both feature vectors and labels. Second, they simplify the learning of base classifiers. As w is randomly generated, there is no need for Cloud to consider sample weights during learning. Meanwhile, the learning of the α_t weights can be individually done by CSP. Finally, this process allows only the CSP to learn the weights of base models, and Cloud to learn the base classifiers, preventing either party learning the complete final model.

SecureBoost Protocol. The SecureBoost learning protocol is defined with a 4-tuple: SB-Learning = (**Setup, BaseApply, ResultEval, Update**). Algorithm 1 depicts the use of these components in the boosting framework. For a boosted model $H(x) = \sum_{t=1}^{\tau} \alpha_t h_t(x)$, Cloud learns the base models $\{h_t(x) = w_t^T x, t = 1..\tau\}$, and CSP learns the model weights $\{\alpha_t, t = 1..\tau\}$.

$(K, E(Z), \{w_i, i = 1..p\}, \delta_1) \leftarrow$ **Setup**$(1^k, \tau, p)$: (1) The key K is generated by a certain party or parties (CSP, Cloud, or both) as required, with the desired security level 1^k; all public keys are published. (2) CSP initializes δ_1 with $1/n$. (3) The training data Z of n instances contains row vectors $z_i = x_i y_i$, which is protected with either a public-key encryption scheme or random masking (e.g., in the secret-sharing construction) to generate $E(Z)$. (4) Data owner sets the desired number of classifiers, τ, and instructs Cloud to generate a pool of prospective RLCs with parameters w_t for $t = 1 \ldots p$, where p is the pool size proportionally larger than τ, e.g., $p = 1.5\tau$.

$\{E(h_t(x_i)), i = 1..n\} \leftarrow$ **BaseApply**$(K, E(Z), w_t)$: With the encrypted training data $E(Z)$ and a model parameter w_t, the procedure will output the model h_t's encrypted prediction results on all training instances.

Algorithm 1. SecureBoost Framework

1: $(K, E(Z), \{w_i, i = 1..p\}, \delta_1) \leftarrow \textbf{Setup}(1^k, \tau, p)$;
2: **for** $t \leftarrow 1$ **to** p **do**
3:      $\{E(h_t(x_i)), i = 1..n\} \leftarrow \textbf{BaseApply}(K, E(Z), w_t)$;
4:      $I_t \leftarrow \textbf{ResultEval}(K, \{E(h_t(x_i)), i = 1..n\})$;
5:      $(\delta_{t+1}, \alpha_t, e_t) \leftarrow \textbf{Update}(K, \delta_t, I_t)$; //by CSP only
6:      **if** τ effective base models have been found **then**
7:          stop the iteration;
8:      **end if**
9: **end for**

$I_t \leftarrow \textbf{ResultEval}(K, \{E(h_t(x_i)), i = 1..n\})$: With the encrypted prediction results, ResultEval allows CSP (not Cloud) to learn the indicator vector I_t of length n, indicating the correctness of h_t's prediction for each training instance.

$(\delta_{t+1}, \alpha_t, e_t) \leftarrow \textbf{Update}(\delta_t, I_t)$: CSP takes I_t, δ_t to compute the weighted error rate $e_t = I_t^T \delta_t$ and if h_t is a valid base classifier i.e. accuracy > 50% (or accuracy < 50% with the RLC decisions reversed), updates its weight $\alpha_t = 0.5ln((1 - e_t)/e_t)$ and computes δ_{t+1} for the next iteration with sample weight updating formula.

In the end, Cloud learns $\{w_t, t = 1..p\}$ and CSP learns $\{\alpha_t, t = 1..p\}$. A two-party function evaluation protocol can be easily developed for Cloud to apply the model for classification, which, however, is not the focus of this paper. The data owner can simply download the model components from the two parties and reconstruct the final model for local application. The design of leaking I_t represents a careful balance between security and efficiency. While it is possible to hide I_t, the complexity of Cloud and CSP processing will be dramatically increased. We have carefully studied the implication of I_t in Sect. 7 and found its impact on security is minimal.

3.2   Security Model

We make some relevant security assumptions here: (1) Both Cloud and CSP are honest-but-curious parties, i.e., they follow the protocols exactly and provide services as expected. However, they are interested in the users' data. (2) Cloud and CSP do not collude, (3) The data owner owns data and models thus is a fully trusted party, (4) All infrastructures and communication channels are secure. While the integrity of data and computation is equally important, we consider it orthogonal to our study. We are mainly concerned with the confidentiality of the following assets.

– **Confidentiality of training data.** User-generated training data may include personal sensitive information. We consider both feature values and the labels sensitive. For example, a user's fitness activity dataset may contain sensitive features such as heart rate and locations, while the labels, i.e., the type of activity, may imply their activity patterns and health conditions.

– **Confidentiality of prediction models.** The learned models are proprietary to the data owner and can link to confidential users' data. Therefore, the model parameters are split and distributed between Cloud and CSP. No single party can learn the complete model.

We adopt the universally composable (UC) security [3,4] to formally define the protocol security. We consider an ideal protocol π implementing the *ideal functionality* $\mathcal{F}$ corresponding to a SecureBoost protocol, involving Cloud and CSP. In the *Real* world, an *honest-but-curious adversary* $\mathcal{A}$ can corrupt any of the parties and gain access to all the inputs and outputs of that party. We say that π securely realizes $\mathcal{F}$ (or π is UC-secure) if for any $\mathcal{A}$ in real world there exists an ideal-process simulator $\mathcal{S}$ in ideal world running probabilistic algorithms in polynomial time (i.e., PPT), such that for any environment $\mathcal{Z}$ and inputs $m = (m_{\mathcal{Z}}, m_{\mathcal{A}/\mathcal{S}}, m_{Cloud/CSP})$,

$$|Pr(Real_{\pi,\mathcal{A},\mathcal{Z}}(k,z,m) = 1) - Pr(Ideal_{\mathcal{F},\mathcal{S},\mathcal{Z}}(k,z,m) = 1)| = negl(k),$$

where $negl(k)$ is a negligible function [23]. In Sect. 7, we propose two theorems that can be proved to show that SecureBoost protocols are UC-secure.

4   Construction with HE and GC

In this section, we present the homomorphic encryption (HE) and GC based construction of SecureBoost. With the HE encrypted data, the **BaseApply** procedure is essentially the homomorphic operation $E(Z)w_t$ that is allowed by both Paillier [32] and RLWE [2] cryptosystems. We use a garbled-circuit based protocol to allow only CSP to learn the indicator vector I_t, without leaking any other information to the parties. In the following, we first describe the construction of the protocol components and then discuss several key technical details.

Setup. CSP generates the HE public and private key and distributes the public key to the users and Cloud. The private key accessible to the data owner when necessary. Users encrypt their submissions. Cloud generates the pool of p prospective weak classifier vectors, $\{w_t, t = 1..p\}$.

BaseApply. With the matrix-vector homomorphic operations enabled by HE, Cloud computes $\{E(u_t) = E(Zw_t), t = 1..p\}$. As this step can be done locally by Cloud, Cloud may choose to conduct this work *offline* before the protocol interactions start.

ResultEval. The problem setting is that Cloud holds $E(u_t)$ and CSP securely identifies the sign of each element of u_t, i.e., $Zw_t > 0$ implying correct prediction by the RLC, which sets the corresponding element of I_t to 1; otherwise to 0. The sign of element is related to the specific integer encoding, which we will elaborate more. With our encoding scheme, we only need to check a specific bit to determine whether $Zw_t > 0$ is true. To satisfy all the security goals, we decide to use a GC protocol for this step that will be discussed in more detail.

As the last step **Update** does not involve crypto operations, we can skip its discussion. Figure 3(a) depicts all the associated Cloud-CSP interactions in this construction.

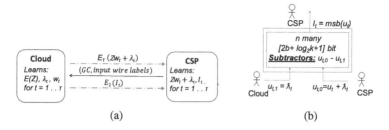

(a)   (b)

Fig. 3. (a) Cloud-CSP interactions in HE+GC construction. E_1 represents HE encryptions whereas E_2 represents GC labels for the GC outputs. (b) GC-based sign checking protocol.

4.1   Technical Detail

Now, we discuss the key problems mentioned in the sketch of the construction above.

Choice of HE Schemes. We consider two choices of HE: Paillier [32] and RLWE [2] in our evaluations. Paillier scheme provides a large bit space allowing to preserve more precisions in floating-integer conversion. Our evaluation shows that with message packing, all RLWE operations including encryption, decryption, addition and one-level multiplication are much faster than Paillier, although the ciphertext size might be larger than that of Paillier.

Integer Conversion. The HE schemes work on integers only. For a floating-point value x, $x \in \mathbb{R}$, to preserve m-digit precision after the decimal point upon conversion and recovery, we have: $v = \lfloor 10^m x \rfloor \mod q$, where q is a large integer such that $10^m x \in (-q/2, q/2)$. Let the modulo operation map the values to $[0, q)$, in such a way that the negative values are mapped to the upper range $(q/2, q)$. It is easy to check that x is recoverable: if $v > q/2$, $x \approx (v - q)/10^m$; otherwise, $x \approx v/10^m$. The modulo additions and multiplications preserve the signs and are thus recoverable. Furthermore, this encoding simplifies the evaluation of the RLC base classifiers, which involves checking the sign of $h_t(x)$. Let b be the total number of bits to represent the values in $[0, q)$. It is trivial to learn that if the b-th bit of a value in the range $[0, q)$ is 1, then the value is in the range $(q/2, q)$, which is negative; otherwise, the value is positive. With large enough q we can accommodate the desired multiplication and addition results without overflow. An n-bit plaintext space that allows one multiplication followed by α additions, as used in our protocol, spares $(n - \alpha)/2$ bits to encode the original value. For easier processing, we normalize the original real values in the same dimension of training data before converting them to b bit integers.

Secure Matrix-Vector Multiplication. The core operation $E(Zw_t)$ involves encrypted $E(Z)$ and Cloud generated random plaintext w_t. Thus, both AHE and SHE schemes can be applied.

Securely Checking Signs of $E(u_t)$. CSP needs to check the result of base classifier prediction, $E(u_t) = E(Zw_t)$ to learn the correctness of prediction on each instance, so that the error rate, the model weight, and the sample weight update can be computed. With the described integer conversion encoding method, the sign checking $u_{t,i} < 0$? is determined by a specific bit in the result. Note that letting CSP know u_t directly may reveal too much information significantly weakening the security. To balance between security and efficiency, we decide to let CSP only learn the signs indicating if the base classifier h_t correctly classified the training instances, and nothing else is leaked. Lu et al. [27] have proposed a comparison protocol based only on RLWE, however, it is extremely expensive to be adapted to our framework. Therefore, we rely on a noise addition procedure to hide the decrypted u_t from CSP and a GC-based de-noising and bit extraction procedure to let CSP learn the specific bit for sign checking. We give the details of these procedures next.

To hide the plaintext u_t from CSP, we use a noise addition method that can be easily implemented by Cloud on the encrypted vector with homomorphic addition: $E(u_{t,0}) = E(u_t) + E(\lambda_t)$, where λ_t is a noise vector generated by the pseudo-random number generator $\mathcal{G}$. Then, CSP can decrypt $E(u_{t,0})$ to learn the noisy result. Let $u_{t,1} = \lambda_t$ held by Cloud. Now the problem is turned to using a GC to securely compute $u_t = u_{t,0} - u_{t,1}$ and return the specific bit of each element of u_t.

Figure 3(b) shows the GC based de-noising and bit extraction protocol. CSP's input to the circuit is the binary form of u'_t elements whereas Cloud's inputs are the binary form of λ_t elements. With associated oblivious transfer (OT) protocol and wire label transfers, the circuit can securely evaluate $u'_t - \lambda_t$ and extract the most significant bit, $msb(u_{t,j}), j = 1..n$, of the result without leaking anything else. Cloud evaluates the circuits and returns the extracted encrypted bits (represented as output labels in GC) to CSP. CSP can then decrypt (re-map) the labels to generate the indicator vector I_t.

5   Construction with SecSh and GC

Alternatively, we design our framework with a mixture of secret sharing and garbled circuit techniques. We call this construction "SecSh + GC". A somewhat similar approach was taken by [29] in constructing confidential gradient-descent based learning. It differs from the HE based construction in two aspects: (1) user data protection uses secret sharing, and (2) matrix-vector multiplication happen over secret random splits of training data held by Cloud and CSP.

Instead of encryption, users randomly split their training data into two shares, one for Cloud and the other for CSP. The sum of shares recovers the original values. Any intermediate results that need protection are also in the form of random shares distributed between Cloud and CSP. As a result, multiplication of two values, say, a and b, each as random shares (e.g., Cloud holds a_0 and b_0 while CSP holds a_1 and b_1, where $a_0 + a_1 = a$ and $b_0 + b_1 = b$), needs the help of AHE encryption to compute each party's random share for ab. As for sign checking, we reuse the GC protocol designed earlier for HE+GC.

Setup. Each user splits their data Z into a random matrix Z_0 and Z_1, where $Z_1 = Z - Z_0$, and securely distributes Z_0 to Cloud and Z_1 to CSP. Cloud also generates a key pair for a chosen AHE scheme and shares the public key with CSP.

BaseApply. With Cloud holding Z_0 and w_t, and CSP holding Z_1, BaseApply will generate random shares of the result $u_t = Zw_t = u_{t,0} - u_{t,1}$: $u_{t,0}$ and $u_{t,1}$ held by Cloud and CSP, respectively. This is implemented with a special matrix-vector multiplication algorithm, which we will describe later.

ResultEval. With the random shares: $u_{t,0}$ and $u_{t,1}$ held by Cloud and CSP respectively, we can apply the same GC protocol presented in the last section for computing $u = u_{t,0} - u_{t,1}$ and extracting the specific bits.

5.1   Technical Detail

The SecSh+GC construction reuses the integer conversion and the GC-based sign checking components. Here, we focus on the major difference: the protocol for computing matrix-vector multiplication with random shares.

Random-Share-Based Matrix-vector Multiplication. To initiate, Cloud and CSP respectively hold the two shares Z_0 and Z_1 of user data in plaintext, and Cloud also holds w_t in plaintext. The goal is to derive random shares of Zw_t and each party learns only one of the shares.

Table 1. BigO estimation for SecureBoost constructions

Construction	Party	Encryption	Decryption	Enc. Mult/Add	Enc. Comm	GC Comm	Storage
HE+GC	User	$O(nk)$	-	-	$O(nk)$	-	-
	Cloud	$O(pn)$	-	$O(pnk)$	$O(pn)$	$O(pnb)$	$O(nk)$
	CSP	-	$O(pn)$	-	-	-	-
SecSh+GC	User	-	-	-	-	-	-
	Cloud	$O(pk)$	$O(pn)$	-	$O(p(n+k))$	$O(pnb)$	$O(nk)$
	CSP	$O(pn)$	-	$O(pnk)$	-	-	$O(nk)$

Cloud computes the part Z_0w_t in plaintext by itself. The challenge is to collect the other part Z_1w_t without CSP knowing w_t and no party knowing the complete result, Zw_t. We use the following procedure to achieve this security goal. (1) Cloud encrypts w_t with an AHE scheme and sends $E(w_t)$ to CSP so that CSP can apply pseudo-homomorphic multiplication to compute $E(Z_1w_t) = Z_1E(w_t)$. (2) CSP generates a random vector λ_t with the pseudo-random number generator $\mathcal{G}$, encrypts it with the public key provided by Cloud, and apply homomorphic addition to get $E(Z_1w_t + \lambda_t)$, which is sent back to Cloud. (3) Cloud decrypts it and sums up with the other part Z_0w_t to get $Zw_t + \lambda_t$. In the end, Cloud gets $u_{t,0} = Zw_t + \lambda_t$ and CSP gets $u_{t,1} = \lambda_t$. At this point, Cloud and CSP use the GC protocol for sign checking in Sect. 4.

6   Cost Analysis

Table 1 summarizes the associated big-O estimation of communication and computation broken down into different operations/components. The notations are the same as defined. In summary, we observe that HE+GC constructions demand no CSP storage and CSP only needs to conduct decryptions and GC constructions. In contrast, the workload and storage are almost equally distributed between Cloud and CSP in SecSh+GC. However, as user-generated data is not encrypted but split into random shares in SecSh+GC, users' costs and overall storage costs are much lower.

7   Security Analysis

According to the security model outlined in Sect. 3.2, we focus on the subcomponents of the protocols that involve both Cloud and CSP and implement a specific ideal function $\mathcal{F}$. The security is proved by finding a simulator $\mathcal{S}$ in the ideal scenario corresponding to the adversary $\mathcal{A}$ in the real scenario such that the environment $\mathcal{Z}$ cannot distinguish the probabilistic outputs of *Ideal* and *Real*.

The major interaction happens in computing the indicator vector I_t for an iteration t. The corresponding ideal function is defined as $\mathcal{F}(m_{Cloud,t}, m_{CSP,t}) \rightarrow I_t$, where $m_{Cloud,t}, m_{CSP,t}$ are Cloud's and CSP's inputs to the function and the function's output is the indicator vector I_t as defined by our protocols. We present two theorems next, the proofs which can be read in the extended version of this paper[2].

Theorem 1. *If the random number generator $\mathcal{G}$ is pseudo-random, and both the HE scheme and GC are CPA-secure, then the HE+GC construction of Secure-Boost is secure in computing I_t with an honest-but-curious adversary.*

Theorem 2. *If the random number generator $\mathcal{G}$ is pseudo-random and both the AHE scheme and GC are CPA-secure, then the SecSH+GC construction is secure in computing I_t with an honest-but-curious adversary.*

7.1   Implication of Revealing I_t to CSP

CSP learns the indicator function $I_{t,i}(h_t(x_i) == y_i)$, for $i = 1..n$ in the iteration t of SecureBoost. It is clear that this leakage does not help CSP learn the complete boosted model $H(x)$ as long as Cloud randomly generates and holds $\{w_t, t = 1..\tau\}$ as secrets. However, we must understand if such leakage may help CSP learn anything about the training data.

Recall that an element of indicator vector $I_t(h_t(x_i) == y_i)$ represent if the base RLC h_t classifies the training instance x_i correctly or incorrectly (1 and 0, respectively). At the end of learning, each record x_i gets p prediction results for p base classifiers $h_t, t = 1..p$, respectively, which is denoted as $c_i = (c_{i,1}, \ldots, c_{i,p})$,

---

[2] https://arxiv.org/abs/1802.08288.

$c_{i,j} \in \{0,1\}$. Let c_i be the *characterization vector* (CV) for the record x_i. The intuition tells that two similar records (i.e., relatively small Euclidean distance) with the same label will lead to similar CVs. However, our experiments show that the reverse is clearly false (Fig. 6 in Sect. 8)—if the reverse was true then adversaries could utilize CV similarity to infer record similarity. In particular, the records having identical CVs have distances (and their standard deviations) not significantly different from those having other types of CVs.

8   Experiments

We design our experiment set on both real and synthetic datasets with three goals: (1) show random linear classifiers are effective weak classifiers for boosting; (2) evaluate associated computation, communication, and storage costs, and their distributions amongst the users, Cloud, and CSP for both the constructions; and (3) understand the trade-off between costs and model quality, including a comparison with another state-of-the-art confidential classification learning framework.

Implementation. We adopt the HELib library [20] for the RLWE encryption scheme, implement the Paillier cryptosystem [32] for the AHE encryption scheme, and use the ObliVM (oblivm.com) library for the garbled circuits. ObliVM has included the state-of-the-art GC optimization techniques such as half AND gates, free XOR gates, and OT extention. The core algorithms for data encoding, encryption, matrix-vector multiplications, and additive perturbation are implemented with C++ using the GMP library. Users' submissions are encoded with the 7-bit floating-integer conversion method (Sect. 4.1). We use the scikit-learn toolkit (scikit-learn.org) to evaluate the model quality for existing classifier learning methods selected for comparison purpose.

Parameter Selection. We pick cryptographic parameters corresponding to 112-bit security. The RLWE parameters allow 32-bit message-space overall, 1 full vector replication, and at least 2 levels of multiplication. The degree of the corresponding cyclotomic polynomial is set to $\phi(m) = 12,000$ and $c = 7$ modulus switching matrices, which gives us $h = 600$ slots for message packing. The Paillier cryptosystem uses 2048-bit key-size to achieve approximately 112-bit security. Our GC-based sign checking protocol accommodates $(2b + \log_2(k))$-bit inputs, where b is the bit-precision (i.e., $b = 7$ in experiments) and k is the dimension of the training data. Note that HELib uses a text format to store the ciphertext which we zip to minimize the costs.

Datasets. We test SecureBoost with both the synthetic and real datasets. Table 2 summarizes the dataset properties. Datasets are selected to cover a disparate range of dimensions and number of instances. All selected datasets contain only two classes to simplify the evaluation. The real datasets come from the UCI Machine Learning Repository [13]. The synthetic dataset is deliberately designed to generate non-linearly separable classes. It is used to conveniently explore and understand the behaviors of RLC-based boosting and the quality of non-linear classification modeling methods.

Table 2. Dataset statistics.

Dataset	Instances	Attributes	Adaboost accuracy	Number of decision stumps
ionosphere	351	34	92.02% ± 4.26%	50
credit	1,000	24	74.80% ± 3.50%	100
spambase	4,601	57	92.31% ± 4.40%	75
epileptic	11,500	179	86.95% ± 3.40%	200
synthetic	150,000	10	89.51% ± 2.10%	75

8.1 Effectiveness of RLC Boosting

The performance of boosting is characterized by the convergence rate and the final accuracy. The speed of convergence is directly related to the overall cost of the SecureBoost protocols. We look at the number of base classifiers (τ) needed to attain a certain level of accuracy. As a randomly generated RLC may fail (i.e., RLCs having $\approx 50\%$ accuracy for the two-class datasets) and be discarded in some of the rounds, we also assess the actual number (p) of RLCs that are tried to generate the final model. All the accuracy results are for 10-fold cross-validation. The following results can be reproduced and verified with the scripts we have uploaded to https://sites.google.com/site/testsboost/.

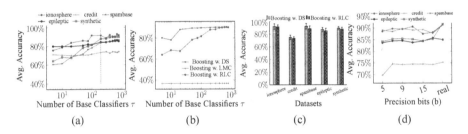

Fig. 4. (a) Convergence of boosting with RLCs. (b) Convergence of boosting with RLCs, LMCs, and DSes for the synthetic dataset. (c) Model quality: boosting with RLCs vs. boosting with DSes. (d) Bit precision vs. model accuracy

Figure 4(a) analyzes the convergence of RLC-based boosting for each dataset. We observe that overall only about 200 base classifiers are sufficient to reach a stable model accuracy level for the considered datasets. Figure 4(b) compares boosting with different base classifiers: RLC, decision stumps (DS), and linear means classifiers (LMC) when learning on the synthetic dataset. Clearly, DS has the advantage of converging faster in about 75–80 rounds. On the other hand, boosting with LMC does not reach the desired accuracy, because the centers of class (i.e., the "means") that are used to define the classification plane stay stable even with changed sample weights. The result is a bunch of highly similar base classifiers in the final boosting model, which does not take advantage of the boosting framework.

Figure 4(c) shows the final model quality produced by RLC boosting and the DS boosting (i.e., the default boosting method). We use 200 RLCs and varying number of DSes as shown in Table 2 as the base classifiers for the datasets. In every case, both methods generate models with almost identical accuracy. All of the above results suggest that RLC boosting is robust and generates high-quality classification models.

Encoding Bits. The number of bits for encoding affects the cost of GC-related components and the precision in floating-integer conversion, which in turn affects the final model quality. Figure 4(d) shows the effect of preserved bits on model accuracy. It seems preserving 7 bits is sufficient to get optimal quality models.

Cost Comparison with DS. As there is no DS learning algorithm on encrypted data (possibly due to its high expense), we develop a DS learning protocol that fits our framework to estimate the costs as shown in Appendix A.2.

8.2   Cost Distribution

We now inspect the associated costs for each involved party in the two constructions. Table 3 shows the parameter settings for different datasets that led to the desired model quality. τ is the number of base classifiers in the final boosting model. p represents the total number of RLCs that are tried in the modeling process, which determines the actual protocol costs. Overall, in about 1–2 tries on average, we can find a valid RLC (with accuracy > 50%).

Table 3. Parameter setting for cost evaluation. τ and p - number of desired and tried RLCs

Dataset	τ	p	Accuracy
ionosphere	200	226	91.5% ± 3.1%
credit	200	342	73.4% ± 2.4%
spambase	200	229	87.4% ± 4.8%
epileptic	200	331	84.41% ± 2.9%
synthetic	200	244	87.91% ± 3.2%

User's Costs. A user's costs depend on the size of training data, i.e. the number of training records n, and the number of dimensions k per record. The Paillier+GC construction requires each user to encrypt their submission element-wise in streaming or batched manner. The RLWE+GC construction requires each user to batch her submissions and encrypt them as a column-wise matrix $E(Z)$ with message packing (see Sect. 2). For the SecSh+GC construction, users simply apply the one-time padding method to generate the masks and distribute the splits to Cloud and CSP, respectively.

Table 4. User's cost for a batch of 600 records

Dataset	HE+GC (RLWE/Paillier)		SecSh+GC
	Enc. (secs)	Upload (MB)	Upload. (MB)
ionosphere	1.54/235.83	38.50/10.25	0.04
credit	1.09/168.45	27.50/7.32	0.03
spambase	2.54/390.80	63.80/16.99	0.07
epileptic	7.91/1,212.84	198.0/52.73	0.09
synthetic	0.48/74.12	12.1/3.22	0.05

Table 4 depicts the user's costs in encrypting and submitting *one batch of records* with the batch size $h = 600$. The HE+GC constructions are more expensive than SecSh+GC in all aspects, but still quite acceptable in most cases. RLWE+GC results in larger ciphertext but far less computations than Paillier+GC.

Cloud and CSP Cost Distribution. As Cloud's and CSP's costs are highly inter-related in the SecureBoost constructions we discuss them together. Note: We use the Paillier cryptosystem in SecSh+GC as the required AHE scheme. Table 5 sums up the costs for all the components. For the smaller datasets, the RLWE+GC construction does not show much benefit over the other two. For datasets with the larger number of records such as the synthetic dataset, both Cloud and CSP take less computational time with RLWE+GC construction in comparison with the other two. For datasets with larger dimensions such as the epileptic dataset, RLWE+GC is more onerous to the Cloud whereas beneficial to the CSP in terms of computation cost. As for storage and communication costs, Paillier+GC and SecSH+GC are favorable across the board. We provide further cost breakdown and analyze cost growth for Cloud and CSP with an increasing number of records and dimensions in Appendix A.3.

Table 5. Overall Cloud and CSP Costs: Storage, Comp. (computation), Comm. (communication)

Dataset	HE+GC (RLWE / Paillier)				SecSh+GC				
	Storage(MB) Cloud	Comp. (minutes) Cloud	CSP	Comm. (MB)	St.(MB) Cloud	CSP	Comp. (minutes) Cloud	CSP	Comm.(MB)
ionosphere	38.5 / 6.0	13.5 / 21.1	3.5 / 16.3	286.2 / 81.0	2.6	2.6	17.8	19.6	84.8
credit	55.0 / 12.2	28.0 / 83.2	12.9 / 70.5	1,119.2 / 537.2	8.1	8.1	72.1	81.6	541.3
spambase	510.4 / 130.3	129.5 / 358.6	33.3 / 268.6	3,842.6 / 1,876.6	76.4	76.4	271.8	355.3	1,885.1
epileptic	3,960.0 / 1,010.7	932.2 / 1,453.0	128.2 / 777.0	12,291.6 / 6,868.3	653.4	653.4	788.1	1,441.8	6897.4
synthetic	3,025.0 / 805.7	1,414.7 / 8,147.3	1,175.4 / 7,424.0	106,891.1 / 57,662.2	383.9	383.9	7,424.5	8,146.8	57,663.5

8.3 Comparing with Other Methods

In this section, we compare SecureBoost with the recently developed SecureML method [29]. It implements the stochastic gradient-descent (SGD) learning based on secret sharing [10], which is then used for logistic regression (LR) and neural network (NN) [21]. We tried different shapes of inner hidden layers and found the minimum-cost setting for satisfactorily handle the non-linearly separable synthetic dataset. SGD is conducted with a mini-batch size of 128 records in training. Both algorithms are run enough iterations until convergence.

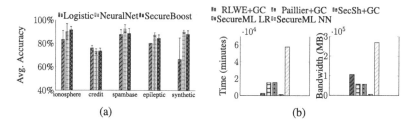

(a)   (b)

Fig. 5. (a) Comparison of model accuracy: Secure-Boost vs. SecureML - Logistic Regression and Neural Network. (b) Overall cost comparison: SecureBoost constructions vs. SecureML neural network and SecureML logistic regression for the synthetic dataset.

Figure 5(a) shows that SecureBoost and SecureML-NN perform similarly, while SecureML-LR due to its inherent linearity [21] underperforms significantly on the non-linearly separable data. This result can also be reproduced and verified with the scripts we have uploaded online[3]. Figure 5(b) shows that Secure-Boost constructions are more efficient than SecureML neural network. The cost patterns will vary for different datasets due to the varying number of training epochs. For this specific dataset, SecureBoost takes 200 iterations, while SecureML NN takes 20 epochs to converge. Logistic regression converges quickly within 10 epochs but gets stuck at a non-optimal result. It appears the per-iteration cost of SecureML NN is much higher.

8.4   Effect of Releasing I_t

We want to verify if similar characterization vectors infer similar training records to understand the leaked information by I_t. Figure 6 measures the average Euclidean distances between the training record pairs corresponding to the characteristic vectors differing by k bits. It is evident that the similarity of characterization vectors does not infer the similarity of training records as shown by similar average distances and standard deviation for all values of k. An attacker may suspect the training records that generate the same characteristic vector as the anchor (attack) record to be closer to the anchor vector as compared to other training records, however it is evident such is not the case. A further analysis on leakage of the indicator vector will be interesting in a malicious cloud setting.

---

[3] https://sites.google.com/site/testsboost/.

Fig. 6. Avg. distance between record-pairs generating characterization vectors differing by k-bits.

9   Related Work

The current implementations of FHE are still too expensive to apply on complex functions. ML Confidential [19] shows that simple linear models can be learned by a semi-honest Cloud from FHE-encrypted data with acceptable costs. However, these simple models are unable to handle non-linearly separable datasets. Lu et al. [27] show that PCA and linear regression can be implemented on FHE encrypted data with reasonable costs for a strictly small number of iterations in the algorithms. Moreover, the comparison operation based on FHE is very expensive [27], which hinders the FHE's application in many algorithms.

Despite new optimization of GC with techniques, such as free XOR gates [24], half AND gates [36], and OT Extension [1], its adaptation in confidential frameworks is still costly. Nikolaenko et al. [30,31] use FastGC [22] and AHE to implement matrix factorization and linear ridge regression solutions. Use of GCs in the expensive operations led these protocols to suffer from unbearable communication costs between CSP and Cloud. In our designs, we carefully craft the primitive operations to minimize the performance impact of the GC-related operations.

Demmler et al. [10] have shown that basic matrix operations can be implemented on random shares held by different parties when using secret sharing secure multi-party computations. SecureML [29] utilized these operations and GC to implement the gradient-descent learning method with a two-server model. However, we note that these models are more expensive than ours to achieve the same level of model quality.

Users may also submit locally perturbed data that satisfy locally differential privacy (e.g., RAPPOR [12]). However, the model quality is significantly affected by the reduced data quality, and the models are also exposed to model-inversion attacks [14,33].

Gamb's et al. [17] proposed algorithms enabling two or more participants to construct a boosting classifier, however, their goal is to train a combined model without sharing the horizontally partitioned training data with one another, not outsourcing it.

Chen and Guo [8] consider using a pool of random linear classifiers in their random space perturbation (RASP) based boosting framework for cloud computing. Unlike our framework, the framework does not provide semantic security.

10 Conclusion

We develop the SecureBoost protocol for data owners to learn high-quality boosted classification models from encrypted or randomly partitioned users' data using public Cloud. The key idea is to use random linear classifiers as the base classifiers to simplify the protocol design. Two constructions: HE+GC and SecSh+GC have been developed, using a novel combination of homomorphic encryption, garbled circuits, and randomized secret sharing to protect the confidentiality and achieve efficiency. We formally analyze the security of the protocol and show that SecureBoost constructions satisfy the universally composable security for multiparty computation. Our experimental evaluation examines the intrinsic relationships among the primitive selection, cost distribution, and model quality. Our results show that the SecureBoost approach is very practical in learning high-quality classification models. Our constructions are the first batch of boosting protocols with practical costs, compared to the expenses of the start-of-the-art implementation of other major predictive modeling methods (e.g., Neural Networks by SecureML). We will extend the study to explore the effect of sub-sampling the training data and differentially private release of the leakage function in the future. Similarly, we will extend the work to multi-class classification problem and other types of boosting.

A Appendix

A.1 Boosting Algorithm

Algorithm 2. Boosting(T, τ)

---

input: training data samples $T = \{(x_i, y_i), i = 1 \ldots n$, where $x_i \in \mathbb{R}$ and $y_i \in \{1, -1\}\}$, number of base classifiers: τ
Initialize the sample weights $\delta_{1i} \leftarrow 1/n$ for $i = 1 \ldots n$;
for $t \leftarrow 1$ **to** τ **do**
  learn a weak classifier $h_t(x)$ with sample weights $\delta_{t,i}, i = 1 \ldots n$;
  for $i \leftarrow 1$ **to** n **do**
    $e_{t,i} = 1$ if $h_t(\delta_{t,i} x_i) == y_i$ else 0;
  end for
  $error = \sum_{i=1}^{n} e_{t,i} \delta_{t,i}$;
  $\alpha_t = ln((1 - error)/error)$;
  $\delta_{t+1,i} = \delta_{t,i} \exp(\alpha_i e_{t,i})$ for $i = 1 \ldots n$;
  $\delta_{t+1} = \delta_{t+1}/|\delta_{t+1}|$;
end for
Output: $H(x) = \sum_{t=1}^{\tau} \alpha_t h_t(x)$

A.2   Confidential Decision Stump Learning

As there is no confidential DS learning algorithm reported, we present our initial design of DS learning that fits our boosting framework. Learning DS involves finding the optimal split for each feature in the training data with maximum information gain. The original algorithm takes $O(n \log n)$ comparisons to sort the values for each feature. However, sorting the dimensions may reveal the ordering information and breach data confidentiality, therefore, sorting may not be used in the confidential version of DS learning. Instead, we use a fixed binning scheme - i.e., partitioning the domain of each normalized dimension (e.g., $(-4, 4)$) into s bins and enumerate all possible decision stumps - for two-class problems and k dimensions, there are $2sk$ such stumps (each split value gets two *conjugate* stumps: e.g., Stump 1: if $X_j < v_j$ return 1 else return 0, Stump 2: if $X_j \geq v_j$ return 1 else return 0). We will describe the HE+GC construction for DS learning here.

The users encrypt their records $E(x_i)$ and labels $E(y_i)$, with $y_i \in \{0, 1\}$, separately with the public key distributed by the CSP. (1) Cloud will start to evaluate each of the sk decision stumps for every record with a slightly modified version of GC described in Sect. 4. Specifically, for each instance (x_i, y_i), it will securely check whether the class label y_i matches the classifier output, e.g., if $X_j < v_j$ return 1 else return 0. Similarly, the evaluation of each DS will give an indicator vector I_r, $r = 1..sk$, where 1 represents prediction error, reverse to the indicator vector described in Sect. 3.1, I_r is known to both Cloud and CSP. We can flip the indicator vector for the conjugate DS. (2) CSP starts a *base classifier selection* process, and computes the weight α_t for each selected DS $h_t(x)$. Specifically, with training sample weights (initialized to $1/n$), w_i, at iteration i, CSP will find one of the sk DSes that minimizes the weighted error, $\arg\min_r (I_r, w_i)$, for $r = 1..sk$. In the end, CSP only knows the index of the DS. It does not know the base classifier parameters, i.e. neither X_j nor v_j. Note that this step does not involve decryption and encryption. (3) The indices of the selected DSes and α_i are submitted by CSP to Data Owner. Data Owner can retrieve the actual DSes from Cloud.

Therefore, the overall cost is dominated by the sk rounds of evaluation in stage (1), not subject to the number of selected base classifiers. To get results close enough to the DS-based boosting model, we may need to take finely divided bins, e.g., $s = 100$. For a 10-dimension dataset, the cost is about equivalent to trying 1000 base classifiers in the RLC protocol. Furthermore, CSP takes a significant amount of storage and computing burden—it will need to keep all the sk indicator vectors for DS selection, the size of which is much larger than the original data, and conduct $sk\tau$ dot products on plaintext if the final model contains τ base classifiers.

A.3   Cloud and CSP Cost Breakdown and Scaling

First, we analyze the shared GC components for the selected real and synthetic datasets in Table 2. Then, we analyze the cost growth of the constructions for with increasing number of records and dimensions.

As all the constructions share the same GC component for sign checking, we list the GC costs together in Table 6. The number of AND gates represents the size of GC. The computational and communication costs include the total of both Cloud's and CSP's. GC's associated costs are linear to n and bit precision b. By comparing Table 5 in Sect. 8.2 and Table 6, it is clear that the GC-component dominates the overall communication cost of our protocols.

Table 6. Costs of the GC component: Computation (comp.) and Communication (Comm.)

Dataset	AND Gates	Comp. (m)	Comm. (MB)
ionosphere	2,016,846	5.1	43.1
credit	8,840,000	20.3	371.2
spambase	37,268,100	47.2	1,202.6
epileptic	87,549,500	101.3	5,009.6
synthetic	695,400,000	927.4	39791.1

Now, we try to understand the relationship between the size of training data and associated costs using synthetic datasets of several sizes and dimensions. First, we fix the number of dimensions $k = 20$ and see how number of records n affects the costs. Figure 7(a) shows that both Cloud's and CSP's costs in RLWE+GC grow much slower than the other two's. CSP's growth rates are almost same for SecSh+GC and Paillier+GC, as they involve the same number of decryption operations.

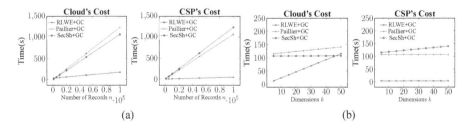

(a)   (b)

Fig. 7. Computation cost. (a) Over increasing records (n) with fixed number of dimensions ($k = 20$). (b) Over increasing dimensions (k) (bottom) and fixed number of records ($n = 10,000$).

Figure 7(b) depicts the effect of increasing the dimensions while fixing the number of records to $n = 10,000$. We observe that RLWE+GC cost for Cloud grows much faster for the larger dimensions. This is due to the associated dimension-wise RLWE replication cost in the matrix-vector multiplication.

On the other hand, CSP's cost when using RLWE+GC is much lower than with the other two constructions, as the RLWE decryptions are much cheaper than that of Paillier. Both Cloud's and CSP's costs when using Paillier+GC and SecSh+GC stay almost flat as only n dominates the overall cost.

References

1. Asharov, G., Lindell, Y., Schneider, T., Zohner, M.: More efficient oblivious transfer and extensions for faster secure computation. In: 2013 ACM SIGSAC Conference on Computer and Communications Security, CCS'13, Berlin, Germany, pp. 535–548 (2013). https://doi.org/10.1145/2508859.2516738, http://doi.acm.org/10.1145/2508859.2516738
2. Brakerski, Z., Gentry, C., Vaikuntanathan, V.: (Leveled) fully homomorphic encryption without bootstrapping. In: Proceedings of the 3rd Innovations in Theoretical Computer Science Conference. ITCS 2012, pp. 309–325. ACM, New York (2012)
3. Canetti, R.: Universally composable security: a new paradigm for cryptographic protocols. In: Proceedings 2001 IEEE International Conference on Cluster Computing, pp. 136–145 (2001)
4. Canetti, R., Cohen, A., Lindell, Y.: A simpler variant of universally composable security for standard multiparty computation (2015)
5. Caruana, R., Niculescu-Mizil, A.: An empirical comparison of supervised learning algorithms. In: Proceedings of International Conference on Machine Learning (ICML), pp. 161–168. ACM, New York (2006)
6. Chapelle, O., Chang, Y.: Yahoo! learning to rank challenge overview. J. Mach. Learn. Res. Proc. Track **14**, 1–24 (2011)
7. Chen, A.: GCreep: Google engineer stalked teens, spied on chats. Gawker (2010). http://gawker.com/5637234/gcreep-google-engineer-stalked-teens-spied-on-chats
8. Chen, K., Guo, S.: Rasp-boost: confidential boosting-model learning with perturbed data in the cloud. IEEE Trans. Cloud Comput. **6**(2), 584–597 (2018)
9. Chen, T., Guestrin, C.: XGBoost: a scalable tree boosting system. In: SIGKDD Conference on Knowledge Discovery and Data Mining (2016)
10. Demmler, D., Schneider, T., Zohner, M.: ABY-a framework for efficient mixed-protocol secure two-party computation. In: 22nd Annual Network and Distributed System Security Symposium, NDSS 2015, San Diego, California, USA, February 8–11, 2015 (2015)
11. Duncan, A.J., Creese, S., Goldsmith, M.: Insider attacks in cloud computing. In: 2012 IEEE 11th International Conference on Trust, Security and Privacy in Computing and Communications (2012)
12. Erlingsson, Ú., Korolova, A., Pihur, V.: RAPPOR: randomized aggregatable privacy-preserving ordinal response. CoRR abs/1407.6981 (2014). http://arxiv.org/abs/1407.6981
13. Frank, A., Asuncion, A.: UCI machine learning repository (2010). http://archive.ics.uci.edu/ml
14. Fredrikson, M., Lantz, E., Jha, S., Lin, S., Page, D., Ristenpart, T.: Privacy in pharmacogenetics: an end-to-end case study of personalized warfarin dosing. In: 23rd USENIX Security Symposium USENIX Security 14, pp. 17–32. USENIX Association, San Diego (2014)

15. Freund, Y., Schapire, R.E.: A short introduction to boosting. In: International Joint Conferences on Artificial Intelligence, pp. 1401–1406. Morgan Kaufmann (1999)
16. Friedman, J.H.: Greedy function approximation: a gradient boosting machine. Ann. Stat. **29**(5), 1189–1232 (2001)
17. Gambs, S., Kégl, B., Aïmeur, E.: Privacy-preserving boosting. Data Min. Knowl. Discov. **14**(1), 131–170 (2007). https://doi.org/10.1007/s10618-006-0051-9
18. Gentry, C.: Fully homomorphic encryption using ideal lattices. In: Annual ACM Symposium on Theory of Computing, pp. 169–178. ACM, New York (2009)
19. Graepel, T., Lauter, K., Naehrig, M.: ML confidential: machine learning on encrypted data. In: Kwon, T., Lee, M.-K., Kwon, D. (eds.) ICISC 2012. LNCS, vol. 7839, pp. 1–21. Springer, Heidelberg (2013). https://doi.org/10.1007/978-3-642-37682-5_1
20. Halevi, S., Shoup, V.: Algorithms in HElib. In: Garay, J.A., Gennaro, R. (eds.) CRYPTO 2014. LNCS, vol. 8616, pp. 554–571. Springer, Heidelberg (2014). https://doi.org/10.1007/978-3-662-44371-2_31
21. Hastie, T., Tibshirani, R., Friedman, J.: The Elements of Statistical Learning. Springer, New York (2001). https://doi.org/10.1007/978-0-387-21606-5
22. Huang, Y., Evans, D., Katz, J., Malka, L.: Faster secure two-party computation using garbled circuits. In: Proceedings of the 20th USENIX Conference on Security. SEC 2011, pp. 35–35. USENIX Association, Berkeley (2011)
23. Katz, J., Lindell, Y.: Introduction to Modern Cryptography. Chapman and Hall/CRC, Boca Raton (2007)
24. Kolesnikov, V., Schneider, T.: Improved garbled circuit: free XOR gates and applications. In: Aceto, L., Damgård, I., Goldberg, L.A., Halldórsson, M.M., Ingólfsdóttir, A., Walukiewicz, I. (eds.) ICALP 2008. LNCS, vol. 5126, pp. 486–498. Springer, Heidelberg (2008). https://doi.org/10.1007/978-3-540-70583-3_40
25. Lazzeretti, R., Barni, M.: Division between encrypted integers by means of garbled circuits. In: 2011 IEEE International Workshop on Information Forensics and Security, pp. 1–6, November 2011. https://doi.org/10.1109/WIFS.2011.6123132
26. LeCun, Y., Bengio, Y., Hinton, G.: Deep learning. Nature **521**(7553), 436 (2015)
27. Lu, W., Kawasaki, S., Sakuma, J.: Using fully homomorphic encryption for statistical analysis of categorical, ordinal and numerical data. IACR Cryptology ePrint Archive **2016**, 1163 (2016)
28. Mansfield-Devine, S.: The Ashley Madison affair. Network Secur. **2015**(9), 8–16 (2015)
29. Mohassel, P., Zhang, Y.: SecureML: a system for scalable privacy-preserving machine learning. In: 2017 IEEE Symposium on Security and Privacy (SP), pp. 19–38, May 2017. https://doi.org/10.1109/SP.2017.12
30. Nikolaenko, V., Ioannidis, S., Weinsberg, U., Joye, M., Taft, N., Boneh, D.: Privacy-preserving matrix factorization. In: Proceedings of the 2013 ACM SIGSAC Conference on Computer and Communications Security, pp. 801–812. ACM, New York (2013)
31. Nikolaenko, V., Weinsberg, U., Ioannidis, S., Joye, M., Boneh, D., Taft, N.: Privacy-preserving ridge regression on hundreds of millions of records. In: Proceedings of the 2013 IEEE Symposium on Security and Privacy, pp. 334–348. IEEE Computer Society (2013)
32. Paillier, P.: Public-key cryptosystems based on composite degree residuosity classes. In: Stern, J. (ed.) EUROCRYPT 1999. LNCS, vol. 1592, pp. 223–238. Springer, Heidelberg (1999). https://doi.org/10.1007/3-540-48910-X_16

33. Shokri, R., Stronati, M., Song, C., Shmatikov, V.: Membership inference attacks against machine learning models. In: 2017 IEEE Symposium on Security and Privacy (SP) (2016)
34. Unger, L.: Breaches to customer account data. Comput. Internet Lawyer **32**(2), 14–20 (2015)
35. Yao, A.C.: How to generate and exchange secrets. In: IEEE Symposium on Foundations of Computer Science, pp. 162–167 (1986)
36. Zahur, S., Rosulek, M., Evans, D.: Two halves make a whole. In: Oswald, E., Fischlin, M. (eds.) EUROCRYPT 2015. LNCS, vol. 9057, pp. 220–250. Springer, Heidelberg (2015). https://doi.org/10.1007/978-3-662-46803-6_8

BDPL: A Boundary Differentially Private Layer Against Machine Learning Model Extraction Attacks

Huadi Zheng[1(✉)], Qingqing Ye[1,2], Haibo Hu[1], Chengfang Fang[3], and Jie Shi[3]

[1] The Hong Kong Polytechnic University, Kowloon, Hong Kong SAR, China
`huadi.zheng@connect.polyu.hk,haibo.hu@polyu.edu.hk`
[2] Renmin University of China, Beijing, China
`yeqq@ruc.edu.cn`
[3] Huawei International, Shanghai, China
`{fang.chengfang,shi.jie1}@huawei.com`

Abstract. Machine learning models trained by large volume of proprietary data and intensive computational resources are valuable assets of
their owners, who merchandise these models to third-party users through
prediction service API. However, existing literature shows that model
parameters are vulnerable to extraction attacks which accumulate a
large number of prediction queries and their responses to train a replica
model. As countermeasures, researchers have proposed to reduce the rich
API output, such as hiding the precise confidence level of the prediction response. Nonetheless, even with response being only one bit, an
adversary can still exploit fine-tuned queries with differential property
to infer the decision boundary of the underlying model. In this paper,
we propose boundary differential privacy (ϵ-BDP) as a solution to protect against such attacks by obfuscating the prediction responses near
the decision boundary. ϵ-BDP guarantees an adversary cannot learn the
decision boundary by a predefined precision no matter how many queries
are issued to the prediction API. We design and prove a perturbation
algorithm called boundary randomized response that can achieve ϵ-BDP.
The effectiveness and high utility of our solution against model extraction attacks are verified by extensive experiments on both linear and
non-linear models.

1 Introduction

Recent advance in deep learning has fostered the business of machine learning
services. Service providers train machine learning models using large datasets
owned or acquired by themselves, and use these models to offer online services,
such as face and voice recognition, through a public prediction API. Popular
products include Microsoft Azure Face API, Google Cloud Speech-to-Text, and
Amazon Comprehend. However, a prediction API call, which consists of a query
and its response, can be vulnerable to adversarial attacks that disclose the internal states of these models. Particularly, a *model extraction* attack [19] is able

© Springer Nature Switzerland AG 2019
K. Sako et al. (Eds.): ESORICS 2019, LNCS 11735, pp. 66–83, 2019.
https://doi.org/10.1007/978-3-030-29959-0_4

to restore important model parameters using the rich information (e.g., model type, prediction confidence) provided by the prediction API. Once the model is extracted, an adversary can further apply model inversion attack [7] to learn the proprietary training data, compromising the privacy of data contributors. Another follow-up attack on the extracted model is *evasion attack* [16,23], which avoids a certain prediction result by modifying its query. For example, a hacker modifies the executable binaries of a malware or the contents of a phishing email in order not to be detected by an antivirus or spam email filter.

There are two state-of-the-art countermeasures against *model extraction* attacks. One is to restrict rich information in the prediction API, for example, by rounding the prediction confidence value to a low granularity. However, even if the service provider completely eliminates this value in the prediction API, that is, to offer prediction label only, an adversary can still defeat this protection by issuing large number of fine-tuned queries and train a replica of the original model with great similarity [13,16,19]. The second countermeasure is to detect malicious extraction by monitoring feature coverage [10] or query distribution [9], and stop the service when a certain threshold is reached. However, since we cannot preclude user collusion, all queries and responses must be considered aggregately, which leads to significant false positive cases and eventually the early termination of service.

To address the disadvantages, in this paper we propose a new countermeasure that obfuscates the output label of a prediction response. There are three main concerns when designing this obfuscation mechanism. First, the accuracy of prediction API is highly correlated with the degree of obfuscation—if obfuscation needs to be applied to most queries, the utility of the machine learning service will degrade severely. Second, the obfuscation mechanism should be independent of both the adversarial attacks stated above and the underlying machine learning models. Third, the obfuscation mechanism should be customizable. That is, it should allow user-defined parameters that can trade utility for model privacy or vice versa.

Our key observation is that most model extraction attacks exploit fine-tuned queries near the decision boundary of a machine learning model. The responses of these queries disclose the details of model parameters and therefore should be obfuscated with priority. To this end, we propose a boundary **differential private layer (BDPL)** for machine learning services. BDPL provides a parameterized approach to obfuscate binary responses whose queries fall in a predefined boundary-sensitive zone. The notion of differential privacy guarantees the responses of all queries in the boundary-sensitive zone are indistinguishable from one another. As such, adversary cannot learn the decision boundary no matter how many queries are issued to the prediction API. On the other hand, the majority of queries from normal users are far away from the decision boundary and therefore are free from obfuscation. In this way, we can make the best use of the obfuscation and retain high utility of the machine learning service. To summarize, our contributions in this paper are as follows.

- We propose a new protection mechanism, namely, boundary differential privacy, against model extraction with fine-tuned queries while balancing service utility and model protection level.
- We develop an efficient method to identify queries in the boundary-sensitive zone, and design a perturbation algorithm called boundary randomized response to guarantee boundary differential privacy.
- We conduct extensive empirical study on both linear and non-linear machine learning models to evaluate the effectiveness of our solution.

The rest of the paper is organized as follows. Section 2 introduces the preliminaries for machine learning and model extraction. Section 3 elaborates on the threat model and problem definition with boundary-sensitive zone and boundary differential privacy. Section 4 presents the details of boundary differentially private layer. Section 5 introduces evaluation metrics and shows the experimental results of BDPL against model extractions. Section 6 reviews the related literature, and Sect. 7 concludes this paper and discusses future work.

2   Preliminaries

2.1   Supervised Machine Learning Model

A dataset $\mathcal{X}$ contains samples in a d-dimensional feature space. Each sample has a membership in a set of predefined classes called *labels*. Supervised machine learning trains a statistical model by such sample-label pairs to make predictions of labels on unknown samples. Without loss of generality, in this paper we focus on binary models which have only two labels—positive and negative. Formally, a binary model f produces a response y to a query sample $\boldsymbol{x}$ as follows.

$$y = f(\boldsymbol{x}) = \begin{cases} \text{"positive" label} \\ \text{"negative" label} \end{cases}$$

Binary models have been widely adopted in many machine learning applications, particularly in spam filtering, malware detection, and disease diagnosis. Depending on the nature of these applications, the model f can be either linear (e.g., logistic regression) or non-linear (e.g., neural network).

2.2   Model Extraction with only Labels

In a model extraction attack, a malicious party attempts to replicate a model from the original one by continuously exploiting the prediction API. Technically any queries can constitute such an attack. However, the more queries the more likely this malicious attack will be exposed. As such, in the literature most model extraction attacks fabricate *fine-tuned queries* by differential techniques such as line search [13,19] and Jacobian augmentation [16]. These queries are carefully selected to capture the information about decision boundary where prediction results vary drastically.

Formally, a model extraction attack selects a set of fine-tuned queries $\mathcal{X}_{diff}$ and obtains their responses $\mathcal{Y}_{diff}$ to train a replica model f'.

$$\mathcal{X}_{diff} = \{\boldsymbol{x}_1, \boldsymbol{x}_2, \ldots, \boldsymbol{x}_n\}, \quad \boldsymbol{x} \in \mathbb{R}^d,$$
$$\mathcal{Y}_{diff} = \{y_1, y_2, \ldots, y_n\}, \quad y \in \mathbb{R}^1,$$
$$\exists \boldsymbol{x}, \ \boldsymbol{x}' \in \mathcal{X}_{diff}, \ dist(\boldsymbol{x}, \boldsymbol{x}') = \delta \ \wedge \ y \neq y',$$

where $dist(\cdot)^1$ measures the distance between two queries and δ is the unit distance adopted in the differential techniques when searching for boundary, i.e., where two corresponding responses $y \neq y'$.

3 Problem Definition

3.1 Motivation and Threat Model

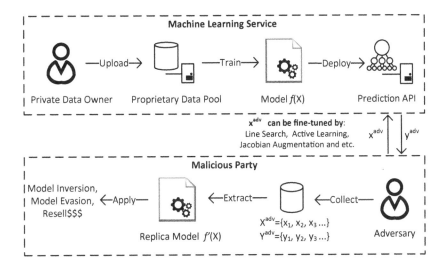

Fig. 1. Motivation and threat model

A machine learning service provides a binary prediction result using a proprietary model as shown in Fig. 1. An adversary wants to produce a replica of this model by continuously querying it through the provided prediction API. We assume he can store all queries and their responses, i.e., labels, and the attack is

---

[1] In general, this notation can be any distance metrics (e.g., Manhattan distance, Euclidean distance). The implications of distance metrics to detailed algorithms will be discussed in Sect. 4.1.

white-box, i.e., he can extract a replicated model using the same model type (e.g., convolutional neural network) and hyperparameters as the original one.[2]

3.2   Boundary-Sensitive Zone

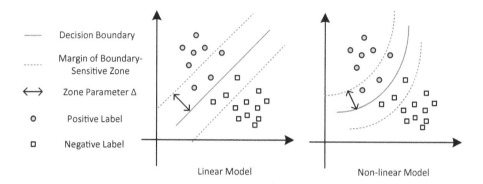

Fig. 2. Illustration of decision boundary and boundary-sensitive zone in 2D

Our problem is to protect against model extraction attacks by obfuscating query responses. Before we formally define the security model, we first introduce the notion of *decision boundary* and *boundary-sensitive zone*. For most supervised models, a decision boundary is a critical borderline in the feature space where labels are different on both sides. Figure 2 illustrates the decision boundaries of a linear and a non-linear model, respectively, in a 2D feature space. In a multi-dimensional feature space, a line boundary becomes a hyperplane, and a curve boundary becomes a hypersurface.

Our key idea is to protect the query responses near the decision boundary against most model extraction attacks. To this end, we introduce the notion of boundary-sensitive zone.

Definition 1 *(Boundary-Sensitive Zone). Given feature space Z, a model f and a parameter Δ chosen by the model owner, all feature vectors adjacent to the decision boundary of f constitute a subspace Z_Δ of Z, where*

$$Z_\Delta = \{\boldsymbol{x} \in \mathbb{R}^d \mid dist(\boldsymbol{x}, f) < \Delta\},$$

where $dist(\cdot)$ measures the distance between a feature vector $\boldsymbol{x}$ and the decision boundary of f. All queries in this zone Z_Δ are considered sensitive and have high risk of revealing the decision boundary of this model.

---

[2] The white-box assumption is based on the fact that state-of-the-art models in specific application domains, such as image classification, are usually public knowledge. Nonetheless, our solution can also work against black-box attacks where such knowledge is proprietary.

3.3 Boundary Differential Privacy

All queries in the boundary-sensitive zone need obfuscation, whose objective is to perturb the responses of any two sensitive queries so that they are indistinguishable for the adversary to determine the true decision boundary within this zone. To this end, we adopt the notion of differential privacy and formally define *boundary differential privacy* as follows.

Definition 2 (ε-*Boundary Differential Privacy*). *A perturbation algorithm* $A(\cdot)$ *achieves ε-boundary differential privacy, if and only if for any two queries* x_1, x_2 *in the boundary-sensitive zone* Z_Δ, *the following inequality always holds for the true responses* y_1 *and* y_2 *and the perturbed ones* $A(y_1)$ *and* $A(y_2)$.

$$e^{-\epsilon} \leq \frac{Pr\big[y_1 = y_2 \big| A(y_1), A(y_2)\big]}{Pr\big[y_1 \neq y_2 \big| A(y_1), A(y_2)\big]} \leq e^{\epsilon}$$

The above inequality guarantees that an adversary cannot deduce whether two perturbed responses $A(y_1)$ and $A(y_2)$ originate from the same ($y_1 = y_2$) or different labels ($y_1 \neq y_2$) with high confidence (controlled by ϵ). As such, the adversary cannot use fine-tuned queries, no matter how many they are, to find the decision boundary within the granule of boundary-sensitive zone.

4 Boundary Differentially Private Layer

In this section, we present our solution to protect against model extraction attacks with respect to ε-boundary differential privacy (ε-BDP) by appending a BDP layer to the model output. According to Definition 2, this layer consists of two major steps—identifying sensitive queries, and perturbing the responses of sensitive queries to satisfy BDP. In what follows, we first introduce a technique to identify sensitive queries with the notion of *corner points*. Then we design a perturbation algorithm called *boundary randomized response* to guarantee ε-BDP. Finally, we summarize the procedures of the boundary differentially private layer in Algorithm 1.

4.1 Identifying Sensitive Queries

A query is identified as sensitive if it falls in the boundary-sensitive zone according to Definition 1. However, in practice the decision boundary may not have a closed form (especially for complex models such as neural networks). In this subsection, we propose a method to determine if a query x_q is sensitive without deriving the boundary-sensitive zone. The idea is to test if a ball centered at x_q with radius Δ intersects with the decision boundary[3]. In theory, this is equivalent to finding if there exists a flipping point x' in the ball that has a different label from that of the query point x_q. Formally,

---

[3] The case of tangency is rarely reached in real life given that the feature space is usually continuous. For simplicity, we mainly consider intersection.

Definition 3 *(Query Sensitivity). A query $\boldsymbol{x}_q$ is sensitive, if and only if:*

$$\exists \boldsymbol{x}' \in B(\boldsymbol{x}_q, \Delta), s.t., f(\boldsymbol{x}') \neq f(\boldsymbol{x}_q),$$

where $B(\boldsymbol{x}_q, \Delta) = \{\boldsymbol{x} \in \mathbb{R}^d \,|dist(\boldsymbol{x}, \boldsymbol{x}_q) \leq \Delta\}$ is the ball centered at $\boldsymbol{x}_q$ with radius Δ.

The above definition needs to test infinite number of points in the ball, which is infeasible. Nonetheless, we observe that if the ball is convex and small enough,[4] a sufficient condition of query $\boldsymbol{x}_q$ being sensitive is that at least one of the *corner points* in each dimension of this ball $B(\boldsymbol{x}_q, \Delta)$ is a flipping point. As such, the sensitivity of query $\boldsymbol{x}_q$ can be approximated by testing the labels of $2d$ corner points of $\boldsymbol{x}_q$ without false negatives. Furthermore, if the distance metric is the $L1$ distance (i.e., Manhattan distance), this is also a necessary condition, which means that testing corner points leads to the exact sensivitity. The following theorem proves this.

Theorem 1 *(Flipping Corner Theorem). A sufficient condition of query $\boldsymbol{x}_q$ being sensitive is that,*

$$\exists \; \boldsymbol{\Delta}_i \in \Delta \cdot \boldsymbol{I}, \; f(\boldsymbol{x}_q \pm \boldsymbol{\Delta}_i) \neq f(\boldsymbol{x}_q),$$

where $\boldsymbol{I}$ is the identity matrix, $\boldsymbol{\Delta}_i$ is the projected interval on some dimension i, and $\boldsymbol{x}_q \pm \boldsymbol{\Delta}_i$ denotes the two corner points in dimension i. If the distance metric is the $L1$ distance, this equation is also a necessary condition.

Proof. Let $\boldsymbol{x}_i$ be one of the corner points in dimension i.

– *(Sufficient Condition)* For any $\boldsymbol{x}_i$, the decision boundary must exist between $\boldsymbol{x}_i$ and $\boldsymbol{x}_q$ where $f(\boldsymbol{x}_i) \neq f(\boldsymbol{x}_q)$. It intersects line $\boldsymbol{x}_i\boldsymbol{x}_q$ at point $\boldsymbol{b}_i$. As $\boldsymbol{x}_i$, $\boldsymbol{x}_q$ and $\boldsymbol{b}_i$ are on the same straight line, we have

$$dist(\boldsymbol{x}_i, \boldsymbol{b}_i) + dist(\boldsymbol{x}_q, \boldsymbol{b}_i) = dist(\boldsymbol{x}_i, \boldsymbol{x}_q) = \Delta.$$

Since $dist(\boldsymbol{x}_q, f)$ is the minimum distance between $\boldsymbol{x}_q$ and any point on the decision boundary, we have

$$dist(\boldsymbol{x}_q, f) \leq dist(\boldsymbol{x}_q, \boldsymbol{b}_i) = \Delta - dist(\boldsymbol{x}_i, \boldsymbol{b}_i) < \Delta.$$

According to Definition 1, query $\boldsymbol{x}_q$ is sensitive and this proves the sufficient condition.
– *(Necessary Condition for L1 Distance)* If $\boldsymbol{x}_q$ is a sensitive query, an $L1$-ball centered at $\boldsymbol{x}_q$ with radius Δ will be given by

$$B(\boldsymbol{x}_q, \Delta) = \{\boldsymbol{x} \in \mathbb{R}^d \mid dist_{L1}(\boldsymbol{x}, \boldsymbol{x}_q) \leq \Delta\}. \tag{1}$$

---

[4] If Δ is small, the decision boundary near the ball can be treated as a hyperplane.

Let $\boldsymbol{b}_m$ be the point which is the closest to $\boldsymbol{x}_q$ on the decision boundary of f. According to Definition 3, we have

$$dist_{L1}(\boldsymbol{x}_q, \boldsymbol{b}_m) = dist_{L1}(\boldsymbol{x}_q, f) < \Delta.$$

Since $\boldsymbol{x}_q$ is sensitive, $\boldsymbol{b}_m$ must be inside this $L1$-ball:

$$\boldsymbol{b}_m \in B(\boldsymbol{x}_q, \Delta).$$

This means that the decision boundary must intersect the ball at $\boldsymbol{b}_m$. As such, at least one convex vertex of the ball is on a different side of the decision boundary than point $\boldsymbol{x}_q$. Since the convex vertices of an $L1$-ball are exactly those corner points, there exists at least one corner point $\boldsymbol{x}_i$ such that $f(\boldsymbol{x}_i) \neq f(\boldsymbol{x}_q)$. And this proves the necessary condition. □

4.2 Perturbation Algorithm: Boundary Randomized Response

Randomized response [22] is a privacy-preserving survey technique developed for surveying sensitive questions. A randomized boolean value is given to the answer and provides plausible deniability. As the perturbation algorithm defined in boundary differential privacy has exactly two output choices, we design the following BRR algorithm based on randomized response to satisfy ϵ-BDP.

Definition 4 *(Boundary Randomized Response, BRR). Given query sample $\boldsymbol{x}_q$ and its true response $y_q \in \{0, 1\}$, the boundary randomized response algorithm $A(y_q)$ perturbs y_q by the following:*

$$A(y_q) = \begin{cases} y_q, & w.p. \quad \frac{1}{2} + \frac{\sqrt{e^{2\epsilon}-1}}{2+2e^{\epsilon}} \\ 1 - y_q, & w.p. \quad \frac{1}{2} - \frac{\sqrt{e^{2\epsilon}-1}}{2+2e^{\epsilon}} \end{cases}$$

Theorem 2. *The boundary randomized response algorithm $A(y_q)$ satisfies ϵ-BDP.*

Proof. To satisfy ϵ-BDP, the following inequality must hold according to Definition 2.

$$\frac{Pr[y_1 = y_2 | A(y_1), A(y_2)]}{Pr[y_1 \neq y_2 | A(y_1), A(y_2)]} \leq e^{\epsilon} \tag{2}$$

We assume p is the probability of retaining y_q and $1 - p$ the probability of flipping y_q. According to algorithm A, for any two responses $y_1, y_2 \in \{0, 1\}$, the four possible cases for the above inequality are:

$$\frac{Pr[y_1 = y_2 | A(y_1) = 0, A(y_2) = 0]}{Pr[y_1 \neq y_2 | A(y_1) = 0, A(y_2) = 0]}, \frac{Pr[y_1 = y_2 | A(y_1) = 1, A(y_2) = 1]}{Pr[y_1 \neq y_2 | A(y_1) = 1, A(y_2) = 1]} = \frac{p^2 + (1-p)^2}{2p \cdot (1-p)},$$

$$\frac{Pr[y_1 = y_2 | A(y_1) = 0, A(y_2) = 1]}{Pr[y_1 \neq y_2 | A(y_1) = 0, A(y_2) = 1]}, \frac{Pr[y_1 = y_2 | A(y_1) = 1, A(y_2) = 0]}{Pr[y_1 \neq y_2 | A(y_1) = 1, A(y_2) = 0]} = \frac{2p \cdot (1-p)}{p^2 + (1-p)^2}.$$

Given $0 \leq p \leq 1$, it is easy to prove that the former two cases are always larger than the latter. If we further use equality instead of ineqaulity in Eq. 2, we can derive the following equation of p:

$$\frac{p^2 + (1-p)^2}{2p \cdot (1-p)} = e^\epsilon$$

By solving the above equation, we can derive p as

$$p = \frac{(2 + 2e^\epsilon) \pm \sqrt{(2 + 2e^\epsilon)^2 - 4(2 + 2e^\epsilon)}}{2(2 + 2e^\epsilon)}$$

$$p_1 = \frac{1}{2} + \frac{\sqrt{e^{2\epsilon} - 1}}{2 + 2e^\epsilon}, \quad p_2 = \frac{1}{2} - \frac{\sqrt{e^{2\epsilon} - 1}}{2 + 2e^\epsilon} \tag{3}$$

Finally, we need to test the validity of both solutions. Let $u = e^\epsilon$, the derivative of p_1 in Eq. 3 with respect to u is:

$$\frac{\partial p}{\partial u} = \frac{(\frac{2}{u-1})(\sqrt{u^2 - 1})}{(2 + 2u)^2} \geq 0$$

As such, p_1 is monotonic with respect to u and ϵ. Since $\epsilon \in [0, +\infty]$, the lower and upper bounds of p_1 are obtained when $\epsilon = 0$ and $\epsilon = +\infty$:

$$\lim_{\epsilon \to 0} \left[\frac{1}{2} + \frac{\sqrt{e^{2\epsilon} - 1}}{2 + 2e^\epsilon} \right] = \frac{1}{2},$$

$$\lim_{\epsilon \to +\infty} \left[\frac{1}{2} + \frac{\sqrt{e^{2\epsilon} - 1}}{2 + 2e^\epsilon} \right] = \lim_{\epsilon \to +\infty} \left[\frac{1}{2} + \frac{\sqrt{1 - \frac{1}{e^{2\epsilon}}}}{\frac{2}{e^\epsilon} + 2} \right] = 1.$$

As such, the derived p_1 in Eq. 3 is in the range of $[\frac{1}{2}, 1)$ and is thus valid. Similarly, we can prove p_2 is in the range of $(0, \frac{1}{2}]$ and is thus invalid. □

4.3   Summary

Algorithm 1 summarizes the detailed procedures of BDP layer that can be tapped to the output of any machine learning model f. When a new query x_q arrives, if it has already been queried before, the layer directly returns the cached response y_q' to prevent attacker from learning multiple perturbed responses of the same query response, which can lead to a less private BDP. Otherwise, the layer first obtains the real result y_q from model f. Then it determines whether x_q is in the boundary-sensitive zone by checking all corner points. As long as one corner point is as a flipping point, the query is identified as sensitive, and the boundary randomized response algorithm $BRR(\cdot)$ with privacy budget ϵ will be invoked. The layer will thus return the perturbed result y_q' and cache it for future use. Otherwise, if x_q is not sensitive after checking all corner points, the real result y_q will be returned.

5   Experiments

In this section, we evaluate the effectiveness of boundary differentially private layer (BDPL) against model extraction attacks. Specifically, we implement those extraction attacks using fine-tuned queries as in [13,19] and compare the success rates of these attacks with and without BDPL. All experiments are implemented with Python 3.6 on a desktop computer running Windows 10 with Intel Core i7-7700 3.6 GHz CPU and 32G DDR4 RAM.

Algorithm 1. Boundary Differentially Private Layer

Input:	Query $x_q \in R^d$
	Model f
	Boundary-Sensitive Zone Parameter Δ
	Boundary Privacy Budget ϵ
Output:	Perturbed Response y

Procedure:

1: **if** x_q is not cached **then**
2:   $y_q = f(x_q)$
3:   $CornerPoints = getCornerPoints(\Delta, x_q)$
4:   **for** x_i in $CornerPoints$ **do**
5:     **if** x_i is a flipping point **then**
6:       $y'_q = \text{BRR}(y_q, \epsilon)$
7:       $\text{Cache}(x_q, y'_q)$
8:       **return** y'_q
9:   **return** y_q
10: **else**
11:   $y'_q = \text{getCached}(x_q)$
12:   **return** y'_q

5.1   Setup

Datasets and Machine Learning Models. We evaluate two datasets and two models used in the literature [19]—a Botany dataset *Mushrooms* (113 attributes, 8124 records) and a census dataset *Adult* (109 attributes, 48842 records), both of which are obtained from UCI machine learning repository [4]. All categorical items are processed by *one-hot-encoding* [8] and missing values are replaced with the mean value of this attribute. We adopt *min-max normalization* to unify all feature domains into $[-1, 1]$. In the *Mushrooms* dataset, the binary label shows whether a mushroom is poisonous or edible, and in the *Adult* dataset, the binary label shows whether the annual income of an adult exceeds 50 K.

We train both a linear model, namely, logistic regression, and a non-linear model, namely, 3-layer neural network, to predict unknown labels on both datasets. Logistic regression is implemented using *cross-entropy* loss with $L2$ regularizer. Neural network is implemented using TensorFlow r1.12 [1]. The hidden layer contains 20 neurons with *tanh* activation. The output layer is implemented with a *sigmoid* function for binary prediction.

Evaluation Metrics. We implement the extraction attack defined in Sect. 2 using fine-tuned queries generated by the line-search technique. It is a full white-box attack which produces an extracted model f' with the same hyperparameters and architectures as the original model f. To compare f and f', we adopt *extraction rate* [10,19] to measure the proportion of matching predictions (i.e., both f and f' predict the same label) in an evaluation query set. Formally,

- **Extraction Rate.** Given an evaluation query set $\mathcal{X}_e$, the extraction rate

$$R = \frac{1}{|\mathcal{X}_e|} \sum_{x_i \in \mathcal{X}_e} \mathbb{1}(f(x_i) = f'(x_i)),$$

where $\mathbb{1}(\cdot)$ is an indicator function that outputs 1 if the input condition holds and 0 otherwise. The extraction rate essentially measures the similarity of model outputs given the same inputs. In our experiments, the evaluation query set could come from either the dataset or uniformly sampled points in the feature space.

- **Utility.** This second metric measures the proportion of responses that are perturbed (i.e., flipped) by BDPL. It indicates how useful these responses are from a normal user's perspective. Formally, given the entire set of queries $\mathcal{X}_q$ issued by clients, and the set of (perturbed) responses $\mathcal{Y}_q$ from the service provider,

$$U = \frac{1}{|\mathcal{X}_q|} \sum_{x_i \in \mathcal{X}_q, y_i \in \mathcal{Y}_q} \mathbb{1}(f(x_i) = y_i).$$

5.2   Overall Evaluation

To evaluate how well the decision boundary can be protected by BDPL, we launch extraction attacks on 4 model/dataset combinations and plot the extraction rate R of sensitive queries in Fig. 3 as the number of queries increases. For BDPL, we set $\Delta = 1/8$, and $\epsilon = 0.01$. In all combinations, except for the initial extraction stage (query size less than 5 K), BDPL exhibits a significant protection effect (up to 12% drop on R) compared with no defense. Furthermore, even though the two models are very diverse (the parameters of the neural network are 20 times more than that of the logistic regression), BDPL shows consistent protection effect by a similar drop of R.

The secondary axis of Fig. 3 also plots the utility of BDPL. We observe that the utility saturates at over 80% after 20 K queries in all combinations except for *Adult w/ Logistic Regression*. This model has the fewest parameters and features, so BDPL has to perturb more sensitive queries to retain the same BDP level as the others. The impact on utility by Δ and ϵ will be shown in Sect. 5.4.

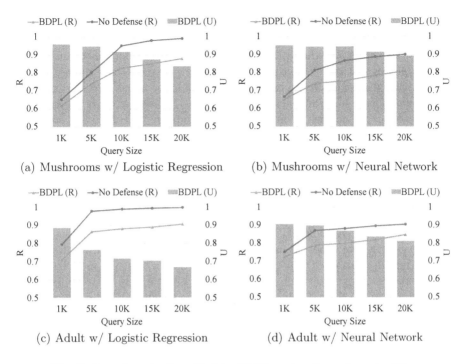

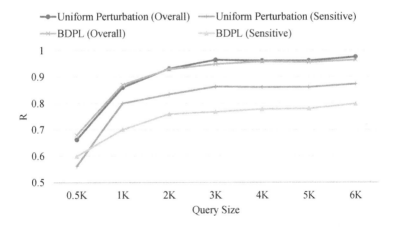

Fig. 3. Overall protection effect by BDPL: extraction rate and utility

5.3   BDPL vs. Uniform Perturbation

Fig. 4. BDPL vs. uniform perturbation

In this experiment, we compare BDPL with a uniform perturbation mechanism that randomly flips the response label by a certain probability, whether the query is sensitive or not. To have a fair comparison, we use trial-and-error[5] to find this probability so that the overall extraction rates of both mechanisms are almost the same. We then plot the extraction rates of both mechanisms for sensitive queries in Fig. 4. Due to space limitation, we only show the results for *Mushrooms with Logistic Regression* with $\Delta = 1/8$ and $\epsilon = 0.01$. We observe that BDPL outperforms uniform perturbation by 5%–7%, which is very significant as this leads to an increase of misclassification rate by 30%–50%. As such, we can conclude that BDPL is very effective in protecting the decision boundary by differentiating sensitive queries from non-sensitive ones, and therefore it retains high utility for query samples that are faraway from the boundary.

5.4   Impact of ϵ and Δ

In this subsection, we evaluate BDPL performance with respect to various values of boundary-sensitive zone parameter Δ and privacy budget ϵ. In each experiment, we fix the value of ϵ (resp. Δ) and vary Δ (resp. ϵ) for all 4 model/dataset combinations. Δ ranges between $1/64$ and $1/8$ while ϵ ranges between 0.01 and 0.64. Figures 5 and 6 show the evaluation results on varying Δ and ϵ respectively.

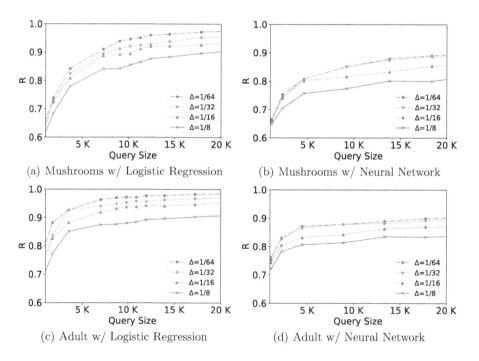

Fig. 5. Impact of varying Δ

---

[5] To do this, we start with 1 random flip out of all responses and measure its overall extraction rate. We then repeatedly increment this number by 1 until the overall extraction rate is very close to that of BDPL.

Impact on Extraction Rate. When Δ increases from $1/64$ to $1/8$, the extraction rate is significantly reduced in both logistic regression (up to 12% drop) and neural network (up to 10% drop). Nonetheless, for neural networks, the extract rate does not change much when Δ increases from $1/64$ to $1/32$, which indicates that if the boundary-sensitive zone is too small, BDPL may not provide effective protection, especially when the decision boundary is non-linear.

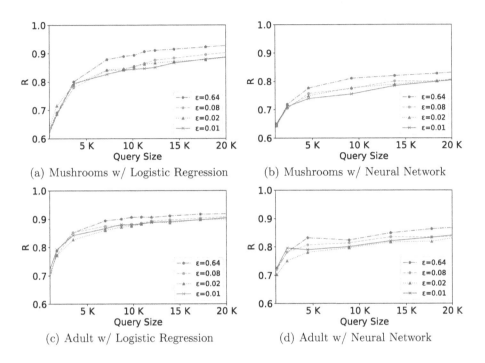

(a) Mushrooms w/ Logistic Regression   (b) Mushrooms w/ Neural Network

(c) Adult w/ Logistic Regression   (d) Adult w/ Neural Network

Fig. 6. Impact of varying ϵ

As for privacy budget ϵ, its impact is not as significant as Δ. We only observe up to 4% drop of extraction rate when ϵ decreases from 0.64 to 0.01 for all 4 model/dataset combinations.

Last but not the least, the extraction rates under all these settings saturate as the query size increases. In most cases, they start to saturate before 5 K queries, and even in the worst case, they saturate at 15 K or 20 K. This indicates that BDPL imposes a theoretical upper bound on the extraction rate no matter how many queries are issued.

Impact on Utility. In Fig. 7, we plot the final utility after 20 K queries for all Δ and ϵ combinations. Except for *Adult w/ Logistic Regression*, all utilities are higher than 80% and most of them are above 90%, which means that BDPL does not severely sacrifice the accuracy of a machine learning service. As expected, the utility reaches peak when $\Delta = 1/64$ (smallest zone size) and $\epsilon = 0.64$ (least probability of perturbation). Furthermore, as is coincided with the extraction rate, the utility is more sensitive to Δ than to ϵ. For example, an increase of Δ from 0.01 to 0.1 leads to a drop of utility by 10%, whereas a decrease of ϵ from 0.1 to 0.01 leads to only 5% drop.

To conclude, BDPL permanently protects decision boundary of both linear and non-linear models with moderate utility loss. The changes of Δ and ϵ (particularly the former) have some modest impact on the extraction rate and utility.

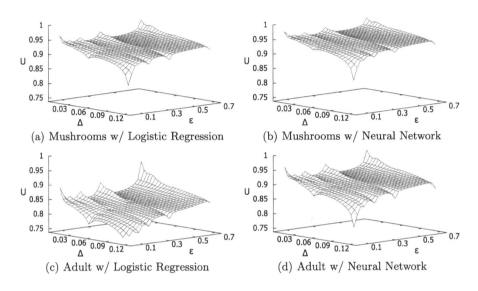

(a) Mushrooms w/ Logistic Regression   (b) Mushrooms w/ Neural Network

(c) Adult w/ Logistic Regression   (d) Adult w/ Neural Network

Fig. 7. Utility vs. Δ and ϵ

6 Related Works

There are three streams of related works, namely, machine learning model extraction, defense, and differential privacy.

Model Extraction. Machine-learning-as-a-service (MLaaS) has furnished model extraction attacks through the rich information available from prediction API. Tramer *et al.* [19] proposed extraction methods that leveraged the confidence information in the API and managed to extract the full set of model parameters using equation-solving. Papernot [16] *et al.* introduced a Jacobian-based data augmentation technique to create synthetic queries and to train a substitute DNN. Similarly, Juuti *et al.* [9] leveraged both optimal hyperparameters and the Jacobian to extract models. Oh *et al.* [14] developed a model-of-model to infer internal information of a neural network such as layer type and kernel sizes. Orekondy *et al.* [15] proposed a knockoff model to steal the functionality of an image classification model with black-box API access. Besides extracting internal parameters, Wang *et al.* [21] also extracted the hyperparamters of a fully trained model by utilizing the zero gradient technique.

Model extraction without confidence is similar to *learning with membership query* [3,20], which learns a concept through querying membership on an oracle. This technique has been exploited by Lowd *et al.* to extract binary classifiers [13]. They used line search to produce optimized queries for linear model extraction. This technique was extended by Tramer *et al.* [19] to non-linear models such as a polynomial kernel support vector machine. They adopted adaptive techniques such as active learning to synthesize fine-tuned queries and to approximate the decision boundary of a model.

Model Extraction Defense. Confidence rounding and ensemble model were shown effective against equation-solving extractions in [19]. Lee *et al.* [12] proposed perturbations using the mechanism of reverse sigmoid to inject deceptive noises to output confidence, which preserved the validity of top and bottom rank labels. Kesarwani *et al.* [10] monitored user-server streams to evaluate the threat level of model extraction with two strategies based on entropy and compact model summaries. The former derived information gain with a decision tree while the latter measured feature coverage of the input space partitioned by source model, both of which were highly correlated to extraction level. Juuti *et al.* [9] adopted a different approach to monitor consecutive queries based on the uniqueness of extraction behavior. A warning would be generated when queries deviated from a benign distribution due to malicious probing. Quiring *et al.* [17] adopted the notion of closeness-to-the-boundary in digital watermarking and applied it to protect against extraction attacks on decision trees. The defense strategy was devised from protection of watermark detector and it monitored the number of queries that fell into security margin.

Differential Privacy. Differential privacy (DP) was first proposed by Dwork [6] to guarantee the privacy of a centralized dataset with standardized mathematical notation. Duchi *et al.* [5] extended this notation to local differential privacy (LDP) for distributed data sources. Randomized response proposed by Warner *et al.* [22] is the baseline perturbation algorithm for LDP, which protects binary answers of individuals. Although differential privacy has not been used in model extraction and defense, it has been applied in several adversarial machine learning tasks. For example, Abadi *et al.* [2] introduced differentially private stochastic gradient descent to deep learning, which can preserve private information of the training set. Lee *et al.* [11] further improved its effectiveness using an adaptive privacy budget. Their approaches are shown effective against model inversion attack [7] or membership inference attack [18].

7   Conclusion and Future Work

In this paper, we propose boundary differential private layer to defend binary machine learning models against extraction attacks by obfuscating the query responses near the decision boundary. This layer guarantees boundary differential privacy (ϵ-BDP) in a user-specified boundary-sensitive zone. To identify sensitive queries that fall in this zone, we develop an efficient approach that use corner points as indicators. We design boundary randomized response as the perturbation algorithm to obfuscate query responses. This algorithm is proved to satisfy ϵ-BDP. Through extensive experimental results, we demonstrate the effectiveness and flexibility of our defense layer on protecting decision boundary while retaining high utility of the machine learning service.

For future work, we plan to generalize our defense layer to a multi-class model and adapt the perturbation algorithm to it. We also plan to extend our defense layer to protect against other machine learning attacks such as model evasion and inversion.

Acknowledgement. This work was supported by National Natural Science Foundation of China (Grant No: 61572413, U1636205, 91646203, 61532010, 91846 204, and 61532016), the Research Grants Council, Hong Kong SAR, China (Grant No: 15238116, 15222118 and C1008-16G), and a research grant from Huawei Technologies.

References

1. Abadi, M., Agarwal, A., Barham, P., et al.: TensorFlow: large-scale machine learning on heterogeneous systems (2015). https://www.tensorflow.org/, software available from tensorflow.org
2. Abadi, M., et al.: Deep learning with differential privacy. In: Proceedings of ACM SIGSAC Conference on Computer and Communications Security, pp. 308–318 (2016)
3. Angluin, D.: Queries and concept learning. Mach. Learn. **2**, 319–342 (1987)
4. Dua, D., Graff, C.: UCI machine learning repository (2017). http://archive.ics.uci.edu/ml
5. Duchi, J.C., Jordan, M.I., Wainwright, M.J.: Local privacy and statistical minimax rates. In: IEEE Symposium on Foundations of Computer Science, pp. 429–438 (2013)
6. Dwork, C.: Differential privacy. In: Bugliesi, M., Preneel, B., Sassone, V., Wegener, I. (eds.) ICALP 2006. LNCS, vol. 4052, pp. 1–12. Springer, Heidelberg (2006). https://doi.org/10.1007/11787006_1
7. Fredrikson, M., Jha, S., Ristenpart, T.: Model inversion attacks that exploit confidence information and basic countermeasures. In: Proceedings of ACM SIGSAC Conference on Computer and Communications Security, pp. 1322–1333 (2015)
8. Harris, D.M., Harris, S.L.: Digital design and computer architecture (2007)
9. Juuti, M., Szyller, S., Dmitrenko, A., Marchal, S., Asokan, N.: Prada: Protecting against DNN model stealing attacks. CoRR abs/1805.02628 (2018)
10. Kesarwani, M., Mukhoty, B., Arya, V., Mehta, S.: Model extraction warning in MLAAS paradigm. In: Annual Computer Security Applications Conference (2018)
11. Lee, J., Kifer, D.: Concentrated differentially private gradient descent with adaptive per-iteration privacy budget. In: ACM SIGKDD Conference on Knowledge Discovery and Data Mining (2018)
12. Lee, T., Edwards, B., Molloy, I., Su, D.: Defending against model stealing attacks using deceptive perturbations. CoRR abs/1806.00054 (2018)
13. Lowd, D., Meek, C.: Adversarial learning. In: Proceedings of the Eleventh ACM SIGKDD International Conference on Knowledge Discovery in Data Mining. KDD 2005, pp. 641–647. ACM (2005)

14. Oh, S.J., Augustin, M., Schiele, B., Fritz, M.: Towards reverse-engineering black-box neural networks. In: International Conference on Learning Representations (2018)
15. Orekondy, T., Schiele, B., Fritz, M.: Knockoff nets: stealing functionality of black-box models. CoRR abs/1812.02766 (2018)
16. Papernot, N., McDaniel, P., Goodfellow, I., Jha, S., Celik, Z.B., Swami, A.: Practical black-box attacks against machine learning. In: Proceedings of the 2017 ACM on Asia Conference on Computer and Communications Security, pp. 506–519 (2017)
17. Quiring, E., Arp, D., Rieck, K.: Forgotten siblings: Unifying attacks on machine learning and digital watermarking. In: IEEE European Symposium on Security and Privacy (EuroS&P), pp. 488–502 (2018)
18. Shokri, R., Stronati, M., Shmatikov, V.: Membership inference attacks against machine learning models. In: IEEE Symposium on Security and Privacy, pp. 3–18 (2017)
19. Tramèr, F., Zhang, F., Juels, A., Reiter, M.K., Ristenpart, T.: Stealing machine learning models via prediction APIS. In: Proceedings of the 25th USENIX Conference on Security Symposium, pp. 601–618 (2016)
20. Valiant, L.G.: A theory of the learnable. In: ACM Symposium on Theory of Computing (1984)
21. Wang, B., Gong, N.Z.: Stealing hyperparameters in machine learning. In: IEEE Symposium on Security and Privacy, pp. 36–52 (2018)
22. Warner, S.L.: Randomized response: a survey technique for eliminating evasive answer bias. J. Am. Stat. Assoc. **60**(309), 63–69 (1965)
23. Xu, W., Qi, Y., Evans, D.: Automatically evading classifiers: a case study on PDF malware classifiers. In: Annual Network and Distributed System Security Symposium (2016)

Information Leakage

The Leakage-Resilience Dilemma

Bryan C. Ward[1], Richard Skowyra[1], Chad Spensky[2], Jason Martin[1],
and Hamed Okhravi[1(✉)]

[1] MIT Lincoln Laboratory, Lexington, USA
{bryan.ward,richard.skowyra,jnmartin,hamed.okhravi}@ll.mit.edu
[2] University of California, Santa Barbara, USA
cspensky@cs.ucsb.edu

Abstract. Many control-flow-hijacking attacks rely on information leakage to disclose the location of gadgets. To address this, several *leakage-resilient* defenses, have been proposed that fundamentally limit the power of information leakage. Examples of such defenses include address-space re-randomization, destructive code reads, and execute-only code memory. Underlying all of these defenses is some form of code randomization. In this paper, we illustrate that randomization at the granularity of a page or coarser is not secure, and can be exploited by generalizing the idea of partial pointer overwrites, which we call the Relative ROP (RelROP) attack. We then analyzed more that 1,300 common binaries and found that 94% of them contained sufficient gadgets for an attacker to spawn a shell. To demonstrate this concretely, we built a proof-of-concept exploit against PHP 7.0.0. Furthermore, randomization at a granularity finer than a memory page faces practicality challenges when applied to shared libraries. Our findings highlight the dilemma that faces randomization techniques: course-grained techniques are efficient but insecure and fine-grained techniques are secure but impractical.

1 Introduction

Memory-corruption attacks continue to be one of the primary attack vectors against modern computer systems [2]. The sophistication of memory-corruption attacks has increased from simple code injection [38] to various forms of code-reuse attacks [11,43] in response to widespread deployment of defenses such as W ⊕ X (a.k.a. Data Execution Prevention – DEP).

Leakage-resilient memory-protection techniques [4,7,12,14,35,50,53] are considered the state-of-the-art in one of several approaches to mitigate the

DISTRIBUTION STATEMENT A. Approved for public release. Distribution is unlimited.

This material is based upon work supported by the Under Secretary of Defense for Research and Engineering under Air Force Contract No. FA8702-15-D-0001. Any opinions, findings, conclusions or recommendations expressed in this material are those of the author(s) and do not necessarily reflect the views of the Under Secretary of Defense for Research and Engineering.

ⓒ Springer Nature Switzerland AG 2019
K. Sako et al. (Eds.): ESORICS 2019, LNCS 11735, pp. 87–106, 2019.
https://doi.org/10.1007/978-3-030-29959-0_5

impact of memory corruption attacks. Such techniques protect the code against various forms of information-leakage attacks (*i.e.,* direct [45,47], indirect [16,41], or side-channel-based [8,42]), thus ensuring that the effects of the underlying randomization cannot be sidestepped by an attacker. Leakage-resilient techniques include various forms of execute-only techniques via memory permissions [4,14] or destructive reads [50], code-pointer protection via code and data decoupling [35], and runtime re-randomization techniques [7,12,53].

All of these leakage-resilient techniques crucially rely on the underlying code-randomization mechanism and its granularity. For example, execute-only memory can be easily bypassed if an attacker knows the code-section layout. Code-randomization techniques fall into two categories: virtual-memory randomization and physical-memory randomization. Virtual-memory randomization only changes the mapping of virtual addresses to physical addresses, and does not change the contents of physical memory. Because such mapping can only be as fine as a page, virtual-memory-randomization mechanisms have page-level granularity or coarser. Examples of such mechanisms include library-level randomization [7,39] and page-level randomization [5]. The second category, physical-memory randomization, is any technique that changes the contents of physical memory. These include function-level [23,31], basic-block-level [12,51], and instruction-level [18,30] randomization mechanisms.

In this paper, we study the security and practicality tradeoffs of code randomization for leakage-resilient defenses. We first show that virtual-memory randomization provides insufficient security guarantees. Extending the idea of partial pointer overwrites, we illustrate an attack, which we call *Relative ROP (Rel-ROP)*, that can bypass such techniques in the absence of additional, protection mechanisms. Specifically, we show that by simply overwriting the least-significant bytes of a pointer, an attacker can address sufficient gadgets within a page to build an exploit, and because the granularity of virtual-memory randomization cannot be finer than a page, this limits their effectiveness in practice.

Although the idea of partial pointer overwrites existed in the literature before [8,19], building a complete attack based on them faces a number of challenges, including the difficulty of chaining gadgets together and the lack of access to many gadgets due to randomization of their addresses. To overcome these challenges, we illustrate how the Procedure Linkage Table (PLT) and the Global Offset Table (GOT) can be abused as a layer of indirection to facilitate exploitation. We show that function pointers within the GOT may be partially overwritten to point instead to gadgets within the page of the original target. We illustrate that numerous gadgets are accessible in each page through partially overwriting GOT entries. We analyze many popular Linux applications and find that many such gadgets can be invoked while the system is protected by code randomization and many different leakage-resilient defenses.

To further demonstrate the realism of RelROP, we build a proof-of-concept exploit against PHP (Sect. 6), which deterministically bypasses many leakage-resilient defenses that rely on virtual-memory randomization.

We then investigate physical-memory randomization mechanisms. While these techniques can be arbitrarily fine-grained, and are thus secure against partial-overwrite attacks, they face many practicality challenges. Among them, is the fact that such techniques require actually moving memory contents, which creates challenges for shared libraries. Such challenges give rise to tradeoffs between security and performance or practicality.

Our findings highlight the dilemma when designing leakage-resilient memory-protection techniques, and illustrate that design choices must consider a fine trade-off between security and practicality in this domain. Since all of the proposed techniques in this domain face either security challenges or practicality challenges (or both), we posit that more research is needed to build effective and efficient leakage-resilient techniques.

The contributions of this paper are as follows:

- We provide an in-depth study of security and practicality implications of code randomization in leakage-resilient memory-protection techniques.
- We illustrate that virtual memory-based code randomization provides insufficient security. We leverage the idea of partial pointer overwrite to build a generic attack, called RelROP, that overwrites one or two least significant byte of a code pointer to access gadgets within the same page as the target.
- We conduct extensive analysis of the prevalence of RelROP gadgets, and find that sufficient RelROP gadgets are found in 94% of analyzed binaries.
- We show the realism of RelROP via a proof-of-concept exploit against PHP.
- We discuss the practicality challenges of physical-memory-based randomization techniques and argue that security and practicality trade-offs need to be considered when leveraging code randomization for leakage resilience.

2 Randomization Granularity

Leakage-resilient techniques, including TASR [7], Shuffler [53], Remix [12], Isomeron [16], Oxymoron [5], Heisenbyte [50], NEAR [52], Morton *et al.* [36], XnR [4], and HideM [22] mitigate the impact of information-leakage attacks on code randomization/diversification. They employ various mechanisms including memory permissions [4,14], destructive reads [50], code pointer protection [35], and runtime re-randomization [7,12,53] to prevent direct memory disclosures (*e.g.,* [4,5,22,52]) and sometimes both direct and indirect memory disclosures (*e.g.,* [7,12,14,16,35,53]).

A key component of every leakage-resilient scheme is a one-time randomization of memory (or more, in the case of re-randomization) in order to obscure the memory layout from the attacker. Once obscured, the remainder of the technique (*e.g.,* execute-only memory) seeks to ensure that the attacker cannot leak memory in order to discover the memory layout.

2.1 Virtual-Memory Randomization

One approach to randomizing memory is to randomize the mapping between virtual- and physical-memory addresses. Attackers relying on code reuse must know the virtual-memory address at which physical code pages are mapped. This is the driving principle behind ASLR [39] and its descendants, for example.

Randomizing virtual addresses is straightforward, as only the page tables for that process need to be changed rather than the underlying physical memory (*i.e.*, no memory moves or copies are required). Therefore, such randomization can be performed efficiently, and ensures that physical pages mapped into multiple processes (*e.g.*, shared libraries) experience no disruption.

Randomization Granularity. Relying on virtual-memory randomization imposes a fundamental limitation on the granularity of randomization. Objects smaller than a page of memory cannot be independently randomized, as page tables cannot be used to reference the addresses of memory objects smaller than a page. Thus, some of the low-order bits of an address remain unchanged after randomization. While the exact size of memory pages is architecture-specific, 4KB is the smallest page size supported by common architectures such as x86, x86-64, and ARM.

In practice, defenses using virtual-memory randomization operate on the library- or page-level. Library-level is the most coarse-grained approach to memory randomization, in which the application binary and base addresses of shared libraries are randomized. It is implemented at load-time by ASLR [39]. TASR [7] provides a leakage-resilient version by re-randomizing in response to input/output system-call pairs. Note that in either case, all memory objects within a library remain at fixed relative offsets to one another, but the relative offsets among libraries are randomized.

Page-level randomization, implemented by Oxymoron [5] at load-time, attempts to provide enhanced security by randomizing at a finer granularity. This ensures that inter-page offsets are randomized, but leaves intra-page offsets fixed.

2.2 Physical-Memory Randomization

Rather than change virtual-to-physical mappings, a randomization technique can instead reorder data/code in physical memory. This requires memory copies that induce overhead, but can operate at an arbitrary level of granularity. Physical memory randomization must also account for how randomization of shared pages is handled, since different processes may be simultaneously attempting to access them. This can have both security and practicality implications.

Randomization Granularity. Unlike virtual-memory randomization, physical-memory randomization may operate at any level of granularity.[1] This can dramatically limit, or entirely remove, the availability of gadgets near code pointers. Recall that low-order bits are fixed in virtual-memory randomization, because

---

[1] In practice, physical-memory randomization has only been applied at the sub-page level, as virtual-memory randomization is more efficient for coarser granularities.

addresses are necessarily page-aligned (*i.e.*, the lower 12 bits are an offset into a page, and the upper bits specify the page in a 4K-size page). Physical memory randomization does not have this constraint (as it does not rely on page tables), and can fully randomize the address of a memory object. For example, it could shift a function by a single byte. This would modify every bit in the address of that function, preventing an attacker from using their local copy of an application to infer anything about the victim's memory layout.

Physical-memory-randomization defenses have been presented at the function [53], basic-block [12,51], and instruction [26] randomization levels. Shuffler [53] randomizes the base address of all functions in a process image. Shared libraries are statically linked at load-time, in order to ensure that their functions can be safely relocated. Remix [12] and Binary Stirring [51] both randomize at the basic-block level. The former re-randomizes periodically, while that latter performs a single load-time randomization. ILR [26] uses process-level virtualization to randomize at the instruction granularity on program load. None of these approaches randomize shared libraries. We will discuss why later in Sect. 8.

3   Threat Model

We assume that a remote attacker has access to a memory-corruption vulnerability that enables arbitrary read and write access to userspace memory. This is consistent with common vulnerabilities that, for example, give attackers control over a buffer index (*e.g.*, CVE-2016-0034), or do not properly safeguard format strings (*e.g.*, CVE-2015-8617).

We make the following assumptions about the defensive configuration of the victim process. (1) $W \oplus X$ is deployed on the system being attacked, so that code injection and code modification are prevented. (2) A leakage-resilient defense is deployed that prevents direct memory disclosures (*i.e.*, leakage of code pages). (3) The Global Offset Table exists. A GOT exists as long as shared libraries are used, and is even present for an isolated binary if it is compiled to be position-independent. Additionally, the majority of leakage-resilient defenses identified in this paper do not extend protections to the GOT, with the exceptions of Oxymoron [5] and Readactor [14]. In Sect. 8, we discuss the implications of requiring GOT protection in more detail. (4) The layout of code regions in memory have been randomized, so that the attacker does not have *a priori* knowledge of the location of code in memory.

This threat model is consistent with that of existing leakage-resilient defenses.

4   Relative ROP Attacks

In this section, we describe a code-reuse attack that generically circumvents many leakage-resilient defenses that rely on virtual-memory randomization. We show that an attacker can use existing code pointers to launch meaningful exploits. This is achieved by partially overwriting the low-order byte of code pointers such that they point to a relative offset within the randomized region, without knowing or needing to corrupt the randomized high-order bytes of that pointer. Thus, we refer to these attacks as *Relative ROP (RelROP)*.

4.1 Partial Pointer Overwriting

A critical assumption to the security of memory randomization is that pointers can only be corrupted *in toto*. However, pointers in modern architectures are not atomic, and in fact require multiple bytes of memory to encode. Furthermore, byte-level memory writes are possible on most common architectures, including x86, x64, ARM, and MIPS. A *partial* pointer overwrite can be used to overwrite select bytes within a word. Partial pointer overwrites have been leveraged in previous exploits [8,19], however, in this work we leverage them in a more general attack technique, RelROP.

In this paper, we assume each memory page is 4 KB, and aligned on 4 KB boundaries. Therefore, the low-order 12 bits of each address represent the offset of the address within the page, while the high-order bits identify the page itself. We define a *memory paragraph* to be the subset of a page that is addressable by overwriting the low-order byte of a pointer. Thus, paragraphs are aligned $2^8 = 256$ byte regions of memory.

If virtual-memory randomization is applied, then the contents of each page are fixed, and can be determined offline by an attacker. Therefore, the memory paragraphs are also fixed, and the attacker can overwrite the low-order byte of an address to point to any gadget within the paragraph. This general concept is depicted in Fig. 1. The question marks denote

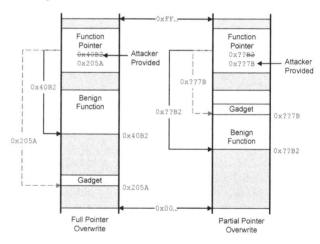

Fig. 1. Partial vs. full pointer overwrites

that those bytes of the pointer are both *unknown* to the attacker (due to the presence of a leakage-resilient technique) and *uncorrupted* by the attacker. The low-order byte, however, which denotes an offset into the paragraph, are corrupted by the attacker by only overwriting a subset of the bits encoding the pointer. The corrupted pointer now points to a gadget within the paragraph, despite the presence of a leakage-resilient technique that protects pointers from disclosure. Note that the attacker-controlled pointer cannot point outside of the page without learning or guessing the value of randomized high-order bytes. Moreover, it cannot point to any other paragraph within the target page because even though bits 9–12 of the address are known to the attacker (from an attacker's local copy), they cannot be overwritten by byte-granularity memory-corruption.

At a high level, all that is required to carry out the attack is the ability to overwrite the low-order byte of the pointer that encodes a position within the pointed-to paragraph, while avoiding any corruption of the randomized higher-order bytes. This can be accomplished using a direct memory-write vulnerability (similar to CVE-2017-0106).[2] Such vulnerabilities arise from unchecked array offset references, for example.

4.2 RelROP Chaining

In order to construct a RelROP gadget chain, we leverage the layer of indirection afforded by the procedure linking table (PLT) and the global offset table (GOT). Each externally linked function, such as those in `libc`, is invoked via a `call` instruction to an absolute address within the PLT. The code within the PLT performs a lookup of the address of the called function within the GOT, and redirects control flow to that address. The GOT and PLT have two key features that enable RelROP chaining.

First, the GOT is in the data region, which is subject to neither the write protections of $W \oplus X$ nor to randomization. Thus, entries in the GOT are vulnerable to partial pointer overwrites. By corrupting GOT entries, the pointer can be offset relative to the function's intended entry point into an attacker-chosen memory region within the paragraph pointed to by that entry.

Second, the PLT is not part of the `.text`/`.code` section, and is therefore not randomized. It does contain code pages, however, so both $W \oplus X$ and leakage-resilience are in effect. Thus, the PLT itself cannot be directly leaked. However, the GOT contains pointers into the PLT in order to support lazy loading of library functions. This standard functionality allows function addresses to be resolved only on use, increasing the speed of program loading. However, it requires pointing un-initialized function pointers (*e.g.*, `_exit` should contain an entry back to its PLT entry) to stub code in the PLT, thus leaking its location.

With these capabilities, a series of pointers to functions in the PLT can be placed on the stack, similar to a standard ROP attack. When these pointers are dereferenced, they will be redirected via the corrupted GOT to attacker-chosen gadgets. This permits chaining of RelROP attacks.

5   RelROP Prevalence Analysis

RelROP attacks leverage GOT entries to address gadgets at a relative offset from that pointer's initial location. In order to investigate the prevalence of gadgets accessible at the paragraph level of granularity, we constructed an analysis tool and applied it to over 1,300 binaries, analyzing the libraries and functions that were dynamically linked by these binaries. In this analysis, we identify all gadgets that are accessible by partially overwriting the low-order byte of a GOT entry.

---

[2] Note that other vulnerability types could also be used. For example, buffer overflows (resp. underflows) could be used, in little-endian (resp. big-endian) architectures.

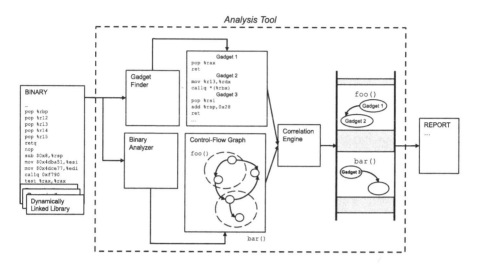

Fig. 2. RelROP gadget prevalence analysis tool architecture

5.1   Analysis-Tool Architecture

The high-level architecture of our analysis tool is depicted in Fig. 2. An input binary is processed in three phases.

First, we leverage **angr** [44], an open-source binary analysis framework, to identify all of the libraries that are linked to a given binary. Then, all conventional ROP gadgets are identified in all of these libraries using an off-the-shelf tool (these are filtered later). We chose to use the open-source tool **rp++** [3] for this purpose, with a search depth of 8 instructions (*i.e.,* each identified gadget is at most 8 instructions long).

Next, we use **angr** to identify all functions from libraries that are actually imported by the binary. That is, we *only* consider functions that actually appear in the binary's PLT, and are thus usable by RelROP. Finally, we use the function information from **angr** to identify all of the gadgets that can be accessed by overwriting the low-order byte of that function's GOT entry. Note that for each case, gadgets can be found within the function (*i.e.,* a positive offset) or within the memory *before* the function (*i.e.,* a negative offset). This is because the physical memory pages of these libraries must remain static during runtime. Thus, in the case of paragraph level randomization we consider every gadget within the memory paragraph (*e.g.,* if the function pointer is 0x11223344, any gadget in the range 0x11223300-0x112233*FF* is accessible).

5.2   Analysis of Real-World Binaries

In order to characterize how prevalent RelROP gadgets are, we ran our tool on every binary contained within the /usr/bin and /usr/sbin directories on a developer machine (Ubuntu 16.04), totaling 1,365 binaries with 577 dynamically linked libraries. The results of this analysis are summarized in Table 1. In this table, the first column represents the major gadget classes, and the next two columns depict the percentage and total, respectively, of analyzed binaries that include a gadget of each class at the paragraph granularity. The percentage of binaries with such gadgets accessible through `libc` is also included alongside the results, as attacks using libc gadgets are more desirable because of their reusability across binaries. These results demonstrate that there are ample gadgets available via partial pointer overwriting even when the attacker is constrained to the gadgets within a single byte of a code pointer.

The results in Table 1 summarize raw metrics on the number of gadgets available, but do not directly address whether there are sufficient gadgets to carry out a RelROP attack. The next step in our evaluation is to identify the fraction of applications that have enough RelROP gadgets to carry out a more complete malicious payload, such as spawning a shell. Specifically, we consider an application vulnerable to a RelROP-spawned shell if it includes either a `mov` or `pop` gadget for all the registers needed for the `execve` syscall (*i.e.*, `rax`, `rdx`, `rsi`, and `rdi`), as well as a syscall gadget. Our analysis determined that *94.4% of the binaries we considered are vulnerable, and 91.4% are vulnerable if gadgets are restricted to libc only*. These results suggest that virtual memory randomization is not, on its own, sufficient to prevent RelROP attacks.

Table 1. Gadgets within paragraph of GOT entry

Gadget	Percentage of binaries with gadgets/libc portion	Total number of gadgets/libc portion
`pop rax`	80.8%/70.2%	64493/12196
`mov rax`	99.7%/99.7%	1118428/378268
`pop rbx`	99.7%/96.3%	2326697/550486
`mov rbx`	82.3%/69.0%	81541/21715
`pop rcx`	79.2%/63.4%	43827/14253
`mov rcx`	90.8%/83.7%	214140/81593
`pop rdx`	66.9%/46.7%	28827/11845
`mov rdx`	99.7%/99.7%	418448/151041
`pop rsi`	95.6%/92.2%	123090/20512
`mov rsi`	99.7%/99.7%	426279/96681
`pop rdi`	95.2%/91.6%	97963/22853
`mov rdi`	93.6%/86.9%	831198/189329
`syscall`	94.8%/93.5%	1067064/814589

We note that in practice, an application may have gadgets that affect all of the necessary registers, but chaining the gadgets together for a successful attack may not be feasible given other side effects present in the gadgets. Additionally, our results are predicated on the completeness of our gadget-analysis tool, and other gadget analyses may identify other gadgets. These results are thus presented as indicative of RelROP prevalence, but are not claimed to be comprehensive.

6 Real-World Exploit

For our real-word exploit, we selected our target based on disclosed CVEs and *not* the availability of gadgets, since our prevalence analysis had already shown that there were likely enough gadgets to construct an exploit payload. Our real-world exploit targets the popular PHP: Hypertext Preprocessor (PHP). Specifically we

Table 2. List of ROP gadgets identified within the entry paragraph of library functions used by PHP 7.0.0

Library	Function	Offset	Gadget
libc-2.23.so	inet_ntoa	0x47	`pop rax; mov rax,rbx;` `pop rdx; pop rbx; ret;`
libc-2.23.so	uname	0x05	`syscall;`
libicuuc.so.55.1	u_isISOControl_55	0x05	`pop rsi; setnbe dl; cmp edi,0x0000009F;` `setbe al; and eax,edx; ret;`
libicuuc.so.55.1	UnicodeString::doCompare	0x03	`pop rdi; or byte [rcx-0x0A],al; ret;`
libxml2.so.2.9.3	xmlParseBalancedChunkMemory	0x04	`pop rcx; add byte [rax],al;` `add byte [rsi+0x06],bh; ret;`

targeted PHP version 7.0.0, and leveraged a known format-string vulnerability (*i.e.*, CVE-2015-8617 [1]) as a proof-of-concept for both leaking and exploiting the GOT.

Note that because of the existence of $W \oplus X$, code regions cannot be written to and data regions cannot be executed. Moreover, because of the deployment of a leakage-resilient defense, code regions cannot be reliably read. As a result, we only assume a read/write capability to *data* pages of memory in our exploit.

6.1 Exploit Details

The goal of our exploit is to achieve control-flow hijacking while PHP is protected by a leakage-resilient defense using virtual-memory randomization up to and including page-level randomization (thus, we are restricted to gadgets within the paragraph of a function pointer). Since PHP is an interpreter, we assume that the attacker is permitted to execute their own malicious PHP file on a remote server, as is common on most hosting providers. To demonstrate a powerful attack, we design an exploit that invokes the `execve` system call to spawn a new shell. This provides the attacker with powerful remote control over the compromised machine with elevated privileges from that of the original PHP script. To accomplish this, we must find a `syscall`-instruction gadget and a set of gadgets to set the necessary argument registers (*i.e.*, `rax`, `rdi`, `rsi`, and `rdx`).

We applied the tool described in Sect. 5 to analyze, offline, a local copy of PHP to identify all of the gadgets that are contained within the entry paragraph (*i.e.*, the paragraph surrounding the pointer to a function's entry point) of every function that is imported by PHP. Note that we can craft our malicious PHP file to specifically call those functions that contain the required gadgets to ensure that the GOT will be populated before our exploit. Our attack is limited to only use gadgets that are contained within entry paragraphs (*i.e.*, the single-byte offset from the function-entry point), which is encoded in the GOT. This constant offset can be added by overwriting only the low-order byte in the GOT entry, which is not affected by randomization at the page-level or coarser granularity. The gadgets identified by our tool are shown in Table 2.

It is worth noting that our `pop rdi` gadget depends on the value of rcx-0x0A being a valid and writable memory region. Similarly, our `pop rcx` gadget requires `rax` and `rsi+0x06` to be writable. Fortunately, we have both `pop rax` and `pop rsi` gadgets that we can use to set these values to known locations in the GOT, which we know to be writable. We can then similarly set `rcx` to a known GOT address to achieve a complete payload.

In traditional ROP attacks, the attacker places the absolute address of the gadgets directly on the stack in order to execute them in the payload. However, in RelROP, we are working with the constraint of virtual-memory randomization and leakage resilience, thus RelROP places the *PLT* addresses on the stack, which will be automatically resolved to our corrupted GOT entries.

To set up the exploit, we leverage the fact that the `.data` segment, including the GOT, is not randomized and is always at a fixed memory location. In the case where this is not true, we could use our memory-read vulnerability (*i.e.,* our format-string vulnerability) to leak the location of the GOT. Given any GOT address, we can trivially calculate the base address, and therefore the address of the functions containing our gadgets, as the order of the GOT entries do not change. This same format string can be leveraged to read the contents of the GOT to obtain the base address of the PLT, as unresolved functions will store pointers to their PLT entry due to lazy binding of library functions.

At this point, we have enough information to modify the GOT entries and build the set of values that need to be placed on the stack when the exploit begins executing.

Next, we modify the lower-order bits of the GOT entries for `gethostbyname`, `php_uname`, `intltz_to_date_time_zone`,

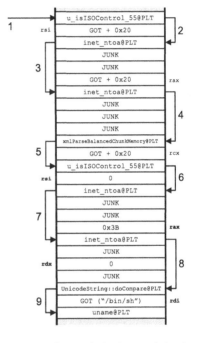

Fig. 3. The stack during exploitation

`IntlChar::isISOControl`, and `DOMDocument::appendXML` (PHP functions that call the functions listed in Table 2) by partially overwriting each entry with the offset of the gadget located in each respective function.

We start by using an assumed arbitrary-write stack-corruption vulnerability to place the proper values on the stack and point the return address to the first gadget. The stack is setup similarly to a traditional ROP payload, containing data that will end up in registers, and addresses of gadgets to be executed. Instead of using the absolute address of the gadgets, however, we use the address of the PLT entries of the functions containing the gadgets. It is important to emphasize that we know the addresses in the PLT from pointers in the GOT used for lazy binding, not from a leakage of the PLT that is prevented by the leakage-resilient defense. The stack during our RelROP attack is shown in Fig. 3. The full exploit is shown in Fig. 4.

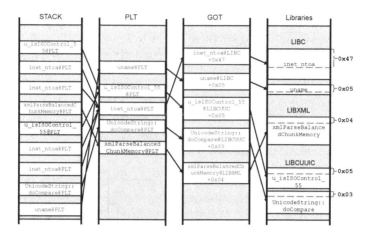

Fig. 4. PHP RelROP exploit

7   Impact on Defenses

In this section, we consider the impact of RelROP attacks on two classes of defenses. Randomization-focused defenses are those whose primary mechanism for mitigating attacks is (re)-randomization of memory at a specific level of granularity. Randomization-dependent defenses are those that require fine-grained memory randomization, but whose primary contribution is orthogonal to randomization (*e.g.*, execute-only memory).

7.1   Randomization-Focused Defenses

Table 3 summarizes the impact of RelROP on leakage-resilient defenses. These include both leakage-resilient defenses that rely on memory re-randomization, and fine-grained randomization mechanisms that may be used by leakage-resilient defenses that are dependent on a fine-grained randomizer. The table also indicates whether the requirements to conduct a RelROP attack are satisfied. We require a GOT to exist and not be *additionally* protected, and that the target be protected by either virtual-memory randomization, or physical-memory randomization that does not extend to shared libraries.

TASR is susceptible RelROP attacks. It is a leakage-resilient defense that re-randomizes code at the library level. Since the GOT is in the data region, it is not randomized by TASR. Re-randomization is applied on every read/write pair to mitigate the effects of memory disclosures. While its coverage does extend to shared libraries, it is implemented via virtual-memory randomization, and is therefore susceptible to RelROP attacks given the analysis presented in Sect. 5.

Remix is a leakage-resilient defense that periodically permutes the basic-block ordering within functions. This necessitates physical memory copies and code patching to ensure that direct jumps point to the correct target. Consequently,

Table 3. Susceptibility of leakage-resilient techniques to RelROP

Defense name	Granularity	Randomization	Unprotected GOT	Unprotected libraries	RelROP
Leakage resilience through memory re-randomization					
TASR [7]	Library	Virtual	Yes	No	Yes
Shuffler [53]	Function	Physical	No	No	No
Remix [12]	Basic Block	Physical	Yes	Yes	Yes
Memory randomization					
Oxymoron [5]	Page	Virtual	No	No	No
Binary Stirring [51]	Basic Block	Physical	Yes	Yes	Yes
ILR [26]	Instruction	Physical	Yes	Yes	Yes

Remix does not protect shared libraries. Since RelROP attacks use only gadgets in shared libraries, Remix is susceptible to RelROP.

Binary Stirring [51] is a load-time basic-block-level randomization technique. It relies on load-time patching of the binary to redirect direct jumps to randomly determined basic-block locations. Consequently, shared libraries are not randomized and can be leveraged to conduct RelROP attacks.

ILR [26] uses process-level virtualization to perform instruction-level randomization. Since this does not extend across processes, shared libraries are not protected and RelROP attacks can bypass it.

Oxymoron [5] randomizes code on the page level, as well as replacing function pointers with trampolines into a protected, GOT-like memory region. This region is isolated via memory segmentation and segment registers. This prevents RelROP attacks due to the inability to partially corrupt function pointers in the GOT. Unfortunately, attacks against it have already been demonstrated [16] and memory segmentation is largely unsupported in 64-bit architectures.

Shuffler is a leakage-resilient defense that is not susceptible to RelROP attacks, as it removes the GOT and relies purely on direct calls to libraries that are statically linked at load time. It periodically re-randomizes code at the function level at a configurable interval. Since functions may be smaller than pages, this randomization requires physical memory copying. This necessitates statically linking shared libraries. Due to the way Shuffler implements re-randomization, the size of each process' code image (including all libraries) is approximately doubled. As a result, the memory overhead on a multi-process system may be prohibitive. Shuffler also requires a dedicated per-process thread to asynchronously perform physical memory copies, which may impact cache and memory performance. Unfortunately, no analysis is provided as to the performance of Shuffler in a multi-process environment, so the true overhead is difficult to estimate.

7.2 Randomization-Dependent Leakage-Resilient Defenses

The defenses considered in this section rely on the existence of a fine-grained randomization mechanism, but their primary contribution is an orthogonal approach to leakage resilience. Since "fine-grained randomization" is often underspecified, the effect of RelROP attacks on each defense cannot be empirically evaluated. Thus, we instead consider whether the GOT/PLT is additionally protected or other implementation details disrupt RelROP attacks.

Multivariant Execution. Multivariant-execution defenses, such as Isomeron [16], are designed to disrupt ROP and JIT-ROP attacks by probabilistically switching program execution among two or more replicas of code, each with different memory layouts. Isomeron specifically applies "fine-grained" code randomization to one of two replicas, and leaves the other unmodified. Execution switches uniformly at random between each replica at the function-call granularity. This disrupts code-reuse attacks that rely on absolute jumps to memory addresses, as the location of gadgets may change at every gadget invocation. However, if the underlying code randomization is virtual-memory randomization, it does not disrupt RelROP attacks. GOT entries in Isomeron are resolved prior to diversification, and Isomeron adds a constant offset to the result if it elects to change the replica being run. Since RelROP attacks corrupt GOT entries prior to this calculation, they are "fixed" by Isomeron to point to the correct replica. If physical-memory randomization is applied to either replica, the partially corrupted pointer would point to a different location in each replica, and therefore the attack would not succeed.

Destructive Code Reads and Execute-Only Memory. Techniques that implement destructive code reads [36,50,52] aim to prevent code-reuse attacks that rely on direct memory disclosure. While all code pages can be both read and executed (in contrast to execute-only memory), attempting to execute code that has previously been read will trigger an error. In response to inference attacks that allow implicit disclosure of code by reading adjacent bytes [46], this approach has recently been combined with semantic-preserving binary re-randomization [36]. Execute-only-memory defenses [4,22] aim to stop the same class of threats as defenses that implement destructive code reads. Rather than destroying code that is read, however, execute-only defenses cause a memory-permission violation at any attempt to read executable memory.

Both of these defense classes rely on the necessity of an attacker reading *code* pages prior to executing that code. However, RelROP attacks rely entirely on reading *data* pages and corrupting code pointers without first disclosing that code (or its address). Only the GOT itself needs to be read, which, as data, does not trigger destruction. Therefore, if virtual-memory randomization is used, then partial pointer overwriting can be used to corrupt code pointers to known gadgets within the containing code paragraph. However, if physical-memory randomization is applied, then the byte value needed for the partial overwrite cannot be determined without first disclosing the randomization, and thus physical-memory randomization would prevent a RelROP attack.

Code-Pointer Protection. Another approach to preventing code-reuse attacks is to protect all pointers to code from disclosure or corruption. Pointguard [13] encrypts pointers and decrypts them just prior to use via a register-stored key. ASLR-Guard [35] uses a combination of encryption and protected lookup tables to hide the value of function pointers. Readactor [14,15] combines execute-only memory, fine-grained code randomization, register randomization, PLT randomization, and replacement of function pointers with trampolines into a protected lookup table. Notably, however, Readactor has been shown vulnerable to profiling-based attacks [41].

Encrypting or otherwise protecting all bytes of function pointers prevents partial overwrites, as low-order bits are no longer vulnerable. In addition, use of trampolines into lookup tables decouples the pointer value from any gadgets near its eventual target, thus making relative-address attacks only able to (at best) change the index into the lookup table. If table randomization and booby traps are used, as in Readactor, even this capability is removed. Thus, code-pointer protection techniques are effective in countering RelROP attacks.

8 Discussion

Physical-memory randomization at the granularity of instruction or basic-blocks, applied ubiquitously to the binary and its linked libraries would not be vulnerable to the RelROP attack described earlier. However, such a technique faces a number of practicality challenges. Furthermore, subsequent design decisions to address those challenges themselves come with security/practicality implications. All of these challenges arise from dealing with shared physical memory pages, such as those in linked libraries. In this section, we first discuss the practical challenges of physical-memory randomization, then we discuss other possible RelROP mitigations.

8.1 Implications of Physical-Memory Randomization

Cross-Process Disclosures. Many physical-memory randomization defenses (see [34] for an overview) apply randomization at compile time, by, for example, inserting NOPs to change relative distances between instructions. These one-time randomization approaches suffer from the fact that a memory disclosure in *any* process using a shared code page (*e.g.,* libc pages) allows the attacker to de-randomize that page in *all* processes using that code page. Thus, leakage-resilient defenses must be applied to every process that links shared libraries.

Shared-Library Synchronization. Physical-memory randomization that takes place at load- or run-time must deal with the fact that multiple processes executing code from shared libraries do not synchronize their accesses, as these pages are traditionally read-only. This becomes problematic when attempting to move that code to another physical memory region. Each process may have stack/heap pointers to different regions of the shared library (especially if library functions call each other), and have instruction pointers at different addresses within that library. All of these pointers must be adjusted to point to the library's new location in a way that is transparent to each running application.

Shuffler [53] addresses the issue by statically linking all libraries into a process image at load time, and maintaining two copies of the process binary and libraries. One copy is active and used for execution, and the other is asynchronously re-randomized by a dedicated thread. When the copy is complete, execution shifts to the new version and re-randomization is applied to the other copy. Unfortunately, this means that if n processes are executing on a system, there are $2n$ copies of libc, $2n$ copies of each application binary, and up to $2n$ copies of other shared libraries. Remix [12], Binary Stirring [51], and ILR [26] address this issue by simply not protecting shared libraries, and limiting themselves to the unshared physical pages corresponding to the main application binary. As shown in Sect. 5, however, this still provides ample attack surface to create a malicious payload. In fact, most valuable gadgets, such as those capable of invoking a system call, are found in libc and not the binary itself.

Memory Thrashing. Runtime re-randomization based on physical-memory randomization, such as Remix [12] and Shuffler [53], periodically perform physical memory copies in order to relocate code regions. This interferes with the performance of the cache and memory subsystem due to large-scale invalidation of cache lines, and additional memory traffic. Depending on the rate at which re-randomization is performed, memory thrashing can become a significant source of overhead. A study of cache and memory performance observed such cache and memory contention can result in slowdowns of a factor of up to 2.5x [32].

8.2 RELRO

A defensive feature in some operating systems called Relocation Read-Only (or RELRO) is sometimes used to protect GOT. Partial RELRO forces GOT to come before BSS, preventing some types of buffer overflows on global variables. Full RELRO marks the entire GOT as read-only.

While partial RELRO has no impact on RelROP, full RELRO breaks it. However, full RELRO has several performance tradeoffs, and is not commonly deployed in practice. A recent study shows that as low as 3% of binaries are protected with full RELRO [48]. There are a few reasons for this. Full RELRO requires all symbols to be resolved at load time, which significantly slows down program startup. Full RELRO is also not a default option in GCC (partial RELRO is). Many Linux distros also do not have RELRO, such a RHEL v6 (and earlier), which will be actively supported until 2021.

9   Related Work

Our work mainly relates to memory-corruption vulnerabilities and mitigation thereof. The literature in these areas is vast. We refer the interested reader to the relevant surveys [10, 34, 49] and focus on closely related work. Since we have already discussed may related efforts in the context of our attack, we limit the work referenced in this section to the remaining closely related ones.

In a concurrent work with ours, a similar attack, PIROP [24], also uses partial pointer overwrites to bypass leakage-resilient defenses. However, PIROP's approach is significantly different from ours in the following aspects. First, PIROP is based on the concept of memory massaging, in which a carefully chosen set of inputs causes the program to place code pointers on the stack. These are then adjusted via partial pointer overwrites. This approach is probabilistic under fine-grained randomization, with probability of success decreasing as the required number of gadgets increases. RelROP attacks, conversely, are deterministic and can scale to arbitrary payload sizes. Second, it is unclear how well PIROP attacks generalize or could be automated. Each proof of concept exploit presented in that work requires study and use of application-specific execution semantics. Rel-ROP attacks only require knowledge of the target binary's GOT. Third, PIROP attacks are only able to bypass memory re-randomization defenses if they are restricted to live pointers that are actively being tracked by the re-randomizer. They cannot rely on stale pointers, such as those remaining from old stack frames whose associated function has already returned. RelROP attacks bypass any virtual memory re-randomization technique. Fourth, PIROP's evaluation focuses on the amount of entropy provided by various existing defenses. Since RelROP attacks are deterministic, this does not apply to our technique. We instead analyze the tradeoffs between virtual and physical memory randomization, and their implications for practical leakage-resilient defenses.

There are also a large number of randomization-based techniques proposed in the literature that perform compile-time [28, 29, 33], load-time [17, 26], or runtime [27, 37] randomization. It has been shown that information-leakage attacks of various types, including direct memory disclosures [47], timing-based and fault-based side-channel attacks [8, 42], script-based leaks [45], indirect pointer leaks [16], profiling attacks [41], and cache-based side-channel attacks [25], can be used to bypass randomization-based defenses. Other orthogonal attacks against many leakage-resilient defenses have also been studied, the details of which are beyond our scope [6, 9, 16, 20, 40, 41, 45, 46].

Control flow integrity (CFI) and all of its variants [10] are another class of memory corruption defenses that are orthogonal to and not impacted by RelROP. They are, however, vulnerable to attacks on the imprecisions of the control flow graph [21].

10 Conclusion

In this paper, we analyzed the security and practicality of memory-randomization mechanisms supporting leakage-resilient defenses. We illustrated an attack, RelROP, that bypasses page-level or coarser virtual-memory randomization via partial overwriting of code pointers. We analyzed the prevalence of RelROP gadgets in popular code bases, and built a proof-of-concept exploit against PHP 7.0.0. In addition, we enumerated the challenges associated with practical deployment of physical-memory randomization defenses that arise from protecting shared memory objects (*e.g.*, shared libraries). Our findings indicate that additional research is needed to design efficient and effective leakage-resilient memory-protection techniques.

References

1. CVE-2015-8617. "Available from MITRE, CVE-ID CVE-2015-8617" (2015). http://cve.mitre.org/cgi-bin/cvename.cgi?name=CVE-2015-8617
2. Threat LandScape Report Q2 2017. Fortinet (2017). https://www.fortinet.com/content/dam/fortinet/assets/threat-reports/Fortinet-Threat-Report-Q2-2017.pdf
3. 0vercl0k: rp++, April 2017. https://github.com/0vercl0k/rp
4. Backes, M., Holz, T., Kollenda, B., Koppe, P., Nürnberger, S., Pewny, J.: You can run but you can't read: preventing disclosure exploits in executable code. In: ACM Conference on Computer and Communications Security. CCS (2014)
5. Backes, M., Nürnberger, S.: Oxymoron: making fine-grained memory randomization practical by allowing code sharing. In: 23rd USENIX Security Symposium. USENIX Sec (2014)
6. Barresi, A., Razavi, K., Payer, M., Gross, T.R.: CAIN: silently breaking ASLR in the cloud. In: 9th USENIX Security Symposium. WOOT 2015 (2015)
7. Bigelow, D., Hobson, T., Rudd, R., Streilein, W., Okhravi, H.: Timely rerandomization for mitigating memory disclosures. In: ACM Conference on Computer and Communications Security. CCS (2015)
8. Bittau, A., Belay, A., Mashtizadeh, A.J., Mazières, D., Boneh, D.: Hacking blind. In: 35th IEEE Symposium on Security and Privacy. S&P (2014)
9. Bosman, E., Razavi, K., Bos, H., Giuffrida, C.: Dedup est machina: Memory deduplication as an advanced exploitation vector. In: 37th IEEE Symposium on Security and Privacy (2016)
10. Burow, N., et al.: Control-flow integrity: precision, security, and performance. ACM Comput. Surv. **50**(1), 16:1–16:33 (2017)
11. Checkoway, S., Davi, L., Dmitrienko, A., Sadeghi, A., Shacham, H., Winandy, M.: Return-oriented programming without returns. In: ACM Conference on Computer and Communications Security. CCS (2010)
12. Chen, Y., Wang, Z., Whalley, D., Lu, L.: Remix: on-demand live randomization. In: Proceedings of the Sixth ACM Conference on Data and Application Security and Privacy, pp. 50–61. ACM (2016)
13. Cowan, C., Beattie, S., Johansen, J., Wagle, P.: Pointguard: protecting pointers from buffer overflow vulnerabilities. In: 12th USENIX Security Symposium. USENIX Sec (2003)
14. Crane, S., et al.: Readactor: practical code randomization resilient to memory disclosure. In: 36th IEEE Symposium on Security and Privacy. S&P (2015)
15. Crane, S., et al.: It's a TRaP: table randomization and protection against function-reuse attacks. In: ACM Conference on Computer and Communications Security. CCS (2015)
16. Davi, L., Liebchen, C., Sadeghi, A.R., Snow, K.Z., Monrose, F.: Isomeron: code randomization resilient to (Just-In-Time) return-oriented programming. In: 22nd Annual Network and Distributed System Security Symposium. NDSS (2015)

17. Davi, L.V., Dmitrienko, A., Nürnberger, S., Sadeghi, A.R.: Gadge me if you can: secure and efficient ad-hoc instruction-level randomization for x86 and ARM. In: ASIACCS, pp. 299–310 (2013)
18. De Sutter, B., Anckaert, B., Geiregat, J., Chanet, D., De Bosschere, K.: Instruction set limitation in support of software diversity. In: Lee, P.J., Cheon, J.H. (eds.) ICISC 2008. LNCS, vol. 5461, pp. 152–165. Springer, Heidelberg (2009). https://doi.org/10.1007/978-3-642-00730-9_10
19. Durden, T.: Bypassing PaX ASLR protection (2002). http://www.phrack.org/issues.html?issue=59&id=9
20. Evans, I., et al.: Missing the point(er): on the effectiveness of code pointer integrity. In: 36th IEEE Symposium on Security and Privacy. S&P (2015)
21. Evans, I., et al.: Control jujutsu: on the weaknesses of fine-grained control flow integrity. In: ACM Conference on Computer and Communications Security. CCS (2015)
22. Gionta, J., Enck, W., Ning, P.: HideM: protecting the contents of userspace memory in the face of disclosure vulnerabilities. In: 5th ACM Conference on Data and Application Security and Privacy. CODASPY (2015)
23. Giuffrida, C., Kuijsten, A., Tanenbaum, A.S.: Enhanced operating system security through efficient and fine-grained address space randomization. In: 21st USENIX Security Symposium. USENIX Sec (2012)
24. Göktas, E., et al.: Position-independent code reuse: on the effectiveness of ASLR in the absence of information disclosure. In: IEEE EuroS&P (2018)
25. Gras, B., Razavi, K., Bosman, E., Bos, H., Giuffrida, C.: ASLR on the line: Practical cache attacks on the MMU. NDSS, February 2017 (2017)
26. Hiser, J., Nguyen, A; Co, M., Hall, M., Davidson, J.: ILR: Where'd my gadgets go. In: 33rd IEEE Symposium on Security and Privacy. S&P (2012)
27. Homescu, A., Brunthaler, S., Larsen, P., Franz, M.: Librando: transparent code randomization for just-in-time compilers. In: ACM Conference on Computer & Communications security, pp. 993–1004 (2013)
28. Homescu, A., Neisius, S., Larsen, P., Brunthaler, S., Franz, M.: Profile-guided automated software diversity. In: International Symposium on Code Generation and Optimization (CGO), pp. 1–11. IEEE (2013)
29. Jackson, T., et al.: Compiler-generated software diversity. In: Moving Target Defense. Advances in Information Security (2011)
30. Jackson, T., Homescu, A., Crane, S., Larsen, P., Brunthaler, S., Franz, M.: Diversifying the software stack using randomized NOP insertion. In: Moving Target Defense. Advances in Information Security (2013)
31. Kil, C., Jun, J., Bookholt, C., Xu, J., Ning, P.: Address space layout permutation (ASLP): towards fine-grained randomization of commodity software. In: 22nd Annual Computer Security Applications Conference. ACSAC (2006)
32. Kim, N., Ward, B.C., Chisholm, M., Anderson, J.H., Smith, F.D.: Attacking the one-out-of-m multicore problem by combining hardware management with mixed-criticality provisioning. Real-Time Syst. **53**(5), 709–759 (2017)
33. Koo, H., Chen, Y., Lu, L., Kemerlis, V.P., Polychronakis, M.: Compiler-assisted code randomization. In: IEEE Symposium on Security & Privacy (SP) (2018)
34. Larsen, P., Homescu, A., Brunthaler, S., Franz, M.: SoK: automated software diversity. In: 35th IEEE Symposium on Security and Privacy. S&P (2014)
35. Lu, K., Song, C., Lee, B., Chung, S.P., Kim, T., Lee, W.: ASLR-Guard: stopping address space leakage for code reuse attacks. In: ACM Conference on Computer and Communications Security. CCS (2015)

36. Morton, M., Koo, H., Li, F., Snow, K.Z., Polychronakis, M., Monrose, F.: Defeating zombie gadgets by re-randomizing code upon disclosure. In: International Symposium on Engineering Secure Software and Systems, pp. 143–160 (2017)
37. Novark, G., Berger, E.D.: Dieharder: securing the heap. In: ACM Conference on Computer and Communications Security. CCS, pp. 573–584 (2010)
38. One, A.: Smashing the stack for fun and profit. Phrack Mag. **7**, 14–16 (1996)
39. PaX: PaX address space layout randomization (2003)
40. Razavi, K., Gras, B., Bosman, E., Preneel, B., Giuffrida, C., Bos, H.: Flip feng shui: hammering a needle in the software stack. In: 25th USENIX Security Symposium. USENIX Sec (2016)
41. Rudd, R., et al.: Address-oblivious code reuse: on the effectiveness of leakage resilient diversity. In: Proceedings of the Network and Distributed System Security Symposium. NDSS 2017, February 2017
42. Seibert, J., Okhravi, H., Söderström, E.: Information leaks without memory disclosures: Remote side channel attacks on diversified code. In: ACM Conference on Computer and Communications Security. CCS (2014)
43. Shacham, H.: The geometry of innocent flesh on the bone: return-into-libc without function calls (on the x86). In: ACM Conference on Computer and Communications Security. CCS (2007)
44. Shoshitaishvili, Y., et al.: SoK: (State of) the art of war: Offensive techniques in binary analysis. In: IEEE Symposium on Security and Privacy (2016)
45. Snow, K.Z., Monrose, F., Davi, L., Dmitrienko, A., Liebchen, C., Sadeghi, A.: Just-in-time code reuse: on the effectiveness of fine-grained address space layout randomization. In: 34th IEEE Symposium on Security and Privacy. S&P (2013)
46. Snow, K.Z., Rogowski, R., Werner, J., Koo, H., Monrose, F., Polychronakis, M.: Return to the zombie gadgets: undermining destructive code reads via code inference attacks. In: 37th IEEE Symposium on Security and Privacy (2016)
47. Strackx, R., Younan, Y., Philippaerts, P., Piessens, F., Lachmund, S., Walter, T.: Breaking the memory secrecy assumption. In: 2nd European Workshop on System Security. EUROSEC (2009)
48. Saito, T., Yokoyama, M., Sugawara, S., Suzaki, K.: Safe trans loader: mitigation and prevention of memory corruption attacks for released binaries. In: Inomata, A., Yasuda, K. (eds.) IWSEC 2018. LNCS, vol. 11049, pp. 68–83. Springer, Cham (2018). https://doi.org/10.1007/978-3-319-97916-8_5
49. Szekeres, L., Payer, M., Wei, T., Song, D.: Sok: eternal war in memory. In: Proceedings of IEEE Symposium on Security and Privacy (2013)
50. Tang, A., Sethumadhavan, S., Stolfo, S.: Heisenbyte: thwarting memory disclosure attacks using destructive code reads. In: ACM Conference on Computer and Communications Security. CCS (2015)
51. Wartell, R., Mohan, V., Hamlen, K.W., Lin, Z.: Binary stirring: self-randomizing instruction addresses of legacy x86 binary code. In: ACM Conference on Computer and Communications Security. CCS (2012)
52. Werner, J., et al.: No-execute-after-read: preventing code disclosure in commodity software. In: 11th ACM Symposium on Information, Computer and Communications Security. ASIACCS (2016)
53. Williams-King, D., et al.: Shuffler: fast and deployable continuous code re-randomization. In: Proceedings of the 12th USENIX Conference on Operating Systems Design and Implementation, pp. 367–382 (2016)

A Taxonomy of Attacks Using BGP Blackholing

Loïc Miller[(⊠)] and Cristel Pelsser

University of Strasbourg, 4 Rue Blaise Pascal, 67081 Strasbourg, France
{loicmiller,pelsser}@unistra.fr

Abstract. BGP blackholing is a common technique used to mitigate DDoS attacks. Generally, the victim sends in a request for traffic to the attacked IP(s) to be dropped. Unfortunately, remote parties may misuse blackholing [29,57] and send requests for IPs they do not own, turning a defense technique into a new attack vector. As DDoS attacks grow in number, blackholing will only become more popular, creating a greater risk this service will be exploited. In this work, we develop a taxonomy of attacks combining hijacks with blackholing: BGP blackjacks (blackhole hijacks). We show that those attacks effectively grant more reach and stealth to the attacker than regular hijacks, and assess the usability of those attacks in various security deployments. We then find that routing security mechanisms for BGP [30,31] do not provide an adequate protection against some of those attacks, and propose additional mechanisms to properly defend against or mitigate them.

Keywords: BGP · Security · Blackholing · DDoS · Communities · Hijacks · Leaks

1 Introduction

DDoS attacks are one of the most potent threats to the Internet. With the rise of the Internet of Things (IoT), the number of connected devices is exploding. The potential of a botnet to launch massive Distributed Denial of Service (DDoS) attacks is taking scary proportions [40]. New attack vectors [1,38] are being discovered and are enabling the largest attacks we have ever seen. In February 2018 for example, Github was under attack, receiving up to 1.3 Tbps of traffic through its CDN, Akamai. Such a high amount of traffic can flood many access links, rendering services behind those links unavailable.

These attacks can be motivated by multiple reasons, including but not limited to revenge [27], activism [41], vandalism [42], financial reasons [32] or political reasons [6].

Fortunately, numerous techniques exist to mitigate DDoS attacks [48,49]. Those techniques can be roughly separated in two categories: proactive mitigation techniques and reactive mitigation techniques. Proactive techniques encompass all the mitigation techniques put in place before an attack happens, like

© Springer Nature Switzerland AG 2019
K. Sako et al. (Eds.): ESORICS 2019, LNCS 11735, pp. 107–127, 2019.
https://doi.org/10.1007/978-3-030-29959-0_6

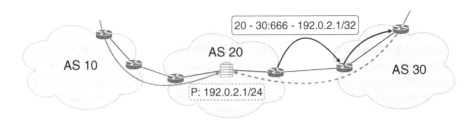

Fig. 1. BGP Blackholing

designing protocols with a reduced amplification factor (the amount of traffic one can get in a response compared to the amount of traffic one has to send in a request), or reducing the number of amplifiers available to attackers. Proactive techniques also include response rate limiting, using sessions for UDP, filtering spoofed packets, making use of anycast or even using Access Control Lists.

DDoS attacks can also be dealt with in a reactive way, by using traffic scrubbing services, where a third party processes the victim's incoming traffic, detects and mitigates the attack, and then forwards the legitimate traffic to the victim.

While filtering provides a great amount of flexibility, it runs into scalability issues in terms of number of entries and packet rate [29], as well as resources and reaction time [14]. A mitigation technique based on forwarding is thus much more scalable, and this is where BGP blackholing shines.

Blackholing [29,57] uses the Border Gateway Protocol (BGP) [43] as a means to announce the need for mitigation. BGP is the de-facto inter-domain routing protocol in the Internet, and it's primary function is to allow Autonomous Systems (ASes) to communicate with others by exchanging reachability information. More specifically, blackholing is announced via BGP communities [8,28], optional transitive BGP attributes which are *"used to pass additional information to both neighboring and remote BGP peers"* [8]. The communities forwarded with an advertisement are interpreted by ASes, which use this information to apply a specific treatment to the route.

Figure 1 depicts blackholing being used to mitigate a DDoS attack. AS 20's server located at 192.0.2.1/32 is under a DDoS attack going through both its neighbors, AS 10 and AS 30. To mitigate the attack, AS 20 sends an advertisement to AS 30, indicating to blackhole prefix 192.0.2.1/32 by adding the community used to signal blackholing to AS 30, '30:666'. The community sent, '30:666' means that AS 30 needs to apply blackholing. In addition to this information, we also usually attach either the NO_EXPORT or the NO_ADVERTISE community to the advertisement, respectively, to keep the scope local to the AS or the router [28].

Blackholing is a very effective mitigation technique [13], but it has a double-edged sword effect: all malicious traffic destined to the blackholed prefix is dropped, but so is legitimate traffic.

The literature highlights shortcomings in BGP communities, namely the lack of standardization and authentication. Firstly, only a handful of communities have a semantic meaning defined in RFCs, the vast majority of them being defined by the AS 'owning' them, making them AS-specific [54]. This lack of standardization makes communities harder to classify [15]. In addition, documentation for communities is scattered and incomplete [54]. In the case of blackholing, Giotsas et al. found 307 different community values used to signal blackholing, with an additionnal 115 labeled as likely [22]. Blackholing is nevertheless frequently used [13], and its use is increasing [22], as it is a very effective way to mitigate DDoS attacks [13,22]. Even though ASes should keep the scope of blackholing local to the AS or the router, it has been shown that 50% (80%) of blackhole communities still traverse up to two (four) ASes, with some blackhole communities traversing as many as eleven ASes [54].

Communities are also vulnerable because they can be altered by third parties: *"Because BGP communities are optional transitive BGP attributes, BGP communities may be acted upon or otherwise used by routing policies in other Autonomous Systems (ASes) on the Internet."* [24]. With other ASes being able to modify communities associated with a BGP advertisement, communities can become a vector of attacks. Solutions to secure Internet routing exist [30,31], but they focus on securing the AS path, leaving other BGP attributes unprotected. Those solutions also suffer from a lack or absence of deployment, due to the lack of incentives to do so [20].

Attacks trying to falsify BGP attributes to gain an advantage are not new. As BGP is a distributed protocol, lacking authentication of route origins and verification of paths, ASes can advertise illegitimate routes for prefixes they do not own, attracting some or all of the traffic to these prefixes. Those advertisements propagate and pollute the Internet, affecting service availability, integrity, and confidentiality of communications [52]. This phenomenon is called prefix hijacking. In this work, we build on top of prefix hijacking to create new attacks through BGP blackholing: blackjacks. Hijacks and blackjacks are similar, in that they both impact reachability of the affected prefix. However, regular hijacks only poison the ASes near the attacker, whereas blackjacks drop traffic directly at the ASes receiving the advertisement, regardless of AS path length. This means blackjacks have more reach, and are stealthier than simple hijacks.

Considering routing attacks and defenses (Sect. 2), we construct an attack taxonomy using blackholing as an attack vector (Sect. 3) and assess the usability of those attacks in different security deployments (Sect. 4). We then detail good practices and implementations to protect against such attacks (Sect. 5). Finally, we review related work (Sect. 6) and conclude in Sect. 7 by reviewing our contributions and describing the possible perspectives and areas of future work.

2   Background

Prefix hijacking can be caused by misconfiguration [47], or with malicious intent, possibly motivated by retaliation [56], information gathering [34], economical reasons [23] or political reasons [35].

On Fig. 2, AS 10 (the victim) advertises a route for the prefix 192.0.2.0/24. The hijacker (AS 40) can fake a direct connection to this network by advertising

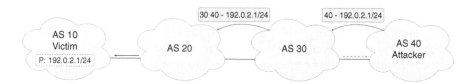

Fig. 2. Prefix hijacking

192.0.2.0/24 to AS 30. Preferring the shorter AS path, AS 30 will choose a new best route going through AS 40, and forward the advertisement to AS 20. AS 20's original route is already the best one, so it does not accept the new route and does not forward the advertisement to AS 10.

We base our work on a hijack taxonomy developed in [52], which is based on three dimensions:

– The manipulation of the AS path.
– The affected prefix.
– The way (hijacked) data traffic is treated.

To illustrate those hijack types, let us reconsider Fig. 2, where AS 10 (the victim) owns and legitimately announces 192.0.2.0/24, and AS 40 is the hijacker. For the sake of simplicity, a BGP advertisement is noted as an announced prefix tagged with an AS path. For example, {AS20, AS10 - 192.0.2.0/24} is a BGP advertisement for prefix 192.0.2.0/24 with AS path {AS20, AS10}, originated by the legitimate AS (AS 10). In their paper, they first classify by AS path manipulation, creating three categories of hijacks:

– **Origin AS (or Type-0) hijacking:** The hijacker announces as its own a prefix that it is not authorized to originate (e.g. {AS40 - 192.0.2.0/24}). This type of hijack is sometimes called prefix re-origination, and is the most commonly observed type of hijack [52].
– **Type-N hijacking ($N \geq 1$):** Also called path manipulation in the literature [10,11,19]. The hijacker announces an illegitimate path for a prefix it does not own, creating fake adjacencies between ASes. The path contains the ASN of the hijacker as the last hop (e.g. {AS40, AS20, AS10 - 192.0.2.0/24}). Here, AS 40 creates a fake adjacency between itself and AS 20. The position of the rightmost fake link in the forged advertisement determines the type. For example, {AS40, AS10 - 192.0.2.0/24} is a Type-1 hijacking, {AS40, AS20, AS10 - 192.0.2.0/24} is a Type-2 hijacking, etc.
– **Type-U hijacking:** The hijacker leaves the legitimate AS path unaltered (but may alter the advertised prefix). In the case both the AS path and the prefix are left unaltered, the event is not a hijack but rather a traffic manipulation attempt, performed by adding communities to the advertisement for example.

The second discriminant is the affected prefix. The hijacker can either perform an exact prefix hijack, where he announces a path for the same prefix that is announced by the legitimate AS, or he can perform a sub-prefix hijack, where he announces a more specific prefix. In the case of an exact prefix hijack, only the part of the Internet that is close to the hijacker (in terms of AS hops) switches to routes towards the hijacker. In the case of a sub-prefix hijack, the entire Internet traffic is sent towards the hijacker to reach the announced sub-prefix. Note that since most routers do not accept BGP advertisements containing a prefix past a certain length (usually /24) to reduce routing table size, a sub-prefix hijack advertising a /25 or more may not be very effective, as the advertisements will be dropped. There is also the case of squatting, where the hijacker announces a prefix owned but not (currently) announced by the legitimate AS. In this work, we disregard squatting as it is not applicable to blackjack attacks.

The last discriminant is the way the data-plane traffic is handled. Once the hijack is accomplished, the attacker attracts some or all of the traffic origi- nally destined to the hijacked prefix to his own AS. The attacker can then drop the packets (blackhole), impersonate the services tied to the hijacked prefix by responding to the victims (imposture), eavesdrop on the traffic and forward it back to the victim (interception) [52,62], and event send spam [59] or carry out other activities.

For example, the hijack depicted in Fig. 2 is a Type-0 exact prefix hijack, as AS 40 re-originates 192.0.2.0/24.

In our work, we will classify the attacks only by AS path manipulation and affected prefix, as blackholing attacks have the sole purpose of dropping traffic. Note that this taxonomy can be extended, as it does not cover cases where, for example, the attacker possesses two or more ASes.

Even though techniques to protect oneself against hijacks lack deployment, they still exist and are the go-to solutions to make BGP more secure.

2.1 BGP Routing Security

When receiving an advertisement, a router might want to verify that the included AS path is legitimate. This process is broken down in two validation steps:

- **Origin validation:** Does the origin AS have a right to announce this prefix?
- **Path validation:** Does the sequence of ASes in the AS path reflect the sequence of ASes crossed by this advertisement?

The Resource Public Key Infrastructure. Origin validation can be achieved through the Resource Public Key Infrastructure [30]. The RPKI is a distributed, hierarchic public key infrastructure. It allows prefix holders (legit- imate holders of IP address space) to emit digitally signed objects, *Route Origin Authorizations (ROAs)*, attesting that a given AS is authorized to originate routes for a set of prefixes.

This way, a given AS can verify that the origin AS present in a given adver- tisement is authorized to originate the prefix (*Route Origin Validation (ROV)*). While the RPKI provides digitally signed routing objects, it does not sign BGP advertisements, and operates separately from BGP. An advantage of RPKI is that the mapping of prefixes to origin ASes is formally verifiable [37].

BGPsec. Path validation can be achieved through BGPsec [31]. BGPsec relies on RPKI as it makes use of certificates.

To secure the path attribute, BGPsec relies on an new optional non-transitive BGP path attribute which replaces the AS_PATH attribute: BGPsec_PATH. The attribute carries digital signatures providing cryptographic assurance that every AS on the path of ASes listed in the advertisement has explicitly authorized the advertisement of the route. BGPsec-compliant BGP speakers (BGPsec speakers) wishing to send BGPsec advertisements to eBGP peers need to possess a private key associated with an RPKI router certificate [46] that corresponds to the BGPsec speakers's ASNs.

Traditional BGP advertisements may still be sent between BGPsec speakers, meaning an attacker can potentially downgrade a BGPsec speaker to regular BGP [33]. BGPsec also does not protect against BGP leaks, which is defined as a violation of the standard model of routing policies, pinpointed by Gao and Rexford [17,18]. Simply put, the Gao-Rexford model states that ASes have incentives to send traffic along customer routes (which generate revenue), as opposed to peer routes (which do not generate revenue) or provider routes (which come at a monetary cost). It also models ASes' willingness to transit traffic from one neighbor to another only when paid to do so by a customer. This is important to keep in mind for one of the attacks we define in Sect. 3.

3   Threat Model and Attack Taxonomy

This section is dedicated to the elaboration of an attack taxonomy. We consider a common and general hijacking threat model [50,52]. An attacker controls a single AS and its border routers. He also has full control of the control plane and the data plane within its own AS. The attacker can arbitrarily manipulate the advertisements that it sends to its neighboring ASes and the traffic that crosses its network. He has no control over advertisements and traffic exchanged between two other ASes.

Even though these attacks can work in numerous configurations, we assume for the sake of explanations that:

Assumption 1. *Every AS uses the Gao-Rexford routing policy model.*

Assumption 2. *Every AS follows the best practices defined in [9] when receiving a blackhole request.*

Those best practices can be summarized as:

1. Set local-preference to 200 (higher preference)
2. Set origin-type to IGP (higher preference)
3. Add the NO_EXPORT community to the advertisement

Following those best practices means that the blackholing advertisement is preferred over other routes and that blackholing is limited to the AS receiving the advertisement.

For the sake of simplicity, a BGP advertisement is noted as an announced prefix tagged with an AS path and communities. For example, {AS20, AS10 - <*blackholer AS*>:666 - 192.0.2.0/24} is an advertisement for prefix 192.0.2.0/24 with AS path {AS20, AS10}, originated by AS 10, and bearing the blackhole community <*blackholer AS*>:666, where <*blackholer AS*>is the AS providing the blackholing service.

Type-0 Blackjack. This first attack is also the simplest. Performing a Type-0 blackjack is done by performing a Type-0 hijack and attaching the blackhole community to the advertisement.

Figure 3 shows AS 30 (the victim) advertising a route for 192.0.2.0/24. AS 10 (the attacker) can perform a Type-0 blackjack by re-originating the prefix 192.0.2.0/24, and attaching the blackhole community to the advertisement. Thus, AS 10 sends {10 - 20:666 - 192.0.2.0/24} to its peer. As AS 20 (the blackholer) follows Assumptions 1 and 2, it blackholes traffic destined to 192.0.2.0/24.

This example highlights two main advantages of blackjack attacks:

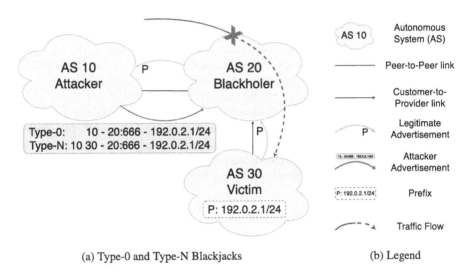

(a) Type-0 and Type-N Blackjacks   (b) Legend

Fig. 3. Type-0 and Type-N Blackjacks

- **Reach:** The attacker can potentially drop more traffic by sending blackholing advertisements to its neighbors than by hijacking the prefix and blackholing the traffic at his AS. If AS 10 tried to do so, it could not have dropped traffic going through AS 20, as AS 20 would prefer the route going through its customer (AS 30). This is not the case anymore with the blackjack attack, since AS 20 now prefers the advertisement of AS 10 per Assumption 2, thus dropping all traffic destined to the blackholed prefix.

Blackholing also grants precedence over AS path length, so the longer AS path that generally comes with hijacks is no longer a problem. Considering this, an attacker can effectively target a specific blackholer multiple AS hops away, by using their specific blackhole community value.

One thing to consider when performing sub-prefix blackjacks with a far away blackholer is that all ASes on the path between the attacker and the blackholer need to forward the advertisement. Since most routers do not accept advertisements containing a prefix past a certain length (usually /24) to reduce routing table size, the blackjack might not reach the blackholer if the targeted prefix is too specific.

Moreover, when the blackholer applies blackholing, a good practice is to add the NO_EXPORT community, which means that a blackjack targeting a prefix advertised in the Internet will stop the blackholer from advertising this prefix, causing even more disruption. In the case of a sub-prefix blackjack, the prefix will still be advertised, but traffic to the target of the attack will still be dropped at the blackholer even though no routes changed.

– **Stealth:** As the attacker is not the one dropping the traffic, he hides himself better from potential onlookers. Note that it may still be possible to retrieve the source of the attack by looking at the advertisements received by the relevant routers at the time of the attack, even though it might be hard to do so, considering those routers are not likely in the network of the victim.

It is also worth noting that an even stealthier attack is possible, if the blackholer(s) is(are) at multiple hops from the attacker. In this case, not only will the attacker not blackhole the traffic himself, but he will also not be the only one that could have sent a blackhole advertisement, as potentially other ASes could have performed the attack. Since an attacker can target a blackholer that is far away, an attack can propagate far from the source of the attack, increasing the difficulty to detect it and identify the attacker.

In our example, AS 20 is blackholing the traffic, even though it was AS 10 that performed the attack.

A disadvantage of Type-0 blackjack attacks is that some defense mechanisms can detect and counter them. By performing Route Origin Validation, either using IRR records or the RPKI, an AS can effectively know which AS is authorized to announce which prefix. Since in a Type-0 blackjack, the attacker is the origin AS, this type of attack is not effective against ASes performing ROV.

Type-N Blackjack. Type-N blackjacks circumvent ROV by creating a false adjacency between the attacker and an AS, in the same way Type-N hijacks work. Indeed, if an AS tries to verify the origin of an AS path, as the origin is legitimate, the AS will deem the origin valid.

Figure 3 depicts a Type-N blackjack. Analogous to our Type-0 blackjack example, AS 30 advertises a route for 192.0.2.0/24. AS 10 can perform a Type-N blackjack by faking an adjacency with AS 30, and attaching the blackhole community to the advertisement. Thus, AS 10 sends {10, 30 - 20:666 - 192.0.2.0/24} to its neighbor. As AS 20 follows Assumptions 1 and 2, it blackholes traffic

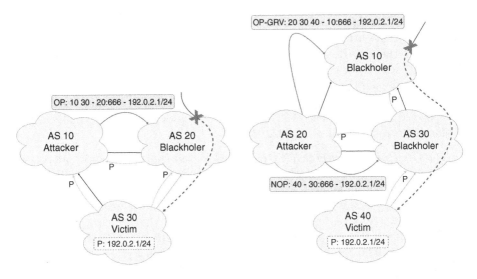

Fig. 4. On Path Blackjack   **Fig. 5.** OP-GRV and NOP Blackjacks

destined to 192.0.2.0/24. A Type-N blackjack has the same reach and stealth properties as a Type-0 blackjack.

Type-N blackjacks can circumvent ROV by creating fake adjacencies, but some defense mechanisms can still detect and counter Type-N blackjacks. By using BGPsec, ASes can verify that the sequence of ASes in the AS path reflects the sequence of ASes crossed by received BGPsec advertisements. In this case, no AS path manipulation is possible, but an attacker can still make use of a subset of Type-U blackjacks.

Type-U Blackjack. The Type-U blackjack category regroups all attacks where the AS path is unaltered, meaning the origin AS is authorized to announce the prefix (not like Type-0 blackjacks), and the adjacencies in the AS path reflect real adjacencies (not like Type-N blackjacks).

This category can be broken down into three sub-categories:

- On Path blackjacks.
- On Path blackjacks which violate the Gao-Rexford export rule.
- Not On Path blackjacks.

1. On Path Blackjack (OP). An on path blackjack is characterized by the attacker being on the path of a legitimate advertisement.

Figure 4 depicts an On Path blackjack. Like in the other examples, AS 30 advertises a route for 192.0.2.0/24. AS 10 can perform an On Path blackjack by sending {10, 30 - 20:666 - 192.0.2.0/24} to AS 20. Normally, AS 20 would prefer the route going through its customer (AS 30), however, the blackhole community in the advertisement of AS 10 makes this advertisement preferable to the advertisement of AS 30. Thus, AS 20 will blackhole all traffic destined to 192.0.2.0/24.

2. On path Blackjack with Gao-Rexford Violation (OP-GRV). In this sub-category, the attacker is also on the path of a legitimate advertisement, but violates the Gao-Rexford export rule when propagating the advertisement, imitating the behavior of a BGP leak.

Figure 5 depicts an On Path blackjack which breaks this rule. AS 20 can perform an On Path blackjack with Gao-Rexford violation by sending the advertisement {20, 30, 40 - 10:666 - 192.0.2.0/24} to its provider (AS 10), making AS 10 blackhole traffic destined to 192.0.2.0/24.

3. Not On Path Blackjack (NOP). The last sub-category contains all other Type-U blackjacks, that is, blackjacks where the attacker is not on the path of an advertisement, but announces a legitimate path. In this sub-category, the origin AS in the AS path is authorized to announce the prefix, the adjacencies in the path reflect real adjacencies, but the attacker is not in the AS path.

Figure 5 gives an example of a NOP blackjack: AS 20 sends the advertisement {40 - 30:666 - 192.0.2.0/24} to AS 30, making AS 30 blackhole traffic destined to 192.0.2.0/24.

On Path blackjacks can be considered stealthier than Type-0 and Type-N blackjacks, as the attacker does not re-originate the prefix and does not create false adjacencies in the AS path. NOP blackjacks are even stealthier, as the attacker is not in the AS path.

Malformed Blackjacks. This last category contains all blackjacks not covered by the other categories. They correspond to blackjacks where the AS path is malformed, meaning all or some of the links between the ASes of the AS path do not exist and/or the origin AS is neither the attacker nor a legitimate AS. We assessed malformed blackjacks to be of little interest when looking for blackhole-based attacks, so we disregard them in the remainder of the paper.

4   Routing Security Deployments

To protect oneself against such attacks, several routing security mechanisms can be employed. Depending on the adoption rate of such mechanisms in the Internet, those attacks have a variable chance of success. In this section, we will consider five such deployments, each implementing those security mechanisms to different extents:

- **No security:** ASes neither use RPKI nor BGPsec.
- **RPKI (partial):** A subset of ASes uses the RPKI, but no AS is using BGPsec.
- **RPKI (full):** All ASes use the RPKI, but no AS is using BGPsec.
- **BGPsec (partial):** A subset of ASes uses both RPKI and BGPsec. The other ASes either use only RPKI or do not use any security mechanisms.
- **BGPsec (full):** All ASes use both RPKI and BGPsec.

It is important to keep in mind that although we consider multiple security deployments, BGPsec is not deployed at all and RPKI is only partially deployed. The RPKI covered around 5–6% of advertised prefixes in 2015 [19,26,61], and covers 13% of advertised prefixes today [39]. Although harder to measure, the deployment status of ROV has also been studied [44,45] and shows that only a few ASes are currently performing ROV. This means the deployment corresponding the most to a real-life scenario is the 'RPKI (partial)' deployment.

Tables 1 and 2 summarize which blackjack attacks can work under those different security deployments, the former against exact prefix blackjacks and the latter against sub-prefix blackjacks. Each row of the table represents a security deployment scenario, and each column represents an attack. Thus, the intersection of a line and a column shows how a particular security deployment fares against a given attack:

- ■   : The security deployment is resistant to the attack.
- □   : The security deployment is not resistant to the attack.
- ▨   : The resistance of the security deployment to the attack is determined by other factors (network topology, where security is deployed, ...)

The next sections go over the different deployments, and describe the attacks possible in each context.

Table 1. Security deployments against exact prefix blackjacks

Security Deployment	Type-0	Type-N	NOP	OP	OP-GRV
BGPsec (full)	■	■	■	□	□
BGPsec (partial)	▨	▨	▨	□	□
RPKI (full)	■	□	□	□	□
RPKI (partial)	▨	□	□	□	□
No security	□	□	□	□	□

Table 2. Security deployments against sub-prefix blackjacks

Security Deployment	Type-0	Type-N	NOP	OP	OP-GRV
BGPsec (full)	■	■	■	■	■
BGPsec (partial)	▨	▨	▨	■	■
RPKI (full)	■	■	■	■	■
RPKI (partial)	▨	▨	▨	■	■
No security	□	□	□	■	■

4.1 Fully Deployed BGPsec

In this subsection, we consider a situation where *every AS has deployed, and uses, BGPsec and RPKI/ROV according to best practices* [7,25,30,31,37].

In this deployment, every AS can be assured that the AS path attribute is protected and legitimate in every advertisement they receive, and that the origin AS is authorized to announce the prefix. Since the attacker needs to send signed BGPsec advertisements for them to be considered by other ASes, he can only potentially perform either variations of On Path blackjacks. There can also be no sub-prefix blackjacks, since all ASes in this deployment can detect the sub-prefix via the RPKI.

4.2 Partially Deployed BGPsec

We now consider a situation where *a subset of AS have deployed, and use, BGPsec and RPKI/ROV according to best practices* [7,25,30,31,37]. *The other ASes either use only RPKI/ROV* [25,30,37] *or do not use any security mechanisms.*

Depending on which ASes on the path of the advertisement from the attacker to the blackholer deployed which security mechanisms, multiple cases arise. If ASes on the path implement no security mechanisms, the case can be assimilated to a 'No Security' deployment. If at least one of the ASes on the path uses ROV, the case can be assimilated to a 'RPKI (partial)' deployment (see Subsect. 4.4). Those two cases can also be assimilated in the case of sub-prefix blackjacks.

If at least one of the ASes on the path uses BGPsec and the RPKI/ROV, then the attacker can potentially make use of both On Path attacks, as well as possibly Type-0 blackjacks (see Subsect. 4.4). The attacker can also potentially make use of Type-N and NOP blackjacks if he can perform downgrade attacks [33] on the ASes using BGPsec.

For sub-prefix blackjacks in this case, the attacker can potentially use Type-0 blackjacks (see Subsect. 4.4). The attacker can also make use of Type-N and NOP sub-prefix blackjacks if he can perform downgrade attacks on the ASes using BGPsec, and the legitimate prefix covering the targeted sub-prefix is either not in the RPKI, or is loose. A prefix is loose *"when not all sub-prefixes of the maximum length allowed by the ROA are advertised in BGP"* [19] (e.g. a ROA allowing a prefix to be advertised up to /24, but the advertised prefix is a /20). The attacker cannot make use of On Path blackjacks in this case, since it would require a prior advertisement of the sub-prefix, which is not possible since we only have one attacker in our attack model.

4.3 Fully Deployed RPKI

In this subsection, *every AS has deployed, and uses, RPKI and ROV according to best practices* [25,30,37].

Here, every AS can verify the association of the advertised prefix and the AS originating it, which means an attacker can potentially carry out all attacks

Table 3. Security detail of the 'RPKI (partial)' deployment against blackjacks

	Prefix in RPKI		Prefix not in RPKI
	ROA is loose	ROA is not loose	
ROV	Type-N/NOP sub-prefix BJ	■	AS policy
no ROV	☐	☐	☐

except Type-0 blackjacks. For sub-prefix blackjacks, no attack is possible since all ASes in this deployment can detect the sub-prefix via the RPKI.

It is important to keep in mind that in a real scenario, it may still be possible to perform Type-0 blackjacks even if ROV is put in place, simply because of the order the router's filter are applied [54]. Instead of discarding an 'invalid' route in case of a Type-0 blackjack, the router might accept the advertisement because blackholing takes precedence.

4.4 Partially Deployed RPKI

In this subsection, *a subset of AS have deployed, and use, RPKI and ROV according to best practices* [25,30,37].

In this deployment, the attacks potentially usable by an attacker depend on three factors:

- The presence (or absence) of ROV at ASes on the path of the advertisement from the attacker to the blackholer.
- The presence (or absence) of the targeted prefix in the RPKI.
- If the prefix is in the RPKI, the fact that the ROA for the prefix is loose or not.

As you can see in Table 3, if ASes on the path of the advertisement do not enforce ROV, the case can be assimilated to a 'No Security' deployment.

Second, if the at least one AS on the path of the advertisement enforces ROV, and the prefix is not in the RPKI, it is up to the AS enforcing ROV to decide what to do (RPKI validation state = 'unknown'). The AS can either diminish its preference of the route, or drop the route. In the former case, exact prefix blackjacks (of all types) will be possible as the AS classifies all routes to this prefix as 'unknown', even the one from the legitimate AS: blackjacks can win the BGP decision process. Sub-prefix blackjacks are also possible (except both On Path variations), and are not even penalized by a diminished preference, as they are more specific than the legitimate advertised prefix. All in all, for prefixes not in the RPKI, an AS enforcing ROV and lowering preferences for 'unknown' route validity states behaves in the same way as an AS not enforcing ROV. In this case, possible attacks are the same as in the 'No Security' deployment. If the AS drops 'unknown' routes, those attacks are no longer possible, but in the current deployment state of RPKI, dropping 'unknown' routes would equate to dropping routes to 87% of the Internet, so for now, a compromise between reachability and security must be made.

Third, if the AS receiving the forged advertisement enforces ROV and the prefix is in the RPKI, two cases arise: either the ROA for the prefix is loose, or it is not. If the ROA is not loose, the deployment can be assimilated to a 'RPKI (full)' deployment. If the ROA is loose, in addition to attacks possible in the 'RPKI (full)' deployment, an attacker can also perform Type-N and NOP sub-prefix blackjacks within the range of maxLength, as the origin AS will match the asID in the ROA.

4.5   No Security

In this subsection, *ASes do not use any of the aforementioned security mechanisms.* If neither BGPsec nor RPKI and ROV are deployed, an attacker can perform all the attacks of the taxonomy. In the case of sub-prefix blackjacks, an attacker can use all the attacks except On Path blackjacks, since it would require a prior advertisement of the sub-prefix, which is not possible since we only have one attacker in our attack model.

5   Good Practices

We highlight two items having an influence on preventing attacks from the taxonomy:

– **Authorized origin:** The origin is authorized if the association between the origin AS and the prefix is 'valid' according to IRRs or the RPKI.
– **Valid path:** The path is considered 'Valid' if the AS path reflects the actual path the advertisement went through. This can be verified using BGPsec.

Even if an AS implements both RPKI and BGPsec, it is still vulnerable to both exact prefix On Path blackjacks, as well as possibly Type-0 exact and sub-prefix blackjacks depending on the state of the prefix in relation to the RPKI (see Table 3).

For an AS not to be vulnerable against Type-0 blackjacks, it needs help from third parties, (e.g. another AS registering its prefixes in the RPKI). However, an AS can protect itself against On Path attacks by adding constraints on advertisements it receives.

5.1   Additional Verification Rules

We suggest two verification steps to protect an AS against On Path blackjacks:

– **Legitimate peer:** The peer sending the blackhole advertisement is legitimate if the leftmost AS in the AS path is the ASN specified in the BGP OPEN message that created the session.

– **Direct connection:** The AS sending the blackhole advertisement is directly connected to the local AS. This can be verified by making sure there is only one AS in the AS path.

If an AS can make sure it has a direct connection to the AS sending the blackhole advertisement, it is then only vulnerable to Type-0 and 1-hop NOP blackjacks (e.g. the one in Fig. 5) by definition. If this AS can also verify this peer is legitimate and authorized to advertise the prefix, then the AS is protected against all the attacks of the taxonomy without needing BGPsec.

It is worth keeping in mind that at this point, acknowledging the deployment state of RPKI and BGPsec, an AS peering through an IXP virtually has no protection against the attacks, as it must trust the IXP to verify the 'Legitimate peer' rule and the route server may not perform ROV[1].

5.2   Additional Good Blackholing Practices

In addition to the rules, other good practices can be put in place. Those good practices help to limit the possible damage caused by an inadvertent blackholing.

A Filter for Less Specific Blackholing Advertisements. The literature specifies that operators should accept blackholing advertisements up to /32 for IPv4, and /128 for IPv6, but does not specify a limit on prefixes which are less specific. We propose that operators reject blackholing advertisements if they are not specific enough, in order to avoid accidental blackholing of large IP blocks.

Acknowledging the distribution of blackholing prefix length [13], we advise to set it to /24, thus only accepting blackholing advertisements from /24 up to /32. This filter can be applied as both an inbound and outbound filter.

Concerning IPv6, observed IXPs put the limit at /19 [12,16]. The literature does not have any specific information enabling us to determine a good limit for IPv6 blackholing prefix specificity, more research needs to be done.

An Outbound Filter for More Specific Blackholing Advertisements. When using blackholing across AS boundaries, an outbound filter should be set on eBGP peering sessions to deny all prefixes longer than the longest prefix expected to be announced, unless that prefix is tagged with a blackhole community. This does not help with accidental blackholing directly, but prevents an AS from advertising more specific prefixes inadvertently.

Considering some of these good practices might not be applicable depending on the situation, or can constrain the blackhole service too much, we propose using a BGPsec extension as a possible alternative to protect against attacks of the taxonomy.

---

[1] This might be changing as several IXPs now seem to implement ROV [3].

5.3   A BGPsec Solution

In a full deployment of BGPsec and RPKI, only On Path attacks are still possible. Thus, the goal of integrating communities to BGPsec is to be able to attribute the changes made to communities to an AS. This attribution is crucial for blackholing, because it allows an AS to accept or reject a blackhole request based on the identity of the AS requesting the blackhole. A blackholing advertisement can then be analyzed, to determine the source of the request, and a decision can be made based on whether or not this AS has a right to blackhole this prefix. Moreover, given an unwanted blackholing event, those responsible for it can be held accountable.

We propose such an extension in [36]. With this extension, as we know which ASes introduced which communities, an AS could simply generate a table associating an AS to a set of prefixes this AS is authorized to blackhole. This table could be populated by RPKI/IRR data, but also manually with trusted peers, or other associations the operator deems relevant. Then, this AS could accept a blackhole request if the AS requesting the blackhole and the prefix in the advertisement matches an association in the table.

6   Related Work

Over the last years, efforts have been made towards characterizing usage and behavior of communities in the Internet. Donnet et al. proposed the first classification of BGP communities [15], and found that community usage increased from 2004 to 2007. The increased popularity of communities has since been established multiple times [13,21,22,54]. Streibelt et al. also found that even though communities are typically relevant only between directly connected ASes, they seem to be propagated beyond, increasing the risks of attacks.

Streibelt et al. also demonstrated that attacks using BGP blackholing are not only possible in theory, but also in an experimental setup and in the wild [54]. In comparison to this paper, they only consider Type-0 blackjacks, so a possible area of future work is to test the other attacks of the taxonomy. Numerous efforts have also been made towards characterizing DDoS attacks, as well as the detection and mitigation techniques that can be used against them [48,49]. Dietzel et al. study the shortcomings of blackholing, and propose Stellar, an advanced blackholing mechanism [14] which can perform fine-grained blackholing using extended communities as a signaling mechanism.

Finally, BGP hijacking has been studied extensively, to characterize them [5,51,52,58,59], to detect them [52,53,60,62], or even to conduct further attacks [2,4,55,59]. A possible area of future work is the adaptation of those detection techniques to blackhole-based attacks.

7   Conclusion

In this paper, we construct a taxonomy using blackholing as an attack vector, and assess the usability of those attacks in various security deployments. We also show those attacks have better reach and stealth than regular hijacks. Namely, blackholing takes precedence over AS relationships and AS path length, meaning a blackjack can affect more ASes than hijacks. By using the specific blackhole community value of a blackholer, an attacker can also drop traffic at ASes much further away than hijacks can. As the attacker is not the one dropping traffic and blackjacks may propagate far, blackjacks are stealthier than hijacks.

We also want to draw attention to the fact that since blackjacks make use of the blackholing service of an AS, making this blackholing information publicly available might not be a good idea without proper standardization and security.

Through attacks suited against the considered security mechanisms (RPKI and BGPsec), we highlight the poor state BGP security deployment is in, and suggest additional rules as well as good practices to protect against the attacks of our taxonomy. In a more general way, we want to emphasize the need for BGP community authentication, either through an extension to BGPsec or another mechanism.

As part of our future work, we want to test the attacks not already covered by Streibelt et al. [54] in a real world setting, to demonstrate those attacks can be carried out and present numerous advantages compared to regular hijacks. Another area to investigate is the existence and characteristics of ASes proposing blackholing services to perform blackhole-based attacks, much like open DNS resolvers can be used to carry out DDoS attacks. More work can also be done to adapt hijack detection techniques to blackhole-based attacks.

The feasibility and subtleties of blackjack attacks remain to be studied in a real-world setting. Since BGPsec has yet to be deployed, and there is still little experience with RPKI, those security mechanisms and their limitations can hardly be tested against at this time. Further research is needed to assess the severity of blackjack attacks in the wild, since actual configuration (e.g. blackholing precedence over other policies, community handling, RTBH provider policy, blackholing propagation, ...) might differ from expectations, and from AS to AS.

Acknowledgments. This project has been made possible in part by a grant from the Cisco University Research Program Fund, an advised fund of Silicon Valley Community Foundation.

References

1. Akamai: Memcached-fueled 1.3 Tbps attacks, March 2018. https://blogs.akamai.com/2018/03/memcached-fueled-13-tbps-attacks.html. Accessed 29 Apr 2019
2. Pilosov, A., Kapela, T.: Stealing The Internet: An Internet-Scale Man In The Middle Attack, August 2008. https://www.defcon.org/images/defcon-16/dc16-presentations/defcon-16-pilosov-kapela.pdf. Accessed 29 Apr 2019
3. Reuter, A., Bush, R., Katz-Bassett, E., Cunha, I., Schmidt, T.C., Wählisch, M.: Measuring Adoption of RPKI Route Origin Validation and Filtering, May 2018. https://ripe76.ripe.net/presentations/63-rov_filtering_update.pdf. Accessed 29 Apr 2019

4. Apostolaki, M., Zohar, A., Vanbever, L.: Hijacking bitcoin: routing attacks on cryptocurrencies. In: 2017 IEEE Symposium on Security and Privacy (SP), pp. 375–392. IEEE (2017)
5. Ballani, H., Francis, P., Zhang, X.: A study of prefix hijacking and interception in the Internet. ACM SIGCOMM Comput. Commun. Rev. **37**(4), 265–276 (2007)
6. Brewster, T.: Cyber Attacks Strike Zimbabweans Around Controversial Election, August 2013. http://www.silicon.co.uk/workspace/zimbabwe-election-cyber-attacks-123938. Accessed 29 Apr 2019
7. Bush, R.: BGPsec Operational Considerations. BCP 211, RFC Editor, September 2017
8. Chandra, R., Traina, P., Li, T.: BGP Communities Attribute. RFC 1997, RFC Editor, August 1996
9. Cisco: Remotely Triggered Black Hole Filtering - Destination Based and Source Based (2005). https://www.cisco.com/c/dam/en/us/products/collateral/security/ios-network-foundation-protection-nfp/prod_white_paper0900aecd80313fac.pdf. Accessed 29 Apr 2019
10. Cohen, A., Gilad, Y., Herzberg, A., Schapira, M.: One hop for RPKI, one giant leap for BGP security. In: Proceedings of the 14th ACM Workshop on Hot Topics in Networks, p. 10. ACM (2015)
11. Cohen, A., Gilad, Y., Herzberg, A., Schapira, M.: Jumpstarting BGP security with path-end validation. In: Proceedings of the 2016 ACM SIGCOMM Conference, pp. 342–355. ACM (2016)
12. DE-CIX: DE-CIX Blackholing Service July 2018. https://www.de-cix.net/_Resources/Persistent/4277e7d4867a78ae923c0f5b3b66d7ff6aeb61f8/DE-CIX-Blackholing-Service.pdf. Accessed 29 Apr 2019; Slide 3
13. Dietzel, C., Feldmann, A., King, T.: Blackholing at IXPs: on the effectiveness of DDoS mitigation in the wild. In: Karagiannis, T., Dimitropoulos, X. (eds.) Passive and Active Measurement, pp. 319–332. Springer International Publishing, Cham (2016)
14. Dietzel, C., Smaragdakis, G., Wichtlhuber, M., Feldmann, A.: Stellar: network attack mitigation using advanced blackholing. In: Proceedings of the 14th International Conference on emerging Networking EXperiments and Technologies, pp. 152–164. ACM (2018)
15. Donnet, B., Bonaventure, O.: On BGP communities. ACM SIGCOMM Comput. Commun. Rev. **38**(2), 55–59 (2008)
16. France-IX: France-IX Blackholing Service, July 2018. https://www.franceix.net/fr/technical/blackholing/. Accessed 29 Apr 2019
17. Gao, L., Griffin, T.G., Rexford, J.: Inherently safe backup routing with BGP. In: Proceedings IEEE INFOCOM 2001. Conference on Computer Communications. Twentieth Annual Joint Conference of the IEEE Computer and Communications Society (Cat. No.01CH37213), vol. 1, pp. 547–556. IEEE, April 2001. https://doi.org/10.1109/INFCOM.2001.916777
18. Gao, L., Rexford, J.: Stable Internet routing without global coordination. IEEE/ACM Trans. Netw. (TON) **9**(6), 681–692 (2001)
19. Gilad, Y., Cohen, A., Herzberg, A., Schapira, M., Shulman, H.: Are We There Yet? On RPKI's Deployment and Security. IACR Cryptology ePrint Archive **2016**, 1010 (2016)
20. Gill, P., Schapira, M., Goldberg, S.: Let the market drive deployment: a strategy for transitioning to BGP security. ACM SIGCOMM Comput. Commun. Rev. **41**(4), 14–25 (2011)

21. Giotsas, V., Dietzel, C., Smaragdakis, G., Feldmann, A., Berger, A., Aben, E.: Detecting peering infrastructure outages in the wild. In: Proceedings of the Conference of the ACM Special Interest Group on Data Communication, pp. 446–459. ACM (2017)

22. Giotsas, V., Smaragdakis, G., Dietzel, C., Richter, P., Feldmann, A., Berger, A.: Inferring BGP blackholing activity in the Internet. In: Proceedings of the 2017 Internet Measurement Conference, pp. 1–14. ACM (2017)

23. Greenberg, A.: Hacker Redirects Traffic From 19 Internet Providers to Steal Bitcoins, August 2014. https://www.wired.com/2014/08/isp-bitcoin-theft/. Accessed 29 Apr 2019

24. Heitz, J., Snijders, J., Patel, K., Bagdonas, I., Hilliard, N.: BGP Large Communities Attribute. RFC 8092, RFC Editor, February 2017

25. Huston, G., Michaelson, G.: Validation of Route Origination Using the Resource Certificate Public Key Infrastructure (PKI) and Route Origin Authorizations (ROAs). RFC 6483, RFC Editor, February 2012

26. Iamartino, D., Pelsser, C., Bush, R.: Measuring BGP route origin registration and validation. In: Mirkovic, J., Liu, Y. (eds.) PAM 2015. LNCS, vol. 8995, pp. 28–40. Springer, Cham (2015). https://doi.org/10.1007/978-3-319-15509-8_3

27. Kandagatla, N.: Disgruntled ex-employees, DDoS attacks and the revenge of the nerds. https://www.wittysparks.com/disgruntled-ex-employees-ddos-attacks-and-the-revenge-of-the-nerds/, November 2017. Accessed 29 Apr 2019

28. King, T., Dietzel, C., Snijders, J., Doering, G., Hankins, G.: BLACKHOLE Community. RFC 7999, RFC Editor, October 2016

29. Kumari, W., McPherson, D.: Remote Triggered Black Hole Filtering with Unicast Reverse Path Forwarding (uRPF). RFC 5635, RFC Editor, August 2009

30. Lepinski, M., Kent, S.: An Infrastructure to Support Secure Internet Routing. RFC 6480, RFC Editor, February 2012. http://www.rfc-editor.org/rfc/rfc6480.txt, http://www.rfc-editor.org/rfc/rfc6480.txt

31. Lepinski, M., Sriram, K.: BGPsec Protocol Specification. RFC 8205, RFC Editor, September 2017

32. Leyden, J.: US credit card firm fights DDoS attack, September 2004. http://www.theregister.co.uk/2004/09/23/authorize_ddos_attack/. Accessed 29 Apr 2019

33. Lychev, R., Goldberg, S., Schapira, M.: BGP security in partial deployment: is the juice worth the squeeze? SIGCOMM Comput. Commun. Rev. **43**(4), 171–182 (2013). https://doi.org/10.1145/2534169.2486010

34. Madory, D.: BackConnect's Suspicious BGP Hijacks, September 2016. https://dyn.com/blog/backconnects-suspicious-bgp-hijacks/. Accessed 29 Apr 2019

35. Madory, D.: Iran Leaks Censorship via BGP Hijacks, January 2017. https://dyn.com/blog/iran-leaks-censorship-via-bgp-hijacks/. Accessed 29 Apr 2019

36. Miller, L., Pelsser, C., Cateloin, S.: DDoS, BGP Leaks and Hijack Mitigation Techniques, August 2018. https://loicmiller.com/documents/hijack_ddos_mitigation.pdf. Accessed 29 Apr 2019

37. Mohapatra, P., Scudder, J., Ward, D., Bush, R., Austein, R.: BGP Prefix Origin Validation. RFC 6811, RFC Editor, January 2013. http://www.rfc-editor.org/rfc/rfc6811.txt, http://www.rfc-editor.org/rfc/rfc6811.txt

38. Morales, C.: NETSCOUT Arbor Confirms 1.7 Tbps DDoS Attack; The Terabit Attack Era Is Upon Us, March 2018. https://www.arbornetworks.com/blog/asert/netscout-arbor-confirms-1-7-tbps-ddos-attack-terabit-attack-era-upon-us/. Accessed 29 Apr 2019

39. National Institute of Standards and Technology: Global Prefix/Origin Validation using RPKI, April 2019. https://rpki-monitor.antd.nist.gov/. Accessed 29 Apr 2019
40. Newman, L.H.: The Botnet That Broke the Internet Isn't Going Away, September 2016. https://www.wired.com/2016/12/botnet-broke-internet-isnt-going-away/. Accessed 29 Apr 2019
41. Pras, A., et al.: Attacks by "Anonymous" WikiLeaks Proponents not Anonymous (2010)
42. Prince, M.: The DDoS That Almost Broke the Internet, March 2013. https://blog.cloudflare.com/the-ddos-that-almost-broke-the-internet/. Accessed 29 Apr 2019
43. Rekhter, Y., Li, T., Hares, S.: A Border Gateway Protocol 4 (BGP-4). RFC 4271, RFC Editor, January 2006. http://www.rfc-editor.org/rfc/rfc4271.txt
44. Reuter, A., Bush, R., Cunha, I., Katz-Bassett, E., Schmidt, T.C., Wählisch, M.: Towards a rigorous methodology for measuring adoption of RPKI route validation and filtering. ACM SIGCOMM Comput. Commun. Rev. **48**(1), 19–27 (2018)
45. Reuter, A., Bush, R., Cunha, I., Katz-Bassett, E., Schmidt, T.C., Wählisch, M.: Measuring RPKI Route Origin Validation Deployment, April 2019. https://rov.rpki.net/. Accessed 29 Apr 2019
46. Reynolds, M., Turner, S., Kent, S.: A Profile for BGPsec Router Certificates, Certificate Revocation Lists, and Certification Requests. RFC 8209, RFC Editor, September 2017
47. RIPE NCC: YouTube Hijacking: A RIPE NCC RIS case study, March 2008. https://www.ripe.net/publications/news/industry-developments/youtube-hijacking-a-ripe-ncc-ris-case-study. Accessed 29 Apr 2019
48. Rossow, C.: Amplification Hell: Revisiting Network Protocols for DDoS Abuse. In: NDSS (2014)
49. Ryba, F.J., Orlinski, M., Wählisch, M., Rossow, C., Schmidt, T.C.: Amplification and DRDoS attack defense-a survey and new perspectives. arXiv preprint arXiv:1505.07892 (2015)
50. Schlamp, J., Holz, R., Jacquemart, Q., Carle, G., Biersack, E.W.: HEAP: reliable assessment of BGP hijacking attacks. IEEE J. Sel. Areas Commun. **34**(6), 1849–1861 (2016)
51. Sermpezis, P., Kotronis, V., Dainotti, A., Dimitropoulos, X.: A survey among network operators on BGP prefix hijacking. ACM SIGCOMM Comput. Commun. Rev. **48**(1), 64–69 (2018)
52. Sermpezis, P., et al.: Artemis: neutralizing BGP hijacking within a minute. IEEE/ACM Trans. Netw. (TON) **26**(6), 2471–2486 (2018)
53. Shi, X., Xiang, Y., Wang, Z., Yin, X., Wu, J.: Detecting prefix hijackings in the internet with argus. In: Proceedings of the 2012 Internet Measurement Conference, pp. 15–28. ACM (2012)
54. Streibelt, F., et al.: BGP communities: even more worms in the routing can. In: Proceedings of the Internet Measurement Conference 2018, pp. 279–292. ACM (2018)
55. Sun, Y., et al.: {RAPTOR}: routing attacks on privacy in Tor. In: 24th {USENIX} Security Symposium ({USENIX} Security 15), pp. 271–286 (2015)
56. Tomlinson, K.: Cyber battle rages on Internet after arrest of cyber crime suspects, September 2016. http://www.archersecuritygroup.com/cyber-battle-rages-internet-arrest-cyber-crime-suspects/. Accessed 29 Apr 2019
57. Turk, D.: Configuring BGP to Block Denial-of-Service Attacks. RFC 3882, RFC Editor, September 2004

58. Vervier, P.A., et al.: Malicious BGP hijacks: appearances can be deceiving. In: 2014 IEEE International Conference on Communications (ICC), pp. 884–889. IEEE (2014)
59. Vervier, P.A., Thonnard, O., Dacier, M.: Mind Your Blocks: On the Stealthiness of Malicious BGP Hijacks. In: NDSS (2015)
60. Wählisch, M., Maennel, O., Schmidt, T.C.: Towards detecting BGP route hijacking using the RPKI. In: Proceedings of the ACM SIGCOMM 2012 Conference on Applications, Technologies, Architectures, and Protocols for Computer Communication, pp. 103–104. Citeseer (2012)
61. Wählisch, M., Schmidt, R., Schmidt, T.C., Maennel, O., Uhlig, S., Tyson, G.: RiPKI: The tragic story of RPKI deployment in the Web ecosystem. In: Proceedings of the 14th ACM Workshop on Hot Topics in Networks. p. 11. ACM (2015)
62. Zheng, C., Ji, L., Pei, D., Wang, J., Francis, P.: A light-weight distributed scheme for detecting IP prefix hijacks in real-time. In: ACM SIGCOMM Computer Communication Review. vol. 37, pp. 277–288. ACM (2007)

Local Obfuscation Mechanisms for Hiding Probability Distributions

Yusuke Kawamoto[1]([✉])[ID] and Takao Murakami[2][ID]

[1] AIST, Tsukuba, Japan
yusuke.kawamoto.aist@gmail.com
[2] AIST, Tokyo, Japan

Abstract. We introduce a formal model for the information leakage of probability distributions and define a notion called distribution privacy as the local differential privacy for probability distributions. Roughly, the distribution privacy of a local obfuscation mechanism means that the attacker cannot significantly gain any information on the distribution of the mechanism's input by observing its output. Then we show that existing local mechanisms can hide input distributions in terms of distribution privacy, while deteriorating the utility by adding too much noise. For example, we prove that the Laplace mechanism needs to add a large amount of noise proportionally to the infinite Wasserstein distance between the two distributions we want to make indistinguishable. To improve the tradeoff between distribution privacy and utility, we introduce a local obfuscation mechanism, called a tupling mechanism, that adds random dummy data to the output. Then we apply this mechanism to the protection of user attributes in location based services. By experiments, we demonstrate that the tupling mechanism outperforms popular local mechanisms in terms of attribute obfuscation and service quality.

Keywords: Local differential privacy · Obfuscation mechanism · Location privacy · Attribute privacy · Wasserstein metric · Compositionality

1 Introduction

Differential privacy [1] is a quantitative notion of privacy that has been applied to a wide range of areas, including databases, geo-locations, and social network. The protection of differential privacy can be achieved by adding controlled noise to given data that we wish to hide or obfuscate. In particular, a number of recent studies have proposed *local obfuscation mechanisms* [2–4], namely, randomized algorithms that perturb each single "point" data (e.g., a geo-location point) by adding certain probabilistic noise before sending it out to a data collector. However, the obfuscation of a probability distribution of points (e.g., a distribution

This work was partially supported by JSPS KAKENHI Grant JP17K12667, JP19H04113, and Inria LOGIS project.

of locations of users at home/outside home) still remains to be investigated in terms of differential privacy.

For example, a location-based service (LBS) provider collects each user's geo-location data to provide a service (e.g., navigation or point-of-interest search), and has been widely studied in terms of the privacy of user locations. As shown in [3,5], users can hide their accurate locations by sending to the LBS provider only approximate location information calculated by an obfuscation mechanism.

Nevertheless, a user's location information can be used for an attacker to infer the user's attributes (e.g., age, gender, social status, and residence area) or activities (e.g., working, sleeping, and shopping) [6–9]. For example, when an attacker knows the distribution of residence locations, he may detect whether given users are *at home* or *outside home* after observing their obfuscated locations. For another example, an attacker may learn whether users are *rich* or *poor* by observing their obfuscated behaviors. These attributes can be used by robbers hence should be protected from them. Privacy issues of such attribute inference are also known in other applications, including recommender systems [10,11] and online social networks [12,13]. However, to our knowledge, no literature has addressed the protection of attributes in terms of local differential privacy.

To illustrate the privacy of attributes in an LBS, let us consider a running example where users try to prevent an attacker from inferring whether they are at home or not. Let λ_{home} and λ_{out} be the probability distributions of locations of the users at home and outside home, respectively. Then the privacy of this attribute means that the attacker cannot learn from an obfuscated location whether the actual location follows the distribution λ_{home} or λ_{out}.

This can be formalized using differential privacy. For each $t \in \{home, out\}$, we denote by $p(y \mid \lambda_t)$ the probability of observing an obfuscated location y when an actual location is distributed over λ_t. Then the privacy of t is defined by:

$$\frac{p(y \mid \lambda_{home})}{p(y \mid \lambda_{out})} \leq e^{\varepsilon},$$

which represents that the attacker cannot distinguish whether the users follow the distribution λ_{home} or λ_{out} with degree of ε.

To generalize this, we define a notion, called *distribution privacy* (DistP), as the differential privacy for probability distributions. Roughly, we say that a mechanism A provides DistP w.r.t. λ_{home} and λ_{out} if no attacker can detect whether the actual location (input to A) is sampled from λ_{home} or λ_{out} after he observed an obfuscated location y (output by A)[1]. Here we note that each user applies the mechanism A locally by herself, hence can customize the amount of noise added to y according to the attributes she wants to hide.

Although existing local differential privacy mechanisms are designed to protect point data, they also hide the distribution that the point data follow. However, we demonstrate that they need to add a large amount of noise to obfuscate distributions, and thus deteriorate the utility of the mechanisms.

---

[1] In our setting, the attacker observes only a sampled output of A, and not the exact histogram of A's output distribution. See Sect. 3.5 for more details.

To achieve both high utility and strong privacy of attributes, we introduce a mechanism, called the *tupling mechanism*, that not only perturbs an actual input, but also adds random dummy data to the output. Then we prove that this mechanism provides DistP. Since the random dummy data obfuscate the shape of the distribution, users can instead reduce the amount of noise added to the actual input, hence they get better utility (e.g., quality of a POI service).

This implies that DistP is a relaxation of differential privacy that guarantees the privacy of attributes while achieving higher utility by weakening the differentially private protection of point data. For example, suppose that users do not mind revealing their actual locations outside home, but want to hide (e.g., from robbers) the fact that they are outside home. When the users employ the tupling mechanism, they output both their (slightly perturbed) actual locations and random dummy locations. Since their outputs include their (roughly) actual locations, they obtain high utility (e.g., learning shops near their locations), while their actual location points are protected only weakly by differential privacy. However, their attributes *at home/outside home* are hidden among the dummy locations, hence protected by DistP. By experiments, we demonstrate that the tupling mechanism is useful to protect the privacy of attributes, and outperforms popular existing mechanisms (the randomized response [14], the planar Laplace [3] and Gaussian mechanisms) in terms of DistP and service quality.

Our Contributions. The main contributions of this work are given as follows:

- We propose a formal model for the privacy of probability distributions in terms of differential privacy. Specifically, we define the notion of distribution privacy (DistP) to represent that the attacker cannot significantly gain information on the distribution of a mechanism's input by observing its output.
- We provide theoretical foundation of DistP, including its useful properties (e.g., compositionality) and its interpretation (e.g., in terms of Bayes factor).
- We quantify the effect of distribution obfuscation by existing local mechanisms. In particular, we show that (extended) differential privacy mechanisms are able to make any two distributions less distinguishable, while deteriorating the utility by adding too much noise to protect all point data.
- For instance, we prove that extended differential privacy mechanisms (e.g., the Laplace mechanism) need to add a large amount of noise proportionally to the ∞-Wasserstein distance $W_{\infty,d}(\lambda_0, \lambda_1)$ between the two distributions λ_0 and λ_1 that we want to make indistinguishable.
- We show that DistP is a useful relaxation of differential privacy when users want to hide their attributes, but not necessarily to protect all point data.
- To improve the tradeoff between DistP and utility, we introduce the *tupling mechanism*, which locally adds random dummies to the output. Then we show that this mechanism provides DistP and hight utility for users.
- We apply local mechanisms to the obfuscation of attributes in location based services (LBSs). Then we show that the tupling mechanism outperforms popular existing mechanisms in terms of DistP and service quality.

All proofs of technical results can be found in [15].

2   Preliminaries

In this section we recall some notions of privacy and metrics used in this paper. Let $\mathbb{N}^{>0}$ be the set of positive integers, and $\mathbb{R}^{>0}$ (resp. $\mathbb{R}^{\geq 0}$) be the set of positive (resp. non-negative) real numbers. Let $[0, 1]$ be the set of non-negative real numbers not grater than 1. Let $\varepsilon, \varepsilon_0, \varepsilon_1 \in \mathbb{R}^{\geq 0}$ and $\delta, \delta_0, \delta_1 \in [0, 1]$.

2.1   Notations for Probability Distributions

We denote by $\mathbb{D}\mathcal{X}$ the *set of all probability distributions* over a set $\mathcal{X}$, and by $|\mathcal{X}|$ the number of elements in a finite set $\mathcal{X}$.

Given a finite set $\mathcal{X}$ and a distribution $\lambda \in \mathbb{D}\mathcal{X}$, the probability of drawing a value x from λ is denoted by $\lambda[x]$. For a finite subset $\mathcal{X}' \subseteq \mathcal{X}$ we define $\lambda[\mathcal{X}']$ by: $\lambda[\mathcal{X}'] = \sum_{x' \in \mathcal{X}'} \lambda[x']$. For a distribution λ over a finite set $\mathcal{X}$, its *support* $\mathsf{supp}(\lambda)$ is defined by $\mathsf{supp}(\lambda) = \{x \in \mathcal{X} : \lambda[x] > 0\}$. Given a $\lambda \in \mathbb{D}\mathcal{X}$ and a $f : \mathcal{X} \to \mathbb{R}$, the expected value of f over λ is: $\mathbb{E}_{x \sim \lambda}[f(x)] \stackrel{\text{def}}{=} \sum_{x \in \mathcal{X}} \lambda[x] f(x)$.

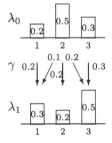

Fig. 1. Coupling γ.

For a randomized algorithm $A : \mathcal{X} \to \mathbb{D}\mathcal{Y}$ and a set $R \subseteq \mathcal{Y}$ we denote by $A(x)[R]$ the probability that given input x, A outputs one of the elements of R. Given a randomized algorithm $A : \mathcal{X} \to \mathbb{D}\mathcal{Y}$ and a distribution λ over $\mathcal{X}$, we define $A^{\#}(\lambda)$ as the distribution of the output of A. Formally, for a finite set $\mathcal{X}$, the *lifting* of A w.r.t. $\mathcal{X}$ is the function $A^{\#} : \mathbb{D}\mathcal{X} \to \mathbb{D}\mathcal{Y}$ such that $A^{\#}(\lambda)[R] \stackrel{\text{def}}{=} \sum_{x \in \mathcal{X}} \lambda[x] A(x)[R]$.

2.2   Differential Privacy (DP)

Differential privacy [1] captures the idea that given two "adjacent" inputs x and x' (from a set $\mathcal{X}$ of data with an adjacency relation Φ), a randomized algorithm A cannot distinguish x from x' (with degree of ε and up to exceptions δ).

Definition 1 (Differential privacy). Let e be the base of natural logarithm. A randomized algorithm $A : \mathcal{X} \to \mathbb{D}\mathcal{Y}$ provides (ε, δ)-*differential privacy (DP)* w.r.t. an adjacency relation $\Phi \subseteq \mathcal{X} \times \mathcal{X}$ if for any $(x, x') \in \Phi$ and any $R \subseteq \mathcal{Y}$,

$$\Pr[A(x) \in R] \leq e^{\varepsilon} \Pr[A(x') \in R] + \delta$$

where the probability is taken over the random choices in A.

2.3   Differential Privacy Mechanisms and Sensitivity

Differential privacy can be achieved by a *privacy mechanism*, namely a randomized algorithm that adds probabilistic noise to a given input that we want to protect. The amount of noise added by some popular mechanisms (e.g., the exponential mechanism) depends on a *utility function* $u : \mathcal{X} \times \mathcal{Y} \to \mathbb{R}$ that maps a pair of input and output to a utility score. More precisely, the noise is added according to the "sensitivity" of u, which we define as follows.

Definition 2 (Utility distance). The *utility distance* w.r.t a utility function $u : (\mathcal{X} \times \mathcal{Y}) \to \mathbb{R}$ is the function d given by: $d(x, x') \overset{\text{def}}{=} \max_{y \in \mathcal{Y}} |u(x, y) - u(x', y)|$.

Note that d is a pseudometric. Hereafter we assume that for all x, y, $u(x, y) = 0$ is logically equivalent to $x = y$. Then the utility distance d is a metric.

Definition 3 (Sensitivity w.r.t. an adjacency relation). The *sensitivity* of a utility function u w.r.t. an adjacency relation $\Phi \subseteq \mathcal{X} \times \mathcal{X}$ is defined as:

$$\Delta_{\Phi,d} \overset{\text{def}}{=} \max_{(x,x') \in \Phi} d(x, x') = \max_{(x,x') \in \Phi} \max_{y \in \mathcal{Y}} |u(x, y) - u(x', y)|.$$

2.4 Extended Differential Privacy (XDP)

We review the notion of *extended differential privacy* [16], which relaxes DP by incorporating a metric d. Intuitively, this notion guarantees that when two inputs x and x' are closer in terms of d, the output distributions are less distinguishable.

Definition 4 (Extended differential privacy). For a metric $d : \mathcal{X} \times \mathcal{X} \to \mathbb{R}$, we say that a randomized algorithm $A : \mathcal{X} \to \mathbb{D}\mathcal{Y}$ provides (ε, δ, d)-*extended differential privacy (XDP)* if for all $x, x' \in \mathcal{X}$ and for any $R \subseteq \mathcal{Y}$,

$$\Pr[A(x) \in R] \le e^{\varepsilon d(x,x')} \Pr[A(x') \in R] + \delta.$$

2.5 Wasserstein Metric

We recall the notion of probability coupling as follows.

Definition 5 (Coupling). Given $\lambda_0 \in \mathbb{D}\mathcal{X}_0$ and $\lambda_1 \in \mathbb{D}\mathcal{X}_1$, a *coupling* of λ_0 and λ_1 is a $\gamma \in \mathbb{D}(\mathcal{X}_0 \times \mathcal{X}_1)$ such that λ_0 and λ_1 are γ's marginal distributions, i.e., for each $x_0 \in \mathcal{X}_0$, $\lambda_0[x_0] = \sum_{x_1' \in \mathcal{X}_1} \gamma[x_0, x_1']$ and for each $x_1 \in \mathcal{X}_1$, $\lambda_1[x_1] = \sum_{x_0' \in \mathcal{X}_0} \gamma[x_0', x_1]$. We denote by $\mathsf{cp}(\lambda_0, \lambda_1)$ the set of all couplings of λ_0 and λ_1.

Example 1 (Coupling as transformation of distributions). Let us consider two distributions λ_0 and λ_1 shown in Fig. 1. A coupling γ of λ_0 and λ_1 shows a way of transforming λ_0 to λ_1. For example, $\gamma[2, 1] = 0.1$ moves from $\lambda_0[2]$ to $\lambda_1[1]$.

We then recall the ∞-Wasserstein metric [17] between two distributions.

Definition 6 (∞-Wasserstein metric). Let d be a metric over $\mathcal{X}$. The ∞-*Wasserstein metric* $W_{\infty,d}$ w.r.t. d is defined by: for any $\lambda_0, \lambda_1 \in \mathbb{D}\mathcal{X}$,

$$W_{\infty,d}(\lambda_0, \lambda_1) = \min_{\gamma \in \mathsf{cp}(\lambda_0,\lambda_1)} \max_{(x_0,x_1) \in \mathsf{supp}(\gamma)} d(x_0, x_1).$$

The ∞-Wasserstein metric $W_{\infty,d}(\lambda_0, \lambda_1)$ represents the minimum largest move between points in a transportation from λ_0 to λ_1. Specifically, in a transportation γ, $\max_{(x_0,x_1)\in\mathsf{supp}(\gamma)} d(x_0, x_1)$ represents the largest move from a point in λ_0 to another in λ_1. For instance, in the coupling γ in Example 1, the largest move is 1 (from $\lambda_0[2]$ to $\lambda_1[1]$, and from $\lambda_0[2]$ to $\lambda_1[3]$). Such a largest move is minimized by a coupling that achieves the ∞-Wasserstein metric. We denote by $\Gamma_{\infty,d}$ the set of all couplings that achieve the ∞-Wasserstein metric.

Finally, we recall the notion of the lifting of relations.

Definition 7 (Lifting of relations). Given a relation $\Phi \subseteq \mathcal{X} \times \mathcal{X}$, the *lifting* of Φ is the maximum relation $\Phi^{\#} \subseteq \mathbb{D}\mathcal{X} \times \mathbb{D}\mathcal{X}$ such that for any $(\lambda_0, \lambda_1) \in \Phi^{\#}$, there exists a coupling $\gamma \in \mathsf{cp}(\lambda_0, \lambda_1)$ satisfying $\mathsf{supp}(\gamma) \subseteq \Phi$.

Note that by Definition 5, the coupling γ is a probability distribution over Φ whose marginal distributions are λ_0 and λ_1. If $\Phi = \mathcal{X} \times \mathcal{X}$, then $\Phi^{\#} = \mathbb{D}\mathcal{X} \times \mathbb{D}\mathcal{X}$.

3 Privacy Notions for Probability Distributions

In this section we introduce a formal model for the privacy of user attributes, which is motivated in Sect. 1.

3.1 Modeling the Privacy of User Attributes in Terms of DP

As a running example, we consider an LBS (location based service) in which each user queries an LBS provider for a list of shops nearby. To hide a user's exact location x from the provider, the user applies a randomized algorithm $A : \mathcal{X} \rightarrow \mathbb{D}\mathcal{Y}$, called a *local obfuscation mechanism*, to her location x, and obtains an approximate information y with the probability $A(x)[y]$.

To illustrate the privacy of attributes, let us consider an example in which users try to prevent an attacker from inferring whether they are *male* or *female* by obfuscating their own exact locations using a mechanism A. For each $t \in \{male, female\}$, let $\lambda_t \in \mathbb{D}\mathcal{X}$ be the prior distribution of the location of the users who have the attribute t. Intuitively, λ_{male} (resp. λ_{female}) represents an attacker's belief on the location of the male (resp. female) users before the attacker observes an output of the mechanism A. Then the privacy of t can be modeled as a property that the attacker has no idea on whether the actual location x follows the distribution λ_{male} or λ_{female} after observing an output y of A.

This can be formalized in terms of ε-local DP. For each $t \in \{male, female\}$, we denote by $p(y \mid \lambda_t)$ the probability of observing an obfuscated location y when an actual location x is distributed over λ_t, i.e., $p(y \mid \lambda_t) = \sum_{x \in \mathcal{X}} \lambda_t[x] A(x)[y]$. Then we can define the privacy of t by:

$$\frac{p(y \mid \lambda_{male})}{p(y \mid \lambda_{female})} \le e^{\varepsilon}.$$

3.2   Distribution Privacy and Extended Distribution Privacy

We generalize the privacy of attributes (in Sect. 3.1) and define the notion of *distribution privacy* (DistP) as the differential privacy where the input is a probability distribution of data rather than a value of data. This notion models a level of obfuscation that hides which distribution a data value is drawn from. Intuitively, we say a randomized algorithm A provides DistP if, by observing an output of A, we cannot detect from which distribution an input to A is generated.

Definition 8 (Distribution privacy). Let $\varepsilon \in \mathbb{R}^{\geq 0}$ and $\delta \in [0,1]$. We say that a randomized algorithm $A : \mathcal{X} \to \mathbb{D}\mathcal{Y}$ provides (ε, δ)-*distribution privacy (DistP) w.r.t.* an adjacency relation $\Psi \subseteq \mathbb{D}\mathcal{X} \times \mathbb{D}\mathcal{X}$ if its lifting $A^{\#} : \mathbb{D}\mathcal{X} \to \mathbb{D}\mathcal{Y}$ provides (ε, δ)-DP w.r.t. Ψ, i.e., for all pairs $(\lambda, \lambda') \in \Psi$ and all $R \subseteq \mathcal{Y}$, we have:

$$A^{\#}(\lambda)[R] \leq e^{\varepsilon} \cdot A^{\#}(\lambda')[R] + \delta.$$

We say A provides (ε, δ)-*DistP w.r.t.* $\Lambda \subseteq \mathbb{D}\mathcal{X}$ if it provides (ε, δ)-DistP w.r.t. Λ^2.

For example, the privacy of a user attribute $t \in \{male, female\}$ described in Sect. 3.1 can be formalized as $(\varepsilon, 0)$-DistP w.r.t. $\{\lambda_{male}, \lambda_{female}\}$.

Mathematically, DistP is not a new notion but the DP for distributions. To contrast with DistP, we refer to the DP for data values as *point privacy*.

Next we introduce an extended form of distribution privacy to a metric. Intuitively, extended distribution privacy guarantees that when two input distributions are closer, then the output distributions must be less distinguishable.

Definition 9 (Extended distribution privacy). Let $d : (\mathbb{D}\mathcal{X} \times \mathbb{D}\mathcal{X}) \to \mathbb{R}$ be a utility distance, and $\Psi \subseteq \mathbb{D}\mathcal{X} \times \mathbb{D}\mathcal{X}$. We say that a mechanism $A : \mathcal{X} \to \mathbb{D}\mathcal{Y}$ provides (ε, d, δ)-*extended distribution privacy (XDistP) w.r.t.* Ψ if the lifting $A^{\#}$ provides (ε, d, δ)-XDP w.r.t. Ψ, i.e., for all $(\lambda, \lambda') \in \Psi$ and all $R \subseteq \mathcal{Y}$, we have:

$$A^{\#}(\lambda)[R] \leq e^{\varepsilon d(\lambda, \lambda')} \cdot A^{\#}(\lambda')[R] + \delta.$$

3.3   Interpretation by Bayes Factor

The interpretation of DP has been explored in previous work [16,18] using the notion of *Bayes factor*. Similarly, the meaning of DistP can also be explained in terms of Bayes factor, which compares the attacker's prior and posterior beliefs.

Assume that an attacker has some belief on the input distribution before observing the output values of an obfuscater A. We denote by $p(\lambda)$ the prior probability that a distribution λ is chosen as the input distribution. By observing an output y of A, the attacker updates his belief on the input distribution. We denote by $p(\lambda|y)$ the posterior probability of λ being chosen, given an output y.

For two distributions λ_0, λ_1, the Bayes factor $K(\lambda_0, \lambda_1, y)$ is defined as the ratio of the two posteriors divided by that of the two priors: $K(\lambda_0, \lambda_1, y) = \frac{p(\lambda_0|y)}{p(\lambda_1|y)} / \frac{p(\lambda_0)}{p(\lambda_1)}$. If the Bayes factor is far from 1 the attacker significantly updates his belief on the distribution by observing a perturbed output y of A.

Assume that A provides $(\varepsilon, 0)$-DistP. By Bayes' theorem, we obtain:

$$K(\lambda_0, \lambda_1, y) = \frac{p(\lambda_0|y)}{p(\lambda_1|y)} \cdot \frac{p(\lambda_1)}{p(\lambda_0)} = \frac{p(y|\lambda_0)}{p(y|\lambda_1)} = \frac{A^\#(\lambda_0)[y]}{A^\#(\lambda_1)[y]} \leq e^\varepsilon.$$

Intuitively, if the attacker believes that λ_0 is k times more likely than λ_1 before the observation, then he believes that λ_0 is $k \cdot e^\varepsilon$ times more likely than λ_1 after the observation. This means that for a small value of ε, DistP guarantees that the attacker does not gain information on the distribution by observing y.

In the case of XDistP, the Bayes factor $K(\lambda_0, \lambda_1, y)$ is bounded above by $e^{\varepsilon d(\lambda_0, \lambda_1)}$. Hence the attacker gains more information for a larger distance $d(\lambda_0, \lambda_1)$.

Table 1. Summary of basic properties of DistP.

Sequential composition $\odot$	A_b is $(\varepsilon_b, \delta_b)$-DistP $\Rightarrow A_1 \odot A_0$ is $(\varepsilon_0 + \varepsilon_1, (\delta_0 + \delta_1) \cdot |\Phi|)$-DistP
Sequential composition $\bullet$	A_b is $(\varepsilon_b, \delta_b)$-DistP $\Rightarrow A_1 \bullet A_0$ is $(\varepsilon_0 + \varepsilon_1, \delta_0 + \delta_1)$-DistP
Post-processing	A_0 is (ε, δ)-DistP $\Rightarrow A_1 \circ A_0$ is (ε, δ)-DistP
Pre-processing (by c-stable T)	A is (ε, δ)-DistP $\Rightarrow A \circ T$ is $(c\varepsilon, \delta)$-DistP

3.4 Privacy Guarantee for Attackers with Close Beliefs

In the previous sections, we assume that we know the distance between two actual input distributions, and can determine the amount of noise required for distribution obfuscation. However, an attacker may have different beliefs on the distributions that are closer to the actual ones, e.g., more accurate distributions obtained by more observations and specific situations (e.g., daytime/nighttime).

To see this, for each $\lambda \in \mathbb{D}\mathcal{X}$, let $\tilde{\lambda}$ be an attacker's belief on λ. We say that an attacker has (c, d)-*close beliefs* if each distribution λ satisfies $d(\lambda, \tilde{\lambda}) \leq c$. Then extended distribution privacy in the presence of an attacker is given by:

Proposition 1 (XDistP with close beliefs). *Let* $A : \mathcal{X} \to \mathbb{D}\mathcal{Y}$ *provide* $(\varepsilon, d, 0)$-*XDistP w.r.t. some* $\Psi \subseteq \mathcal{X} \times \mathcal{X}$. *If an attacker has* (c, d)-*close beliefs, then for all* $(\lambda_0, \lambda_1) \in \Psi$ *and all* $R \subseteq \mathcal{Y}$, *we have* $A^\#(\tilde{\lambda}_0)[R] \leq e^{\varepsilon(d(\lambda_0, \lambda_1) + 2c)} \cdot A^\#(\tilde{\lambda}_1)[R]$.

When the attacker's beliefs are closer to ours, then c is smaller, hence a stronger distribution privacy is guaranteed. See [15] for a proposition with DistP. Note that assuming some attacker's beliefs are inevitable also in many previous studies, e.g., when we want to protect the privacy of correlated data [19–21].

3.5   Difference from the Histogram Privacy

Finally, we present a brief remark on the difference between DistP and the *differential privacy of histogram publication* (e.g., [22]). Roughly, a histogram publication mechanism is a *central* mechanism that aims at *hiding a single record* $x \in \mathcal{X}$ and outputs an obfuscated histogram, e.g., a distribution $\mu \in \mathbb{D}\mathcal{Y}$, whereas a DistP mechanism is a *local* mechanism that aims at *hiding an input distribution* $\lambda \in \mathbb{D}\mathcal{X}$ and outputs a single perturbed value $y \in \mathcal{Y}$.

Note that neither of these implies the other. The ε-DP of a histogram publication mechanism means that for any two adjacent inputs $x, x' \in \mathcal{X}$ and any histogram $\mu \in \mathbb{D}\mathcal{Y}$, $\frac{p(\mu|x)}{p(\mu|x')} \le e^{\varepsilon}$. However, this does not derive ε-DistP, i.e., for any adjacent input distributions $\lambda, \lambda' \in \mathbb{D}\mathcal{X}$ and any output $y \in \mathcal{Y}$, $\frac{p(y|\lambda)}{p(y|\lambda')} \le e^{\varepsilon}$.

4   Basic Properties of Distribution Privacy

In Table 1, we show basic properties of DistP. (See the arXiv version [15] for the full table with XDistP and their detailed proofs.)

The composition $A_1 \odot A_0$ means that an identical input x is given to two DistP mechanisms A_0 and A_1, whereas the composition $A_1 \bullet A_0$ means that independent inputs x_b are provided to mechanisms A_b [23]. The compositionality can be used to quantify the attribute privacy against an attacker who obtains multiple released data each obfuscated for the purpose of protecting a different attribute. For example, let $\Psi = \{(\lambda_{male}, \lambda_{female}), (\lambda_{home}, \lambda_{out})\}$, and A_0 (resp. A_1) be a mechanism providing ε_0-DistP (resp. ε_1-DistP) w.r.t. Ψ. When A_0 (resp. A_1) obfuscates a location x_0 for the sake of protecting *male/female* (resp. *home/out*), then both *male/female* and *home/out* are protected with $(\varepsilon_0 + \varepsilon_1)$-DistP.

As for pre-processing, the stability notion is different from that for DP:

Definition 10 (Stability). Let $c \in \mathbb{N}^{>0}$, $\Psi \subseteq \mathbb{D}\mathcal{X} \times \mathbb{D}\mathcal{X}$, and W be a metric over $\mathbb{D}\mathcal{X}$. A transformation $T : \mathbb{D}\mathcal{X} \to \mathbb{D}\mathcal{X}$ is (c, Ψ)-*stable* if for any $(\lambda_0, \lambda_1) \in \Psi$, $T(\lambda_0)$ can be reached from $T(\lambda_1)$ at most c-steps over Ψ. Analogously, $T : \mathbb{D}\mathcal{X} \to \mathbb{D}\mathcal{X}$ is (c, W)-*stable* if for any $\lambda_0, \lambda_1 \in \mathbb{D}\mathcal{X}$, $W(T(\lambda_0), T(\lambda_1)) \le c\,W(\lambda_0, \lambda_1)$.

We present relationships among privacy notions in [15]. An important property is that when the relation $\Psi \subseteq \mathbb{D}\mathcal{X} \times \mathbb{D}\mathcal{X}$ includes pairs of point distributions (i.e., distributions having single points with probability 1), DistP (resp. XDistP) implies DP (resp. XDP). In contrast, if Ψ does not include pairs of point distributions, DistP (resp. XDistP) may not imply DP (resp. XDP), as in Sect. 6.

5   Distribution Obfuscation by Point Obfuscation

In this section we present how the point obfuscation mechanisms (including DP and XDP mechanisms) contribute to the obfuscation of probability distributions.

5.1   Distribution Obfuscation by DP Mechanisms

We first show every DP mechanism provides DistP. (See Definition 7 for $\Phi^{\#}$.)

Theorem 1 $((\varepsilon, \delta)$-DP $\Rightarrow (\varepsilon, \delta \cdot |\Phi|)$-DistP). *Let $\Phi \subseteq \mathcal{X} \times \mathcal{X}$. If $A : \mathcal{X} \to \mathbb{D}\mathcal{Y}$ provides (ε, δ)-DP w.r.t. Φ, then it provides $(\varepsilon, \delta \cdot |\Phi|)$-DistP w.r.t. $\Phi^{\#}$.*

This means that the mechanism A makes any pair $(\lambda_0, \lambda_1) \in \Phi^{\#}$ indistinguishable up to the threshold ε and with exceptions $\delta \cdot |\Phi|$. Intuitively, when λ_0 and λ_1 are adjacent w.r.t. the relation $\Phi^{\#}$, we can construct λ_1 from λ_0 only by moving mass from $\lambda_0[x_0]$ to $\lambda_1[x_1]$ where $(x_0, x_1) \in \Phi$ (i.e., x_0 is adjacent to x_1).

Example 2 (Randomized response). By Theorem 1, the $(\varepsilon, 0)$-DP randomized response [14] and RAPPOR [4] provide $(\varepsilon, 0)$-DistP. When we use these mechanisms, the estimation of the input distribution is harder for a smaller ε. However, these DP mechanisms tend to have small utility, because they add much noise to hide not only the input distributions, but everything about inputs.

5.2   Distribution Obfuscation by XDP Mechanisms

Compared to DP mechanisms, XDP mechanisms are known to provide better utility. Alvim et al. [24] show the planar Laplace mechanism [3] adds less noise than the randomized response, since XDP hides only closer locations. However, we show XDP mechanisms still need to add much noise proportionally to the ∞-Wasserstein distance between the distributions we want make indistinguishable.

The ∞-Wasserstein Distance $W_{\infty,d}$ as Utility Distance. We first observe how much ε' is sufficient for an ε'-XDP mechanism (e.g., the Laplace mechanism) to make two distribution λ_0 and λ_1 indistinguishable in terms of ε-DistP.

Suppose that λ_0 and λ_1 are point distributions such that $\lambda_0[x_0] = \lambda_1[x_1] = 1$ for some $x_0, x_1 \in \mathcal{X}$. Then an ε'-XDP mechanism A satisfies:

$$D_\infty(A^{\#}(\lambda_0) \,\|\, A^{\#}(\lambda_1)) = D_\infty(A(x_0) \,\|\, A(x_1)) \le \varepsilon' d(x_0, x_1).$$

In order for A to provide ε-DistP, ε' should be defined as $\frac{\varepsilon}{d(x_0, x_1)}$. That is, the noise added by A should be proportional to the distance between x_0 and x_1.

To extend this to arbitrary distributions, we need to define a utility metric between distributions. A natural possible definition would be the largest distance between values of λ_0 and λ_1, i.e., the *diameter* over the supports defined by:

$$\mathsf{diam}(\lambda_0, \lambda_1) = \max_{x_0 \in \mathsf{supp}(\lambda_0), x_1 \in \mathsf{supp}(\lambda_1)} d(x_0, x_1).$$

However, when there is an outlier in λ_0 or λ_1 that is far from other values in the supports, then the diameter $\mathsf{diam}(\lambda_0, \lambda_1)$ is large. Hence the mechanisms that add noise proportionally to the diameter would lose utility too much.

To have better utility, we employ the ∞-Wasserstein metric $W_{\infty,d}$. The idea is that given two distributions λ_0 and λ_1 over $\mathcal{X}$, we consider the cost of a transportation of weights from λ_0 to λ_1. The transportation is formalized as a coupling γ of λ_0 and λ_1 (see Definition 5), and the cost of the largest move is $\Delta_{\mathsf{supp}(\gamma),d} = \max\limits_{(x_0,x_1)\in\mathsf{supp}(\gamma)} d(x_0,x_1)$, i.e., the sensitivity w.r.t. the adjacency relation $\mathsf{supp}(\gamma) \subseteq \mathcal{X} \times \mathcal{X}$ (Definition 3). The minimum cost of the largest move is given by the ∞-Wasserstein metric: $W_{\infty,d}(\lambda_0,\lambda_1) = \min\limits_{\gamma\in\mathsf{cp}(\lambda_0,\lambda_1)} \Delta_{\mathsf{supp}(\gamma),d}$.

XDP implies XDistP. We show every XDP mechanism provides XDistP with the metric $W_{\infty,d}$. To formalize this, we define a lifted relation $\Phi^{\#}_{W_\infty}$ as the maximum relation over $\mathbb{D}\mathcal{X}$ s.t. for any $(\lambda_0,\lambda_1) \in \Phi^{\#}_{W_\infty}$, there is a coupling $\gamma \in \mathsf{cp}(\lambda_0,\lambda_1)$ satisfying $\mathsf{supp}(\gamma) \subseteq \Phi$ and $\gamma \in \Gamma_{\infty,d}(\lambda_0,\lambda_1)$. Then $\Phi^{\#}_{W_\infty} \subseteq \Phi^{\#}$ holds.

Theorem 2 ((ε,d,δ)-XDP $\Rightarrow$ $(\varepsilon, W_{\infty,d}, \delta\cdot|\Phi|)$-XDistP). *If $A : \mathcal{X} \to \mathbb{D}\mathcal{Y}$ provides (ε,d,δ)-XDP w.r.t. $\Phi \subseteq \mathcal{X} \times \mathcal{X}$, it provides $(\varepsilon, W_{\infty,d}, \delta\cdot|\Phi|)$-XDistP w.r.t. $\Phi^{\#}_{W_\infty}$.*

Algorithm 1. Tupling mechanism $Q^{\mathsf{tp}}_{k,\nu,A}$

Input: x: input, k: #dummies, ν: distribution of dummies, A: randomized algorithm
Output: $y = (r_1,\ldots,r_i,s,r_{i+1},\ldots,r_k)$: the output value of the tupling mechanism

$s \xleftarrow{\$} A(x)$; // Draw an obfuscated value s of an input x

$r_1,r_2,\ldots,r_k \xleftarrow{\$} \nu$; // Draw k dummies from a given distribution ν

$i \xleftarrow{\$} \{1,2,\ldots,k+1\}$; // Draw i to decide the order of the outputs

return $(r_1,\ldots,r_i,s,r_{i+1},\ldots,r_k)$;

By Theorem 2, when $\delta > 0$, the noise required for obfuscation is proportional to $|\Phi|$, which is at most the domain size squared $|\mathcal{X}|^2$. This implies that for a larger domain $\mathcal{X}$, the Gaussian mechanism is not suited for distribution obfuscation. We will demonstrate this by experiments in Sect. 7.4.

In contrast, the Laplace/exponential mechanisms provide $(\varepsilon, W_{\infty,d}, 0)$-DistP. Since $W_{\infty,d}(\lambda_0,\lambda_1) \leq \mathsf{diam}(\lambda_0,\lambda_1)$, the noise added proportionally to $W_{\infty,d}$ can be smaller than diam. This implies that obfuscating a distribution requires less noise than obfuscating a set of data. However, the required noise can still be very large when we want to make two distant distributions indistinguishable.

6   Distribution Obfuscation by Random Dummies

In this section we introduce a local mechanism called a *tupling mechanism* to improve the tradeoff between DistP and utility, as motivated in Sect. 1.

6.1   Tupling Mechanism

We first define the *tupling mechanism* as a local mechanism that obfuscates a given input x by using a point perturbation mechanism A (not necessarily in terms of DP or XDP), and that also adds k random dummies $r_1, r_2, \ldots, r_k$ to the output to obfuscate the input distribution (Algorithm 1). The probability that given an input x, the mechanism $Q^{\text{tp}}_{k,\nu,A}$ outputs $\bar{y}$ is given by $Q^{\text{tp}}_{k,\nu,A}(x)[\bar{y}]$.

6.2   Privacy of the Tupling Mechanism

Next we show that the tupling mechanism provides DistP w.r.t. the following class of distributions. Given $\beta, \eta \in [0, 1]$ and $A : \mathcal{X} \to \mathbb{D}\mathcal{Y}$, we define $\Lambda_{\beta, \eta, A}$ by:

$$\Lambda_{\beta,\eta,A} = \left\{ \lambda \in \mathbb{D}\mathcal{X} \mid \Pr\left[y \xleftarrow{\$} \mathcal{Y} : A^{\#}(\lambda)[y] \le \beta \right] \ge 1 - \eta \right\}.$$

For instance, a distribution λ satisfying $\max_x \lambda[x] \le \beta$ belongs to $\Lambda_{\beta,0,A}$.

Theorem 3 (DistP of the tupling mechanism). *Let* $k \in \mathbb{N}^{>0}$, ν *be the uniform distribution over* $\mathcal{Y}$, $A : \mathcal{X} \to \mathbb{D}\mathcal{Y}$, *and* $\beta, \eta \in [0, 1]$. *Given an* $0 < \alpha < \frac{k}{|\mathcal{Y}|}$, *let* $\varepsilon_\alpha = \ln \frac{k + (\alpha + \beta) \cdot |\mathcal{Y}|}{k - \alpha \cdot |\mathcal{Y}|}$ *and* $\delta_\alpha = 2e^{-\frac{2\alpha^2}{k\beta^2}} + \eta$. *Then the* (k, ν, A)-*tupling mechanism provides* $(\varepsilon_\alpha, \delta_\alpha)$-*DistP w.r.t.* $\Lambda^2_{\beta,\eta,A}$.

This claim states that just adding random dummies achieves DistP without any assumption on A (e.g., A does not have to provide DP). For a smaller range size $|\mathcal{Y}|$ and a larger number k of dummies, we obtain a stronger DistP.

Note that the distributions protected by $Q^{\text{tp}}_{k,\nu,A}$ belong to the set $\Lambda_{\beta,\eta,A}$.

– When $\beta = 1$, $\Lambda_{\beta,\eta,A}$ is the set of all distributions (i.e., $\Lambda_{1,\eta,A} = \mathbb{D}\mathcal{X}$) while ε_α and δ_α tend to be large.
– For a smaller β, the set $\Lambda_{\beta,\eta,A}$ is smaller while ε_α and δ_α are smaller; that is, the mechanism provides a stronger DistP for a smaller set of distributions.
– If A provides ε_A-DP, $\Lambda_{\beta,\eta,A}$ goes to $\mathbb{D}\mathcal{X}$ for $\varepsilon_A \to 0$. More generally, $\Lambda_{\beta,\eta,A}$ is larger when the maximum output probability $\max_y A^{\#}(\lambda)[y]$ is smaller.

In practice, even when ε_A is relatively large, a small number of dummies enables us to provide a strong DistP, as shown by experiments in Sect. 7.

We note that Theorem 3 may not imply DP of the tupling mechanism, depending on A. For example, suppose that A is the identity function. For small ε_α and δ_α, we have $\beta \ll 1$, hence no point distribution λ (where $\lambda[x] = 1$ for some x) belongs to $\Lambda_{\beta,\eta,A}$, namely, the tupling mechanism does not provide $(\varepsilon_\alpha, \delta_\alpha)$-DP.

6.3   Service Quality Loss and Cost of the Tupling Mechanism

When a mechanism outputs a value y closer to the original input x, she obtains a larger *utility*, or equivalently, a smaller *service quality loss* $d(x, y)$. For example, in an LBS (location based service), if a user located at x submits an obfuscated location y, the LBS provider returns the shops near y, hence the service quality loss can be expressed as the Euclidean distance $d(x,y) \stackrel{\text{def}}{=} \|x - y\|$.

Since each output of the tupling mechanism consists of $k + 1$ elements, the quality loss of submitting a tuple $\bar{y} = (y_1, y_2, \ldots, y_{k+1})$ amounts to $d(x, \bar{y}):=\min_i d(x, y_i)$. Then the expected quality loss of the mechanism is defined as follows.

Definition 11 (Expected quality loss of the tupling mechanism). For a $\lambda \in \mathbb{D}\mathcal{X}$ and a metric $d : \mathcal{X} \times \mathcal{Y} \to \mathbb{R}$, the *expected quality loss* of $Q^{\text{tp}}_{k,\nu,A}$ is:

$$L\left(Q^{\text{tp}}_{k,\nu,A}\right) = \sum_{x \in \mathcal{X}} \sum_{\bar{y} \in \mathcal{Y}^{k+1}} \lambda[x] \; Q^{\text{tp}}_{k,\nu,A}(x)[\bar{y}] \min_i d(x, y_i).$$

For a larger number k of random dummies, $\min_i d(x, y_i)$ is smaller on average, hence $L\left(Q^{\text{tp}}_{k,\nu,A}\right)$ is also smaller. Furthermore, thanks to the distribution obfuscation by random dummies, we can instead reduce the perturbation noise added to the actual input x to obtain the same level of DistP. Therefore, the service quality is much higher than existing mechanisms, as shown in Sect. 7.

6.4 Improving the Worst-Case Quality Loss

As a point obfuscation mechanism A used in the tupling mechanism $Q^{\text{tp}}_{k,\nu,A}$, we define the *restricted Laplace (RL) mechanism* below. Intuitively, (ε_A, r)-RL mechanism adds ε_A-XDP Laplace noise only within a radius r of the original location x. This ensures that the worst-case quality loss of the tupling mechanisms is bounded above by the radius r, whereas the standard Laplace mechanism reports a location y that is arbitrarily distant from x with a small probability.

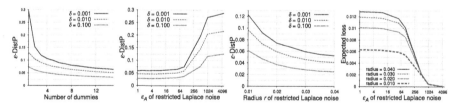

(a) #dummies and ε-DistP (when using $(100, 0.020)$-RL mechanism).

(b) ε_A of $(\varepsilon_A, 0.020)$-RL mechanism and ε-DistP (with 10 dummies).

(c) A radius r of $(100, r)$-RL mechanism and ε-DistP (with 10 dummies).

(d) ε_A of (ε_A, r)- RL mechanism and the expected loss (with 5 dummies).

Fig. 2. Empirical DistP and quality loss of $Q^{\text{tp}}_{k,\nu,A}$ for the attribute *male/female*.

Definition 12 (RL mechanism). Let $\mathcal{Y}_{x,r} = \{y' \in \mathcal{Y} \mid d(x, y') \leq r\}$. We define (ε_A, r)-*restricted Laplace (RL) mechanism* as the $A : \mathcal{X} \to \mathbb{D}\mathcal{Y}$ defined by:

$$A(x)[y] = \frac{e^{-\varepsilon d(x,y)}}{\sum_{y' \in \mathcal{Y}_{x,r}} e^{-\varepsilon d(x,y')}} \text{ if } y \in \mathcal{Y}_{x,r}, \text{ and } A(x)[y] = 0 \text{ otherwise.}$$

Since the support of A is limited to $\mathcal{Y}_{x,r}$, A provides better service quality but does not provide DP. Nevertheless, as shown in Theorem 3, $Q^{\mathsf{tp}}_{k,\nu,A}$ provides DistP, due to dummies in $\mathcal{Y} \setminus \mathcal{Y}_{x,r}$. This implies that DistP is a relaxation of DP that guarantees the privacy of attributes while achieving higher utility by weakening the DP protection of point data. In other words, DistP mechanisms are useful when users want both to keep high utility and to protect the attribute privacy more strongly than what a DP mechanism can guarantee (e.g., when users do not mind revealing their actual locations outside home, but want to hide from robbers the fact that they are outside home, as motivated in Sect. 1).

7   Application to Attribute Privacy in LBSs

In this section we apply local mechanisms to the protection of the attribute privacy in location based services (LBSs) where each user submits her own location x to an LBS provider to obtain information relevant to x (e.g., shops near x).

7.1   Experimental Setup

We perform experiments on location privacy in Manhattan by using the Foursquare dataset (Global-scale Check-in Dataset) [25]. We first divide Manhattan into 11×10 regions with $1.0\,\mathrm{km}$ intervals. To provide more useful information to users in crowded regions, we further re-divide these regions to 276 regions by recursively partitioning each crowded region into four until each resulting region has roughly similar population density.[2] Let $\mathcal{Y}$ be the set of those 276 regions, and $\mathcal{X}$ be the set of the 228 regions inside the central $10\,\mathrm{km} \times 9\,\mathrm{km}$ area in $\mathcal{Y}$.

As an obfuscation mechanism Q, we use the tupling mechanism $Q^{\mathsf{tp}}_{k,\nu,A}$ that uses an (ε_A, r)-RL mechanism A and the uniform distribution ν over $\mathcal{Y}$ to generate dummy locations. Note that ν is close to the population density distribution over $\mathcal{Y}$, because each region in $\mathcal{Y}$ is constructed to have roughly similar population density. In the definitions of the RL mechanism and the quality loss, we use the Euclidean distance $\| \cdot \|$ between the central points of the regions.

In the experiments, we measure the privacy of user attributes, formalized as DistP. For example, let us consider the attribute $male/female$. For each $t \in \{male, female\}$, let $\lambda_t \in \mathbb{D}\mathcal{X}$ be the prior distribution of the location of the users having the attribute t. Then, λ_{male} (resp. λ_{female}) represents an attacker's belief on the location of the male (resp. female) users. We define these as the empirical distributions that the attacker can calculate from the above Foursquare dataset.

7.2   Evaluation of the Tupling Mechanism

Distribution Privacy. We demonstrate by experiments that the *male* users cannot be recognized as which of *male* or *female* in terms of DistP. In Fig. 2,

---

[2] This partition may be useful to achieve smaller values (ε, δ) of DistP, because β tends to be smaller when the population density is closer to the uniform distribution.

we show the experimental results on the DistP of the tupling mechanism $Q_{k,\nu,A}^{tp}$. For a larger number k of dummy locations, we have a stronger DistP (Fig. 2a). For a larger ε_A, $(\varepsilon_A, 0.020)$-RL mechanism A adds less noise, hence the tupling mechanism provides a weaker DistP (Fig. 2b)[3]. For a larger radius r, the RL mechanism A spreads the original distribution λ_{male} and thus provides a strong DistP (Fig. 2c). We also show the relationship between k and DistP in the eastern/western Tokyo and London, which have different levels of privacy (Fig. 3).

These results imply that if we add more dummies, we can decrease the noise level/radius of A to have better utility, while keeping the same level ε of DistP. Conversely, if A adds more noise, we can decrease the number k of dummies.

Expected Quality Loss. In Fig. 2d, we show the experimental results on the expected quality loss of the tupling mechanism. For a larger ε_A, A adds less noise, hence the loss is smaller. We confirm that for more dummy data, the expected quality loss is smaller. Unlike the planar Laplace mechanism (PL), A ensures that the worst quality loss is bounded above by the radius r. Furthermore, for a smaller radius r, the expected loss is also smaller as shown in Fig. 2d.

7.3 Appropriate Parameters

We define the *attack success rate (ASR)* as the ratio that the attacker succeeds to infer a user has an attribute when she does actually. We use an inference algorithm based on the Bayes decision rule [26] to minimize the identification error probability when the estimated posterior probability is accurate [26].

In Fig. 4, we show the relationships between DistP and ASR in Manhattan for the attribute *home*, meaning the users located at their home. In theory, ASR = 0.5 represents the attacker learns nothing about the attribute, whereas

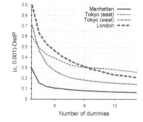
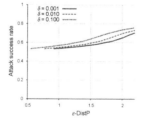
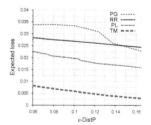

Fig. 3. k and DistP for *male/female* in different cities.

Fig. 4. DistP and ASR of the tupling ($k = 10$, $r = 0.020$).

Fig. 5. $(\varepsilon, 0.001)$-DistP and expected loss for *male/female* and TM using $k = 10$, $r = 0.020$.

---

[3] In Fig. 2b, for $\varepsilon_A \to 0$, ε does not converge to 0, since the radius $r = 0.020$ of RL does not cover the whole $\mathcal{Y}$. However, if $r \geq \max_{x,y} \|x - y\|$, ε converges to 0.

the empirical ASR in our experiments fluctuates around 0.5. This seems to be caused by the fact that the dataset and the number of locations are finite. From Fig. 4, we conclude that $\varepsilon = 1$ is an appropriate parameter for $(\varepsilon, 0.001)$-DistP to achieve ASR $= 0.5$ in our setting, and we confirm this for other attributes. However, we note that this is an empirical criterion possibly depending on our setting, and the choice of ε for DistP can be as controversial as that for DP and should also be investigated using approaches for DP (e.g., [27]) in future work.

7.4   Comparison of Obfuscation Mechanisms

We demonstrate that the tupling mechanism (TM) outperforms the popular mechanisms: the randomized response (RR), the planar Laplace (PL), and the planar Gaussian (PG). In Fig. 5 we compare these concerning the relationship between ε-DistP and expected quality loss. Since PG always has some δ, it provides a weaker DistP than PL for the same quality loss. We also confirm that PL has smaller loss than RR, since it adds noise proportionally to the distance.

Finally, we briefly discuss the computational cost of the tupling mechanism $Q_{k,\nu,A}^{\mathsf{tp}}$, compared to PL. In the implementation, for a larger domain $\mathcal{X}$, PL deals with a larger size $|\mathcal{X}| \times |\mathcal{Y}|$ of the mechanism's matrix, since it outputs each region with a non-zero probability. In contrast, since the RL mechanism A used in $Q_{k,\nu,A}^{\mathsf{tp}}$ maps each location x to a region within a radius r of x, the size of A's matrix is $|\mathcal{X}| \times |\mathcal{Y}_{x,r}|$, requiring much smaller memory space than PL.

Furthermore, the users of TM can simply ignore the responses to dummy queries, whereas the users of PL need to select relevant POIs (point of interests) from a large radius of x, which could cost computationally for many POIs. Therefore, TM is more suited to be used in mobile environments than PL.

8   Related Work

Differential Privacy. Since the seminal work of Dwork [1] on DP, a number of its variants have been studied to provide different privacy guarantees; e.g., f-divergence privacy [28], d-privacy [16], Pufferfish privacy [20], local DP [2], and utility-optimized local DP [29]. All of these are intended to protect the input data rather than the input distributions. Note that distribution*al* privacy [30] is different from DistP and does not aim at protecting the privacy of distributions.

To our knowledge, this is the first work that investigates the *differential privacy* of probability distributions lying behind the input. However, a few studies have proposed related notions. Jelasity et al. [31] propose *distributional differential privacy* w.r.t. parameters θ and θ' of two distributions, which aims at protecting the privacy of the distribution parameters but is defined in a Bayesian style (unlike DP and DistP) to satisfy that for any output sequence y, $p(\theta|y) \leq e^{\varepsilon} p(\theta'|y)$. After a preliminary version of this paper appeared in arXiv [15], a notion generalizing DistP, called *profile based privacy*, is proposed in [32].

Some studies are technically related to our work. Song *et al.* [21] propose the Wasserstein mechanism to provide Pufferfish privacy, which protects correlated inputs. Fernandes *et al.* [33] introduce Earth mover's privacy, which is technically different from DistP in that their mechanism obfuscates a vector (a bag-of-words) instead of a distribution, and perturbs each element of the vector. Sei *et al.* [34] propose a variant of the randomized response to protect individual data and provide high utility of database. However, we emphasize again that our work differs from these studies in that we aim at protecting input distributions.

Location Privacy. Location privacy has been widely studied in the literature, and its survey can be found in [35]. A number of location obfuscation methods have been proposed so far, and they can be broadly divided into the following four types: perturbation (adding noise) [3,5,36], location generalization (merging regions) [37,38], and location hiding (deleting) [37,39], and adding dummy locations [40–42]. Location obfuscation based on DP (or its variant) have also been widely studied, and they can be categorized into the ones in the centralized model [43,44] and the ones in the local model [3,5]. However, these methods aim at protecting locations, and neither at protecting users' attributes (e.g., age, gender) nor activities (e.g., working, shopping) in a DP manner. Despite the fact that users' attributes and activities can be inferred from their locations [6–8], to our knowledge, no studies have proposed obfuscation mechanisms to provide rigorous DP guarantee for such attributes and activities.

9   Conclusion

We have proposed a formal model for the privacy of probability distributions and introduced the notion of distribution privacy (DistP). Then we have shown that existing local mechanisms deteriorate the utility by adding too much noise to provide DistP. To improve the tradeoff between DistP and utility, we have introduced the tupling mechanism and applied it to the protection of user attributes in LBSs. Then we have demonstrated that the tupling mechanism outperforms popular local mechanisms in terms of attribute obfuscation and service quality.

Acknowledgment. We thank the reviewers, Catuscia Palamidessi, Gilles Barthe, and Frank D. Valencia for their helpful comments on preliminary drafts.

A   Experimental Results

In this section we present some of the experimental results on the following four attributes. See [15] for further experimental results.

- *social/less-social* represent whether a user's social status [45] (the number of followers divided by the number of followings) is greater than 5 or not.
- *workplace/non-workplace* represent whether a user is at office or not. This attribute can be thought as sensitive when it implies users are unemployed.
- *home/out* represent whether a user is at home or not.

– *north/south* represent whether a user's home is located in the northern or southern Manhattan. This attribute needs to be protected from stalkers.

First, we compare different obfuscation mechanisms for various attributes in Figs. 5, 6a, and b. We also compare different time periods: 00 h–05 h, 06 h–11 h, 12 h–17 h, 18 h–23 h in Manhattan in Fig. 7.

Next, we compare the experimental results on five cities: Manhattan, eastern Tokyo, western Tokyo, London, and Paris. In Table 2 we show examples of parameters that achieve the same levels of DistP in different cities. More detailed can be found in Fig. 8 (*male/female*).

Finally, we compare theoretical/empirical values of ε-DistP as follows. In Table 3, we show the theoretical values of ε calculated by Theorem 3 for $\delta = 0.001, 0.01, 0.1$. Compared to experiments, those values can only give loose upper bounds on ε, because of the concentration inequality used to derive Theorem 3.

Table 2. The number k of dummies required for achieving DistP in different cities (MH = Manhattan, TKE = Tokyo (east), TKW = Tokyo (west), LD = London, PR = Paris) when $\varepsilon_A = 100$ and $r = 0.020$. Note that the data of Paris for *male/female* are excluded because of the insufficient sample size.

	MH	TKE	TKW	LD	PR
$(0.25, 0.001)$-DistP for **male/female**	2	>20	5	10	—
$(0.50, 0.001)$-DistP for **social/less social**	2	3	>20	2	3
$(1.00, 0.001)$-DistP for **work/non-work**	2	2	>20	1	2
$(1.50, 0.001)$-DistP for **home/outside**	3	5	>20	>20	4

Table 3. Theoretical/empirical ε-DistP of $Q_{k,\nu,A}^{\mathrm{tp}}$ ($k = 10$, $\varepsilon_A = 10$, $r = 0.020$).

	$\delta = 0.001$	$\delta = 0.01$	$\delta = 0.1$
Theoretical bounds	2.170	1.625	1.140
Empirical values	0.04450	0.03534	0.02295

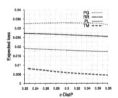

(a) $(\varepsilon, 0.001)$-DistP and expected loss for *social/less-social* in Manhattan.

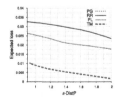

(b) $(\varepsilon, 0.001)$-DistP and expected loss for *home/out* in Manhattan.

Fig. 6. Comparison of the randomized response (RR), the planar Laplace mechanism (PL), the planar Gaussian mechanism (PG), and the tupling mechanism (TM) $Q_{k,\nu,A}^{\mathrm{tp}}$ with $k = 10$ dummies and a radius $r = 0.020$.

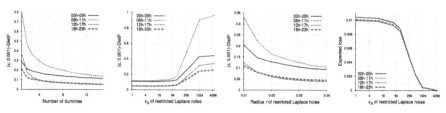

(a) #dummies and ε-DistP (when using (100, 0.020)-RL mechanism).

(b) ε_A of $(\varepsilon_A, 0.020)$-RL mechanism and ε-DistP (with 10 dummies).

(c) A radius r of $(100, r)$-RL mechanism and ε-DistP (with 10 dummies).

(d) ε_A of (ε_A, r)-RL mechanism and the expected loss (with 5 dummies).

Fig. 7. Empirical DistP and loss for *male/female* in different hours.

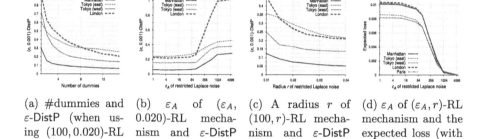

(a) #dummies and ε-DistP (when using (100, 0.020)-RL mechanism).

(b) ε_A of $(\varepsilon_A, 0.020)$-RL mechanism and ε-DistP (with 10 dummies).

(c) A radius r of $(100, r)$-RL mechanism and ε-DistP (with 10 dummies).

(d) ε_A of (ε_A, r)-RL mechanism and the expected loss (with 5 dummies).

Fig. 8. Empirical DistP and loss for *male/female* in different cities.

References

1. Dwork, C.: Differential privacy. In: Bugliesi, M., Preneel, B., Sassone, V., Wegener, I. (eds.) ICALP 2006. LNCS, vol. 4052, pp. 1–12. Springer, Heidelberg (2006). https://doi.org/10.1007/11787006_1

2. Duchi, J.C., Jordan, M.I., Wainwright, M.J.: Local privacy and statistical minimax rates. In: Proceedings of FOCS, pp. 429–438 (2013)

3. Andrés, M.E., Bordenabe, N.E., Chatzikokolakis, K., Palamidessi, C.: Geo-indistinguishability: differential privacy for location-based systems. In: Proceedings of CCS, pp. 901–914. ACM (2013)

4. Erlingsson, Ú., Pihur, V., Korolova, A.: RAPPOR: randomized aggregatable privacy-preserving ordinal response. In: Proceedings of CCS, pp. 1054–1067 (2014)

5. Bordenabe, N.E., Chatzikokolakis, K., Palamidessi, C.: Optimal geo-indistinguishable mechanisms for location privacy. In: Proceedings of CCS, pp. 251–262 (2014)

6. Liao, L., Fox, D., Kautz, H.: Extracting places and activities from GPS traces using hierarchical conditional random fields. Int. J. Robot. Res. **1**(26), 119–134 (2007)

7. Zheng, V.W., Zheng, Y., Yang, Q.: Joint learning user's activities and profiles from GPS data. In: Proceedings of LBSN, pp. 17–20 (2009)

8. Matsuo, Y., Okazaki, N., Izumi, K., Nakamura, Y., Nishimura, T., Hasida, K.: Inferring long-term user properties based on users' location history. In: Proceedings of IJCAI, pp. 2159–2165 (2007)
9. Yang, D., Qu, B., Cudré-Mauroux, P.: Privacy-preserving social media data publishing for personalized ranking-based recommendation. IEEE Trans. Knowl. Data Eng. **31**(3), 507–520 (2019)
10. Otterbacher, J.: Inferring gender of movie reviewers: exploiting writing style, content and metadata. In: Proceedings of CIKM, pp. 369–378 (2010)
11. Weinsberg, U., Bhagat, S., Ioannidis, S., Taft, N.: BlurMe: inferring and obfuscating user gender based on ratings. In: Proceedings of RecSys, pp. 195–202 (2012)
12. Gong, N.Z., Liu, B.: Attribute inference attacks in online social networks. ACM Trans. Priv. Secur. **21**(1), 3:1–3:30 (2018)
13. Mislove, A., Viswanath, B., Gummadi, P.K., Druschel, P.: You are who you know: inferring user profiles in online social networks. In: Proceedings of WSDM, pp. 251–260 (2010)
14. Kairouz, P., Bonawitz, K., Ramage, D.: Discrete distribution estimation under local privacy. In: Proceedings of ICML, pp. 2436–2444 (2016)
15. Kawamoto, Y., Murakami, T.: Local obfuscation mechanisms for hiding probability distributions, CoRR, vol. abs/1812.00939 (2018). arXiv:1812.00939
16. Chatzikokolakis, K., Andrés, M.E., Bordenabe, N.E., Palamidessi, C.: Broadening the scope of differential privacy using metrics. In: De Cristofaro, E., Wright, M. (eds.) PETS 2013. LNCS, vol. 7981, pp. 82–102. Springer, Heidelberg (2013). https://doi.org/10.1007/978-3-642-39077-7_5
17. Vaserstein, L.: Markovian processes on countable space product describing large systems of automata. Probl. Peredachi Inf. **5**(3), 64–72 (1969)
18. Dwork, C., McSherry, F., Nissim, K., Smith, A.: Calibrating noise to sensitivity in private data analysis. In: Halevi, S., Rabin, T. (eds.) TCC 2006. LNCS, vol. 3876, pp. 265–284. Springer, Heidelberg (2006). https://doi.org/10.1007/11681878_14
19. Kifer, D., Machanavajjhala, A.: No free lunch in data privacy. In: Proceedings of SIGMOD, pp. 193–204 (2011)
20. Kifer, D., Machanavajjhala, A.: A rigorous and customizable framework for privacy. In: Proceedings of PODS, pp. 77–88 (2012)
21. Song, S., Wang, Y., Chaudhuri, K.: Pufferfish privacy mechanisms for correlated data. In: Proceedings of SIGMOD, pp. 1291–1306 (2017)
22. Xu, J., Zhang, Z., Xiao, X., Yang, Y., Yu, G., Winslett, M.: Differentially private histogram publication. VLDB J. **22**(6), 797–822 (2013)
23. Kawamoto, Y., Chatzikokolakis, K., Palamidessi, C.: On the compositionality of quantitative information flow. Log. Methods Comput. Sci. **13**(3) (2017)
24. Alvim, M.S., Chatzikokolakis, K., Palamidessi, C., Pazii, A.: Invited paper: local differential privacy on metric spaces: optimizing the trade-off with utility. In: Proceedings of CSF, pp. 262–267 (2018)
25. Yang, D., Zhang, D., Qu, B.: Participatory cultural mapping based on collective behavior data in location based social networks. ACM Trans. Intell. Syst. Technol. **7**(3), 30:1–30:23 (2015)
26. Duda, R.O., Hart, P.E., Stork, D.G.: Pattern Classification. Wiley, Hoboken (2000)
27. Hsu, J., et al.: Differential privacy: an economic method for choosing epsilon. In: Proceedings of CSF, pp. 398–410 (2014)

28. Barthe, G., Olmedo, F.: Beyond differential privacy: composition theorems and relational logic for f-divergences between probabilistic programs. In: Fomin, F.V., Freivalds, R., Kwiatkowska, M., Peleg, D. (eds.) ICALP 2013. LNCS, vol. 7966, pp. 49–60. Springer, Heidelberg (2013). https://doi.org/10.1007/978-3-642-39212-2_8

29. Murakami, T., Kawamoto, Y.: Utility-optimized local differential privacy mechanisms for distribution estimation. In: Proceedings of USENIX Security (2019, to appear)

30. Blum, A., Ligett, K., Roth, A.: A learning theory approach to noninteractive database privacy. J. ACM **60**(2), 12:1–12:25 (2013)

31. Jelasity, M., Birman, K.P.: Distributional differential privacy for large-scale smart metering. In: Proceedings of IH&MMSec, pp. 141–146 (2014)

32. Geumlek, J., Chaudhuri, K.: Profile-based privacy for locally private computations, CoRR, vol. abs/1903.09084 (2019)

33. Fernandes, N., Dras, M., McIver, A.: Generalised differential privacy for text document processing. In: Nielson, F., Sands, D. (eds.) POST 2019. LNCS, vol. 11426, pp. 123–148. Springer, Cham (2019). https://doi.org/10.1007/978-3-030-17138-4_6

34. Sei, Y., Ohsuga, A.: Differential private data collection and analysis based on randomized multiple dummies for untrusted mobile crowdsensing. IEEE Trans. Inf. Forensics Secur. **12**(4), 926–939 (2017)

35. Chatzikokolakis, K., ElSalamouny, E., Palamidessi, C., Anna, P.: Methods for location privacy: a comparative overview. Found. Trends® Priv. Secur. **1**(4), 199–257 (2017)

36. Shokri, R., Theodorakopoulos, G., Troncoso, C., Hubaux, J.-P., Boudec, J.-Y.L.: Protecting location privacy: optimal strategy against localization attacks. In: Proceedings of CCS, pp. 617–627. ACM (2012)

37. Shokri, R., Theodorakopoulos, G., Boudec, J.-Y.L., Hubaux, J.-P.: Quantifying location privacy. In: Proceedings of S&P, pp. 247–262. IEEE (2011)

38. Xue, M., Kalnis, P., Pung, H.K.: Location diversity: enhanced privacy protection in location based services. In: Choudhury, T., Quigley, A., Strang, T., Suginuma, K. (eds.) LoCA 2009. LNCS, vol. 5561, pp. 70–87. Springer, Heidelberg (2009). https://doi.org/10.1007/978-3-642-01721-6_5

39. Hoh, B., Gruteser, M., Xiong, H., Alrabady, A.: Preserving privacy in GPS traces via uncertainty-aware path cloaking. In: Proceedings of CCS, pp. 161–171. ACM (2007)

40. Bindschaedler, V., Shokri, R.: Synthesizing plausible privacy-preserving location traces. In: Proceedings of S&P, pp. 546–563 (2016)

41. Chow, R., Golle, P.: Faking contextual data for fun, profit, and privacy. In: Proceedings of PES, pp. 105–108. ACM (2009)

42. Kido, H., Yanagisawa, Y., Satoh, T.: Protection of location privacy using dummies for location-based services. In: Proceedings of ICDE Workshops, p. 1248 (2005)

43. Machanavajjhala, A., Kifer, D., Abowd, J.M., Gehrke, J., Vilhuber, L.: Privacy: theory meets practice on the map. In: Proceedings of ICDE, pp. 277–286. IEEE (2008)

44. Ho, S.-S., Ruan, S.: Differential privacy for location pattern mining. In: Proceedings of SPRINGL, pp. 17–24. ACM (2011)

45. Cheng, Z., Caverlee, J., Lee, K., Sui, D.Z.: Exploring millions of footprints in location sharing services. In: Proceedings of ICWSM (2011)

A First Look into Privacy Leakage in 3D Mixed Reality Data

Jaybie A. de Guzman[1,2(✉)] ⓘ, Kanchana Thilakarathna[2,3] ⓘ,
and Aruna Seneviratne[1,2] ⓘ

[1] University of New South Wales, Sydney, NSW 2052, Australia
j.deguzman@student.unsw.edu.au, a.seneviratne@unsw.edu.au
[2] Data61 | CSIRO, Sydney, NSW 2015, Australia
[3] University of Sydney, Sydney, NSW 2006, Australia
kanchana.thilakarathna@sydney.edu.au

Abstract. We have seen a rise in *mixed* (MR) and *augmented reality* (AR) applications and devices in recent years. Subsequently, we have become familiar with the sensing power of these applications and devices, and we are only starting to realize the nascent risks that these technology puts over our privacy and security. Current privacy protection measures are primarily aimed towards known and well-utilised data types (i.e. location, on-line activity, biometric, and so on) while a few works have focused on looking into the security and privacy risks of and providing protection on MR data, particularly on 3D MR data. In this work, we primarily reveal the privacy leakage from released 3D MR data and how the leakage persist even after implementing spatial generalizations and abstractions. Firstly, we formalize the *spatial privacy* problem in 3D mixed reality data as well as the adversary model. Then, we demonstrate through an inference model how adversaries can identify 3D spaces and, potentially, infer more spatial information. Moreover, we also demonstrate how *compact* 3D MR Data can be in terms of memory usage which allows adversaries to create lightweight 3D inference models of user spaces.

Keywords: Mixed and augmented reality · 3D data ·
Point cloud data · Security and privacy

1 Introduction

Pokémon Go's release in 2016 arguably marked the beginning of augmented reality (AR) and mixed reality (MR) to be part of the mainstream mobile market. Soon after, Apple launched the ARKit in 2017 and, halfway through 2018, Google followed with the ARCore.[1] Microsoft, on the other hand, focused on the head-mounted displays (or HMDs) with the HoloLens and other OEM headsets running their Windows Mixed Reality platform.[2] These developments

---

[1] See https://developer.apple.com/documentation/arkit for Apple's ARKit See https://developers.google.com/ar/ for Google's ARCore.
[2] https://developer.microsoft.com/en-us/windows/mixed-reality.

K. Sako et al. (Eds.): ESORICS 2019, LNCS 11735, pp. 149–169, 2019.
https://doi.org/10.1007/978-3-030-29959-0_8

undoubtedly signifies the very near future with AR and MR being ubiquitous. (Henceforth, following Milgram's definition [18], we will be collectively calling both augmented and mixed reality as mixed reality or MR.)

Most mobile MR development platforms (i.e. ARCore, and ARKit) utilise a form of *visual odometry* combined with motion or inertial information to map the device's position relative to the real-world, while dedicated HMDs (i.e. HoloLens), leverage multiple cameras with depth sensors to understand the environment and create a virtual 3D map. Once a good mapping has been created, the virtual space (or a coordinate system) is shared with applications to allow synthetic or augmented content to interact with the physical world such as *anchoring* a virtual object on your desk.

However, this environment understanding capability required by MR poses unforeseen privacy risks for users. Once these captured 3D maps have been revealed to untrusted parties, potentially sensitive spatial information about the users' space are disclosed. Adversaries can vary from a background service that delivers unsolicited ads based on the objects detected from the user's surroundings to burglars who are able to map the user's house, and, perhaps, the locations and dimensions of specific objects in their house based on the released 3D data. Furthermore, turning off GPS tracking for location privacy may no longer be sufficient once the user starts using MR applications that can expose their locations through the 3D and visual data that are exposed.[3]

The recent EU-GDPR ruling aims to address these issues from a policy approach. It aims to empower the users and protect their data privacy. This highlights the importance of designing and developing *privacy-enhancing technologies* (PETs). Currently, there are numerous PETs designed for structured data such as k-anonymity [23], and *differential privacy* [4], as well as techniques for data aggregation during information collection [9]. However, current techniques protecting media are mostly for conventional data types, and are primarily focusing on *facial de-identification* for *identity privacy* [7,19,27] as well as protection against visual capture recording mechanisms [1,28]. (See [8] for a survey of MR-related security and privacy protection approaches.)

In this work, we focus on the *nascent risks* from captured and collected 3D data used for MR processing. To demonstrate the privacy leakage, we utilize actual 3D point cloud data, captured by a Microsoft HoloLens, to construct an adversarial inferrer that can identify spaces from the revealed 3D data. The inference performance is evaluated over both raw data and different 3D data generalizations. And we show how such generalizations are ineffective even with a simple *matching-based* inference attack. To the best of our knowledge, this

---

[3] For example, Google has unveiled their *Visual Positioning Service* (or VPS) using 3D data to locate users in space – an offshoot of Project Tango – during their 2018 I/O keynote event.

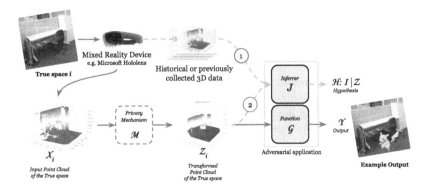

Fig. 1. Information flow (following the green solid arrows) for a desired MR functionality G with an intermediate privacy-preserving mechanism M; while an MR adversarial process (represented by the red broken arrows) may be done off line: (1) adversarial inference *modeling* or *learning* from, say, historical 3D data, and (2) adversarial inference or *matching* over released 3D data (Color figure online)

is the first work that aims to expose these risks. Consequently, we make the following specific contributions in this work:

1. We formalize the *3D spatial privacy problem* and define the privacy and utility metrics specific to 3D MR data.
2. We present a *3D adversarial inference model* to reveal the spatial privacy leakage and their effectiveness.
3. Using 3D point cloud data collected from Microsoft HoloLens, which is also the same 3D data representation format for Google's ARCore and Apple's ARKit, we demonstrate that 3D spatial inference attacks are possible on these MR platforms.
4. Lastly, results show the *insufficient protection* provided by spatial generalizations even by only using simple descriptor-matching for adversarial inference.

The rest of the paper is organized follows. Section 2 elaborates on the 3D MR data, i.e. point cloud data, and presents the theoretical framework of our *3D privacy problem*. In Sect. 4, we describe the evaluation methodology used to determine the privacy leakage in 3D data with and without spatial generalizations. The results are presented in Sect. 5 and the related work in Sect. 6. We conclude the paper in Sect. 7.

2   3D Privacy Problem

2.1   Why 3D?

With images and video, what the machine sees is practically what the user sees and a great deal of privacy work have been done on these data forms. Contrariwise, in MR, the experience is exported as visual data (e.g. objects augmented

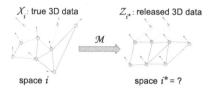

Fig. 2. A privacy preserving mechanism M transforms the raw point clouds X to a *potentially* privacy-preserving version Z to *hide* location identity ($i^* = ?$).

on the user's view) while its 3D nature, especially of the underlying data, is not exposed to the users: what the machine sees is different (arguably, even more) than what the user sees. That is, the digital representation of the physical world, the 3D point cloud data, is not exposed to the user. This inherent perceptual difference creates a disconnect and, perhaps, affects (or the lack thereof) how users perceive the sensitivity of 3D information. Furthermore, current MR platforms (i.e. Windows MR, ARCore and ARKit) directly operates on these 3D spatial maps or point clouds and, so far, no privacy preservation is applied before providing these data to third party applications.

3D Point Cloud Data. The 3D points comprising the 3D point cloud can be described by their $\{x, y, z\}$-position in space with an accompanying normal vector $\{n_x, n_y, n_z\}$. Figure 2 shows the point clouds as a mesh of 3D points with associated orientations represented by normal vectors. These are the minimum information necessary to capture the *geometric* properties of 3D spaces. Where normal vectors are not readily available, it is estimated from the points themselves. Sometimes, point clouds may also be accompanied by *photometric* information such as RGB or light intensity extracted from associated images or videos. For this work, we will only be focusing on the use of geometric information and leverage them for 3D description for emulating adversarial inference.

2.2   Defining the 3D Privacy Problem

We define the elements shown in Fig. 1: the space represented by a point cloud X identified by a label i; the privacy preserving mechanism M that transforms X to a privacy-preserved point cloud Z, i.e. $M : X \mapsto Z$ as shown in Fig. 2; an intended functionality G that produces an intended output Y, and from which we derive the utility function U; and an adversarial inferrer J that produces a hypothesis H to reveal the identity of a given unknown space. The adversarial processes may be done off line and not necessarily during MR function runtime. (See Appendix A for detailed definitions on X, M, Z, and G.)

Defining the Function Utility. For a given functionality G, an effective mechanism M aims to make the resulting outputs y_i from the raw point cloud x_i and its privacy-preserving version $z_{(i)}$ similar, i.e. $y_{x_i} \simeq y_{z_{(i)}}$, or their difference is small, $D_{Z;X} = |y_{x_i} - y_{z_{(i)}}| \to 0$. Or in terms of a utility function U which we intend to maximize (i.e. as close to 1 as possible if we assume that $D_{Z;X} \leq 1$),

$$U(Z; X) = 1 - D_{Z;X}, \ where \ Z = M(X). \tag{1}$$

The most common functionality in MR is the *anchoring* of virtual 3D objects on to real-world surfaces (e.g. the floor, walls, or tables) which requires near-truth 3D point cloud representations to provide consistent anchored augmentations.

Defining the Adversarial Inferrer. An inferrer J produces a hypothesis $h : i^* = i$ about the true location i of a given set of point clouds, x_{i^*} or $z_{(i^*)}$, for any query space i^* (i.e. $J : x_{i^*}$ or $z_{(i^*)}$ for any $i^* \rightarrow h : i^* = i$) where the following inequality holds

$$P(h : i^* = i | x_{i^*} \ or \ z_{(i^*)}) > P(h : i^* = i^o, \ for \ any \ i^o \neq i | x_{i^*} \ or \ z_{(i^*)}). \tag{2}$$

The Privacy-Utility Problem. Consequently, we can now pose the following *privacy* function Π in terms of the error rate of the inferrer,

$$\Pi(Z; X) = \underset{iterations}{mean} \frac{|h : i_z \neq i_x|}{|\forall i|}, \tag{3}$$

which is simply the *mean misclassification rate* of an inferrer J about the query space i_z whose true identity is i_x. A few works in the literature uses the same error-based metric for privacy [22,26]. A desired M produces Z that maximizes both the privacy Π and the utility function U.

Privacy and Utility Metrics. Now, we define the specific privacy and utility metrics for this work. For privacy, we use the same notion of a high error rate as high privacy; thus, the same metric defined by Eq. 3 holds. For utility, we use the same similarity definition defined by Eq. 1 but define the specific components of the similarity function as,

$$U(Z; X) = mean(\alpha \cdot (1 - ||x - z||) + \beta \cdot (\boldsymbol{n_x} \cdot \boldsymbol{n_z})) \tag{4}$$

where the first component is the 3D point similarity of the true/raw point x from the transformed point z, the second component are their normal vector similarity, and α and β are contribution weights where $\alpha, \beta \in [0,1]$ and $\alpha + \beta = 1$. We set $\alpha, \beta = 0.5$. We also insert a subjective acceptability metric $\gamma \in [0,1]$ like so,

$$U(Z; X) = mean \left[\alpha \cdot \left(1 - \frac{\lceil ||x - z|| \rceil_\gamma}{\gamma} \right) + \beta \cdot \left(\lfloor \boldsymbol{n_x} \cdot \boldsymbol{n_z} \rfloor_{1-\gamma} - \frac{1 - \gamma}{\gamma} \right) \right]. \tag{5}$$

γ allows us to specify the level of error or deviation of the released (i.e. generalized) spaces from the true space – any deviation beyond the set γ results to a zero utility. The range of $U(X, Z) \in [0,1]$.

2.3   Adversary Model

Adversaries may desire to, at the very least, infer the location of the users using released 3D data. They may further infer user poses, movement in space, or, even, detect changes in user environment. Furthermore, in contrast to video and image capture, 3D data, when generalized, can provide a much more lightweight and near-truth representation of user spaces which we will see later (Sect. 5.5). For our evaluation, we will focus on the minimum attack where the adversary infers the spatial location of the user given historical 3D raw data of user spaces. We also assume that the adversary is not aware of the generalizations that an MR platform can perform over 3D data before it is released.

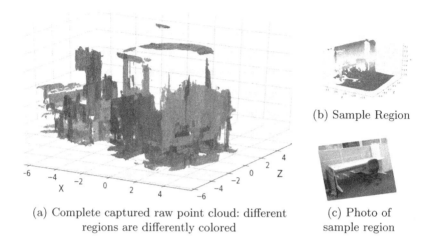

(a) Complete captured raw point cloud: different
regions are differently colored

(b) Sample Region

(c) Photo of
sample region

Fig. 3. Render of the gathered point cloud (1 unit is roughly 1 m in the real-world)

Using the definitions in Sect. 2.2, we can formalize the adversary models as previously shown in Fig. 1. We assume that the adversary has *prior knowledge* about the spaces which they can use as reference for building their inference model J. Prior knowledge can be made available through (1) *historical* or publicly available 3D spatial data of the user spaces, (2) *previously provided* data by the user themselves or other users, or (3) from a *colluding application* or service that has access to raw or higher resolution 3D data.

Adversarial Inference. Our adversarial inference is a two-step process as labelled in Fig. 1: (1) the creation of a reference description model or dictionary using the 3D descriptor algorithms (Sect. 3.2) over the previously known spaces as reference, (2) and the inference of unknown spaces by *matching* their 3D descriptors to that of the reference descriptors from step 1. The construction of the inference model is detailed in the next section.

3   3D Description and Inference

3.1   3D MR Data

We gathered real 3D point cloud data using the Microsoft HoloLens in an office environment to demonstrate the leakage from actual human-scale spaces in which an MR device is usually used.[4] The render of the gathered 3D space is shown in Fig. 3a. We sliced our gathered point cloud into roughly 2.5 × 2.5 squares about the xz-plane (i.e. the floor plane) to create a synthetic set of multiple spaces.[5] The resulting number of spaces after slicing is 38. Also, we treat the spaces to be non-contiguous – specifically, spaces that are truly adjacent do not inform adversarial inference.

3.2   Describing the 3D Space

The 3D point clouds can then be used by the adversary to train an inference model. Features that describe and discriminate among 3D spaces are usually used for inference modelling. There are considerable features in 3D point clouds for it to be directly used as a 3D descriptor, albeit a crude one, and it won't be translation- and rotation-invariant by itself. Hence, invariant descriptors are necessary for adversarial inference models to be resilient.

To provide invariance, we utilize existing 3D description algorithms.[6] The curvature-reliant self-similarity (SS) descriptors [10] are very sensitive to point cloud variations, due to the curvature estimation. To counter this, we explored the use of non-curvature reliant spin image (SI) descriptors [13,14]. SI descriptors only use the normal vector unlike the SS approach which uses *local curvature maxima* for key point selection. Thus, a vanilla SI computes the descriptor for every point in the point cloud which produces a dense descriptor space. For our SI implementation, we extract key points and descriptors from the subsampled space by factor of 3 (Fig. 5 shows that significant errors only appear at resolutions < 3) to create a lighter weight descriptor set. Also, the spinning effect reduces the impact of variations within that spin which makes SI descriptors more robust compared to SS descriptors. Furthermore, as we will describe in Sect. 4.1, plane generalization removes curvatures which makes its use as a geometric description information impractical. Validation of the inference performance of these descriptors are detailed in Sect. 3.3.

3.3   Inferring the 3D Space

For the adversarial inference model, we built two types of *inferrers*: (1) a *baseline 3D Bayesian* inference model using directly the 3D point cloud data, and (2) a *matching-based* inference model using the rotation-invariant descriptors.

---

[4] There are numerous 3D point cloud datasets such as those listed in http://cvgl. stanford.edu/resources.html but most of these available 3D data sets are models of objects or of city-scale models.

[5] Note: the resulting surface are of the slice varies due to the walls, and objects within a slice. It can also be less than 2.5 × 2.5 due to gaps on the space.

[6] For a concise discussion and bench marking of different 3D description algorithms, we direct the reader to [3].

Inference Using the Rotation-Invariant Descriptors. It is challenging to create a straightforward 3D inference model as we would have in a 3D Bayesian model.[7] As a work around, we utilize the standard matching-based approach that is used over high-dimensional descriptors. This approach is rather *deterministic* as opposed to the *probabilistic* Bayesian inference model.

This deterministic approach used for the rotation-invariant descriptors utilizes a *matching-based voting mechanism* with a reference set of descriptors to determine a match; then, *nearest neighbor distance ratio* (or NNDR) is used to qualify a match. Thus, instead of the probabilistic maximization described in Eq. 2, we utilize this NNDR-based approach for deterministic inference. See Appendix B for more details on this descriptor matching process.

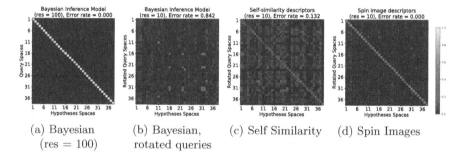

(a) Bayesian   (b) Bayesian,   (c) Self Similarity   (d) Spin Images
(res = 100)   rotated queries

Fig. 4. Inference performance heatmaps of the different 3D description approaches

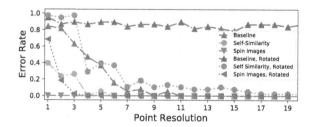

Fig. 5. Performance of the different 3D description/inference for different resolutions

Validating the Inference Models. We conducted a preliminary validation to check the effectiveness of the chosen description and inference approaches. To validate our inference models, we feed them the same data as queries.

---

[7] For example, our spin image description implementation have 200 (i.e. 10×20) dimensions; it'll require 10^{200} bins for every key point to be described if we are to approximate that each dimension will have 10 bins.

Using the Bayesian Inference Model. When complete versions of the set of points x_i for each space i is given as a query data, the baseline Bayesian inference model performs very well as shown by the solid yellow diagonal in the heatmap/confusion matrix in Fig. 4a. Figure 5 shows the results of varying the resolution from $1 \leq res < 20$. For un-rotated query spaces, the Bayesian inference model only starts to have errors at resolutions ≤ 10, while its error rate for rotated query spaces is ≥ 0.8 for all resolutions. As we have indicated earlier in Sect. 3.2, the baseline inference model is not rotation-invariant and it is clearly observed here. For example, Fig. 4b shows a heat-map for a lower resolution of $res = 10$ with rotated query spaces; we can not see a distinguishable diagonal to signify good inference performance.

Using the Rotation-Invariant Descriptors. With un-rotated query spaces, the SS descriptors' maximum error rate is only 0.4 as shown in Fig. 5, while the SI descriptors stays 0 even at the smallest resolution of 1. With rotated query spaces, errors increased for both but significant errors (i.e. ≥ 0.1) only appear at $res \leq 3$ for the SI descriptors, while errors for the SS descriptors already appear even at higher resolutions of $res \leq 14$.

The excellent performance of the spin image descriptors can be better visualized with the heatmaps shown in Fig. 4 with $res = 10$. As can be observed, the spin images discriminates well as demonstrated by the clearer diagonal in Fig. 4d as compared to Fig. 4c. Thus, in the succeeding experiments described in the next section (with results in Sect. 5), we will only be using spin image descriptors.

Fig. 6. Surface generalization, i.e. plane fitting, example: (left) sample raw space, (center) RANSAC generalization, and (right) locally-originated generalization.

4   Evaluation Setup

For evaluating the performance of an adversary as described in Sect. 2.3, we check its inference performance over released modified point clouds. We use the descriptor set extracted from the 3D raw point cloud data as the reference set available to the adversary (labelled 1 in Fig. 1). We, then, implement various information reduction techniques to investigate how well can the adversary infer the identity, i.e. spatial location, of the released and modified point cloud.

4.1   3D Information Reduction Strategies

To limit the amount of information released with the point clouds, (1) plane generalizations and (2) partial releasing can be utilised to provide MR applications the least information necessary to deliver the desired functionality.

Plane Fitting Generalization. For the generalizations, as we do not intend to determine an efficient 3D generalization algorithm for our data, we have employed two simple techniques: the popular Random Sample Consensus (or RANSAC) plane fitting method [6], and a simple locally-originated plane generalization (we use label LOCAL henceforth). Figure 2 earlier shows what structurally occurs during plane-fitting generalization which can potentially preserve spatial privacy. Please see Appendix C for the generalization pseudo-code (Algorithms 1 and 2).

RANSAC. For our implementation, we directly utilize the accompanying normal vector of each point to estimate the planes in the plane fitting process instead of computing or estimating them from the neighbouring points. Algorithm 1 (in Appendix C) shows the pseudo-code of our RANSAC implementation, while an example RANSAC spatial generalization is shown in Fig. 6-center.

LOCAL. On the other hand, LOCAL generalization is an oversimplification of RANSAC as can be seen in Algorithm 2. We removed the point and plane test (i.e. Lines 12 and 14 in Algorithm 1) which ensures that a point is a valid member of the candidate plane and that the candidate plane is the best, i.e. largest, among all candidate planes. This results in more inaccurate generalizations as we go further away from the initial test point from which the candidate plane originated. Figure 6-right shows a sample LOCAL generalization.

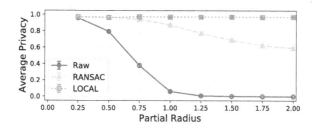

Fig. 7. Average privacy (i.e. *mean error rate ± margin of error with 95% confidence*) over one-time released partial spaces with varying radii and generalizations

Partial Spaces. In partial spaces, we only release *segments* of the space with varying radius. This demonstrates the case when an MR application is provided with limited 3D spatial information *only once*, such as a specific surface, a plane or an anchor point. We apply this technique to both raw and generalized point clouds. For every partial space level (i.e. radius), we get 10 sample random iterations per space as a user can initiate an MR application from any point within a space; to demonstrate rotation-invariance, we further vary the spaces by doing 5 random rotations which results to a total of 50 iterations per space. We, then, get the mean error rate (with confidence intervals) over these iterations.

4.2 Successive Release of Partial Spaces

We use the information reduction techniques described in Sect. 4.1 as strategies for privacy protection. First, we evaluated adversarial performance over *one-time* released partial spaces as described in Sect. 4.1. Then, we introduced more information by successively releasing partial spaces.

To demonstrate the case when users are moving around and their physical space is gradually revealed, we included an experimental setup that successively releases partial spaces. Following the described abstraction strategies in Sect. 4.1, we have the following different 3D data setups for successively releasing of partial spaces: (1) from collected raw points, (2) from RANSAC generalized planes, and (3) from LOCAL generalized planes. Similar to the one-time partial release case, we do 10 sample iterations, and 5 random rotations for each case in the successive release setup. (For the extended LOCAL shown in Fig. 8d, we do 10 sample iterations but only did one random rotation for demonstration purposes.)

5 Results and Discussion

In the succeeding discussions, we would like to emphasize the trends and relative values rather than absolute empirical values themselves. We also presented takeaways whose discussions on trends and relationships can be generalized.

5.1 Inference of Partial Spaces

Figure 7 shows the performance of our adversarial inference over partial spaces with raw points and of the two generalized cases. For the raw-points case, at radius $r = 0.25$, the average privacy Π_{Raw} is very high, but immediately drops below $\Pi_{Raw} < 0.8$ at $r \geq 0.5$. With RANSAC generalization applied, it can be seen that the inference success is reduced, or essentially prevented, with radii $r \leq 1.0$, but average privacy Π_{RANSAC} starts to decrease for $r > 1.0$; thus, RANSAC generalizations are not effective protection strategies. This should not come as a surprise, since the RANSAC algorithm will try to fit planes as close to the true/raw space.

On the other hand, locally-originated plane generalizations can prevent inference for this one-time partial release case. Regardless of the size of the revealed space, the average privacy stays at $\Pi_{LOCAL} > 0.9$ as shown in Fig. 7. In fact, contrary to RANSAC generalizations, locally-originated plane generalizations will maintain a high Π_{LOCAL} with larger revealed spaces because the LOCAL algorithm will only produce a generalized plane from a *singular* local reference point which may not even be from a true plane or have a normal vector consistent with its neighbours. This results in plane generalizations that are more likely to be very different from the surfaces of the true spaces.

5.2   Successive Release of Partial Spaces

Following the partial spaces performance, it is tempting to say that we can maintain privacy by only releasing partial spaces of $r \leq 0.25$ even with raw captured data, but that is only for the single one-time release case. In this section, as described in Sect. 4.2, we will now show the privacy or inference performance when we *successively* release partial spaces.

Raw-Points Spaces. Figure 8a shows the inference performance of successively released partial raw-points spaces. This is consistent with the results presented in Fig. 7. After a good number of releases, the space is slowly revealed; thus, the dropping average privacy. For $r = 0.25$, the Π_{Raw} drops below 0.8 after 4 or more releases, while for the larger radii, $r \geq 0.5$, the average privacy quickly drops and even starts at $\Pi_{Raw} < 0.8$ at the first release.

RANSAC Generalized Planes. For the successively released, RANSAC generalized partial spaces, as shown in Fig. 8b, after 4 releases, $\Pi_{RANSAC} \leq 0.8$ for radius $r = 0.75$. Similar to the performance shown in Fig. 7, at higher radii, Π_{RANSAC} for successive release eventually falls below ≤ 0.6 after a good number of releases. Specifically, for $r \geq 0.5$, $\Pi_{RANSAC} \leq 0.6$ after about 14 releases.

Compared to the successively released partial spaces from raw points, the RANSAC generalization already contributes some errors to the released spaces. This reflects on the rather slow drop of Π_{RANSAC}. Nonetheless, if RANSAC spaces are continuously released, regardless of its size, the space will be revealed. However, keeping RANSAC spaces to a small size, i.e. $r \leq 0.5$, and limiting release, e.g. no more than 10 releases, RANSAC can be a potential inference protection aside from being a generalization technique.

Local Generalized Planes. Similar to the results in Fig. 7, the inference performance from successively released and locally generalized partial spaces, as shown in Fig. 8c, presents error rates above 0.8 within 20 releases. To check inference performance for more releases using LOCAL, we extend the number of releases to 96 and checked the inference performance every multiple of 5 successive releases as shown in Fig. 8d. Now, the average Π_{LOCAL} do drop to ≤ 0.8 for $r = 0.25$ ($r = 0.75$ approaches 0.8 at release 10) but eventually increases with more releases. Due to the high inaccuracy provided by localized generalizations, especially at larger partial spaces, more releases do not contribute to improved inference and only *misleads* adversarial inference. Partially released planes with nearby originating points with different normals will produce planes within the same vicinity but of different orientations. This confuses the inferrer. Thus, if spatial privacy is a priority, localized generalizations can be used.

Takeaway. *Privacy can be arranged as $\Pi_{Raw} < \Pi_{RANSAC} < \Pi_{LOCAL}$, based on the form of released data; for continuously released large spaces ($r > 0.5$), RANSAC cannot provide adequate privacy, but for small enough spaces ($r \leq 0.5$), it can be a potential form of inference protection coupled with limited or controlled releasing.*

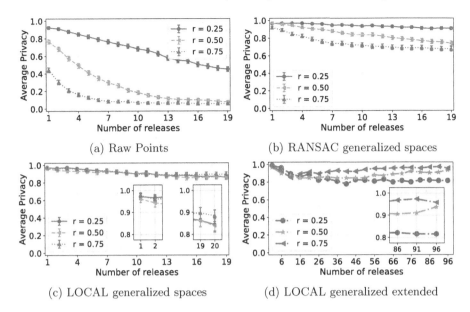

(a) Raw Points

(b) RANSAC generalized spaces

(c) LOCAL generalized spaces

(d) LOCAL generalized extended

Fig. 8. Average privacy (*mean error rate ± margin of error with 95% confidence*) over *successively* released partial spaces. For Fig. 8a–c, we perform up to 20 releases per iteration. For Fig. 8c, we extend the LOCAL case to see long-term inference.

5.3 Inference Trends with Spatial Properties

Precision and Recall. We also checked the precision and recall as an inference performance metric. These values were checked for every space as well as the impacts of spatial properties on inference and/or privacy. Figure 9a shows the average precision and recall of our adversarial inferrer as we vary the radius of partial spaces. As expected, for raw-points and RANSAC-generalized spaces, precision and recall increases as the radius increases. On the other hand, precision and recall of LOCAL stays low, < 0.1, and only ever so slightly increases –

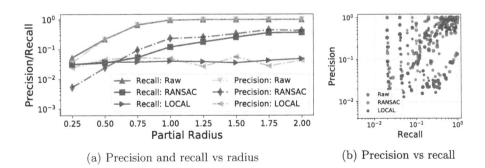

(a) Precision and recall vs radius

(b) Precision vs recall

Fig. 9. Precision and recall over partial spaces

from 0.032 to 0.048 for recall, and from 0.024 to 0.043 for precision – but not consistently (as we can see with the dips in precision at $r = 1.25$ & 1.75).

Figure 9b shows the scatter plot of the precision and recall values for all spaces and iterations (averaged in Fig. 9a) with the radius (relatively) depicted by the size of the circle. We can see that the values for the raw-points spaces crowd on the upper right quadrant, i.e. high precision and recall area, while that of RANSAC generalized spaces is slightly more scattered but also crowds on the upper right quadrant. For the locally-generalized spaces, most of the green circles reside on the lower half which means that recall is spread from low to mid-high but precision values are mostly very low.

Despite the bad performance of our adversarial inferrer, looking more closely in to the spaces reveals some consistency. We looked into the top 10 spaces for raw points, RANSAC generalized, and LOCAL generalized in terms of *number of false positives, precision, recall,* and *least errors/privacy*. (In the interest of space, we no longer show the list of top 10 spaces.) The list reveals that the spaces with high recall and least errors are almost the same; thus, high recall and least errors have a high correlation (i.e. $\rho_{recall,least-errors} \approx 0.964$).

Furthermore, for the raw and RANSAC cases, the average number of planes of the top 10 spaces with high false positives are small, i.e. 4.21 and 4.38, respectively, while those of the top 10 spaces in terms of precision have higher averages at 14.44 and 13.77, respectively. Thus, raw or RANSAC spaces with more planes have lower uncertainty in being inferred or identified, and, perhaps, if privacy is desired, we may only release a lower number of planes, i.e. < 5. However, for the LOCAL generalized case, there is no observable trend among the inference performance and that of the number of planes.

Takeaway. Raw and RANSAC spaces with higher number of observable or generalized planes are more likely to be inferred with higher precision; thus, releasing spatial generalizations with lower number of planes (i.e. < 5) can confuse adversarial inference.

5.4   Computing Utility of Generalizations

Plane-fitting generalizations contribute variations to the released point clouds from true spaces. Figure 10a shows the computed average utility based on Eq. 5 for the different generalizations with varying partial radius and acceptability metric γ. A γ value of 1 means that we accept variations for up to 1 unit-combined-difference (see Eq. 5) of the true point from the released point and the true normal from the released normal.

For reference, we include the point-level (synonymous to $r = 0$) utility computation from RANSAC points which produces the highest utility trend, while other RANSAC generalizations of partial spaces with $r > 0$ comes close second. The average utility provided by RANSAC generalizations are consistent regardless of the size of the released generalized spaces. It does decrease as we decrease the acceptability value γ, but it does not go too low, i.e $U_{RANSAC} \geq 0.5$ for $\gamma \geq 0.1$, such that the generalizations are rendered unacceptable. This is due to how RANSAC generalizations tries to approach the true spaces.

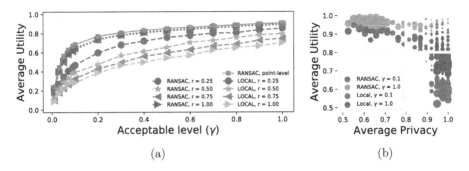

Fig. 10. (a) Utility of the generalizations (Note: Utility of true points and planes are always 1.); (b) Scatter plot of utility and error rate of different partial spaces (radius is relatively indicated by marker size)

On the other hand, LOCAL generalizations have lower utility trends and go much lower as the radius increases. This is due to the increased inaccuracies in the localized generalizations as it disregards point locations and normals other than the randomly chosen origin point. As a result, the utility trend further decreases as we increase the radius, and this is true for any γ. In fact, at $\gamma = 0.1$, $U_{LOCAL} \leq 0.5$ at $r = 0.25$. As expected, if we are to set the acceptable utility at ≥ 0.8, only localized generalizations of radius $r \leq 0.5$ can provide such utility and $r = 0.5$ barely makes the cutoff at $\gamma = 1.0$. Any γ lower than that, only generalizations with $r \leq 0.25$ can provide an average utility ≥ 0.8.

In reality, these U_{LOCAL} values are unacceptable. If we are to set an acceptability level of $\gamma \leq 0.2$, there is only at most 0.6 chance of getting a locally generalized point that is close to the true point including its orientation. Thus, for the rest of the points from a locally generalized point cloud, augmentations are translated by at most 0.2 m (in any direction) and/or rotated by at most $cos^{-1}(0.2)$ or 78.5°.

The difference in utility and error rate as we vary the radius of partial spaces is better visualized by the scatter plot in Fig. 10b. U_{RANSAC} stays ≥ 0.8 and

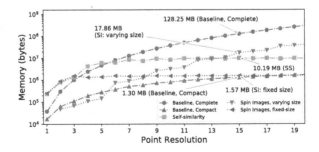

Fig. 11. Used memory by inference models and descriptors extracted from different point cloud resolutions.

privacy drops as we increase the size, while U_{LOCAL} is only ≥ 0.8 for smaller partial size and the privacy is consistently ≥ 0.8. The relatively higher utility of smaller LOCAL releases is further corroborated by the average privacy values of the successive release case shown in Fig. 8c and d which shows smaller spaces having lower privacy compared to larger spaces with more releases.

For LOCAL, points nearby the reference point will most likely have similar normal vector directions, but as we go further away from the reference point on the same locally generalized plane the variation increases, and thus the utility drops. Conversely, RANSAC contributed variations are fairly consistent and low regardless of a point's distance from a reference point with which the generalized plane was produced, since it tries to do a good representation of the true space.

Takeaway. *Overall, **LOCAL** generalizations provides high average privacy but can only provide adequate utility for smaller spaces; for example, utility of $U >$ 0.5 for $\gamma \leq 0.2$ can only be achieved with spaces of small radius $r \leq 0.25$.*

5.5 Memory Compactness of Descriptors and Inference Models

Another interesting aspect is how a very good inferrer can be constructed at a low resolution $res \leq 10$ with discriminative performance similar to that of higher resolutions (see Fig. 5). As shown in Fig. 11, the memory size exponentially increases as we increase the resolution. A baseline Bayesian inference model with a low resolution of 15 requires a memory size of about 128 MB. This memory usage is undesirably huge due to the almost complete representation of the point probabilities in 3D space. However, we can take advantage of the sparsity of the data points to make it compact. The memory usage by the compact representation is also shown in Fig. 11. At res = 15, the compact memory usage is now just 1.30 MB from the original 128 MB – almost 2 orders of magnitude smaller.

For the rotation-invariant descriptors, at res = 15, a corresponding set of SS descriptors takes about 10.19 MB, but a corresponding set of SI descriptors – which, anyway, performs better than SS descriptors – with a fixed descriptor size is as compact as the baseline inference model (that is not rotation-invariant) at only 1.58 MB. In fact, we used res = 3 (as previously stated in Sect. 3.2) for the descriptors used in the inference evaluation discussed in the previous subsections.

Thus, any MR application (trusted or not) with access to 3D data produced by the user's MR device can efficiently create a lightweight inference model of the user's space. (For reference, the original point-cloud data is about 13 MB; thus, our inferrer is a much more compact representation of the point-cloud data at res = 15.)

Takeaway. *A compact and efficient inferrer of 3D spaces can be created from raw point cloud data released by any MR-capable device (which, now, can be any device with a vision sensor and adequate processing power).*

6 Related Work

Most privacy work for MR were primarily focused on *visual* information or media (i.e. image and video) sanitization [12,20,21]. Aside from that are *abstraction* approaches to privacy protection. In the specific 3D use case, significant work have been done on protecting physiological information using abstractions [5,11] using the idea of *least privilege* [25]. The same approach has also been used for providing visual privacy when using 3D MR browsers [24]. However, these works did not specifically work on protecting 3D MR data against spatial inference.

Other recent works have focused on protecting MR outputs specifically in ensuring user safety [15,16]. Furthermore, as MR devices allow for new modes of *collaboration*, issues on *power imbalance* brought by the *directionality* of MR interfaces [2] are now being studied as well [17]. Again, these works do not focus on spatial inference using 3D MR data.

7 Conclusion

In this work, we demonstrated how we can infer and reveal spaces employing descriptor-based inference over 3D point cloud data collected using the Microsoft HoloLens. The same point cloud data representation is also used by Google's ARCore and Apple's ARKit. Therefore, it is possible to easily extend this work to these mobile MR platforms as well. Currently, these MR platforms do not apply privacy preservation on released 3D MR data to third party applications which can allow adversaries to easily perform spatial inference attacks similar to what we have demonstrated. In addition, we have demonstrated how leakage can persist even after implementing spatial generalizations: RANSAC generalizations can't provide adequate protection when continuous successive generalizations are released, while LOCAL generalizations provide promise in protecting spatial privacy but utility is currently undesirably low. If directly applied, LOCAL generalizations cause augmentations to be shifted, translated, and/or rotated by a great degree, i.e. a maximum combined error of 0.2 with maximum average utility of only 0.6.[8] Moreover, we show how compact in terms of memory usage these 3D inference models can be, which allows adversaries to keep models for every users' set of 3D spaces.

In our future work, we aim to develop a hybrid generalization technique as a potential privacy solution combining desirable properties from RANSAC and LOCAL to; perhaps, in conjunction with *controlled releasing*, where we do not release a new portion of the space if the requested 3D space overlaps with those released earlier. Moreover, limiting released generalizations to no more than 4 planes, and/or limiting the number of partial successive releases may also provide inference protection. Furthermore, we intend to extend the proposed *geometric information* based inference strategy to use additional *photometric* information such as (RGB) color profile as well as employing advanced techniques for adversarial inference.

---

[8] Combined error in terms of rotation ($\cos \Delta\theta$) and translation (Δx); see Eq. 5.

A   3D Spatial Definitions

Defining the Input Space. Let X_i be the raw representation of space i in the physical world. A point-cloud extractor F takes pose information vector $v \in R^3$ and releases a point cloud $x_{i,v}$ relative to that pose, $F : X_i, v \rightarrow x_{i,v}$, for any 3D space with location i and a reference pose v.

Combining $x_{i,v}$ produces a complete point-cloud representation of space X_i, which we label as $\hat{X}_i = \bigcup_v x_{i,v} \; \forall v$. An extension of this is that for any pose $v \in R^3$, we get a partial point-cloud representation $X_{i,v}$ of the true space. And that there exists a set of poses $v_s \subset V$ such that $\hat{X}_{i,v_s} = \bigcup_{v \in v_s} x_{i,v}$ spans X_i or $\hat{X}_{i,v_s} = X_i$.

Defining the Abstraction. A privacy-preserving mechanism M transforms any released point cloud $x_{i,v}$ to a privacy-preserving version $z_{(i),v}$, $M : x_{i,v} \rightarrow z_{(i),v}$, where we denote the privacy-preservation of i by (i) – that is, the true i of a released z is not divulged or kept secret. Figure 2 shows a simple visualization of the transformation that can occur. In this specific case, the normal vectors of the adjacent points are aligned to create a flat surface.

Similar to the raw point-clouds $x_{i,v}$, combining the privacy-preserving point-cloud representations $z_{(i),v}$ produces $\hat{Z}_{(i)} = \bigcup_v z_{(i),v}$ for all $v \in V$, or $Z_{(i)} = \bigcup_v z_{(i),v}$.

Defining the Intended Functionality. An intended deterministic output y produced by an intended application or functionality G upon taking point clouds as the input, expressed as $G : x_i, or\, z_{(i)} \rightarrow y_{(i)}$.

B   Defining the Feature Matching Process Using Rotation-Invariant Descriptors

A matching function Υ maps two sets of features f_a and f_b, of spaces a and b, like so: $\Upsilon : f_a \mapsto f_b$.

To determine good matches, we use the descriptor Euclidean distance as a measure of their similarity. To *accept* a match for a key point $x_{a,1}$ with feature $f_{a,1}$ of an unknown query space $a = i^*$, we get the *nearest neighbor distance ratio* (NNDR) of the features like so: $\frac{||f_{a,1} - f_{b,1}||}{||f_{a,1} - f_{b,2}||} < threshold$, where descriptor $f_{b,1}$ of $x_{b,1}$ (i.e. key point x_1 of known space $b = i$) is the nearest neighbor of descriptor $f_{a,1}$ of $x_{a,1}$ (i.e. key point x_1 of unknown query space $a = i^*$) and $f_{b,2}$ is the second nearest neighbor, and see if the NNDR falls below a set threshold (e.g. 0.75 for the self-similarity, or 0.9 for the spin-image descriptors). Then, we maximum-normalize the distance of the accepted matches to make the maximum distance be 1. The mean of the distances is multiplied with a Bayesian-inspired weight, $\frac{|\{f_{x_{i^*}} \mapsto f_{x_i}\}|}{|\{f_{x_{i^*}}\}|}$, where $|\{f_{x_{i^*}} \mapsto f_{x_i}\}|$ is the number of matched descriptors of an unknown query space $x_{a=i^*}$ from one of the known reference spaces $x_{b=i}, i \in \forall i$, and $|\{f_{x_{i^*}}\}|$ is the number of key points or descriptors extracted from the query space x_{i*}. This allows us to create a hypothesis, i.e. $h : i^* = i$, also via argument-maximization as follows,

$$\arg \max_i \left(1 - \underset{\{f_{x_{i*}} \mapsto f_{x_i}\}}{\text{mean}} \{||f_{x_{i*}} - f_{x_i}||\} \right) \cdot \frac{|\{f_{x_{i*}} \mapsto f_{x_i}\}|}{|\{f_{x_{i*}}\}|}, \tag{6}$$

where the first product term is the mean similarity (i.e. 1 - *mean difference*) while the second term is the Bayesian-inspired weight.

C   Plane Generalization

Our RANSAC plane generalization, shown in Algorithm 1, mainly follows the described algorithm in [6] except for the normal estimation which we skip and instead use the estimated normal vectors directly provided by the spatial mesh produced by the HoloLens. On the other hand, the algorithm for the locally-originated plane generalization, shown in Algorithm 2, is a crude and simplified generalization which removes the point (Line 12) and plane (Line 14) discrimination process from RANSAC.

Algorithm 1. RANSAC algorithm [6]

---

1 **F** the number of planes to find = 30
2 **T** the point-plane distance threshold = 0.05
3 **R** the number of RANSAC trials = 100
   Data: $X = \{x_1, x_2, ..., x_n\}$, a set of 3D points
   Result: $P = \{p_{x_m} : \{x_{p_1}, x_{p_2}, ...\}\}$, a set of planes (a 3D point, and a normal) and their associated co-planar points

4 **for** $f \leftarrow 1$ **to** F **do**
5 | bestPlane = $\{0, 0\}$
6 | bestPoints = $\{\}$
7 | **for** $r \leftarrow 1$ **to** R **do**
8 | | $S = s_1 =$ a point at random from X
9 | | $thisPlane = \{s_1, normal_{s_1}\}$
10 | | $thisPoints = \{\}$
11 | | **for** $x_i \in X$ **do**
12 | | | **if** $(distance(thisPlane, x_i) \leq T)$ **then**
13 | | | | $thisPoints \leftarrow thisPoints + x_i$
14 | | **if** $|thisPoints| > |bestPoints|$ **then**
15 | | | bestPlane $\leftarrow$ thisPlane
16 | | | bestPoints $\leftarrow$ thisPoints
17 | $P \leftarrow P + \{bestPlane, coPlanarTransformed(bestPoints)\}$
18 | $X \leftarrow X - bestPoints$

Algorithm 2. Locally-originated plane generalization

---

1 **F** the number of planes to find = 30
2 **r** the radius of the local region (e.g. 0.5)
   Data: $X = \{x_1, x_2, ..., x_n\}$, a set of 3D points
   Result: $P = \{p_{x_m} : \{x_{p_1}, x_{p_2}, ...\}\}$, a set of planes (a 3D point, and a normal) and their
          associated co-planar points
3 **for** $f \leftarrow 1$ **to** F **do**
4 | $S = s_1 =$ a point at random from X
5 | $thisPlane = \{s_1, normal_{s_1}\}$
6 | $thisPoints = \{x_i \in X : |x_i - s_1| \leq r\}$
7 | $P \leftarrow P + \{thisPlane, coPlanarTransformed(thisPoints)\}$
8 | $X \leftarrow X - thisPoints$

References

1. Acquisti, A.: Privacy in the age of augmented reality (2011)
2. Benford, S., Greenhalgh, C., Reynard, G., Brown, C., Koleva, B.: Understanding and constructing shared spaces with mixed-reality boundaries. ACM Trans. Comput. Hum. Interact. (TOCHI) **5**(3), 185–223 (1998)
3. Bronstein, A.M., et al.: SHREC 2010: robust feature detection and description benchmark. In: Proceedings of EUROGRAPHICS Workshop on 3D Object Retrieval (3DOR) (2010)
4. Dwork, C., Roth, A., et al.: The algorithmic foundations of differential privacy. Found. Trends® Theor. Comput. Sci. **9**(3–4), 211–407 (2014)
5. Figueiredo, L.S., Livshits, B., Molnar, D., Veanes, M.: Prepose: privacy, security, and reliability for gesture-based programming. In: 2016 IEEE Symposium on Security and Privacy (SP), pp. 122–137. IEEE (2016)
6. Fischler, M.A., Bolles, R.C.: Random sample consensus: a paradigm for model fitting with applications to image analysis and automated cartography. Commun. ACM **24**(6), 381–395 (1981)
7. Gross, R., Sweeney, L., de la Torre, F., Baker, S.: Semi-supervised learning of multi-factor models for face de-identification. In: 2008 IEEE Conference on Computer Vision and Pattern Recognition, pp. 1–8, June 2008. https://doi.org/10.1109/CVPR.2008.4587369
8. de Guzman, J.A., Thilakarathna, K., Seneviratne, A.: Security and privacy approaches in mixed reality: a literature survey. arXiv preprint arXiv:1802.05797 (2018)
9. He, W., Liu, X., Nguyen, H.V., Nahrstedt, K., Abdelzaher, T.: PDA: privacy-preserving data aggregation for information collection. ACM Trans. Sens. Netw. (TOSN) **8**(1), 6 (2011)
10. Huang, J., You, S.: Point cloud matching based on 3d self-similarity. In: 2012 IEEE Computer Society Conference on Computer Vision and Pattern Recognition Workshops (CVPRW), pp. 41–48. IEEE (2012)
11. Jana, S., et al.: Enabling fine-grained permissions for augmented reality applications with recognizers. In: USENIX Security (2013)
12. Jana, S., Narayanan, A., Shmatikov, V.: A scanner darkly: protecting user privacy from perceptual applications. In: 2013 IEEE Symposium on Security and Privacy (SP), pp. 349–363. IEEE (2013)
13. Johnson, A.E., Hebert, M.: Using spin images for efficient object recognition in cluttered 3d scenes. IEEE Trans. Pattern Anal. Mach. Intell. **5**, 433–449 (1999)

14. Johnson, A.E., Hebert, M.: Surface matching for object recognition in complex three-dimensional scenes. Image Vis. Comput. **16**(9–10), 635–651 (1998)
15. Lebeck, K., Kohno, T., Roesner, F.: How to safely augment reality: challenges and directions. In: Proceedings of the 17th International Workshop on Mobile Computing Systems and Applications, pp. 45–50. ACM (2016)
16. Lebeck, K., Ruth, K., Kohno, T., Roesner, F.: Securing augmented reality output. In: 2017 IEEE Symposium on Security and Privacy (SP), pp. 320–337. IEEE (2017)
17. Lebeck, K., Ruth, K., Kohno, T., Roesner, F.: Towards security and privacy for multi-user augmented reality: foundations with end users. In: Towards Security and Privacy for Multi-User Augmented Reality: Foundations with End Users, p. 0. IEEE (2018)
18. Milgram, P., Kishino, F.: A taxonomy of mixed reality visual displays. IEICE Trans. Inf. Syst. **77**(12), 1321–1329 (1994)
19. Newton, E.M., Sweeney, L., Malin, B.: Preserving privacy by de-identifying face images. IEEE Trans. Knowl. Data Eng. **17**(2), 232–243 (2005)
20. Raval, N., Srivastava, A., Razeen, A., Lebeck, K., Machanavajjhala, A., Cox, L.P.: What you mark is what apps see. In: Proceedings of the 14th Annual International Conference on Mobile Systems, Applications, and Services, pp. 249–261. ACM (2016)
21. Roesner, F., Molnar, D., Moshchuk, A., Kohno, T., Wang, H.J.: World-driven access control for continuous sensing. In: Proceedings of the 2014 ACM SIGSAC Conference on Computer and Communications Security, pp. 1169–1181. ACM (2014)
22. Shokri, R., Theodorakopoulos, G., Le Boudec, J.Y., Hubaux, J.P.: Quantifying location privacy. In: 2011 IEEE Symposium on Security and Privacy, pp. 247–262. IEEE (2011)
23. Sweeney, L.: k-anonymity: a model for protecting privacy. Int. J. Uncertain. Fuzziness Knowl. Based Syst. **10**(05), 557–570 (2002)
24. Vilk, J., et al.: SurroundWeb: mitigating privacy concerns in a 3d web browser. In: 2015 IEEE Symposium on Security and Privacy (SP), pp. 431–446. IEEE (2015)
25. Vilk, J., et al.: Least privilege rendering in a 3d web browser. Technical report (2014)
26. Wagner, I., Eckhoff, D.: Technical privacy metrics: a systematic survey. ACM Comput. Surv. **51**(3), 57:1–57:38 (2018). https://doi.org/10.1145/3168389, http://doi.acm.org/10.1145/3168389
27. Wu, Y., Yang, F., Ling, H.: Privacy-protective-gan for face de-identification. arXiv preprint arXiv:1806.08906 (2018)
28. Zarepour, E., Hosseini, M., Kanhere, S.S., Sowmya, A.: A context-based privacy preserving framework for wearable visual lifeloggers. In: 2016 IEEE International Conference on Pervasive Computing and Communication Workshops (PerCom Workshops), pp. 1–4. IEEE (2016)

Signatures and Re-encryption

Flexible Signatures: Making Authentication Suitable for Real-Time Environments

Duc V. Le[1][✉], Mahimna Kelkar[2], and Aniket Kate[1]

[1] Purdue University, West Lafayette, USA
{le52,aniket}@purdue.edu
[2] Cornell University, Ithaca, USA
mahimna@cs.cornell.edu

Abstract. This work introduces the concept of flexible signatures. In a flexible signature scheme, the verification algorithm quantifies the validity of a signature based on the number of computations performed, such that the signature's validation (or confidence) level in $[0, 1]$ improves as the algorithm performs more computations. Importantly, the definition of flexible signatures does *not* assume the resource restriction to be known in advance, a significant advantage when the verification process is hard stopped by a system interrupt. Prominent traditional signature schemes such as RSA, (EC)DSA seem unsuitable towards building flexible signatures because rigid all-or-nothing guarantees offered by the traditional cryptographic primitives have been particularly unattractive in these unpredictably resource-constrained environments.

In this work, we find the use of the Lamport-Diffie one-time signature and Merkle authentication tree to be suitable for building flexible signatures. We present a flexible signature construction based on these hash-based primitives and prove its security with concrete security analysis. We also perform a thorough validity-level analysis demonstrating an attractive computation-vs-validity trade-off offered by our construction: a security level of 80 bits can be ensured by performing only around $\frac{2}{3}$rd of the total hash computations for our flexible signature construction with a Merkle tree of height 20. Finally, we have implemented our constructions in a resource-constrained environment on a Raspberry Pi. Our analysis demonstrates that the proposed flexible signature design is comparable to other standard signature schemes in terms of running time while offering a quantified level of security at each step of the verification algorithm.

We see this work as the first step towards realizing the flexible-security cryptographic primitives. Beyond flexible signatures, our flexible-security conceptualization offers an interesting opportunity to build similar primitives in the asymmetric as well as symmetric cryptographic domains.

Mahimna Kelkar—This research was completed at Purdue University.

K. Sako et al. (Eds.): ESORICS 2019, LNCS 11735, pp. 173–193, 2019.
https://doi.org/10.1007/978-3-030-29959-0_9

1   Introduction

Security for embedded and real-time systems has become a greater concern with manufacturers increasing connectivity of these traditionally isolated control networks to the outside world. The computerization of hitherto purely mechanical elements in vehicular networks, such as connections to the brakes, throttle, and steering wheel, has led to a life-threatening increase of exploitation power. In the event that an attacker gains access to an embedded control network, safety-critical message traffic can be manipulated inducing catastrophic system failures. In recent years, numerous attacks have impressively demonstrated that the software running on embedded controllers could be successfully exploited, often even remotely [17,24,27]. With the rise of the Internet of Things (IoT), more non-traditional embedded devices have started to get integrated into personal and commercial computing infrastructures, and security will soon become a paramount issue for the new-age embedded systems [10,29].

Well-established authentication and integrity protection mechanisms such as digital signatures or MACs can effectively solve many of the security issues with embedded systems. However, the industry is hesitant to adopt those as most embedded devices pose severe resource constraints on the security architecture regarding memory, computational capacity, energy and time. Given the real-time deadlines, the embedded devices might not be able complete verifications by the deadline rendering *all* verification efforts useless.

Indeed, traditional cryptographic primitives are not designed for such uncertain settings with unpredictable resource constraints. Consider prominent digital signature schemes (such as RSA and ECDSA) that allow a signer who has created a pair of private and public keys to sign messages so that any verifier can later verify the signature with the signer's public key. The verification algorithms of those signature schemes are deterministic and only return a binary answer for the validity of the signature (i.e., 0 or 1). Such verification mechanisms may be unsatisfactory for an embedded module with unpredictable computing resources or time to perform the verification: if the module can only partially complete the verification process due to resource constraints or some *unplanned* real-time system interrupt, there are no partial validity guarantees available.

This calls for a signature scheme that can quantify the validity of the signature based on the number of computations performed during the verification. In particular, for a signature scheme instantiation with 128-bit security, we expect the verification process to be flexible enough to offer a validity (or confidence) level in $[0, 1]$ based on the resources available during the verification process. We observe that none of the existing signature schemes offer such a trade-off between the computation time/resource and the security level in a flexible manner.

Contribution. This paper initiates the study of cryptographic primitives with flexible security guarantees that can be of tremendous interest to real-time systems. In particular, we investigate the notion of a flexible signature scheme that offers partial security for an unpredictably partial verification.

As the first step, based on the standard definition of digital signatures, we propose a new definition of a signature scheme with a flexible verification algorithm. Here, instead of returning a binary answer, the verification algorithm returns a value, $\alpha \in [0,1] \cup \perp$ that quantifies the validity of the signature based on a number of computations performed.

Next, we provide a provably secure construction of the flexible signature scheme based on the Lamport-Diffie one-time signature construction [19] and the Merkle authentication tree [22]. The security of our signature relies on the difficulty of finding a ℓ-near-collision pair for a collision-resistant hash function. Through our analysis, we demonstrate that our construction still offers a high-security level against adaptive chosen message attacks despite performing fewer computations during verification. For example, a security level of 80 bits requires performing only around $\frac{2}{3}$rd of the total required hash computations for a Merkle tree of height 20.

Finally, we prototype our constructions in a resource-constrained environment by implementing those on a Raspberry Pi. We find that the performance of the proposed constructions is comparable to other prominent signature schemes in terms of running time while offering a flexible trade-off between the security level and the number of computations. Importantly, neither the security level nor the number of computations has to be pre-determined during verification.

Related Work. Fischlin [13] proposed a similar framework for progressively verifiable message authentication codes (MACs). In particular, the author presented two concrete constructions for progressively verifiable MACs that allow the verifier to spot errors or invalid tags after a reasonable number of computations. Also, the paper introduced the concept of detection probability to denote the probability that the verifier detects errors after verifying a certain number of blocks. In this work, we address the open problem of a progressively verifiable digital signature scheme, and we incorporate the detection probability concept into the security analysis of our schemes.

Bellare, Goldreich, and Goldwasser [3] introduced incremental signatures. Here, given a signature on a document, a signer can obtain a (new) signature on a similar document by partially updating the available signature. The incremental signature computation is more efficient than computing a signature from scratch and thus can offer some advantage to a resource-constrained signer. However, it provides no benefit for a resource-constrained verifier; the verifier still needs to perform a complete verification of the signature.

Signature scheme with batch verification [2,8] is a cryptographic primitive that offers an efficient verifying property. Namely, after receiving multiple signatures from different sources, a verifier can efficiently verify the entire set of signatures at once. Batch verification signature scheme and flexible signature scheme are similar in that they offer an efficient and flexible verification mechanism. However, while the batch verification signature merely seeks to reduce the load on a busy server, the flexible signature focuses on a resource-constrained verifier who can tolerate a partial security guarantee from a signature.

Freitag et al. [14] proposed the concept of signatures with randomized verification. Here, the verifying algorithm takes as input the public key along with some random coin to determine the validity of the signature. In those schemes, the attacker's advantage of forging a valid message-signature pair, (m^*, σ^*), is determined by the fraction of coins that accept (m^*, σ^*). Freitag et al. constructed a signature scheme with randomized identity-based encryption (IBE) schemes using Naor's transformation and show that the security level of their signature scheme is fixed to the size of the underlying IBE scheme's identity space. While our work can be formally defined as a signature scheme with randomized verification, our scheme offers a more flexible verification in which the security level of the scheme can be efficiently computed based on the output of the verifying algorithm.

Finally, Fan, Garay, and Mohassel [11] proposed the concept of short and adjustable signatures. They offered three variants, namely setup adjustable, signing adjustable, and verification adjustable signatures offering different trade-offs between the length and the security of the signature. The first two variants allow the signer to adjust the length of the signature, while the last variant allows the verifier to shorten the signature during the verification phase. They presented three constructions for each variant based on indistinguishably obfuscation ($i\mathcal{O}$), and one concrete construction *only* for the setup-adjustable variant based on the BLS Signature Scheme [5]. Unfortunately, none of those constructions is suitable for constructing flexible signatures tolerating unpredictable interrupts.

2   Preliminaries

Figure 1 presents prominent notational conventions that we use throughout this work. Our constructions employ the following standard properties of cryptographic hash functions. We use $H : \mathcal{K} \times \mathcal{M} \rightarrow \{0,1\}^n$ to denote a family of hash functions that is parameterized by a key $k \in \mathcal{K}$ and message $m \in \mathcal{M}$ and outputs a binary string of length n. For this work, we consider two security properties for hash functions from [26], preimage resistance, collision resistance, and one weaker security notion from [18,21], ℓ-near collision resistance.

Preimage Resistance: We call a family H of hash functions (t_{ow}, ϵ_{ow})-preimage resistant, if for any $\mathcal{A}$ that runs for at most t_{ow}, the adversary's advantage is:

$$\mathsf{Adv}_H^{ow}(\mathcal{A}) = \Pr\left[\begin{array}{l} k \xleftarrow{\$} \mathcal{K}, x \xleftarrow{\$} \mathcal{M} \\ y \leftarrow H(k,x), x' \leftarrow \mathcal{A}(k,y) \end{array} : H(k,x') = y\right] \leq \epsilon_{ow}$$

Collision Resistance: We call a family H of hash functions (t_{cr}, ϵ_{cr})-collision resistant, if for any $\mathcal{A}$ that runs for at most t_{cr}, the adversary's advantage is:

$$\mathsf{Adv}_H^{cr}(\mathcal{A}) = \Pr\left[\begin{array}{l} k \xleftarrow{\$} \mathcal{K} \\ (x,x') \leftarrow \mathcal{A}(k) \end{array} : (x \neq x') \wedge (H(k,x) = H(k,x'))\right] \leq \epsilon_{cr}$$

n	Security parameter
$[m]$	$\{1,\ldots,m\}$
$m_1\|m_2$	Concatenation of strings m_1 and m_2
$(d_i)_{i\in[m]}$	Concatenation of m elements, $d_1\|d_2\|...\|d_m$
$x \xleftarrow{\$} \mathcal{X}$	x is chosen uniformly at random from some set $\mathcal{X}$
$\Delta(x,y)$	Hamming distance between two binary strings x and y
$f(m) = \mathsf{poly}(m)$	$f(m)$ is a polynomial function in m
$f(m) = \mathsf{negl}(m)$	$f(m)$ is a negligible function in m, if $f(m) = o(1/m^c)\ \forall c \in \mathbb{N}$
$[\![r]\!]$	Optional parameter r in an algorithm definition

Fig. 1. Notations

ℓ-near-collision Resistance: We call a family H of hash functions $(t_{\ell\text{-}ncr}, \epsilon_{\ell\text{-}ncr})$-$\ell$-near-collision resistant, if for any $\mathcal{A}$ that runs for at most $t_{\ell\text{-}ncr}$ and $0 \leq \ell \leq n$, the adversary's advantage is:

$$\mathsf{Adv}_{H,\ell}^{ncr}(\mathcal{A}) = \Pr\left[\begin{array}{l} k \xleftarrow{\$} \mathcal{K}; \\ (x,x') \leftarrow \mathcal{A}(k,\ell) \end{array} : (x \neq x') \wedge (\Delta(H(k,x),H(k,x')) \leq \ell) \right] \leq \epsilon_{\ell\text{-}ncr}$$

Generic Attacks. To find the preimage $t_{ow} = 2^q$ is required to achieve $\epsilon_{ow} = 1/2^{n-q}$ using exhaustive search. Due to the birthday paradox, however, only $t_{cr} = 2^{n/2}$ is required to find a collision with a success probability of $\epsilon_{cr} \approx 1/2$. Finally, Lamberger et al. showed in [18] that at least $t_{\ell\text{-}ncr} = 2^{n/2}/\sqrt{\sum_{i=0}^{\ell} \binom{n}{i}}$ is required to find a ℓ-near-collision with a success probability of $\epsilon_{\ell\text{-}ncr} \approx 1/2$.

Unkeyed Hash Functions. In practice, the key for standard hash functions is public; therefore, from this point, we refer to the cryptographic hash function H as a fixed function $H : \mathcal{M} \to \{0,1\}^n$.

3   Security Definition

In this section, we define our flexible signature scheme. We adopt the standard definition of a signature scheme [16] to the flexible security setting. An instance of an interrupted flexible signature verification is expected to return a validity value, α, in the range $[0,1]$. To model the notion of runtime interruptions in the signature definition, we introduce the concept of an interruption oracle iOracle$_\Sigma(1^n)$ for signature scheme Σ and give the verification algorithm access to it. The interruption oracle outputs an interruption position r in the sequence of computation steps involved the verification algorithm. For simplicity, if we denote max to be the maximum number of computations needed (e.g. clock cycles, number of hash computations, or modular exponentiations) for a signature verification, then iOracle$_\Sigma(1^n)$ outputs a value $r \in \{0,\ldots,\mathsf{max}\}$. The specification of the interruption position may vary depending on the choice of the signature scheme; e.g., in this work, we define the interruption position as the number of hash computations performed in the verification algorithm.

Definition 1. *A flexible signature scheme,* Σ = (Gen, Sign, Ver)*, consists of three algorithms:*

- Gen(1^n) *is a probabilistic algorithm that takes a security parameter 1^n as input and outputs a pair (pk, sk) of public key and secret key.*
- Sign(sk, m) *is a probabilistic algorithm that takes a private key sk and a message m from a message space $\mathcal{M}$ as inputs and outputs a signature σ from signature space $\mathcal{S}$.*
- Ver($pk, m, \sigma, [\![r]\!]$) *is a probabilistic algorithm that takes a public key pk, a message m, a signature σ, an optional interruption position $r \in \{0, \ldots, \text{max}\}$ as inputs. If r is not provided, then the algorithm will query an interruption oracle,* iOracle$_\Sigma(1^n)$ *to determine $r \in \{0, \ldots, \text{max}\}$. The algorithm outputs a real value $\alpha \in [0, 1] \cup \{\bot\}^1$. The signature is invalid if $\alpha = \bot$.*

The following correctness condition must hold: For $\forall (pk, sk) \leftarrow$ Gen(1^n)$, \forall m \in \mathcal{M}, \forall r \in \{0, ..., \text{max}\} : \Pr[\text{Ver}(pk, m, \text{Sign}(sk, m), r) = \bot] = 0$.

Remark 1. The interruption oracle only serves as a virtual party for definitional reasons. In practice, the verification algorithm does not receive the interruption position r as an input, and the algorithm continues to perform computations until it receives an interruption. To model runtime interruptions using the interruption oracle iOracle$_\Sigma(1^n)$, in this work, we expect the flow of the verification algorithm to *not* be affected/biased by the r value offered by iOracle$_\Sigma(1^n)$ at the beginning of the verification. Also, we note that depending on signature schemes, there can be more than one way to define the interruption position, r (e.g. clock cycles, number of hash computations, or modular exponentiations).

Extracting Function. We assume that for a flexible signature scheme, there exists an efficient function, iExtract$_\Sigma(\cdot)$, that takes as input the validity of the signature α and outputs the interruption position r. Intuitively, for the case of an unexpected interruption, the verifier need not know when the verification algorithm is interrupted. However, based on the validity output α, the verifier should be able to use iExtract$_\Sigma(\cdot)$ to learn the interruption position, r. The definition of extracting function depends on the specification of the interruption position and signature scheme. We will define our iExtract$_\Sigma(\cdot)$ for each of our proposed constructions in Sects. 4 and 5.

Security of Flexible Signature Scheme. We present a corresponding definition to the existential unforgeability under adaptive chosen message attack (EUF-CMA) experiment in order to prove the security of our scheme. For a given flexible signature scheme Σ = (Gen, Sign, Ver) and $\alpha \in [0, 1]$, the attack experiment is defined as follows:

Experiment FlexExp$_{\mathcal{A}, \Sigma}(1^n, \alpha)$:

1. The challenger $\mathcal{C}$ runs Gen(1^n) to obtain (pk, sk) and iExtract$_\Sigma(\alpha)$ to obtain position r. $\mathcal{C}$ sends (pk, r) to $\mathcal{A}$.

---

[1] $\alpha = 0$ means that no operations are performed in the verification algorithm.

2. Attacker $\mathcal{A}$ queries $\mathcal{C}$ for signatures of its adaptively chosen messages. Let $Q_{\mathcal{A}}^{\mathsf{Sign}(sk,\cdot)} = \{m_i\}_{i\in[q]}$ be the set of all messages that $\mathcal{A}$ queries $\mathcal{C}$ where the ith query is a message $m_i \in \mathcal{M}$. After receiving m_i, $\mathcal{C}$ computes $\sigma_i \leftarrow \mathsf{Sign}(sk, m_i)$, and sends σ_i to $\mathcal{A}$.
3. Eventually, $\mathcal{A}$ outputs a pair $(m^*, \sigma^*) \in \mathcal{M} \times \mathcal{S}^2$, where message $m^* \notin Q_{\mathcal{A}}^{\mathsf{Sign}(sk,\cdot)}$ and sends the pair to $\mathcal{C}$.
4. $\mathcal{C}$ computes $\alpha^* \leftarrow \mathsf{Ver}(pk, m^*, \sigma^*, r)$. If $(\alpha^* \neq \bot)$ and $(\alpha^* \geq \alpha)$, the experiment returns 1; else, it returns 0.

Definition 2. *For the security parameter n and $\alpha \in [0,1]$, a flexible signature scheme Σ is (t, ϵ, q) existential unforgeable under adaptive chosen-message attack if for all efficient adversaries $\mathcal{A}$ that run for at most time t and query $\mathsf{Sign}(sk, \cdot)$ at most q times, the success probability is:*

$$\mathsf{Adv}_{\mathcal{A},\Sigma}^{\mathsf{flex}}(n) = \Pr[\mathsf{FlexExp}_{\mathcal{A},\Sigma}(1^n, \alpha) = 1] \leq \epsilon$$

Here, t and ϵ are functions of α and n, and $q = \mathsf{poly}(n)$.

4 Flexible Lamport-Diffie One-Time Signature

In this section, we present our concrete construction of the flexible one-time signature scheme. This construction is based on the Lamport-Diffie one time signature construction introduced in [19].

4.1 Construction

We show the concrete construction of the flexible Lamport-Diffie one-time signature in Fig. 2. Here, we use the same key generation and signing algorithms from the Lamport-Diffie signature and modify the verification algorithm.

Key Generation Algorithm. The key generation algorithm takes a parameter 1^n as input, and generates a private key by choosing $2n$ bit strings each of length n uniformly at random from $\{0,1\}^n$, namely, $\mathsf{SK} = (sk_i[b])_{i\in[n],b\in\{0,1\}} \in \{0,1\}^{2n^2}$. The public key is obtained by evaluating the preimage-resistant hash function on each of the private key's n bit string, such that $\mathsf{PK} = (pk_i[b])_{i\in[n],b\in\{0,1\}}$ where $pk_i[b] = F(sk_i[b])$ and $F(\cdot)$ is the preimage-resistant hash function.

Signing Algorithm. The signing algorithm takes as input the message m and the private key SK. First, it computes the digest of the message $d = G(m) = (d_i)_{i\in[n]}$ where $d_i \in \{0,1\}$ and $G(\cdot)$ is a collision-resistant hash function that outputs digests of length n. The signature is generated based on the digest d as $\sigma = (sk_i[d_i])_{i\in[n]}$.

---

[2] The higher validity implies a higher interruption position. Hence, the best strategy for the adversary is to use the initial position defined by the challenger.

Flexible Verification Algorithm. This algorithm takes as input a message m, a public key PK, a signature σ, and an optional interruption position $[\![r]\!]$ and outputs the validity of the signature α. In this construction, we model the interruption condition $r \in \{0, 1, \ldots, n\}$, as the number of hash $F(\cdot)$ computations performed during verification. As mentioned earlier in Sect. 3, to faithfully model the interruption process, the flow of the verification algorithm should not be biased by the r value in any intelligent manner. First, the verification algorithm will query the interruption oracle to determine the interruption position r. The algorithm then computes the digest of the message, $d = G(m) = (d_i)_{i \in [n]}$. Now, instead of sequentially verifying the signature bits like the verification in the standard scheme, the flexible verification algorithm randomly selects a position i of the signature and checks whether $F(\sigma_i[d_i]) = pk_i[d_i]$. If there is one invalid preimage, the verification aborts and returns $\alpha = \bot$. Otherwise, once the interruption condition is met or all positions are verified, the algorithm returns the validity as the fraction of the number of bits that passed the verification check over the length of the signature. In this Lamport-Diffie construction, given the validity α value output by the verification algorithm, the verifier simply computes the interruption position as follows: $\mathsf{iExtract}_{\Sigma_{fots}}(\alpha) = \lfloor \alpha \cdot n \rfloor$

Flexible Lamport-Diffie One-time Signature

Given the security parameter n, a preimage resistant hash function $F : \{0,1\}^n \to \{0,1\}^n$, a collision resistant hash function $G : \{0,1\}^* \to \{0,1\}^n$, the flexible Lamport-Diffie one-time signature scheme Σ_{fots} works as follows:

$\mathsf{Gen}(1^n)$: *for each $i \in [n], b \in \{0,1\}$:*

$$\text{choose } sk_i[b] \xleftarrow{\$} \{0,1\}^n, \text{ set } pk_j[b] = F(sk_i[b])$$

$\qquad output :$ $\mathsf{SK} = (sk_i[b])_{i \in [n], b \in \{0,1\}}$, $\mathsf{PK} = (pk_i[b]))_{i \in [n], b \in \{0,1\}}$

$\mathsf{Sign}(\mathsf{SK}, m)$:*compute $d = G(m) = (d_i)_{i \in [n]}$, parse $\mathsf{SK} = (sk_i[b])_{i \in [n], b \in \{0,1\}}$.*

$\qquad output :$ $\sigma = (sk_i[d_i])_{i \in [n]}$

$\mathsf{Ver}(\mathsf{PK}, m, \sigma, [\![r]\!])$: *if r is not provided: set $r \leftarrow \mathsf{iOracle}(1^n)$,*

$\qquad k_F = 0, \ N = [n]$

$\qquad compute \ d = G(m) = (d_i)_{i \in [n]}$

$\qquad write \ \mathsf{PK} = (pk_i[b])_{i \in [n], b \in \{0,1\}}, \ \sigma = (\sigma_i)_{i \in [n]}$

$\qquad while \ (r > 0) \ and \ (N \neq \emptyset) :$

$\qquad\qquad choose \ i \xleftarrow{\$} N$

$\qquad\qquad if \ F(\sigma_i) \neq pk_i(d_i), \ return \ \alpha = \bot$

$\qquad\qquad N = N - \{i\}, k_F = k_F + 1, r = r - 1$

$\qquad output :$ $\alpha = k_F/n$

Fig. 2. Construction of the flexible Lamport-Diffie one-time signature

4.2   Security Analysis

In the flexible Lamport-Diffie one-time signature setting, as the verification algorithm does not perform verification at every position of the signature, the adversary can increase the probability of winning by outputting two messages whose hash digests are close. This is equivalent to finding an ℓ-near-collision pair where ℓ is determined by the adversary. Theorem 1 offers the trade-off between computation time and success probability for the adversary.

Theorem 1. *Let F be (t_{ow}, ϵ_{ow}) preimage-resistant hash function, G be $(t_{\ell\text{-}ncr}, \epsilon_{\ell\text{-}ncr})$ ℓ-near-collision-resistant hash function, k_F, k_G be the number of times $F(\cdot), G(\cdot)$ evaluated in the verification respectively, d be the Hamming distance between two message digests output by $\mathcal{A}$, and $t_{gen}, t_{sign}, t_{ver}$ be the time it takes to generate keys, sign the message, and verify the signature respectively. With $1 \leq k_F \leq n$, $k_G = 1$, the flexible Lamport-Diffie one-time signature Σ_{fots} is $(t_{fots}, \epsilon_{fots}, 1)$ EUF-CMA where:*

$$\alpha = k_F/n$$

$$t_{fots} = \min\{t_{ow}, t_{\ell\text{-}ncr}\} - t_{sign} - t_{ver} - t_{gen} \text{ where } 0 \leq \ell \leq n - k_F$$

$$\epsilon_{fots} \leq \min\left\{1, 2 \cdot \max\left\{\prod_{i=0}^{k_F-1}\left(1 - \frac{d}{n-i}\right), 4n \cdot \epsilon_{ow}\right\}\right\} \text{ where } 0 \leq d \leq \ell$$

The proof of Theorem 1 is shifted to Appendix A.

Security Level. Towards making the security of flexible Lamport-Diffie one-time signatures more comprehensible, we adapt the security level computation from [7]. For any (t, ϵ) signature scheme, we define the security of the scheme to be $\log_2(t/\epsilon)$. As, in the flexible setting, the value of the pair (t, ϵ) may vary as the adversary decides the Hamming distance ℓ, for each value of $k_F \in \{0, \ldots, n\}$, we compute the adversarial advantage for all values $0 \leq \ell \leq n - k_F$ and output the minimum value of $\log_2(t_{fots}/\epsilon_{fots})$ as the security level of our scheme. A detailed security level analysis for the Lamport-Diffie one-time signature is available in Sect. 6.1.

5   Flexible Merkle Tree Signature

We use the Merkle authentication tree [22] to convert the flexible Lamport-Diffie one-time signature scheme into a flexible many-time signature scheme.

5.1   Construction

In the Merkle tree signature scheme, in addition to verifying the validity of the signature, the verifier uses the authentication nodes provided by the signer to check the authenticity of the one-time public key. We are interested in quantifying such values under an interruption. To achieve such a requirement, we require the signer to provide additional nodes in the authentication path.

Key Generation Algorithm. Our key generation remains the same as the one proposed in the original Merkle tree signature scheme [22]. For a tree of height h, the generation algorithm generates 2^h Lamport-Diffie one-time key pairs, $(\mathsf{PK}_i, \mathsf{SK}_i)_{i \in [2^h]}$. The leaves of the tree are digests of one-time public keys, $H(\mathsf{PK}_i)$, where $H(\cdot)$ is a collision-resistant hash function. An inner node of the Merkle tree is the hash digest of the concatenation of its left and right children. Finally, the public key of the scheme is the root of the tree, and the secret key is the set of 2^h one-time secret keys.

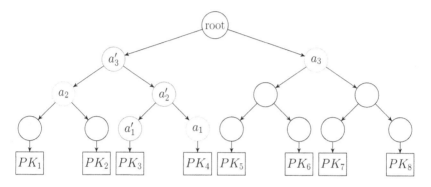

Fig. 3. An example of new authentication nodes for PK_3 where $\mathsf{Auth}_3 = (a_1, a_2, a_3)$ is the set of authentication nodes in the original scheme and $\mathsf{Auth}_3^c = (a_1', a_2', a_3')$ is the set of additional authentication nodes

Modified Signing Algorithm. In the original Merkle signature scheme, a signature consists of four parts: the signature state s, a one-time signature σ_s, a one-time public key PK_s and a set of authentication nodes $\mathsf{Auth}_s = (a_i)_{i \in [h]}$. The verifier can use PK_s to verify the validity of the σ_s and use nodes in Auth_s and state s to efficiently verify the authenticity of PK_s. For our signing algorithm, along with authentication nodes in the old construction, we require the signer to send the nodes that complete the direct authentication path from the one-time public key to the root. We call this set of nodes complement authentication nodes, $\mathsf{Auth}_s^c = (a_i')_{i \in [h]}$. The reason for including additional authentication nodes is to allow the verifier to randomly verify any level of the tree. Moreover, with additional authentication nodes, verifier can verify different levels of the tree in parallel. Figure 3 describes an example of the new requirement for a tree of height three. The modified signature now consists of five parts: a state s, a Lamport-Diffie one-time signature σ_s, a one-time public key PK_s, a set of authentication nodes Auth_s, and a set of complement authentication nodes Auth_s^c.

Flexible Verification Algorithm. With additional authentication nodes, the verification algorithm can verify the authenticity of the public key at arbitrary levels of the authentication tree as well as use the flexible verification described in Sect. 4 to partially verify the validity of the one-time signature. In the end,

Flexible Merkle Tree Signature Scheme

Given the security parameter n, the height of the tree h, a preimage resistant hash function $F : \{0,1\}^n \to \{0,1\}^n$, a collision resistant hash function $H : \{0,1\}^* \to \{0,1\}^n$, $G : \{0,1\}^* \to \{0,1\}^n$, and a flexible Lamport-Diffie one-time signature scheme $\Sigma_{fots} = (\mathsf{Gen}_{fots}, \mathsf{Sign}_{fots}, \mathsf{Ver}_{fots})$. The stateful flexible Merkle scheme Σ_{fms} works as follows:

$\mathsf{Gen}(1^n)$: *generate 2^h ots pairs $\{(\mathsf{PK}_i, \mathsf{SK}_i)\}_{i \in [2^h]}$ using $\mathsf{Gen}_{fots}(1^n)$*

    compute the inner nodes of the Merkle tree as follows:

$$node_i[j] = H(node_{i-1}[2j-1] \| node_{i-1}[2j])$$
$$2 \le i \le h+1, 1 \le j \le 2^{h+1-i}$$
$$node_1[i] = H(PK_i), 1 \le i \le 2^h$$

    output : $\mathsf{SK} = \{\mathsf{SK}_i\}_{i \in [2^h]}, \mathsf{PK} = root$ *(i.e. $node_{h+1}[1]$),* $s = 1$

$\mathsf{Sign}(\mathsf{SK}, m, s)$: *compute $\sigma_s = \mathsf{Sign}_{fots}(\mathsf{SK}_s, m)$*

    compute $\mathsf{Auth_s} = (a_i)_{i \in [h]}$, where

$$a_i = \begin{cases} node_i[\lceil s/2^{i-1} \rceil + 1] & if \ \lceil s/2^{i-1} \rceil \equiv 1 \ mod \ 2 \\ node_i[\lceil s/2^{i-1} \rceil - 1] & if \ \lceil s/2^{i-1} \rceil \equiv 0 \ mod \ 2 \end{cases}$$

    compute $\mathsf{Auth_s^c} = (a_i')_{i \in [h]}$, where $a_i' = node_i[\lceil s/2^{i-1} \rceil]$

    output : $\sigma = (s, \sigma_s, \mathsf{PK_s}, \mathsf{Auth_s}, \mathsf{Auth_s^c}), s = s+1$

$\mathsf{Ver}(\mathsf{PK}, m, \sigma, [\![r]\!])$: *if r is not provided: set $r \leftarrow \mathsf{iOracle}(1^n)$,*

    set $N = [n], T = [h+1], k_F = 0, k_H = 0$

    compute $G(m) = d = (d_i)_{i \in [n]}$

    extract $(s, \sigma_{fots}, \mathsf{PK_{fots}}, \mathsf{Auth}, \mathsf{Auth^c}) \leftarrow \sigma$

    write $\sigma_{ots} = (\sigma_i)_{i \in [n]}$, $\mathsf{PK_{fots}} = (pk_i[b])_{i \in [n], b \in \{0,1\}}$,

        $\mathsf{Auth_s} = (a_i)_{i \in [h]}$, $\mathsf{Auth_s^c} = (a_i')_{i \in [h]}$

    while $r > 0$ and $H \ne \emptyset$ and $N \ne \emptyset$ do :

        if $1 - 1/2^{k_F/2} \le k_H/(h+1)$:

            choose $i \xleftarrow{\$} N$, if $F(\sigma_i) \ne pk_i(d_i)$, output : $\alpha = \perp$

            $N = N - \{i\}, \ k_F = k_F + 1$

        else : choose $j \xleftarrow{\$} T$, set $a_{h+1}' = \mathsf{PK}$

        if $j = 1$: if $a_1' \ne H(\mathsf{PK_s})$, output : $\alpha = \perp$

        if $j > 1$: if a_j' is not a parent of a_{j-1} and a_{j-1}' :

            output $\alpha = \perp$.

        $T = T - \{j\}, k_H = k_H + 1$

    $r = r - 1$

    output : $\alpha = (k_F/n, k_H/(h+1))$

Fig. 4. The flexible merkle signature construction

the verification returns $\alpha = (\alpha_v, \alpha_a)$ that contains both the validity of the signature and the authenticity of the public key. In this construction, we define the interruption $r \in \{0, 1, \ldots, n + h + 1\}$, as the number of computations performed during the verification step.

In contrast to the verification performed in the one-time signature scheme, the security guarantee the verifier gains from the authenticity verification of the one-time public key only increases linearly as the number of computations performed on the authentication path increase: The adversary can always generate a new one-time key pair to sign the message that is not a part of one-time key pairs created by the generation algorithm. In the original Merkle scheme, such a key-pair will fail the authenticity check with overwhelming probability because the verifier can use the authentication nodes to compute and verify the root. However, in the flexible setting, the verifier may not be able to complete the authenticity verification, and there is a non-negligible probability that an invalid one-time public key will be used to verify the validity of the signature. Therefore, the verifier gains an exponential security guarantee about the validity of the one-time signature but only a linear guarantee about the authenticity of the public key as the number of computations increases.

To address this issue, the verification algorithm needs to balance the computations performed on the authentication path and the computations performed on the one-time signature. We define the confidence for the validity of the one-time signature as $1 - 1/2^{k_F/2}$ and the confidence for authenticity of the one-time public key as $k_H/(h + 1)$, where k_F is the number of computations performed on the one-time signature, k_H is the number of computations performed on the one-time public key, and h is the height of the Merkle tree. To balance the number of computations, the verifier needs to maintain $1 - 1/2^{k_F/2} \approx k_H/(h + 1)$. With the new signing and verifying algorithms described above, we present a detailed construction of the flexible Merkle signature scheme in Fig. 4. In this Merkle signature construction, given the validity $\alpha = (\alpha_v, \alpha_a)$ value output by the verification algorithm, the verifier can compute the interruption position as follow: $\mathsf{iExtract}_{\Sigma_{fms}}(\alpha) = \lfloor \alpha_v n \rfloor + \lfloor \alpha_a(h + 1) \rfloor$.

5.2   Security Analysis

Theorem 2 presents the trade-off between computation time and success probability for the adversary $\mathcal{A}$.

Theorem 2. *Let F be (t_{ow}, ϵ_{ow}) preimage-resistant hash function, G be $(t_{\ell\text{-}ncr}, \epsilon_{\ell\text{-}ncr})$ ℓ-near-collision-resistant hash function, H be (t_{cr}, ϵ_{cr}) collision-resistant hash function, k_F, k_G, k_H be the number of times $F(\cdot), G(\cdot), H(\cdot)$ performed respectively, d be the smallest Hamming distance between the forged message digest and other queried message digests, and $t_{gen}, t_{sign}, t_{ver}$ be the time it takes to generate keys, sign the message, and verify the signature respectively. With $1 \leq k_F \leq n$, $0 \leq k_H \leq h + 1$, and $k_G = 1$, the flexible Merkle signature construction (Σ_{fms}) from flexible Lamport-Diffie one-time signature scheme is $(t_{fms}, \epsilon_{fms}, 2^h)$ EU-CMA, where*

$$\alpha = (k_F/n, k_H/(h+1))$$

$$t_{fms} = \begin{cases} \mathcal{O}(1) & \text{when } k_H < h+1, \\ \min\left\{t_{ow}, t_{\ell\text{-}ncr}, t_{cr}\right\} - 2^h \cdot t_{sign} - t_{ver} - t_{gen} & \text{where } 0 \le \ell \le n - k_F \end{cases}$$

$$\epsilon_{fms} \le \min\left\{1, 4 \cdot \max\left\{1 - \frac{k_H}{(h+1)}, 2^h \prod_{i=0}^{k_F-1}\left(1 - \frac{d}{n-i}\right), 2^{h+\log_2 4n} \cdot \epsilon_{ow}, \epsilon_{cr}\right\}\right\}$$

$$\text{where } 0 \le d \le \ell$$

The proof of Theorem 2 is shifted to Appendix A. A more detailed version of the proof will be included in the extended version [20].

5.3   Other Signature Schemes

Over the last few years, several optimized versions of Merkle tree signature and one-time signature schemes have been proposed. This includes XMSS [6] and SPHINCS [4] for the tree signatures, and HORS [23], BIBA [25], HORST [4] and Winternitz [22] for one-time signatures. While the security analysis for each scheme may vary, we can use the same technique described above to transform those schemes into signature schemes with a flexible verification. In this work, we choose to use Lamport-Diffie One-time signatures in our construction for two reasons. First, the number of hash evaluations in Lamport-Diffie Signature verification is fixed for constant size messages, and this gives better and more precise security proofs. Second, Lamport-Diffie one-time signature has better performance in terms of the running time. Thus, according to our experiment and analysis, the Lamport-Diffie One-time signature scheme combined with Merkle Tree provides a better speed performance and more concrete security proofs.

We also investigate number-theoretic signature schemes and observe that the similar verification technique can be applied to the Fiat-Shamir Signature Scheme [12] as its signature is partitioned into different verifiable sets. However, compared to hash function evaluations, the computation of modular exponentiation is significantly more expensive and thus may not be suitable for flexible security application environments. On the other hand, lattice-based signature schemes such as GPV signatures [15] can be an interesting candidate for a flexible signature construction. For GPV signatures, a public key is a matrix output by a trapdoor sampling algorithm, and a signature is output by a pre-image sampling algorithm. The signature verification is performed using a matrix and vector multiplication. The same randomized verification technique seems to be applicable here on different rows of the matrix. In the future, we plan to explore a flexible version of GPV signatures.

6   Evaluation, Performance Analysis, and Discussion

In this section, we evaluate the performance and the security level of the flexible Lamport-Diffie one-time signature and flexible Merkle signature schemes.

For both schemes, the validity value α suggests the number of computations performed (i.e., k_H, k_F) during verification. Based on the value α, the verifier determines the security level achieved by the (interrupted) verification instance.

6.1   Security Level of Flexible Lamport-Diffie One-Time Signature

The security level of a flexible Lamport-Diffie signature depends on the actual Hamming distance between two message digests output by the adversary and it can increase its advantage by spending more time to find a near-collision pair. However, it is unclear how to precisely measure the exact Hamming distance between those two digests. Therefore, we outline some possible assumptions in order to estimate precisely the value of $\Delta(G(m), G(m^*))$. Using the generic attack on finding near collision pair [18], we can assume that an adversary $\mathcal{A}$ who uses a generic birthday attack can always output a pair (m, m^*) such that $\Delta(G(m), G(m^*)) \leq \ell$ after spending $t_{\ell\text{-}ncr} = 2^{n/2}/\sqrt{\sum_{i=0}^{\ell}\binom{n}{i}}$. Second, for a fixed value ℓ, if the adversary finds a pair (m, m^*) such that $\Delta(G(m), G(m^*)) \leq \ell$, we let $d = \Delta(G(m), G(m^*))$ is equal to the expected value of $\Delta(G(m), G(m^*))$. The intuition behind the second assumption is that as we let the Hamming distance d decrease by 1, the probability that $\Delta(G(m), G(m^*)) = d$ decreases by factor of n; therefore, the actual value of d should be closer to ℓ than to 0.

We define the set $B_\ell(G(m)) = \{x \mid x \in \{0,1\}^n \wedge \Delta(x, G(m)) \leq \ell\}$. If $G(m)$ and $G(m^*)$ is a ℓ-near-collision pair, then $G(m^*) \in B_\ell(G(m))$. If $G(\cdot)$ behaves as an uniformly random function, then given ℓ, the expected value of $\Delta(G(m), G(m^*))$ is:

$$\mathbb{E}(\Delta(G(m), G(m^*))) = \sum_{j=0}^{\ell} j \cdot \frac{\binom{n}{j}}{|B_\ell(G(m))|} = \sum_{j=0}^{\ell} j \cdot \frac{\binom{n}{j}}{\sum_{i=0}^{\ell}\binom{n}{i}} \tag{1}$$

For the case of Lamport-Diffie one-time signature, we have $t_{gen} = 2n, t_{sign} = t_{ver} = n$. Combining Theorem 1 and Eq. 1, we have:

$$t_{fots} = \max\left\{1, \frac{2^{n/2}}{\sqrt{\sum_{i=0}^{\ell}\binom{n}{i}}} - 4 \cdot n\right\} \text{ for } \ell \leq n - k_F$$

$$\epsilon_{fots} \leq \min\left\{1, 2 \cdot \prod_{i=0}^{k_F-1}\left(1 - \frac{d}{n-i}\right)\right\} \text{ where } d = \mathbb{E}(\Delta(G(m), G(m^*))),$$

$$\text{given } \Delta(G(m), G(m^*)) \leq \ell$$

Finally, the adversary's advantage varies depending on the value of ℓ. Therefore, for a fixed value k_F, we compute the adversarial advantage all values $\ell \leq n - k_F$ and output the minimum value of $\log_2\left(t_{fots}/\epsilon_{fots}\right)$ as the security level of the scheme.

Figure 5 gives the trade-off between the number of computations and the security level of the flexible Lamport-Diffie scheme. Compared to the original

Lamport-Diffie scheme, our construction offers a reasonable security level despite a smaller number of computations. For example, while a complete verification requires 256 evaluations of $F(\cdot)$ to achieve the 128-bit security level, with only 128 evaluations of $F(\cdot)$, the scheme still offers around the 92-bit security level.

6.2   Security Level of Flexible Merkle Tree Signature

For the Merkle tree signature scheme, using the results from [9, 28], we have $t_{gen} = 2^h \cdot 2n + 2^{h+1} - 1, t_{ver} = n + h + 1, t_{sign} = (h + 1) \cdot n$. There are two cases for the Merkle tree signature: (1) The authenticity check is complete, $k_H = h + 1$ and (2) The authenticity check is not complete, $k_H < h + 1$.

When $k_H < h + 1$, the adversary's probability of winning is non-negligible, and the time it needs to spend on the attack is constant; therefore, when the authenticity check is not complete, we simply let: $t_{fms} = 1, \epsilon_{fms} = 1 - k_H/(h+1)$. When the authenticity verification is complete, $k_H = h + 1$, using the equation described in Theorem 2, we obtain the following parameters for the flexible Merkle tree scheme:

$$t_{fms} = \max\left\{1, t_{\ell\text{-}ncr} - 2^{h+\log_2(h+1)n} - 2^{h\cdot\log_2 2n} - 2^{\log_2(n-h-1)}\right\} \text{ for } \ell \leq n - k_F$$

$$\epsilon_{fms} \leq \min\left\{1, 2^h \cdot \prod_{i=0}^{k_F-1}\left(1 - \frac{d}{n-i}\right)\right\} \text{ where } d = \mathbb{E}(\Delta(G(m), G(m^*)))$$

Using those formulas, we compute the security level of the flexible Merkle signature as $\log_2(t_{fms}/\epsilon_{fms})$. Figure 6 shows the trade-off between the security level of the scheme and the number of computations of the flexible Merkle tree signature with $h = 20$. Notice that, for small number of computations, the security level of Merkle tree construction does not increase. The reason is that if the authenticity of the public key is not completely checked, the probability that the adversary wins the forgery experiment is always the fraction of the number of computations on the authentication path over the height of the tree,

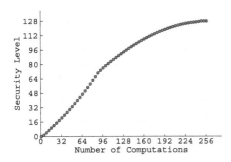

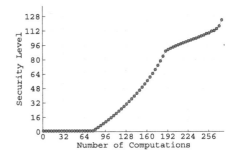

Fig. 5. Security level of flexible Lamport-Diffie one-time signature

Fig. 6. Security level of flexible merkle tree signature

and the forging time remains constant. Moreover, for a tree of height h, there are 2^h instances of flexible Lamport-Diffie one-time signature. Therefore, if $F(\cdot)$ evaluated only for a small number of times, the cost of finding an ℓ-near-collision pair (for $\ell \leq n - k_F$) is cheap. The probability that such a pair passes the one-time verification step in one instance of 2^h instances of flexible Lamport-Diffie one-time signature is high. This leads to an undesirable security level during the first few computations.

6.3   Implementation and Performance

We have implemented prototypes of our proposed constructions in C, using the SHA-256 implementation of OpenSSL. We evaluated the performance of our proposed constructions on a Raspberry Pi 3, Model B equipped with 1 GB RAM.

Table 1 gives the performance and security levels of the flexible verification algorithm of both schemes compared to other standard signature schemes (i.e., RSA, DSA, ECDSA, and EdDSA) based on the percentage of computations $p = 20\%, 40\%, 60\%, 80\%$, and 100% for messages of size 256^3. For other signature schemes, we obtain the performance of those schemes using the OpenSSL library. More specifically, for ECDSA, we used two standard curves: Ed25519 and nistp256. For the RSA signature scheme, we used the smallest recommended public key $2^{16} + 1$ for the verification algorithm. For the security levels of other signature schemes, we use the information from [1,6]. As shown in Table 1, the performance of both flexible signature schemes is comparable to other standard schemes in terms of the verification running time. More importantly, both constructions offer an increasing security level at each step of the algorithm while

Table 1. Comparing flexible signature schemes performance for different levels of signature verification with other signature schemes.

	Signature Verification; Output Format: (**Timings, Security Level**)				
Percentage of computations	20%	40%	60%	80%	100%
RSA 3072, $pk = 2^{16} + 1$	-	-	-	-	$(1.43\,\text{ms}, 128)$
DSA 2048	-	-	-	-	$(4.93\,\text{ms}, 87)$
EdDSA (Ed25519 curve)	-	-	-	-	$(3.21\,\text{ms}, 128)$
ECDSA (nistp256 curve)	-	-	-	-	$(3.39\,\text{ms}, 128)$
Lamport-Diffie OTS verification, $n = 256$	$(0.16\,\text{ms}, 35)$	$(0.31\,\text{ms}, 79)$	$(0.43\,\text{ms}, 105)$	$(0.47\,\text{ms}, 121)$	$(0.54\,\text{ms}, 127)$
Merkle signature verification, $n = 256, h = 20$	$(0.85\,\text{ms}, 1)$	$(0.93\,\text{ms}, 19)$	$(1.00\,\text{ms}, 61)$	$(1.06\,\text{ms}, 99)$	$(1.23\,\text{ms}, 127)$

---

[3] We focus on the verification algorithm in this work. For the performance of signing, generation algorithms, and the size of the signature we refer readers to [6,7].

other signature schemes can only provide such information at the end of the verification algorithm, and Table 1 demonstrates that in the form of (Timings, Security Level) pairs. Also, notice that as the number of verification computations increases, the Lamport-Diffie OTS gives a higher security level than the signing shorter hash digest approach which offers the security level that is equal to half of the length of the hash digest. The main reason is that the verification algorithm verifies the signature at random locations, and while the adversary may learn about the number of computations performed, the adversary does not know which indices of the signature get verified. Thus, the adversary has to decide how close the two digests should be to maximize his adversarial advantage. For the case of Merkle tree signatures, we do not see a huge improvement in the performance of the verification despite a smaller number of computations. This is because the computation of $H(\mathsf{PK_{fots}})$ and $G(m)$ can be expensive, because of the use the Merkle-Damgård transformation in SHA2 hash family, as those computations requires more calls to the compression function depending on the input size. Nevertheless, for real-time environments, we expect messages to be smaller in size.

7   Conclusion

In this paper, we defined the concept of a signature scheme with a flexible verification algorithm. We presented two concrete constructions based on the Lamport-Diffie one-time signature scheme and the Merkle signature scheme and formally proved their security. We also implemented prototypes of our proposed constructions and showed that the running time performance of our proposed designs is comparable to other signature schemes in a resource-constrained environment. More importantly, compared to standard signature schemes with deterministic verification, our schemes allow the verifier to put different constraints on the verification algorithm in a spontaneous manner and still guarantee a reasonable security level. Our proposed signature scheme is one of the few cryptographic primitives that offers a trade-off between security and resources. It can be highly useful for cryptographic mechanisms in unpredictably resource constrained environments such as real-time systems.

In the long run, significant research will be required in this challenging flexible security area. We plan to explore similar ideas for confidentiality in (symmetric or asymmetric) encryptions, integrity with MACs, and possibly beyond. We believe these cryptographic protocols will make security mechanisms more prevalent in the real-time systems.

Acknowledgment. We thank Mikhail Atallah, Dominique Schröder, and the anonymous reviewers for encouraging discussions and suggestions.

A   Proofs

In this section, we provided the formal proofs of two stated theorems.

Proof of Theorem 1. Let m be the message asked by $\mathcal{A}$ during the experiment $\mathsf{FlexExp}_{\Sigma,\mathcal{A}}(1^n, \alpha)$, and (m^*, σ^*) be the forgery pair. We define the distance, $d = \Delta(G(m), G(m^*))$. We notice that for a pair (m, m^*) output by the adversary during the forgery experiment, if $\Delta(G(m), G(m^*)) > n - k_F$, then by pigeonhole principle, at least one of different positions will be checked. Therefore, in order to maximize the success probability, the adversary has to choose ℓ and find a ℓ-near-collision pair where the Hamming distance of $G(m)$ and $G(m^*)$ is less than ℓ where $\ell \le (n - k_F)$. In order to output such near-collision pair, $\mathcal{A}$ requires at least $t = t_{\ell\text{-}ncr} = 2^{n/2}/\sqrt{\sum_{i=0}^{\ell} \binom{n}{i}}$. Also, on the other hand, $\mathcal{A}$ may win the forgery experiment by spending t_{ow} to break the underlying preimage resistant hash function. Thus, subtracting the running time of generating, signing, and verifying algorithms, we have: $t_{fots} = \min\{t_{ow}, t_{\ell\text{-}ncr}\} - t_{sign} - t_{gen} - t_{ver}$ where $0 \le \ell \le n - k_F$. For the success probability, we let Miss be the event that no different bit gets verified. Since d is the Hamming distance between 2 message digests, either none of those different positions were checked, or some of those positions passed the check (i.e. the preimage was found). Thus, we rewrite $\mathcal{A}$'s advantage for the forging experiment as follows: $\Pr[\mathsf{FlexExp}_{\mathcal{A},\Sigma}(1^n, \alpha) = 1] \le \Pr[\mathsf{Miss}] + \Pr[\mathsf{FlexExp}_{\mathcal{A},\Sigma}(1^n, \alpha) = 1 \wedge \overline{\mathsf{Miss}}]$.

The event $(\mathsf{FlexExp}_{\mathcal{A},\Sigma}(1^n, \alpha) = 1 \wedge \overline{\mathsf{Miss}})$ implies that $\mathcal{A}$ wins the forgery experiment by providing a preimage of $F(\cdot)$. Therefore, we can use $\mathcal{A}$ to construct a preimage finder $\mathcal{B}$. The reduction is presented in [7]. One can show:

$$\Pr[\mathsf{FlexExp}_{\mathcal{A},\Sigma}(1^n, \alpha) = 1 \wedge \overline{\mathsf{Miss}}] \le 4n \cdot \mathsf{Adv}_{\mathcal{B},\mathsf{F}}^{\mathsf{pre}}(n) = 4n \cdot \epsilon_{ow} \qquad (2)$$

Finally, $\Pr[\mathsf{Miss}]$ implies the adversary can win the forging experiment if the challenger does not perform verification on the different bits. Since d is the number of different bits between two digests, the probability that the challenger does not perform verification on those positions is:

$$\Pr[\mathsf{Miss}] = \prod_{i=0}^{k_F - 1} \frac{n - d - i}{n - i} = \prod_{i=0}^{k_F - 1} \left(1 - \frac{d}{n - i}\right) \qquad (3)$$

From Eqs. (2) and (3), we have:

$$\Pr[\mathsf{FlexExp}_{\mathcal{A},\Sigma}(1^n, \alpha) = 1] \le \min\left\{1, 2 \cdot \max\left\{\prod_{i=0}^{k_F - 1}\left(1 - \frac{d}{n - i}\right), 4n \cdot \epsilon_{ow}\right\}\right\}$$

which completes the proof.   ∎

Proof of Theorem 2. Intuitively, if adversary $\mathcal{A}$ provides an invalid one-time public key, the verification must fail for at least one level of tree. Otherwise, $\mathcal{A}$ successfully finds a collision of H. However, in our scheme, since every level of the tree may not be verified, there is a possibility that the forged level is not checked. We formalize the intuition as following; we let $\mathsf{InvalidOPK}$ be the event that $\mathcal{A}$ provides an invalid one-time public key. Consider the Merkle tree construction based on the one-time signature construction.

$$\Pr[\mathsf{FlexExp}_{\mathcal{A},\Sigma}(1^n,\alpha) = 1] = \Pr[\mathsf{FlexExp}_{\mathcal{A},\Sigma}(1^n,\alpha) = 1 \wedge \mathsf{InvalidPK}] \\ + \Pr[\mathsf{FlexExp}_{\mathcal{A},\Sigma}(1^n,\alpha) = 1 \wedge \overline{\mathsf{InvalidPK}}] \tag{4}$$

The $\mathsf{FlexExp}_{\mathcal{A},\Sigma}(1^n,\alpha) = 1 \wedge \mathsf{InvalidPK}$ implies that $\mathcal{A}$ provided an invalid one-time public key but won the forgery experiment. Thus, either the verifier failed to check a "bad" level of the tree or $\mathcal{A}$ found a collision of $H(\cdot)$. For a tree of height h, there are $h + 1$ levels that one needs to verify for the complete authentication. Since k_H is the number of times $H(\cdot)$ is evaluated, using a union bound, we have:

$$\Pr[\mathsf{FlexExp}_{\mathcal{A},\Sigma}(1^n,\alpha) = 1 \wedge \mathsf{InvalidPK}] \leq 2 \cdot \max\left\{1 - \frac{k_H}{h+1}, \epsilon_{cr}\right\} \tag{5}$$

If $\mathcal{A}$ found a collision of $H(\cdot)$, then we can construct a collision finder [7].

The event $\mathsf{FlexExp}_{\mathcal{A},\Sigma}(1^n,\alpha) = 1 \wedge \overline{\mathsf{InvalidPK}}$ implies that $\mathcal{A}$ won the flexible forgery experiment for one-time signature scheme. Since we defined k_F to be the number of $F(\cdot)$ evaluated, the underlying flexible one-time signature is $(t_{fots}, \epsilon_{fots}, 1)$. Therefore, using Theorem 1, we get:

$$\epsilon_{fots} \leq 2 \cdot \max\left\{\prod_{i=0}^{k_F-1}\left(1 - \frac{d}{n-i}\right), 4n \cdot \epsilon_{ow}\right\} \text{ where } 0 \leq d \leq \ell \leq n - k_F$$

Since there are 2^h instances of the flexible Lamport-Diffie one-time signature, it means that for $0 \leq d \leq \ell \leq n - k_F$, $\mathcal{A}$ wins the forgery game with probability:

$$\Pr[\mathsf{FlexExp}_{\mathcal{A},\Sigma}(1^n,\alpha) = 1 \wedge \overline{\mathsf{InvalidPK}}]$$

$$\leq 2 \cdot \max\left\{2^h \cdot \prod_{i=0}^{k_F-1}\left(1 - \frac{d}{n-i}\right), 2^{h+\log_2 4n} \cdot \epsilon_{ow}\right\} \tag{6}$$

From Eqs. (4), (5) and (6), for $0 \leq d \leq \ell \leq n - k_F$, we have:

$$\epsilon_{fms} \leq 4 \cdot \max\left\{1 - k_H/(h+1), 2^h \cdot \prod_{i=0}^{k_F-1}\left(1 - \frac{d}{n-i}\right), 2^{h+\log_2 4n} \cdot \epsilon_{ow}, \epsilon_{cr}\right\}$$

When $k_H < h + 1$, we simply let $t_{fms} = \mathcal{O}(1)$ because $\mathcal{A}$ will win the forgery experiment with probability $1 - k_H/(h+1)$. When $k_H = h + 1$, we have:

$$\epsilon_{fms} \leq 4 \cdot \max\left\{2^h \cdot \prod_{i=0}^{k_F-1}(1 - \frac{d}{n-i}), 2^{h+\log_2 4n} \cdot \epsilon_{ow}, \epsilon_{cr}\right\} \text{ where } 0 \leq d \leq \ell \leq n - k_F$$

and using [7, Theorem 5], we have $t_{fms} = \min\{t_{cr}, t_{fots}\} - 2^h \cdot t_{sign} - t_{ver} - t_{gen}$. Now, using Theorem 1, we get: $t_{fms} = \min\{t_{ow}, t_{\ell-ncr}, t_{cr}\} - 2^h \cdot t_{sign} - t_{ver} - t_{gen}$ where $0 \leq \ell \leq n - k$. This completes the proof. ∎

References

1. Barker, E.: Recommended for key management-part 1: General. https://nvlpubs. nist.gov/nistpubs/SpecialPublications/NIST.SP.800-57pt1r4.pdf
2. Bellare, M., Garay, J.A., Rabin, T.: Fast batch verification for modular exponentiation and digital signatures. In: Nyberg, K. (ed.) EUROCRYPT 1998. LNCS, vol. 1403, pp. 236–250. Springer, Heidelberg (1998). https://doi.org/10.1007/BFb0054130
3. Bellare, M., Goldreich, O., Goldwasser, S.: Incremental cryptography: the case of hashing and signing. In: Desmedt, Y.G. (ed.) CRYPTO 1994. LNCS, vol. 839, pp. 216–233. Springer, Heidelberg (1994). https://doi.org/10.1007/3-540-48658-5_22
4. Bernstein, D.J., et al.: SPHINCS: practical stateless hash-based signatures. In: Oswald, E., Fischlin, M. (eds.) EUROCRYPT 2015. LNCS, vol. 9056, pp. 368–397. Springer, Heidelberg (2015). https://doi.org/10.1007/978-3-662-46800-5_15
5. Boneh, D., Lynn, B., Shacham, H.: Short signatures from the weil pairing. J. Cryptol. **17**(4), 297–319 (2004)
6. Buchmann, J., Dahmen, E., Hülsing, A.: XMSS - a practical forward secure signature scheme based on minimal security assumptions. In: Yang, B.-Y. (ed.) PQCrypto 2011. LNCS, vol. 7071, pp. 117–129. Springer, Heidelberg (2011). https://doi.org/10.1007/978-3-642-25405-5_8
7. Buchmann, J., Dahmen, E., Szydlo, M.: Hash-based digital signature schemes. In: Bernstein, D.J., Buchmann, J., Dahmen, E. (eds.) Post-Quantum Cryptography. Springer, Heidelberg (2009). https://doi.org/10.1007/978-3-540-88702-7_3
8. Camenisch, J., Hohenberger, S., Pedersen, M.Ø.: Batch verification of short signatures. In: Naor, M. (ed.) EUROCRYPT 2007. LNCS, vol. 4515, pp. 246–263. Springer, Heidelberg (2007). https://doi.org/10.1007/978-3-540-72540-4_14
9. Dahmen, E., Okeya, K., Takagi, T., Vuillaume, C.: Digital signatures out of second-preimage resistant hash functions. In: Buchmann, J., Ding, J. (eds.) PQCrypto 2008. LNCS, vol. 5299, pp. 109–123. Springer, Heidelberg (2008). https://doi.org/10.1007/978-3-540-88403-3_8
10. Denning, T., Kohno, T., Levy, H.M.: Computer security and the modern home. Commun. ACM **1**, 94–103 (2013)
11. Fan, X., Garay, J., Mohassel, P.: Short and adjustable signatures. Cryptology ePrint Archive, Report 2016/549 (2016)
12. Fiat, A., Shamir, A.: How to prove yourself: practical solutions to identification and signature problems. In: Odlyzko, A.M. (ed.) CRYPTO 1986. LNCS, vol. 263, pp. 186–194. Springer, Heidelberg (1987). https://doi.org/10.1007/3-540-47721-7_12
13. Fischlin, M.: Progressive verification: the case of message authentication. In: Johansson, T., Maitra, S. (eds.) INDOCRYPT 2003. LNCS, vol. 2904, pp. 416–429. Springer, Heidelberg (2003). https://doi.org/10.1007/978-3-540-24582-7_31
14. Freitag, C., et al.: Signature schemes with randomized verification. In: Gollmann, D., Miyaji, A., Kikuchi, H. (eds.) ACNS 2017. LNCS, vol. 10355, pp. 373–389. Springer, Cham (2017). https://doi.org/10.1007/978-3-319-61204-1_19
15. Gentry, C., Peikert, C., Vaikuntanathan, V.: Trapdoors for hard lattices and new cryptographic constructions. In: STOC 2008, pp. 197–206 (2008)
16. Katz, J., Lindell, Y.: Introduction to Modern Cryptography, chap. 12, pp. 442–443 (2007)
17. Koscher, K., et al.: Experimental security analysis of a modern automobile. In: IEEE S&P 2010, pp. 447–462 (2010)
18. Lamberger, M., Teufl, E.: Memoryless near-collisions, revisited. CoRR (2012)

19. Lamport, L.: Constructing digital signatures from a one way function. SRI intl. CSL-98 (1979)

20. Le, D.V., Kelkar, M., Kate, A.: Flexible signatures: towards making authentication suitable for real-time environments. Cryptology ePrint Archive, Report 2018/343 (2018)

21. Menezes, A.J., Vanstone, S.A., Oorschot, P.C.V.: Handbook of Applied Cryptography, 1st edn. CRC Press, Inc., Boca Raton (1996)

22. Merkle, R.C.: A certified digital signature. In: Brassard, G. (ed.) CRYPTO 1989. LNCS, vol. 435, pp. 218–238. Springer, New York (1990). https://doi.org/10.1007/0-387-34805-0_21

23. Perrig, A.: The BiBa one-time signature and broadcast authentication protocol. In: CCS 2001, pp. 28–37 (2001)

24. Petit, J., Stottelaar, B., Feiri, M., Kargl, F.: Remote attacks on automated vehicles sensors: experiments on camera and liDAR. In: Black Hat Europe, November 2015

25. Reyzin, L., Reyzin, N.: Better than BiBa: short one-time signatures with fast signing and verifying. In: Batten, L., Seberry, J. (eds.) ACISP 2002. LNCS, vol. 2384, pp. 144–153. Springer, Heidelberg (2002). https://doi.org/10.1007/3-540-45450-0_11

26. Rogaway, P., Shrimpton, T.: Cryptographic hash-function basics: definitions, implications, and separations for preimage resistance, second-preimage resistance, and collision resistance. In: Roy, B., Meier, W. (eds.) FSE 2004. LNCS, vol. 3017, pp. 371–388. Springer, Heidelberg (2004). https://doi.org/10.1007/978-3-540-25937-4_24

27. Sadeghi, A.R., Wachsmann, C., Waidner, M.: Security and privacy challenges in industrial internet of things. In: DAC 2015, pp. 1–6 (2015)

28. Szydlo, M.: Merkle tree traversal in log space and time. In: Cachin, C., Camenisch, J.L. (eds.) EUROCRYPT 2004. LNCS, vol. 3027, pp. 541–554. Springer, Heidelberg (2004). https://doi.org/10.1007/978-3-540-24676-3_32

29. Yu, T., Sekar, V., Seshan, S., Agarwal, Y., Xu, C.: Handling a trillion (unfixable) flaws on a billion devices: rethinking network security for the internet-of-things. In: HotNets XIV, pp. 5:1–5:7 (2015)

DGM: A Dynamic and Revocable Group Merkle Signature

Maxime Buser[1]([⊠]), Joseph K. Liu[1], Ron Steinfeld[1], Amin Sakzad[1],
and Shi-Feng Sun[1,2]

[1] Faculty of Information Technology, Monash University, Melbourne, Australia
{maxime.buser,joseph.liu,ron.steinfeld,amin.sakzad,
shifeng.sun}@monash.edu
[2] Data61, CSIRO, Melbourne/Sydney, Australia

Abstract. Group signatures are considered as one of the most prominent cryptographic primitives to ensure privacy. In essence, group signatures ensure the authenticity of messages while the author of the message remains anonymous. In this study, we propose a dynamic post-quantum group signature (GS) extending the static G-Merkle group signature (PQCRYPTO 2018). In particular, our dynamic G-Merkle (DGM) allows new users to join the group at any time. Similar to G-Merkle scheme, our DGM only involves symmetric primitives and makes use of a One-Time Signature scheme (OTS). Each member of the group receives a certain amount of OTS key pairs and can ask the Manager $\mathcal{M}$ for more if needed. Our DGM also provides an innovative way of signing revocation by employing Symmetric Puncturable Encryption (SPE) recently appeared in (ACM CCS 2018). DGM provides a significantly smaller signature size than other GSs based on symmetric primitives and also reduces the influence of the number of group members on the signature size and on the limitations of the application of G-Merkle.

Keywords: Group signature · Symmetric cryptography ·
Post-quantum cryptography · Hash-based signature

1 Introduction

Group signature (GS) schemes firstly introduced in 1991 by Chaum and van Heyst [10], have attracted a considerable research attention due their promise to allow members of a group to anonymously sign a digital message on behalf of the whole group. A manager is responsible for the good functioning of the group. The literature defines two main different types of GS: static and dynamic. By a statics GS, we mean that the members are fixed after the setup phase, while the dynamic configuration allows new members to join the group even after the setup phase is completed. Moreover, GS can provide revocation, which basically means that the manager could revoke the ability of signing a message by a group member.

© Springer Nature Switzerland AG 2019
K. Sako et al. (Eds.): ESORICS 2019, LNCS 11735, pp. 194–214, 2019.
https://doi.org/10.1007/978-3-030-29959-0_10

Another area which is currently receiving a great research attention is the post-quantum security given, among others, the launch of the NIST project [1]. By definition, a scheme offers post-quantum security if it is secured against an adversary who has access to a quantum computer.

Thanks to the relevance of both above-mentioned areas, the research interest for designing GS schemes achieving post-quantum security is increasing. However, in their goal of creating post-quantum GS, researchers face several challenges. This includes achieving (practical and) acceptable post-quantum signature sizes and providing dynamicity. When it comes to post-quantum security, lattice-based cryptography is commonly used. However, there exists other approaches like the code-based cryptography, or the use supersingular isogenies. In this work, we achieve post-quantum security by using symmetric primitives as in [6,9]. Our construction contributes to complete the actual lack of research, that is providing dynamicity and revocation to efficient post-quantum group signatures based on symmetric primitives only. One of the main issues of the previous post-quantum symmetric solutions is in fact the size of the generated signatures. Since the standard symmetric cryptographic algorithms like AES or SHA are efficient and short, our DGM design and algorithms will also be simple and efficient and signature sizes will be short compared to other GS based on symmetric primitives.

1.1 Contributions

In this paper, we introduce a dynamic post-quantum group signature using only symmetric primitives like hash functions and block ciphers. Our starting point is the static GS G-Merkle, designed by El Bansarkhani and Misoczki [11]. Our specific contributions are listed below:

- **Introducing DGM:** We propose a dynamic G-Merkle (DGM) GS and solve the problem of G-Merkle to deal with large group by using multiple parallel Merkle trees (Sects. 4 and 5) (See Fig. 3). Moreover, our extension assures that each correctly generated signature will go through the verification process. This is in contrast to dynamic GS of [6], in which a signature will be rejected if a new member has joined the group after the last update of parameters with the manager (Sect. 5).
- **Competitive signature size:** Our DGM signatures are significantly shorter (in term of size) than other dynamic GSs based on symmetric primitives. Moreover, the influence of the number of group members on the size (length) of the signature is diminished comparing to G-Merkle. All these have also been verified by numerical results derived from GS application (See Tables 1 and 3).
- **Innovative revocation process:** We also propose an innovative way of revoking the ability to sign of a misbehaved group member with the use of symmetric puncturable encryption (See Sect. 4.2).

Table 1 compares DGM with other Post-Quantum GS schemes and their functionalities. It shows that more than providing dynamicity and revocation, DGM's

Table 1. Comparison of different GSs and their functionalities for $N = 2^l$ being the number of group members, B be the number of OTS keys per member, λ be the security parameters, and rvk be the number of revoked OTS keys.

GS	Sig. size	Group PK size	Dynamicity	Revocation
Laguillaumie et al. [20]	$\mathcal{O}(\lambda^2 \cdot \log N)$	$\mathcal{O}(\lambda^2 \cdot \log N)$	Yes	No
Gordon et al. [15]	$\mathcal{O}(\lambda^2 \cdot N)$	$\mathcal{O}(\lambda^2 \cdot N)$	No	No
Katz et al. [19]	$\mathcal{O}(\lambda \cdot \log N)$	$\mathcal{O}(\lambda)$	No	No
Boneh et al. [6]	$\mathcal{O}(\lambda \cdot \log N)$	$\mathcal{O}(\lambda)$	Yes	Yes
G-Merkle [11]	$\mathcal{O}(\log(N \cdot B))$	$\mathcal{O}(\lambda)$	No	No
Ling et al. [26]	$\mathcal{O}(\lambda)$	$\mathcal{O}(\lambda)$	Yes	No
DGM	$\mathcal{O}(\lambda)$	$\mathcal{O}(\lambda \cdot \text{rvk})$	Yes	Yes

main advantage is to remove the dependency of the signature size on number of group members N. Indeed, the size of the group signature is set during the setup phase and will remain unchanged afterwards.

1.2 Related Works

Chaum et al. [10] were the firsts to theorize the concept of anonymously signing on behalf of a group. However, the most commonly used definition for dynamic GS is the one presented by Bellare et al. in [5]. In the field of post-quantum security, the first hash-based signature scheme designed are one-time signature schemes (OTS) presented in [21], or more recently in [17]. The work of [28] transformed OTS to a multi-signature scheme thanks to a Merkle tree. However, the weakness with the Merkle signature is that the number of possible signatures is fixed after setup phase. Therefore, Chalkias et al. [8] proposed to add a fall back mechanism along with the Merkle tree to add more flexibility. Even if there exist hash-based signatures, when it comes to design post-quantum GS, most researchers choose lattice-based cryptography rather than using symmetric primitives. The works of Libert et al. [22,23], Gordon et al. [15], and Ling et al. [24,25] demonstrate this trend.

Nevertheless, the construction of the Zero-Knowledge proof [14] ZKBoo [13], constructed only with symmetric primitives, shows that symmetric primitive can also be used to design post-quantum signature and group signature. ZKBoo uses the concept presented by Ishai et al, namely the "MPC in the head" [18]. From this, one can achieve new optimized Zero-Knowledge proofs such as [2,9] or [19]. The state-of-the-art post-quantum signatures based on symmetric primitives are constructed by Chase et al., who built digital signature schemes by designing ZKB++ [9], an optimization of ZKBoo. Alongside ZKB++, either Fiat-Shamir Transform [12] or Unruh Transform [30] were employed to construct an Non-Interactive Zero-Knowledge proof (NIZK) [3].

A dynamic GS constructed with symmetric primitives is proposed first by Boneh et al. [6]. Recently, a new draft of post-quantum GS has been proposed by

Katz et al. [19], with an optimized NIZK based on symmetric primitives and "MPC in the head". El Bansarkhani and Misoczki [11] presented G-Merkle a static GS, which is basically a modification of the Merkle signature.

2 Preliminaries

This section aims to introduce all of the theoretical concepts on which our GS is constructed. We also formally define a GS in this Section. Our scheme relies on Merkle tree [28] and is based on two main symmetric primitives: hash function H and symmetric encryption SE composed by a tuple of polynomial-time algorithms SE = (SE.KeyGen, SE.Enc, SE.Dec) (See Appendix B for more details). We also use a One-Time Signature scheme OTS, that can be easily constructed by symmetric primitives, only is defined by a tuple of polynomial-time algorithms OTS = (OTS.KeyGen, OTS.Sign, OTS.Verify) (See Appendix B for details).

2.1 Puncturable Pseudorandom Function

We first introduce the syntax of a keyed puncturable Pseudorandom function (PRF) [16,29] $F : K \times X \leftarrow Y$, where K is the key space, X is the input space, and Y is to the output space. This function takes an input $x \in X$ and a key $k \in K$ and outputs $y = F(k, x)$. Furthermore, it has the following two functions

- F.Punc$(k, x) = k_x$: takes as input a PRF key $k \in K$ and an element $x \in X$, and outputs a punctured secret key $k_x \in K_p$ and
- F.Eval$(k_x, x) = y$: takes as input a punctured key $k_x \in K_p$ and an element $x \in X$, and outputs an element y, where

$$\mathsf{F.Eval}(k_{x'}, x) = \begin{cases} F(k, x) & \text{if } x \neq x' \\ \bot & \text{else.} \end{cases} \quad (1)$$

2.2 Puncturable Encryption

In this work, we use another symmetric primitive called symmetric puncturable encryption (SPE) [29]. This was used in the context of searchable encryption. The term "puncture" is used because the secret key has been revoked the ability to decrypt some ciphertext. A d-puncturable SPE with message space $\mathcal{PM}$ and tag space $\mathcal{T}$, is defined by the following four polynomial time algorithms:

- SPE.KeyGen$(1^\lambda, d) = $ SPE.msk: take as inputs a security parameter λ and a positive integer d, which indicates the maximum number of allowed punctured tags. It outputs a random secret key SPE.sk$_0$ and sets SPE.msk = (SPE.sk$_0$, d),
- SPE.Enc$(m, $ SPE.msk, $t) = $ SPE.ct: the encryption algorithm taking SPE.msk, a message m, and a tag t as inputs and outputs a ciphertext SPE.ct,
- Punc(SPE.sk$_{i-1}$, $t') = $ SPE.sk$_i$: the puncture algorithm, which takes as inputs SPE.sk$_{i-1}$ and a new tag t' and outputs a new key SPE.sk$_i$. The new SPE.sk$_i$ can decrypt every ciphertext that SPE.sk$_{i-1}$ can except the one encrypted with t', and

- SPE.Enc(SPE.ct, SPE.sk$_i$, t) = $m/\perp$: a deterministic decryption algorithm, which takes as inputs a punctured key SPE.sk$_i$, a ciphertext SPE.ct, and a tag t, and finally outputs a plaintext m.

A security model for SPE is formalized in [29], however, we only use the correctness of SPE in our setting with a security parameters λ, which is defined as:

$$\Pr[\text{SPE.Dec}(\text{SPE.Enc}(\text{SPE.msk}, m, t), \text{SPE.sk}_i, t) = m] = 1. \tag{2}$$

where $t \in T \setminus T_i$, where $T_i = \{t_1, t_2, \ldots, t_n\}$ is an arbitrary set of distinct tags punctured at SPE.sk$_i$.

2.3 Group Signature (GS)

A GS is composed of three different identities/parties:

- Manager $\mathcal{M}$: the central authority of group responsible for the perfect functioning of the group, allows new members to join the group, can reveal the identity of a signer, and can revoke the ability to sign to a misbehaved member.
- Member: one of the identities/users of the group, who can anonymously generate a signature, and
- Verifier: is an outsider (which can be a member or manager of the group as well), who can only verify the validity of a group signature using public parameters.

Our definition of a dynamic GS (DGS) is based on, [5–7]. A DGS is specified by the following polynomial time algorithms:

- DGS.Setup(1^λ, DGS.set) = (DGS.param, DGS.msk): The manager $\mathcal{M}$ on input of the security parameter λ and setup parameters DGS.set executes this algorithm and outputs the public parameters DGS.param and the manager's secret key DGS.msk.
- DGS.Join: This is an interactive process that takes place between $\mathcal{M}$ and an individual user id$_\mathcal{U}$, who desires to join the group. Similar to [7], we assume that all interactions between parties take place over a secure channel.
- DGS.Sign(m, param$_{\text{id}_\mathcal{U}}$) = DGS.σ: This algorithm is run by the member id$_\mathcal{U}$ with its private parameters param$_{\text{id}_\mathcal{U}}$ and outputs a valid anonymous signature DGS.σ.
- DGS.Verify(m, DGS.σ, DGS.param) = 0/1: is a deterministic algorithm that checks the validity of the signature. It outputs 1 if the signature is a valid signing of m and 0 otherwise.
- DGS.Open(DGS.σ, DGS.msk) = id$_\mathcal{U}$: is an algorithm ran by $\mathcal{M}$ to reveal the identity of the signer of DGS.σ.
- DGS.Revoke(id$_\mathcal{U}$) = DGS.param: is an algorithm that updates the public parameters DGS.param based on the misbehaved group member id$_\mathcal{U}$. It revokes the ability of user id$_\mathcal{U}$ to generate valid signature.

A DGS achieves the following security requirements:

Definition 1 *(Correctness). Let* DGS.σ *be a signature produced by an honest member* id$_\mathcal{U}$ *of* DGS *and message* m. *This* DGS *achieves correctness if and only if*

$$\Pr[\mathsf{DGS.Verify}(m, \mathsf{DGS}.\sigma, \mathsf{DGS.param}) = 0] < negl(\lambda). \tag{3}$$

Definition 2 *(Unforgeability) [6]. A* DGS *achieves unforgeability if an adversary cannot construct a valid signature* DGS.σ' *which can be linked to an honest member* id$_\mathcal{U}$. *A* DGS *achieves unforgeability if and only if for a security parameter* λ *the advantage* $\mathbf{Adv}_\mathcal{A}^{Forge}$ *of an adversary* $\mathcal{A}$ *is*

$$\mathbf{Adv}_\mathcal{A}^{Forge} = \Pr[\boldsymbol{Exp}_{\mathcal{A},\mathsf{DGS}}^{Forge}(\lambda) = 1] < negl(\lambda), \tag{4}$$

where $\boldsymbol{Exp}_{\mathcal{A},\mathsf{DGS}}^{Forge}(\lambda)$ *is defined in Appendix A.*

Definition 3 *(Anonymity) [7]. A* DGS *achieves anonymity if and only if the signature does not reveal the identity of the signer. A* DGS *achieves anonymity if and only if for a security parameter* λ *the advantage* $\mathbf{Adv}_\mathcal{A}^{Anon}$ *of an adversary* $\mathcal{A}$ *is*

$$\mathbf{Adv}_\mathcal{A}^{Anon} = |\Pr[\boldsymbol{Exp}_{\mathcal{A},\mathsf{DGS}}^{Anon-0}(\lambda) = 1] - \Pr[\boldsymbol{Exp}_{\mathcal{A},\mathsf{DGS}}^{Anon-1}(\lambda) = 1]| < negl(\lambda), \tag{5}$$

where $\boldsymbol{Exp}_{\mathcal{A},\mathsf{DGS}}^{Anon-b}(\lambda)$ *is defined in Appendix A.*

Definition 4 *(Traceability) [4]. A* DGS *achieves traceability if and only if no adversary can generate a valid signature* DGS.σ *which cannot be associated with an active member of the group, so* DGS.Open(DGS.σ, DGS.msk) $= 0$. *A* DGS *achieves traceability if and only if for a security parameter* λ *the advantage* $\mathbf{Adv}_\mathcal{A}^{Trace}$ *of an adversary* $\mathcal{A}$ *is*

$$\mathbf{Adv}_\mathcal{A}^{Trace} = \Pr[\boldsymbol{Exp}_{\mathcal{A},\mathsf{DGS}}^{Trace}(\lambda) = 1] < negl(\lambda), \tag{6}$$

where $\boldsymbol{Exp}_{\mathcal{A},\mathsf{DGS}}^{Trace}(\lambda)$ *is defined in Appendix A.*

3   G-Merkle (GM) [11]

G-Merkel (GM) is a post-quantum GS constructed from symmetric primitives and based on the idea of the Merkle signature [28]. GM uses a hash function H, an OTS scheme, and a symmetric encryption scheme SE. In the following, we give an overview of such a scheme.

GM Overview: The manager $\mathcal{M}$ has the responsibility for a group of N users, and each user will be allowed to sign B messages. This means that each user possesses B OTS key pairs. Therefore, the group public key GM.gpk will be the Merkle root of the tree generated over $B \cdot N$ leaves where each leaf is an OTS public key. Each leaf is labelled from 1 to $B \cdot N$ and the i-th member will receive the OTS keys corresponding to leaves $\{B \cdot (i-1) + 1, \ldots, B \cdot i\}$. Similar to traditional Merkle signature, a signature is composed of an OTS signature and the path from OTS.pk to GM.gpk. However, in order to ensure user anonymity, $\mathcal{M}$ "Shuffles" the set of leaves L. During the "Shuffle" process, the set L is composed of tuples $\{(\mathsf{OTS.pk}_1, \mathsf{GM.pos}_1), \ldots, (\mathsf{OTS.pk}_{B \cdot N}, \mathsf{GM.pos}_{B \cdot N})\}$, where $\mathsf{GM.pos}_i = \mathsf{SE.Enc}(i, \mathsf{GM.msk})$ and GM.msk is the $\mathcal{M}$'s secret key. The "Shuffle" procedure ends by ordering the set L according to GM.pos. Another modification of the first layer of nodes is then built by not only including the leaves in the hashes, but also the encrypted values of the respective leaves, e.g. $H(\mathsf{OTS.pk}_i || \mathsf{GM.pos}_i)$ (see Fig. 1). Finally, $\mathcal{M}$ generates the Merkle tree which gives GM.gpk. The "Shuffle" process prevents an adversary from identifying sub-tree and hence guessing the identity of the signer. Figure 1 shows the GM tree structure for $N = 2$ and $B = 2$, where $\mathsf{GM.pos}_3 \leq \mathsf{GM.pos}_2 \leq \mathsf{GM.pos}_4 \leq \mathsf{GM.pos}_1$.

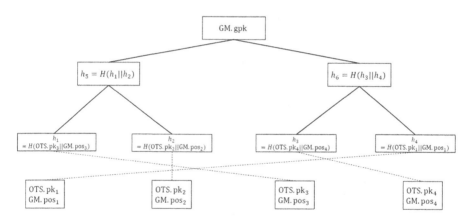

Fig. 1. G-Merkle: tree structure

GM Limitations: The lack of flexibility of GM appears to be its main limitation. Undeniably, GM is reserved for static groups because the maximum number of available OTS key pairs will be fixed, and so will the number of members after the setup phase. We address this issue by introducing DGM as follows. Another issue of GM, already mentioned in [6], is the lack of efficiency in the setup process for large groups, which limits its application in practical scenarios. We further demonstrate that our DGM solves this lack of efficiency in GM with respect to time taken to perform the setup phase (see Fig. 3).

4   DGM

This section aims to present our GS and starts with an overview of DGM by highlighting the differences with GM. Then, we will present the construction of DGM explicitly. DGM is constructed with a hash-based OTS scheme OTS, a symmetric encryption SE, a symmetric puncturable encryption SPE, and a hash function H. It follows the definition of dynamic GS presented in Sect. 2.3.

4.1   DGM Overview

DGM is a dynamic extension of GM by allowing new members to join the group after the setup phase. Contrary to GM, DGM members are not limited to have only B OTS key pairs and therefore to generate B signatures. Indeed, when a member is running out of OTS key pairs he can request new ones from the manager $\mathcal{M}$.

Two Types of Merkle Tree: To achieve dynamicity, we change the tree structure (See Fig. 2). Indeed, DGM distinguishes two types of Merkle trees. There is a unique Merkle tree named *Initial Merkle tree* (IMT), which is generated during the setup phase. The IMT is generated on randomly choosing leaves and its Merkle root is the group public key DGM.gpk. An example of an IMT is shown in Fig. 2, where the elements l_1 to l_8 are randomly chosen strings. The second type of Merkle trees are the *Signing Merkle Tree* (SMT). Those trees are parallel trees to IMT and linked with an internal node of IMT called "fallback node" and denoted with Fn. The link between a SMT and the IMT is created with Fn and a "fallback key" Fk. After the generation of a SMT, Fk is computed

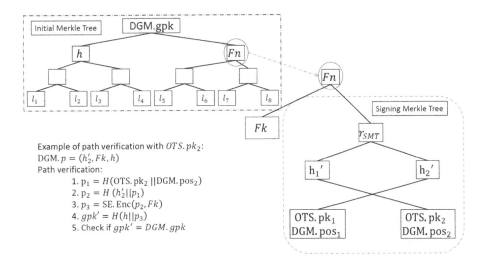

Fig. 2. DGM Merkle trees example

as $\mathsf{SE.Dec}(Fn, r_{SMT}) = Fk$, where r_{SMT} is the root of the SMT. Therefore, for the path verification from an OTS key to $\mathsf{DGM.gpk}$, $\mathsf{SE.Enc}(Fk, r_{SMT}) = Fn$ should be computed. SMTs are generated when a group member requests new OTS key pairs and constructed in a similar manner to GM tree. Their leaves are kept secret to hide the time of the generation. Each of its leaves have an index $\mathsf{DGM.i} = (t, l)$, where t is the SMT number and l is the leaf number. DGM "Shuffles" the leaves with a symmetric encryption scheme. All leaves of the SMT are sorted by $\mathsf{DGM.pos}$, where $\mathsf{DGM.pos} = \mathsf{SE.Enc}(\mathsf{DGM.i}, \mathsf{DGM.msk})$. In Fig. 2, we have $\mathsf{DGM.pos}_2 < \mathsf{DGM.pos}_1$.

Join and Request OTS Keys: DGM separates the join process from the request of OTS keys. A prospective user needs to first join the group and then it will have the possibility to request OTS keys. The request for new OTS keys is a subroutine (See Algorithms 1 and 2) of the signing algorithms which is executed when the signer does not have an available an OTS key pair. When $\mathcal{M}$ receives a request for a new OTS keys, she selects randomly an internal IMT node n_i. If n_i is a fallback node, then it takes the next available key pair of the corresponding SMT. Otherwise, she needs to generate a new SMT. All trees are generated by $\mathcal{M}$, who owns the manager secret key $\mathsf{DGM.msk}$ owns and her private parameters $\mathsf{DGM.param}$ composed of all private lists. When the SMT associated with n_i has used all its leafs, n_i is not considered as a fallback node. A new SMT will be generated when n_i will be selected.

The DGM Signature $\mathsf{DGM.}\sigma$: The format of $\mathsf{DGM.}\sigma$ is identical to GM. Therefore, $\mathsf{DGM.}\sigma = (m, \mathsf{OTS.}\sigma, \mathsf{OTS.pk}, \mathsf{DGM.pos}, \mathsf{DGM.p})$, where $\mathsf{OTS.}\sigma$ is the OTS signature of the message m, which can be verified with $\mathsf{OTS.pk}$. $\mathsf{DGM.pos}$ is the corresponding position of $\mathsf{OTS.pk}$ in the tree and $\mathsf{DGM.p}$ is the path from the $\mathsf{OTS.pk}$ to $\mathsf{DGM.gpk}$. The only difference between $\mathsf{DGM.}\sigma$ and $\mathsf{GM.}\sigma$ is the fallback key Fk, which is an element of the path. In order to verify the path, the verifier needs to use $\mathsf{SE.Enc}$ instead of H and also verify the validity of Fk with $\mathcal{M}$, because SE does not provide collision resistance. An example of path verification is illustrated in the Fig. 2.

Revocation Using SPE: DGM provides an innovative way of revoking the ability to a group member to sign. The $\mathsf{DGM.pos}$ is an element of the signature specific to a member allowing $\mathcal{M}$ to perform such a task. To revoke a member $\mathsf{id}_{\mathcal{U}}$, $\mathcal{M}$ will first generate a new $\mathsf{DGM.rvk}_0 = \mathsf{SPE.msk}$, then she will puncture the key with every $\mathsf{DGM.pos}$ of all revoked members producing the punctured key $\mathsf{DGM.rvk}_1 = \mathsf{SPE.sk}$. During the verification, the verifier runs $\mathsf{SPE.Dec}(\mathsf{SPE.Enc}(m, \mathsf{DGM.rvk}_0, \mathsf{DGM.pos}), \mathsf{DGM.rvk}_1, \mathsf{DGM.pos})$ (line 1 of $\mathsf{DGM.Verify}$ in Algorithm 1) and if it outputs something rather than m, then it means that by the correctness of SPE (See Sect. 2.2), that $\mathsf{DGM.pos}$ has been punctured so the signer has been revoked. SPE offers a revocation alternative compared to the traditional use of lists. Previously, the only way to revoke members for GS constructed with symmetric primitives was the use of lists. For example, Boneh et al. [6] used two lists, one of revoked signature and another with the secret key of revoked members, which leads to their identities. In contrary to their work, DGM preserves anonymity of revoked members (See Sect. 4.3). Furthermore, it allows the verifier to work with only the signature and $\mathcal{M}$'s public parameter to perform and check the revocation.

4.2 Detailed DGM Construction

Our GS follows the definition presented in Sect. 2.2. The main parameters are summarized in the Table 2. All algorithms are presented in Algorithm 1. The parts in Algorithm 1 highlighted in red are the ones which differ from GM [11]. In the following, we describe each algorithm in more details:

DGM.Setup(1^λ, DGM.set) = (DGM.param, DGM.msk): For the DGM setup algorithm the setup parameters are DGM.set = h_{IMT}. It outputs the public parameters DGM.param meaning the group public key DGM.gpk and the manager secret key DGM.msk. It also initializes all M's private list $\mathcal{M}$.param =(**OTS**, **FN**, **FK**, **members**). The algorithm generates $2^{h_{\mathsf{IMT}}}$ random leaves and then constructs IMT. Figure 2 shows an example with the parameter $h_{\mathsf{IMT}} = 3$.

DGM.Join: This interactive protocol is taking place between $\mathcal{M}$ and a prospective member $\mathsf{id}_{\mathcal{U}}$. $\mathcal{M}$ will add $\mathsf{id}_{\mathcal{U}}$ to **members** and $\mathsf{id}_{\mathcal{U}}$ stores the challenges

Table 2. DGM parameters summary

IMT	Initial Merkle tree
SMT_t	t-th Signing Merkle tree
DGM.msk	Manager's secret key
DGM.rvk	The public revocation key, which is equal to $(\mathrm{DGM.rvk}_0 = \mathrm{SPE.msk}, \mathrm{DGM.rvk}_1 = \mathrm{SPE.sk}_{rvks})$
DGM.param	Group public parameters composed of DGM.gpk and DGM.rvk
$\mathrm{DGM.pos}_i$	SE.Enc(DGM.i, DGM.msk)
DGM.i	Tuple (t, i) denoting the i-th OTS key of the t-th SMT
members	List of members composed of all identities with their associated DGM.i
OTS	List of non-assigned OTS keys
FK	List of fallback keys
FN	List of fallback nodes
$\mathcal{M}$.param	The $\mathcal{M}$'s private lists, (**OTS**, **FN**, **FK**, **members**)
h_{IMT}	The height of IMT
$\mathrm{param}_{\mathsf{id}_{\mathcal{U}}}$	The private parameters of $\mathsf{id}_{\mathcal{U}}$ including its OTS **keys** and a variable $state$
$rvks$	Total number of revoked OTS keys
$n_i.level$	Level of the fallback node n_i in IMT, for example the node FN in Fig. 2 is $Fn.level = 1$ and DGM.gpk is at level 0

sent by $\mathcal{M}$. The user uses these to prove its own identity when requesting OTS keys. During this process, $\mathrm{id}_{\mathcal{U}}$ will receive a challenge c which will be used for the request of new OTS key pairs.

$\mathsf{DGM.Sign}(m, \mathsf{param}_{\mathrm{id}_{\mathcal{U}}}) = \mathsf{DGM}.\sigma$: The signing algorithm is similar as in GM [11], it takes as input the message m and the private parameters $\mathsf{param}_{\mathrm{id}_{\mathcal{U}}}$ of the user SE.Enc composed of a private list of OTS key pairs and an integer $state$ which protects $\mathrm{id}_{\mathcal{U}}$ to use twice the same OTS key pair. The difference with GM [11] is the subroutine named $\mathsf{DGM.OTSRequest}$ (See Algorithm2) and that is executed if $\mathrm{id}_{\mathcal{U}}$ needs new OTS keys.

Algorithm 1 DGM algorithms

DGM.Setup
Input: λ, DGM.set
Output: DGM.param, DGM.msk
1: DGM.msk = SE.KeyGen(1^λ)
2: Initialize **FK**, **FN**, **members**, **OTS**.
3: Generate of a set $2^{h_{\mathrm{IMT}}}$ (element l_1 to l_8 in Fig. 2) of random leaves of size λ. Generate IMT where the Merkle root is the group public key DGM.gpk
4: **return** DGM.param, DGM.msk

DGM.Join
1: $\mathrm{id}_{\mathcal{U}}$ sends a request to join the group
2: $\mathcal{M}$ generates a challenge $c \in \{0,1\}^\lambda$ sends it to $\mathrm{id}_{\mathcal{U}}$
3: $\mathrm{id}_{\mathcal{U}}$ stores c
4: $\mathcal{M}$ adds $\mathrm{id}_{\mathcal{U}}$ to the list **members**

DGM.Sign
Input: m, $\mathsf{param}_{\mathrm{id}_{\mathcal{U}}}$
Output: DGM.σ
1: **if** $\mathrm{id}_{\mathcal{U}}$ has no OTS key available **then**
2:    DGM.OTSRequest (Algorithm 2)
3: **end if**
4: OTS.σ = OTS.Sign(m, OTS.priv$_{state}$).
5: Construct the signature DGM.σ = (m, OTS.σ, OTS.pk$_{state}$, DGM.pos, DGM.p)
6: $state = state + 1$
7: **return** DGM.σ

DGM.Verify
Input: m, DGM.σ, DGM.param
Output: 0/1
1: **if** SPE.Dec(SPE.Enc(m, DGM.rvk$_0$, DGM.pos),

DGM.rvk$_1$, DGM.pos) $= \perp$ **then**
2:    **return** 0
3: **end if**
4: **if** OTS.Verify(m, OTS.σ, OTS.pk) $= 0$ **then**
5:    **return** 0
6: **end if**
7: Verify the path DGM.p starting with H(OTS.pk$\|$DGM.pos). (See Fig. 2)
8: **if** $gpk' \neq$ DGM.gpk **then**
9:    **return** 0
10: **end if**
11: verification of validity of Fk with $\mathcal{M}$
12: **return** 1

DGM.Open
Input: DGM.σ, DGM.msk
Output: $\mathrm{id}_{\mathcal{U}}$
1: DGM.i = SE.Dec(DGM.pos, DGM.msk)
2: **return** $\mathrm{id}_{\mathcal{U}}$ from **members** corresponding to DGM.i

DGM.Revoke
Require: $\mathrm{id}_{\mathcal{U}}$
Ensure: DGM.param
1: $rvks = rvks+$ number of DGM.pos associated with $\mathrm{id}_{\mathcal{U}}$
2: DGM.rvk$_0$ = SPE.KeyGen(1^λ, $rvks$)
3: **for** 1 to $rvks$ **do**
4:    rvk_i = SPE.Punc(rvk_{i-1}, DGM.pos$_i$)
      // Puncture of all DGM.poss belonging to revoked members
5: **end for**
6: DGM.rvk$_1$ = rvk_i
7: **return** DGM.param

DGM.OTSRequest is interactive protocol takes place over a secure channel between a group member $id_\mathcal{U}$ who desires B new OTS key pairs and $\mathcal{M}$. When receiving request for new OTS key pairs, $\mathcal{M}$ will call the procedure DGM.Update which will assign B new OTS key to $id_\mathcal{U}$. From already generated SMT or from newly generated SMT ones. The detail of DGM.Update procedure is presented in Algorithm 2, where the part written in blue is the "Shuffle" process similar to GM [11] (See Sect. 3). As an example, in Fig. 2, if the node Fn is selected at step 2 and the first OTS key pair have already been assigned, the second OTS key pair will be assigned to the members, if she is not the second leaf of the tree because of the "Shuffle" process. If another node is selected, we need to generate a new SMT.

DGM.Verify$(m, DGM.\sigma, \mathcal{M}.param) = 0/1$: This deterministic verification algorithm is very similar to the one from GM. The first difference is the path verification (See Fig. 2). The second is the interaction between $\mathcal{M}$ and the verifier, to assure the validity of Fk in the path and the last one is the execution of SPE.Enc and SPE.Dec procedures to verify that the signer was not revoked. The DGM.pos of all revoked signatures have been used to generate a new punctured key such that DGM.Enc will not output a valid plaintext if DGM.pos has been punctured.

Algorithm 2 DGM subroutines

DGM.OTSRequest
1: $id_\mathcal{U}$ generates $n = H(B||c)$.
2: $id_\mathcal{U}$ sends (B, n) to $\mathcal{M}$
3: $\mathcal{M}$ verifies the validity of n
4: If the verification succeeds, then $\mathcal{M}$ runs the Update$(B, id_\mathcal{U})$ subroutine resolving new assigned OTS keys OTS.Keys to $id_\mathcal{U}$ and updated $\mathcal{M}.param$.
5: $\mathcal{M}$ sends the OTS.Keys to $id_\mathcal{U}$ and stores all indexes of the OTS.Keys in the list **members** at the entry $id_\mathcal{U}$.

DGM.Update
Input: $B, id_\mathcal{U}$
Output: Updated $\mathcal{M}.param$
1: Select B random internal Nodes n_i of IMT
2: **for** $i = 1$ to B **do**
3:    **if** $n_i \in$ **FN then**
4:       Assign the next available leaf to $id_\mathcal{U}$ of the corresponding SMT associated with n_i
5:       **if** n_i has no leaf left **then**

6:       Remove n_i from **FN**
7:    **end if**
8:   **else**
9:     Create a new SMT t for n_i
10:     $newOTS = 2^{h_{IMT} - n_i.level - 1}$
11:     **for** $i = 1$ to $newOTS$ **do**
12:       $(OTS.pk_i, OTS.priv_i)$ $= OTS.KeyGen(1^\lambda)$
13:       $DGM.i = (t, i)$
14:       $l_i = (OTS.pk_i, DGM.i)$
15:     **end for**
16:     Generate Merkle tree on the shuffled *leaves* $l_1, \ldots, l_{newOTS}$ which give the Merkle root r_{SMT} (See Fig. 2)
17:     $Fk = SE.Dec(n_i, r_{SMT})$
18:     assign the first of OTS key pair to $id_\mathcal{U}$
19:     add all other OTS keys to **OTS**
20:     add Fk to **FK**
21:     add n_i to **FN**
22:   **end if**
23: **end for**

$\overline{\text{DGM.Open}(\text{DGM}.\sigma, \text{DGM.msk}) = \text{id}_\mathcal{U}}$: This algorithm executed by $\mathcal{M}$ returns the identity of a group member, who provides $\text{DGM}.\sigma$.

$\overline{\text{DGM.Revoke}(\text{id}_\mathcal{U}) = \text{DGM.param}}$: This algorithm, executed by $\mathcal{M}$, revokes the ability of a malicious member to sign a message by puncturing (See Sect. 2.2 on SPE) all DGM.poss associated with $\text{id}_\mathcal{U}$ and all previous revoked members.

4.3　Correctness and Security Analysis

DGM assumes that the manager $\mathcal{M}$ is trusted. Therefore, $\mathcal{M}$ is available, generates trees and OTS keys correctly and will not collide with the adversary. We also assume than the communications for DGM.Join and DGM.OTSRequest take place over secure channels. The adversary $\mathcal{A}$ follows the security games presented in Appendix A in the Fig. 4. She has access to private information of corrupted members and to the private list **members**. DGM achieves correctness, unforgeability, anonymity and traceability (Sect. 2.3).

Theorem 1 (Correctness). *Let* DGM *be the construction provided in Algorithm 1 with a secure hash function H, an* IND − CPA *secure symmetric encryption* SE, *a secure* OTS *scheme, and a secure symmetric puncturable encryption* SPE. DGM *achieves correctness in Definition 1.*

Proof. The correctness of DGM is ensued from the correctness of its underlying primitives H, SE and SPE.　　　　　　　　　　　　　　　　　　　　　　　□

Theorem 2 (Unforgeability). *Let* DGM *be the construction provided in Algorithm 1 with a secure hash function H, a* IND − CPA *secure symmetric encryption* SE, *a secure* OTS *scheme, and a secure symmetric puncturable encryption* SPE. DGM *achieves unforgeability based on Definition 2.*

Proof. To forge a signature, $\mathcal{A}$ (Fig. 4) needs to have a valid path from OTS.pk to DGM.gpk by the properties of a collision-resistant hash function, it is computationally not feasible instead knowing every single element of DGM.p and the DGM.pos of OTS.pk in the tree. The first possibility consists of $\mathcal{A}$ taking a valid path of a corrupted member and trying to find DGM.pos′ associated with a non-corrupted member such that $H(\text{OTS.pk}′||\text{DGM.pos}′) = H(\text{OTS.pk}||\text{DGM.pos})$. By the collision resistance property of H, it is not computationally feasible (See Appendix B). If $\mathcal{A}$ has access to a valid OTS.pk, she needs to recover OTS.priv to generate a valid OTS.σ and thanks to the security property of OTS, it not feasible. Therefore the probability of forging a signature is negligible as $\Pr[\text{DGM.Verify}(m, \text{DGM}.\sigma′, \text{DGM.param}) = 1] < \text{negl}(\lambda)$. Another possibility for $\mathcal{A}$ is to create her own path to DGM.gpk by generating her own Fk. However, because of the assumption that $\mathcal{M}$ is trusted, the Fk verification will not pass. Moreover, if she uses the parameters of corrupted members, DGM.Verify would still reject DGM.$\sigma′$ because we assumed that $\mathcal{M}$ is trusted and works correctly. Therefore, all DGM.poss of corrupted member has been punctured. Thanks to the correctness of SPE (See Sect. 2.2), the execution of DGM.Verify outputs 0 (see line 1 of Algorithm 1).　　　　　　　　　　　　　　　　　　　□

Theorem 3 (Anonymity). *Let* DGM *be the construction provided in Algorithm 1 with a secure hash function* H, *an* IND $-$ CPA *secure symmetric encryption* SE, *a secure* OTS *scheme, and a secure symmetric puncturable encryption* SPE. DGM *achieves anonymity based on Definition 3.*

Proof. $\mathcal{A}$ (see Fig. 4) has access to all OTS key pairs and paths except for two pairs of two different non-corrupted members and the private lists of $\mathcal{M}$. Therefore, when calling the challenge, she knows the index associated with the non-corrupted members. The only element of the signature DGM.σ, which reveals information about the identity of the signer is DGM.pos, which corresponds to SE.Enc(DGM.i, DGM.msk). Thanks to the IND $-$ CPA security (See Appendix B) of SE, $\mathcal{A}$ can only guess the identity if she breaks the scheme SE. Therefore, if we assume that SE is secure and that $\mathcal{M}$ does not reveal DGM.msk, then $\mathcal{A}$ can not distinguish between associated DGM.pos$'$ with the ones from the member. Moreover, to insure anonymity the trusted $\mathcal{M}$ has to keep secret the list of **FN** and **FK** to not give precisely the apparition time of new Fks which could lead to leak some information on the call DGM.OTSRequest of a member id$_\mathcal{U}$. This secrecy added with the "Shuffle" process hide the creation of a new SMT. Moreover, revoked members preserved their anonymity because the revocation process works on the DGM.pos elements of revoked members. In this framework, $\mathcal{A}$ cannot find the identity of the revoked users due to the security of SE scheme. □

Theorem 4. (Traceability). *Let* DGM *be the construction provided in Algorithm 1 with a secure hash function* H, *an* IND $-$ CPA *secure symmetric encryption* SE, *a secure* OTS *scheme, and a secure symmetric puncturable encryption* SPE. DGM *achieves traceability based on Definition 4.*

Proof. $\mathcal{A}$ (see Fig. 4) needs to construct a valid signature which cannot be attributed to any members. Therefore, she needs to change DGM.pos in DGM.σ. As $\mathcal{A}$ can corrupt members, she has access to private parameters of corrupted members, hence she knows the valid path to DGM.gpk. The needs to generate a valid OTS signature first, which can be successfully done by using an OTS key pair of corrupted members. Secondly, she needs to change the variable DGM.pos associated with the OTS key pair that she used to sign the message m by a random element DGM.pos$'$, such that $H(\text{OTS.pk}\|\text{DGM.pos}) = H(\text{OTS.pk}\|\text{DGM.pos}')$ However, because of the collision resistance property of H (see Appendix B) it is not computationally feasible. Therefore, the probability that $Pr[\text{DGM.Verify}(m, \text{DGM}.\sigma, \text{DGM.param}) = 1] < negl(\lambda)$ with DGM.σ, $= (\text{OTS}.\sigma, \text{OTS.pk}, \text{DGM.p}, \text{DGM.pos}')$. □

5   Evaluation

In this section, we compare the performance of different phases of our DGM algorithm. We also evaluate the numerical performance of our DGM setup algorithm DGM.Setup and show its advantage compared to GM.Setup.

Table 3. Signature size comparison.

GS	Signature size (KB)	Max message size (KB)
Boneh et al. [6]	1331	-
Katz et al. [19]	315	-
DGM[a]	2.72	5.03
DGM[b]	9.54	2.51

[a]SHA-256, AES-256, W-OTS, message size = 256 bits
[b]SHA3-512, AES-512, W-OTS, message size = 512 bits

DGM.σ's size: The main advantage of DGM is its constant signature size (with respect to the number of group members N) compared to the current state of art. Table 1 demonstrates this trend. Although, Ling et al. [26] proposed a lattice-based GS with a signature size independent of the number of group members, they have not explored the applicability of their results. A weakness of our scheme is the size of the public parameters, which are increasing when members are revoked, because the size of DGM.rvk increases after each revocation if we use the SPE proposed in [29]. Moreover, in terms of practical application, we also compare our scheme with the GS provided in [19], which has the current dynamic GS benchmark with symmetric primitives. Although the GS given by Katz et al. [19] does not explicitly provide a dynamic GS, their construction is similar to the Boneh et al. [6] GS, so it could be considered as a dynamic GS. The smallest signature size provided by Katz et al. is 315KB for a group of 2^7 members. The size $|DGM.\sigma|$ of DGM.σ is $|OTS.\sigma| + |OTS.pk| + |H| \cdot h_{IMT} + |DGM.pos|$. Using all symmetric standard and we set $h_{IMT} = 20$, which is the maximum applicable h_{IMT} size. Table 3 compares signature sizes of two different instances of DGM, achieving different levels of security, with those GS from [6,19]. It shows that our instance approximately achieves a signature size 115 times smaller than Katz et al. GS [19]. The third column presents the maximum message size for which our DGM.σ can achieve a smaller signature size compared to those in [19].

DGM Signature Verification: Another advantage of our scheme is that a valid signature will remain valid during the whole life of the group. In DGM, DGM.gpk and the element DGM.p of a signature allow a member to prove its membership, although other schemes work with accumulators to prove membership in a group [6]. To sign, a member has to be updated about the state of accumulators in order to generate a valid membership proof in the signature. Nevertheless, when a new member joins the group, the membership proof will be updated. This update has as consequence that all of the other members of the group need to update to prove their membership in their next signature. Although a member keeps updating regularly, the risk of generating a signature with a non-valid proof of membership still exists because if a new member joins between the last update and the signing time then it will have an invalid signature. This interactive process DGM.OTSRequest can be seen as an update

Table 4. Verification: DGM vs GM

	Dynamicity	Revocation
DGM overhead	Path verification (Fig. 2)	Execution of SPE.Enc
	Interaction with $\mathcal{M}$	and SPE.Dec

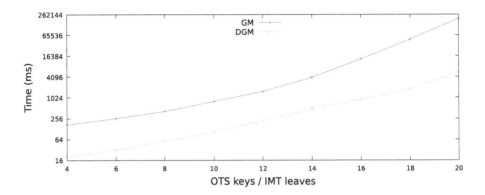

Fig. 3. Setup performance comparison: GM.Setup vs DGM.Setup

process and hence the risk of generating a signature with a non-valid DGM.p does not exist in our scheme. The reason why this risk is lifted is that the joining of new members in the group has no influence on the older members. However, the DGM verification has a major cost due to the extension (see Table 4). The dynamicity brings an interaction between $\mathcal{M}$ and the verifier, which could be an important limitation for possible application. Our futures objectives will be to suppress the interaction without jeopardizing the security of DGM. Furthermore, the use of SPE to provide revocation generates another additional cost, which we will evaluate in our futures works.

DGM Setup Phase Time: Figure 3 shows the difference in numerical performances of both setup phases of GM and DGM implemented in Java. The implementation relies on the SHA-256 as hash functions. For OTS purpose, we decided to implement W-OTS [17]. The "Shuffle" of the leaves was done with the block cipher AES and the Java Interface Comparator with the Timsort algorithm inspired from [27]. The results of our implementation are shown in Fig. 3, comparing the time (ms) needed for setup processes with different size of Merkle trees. A difference between GM and DGM is the time of OTS key pairs generation. During the setup, GM needs to generates all $N \cdot B$ OTS keys for a group of N members with B possible signature for each of the members. While DGM delays and divides the generation of the OTS keys over the time and needs only to generate IMT. Our results presented in Fig. 3 shows that this delay improves the applicability of the GS.

6   Conclusion

In this paper, we presented a dynamic post-quantum GS (called DGM), extending the static GM approach to allow new users to join the group at any time. Similar to GM, our scheme relies only on symmetric primitives. While other dynamic post-quantum groups are often criticized for generating signatures of large signature sizes, our proposal suggests that the size of a signature can be reduced by using only symmetric primitives. Moreover, our competitive signature sizes do not rely on the number of group members outperforming other state-of-the-art GSs like [19]. This can be considered as the current benchmark for application of post-quantum dynamic GS constructed with symmetric primitives. DGM also provides a new approach for signature revocation with the use of symmetric puncturable encryption (SPE). Practical analysis were conducted to show and evaluate the applicability of our constructed DGM.

A   Security Games

To prove the security of a DGS, we defined games (see Fig. 4, where unrestricted queries means that the oracle can be called multiple time). An adversary $\mathcal{A}$ can call the following oracles:

Oracles:

- $Setup(\lambda, \mathsf{DGS.set})$: runs the set up algorithm according to the parameters λ and $\mathsf{DGS.set}$.
- $Chal_b(\mathsf{id}_{\mathcal{U}}^1, \mathsf{id}_{\mathcal{U}}^2, m, \mathsf{DGS.param})$: returns the signature of $\mathsf{id}_{\mathcal{U}}^b$ for $b \in \{0, 1\}$
- $AddMember(\mathsf{id}_{\mathcal{U}})$: adds a new honest member $\mathsf{id}_{\mathcal{U}}$ to the group.
- $addCorruptMember(\mathsf{id}_{\mathcal{U}})$: creates a new corrupted member. $\mathcal{A}$ will have access to all private information of corrupted members.
- $Corrupt(\mathsf{id}_{\mathcal{U}})$: returns one OTS key pair of the non-corrupted member $\mathsf{id}_{\mathcal{U}}$.
- $Open(m, \mathsf{DGS}.\sigma)$: returns the identity of the author of $\mathsf{DGS}.\sigma$.
- $Sign(m, \mathsf{id}_{\mathcal{U}})$: returns a valid signature from the user $\mathsf{id}_{\mathcal{U}}$ for the message m.

B   Symmetric Primitives

The second part of the Appendix provides the definition of symmetric primitives used.

Hash Function: A hash function $H : \{0, 1\}^* \to \{0, 1\}^\lambda$ is a function which takes as input a message x of any length and outputs the hash value h with the length n of x. A hash function is characterized by three properties:

- One-wayness: A function is one way if and only if knowing a hash value h is unfeasible in polynomial time to find x such that $h = H(x)$.

$\mathbf{Exp}_{\mathcal{A},\mathsf{DGS}}^{Forge}(\lambda):$

- $Setup(\lambda, \mathsf{DGS}.\mathsf{set})$
- Unrestricted Queries:
  - $AddMember(\mathsf{id}_\mathcal{U})$
  - $addCorruptMember(\mathsf{id}_\mathcal{U})$
  - $Corrupt(\mathsf{id}_\mathcal{U})$
  - $Open(m, \mathsf{DGS}.\sigma)$
  - $Sign(m, \mathsf{id}_\mathcal{U})$
- Generate $\mathsf{DGS}.\sigma'$
- **Return** $\mathsf{DGS}.\mathsf{Verify}(m, .\mathsf{DGS}.\sigma, \mathsf{DGS}.\mathsf{param})$

$\mathbf{Exp}_{\mathcal{A},\mathsf{DGS}}^{Anom}(\lambda):$

- $Setup(\lambda, \mathsf{DGS}.\mathsf{set})$
- Unrestricted Queries:
  - $AddMember(\mathsf{id}_\mathcal{U})$
  - $addCorruptMember(\mathsf{id}_\mathcal{U})$
  - $Corrupt(\mathsf{id}_\mathcal{U})$
  - $Open(m, \mathsf{DGS}.\sigma)$
  - $Sign(m, \mathsf{id}_\mathcal{U})$

- $\mathsf{DGS}.\sigma' \leftarrow$
  $Chal_b(\mathsf{id}_\mathcal{U}^1, \mathsf{id}_\mathcal{U}^2, m, \mathsf{DGS}.\mathsf{param})$
- **Return** b'

$\mathbf{Exp}_{\mathcal{A},\mathsf{DGS}}^{Trace}(\lambda):$

- $Setup(\lambda, \mathsf{DGS}.\mathsf{set})$
- Unrestricted Queries:
  - $AddMember(\mathsf{id}_\mathcal{U})$
  - $addCorruptMember(\mathsf{id}_\mathcal{U})$
  - $Corrupt(\mathsf{id}_\mathcal{U})$
  - $Open(m, \mathsf{DGS}.\sigma)$
  - $Sign(m, \mathsf{id}_\mathcal{U})$
- Generate $\mathsf{DGS}.\sigma'$
- **Return**
  $\mathsf{DGS}.\mathsf{Verify}(m, \mathsf{DGS}.\sigma, \mathsf{DGS}.\mathsf{param})$
  $== 1$
  $\&\&$
  $\mathsf{DGS}.\mathsf{Open}(\mathsf{DGS}.\sigma, \mathsf{DGS}.\mathsf{msk}) == \perp$

Fig. 4. Security games

- Collision Resistance: A function achieves collision resistance if and only if a polynomial time algorithm which finds x_0 and x_1 such that $x_0 \neq x_1$ and $H(x_0) = H(x_1)$ do not exist.
- Second Pre-image Resistance: A function achieves second pre-image resistance if and only if knowing a pair $(x_0, H(x_0))$ it is unfeasible for a polynomial time algorithm to find another input x_1 such that $H(x_1) = H(x_0)$.

Symmetric Encryption: [29] is composed of the following algorithms:

- $\mathsf{SE}.\mathsf{KeyGen}(1^\lambda) = \mathsf{SE}.\mathsf{sk}$: This algorithm takes as input the security parameter and outputs a secret key $\in \{0,1\}^\lambda$
- $\mathsf{SE}.\mathsf{Enc}(p, \mathsf{SE}.\mathsf{sk}) = c$: the encryption takes as input the secret key $\mathsf{SE}.\mathsf{sk} \in \{0,1\}^\lambda$ and a plaintext $p \in \{0,1\}^\lambda$, outputs the ciphertext $c \in \{0,1\}^\lambda$.
- $\mathsf{SE}.\mathsf{Dec}(c, \mathsf{SE}.\mathsf{sk}) = p$: the decryption takes as input the secret key $sk \in \{0,1\}^\lambda$ and a ciphertext $c \in \{0,1\}^\lambda$, outputs the plaintext $p \in \{0,1\}^\lambda$.

Semantical Security: Let be $\mathsf{SE} = (\mathsf{SE}.\mathsf{KeyGen}, \mathsf{SE}.\mathsf{Enc}, \mathsf{SE}.\mathsf{Dec})$ be symmetric cryptosystem. We say that SE is $\mathsf{IND} - \mathsf{CPA}$ secure if the advantage of an adversary

$$\mathsf{Adv}_{\mathsf{SE}.\mathsf{sk}}^{\mathsf{IND}-\mathsf{CPA}} = |\Pr[\mathcal{A}(\mathsf{SE}.\mathsf{Enc}(p_0, \mathsf{SE}.\mathsf{sk}) = 1] - \Pr[\mathcal{A}(\mathsf{SE}.\mathsf{Enc}(p_1, \mathsf{SE}.\mathsf{sk}) = 0]|$$
$$< \mathsf{negl}(\lambda), \tag{7}$$

when $\mathcal{A}$ can choose p_0 and p_1 and for a security parameters λ.

One-Time Signature (OTS): One-Time Signature schemes (OTS) can sign a message once. An OTS scheme is a digital signature scheme constructed with the help of three algorithms: OTS.KeyGen, OTS.Sign and OTS.Verify.

- OTS.KeyGen(1^λ) = (OTS.pk, OTS.priv) generates one key pair, one public key OTS.pk, and one private key OTS.priv, depending on the security wanted λ.
- OTS.Sign$(m, \text{OTS.priv})$ = OTS.σ signs a digital message m with the private key OTS.priv. It outputs a valid digital signature OTS.σ.
- OTS.Verify$(m, \text{OTS.}\sigma, \text{OTS.pk})$ = 0/1 is a deterministic algorithm which verifies the validity of a signature OTS.σ for a message m with the public key OTS.pk.

OTS security: We assume that a secure OTS scheme achieves unforgeability and key one-wayness.

Unforgeability means that for a security parameter λ

$$\Pr[\text{OTS.Verify}(m, \text{OTS.}\sigma', \text{OTS.pk})] = 1 < \text{negl}(\lambda)$$

if an adversary generates a signature OTS.σ' from OTS.pk.

Key one-wayness means that knowing OTS.pk it is unfeasible in polynomial time to recover the corresponding OTS.priv.

References

1. PQC. https://csrc.nist.gov/projects/post-quantum-cryptography
2. Ames, S., Hazay, C., Ishai, Y., Venkitasubramaniam, M.: Ligero: lightweight sublinear arguments without a trusted setup. In: ACM CCS, pp. 2087–2104. ACM (2017)
3. Bellare, M., Goldreich, O.: On defining proofs of knowledge. In: Brickell, E.F. (ed.) CRYPTO 1992. LNCS, vol. 740, pp. 390–420. Springer, Heidelberg (1993). https://doi.org/10.1007/3-540-48071-4_28
4. Bellare, M., Micciancio, D., Warinschi, B.: Foundations of group signatures: formal definitions, simplified requirements, and a construction based on general assumptions. In: Biham, E. (ed.) EUROCRYPT 2003. LNCS, vol. 2656, pp. 614–629. Springer, Heidelberg (2003). https://doi.org/10.1007/3-540-39200-9_38
5. Bellare, M., Shi, H., Zhang, C.: Foundations of group signatures: the case of dynamic groups. In: Menezes, A. (ed.) CT-RSA 2005. LNCS, vol. 3376, pp. 136–153. Springer, Heidelberg (2005). https://doi.org/10.1007/978-3-540-30574-3_11
6. Boneh, D., Eskandarian, S., Fisch, B.: Post-quantum EPID group signatures from symmetric primitives. Technical report, Cryptology ePrint Archive, report 2018/261 (2018). https://eprint.iacr.org/2018/261
7. Bootle, J., Cerulli, A., Chaidos, P., Ghadafi, E., Groth, J.: Foundations of fully dynamic group signatures. In: Manulis, M., Sadeghi, A.-R., Schneider, S. (eds.) ACNS 2016. LNCS, vol. 9696, pp. 117–136. Springer, Cham (2016). https://doi.org/10.1007/978-3-319-39555-5_7
8. Chalkias, K., Brown, J., Hearn, M., Lillehagen, T., Nitto, I., Schroeter, T.: Blockchained post-quantum signatures (2018)

9. Chase, M., et al.: Post-quantum zero-knowledge and signatures from symmetric-key primitives. In: ACM CCS, pp. 1825–1842. ACM (2017)
10. Chaum, D., van Heyst, E.: Group signatures. In: Davies, D.W. (ed.) EUROCRYPT 1991. LNCS, vol. 547, pp. 257–265. Springer, Heidelberg (1991). https://doi.org/10.1007/3-540-46416-6_22
11. El Bansarkhani, R., Misoczki, R.: G-Merkle: a hash-based group signature scheme from standard assumptions. In: Lange, T., Steinwandt, R. (eds.) PQCrypto 2018. LNCS, vol. 10786, pp. 441–463. Springer, Cham (2018). https://doi.org/10.1007/978-3-319-79063-3_21
12. Fiat, A., Shamir, A.: How to prove yourself: practical solutions to identification and signature problems. In: Odlyzko, A.M. (ed.) CRYPTO 1986. LNCS, vol. 263, pp. 186–194. Springer, Heidelberg (1987). https://doi.org/10.1007/3-540-47721-7_12
13. Giacomelli, I., Madsen, J., Orlandi, C.: ZKBoo: faster zero-knowledge for Boolean circuits. In: USENIX Security, pp. 1069–1083 (2016)
14. Goldreich, O., Micali, S., Wigderson, A.: Proofs that yield nothing but their validity or all languages in NP have zero-knowledge proof systems. J. ACM (JACM) 38(3), 690–728 (1991)
15. Gordon, S.D., Katz, J., Vaikuntanathan, V.: A group signature scheme from lattice assumptions. In: Abe, M. (ed.) ASIACRYPT 2010. LNCS, vol. 6477, pp. 395–412. Springer, Heidelberg (2010). https://doi.org/10.1007/978-3-642-17373-8_23
16. Hohenberger, S., Koppula, V., Waters, B.: Adaptively secure puncturable pseudo-random functions in the standard model. In: Iwata, T., Cheon, J.H. (eds.) ASIACRYPT 2015. LNCS, vol. 9452, pp. 79–102. Springer, Heidelberg (2015). https://doi.org/10.1007/978-3-662-48797-6_4
17. Hülsing, A.: W-OTS+ – shorter signatures for hash-based signature schemes. In: Youssef, A., Nitaj, A., Hassanien, A.E. (eds.) AFRICACRYPT 2013. LNCS, vol. 7918, pp. 173–188. Springer, Heidelberg (2013). https://doi.org/10.1007/978-3-642-38553-7_10
18. Ishai, Y., Kushilevitz, E., Ostrovsky, R., Sahai, A.: Zero-knowledge proofs from secure multiparty computation. SIAM J. Comput. 39(3), 1121–1152 (2009)
19. Katz, J., Kolesnikov, V., Wang, X.: Improved non-interactive zero knowledge with applications to post-quantum signatures. Technical report, Cryptology ePrint Archive, report 2018/475 (2018)
20. Laguillaumie, F., Langlois, A., Libert, B., Stehlé, D.: Lattice-based group signatures with logarithmic signature size. In: Sako, K., Sarkar, P. (eds.) ASIACRYPT 2013. LNCS, vol. 8270, pp. 41–61. Springer, Heidelberg (2013). https://doi.org/10.1007/978-3-642-42045-0_3
21. Lamport, L.: Constructing digital signatures from a one-way function. Technical report CSL-98, SRI International Palo Alto (1979)
22. Libert, B., Ling, S., Mouhartem, F., Nguyen, K., Wang, H.: Signature schemes with efficient protocols and dynamic group signatures from lattice assumptions. In: Cheon, J.H., Takagi, T. (eds.) ASIACRYPT 2016. LNCS, vol. 10032, pp. 373–403. Springer, Heidelberg (2016). https://doi.org/10.1007/978-3-662-53890-6_13
23. Libert, B., Ling, S., Nguyen, K., Wang, H.: Zero-knowledge arguments for lattice-based accumulators: logarithmic-size ring signatures and group signatures without trapdoors. In: Fischlin, M., Coron, J.-S. (eds.) EUROCRYPT 2016. LNCS, vol. 9666, pp. 1–31. Springer, Heidelberg (2016). https://doi.org/10.1007/978-3-662-49896-5_1
24. Ling, S., Nguyen, K., Wang, H.: Group signatures from lattices: simpler, tighter, shorter, ring-based. In: Katz, J. (ed.) PKC 2015. LNCS, vol. 9020, pp. 427–449. Springer, Heidelberg (2015). https://doi.org/10.1007/978-3-662-46447-2_19

25. Ling, S., Nguyen, K., Wang, H., Xu, Y.: Lattice-based group signatures: achieving full dynamicity with ease. In: Gollmann, D., Miyaji, A., Kikuchi, H. (eds.) ACNS 2017. LNCS, vol. 10355, pp. 293–312. Springer, Cham (2017). https://doi.org/10.1007/978-3-319-61204-1_15

26. Ling, S., Nguyen, K., Wang, H., Xu, Y.: Constant-size group signatures from lattices. In: Abdalla, M., Dahab, R. (eds.) PKC 2018. LNCS, vol. 10770, pp. 58–88. Springer, Cham (2018). https://doi.org/10.1007/978-3-319-76581-5_3

27. McIlroy, P.: Optimistic sorting and information theoretic complexity. In: Proceedings of the Fourth Annual ACM-SIAM Symposium on Discrete algorithms, pp. 467–474. Society for Industrial and Applied Mathematics (1993)

28. Merkle, R.C.: A certified digital signature. In: Brassard, G. (ed.) CRYPTO 1989. LNCS, vol. 435, pp. 218–238. Springer, New York (1990). https://doi.org/10.1007/0-387-34805-0_21

29. Sun, S.-F., et al.: Practical backward-secure searchable encryption from symmetric puncturable encryption. In: ACM CCS 2018, pp. 763–780. ACM (2018)

30. Unruh, D.: Non-interactive zero-knowledge proofs in the quantum random Oracle model. In: Oswald, E., Fischlin, M. (eds.) EUROCRYPT 2015. LNCS, vol. 9057, pp. 755–784. Springer, Heidelberg (2015). https://doi.org/10.1007/978-3-662-46803-6_25

Puncturable Proxy Re-Encryption Supporting to Group Messaging Service

Tran Viet Xuan Phuong[1,2](✉), Willy Susilo[1], Jongkil Kim[1], Guomin Yang[1], and Dongxi Liu[2]

[1] Institute of Cybersecurity and Cryptology School of Computing and Information Technology, University of Wollongong, Wollongong, Australia
{txuan,wsusilo,jongkil,gyang}@uow.edu.au
[2] Data61, CSIRO, Syndey, Australia
Dongxi.Liu@data61.csiro.au

Abstract. This work envisions a new encryption primitive for many-to-many paradigms such as group messaging systems. Previously, puncturable encryption (PE) was introduced to provide forward security for asynchronous messaging services. However, existing PE schemes were proposed only for one-to-one communication, and causes a significant overhead for a group messaging system. In fact, the group communication over PE can only be achieved by encrypting a message multiple times for each receiver by the sender's device, which is usually suitable to restricted resources such as mobile phones or sensor devices. Our new suggested scheme enables to re-encrypt ciphertexts of puncturable encryption by a message server (i.e., a proxy) so that computationally heavy operations are delegated to the server who has more powerful processors and a constant power source. We then proposed a new Puncturable Proxy Re-Encryption (PPRE) scheme. The scheme is inspired by unidirectional proxy re-encryption (UPRE), which achieves forward secrecy through fine-grained revocation of decryption capability by integrating the PE scheme. This paper first presents a forward secure PPRE in the group messaging service. Our scheme is IND-CCA secure under 3-weak Decision Bilinear Diffie-Hellman Inversion assumption.

Keywords: Puncturable encryption · Proxy Re-Encryption · Group messaging service · CCA security

1 Introduction

Green and Miers introduced Puncturable Encryption (PE) [15] to produce efficient forward-secure encryption for asynchronous communication with low overhead. Forward secrecy is a crucial trend on secure communication. For example, a new version of TLS v1.3 mandates forward secrecy for its key exchange. The protocols that do not support forward secrecy will be gradually deprecated in the near future. PE enables users to utilize forward secure asynchronous communication such as a messaging service.

© Springer Nature Switzerland AG 2019
K. Sako et al. (Eds.): ESORICS 2019, LNCS 11735, pp. 215–233, 2019.
https://doi.org/10.1007/978-3-030-29959-0_11

A group messaging service in real-world applications such as Snapchat and Whatsapp is essential since the communication between users is not always one-to-one. Many-to-many communication (e.g., a group messaging service) has a capability to boost customer convenience in the business/private conversation for a group of users. Therefore, supporting group messaging service makes a conversation more specific and focused. Forward secrecy and asynchronous properties that PE offers are still important in a group messaging service. However, messages in group communication are not always synchronized. Participants who are traveling or on-the-go will receive the messages with a significant delay. Furthermore, in the event that a user key in group communication is compromised; the confidentiality of past messages will fail.

In the existing work, the proposed PE schemes are constructed only for one-to-one communication between a sender and a receiver. How to use those PE schemes for many-to-many communication such as a group messaging service remains daunting. One of the most trivial ways is a participant of a group communication encrypts a message for all other participants in the communication one-by-one using PE, but this requires significant computation overhead to the sender. Particularly, if a message is sent from resource-constraint devices such as mobiles and sensor devices, this causes a substantial amount of battery consumption and delay as the number of participants grows.

To mitigate the delay time or support messaging for individuals who are away, we revisit the Proxy Re-Encryption (PRE) [2,3,17]. Suppose that Alice makes a group chatting room and invites multiple users, every time a new user joins in the group chatting, Alice computes the re-encryption key for this user by his public key and uploads to a messaging server, which is considered as a proxy. If anyone sends a message in this room, the message is encrypted only for Alice and send to the message server. The message server re-encrypts the encrypted message for all participants one-by-one using the re-encryption keys that Alice uploaded, then delivers it to the participants. Because the message server has more powerful processors and constant power source, it will reduce the delay caused by multiple encryptions. Moreover, each participant will encrypt the message only once as a general PE scheme; it prolongs the battery life of participant devices, significantly.

Contribution: Motivated by the aforementioned scenario, we investigate the fine-grained revocation of decryption capability only for specific messages while all other messages are decryptable in [15], then incorporate the unidirectional proxy re-encryption (UPRE) to firstly propose Puncturable Proxy Re-Encryption (PPRE). In a nutshell, PPRE scheme has both PE and UPRE scheme; however, it is not straightforward to deploy both schemes into the typical proxy re-encryption. At a high-level idea, each message is attached to a tag $t \in \{t_1, \ldots, t_d\}$, which can be time stamps or message identifiers. The ciphertext also includes the set of tags corresponding to the stamped messages. The delegator applies the puncture algorithm to puncture her secret key by tag $t \in \{t_1, \ldots, t_d\}$ if she wants to revoke the capability of decryption tag t. This addressing issue is achieved the forward secrecy in the messaging system.

Next to delegate the decryption right, the delegator sends the template of puncture key TK and the re-encryption key $R_{B \leftarrow A}$ to the proxy server, then the proxy uses the $R_{B \leftarrow A}$ to re-encrypt the ciphertext. The proxy will delegate TK and ciphertext to the delegatee. From the template key TK, the delegatee can derive his/her own puncture keys. The decryption of delegatee is input of the puncture key and his secret key. The proposed scheme first achieve IND-CCA security, which is a considerable security assumption to provide a more realistic adversarial model. We are inspired by the papers of [7,9,17] which present scheme to apply a strongly unforgeable one-time signature to bind ciphertext components altogether and offer a secure against chosen ciphertext attacks in the manner of [8].

Table 1. Performance comparison between our proposed scheme and [17] scheme.

Scheme	Level 1 - ciphertext	Level 2 - ciphertext	Level 1 dec	Level 2 dec	Attack
[17]	2 Sig + 4$|\mathbb{G}|$ + 1$|\mathbb{G}_T|$	2 Sig + 2$|\mathbb{G}|$ + 1$|\mathbb{G}_T|$	1p	1p	IND-CCA
PPRE	2 Sig + $(7+d)|\mathbb{G}|$ + 1$|\mathbb{G}_T|$	2 Sig + $(2+d)|\mathbb{G}|$ + 1$|\mathbb{G}_T|$	tp	tp	IND-CCA

We highlight a detailed computation of our Puncturable Proxy Re-Encryption and typical Unidirectional PRE of [17]. The schemes are compared in terms of the order of the underlying group, ciphertext size, decryption cost, and security assumption. We use d to denote the number of tags, and t the number of puncture tags.

Related Work. In the early concept presented in [18], the original recipient must be available for re-encrypting ciphertexts when needed, which is not always feasible. Later, [4] first proposed a proxy re-encryption, which establishes an actual notion with the elegance of the construction. This scheme is based on Elgamal, and it is constructed upon a group $\mathbb{G}$ of prime order p. [2,3] proposed the first unidirectional PRE scheme, based on bilinear pairings. These schemes are also the first to present the idea of multiple ciphertext space. Apart from [2,3,9] presents the first CCA-secure bidirectional scheme in the standard model, while the unidirectional case, [16,17] achieve the chosen ciphertext security in the standard model. [24] then proposed bidirectional schemes without pairings under CCA-secure in the random oracle model. [14] proposed a new fashion of PRE scheme as the first identity-based encryption proxy encryption (IBPRE) scheme. Using the identity-based, this scheme uses the identities of the delegator and delegatee as their public keys. Another interesting proposal proposed by [1] defines the notion of key privacy in the context of PRE, which prevents the proxy to derive the identities of both sender and receiver from a re-encryption key. As the new variances of IBPRE, [10] presented IB-PRE scheme built upon the reductions to the security of IBE [22]. [19] proposed Hybrid proxy re-encryption, which ciphertext encrypted by public key encryption scheme can be re-encrypted to ciphertexts under an identity-based encryption scheme. Recently, [20] introduces proxy re-encryption with the scenario of key rotation of data stored on the cloud to reduce the rotating cost. Several works proposed as condition [23], type-based proxy re-encryption [21] to produce the diversity for PRE. In addition, PRE is appropriate to deploy in the cloud services. [13] proposed the variant of proxy re-encryption schemes in the dropbox, and [5] produced efficient and secure shared storage.

2 Preliminaries

2.1 Bilinear Map

Let $\mathbb{G}$ and $\mathbb{G}_T$ be two multiplicative cyclic groups of same prime order p, and g a generator of $\mathbb{G}$. We define $e : \mathbb{G} \times \mathbb{G} \to \mathbb{G}_T$ be a bilinear map with the following properties: (1) Bilinearity : $e(u^a, v^b) = e(u^b, v^a) = e(u, v)^{ab}$ for all $u, v \in \mathbb{G}$ and $a, b \in \mathbb{Z}_p$. (2) Non-degeneracy : $e(g, g) \neq 1$. Notice that the map e is symmetric since $e(g^a, g^b) = e(g, g)^{ab} = e(g^b, g^a)$.

2.2 The 3-Weak Decision Bilinear Diffie-Hellman Inversion (3-WDBDHI)

The Decision 3-wDBDHI problem is the intractability of a variant of Decisional Bilinear Diffie-Hellman [6] assumption, which consider the indistinguishable computational of $e(g, g)^{b/a}$ from tuple of random elements $(g, g^a, g^{a^2}, g^{a^q}, g^b)$. There is a distinguisher $A t, \epsilon$- breaks the assumption if it runs in poly-nomial t time and $|\Pr[A(g, g^a, g^{a^2}, g^{a^3}, g^b, e(g, g)^{b/a}) = 1 | a, b \in_R \mathbb{Z}_p^*] - \Pr[A(g, g^a, g^{a^2}, g^{a^3}, g^b, e(g, g)^z) = 1 | a, b, z \in_R \mathbb{Z}_p^*] \leq \epsilon(k)$. In the works of [12,17], the 3-wDBDHI problem is shown obviously that it is not easier than the (q-DBDHI) problem [6] for $q \leq 3$, which is to recognize $e(g, g)^{1/a}$ given $(g, g^a, \ldots, g^{a^q}) \in \mathbb{G}^{q+1}$.

2.3 One-Time Signatures

We apply the CHK method [8] to use one-time signatures, which consist of a triple of algorithms $\mathsf{Sig} = (\mathcal{G}, \mathcal{S}, \mathcal{V})$. The algorithm inputs of a security param-eter λ, $\mathcal{G}$ generates a one-time key pair (ssk, svk) while, for any message M, $\mathcal{V}(\sigma, svk, M)$ outputs 1 whenever $\sigma = \mathcal{S}(ssk, M)$ and 0 otherwise. The strongly unforgetable one-time signatures are presented [8], which means that no PPT adversary can create a new signature for a previously signed message.

Definition 1. $\mathsf{Sig} = (\mathcal{G}, \mathcal{S}, \mathcal{V})$ is a strong one time signature if the probability is negligible for any PPT forger $\mathcal{F}$

$$Adv^{\mathsf{OTS}} = Pr[(ssk, svk) \leftarrow \mathcal{G}(\lambda); (M, St) \leftarrow \mathcal{F}(svk); \sigma \leftarrow \mathcal{S}(ssk, M); (M', \sigma')$$
$$\leftarrow \mathcal{F}(M, \sigma, svk, St) : \mathcal{V}(\sigma', svk, M') = 1 \wedge (M', \sigma') \neq (M, \sigma)],$$

where St denotes $\mathcal{F}$'s state information across stages.

2.4 Lagrange Polynomial and Interpolation

Suppose that a polynomial of degree d is uniquely defined by a set of points $(x_0, y_0), (x_1, y_1), \ldots, (x_{d+1}, y_{d+1})$. The Lagrange form of the polynomial allows the computation of a point x on the polynomial using only $d+1$ points as follows:

$$q(x) = L(x, xc, yc) = \sum_{j=0}^{d} (yc[j] \cdot \ell(x, j, xc)),$$

where, $xc = [x_0, \ldots, x_{d+1}]$ and $yc = [y_0, \ldots, y_{d+1}]$ and the Lagrange basis polynomial $\ell(\ldots)$ is:

$$\ell(x, j, xc) = \prod_{0 \leq m, m \neq j \leq d} \frac{x - xc[m]}{xc[j] - xc[m]}.$$

Applying the Lagrange polynomial form, a random degree d polynomial $q(x)$ is selected, which consists of sampling d random values $r_1 \ldots, r_d$ from $\mathbb{Z}_p$, setting points $(1, r_1), (2, r_2), \ldots, (d, r_d)$ and setting the final point to $(0, \beta)$ to guarantee $q(0) = \beta$. Lagrange interpolation can compute $V(x)$ without knowledge of the polynomial coefficients by only the public values $g^{q(0)}, \ldots, g^{q(d)}$ as:

$V(x) = g^{q(x)} = g^{\sum_{j=0}^{d} y_j \ell(x,j,xc)} = \prod_{j=0}^{d} (g^{q(j)})^{\ell(x,j,xc)}$, where $\ell(x, j, xc)$ is already defined.

3 Model and Security Notions

3.1 Puncturable Proxy Re-Encryption

Puncturable Proxy Re-Encryption scheme has Global-setup, KeyGeneration, Re-KeyGen, Puncture, Encryption$_1$ (is not re-encrypt-able), Encryption$_2$, Re-Encryption, and Decryption$_1$, Decryption$_2$ algorithms defined in the following.

▶ Global-setup($1^k, d$). On input a security parameter k, a maximum number of tags per ciphertext d, the algorithm outputs the public parameter param, and initial puncture key PSK$_0$.

▶ Key-Generation(param, PSK$_0$). On input the public parameter param and an initial puncture key PSK$_0$, the algorithms generates the public/secret key pair for a user A, then combines the secret key A and PSK$_0$ to produce new puncture key PSK$_0'$.

▶ Puncture(param, TK, PSK$_{i-1}, t$). On input an existing key PSK$_{i-1}$ as $\{$PSK$_0'$, PSK$_1, \ldots,$ PSK$_{i-1}\}$, and a tag t, the algorithm outputs PSK$_i$.

▶ Re-KeyGen(param, sk$_A$, pk$_B$). On input the public parameter param, secret key A, and public key B. A first generates a template puncture key TK by the param and sk$_A$. Then A then publicly delegates to user B a re-encryption key R$_{B \leftarrow A}$, and encrypted form Enc$_{pk_B}$(TK).

▶ $\mathsf{Encryption}_1(\mathsf{param}, \mathsf{pk}_A, M, t_1, \ldots, t_d)$. On input the param, public key of the user A, a message M, and a set of tags $(t_1, \ldots, t_d)$, the algorithm outputs the first level ciphertext CT_1 along with the tags $(t_1, \ldots, t_d)$.

▶ $\mathsf{Encryption}_2(\mathsf{param}, \mathsf{pk}_A, M, t_1, \ldots, t_d)$. On input the param, public key of user A, a message M, and a set of tags $(t_1, \ldots, t_d)$, the algorithm outputs the second level ciphertext CT_2 along with the tags $t_1, \ldots, t_d$.

▶ $\mathsf{Re\text{-}Encryption}(\mathsf{CT}_2, \mathsf{R}_{B\leftarrow A})$. On input the second level ciphertext CT_2 along with the tags $t_1, \ldots, t_d$, a re-key $\mathsf{R}_{A\leftarrow B}$. The algorithm first checks the validity of CT_2. If CT_2 is well-formed, the algorithm computes from CT_2 by the re-encryption key $\mathsf{R}_{B\leftarrow A}$, and produce the ciphertext CT_1, along with the tags $t_1, \ldots, t_d$. Otherwise, CT_2 is declared 'invalid.'

▶ $\mathsf{Decryption}_1(\mathsf{param}, \mathsf{sk}_B, \mathsf{CT}_1, t_1, \ldots, t_d)$. On the input param, the secret key of user B, punctured key PSK_i, ciphertext CT_1 along with $(t_1, \ldots, t_d)$, the algorithm outputs message M or 'invalid.'

▶ $\mathsf{Decryption}_2(\mathsf{param}, \mathsf{sk}_A, \mathsf{PSK}_i, \mathsf{CT}_2, t_1, \ldots, t_d)$. On the input param, the secret key of user A, punctured key PSK_i, second ciphertext CT_2 along with $(t_1, \ldots, t_d)$, the decryption outputs message as M or 'invalid.'

Correctness. For any common public parameters param, for any message $m \in \{0,1\}^*$ and any couple of public/secret key pair $(\mathsf{pk}_A, \mathsf{sk}_A), (\mathsf{pk}_B, \mathsf{sk}_B)$ these algorithms should satisfy the following conditions:

$$\mathsf{Decryption}_1(\mathsf{param}, \mathsf{sk}_A, \mathsf{PSK}_i, \mathsf{CT}_1) = M;$$
$$\mathsf{Decryption}_2(\mathsf{param}, \mathsf{sk}_A, \mathsf{PSK}_i, \mathsf{CT}_2) = M;$$
$$\mathsf{Decryption}_1(\mathsf{param}, \mathsf{sk}_B, \mathsf{Re\text{-}Encryption}(\mathsf{CT}_2, \mathsf{R}_{B\leftarrow A}),$$
$$\mathsf{Re\text{-}KeyGen}(\mathsf{param}, \mathsf{sk}_A, \mathsf{pk}_B), \mathsf{PSK}_i) = M.$$

We use the standard security notions of proxy re-encryption schemes [2,3,11,17], which initializes empty lists of corrupted users CU and honest users HU. In addition, we define two empty sets P, C, a counter n, a targeted user x^*, and a set of tags $t_1^*, \ldots, t_d^*$. Then, A Puncturable Proxy Re-Encryption scheme is replayable chosen-ciphertext attack (RCCA) secure at level 2 ciphertexts for any PPT adversary $\mathcal{A}$ if the probability

$$\Pr[\mathsf{param} \leftarrow \mathsf{Global\text{-}setup}(1^k, d); (\mathsf{pk}_{x^*}, \mathsf{sk}_{x^*}) \leftarrow \mathsf{Key\text{-}Generation}_{x^*}(\mathsf{param});$$
$$\{(\mathsf{pk}_x, \mathsf{sk}_x) \leftarrow \mathsf{Key\text{-}Generation}_{HU}(\mathsf{param})\}; \{(\mathsf{pk}_y, \mathsf{sk}_y) \leftarrow \mathsf{Key\text{-}Generation}_{CU}(\mathsf{param})\};$$
$$\{\mathsf{R}_{x \leftarrow x^*} \leftarrow \mathsf{Re\text{-}KeyGen}(\mathsf{sk}_{x^*}, \mathsf{pk}_x)\}, \{\mathsf{R}_{x^* \leftarrow x} \leftarrow \mathsf{Re\text{-}KeyGen}(\mathsf{sk}_x, \mathsf{pk}_{x^*})\};$$
$$\{\mathsf{R}_{x' \leftarrow x} \leftarrow \mathsf{Re\text{-}KeyGen}(\mathsf{sk}_x, \mathsf{pk}'_x)\}, \{\mathsf{R}_{x \leftarrow y} \leftarrow \mathsf{Re\text{-}KeyGen}(\mathsf{sk}_y, \mathsf{pk}_x)\};$$
$$\{n{+}{+}, \mathsf{PSK}_n = \mathsf{Puncture}_{x^*}(\mathsf{param}, \mathsf{TK}, \mathsf{PSK}'_{n-1}, t), P \leftarrow t\};$$
$$\{n{+}{+}, \mathsf{PSK}_n = \mathsf{Puncture}_{HU}(\mathsf{param}, \mathsf{TK}, \mathsf{PSK}'_{n-1}, t), P \leftarrow t\};$$
$$\{n{+}{+}, \mathsf{PSK}_n = \mathsf{Puncture}_{CU}(\mathsf{param}, \mathsf{TK}, \mathsf{PSK}'_{n-1}, t), P \leftarrow t\}; \mathbf{Corrupt}();$$
$$(m_1, m_0, St) \leftarrow \mathcal{A}^{\mathcal{O}_{1-dec}, \mathcal{O}_{reenc}}(\mathsf{pk}_{x^*}, \{(\mathsf{pk}_x, \mathsf{sk}_x)\},$$
$$\{\mathsf{R}_{x \leftarrow x^*}\}, \{\mathsf{R}_{x \leftarrow x^*}\}, \{\mathsf{R}_{x' \leftarrow x}\}, \{\mathsf{R}_{x \leftarrow y}\}, (t_1, \ldots, t_d), (t_1^*, \ldots, t_d^*));$$
$$\mu \xleftarrow{R} \{0,1\}, \mathsf{CT}_2^* = \mathsf{Encryption}_2(m_{\mu^*}, \mathsf{pk}_{x^*}, (t_1^*, \ldots, t_d^*));$$
$$\mu' \leftarrow \mathcal{A}^{\mathcal{O}_{1-dec}, \mathcal{O}_{reenc}}(\mathsf{CT}_2^*, St)) : \mu' = \mu] - \frac{1}{2} < \epsilon(k),$$

with St is the state information, $\{x'\}$ are honest users.

- **Corrupt()**is invoked in the first time; the adversary issues this query. Then, the challenger returns the most recent punctured key PSK_n to the adversary, and sets $C \leftarrow P$. All subsequent queries return $\perp$.
- $\mathcal{O}(\text{reenc})$: Responding a re-encryption query from user pk_x to user pk_y, PSK, and tags $(t_1, \ldots, t_d)$ for a second level ciphertext CT_2, this oracle returns 'invalid' if CT_2 is not encrypted by $\mathsf{pk}_x, (t_1, \ldots, t_d)$. It returns $\perp$ if $\mathsf{pk}_y \in$ CU and $(\mathsf{pk}_{x^*}, \mathsf{CT}_2^*, (t_1^*, \ldots, t_d^*)) = (\mathsf{pk}_x, \mathsf{CT}_2, (t_1, \ldots, t_d))$. Otherwise, $\mathsf{CT}_1 = \mathsf{Re\text{-}Encryption}(\mathsf{CT}_2, \mathsf{sk}_x, \mathsf{pk}_y)$ is returned to $\mathcal{A}$.
- $\mathcal{O}(\text{1-dec})$: Given $\mathsf{pk}_{x'}, \mathsf{CT}_1, (t_1, \ldots, t_d)$, this oracle returns 'invalid' if CT_1 is not belongs to $\mathsf{pk}_{x'}$ and $(t_1, \ldots, t_d)$. If the condition in 'guess' stage occurs similarly in the 'queries' stage, $\mathcal{B}$ outputs $\perp$. If $(\mathsf{pk}_{x'}, \mathsf{CT}_1, (t_1, \ldots, t_d))$ is Derivative of challenge pair $(\mathsf{pk}_{x^*}, \mathsf{CT}_1^*, (t_1^*, \ldots, t_d^*))$ as CT_1 is the first level ciphertext and $\mathsf{pk}_{x'} = \mathsf{pk}_{x^*}$ or $x' \in \mathsf{HU}$, it returns $\perp$. If Decryption$_1(\text{param}, \mathsf{sk}_{x'}, \mathsf{CT}_1, \mathsf{PSK}_i, t_1, \ldots, t_d) \in \{m_0, m_1\}$, it returns $\perp$. Otherwise, $m = \mathsf{Decryption}_1(\text{param}, \mathsf{sk}_{x'}, \mathsf{PSK}_i, \mathsf{CT}_1,)$.

A Puncturable Proxy Re-Encryption scheme is also replayable chosen-ciphertext attack (RCCA) secure at level 1 ciphertexts. In fact, the adversary is guaranteed to access to re-encryption keys. Since first level ciphertexts cannot be re-encrypted, the attackers is not equipped to obtain the honest-to-corrupt re-encryption keys. The $\mathcal{O}_{reenc}$ oracle is unusable since all re-encryption keys are available to $\mathcal{A}$, $\mathcal{O}_{2-dec}$ is also unnecessary. Finally, Derivative of the challenge ciphertext is simply defined as encryptions of either m_0 or m_1 with the target public key pk_{x^*}.

4 Puncturable Proxy Re-Encryption Under Chosen Ciphertext Attack

The main construction of Puncturable Proxy Re-Encryption (PPRE) applies the inherent Unidirectional Proxy Re-Encryption (UPRE) [3], where the second ciphertext is $((g^a)^s, M \cdot e(g, g)^s)$; g^a is public key of Alice. Then the proxy re-encrypts the second ciphertext into the first ciphertext as $(e((g^a)^s, g^{b/a}), M \cdot e(g, g)^s) = (e(g, g)^{bs}, M \cdot e(g, g)^s)$, which $g^{b/a}$ is the re-encryption key between Alice and Bob.

Hence, [16,17] employs the CHK transform [8] to product the re-encrypted ciphertext by the following fashion. The proxy replaces g^{as} by a randomized pair $(g^{b/ar}, g^{ars})$, for a blinding random $r \in_R \mathbb{Z}_p$. All components in second ciphertext remain in $\mathbb{G}$. Bob can eventually decrypt the message $M \cdot e(g, g)^s / (e(g, g)^{bs})^{1/b}$. Firstly, we are inspired [17]'s method incorporating the Puncturable Encryption (PE) and URPE schemes. The global setup algorithm initially shares a master secret key α as α_1, α_2, which are used as the master secret keys of PE, UPRE schemes respectively. In order to recover α_1, α_2 in decryption process, we produce a delegation key $\mathsf{DK} = g^{\alpha_2 + r_2}$ and puncture key $\mathsf{PSK} = g^{\alpha_1 + r_1 - r_2}$ as the mode of [15]. The second ciphertext is generated to $((\mathsf{DK}^a)^s, M \cdot e(g, g)^{(\alpha_1 + \alpha_2)s}, F(t)^s)$, in which $F(t)$ is the arbitrary formula to compute the tags in Puncturable Encryption. Secondly, the component of ciphertext includes the $F(t)^s$, then the first ciphertext should have $F(t)^{rs}$. Consequently, the proxy should replace DK^{as} by a randomized pair $(\mathsf{DK}^{b/ak}, g^{arsk})$ for "*double blinding randoms*" $r, k \in_R \mathbb{Z}_p$. By this way, $e(\mathsf{DK}^{b/ak}, g^{arsk}) = e(\mathsf{DK}, g)^{brs}$ can be cancel out with the exponent's components including rs. In this manner, Bob can recover the $e(g, g)^{(\alpha_1 + \alpha_2)s}$ to read message M by computing the α_1, α_2 in term of puncture key, re-encryption form, respectively. In addition, we produce $(\mathsf{ct}_{12}, \mathsf{ct}'_{12}, \mathsf{ct}''_{12}) = (g^r, g^{ark}, g^{ak})$ in order to check whether the safety of ciphertext is, meanwhile the verifying step is required to achieve the IND-CCA security. We will elaborate PPRE scheme in the next description.

4.1   Description

We elaborate the Global-setup, Key-Generation, Puncture, Re-KeyGen, Encryption$_1$ (is not re-encryptable), Encryption$_2$, Re-Encryption, Decryption$_1$, and Decryption$_2$ algorithms defined in the following.

▶ Global-setup($1^k, d$). On input a security parameter k, a maximum number of tags per ciphertext d, the algorithm firstly chooses a group $\mathbb{G}$ of prime order p, a bilinear map $e : \mathbb{G} \times \mathbb{G} \rightarrow \mathbb{G}_T$, a generator g, w, v, a hash function $H : \{0,1\}^* \rightarrow \mathbb{Z}_p$, and a strongly unforgeable one-time signature scheme $\mathsf{Sig} = (\mathcal{G}, \mathcal{S}, \mathcal{V})$. Then the algorithm randomly selects exponents $r_1, r_2, \alpha_1, \alpha_2 \in \mathbb{Z}_p$. It samples polynomial $q(x)$ of degree d. From $i = 1$ to d, it computes $q(i)$, subjects to the constraint that $q(0) = 1$.
Secondly, the algorithms defines $V(x) = g^{q(x)}$, and let t_0 be a distinguished tag not used during normal operation. Next, it computes the initial puncture key using the master key α_1, and distinguished tag t_0: $\mathsf{PSK}_0 = (\mathsf{PSK}_{01}, \mathsf{PSK}_{02}, \mathsf{PSK}_{03}, \mathsf{PSK}_{04}) = (g^{\alpha_1 + r_1 - r_2}, V(H(t_0))^{r_1}, g^{r_1}, t_0)$. Using the master key α_2, the algorithm generates the global key for user key generation: $\mathsf{DK} = g^{\alpha_2 + r_2}$. Finally, it outputs the public parameter: $\mathsf{param} = (g, Y = e(g, g^{\alpha_1 + \alpha_2}), \mathsf{Sig}, \mathsf{DK}, g^{q(1)}, \dots, g^{q(d)}, t_0)$, and initial puncture key PSK_0.
▶ Key-Generation($\mathsf{param}, \mathsf{PSK}_0$). To generate the public/secret key pair for a user A, the algorithm randomly picks $a \in_R \mathbb{Z}_p$. Then, it sets the public key, the secret key, and new initial puncture key from SK_0 to be: $\mathsf{pk_A} = \mathsf{DK}^a, \mathsf{sk_A} = a, \mathsf{PSK}'_0 = (\mathsf{PSK}'_{01}, \mathsf{PSK}'_{02}, \mathsf{PSK}'_{03}, \mathsf{PSK}'_{04}) = ((g^{\alpha_1 + r_1 - r_2})^{1/a}, (V(H(t_0))^{r_1})^{1/a}, g^{r_1}, t_0)$.
▶ Re-KeyGen($\mathsf{param}, \mathsf{DK}, \mathsf{PSK}_i$). A user A delegates to B as follows:
 • B chooses and stores a random value $u \in \mathbb{Z}_p$, then publishes (g^u, DK^u).
 • A creates ($\mathsf{R}_{\mathsf{B} \leftarrow \mathsf{A}} = \mathsf{DK}^{u/a}$).
 • A create $\mathsf{TK} = \{g^{1/a}, g^{q(1)/a}, \dots, g^{q(d)/a}\}$.
 • A uses public key B to encrypt A's puncture keys as $\mathsf{Enc}_{pk_\mathsf{B}}(\mathsf{PSK}_i)$.
 • A then delegates ($\mathsf{R}_{\mathsf{B} \leftarrow \mathsf{A}}, \mathsf{Enc}_{pk_\mathsf{B}}(\mathsf{TK})$) to B.

▶ Puncture$(\mathsf{param}, \mathsf{TK}, \mathsf{PSK}'_i, t)$. On input an existing key PSK_{i-1} as $\{\mathsf{PSK}_0, \mathsf{PSK}_1, \ldots, \mathsf{PSK}_{i-1}\}$, the algorithm chooses λ', r', r_t randomly from $\mathbb{Z}_p$, and computes:

$$\mathsf{PSK}'_0 = (\mathsf{PSK}'_{01} \cdot (g^{1/a})^{r'-\lambda'}, \mathsf{PSK}'_{02} \cdot (V(H(t_0))^{1/a})^{r'}, \mathsf{PSK}'_{03} \cdot g^{r'}, t_0)$$
$$\mathsf{PSK}_i = ((g^{1/a})^{\lambda'+r_t}, (V(H(t))^{1/a})^{r_t}, g^{r_t}, t).$$

Then it outputs: $\mathsf{PSK}_i = (\mathsf{PSK}'_0, \mathsf{PSK}_1, \ldots, \mathsf{PSK}_{i-1}, \mathsf{PSK}_i)$.

▶ Encryption$_1(\mathsf{param}, \mathsf{pk}_A, M, t_1, \ldots, t_d)$. On input the param, public key of user A, a message M, and a set of tags $t_1, \ldots, t_d \in \{0,1\}^* \backslash \{t_0\}$, the algorithm first randomly chooses s, r, k in $\mathbb{Z}_p$. Secondly, the algorithm selects a one-time signature key pair (ssk, svk) randomly from $\mathcal{G}(\lambda)$. It outputs:

$$\begin{aligned}
\mathsf{CT}_1 &= (\mathsf{ct}_{10}, \mathsf{ct}_{11}, \mathsf{ct}_{12}, \mathsf{ct}'_{12}, \mathsf{ct}''_{12}, \mathsf{ct}'''_{12}, \mathsf{ct}_{13}, \mathsf{ct}_{14}, \mathsf{ct}_{15_i}, \mathsf{ct}_{16}, \sigma) \\
&= (svk, M \cdot Y^{rs}, g^{ars}, g^r, g^{ark}, g^{ak}, \mathsf{DK}^{1/k}, g^{akrs}, \{V(H(t_i))^{rs}\}_{i \in \{1,\ldots,d\}}, \\
&\quad (u^{svk} \cdot v)^{rs}, \mathcal{S}(ssk, (\mathsf{ct}_{11}, \mathsf{ct}_{15_i}, \mathsf{ct}_{16})))
\end{aligned}$$

along with the tags $t_1, \ldots, t_d$. In such a way, the ciphertext can be decrypted by only the user A.

▶ Encryption$_2(\mathsf{param}, \mathsf{pk}_A, M, t_1, \ldots, t_d)$. On input the param, public key of user A, a message M, and a set of tags $t_1, \ldots, t_d \in \{0,1\}^* \backslash \{t_0\}$, the algorithm first randomly chooses s in $\mathbb{Z}_p$. Secondly, the algorithm selects a one-time signature key pair (ssk, svk) randomly from $\mathcal{G}(\lambda)$. It outputs:

$$\begin{aligned}
\mathsf{CT}_2 &= (\mathsf{ct}_{20}, \mathsf{ct}_{21}, \mathsf{ct}_{22}, \mathsf{ct}_{23_i}, \mathsf{ct}_{24}, \sigma) \\
&= (svk, M \cdot Y^s, g^{as}, \{V(H(t_i))^s\}_{i \in \{1,\ldots,d\}}, (u^{svk} \cdot v)^s, \mathcal{S}(ssk, (\mathsf{ct}_{21}, \mathsf{ct}_{23_i}, \mathsf{ct}_{24_i}))),
\end{aligned}$$

along with the tags $t_1, \ldots, t_d$. In such a way, the ciphertext can be decrypted by user A and her delegatees.

▶ Re-Encryption$(\mathsf{CT}_2, \mathsf{R}_{B \leftarrow A})$. On input the second level ciphertext CT_2, a re-key $\mathsf{R}_{A \leftarrow B}$, and a set of tags $t_1, \ldots, t_d \in \{0,1\}^* \backslash \{t_0\}$. The algorithm first checks the validity of CT_2 by verifying the following conditions:

$$e(\mathsf{ct}_{22}, u^{\mathsf{ct}_{20}} \cdot w) \overset{?}{=} e(g^a, \mathsf{ct}_{24}), \tag{1}$$

$$\mathcal{V}(\mathsf{ct}_{20}, \sigma, (\mathsf{ct}_{21}, \mathsf{ct}_{23_i}, \mathsf{ct}_{24})) \overset{?}{=} 1. \tag{2}$$

If CT_2 is well-formed, the algorithm chooses r, k randomly from $\mathbb{Z}_p$, then computes from CT_2 :

$$\begin{aligned}
\mathsf{CT}_1 &= (\mathsf{ct}_{10}, \mathsf{ct}_{11}, \mathsf{ct}_{12}, \mathsf{ct}'_{12}, \mathsf{ct}''_{12}, \mathsf{ct}'''_{12}, \mathsf{ct}_{13}, \mathsf{ct}_{14}, \mathsf{ct}_{15_i}, \mathsf{ct}_{16}, \sigma) \\
&= (svk, M \cdot Y^{rs}, g^{ars}, g^r, g^{ark}, g^{ak}, (\mathsf{DK}^{u/a})^{1/k}, g^{akrs}, \{V(H(t_i))^{rs}\}_{i \in \{1,\ldots,d\}}, \\
&\quad (u^{svk} \cdot v)^{rs}, \mathcal{S}(ssk, (\mathsf{ct}_{11}, \mathsf{ct}_{15_i}, \mathsf{ct}_{16}))),
\end{aligned}$$

along with the tags $t_1, \ldots, t_d$. Otherwise, CT_2 is declared 'invalid'.

▶ Decryption$_1(\mathsf{param}, \mathsf{sk}_B, \mathsf{Enc}_{\mathsf{pk}_B}(\mathsf{PSK}_i), \mathsf{CT}_1, t_1, \ldots, t_d)$. On the input param, the secret key of user B, encrypted form $\mathsf{Enc}_{\mathsf{pk}_B}(\mathsf{PSK}_i)$, re-encrypted ciphertext

CT_1 along with $\{t_1, \ldots, t_d\}$, the algorithm first checks the validity of CT_1 by verifying the following conditions:

$$e(\mathsf{ct}''_{12}, \mathsf{ct}_{14}) \overset{?}{=} e(\mathsf{DK}^u, \mathsf{ct}'_{12}), \tag{3}$$

$$e(\mathsf{ct}_{13}, u^{\mathsf{ct}_{10}} \cdot w) \overset{?}{=} e(\mathsf{ct}''_{12}, \mathsf{ct}_{16}), \tag{4}$$

$$\mathcal{V}(\mathsf{ct}_{10}, \sigma, (\mathsf{ct}_{11}, \mathsf{ct}_{15_i}, \mathsf{ct}_{16})) \overset{?}{=} 1. \tag{5}$$

If (3)-(5) hold, then for $j = 0, \ldots, i$, the punctured key PSK_i is parsed as $(\mathsf{PSK}_{i1}, \mathsf{PSK}_{i2}, \mathsf{PSK}_{i3}, \mathsf{PSK}_{i4})$. Next, it computes a set of coefficients $w_1, \ldots, w_d, w^*$ such that: $w^* \cdot q(H(\mathsf{PSK}_{i4})) + \sum_{k=1}^{d}(w_k \cdot q(H(t_k))) = q(0) = 1$
Finally, it computes:

$$A = \prod_{j=0}^{i} \frac{e(\mathsf{PSK}_{j1}, \mathsf{ct}_{12})}{e(\mathsf{PSK}_{j3}, \prod_{k=1}^{d} \mathsf{ct}_{15,k}^{w_k}) \cdot e(\mathsf{PSK}_{j2}, \mathsf{ct}_{12})^{w^*}}$$

$$= \frac{e((g^{\alpha_1 + r_1 - r_2 + r' - \lambda'})^{1/a}, g^{ars})}{e(g^{r_1 + r'}, \prod_{k=1}^{d} V(H(t_k))^{rsw_k}) \cdot e((V(H(t_0))^{r' + r_0})^{1/a}, g^{ars})^{w^*}}$$

$$\cdots \frac{e(g^{\lambda' + r_t}, g^{rs})}{e(g^{r_t}, \prod_{k=1}^{d} V(H(t_k))^{w_k}) \cdot e(V(H(t))^{r_t}, g^{rs})^{w^*}}$$

$$= \frac{e(g,g)^{(\alpha_1 + r_1 - r_2 + r' - \lambda')rs}}{e(g,g)^{rs(r_1 + r')}} \cdots \frac{e(g,g)^{(r_t + \lambda')rs}}{e(g,g)^{r_t sr}} = e(g,g)^{(\alpha_1 - r_2)rs}.$$

$$B = e(\mathsf{ct}_{13}, \mathsf{ct}_{14}) = e(g^{(\alpha_2 + r_2)u/ak}, g^{arks}) = e(g,g)^{(\alpha_2 + r_2)rus},$$

and outputs message as: $M = \frac{\mathsf{ct}_{11}}{A \cdot B^{1/u}}$.

▶ $\mathsf{Decryption}_2(\mathsf{param}, \mathsf{sk}_A, \mathsf{PSK}_i, \mathsf{CT}_2, t_1, \ldots, t_d)$. On the input param, the secret key of user A, puncture key PSK_i, ciphertext CT_2 along with $\{t_1, \ldots, t_d\}, t$, the decryption algorithm first computes: for $j = 0, \ldots, i$, the punctured key PSK_i is parsed as $(\mathsf{PSK}_{i1}, \mathsf{PSK}_{i2}, \mathsf{PSK}_{i3}, \mathsf{PSK}_{i4})$. Next, it computes a set of coefficients $w_1, \ldots, w_d, w^*$ such that $w^* \cdot q(H(\mathsf{PSK}_{i4})) + \sum_{k=1}^{d}(w_k \cdot q(H(t_k))) = q(0) = 1$. Finally, it computes:

$$A = \prod_{j=0}^{i} \frac{e(\mathsf{PSK}_{j1}, \mathsf{ct}_{22})}{e(\mathsf{PSK}_{j3}, \prod_{k=1}^{d} \mathsf{ct}_{23,k}^{w_k}) \cdot e(\mathsf{PSK}_{j2}, \mathsf{ct}_{22})^{w^*}}$$

$$= \frac{e((g^{\alpha_1+r_1-r_2+r'-\lambda'})^{1/a}, g^{as})}{e(g^{r_1+r'}, \prod_{k=1}^{d} V(H(t_k))^{sw_k}) \cdot e((V(H(t_0))^{r'+r_0})^{1/a}, g^{as})^{w^*}}$$

$$\cdots \frac{e(g^{\lambda'+r_t}, g^s)}{e(g^{r_t}, \prod_{k=1}^{d} V(H(t_k))^{w_k}) \cdot e(V(H(t))^{r_t}, g^s)^{w^*}}$$

$$= \frac{e(g,g)^{(\alpha_1+r_1-r_2+r'-\lambda')s}}{e(g,g)^{s(r_1+r')}} \cdots \frac{e(g,g)^{(r_t+\lambda')rs}}{e(g,g)^{r_ts}} = e(g,g)^{\alpha_1 s} e(g,g)^{-r_2 s}.$$

$$B = e(\mathsf{ct}_{22}, \mathsf{DK}) = e(g^{as}, g^{\alpha_2+r_2}),$$

and outputs message as: $M = \frac{\mathsf{ct}_{11}}{A \cdot B^{1/a}}$.

4.2 Security

Theorem 1. *Assuming the strong unforgebility of the one-time signature, our Puncturable Proxy Re-Encryption scheme is* RCCA−*secure at level 2 under the* $3 - wDBDHI$ *assumption.*

Proof. Let $(g, A_{-1} = g^{1/a}, A_1 = g^a, A_2 = g^{a^2}, B = g^b, T)$ be modified $3 - wDBDHI$ instance. We build an algorithm $\mathcal{B}$ deciding if $T = (g,g)^{b/a^2}$ out of a successful RCCA adversary $\mathcal{A}$.

We define an event F_{OTS} and bound its probability to occur. Let $\mathsf{CT}_2^* = (\mathsf{ct}_{20}^*, \mathsf{ct}_{21}^*, \mathsf{ct}_{22}^*, \mathsf{ct}_{23_i}^*, \mathsf{ct}_{24}^*, \sigma^*)$ be the challenge ciphertext received by $\mathcal{A}$, and the set $(t_1^*, \ldots, t_d^*)$ be the target set initially output by $\mathcal{A}$. At some points in the process, F_{OTS} is the even that $\mathcal{A}$ issues a decryption query for a first level ciphertext $\mathsf{CT}_1 = (svk^*, \mathsf{ct}_{11}, \mathsf{ct}_{12}, \mathsf{ct}_{12}', \mathsf{ct}_{12}'', \mathsf{ct}_{12}''', \mathsf{ct}_{13}, \mathsf{ct}_{14}, \mathsf{ct}_{15_i}, \mathsf{ct}_{16}, \sigma)$ or a re-encryption query $\mathsf{RC}^* = (svk^*, \mathsf{rc}_1, \mathsf{rc}_2, \mathsf{rc}_{3_i}, \mathsf{rc}_4, \sigma)$ where $(\mathsf{ct}_{11}, \mathsf{ct}_{15_i}, \mathsf{ct}_{16}, \sigma) \neq (\mathsf{ct}_{21}^*, \mathsf{ct}_{23_i}^*, \mathsf{ct}_{24}^*, \sigma^*)$ but $\mathcal{V}(\sigma, svk, (\mathsf{ct}_{11}, \mathsf{ct}_{15_i}, \mathsf{ct}_{16})) = 1$ (resp. $\mathcal{V}(\sigma, svk, (\mathsf{ct}_{11}, \mathsf{ct}_{15_i}, \mathsf{ct}_{16})) = 1$). In the *queries* stage, $\mathcal{A}$ has simply no information on svk^*. Therefore, the probability of a pre-challenge occurrence of F_{OTS} does not exceed $q_0 \cdot \delta$ if q_0 is the overall number of oracle queries and δ denotes the maximal probability. In the guess stage, F_{OTS} is enhanced to an algorithm breaking the strong unforgeability of the one-time signatures. Therefore, the probability $Pr[F_{\mathsf{OTS}}] \leq q_0/p + Adv^{\mathsf{OTS}}$, where $q_0/p + Adv^{\mathsf{OTS}}$ must be negligible by assumption.

Global Setup Phase. $\mathcal{B}$ generates a one-time signature key pair $(ssk^*, svk^*) \leftarrow \mathcal{G}(\lambda)$ and provides $\mathcal{A}$ with public parameters including $w = A_1^{\beta_1(\alpha_1+\alpha_2)}$ and $v = A_1^{(-\beta_1 svk^*)((\alpha_1+\alpha_2))} \cdot A_2^{\beta_2(\alpha_1+\alpha_2)}$ for random $\beta_1, \beta_2, \alpha_1, \alpha_2$ in $\mathbb{Z}_p$. Observe that w and v define a hash function $F(svk) = w^{svk} \cdot v = A_1^{\alpha_1(svk-svk^*)} \cdot A_2^{\alpha_2}$, and computes $g^{\alpha_1}, g^{\alpha_2}$. $\mathcal{B}$ chooses $d+1$ points $\theta_0, \theta_1, \ldots, \theta_d$ uniformly at random from $\mathbb{Z}_p$, in which θ_0 is a distinguished value not used normal simulation. Then it implicitly sets $q(0) = 1$, while $q(t_i) = \theta_i$, then $V(H(t_i)) = A_2^{q(t_i)} = g^{a^2 \theta_i}$. $\mathcal{B}$ continuously initializes two empty sets P, C and a counter $\tau = 0$.

$\mathcal{B}$ generates the initial puncture key as $\mathsf{PSK}_0 = (\mathsf{PSK}_{01}, \mathsf{PSK}_{02}, \mathsf{PSK}_{03}, \mathsf{PSK}_{04}) = (A_1^{\alpha_1 + r_1 + r_2}, V(H(t_0))^{r_1}, g^{r_1}, t_0)$, and the global key for user key generation $\mathsf{DK} = g^{\alpha_2 + r_2}$, with $r_1, r_2, \in_R \mathbb{Z}_p$.

Phase 1. $\mathcal{A}$ can repeatedly issue any of the following queries: Hereafter, we call HU the set of honest parties, including user x^* that is assigned the target public key pk_{x^*}, and CU the set of corrupt parties. Throughout the game, $\mathcal{A}$'s environment is simulated as follows:

– Key-Generation: public keys of honest users $x \in \mathsf{HU}\backslash x^*$ are defined as $\mathsf{pk}_x = A_1^x = g^{ax}$ for a randomly chosen x in $\mathbb{Z}_p$, also implicitly sets $\mathsf{sk}_x = x$. In addition, user x will generate the PSK_0':

$$\mathsf{PSK}_0' = (\mathsf{PSK}_{01}', \mathsf{PSK}_{02}', \mathsf{PSK}_{03}', \mathsf{PSK}_{04}') = (A_1^{(\alpha_1 + r_1 - r_2)1/x}, A_1^{\theta_0 r_1 1/x}, g^{r_1}, t_0).$$

The target user's public key is set as $A_2^{x^*} = g^{x^* a^2}$, also implicitly sets $\mathsf{sk}_{x^*} = ax^*$ with $x^* \in_R \mathbb{Z}_p$. User x^* generates the key PSK_0'

$$\mathsf{PSK}_0' = (\mathsf{PSK}_{01}', \mathsf{PSK}_{02}', \mathsf{PSK}_{03}', \mathsf{PSK}_{04}') = (A_1^{(\alpha_1 + r_1 - r_2)1/x^*}, A_1^{\theta_0 r_1 1/x^*}, g^{r_1}, t_0).$$

The key pair of a corrupted user $x \in \mathsf{CU}$ is set as (g^x, x), for a random $x \in_R \mathbb{Z}_p$. The key PSK_0' of corrupted user is generated

$$\mathsf{PSK}_0' = (\mathsf{PSK}_{01}', \mathsf{PSK}_{02}', \mathsf{PSK}_{03}', \mathsf{PSK}_{04}') = (A_1^{(\alpha_1 + r_1 - r_2)1/x}, A_1^{\theta_0 r_1 1/x}, g^{r_1}, t_0).$$

So that all pairs of keys can be given to $\mathcal{A}$.

To generate re-encryption keys from player x to player y, $\mathcal{B}$ has to distinguish several situations:

- If $x \in \mathsf{HU}\backslash\{x^*\}$ and $y = x^*$, $\mathcal{B}$ returns $R_{x \leftarrow x^*} = (g^{\alpha_2 + r_2})^{x^* \cdot a^2/(ax)} = A_1^{(\alpha_2 + r_2)x^*/x}$, and $\mathsf{TK} = \{g^{1/x}, g^{a^2 \theta_i/x}\}$, which is a valid re-encryption key.
- If $x = x^*$ and $y \in \mathsf{HU}\backslash\{x^*\}$, $\mathcal{B}$ responds with $R_{x^* \leftarrow y} = (g^{\alpha_2 + r_2})^{ax/x^* a^2} = A_{-1}^{(\alpha_2 + r_2)x/x^*}$, and $\mathsf{TK} = \{g^{1/x^*}, g^{a^2 \theta_i/x^*}\}$, that also has the correct distribution.
- If $x, y \in \mathsf{HU}\backslash\{x^*\}$, $\mathcal{B}$ returns $R_{x \leftarrow y} = (g^{\alpha_2 + r_2})^{(ay)/(ax)} = g^{(\alpha_2 + r_2)y/x}$, and $\mathsf{TK} = \{g^{1/x}, g^{a^2 \theta_i/x}\}$,.
- If $x \in \mathsf{HU}\backslash\{x^*\}$ and $y \in \mathsf{CU}$, $\mathcal{B}$ outputs $R_{x \leftarrow y} = (g^{\alpha_2 + r_2})^{y/(ax)} = A_{-1}^{(\alpha_2 + r_2)y/x}$, and $\mathsf{TK} = \{g^{1/x}, g^{a^2 \theta_i/x}\}$, which is also computable.
- Finally, $\mathcal{B}$ uses public key y to encrypt $\mathsf{Enc}_{\mathsf{pk}_y}(\mathsf{TK})$ x's puncture key.

– Puncture: $\mathcal{B}$ increments n, and computes: $\mathsf{PSK}_n = \mathsf{Puncture}(\mathsf{param}, \mathsf{PSK}_{n-1}', \mathsf{TK}, t)$, and adds t to set P, we consider:

Corrupt() query and $\{t_1^*, \ldots, t_d^*\} \cap C = \emptyset$. $\mathcal{B}$ now chooses randomly $r', r_t, \lambda \in \mathbb{Z}_p$. Thus, it outputs the following:

$$\mathsf{PSK}_0'' = ((\mathsf{PSK}_{01}' \cdot A_1^{r'-\lambda'})^{1/x}, \mathsf{PSK}_{02}' \cdot (A_1^{\theta_0 r'})^{1/x}, \mathsf{PSK}_{03}' \cdot g^{r'}, t_0),$$
$$\mathsf{PSK}_i = ((A_1^{\lambda'+r_t})^{1/x}, (V(H(t))^{r_t})^{1/x}, g^{r_t}, t) = ((A_1)^{(\lambda'+r_t)1/x}, A_1^{\theta_t r_t 1/x}, g^{r_t}, t)$$

Corrupt() is invoked at the first time; the adversary issues this query. Then, the challenger returns the most recent punctured key PSK_n to the adversary and sets $C \leftarrow P$. All subsequent queries return $\perp$.

- Re-Encryption queries: Responding to a re-encryption query from user x to user y for a second level ciphertext $\mathsf{CT}_2 = (\mathsf{ct}_{20}, \mathsf{ct}_{21}, \mathsf{ct}_{22}, \mathsf{ct}_{23_i}, \mathsf{ct}_{24}, \sigma)$, $\mathcal{B}$ returns 'invalid' if the following testing is not bypassed (1)–(2)
  - If $x \neq x^*$ or if $x = x^*$ and $y \in \mathsf{HU} \backslash \{x^*\}$, $\mathcal{B}$ simply re-encrypts using the re-encryption key which is available in either case.
  - If $x = x^*$, and $y \in \mathsf{CU}$,
    * If $\mathsf{ct}_{20} = svk^*$, $\mathcal{B}$ encounters an occurrence of F_{OTS} and halts. Indeed, re-encryptions of the challenge ciphertext towards corrupt users are disallowed in the 'guess' stage. Therefore, $(\mathsf{ct}_{21}, \mathsf{ct}_{23_i}, \mathsf{ct}_{24}, \sigma) \neq (\mathsf{ct}_{21}^*, \mathsf{ct}_{23_i}^*, \mathsf{ct}_{24}^*, \sigma^*)$ since we would have $\mathsf{CT}_2 \neq \mathsf{CT}_2^*$ and $x \neq x^*$ if $(\mathsf{ct}_{21}, \mathsf{ct}_{23_i}, \mathsf{ct}_{24}, \sigma) \neq (\mathsf{ct}_{21}^*, \mathsf{ct}_{23_i}^*, \mathsf{ct}_{24}^*, \sigma^*)$.
    * With the case $\mathsf{ct}_{20} \neq svk^*$, $x = x^*$ and $y \in \mathsf{CU}$. Given $\mathsf{ct}_{22}^{1/x^*} = A_2^s$, from $\mathsf{ct}_{16} = \mathsf{ct}_{24} = F(svk)^s = (A_1^{\beta(svk-svk^*)} \cdot A_2^{\beta_2})^s$, $\mathcal{B}$ can compute: $A_1^s = g^{as} = (\frac{\mathsf{ct}_{24}}{\mathsf{ct}_{22}^{\beta_2/x^*}})^{\frac{1}{\beta_1(svk-svk^*)}}$.
    * Knowing g^{as} and user y's private key, $\mathcal{B}$ picks $r, k \in_R \mathbb{Z}_p$ to compute: $\mathsf{ct}_{12} = A_1^{rs} = g^{ars}, \mathsf{ct}_{12}' = g^r, \mathsf{ct}_{12}'' = g^{ark}, \mathsf{ct}_{12}''' = g^{ak}, \mathsf{ct}_{13} = (A_{-1})^{(\alpha_2+r_2)y/x^*k} = (g^{y/x^*})^{(\alpha_2+r_2)/k} \mathsf{ct}_{14} = A_1^{rsk} = g^{ars}, \mathsf{ct}_{15_i} = A_2^{\theta_i sr}$, and return $\mathsf{CT}_1 = (\mathsf{ct}_{10}, \mathsf{ct}_{11}, \mathsf{ct}_{12}, \mathsf{ct}_{12}', \mathsf{ct}_{12}'', \mathsf{ct}_{12}''', \mathsf{ct}_{13}, \mathsf{ct}_{14}, \mathsf{ct}_{15_i}, \mathsf{ct}_{16}, \sigma)$ which has the proper distribution.
- First level decryption queries: $\mathcal{A}$ may ask the decryption of a first level ciphertext $\mathsf{CT}_1 = (\mathsf{ct}_{10}, \mathsf{ct}_{11}, \mathsf{ct}_{12}, \mathsf{ct}_{12}', \mathsf{ct}_{12}'', \mathsf{ct}_{12}''', \mathsf{ct}_{13}, \mathsf{ct}_{14}, \mathsf{ct}_{15_i}, \mathsf{ct}_{16}, \sigma)$ under the public key g^x. For such a request, $\mathcal{B}$ returns 'invalid' if (3)–(5) do not hold. We assume $y \in \mathsf{HU}$ since $\mathcal{B}$ can decrypt using the known private key, then $\mathcal{B}$ can decrypt $\mathsf{Dec}_{\mathsf{sk}_y}(\mathsf{Enc}_{\mathsf{pk}_y}(\mathsf{PSK}_i))$ to receive the PSK_i. In the next step, let us first assume that $\mathsf{ct}_{10} = \mathsf{ct}_{10}^* = svk^*$. If $(\mathsf{ct}_{11}, \mathsf{ct}_{15_i}, \mathsf{ct}_{16}, \sigma) \neq (\mathsf{ct}_{11}^*, \mathsf{ct}_{15_i}^*, \mathsf{ct}_{16}^*, \sigma)$, $\mathcal{B}$ is presented with occurrence of F_{OTS} and halts. If $(\mathsf{ct}_{11}, \mathsf{ct}_{15_i}, \mathsf{ct}_{16}, \sigma) = (\mathsf{ct}_{11}^*, \mathsf{ct}_{15_i}^*, \mathsf{ct}_{16}^*, \sigma)$, $\mathcal{B}$ outputs $\perp$ which deem CT_1 as a derivative of the challenge pair of CT^*, x^*. Additionally, we reduce the computation of $e(\mathsf{ct}_{13}, \mathsf{ct}_{14}) = e(\mathsf{DK}_y, g)^{rs}$ to simulate conveniently in the next step. Lets $\mathsf{ct}_{10} \neq svk^*$, we assume that $y = x^*$, then we $\mathsf{pk}_y = g^{a^2 x^*}$ since $\mathcal{B}$ can decrypt using the known private key y. The validity of the ciphertext guarantees : $e(\mathsf{ct}_{13}, \mathsf{ct}_{14}) = e(\mathsf{DK}, g)^{a^2 yrs}, \mathsf{ct}_{16} = F(svk)^{rs} = g^{\beta_1 ars(svk-svk^*)(\alpha_1+\alpha_2)} \cdot g^{a^2 r \beta_2(\alpha_1+\alpha_2)}$.

$$A = \prod_{j=0}^{i} \frac{e(\mathsf{PSK}_{j1}, \mathsf{ct}_{12})^{x^*}}{e(\mathsf{PSK}_{j3}, \prod_{k=1}^{d} \mathsf{ct}_{15,k}^{w_k}) \cdot e(\mathsf{PSK}_{j2}, \mathsf{ct}_{12})^{x^* w^*}}$$

$$= \frac{e((A_1^{\alpha_1 + r_1 - r_2 + r' - \lambda'})^{1/x^*}, g^{ars})^{x^*}}{e(g^{r_1 + r'}, \prod_{k=1}^{d} (A_2^{\theta_0})^{r s w_k}) \cdot e(A_1^{\theta_0 r_1 1/x}, g^{ars})^{x^* w^*}}$$

$$\cdots \frac{e(g^{\lambda' + r_t}, g^{ars})^{x^*}}{e(g^{r_t}, \prod_{k=1}^{d} V(H(t_k))^{w_k}) \cdot e(A_1^{\theta_t r_1 1/x}, g^{ars})^{x^* w^*}} = e(g,g)^{a^2(\alpha_1 - r_2) rs}.$$

Next, $\mathcal{B}$ computes:

$$\gamma = e(g,g)^{ars(\alpha_1 + \alpha_2)} = \left(\frac{e(\mathsf{ct}_{16}, g)}{A^{\beta_2} \cdot (\mathsf{ct}_{13}, \mathsf{ct}_{14})^{\beta_2 / y(\alpha_2 + r_2)}} \right)^{\frac{1}{\beta_1(svk - svk^*)}}.$$

$\mathcal{B}$ continually computes: $e(\mathsf{ct}_{16}, A_{-1}) = e(\mathsf{ct}_{16}, g^{1/a}) = e(g,g)^{\beta_1 rs(svk - svk^*)(\alpha_1 + \alpha_2)}$.

$e(g,g)^{ars\beta_2(\alpha_1 + \alpha_2)}$. γ uncovers: $e(g,g)^{rs(\alpha_1 + \alpha_2)} = \left(\frac{e(\mathsf{ct}_{16}, A_{-1})}{\gamma^{\beta_2/x^*}} \right)^{\frac{1}{\beta_1(svk - svk^*)}}$,

and the plaintext $m = \mathsf{ct}_{11}/e(g,g)^{rs(\alpha_1 + \alpha_2)}$.

In the next phases, $\mathcal{B}$ must check that m differs from messages m_0, m_1 involved in the challenge query. If $m \in \{m_0, m_1\}$. $\mathcal{B}$ returns $\perp$ according to the RCCA-security rules.

Challenge. $\mathcal{A}$ chooses messages m_0, m_1. At this stage, $\mathcal{B}$ flips a coin $\mu^* \in_R \{0,1\}$, and generates the challenge ciphertext ct_2^* as:

$$\mathsf{ct}_{20}^* = svk^*, \mathsf{ct}_{21}^* = m_{\mu^*} \cdot T^{\alpha_1 + \alpha_2}, \mathsf{ct}_{22}^* = B^{x^*}, \mathsf{ct}_{23_i}^* = B^{\theta_i}, \mathsf{ct}_{24}^* = B^{\beta_2},$$

and $\sigma^* = \mathcal{S}(ssk^*, (\mathsf{ct}_{21}^*, \mathsf{ct}_{23}^*, \mathsf{ct}_{24_i}^*))$. With $\mathsf{pk}_x = g^{x^* a^2}$, $B = g^b$, and the random exponent $s = b/a^2$.

Phase 2. It is identical to Phase 1 with the following restrictions: (1) Corrupt() returns $\perp$ if $\{t_1^*, \ldots, t_d^*\} \cap P = \emptyset$; (2) Re-Encryption queries if (1)–(2) is bypassed and $\mathsf{CT}_2 \neq \mathsf{CT}_2^* \wedge x \neq x^*$. (3) $\mathsf{Decrypt}_1(\mathsf{param}, \mathsf{sk}_x, \mathsf{PSK}_i, \mathsf{CT}_1, t_1, \ldots, t_d)$ is queried.

Guess. CT_2^* is a valid encryption of m_{μ^*} if $T = e(g,g)^{b/a^2}$. In contrast, if T is random in $\mathbb{G}_T$, CT_2^* perfectly hides m_{μ^*} and $\mathcal{A}$ cannot guess μ^* with better probability than $1/2$. When $\mathcal{A}$ eventually outputs her result $\mu' \in \{0,1\}$, $\mathcal{B}$ decides $T = e(g,g)^{b/a^2}$ if $\mu' = \mu$ and that T is randomly chosen. □

Theorem 2. *Assuming the strong unforgebility of the one-time signature, Puncturable Proxy Re-Encryption scheme is RCCA$-$secure at level 1 under the $3 - wDBDHI$ assumption.*

Proof. The proof of Theorem 2 will be provided in Appendix A. □

5   Conclusion

We present a Puncturable Proxy Re-Encryption Scheme supporting forward secrecy for asynchronous communication. Particularly, the proposed scheme is well-suited to many-to-many communication such as a group messaging service since a participant securely delegates computational demand operations to communicate with multiple parties to a proxy (i.e. a message server). Therefore, it allows many participants to exchange messages efficiently in group communication. One opening problem is the transformation of these schemes to obtain adaptive security. We leave it as our future work.

A   Proof of Theorem 2

Let $(g, A_{-1} = g^{1/a}, A_1 = g^a, A_2 = g^{a^2}, B = g^b, T)$ be modified $3 - wDBDHI$ instance. We build an algorithm $\mathcal{B}$ deciding if $T = (g, g)^{b/a^2}$ out of a successful RCCA adversary $\mathcal{A}$.

In this proof, our simulator $\mathcal{B}$ simply halts and outputs a random bit if F_{OTS} ever occurs. Let $\mathsf{CT}_1^* = (svk^*, \mathsf{ct}_{11}^*, \mathsf{ct}_{12}^*, \mathsf{ct}_{13}^*, \mathsf{ct}_{14}^*, \mathsf{ct}_{15}^*, \mathsf{ct}_{16}^*, \sigma^*)$ denotes the challenge ciphertext at the first level received by $\mathcal{A}$, and the set $(t_1^*, \ldots, t_d^*)$ be the target set initially output by $\mathcal{A}$.

Global setup phase. $\mathcal{B}$ generates a one-time signature key pair $(ssk^*, svk^*) \leftarrow \mathcal{G}(\lambda)$ and provides $\mathcal{A}$ with public parameters including $w = A_1^{\beta_1}$ and $v = A_1^{-\beta_1 svk^*} \cdot A_2^{\beta_2}$ for random β_1, β_2 in $\mathbb{Z}_p$. Observe that w and v define a hash function $F(svk) = w^{svk} \cdot v = A_1^{\alpha_1(svk - svk^*)} \cdot A_2^{\alpha_2}$.
$\mathcal{B}$ also selects randomly $\alpha_1, \alpha_2 \in \mathbb{Z}_p$, and computes $g^{\alpha_1}, g^{\alpha_2}$. $\mathcal{B}$ chooses $d + 1$ points $\theta_0, \theta_1, \ldots, \theta_d$ uniformly at random from $\mathbb{Z}_p$, in which θ_0 be a distinguished value not used normal simulation. Then, $\mathcal{B}$ implicitly sets $q(0) = 1$, while $q(t_i) = \theta_{t_i}$, then $V(H(t_i)) = gA_1^{q(t_i)} = g^{a\theta_{t_i}}$. $\mathcal{B}$ continuously initializes two empty sets P, C and a counter $\tau = 0$.
$\mathcal{B}$ generates the initial puncture key as $\mathsf{PSK}_0 = (\mathsf{PSK}_{01}, \mathsf{PSK}_{02}, \mathsf{PSK}_{03}, \mathsf{PSK}_{04}) = (A_1^{\alpha_1 + r_1 + r_2}, V(H(t_0))^{r_1}, g^{r_1}, t_0)$, and the global key for user key generation $\mathsf{DK} = g^{\alpha_2 + r_2}$, with $r_1, r_2, \in_R \mathbb{Z}_p$.

Phase 1. $\mathcal{A}$ can repeatedly issue any of the following queries: we call HU the set of honest parties, including user $x*$ that is assigned the target public key pk_{x^*}, and CU the set of corrupt parties. Throughout the game, $\mathcal{A}$'s environment is simulated as follows:

– Key-Generation: public keys of honest users $x \in \mathsf{HU} \backslash x^*$ and corrupt users $x \in \mathsf{CU}$ are defined as $\mathsf{pk}_x = g^x$ for a randomly chosen x in $\mathbb{Z}_p$. In addition, user x will generate the PSK_0':

$$\mathsf{PSK}_0' = (\mathsf{PSK}_{01}', \mathsf{PSK}_{02}', \mathsf{PSK}_{03}', \mathsf{PSK}_{04}') = (A_1^{(\alpha_1 + r_1 - r_2)1/x}, A_1^{\theta_0 r_1 1/x}, g^{r_1}, t_0).$$

The target user's public key is set as $A_1^{x^*} = g^a$.

$$\mathsf{PSK}_0' = (\mathsf{PSK}_{01}', \mathsf{PSK}_{02}', \mathsf{PSK}_{03}', \mathsf{PSK}_{04}') = (g^{(\alpha_1 + r_1 - r_2)}, g^{\theta_0 r_1}, g^{r_1}, t_0).$$

For corrupt users $i \in \mathsf{CU}$, public key and secret key are both disclosed To generate re-encryption keys from player x to player y, all re-encryption keys are computed:

- If $x, y \neq x^*, \mathsf{R}_{x \leftarrow y} = g^{(\alpha_2 + r_2)y/x}$
- If $y \neq x^*, \mathsf{R}_{x^* \leftarrow y} = A_{-1}^{(\alpha_2 + r_2)y}$ and $\mathsf{R}_{y \leftarrow x^*} = A_1^{(\alpha_2 + r_2)1/y}$.

- Puncture: . $\mathcal{B}$ increments n, and computes: $\mathsf{PSK}_n = \mathsf{Puncture}(\mathsf{param},$ $\mathsf{PSK}'_{n-1}, \mathsf{TK}, t)$, and adds t to set P, we consider: **Corrupt()** is queried and $\{t_1^*, \ldots, t_d^*\} \cap C = \emptyset$. $\mathcal{B}$ now chooses randomly $r', r_t, \lambda \in \mathbb{Z}_p$. Thus it outputs the following:

$$\mathsf{PSK}''_0 = (\mathsf{PSK}'_{01} \cdot (A_1^{r'-\lambda'})^{1/x}, \mathsf{PSK}'_{02} \cdot (V(H(t_0))^{r'})^{1/x}, \mathsf{PSK}'_{03} \cdot g^{r'}, t_0)$$
$$= (\mathsf{PSK}'_{01} \cdot (A_1^{r'-\lambda'})^{1/x}, \mathsf{PSK}'_{02} \cdot (A_1^{\theta_0 r'})^{1/x}, \mathsf{PSK}'_{03} \cdot g^{r'}, t_0),$$
$$\mathsf{PSK}_i = ((A_1^{\lambda'+r_t})^{1/x}, (A_1^{\theta_t r_t})^{1/x}, g^{r_t}, t).$$

Corrupt() is called at the first time; the adversary issues this query. Then the challenger returns the most recent punctured key PSK_n to the adversary and sets $C \leftarrow P$. All subsequent queries return $\bot$.

- First level decryption queries: $\mathcal{A}$ may ask the decryption of a first level ciphertext $\mathsf{CT}_1 = (\mathsf{ct}_{10}, \mathsf{ct}_{11}, \mathsf{ct}_{12}, \mathsf{ct}'_{12}, \mathsf{ct}''_{12}, \mathsf{ct}'''_{12}, , \mathsf{ct}_{13}, \mathsf{ct}_{14}, \mathsf{ct}_{15_i}, \mathsf{ct}_{16}, \sigma)$ under the public key g^x. For such a request, $\mathcal{B}$ returns 'invalid' if $(3)-(5)$ do not hold. We assume $y \in \mathsf{HU}$ since $\mathcal{B}$ can decrypt using the known private key, then $\mathcal{B}$ can decrypt $\mathsf{Dec}_{\mathsf{sk}_y}(\mathsf{Enc}_{\mathsf{pk}_y}(\mathsf{PSK}_i))$ to receive the PSK_i. In the next step, let us first assume that $\mathsf{ct}_{10} = \mathsf{ct}_{10}^* = svk^*$. If $(\mathsf{ct}_{11}, \mathsf{ct}_{15_i}, \mathsf{ct}_{16}, \sigma) \neq (\mathsf{ct}_{11}^*, \mathsf{ct}_{15_i}^*, \mathsf{ct}_{16}^*, \sigma)$, $\mathcal{B}$ is presented with occurence of F_{OTS} and halts. If $(\mathsf{ct}_{11}, \mathsf{ct}_{15_i}, \mathsf{ct}_{16}, \sigma) = (\mathsf{ct}_{11}^*, \mathsf{ct}_{15_i}^*, \mathsf{ct}_{16}^*, \sigma)$, $\mathcal{B}$ outputs $\bot$ which deem CT_1 as a derivative of the challenge pair of CT^*, x^*. We have to compute:

$$\mathsf{ct}_{12} = A_1^{rs} = g^{ars}, \mathsf{ct}'_{12} = g^r, \mathsf{ct}''_{12} = g^{ark}, \mathsf{ct}'''_{12} = g^{ak}, \mathsf{ct}_{13} = (A_{-1})^{(\alpha_2 + r_2)y/k}$$
$$= (g^{1/y})^{(\alpha_2 + r_2)/k}, \mathsf{ct}_{14} = A_1 rsk = g^{ars}, \mathsf{ct}_{15_i} = A_2^{\theta_i sr},$$

for unknown exponents $r, k \in_R \mathbb{Z}_p$. We reduce the computation of $e(\mathsf{ct}_{13}, \mathsf{ct}_{14})$ equals to $e(\mathsf{DK}_y, g)^{rs}$ to simulate conveniently in the next step. Lets $\mathsf{ct}_{10} \neq svk^*$, we assume that $y = x^*$, then we $\mathsf{pk}_y = g^a$ since $\mathcal{B}$ can decrypt using the known private key y. The validity of the ciphertext guarantees

$$e(\mathsf{ct}_{13}, \mathsf{ct}_{14}) = e(\mathsf{DK}, g)^{ars},$$
$$\mathsf{ct}_{16} = F(svk)^{rs} = g^{\beta_1 ars(svk - svk^*)(\alpha_1 + \alpha_2)} \cdot g^{a^2 r \beta_2 (\alpha_1 + \alpha_2)}.$$

Then,

$$A = \prod_{j=0}^{i} \frac{e(\mathsf{PSK}_{j1}, \mathsf{ct}_{12})^{x^*}}{e(\mathsf{PSK}_{j3}, \prod_{k=1}^{d} \mathsf{ct}_{15,k}^{w_k}) \cdot e(\mathsf{PSK}_{j2}, \mathsf{ct}_{12})^{x^* w^*}}$$

$$= \frac{e((g^{\alpha_1 + r_1 - r_2 + r' - \lambda'})^{1/x^*}, g^{ars})^{x^*}}{e(g^{r_1 + r'}, \prod_{k=1}^{d} (A_1^{\theta_0})^{rsw_k}) \cdot e(g^{\theta_0 r_1 1/x}, g^{ars})^{x^* w^*}}$$

$$\cdots \frac{e(g^{\lambda' + r_t}, g^{ars})^{x^*}}{e(g^{r_t}, \prod_{k=1}^{d} V(H(t_k))^{w_k}) \cdot e(g^{\theta_t r_1 1/x}, g^{ars})^{x^* w^*}} = e(g,g)^{a(\alpha_1 - r_2) rs}.$$

$\mathcal{B}$ computes: $e(g,g)^{rs(\alpha_1 + \alpha_2)} = \left(\dfrac{e(\mathsf{ct}_{16}, A_{-1})}{A^{\beta_2} \cdot (\mathsf{ct}_{13}, \mathsf{ct}_{14})^{\beta_2 / y(\alpha_2 + r_2)}} \right)^{\frac{1}{\beta_1(svk - svk^*)}}$, and

recovers the plaintext $m = \mathsf{ct}_{11} / e(g,g)^{rs(\alpha_1 + \alpha_2)}$.

- If $e(\mathsf{ct}_{13}, \mathsf{ct}_{14}) = e(\mathsf{ct}_{13}^*, \mathsf{ct}_{14}^*)$, $\mathcal{B}$ returns $\perp$ meaning that CT_1 is simply a re-randomization of the challenge ciphertext.
- We require $(\mathsf{ct}_{11}, \mathsf{ct}_{15_i}, \mathsf{ct}_{16}, \sigma) \neq (\mathsf{ct}_{11}^*, \mathsf{ct}_{15_i}^*, \mathsf{ct}_{16}^*, \sigma)$, which is an occurence of F_{OTS} and implies $\mathcal{B}$'s termination.

In the next phases, $\mathcal{B}$ must check that m differs from messages m_0, m_1 involved in the challenge query. If $m \in \{m_0, m_1\}$. $\mathcal{B}$ returns $\perp$ according to the RCCA-security rules.

Challenge. $\mathcal{A}$ chooses messages m_0, m_1. At this stage, $\mathcal{B}$ flips a coin $\mu^* \in_R \{0,1\}$, and generates the challenge ciphertext ct_1^* as:

$$\mathsf{ct}_{10}^* = svk^*, \mathsf{ct}_{11}^* = m_{\mu^*} \cdot T^{\alpha_1 + \alpha_2}, \mathsf{ct}_{12}^* = B^{\gamma x^*}, \mathsf{ct}_{12}'^* = A_1^{\gamma}, \mathsf{ct}_{12}''^* = A_2^{\gamma k}, \mathsf{ct}_{12}'''^* = A_1^k,$$

$$\mathsf{ct}_{13}^* = A_{-1}^{k(\alpha_2 + r_2)}, \mathsf{ct}_{14}^* = B^{k\gamma}, \mathsf{ct}_{15_i}^* = B^{\theta_i \gamma}, \mathsf{ct}_{16}^* = B^{\beta_2},$$

and $\sigma^* = \mathcal{S}(ssk, (\mathsf{ct}_{11}^*, \mathsf{ct}_{14_i}^*, \mathsf{ct}_{15}^*, \mathsf{ct}_{16}^*))$. With $\mathsf{pk}_x = g^{x^* a}$, $B = g^b$, and $r = a\gamma, k, s = b/a^2$ with the random numbers $\gamma, k \in \mathbb{Z}_p$.

Phase 2. This phase is identical to Phase 1 with following restrictions: (1) Corrupt() returns $\perp$ if $\{t_1^*, \ldots, t_d^*\} \cap P = \emptyset$. (2) $\mathsf{Decrypt}_1(param, \mathsf{sk}_A, \mathsf{PSK}_i, \mathsf{CT}_1, t_1, \ldots, t_d)$ returns $\perp$ if $(\mathsf{CT}_1, t_1, \ldots, t_d) \neq (\mathsf{CT}_1^*, t_1^*, \ldots, t_d^*)$.

Guess. CT_1^* is a valid encryption of m_{μ^*} if $T = e(g,g)^{b/a^2}$. In contrast, if T is random in $\mathbb{G}_T$, CT_1^* perfectly hides m_{μ^*} and $\mathcal{A}$ cannot guess μ^* with better probability than $1/2$. When $\mathcal{A}$ eventually outputs her result $\mu' \in \{0,1\}$, $\mathcal{B}$ decides $T = e(g,g)^{b/a^2}$ if $\mu' = \mu$ and that T is randomly chosen.

References

1. Ateniese, G., Benson, K., Hohenberger, S.: Key-private proxy re-encryption. In: Fischlin, M. (ed.) CT-RSA 2009. LNCS, vol. 5473, pp. 279–294. Springer, Heidelberg (2009). https://doi.org/10.1007/978-3-642-00862-7_19
2. Ateniese, G., Fu, K., Green, M., Hohenberger, S.: Improved proxy re-encryption schemes with applications to secure distributed storage. ACM Trans. Inf. Syst. Secur. 9, 1–30 (2006)
3. Ateniese, G., Fu, K., Green, M., Hohenberger, S.: Improved proxy re-encryption schemes with applications to secure distributed storage. In: NDSS (2015)
4. Blaze, M., Bleumer, G., Strauss, M.: Divertible protocols and atomic proxy cryptography. Adv. Cryptol. - EUROCRYPT **1403**, 127–144 (1998)
5. Blazy, O., Bultel, X., Lafourcade, P.: Two secure anonymous proxy-based data storages. In: Proceedings of the 13th ICETE. pp. 251–258 (2016)
6. Boneh, D., Boyen, X.: Efficient selective identity-based encryption without random oracles. J. Cryptol. **24**, 659–693 (2011)
7. Canetti, R., Halevi, S., Katz, J.: A forward-secure public-key encryption scheme. In: Biham, E. (ed.) EUROCRYPT 2003. LNCS, vol. 2656, pp. 255–271. Springer, Heidelberg (2003). https://doi.org/10.1007/3-540-39200-9_16
8. Canetti, R., Halevi, S., Katz, J.: Chosen-ciphertext security from identity-based encryption. In: Cachin, C., Camenisch, J.L. (eds.) EUROCRYPT 2004. LNCS, vol. 3027, pp. 207–222. Springer, Heidelberg (2004). https://doi.org/10.1007/978-3-540-24676-3_13
9. Canetti, R., Hohenberger, S.: Chosen-ciphertext secure proxy re-encryption. In: Proceedings of the 14th ACM CCS (2007)
10. Chu, C.-K., Tzeng, W.-G.: Identity-based proxy re-encryption without random oracles. In: Garay, J.A., Lenstra, A.K., Mambo, M., Peralta, R. (eds.) ISC 2007. LNCS, vol. 4779, pp. 189–202. Springer, Heidelberg (2007). https://doi.org/10.1007/978-3-540-75496-1_13
11. Derler, D., Krenn, S., Lorünser, T., Ramacher, S., Slamanig, D., Striecks, C.: Revisiting proxy re-encryption: forward secrecy, improved security, and applications. In: Abdalla, M., Dahab, R. (eds.) PKC 2018. LNCS, vol. 10769, pp. 219–250. Springer, Cham (2018). https://doi.org/10.1007/978-3-319-76578-5_8
12. Dodis, Y., Yampolskiy, A.: A verifiable random function with short proofs and keys. In: Proceedings of the 8th PKC. pp. 416–431 (2005)
13. Ge, C., Susilo, W., Fang, L., Wang, J., Shi, Y.: A cca-secure key-policy attribute-based proxy re-encryption in the adaptive corruption model for dropbox data sharing system. Des. Codes Crypt. **86**(11), 2587–2603 (2018)
14. Green, M., Ateniese, G.: Identity-based proxy re-encryption. In: Katz, J., Yung, M. (eds.) ACNS 2007. LNCS, vol. 4521, pp. 288–306. Springer, Heidelberg (2007). https://doi.org/10.1007/978-3-540-72738-5_19
15. Green, M.D., Miers, I.: Forward secure asynchronous messaging from puncturable encryption. In: Proceedings of the 2015 IEEE S and P, pp. 305–320. IEEE Computer Society (2015)
16. Libert, B., Vergnaud, D.: Unidirectional chosen-ciphertext secure proxy re-encryption. IEEE Trans. Inf. Theor. **57**(3), 1786–1802 (2011)
17. Libert, B., Vergnaud, D.: Unidirectional chosen-ciphertext secure proxy re-encryption. In: Cramer, R. (ed.) PKC 2008. LNCS, vol. 4939, pp. 360–379. Springer, Heidelberg (2008). https://doi.org/10.1007/978-3-540-78440-1_21

18. Mambo, M., Okamoto, E.: Proxy cryptosystems: delegation of the power to decrypt ciphertexts. IEICE Trans. Fundam. **80**–**A**, 54–63 (1997)
19. Matsuo, T.: Proxy re-encryption systems for identity-based encryption. In: Takagi, T., Okamoto, T., Okamoto, E., Okamoto, T. (eds.) Pairing 2007. LNCS, vol. 4575, pp. 247–267. Springer, Heidelberg (2007). https://doi.org/10.1007/978-3-540-73489-5_13
20. Myers, S., Shull, A.: Efficient hybrid proxy re-encryption for practical revocation and key rotation. Cryptology ePrint Archive, Report 2017/833 (2017). https://eprint.iacr.org/2017/833
21. Tang, Q.: Type-based proxy re-encryption and its construction. In: Proceedings of the 9th INDOCRYPT. pp. 130–144. Berlin, Heidelberg (2008)
22. Waters, B.: Efficient identity-based encryption without random oracles. In: Cramer, R. (ed.) EUROCRYPT 2005. LNCS, vol. 3494, pp. 114–127. Springer, Heidelberg (2005). https://doi.org/10.1007/11426639_7
23. Weng, J., Deng, R.H., Ding, X., Chu, C.K., Lai, J.: Conditional proxy re-encryption secure against chosen-ciphertext attack. In: Proceedings of the 4th ASIACCS. pp. 322–332 (2009)
24. Weng, J., Deng, R.H., Liu, S., Chen, K.: Chosen-ciphertext secure bidirectional proxy re-encryption schemes without pairings. Inf. Sci. **180**(24), 5077–5089 (2010)

Generic Traceable Proxy Re-encryption and Accountable Extension in Consensus Network

Hui Guo[1,2], Zhenfeng Zhang[3], Jing Xu[3(✉)], and Mingyuan Xia[4]

[1] State Key Laboratory of Cryptology, P.O. Box 5159, Beijing 100878, China
guohtech@foxmail.com
[2] Guangdong Provincial Key Laboratory of Data Security and Privacy Protection,
Guangzhou 510632, People's Republic of China
[3] Institute of Software, Chinese Academy of Sciences, Beijing, China
{zfzhang,xujing}@tca.iscas.ac.cn
[4] Statistics Department, Tianjin University of Finance and Economics,
Tianjin City, China
xiamingyuan1213@163.com

Abstract. Proxy re-encryption provides a promising solution to share encrypted data in consensus network. When the data owner is going to share her encrypted data with some receiver, he will generate re-encryption key for this receiver and distribute the key among the consensus network nodes following some rules. By using the re-encryption key, the nodes can transform the ciphertexts for the receiver without learning anything about the underlying plaintexts. However, if malicious nodes and receivers collude, they can obtain the capability to decrypt all transformable ciphertexts of the data owner, especially for multi-nodes setting of consensus network. In order to address this problem, some "tracing mechanisms" are naturally required to identify misbehaving nodes and foster accountability when the re-encryption key is abused for distributing the decryption capability.

In this paper, we propose a generic traceable proxy re-encryption construction from any proxy re-encryption scheme, with the twice size ciphertext as the underlying proxy re-encryption scheme. Then our construction can be instantiated properly to yield the first traceable proxy re-encryption with constant size ciphertext, which greatly reduces both the communication and storage costs in consensus network. Furthermore, we show how to generate an undeniable proof for node's misbehavior and support accountability to any proxy re-encryption scheme. Our construction is the first traceable proxy re-encryption scheme with accountability, which is desirable in consensus network so that malicious node can be traced and cannot deny his leakage of re-encryption capabilities.

Keywords: Proxy re-encryption · Traceability · Accountability · Consensus network

© Springer Nature Switzerland AG 2019
K. Sako et al. (Eds.): ESORICS 2019, LNCS 11735, pp. 234–256, 2019.
https://doi.org/10.1007/978-3-030-29959-0_12

1   Introduction

Proxy re-encryption (PRE) [4], proposed by Blaze, Bleumer and Strauss in Eurocrypt 1998, provides a compelling solution to the encrypted data sharing problem. In a PRE scheme, a proxy is given a re-encryption key and has the ability to translate a data owner's ciphertext into a receiver's, without learning anything about the plaintext data. Due to its ciphertext transformation property, PRE has got lots of attention and applications, including email forwarding [7], distributed files systems [3,37], digital rights management [32], publish-subscribe systems [6], cloud data sharing [27,35,39].

One of the most important applications of PRE is NuCypher [1], a decentralized key management system (KMS), which addresses the limitations of using consensus network to store and manipulate encrypted data. Using PRE and consensus networks as major building blocks, NuCypher KMS supports various products such as medical & biotech data platform, key management and decentralized database. In NuCypher KMS, each node of the consensus network acts as a proxy to accomplish the task of re-encryption. If the data owner is going to share his data with some receiver, he will generate re-encryption keys for this receiver and distribute the keys among the nodes following some rules. When the receiver needs some specific data, he applies to the data owner for permission on these data. After receiving the permission, the nodes re-encrypt these data's ciphertext to the receiver. The receiver applies to the data owner for permissions every time upon his need of different data.

However, like all other consensus networks, nodes in NuCypher KMS may cheat. One of the cheating behaviors is revealing re-encryption keys to the data receiver. With the re-encryption key, the receiver can decrypt all the data owner's ciphertext and he needn't apply to the data owner for permissions any more. What's worse, the data receiver could generate decryption device of the data owner and sell it online or offline, which may cause the data owner's economic loss. This weakness is also known as re-encryption key abuse problem.

To mitigate the above security concern in multi-proxies setting, Libert and Vergnaud [23] proposed traceable PRE, where there is a tracing algorithm for tracing malicious proxies leaking re-encryption keys. Specifically, every re-encryption key is linked to a particular proxy, and by observing the leaked re-encryption key or partial of it, the tracing algorithm can identify the proxy who is cheating. NuCypher KMS adopts traceable PRE scheme [23], which discourages nodes from leaking re-encryption keys by forfeiting the cheating node's collateral. However, in traceable PRE scheme [23], the computational overhead and the size of ciphertexts are linear with the length of the underlying code, and thus both the communication and storage costs of the consensus network are significantly increased.

In many cases, only identifying revealed re-encryption key is not enough for applications, as the data owner itself may already leak it. In the above NuCypher KMS example, even though there exists tracing algorithm identifying which re-encryption key is revealed, the malicious node still does not have any risk of being caught as the traitor (even in a court) and he can confidently deny his misbehavior and claim that the tracing result is not an non-repudiable proof thus cannot be considered as an evidence. This is due to the fact that there is no conclusive proof about who is guilty between malicious node and data owner. In order to address the above problem, Guo et al. [16] introduced accountable PRE where there exists a judge algorithm establishing an un-deniable proof once a misbehaving proxy is caught, and they also proposed a concrete scheme with constant ciphertext. However, their construction does not consider traceability and cannot be accountable with more than one node/proxy, which is unsuitable for the consensus network.

In this paper, we are trying to answer the following open and fundamental questions:

- *Is it possible to construct traceable PRE scheme with constant ciphertext?*
  It will significantly decrease the computation and storage costs in consensus network.
- *Is it possible to construct PRE schemes supporting both traceability and accountability?*
  It will trace malicious node/proxy and generate undeniable proof for a court of law to carry out punishment.
- *Is it possible to enable any PRE scheme to support traceability/accountability?*
  It may potentially stimulate the adoption of PRE schemes in practice.

1.1   Our Contribution

In this work, we aim to provide a systematic study of re-encryption key abuse problems in proxy re-encryption schemes. First, motivated by the traitor tracing scheme, we propose a generic construction that converts any existing ordinary PRE scheme into a traceable PRE scheme. Our construction utilizes collusion resistant fingerprinting codes and embeds them in re-encryption keys. A tracing algorithm can recover a pirate codeword from a suspected decryption device and further identify a source codeword from such a pirate codeword based on the security of fingerprinting codes. By this way, the re-encryption key embedded in such a source codeword would be traced to create the suspected decryption device. The traceability is done in a standard black-box way that the tracing algorithm only need oracle access to the unauthorized (or pirate) decoder. In addition, our generic construction only doubles the ciphertext size of the underlying PRE scheme and can be instantiated efficiently. The instantiation is the first traceable PRE scheme with constant size ciphertext.

Second, we further transform our generic traceable PRE to be accountable. Specifically, the data owner/delegator cannot be aware of the proxy's re-encryption key completely, and thus an un-deniable proof can be formed if a traitor is caught from a pirate decoder, which is performed by a new Judge protocol. Our primary challenge in this construction is to ensure consistency between the Trace and the Judge protocol, i.e., an identified traitor cannot evade the confirmation from the judge, which heavily relies on the security of the asymmetric fingerprinting scheme. Our construction is not only generic but also the

Table 1. Comparison of PRE schemes related to defend against re-encryption key abuse attack, where we instantiate our generic construction with the AFGH PRE scheme [3]. N denotes the maximum number of delegatees for each delegator in [23]. poly(λ) denotes the computational cost is polynomial with respect to the security parameter λ.

Schemes		[23]	[17]	[15]	[16]	Our instantiation
Traceability		$\checkmark$	$\times$	$\times$	$\times$	$\checkmark$
Accountability		$\times$	$\times$	$\times$	$\checkmark$	$\checkmark$
Constant ciphertext size		$\times$	$\checkmark$	$\times$	$\checkmark$	$\checkmark$
Computational cost (ms)	Enc_1	1.24	3.64	poly(λ)	3.64	1.24
	Enc_2	$O(\log N)$	10.22	poly(λ)	6.04	9.6
	ReEnc	12.1	14.5	poly(λ)	6.67	6.05
	Dec_1	0.62	6.67	poly(λ)	6.67	0.62
	Dec_2	6.67	6.67	poly(λ)	6.67	6.67

first traceable PRE with accountability in multi-proxies setting. Moreover, black-box traceability is also supported and the instantiated scheme has constant size ciphertext.

We use an implementation [36] of MIRACL CryptoSDK at 80-bit security level as a benchmark to estimate the overhead of our construction instantiated with AFGH PRE scheme [3] and existing PRE schemes related to defend against re-encryption key abuse attack. Table 1 illustrates the comparison and the results show that the resulting scheme performs substantially better on re-encryption and first level encryption/decryption efficiency, significantly on ciphertext size, which reduces both communication and computation complexity. More comparison details can be seen in Sect. 6.

1.2   Related Work

In 1998, Blaze et al. [4] first proposed the concept of PRE. Afterwards, a lot of works followed up to enhance its security and functionalities, including CPA secure PREs [8,9,19], CCA secure PREs [7,12,24,36] and secure PRE under honest re-encryption attacks (HRA) [10], type-based (conditional) PREs [33,34, 37], forward secure PRE [11] and PRE for revocation and key rotation [26], etc.

Re-Encryption Key Abuse of PRE. Addressing re-encryption key abuse problem of PRE scheme was started with the work of Ateniese et al. [3]. They proposed the concept of non-transferability but left it as an open problem to give a concrete construction. Since then, there has been several works towards addressing this problem. Libert and Vergnaud [23] proposed a traceable proxy re-encryption scheme, where the delegator can identify the malicious proxy leaking re-encryption keys. To achieve this property, they borrowed ideas from an identity-based traitor tracing scheme based on wildcard identity-based encryption (IBE) [2] and inherited its disadvantages: the computational overhead and the size of ciphertexts are linear with the length of the underlying code. Later, Hayashi et al. [18] and Guo et al. [17] tried to construct secure PRE schemes against re-encryption key forging attacks. Unfortunately, neither of the two schemes is able to capture all re-encryption key abusing attacks. Recently, Guo et al. [15] formalized the notion of non-transferability, and proposed a concrete construction using an indistinguishability obfuscator for circuits and a k-unforgeable authentication scheme as main tools. However, due to inefficiency of the current indistinguishability obfuscator, their scheme is impractical till now. Later, Guo et al. [16] proposed the notion of accountable PRE and gave an efficient construction under standard model. In accountable PRE, if the proxy is accused to abuse the re-encryption key for distributing the decryption capability, a judge algorithm can decide whether it is innocent or not. However, their scheme only allows one proxy to re-encrypt ciphertext, and thus cannot be applied to the consensus network.

Accountable Authority IBE/ABE. In order to mitigate the key escrow problem in IBE and attribute based encryption (ABE), accountable authority IBE/ABE has been studied in various works [13,14,20–22,25,28,31,38]. Our work has similarities with accountable IBE/ABE. Informally, accountable IBE/ABE aims at solving the key abuse problem of the PKG, while we try to address the key abuse issue of the proxy in this paper. However, different from the PKG considered to be a trusted party unconditionally in most IBE/ABE, the proxy is only a semi-honest party in PRE, and thus it is of great practical significance to restrict misbehavior of the proxy.

2   Preliminary

2.1   Fingerprinting Codes

We are only interested in binary codes, i.e. codes defined over $\{0,1\}$. Let the symbol of '?' denotes an unknown bit, either 0 or 1. For a word $\bar{w} \in \{0,1\}^l$, we write $\bar{w} = w_1, \cdots, w_l$, where $w_i \in \{0,1\}$ is the ith letter of $\bar{w}$ for $i = 1, \cdots, l$. Let n be an integer, λ be the security parameter and $\mathsf{negl}(\cdot)$ be a negligible function.

Fingerprinting codes are defined by two algorithms [5]:

- CodeGen(n, λ) : This algorithm is called a code generator. It outputs a pair (Γ, tk), where Γ denote a code containing n words in $\{0,1\}^l$ for some $l > 0$ and tk is called a tracing key.
- Identify$(tk, \bar{w}^*)$: This algorithm takes as input a pair $(\bar{w}^*, tk)$ where $\bar{w}^* \in \{0,1\}^l$. The algorithm outputs a subset U of $\{1, \cdots, n\}$. Informally, an element in U is "accused" of being an index of a traitor for creating the word $\bar{w}^*$.

Before formalizing the security definition for fingerprinting codes, recall the definition of feasible set [5]:

- Let $W = \{\bar{w}^{(1)}, \cdots, \bar{w}^{(t)}\}$ be a set of words in $\{0,1\}^l$. We say that a word $\bar{w} \in \{0,1\}^l$ is feasible for W if there is a $j \in [t]$ such that $\bar{w}_i = \bar{w}_i^{(j)}, \forall i \in [l]$.
- For a set of words $W \subset \{0,1\}^l$, we say that the feasible set of W, denoted $F(W)$, is the set of all words that are feasible for W.
- We say that the extended feasible set for W, denoted $F_?(W)$, is the set of all feasible words for $W \subset \{0,1,?\}^l$.

The security of fingerprinting codes is defined using a game between a challenger and an adversary as follows.

Definition 1. [5] Fingerprinting code (CodeGen, Identify) is said to be fully collusion resistant if for any adversary $\mathcal{A}$, any $n > 0$ and any subset $C \subset \{1, \cdots, n\}$, the following holds:

$$\Pr\begin{bmatrix} (\Gamma, tk) \leftarrow \text{CodeGen}(n, \lambda) \text{ where } \Gamma = \{\bar{w}^{(1)}, \cdots, \bar{w}^{(n)}\}; \\ \bar{w}^* \in F(\{\bar{w}^{(i)}\}_{i \in C}) \leftarrow \mathcal{A}(n, \lambda, \{\bar{w}^{(i)}\}_{i \in C}) : \\ \text{Identify}(\bar{w}^*, tk) = \emptyset \text{ or Identify}(\bar{w}^*, tk) \not\subset C \end{bmatrix} < \text{negl}(\lambda)$$

Definition 2. [5] Fingerprinting code is δ-robust if the pirate code $\bar{w}^*$ in the above definition is allowed to contain no more than δl symbols of '?', where l is the code length.

Note that Definition 2 is an extension of collusion resistant fingerprinting codes from Definition 1. It allows tracing noisy codewords that we fail to determine which bits are in the adversary's possession on several coordinates.

3   Definition and Security Model

3.1   Basic PRE

In this paper, we use λ to denote the security parameter. First, recall the definition of a basic PRE scheme [23], which is a tuple of algorithms (Setup, KeyGen, ReKeyGen, Enc$_1$, Enc$_2$, ReEnc, Dec$_1$, Dec$_2$):

- Setup(λ): Taking a security parameter λ as input, this algorithm outputs public parameter param which specifies plaintext space M, ciphertext space C and randomness space R.
- KeyGen(param): Taking the security parameter λ as input, this algorithm outputs the user's public key and secret key pair $(\text{pk}_i, \text{sk}_i)$. We omit param in the following algorithms' inputs.
- ReKeyGen(sk_i, pk_j): Taking a delegator's secret key sk_i and a delegatee's public key pk_j as input, this algorithm outputs a re-encryption key $\text{rk}_{i \to j}$.
- Enc$_1$(pk_j, m): Taking a user's public key pk_j and a message $m \in M$ as input, this algorithm outputs a ciphertext C'_j. It is a first level ciphertext and cannot be re-encrypted for another user.

- $\text{Enc}_2(\mathsf{pk}_i, m)$: Taking a user's public key pk_i and a message $m \in \mathsf{M}$ as input, this algorithm outputs a ciphertext C_i. It is a second level ciphertext and can be re-encrypted for another user.
- $\text{ReEnc}(\mathsf{rk}_{i \to j}, C_i)$: Taking the re-encryption key $\mathsf{rk}_{i \to j}$ and a second level ciphertext C_i as input, this algorithm outputs a re-encrypted ciphertext C_j'.
- $\text{Dec}_1(\mathsf{sk}_j, C_j')$: Taking the secret key sk_j and a first level ciphertext or a re-encrypted ciphertext C_j' as input, this algorithm outputs a message $m \in \mathsf{M}$.
- $\text{Dec}_2(\mathsf{sk}_i, C_i)$: Taking the secret key sk_i and a second level ciphertext C_i as input, this algorithm outputs a message $m \in \mathsf{M}$.

Correctness. For any message $m \in \mathsf{M}$, any users' key pairs $(\mathsf{pk}_i, \mathsf{sk}_i), (\mathsf{pk}_j, \mathsf{sk}_j) \leftarrow$ KeyGen(param) and any re-encryption key $\mathsf{rk}_{i \to j} \leftarrow$ ReKeyGen($\mathsf{sk}_i, \mathsf{pk}_j$), the following conditions hold:

$$\text{Dec}_1(\mathsf{sk}_j, \text{Enc}_1(\mathsf{pk}_j, m)) = m; \ \text{Dec}_2(\mathsf{sk}_i, \text{Enc}_2(\mathsf{pk}_i, m)) = m;$$
$$\text{Dec}_1(\mathsf{sk}_j, \text{ReEnc}(\mathsf{rk}_{i \to j}, \text{Enc}_2(\mathsf{pk}_i, m))) = m.$$

3.2 CPA Security

An adversary has access to the following oracles:

- Uncorrupted key generation oracle $\mathcal{O}_{\text{hkg}}(i)$: Compute $(\mathsf{pk}_i, \mathsf{sk}_i) \leftarrow$ KeyGen(i), return pk_i.
- Corrupted key generation oracle $\mathcal{O}_{\text{ckg}}(i)$: Compute $(\mathsf{pk}_i, \mathsf{sk}_i) \leftarrow$ KeyGen(i), return $(\mathsf{sk}_i, \mathsf{pk}_i)$.
- Re-encryption key generation oracle $\mathcal{O}_{\text{rkg}}(\mathsf{pk}_i, \mathsf{pk}_j)$: On input of $(\mathsf{pk}_i, \mathsf{pk}_j)$, where $\mathsf{pk}_i, \mathsf{pk}_j$ were generated before by KeyGen, return a re-encryption key $\mathsf{rk}_{i \to j} \leftarrow$ ReKeyGen($\mathsf{sk}_i, \mathsf{pk}_j$).

To capture the CPA security notion for PRE schemes, we associate a CPA adversary $\mathcal{A}$ with the following template security experiment:

$$\begin{aligned}
&\text{Experiment } \text{Exp}_{\Pi, \mathcal{A}}^{\text{cpa-}\gamma}(\lambda) \\
&\quad \text{param} \leftarrow \text{Setup}(\lambda); \\
&\quad (\mathsf{pk}^*, m_0, m_1) \leftarrow \mathcal{A}^{\mathcal{O}'}(\text{param}); \\
&\quad d^* \leftarrow \{0, 1\}; \\
&\quad C^* = \text{Enc}_\gamma(\mathsf{pk}^*, m_{d^*}); \\
&\quad d' \leftarrow \mathcal{A}^{\mathcal{O}'}(\text{param}, C^*); \\
&\quad \text{If } d' = d^* \text{ return } 1; \\
&\quad \text{else return } 0.
\end{aligned}$$

In the above experiment, $\gamma \in \{1, 2\}$ specifies which level ciphertext that $\mathcal{A}$ attacks and $\mathcal{O}' = \{\mathcal{O}_{\text{hkg}}, \mathcal{O}_{\text{ckg}}, \mathcal{O}_{\text{rkg}}\}$. The advantage of $\mathcal{A}$ is defined as

$$\text{Adv}_{\Pi, \mathcal{A}}^{\text{cpa-}\gamma}(\lambda) = |\Pr[\text{Exp}_{\Pi, \mathcal{A}}^{\text{cpa-}\gamma}(\lambda) = 1] - \frac{1}{2}|.$$

Formally, we present the CPA security as follows.

Definition 3 *(CPA Security at the Second Level* [17].*)* For any PRE scheme Π_s, we instantiate the experiment with a CPA adversary $\mathcal{A}$ and $\gamma = 2$. It is required that pk^* is uncorrupted and $|m_0| = |m_1|$. If C^* denotes the challenge ciphertext, $\mathcal{A}$ can never make re-encryption key generation query $\mathcal{O}_{\mathrm{rkg}}(\mathsf{pk}^*, \mathsf{pk}_j)$, where pk_j is corrupted.

Π_s is said to be secure against chosen plaintext attacks at the second level ciphertext if for any polynomial time adversary $\mathcal{A}$, the advantage function $\mathrm{Adv}_{\Pi_s, \mathcal{A}}^{\mathrm{cpa\text{-}2}}(\lambda)$ is negligible in λ.

Definition 4 *(CPA Security at the First Level* [17].*)* For any PRE scheme Π_s, we instantiate the experiment with a CPA adversary $\mathcal{A}$ and $\gamma = 1$. It is required that pk^* is uncorrupted and $|m_0| = |m_1|$.

Π_s is said to be secure against chosen plaintext attacks at the first level ciphertext if for any polynomial time adversary $\mathcal{A}$, the advantage function $\mathrm{Adv}_{\Pi_s, \mathcal{A}}^{\mathrm{cpa\text{-}1}}(\lambda)$ is negligible in λ.

Remark 1. Recently, [10] shows CPA security is not an appropriate security definition for PRE when the delegatee is not trusted. But since CPA security is simple and it is the basis for CCA security and HRA security, we use it to demonstrate how to give a generic construction. Note that, CPA security can be replaced by CCA security or HRA security without changing our generic construction.

3.3   Traceable PRE

Compared to the basic PRE scheme, traceable PRE [23] has one more algorithm, Trace algorithm, for identifying malicious proxy. Moreover, in order to trace the malicious proxy, ReKeyGen algorithm would output a tracing key as well as a re-encryption key. Specifically,

- ReKeyGen($\mathsf{sk}_i, \mathsf{pk}_j$): Taking a delegator's secret key sk_i and a delegatee's public key pk_j as input, this algorithm outputs a re-encryption key $\mathsf{rk}_{i \to j}$ and a tracing key tk_i.
- Trace$^{D_{i,\mu}}$($\mathsf{pk}_i, \mathsf{tk}_i$): This algorithm is run by delegator. With black-box access to a μ-useful decryption device $D_{i,\mu}$[1] and taking the tracing key tk_i as input, this algorithm outputs at least one tag of the re-encryption keys.

3.4   Black Box Traceability

Consider the case that a delegator has multiple proxies and multiple delegatees. Informally speaking, a PRE scheme is called traceable if at least one of the colluded proxies creating a pirate decryption device can be identified.

---

[1] For non-negligible probability value μ, a PPT algorithm $D_{i,\mu}$ is a μ-useful decryption device for user i, if $\Pr[m \leftarrow \mathsf{M}, C_i \leftarrow \mathsf{Enc}_2(\mathsf{pk}_i, m), m' \leftarrow D_{i,\mu}(C_i) : m = m'] \geq \mu$, where M is the plaintext space.

In traceable PRE, ReKeyGen algorithm additionally generates a tracing key, and the re-encryption key generation oracle is accordingly adapted as follows.

– Re-encryption key generation oracle $\mathcal{O}_{\mathrm{rkg}}^{(t)}(\mathsf{pk}_i, \mathsf{pk}_j)$: On input of $(\mathsf{pk}_i, \mathsf{pk}_j)$, run $(\mathsf{rk}_{i \to j}, \mathsf{tk}_i) \leftarrow \mathrm{ReKeyGen}(\mathsf{sk}_i, \mathsf{pk}_j)$ and return re-encryption key $\mathsf{rk}_{i \to j}$.

In the oracle $\mathcal{O}_{\mathrm{rkg}}^{(t)}$, the challenger also generates a tracing key, but does not output it to the adversary.

With oracles $\mathcal{O}_{\mathrm{hkg}}, \mathcal{O}_{\mathrm{ckg}}, \mathcal{O}_{\mathrm{rkg}}^{(t)}$, the security experiment is defined as follows:

$$
\begin{aligned}
&\text{Experiment } \mathrm{Exp}_{\Pi,\mathcal{A}}^{\mathrm{Trace}}(\lambda) \\
&\quad \mathsf{param} \leftarrow \mathrm{Setup}(\lambda); \\
&\quad \mathsf{pk}^*, D_{*,\mu} \leftarrow \mathcal{A}^{\mathcal{O}_{\mathrm{hkg}}, \mathcal{O}_{\mathrm{ckg}}, \mathcal{O}_{\mathrm{rkg}}^{(t)}}(\mathsf{param}) \\
&\quad \text{where } \mathsf{pk}^* \text{ is generated by } \mathcal{O}_{\mathrm{hkg}} \\
&\quad \text{and } \mu \text{ is a non-negligible probability value;} \\
&\quad \text{If } \mathrm{Trace}^{D_{*,\mu}}(\mathsf{pk}^*, \mathsf{tk}^*) = \emptyset \text{ or } \mathrm{Trace}^{D_{*,\mu}}(\mathsf{pk}^*, \mathsf{tk}^*) \not\subset C \\
&\quad \text{where } \mathsf{tk}^* \text{ is generated by } \mathcal{O}_{\mathrm{rkg}} \text{ and } C \text{ is the tag set} \\
&\quad \text{of re-encryption keys queried by } \mathcal{A}. \\
&\quad \text{return 1;} \\
&\quad \text{else return 0.}
\end{aligned}
$$

The advantage of $\mathcal{A}$ is defined as

$$
\mathrm{Adv}_{\Pi,\mathcal{A}}^{\mathrm{Trace}}(\lambda) = \mid \mathrm{Pr}[\mathrm{Exp}_{\Pi,\mathcal{A}}^{\mathrm{Trace}}(\lambda) = 1] \mid.
$$

Definition 5 *(Traceability.)* A PRE scheme Π_s is said to be μ-traceable if for any polynomial time adversary $\mathcal{A}$, the advantage function $\mathrm{Adv}_{\Pi,\mathcal{A}}^{\mathrm{Trace}}(\lambda)$ is negligible in λ.

4   Generic Traceable Construction

Intuition. The existing traceable PRE scheme [23] might be seen as using a multi-receiver encryption scheme derived from the single level *Wa-WIBE* of [2]. The re-encryption keys are generated by selecting a unique identifier and binding decryption keys of the multi-receiver scheme to delegatees' public keys. [23] shows how to construct traceable PRE based on concrete algebraic structure. However, it is not clear whether it is possible to give a generic construction based on any basic PRE scheme.

We observe that several properties should be satisfied to gain traceability:

– Each re-encryption key should be bound to a unique identifier that can be traced back to.
– For a suspected decryption device, the tracing algorithm could recover partial information about the identifier of the re-encryption key involved in creating the device.
– The re-encryption key involved in creating the device could be identified from the partial information.

- In addition, to obtain black-box tracing property, the ciphertext should have two forms, one is for usual decryption and the other is for tracing. In more detail, for normal encryption, all delegatees should obtain the re-encrypted ciphertext of the same message. However, for traitor-tracing purpose, it is not the case since the tracing algorithm need to distinguish which re-encryption key being involved in a given pirate decryption device.

Motivated by the traitor tracing scheme [5], we observe that such properties can be achieved by using fingerprinting codes. At high level, we embed collusion resistant fingerprinting codeword in each re-encryption key. A tracing algorithm is designed to first recover a pirate codeword from a suspected decryption device, and then identify a source codeword from such a pirate codeword based on the security of fingerprinting codes. As a result, the re-encryption key embedded in such a source codeword would be involved in creating the suspected decryption device. Therefore, the crux here is how to design the tracing algorithm, as well as the ciphertexts and the re-encryption keys to support the tracing algorithm. We use basic PRE and fingerprinting codes as building blocks.

- For generating the re-encryption key, we embed fingerprinting codes as follows. Assume the fingerprinting code's length is l, and every user's public/secret pair includes l pairs of the original PRE scheme. Delegator prepares l pairs of re-encryption key elements, denoted as $\{rk_{k,b}\}_{k=1,\cdots,l,b=0,1}$, which are generated by l secret keys. When generating a new re-encryption key, he chooses an unemployed codeword at random, denoted as $\{b_k\}_{k=1,\cdots,l}$ where $b_k \in \{0,1\}$. For each pair of the re-encryption key elements, he picks one element according to the corresponding bit of codeword. At last, he collects l re-encryption key element $\{rk_{k,b_k}\}_{k=1,\cdots,l,b_k\in\{0,1\}}$ and sends them to the proxy. Note that, for a single bit of the codeword, the proxy holds either of $rk_{k,0}$ and $rk_{k,1}$.
- For the ciphertext, it can be designed into two parts. Each part can be re-encrypted by either $rk_{k,0}$ or $rk_{k,1}$. In normal encryption algorithm, both parts encrypt the same plaintext, while in tracing algorithm, the two parts encrypt different plaintext for distinguishing one bit of the suspected codeword.
- For tracing algorithm, as mentioned above, it can be implemented by feeding the pirate decryption device with training ciphertext. Based on the responses, the tracer can recover a pirate codeword. The fingerprinting code then can be used to find one corrupted codeword, and finally the traitor. See more details in the following construction.

Construction. Let $(\mathsf{CodeGen},\mathsf{Identify})$ be a fingerprinting code, which contains n words in $\{0,1\}^l$. For a given PRE scheme $\Pi = (\overline{\mathsf{Setup}}, \overline{\mathsf{KeyGen}}, \overline{\mathsf{ReKeyGen}}, \overline{\mathsf{Enc_1}}, \overline{\mathsf{Enc_2}}, \overline{\mathsf{ReEnc}}, \overline{\mathsf{Dec_1}}, \overline{\mathsf{Dec_2}})$, the generic traceable PRE construction is as follows:

- **Setup**(λ): Taking the security parameter λ as input, run $\overline{\mathsf{Setup}}$ algorithm of Π and output the system parameters param.

- **KeyGen(param)**: For user i, run $2l$ times $\overline{\text{KeyGen}}$ algorithm of Π to generate $\{(sk_{i,k,b}, pk_{i,k,b})\}_{k=1,\cdots,l,b=0,1}$. Set $\mathbf{sk_i} = \{sk_{i,k,b}\}_{k=1,\cdots,l,b=0,1}$ and $\mathbf{pk_i} = \{pk_{i,k,b}\}_{k=1,\cdots,l,b=0,1}$.

- **ReKeyGen($\mathbf{sk_i}, \mathbf{pk_j}$)**: Given user i's secret key $\mathbf{sk_i} = \{sk_{i,k,b}\}_{k=1,\cdots,l,b=0,1}$ and user j's public key $\mathbf{pk_j} = \{pk_{j,k,b}\}_{k=1,\cdots,l,b=0,1}$ as input,, user i proceeds as follows:
  - First, check whether it is the first time for user i to generate re-encryption keys. If it is, generate fingerprinting code by running $(\Gamma_i, tk_i) \leftarrow \text{CodeGen}(n, \lambda)$, where $\Gamma = \{\bar{w}^{(1)}, \cdots, \bar{w}^{(n)}\} \subset \{0,1\}^l$, tk_i is the tracing key and n denotes the maximum number of the delegatees. Set $\mathbf{tk_i} = tk_i$.
  - Then, choose a previously unemployed bit string $\bar{w}^{(u)} = w_1, \cdots, w_l \in \Gamma_i$ and generate the re-encryption key $\mathbf{rk} = (\bar{w}^{(u)}, \{rk_{k,w_k}^{(i \rightarrow j)}\}_{k=1,\cdots,l})$, where u denotes the tag of the re-encryption key and $rk_{k,w_k}^{(i \rightarrow j)}$ is the output by running algorithm $\overline{\text{ReKeyGen}}(sk_{i,k,w_k}, pk_{j,1,0})$ of Π.

- **$\text{Enc}_1(\mathbf{pk_j}, m)$**: Given $\mathbf{pk_j} = \{pk_{j,k,b}\}_{k=1,\cdots,l,b=0,1}$ and a message m, run the $\overline{\text{Enc}_1}$ algorithm of Π and return $\mathbf{C'_j} = \overline{\text{Enc}_1}(pk_{j,1,0}, m)$.

- **$\text{Enc}_2(\mathbf{pk_i}, m)$**: Given $\mathbf{pk_i} = \{pk_{i,k,b}\}_{k=1,\cdots,l,b=0,1}$, randomly choose $r \leftarrow \{1, \cdots, l\}$. Run the $\overline{\text{Enc}_2}$ algorithm of Π, and set $c_{r,0} = \overline{\text{Enc}_2}(pk_{i,r,0}, m)$ and $c_{r,1} = \overline{\text{Enc}_2}(pk_{i,r,1}, m)$. Return the second level ciphertext $\mathbf{C_i} = (c_{r,0}, c_{r,1}, r)$.

- **$\text{ReEnc}(\mathbf{rk_{i \rightarrow j}}, \mathbf{C_i})$** : On input re-encryption key $\mathbf{rk} = (\bar{w}, \{rk_{k,w_k}^{(i \rightarrow j)}\}_{k=1,\cdots,l})$ and ciphertext $\mathbf{C_i}$, parse the ciphertext $\mathbf{C_i} = (c_{r,0}, c_{r,1}, r)$ and run the $\overline{\text{ReEnc}}$ algorithm of Π with $rk_{r,w_r}^{(i \rightarrow j)}$, it outputs a re-encrypted ciphertext $\mathbf{C'_j} = \overline{\text{ReEnc}}(rk_{r,w_r}^{(i \rightarrow j)}, c_{r,w_r})$.

- **$\text{Dec}_1(\mathbf{sk_j}, \mathbf{C'_j})$**: On input secret key $\mathbf{sk_j} = \{sk_{j,k,b}\}_{k=1,\cdots,l,b=0,1}$ and a ciphertext $\mathbf{C'_j} = c'_j$ as input, run the $\overline{\text{Dec}_1}$ algorithm of the underlying PRE and return $m = \overline{\text{Dec}_1}(sk_{j,1,0}, c'_j)$.

- **$\text{Dec}_2(\mathbf{sk_i}, \mathbf{C_i})$**: On input secret key $\mathbf{sk_i} = \{sk_{i,k,b}\}_{k=1,\cdots,l,b=0,1}$ and a second level ciphertext $\mathbf{C_i} = (c_{r,0}, c_{r,1}, r)$, run $\overline{\text{Dec}_2}(sk_{i,r,w_r}, c_{r,w_r})$ and output the result.

- **$\text{Trace}^{D_{i,\mu}}(\mathbf{pk_i}, \mathbf{tk_i})$**: With black-box access to a μ-useful decryption device $D_{i,\mu}$ and taking the pubic key $\mathbf{pk_i} = \{pk_{i,k,b}\}_{k=1,\cdots,l,b=0,1}$ and $\mathbf{tk_i} = tk_i$ as input, proceed as following steps.
  1. For each $k \in \{1, \cdots, l\}$,
     (a) Repeat the following steps λ^2 times, and let p_k be the fraction of times such that $m = \hat{m}$:

$$m \leftarrow M$$
$$c_0 \leftarrow \overline{\text{Enc}_2}(pk_{i,k,0}, m), c_1 \leftarrow \overline{\text{Enc}_2}(pk_{i,k,1}, 0)$$
$$c^* \leftarrow (c_0, c_1, k)$$
$$\hat{m} \leftarrow D_{i,\mu}(c^*).$$

(b) Repeat the following steps λ^2 times, and let q_k be the fraction of times such that $m = \hat{m}$:

$$m \leftarrow \mathsf{M}$$
$$c_0 \leftarrow \overline{\mathsf{Enc_2}}(pk_{i,k,0}, m), c_1 \leftarrow \overline{\mathsf{Enc_2}}(pk_{i,k,1}, m)$$
$$c^* \leftarrow (c_0, c_1, k)$$
$$\hat{m} \leftarrow D_{i,\mu}(c^*).$$

2. After the repetitions for each k, let $w_k \in \{0,1\}$ be

$$w_k = \begin{cases} 0 & \text{if } p_k > 0 \\ 1 & \text{if } p_k = 0 \text{ and } q_k > \frac{1}{\sqrt{\lambda}} \\ ? & \text{otherwise} \end{cases}$$

3. Set $\bar{w}^* = w_1 \cdots w_l$. Run Identify$(tk_i, \bar{w}^*)$ and output the traitor set.

Correctness. For a given ciphertext, the re-encryption and decryption algorithms of the above generic construction actually runs re-encryption and decryption algorithms of an underlying PRE scheme Π, and thus the correctness is implied.

Theorem 1. *The above generic construction is a μ-traceable PRE under the assumption that the underlying PRE scheme Π is CPA secure and* (CodeGen, Identify) *is a δ-robust fully collusion resistant fingerprinting code, where $\delta = \mu/(1 - 2/\sqrt{\lambda})$ and λ denotes the security parameter.*

Proof Sketch. Since the encryption algorithm of generic construction simply runs that of the underlying PRE scheme twice, CPA security is implied[2]. Then we give some intuitions on traceability. Note that traceability here does not allow adversary to obtain the delegator's secret keys. To prove the traceability, we observe the quantities p_k and q_k computed in the **Trace** algorithm. First, if $p_k > 0$ then the adversary must possess $(rk_{k,0}^{(i \to j)}, sk_{j,1,0})$ for some j with high probability, since otherwise the underlying PRE is not CPA secure. Second, if there is a gap between p_k and q_k, the adversary must possess $(rk_{k,1}^{(i \to j)}, sk_{j,1,0})$ for some j with high probability, since otherwise the underlying PRE is not CPA secure. In summary, $\bar{w}^* = w_1 \cdots w_l$ computed in the **Trace** algorithm is contained in $F_?(\{\bar{w}^{(i)}\}_{i \in C})$ with high probability, where C denotes the set of codewords of re-encryption keys queried by $\mathcal{A}$. Therefore, Identify$(tk_i, \bar{w}^*)$ outputs a member of C with overwhelming probability. The equation $\delta = \mu/(1 - 2/\sqrt{\lambda})$ can be proved via a standard probabilistic argument, see more details in [5].

---

[2] Similarly, if the underlying PRE scheme is HRA/CCA secure, then the generic construction is also HRA/CCA secure.

5   Enforcing Accountability

In traceable PRE, though a proxy is identified from a pirate decryption device, there is still possibility that it is generated by the delegator. Therefore, it is necessary to distinguish whether the proxy is involved in generating the device or not. Accountability can provide such functionality.

This property would be supported only if the delegator does not know the whole re-encryption key, since otherwise he is able to incriminate an honest proxy. In order to achieve this goal, it is a possible way that the proxy chooses an additional private input in re-encryption key generation algorithm. Specifically,

- ReKeyGen($\mathsf{sk}_i, \mathsf{pk}_j, u, s_u$): It is a secure 2-party protocol between the delegator and a proxy, where u denotes the tag of re-encryption key and s_u is a private input chosen by the proxy. At the end of this algorithm, the proxy obtains a re-encryption key $\mathsf{rk}_{i \to j}^{(u)}$ and the delegator obtains a tracing key tk_i. A delegator can generate at most n re-encryption keys.

To support accountability, Trace algorithm outputs a proof in addition to the suspected re-encryption key's tag, as the evidence of the malicious proxy's misbehavior. Specifically,

- Trace$^{D_{i,\mu}}$($\mathsf{pk}_i, \mathsf{tk}_i$): This algorithm is run by delegator. With black-box access to a μ-useful decryption device $D_{i,\mu}$, and taking the tracing key tk_i as input, it outputs a re-encryption key tag $u \in [n]$ along with a proof Ω.

Compared to traceable PRE, accountable PRE has an extra Judge algorithm, which is run after the Trace algorithm for deciding whether the suspected re-encryption key has been involved in creating the pirate decryption device. It takes both the proxy's private input and the proof as input. Specifically,

- Judge($\mathsf{pk}_i, \mathsf{tk}_i, u, \Omega, s_u$): Taking the pubic key pk_i, tracing key tk_i, a suspected re-encryption key tag u, a proof Ω and the private input s_u chosen by the corresponding proxy as input, this algorithm outputs Proxy or Delegator, indicating the one who is responsible for the decryption device.

5.1   Security of Accountable PRE in Multi-proxies Setting

Because of the change of inputs in ReKeyGen algorithm, the re-encryption key generation oracle is accordingly modified as follows.

- Re-encryption key generation oracle $\mathcal{O}_{\mathrm{rkg}}^{(a)}(\mathsf{pk}_i, \mathsf{pk}_j, u, s_u)$: On input of ($\mathsf{pk}_i, \mathsf{pk}_j, u, s_u$), where $\mathsf{pk}_i, \mathsf{pk}_j$ are generated by KeyGen, u denotes the tag of re-encryption key and s_u is selected by $\mathcal{A}$ as the proxy's secret input, this oracle generates a re-encryption key $\mathsf{rk}_{i \to j}^{(u)}$ and a tracing key tk_i. Return the re-encryption key $\mathsf{rk}_{i \to j}^{(u)}$.

Notice that CPA security can be easily adapted from standard definitions, and thus we focus more on the security regarding traceability and accountability.

Strong Traceability. With the oracles $\mathcal{O}_{hkg}, \mathcal{O}_{ckg}$ described in Sect. 3.2 and $\mathcal{O}_{rkg}$ defined above, the security experiment is as follows:

Experiment $\mathrm{Exp}_{\Pi,\mathcal{A}}^{sTrace}(\lambda)$
 param $\leftarrow$ Setup(λ);
 $\mathsf{pk}^*, D_{*,\mu} \leftarrow \mathcal{A}^{\mathcal{O}_{hkg}, \mathcal{O}_{ckg}, \mathcal{O}_{rkg}^{(a)}}(\mathsf{param}, \{s_u\}_{u \in C})$
 where pk^* is generated by $\mathcal{O}_{hkg}$, μ is a non-negligible probability value
 and C denotes the tag set of re-encryption keys queried by $\mathcal{A}$;
 $(u^*, \Omega) \leftarrow \mathrm{Trace}^{D_{*,\mu}}(\mathsf{pk}^*, \mathsf{tk}^*)$
 where tk^* is the tracing key generated by $\mathcal{O}_{rkg}^{(a)}$;
 If $u^* = \bot$ or $u^* \notin C$
 return 1;
 else return 0.

Definition 6 *(Strong Traceability.)* A PRE scheme Π_s is said to support strong traceability if for any polynomial time adversary $\mathcal{A}$, the advantage function $\mathrm{Adv}_{\Pi,\mathcal{A}}^{sTrace}(\lambda)$ is negligible in λ.

We call it *Strong Traceability* since the tracing algorithm outputs a proof Ω as well as a suspected tag u.

Accountability. Informally speaking, accountability has two folds. (i) Non-repudiation: a proxy involved in creating a pirate decryption device cannot deny its responsibility. (ii) Non-framing: an honest proxy cannot be framed by a malicious delegator by generating a pirate decryption device, even though the delegator may collude with other proxies and delegatees.

First, let's consider the non-repudiation security. In the security experiment, the adversary can query and obtain a polynomial number of users' secret keys and re-encryption keys. He can also choose the proxies' secret inputs. We say that the adversary is successful if, it outputs a decryption device which misleads a judge to believe an honest delegator is guilty. The experiment is defined as follows:

Experiment $\mathrm{Exp}_{\Pi,\mathcal{A}}^{NR}(\lambda)$
 param $\leftarrow$ Setup(λ);
 $\mathsf{pk}^*, D_{*,\mu} \leftarrow \mathcal{A}^{\mathcal{O}_{hkg}, \mathcal{O}_{ckg}, \mathcal{O}_{rkg}^{(a)}}(\mathsf{param}, \{s_u\}_{u \in C})$
 where pk^* is generated by $\mathcal{O}_{hkg}$, μ is a non-negligible probability value
 and C denotes the tag set of re-encryption keys queried by $\mathcal{A}$;
 $(u^*, \Omega) \leftarrow \mathrm{Trace}^{D_{*,\mu}}(\mathsf{pk}^*, \mathsf{tk}^*)$
 where tk^* is the tracing key generated by $\mathcal{O}_{rkg}^{(a)}$;
 If $\mathrm{Judge}(\mathsf{pk}^*, \mathsf{tk}^*, u^*, \Omega, s_{u^*}) = \mathrm{Delegator}$
 return 1;
 else return 0.

The advantage of $\mathcal{A}$ is defined as

$$\mathrm{Adv}_{\Pi,\mathcal{A}}^{\mathrm{NR}}(\lambda) = |\Pr[\mathrm{Exp}_{\Pi,\mathcal{A}}^{\mathrm{NR}}(\lambda) = 1]|.$$

Definition 7 *(Non-Repudiation Security.)* A PRE scheme Π_s is said to be non-repudiation secure if for any polynomial time adversary $\mathcal{A}$, the advantage function $\mathrm{Adv}_{\Pi_s,\mathcal{A}}^{\mathrm{NR}}(\lambda)$ is negligible in λ.

Similarly, we consider the non-framing security. In the security experiment, the adversary can query and obtain a polynomial number of users' secret keys and re-encryption keys. He also can choose some re-encryption keys' secret inputs of proxies. We say that the adversary is successful if, it outputs a decryption device which misleads a judge to believe the honest proxy is guilty. To formulate this security definition, we define the experiment as follows:

Experiment $\mathrm{Exp}_{\Pi,\mathcal{A}}^{\mathrm{NF}}(\lambda)$
  param, $u', s_{u'} \leftarrow \mathrm{Setup}(\lambda)$;
  $\mathsf{pk}^*, D_{*,\mu} \leftarrow \mathcal{A}^{\mathcal{O}_{\mathrm{hkg}}, \mathcal{O}_{\mathrm{ckg}}, \mathcal{O}_{\mathrm{rkg}}^{(a)}}(\mathsf{param}, \{u, s_u\}_{u \neq u'})$
  where pk^* is generated by $\mathcal{O}_{\mathrm{ckg}}$
  and μ is a non-negligible probability value;
  If $\mathrm{Judge}^{D_{*,\mu}}(\mathsf{pk}^*, \mathsf{tk}^*, u', s_{u'}) = \mathrm{Proxy}$
  where tk^* is generated by $\mathcal{O}_{\mathrm{rkg}}^{(a)}$
  return 1;
  else return 0.

The advantage of $\mathcal{A}$ is defined as

$$\mathrm{Adv}_{\Pi,\mathcal{A}}^{\mathrm{NF}}(\lambda) = |\Pr[\mathrm{Exp}_{\Pi,\mathcal{A}}^{\mathrm{NF}}(\lambda) = 1]|.$$

Definition 8 *(Non-Framing Security.)* A PRE scheme Π_s is said to be non-framing secure if for any polynomial time adversary $\mathcal{A}$, the advantage function $\mathrm{Adv}_{\Pi_s,\mathcal{A}}^{\mathrm{NF}}(\lambda)$ is negligible in λ.

A PRE scheme is said to be accountable, if it is both non-repudiation secure and non-framing secure.

5.2   Construction

The main challenge in constructing accountable PRE is to ensure consistency between the Trace and the Judge protocol, i.e., an identified traitor cannot evade the confirmation from the judge. Inspired by the concept of asymmetric fingerprinting codes [29,30], we upgrade the above generic traceable PRE to achieve accountability.

For a given PRE scheme $\Pi = (\overline{\mathsf{Setup}}, \overline{\mathsf{KeyGen}}, \overline{\mathsf{ReKeyGen}}, \overline{\mathsf{Enc}_1}, \overline{\mathsf{Enc}_2}, \overline{\mathsf{ReEnc}}, \overline{\mathsf{Dec}_1}, \overline{\mathsf{Dec}_2})$, we use an asymmetric fingerprinting code $(\mathsf{AsymCodeGen}, \mathsf{AsymIdentify}, \mathsf{ArbiterPredicate})$ and an oblivious transfer (OT) protocol as major building blocks. Let l be the code length of the asymmetric fingerprinting code. Our generic accountable PRE construction works as follows:

- **Setup**(λ), **KeyGen**(param): These algorithms are the same as those of the above generic traceable PRE.
- **ReKeyGen**$(\mathbf{sk_i}, \mathbf{pk_j}, u, s_u)$. It is a protocol between the delegator and the proxy:
  1. Given user i's secret key $\mathbf{sk_i} = (\{sk_{i,k,b}\}_{k=1,\cdots,l,b=0,1})$ and user j's public key $\mathbf{pk_j} = \{pk_{j,k,b}\}_{k=1,\cdots,l,b=0,1}$ as input, if it is the first time for user i to generate re-encryption keys for user j, he prepares the re-encryption key elements $\{rk_{k,b}^{(i\rightarrow j)}\}_{k=1,\cdots,l,b=0,1}$ where $rk_{k,b}^{(i\rightarrow j)}$ is the output by running algorithm $\overline{\mathsf{ReKeyGen}}(sk_{i,k,b}, pk_{j,1,0})$ of Π.
  2. Proxy chooses s_u as his private input for running $\mathsf{AsymCodeGen}$ with the delegator to generate the u-th word of the code Γ_i. At the end of this protocol, the proxy gets a word $\bar{w}^{(u)} = w_1, \cdots, w_l$ and the delegator obtains a tracing key tk_i if it is the first time for user i to generate re-encryption keys. Set $\mathbf{tk_i} = tk_i$.
  3. Delegator uses $\{rk_{k,b}^{(i\rightarrow j)}\}_{k=1,\cdots,l,b=0,1}$ as input and proxy uses $\bar{w}^{(u)} = w_1, \cdots, w_l$ as input to run l times OT protocol. At the end of the protocol, the proxy obtains $rk_{k,w_k}^{(i\rightarrow j)}$ for $k = 1, \cdots, l$. The re-encryption key is set as $\mathbf{rk} = (\bar{w}^{(u)}, \{rk_{k,w_k}^{(i\rightarrow j)}\}_{k=1,\cdots,l})$.
- **Enc$_1$**$(\mathbf{pk_j}, m)$, **Enc$_2$**$(\mathbf{pk_i}, m)$, **ReEnc**$(\mathbf{rk_{i\rightarrow j}}, \mathbf{C_i})$, **Dec$_1$**$(\mathbf{sk_j}, \mathbf{C'_j})$, **Dec$_2$**$(\mathbf{sk_i}, \mathbf{C_i})$:These algorithms are the same as those of the above generic traceable PRE.
- **Trace**$^{D_{i,\mu}}(\mathbf{pk_i}, \mathbf{tk_i})$: This algorithms is the same as that of the above generic traceable PRE construction except for replacing $\mathsf{Identify}(tk_i, \bar{w}^*)$ with $\mathsf{AsymIdentify}(tk_i, \bar{w}^*)$ in Step 3. The output is (u, Ω), where u is the tag of the re-encryption key and Ω is a proof.
- **Judge**$(\mathbf{pk_i}, \mathbf{tk_i}, u, \Omega, s_u)$. This is a protocol among the judge, the delegator, and a suspected proxy who owns the re-encryption key with tag u. The delegator is with input $(\mathbf{pk_i}, \mathbf{tk_i}, u, \Omega)$, and the proxy is with input s_u.
  1. The proxy reveals its private input s_u to the judge, and proves its correctness according to **ReKeyGen**$(\mathbf{sk_i}, \mathbf{pk_j}, u, s_u)$.
  2. The delegator sends the judge the tracing key tk_i and proves its validity to **ReKeyGen**$(\mathbf{sk_i}, \mathbf{pk_j}, u, s_u)$.
  3. The judge runs $\mathsf{ArbiterPredicate}(tk_i, u, \Omega, s_u)$. If $\mathsf{ArbiterPredicate}(tk_i, u, \Omega, s_u) = 1$ he outputs "Proxy" and otherwise outputs "Delegator".

Similar to the traceable PRE case, CPA security is straightforward assuming the underlying scheme Π is CPA secure. Thus, we only focus on the traceability and accountability properties here. Intuitively, these two properties inherit from the asymmetric fingerprinting codes, which was formally demonstrated in [29].

In order to establish the security reduction to the underlying codes, we first use OT protocol to generate the re-encryption key. The security of OT protocol ensures that the proxy can only obtain the re-encryption key fragments related to its codeword, while the delegator does not know the codeword held by the proxy. Another possibility of reduction failure could be inconsistent inputs during the Judge protocol. That is, either the delegator or the proxy may cheat the judge about his input in the **ReKeyGen** protocol. Fortunately, it can be avoided by letting both the delegator and the proxy prove their inputs consistent with the **ReKeyGen** algorithm.

With the above security intuition and due to space limit, we defer detailed security proof to the full version, and we summarize the security as follows.

Theorem 2 *(Informal).* The above construction has strong traceability and accountability based on CPA secure PRE scheme Π, secure asymmetric fingerprinting code (AsymCodeGen, AsymIdentify, ArbiterPredicate), and secure OT protocol.

6   Instantiation and Discussion

We instantiate the generic constructions with the well-known AFGH PRE scheme [3]. The scheme is unidirectional and CPA secure under the extended Decisional Bilinear Diffie-Hellman (eDBDH) assumption. When the AFGH scheme is made traceable, the comparison is as in Tables 2 and 3.

Table 2 compares our instantiation with those in [15–17,23] in terms of security and performance, all of which are related to defend against re-encryption key abuse attack. From Table 2, it is clear that only our scheme achieves traceability and accountability with constant computational cost and ciphertext/key size.

Next, we look into the efficiency comparison in more detail in Table 3. t_p, t'_e and t_e denote the time for computing a bilinear pairing, an exponentiation in group $\mathbb{G}_T$ and an exponentiation in group $\mathbb{G}$, respectively. $|\mathbb{G}|$, $|\mathbb{G}_T|$ and $|\mathbb{Z}_p|$ denote the bit-length of an element in $\mathbb{G}$, an element in $\mathbb{G}_T$ and an integer in $\mathbb{Z}_p$, respectively. l denotes the length of the underlying code. N denotes the maximum number of delegatees for each delegator in [23]. $\mathrm{poly}(\lambda)$ denotes the computational cost or ciphertext/key size is polynomial with respect to the security parameter λ.

For all the compared schemes, we take similar optimizations by precomputing some bilinear pairings offline. To make it more clearly, we use an implementation [36] of MIRACL CryptoSDK at 80-bit security level as a benchmark to estimate efficiency of pairings and exponentiations, where $t_p = 6.05\,\mathrm{ms}$, $t_m = 3.04\,\mathrm{ms}$, $t'_e = 0.62\,\mathrm{ms}$ and $t_e = 2.4\,\mathrm{ms}$.

Table 2. General comparison

	[23]	[17]	[15]	[16]	Our instantiation
Security of ciphertext	CPA	CPA	CPA	CPA	CPA
Assumption	augmented DBDH	DBDH	$i\mathcal{O}$, k-authentication, PRG	DBDH	eDBDH
Traceability	✓	✗	✗	✗	✓
Accountability	✗	✗	✗	✓	✓
Multi-proxies setting	✓	✗	✗	✗	✓
Constant ciphertext size	✗	✓	✗	✓	✓
Constant computational cost	✗	✓	✗	✓	✓

Table 3. Efficiency comparison

Schemes	Key and ciphertext size				Computational cost				
	PK	RK	First level	Second level	Enc First level (ms)	Enc Second level (ms)	ReEnc (ms)	Dec First level (ms)	Dec Second level (ms)
[23]	$O(\log N)$	$2\lvert G_2\rvert$	$2\lvert G_T\rvert$	$O(\log N)$	$2t'_e$ / 1.24	– / $O(\log N)$	$2t_p$ / 12.10	t'_e / 0.62	$t_p+t'_e$ / 6.67
[17]	$3\lvert G\rvert$	$\lvert G\rvert+2\lvert Z_p\rvert$	$2\lvert G_T\rvert+\lvert G\rvert$	$\lvert G_T\rvert+4\lvert G\rvert$	$2t'_e+t_e$ / 3.64	t'_e+4t_e / 10.22	$2t_p+t_e$ / 14.5	$t_p+t'_e$ / 6.67	$t_p+t'_e$ / 6.67
[15]	$\mathrm{poly}(\lambda)$	$\mathrm{poly}(\lambda)$	$\mathrm{poly}(\lambda)$	$\mathrm{poly}(\lambda)$	– / $\mathrm{poly}(\lambda)$	– / $\mathrm{poly}(\lambda)$	– / $\mathrm{poly}(\lambda)$	– / $\mathrm{poly}(\lambda)$	– / $\mathrm{poly}(\lambda)$
[16]	$2\lvert G\rvert$	$\lvert G\rvert$	$2\lvert G_T\rvert+\lvert G\rvert$	$2\lvert G_T\rvert+2\lvert G\rvert$	$2t'_e+t_e$ / 3.64	$2t'_e+2t_e$ / 6.04	$t_p+t'_e$ / 6.67	$t_p+t'_e$ / 6.67	$t_p+t'_e$ / 6.67
Our instantiation	$2l\lvert G\rvert$	$l\lvert G\rvert$	$2\lvert G_T\rvert$	$2\lvert G\rvert$	$2t'_e$ / 1.24	$4t_e$ / 9.6	t_p / 6.05	t'_e / 0.62	$t_p+t'_e$ / 6.67

The results show that our scheme has competing computation and communication efficiency, performing substantially better on re-encryption and first level encryption/decryption efficiency, significantly on ciphertext size, meanwhile it also provides both traceability and accountability under the standard security assumption.

7   Conclusion

Due to the nature of PRE schemes, proxy can collude with the data receiver to derive and distribute the data owner's decryption capability, which has been the major concerns for users sharing encrypted data in consensus network. In this paper, we proposed the generic construction for traceable PRE and accountable PRE. With proper instantiation, it yields the first traceable PRE scheme with constant ciphertext and the first accountable PRE construction in multi-proxies setting, so that malicious node can be traced and moreover cannot deny his leakage of re-encryption capabilities, which may potentially stimulate the adoption of PRE schemes in practice.

Acknowledgement. This work is supported by the National Key R&D Program of China (Grant Nos 2018YFB0804105, 2017YFB0802500), the National Natural Science Foundation of China (Grant Nos 61802021, U1536205, 61572485) and the Opening Project of Guangdong Provincial Key Laboratory of Data Security and Privacy Protection (Grant No. 2017B030301004).

A   Asymmetric Fingerprinting Codes

In fingerprinting schemes, since both the provider and the receiver know the fingerprinted copy, it cannot be proved that a found copy was leaked by the receiver instead of the provider. While in asymmetric fingerprinting schemes, introduced by [30] and further studied by [29], only the receiver knows the fingerprinted copy, and a found copy can be proved to third parties whose copy it was.

Asymmetric fingerprinting is defined by the following algorithms [29]:

- AsymCodeGen(n, λ, s_u) : This is a two party protocol between the provider and the receiver. λ is the security parameter. The receiver chooses a private input s_u to generate the u-th word of the code Γ, containing up to n codewords. At the end of this algorithm, the provider obtains a tracing key tk and the receiver gets a word $\bar{w}^{(u)}$.
- AsymIdentify$(tk, \bar{w}^*)$: On input of a pirate word $\bar{w}^* \in \{0, 1\}^l$, this algorithm either fails to identify and outputs $\perp$, or outputs a codeword index $u \in \{1, \cdots, n\}$ along with a proof Ω. Informally, the u-th user is "accused" of being a traitor for creating the word $\bar{w}^*$.
- ArbiterPredicate(tk, u, Ω, s_u) This is a 3-party protocol between the arbiter, the provider and the receiver. The provider inputs (tk, u, Ω), where u denotes

an index of a traitor being "accused" for creating the word $\bar{w}^*$. The receiver inputs s_u, which is his private input for creating the u-th word of the code Γ. This predicate returns 1 if proof Ω contains some non-trivial information on s_u and returns 0 otherwise.

For simplifying, we consider AsymCodeGen is a secure 2-party protocol as [29]. That is, the provider obtains no more than the tracing key tk and the receiver obtains no more than the word $\bar{w}^{(u)}$.

In addition to the tracing capability, an asymmetric fingerprinting code supports two additional features, non-repudiation and non-framing. We recall the security properties of asymmetric fingerprinting codes as follows [29]:

- Traceability: For any adversary $\mathcal{A}$, any $n > 0$ and any subset $C \subset \{1, \cdots, n\}$, the following holds

$$\Pr \begin{bmatrix} \{(\bar{w}^{(i)}, tk) \leftarrow \text{AsymCodeGen}(n, \lambda, s_i)\}_{i=1,\cdots,n}; \\ \bar{w}^* \in F(\{\bar{w}^{(i)}\}_{i \in C}) \leftarrow \mathcal{A}(n, \lambda, \{s_i, \bar{w}^{(i)}\}_{i \in C}) : \\ (u, \Omega) \leftarrow \text{AsymIdentify}(tk, \bar{w}^*) : \\ u = \perp \text{ or } u \notin C \end{bmatrix} < \text{negl}(\lambda)$$

- Non-repudiation: It further holds that

$$\Pr\left[0 \leftarrow \text{ArbiterPredicate}(tk, u, \Omega, s_u)\right] < \text{negl}(\lambda)$$

- Non-framing: For any adversary $\mathcal{A}$, any $n > 0$ and any $u' \in [n]$, the following holds

$$\Pr \begin{bmatrix} \{(\bar{w}^{(i)}, tk) \leftarrow \text{AsymCodeGen}(n, \lambda, s_i)\}_{i=1,\cdots,n}; \\ \Omega' \leftarrow \mathcal{A}(n, \lambda, tk, \{s_i\}_{i \in [n] \setminus \{u'\}}) : \\ 1 \leftarrow \text{ArbiterPredicate}(tk, u', \Omega', s_{u'}) \end{bmatrix} < \text{negl}(\lambda)$$

Remark 2. Pehlivanoglu [29] introduced an asymmetric binary fingerprinting code based on Boneh-Shaw code and proved it satisfying the above properties. Despite that the above definition seems slightly different from [29] in expression, the functionality and security remain unchanged.

References

1. Nucypher. https://www.nucypher.com/
2. Abdalla, M., Catalano, D., Dent, A.W., Malone-Lee, J., Neven, G., Smart, N.P.: Identity-based encryption gone wild. In: Bugliesi, M., Preneel, B., Sassone, V., Wegener, I. (eds.) ICALP 2006. LNCS, vol. 4052, pp. 300–311. Springer, Heidelberg (2006). https://doi.org/10.1007/11787006_26
3. Ateniese, G., Fu, K., Green, M., Hohenberger, S.: Improved proxy re-encryption schemes with applications to secure distributed storage. In: NDSS (2005)
4. Blaze, M., Bleumer, G., Strauss, M.: Divertible protocols and atomic proxy cryptography. In: Nyberg, K. (ed.) EUROCRYPT 1998. LNCS, vol. 1403, pp. 127–144. Springer, Heidelberg (1998). https://doi.org/10.1007/BFb0054122

5. Boneh, D., Naor, M.: Traitor tracing with constant size ciphertext. In: Proceedings of the 15th ACM conference on Computer and communications security, pp. 501–510. ACM (2008)
6. Borcea, C., Polyakov, Y., Rohloff, K., Ryan, G., et al.: Picador: end-to-end encrypted publish-subscribe information distribution with proxy re-encryption. Future Gener. Comput. Syst. **71**, 177–191 (2017)
7. Canetti, R., Hohenberger, S.: Chosen-ciphertext secure proxy re-encryption. In: Proceedings of the 14th ACM conference on Computer and communications security, pp. 185–194. ACM (2007)
8. Chandran, N., Chase, M., Liu, F.-H., Nishimaki, R., Xagawa, K.: Re-encryption, functional re-encryption, and multi-hop re-encryption: a framework for achieving obfuscation-based security and instantiations from lattices. In: Krawczyk, H. (ed.) PKC 2014. LNCS, vol. 8383, pp. 95–112. Springer, Heidelberg (2014). https://doi.org/10.1007/978-3-642-54631-0_6
9. Chandran, N., Chase, M., Vaikuntanathan, V.: Functional re-encryption and collusion-resistant obfuscation. In: Cramer, R. (ed.) TCC 2012. LNCS, vol. 7194, pp. 404–421. Springer, Heidelberg (2012). https://doi.org/10.1007/978-3-642-28914-9_23
10. Cohen, A.: What about Bob? the inadequacy of CPA security for proxy reencryption. In: Lin, D., Sako, K. (eds.) PKC 2019. LNCS, vol. 11443, pp. 287–316. Springer, Cham (2019). https://doi.org/10.1007/978-3-030-17259-6_10
11. Derler, D., Krenn, S., Lorünser, T., Ramacher, S., Slamanig, D., Striecks, C.: Revisiting proxy re-encryption: forward secrecy, improved security, and applications. In: Abdalla, M., Dahab, R. (eds.) PKC 2018. LNCS, vol. 10769, pp. 219–250. Springer, Cham (2018). https://doi.org/10.1007/978-3-319-76578-5_8
12. Fuchsbauer, G., Kamath, C., Klein, K., Pietrzak, K.: Adaptively secure proxy re-encryption. In: Lin, D., Sako, K. (eds.) PKC 2019. LNCS, vol. 11443, pp. 317–346. Springer, Cham (2019). https://doi.org/10.1007/978-3-030-17259-6_11
13. Goyal, V.: Reducing trust in the PKG in identity based cryptosystems. In: Menezes, A. (ed.) CRYPTO 2007. LNCS, vol. 4622, pp. 430–447. Springer, Heidelberg (2007). https://doi.org/10.1007/978-3-540-74143-5_24
14. Goyal, V., Lu, S., Sahai, A., Waters, B.: Black-box accountable authority identity-based encryption. In: Proceedings of the 15th ACM conference on Computer and communications security, pp. 427–436. ACM (2008)
15. Guo, H., Zhang, Z., Xu, J., An, N.: Non-transferable proxy re-encryption. Comput. J. **62**(4), 490–506 (2019). https://doi.org/10.1093/comjnl/bxy096
16. Guo, H., Zhang, Z., Xu, J., An, N., Lan, X.: Accountable proxy re-encryption for secure data sharing. IEEE Trans. Dependable Secure Comput. (2018)
17. Guo, H., Zhang, Z., Zhang, J.: Proxy re-encryption with unforgeable re-encryption keys. In: Gritzalis, D., Kiayias, A., Askoxylakis, I. (eds.) CANS 2014. LNCS, vol. 8813, pp. 20–33. Springer, Cham (2014). https://doi.org/10.1007/978-3-319-12280-9_2
18. Hayashi, R., Matsushita, T., Yoshida, T., Fujii, Y., Okada, K.: Unforgeability of re-encryption keys against collusion attack in proxy re-encryption. In: Iwata, T., Nishigaki, M. (eds.) IWSEC 2011. LNCS, vol. 7038, pp. 210–229. Springer, Heidelberg (2011). https://doi.org/10.1007/978-3-642-25141-2_14
19. Hohenberger, S., Rothblum, G.N., Shelat, A., Vaikuntanathan, V.: Securely obfuscating re-encryption. In: Vadhan, S.P. (ed.) TCC 2007. LNCS, vol. 4392, pp. 233–252. Springer, Heidelberg (2007). https://doi.org/10.1007/978-3-540-70936-7_13

20. Kiayias, A., Tang, Q.: Making *any* identity-based encryption accountable, efficiently. In: Pernul, G., Ryan, P.Y.A., Weippl, E. (eds.) ESORICS 2015. LNCS, vol. 9326, pp. 326–346. Springer, Cham (2015). https://doi.org/10.1007/978-3-319-24174-6_17

21. Lai, J., Deng, R.H., Zhao, Y., Weng, J.: Accountable authority identity-based encryption with public traceability. In: Dawson, E. (ed.) CT-RSA 2013. LNCS, vol. 7779, pp. 326–342. Springer, Heidelberg (2013). https://doi.org/10.1007/978-3-642-36095-4_21

22. Lai, J., Tang, Q.: Making *any* attribute-based encryption accountable, efficiently. In: Lopez, J., Zhou, J., Soriano, M. (eds.) ESORICS 2018. LNCS, vol. 11099, pp. 527–547. Springer, Cham (2018). https://doi.org/10.1007/978-3-319-98989-1_26

23. Libert, B., Vergnaud, D.: Tracing malicious proxies in proxy re-encryption. In: Galbraith, S.D., Paterson, K.G. (eds.) Pairing 2008. LNCS, vol. 5209, pp. 332–353. Springer, Heidelberg (2008). https://doi.org/10.1007/978-3-540-85538-5_22

24. Libert, B., Vergnaud, D.: Unidirectional chosen-ciphertext secure proxy re-encryption. In: Cramer, R. (ed.) PKC 2008. LNCS, vol. 4939, pp. 360–379. Springer, Heidelberg (2008). https://doi.org/10.1007/978-3-540-78440-1_21

25. Libert, B., Vergnaud, D.: Towards black-box accountable authority IBE with short ciphertexts and private keys. In: Jarecki, S., Tsudik, G. (eds.) PKC 2009. LNCS, vol. 5443, pp. 235–255. Springer, Heidelberg (2009). https://doi.org/10.1007/978-3-642-00468-1_14

26. Myers, S., Shull, A.: Efficient hybrid proxy re-encryption for practical revocation and key rotation. Technical report, Cryptology ePrint Archive, Report 2017/833 (2017)

27. Myers, S., Shull, A.: Practical revocation and key rotation. In: Smart, N.P. (ed.) CT-RSA 2018. LNCS, vol. 10808, pp. 157–178. Springer, Cham (2018). https://doi.org/10.1007/978-3-319-76953-0_9

28. Ning, J., Dong, X., Cao, Z., Wei, L.: Accountable authority ciphertext-policy attribute-based encryption with white-box traceability and public auditing in the cloud. In: Pernul, G., Ryan, P.Y.A., Weippl, E. (eds.) ESORICS 2015. LNCS, vol. 9327, pp. 270–289. Springer, Cham (2015). https://doi.org/10.1007/978-3-319-24177-7_14

29. Pehlivanoglu, S.: An asymmetric fingerprinting code for collusion-resistant buyer-seller watermarking. In: Proceedings of the first ACM workshop on Information hiding and multimedia security, pp. 35–44. ACM (2013)

30. Pfitzmann, B., Schunter, M.: Asymmetric fingerprinting. In: Maurer, U. (ed.) EUROCRYPT 1996. LNCS, vol. 1070, pp. 84–95. Springer, Heidelberg (1996). https://doi.org/10.1007/3-540-68339-9_8

31. Sahai, A., Seyalioglu, H.: Fully Secure accountable-authority identity-based encryption. In: Catalano, D., Fazio, N., Gennaro, R., Nicolosi, A. (eds.) PKC 2011. LNCS, vol. 6571, pp. 296–316. Springer, Heidelberg (2011). https://doi.org/10.1007/978-3-642-19379-8_19

32. Taban, G., Cárdenas, A.A., Gligor, V.D.: Towards a secure and interoperable drm architecture. In: Proceedings of the ACM workshop on Digital rights management, pp. 69–78. ACM (2006)

33. Tang, Q.: Type-based proxy re-encryption and its construction. In: Chowdhury, D.R., Rijmen, V., Das, A. (eds.) INDOCRYPT 2008. LNCS, vol. 5365, pp. 130–144. Springer, Heidelberg (2008). https://doi.org/10.1007/978-3-540-89754-5_11

34. Weng, J., Chen, M., Yang, Y., Deng, R., Chen, K., Bao, F.: CCA-secure unidirectional proxy re-encryption in the adaptive corruption model without random oracles. Sci. China Inf. Sci. **53**(3), 593–606 (2010)

35. Xu, P., Xu, J., Wang, W., Jin, H., Susilo, W., Zou, D.: Generally hybrid proxy re-encryption: a secure data sharing among cryptographic clouds. In: Proceedings of the 11th ACM on Asia Conference on Computer and Communications Security, pp. 913–918. ACM (2016)
36. Zhang, J., Zhang, Z., Chen, Y.: PRE: Stronger security notions and efficient construction with non-interactive opening. In: Theoretical Computer Science (2014)
37. Zhang, J., Zhang, Z., Guo, H.: Towards secure data distribution systems in mobile cloud computing. IEEE Trans. Mob. Comput. **16**(11), 3222–3235 (2017)
38. Zhang, Y., Li, J., Zheng, D., Chen, X., Li, H.: Accountable large-universe attribute-based encryption supporting any monotone access structures. In: Liu, J.K.K., Steinfeld, R. (eds.) ACISP 2016. LNCS, vol. 9722, pp. 509–524. Springer, Cham (2016). https://doi.org/10.1007/978-3-319-40253-6_31
39. Zuo, C., Shao, J., Liu, J.K., Wei, G., Ling, Ý.: Fine-grained two-factor protection mechanism for data sharing in cloud storage. IEEE Trans. Inf. Forensics Secur. **13**(1), 186–196 (2018)

Side Channels

Side-Channel Aware Fuzzing

Philip Sperl[(⊠)] and Konstantin Böttinger

Fraunhofer Institute for Applied and Integrated Security,
Garching bei München, Germany
{philip.sperl,konstantin.boettinger}@aisec.fraunhofer.de

Abstract. Software testing is becoming a critical part of the development cycle of embedded devices, enabling vulnerability detection. A well-studied approach of software testing is fuzz-testing (fuzzing), during which mutated input is sent to an input-processing software while its behavior is monitored. The goal is to identify faulty states in the program, triggered by malformed inputs. Even though this technique is widely performed, fuzzing cannot be applied to embedded devices to its full extent. Due to the lack of adequately powerful I/O capabilities or an operating system the feedback needed for fuzzing cannot be acquired. In this paper we present and evaluate a new·approach to extract feedback for fuzzing on embedded devices using information the power consumption leaks. Side-channel aware fuzzing is a threefold process that is initiated by sending an input to a target device and measuring its power consumption. First, we extract features from the power traces of the target device using machine learning algorithms. Subsequently, we use the features to reconstruct the code structure of the analyzed firmware. In the final step we calculate a score for the input, which is proportional to the code coverage.

We carry out our proof of concept by fuzzing synthetic software and a light-weight AES implementation running on an ARM Cortex-M4 microcontroller. Our results show that the power side-channel carries information relevant for fuzzing.

Keywords: Embedded systems security · Side-channel analysis · Fuzzing

1 Introduction

Embedded systems are nowadays used in a wide range of domains and applications. The employed devices are often connected to information exchanging networks like the Internet of Thisngs (IoT). As the number of connected devices is continuously growing, the security of the employed software is gaining impact on our daily life.

Vulnerabilities in embedded devices can be classified by their cause of occurrence, e.g., programming errors, web-based vulnerabilities, weak access control or authentication, and improper use of cryptography [20]. In the following we

© Springer Nature Switzerland AG 2019
K. Sako et al. (Eds.): ESORICS 2019, LNCS 11735, pp. 259–278, 2019.
https://doi.org/10.1007/978-3-030-29959-0_13

will focus on the security threats emerging from programming errors. Such errors often lead to memory corruptions like buffer overflows, which attackers make use of in targeted exploits. To prevent or find errors leading to such vulnerabilities, several measures exist. For instance, source code analysis during the development of the system, or subsequent reverse engineering. Both techniques require either the source code or at least deep understanding of the system. Furthermore, both approaches cannot be automated or executed large-scale, which increases cost, either during the development or security evaluation phase.

From the realm of general purpose computers and software testing, the approach of fuzz-testing (fuzzing) is widely accepted and even executed during commercial software development [11]. During fuzzing, automatically generated input is sent to the input-processing software under test (SUT) while its behavior is examined. Different instrumentation techniques and mechanisms provided by the operating system (OS) allow evaluation of the impact of the input, leading to an effective and automated vulnerability detection tool. Because of the I/O-limitations, restricted computing power, and missing OS, embedded systems lack the possibility of returning enough information required during fuzzing [18]. This restrains fuzzing on embedded devices to a black-box manner.

To circumvent this problem, we present a novel and unexplored technique using the power side-channel of embedded devices as source of feedback for fuzzing. We show that the process of sending an input vector to the device, measuring the power consumption, and extracting information from the power traces enables us to deduce the control flow graph (CFG) of the software. Subsequently, we present a method of using this representation of the control flow to evaluate the impact of the input on the behavior of the device in terms of code coverage. We show that this approach is a significant step towards white-box fuzzing on embedded devices.

In summary, we make the following contributions:

- We present the novel idea of extracting feedback from the power side-channel to enhance fuzzing of embedded devices.
- In the proof of concept we successfully fuzz synthetic software and a lightweight advanced encryption standard (AES) [19] implementation and evaluate our results.
- Finally, we provide a base line for future work on side-channel-based feature extraction.

The rest of this paper is organized as follows. In Sect. 2 we review related work and summarize latest findings in embedded device fuzzing. We present our concept of extracting feedback from the power side-channel to enable white-box fuzzing of embedded devices in Sect. 3. In Sect. 4 we present our proof-of-concept and evaluation results. We conclude the paper in Sect. 5.

2 Related Work

We divide this section into four parts. First we show challenges in embedded device fuzzing before we introduce state-of-the-art techniques. Subsequently we present latest findings in side-channel based reverse engineering. Finally, we present the first contributions using side-channel information to assess the program flow of embedded devices.

Muench et al. [18] split the challenges encountered when fuzzing embedded devices into three categories. We adopt this categorization for devices without an OS and explain it in the following.

Fault Detection: Faults during program execution often lead to program crashes, which need to be detected during fuzzing. For fuzzing on a PC, the OS offers mechanisms for detecting crashes, e.g., a segmentation fault communicated to the fuzzing tool by console output. Even though some embedded processors contain Memory Management Units (MMU), the lack of an OS hinders the possibility to communicate faults to the outer world. Hence, possible program crashes or subsequent reboot sequences may remain undetected.

Performance, Throughput, and Scalability: Profiting from the multitasking capabilities of OS-based systems, multiple instances of the SUT can run simultaneously, increasing the fuzzing throughput. Transferring this knowledge to embedded systems suffers limitations, because of the missing OS or single-core architecture of the devices. A solution is the application of multiple devices executing the same firmware, which may be limited due to financial restrictions.

Instrumentation: Both, compile-time and run-time approaches suffer in feasibility due to the restrictions in embedded systems. Recompiling binaries, like on PCs, is not possible if the source code is not available. Besides the difficult task of binary rewriting, run-time instrumentation techniques as well as virtualization are not applicable due to the missing OS.

Because of the difficulties presented above, research concerning fuzzing of OS-free embedded devices exclusively deals with a black-box approach. Even though we present a white-box solution, some findings in black-box fuzzing are worth mentioning. Koscher et al. [13] and Lee et al. [14] carry out fuzzing of CAN packets. Alimi et al. [1] made use of black-box fuzzing when looking for vulnerabilities in applets on smart cards. Muench et al. [18] try to improve fuzzing by partial and full emulation of embedded devices. Zaddach et al. [26] propose a related approach and improve the emulation-based testing process by forwarding memory accesses on the emulated target to the physical device.

Symbolic execution poses an alternative approach. Davidson et al. [6] show the possibility to find bugs in firmware using a specification of the memory layout of the target device, the source code, and their KLEE-based [3] symbolic execution engine. With this setup the authors are able to perform fuzzing of the target device. Further improvements to this approach were shown by Corteggiani et al. [5], in which access to the source code is required as well.

Ever since the introduction of the Differential Power Analysis by Kocher et al. [12] numerous publications picked up the concept of analyzing information leaked over the power or electromagnetic (EM) side-channel of embedded devices. As we link the concepts of side-channel analysis and fuzzing, we profit from research in the field of side-channel based reverse engineering. Strobel et al. [24] show an effective way to reconstruct the assembly code executed by CPUs using EM emanations. By decapsulating the attacked chip and using eight measurement probes, the authors achieve an instruction recognition rate of 87,69% targeting real code. Msgna et al. [17] use a k-nearest neighbors (*kNN*) classification for reverse engineering. The authors exploit the fact that the power consumption of digital circuits depends on the processed data and executed instructions [15]. Targeting test code the authors achieve an instruction recognition rate of 100%.

The first method using side-channel information to gain insights into the executed code paths of an embedded device is presented by Callan et al. [4]. In the training phase the authors measure the EM emanations of a target device while it executes instrumented code. During the profiling phase EM traces are measured while the device executes the original source code. The authors compare both sets of EM traces to identify the currently executed program path. If further refined, this approach poses a possible source of information to fuzz firmware for which the source code is available. Nonetheless, the authors do not evaluate the scenario in which the source code is not available. Similarly, Han et al. [9] use the EM emanations of embedded controllers to identify the current control flow. The authors are able to detect malicious executions with high confidence. Van Aubel et al. [25] use EM traces and methods from the classical side-channel analysis to build an intrusion detection tool for industrial control systems.

3 Elements of Side-Channel Aware Fuzzing

In this section we present our main contribution, a novel technique for extracting feedback from an embedded device using the power side-channel to make white-box fuzzing possible. In particular, we calculate scores for the inputs proportional to the provoked code coverage. The calculation of the scores is inspired by the procedure implemented in the widely used and accepted American Fuzzy Lop (AFL) fuzzing tool. By instrumenting the code, AFL counts the basic block transitions during the processing of each input. The number of newly executed basic block transitions is then directly used as score for the inputs, see [27]. In subsequent fuzzing runs, AFL mutates inputs with the highest scores and feeds them back to the SUT. The goal is to accumulate a series of inputs for which a code coverage of 100% is reached. In this paper we neglect the prioritization and mutation of the inputs and solely provide code coverage scores. The scores can then be fed to a tool like AFL, to perform the remaining actions required for a closed fuzzing loop.

We carry out the illustration of our concept in a bottom-up manner. First, we explain all underlying building blocks, before we present the complete concept as well as the overall schematic of the side-channel aware fuzzing loop. In Fig. 1 we show the setup and required equipment. During the feedback-driven loop, we use an oscilloscope to measure the power consumption of the target device and send the power traces to the evaluation computer. Using this PC we process the traces and conduct the side-channel analysis (SCA) consisting of three steps. First, we identify the individual basic blocks of the software. In the second step we characterize the found basic blocks and the transition sequence. Finally, we calculate code coverage scores for each input.

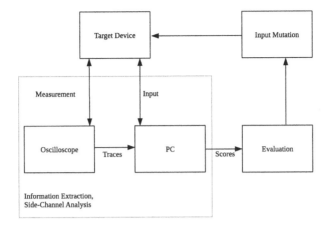

Fig. 1. Side-channel driven fuzzing feedback loop.

Throughout the discussion of the SCA building blocks we assume that for each input sent to the device, its power consumption is measured. The lengths of the power traces cover the exact time the device requires to process the currently evaluated input. For the sake of simplicity, we examine one input and its corresponding trace in the following. In a real world application and during our proof of concept, we perform the analysis for each input sent to the target device.

3.1   Feature Extraction Using the Power Side-Channel

A power trace is an array of n quantized measurement points of the physical power consumption of the target device. The number of points depends on the measurement period and the sampling rate of the used oscilloscope. Even though side-channel aware fuzzing is based on power traces, we convey our concept without illustration of actual power measurements. We decided to do so in order to provide a general introduction of our approach, which can be transferred to a wide range of devices. The central goal of our concept is to estimate the code coverage triggered during the processing of the current input. A widely used metric to express code coverage is the number of basic block transitions. In this paper we make use of this idea, therefore we define basic blocks and the separation of such in the following.

Basic blocks are lines of code which are executed without interruption of a branch instruction [10]. Hence, if the execution of a basic block begins, it will be executed completely before another basic block is triggered. Branch instructions at the end of each basic block coordinate the transitions.

This observation builds the core of our concept. If we detect the moment in which a target device executes a branch instruction, we find the borders between the basic blocks. As a consequence, we focus on this class of instructions and present a method to detect branch instructions using the collected power traces.

Subsequently we provide methods to characterize the basic blocks, so that we can estimate the number of individual basic block transitions per input.

Branch Detection. The power consumption of digital circuits consists of four components. Each sample of a power trace is determined by the executed instruction, processed data, electronic noise characteristics of the device, and a constant component. To detect branches we exploit the operation-dependent component of the power consumption.

We interpret the branch detection as a binary classification problem, since all remaining instructions executed by the device are not of interest. During initialization we split the examined power trace into k windows. Note that the beginning of each window matches the beginning of a potential branch instruction. Moreover, the windows and the branch instructions share the same length. After this initialization, we carry out the binary classification, which we execute k times per trace. In this classification procedure a predictor decides which window shows a branch instruction. Machine learning algorithms with a previous training phase can build the basis for the predictor. If the prediction indicates that the currently analyzed window shows a branch, we add the location to the result list $B_{locations}$.

To create train data on which the machine learning algorithm can be trained, we need an identical and programmable target device. We let this training device execute branch instructions with various offsets and distances, while we measure its power consumption. During the supervised training, we use the labeled power traces to create the branch detection model.

Branch Distance Classification. A feature providing evidence whether a transition was already executed before is the distance between a found basic block and its predecessor. Here, we define this distance as the number of instructions which the device under test (DUT) skips due to the branch instruction.

In order to estimate the number of skipped instructions we exploit the data-dependent component of power traces and the following insight. Branch instructions contain labels to which they should jump. The CPU calculates the distance between the current location and the label and adds it to the program counter. Since this process is data-dependent, the power side-channel leaks information about this distance.

We again use a supervised machine learning algorithm to estimate the distances of the found branches. In the training phase our train device performs branches with known distances while we measure its power consumption. We use the resulting labeled data to train the algorithm and create the branch distance model.

In the branch distance classification we first cut the traces, such that we only evaluate samples measured during the execution of branch instructions. We apply our previously created model and store the classification output in the result list $B_{distances}$.

As an alternative to the branch distance classification which might not be successful for every branch or device, we present an additional approach to distinguish the basic blocks in the following.

Basic Block Fingerprinting. To distinguish basic blocks we assign side-channel based fingerprints to each. For this purpose we use the slices of the power traces between the previously found branch instructions. These parts represent the power consumption during the execution of basic blocks. Hence, we conduct an initialization phase in which we cut the traces accordingly. In the first step of our algorithm we extract four features from each analyzed power trace window. Subsequently we use the features to fingerprint the basic blocks. We present the extracted features and illustrate the purpose of each in terms of contributed information.

Basic blocks often differ in their required execution time. Evaluating this feature allows an easy-to-implement distinction. Therefore, the first metric we consider is the length P_{length} of the individual slices.

For the calculation of the second feature P_{peaks}, the algorithm evaluates the number of peaks for each trace segment. For the majority of embedded devices, the power traces consist of periodically occurring peaks. Internal clocks which may have the frequency of the system clock or other clocks like the flash clock have the major impact on the number of peaks. Additional peaks can occur in the power traces due to complex instructions. The additionally required computational power increases the power consumption resulting in spikes in the traces. Thus, the number of peaks in the trace windows shows the approximate duration and indicate the complexity of the executed instructions.

The third metric is the mean P_{mean}, of the windows, which is the mean power consumption during the basic block execution.

The last metric we calculate is the skewness, $P_{skewness}$. Translated to the power consumption, this metric enables the following distinction of cases. Assume two basic blocks A and B sharing the same number of instructions, with identical mean power consumption. Basic block A consists of instructions with evenly distributed computational cost and resulting power consumption. In contrast to that, basic block B contains one significantly more complex instruction than the instructions found in A. Furthermore, the remaining instructions in B are less complex than the ones found in A, resulting in a the same mean power consumption. By analyzing the skewness of the power traces, we are able to distinguish basic blocks A and B.

In the final step of the basic block fingerprinting, we superpose the four extracted features to create the fingerprints. We present two approaches to achieve this superposition.

In our first approach we take all four values of the currently analyzed basic block and store them in a four-dimensional vector. We call this method *separated*. This approach is easy to implement, however, in subsequent calculations the dimension of the feature vector can lead to increased execution times compared to a scalar value representing the fingerprint.

Therefore, in the second approach, which we call *summed*, we adopt this idea and sum up the four previously calculated values. Alternatively, a hash function can be applied to generate a fingerprint. This approach is very effective if the underlying values already lead to a strong distinction between the basic blocks. For both approaches we store the fingerprints of the basic blocks in the result table B_{prints}.

3.2   Control Flow Reconstruction

In this section we use our knowledge of the basic block transitions to reconstruct the program flow of the analyzed firmware. We present two algorithms for this purpose. Both use the previously found branch locations. The first algorithm uses the branch distances, while the second one uses the basic block fingerprints to further characterize the transitions. For both approaches we give an exemplary control flow in Fig. 2 to visualize the concepts of the reconstruction. Each control flow represents the processing of one input by the target device.

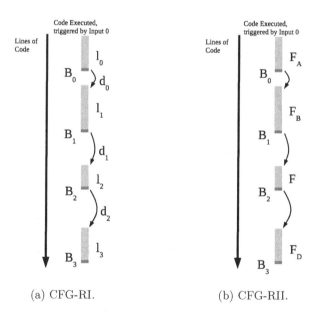

(a) CFG-RI.   (b) CFG-RII.

Fig. 2. Illustration of the two control flow reconstruction algorithms and the required information.

Furthermore, we introduce the following notation. B_x indicates the branch location with the index x. The corresponding distance of the branch to its successor is d_x. The length of the executed basic block with index i is l_i. The fingerprint for the basic block A is F_A.

We store the results of the control flow reconstruction in the table T_{CFG}. Table 1 shows the results according to the examples from Fig. 2. The left column holds the branch IDs for all inputs, while the columns to the right hold the results of the control flow reconstruction. In the following we convey both algorithms and explain the results from Table 1.

CFG Reconstruction I (CFG-RI). In this CFG reconstruction algorithm we use our knowledge of the branch locations $B_{\text{locations}}$ and their corresponding distances $B_{\text{distances}}$. For each branch we calculate a two-dimensional vector which characterizes the subsequent basic block and store it in T_{CFG}. Thereby we sufficiently describe the control flow of the tested software in order to evaluate the sequence of performed basic block transitions. In the following we describe the creation of the vectors using Fig. 2(a).

We build the vector $[B_{\text{offset}}, C_{\text{length}}]$ by stacking two characteristic values for each basic block. B_{offset} indicates the offset of the branch location in the code, expressed in number of instructions executed or skipped until the branch itself is executed. In Fig. 2(a), for branch B_0 this value is l_0. For branch B_1 this value depends on the following intermediate results. Until B_1 is executed, the two basic blocks with the lengths l_0 and l_1 are executed. In addition to that, we estimate the distance of branch B_0 to be d_0. Hence, with the sum of the discovered distances $(l_0 + l_1 + d_0)$ we express the offset for branch B_1. The second result value C_{length} is the length of the code after each branch, l_i. For the branches B_0 and B_1 these values are l_1 and l_2, respectively.

With the location of a specific branch with respect to the previously executed code and the length of the following basic block, we sufficiently describe the control flow of the code to evaluate if we triggered a new basic block transition.

CFG Reconstruction II (CFG-RII). In this approach we use the unique fingerprints B_{prints}. Each fingerprint describes one basic block, which enables us to distinguish them. Hence, we directly store the fingerprints in the result table next to the according branch ID. Note that we assume the code started without an initial branch. Therefore the first fingerprint is stored without an associated branch ID. With this result table we provide the sequence of transitions and fully reconstruct the program flow on the basic block level.

Theoretical Comparison. Both algorithms reconstruct the analyzed software to such an extent, that we are able to calculate scores for each input representing the number of newly triggered basic block transitions. The two approaches differ in the used side-channel information. Hence, each algorithm has advantages depending on the attacked device and measurement quality. In the following we give a recommendation on when to use either of the algorithms.

CFG-RI can lead to an accurate reconstruction of the examined code. The drawback of this approach is the additional training phase we need to perform prior to the branch distance classification. This leads to a more time and memory consuming process before the actual fuzzing. In order to classify the branch distances, the corresponding machine learning model has to be loaded in the evaluation computer in addition to the model for the branch detection and the analyzed

Table 1. Result table T_{CFG} showing the results for both control flow reconstruction algorithms.

Branch ID	Results CFG-RI	Results CFG-RII
-	$[B_{offset,start}, C_{length,start}]$	$B_{prints,start}$
0	$[B_{offset,0}, C_{length,0}]$	$B_{prints,0}$
1	$[B_{offset,1}, C_{length,1}]$	$B_{prints,1}$
⋮	⋮	⋮
⋮	⋱	⋱

power traces. Moreover, the measurement quality and target device properties highly influence the accuracy during the estimation of the branch distances. Different test devices and measurement equipment may lead to poor results preventing a correct estimation. Additionally, we emphasize the fault propagation concerning this algorithm. If one branch distance is classified wrongly, the remaining code reconstruction process results in a flawed CFG.

In CFG-RII the results during the fingerprint calculations do not depend on the quality of the measurement setup and the attacked device as it is the case during the branch distance classification. Furthermore, a potential error does not corrupt all following results. As drawback, regardless of the complexity of the fingerprints, the probability of collisions is not fully ruled out. A collision occurs if for two or more different basic blocks the same fingerprint is generated. The consequence of such an error would be in the worst case, that one yet unknown basic block transition would not be detected as such. The resulting score of the analyzed input would be smaller than the actual score.

We sum up the findings of the comparison as follows. With algorithm CFG-RI we can precisely reconstruct the structure of the tested firmware. Because of the error propagation property, we exclusively recommend using it if a strong recognition rate during the branch distance classification is reached. In contrast to that, we present CFG-RII as an easy to implement and intuitive backup strategy. We will present a quantitative comparison of both algorithms in Sect. 4.

3.3   Score Calculation

In the final step of our approach we calculate the score which is the number of newly triggered basic block transitions per input. The list Ω, that is empty at the beginning of the fuzzing process, holds all known basic block transitions. For the score calculation we use the result table we gained during the control flow reconstruction. We analyze the neighboring pairs of basic blocks and their corresponding representation, realized either with the fingerprints or the branch distances. If the currently analyzed pair is already stored in Ω, we will not increase the score. In contrast to that, if the pair is not in Ω, we add it to the list and increase the score for the corresponding input by 1. With this procedure we adopt the concept of estimating the code coverage in terms of basic block transitions, similar to the AFL fuzzing tool.

3.4 Error Prevention and Trace Preprocessing

To prevent errors, we aim to increase the signal-to-noise-ratio (SNR) of the measured power consumption. Since the electronic noise follows a normal distribution [15], a widely performed approach is to increase the number of measurements showing the same operations and form superposed traces. We adopt this concept and present three different approaches to achieve this. For all approaches, we send the same input to the device multiple times and capture the power traces. Note that the traces need to be aligned correctly in order to allow valid calculations. For this purpose we use a precise trigger, which depends on the system clock of the DUT to start the measurement.

In the first approach, for every sample point in the power traces, we calculate the average to form a *mean* trace. Alternatively, we continuously average over the measured samples and assign higher weights to later recorded traces. We call this approach *sweep*. Using either of the superposed traces we carry out all calculations as explained in Sect. 3 resulting in one score per input.

Alternatively, in the second approach we execute the feature extraction and score calculation for every trace showing the same operations separately. After a following majority vote we accept the most probable results.

In addition, a hybrid version poses a third alternative. Here we calculate multiple scores for the same input using either *mean* or *sweep* traces.

3.5 Overall Side-Channel Driven Fuzzing Algorithm

Above we described all building blocks of our approach. In this section we link them and present an overview. Assume we sent multiple inputs to the DUT while we recorded the power consumption during the processing of each input.

In the first step, we load a batch of power traces and calculate the pairwise mean-squared-error (MSE) among them. With this measure we perform a first refinement prior to the actual SCA calculations to exclude multiple traces showing the same sequence of instructions. If for a pair of traces, the MSE is below a certain threshold, we can assume the same sequence of operations and hence basic blocks were triggered. We exclude such traces and increase the overall fuzzing throughput. Note that we need to analyze the noise properties of the tested DUT to define the MSE threshold.

For the remaining traces, we calculate the scores using our previously introduced algorithms. To complete the fuzzing loop, we suggest using a state-of-the-art fuzzing tool like AFL or SAGE [8]. The analyst can feed the calculated scores to a tool, which prioritizes the inputs and further mutates promising examples. Figure 3 shows the overall setup. The different loops indicate operations which we execute in parallel to further increase the throughput of the framework.

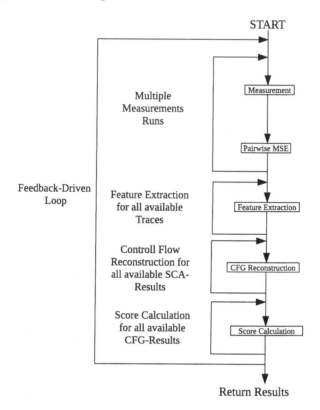

Fig. 3. Overview of the building blocks of side-channel aware fuzzing.

4   Experiments and Evaluation

The lack of a base line to which different fuzzing techniques can be compared to is a known problem in software testing picked up by Dolan-Gavitt et al. [7]. The authors present a system, which injects bugs into C code. This modified code enables the comparison of various testing tools.

Regarding embedded device fuzzing, we face a similar but more fundamental challenge. Prior to evaluating the actual fuzzing success, we need to assess the underlying feedback itself. Therefore, we present a test environment, which allows the calculation of theoretical scores. Furthermore, we introduce three evaluation metrics to assess the quality of the calculated scores. This framework forms a possible base line for future work on feedback extraction, aiming to enhance embedded device fuzzing.

Additionally we show implementation details essential for our proof of concept and information about the achieved results, gained during fuzzing of synthetic software and a light-weight AES implementation. Finally we discuss the transferability of side-channel aware fuzzing to a broader range of embedded devices.

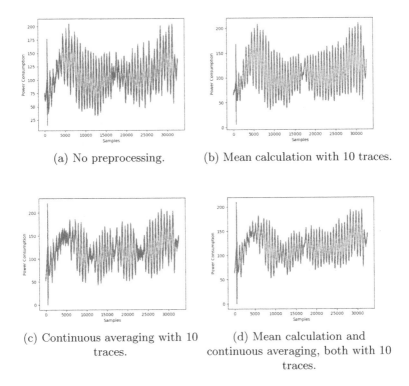

(a) No preprocessing.

(b) Mean calculation with 10 traces.

(c) Continuous averaging with 10 traces.

(d) Mean calculation and continuous averaging, both with 10 traces.

Fig. 4. Four power traces measured during the execution of the same instructions, showing the impact of different preprocessing techniques.

4.1 Evaluation Code

During the proof of concept the analyzed target device executes a test software, which allows the calculation of theoretical code coverage scores for the inputs. The test software takes 16 bytes as input so that 16 binary decision stages are passed throughout the processing. We test five versions of the software, which differ in the decision probability at the binary decision stages. Each version covers 48 basic blocks and 60 possible basic block transitions. The evaluation code hence provides 300 different basic block transitions, our implementation of side-channel aware fuzzing needs to detect. The distances of the branches between the basic blocks range from 10 to 150 skipped instructions. For the individual basic blocks we chose a randomized implementation such that they differ in length, instruction types, used operands, and complexity. Since embedded devices often operate in sensing-actuating loops, some basic blocks in real-world code may only contain a small and simple sequence of instructions. Therefore, to emulate this case the shortest basic blocks contain 10 instructions, whereas we use 110 instructions to form the longest blocks. A further motivation to include short basic blocks is to show the sufficient detail among the power traces which we are able to exploit. If we are able to separate even small basic blocks, our concept does not lack applicability regarding real software.

4.2 Benchmark Metrics

We consider three metrics as measures for the performance of our concept. To allow the following evaluation we interpret multiple scores as arrays or result-traces, respectively. This holds true for the calculated as well as for the theoretical scores. We evaluate the MSE and correlation coefficient between the result-traces. In addition we calculate the number of crucial errors. Such errors occur if for a certain input which triggers the execution of at least one new basic block transition, a score of 0 is returned. In this case the according input would be discarded and not be considered for further mutations. This error type leads to a major decrease in the fuzzing success.

4.3 Implementation Decisions - Classification Approach

The main decision during the implementation is the choice of a machine learning-based classifier for the branch detection and branch distance classification. To perform a comparison of different classification algorithms we record 50 000 traces for the two classes (branch vs. no branch) and use them to train the machine learning models. We compare eight different machine learning algorithms to detect branches. To view the performance of each algorithm, we calculate Matthew's correlation coefficient (MCC) [16], which is well suited for the evaluation of binary classifications of imbalanced data sets [21].

We achieve best results using a *kNN* classification with $k = 3$ and an MCC of 0.93. This result corresponds to the latest findings in related work, see Sect. 2. Therefore, we apply this approach during the proof of concept in which we were able to reach an MCC of 0.78 for the branch detection.

4.4 Test Scenario and Power Traces

In this section we outline important facts about our proof of concept. We show power traces to illustrate the actual application of the algorithms from Sect. 3. We particularly focus on the branch detection and branch distance classification.

During the evaluation phase, our test software (see Sect. 4.1) runs on an STM32F417 [23] microcontroller. This reduced instruction set computer (RISC) based controller uses the ARM Cortex-M4 [2] processor. We set the clock frequency of the DUT to 84 MHz. The DUT processes a batch of 100 random inputs while we measure its power consumption using a shunt resistor of $47\,\Omega$. From the Nyquist-Shannon sampling theorem [22] we know that the sampling rate needs to be at least twice as high as the frequency of the measured signal to prevent a loss of information. Hence, we set the sampling rate of our *LeCroy Wave-Pro 760Zi-A* oscilloscope to 5 GS/s. After all steps of side-channel aware fuzzing our implementation returns a result-trace containing 100 scores. Each score corresponds to one input sent to the DUT. Figure 4 shows four power traces we measured with a differential probe. The individual traces differ in the applied preprocessing technique and give the reader an intuition about the form of the analyzed data.

Figure 5 shows a power trace during the branch detection. For a simple illustration, we chose to implement one branch instruction in the code executed by the DUT. In the first step we slice the power trace into equally sized windows, using a peak detection. Each peak, marked with a red cross is a potential beginning of a branch instruction. The windows have the length of one branch instruction, which we characterized in the training phase. After the binary classification on each window, only one peak is detected as the beginning of a branch, marked with a black circle.

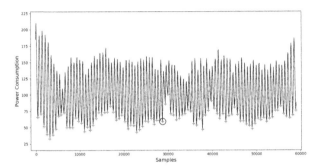

Fig. 5. Power trace during the branch detection, consisting of a peak detection and binary classifications.

Figure 6 shows two power traces during the branch distance classification. The traces show the power consumption of the target device during the execution of two branches with different distances. We can clearly distinguish the power traces and hence the distances of the branches. Note that both traces still show a large similarity, such that we are able to detect both branches.

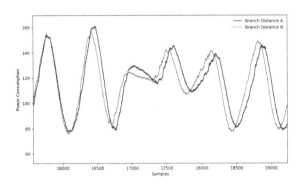

Fig. 6. Two power traces during the execution of two branches with different distances.

4.5 Results

We sum up the results of our proof of concept in Table 2. The result values show the effects of the different preprocessing techniques, the two CFG reconstruction approaches, and impacts of a majority vote in the feature extraction. We emphasize that preprocessing is a necessary step as we achieved better results compared to an analysis using unprocessed traces. The various CFG reconstruction algorithms perform comparably, this allows a selection depending on the analyzed device and measurement quality. Regarding our test environment, no majority vote in the feature extraction reaches superior results compared to a majority vote-based approach.

With our results we can report that the power side-channel of embedded devices carries information relevant for fuzzing. We are able to calculate result traces, which strongly correlate with the actual result values. The maximum correlation coefficient is 0.95. Furthermore, our framework makes on average 0.69 crucial errors per 100 inputs.

4.6 Fuzzing an AES Implementation

In order to provide first test results on real-world code we implemented AES on our DUT for data encryption. The AES algorithm does not perform input-dependent branches. Hence, we can easily compare our calculated scores to the actual number of basic block transitions in our AES implementation. Furthermore, AES is commonly performed by embedded devices, resulting in realistic power traces. For our tests we encrypted randomly chosen plaintexts using one

Table 2. Results during the proof of concept. The target devices executes synthetic code and handles 100 random inputs.

Performance Metrics	Preprocessing, number of used traces		CFG Reconstruction majority (white) vs. non-majority vote (gray)			
	mean	*sweep*	*CFG-RI*		*CFG-RII (separate)*	*CFG-RII (summed)*
Mean Squared Error	1	1	6.16	3.21	6.73 4.13	5.96 5.23
	10	1	4.11	2.81	4.63 3.80	7.38 5.20
	1	10	4.66	3.33	6.05 4.65	4.49 3.37
	10	10	4.77	3.54	4.75 4.33	5.58 4.08
Correlation Coefficient	1	1	0.85	0.93	0.91 0.94	0.86 0.91
	10	1	0.91	0.93	0.94 0.95	0.84 0.92
	1	10	0.90	0.92	0.94 0.94	0.91 0.94
	10	10	0.89	0.92	0.95 0.95	0.90 0.93
Number of Crucial Errors	1	1	0.5	0.9	0.4 0.7	0.4 0.6
	10	1	0.5	0.5	0.6 1.2	0.3 0.8
	1	10	0.4	0.8	0.5 0.6	0.6 0.7
	10	10	1.2	1.3	1.1 1.2	0.5 0.3

random key. During each encryption run, we let our implementation of side-channel aware fuzzing estimate the number of basic block transitions, which have been triggered at least once. Hence, we calculate the scores for each encryption and plaintext. Our AES implementation triggers 41 unique basic block transitions during its ten rounds of encryption. We identified this number during a static code analysis of the compiled binary. Over 100 encryption runs, our framework detects 38 transitions on average. This shows the applicability of our concept, regarding code commonly found on embedded devices. In future work we will extend our tests to a broader range of software including more complex examples containing input-dependent branches.

4.7 Transferability and Generalization

We carried out the description of the concept in a generic way. The motivation to do so is to give software engineers and testers the opportunity to adopt the concept, but implement it in a way fitting to their needs, attacked device, and measurement environment. These factors influence the quality of the power traces and hence the quality of the results. During the evaluation of different aspects of the concept and its implementation we payed attention to the transferability of side-channel aware fuzzing. Even though we fuzzed solely one specific DUT, a broader range of embedded devices can be analyzed with our concept. As can be seen in Sect. 2, considerable success has been achieved in side-channel based reverse engineering. In related work a significant part of the instruction sequence executed by different RISC-based target devices was successfully reconstructed. With this state-of-the art research and the fact, that our concept is based on a successful branch detection we suffer no limitations regarding transferability to other RISC-based target devices. In future work we will further investigate this assumption.

Furthermore we plan to target the challenge of detecting faults in embedded devices during fuzzing. Such faults often trigger a reboot of the device which is a known sequence of actions resulting in characteristic power traces. In an additional preprocessing step prior to the SCA calculations a machine learning based classifier could detect reboot sequences. This information could then be sent to the fuzzing tool.

5 Conclusion

In this paper we combine the two yet unlinked but well studied research fields of fuzzing and side-channel analysis to enable white-box fuzzing of software on embedded devices. With the results we gained from our proof of concept we show that the power side-channel provides sufficient information for a feedback-driven fuzzing loop.

Side-channel aware fuzzing is a threefold concept in which we ultimately assign scores to fuzzing inputs. The scores are proportional to the code coverage during the processing of the individual inputs. We use the number of basic block transitions to assess the code coverage and calculate the scores. In the machine learning based feature extraction approach we analyze the power consumption of the targeted embedded device. With the extracted features we discover the time when the device executes branch instructions which are the borders between basic blocks. Furthermore, we reconstruct the jump distances of the branches. In addition to that, we calculate fingerprints of the trace segments showing the basic blocks. We secondly conduct a control flow reconstruction using the extracted features. By evaluating either the branch distances or fingerprints of the trace parts between the branches, we are able to determine if we triggered a new basic block transition. In the final score calculation, we use the control flow of the software to calculate the score of the inputs sent to the target device.

We carried out the proof of concept on a state-of-the-art ARM Cortex-M4 microcontroller. The structure of our synthetic test code allows calculation of the code coverage triggered by an input so that future work may employ it as a base line. Using this test code and an implementation of our concept, we are able to see a strong correlation between our calculated scores and the theoretical scores. The maximal correlation coefficient we achieved is 0.95. Additionally we correctly estimated the number of basic block transitions in a light-weight AES implementation using our framework. This states a significant step towards white-box fuzzing for vulnerability detection on embedded devices.

References

1. Alimi, V., Vernois, S., Rosenberger, C.: Analysis of embedded applications by evolutionary fuzzing. In: 2014 International Conference on High Performance Computing Simulation (HPCS), pp. 551–557, July 2014
2. Arm Holdings: Cortex-M4 Technical Reference Manual. http://infocenter.arm. com/help/topic/com.arm.doc.ddi0439b/DDI0439B_cortex_m4_r0p0_trm.pdf
3. Cadar, C., Dunbar, D., Engler, D.: KLEE: unassisted and automatic generation of high-coverage tests for complex systems programs. In: Proceedings of the 8th USENIX Conference on Operating Systems Design and Implementation, OSDI 2008, pp. 209–224. USENIX Association, Berkeley (2008). http://dl.acm. org/citation.cfm?id=1855741.1855756
4. Callan, R., Behrang, F., Zajic, A., Prvulovic, M., Orso, A.: Zero-overhead profiling via EM emanations. In: Proceedings of the 25th International Symposium on Software Testing and Analysis, SSTA 2016, pp. 401–412. ACM, New York (2016). https://doi.org/10.1145/2931037.2931065, http://doi.acm.org/ 10.1145/2931037.2931065
5. Corteggiani, N., Camurati, G., Francillon, A.: Inception: system-wide security testing of real-world embedded systems software. In: 27th USENIX Security Symposium (USENIX Security 2018), pp. 309–326. USENIX Association, Baltimore (2018). https://www.usenix.org/conference/usenixsecurity18/presentation/ corteggiani
6. Davidson, D., Moench, B., Ristenpart, T., Jha, S.: FIE on firmware: finding vulnerabilities in embedded systems using symbolic execution. In: Presented as part of the 22nd USENIX Security Symposium (USENIX Security 2013), pp. 463–478. USENIX, Washington, D.C. (2013). https://www.usenix.org/conference/ usenixsecurity13/technical-sessions/paper/davidson

7. Dolan-Gavitt, B., et al.: LAVA: large-scale automated vulnerability addition. In: IEEE Symposium on Security and Privacy, pp. 110–121. IEEE Computer Society (2016)
8. Godefroid, P., Levin, M.Y., Molnar, D.: Automated whitebox fuzz testing. In: Network and Distributed System Security (NDSS) Symposium, NDSS 2008 (2008)
9. Han, Y., Etigowni, S., Liu, H., Zonouz, S., Petropulu, A.: Watch me, but don't touch me! contactless control flow monitoring via electromagnetic emanations. In: Proceedings of the 2017 ACM SIGSAC Conference on Computer and Communications Security, pp. 1095–1108. ACM (2017)
10. Hennessy, J.L., Patterson, D.A.: Computer Architecture: A Quantitative Approach, 5th edn. Morgan Kaufmann Publishers Inc., San Francisco (2011)
11. Howard, M., Lipner, S.: The Security Development Lifecycle. Microsoft Press, Redmond (2006)
12. Kocher, P., Jaffe, J., Jun, B.: Differential power analysis. In: Wiener, M. (ed.) CRYPTO 1999. LNCS, vol. 1666, pp. 388–397. Springer, Heidelberg (1999). https://doi.org/10.1007/3-540-48405-1_25
13. Koscher, K., et al.: Experimental security analysis of a modern automobile. In: Proceedings of the 2010 IEEE Symposium on Security and Privacy, SP 2010, pp. 447–462. IEEE Computer Society, Washington, DC (2010). https://doi.org/10.1109/SP.2010.34
14. Lee, H., Choi, K., Chung, K., Kim, J., Yim, K.: Fuzzing CAN packets into automobiles. In: 2015 IEEE 29th International Conference on Advanced Information Networking and Applications, pp. 817–821, March 2015
15. Mangard, S., Oswald, E., Popp, T.: Power Analysis Attacks: Revealing the Secrets of Smart Cards (Advances in Information Security). Springer, Heidelberg (2007). https://doi.org/10.1007/978-0-387-38162-6
16. Matthews, B.: Comparison of the predicted and observed secondary structure of T4 phage lysozyme. Biochim. Biophys. Acta (BBA) Protein Struct. **405**(2), 442–451 (1975)
17. Msgna, M., Markantonakis, K., Mayes, K.: Precise instruction-level side channel profiling of embedded processors. In: Huang, X., Zhou, J. (eds.) ISPEC 2014. LNCS, vol. 8434, pp. 129–143. Springer, Cham (2014). https://doi.org/10.1007/978-3-319-06320-1_11
18. Muench, M., Stijohann, J., Kargl, F., Francillon, A., Balzarotti, D.: What you corrupt is not what you crash: challenges in fuzzing embedded devices. In: Network and Distributed System Security (NDSS) Symposium, NDSS 2018, February 2018
19. National Institute of Standards and Technology: Advanced encryption standard. NIST FIPS PUB 197 (2001)
20. Papp, D., Ma, Z., Buttyan, L.: Embedded systems security: threats, vulnerabilities, and attack taxonomy. In: 2015 13th Annual Conference on Privacy, Security and Trust (PST), pp. 145–152, July 2015
21. Powers, D.: Evaluation: From Precision, Recall and F-Factor to ROC, Informedness, Markedness & Correlation (2011)
22. Shannon, C.E.: Communication in the presence of noise. Proc. IRE **37**(1), 10–21 (1949)
23. STMicroelectronics: STM32F417xx Datasheet. https://www.st.com/resource/en/datasheet/dm00035129.pdf
24. Strobel, D., Bache, F., Oswald, D., Schellenberg, F., Paar, C.: SCANDALee: a side-ChANnel-based DisAssembLer using local electromagnetic emanations. In: 2015 Design, Automation Test in Europe Conference Exhibition (DATE), pp. 139–144, March 2015

25. Van Aubel, P., Papagiannopoulos, K., Chmielewski, Ł., Doerr, C.: Side-channel based intrusion detection for industrial control systems. In: D'Agostino, G., Scala, A. (eds.) Critical Information Infrastructures Security, pp. 207–224. Springer, Cham (2018). https://doi.org/10.1007/978-3-319-99843-5_19
26. Zaddach, J., Bruno, L., Francillon, A., Balzarotti, D.: AVATAR: a framework to support dynamic security analysis of embedded systems' firmwares. In: Network and Distributed System Security Symposium, San Diego, USA, 23–26 February 2014, NDSS 2014, February 2014. https://doi.org/10.14722/ndss.2014.23229, http://www.eurecom.fr/publication/4158
27. Zalewski, M.: American Fuzzy Lop. http://lcamtuf.coredump.cx/afl/

NetSpectre: Read Arbitrary Memory over Network

Michael Schwarz[1($\boxtimes$)], Martin Schwarzl[1], Moritz Lipp[1], Jon Masters[2], and Daniel Gruss[1]

[1] Graz University of Technology, Graz, Austria
michael.schwarz@iaik.tugraz.at
[2] Red Hat, Cambridge, MA, USA

Abstract. All Spectre attacks so far required local code execution. We present the first fully remote Spectre attack. For this purpose, we demonstrate the first access-driven remote Evict+Reload cache attack over the network, leaking 15 bits per hour. We present a novel high-performance AVX-based covert channel that we use in our cache-free Spectre attack. We show that in particular remote Spectre attacks perform significantly better with the AVX-based covert channel, leaking 60 bits per hour from the target system. We demonstrate practical NetSpectre attacks on the Google cloud, remotely leaking data and remotely breaking ASLR.

1 Introduction

Over the past 20 years, software-based microarchitectural attacks have evolved from theoretical attacks [36] on implementations of cryptographic algorithms [49], to more generic practical attacks [25,60], and recently to high potential threats [35,38,47,55,58] breaking the fundamental memory and process isolation. Spectre [35] is a microarchitectural attack, tricking another program into speculatively executing an instruction sequence which leaves microarchitectural side effects. Except for SMoTherSpectre [10], all Spectre attacks demonstrated so far [12] exploit timing differences caused by the pollution of data caches.

By manipulating the branch prediction, Spectre tricks a process into performing a sequence of memory accesses which leak secrets from chosen virtual memory locations to the attacker. Spectre attacks have so far been demonstrated in JavaScript [35] and native code [14,27,35,37,41,59], but it is likely that any environment allowing sufficiently accurate timing measurements and some form of code execution enables these attacks. Attacks on Intel SGX enclaves showed that enclaves are also vulnerable to Spectre attacks [14]. However, there are many devices which never run any attacker-controlled code, *i.e.*, no JavaScript, no native code, and no other form of code execution on the target system. Until now, these systems were believed to be safe against such attacks. In fact, while some vendors discuss remote targets [8,43] others are convinced that these systems are still safe and recommend to not take any action on these devices [32].

© Springer Nature Switzerland AG 2019
K. Sako et al. (Eds.): ESORICS 2019, LNCS 11735, pp. 279–299, 2019.
https://doi.org/10.1007/978-3-030-29959-0_14

In this paper, we present NetSpectre, a new attack based on Spectre, requiring no attacker-controlled code on the target device, thus affecting billions of devices. Similar to a local Spectre attack, our remote attack requires the presence of a Spectre gadget in the code of the target. We show that systems containing the required Spectre gadgets in an exposed network interface or API can be attacked with our generic remote Spectre attack, allowing to read arbitrary memory over the network. The attacker only sends a series of requests and measures the response time to leak a secret from the victim.

We show that memory access latency, in general, is reflected in the latency of network requests. Hence, we demonstrate that it is possible for an attacker to distinguish cache hits and misses on specific cache lines remotely, by measuring and averaging over a larger number of measurements (law of large numbers). Based on this, we implemented the first access-driven remote cache attack, a remote variant of Evict+Reload called *Thrash+Reload*. We facilitate this technique to retrofit existing Spectre attacks to a network-based scenario and leak 15 bits per hour from a vulnerable target system.

By using a novel side channel based on the execution time of AVX2 instructions, we demonstrate the first Spectre attack which does not rely on a cache covert channel. Our AVX-based covert channel achieves a native code performance of 125 bytes per second at an error rate of 0.58%. This covert channel achieves a higher performance in our NetSpectre attack than the cache covert channel. As cache eviction is not necessary anymore, we increase the speed to leaking 60 bits per hour from the target system in a local area network. In the Google cloud, we leak around 3 bits per hour from another virtual machine (VM).

We demonstrate that using previously ignored gadgets allows breaking address-space layout randomization in a remote attack. Address-space layout randomization (ASLR) is a defense mechanism deployed on most systems today, randomizing virtually all addresses. An attacker with local code execution can easily bypass ASLR since ASLR mostly aims at defending against remote attacks but not local attacks. Hence, many weaker gadgets for Spectre attacks were ignored so far, since they do not allow leaking actual data, but only address information. However, in the remote attack scenario weaker gadgets are still very powerful.

Spectre gadgets can be more versatile than anticipated in previous work. This not only becomes apparent with the weaker gadgets we use in our remote ASLR break but even more so with the value-thresholding technique we propose. Value-thresholding leaks bit-by-bit by through comparisons, by using a divide-and-conquer approach similar to a binary search.

Contributions. The contributions of this work are:

1. We present the first access-driven remote cache attack (Evict+Reload) and the first remote Spectre attack.
2. We demonstrate the first Spectre attack which does not use the cache but a new and fast AVX-based covert channel.
3. We use simpler Spectre gadgets in remote ASLR breaks.

Outline. Section 2 provides background. Section 3 overviews NetSpectre. Section 4 presents new remote covert channels. Section 5 details our attack. Section 6 evaluates the performance of NetSpectre. We conclude in Sect. 7.

2   Background

Modern CPUs have multiple execution units operating in parallel and precomputing results. To retain the architecturally defined execution order, a reorder buffer stores results until they are ready to be retired (made visible on the architectural level) in the order defined by the instruction stream. To keep precomputing, predictions are often necessary using e.g., on branch prediction. To optimize the prediction quality, modern CPUs incorporate several branch prediction mechanisms. If an interrupt occurs or a misprediction is unrolled, any precomputed results are architecturally discarded, however, the microarchitectural state is not reverted. Executed instructions that are not retired are called transient instructions [12,35,38].

Microarchitectural side-channel attacks exploit different microarchitectural elements. They were first explored for attacks on cryptographic algorithms [36,49,60] but today are generic attack techniques for a wide range of attack targets. Cache attacks exploit timing differences introduced by small in-CPU memory buffers. Different cache attack techniques have been proposed in the past, including Prime+Probe [49,52], and Flush+Reload [60]. In a covert channel, the attacker controls both, the part that induces the side effect, and the part that measures the side effect. Both Prime+Probe and Flush+Reload have been used in high-performance covert channels [24,39,45].

Meltdown [38] and Spectre [35] use covert channels to transmit data from the transient execution to a persistent state. Meltdown exploits vulnerable deferred permission checks. Spectre [35] exploits speculative execution in general. Hence, they do not rely on any vulnerability, but solely on optimizations. Through manipulation of the branch prediction mechanisms, an attacker lures a victim process into executing attacker-chosen code gadgets. This enables the attacker to establish a covert channel from the speculative execution in the victim process to a receiver process under attacker control.

SIMD (single instruction multiple data) instructions enable parallel operation on multiple data values. They are available as instruction set extensions on modern CPUs, e.g., Intel MMX [28–30,51], AMD 3DNow! [4,48], and ARM VFP and NEON [3,6,7]. On Intel, some of the SIMD instructions are processed by a dedicated SIMD unit within the CPU core. However, to save energy, the SIMD unit is turned off when not used. Consequently, to execute such instructions, the SIMD unit is first powered up, introducing a small latency on the first few instructions [18]. Liu [40] noted that some SIMD instructions can be used to improve bus-contention covert channels. However, so far, SIMD instructions have not yet been used for pure SIMD covert channels or side-channel attacks.

One security mechanism present in modern operating systems is address-space layout randomization (ASLR) [50]. It randomizes the locations of objects or regions in memory, e.g., heap objects and stacks, so that an attacker cannot predict correct addresses. Naturally, this is a probabilistic approach, but it provides a significant gain in security in practice. ASLR especially aims at mitigating control-flow-hijacking attacks, but it also makes other remote attacks difficult where the attacker has to provide a specific address.

3   Attack Overview

The building blocks of a NetSpectre attack are two *NetSpectre gadgets*: a *leak gadget*, and a *transmit gadget*. We discuss the roles of these gadgets, which allow an attacker to perform a Spectre attack without any local code execution or access, based on their type (leak or transmit) and the microarchitectural element they use (e.g., cache).

Spectre attacks induce a victim to speculatively perform operations that do not occur in strict in-order processing of the program's instructions, and which leak a victim's confidential information via a covert channel to an attacker. Multiple Spectre variants are exploiting different prediction mechanisms. Spectre-PHT (also known as Variant 1) [34,35] mistrains a conditional branch, e.g., a bounds check. Spectre-BTB (also known as Variant 2) [35] exploits mispredictions of indirect calls, Spectre-STL (also known as Variant 4) speculatively bypasses stores [27], and Spectre-RSB misuses the return stack buffer [37,41]. While attack works with any Spectre variant, we focus on Spectre-PHT as it is widespread, illustrative, and difficult to fix in hardware [12,31].

Before the value of a branch condition is known (resolved), the CPU predicts the most likely outcome and then continues with the corresponding code path. There are several reasons why the result of the condition is not known at the time of evaluation, e.g., a cache miss on parts of the condition, complex dependencies which are not yet satisfied, or a bottleneck in a required execution unit. By hiding these latencies, speculative execution leads to faster overall execution if the branch condition was predicted correctly. Intermediate results of a wrongly predicted condition are simply not committed to the architectural state, and the effective performance is similar to that which would have occurred had the CPU never performed any speculative execution. However, any modifications of the microarchitectural state that occurred during speculative execution, such as the cache state, are not reverted.

As our NetSpectre attack is mounted over the network, the victim device requires a network interface an attacker can reach. While this need not necessarily be Ethernet, a wireless or cellular link are also possible. Moreover, the target of the attack could also be baseband firmware running within a phone [5,8]. The attacker must be able to send a large number of network packets to the victim but not necessarily within a short time frame. Furthermore, the content of the packets in our attack is not required to be attacker-controlled.

In contrast to local Spectre attacks, our NetSpectre attack is not split into two phases. Instead, the attacker constantly performs operations to mistrain the CPU, which will make it constantly run into exploitably erroneous speculative execution. NetSpectre does not mistrain across process boundaries, but

```
if (x < length)
    if(array[x] > y)
        flag &= true
```

Listing 1.1. Excerpt of a function executed when a network packet is processed.

instead trains in-place by passing in-bounds and out-of-bounds values alternatingly to the exposed interface. For our NetSpectre attack, the attacker requires two Spectre gadgets, which are executed if a network packet is received: a *leak gadget*, and a *transmit gadget*. The *leak gadget* accesses an array offset at an attacker-controlled index, compares it with a user provided value, and changes some microarchitectural state depending on the result of the comparison. The *transmit gadget* performs an arbitrary operation where the runtime depends on the microarchitectural state modified by the *leak gadget*. Hidden in a significant amount of noise, this timing difference can be observed in the network packet response time. Spectre gadgets can be found in modern network drivers, network stacks, and network service implementations.

To illustrate the working principle of our NetSpectre attack, we consider a basic example similar to the original Spectre-PHT example [35] in an adapted scenario: the code in Listing 1.1 is part of a function that is executed when a network packet is received. Note that this just one variant to enable bit-wise leakage, there is an abundance of other gadgets that leak a single bit. We assume that x is attacker-controlled, e.g., a field in a packet header or an index for some API. This code forms our *leak gadget*.

The code fragment begins with a bound check on x, a best practice for secure software. The attacker can remotely exploit speculative execution as follows:

1. The attacker sends multiple network packets with the value of x always in bounds. This trains the branch predictor, increasing the chance that the outcome of the comparison is predicted as true.
2. A packet where x is out of bounds is sent, such that array[x] is a secret value in the target's memory. However, the branch predictor still assumes the bounds check to be true, and the memory access is speculatively executed.
3. If the attacker-controlled value y is less than the secret value array[x], the flag variable is accessed.

While changes are not committed architecturally after the condition is resolved, microarchitectural state changes are not reverted. Thus, in Listing 1.1, the cache state of flag changes although the value of flag does not change. Only if the attacker guessed y such that it is less than array[x], flag is cached. Note that the operation on flag is not relevant as long as flag is accessed.

The *transmit gadget* is much simpler, as it only has to use flag in an arbitrary operation. Consequently, the execution time of the gadget will depend on the cache state of flag. In the most simple case, the *transmit gadget* simply returns the value of flag, which is set by the *leak gadget*. As the architectural state of flag (*i.e.*, its value) does not change for out-of-bounds x, it does not leak secret information. However, the response time of the *transmit gadget* depends on the microarchitectural state of `flag` (*i.e.*, whether it is cached), which leaks one secret bit of information.

To complete the attack, the attacker performs a binary search over the value range. Each tested value leaks one secret bit. As the difference in the response time is in the range of nanoseconds, the attacker needs to average over a large number of measurements to obtain the secret value with acceptable confidence. Indeed, our experiments show that the difference in the microarchitectural state becomes visible when performing a large number of measurements. Hence, an attacker can first measure the two corner cases (*i.e.*, cached and uncached) and afterward, to extract a real secret bit, perform as many measurements as necessary to distinguish which case it is with confidence, e.g., using a threshold or a Bayes classifier.

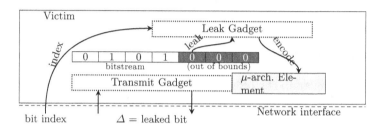

Fig. 1. The interaction of the *NetSpectre gadget* types.

We refer to the two gadgets, the *leak gadget* and the *transmit gadget*, as *NetSpectre gadgets*. Running a *NetSpectre gadget* may require sending more than one packet. Furthermore, the *leak gadget* and *transmit gadget* may be reachable via different independent interfaces, *i.e.*, both interfaces must be attacker-accessible. Figure 1 illustrates the two gadgets types that are detailed in Sect. 3.2.

From the listings illustrating gadgets, it is clear that such code snippets exist in real-world code (cf. Listing 1.3). However, as they can potentially be spread across many instructions and might not be visible in the source code, identifying such gadgets is currently an open problem which is also discussed in other Spectre papers [34,35,37,41]. Moreover, the reachability of a gadget with specific constraints is an orthogonal problem and out of scope for this paper. As a consequence, we follow best practices by introducing Spectre gadgets into software run by the victim to evaluate the attack in the same manner as other Spectre papers [34,37,41]. Suitable gadgets can be located in real-world software applications through static analysis of source code or through binary inspection.

3.1   Gadget Location

The set of attack targets depends on the location of the *NetSpectre gadgets*. As illustrated in Fig. 2, on a high level, there are two different gadget locations: in the user space or in the kernel space. However, they can also be found in software running below, e.g., hypervisor, baseband or firmware.

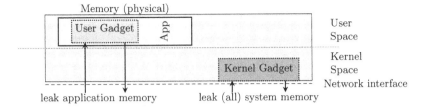

Fig. 2. Depending on the gadget location, the attacker can access memory of the application or the entire kernel, typically including all system memory.

Attacks on the Kernel. The network driver is usually implemented in the kernel of the operating system, either as a fixed component or as a kernel module. In either case, kernel code is executed when a network packet is received. If any kernel code processed during the handling of the network packet contains a *NetSpectre gadget*, *i.e.*, an attacker-controlled part of the packet is used as an index, comparing the array value with a second user-controlled value, a NetSpectre attack is possible.

An attack on the kernel code is particularly powerful, as the kernel does not only have the kernel memory mapped but typically also the entire physical memory. On Linux and macOS, the physical memory can be accessed via the direct-physical map, *i.e.*, every physical memory location is accessible via a predefined virtual address in the kernel address space. Windows does not use a direct-physical map but maintains memory pools, which typically also map a large fraction of the physical memory. Thus, a NetSpectre attack using a *NetSpectre gadget* in the kernel can in general leak arbitrary values from memory.

Attacks on the User Space. Usually, network packets are not only handled by the kernel but are passed on to a user-space application which processes the content of the packet. Hence, not only the kernel but also user-space applications can contain *NetSpectre gadgets*. In fact, all code paths that are executed when a network packet arrives are candidates to look for *NetSpectre gadgets*. This does include code both on the server side and the client side.

An advantage in attacking user-space applications is the significantly larger attack surface, as many applications process network packets. Especially on servers, there are an abundance of services processing user-controlled network packets, e.g., web servers, FTP servers, or SSH daemons. Moreover, a remote server can also attack a client machine, e.g., via web sockets, or SSH connections. In contrast to attacks on the kernel space, which in general can leak any data stored in the system memory, attacks on a user-space application can only leak secrets of the attacked application.

Such application-specific secrets include secrets of the application itself, e.g., credentials and keys. Thus, a NetSpectre attack using a *NetSpectre gadget* in an application can access arbitrary data processed by the application. Furthermore, if the victim is a multi-user application, e.g., a web server, it also contains the secrets of multiple users. This is especially interesting for popular websites with many users.

3.2 Gadget Type

We now discuss the different *NetSpectre gadgets*; the *leak gadget* to encode a secret bit into a microarchitectural state, and the *transmit gadget* to transfer the microarchitectural state to a remote attacker.

Leak Gadget. A *leak gadget* leaks secret data by changing a microarchitectural state depending on the value of a memory location that is not directly accessible to the attacker. The state changes on the victim device, not directly observable over the network. A NetSpectre *leak gadget* only leaks a single bit. Single-bit gadgets are the most versatile, as storing a one-bit (binary) state can be accomplished with many microarchitectural states, as only two cases have to be distinguished (cf. Sect. 4). Thus, we focus on single-bit *leak gadgets* in this paper as they can be as simple as shown in Listing 1.1. In this example, a value (flag) is cached if the value at the attacker-chosen location is larger than the attacker-chosen value y. The attacker can use this gadget to leak secret bits into the microarchitectural state.

Transmit Gadget. In contrast to Spectre, NetSpectre requires an additional gadget to transmit the leaked information to the attacker. As the attacker does not control any code on the victim device, the recovery process, *i.e.*, observing the microarchitectural state, cannot be implemented by the attacker. Furthermore, the architectural state can usually not be accessed via the network and, thus, it would not even help if the gadget converts the state.

From the attacker's perspective, the microarchitectural state must become visible over the network. This may not only happen directly via the content of a network packet but also via side effects. Indeed, the microarchitectural state will in some cases become visible, e.g., in the form of the response time. We refer to a code fragment which exposes the microarchitectural state to a network-based attacker and which can be triggered by an attacker, as a *transmit gadget*. Naturally, the *transmit gadget* has to be located on the victim device. With a *transmit gadget*, the microarchitectural state measurement happens on a remote machine but exposes the microarchitectural state over a network-reachable interface.

In the original Spectre attack, Flush+Reload is used to transfer the microarchitectural state to an architectural state, which is then read by the attacker to leak the secret. The ideal case would be if such a Flush+Reload gadget is available on the victim, and the architectural state can be observed over the network. However, as it is unlikely to locate an exploitable Flush+Reload gadget on the victim and access the architectural state, regular Spectre gadgets cannot simply be retrofitted to mount a NetSpectre attack.

In the most direct case, the microarchitectural state becomes visible for a remote attacker, through the latency of a network packet. A simple *transmit gadget* for the *leak gadget* shown in Listing 1.1 just accesses the variable `flag`. The response time of the network packet depends on the cache state of the variable, *i.e.*, if the variable was accessed, the response takes less time. Generally, an attacker can observe changes in the microarchitectural state if such differences are measurable via the network.

4   Remote Microarchitectural Covert Channels

A cornerstone of our NetSpectre attack is building a microarchitectural covert channel that exposes information to a remote attacker (cf. Sect. 3). Since in our scenario the attacker cannot run any code on the target system, we use a *transmit gadget* whose execution can be triggered by the attacker. In this section, we present the first remote access-driven cache attack, *Thrash+Reload*, a variant of Evict+Reload. We show that with *Thrash+Reload*, an attacker can build a covert channel from the speculative execution on the target device to a remote receiving end on the attacker's machine. Furthermore, we also present a previously unknown microarchitectural covert channel based on AVX2 instructions. We show that this covert channel can be used in NetSpectre attacks, yielding even higher transmission rates than the remote cache covert channel.

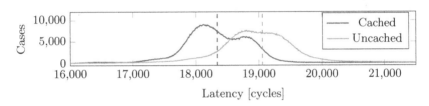

Fig. 3. Measuring the response time of a *transmit gadget* accessing a certain variable. Only by performing a large number of measurements, the difference in the response timings depending on the cache state becomes visible. The distribution's average values are shown as dashed lines.

4.1   Remote Cache Covert Channel

Kocher et al. [35] use the cache as the microarchitectural element to encode the leaked data. This allows using well-known cache side-channel attacks, such as Flush+Reload [60] or Prime+Probe [49,52] to deduce the microarchitectural state and thus the encoded data. However, not only caches keep microarchitectural states which can be used for covert channels [11,16,19,53,56].

Mounting a Spectre attack by using the cache has three main advantages: there are powerful methods to make the cache state visible, many operations modify the cache state and are thus visible in the cache, and the timing difference between a cache hit and cache miss is comparably large. Flush+Reload is usually considered the most fine-grained and accurate cache attack, with almost zero noise [19,24,60]. If shared memory is not available, Prime+Probe is considered the next best choice [45,57]. Consequently, all Spectre attacks published so far use either Flush+Reload [14,35] or Prime+Probe [59].

For the first NetSpectre attack, we need to adapt local cache covert channel techniques. Instead of measuring the memory access time directly, we measure the response time of a network request which uses the corresponding memory location. Hence, the response time is influenced by the cache state of the variable used for the attack. The difference in the response time due to the cache state is in the range of nanoseconds since memory accesses are comparably fast.

The network latency is subject to many factors, leading to noisy results. However, the law of large numbers applies: no matter how much statistically independent noise is included, averaging over a large number reveals the signal [1,2,9,33,61]. Hence, an attacker can still obtain the secret value with confidence.

Figure 3 shows that the difference in the microarchitectural state is indeed visible when performing a large number of measurements. The average values of the two distributions are illustrated as dashed vertical lines. An attacker can either use a classifier on the measured values, or first measure the two corner cases (cached and uncached) to get a threshold for the real measurements.

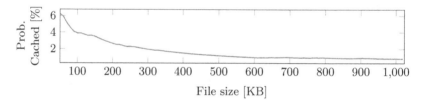

Fig. 4. The probability that a specific variable is evicted from the victim's last-level cache by downloading a file from the victim (Intel i5-6200U). The larger the downloaded file, the higher the probability that the variable is evicted.

Still, as the measurement destroys the cache state, *i.e.*, the variable is always cached after the first measurement, the attacker requires a method to evict (or flush) the variable from the cache. As it is unlikely that the victim provides an interface to flush or evict a variable directly, the attacker cannot use well-known cache attacks but has to resort to more crude methods. Instead of the targeted eviction in Evict+Reload, we simply evict the entire last-level cache by thrashing the cache, similar to Maurice et al. [44]. Hence, we call this technique *Thrash+Reload*. To thrash the entire cache without code execution, we use a network-accessible interface. In the simplest form, any packet sent from the victim to the attacker, e.g., a file download, can evict a variable from the cache.

Figure 4 shows the probability of evicting a specific variable (*i.e.*, the `flag` variable) from the last-level cache by requesting a file from the victim. The victim is running on an Intel i5-6200U with 3 MB last-level cache. Downloading a 590 kilobytes file evicts our variable with a probability of ≥99%.

With a mechanism to distinguish hits and misses, and a mechanism to evict the cache, we have all building blocks required for a cache side-channel attack or a cache covert channel. *Thrash+Reload* combines both mechanisms over a network interface, forming the first remote cache covert channel. In our experiments on a local area network, we achieve a transmission rate of up to 4 bit per minute, with an error rate of <0.1 %. This is significantly slower than cache covert channels in a local native environment, e.g., the most similar attack (Evict+Reload) achieves a performance of 13.6 kb/s with an error rate of 3.79%.

We use our remote cache covert channel for remote Spectre attacks. However, remote cache covert channels and especially remote cache side-channel attacks are an interesting object of study. Many attacks that were presented previously would be devastating if mounted over a network interface [22,25,60].

4.2   Remote AVX-Based Covert Channel

To demonstrate the first Spectre variant which does not rely on the cache as the microarchitectural element, we require a covert channel which allows transmitting information from speculative execution to an architectural state. Thus, we build a novel covert channel based on timing differences in AVX2 instructions. This covert channel has a low error rate and high performance, and it allows for a significant performance improvement in our NetSpectre attack as compared to the remote cache covert channel.

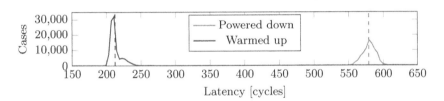

Fig. 5. If the AVX2 unit is inactive (powered down), executing an AVX2 instruction takes on average 366 cycles longer than on an active AVX2 unit (Intel i5-6200U). Average values shown as dashed lines.

To save power, the CPU can power down the upper half of the AVX2 unit which is used to perform operations on 256-bit registers. The upper half of the unit is powered up as soon as an instruction is executed which uses 256-bit values [46]. If it is not used for more than 1 ms, it is powered down [17].

Performing a 256-bit operation when the upper half is powered down incurs a significant performance penalty. For example, we measured the execution (including measurement overhead) of a simple bit-wise AND of two 256-bit registers (VPAND) on an Intel i5-6200U (cf. Fig. 5). If the upper half is active, the operation takes on average 210 cycles, whereas if the upper half is powered down (*i.e.*, it is inactive), the operation takes on average 576 cycles. The difference of 366 cycles is even larger than the difference between cache hits and misses, which is only 160 cycles on the same system. Hence, the timing difference in AVX2 instructions is better for remote microarchitectural attacks.

Similarly to the cache, reading the latency of an AVX2 instruction also destroys the encoded information. Therefore, an attacker requires a method to reset the AVX2 unit, *i.e.*, power down the upper half. In contrast to the cache, this is easier, as the upper half of the AVX2 unit is automatically powered down after 1 ms of inactivity. Thus, an attacker only has to wait at least 1 ms.

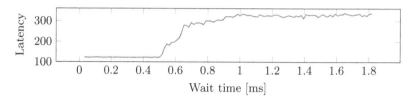

Fig. 6. The number of cycles it takes to execute the VPAND instruction (with measurement overhead) after not using the AVX2 unit. After 0.5 ms, the upper half of the AVX2 unit powers down, which increases the latency for subsequent AVX2 instructions. After 1 ms, it is fully powered down, and we see the maximum latency for subsequent AVX2 instructions.

```
if (x < length)
    if(array[x] > y)
        _mm256_instruction();
```

Listing 1.2. AVX2 NetSpectre gadget which encodes one bit of information.

Figure 6 shows the execution time of an AVX2 instruction (specifically VPAND) after inactivity of the AVX2 unit. If the inactivity is shorter than 0.5 ms, *i.e.*, the last AVX2 instruction was executed not more than 0.5 ms ago, there is no performance penalty when executing an AVX2 instruction which uses the upper half of the AVX2 unit. After that, the AVX2 unit begins powering down, increasing the execution time for any subsequent AVX2 instruction, as the unit has to be powered up again while emulating AVX2 in the meantime [17]. It is fully powered down after approximately 1 ms, leading to the highest performance penalty if any AVX2 instruction is executed in this state.

A *leak gadget* using AVX2 is similar to a *leak gadget* using the cache. Listing 1.2 shows (pseudo-)code of an AVX2 *leak gadget*. The _mm256_instruction represents an arbitrary 256-bit AVX2 instruction, e.g., _mm256_and_si256. If the referenced element x is larger than the user-controlled value y, the instruction is executed, and as a consequence, the upper half of the AVX2 unit is powered on. The power up also happens if the branch-prediction outcome of the bounds check was incorrect and the AVX2 instruction is accessed speculatively. Note that there is no data dependency between the AVX2 instruction and the array lookup. Only the information whether an AVX2 instruction was executed is used to transmit the secret bit of information through the covert channel.

The *transmit gadget* is again similar to the *transmit gadget* for the cache. Any function that uses an AVX2 instruction, and has thus a measurable runtime difference observable over the network, can be used as a *transmit gadget*. Even the *leak gadget* shown in Listing 1.2 can act as a *transmit gadget*. By providing an in-bounds value for x, the runtime of the function depends on the state of the upper half of the AVX2 unit. If the upper half of the unit was used before, *i.e.*, a '1'-bit (`array[x] > y`) was leaked, the function executes faster than if the upper half was not used before, *i.e.*, a '0'-bit (`array[x] <= y`) was leaked.

With these building blocks, we build the first pure-AVX covert channel and the first AVX-based remote covert channel. In our experiments in a native local environment, we achieve a transmission rate of 125 B/s with an error rate of 0.58%. In a local area network, we achieve a transmission rate of 8 B/min, with an error rate of <0.1%. Since the true capacity of this remote covert channel is higher than the true capacity of our remote cache covert channel, it yields higher performance in our NetSpectre attack.

5   Attack Variants

In this section, we first describe an attack to extract secret data via value-thresholding bit-by-bit from the memory of the target system. We then describe how to defeat ASLR on the remote machine, paving the way for remote exploitation. We use gadgets based on Spectre-PHT for illustrative purposes, but this can naturally be done with any Spectre gadget that lies in a code path reached from handling a remote packet.

5.1   Extracting Data from the Target

With typical *NetSpectre gadgets* (cf. Sect. 3), the attack consists of 4 steps. Depending on the gadgets, the *leak gadget* and *transmit gadget* can be the same.

1. Mistrain the branch predictor.
2. Reset the state of the microarchitectural element.
3. Leak a bit via value-thresholding to the microarchitectural element.
4. Expose the element state to the network.

In step 1, the attacker mistrains the branch predictor of the victim to run a Spectre attack by using the *leak gadget* with valid indices. The valid indices ensure that the branch predictor learns always to take the branch, *i.e.*, speculating that the condition is true. With no feedback to the attacker, the microarchitectural state does not have to be reset or transmitted.

In step 2, the attacker resets the microarchitectural state to enable encoding leaked bits using a microarchitectural element. This step depends on the used microarchitectural element, e.g., when using the cache, the attacker downloads a large file from the victim; for AVX2, the attacker waits for about 1 ms.

In step 3, the attacker exploits Spectre to leak a single bit from the victim. As the branch predictor is mistrained in step 1, providing an out-of-bounds index to the *leak gadget* will run the in-bounds path and modify the microarchitectural element, *i.e.*, the bit is encoded in the microarchitectural element.

In step 4, the attacker has to transmit the encoded information via the network. This step corresponds to the second phase of the original Spectre attack. In contrast to the original Spectre attack, which uses a cache attack, the attacker uses the *transmit gadget* for this step as described in Sect. 4. The attacker sends a network packet which is handled by the *transmit gadget* and measures the time from sending the packet until the response arrives. As described in Sect. 4, this round-trip time depends on the state of the microarchitectural element, and thus on the leaked bit.

As the network latency varies, the four steps have to be repeated to eliminate the noise caused by these fluctuations. Typically, the variance in latency follows a certain distribution depending on multiple factors, e.g., distance, number of hops, network congestion [13,21,26]. The number of repetitions depends mainly on the variance in network connection latency. Thus, depending on the latency distribution, the number of repetitions can be deduced using statistical methods. In Sect. 6.1, we evaluate this variant and provide empirically determined numbers for our attack setup.

```
if (x < array_length)
    access(array[x])
```

Listing 1.3. A NetSpectre gadget which can be used to break ASLR.

5.2   Remotely Breaking ASLR on the Target

If the attacker has no access to bit-leaking *NetSpectre gadgets*, it is possible to use a weaker *NetSpectre gadget* which does not leak the actual data but only information about the corresponding address. Such gadgets were not considered harmful for Spectre attacks, which already have local code execution, as ASLR does not protect against local attacks. However, in a remote scenario, it is very valuable to break ASLR. If such a *NetSpectre gadget* is found in a user-space program, it breaks ASLR for this process.

Listing 1.3 shows a *leak gadget* which we use to break ASLR in 3 steps:

1. Mistrain the branch predictor.
2. Out-of-bounds access to cache a known memory location.
3. Measure the execution time of a function via network to deduce whether the out-of-bounds access cached it.

The mistraining step is the same as for any Spectre attack, leading to speculative out-of-bounds accesses relative to the array. If the attacker provides an out-of-bounds value for x after mistraining, the array element indexed is speculatively accessed. Assuming a byte array and an (unsigned) 64-bit index, an attacker can (speculatively) access any memory location, as the index wraps around if the base address plus the index is larger than the virtual memory.

If the byte at this memory location is valid and cacheable, the speculative execution will fetch the corresponding memory location into the cache. Thus, this gadget allows caching arbitrary memory locations which are valid in the current virtual memory, *i.e.*, every mapped memory location of the current application.

The attacker uses this gadget to cache a memory location at a known location, e.g., the vsyscall page which is mapped into every application at the same virtual address [15]. The attacker measures the execution time of a function accessing the now cached memory location. If it is faster, the out-of-bounds index actually cached an address used by this function. From the known address and the index value, *i.e.*, the relative offset to the known address, the address of the *leak gadget* can be calculated.

With an ASLR entropy of 30 b on Linux [42], there are 2^{30} possible offsets the attacker has to check. Due to the KPTI (formerly KAISER [23]) patches, no other page close to the vsyscall page is mapped in the user space. Consequently, in the 2^{30} possible offsets, there is only a single valid, and thus cacheable, offset. Hence, we can perform a binary search to find the correct offset, *i.e.*, speculatively try to load half of the possible offsets into the cache and check a single time. If the single valid offset was cached, the attacker chose the correct half. Otherwise, the attacker continues with the other half. This reduces the number of checks to defeat ASLR to only 30.

Although vsyscall is a legacy feature, we found it to be still enabled on Ubuntu 17.10 and Debian 9.4, the default operating system for VMs on the Google Cloud. Moreover, any other function or data can be used instead of vsyscall if the address is known. If the address of the *leak gadget* is known, it can be repeated to de-randomize any other function where its execution time of can be measured via the network. If the attacker knows a memory page at a fixed offset in the kernel, the same attack can be run on a *NetSpectre gadget* in the kernel to break KASLR.

6   Evaluation

In this section, we evaluate NetSpectre and the performance of our proof-of-concept implementation. Section 6.1 provides a qualitative evaluation and Sect. 6.2 a quantitative evaluation of our NetSpectre attacks. For the evaluation, we used laptops (Intel i5-4200M, i5-6200U, i7-8550U), as well as desktop PCs (Intel i7-6700K, i7-8700K), an unspecified Intel Xeon Skylake in the Google Cloud Platform, and an ARM A75.

6.1   Leakage

To evaluate NetSpectre on the different devices, we constructed a victim program which contains the same *leak gadget* and *transmit gadget* on all test platforms (cf. Sect. 3). We leaked known values from the victim to verify that our attack was successful and to determine how many measurements are necessary. Except for the cloud setup, all evaluations were done in a local lab environment.

We used Spectre-PHT for all evaluations. However, other Spectre variants can be used in the same manner.

Desktop and Laptop Computers. Like other microarchitectural attacks, NetSpectre requires a large number of measurements to distinguish bits with a certain confidence (law of large numbers). On a local network, around 100 000 measurements are required to observe a difference clearly.

For our local attack, we had a gigabit connection between victim and attacker, a typical scenario in local networks and for network connections of dedicated and virtual servers. We measured a standard deviation of the network latency of 15.6 μs. Applying the three-sigma rule [54], in at least 88.8% cases, the latency deviates ±46.8 μs from the average. This is nearly 3 orders of magnitude larger than the actual timing difference the attacker wants to measure, explaining the large number of measurements required.

Our proof-of-concept NetSpectre implementation leaks arbitrary bits from the victim by specifying an out-of-bounds index and comparing it with a user-provided value. Figure 7 shows the leakage of one byte using our proof-of-concept implementation. For every bit, we repeated the measurements 1 000 000 times. Although we only use a naïve threshold on the maximum of the histograms, we can clearly distinguish '0'-bits from '1'-bits (`array[x]` `<=` y and `array[x]` `>` y). More sophisticated methods, e.g., machine learning approaches, might be able to reduce the number of measurements further.

ARM Devices. Also in our evaluation on ARM devices, we used a wired network, as the network-latency varies too much in today's wireless connections. The ARM core we tested turned out to have a significantly higher variance in the network latency. We measured a standard deviation of the network latency of 128.5 μs. Again, with the three-sigma rule, we estimate that at least 88.8% of the measurements are within ±385.5 μs.

Figure 8 shows two leaked bits, a '0'- and a '1'-bit (`array[x]` `<=` y and `array[x]` `>` y), of an ARM Cortex-A75 victim. Even with the higher variance in latency, thresholding allows separating the maxima of the histograms, *i.e.*, the attack works on ARM devices.

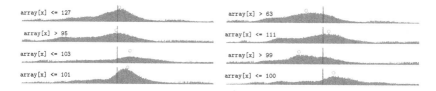

Fig. 7. Leaking the byte 100 (`01100100` in binary) bit by bit using a NetSpectre attack. The maximum of the histograms (green circle) can be separated using a simple threshold (red line). If the maximum is left of the threshold, the bit is interpreted as '1', otherwise as '0'. (Color figure online)

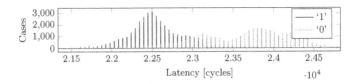

Fig. 8. Histogram of the measurements for a '0'-bit and a '1'-bit (`array[x] <= y` and `array[x] > y`) on an ARM Cortex A75. Although the times for both cases overlap, they are clearly distinguishable.

Cloud Instances. For the cloud instance, we tested our proof-of-concept implementation on the Google Cloud Platform. We created two VMs in the same region, one as the attacker, one as the victim. For both VMs, we used a default Ubuntu 16.04.4 LTS as the operating system. The measured standard deviation of the network latency was $52.3\,\mu s$. Thus, we estimate that at least 88.8% of the measurements are in a range of $\pm 156.9\,\mu s$.

To adapt for the higher variance in network latency, we increased the number of measurements to 20 000 000 per comparison. Figure 9 shows a (smoothed) histogram for both a '0'-bit and a '1'-bit (`array[x] <= y` and `array[x] > y`) on the Google Cloud VMs. Although there is still noise visible, it is possible to distinguish the two cases and thus perform a binary search to leak bit-by-bit of the value from the victim cloud VM.

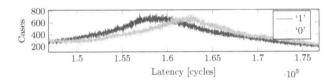

Fig. 9. Histogram of the measurements for the cases `array[x] <= y` and `array[x] > y` on two Google Cloud VMs with 20 000 000 measurements.

6.2   NetSpectre Performance

We evaluate the throughput and error rate of NetSpectre in this section.

Local Network. Attacks on the local network perform best, as the variance in network latency is significantly smaller than over the internet (cf. Sect. 6.1). In our setup, we repeat the measurement 1 000 000 times per bit to reliably leak bytes from the victim. On average, leaking one byte takes 30 min, which amounts to approximately 4 min per bit. Using the AVX covert channel instead of the cache reduces the required time to leak an entire byte to only 8 min. On average, we can break ASLR remotely within 2 h using the cache covert channel.

We used `stress -i 1 -d 1` for the experiments, to simulate a realistic environment. Although we expected our attack to work best on a completely idle server, we did not see any negative effects from the moderate server loads. In fact, they even slightly improved the performance. One reason for this is that a higher server load incurs a higher number of memory and cache accesses [1] and thus facilitates the cache thrashing (cf. Sect. 4), which is the performance bottleneck of our attack. Another reason is that a higher server load might exhaust execution ports required to calculate the bounds check in the leak gadget, thus increasing the chance that the CPU has to execute the condition speculatively.

Our NetSpectre attack in local networks is comparably slow. However, in particular, specialized malware attacks are often active over several months in local networks. Over such a time frame, the attacker can indeed leak all data of interest from a target system on the same network.

Cloud Network. We evaluated the performance in the Google cloud using two VMs. The two VMs have 2 virtual CPUs each, which enabled a 4 Gbit/s connection [20]. In this setup, we repeat the measurement 20 000 000 times per bit to get an error-free leakage of bytes. On average, leaking one byte takes 8 h for the cache covert channel, and 3 h for the AVX covert channel.

Despite the low performance, it shows that remote Spectre attacks are feasible between independent VMs in the public cloud. As specialized malware attacks often run for several weeks or months, such an extended time frame is sufficient to leak sensitive data, e.g., encryption keys or passwords.

Performance Improvements. For all measurements, we used commodity hardware in off-the-shelf laptops to measure the network-packet response time. Thus, there is additional latency (*i.e.*, noise) due to the latency of the operating system and network hardware of the attacker. Measuring the response time directly on the ethernet (or fiber) connection using dedicated hardware can drastically improve the attack performance. We expect that such a setup can easily reduce the time by a factor of 2 to 10.

7   Conclusion

In this paper, we presented NetSpectre, the first remote Spectre attack and the first Spectre attack which does not use a cache covert channel. With a remote Evict+Reload cache attack over network we can leak 15 bits per hour, with our new AVX-based covert channel even 60 bits per hour. We demonstrated NetSpectre on the Google cloud and in local networks, remotely leaking data and remotely breaking ASLR.

Acknowledgments. We would like to thank our anonymous reviewers for their feedback and Anders Fogh, Halvar Flake, Jann Horn, Stefan Mangard, Jo Van Bulck, and Matt Miller for feedback on an early draft.

This work has been supported by the European Research Council (ERC) under the European Union's Horizon 2020 research and innovation programme (grant agreement No 681402).

References

1. Acıiçmez, O., Schindler, W., Koç, Ç.K.: Cache based remote timing attack on the AES. In: Abe, M. (ed.) CT-RSA 2007. LNCS, vol. 4377, pp. 271–286. Springer, Heidelberg (2006). https://doi.org/10.1007/11967668_18
2. Aly, H., ElGayyar, M.: Attacking AES using Bernstein's attack on modern processors. In: Youssef, A., Nitaj, A., Hassanien, A.E. (eds.) AFRICACRYPT 2013. LNCS, vol. 7918, pp. 127–139. Springer, Heidelberg (2013). https://doi.org/10.1007/978-3-642-38553-7_7
3. AMD Inc: Realview® Compilation Tools (2002)
4. AMD Inc: AMD64 Architecture Programmer's Manual (2017)
5. ARM Limited: CPU CORTEX-R8 (2009). https://www.arm.com/products/silicon-ip-cpu/cortex-r/cortex-r8
6. ARM Limited: ARM Architecture Reference Manual. ARMv7-A and ARMv7-R edition. ARM Limited (2012)
7. ARM Limited: ARM Architecture Reference Manual ARMv8. ARM Limited (2013)
8. ARM Limited: Vulnerability of Speculative Processors to Cache Timing Side-Channel Mechanism (2018)
9. Bernstein, D.J.: Cache-Timing Attacks on AES (2005). http://cr.yp.to/antiforgery/cachetiming-20050414.pdf
10. Bhattacharyya, A., et al.: SMoTherSpectre: exploiting speculative execution through port contention. arXiv:1903.01843 (2019)
11. Bulygin, Y.: CPU side-channels vs. virtualization malware: The good, the bad, or the ugly. ToorCon (2008)
12. Canella, C., et al.: A systematic evaluation of transient execution attacks and defenses. In: USENIX Security Symposium (2019)
13. Charneski, A.: Modeling network latency (2015). https://blog.simiacryptus.com/2015/10/modeling-network-latency.html
14. Chen, G., Chen, S., Xiao, Y., Zhang, Y., Lin, Z., Lai, T.H.: SGXPECTRE Attacks: Leaking Enclave Secrets via Speculative Execution. arXiv:1802.09085 (2018)
15. Corbet, J.: On vsyscalls and the vDSO (2011). https://lwn.net/Articles/446528/
16. Evtyushkin, D., Ponomarev, D., Abu-Ghazaleh, N.: Jump over ASLR: attacking branch predictors to bypass ASLR. In: MICRO (2016)
17. Fog, A.: Test results for broadwell and skylake (2015). http://www.agner.org/optimize/blog/read.php?i=415#415
18. Fog, A.: The microarchitecture of Intel, AMD and VIA CPUs: An optimization guide for assembly programmers and compiler makers (2016)
19. Ge, Q., Yarom, Y., Cock, D., Heiser, G.: A survey of microarchitectural timing attacks and countermeasures on contemporary hardware. J. Cryptogr. Eng. **8**, 1–27 (2016)
20. Google: Egress throughput caps (2018). https://cloud.google.com/compute/docs/networks-and-firewalls#egress_throughput_caps
21. Goonatilake, R., Bachnak, R.A.: Modeling latency in a network distribution. Netw. Commun. Technol. **1**(2), 1 (2012)

22. Gras, B., Razavi, K., Bosman, E., Bos, H., Giuffrida, C.: ASLR on the line: practical cache attacks on the MMU. In: NDSS (2017)
23. Gruss, D., Lipp, M., Schwarz, M., Fellner, R., Maurice, C., Mangard, S.: KASLR is dead: long live KASLR. In: Bodden, E., Payer, M., Athanasopoulos, E. (eds.) ESSoS 2017. LNCS, vol. 10379, pp. 161–176. Springer, Cham (2017). https://doi.org/10.1007/978-3-319-62105-0_11
24. Gruss, D., Maurice, C., Wagner, K., Mangard, S.: Flush+Flush: a fast and stealthy cache attack. In: Caballero, J., Zurutuza, U., Rodríguez, R.J. (eds.) DIMVA 2016. LNCS, vol. 9721, pp. 279–299. Springer, Cham (2016). https://doi.org/10.1007/978-3-319-40667-1_14
25. Gruss, D., Spreitzer, R., Mangard, S.: Cache template attacks: automating attacks on inclusive last-level caches. In: USENIX Security Symposium (2015)
26. Hopper, N., Vasserman, E.Y., Chan-Tin, E.: How much anonymity does network latency leak? TISSEC (2010)
27. Horn, J.: Speculative execution, variant 4: speculative store bypass (2018)
28. Intel: Intel® 64 and IA-32 Architectures Software Developer's Manual Volume 2 (2A, 2B & 2C): Instruction Set Reference, A-Z 253665 (2014)
29. Intel: Intel® 64 and IA-32 Architectures Software Developer's Manual, Volume 1: Basic Architecture 253665 (2016)
30. Intel: Intel® 64 and IA-32 Architectures Software Developer's Manual, Volume 3 (3A, 3B & 3C): System Programming Guide (325384) (2016)
31. Intel Newsroom: Advancing security at the silicon level, March 2018. https://newsroom.intel.com/editorials/advancing-security-silicon-level/
32. Intel Newsroom: Microcode revision guidance, April 2018. https://newsroom.intel.com/wp-content/uploads/sites/11/2018/04/microcode-update-guidance.pdf
33. Jayasinghe, D., Fernando, J., Herath, R., Ragel, R.: Remote cache timing attack on advanced encryption standard and countermeasures. In: ICIAFs (2010)
34. Kiriansky, V., Waldspurger, C.: Speculative Buffer Overflows: Attacks and Defenses. arXiv:1807.03757 (2018)
35. Kocher, P., et al.: Spectre attacks: exploiting speculative execution. In: S&P (2019)
36. Kocher, P.C.: Timing attacks on implementations of Diffie-Hellman, RSA, DSS, and other systems. In: Koblitz, N. (ed.) CRYPTO 1996. LNCS, vol. 1109, pp. 104–113. Springer, Heidelberg (1996). https://doi.org/10.1007/3-540-68697-5_9
37. Koruyeh, E.M., Khasawneh, K., Song, C., Abu-Ghazaleh, N.: Spectre returns! speculation attacks using the return stack buffer. In: WOOT (2018)
38. Lipp, M., et al.: Meltdown: reading Kernel memory from user space. In: USENIX Security Symposium (2018)
39. Liu, F., Yarom, Y., Ge, Q., Heiser, G., Lee, R.B.: Last-level cache side-channel attacks are practical. In: S&P (2015)
40. Liu, W., Gao, D., Reiter, M.K.: On-demand time blurring to support side-channel defense. In: Foley, S.N., Gollmann, D., Snekkenes, E. (eds.) ESORICS 2017. LNCS, vol. 10493, pp. 210–228. Springer, Cham (2017). https://doi.org/10.1007/978-3-319-66399-9_12
41. Maisuradze, G., Rossow, C.: ret2spec: speculative execution using return stack buffers. In: CCS (2018)
42. Marco-Gisbert, H., Ripoll-Ripoll, I.: Exploiting Linux and PaX ASLR's weaknesses on 32-and 64-bit systems. BlackHat Asia (2016)
43. Masters, J.: Thoughts on NetSpectre (2018). https://www.redhat.com/en/blog/thoughts-netspectre

44. Maurice, C., Neumann, C., Heen, O., Francillon, A.: C5: cross-cores cache covert channel. In: Almgren, M., Gulisano, V., Maggi, F. (eds.) DIMVA 2015. LNCS, vol. 9148, pp. 46–64. Springer, Cham (2015). https://doi.org/10.1007/978-3-319-20550-2_3

45. Maurice, C., et al.: Hello from the other side: SSH over robust cache covert channels in the cloud. In: NDSS (2017)

46. McCalpin, J.D.: Test results for Intel's Sandy Bridge processor (2015). http://agner.org/optimize/blog/read.php?i=378#378

47. Minkin, M., et al.: Fallout: Reading Kernel Writes From User Space. arXiv:1905.12701 (2019)

48. Oberman, S., Favor, G., Weber, F.: AMD 3DNow! technology: architecture and implementations. IEEE Micro **19**(2), 37–48 (1999)

49. Osvik, D.A., Shamir, A., Tromer, E.: Cache attacks and countermeasures: the case of AES. In: Pointcheval, D. (ed.) CT-RSA 2006. LNCS, vol. 3860, pp. 1–20. Springer, Heidelberg (2006). https://doi.org/10.1007/11605805_1

50. PaX Team: Address space layout randomization (ASLR) (2003)

51. Peleg, A., Weiser, U.: MMX technology extension to the Intel architecture. IEEE Micro **16**(4), 42–50 (1996)

52. Percival, C.: Cache missing for fun and profit. In: BSDCan (2005)

53. Pessl, P., Gruss, D., Maurice, C., Schwarz, M., Mangard, S.: DRAMA: exploiting DRAM addressing for cross-CPU attacks. In: USENIX Security Symposium (2016)

54. Pukelsheim, F.: The three sigma rule. The American Statistician (1994)

55. van Schaik, S., et al.: RIDL: rogue in-flight data load. In: S&P (2019)

56. Schwarz, M., Canella, C., Giner, L., Gruss, D.: Store-to-Leak Forwarding: Leaking Data on Meltdown-resistant CPUs. arXiv:1905.05725 (2019)

57. Schwarz, M., Weiser, S., Gruss, D., Maurice, C., Mangard, S.: Malware guard extension: using SGX to conceal cache attacks. In: Polychronakis, M., Meier, M. (eds.) DIMVA 2017. LNCS, vol. 10327, pp. 3–24. Springer, Cham (2017). https://doi.org/10.1007/978-3-319-60876-1_1

58. Schwarz, M., et al.: ZombieLoad: cross-privilege-boundary data sampling. arXiv:1905.05726 (2019)

59. Trippel, C., Lustig, D., Martonosi, M.: MeltdownPrime and SpectrePrime: Automatically-Synthesized Attacks Exploiting Invalidation-Based Coherence Protocols. arXiv:1802.03802 (2018)

60. Yarom, Y., Falkner, K.: Flush+Reload: a high resolution, low noise, L3 cache side-channel attack. In: USENIX Security Symposium (2014)

61. Zhao, X.j., Wang, T., Zheng, Y.: Cache Timing Attacks on Camellia Block Cipher (2009)

maskVerif: Automated Verification of Higher-Order Masking in Presence of Physical Defaults

Gilles Barthe[1], Sonia Belaïd[2(✉)], Gaëtan Cassiers[3], Pierre-Alain Fouque[4], Benjamin Grégoire[5], and Francois-Xavier Standaert[3]

[1] MPI-SP and IMDEA Software Institute, Madrid, Spain
gjbarthe@gmail.com
[2] CryptoExperts, Paris, France
sonia.belaid@cryptoexperts.com
[3] Université Catholique de Louvain, Ottignies-Louvain-la-Neuve, Belgium
{gaetan.cassiers,francois-xavier.standaert}@uclouvain.be
[4] Université de Rennes, Rennes, France
pierre-alain.fouque@univ-rennes1.fr
[5] Inria Sophia-Antipolis Méditerranée, Valbonne, France
benjamin.gregoire@sophia.inria.fr

Abstract. Power and electromagnetic based side-channel attacks are serious threats against the security of cryptographic embedded devices. In order to mitigate these attacks, implementations use countermeasures, among which masking is currently the most investigated and deployed choice. Unfortunately, commonly studied forms of masking rely on underlying assumptions that are difficult to satisfy in practice. This is due to physical defaults, such as glitches or transitions, which can recombine the masked data in a way that concretely reduces an implementation's security.

We develop and implement an automated approach for verifying security of masked implementations in presence of physical defaults (glitches or transitions). Our approach helps to recover the main strengths of masking: rigorous foundations, composability guarantees, automated verification under more realistic assumptions. Our work follows the approach of (Barthe et al. EUROCRYPT 2015) and thus contributes to demonstrate the benefits of language-based approaches (specifically probabilistic information flow) for masking.

Keywords: Side-channel attacks · Masking countermeasure · Physical defaults · Glitches · Automated verification · Composability · maskVerif

1 Introduction

While the design of cryptographic algorithms such as block ciphers is a relatively well-understood problem [26], the secure implementation of such algorithms is

© Springer Nature Switzerland AG 2019
K. Sako et al. (Eds.): ESORICS 2019, LNCS 11735, pp. 300–318, 2019.
https://doi.org/10.1007/978-3-030-29959-0_15

still a quite open topic. For example, the last two decades have shown that a wide range of side-channel attacks can be performed against cryptographic implementations, exploiting physical sources of leakage such as timing [27], power consumption [28] or electromagnetic radiation [20]. If no attention is paid, measuring such physical information enables retrieving cryptographic keys extremely efficiently. As a result, various types of countermeasures have been introduced to mitigate side-channel leakages, ranging from heuristic to more formal.

In general, checking that an implementation is protected against side-channel attacks is a complex and error-prone process (see [29] for an overview). As a result, countermeasures relying on a more established theory have gained in relevance over the last years, in order to simplify both the design and the evaluation of protected implementations. The masking countermeasure (which consists in performing the sensitive computations on secret-shared data) has been shown to be a particularly interesting candidate in this landscape [11]. The main reason is that practical security against physical leakages via masking can be reduced (under some noise and independence assumptions) to a much simpler (and abstract) security model, where the adversary just observes intermediate values during execution of the implementation [14]. We will next refer to this simpler abstract model as *ISW model*, after its inventors [25].

One advantage of the ISW model is that its conceptual simplicity makes it amenable to formal verification. This has been demonstrated in a series of works, including [2,3,6,9,10,12,17,31,34]. The most immediate benefit of formal verification is its automation, allowing to deal with the combinatorial complexity of proving masked implementations secure. This complexity is specially significant for implementations where secrets are split into a large number of shares; we call such implementations higher-order. Perhaps more importantly, formal verification has also been instrumental for advancing the state-of-the-art in masking. First, formal verification tools have been used to reduce the randomness cost of existing schemes. Second, strong non-interference, which solves a long-standing problem of compositional reasoning for masking, has first emerged in the context of formal verification, before being adopted in the literature on masking.

However, and to the exception of [9,10], the abstractions in these tools still do not prevent the risks due to specific physical defaults that may happen when trying to implement masking in hardware or software devices. In fact, many masking schemes that are secure in the abstract ISW model become insecure (or at least less secure) when concretely implemented.

This is usually due to physical defaults which contradict the independence assumption required for secure masking. For instance, *glitches* are a form of physical default occurring when the information does not propagate simultaneously throughout execution. They introduce dependencies between the leakage of an instruction and of its predecessors (in the sense of dataflow analysis). These dependencies may cause hardware implementations proved secure in the ISW model to be practically vulnerable against side-channel attacks [30]. *Transitions* are another example of physical default which more typically happen in software implementations, where the value in a register is overwritten by another value and leads the leakages to depend on both [1,13].

As a consequence, it is necessary to develop models and verification methods for proving security in presence of physical defaults. Bloem et al. [9] and Faust et al. [19] independently extend the ISW model in order to capture physical defaults such as glitches—we will next denote this model as the *ISW model with glitches*. In addition, Bloem et al. propose an automated method based on an estimation of Fourier coefficients for proving that an implementation is secure in their model. They also use their verification method on a set of examples, including the S-Boxes of the AES and Keccak. Due to the computational cost of their approach, the tool primarily applies to the first-order setting, where secrets are split into two shares. Moreover, their method does not consider strong non-interference, which is key to verify complete implementations. By contrast, Faust et al. provide a hand-made analysis of some masking gadgets and prove their strong non-interference with glitches for arbitrary number of shares (at the cost of higher randomness requirements), and discuss simple conditions under which the composability rules from [3] apply to implementations with glitches. As for [10], it is built on top of this submission (from on an earlier version of the current paper) and is still restricted to the verification of probing security only.

Contributions. We implement an efficient method for reasoning about security of higher-order masked implementations in presence of physical defaults. Our method follows a language-based approach based on probabilistic information flow for proving security of masked implementations [2], and so provides further evidence of the benefits of language-based approaches.

As in [2], our method follows a divide-and-conquer approach, embodied in two algorithms. Our first algorithm checks if leakages are independent of secrets for a fixed admissible set of observations. The algorithm repeatedly applies semantic-preserving simplifications to the symbolic representation of the leakages, until it does not depend on secrets or it fails. One significant improvement over [2] is that our algorithm (i) is sound and complete (no attack missed and no false negative) for linear systems of equations; (ii) it minimizes false negatives for non-linear cases. Our second algorithm explores all admissible observation sets, calling the first algorithm on each of them. This algorithm is carefully designed to minimize the number of sets to explore, using the idea of large sets from [2]. One significant improvement over [2] is that our algorithm (i) minimizes the number of large sets (ii) uses more sophisticated data structures that improve overall efficiency.

In addition, both algorithms are specifically tailored to a rich programming model, which we introduce to maximize applicability. The critical feature of our new programming model is that all instructions are annotated with a symbolic representation of leakage. Our programming model neatly subsumes several models from the literature, including the ISW model, the recently proposed ISW model with glitches, and a version of the ISW model with transitions. Moreover, our tool applies to three main security notions: probing security, threshold non-interference, and strong non-interference (which is essential for compositional reasoning). Our coverage of models and properties is displayed in Table 1.

Table 1. Verification of higher-order masked implementations in the ISW model (1), the ISW model with glitches (2), and a version of the ISW model with transitions (3)

Tools	probing security			threshold non-interference			threshold strong non-interference		
	(1)	(2)	(3)	(1)	(2)	(3)	(1)	(2)	(3)
maskVerif [2,3]	✓	✗	✓	✓	✗	✓	✓	✗	✓
Bloem *et al.* [9]	✓	✓	✗	✗	✗	✗	✗	✗	✗
this work	✓	✓	✓	✓	✓	✓	✓	✓	✓

We implement our method on top of `maskVerif` and evaluate our tool on existing benchmarks. Our tool is able to verify programs efficiently for security notions that bring stronger compositional guarantees than [9] and faster than state-of-the-art tools. For instance, checking probing security for the ISW multiplication at order 4 (resp. order 5) takes 1 (resp. 45) second using [2], while it takes only 0.1 (resp. 2.6) second with our tool. And checking probing security with glitches for DOM Keccak S-box at order 3 takes only 0.49 s when it takes more than 25 min in [9].

2 Motivating Examples

Consider the logical **and**, which takes as input bits a and b and produces as output a bit c such that $c = a \times b$ (we use arithmetic notation). A (first-order) masked implementation of this algorithm takes as input bits $a[0]$, $a[1]$, $b[0]$ and $b[1]$, called input shares, and outputs bits $c[0]$ and $c[1]$, called output shares. Couples of shares are initially built from a uniform value r generated at random and the sum of this random value with the secret one. Doing so, any single share remains completely independent from the secret. We consider two families of masked implementations and outline their verification. The first family is intended to provide protection against glitches. The second family is intended to provide protection against transitions.

2.1 Glitches

Figure 1 introduces a first-order masked implementation of logical **and** from [22] in an idealized hardware language. The program is given as a sequence of assignments. The instruction $r \leftarrow_\$ \{0,1\}$ is a random assignment, i.e. r is sampled uniformly from $\{0,1\}$. The assignments $t_2 \leftarrow_{ff} t_1$ and $t_6 \leftarrow_{ff} t_5$ are flip-flop assignments; they are used to store stable computations (so have no computational content), and stop the propagation of leakage. The remaining instructions are standard arithmetic assignments. The masked implementation must satisfy:

correctness: the masked implementation coincides with the original algorithm, i.e. $c = a \times b$, with $a = a[0] + a[1]$, $b = b[0] + b[1]$, $c = c[0] + c[1]$;
security: leakage does not reveal information about secrets. We make the definition of leakage precise below and sketch a proof of security.

We first consider correctness. We symbolically execute the program to compute for each program point an expression over input shares $a[0], a[1], b[0], b[1]$ and probabilistic variable r, see the second column of Fig. 1. We use $b[i] \times a$ as shorthand for $b[i] \times a[0] + b[i] \times a[1]$.

We now turn to security. We first define a symbolic representation of leakage, shown in the third column of Fig. 1. The representation assigns to each program point a tuple of expressions over input shares $a[0], a[1], b[0], b[1]$ and probabilistic variable r. Random assignment $r \leftarrow_\$ \{0, 1\}$ leaks singleton $\{r\}$. Flip-flop assignments $t_2 \leftarrow_{ff} t_1$ and $t_6 \leftarrow_{ff} t_5$ leak singletons $\{b[1] \times a[0] + r\}$ and $\{b[0] \times a[1] + r\}$, i.e. the expressions they compute. Arithmetic assignments propagate transient leakages (due to glitches). For instance, assignment $t_1 \leftarrow t_0 + r$ leaks the union of the leakage of the first two assignments. More generally, the leakage of an arithmetic assignment is defined as the leakage of its two operands (with the convention that an input share $a[i]$ leaks $\{a[i]\}$).

The symbolic representation of leakage can be simplified by applying rules that preserve their semantics (defined formally in later sections). One commonly used rule is optimistic sampling, which replaces an expression of the form $e + r$, where r only occurs once in the tuple, by r. We show the simplified leakage on the last column of Fig. 1. Note that (simplified) leakage at each program point depends on at most one share of a (either $a[0]$ or $a[1]$) and one share of b (either $b[0]$ or $b[1]$). This suffices to conclude that the implementation is thus secure. We will make this claim precise in the next sections. For now, it suffices to get the following intuition: assume that a and b are the secrets, and $(a[0], a[1])$ is a secret sharing of a, i.e. $a[0]$ and $a[1]$ taken individually are uniformly distributed, and $a[0] + a[1] = a$. Then knowledge of $a[0]$ or $a[1]$ does not reveal any information about a. The situation is similar for b. Thus, knowledge of a single share of a and a single share of b does not reveal anything about them.

Instruction	Symbolic value	Symbolic leakage	Simplified
$t_0 \leftarrow b[1] \times a[0]$	$b[1] \times a[0]$	$\{b[1], a[0]\}$	$\{b[1], a[0]\}$
$r \leftarrow_\$ \{0, 1\}$	r	$\{r\}$	$\{r\}$
$t_1 \leftarrow t_0 + r$	$b[1] \times a[0] + r$	$\{\mathbf{b[1]}, \mathbf{a[0]}, \mathbf{r}\}$	$\{\mathbf{b[1]}, \mathbf{a[0]}, \mathbf{r}\}$
$t_2 \leftarrow_{ff} t_1$	$b[1] \times a[0] + r$	$\{b[1] \times a[0] + r\}$	$\{r\}$
$t_3 \leftarrow b[1] \times a[1]$	$b[1] \times a[1]$	$\{b[1], a[1]\}$	$\{b[1], a[1]\}$
$c[1] \leftarrow t_3 + t_2$	$b[1] \times a + r$	$\{\mathbf{b[1]}, \mathbf{a[1]}, b[1] \times a[0] + r\}$	$\{\mathbf{b[1]}, \mathbf{a[1]}, \mathbf{r}\}$
$t_4 \leftarrow b[0] \times a[1]$	$b[0] \times a[1]$	$\{b[0], a[1]\}$	$\{b[0], a[1]\}$
$t_5 \leftarrow t_4 + r$	$b[0] \times a[1] + r$	$\{\mathbf{b[0]}, \mathbf{a[1]}, \mathbf{r}\}$	$\{\mathbf{b[0]}, \mathbf{a[1]}, \mathbf{r}\}$
$t_6 \leftarrow_{ff} t_5$	$b[0] \times a[1] + r$	$\{b[0] \times a[1] + r\}$	$\{r\}$
$t_7 \leftarrow b[0] \times a[0]$	$b[0] \times a[0]$	$\{b[0], a[0]\}$	$\{b[0], a[0]\}$
$c[0] \leftarrow t_7 + t_6$	$b[0] \times a + r$	$\{\mathbf{b[0]}, \mathbf{a[0]}, b[0] \times a[1] + r\}$	$\{\mathbf{b[0]}, \mathbf{a[0]}, \mathbf{r}\}$

Fig. 1. Masked implementation of logical bit **and** against glitches. The second column contains the symbolic expression computed for each program point. The third and fourth columns are symbolic representations of leakage, before and after simplification. Maximal sets are written in bold. It is easy to check that $c[0] + c[1] = a \times b$.

Now consider the variant of the algorithm that omits the second flip-flop assignment in Fig. 2. The leakage at the last program point is no longer independent of a, since both $a[0]$ and $a[1]$ appear in the tuple. Concretely, an attacker with access to the joint distribution $\{b[0], a[0], a[1], r\}$ can retrieve the second and third components and add them to obtain a.

Instruction	Symbolic value	Symbolic leakage	Simplified
$t_0 \leftarrow b[1] \times a[0]$	$b[1] \times a[0]$	$\{b[1], a[0]\}$	$\{\mathbf{b}[1], \mathbf{a}[0]\}$
$r \leftarrow_\$ \{0,1\}$	r	$\{r\}$	$\{r\}$
$t_1 \leftarrow t_0 + r$	$b[1] \times a[0] + r$	$\{\mathbf{b}[1], \mathbf{a}[0], \mathbf{r}\}$	$\{\mathbf{b}[1], \mathbf{a}[0], \mathbf{r}\}$
$t_2 \leftarrow_{ff} t_1$	$b[1] \times a[0] + r$	$\{b[1] \times a[0] + r\}$	$\{r\}$
$t_3 \leftarrow b[1] \times a[1]$	$b[1] \times a[1]$	$\{b[1], a[1]\}$	$\{\mathbf{b}[1], \mathbf{a}[1]\}$
$c[1] \leftarrow t_3 + t_2$	$b[1] \times a + r$	$\{\mathbf{b}[1], \mathbf{a}[1], b[1] \times a[0] + r\}$	$\{\mathbf{b}[1], \mathbf{a}[1], \mathbf{r}\}$
$t_4 \leftarrow b[0] \times a[1]$	$b[0] \times a[1]$	$\{b[0], a[1]\}$	$\{\mathbf{b}[0], \mathbf{a}[1]\}$
$t_5 \leftarrow t_4 + r$	$b[0] \times a[1] + r$	$\{\mathbf{b}[0], \mathbf{a}[1], \mathbf{r}\}$	$\{\mathbf{b}[0], \mathbf{a}[1], \mathbf{r}\}$
$t_6 \leftarrow b[0] \times a[0]$	$b[0] \times a[0]$	$\{b[0], a[0]\}$	$\{\mathbf{b}[0], \mathbf{a}[0]\}$
$c[0] \leftarrow t_5 + t_6$	$b[0] \times a + r$	$\{\mathbf{b}[0], \mathbf{a}[0], \mathbf{a}[1], \mathbf{r}\}$	$\{\mathbf{b}[0], \mathbf{a}[0], \mathbf{a}[1], \mathbf{r}\}$

Fig. 2. Insecure masked implementation of logical bit **and** against glitches. The second column contains the symbolic expression computed for each program point. The third and fourth columns are symbolic representations of leakage, before and after simplification. Maximal sets are written in bold. It is easy to check that $c[0] + c[1] = a \times b$.

We next describe how these examples are handled in our tool. The user provides a masked Verilog implementation of these algorithms and sets various parameters, including a security property (explained later). We first use an off-the-shelf tool (yosis) which generates an implementation in the ilang intermediate format (.ilang). The .ilang implementation is manually annotated to specify the public variables, the secret input variables, the secret output variables, and the random variables. Next, our tool generates from the annotated .ilang implementation an internal representation with a symbolic representation of leakage at each program point. At this point, verification starts. Our implementation exploits the fact that tuples of expressions are naturally ordered w.r.t the subset relation, e.g. the tuple $\{b[1], a[0], r\}$ leaks more than the singleton $\{b[1], a[0]\}$. Thus, it suffices to consider maximal leakage sets, which appear in bold in Fig. 1. Whenever verification fails, i.e. a potentially flawed tuple is detected, our tool computes the joint distribution of this tuple, so as to verify exactly whether this tuple is an attack for the weakest security notion considered. This step is exact, therefore all false negatives are removed. Our tool successfully concludes for the secure examples, and outputs and checks the flawed tuple of intermediate computations for the insecure examples.

2.2 Transitions

For simplicity of exposition, we consider a model with transitions but no glitches (and thus do not use flip-flop gates). Figure 3 introduces another first-order masked implementation of logical **and**. The difference with the previous implementation is that variable t_0 is reused in the last but one instruction. As a consequence, observing the last but one instruction reveals both values of t_0, and depend on b. This is easily fixed by using a fresh variable t_5 in place of t_0. Interestingly, replacing t_0 with t_5 places us in a model in which every instruction leaks its symbolic expression, i.e. the abstract ISW model. In both cases, verification with our tool then proceeds as described in the previous subsection.

Instruction	Symbolic value	Leakage
$t_0 \leftarrow b[1] \times a[0]$	$b[1] \times a[0]$	$\{b[1] \times a[0]\}$
$r \leftarrow_\$ \{0, 1\}$	r	$\{r\}$
$t_1 \leftarrow t_0 + r$	$b[1] \times a[0] + r$	$\{b[1] \times a[0] + r\}$
$t_2 \leftarrow b[1] \times a[1]$	$b[1] \times a[1]$	$\{b[1] \times a[1]\}$
$c[1] \leftarrow t_1 + t_2$	$b[1] \times a + r$	$\{b[1] \times a + r\}$
$t_3 \leftarrow b[0] \times a[1]$	$b[0] \times a[1]$	$\{b[0] \times a[1]\}$
$t_4 \leftarrow t_3 + r$	$b[0] \times a[1] + r$	$\{b[0] \times a[1] + r\}$
$t_0 \leftarrow b[0] \times a[0]$	$b[0] \times a[0]$	$\{b[1] \times a[0], b[0] \times a[0]\}$
$c[0] \leftarrow t_4 + t_0$	$b[0] \times a + r$	$\{b[0] \times a + r\}$

Fig. 3. Masked implementation of logical bit **and** against transitions. The second column contains the symbolic expression computed for each program point. The third column contains leakage. It is easy to check that $c[0] + c[1] = a \times b$.

3 Programming Model and Security Definitions

This section introduces an intermediate representation which captures different security models and notions, and presents algorithmic tools for checking that programs are secure. For the clarity of exposition, we focus on a simple setting without public variables. Adding public variables poses no technical difficulty, but clutters presentation.

3.1 Syntax and Semantics of Programs

Our intermediate representation abstracts away from the specifics of a particular security model, by requiring that all leakage is made explicit through program annotations. This eliminates the need to consider flip-flop assignments.

We assume throughout this paper that programs operate over Booleans. Figure 4 presents the syntax of programs as sequences of annotated instructions. An annotated instruction is an instruction annotated with a unique program point $p \in \mathcal{P}$, and a tuple ℓ of expressions which model its leakage. Instructions are probabilistic or deterministic assignments. We assume code to be written in 3-address form, i.e. the right-hand side of a deterministic assignment is of the form $v_1 + v_2$ or $v_1 \times v_2$, where v_i is either a share $a[i]$, a deterministic variable x, or a probabilistic variable r. The left-hand side of an deterministic assignment

$$v ::= r \mid x \mid a[i]$$
$$e ::= r \mid a[i] \mid e + e \mid e \times e$$
$$\ell ::= \{e_1, \ldots, e_n\}$$

$$
\begin{array}{lll}
I ::= x \leftarrow v_1 \circ v_2 & & \text{deterministic assignment} \\
\mid a[i] \leftarrow v_1 \circ v_2 & & \text{output assignment} \\
\mid r \leftarrow_\$ \mathcal{K} & & \text{probabilistic assignment} \\
C ::= p : I \mid \ell & & \text{instruction} \\
\mid C; C & & \text{sequential composition}
\end{array}
$$

Fig. 4. Syntax of expressions, instructions and commands. $\circ$ ranges over $\{+, \times\}$. x ranges over a set of deterministic variables $\mathcal{V}$, r ranges over a set of probabilistic variables $\mathcal{R}$. $a[i]$ is called a share; a is drawn from a set $\mathcal{A}$ and $i \in \{0, \ldots, t\}$ for some fixed value t, generally called order.

is either a share $a[i]$ or a deterministic variable x. A probabilistic assignment is of the form $r \leftarrow_\$ \mathcal{K}$, where r is drawn from a set $\mathcal{R}$ of probabilistic variables.

We now define the leakage. Let $\mathcal{L} = \bigcup_i \mathcal{K}^i$. For every discrete set X, $\mathsf{Distr}(X)$ denotes the set of distributions over X. A memory is a map that assigns to every share $a[i]$ a value in $\mathcal{K}$. We let $\mathcal{M}$ denote the set of memories. Now consider an observation set O, i.e. a subset of $\mathcal{P}$ such that $|O| \leq t$. We define the function:

$$[\![s]\!]_O : \mathcal{M} \to \mathsf{Distr}(O \to \mathcal{L})$$

which computes the joint leakage of s on observation set O on input memory $m \in \mathcal{M}$. The definition of $[\![s]\!]_O$ is obtained by pushing forward the instrumented semantics $[\![s]\!] : \mathcal{M} \to \mathsf{Distr}(\mathcal{P} \to (\mathcal{K} \times \mathcal{L}))$ along the obvious projection function. The definition is standard, and omitted. The function $[\![s]\!]_O$ is naturally extended to distributions over memories; we abuse notation and still write $[\![s]\!]_O$.

3.2 Security Notions

We recall three increasingly strong notions of security from the literature: probing security, threshold non-interference, and threshold strong non-interference. All notions capture some form of probabilistic non-interference.

Probing security is a notion of non-interference under uniform inputs. Formally, we define a set of universally uniform distributions and say that a command s is t-probing secure iff for every observation set O such that $|O| \leq t$ and universally uniform distributions μ and μ', we have $[\![s]\!]_O(\mu) = [\![s]\!]_O(\mu')$. Probing security considers a scenario where secret sharing is used to encode secret inputs, and the masked program is executed on encoded inputs. Since encodings are universally uniform, probing security entails that leakage does not depend on secrets.

For a concrete definition of universal uniformity, we consider the case of memories over inputs $a[0]$, $a[1]$, $b[0]$, and $b[1]$. In this setting, a distribution over memories is universally uniform iff it is the image of the function mapping pairs (a, b) to the distribution

$$a_0 \leftarrow_\$ \mathcal{K}; b_0 \leftarrow_\$ \mathcal{K}; \mathsf{return} \; \langle a[0] \mapsto a_0, a[1] \mapsto a + a_0, b[0] \mapsto b_0, b[1] \mapsto b + b_0 \rangle$$

Probing security guarantees that leakage does not depend on secrets. Indeed, it is always possible to simulate leakage by generating an encoding of arbitrary values a' and b', and then executing the command on this encoding. This will result in an identical leakage.

(Threshold) non-interference can be understood as a notion of non-interference under cardinality constraints. A command s is t-non-interfering (t-NI) if and only if any set of at most t intermediate variables can be perfectly simulated from at most t shares of each input. Concretely, a command s is (threshold) non-interfering at order t iff for every observation set O such that $|O| \leq t$, there exists an indexed family of sets $(I_a)_{a \in \mathcal{A}} \subseteq \{0, \dots, t\}$ such that $|I_a| \leq t$ and for every initial memories m and m',

$$m \simeq_{(I_a)_{a \in \mathcal{A}}} m' \implies [\![s]\!]_O(m) = [\![s]\!]_O(m')$$

where $m \simeq_{(I_a)_{a \in \mathcal{A}}} m'$ iff for every $a \in \mathcal{A}$ and $i \in I_a$, we have $m(a[i]) = m'(a[i])$. The intuition behind threshold non-interference is similar to the one behind probing security. In particular, threshold non-interference entails probing security.

For a realization of threshold non-interference, consider a masked implementation that takes as inputs $a[0]$, $a[1]$, $b[0]$, and $b[1]$. Threshold non-interference ensures that leakage only depends on one of the sets $(\{a[i], b[j]\})_{i,j \in \{0,1\}^2}$. Given that the secret a is independent from $a[i]$ and similarly for b, it follows that leakage does not give any information about the secrets.

(Threshold) strong non-interference [3] is a very technical strengthening of (threshold) non-interference. It brings very strong composability guarantees that do not hold for (threshold) non-interference. Technically, strong non-interference imposes more stringent cardinality constraints. For every observation set O, we distinguish between internal observations O_{in} (program points where the lhs of the assignment is a variable) and output observations O_{out} (program points where the left-hand side of the assignment is a share $a[i]$). We say that a command s is t-strong non-interfering (t-SNI) iff for every observation set O such that $|O| \leq t$, there exists an indexed family of sets $(I_a)_{a \in \mathcal{A}} \subseteq \{0, \dots, t\}$, such that $|I_a| \leq |O_{in}|$ and for every initial memories m and m',

$$m \simeq_{(I_a)_{a \in \mathcal{A}}} m' \implies [\![s]\!]_O(m) = [\![s]\!]_O(m').$$

It is put forward in [19] that if a gadget is strongly non-interfering with glitches (which requires storing its outputs in flip flops so that they are stable and cannot propagate glitches), then the general composition rules introduced in [3] apply to hardware implementations with glitches. Being able to verify such stronger security notions is therefore helpful to analyze full ciphers and high number of shares, since it allows analyzing smaller (computationally tractable) parts of them independently, with global security guarantees thanks to composition.

4   Algorithmic Verification

Checking probing or (S)NI security requires to verify a probabilistic non-interference property for all observation sets of size t. We define a generic verification parameterized by a test specific to each security property. The algorithm follows the same overall structure as `maskVerif` and relies on two functions. The first function Check is a *verification* algorithm for proving the probabilistic non-interference property of a fixed observation set. The function CheckAll is an *exploration* algorithm which (adaptively) scans all the possible sets of observations. Verification succeeds if the algorithm proves absence of leakage for all observation sets.

To verify that an observation set O (a tuple of expressions) is independent from some secret, the key idea is to apply successive transformation on O into O', preserving its distribution, until a termination condition Test is able to syntactically decide the independence. The Test function depends on the property:

- For probing security, we check if the tuple is independent from the initial mapping by checking syntactically if the secret inputs do not appear in O'.
- For non-interference, we check if for each input parameter a, at most t shares $a[i]$ occur in the tuple O'.
- For strong non-interference, the condition is similar: for each parameter a, at most $|O_{in}|$ shares $a[i]$ should occur in O'.

The transformation of O is based on optimistic sampling rule: if $r \not\in e$ then r and $e + r$ follow the same distribution, as well as O and O' where r is replaced by $e + r$ ($O\{r \leftarrow e+r\}$). The condition $r \not\in e$ (i.e r is not a variable of e) ensures that the distributions of r and e are independent. The critical step is to select a substitution that will guarantee that the method terminates. Take for example $O = (r, x + r)$. If we replace r by $x + r$, we obtain after simplification $(x + r, r)$ on which we could apply the same transformation again and again.

Verification of Single Observation Set. The Check verification algorithm is summarized in Fig. 5: it takes as input an observation set represented as a tuple O of expressions. If Test is satisfied then Check succeeds. Otherwise, it uses the Select procedure to perform a transformation of O into O'. To guarantee termination, the algorithm first attempts to check if O can be rewritten (modulo associativity and commutativity of $+$) as $C[e + r]$ where $C[\cdot]$ is a context, and $r \not\in e \cup C$, i.e. r does not occur in e and C). If it is the case, we apply the optimistic sampling rule and get $C[e + r]\{r \leftarrow e + r\} = C[e + (e + r)] = C[r]$. Notice that in that case the size of $C[r]$ is less than the size of O (i.e the size of the resulting O' decreases).

If the algorithm cannot exhibit such a context, it tries to apply the general optimistic sampling rule (removing the condition $r \not\in C$). The resulting expression is the simplification of $O\{r \leftarrow e+r\}$. For the simplification, we basically use the ring laws but the distributivity makes harder the detection of new simplifications. Notice that this time the size of the resulting $O' = O\{r \leftarrow e+r\}$ does not

Verification algorithm	
proc Select$(R, O) =$	**proc** Check$(R, B, O) =$
if $\exists r, e, C \mid O = C[e + r] \wedge r \notin e \cup C$ **then**	**if** Test(O) **then return** B;
return $(R, (e, r), C[r])$;	$(R', b, O') =$ Select(R, O);
if $\exists r, e, C \mid O = C[e + r] \wedge r \notin e \cup R$ **then**	Check$(R', B :: b, O')$;
$O' =$ Simplify$(O\{r \leftarrow e + r\})$;	
return $(R \cup \{r\}, (e, r), O')$;	
else fail ;	

Exploration algorithm	
proc Replay$(B, O) =$	**proc** Extend$(B, X) =$
if $B = []$ **then return** Test(Simplify(O))	$\{O \in X \mid$
if $B = (e, r) :: B'$ **then**	Replay$(B, O)\}$
Replay$(B', O\{r \leftarrow e + r\})$	
proc OptSampling$(X) =$	**proc** CheckAll$(X) =$
if $\exists r, e, C_X \mid X = C_X[e + r] \wedge r \notin e \cup C_X$ **then**	**if** $X = \emptyset$ **return** true;
OptSampling$(C_X[r])$;	$X =$ OptSampling(X);
else return X;	$O =$ Choose(X);
	$B =$ Check$(\emptyset, [], O)$;
	$X_0 =$ Extend(B, X);
	CheckAll$(X \setminus X_0)$;

Fig. 5. Verification algorithm for probing security

necessarily decrease. To ensure termination, we add a set R of random variables on which the general rule has already been used. The application of the rule is conditioned by the fact that $r \notin R$. The termination of the Check algorithm is ensured since either R increases or the size of O decreases (lexicographic order).

When more than one r allow to apply the rules (i.e for the selection of the context), we define the multiplicative depth of a random variable and we rewrite in increasing order of multiplicative depth. For instance, in the expression $r + (r' + e) \times e'$ we assign multiplicative depth 0 to r and 1 to r'.

We can prove that our new algorithm always terminates and is sound, i.e. it can detect all the attacks in our models. Note that considering only the first rule (first **if** statement of Select) makes our algorithm equivalent to the one of [2]. When we apply both rules (the two **if** statements of Select), our algorithm is equivalent to the one of [4], inspired from Gaussian elimination: contrary to this last one, we do not require the expressions to be linear. An additional advantage is the absence of false negatives when all the expressions are linear (completeness), it is no more the case if we remove the second **if** in Select.

Both algorithms return the list B of optimistic sampling rules that have been applied: successive transformations in the exploration algorithm can be replayed.

Exploration. The exploration algorithm ensures that the verification algorithm analyzes all the possible sets of at most t intermediate variables. However, rather than verifying each set separately, the exploration algorithm recursively checks larger sets, as in [2]. The idea behind the exploration algorithm is that if a tuple O is probabilistic non-interfering then all sub-tuples of O are. We present a very high level description of the algorithm to highlight the main differences with [2].

The algorithm CheckAll is presented in Fig. 5. Let X be the set of all tuples that need to be checked. If X is empty all tuples are trivially checked and the algorithm returns true. Else, it first tries to simplify as much as possible the set X by applying the simple optimistic sampling rule, as in the first if of Select. This point is really crucial because it allows to share simplifications between all tuples in X and was not done in [2]. Then, the algorithm chooses an element O in X and tries to check it. If O is successfully verified, the result B is a list of optimistic sampling transformations that can be applied to prove independence of O. Next, the algorithm selects all the elements of X that can be checked using the transformation B using Extend[1]. At this point all elements in X_0 are known to satisfy the desired properties. Finally the algorithm needs to check the remaining tuples $X \setminus X_0$.

Initially, X represents the set of all tuples of t elements that can be generated within the set of m possible observations. Its size is $\binom{m}{t}$. A naive implementation would thus be exponential in t and it is crucial to have efficient data structures to represent X and to implement the functions OptSampling, Extend, and $X \setminus X_0$. We use the data structures presented in [2] (worklist base space splitting).

Moreover, we use a representation of expressions as imperative graphs. This allows to detect easily if the simplest version of optimistic sampling rule can be applied (used in the first conditional of Select and OptSampling), and to compute efficiently the resulting expression.

5   Experiments

This section reports on experimental evaluation of our approach.

Examples. Our examples are mainly extracted from the available database provided by the authors of [9]. It gathers four different Verilog implementations of a masked multiplication. Three of them are implemented at the first masking order only, while DOM AND, designed in [22], is available up to order $t = 4$, i.e. when sensitive data is split into $t + 1 = 5$ shares. For the latter, we also consider modified versions that achieve non-interference and strong non-interference. Larger implementations are also provided, namely three S-boxes. AES S-box as designed in [22] and both versions of FIDES S-box as designed in [8] are implemented at the first order. We also consider a second-order and third-order AES S-box [21], and a Keccak S-box as designed in [23] and implemented from the first to the third order. In addition to this existing set of examples, Keccak S-box is analyzed at two extra orders, namely $t = 4$ and $t = 5$, and two versions of a different multiplication PARA AND [5] are verified from the first to the fourth order.

---

[1] Missing tuples with Extend does not impact the correctness of the algorithm.

Benchmarks. First of all, we compare our tool with [2] which can only check probing security without glitches. While our tool is a variant, the resulting implementation is much more efficient. For example, checking probing security for the ISW multiplication at order 4 (resp. order 5) takes 1 (resp. 45) second using [2], while it takes only 0.1 (resp. 2.6) second with our tool.

Table 2 summarizes the verification outcome of the examples[2]. We use a 2.6 GHz Intel Core i7 with 16 GB of RAM running on macOS High Sierra, while Bloem et al. [9] use a Intel Xeon E5-2699v4 CPU with a clock frequency of 3.6 GHz and 512 GB of RAM running in a 64-bit Linux OS environment. The table reports on verification for the three main security properties, namely SNI, NI, and probing security, and for two scenarios: a hardware scenario (HW) with glitches, and a software scenario (SW) without physical defaults. While the tool can also take into account transitions, we omit such examples as most of our implementations come from hardware where each wire is assigned only once (and so do not have transition).

The first column of the table (# obs) indicates the number of possible observations in the targeted implementation. In the software scenario, it corresponds to the number of intermediate variables. In the hardware scenario with glitches, it corresponds to the number of optimal observations. Note the latter is much lower than in the software scenario since non-maximal observation sets are ignored. Also note that while this first column displays the number of observations n that will be further treated, verification at order t requires the analysis of $\binom{n}{t}$ tuples. For instance, the verification of Keccak S-box in the software scenario at order 4 requires the analysis of $\binom{450}{4} \approx 2^{31}$ tuples. The second, third, and fourth columns report on the verification times in the 6 modes. We report 0.01 s when the result is instantaneous and ∞ when the computations take more than 10 h. When an implementation is insecure in a weaker model, then its verification time is equal for the stronger model. To report the outcome, a cross is displayed when a concrete attack is exhibited. Otherwise, the verification ends up successfully, indicating that the implementation is secure.

Comparison with Bloem et al. (EUROCRYPT 2018). Bloem *et al.* [9] present a formal technique for proving security of implementations in the ISW model with glitches. Their method is based on Xiao-Massey lemma, which provides a necessary and sufficient condition for a boolean function to be statistically independent from a subset of its variables. Informally, the lemma states that a boolean function f is statistically independent of a set of variables X iff the so-called Fourier coefficients of every non-empty subset of X is null. However, since the computation of Fourier coefficients is computationally expensive, they use instead an approximation method whose correctness is established in their paper. By encoding their approximation in logical form, they are able to instantiate their approach using SAT-based solvers. Their tool can verify implementations of AES, Keccak and FIDES S-Boxes, but the verification cost is significant.

---

[2] Programs/logs are available at https://gitlab.com/benjgregoire/maskverif/.

The last column indicates the timings from [9] which are only available for probing security with and without glitches[3]. A dash is displayed when the example is not tested in [9]. The results show that our tool performs significantly better than the algorithm provided in [9]. For instance, the verification of the hardware first-order masked implementation of AES S-box is at the very least 7826 times much faster with our tool. In particular, note that some of the benchmarks provided for the tool of Bloem et al. only concern the verification of one secret (the ranking corresponds to the fastest and the lowest verification of the secrets). They are highlighted with a symbol *. As a consequence, without parallelization, these timings would probably be significantly higher. Our algorithm can also be parallelized (it is an option of our tool), but we only use this option for Keccak at order 5 since it makes the timing measurement less accurate.

6   Related Work

This section reviews the state-of-the-art verification tools for software (without physical defaults but transitions) and hardware masked implementations.

Software Implementations. Moss et al. [31] were the first to consider the use of automated methods to build or verify masked implementations. Specifically, they implement a type-based masking compiler that tracks which variables are masked by random values and iteratively modifies an unprotected program until all secrets are masked. This strategy ensures security against first-order DPA.

While type-based verification is generally efficient and scalable, it is also often overly conservative, i.e. it rejects secure programs. Logic-based verification often strikes interesting trade-offs between efficiency and expressiveness. This possibility was first explored in the context of masked implementations by Bayrak et al. [6]. Concretely, they propose a SMT-based method for analyzing the security of masked implementations against first-order DPA. Contrary to [31] which targets proving a stronger property of programs, their method directly targets proving statistical independence between secrets and leakage. While it is limited to first-order masking, it was extended to higher orders by Eldib, Wang and Schaumont [17]. Their approach is based on a logical characterization of security, akin to non-interference, and is based on model counting. While model counting incurs an exponential blow-up in the security order, and becomes infeasible even for relatively small orders, Eldib *et al.* circumvent the issue using incremental verification. Although such methods help, the scope of application of their methods remains limited. Recently, Zhang et al. [34] show how abstraction-refinement techniques provide significant improvement in terms of precision and scalability. Their tool, called SCInfer, alternates between fast and moderately precise approaches (partly inspired from [2] below) and computationally expensive but precise approaches.

---

[3] Note that the timings of [9] are obtained with a more powerful machine than ours.

Table 2. Overview of verification of masked hardware circuits

	# obs		SNI		NI		probing		probing [9]	
	HW	SW	HW	SW	HW	SW	HW	SW	HW	SW
first-order verification										
Trichina AND [33]	2	13	0.01s ✗	0.01s ✗	0.01s ✗	0.01s ✗	0.01s ✗	0.01s ✗	≤ 2s ✗	≤ 1s ✗
ISW AND [25]	1	13	0.01s ✗	0.01s	0.01s ✗	0.01s	0.01s ✗	0.01s	≤2s ✗	≤1s
TI AND [32]	3	21	0.01s ✗	0.01s ✗	0.01s	0.01s	0.01s	0.01s	≤3s	≤1s
DOM AND [22]	4	13	0.01s ✗	0.01s	0.01s	0.01s	0.01s	0.01s	≤2s	≤1s
DOM AND SNI	6	13	0.01s	0.01s	0.01s	0.01s	0.01s	0.01s	-	-
PARA AND [5]	6	16	0.01s	0.01s	0.01s	0.01s	0.01s	0.01s	-	-
DOM Keccak S-box [23]	20	76	0.01s ✗	0.01s	0.01s	0.01s	0.01s	0.01s	≤20s	≤1s
DOM AES S-box [22]	96	571	0.02s ✗	0.04s ✗	0.02s ✗	0.04s ✗	0.06s	0.6s	≤5-10h*	≤30s*
TI Fides-160 S-box [8]	192	6657	0.2s ✗	0.2s ✗	0.3s	57s	0.3s	2.8s	≤1-3s*	≤1-2s*
TI Fides-192 APN [8]	128	69281	2.3s ✗	2.46s ✗	2.25s	∞	2.3s	3m49s	≤ 5s-2h	≤2s-20m
second-order verification										
DOM AND [22]	12	30	0.01s ✗	0.01s	0.01s	0.01s	0.01s	0.01s	≤1s	≤1s
DOM AND SNI	15	30	0.01s	0.01s	0.01s	0.01s	0.01s	0.01s	-	-
PARA AND [5]	15	30	0.01s	0.01s	0.01s	0.01s	0.01s	0.01s	-	-
DOM Keccak S-box [23]	60	165	0.01s ✗	0.2	0.07s	0.14s	0.03s	0.03s	≤40s*	≤10s*
DOM AES S-box [21]	168	1205	3s ✗	3m9s ✗	3s ✗	3m9s ✗	10.7s	15m45s	-	-
third-order verification										
DOM AND [22]	20	54	0.01s ✗	0.04s	0.02s	0.05s	0.02s	0.03s	≤20s	≤4s
DOM AND SNI	24	54	0.04s	0.04s	0.03s	0.05s	0.03s	0.03s	-	-
PARA AND NI [5]	20	48	0.01s ✗	0.01s ✗	0.02s	0.03s	0.02s	0.02s	-	-
PARA AND SNI [5]	28	53	0.04s	0.05s	0.02s	0.04s	0.02s	0.02s	-	-
DOM Keccak S-box [23]	100	290	0.01s ✗	41s	3.6s	11.6s	0.49s	0.68s	≤25m*	≤4m*
DOM AES S-box [21]	296	2011	0.05s ✗	0.05s ✗	0.05s ✗	0.05s ✗	12m36s	∞	-	-
fourth-order verification										
DOM AND [22]	30	87	0.03s ✗	0.34s	0.1s	0.15s	0.1s	0.1s	≤7m	≤2m
PARA AND NI [5]	35	75	0.01s ✗	0.01s ✗	0.15s	0.42s	0.18s	0.15s	-	-
PARA AND SNI [5]	40	85	0.34s	0.81s	0.17s	0.47s	0.16s	0.16s	-	-
DOM Keccak S-box [23]	150	450	0.02s ✗	∞	4m	13m20	20s	41s	-	-
fifth-order verification										
DOM Keccak S-box [23]	210	618	0.02s ✗	∞	1h6m	∞	3m59s	14m6s	-	-

Independently, Barthe et al. [2] propose a different approach for proving probing security. They establish and leverage a tight connection between the security of masked implementations and probabilistic non-interference, for which they propose efficient verification methods. Specifically, they show how a relational program logic previously used for mechanizing proofs of provable security can be specialized into an efficient procedure for proving probabilistic non-interference, and develop techniques that overcome the combinatorial explosion of observation sets for high orders. The concrete outcome of their work is the maskVerif framework, which achieves practicality at reasonably high orders, and prove security in all introduced non-interference security notions. A tweaked version additionally handles verification in presence of transitions, but hardware physical defaults (e.g., glitches) are not supported. This work remains also permissive to false negatives. In the same line of work, Coron [12] presents an alternative tool, called checkMasks, which achieves similar functionalities as maskVerif, but exploits a more extensive set of transformations for operating on tuples of expressions. This is useful to achieve better verification times on selected examples.

A follow-up work by Barthe et al. [3] addresses the problem of compositional reasoning by introducing the notion of strong non-interference (SNI), and adapts maskVerif to check SNI. The adaptation achieves similar coverage as the original tool, i.e. it achieves practicality at reasonably high-orders. In addition, [3] proposes an information flow type system with cardinality constraints, which forms the basis of a compiler, called maskComp. This compiler transforms an unprotected implementation into an implementation that is protected at any desired order. Somewhat similar to the masking compiler of [31], maskComp uses typing information to control and to minimize the insertion of mask refreshing gadgets. In the same line of work, Belaïd, Goudarzi, and Rivain recently propose tightPROVE [7] which exactly and directly verifies the software probing security of a circuit based on standard gadgets at any order.

Hardware Implementations. As recalled in the previous section, Bloem et al. [9] provide a tool for proving probing security of masked implementations in the ISW model with glitches. While this tool benefits from the new treatment of physical defaults, it faces efficiency issues and cannot handle classical higher-order examples. Recently Bloem, Iusupov, Krenn, and Mangard [10] provide some technical optimizations based on an earlier version of this paper (using our same tool), but that are still restricted to proofs on probing security. Namely, proven implementations thus cannot be safely composed to achieve larger secure ones. The work of Faust et al. follows the alternative approach of proving the strong non-interference of some basic gadgets with glitches, which allows composing circuits at arbitrary orders (but less efficiently) [19].

7 Conclusions

We have developed and implemented an automated method for verifying masked implementations in presence of physical defaults. Our tool is based on novel and efficient algorithms for proving probabilistic non-interference for all admissible observation sets by an attacker. Our tool conveniently supports the three main notions of security (probing security, threshold non-interference and strong non-interference) and is able to verify efficiently implementations at high orders.

In the future, it would be interesting to extend our work beyond purely qualitative security definitions, and to consider quantitative definitions that upper bound how much leakage reveals about secrets—using total variation distance [18] or more recent metrics that directly or indirectly relate to noisy leakage security [15,16]. More speculatively, it would also be interesting to extend our framework and verification methodologies to active adversaries, who can tamper with computations [24]. A first step would be to extend the correspondence between information flow and simulation-based security to the case of active adversaries. An appealing possibility would be to exploit the well-known dual view of information flow security for confidentiality and integrity. It would also be interesting to build tools based on our algorithms to synthesize masked implementations.

Acknowledgements. This work is partially supported by the French FUI-AAP25 VeriSiCC project and ONR project N00014-19-1-2292. Gaëtan Cassiers and François-Xavier Standaert are resp. Research Fellow and and Senior Associate Researcher of the Belgian Fund for Scientific Research (FNRS-F.R.S.).

References

1. Balasch, J., Gierlichs, B., Grosso, V., Reparaz, O., Standaert, F.-X.: On the cost of lazy engineering for masked software implementations. In: Joye, M., Moradi, A. (eds.) CARDIS 2014. LNCS, vol. 8968, pp. 64–81. Springer, Cham (2015). https://doi.org/10.1007/978-3-319-16763-3_5

2. Barthe, G., Belaïd, S., Dupressoir, F., Fouque, P.-A., Grégoire, B., Strub, P.-Y.: Verified proofs of higher-order masking. In: Oswald, E., Fischlin, M. (eds.) EUROCRYPT 2015, Part I. LNCS, vol. 9056, pp. 457–485. Springer, Heidelberg (2015). https://doi.org/10.1007/978-3-662-46800-5_18

3. Barthe, G., et al.: Strong non-interference and type-directed higher-order masking. In: Weippl, E.R., Katzenbeisser, S., Kruegel, C., Myers, A.C., Halevi, S. (eds.) ACM CCS 2016, pp. 116–129. ACM Press, October 2016

4. Barthe, G., Daubignard, M., Kapron, B., Lakhnech, Y., Laporte, V.: On the equality of probabilistic terms. In: Clarke, E.M., Voronkov, A. (eds.) LPAR 2010. LNCS (LNAI), vol. 6355, pp. 46–63. Springer, Heidelberg (2010). https://doi.org/10.1007/978-3-642-17511-4_4

5. Barthe, G., Dupressoir, F., Faust, S., Grégoire, B., Standaert, F.-X., Strub, P.-Y.: Parallel implementations of masking schemes and the bounded moment leakage model. In: Coron, J.-S., Nielsen, J.B. (eds.) EUROCRYPT 2017, Part I. LNCS, vol. 10210, pp. 535–566. Springer, Cham (2017). https://doi.org/10.1007/978-3-319-56620-7_19

6. Bayrak, A.G., Regazzoni, F., Novo, D., Ienne, P.: Sleuth: automated verification of software power analysis countermeasures. In: Bertoni, G., Coron, J.-S. (eds.) CHES 2013. LNCS, vol. 8086, pp. 293–310. Springer, Heidelberg (2013). https://doi.org/10.1007/978-3-642-40349-1_17

7. Belaïd, S., Goudarzi, D., Rivain, M.: Tight private circuits: achieving probing security with the least refreshing. In: Peyrin, T., Galbraith, S. (eds.) ASIACRYPT 2018, Part II. LNCS, vol. 11273, pp. 343–372. Springer, Cham (2018). https://doi.org/10.1007/978-3-030-03329-3_12

8. Bilgin, B., Bogdanov, A., Knežević, M., Mendel, F., Wang, Q.: FIDES: lightweight authenticated cipher with side-channel resistance for constrained hardware. In: Bertoni, G., Coron, J.-S. (eds.) CHES 2013. LNCS, vol. 8086, pp. 142–158. Springer, Heidelberg (2013). https://doi.org/10.1007/978-3-642-40349-1_9

9. Bloem, R., Gross, H., Iusupov, R., Könighofer, B., Mangard, S., Winter, J.: Formal verification of masked hardware implementations in the presence of glitches. In: Nielsen, J.B., Rijmen, V. (eds.) EUROCRYPT 2018, Part II. LNCS, vol. 10821, pp. 321–353. Springer, Cham (2018). https://doi.org/10.1007/978-3-319-78375-8_11

10. Bloem, R., Iusupov, R., Krenn, M., Mangard, S.: Sharing independence & relabeling: efficient formal verification of higher-order masking. Cryptology ePrint Archive, Report 2018/1031 (2018). https://eprint.iacr.org/2018/1031

11. Chari, S., Jutla, C.S., Rao, J.R., Rohatgi, P.: Towards sound approaches to counteract power-analysis attacks. In: Wiener, M. (ed.) CRYPTO 1999. LNCS, vol. 1666, pp. 398–412. Springer, Heidelberg (1999). https://doi.org/10.1007/3-540-48405-1_26

12. Coron, J.-S.: Formal verification of side-channel countermeasures via elementary circuit transformations. In: Preneel, B., Vercauteren, F. (eds.) ACNS 2018. LNCS, vol. 10892, pp. 65–82. Springer, Cham (2018). https://doi.org/10.1007/978-3-319-93387-0_4

13. Coron, J.-S., Giraud, C., Prouff, E., Renner, S., Rivain, M., Vadnala, P.K.: Conversion of security proofs from one leakage model to another: a new issue. In: Schindler, W., Huss, S.A. (eds.) COSADE 2012. LNCS, vol. 7275, pp. 69–81. Springer, Heidelberg (2012). https://doi.org/10.1007/978-3-642-29912-4_6

14. Duc, A., Dziembowski, S., Faust, S.: Unifying leakage models: from probing attacks to noisy leakage. In: Nguyen, P.Q., Oswald, E. (eds.) EUROCRYPT 2014. LNCS, vol. 8441, pp. 423–440. Springer, Heidelberg (2014). https://doi.org/10.1007/978-3-642-55220-5_24

15. Duc, A., Dziembowski, S., Faust, S.: Unifying leakage models: from probing attacks to noisy leakage. J. Cryptol. 32(1), 151–177 (2019)

16. Duc, A., Faust, S., Standaert, F.-X.: Making masking security proofs concrete. In: Oswald, E., Fischlin, M. (eds.) EUROCRYPT 2015, Part I. LNCS, vol. 9056, pp. 401–429. Springer, Heidelberg (2015). https://doi.org/10.1007/978-3-662-46800-5_16

17. Eldib, H., Wang, C., Schaumont, P.: Formal verification of software countermeasures against side-channel attacks. ACM Trans. Softw. Eng. Methodol. 24(2), 11:1–11:24 (2014)

18. Eldib, H., Wang, C., Taha, M.M.I., Schaumont, P.: Quantitative masking strength: quantifying the power side-channel resistance of software code. IEEE Trans. CAD Integr. Circuits Syst. 34(10), 1558–1568 (2015)

19. Faust, S., Grosso, V., Pozo, S.M.D., Paglialonga, C., Standaert, F.-X.: Composable masking schemes in the presence of physical defaults & the robust probing model. IACR TCHES 2018(3), 89–120 (2018). https://tches.iacr.org/index.php/TCHES/article/view/7270

20. Gandolfi, K., Mourtel, C., Olivier, F.: Electromagnetic analysis: concrete results. In: Koç, Ç.K., Naccache, D., Paar, C. (eds.) CHES 2001. LNCS, vol. 2162, pp. 251–261. Springer, Heidelberg (2001). https://doi.org/10.1007/3-540-44709-1_21

21. Groß, H., Krenn, M., Mangard, S.: Second and third order verilog implementations of AES s-box (2018)

22. Gross, H., Mangard, S., Korak, T.: An efficient side-channel protected AES implementation with arbitrary protection order. In: Handschuh, H. (ed.) CT-RSA 2017. LNCS, vol. 10159, pp. 95–112. Springer, Cham (2017). https://doi.org/10.1007/978-3-319-52153-4_6

23. Gross, H., Schaffenrath, D., Mangard, S.: Higher-order side-channel protected implementations of keccak. Cryptology ePrint Archive, Report 2017/395 (2017). http://eprint.iacr.org/2017/395

24. Ishai, Y., Prabhakaran, M., Sahai, A., Wagner, D.: Private circuits II: keeping secrets in tamperable circuits. In: Vaudenay, S. (ed.) EUROCRYPT 2006. LNCS, vol. 4004, pp. 308–327. Springer, Heidelberg (2006). https://doi.org/10.1007/11761679_19

25. Ishai, Y., Sahai, A., Wagner, D.: Private circuits: securing hardware against probing attacks. In: Boneh, D. (ed.) CRYPTO 2003. LNCS, vol. 2729, pp. 463–481. Springer, Heidelberg (2003). https://doi.org/10.1007/978-3-540-45146-4_27

26. Knudsen, L.R., Robshaw, M.: The Block Cipher Companion. Information Security and Cryptography. Springer, Heidelberg (2011). https://doi.org/10.1007/978-3-642-17342-4

27. Kocher, P.C.: Timing attacks on implementations of Diffie-Hellman, RSA, DSS, and other systems. In: Koblitz, N. (ed.) CRYPTO 1996. LNCS, vol. 1109, pp. 104–113. Springer, Heidelberg (1996). https://doi.org/10.1007/3-540-68697-5_9

28. Kocher, P., Jaffe, J., Jun, B.: Differential power analysis. In: Wiener, M. (ed.) CRYPTO 1999. LNCS, vol. 1666, pp. 388–397. Springer, Heidelberg (1999). https://doi.org/10.1007/3-540-48405-1_25

29. Mangard, S., Oswald, E., Popp, T.: Power Analysis Attacks - Revealing The Secrets of Smart Cards. Springer, New York (2007). https://doi.org/10.1007/978-0-387-38162-6

30. Mangard, S., Popp, T., Gammel, B.M.: Side-channel leakage of masked CMOS gates. In: Menezes, A. (ed.) CT-RSA 2005. LNCS, vol. 3376, pp. 351–365. Springer, Heidelberg (2005). https://doi.org/10.1007/978-3-540-30574-3_24

31. Moss, A., Oswald, E., Page, D., Tunstall, M.: Compiler assisted masking. In: Prouff, E., Schaumont, P. (eds.) CHES 2012. LNCS, vol. 7428, pp. 58–75. Springer, Heidelberg (2012). https://doi.org/10.1007/978-3-642-33027-8_4

32. Nikova, S., Rechberger, C., Rijmen, V.: Threshold implementations against side-channel attacks and glitches. In: Ning, P., Qing, S., Li, N. (eds.) ICICS 2006. LNCS, vol. 4307, pp. 529–545. Springer, Heidelberg (2006). https://doi.org/10.1007/11935308_38

33. Trichina, E.: Combinational logic design for AES subbyte transformation on masked data. Cryptology ePrint Archive, Report 2003/236 (2003). http://eprint.iacr.org/2003/236

34. Zhang, J., Gao, P., Song, F., Wang, C.: SCInfer: refinement-based verification of software countermeasures against side-channel attacks. In: Chockler, H., Weissenbacher, G. (eds.) CAV 2018, Part II. LNCS, vol. 10982, pp. 157–177. Springer, Cham (2018). https://doi.org/10.1007/978-3-319-96142-2_12

Automated Formal Analysis
of Side-Channel Attacks on Probabilistic
Systems

Chris Novakovic$^{(\boxtimes)}$ ⓘ and David Parker ⓘ

School of Computer Science, University of Birmingham, Birmingham, UK
{c.novakovic,d.a.parker}@cs.bham.ac.uk

Abstract. The security guarantees of even theoretically-secure systems can be undermined by the presence of side channels in their implementations. We present SCH-IMP, a probabilistic imperative language for side channel analysis containing primitives for identifying secret and publicly-observable data, and in which resource consumption is modelled at the function level. We provide a semantics for SCH-IMP programs in terms of discrete-time Markov chains. Building on this, we propose automated techniques to detect worst-case attack strategies for correctly deducing a program's secret information from its outputs and resource consumption, based on verification of partially-observable Markov decision processes. We implement this in a tool and show how it can be used to quantify the severity of worst-case side-channel attacks against a selection of systems, including anonymity networks, covert communication channels and modular arithmetic implementations used for public-key cryptography.

1 Introduction

Side channels are covert channels that convey information about the behaviour of a hardware or software system implementation beyond what was intended by its design. Information from a system's side channels—most commonly via their use of resources such as time or power, or their production of emissions such as electromagnetic radiation or sound—may be combined with information gained via the system's regular output channels in such a way that an observer may be able to correlate the system's overt behaviour with information they are unable to directly observe, such as data stored in a program's memory.

Side channels are most impactful in systems that attempt to ensure the confidentiality of some secret data being processed, even in systems that are theoretically secure. Software-level attacks often leverage authorised access or exposure to the system that the attacker already has, making them particularly potent: for instance, a *timing side channel* may be exploitable by an attacker with a user account on the same system, or with a virtual machine running on the same hypervisor (e.g. [19,22]). Hardware-level attacks—such as *power analysis*—were once prohibitively expensive to mount, but thanks to the ever-increasing quality of consumer-level gadgets and falling cost of specialist hardware, even they are

© Springer Nature Switzerland AG 2019
K. Sako et al. (Eds.): ESORICS 2019, LNCS 11735, pp. 319–337, 2019.
https://doi.org/10.1007/978-3-030-29959-0_16

now within reach of attackers with modest resources; e.g., it is now possible to use \$50 software-defined radios to break widely-used cryptosystems [8,9].

Given the potential severity and relative ease of performing successful side-channel attacks, there is a need to be able to verify that implementations of theoretically-secure systems are free of such vulnerabilities—or, in cases where side channels are an unavoidable consequence of the system's intended behaviour, that they do not leak more than a maximum permitted amount of information about the secret data being processed. When an undesirable side-channel does exist, we also want to know the execution path through the system that causes the side channel to arise, so that it can be eliminated or mitigated.

This paper presents a framework for automatically analysing systems for the presence of side channels in the face of an adversary with knowledge of the system's behaviour (although not necessarily the secret information it is processing) and the capability to observe its outputs; this is analogous to a physical attacker with (e.g.) a hardware schematic or program source code and the ability to time certain operations or empirically measure their power consumption. Since probability is an important factor in the design and implementation of many security protocols and systems, we focus on the analysis of probabilistic systems.

We have developed SCH-IMP, a probabilistic language featuring control flow structures (functions, conditionals and loops), scoped variable declaration and assignment, and the ability to indicate that certain values are output publicly. The language is expressive enough that non-trivial models can be encoded succinctly. The program's secret information is stored in variables defined with the keyword initial. As with regular variables in SCH-IMP, the values of initial variables are assigned according to a probability mass function (p.m.f.); however, the attacker does not necessarily know which concrete value was drawn from each p.m.f. and assigned to each initial variable, and the attacker's goal is therefore to maximise what they learn about these concrete values by observing the program's externally-visible behaviour.

A novelty of this framework is the ability to reason about the resource usage of SCH-IMP programs. A *resource function* is declared alongside a SCH-IMP program, which defines how (a subset of) functions declared in the program make use of resources when invoked. While our focus in this paper is on how functions consume time and power, the framework is flexible enough that any other consumable resource could be considered. We assume that the attacker is capable of monitoring the program's resource usage as it executes, and may exploit it in an effort to compromise the secrecy of its initial variables.

We provide a semantics for the execution of SCH-IMP programs that is parameterised by the resource function and defined in terms of a discrete-time Markov chain (DTMC). The states of the DTMC capture two constructs of relevance to side-channel analysis: the set of concrete mappings for each initial variable declared in the program, and an *observation function* encoding all of the information about the program's behaviour that is exposed to the attacker.

First, we systematically explore and construct this DTMC representing the (probabilistic) behaviour of the system. We then use this to construct a partially-observable Markov decision process (POMDP) in which the initial variable information from each terminating state is hidden. The partial observability property of a POMDP is ideal for modelling the uncertain knowledge of the SCH-IMP program's internal state (specifically, the concrete value of each initial variable for a particular execution trace) from the attacker's perspective. We then solve the POMDP to identify the attacker's optimal strategies for learning the hidden initial variable information by observing the outputs and resource usage. In doing so, we compute the (worst-case) probability of such an attack succeeding, thus meaningfully quantifying the worst-case exposure of the program's secrets.

Our approach is fully automated and we have implemented it in a tool [1]. An analyst need only encode their system in SCH-IMP, along with the resource usage of its functions (which could be empirically measured). The tool then explores the DTMC representing the system's state space and constructs and solves the POMDP modelling the attacker's uncertain knowledge of this state space using an extension [17] of the PRISM [13] model checker. The two phase construction of the POMDP (via a DTMC) provides opportunities to aggressively minimise the state space of the models. This is an important consideration for any technique based on exhaustive state space exploration. We illustrate the practicality and applicability of our techniques and tool by applying them to a selection of case studies: an anonymity network, a covert communication channel, and a modular arithmetic implementation used for public-key cryptography.

1.1 Related Work

The leakage of information from a secret channel to a public channel in insecure systems is a well-known problem, and has been studied extensively. Many existing approaches use concepts from information theory to quantify the leakage; common measures include Shannon entropy, min-entropy, and mutual information. (Smith [20] performs a brief survey.) There is no single measure that is appropriate for use in all scenarios [2], and it is often difficult to interpret their concrete effect on the system's security. In contrast, our framework provides an easily-understood metric: the probability that the attacker's best possible strategy successfully manages to compromise the system's secret information.

We consider the effect of side channels on probabilistic systems in which the secret information is present at initialisation and outputs (including the use of resources) occur as the system executes and eventually terminates. Information flow and side-channel analysis frameworks for several other types of system exist, including non-terminating [3,23] and interactive [12] systems. Although our framework does not currently consider the case where the attacker is able to interact with and observe the system simultaneously, it is intended to be extendable to this case by modelling the entire execution of the system as a POMDP and the attacker's inputs as nondeterministic choices.

There are many examples of probabilistic languages in the literature, e.g. in artificial intelligence, where reasoning under uncertainty in probabilistic environments is common. These languages are inappropriate for use in our work, as either they are too low-level to succinctly encode the systems (and their resource usage) described in Sect. 4 (e.g. [7]), or because uncertainty of and belief about the program's state are an inherent aspect of the language (e.g. [18]); our work infers the attacker's uncertainty as the POMDP is constructed, and does not require that complexity to be part of the language encoding the system itself. SCH-IMP is most closely related to CH-IMP, a probabilistic language for information flow analysis that features in our earlier work [6]. As in SCH-IMP, the execution of CH-IMP programs is defined as a semantics that induces a DTMC; however, CH-IMP has no notion of subroutines or functions that define their resource usage, which are needed for side-channel analysis.

While POMDPs are widely used in other areas of research, their application to quantitative information flow analysis is less well-studied. Marecki et al. [15] analyse unauthorised information leaks in one-to-many broadcast systems, using POMDPs to model the sender's uncertainty about the recipient's subsequent handling of the secret information; Tschantz et al. [21] have a similar concern. The covert channel example that we use as an example in Sect. 4 was analysed as a POMDP in [17], but that does not explicitly consider side channels or attack strategies. To the best of our knowledge, our framework is the first to use POMDPs for the formal analysis of side-channel attacks.

2   A Language for Formal Side-Channel Analysis

We now present SCH-IMP, the probabilistic language used by our framework. In this section, we give the syntax of the language, explain how resource usage is modelled in SCH-IMP programs, and give a formal definition of the semantics.

2.1   The SCH-IMP Language

The grammar for SCH-IMP is shown in Fig. 1 and we give an illustrative example program in Fig. 2 (a larger example for one of our case studies can also be found in Appendix A). Values of variables are rational numbers, assigned according to a p.m.f. over $\mathbb{Q}$. There are two types of variables: *initial variables* (declared with the initial command at the start of the program, whose initial values are considered "secret" and therefore of interest to an attacker), and regular variables (declared with the new command, and which have no secrecy connotations). Initial variables, and regular variables declared immediately afterward, are visible to all functions, while variables declared inside function bodies and if and while blocks are in scope only within those constructs. We consider programs that declare a variable with the same name twice in the same scope or that refer to undefined variables to be badly-formed.

Following the declaration of top-level variables, a program consists of at least one function definition followed by the invocation of one of these functions. Function bodies may invoke other functions, subject to the limitations described in Sect. 2.2. Before a function returns control to its caller, it may output the result of evaluating one or more arithmetic expressions with the output command; these values are considered "public" and visible to the attacker.

$$\mathbb{P} ::= \text{[initial } V := \rho;]^*$$
$$\text{[new } V := \rho;]^*$$
$$\text{[function } F([V]^*) \text{ \{ } C; \text{ [output } [A]^+;]^? \text{ return };]^+$$
$$F([A]^*); \text{ end}$$

$$C ::= \text{skip} \mid \text{new } V := \rho \mid V := \rho \mid F([A]^*)$$
$$\mid \text{if } (B) \text{ \{ } C \text{ \} [else \{ } C \text{ \}]}^?$$
$$\mid \text{while } (B) \text{ \{ } C \text{ \} } \mid C; C$$

Fig. 1. The SCH-IMP grammar. V is a variable name, A is an arithmetic expression, B is a Boolean expression, and ρ is a p.m.f. over arithmetic expressions.

```
initial i := {                              {
    0 → 1/4, 1 → 1/4, 2 → 1/4, 3 → 1/4        f → {
};                                              (0) → {
function f(x) {                                     (5, 7) → 1/2, (6, 7) → 1/2
    new o := 1;                                 },
    if (x > 0) { o := x / x };                  (_) → {
    output o;                                       (6, 7) → 1/2, (7, 7) → 1/2
    return                                      }
};                                            }
f(i);                                       }
end
```

Fig. 2. A SCH-IMP program and resource function containing a side channel when i = 0. _ represents any arithmetic constant permitted by SCH-IMP (i.e., a rational number).

2.2   Resource Usage in SCH-IMP Programs

While the overt behaviour of SCH-IMP programs is expressed by the syntax in Fig. 1, we are primarily interested in the covert information about the program's behaviour that is revealed during its execution. In reality, this covert information is most often revealed through a system's use of available resources, typically time and power. Since functions represent the broadest level of control flow within SCH-IMP programs, and because the behaviour of a function typically varies depending on the arguments passed to it, it is natural to reason about the resource usage of a program's functions based on how they are called. We therefore employ a *resource function* that defines how functions in the SCH-IMP program consume time and power based on the arguments passed to them.

Definition 1 (resource function). *A resource function $\mathcal{R}$ for a SCH-IMP program $\mathbb{P}$ ranges over a subset of the functions declared in $\mathbb{P}$ and, for each such function F, partially maps sequences of arguments $(q_1, \ldots, q_n)$ to probability distributions over tuples $(\mathbb{N} \times \mathbb{N})$ that define the number of units of time that elapse and of power that are consumed when $F(q_1, \ldots, q_n)$ is executed.*

Similarly to how a SCH-IMP program can be seen as a formal encoding of a system, a resource function can be seen as a formal encoding of a system's resource usage; as such, the information in a resource function could (e.g.) be determined empirically from the resource usage of a system's implementation.

An example SCH-IMP program and its resource function are given in Fig. 2. While the program theoretically does not overtly leak information about the secret value of the initial variable i—it ultimately has no effect on the value of o that is output and visible to the attacker—the resource function indicates that the function f() on average executes slightly faster when its parameter x is 0, perhaps because of the extra operation that is performed when x > 0. Because the value of x is directly related to that of i when it was declared, this in fact presents a timing side channel that leaks information about i to the attacker.

Although function bodies consist of one or more commands, we take a high-level view of their resource consumption: their commands consume resources as a single unit, rather than discretely. From the perspective of the attacker, a function that consumes a non-zero amount of time or power when it executes does so atomically, regardless of the size or complexity of its body. In order to provide a clean definition of resource usage, we introduce the notion of an *instantaneous* function, whose execution takes no time and consumes no power from the perspective of the attacker; this is defined formally below. Any other function is referred to as *non-instantaneous*.

Definition 2 (instantaneous function). *A* SCH-IMP *function F with n parameters is* instantaneous *with respect to a resource function $\mathcal{R}$ iff $F \notin \mathrm{dom}\,(\mathcal{R})$ or $\mathcal{R}\,(F)\,(q_1, \ldots, q_n) = \{(0,0) \rightarrow 1\}$ for any argument sequence $(q_1, \ldots, q_n)$.*

Because function bodies may themselves invoke functions, it is unclear what information an attacker would learn about a program if a non-instantaneous function A were to invoke another non-instantaneous function B given the above definitions: because the commands in a non-instantaneous function body consume resources as a single unit, the resources consumed by B would also appear to be consumed during its invocation in A, at which point A would no longer necessarily consume the resources dictated by the resource function, thus creating a contradiction. To simplify matters, we consider programs in which non-instantaneous functions invoke non-instantaneous functions to be badly-formed. All other forms of invocation, including (bounded) recursive invocation of instantaneous functions, are permitted.

Information Leakage Model. The presence of side channels in a system can be characterised as a special case of information leakage in which the "public information" in the system consists not only of the overt outputs that the system produces on the public channel, but also information on other visible channels that can be correlated with the information from the public channel to form a new *multiplex* channel with a greater capacity. This creates a best-case scenario in which an attacker observing the multiplex channel learns nothing more about the system's secret information than they do by observing only the public channel; this indicates that the system is free from side channels. Alternatively, the worst-case scenario is the one in which the attacker learns nothing about the system's secret information by observing the public channel, but learns all of the secret information when observing the multiplex channel.

2.3   Semantics for the SCH-IMP Language

The execution of a SCH-IMP program is defined in terms of a discrete-time Markov chain (DTMC):

Definition 3 (discrete-time Markov chain). *A DTMC $\mathcal{D}$ is a tuple $(S, \bar{s}, \mathbf{P})$, where S is a finite set of states, $\bar{s} \in S$ is an initial state, and $\mathbf{P} : S \times S \to [0,1]$ is a transition probability matrix such that $\sum_{s' \in S} \mathbf{P}(s, s') = 1$ for all $s \in S$.*

In the context of SCH-IMP, the states in S define the execution status of the program at any given moment, providing a notion of a program counter, storage for bindings for in-scope variables, and information about the secret data, observable data and resource usage that has occurred up to that point during the program's execution. More formally:

Definition 4 (state). *A SCH-IMP state is a tuple $(\mathcal{F}, \mathbb{I}, t, p, \Delta)$, where:*

- *$\mathcal{F} : C \times \text{seq}(\mathbf{Var} \to \mathbb{Q})$ is a stack of commands (with their associated variable scope frames) that remain to be executed;*
- *$\mathbb{I} : \mathbf{Var} \to \mathbb{Q}$ is a mapping consisting of the initial variables defined during the program's execution along with their values;*
- *$t : \mathbb{N}$ is the total time that has elapsed so far during the program's execution;*
- *$p : \mathbb{N}$ is the cumulative amount of power that has been consumed so far during the program's execution;*
- *$\Delta : \mathbb{N} \to \mathbb{N} \times \text{seq}(\mathbb{Q})$ is an observation function defining the cumulative amount of power consumed by and values that were output from the program at a given time.*

$\mathcal{F}$ behaves like a call stack: each element in $\mathcal{F}$ represents the commands to be executed during invocation of a single function, along with a sequence of bindings for variables that are visible to that function, which we denote with σ. The first element in $\mathcal{F}$ represents the function currently being executed. Within σ, the last element represents the program's global scope (i.e., it contains bindings for the top-level variables declared at the start of the program); the penultimate element contains bindings for the function's parameters based on the arguments present when the function was invoked, and the remaining elements represent block-level scope frames within the function, becoming narrower toward the start of the sequence. $\mathbb{I}$ maintains the secret values of the initial variables at the point at which they were declared, while the observation function Δ represents the attacker's knowledge of the program's execution status; they are respectively formalisations of the program's secret and multiplex channels described earlier.

The semantic rules for the SCH-IMP commands relevant to side-channel analysis are shown in Fig. 3; the remaining rules are intuitive or result in deterministic transitions between states that are not relevant to side-channel analysis, and are omitted for brevity. We write $s \xrightarrow{p} s'$ to denote the existence of a DTMC transition from state s to state s' with probability p (i.e. $\mathbf{P}(s, s') = p$). Formally, therefore, the semantics of a SCH-IMP program is a DTMC (per Definition 3), where S is a finite set of SCH-IMP states (per Definition 4), $\bar{s} = ((\mathbb{P}, (\{\})), \{\}, 0, 0, \{\})$, and $\mathbf{P}$ is defined by the rules in Fig. 3 (amongst others).

There are two sources of probabilistic behaviour in SCH-IMP. The first is the initial, new and assignment commands, which bind a value to a variable according to a p.m.f. ρ. Variable scope is maintained as functions and command blocks (i.e., branches of if commands and bodies of while loops) execute via the creation and destruction of scope frames. We note that the value of a variable declared with the initial command is only considered secret *at the point at which it is declared*; thus, secrecy is a property of the *specific value* of an initial variable, rather than of the variable itself.

The second source of probabilistic behaviour is the resource function $\mathcal{R}$: when a function is invoked, the cumulative elapsed time and power consumption of the program are incremented probabilistically according to the p.m.f. $\mathcal{R}(F, (q_1, \ldots, q_n))$ (where $(q_1, \ldots, q_n)$ are the arguments passed to F after evaluation) and are stored in s'. The new time and power information is also stored in the observation function Δ, indicating that the attacker is able to observe how the program is consuming resources as it executes.

The output command indicates that the given sequence of values (following evaluation of the expressions) is revealed on the program's public channel. This sequence is associated with the current amount of elapsed time in the observation function; if values have already been output by the program at this time point, the new outputs are appended to the existing sequence. This means that the

$$\frac{[\![A]\!]o :: \sigma \to q}{((\text{initial } V := \rho;\, C, o :: \sigma) :: \mathcal{F}, \mathbb{I}, t, p, \Delta) \xrightarrow{\rho(A)}} $$
$$((C, o \cup \{V \to q\} :: \sigma) :: \mathcal{F}, \mathbb{I} \cup \{V \to q\}, t, p, \Delta)$$

$$\frac{[\![A_i]\!]\sigma \to q_i}{((\text{output } V_1, \ldots, V_n;\, C, \sigma) :: \mathcal{F}, \mathbb{I}, t, p, \Delta) \xrightarrow{1}}$$
$$((C, \sigma) :: \mathcal{F}, \mathbb{I}, t, p, \Delta \cup \{t \to (\Delta_p(t), \Delta_o(t) :: (q_1, \ldots, q_n))\})$$

$$\frac{[\![A_i]\!]\sigma \to q_i}{((F(A_1, \ldots, A_n);\, C, \sigma) :: \mathcal{F}, \mathbb{I}, t, p, \Delta) \xrightarrow{\mathcal{R}(F, (q_1, \ldots, q_n), (t', p'))}}$$
$$(((\mathbf{C}(F), \{\mathbf{V}(F)_1 \to q_1, \ldots, \mathbf{V}(F)_n \to q_n\} :: \sigma_G), (C, \sigma)) :: \mathcal{F},$$
$$\mathbb{I}, t + t', p + p', \Delta \cup \{t \to (\Delta_p(t) + p', ())\})$$

Fig. 3. The side-channel semantic rules of SCH-IMP. σ_G is the global variable scope frame, $\mathbf{V}(F)$ and $\mathbf{C}(F)$ are the parameter names and body of function F respectively, $\Delta_p(t)$ and $\Delta_o(t)$ are the power consumption and the list of values output at time t.

invocation of multiple instantaneous functions, all producing outputs, will appear to the attacker as an instantaneous stream of outputs on the public channel.

In this work, we assume that SCH-IMP programs always eventually terminate (with probability 1) and that their semantics yields a finite state space. We define *terminating* states as those in which an end command is executed, and denote the set of all such states $\underline{S}$.

3 Automated Detection of Side-Channel Attacks

Using the semantics defined above, we can construct a DTMC representing all possible executions of a SCH-IMP program. From this, we describe how to build and analyse a partially-observable Markov decision process to detect and quantify side-channel attacks that compromise the program's secret information.

3.1 POMDPs

We model the attacker's capabilities using *partially-observable Markov decision processes* (POMDPs), which are an extension of a Markov decision processes (MDPs). POMDPs model decision-making in the context of a probabilistic system where decisions can only be made based on observable parts of the system. We summarise the key concepts below, adopting the notation of [17].

Definition 5 (POMDP). *A POMDP is a tuple* $\mathcal{P} = (S, \bar{s}, A, T, O, \mathbf{O})$, *where: S is a finite set of states; $\bar{s} \in S$ is an initial state; A is a set of actions; $T : S \times A \to (S \to [0,1])$ is a (partial) transition probability function; O is a finite set of observations; and $\mathbf{O} : S \to O$ is a labelling of states with observations.*

In each state $s \in S$ of a POMDP, there is a choice between the set of available actions $A(s) \stackrel{\text{def}}{=} \{a \in A \mid T(s,a) \text{ is defined}\}$. States with the same observation must have the same available actions, i.e., for states $s, s' \in S$ with $\mathbf{O}(s) = \mathbf{O}(s')$, we have $A(s) = A(s')$. Once an action $a \in A(s)$ is chosen in state s, the next state of the POMDP is determined by the probability distribution $T(s,a)$, i.e. it transitions to state s' with probability $T(s,a)(s')$.

A *strategy* (also known as a policy) of a POMDP $\mathcal{P}$ resolves the choice of action taken in each state, based on the history of its execution so far. Formally, it is defined as a function from any finite path of $\mathcal{P}$ to one of the actions available in the final state of the path. We are only interested in *observation-based* strategies which make decisions based purely on the observation $\mathbf{O}(s)$ for each state s of the POMDP's history. In this work, we only need *finite-memory* strategies, whose choices depend not on the full history of the POMDP, but on one of a finite set of modes, which are switched between over time. Under a given strategy σ for $\mathcal{P}$, we can define a probability measure $Pr_{\mathcal{P}}^{\sigma}$ over the set of possible paths (executions) through the POMDP [11] and use this to quantify various measures of interest. In this paper, we concern ourselves with the probability $Pr_{\mathcal{P}}^{\sigma}(\Diamond T)$ of reaching a set $T \subseteq S$ of target states. We then wish to compute the maximum probability, over all possible strategies, of reaching T, and an optimal strategy σ^* which achieves this. While this problem is known to be undecidable [14], a variety of practical techniques exist to approximate the optimal probability.

3.2 Detecting Side Channels Using POMDPs

We represent the interaction of a SCH-IMP program and an attacker as a POMDP. Probabilities in the POMDP are used to model the initial assignment of values to initial variables. We use partial observation to accurately model the capabilities of an attacker, who can observe the program's multiplex channel and must make decisions about how to proceed based only on this information.

The partial observability property restricts the knowledge of the POMDP's current state s to its observations $\mathbf{O}(s) \in O$. This is useful for the purpose of modelling an attacker in SCH-IMP, as it allows privileged parts of the program's status (e.g., the concrete value of each initial variable) to be hidden while exposing information available on the program's multiplex channel via O.

For a SCH-IMP program $\mathbb{P}$, we will denote by $\mathcal{P}_{\mathbb{P}}$ the POMDP constructed to analyse it. The starting point for this is the DTMC representing the semantics of $\mathbb{P}$, which we denote $\mathcal{D}_{\mathbb{P}}$. Intuitively, $\mathcal{D}_{\mathbb{P}}$ represents the execution of $\mathbb{P}$, parts of which are observable by the attacker; we then allow the attacker to guess the value of the program's initial variables based on these observations.

The DTMC has a set of *terminating* states $\underline{S}$ in which an end command is executed; we assume that these states are reached with probability 1. Each state in $\underline{S}$ contains two constructs relevant to side-channel analysis of the program: $\mathbb{I}$, which contains the original (secret) value of each of its initial variables, and Δ, which contains all of its publicly-observable information—a record of when it produced its outputs, and when it consumed power.

States of $\mathcal{P}_{\mathbb{P}}$ consist of references to the representations of $\mathbb{I}$ and Δ found in the DTMC's state, along with Boolean values indicating whether the attacker's guess for the value of each initial variable in $\mathbb{I}$ is correct. The observation function $\mathbf{O}$ is used to hide $\mathbb{I}$.

The POMDP is constructed in two phases. In the first phase, each unique representation of both $\mathbb{I}$ and Δ is extracted from $\underline{S}$ and a new state for $\mathcal{P}_{\mathbb{P}}$ is constructed from each of them, with the Boolean correctness values remaining undefined. A transition from the POMDP's initial state to each of these "phase-1" states is then added, and assigned a probability equal to the probability in $\mathcal{D}_{\mathbb{P}}$ of reaching states in $\underline{S}$ containing each particular representation of $\mathbb{I}$ and Δ. The probability for all possible such values can be determined simultaneously by computing the steady-state probability distribution of $\mathcal{D}_{\mathbb{P}}$.

In the second phase, another set of states is generated in which the representations of $\mathbb{I}$ and Δ are undefined, and each of the Boolean correctness values is set to either *true* or *false*; the number of "phase-2" states is therefore 2^n, where n is the number of initial variables declared in the SCH-IMP program. The actions between the "phase-1" and "phase-2" states represent the attacker guessing a concrete value for each of the initial variables; the set of available actions between the first and second phases is therefore the Cartesian product of the sets of possible values for each initial variable. Each action results in a single deterministic transition to a "phase-2" state in which the correctness variables are assigned depending on whether each guess is correct.

Finally, we compute (or approximate) the maximum probability, in $\mathcal{P}_{\mathbb{P}}$, of reaching "phase-2" states where the guesses for all (or, if preferred, a subset) of the initial variables are correct. A corresponding POMDP strategy that achieves these values represents the attacker strategy for optimally guessing the program's secret information based on its observations.

4   Experimental Results

We have implemented the SCH-IMP language and our side channel detection techniques in a software tool. Here, we describe its implementation and demonstrate the applicability of our approach by using it to detect and quantify side channels in three case studies. The tool, as well as the SCH-IMP code for these examples, is available online [1].

4.1   Implementation

Our tool is primarily implemented in Java. Parsers for the SCH-IMP language and resource function definitions are developed in ANTLR. Construction and analysis of DTMCs and POMDPs is achieved by building upon the PRISM model checker [13], in particular the POMDP extension presented in [17].

Construction of the DTMC for a SCH-IMP program is achieved by implementing the semantic rules shown in Fig. 3 as well as the ones omitted from this paper for brevity. These are used in conjunction with PRISM's *model generator* interface, used to systematically construct probabilistic models in its "explicit" model checking engine. A number of optimisations are employed here to reduce the amount of time and memory required to fully explore the DTMC's state space. The most effective optimisation drastically reduces the total number of states in the model altogether: since many commands in SCH-IMP result in deterministic transitions between states, paths of deterministic transitions between more than two states are collapsed into a single deterministic transition between the states at the start and end of the path. This allows our tool to be a faithful representation of the formal model presented in this paper, while still being able to analyse systems that it otherwise could not.

The construction of the POMDP representing the attack model of a SCH-IMP is achieved using a second phase of the model generator interface. Transition probabilities are computed using a steady-state analysis of the DTMC. The resulting POMDP is then (approximately) solved to determine an optimal attack strategy. This is done using the approach of [17], which is based on the construction and solution of a grid-based discretisation of the *belief space* of the POMDP. For our experiments, we fixed a grid resolution of 8 (see [17] for details), which sufficed to give accurate approximations (see Sect. 4.5).

4.2   Traceability in Anonymous Communication Networks

Our first case study is the *DC-net* [4] communication network protocol, which provides for the anonymous transmission of a single bit of information per round amongst its constituent nodes. Assuming the nodes are arranged in a ring, each round proceeds as follows. Each pair of adjacent nodes randomly generates a single bit that is known only to them; this is achieved by each of the nodes randomly generating a single bit and transmitting it to the other node over a private secure channel, allowing each node to independently compute the shared bit by XORing the bit they generated with the bit they received from the other node. After this process is complete, each node has knowledge of two shared bits (one shared with each node adjacent to them). Each node then XORs these two known shared bits and publicly broadcasts the output of this operation to the other nodes, with the exception of the node that wants to transmit one extra bit anonymously during this round; this node instead broadcasts the inversion of their XOR output. When all nodes have broadcasted, each node can independently verify whether one of the nodes transmitted an extra bit in this round by XORing together all of the broadcasted bits: a result of 1 indicates the transmission of an extra bit; 0 indicates the absence of an extra bit.

While the DC-net is theoretically secure—the identity of the node transmitting the extra bit of information is concealed both to other nodes in the DC-net and to external observers—a faulty implementation may nevertheless leak information about the transmitting node's identity. Many different implementation errors could cause this situation. For example, since the node attempting to communicate anonymously must perform an additional computation compared to the other nodes, an implementation that fails to account for the additional processing time this computation incurs may cause a noticeable delay before the transmitting node broadcasts. This would therefore introduce a timing side-channel into the protocol that reveals the identity of the transmitting node.

A Sch-imp encoding of one round of a four-node DC-net is shown in Appendix A. One of the nodes is chosen uniformly to become the transmitting node in this round; its identity is stored in the initial variable transmitter, indicating that the transmitting node's identity should be concealed from the attacker. Since we assume that the model itself is known to the attacker, we are also implicitly stating that the attacker knows that each node is equally likely to be the transmitter. The broadcast() function executes the protocol from the perspective of one node (whose identity is given by the index parameter), and is invoked four times by the main() function; whether or not this node is the transmitter is given by the is_transmitter parameter. The single-bit value stored in b, which is revealed publicly at the end of the function, is computed by XORing the values of my_bit and their_bit; if this node is the transmitter, the value of b is then XORed with 1 to invert its value. The extra time taken to perform the additional computation in the case of the transmitting node is reflected in the resource function definition for broadcast(), in which broadcast()'s execution consumes a constant amount of power, but which takes differing amounts of time to execute depending on whether the node is the transmitter. The question of interest, therefore, is how much information about the identity of the transmitting node is revealed to the attacker as a result of the attacker observing the timing of the four executions of the broadcast() function, and how the attacker can improve upon their *a priori* random guess (a strategy that succeeds with probability 0.25, as each node is equally likely to be the transmitter).

We consider the scenario in which the elapsed time is drawn from an approximately binomial distribution centred on 4 units of time when the broadcasting node is the transmitter and 3 units of time otherwise, modelling a situation in which the transmitter will on average take longer to broadcast but with enough of an intersection between the two distributions that the attacker cannot be sure of their identity based solely on the timing side channel. In this scenario, SCH-IMP identifies an attacker strategy that successfully deanonymises the transmitter with probability ≈ 0.527, a significant improvement over the probability of 0.25 expected of the ideal implementation.

4.3   Covert Information Flows over a Unidirectional Network

The purpose of a *unidirectional network* is to provide a means for, and enforcement of, one-way communication between hosts. An example is the National Research Laboratory's Network Pump [10], intended for use in classified networks: it divides the network into "low-security" and "high-security" partitions and, while hosts in the low-security partition may send messages to hosts in the high-security partition, it forbids information from being communicated in the opposite direction. However, the Network Pump also provides confirmation of receipt of messages, which introduces the possibility of a covert channel being created between the partitions via collusive timing delays in message receipt confirmations: if hosts in each partition can mutually agree on a scheme for encoding bits of information in the time taken between the low-security node sending its message and the high-security node confirming receipt of that message, a forbidden side channel from the high-security node to the low-security node can be created. Although a well-designed unidirectional network will introduce noise into this side channel by probabilistically inserting its own delay between receiving the confirmation from the high-security node and forwarding it on to the low-security node, the nodes will always be able to defeat the network by agreeing on a sufficiently long delay; there is therefore a trade-off to be made between limiting the capacity of the side channel (i.e., by maximising the delay) and maintaining network performance.

In the SCH-IMP model of this scenario, a high-security node attempts to covertly communicate a secret value in an initial variable h (which is equally likely to be 0 or 1) to a low-security node via a unidirectional network. The acknowledgement delay introduced by the high-security node lasts for h0 units of time when h is 0 and h1 units of time when h is 1. The network introduces its own probabilistic delay of $1/2^{hn}$ units of time, where n is the value of h. If the low-security node does not receive an acknowledgement after 10 units of time, it assumes the message has been lost. The nodes may exchange up to m messages in an attempt to communicate the value of h. By fixing the value of h0 and varying the values of h1 and m, we can identify the artificial delays that the high-security node can choose to insert to maximise the probability that the value of h is leaked successfully within the permitted number of messages while maintaining network performance.

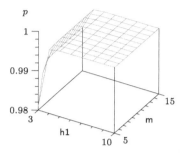

Fig. 4. The vulnerability of the unidirectional network to side-channel attacks for a fixed value of h0 (2) and varying values of h1 and m.

Figure 4 shows the probability of h successfully being communicated for a fixed value of 2 for h0, values of h1 from 3–10, and values of m from 5–15. The colluding nodes quickly benefit from diminishing returns as h1 and m both increase: when h1 = 4, the nodes can already leak h with probability ≈ 0.997 within 4 messages, and the success rate does not improve significantly either by increasing the artificial delay or by exchanging more messages.

4.4 Power Consumption of Square-and-Multiply Algorithms

Modular exponentiation—a modular arithmetic variant of the exponentiation operation—is a fundamental operation in public-key cryptography. Operations are of the form $b^n \bmod m$. While it is cheap to compute directly for small values of n, more efficient algorithms are required when computing modular exponentiations for larger values of n, such as those used as private or public keys in public-key cryptography. *Square-and-multiply* is one such algorithm: starting with $r = 1$, for each bit n_i in n, r is squared modulo m and then multiplied by b modulo m if bit n_i is 1; the result of the modular exponentiation is the final value of r. While this algorithm is able to compute modular exponentiations with lower space and time complexities than the direct method due to the efficiency with which the squaring operation can be performed in hardware, the multiplication operation is still comparatively expensive. Crucially, because this expense only occurs for certain bits of n, naive implementations of the algorithm leak information about n. This has been the basis of power analysis side-channel attacks against cryptosystems that rely on the impracticality of inverting the modular exponentiation by computing the discrete logarithm (e.g., [16]).

In the SCH-IMP modelling of this scenario, we assume a naive implementation of square-and-multiply is being used to compute a ciphertext for a public-key cryptosystem, so the exponent n is in fact a private key e whose value is secret;

we select values of n from a uniform distribution over 0–7. The values of b and m are unimportant in this scenario, so we arbitrarily fix them at $b = 42$ and $m = 13$. The core of the algorithm is implemented in the sq_mult() function, which in turn calls the functions sq_mod() and mult_mod() depending on the values of the individual bits of e. Since modular multiplication is a more expensive operation than modular squaring, the resource function assigns a greater consumption of power to mult_mod() than to sq_mod(). The function outputs the result of the exponentiation.

Even in an implementation free of side channels, the sq_mult() function necessarily leaks information, as our attacker model assumes that the attacker knows the value of m and the range of values for b (because of their knowledge of the system's behaviour) as well as the result of the exponentiation (by observing the outputs). The question is therefore how much *more* likely it is that the system leaks information about n due to the presence of side channels. In the ideal case—i.e., in which there is no time or power cost to invoking either sq_mod() or mult_mod(), and therefore no side channel to exploit—the attacker finds a strategy that successfully recovers e with probability ≈ 0.406. On the other hand, when sq_mod() draws power from an approximately binomial distribution centred on 3 units and mult_mod() from another centred on 5 units—simulating not only the additional power draw of the more complex function, but also the imprecise nature of power consumption and power analysis—the probability of finding an attack strategy that successfully recovers e increases to ≈ 0.964, almost certainly compromising the secrecy of the key.

There are various alternative modular exponentiation algorithms that mitigate this side channel, usually at the expense of efficiency. One example is *square-and-multiply-always*, in which the modular multiplication is performed for every bit of n and the result discarded if it is not needed. While SCH-IMP verifies that this algorithm is free of side channels—a successful attack is found with probability ≈ 0.406, indicating that it is an ideal implementation—it is clearly wasteful. Chevallier-Mames et al. [5] propose a number of more efficient side-channel-resistant alternatives that rely on modular multiplication alongside standard arithmetic operations such as addition and bitwise XOR; they assume that these standard operations are side-channel-equivalent, assumptions that we also make for SCH-IMP's model (i.e., that they consume the same resources when executing regardless of their operands). SCH-IMP is able to verify that the algorithms in Figs. 2(b) and 4(b) of [5] are also equivalent to the ideal square-and-multiply implementation.

4.5 Evaluation

Table 1 summarises the performance of our tool with these case studies. The "Result" columns show the approximate probability p of the attacker's best possible strategy succeeding. The "error" values refer to the absolute difference between the lower and upper bounds returned by the approximate POMDP solution technique of [17] used in our tool. The largest error we encountered was 0.03 (in the unidirectional network examples where h1 $\geq$ 8). Tighter bounds can be obtained if required using a finer grid resolution, at a cost of additional time and memory. The table also shows the size of both the DTMC and POMDP constructed, and the time required for the full process (we ran our experiments on a 2.1 GHz machine with the Java virtual machine allocated 8 GB of memory).

Table 1. The DTMC and POMDP sizes for a selection of examples, along with the result of (and total time taken for) the analysis.

Example	States		Result		Time (min)
	DTMC	POMDP	p	Error	
DC-net	93333	20003	0.527	0.017	63
Uni. network: h1 = 3, m ≤ 15	142547	36009	0.991	0.000	13
Uni. network: h1 = 10, m ≤ 5	43461	12403	0.997	0.003	1
Square-and-multiply: naive	60749	27003	0.964	0.000	16

The framework and tool both rely on the ability to identify the SCH-IMP program's terminating states and the probability of reaching each of them; this requires the exploration of the program's entire state space, which is infeasible in practice for large systems due to the excessive time and space complexities. However, our tool makes a number of aggressive optimisations to reduce the complexity of the DTMC model of a program's execution; most significantly, paths consisting of multiple deterministic transitions are collapsed into a single transition, reducing both the number of states and transitions without affecting the accuracy of the analysis. This explains the much larger analysis time for the DC-net example in Table 1 compared to the other examples, even though the number of states is similar: the DC-net program induces several orders of magnitude more deterministic transitions than the others, and while these transitions must be explored (hence the higher execution time), the tool only stores states and transitions that affect the side-channel analysis. Without such optimisations, the DC-net example would otherwise be infeasible to analyse.

5   Conclusion

We have presented a framework for formally analysing probabilistic systems for the presence of side channels; systems are specified in SCH-IMP, an imperative probabilistic language, and are then systematically analysed through the construction and solution of a POMDP. This identifies possible side-channel attacks in the face of an adversary with knowledge of the system's behaviour, outputs and resource usage, and culminates in an easily-understood metric: the probability that the adversary's most effective attack successfully compromises the system's secret information, plus the strategy it employs to do so. We implemented our approach in a tool and applied it to several case studies. Future work will analyse extended attack models, for example where we also consider the most efficient way in which an attacker can observe the system.

Acknowledgements. This work was supported by the PRINCESS project (contract FA8750-16-C-0045) funded by the DARPA BRASS programme.

A   Appendix SCH-IMP Model for Sect. 4.2

SCH-IMP program:

```
initial transmitter := { 1 → 1/4, 2 → 1/4, 3 → 1/4, 4 → 1/4 };
new nodes := 4;
new last_my_bit := { 0 → 1/2, 1 → 1/2 };
new last_their_bit := 0;
function broadcast(index, is_transmitter, their_bit) {
   new my_bit := 0;
   if (index == nodes - 1) {
     my_bit := last_my_bit
   } else {
     my_bit := { 0 → 1/2, 1 → 1/2 }
   };
   new b := my_bit xor their_bit;
   if (is_transmitter == 1) { b := b xor 1 };
   last_their_bit := my_bit;
   output b;
   return
};
function main() {
   new i := 0;
   while (i < nodes) {
     new is_transmitter := 0;
     if (i + 1 == transmitter) { is_transmitter := 1 };
     if (i == 0) {
       broadcast(i, is_transmitter, last_my_bit)
     } else {
       broadcast(i, is_transmitter, last_their_bit)
     };
     i := i + 1
   };
   return
};
main();
end
```

Resource function:
{
  broadcast → {
    $(\_, 0, \_) \to \{(1,1) \to {}^{1}/_{10}, (2,1) \to {}^{1}/_{5}, (3,1) \to {}^{2}/_{5}, (4,1) \to {}^{1}/_{5}, (5,1) \to {}^{1}/_{10}\},$
    $(\_, 1, \_) \to \{(2,1) \to {}^{1}/_{10}, (3,1) \to {}^{1}/_{5}, (4,1) \to {}^{2}/_{5}, (5,1) \to {}^{1}/_{5}, (6,1) \to {}^{1}/_{10}\}$
  }
}

References

1. The SCH-IMP Tool (2019). https://www.cs.bham.ac.uk/research/projects/schimp/
2. Alvim, M.S., Chatzikokolakis, K., McIver, A., Morgan, C., Palamidessi, C., Smith, G.: Axioms for Information Leakage. In: Proceedings of the 29th IEEE Computer Security Foundations Symposium (CSF 2016), pp. 77–92 (2016)
3. Biondi, F., Legay, A., Nielsen, B.F., Malacaria, P., Wasowski, A.: Information leakage of non-terminating processes. In: Proceedings of the 34th International Conference on Foundation of Software Technology and Theoretical Computer Science (FSTTCS 2014), pp. 517–529 (2014)
4. Chaum, D.: The dining cryptographers problem: unconditional sender and recipient untraceability. J. Cryptol. **1**, 65–75 (1988)
5. Chevallier-Mames, B., Ciet, M., Joye, M.: Low-cost solutions for preventing simple side-channel analysis: side-channel atomicity. IEEE Trans. Comput. **53**(6), 760–768 (2004)
6. Chothia, T., Kawamoto, Y., Novakovic, C., Parker, D.: Probabilistic point-to-point information leakage. In: Proceedings of the IEEE 26th Computer Security Foundations Symposium (CSF 2013), pp. 193–205 (2013)
7. Dekhtyar, M.I., Dekhtyar, A., Subrahmanian, V.S.: Hybrid probabilistic programs: algorithms and complexity. In: Proceedings of the 15th Conference on Uncertainty in Artificial Intelligence (UAI 1999), pp. 160–169 (1999)
8. Genkin, D., Pachmanov, L., Pipman, I., Tromer, E.: Stealing keys from PCs using a radio: cheap electromagnetic attacks on windowed exponentiation. In: Güneysu, T., Handschuh, H. (eds.) CHES 2015. LNCS, vol. 9293, pp. 207–228. Springer, Heidelberg (2015). https://doi.org/10.1007/978-3-662-48324-4_11
9. Genkin, D., Shamir, A., Tromer, E.: RSA key extraction via low-bandwidth acoustic cryptanalysis. In: Garay, J.A., Gennaro, R. (eds.) CRYPTO 2014. LNCS, vol. 8616, pp. 444–461. Springer, Heidelberg (2014). https://doi.org/10.1007/978-3-662-44371-2_25
10. Kang, M.H., Moore, A.P., Moskowitz, I.S.: Design and assurance strategy for the NRL pump. IEEE Comput. **31**(4), 56–64 (1998)
11. Kemeny, J., Snell, J., Knapp, A.: Denumerable Markov Chains, 2nd edn. Springer, New York (1976). https://doi.org/10.1007/978-1-4684-9455-6
12. Köpf, B., Basin, D.: An information-theoretic model for adaptive side-channel attacks. In: Proceedings of the 2007 ACM Conference on Computer and Communications Security (CCS 2007), pp. 286–296 (2007)
13. Kwiatkowska, M., Norman, G., Parker, D.: PRISM 4.0: verification of probabilistic real-time systems. In: Gopalakrishnan, G., Qadeer, S. (eds.) CAV 2011. LNCS, vol. 6806, pp. 585–591. Springer, Heidelberg (2011). https://doi.org/10.1007/978-3-642-22110-1_47
14. Madani, O., Hanks, S., Condon, A.: On the undecidability of probabilistic planning and related stochastic optimization problems. Artif. Intell. **147**(1–2), 5–34 (2003)

15. Marecki, J., Srivatsa, M., Varakantham, P.: A decision theoretic approach to data leakage prevention. In: Proceedings of the 2010 IEEE Second International Conference on Social Computing (PASSAT 2010), pp. 776–784 (2010)
16. Messerges, T.S., Dabbish, E.A., Sloan, R.H.: Power analysis attacks of modular exponentiation in smartcards. In: Koç, Ç.K., Paar, C. (eds.) CHES 1999. LNCS, vol. 1717, pp. 144–157. Springer, Heidelberg (1999). https://doi.org/10.1007/3-540-48059-5_14
17. Norman, G., Parker, D., Zou, X.: Verification and control of partially observable probabilistic systems. R. Time Syst. **53**(3), 354–402 (2017)
18. Pfeffer, A.: IBAL: a probabilistic rational programming language. In: Proceedings of the 17th International Joint Conference on Artificial Intelligence (IJCAI 2001), pp. 733–740 (2001)
19. Ristenpart, T., Tromer, E., Shacham, H., Savage, S.: Hey, you, get off of my cloud: exploring information leakage in third-party compute clouds. In: Proceedings of the 2009 ACM Conference on Computer and Communications Security (CCS 2009), pp. 199–212 (2009)
20. Smith, G.: On the foundations of quantitative information flow. In: de Alfaro, L. (ed.) FoSSaCS 2009. LNCS, vol. 5504, pp. 288–302. Springer, Heidelberg (2009). https://doi.org/10.1007/978-3-642-00596-1_21
21. Tschantz, M.C., Datta, A., Wing, J.M.: Purpose restrictions on information use. In: Crampton, J., Jajodia, S., Mayes, K. (eds.) ESORICS 2013. LNCS, vol. 8134, pp. 610–627. Springer, Heidelberg (2013). https://doi.org/10.1007/978-3-642-40203-6_34
22. Yarom, Y., Falkner, K.: FLUSH+RELOAD: a high resolution, low noise, L3 cache side-channel attack. In: Proceedings of the 23rd USENIX Security Symposium, pp. 719–732 (2014)
23. Zhang, D., Askarov, A., Myers, A.C.: Predictive mitigation of timing channels in interactive systems. In: Proceedings of the 18th ACM Conference on Computer and Communications Security (CCS 2011), pp. 563–574 (2011)

Formal Modelling and Verification

A Formal Model for Checking Cryptographic API Usage in JavaScript

Duncan Mitchell[1]([⊠]) [ID] and Johannes Kinder[2] [ID]

[1] Department of Computer Science, Royal Holloway, University of London,
Egham, UK
`duncan.mitchell.2015@rhul.ac.uk`
[2] Research Institute CODE, Bundeswehr University Munich, Neubiberg, Germany
`johannes.kinder@unibw.de`

Abstract. Modern JavaScript implementations include APIs offering strong cryptography, but it is easy for non-expert developers to misuse them and introduce potentially critical security bugs. In this paper, we formalize a mechanism to rule out such bugs through runtime enforcement of cryptographic API specifications. In particular, we construct a dynamic variant of Security Annotations, which represent security properties of values via type-like information. We formalize Security Annotations within an existing JavaScript semantics and mechanize it to obtain a reference interpreter for JavaScript with embedded Security Annotations. We provide a specification for a fragment of the W3C WebCrypto standard and demonstrate how this specification can reveal security vulnerabilities in JavaScript code with the help of a case study. We define a notion of safety with respect to Security Annotations and extend this to security guarantees for individual programs.

1 Introduction

The standardization of cryptographic APIs in JavaScript through the W3C Web Cryptography API, *WebCrypto* [31], has made strong cryptography available to web developers. In theory, this allows non-experts to implement true end-to-end encryption of confidential data. However, mistakes are easily made when developers use cryptographic APIs. For example, the JavaScript snippet in Listing 1 generates secure keys and then encrypts and signs a message before sending it. Here, the developer made the mistake of appending a signature of the plaintext to the message, allowing an observer to identify retransmissions of the same message. Mistakes like this undermine the security of the overall system, even when the implementation of the cryptographic API itself is correct.

Such mistakes are not exclusive to JavaScript, but in fact common across languages [8,16,20]. Alas, JavaScript exacerbates the problem, due to its dynamic nature and unconventional semantics [22], which thwart traditional analysis techniques and offer plenty of opportunities to violate API specifications. Existing work on JavaScript focuses on the verification of protocol implementations through restriction to small subsets of the language [2,14]. There is currently

© Springer Nature Switzerland AG 2019
K. Sako et al. (Eds.): ESORICS 2019, LNCS 11735, pp. 341–360, 2019.
https://doi.org/10.1007/978-3-030-29959-0_17

little support to help non-expert developers avoid introducing critical security bugs into applications built on full JavaScript.

```
1   const c = window.crypto.subtle;
2   const hmac = async (msg) => {
3     const alg = { name: "HMAC", hash: {name: "SHA-256"} };
4     const key = await c.generateKey(alg, false, ["sign", "verify"]);
5     return await c.sign({ name: "HMAC" }, key, msg);
6   }
7   const enc = async (msg) => {
8     const iv = crypto.getRandomValues(new Uint8Array(12));
9     const alg = { name: "AES-GCM", iv: iv };
10    const key = c.generateKey({name: "AES-GCM",
11      length: 256}, false, ["encrypt", "decrypt"]);
12    return await { iv: iv, ct: c.encrypt(alg, key, msg) };
13  }
14  let msg = new TextEncoder().encode("my message");
15  send({ct: enc(msg), sig: hmac(msg)});
```

Listing 1: Application code: signing before encrypting.

In this work, we introduce a mechanism which rules out misuse of trusted APIs in JavaScript code through runtime enforcement. We extend the concept of Security Annotations [19], type-like tags which represent security properties, such as whether a value is ciphertext or a cryptographic key. Security Annotations are orthogonal to the existing type system and composable to allow for the expression of multiple distinct security properties.

In particular, we make the following contributions:

- We formalize a runtime semantics for Security Annotations in JavaScript by extending an existing formal semantics for a core of JavaScript, S5 [22] (Sect. 4).
- We mechanize Security Annotations, building upon an existing implementation of S5. We extend this to a reference interpreter for JavaScript programs through extending the JavaScript-to-S5 desugaring relation (Sect. 5).
- We provide an annotated fragment of the WebCrypto API which defines safe usage of the API through Security Annotations. Developers can replace the WebCrypto API with this annotated copy, which allows our mechanism to report violations of the otherwise implicit API specifications. We demonstrate how this approach can be used to avoid common cryptographic pitfalls by detecting violations of security properties in a case study (Sect. 5.3).
- We provide safety guarantees for this Security Annotation mechanism, and extend these to describe resulting security guarantees for programs using the annotated WebCrypto fragment (Sect. 6).

$$\text{[S-Refl]} \quad \frac{}{S \prec: S} \qquad \text{[S-Top]} \quad \frac{}{S \prec: \mathsf{Top}}$$

$$\text{[S-Trans]} \quad \frac{S_1 \prec: S_2 \qquad S_2 \prec: S_3}{S_1 \prec: S_2} \qquad \text{[S-Perm]} \quad \frac{S_1 * \ldots * S_n \text{ permutes } R_1 * \ldots * R_n}{S_1 * \ldots * S_n \prec: R_1 * \ldots * R_n}$$

$$\text{[S-Width]} \quad \frac{}{*_{i=1}^{n+k} S_i \prec: *_{i=1}^{n} S_i} \qquad \text{[S-Depth]} \quad \frac{\text{for each } i,\ S_i' \prec: S_i}{*_{i=1}^{n} S_i' \prec: *_{i=1}^{n} S_i}$$

Fig. 1. Hierarchical Security Annotation judgments [19].

2 Background

We begin by introducing necessary background on Security Annotations (Sect. 2.1) and our underlying JavaScript semantics (Sect. 2.2).

2.1 Security Annotations

Security Annotations represent security properties valid on objects or values within a program [19]. For example, the return value of a trusted key generation API is a valid cryptographic key, so could carry an annotation CryptKey. Annotations are composable: if the value has also been generated as a cryptographically secure random value (CSRV), then it can be annotated through composition CSRV * CryptKey, via the commutative operator $*$. Security properties are hierarchical: for example, PrivKey is more specific than CryptKey. Security Annotations therefore have a notion of subannotation judgments, e.g., PrivKey $\prec:$ CryptKey. Combined with the composition operator, this yields a lattice of security annotations. We include the rules defining this lattice in Fig. 1. These judgments follow those given in Mitchell et al. [19]; additional rules governing reflexivity, transitivity and permutations are included for completeness. In these rules, S_i are arbitrary Security Annotations and Top is the least specific Security Annotation, representing a lack of security properties.

Mitchell et al. [19] enforce Security Annotations statically within a small lambda calculus. The expression v **as** S adds S as an annotation to v, representing newly valid security properties. Similarly, v **drop** S discards S from v, using a cut operator to remove an annotation whilst ensuring super-properties remain valid. We cut the annotation S_2 from S_1 via the following definition: $\mathsf{cut}(S_1, S_2)$ is the annotation R with (i) $S_1 \prec: R$ and (ii) $R \not\prec: S_2$ such that whenever R' also satisfies (i) and (ii) in place of R, then $R \prec: R'$ and $R' \not\prec: R$ [19].

2.2 S5: A Semantics for JavaScript

S5 [22] is a lambda calculus-like language which reflects the semantics of the strict mode of EcmaScript 5.1 (ES5). S5 is accompanied by a desugaring function, which takes native JavaScript source programs and translates them to

[E-COMPAT]	$\dfrac{e \implies e'}{\sigma\Theta; E\langle e\rangle \to \sigma\Theta; E\langle e'\rangle}$	[E-ENVSTORE]	$\dfrac{\sigma; e \to^{\sigma} \sigma'; e'}{\sigma\Theta; E\langle e\rangle \to \sigma'\Theta; E\langle e'\rangle}$
[E-CONTROL]	$\dfrac{e \to^{e} e'}{\sigma\Theta; E\langle e\rangle \to \sigma\Theta; E\langle e'\rangle}$	[E-OBJECTS]	$\dfrac{\Theta; e \to^{\Theta} \Theta'; e'}{\sigma\Theta; E\langle e\rangle \to \sigma\Theta'; E\langle e'\rangle}$

Fig. 2. The reduction relations for S5 [22].

S5 programs. S5 itself is described via small-step semantics, incorporating ES5 features such as getters, setters and eval. The language is not a complete reference implementation for the entire standard but is tested against the official ES5 test suite.

Terms in S5 are 3-tuples comprised of an expression, e, a store σ (mapping locations to values) and an object store Θ (mapping references to object literals); the evaluation context is denoted E. The reduction relation $\to$ is split into four parts dependent on which portions of the term are manipulated; their definitions are given in Fig. 2. For ease of reference, S5's syntax is given in Appendix A; full details of S5 are contained in the work of Politz et al. [22].

3 Overview

We present an overview of our approach. First, we discuss how Security Annotations express properties of cryptography APIs (Sect. 3.1). We describe, through example, how such properties are enforced without changes to client code (Sect. 3.2).

3.1 Annotating APIs with Security Annotations

We provide a thin layer of JavaScript code (a *shim*) which adds pre- and post-conditions to WebCrypto APIs. Listing 2 gives an example of such a shim for the encrypt API, which encodes the runtime specification for the API. This shim is included directly into application code via require; line 15 redefines WebCrypto's encrypt. This is the only addition an application developer need make to their codebase; the propagation of these annotations is governed by the mechanisms formalized in Sect. 4. Security Annotations on arguments are checked against the API's preconditions, made explicit through annotation guards. Security Annotations are then attached to return values of functions when these API calls contain specific postconditions.

Lines 1–3 define the annotation lattice for this API; this implicitly contains Top, which represents a lack of security properties. The syntax **SecAnn** $S_1 * \ldots * S_n$ defines orthogonal annotations $S_1, \ldots, S_n$. Lines 2–3 use the syntax **SecAnn** $S_1 * \ldots * S_n$ **Extends** S, to define new annotations $S_1, \ldots, S_n$ with $S_i \prec: S$ for each i.

```
1   SecAnn <CSRV * Message * CryptKey>;
2   SecAnn <PrivKey * PubKey * SymKey> Extends <CryptKey>;
3   SecAnn <Plaintext * Ciphertext> Extends <Message>;
4
5   window.oldCrypto = window.crypto;
6   const encShim = async function(alg :S ["iv", <CSRV>], key, data) {
7     if (/AES/.test(alg.name)) {
8       (function(arg : <SymKey>) {})(key);
9     } else if (/RSA/.test(alg.name)) {
10      (function(arg : <PubKey>) {})(key);
11    } else { throw FailedSecurityCheck; }
12    var res = await window.oldCrypto.subtle.encrypt(alg, key, data);
13    return (cpAnn(data, res) drop <Plaintext>) as <Ciphertext>;
14  }
15  Object.defineProperty(window.crypto.subtle, "encrypt", {value: encShim});
```

Listing 2: An annotated shim of WebCrypto's encrypt API.

Security Annotations are enforced at function boundaries via arg : S, which ensures arg meets the annotation guard S. For example, on line 8, we enforce that if the symmetric encryption algorithm AES is selected, then the key argument to the function is annotated with SymKey. On line 6, :E checks that the specified object property meets its guard. In this case, we check that the initialization vector supplied as part of the alg object is a properly generated random value.

Postconditions are attached as annotations to return values. Encryption is performed by the original API (line 12); annotations representing newly valid security properties are then attached (line 13). First, **cpAnn** attaches all annotations from the data argument to res: security properties of the data are not invalidated as a result of encryption. The advantage of **cpAnn** is that we do not need to know the precise annotations of data. The exception is that if data was annotated with Plaintext (e.g., if it had been previously decrypted), we discard this annotation via the **drop** operator. Finally, we attach Ciphertext to the return value via the **as** operator.

3.2   Transparent Property Enforcement

The application in Listing 1 sends an encrypted, signed message across a network via the send method (line 15). The application developer uses WebCrypto in order to encrypt and sign this message; without our drop-in WebCrypto shim this application will execute and the developer will be unaware of a security flaw. Although individual wrapper functions for signing and encryption are correct, there is a logical error that causes a security bug. In particular, a signature is generated of the plaintext and sent alongside the corresponding ciphertext. This undermines the security of the application: attacks against this signature can reveal details about the underlying plaintext.

At runtime, the application builds the object to send: the ct property is constructed by calling the developer's enc function. This function is correct: the array stored in iv is annotated with CSRV, the postcondition of WebCrypto's

$$
\begin{array}{rl}
a := & \textit{Atomic Annotations} \\
S := & a \mid S * S \mid \mathsf{Top} \\
w := & \mathsf{str} \mid \mathsf{num} \mid \mathbf{true} \mid \mathbf{false} \\
w' := & \mathbf{null} \mid \mathbf{undefined} \mid \mathsf{func}(x : S, \ldots)\{e\} \\
r := & \textit{object references} \\
l := & \textit{locations} \\
v := & w{<}S{>} \mid r \mid w' \\
e := & \ldots \mid e \ \mathbf{as} \ S \mid e \ \mathbf{drop} \ S \mid \mathsf{cpAnn}(e, e) \\
\cdots & \\
\theta' := & \{[av] \ \mathsf{str} : pv, \ldots\} \\
\theta := & \theta'{<}S{>} \\
\sigma := & \cdot \mid \sigma, l : v \\
\Theta := & \cdot \mid \Theta, r : \theta \\
\cdots & \\
E' := & \ldots \mid E' \ \mathbf{as} \ S \mid E' \ \mathbf{drop} \ S \mid \mathsf{cpAnn}(E', e) \mid \mathsf{cpAnn}(v, E')
\end{array}
$$

Fig. 3. Syntax modifications to add Security Annotations to S5.

getRandomValues. The generateKey API, when the algorithm is symmetric (i.e., in the case of both HMAC and AES), returns a valid symmetric key (annotated with SymKey). The call to WebCrypto's encrypt succeeds since each argument satisfies the specification (Listing 2). Next, the developer calls hmac with argument the unencrypted msg. Similarly, the key is correctly generated via the API. However, there is an implicit precondition of sign—data to be signed must be ciphertext to avoid common attacks against the signature revealing information about it. By using our drop-in shim for WebCrypto, this bug is detected: since msg is not annotated with Ciphertext an error is thrown on entry to sign, reporting the violation to the developer.

4   Security Annotations for S5

We formalize Security Annotations within S5 [22], starting with modifications to the syntax (Sect. 4.1). We describe mechanisms for manipulating annotations (Sect. 4.2), runtime enforcement (Sect. 4.3), and their effect on the rest of S5 (Sect. 4.4).

4.1   Syntax

The additions and modifications to the syntax of S5 (given in Appendix A) to incorporate Security Annotations are contained in Fig. 3. We introduce atomic annotations a, which represent a single security property, and general annotations S, which are either Top, the least specific annotation, an atomic annotation, or the composition of two annotations, given by $*$. Annotations are only attached to certain prevalues w. Prevalues which should not be annotated are given by w', values are then either references $r,w <S>$ or w', where $w <S>$ is syntactic sugar for the pair of an annotatable value w along with its corresponding Security Annotation S. An additional modification to the syntax reflects the addition of annotations to objects: we consider pre-objects, θ', which form objects when annotated with a Security Annotation S. We annotate objects directly as opposed to their references; properties within objects are annotated in the same manner as values. When an object is modified, previously valid security properties on the object are no longer guaranteed: modifying an object field should alter the annotations associated to the field, and also the annotations of the overall object.

Additional expressions, e, based on manipulating security annotations, cover the **as**, **drop** and **cpAnn** constructs. We add evaluation contexts, E', to cover these cases, where these are built in the same manner as in S5 (see Appendix A). Finally, enforcement of Security Annotations is added to functions via the form func$(x : S, \ldots)$; this does not require modification of the evaluation contexts.

4.2 Coercing Security Annotations

The evaluation judgments for coercion of annotations on values and objects are given in Fig. 4, distinguished by case analysis on values. The expression v **as** S upcasts v to a more specific annotation, achieved by composing the previously valid annotation with S. Dependent on whether we treat $w <S>$ (in [E-AsW]), or a reference r ([E-AsR]), we make use of distinct reduction relations (Fig. 2). In the former case, [E-COMPAT] is used to govern the evaluation. In the latter, [E-OBJECTS] is used to modify the object's annotation in the object store. Finally, we throw an error whenever a function, **null** or **undefined** is passed to one of these expressions treating coercion of annotations (e.g., [E-AsW']). The case analysis for **drop** are similar; v **drop** S downcasts v to a less specific annotation. This is accomplished via the cut operator (Sect. 2.1) to prune the S from the annotation of v. Listing 2 illustrates the use of **cpAnn** to ensure properties of data are still valid after encryption by copying annotations from one value (or object) to another. As with **as**, the addition of newly valid annotations does not render previous annotations invalid, so composition unifies them; the evaluation rules are therefore similar in structure.

4.3 Checking Security Annotations

Figure 5 codifies the enforcement of Security Annotations at function boundaries. [E-APP] governs the case when arguments meet their annotation-guards and the function is evaluated. This rule inspects the object store (to look up object annotations when arguments are references) and modifies the variable store (to bind arguments to the corresponding variables); we therefore use the standard reduction relation rather than the split components (Fig. 2). To

$$[\text{E-AsW}] \quad \frac{v = w\text{<}S\text{>}}{v \text{ as } S' \implies w\text{<}S * S'\text{>}}$$

$$[\text{E-AsR}] \quad \frac{v = r \quad \Theta(r) = \theta'\text{<}R\text{>} \quad \Theta' = \Theta[^r/\theta'\text{<}R * S'\text{>}]}{\Theta; v \text{ as } S' \to^\Theta \Theta'; v}$$

$$[\text{E-AsW'}] \quad \frac{v = w'}{v \text{ as } S \implies \textbf{throw NotAnnotatable}}$$

$$[\text{E-DropW}] \quad \frac{v = w\text{<}S\text{>}}{v \text{ drop } S' \implies w\text{<cut}(S, S')\text{>}}$$

$$[\text{E-DropR}] \quad \frac{v = r \quad \Theta(r) = \theta'\text{<}R\text{>} \quad \Theta' = \Theta[^r/\theta'\text{<cut}(R, S')\text{>}]}{\Theta; v \text{ drop } S' \to^\Theta \Theta'; v}$$

$$[\text{E-DropW'}] \quad \frac{v = w'}{v \text{ drop } S \implies \textbf{throw NotAnnotatable}}$$

$$[\text{E-CpWW}] \quad \frac{v_1 = w_1\text{<}S_1\text{>} \quad v_2 = w_2\text{<}S_2\text{>}}{\textbf{cpAnn}(v_1, v_2) \implies v_2\text{<}S_1 * S_2\text{>}}$$

$$[\text{E-CpWR}] \quad \frac{v_1 = w\text{<}S_1\text{>} \quad v_2 = r \quad \Theta(r) = \theta'\text{<}S_2\text{>} \quad \Theta' = \Theta[^r/\theta'\text{<}S_1 * S_2\text{>}]}{\Theta; \textbf{cpAnn}(v_1, v_2) \to^\Theta \Theta'; v_2}$$

$$[\text{E-CpRW}] \quad \frac{v_1 = r \quad \Theta(r) = \theta'\text{<}S_1\text{>} \quad v_2 = w\text{<}S_2\text{>}}{\Theta; \textbf{cpAnn}(v_1, v_2) \to^\Theta \Theta; w\text{<}S_1 * S_2\text{>}}$$

$$[\text{E-CpRR}] \quad \frac{v_1 = r_1 \quad v_2 = r_2 \quad \Theta(r_1) = \theta_1'\text{<}S_1\text{>} \quad \Theta(r_2) = \theta_2'\text{<}S_2\text{>}}{\Theta' = \Theta[^{r_2}/\theta_2'\text{<}S_1 * S_2\text{>}]}{\Theta; \textbf{cpAnn}(v_1, v_2) \to^\Theta \Theta'; v_2}$$

$$[\text{E-CpW'V}] \quad \frac{v_1 = w'}{\textbf{cpAnn}(v_1, v_2) \implies \textbf{throw NotAnnotatable}}$$

$$[\text{E-CpVW'}] \quad \frac{v_2 = w'}{\textbf{cpAnn}(v_1, v_2) \implies \textbf{throw NotAnnotatable}}$$

Fig. 4. Judgments for coercing annotations: **as**, **drop** and **cpAnn**.

reflect the hierarchy of the annotation lattice, this rule bakes in subsumption, e.g., enforcement of CryptKey would accept the more specific PrivKey. A common JavaScript paradigm is for non-annotatable values, e.g., functions, to be passed as arguments; we insist the guard for such arguments is Top, i.e., no security precondition. For any annotatable values, $w \text{ <}S\text{>}$, we insist S satisfies the guard S'. For references r, we look up the corresponding object and insist the annotation meets the guard. Direct checking of object properties and the **this** argument is achieved via source-to-source rewritings, described in Sect. 5.2. [E-APPFAIL] describes what happens when annotation-checking fails, i.e., whenever an argument carries a less precise annotation than its guard. FailedSecurityCheck is thrown to report the potential security vulnerability to the user, rather than simply halting evaluation.

$$[\text{E-App}] \quad \begin{array}{c} \forall i \in \{1, \ldots, n\} \ : \ \big(\neg(v_i = w_i') \vee (S_i' = \textsf{Top})\big) \\ \forall i \in \{1, \ldots, n\} \ : \ \big(\neg(v_i = w_i\langle S_i\rangle) \vee (S_i \prec: S_i')\big) \\ \forall i \in \{1, \ldots, n\} \ : \ \big(\neg(v_i = r_i \wedge \Theta(r) = \theta\langle S_i\rangle) \vee (S_i \prec: S_i')\big) \\ \sigma' = \sigma, l_1 : v_1, \ldots, l_n : v_n \text{ where } l_1 \ldots l_n \text{ fresh in } \sigma, e, v_1, \ldots, v_n \\ \hline \Theta\sigma; \textsf{func}(x_1 : S_1', \ldots, x_n : S_n')\{e\}(v_1, \ldots, v_n) \rightarrow \Theta\sigma'; e[^{x_1}/_{l_1}, \ldots, ^{x_n}/_{l_n}] \end{array}$$

$$[\text{E-AppFail}] \quad \begin{array}{c} \exists i \in \{1, \ldots, n\} \ : \ (v_i = w_i' \wedge S_i' \neq \textsf{Top}) \\ \vee \exists i \in \{1, \ldots, n\} \ : \ (v_i = w_i\langle S_i\rangle \wedge S_i \not\prec: S_i') \\ \vee \ \exists i \in \{1, \ldots, n\} \ : \ (v_i = r_i \wedge \Theta(r) = \theta\langle S_i\rangle \wedge S_i \not\prec: S_i') \\ \hline \Theta; \textsf{func}(x_1 : S_1', \ldots, x_n : S_n')\{e\}(v_1, \ldots, v_n) \\ \implies \Theta; \textbf{throw } \textsf{FailedSecurityCheck} \end{array}$$

Fig. 5. Function application with Security Annotation enforcement.

4.4 Completing S5 with Security Annotations

The rest of S5 remains largely unchanged. After object fields are manipulated, there is no guarantee the object annotation remains valid. For example, modifying the keyUsages field of a key object returned from the generateKey API may undermine the security of any future operation involving the key. Any previously valid security properties on the object can no longer be guaranteed; Top is therefore associated as the object's annotation. Figure 6 includes judgments for field manipulation, including adding fields which do not exist and writable 'shadow' fields. These semantics are transparent to annotations to allow prevalues to govern control flow, e.g., the configurable property must be **true** in [E-DeleteField].

5 Security Annotations for JavaScript

We describe the mechanization of this model (Sect. 5.1) and a desugaring relation which allows the execution of JavaScript with Security Annotations[1]. We discuss the annotation checking of object internals (Sect. 5.2) and demonstrate its operation on a case study (Sect. 5.3).

5.1 Implementing Security Annotations in S5

We mechanize Security Annotations on top of the existing reference implementation of S5 [22]. Alongside object and variable stores, we maintain a third *annotation store*, the lattice of valid annotations in the program. Security Annotations are declared via the **SecAnn** and **Extends** expressions described in Sect. 3.1. These expressions modify the annotation store to reflect additions to the lattice and evaluate to **undefined**. Using an annotation prior to declaration results in

---

[1] An accompanying implementation is available at: https://github.com/duncan-mitchell/SecAnnRefInterpreter.

[E-ADDFIELD] $\dfrac{\begin{array}{c} \Theta(r) = \{[\text{extensible} : \textbf{true}\!<\!S_1\!>\ldots]\,\text{str}'\!<\!S_2\!> : av,\ldots\} \qquad \Theta; r[\text{str}\!<\!S_3\!>] \Downarrow [] \\ pv = [\text{config} : \textbf{true}\!<\!\text{Top}\!>, \text{enum} : \textbf{true}\!<\!\text{Top}\!>, \text{value} : v, \text{writable} : \textbf{true}\!<\!\text{Top}\!>] \\ \Theta' = \Theta[^r/\{[\text{extensible} : \textbf{true}\!<\!S_1\!>\ldots]\,\text{str}\!<\!S\!> : pv,\, \text{str}'\!<\!S_2\!> : av,\ldots\}] \end{array}}{\Theta; r[\text{str}\!<\!S\!> = v]^{v_a} \to^{\Theta} \Theta'; v}$

[E-SETFIELD] $\dfrac{\begin{array}{c} \Theta(r) = \{pv \ldots \text{str}\!<\!S_1\!> : [\ldots \text{value} : v', \text{writable} : \textbf{true}\!<\!S_2\!>], \ldots\}\!<\!S\!> \\ \Theta' = \Theta[^r/\{pv \ldots \text{str}\!<\!S_1\!> : [\ldots \text{value} : v, \text{writable} : \textbf{true}\!<\!S_2\!>], \ldots\}\!<\!\text{Top}\!>] \end{array}}{\Theta; r[\text{str}\!<\!S_3\!> = v]^{v_a} \to^{\Theta} \Theta'; v}$

[E-DELETENOTFOUND] $\dfrac{\Theta(r) = \{av\,\text{str}_1\!<\!S'\!> : pv_1, \ldots\} \qquad \text{str} \notin \{\text{str}_1, \ldots\}}{\Theta; r[\textbf{delete}\ \text{str}\!<\!S\!>] \to^{\Theta} \Theta; \textbf{false}\!<\!\text{Top}\!>}$

[E-DELETEFOUND] $\dfrac{\begin{array}{c} \Theta(r) = \{av\,\text{str}_1\!<\!S_1\!> : pv_1, \ldots, \text{str}\!<\!S'\!> : [\ldots \text{configurable} : \textbf{true}\!<\!S'\!>, \ldots], \text{str}_n\!<\!S_n\!> : pv_n, \ldots\}\!<\!S\!> \\ \Theta' = \Theta[^r/\{av\,\text{str}_1\!<\!S_1\!> : pv_1, \ldots \text{str}_n\!<\!S_n\!> : pv_n, \ldots\}\!<\!\text{Top}\!>] \end{array}}{\Theta; r[\text{delete}\ \text{str}\!<\!S''\!>] \to^{\Theta} \Theta'; \textbf{true}\!<\!\text{Top}\!>}$

[E-SHADOWFIELD] $\dfrac{\begin{array}{c} \Theta(r) = \{[\text{extensible} : \textbf{true}\!<\!S_1\!>\ldots]\,\text{str}'\!<\!S_2\!> : av,\ldots\} \qquad \Theta; r[\text{str}\!<\!S_3\!>] \Downarrow [\ldots \text{writable} : \textbf{true}\!<\!S_4\!>\ldots] \\ pv = [\text{config} : \textbf{true}\!<\!\text{Top}\!>, \text{enum} : \textbf{true}\!<\!\text{Top}\!>, \text{value} : v, \text{writable} : \textbf{true}\!<\!\text{Top}\!>] \\ \Theta' = \Theta[^r/\{[\text{extensible} : \textbf{true}\!<\!S_1\!>\ldots]\,\text{str}\!<\!S\!> : pv,\, \text{str}'\!<\!S_2\!> : av,\ldots\}] \end{array}}{\Theta; r[\text{str}\!<\!S\!> = v]^{v_a} \to^{\Theta} \Theta'; v}$

Fig. 6. Judgments for setting, deleting and adding fields.

an exception. The lattice is also inspected in function application (Fig. 5) to compare annotations with respect to subsumption. Section 4 describes functions in which each argument is checked against some annotation guard. In implementation, we retain enforcement-free functions and do not insist every argument has an annotation-guard. This allows reuse of existing ES5 environment implementations described in the work of Politz et al. [22].

5.2 A Reference Interpreter for Security Annotations in JavaScript

We execute JavaScript code with Security Annotations by extending the JavaScript-to-S5 desugaring relation. We extend the syntax of JavaScript by adding Security Annotations and function guards, as well as the expressions **as**, **drop**, **cpAnn**, **SecAnn** and **SecAnn Extends**. Our desugaring rewrites these expressions into their S5 equivalents, which are then executed in the reference interpreter.

Checking Object Properties. Listing 2 demonstrates the need for checking properties of objects. We achieve this via source-to-source rewritings at the JavaScript level; these are simplified by an assert function

```
let assert = function(arg, ann){ (function(x : ann) {})(arg); }.
```

There are three possible cases; first, obj :S [prop, S] checks obj[prop] meets S. We check the specified property exists, and insist it satisfies the guard S:

```
if (typeof obj == 'object' &&
    Object.getOwnPropertyNames(obj).indexOf(prop) >= 0) {
    assert(x[prop], S);
} else { throw 'FailedSecurityCheck'; }
```

Second, obj :A S checks all properties meet the guard S; to achieve this we iterate over all object properties:

```
if (typeof obj == 'object') {
    let props = Object.getOwnPropertyNames(obj);
    for (let iter = 0; iter < props.length; iter++) {
        assert(obj[props[iter]], S);
    }
} else { throw 'FailedSecurityCheck'; }.
```

Finally, obj :E [N, S] checks at least N properties satisfy S. As before, we iterate over object properties, counting the number that meet the guard:

```
if (typeof obj == 'object') {
    let props = Object.getOwnPropertyNames(x), successes = 0;
    for (let iter = 0; iter < props.length; iter++) {
        try { assert(x[props[iter]], S); successes++; } catch (e) { };
    }
    if (successes < N) { throw 'FailedSecurityCheck'; }
} else { throw 'FailedSecurityCheck'; }
```

Checking **this**. Functions have an implicit **this** argument, the context object in which the current code is executing. In the manner of checking object properties, we check this via the syntax **function(:** S, ...) { body(); } which is rewritten to **function(**...){ assert(**this**, S); body(); }..

5.3   Using the Reference Interpreter

We provide a reference implementation of Security Annotations for the correctness of future implementations in native JavaScript. Our interpreter translates a subset of Node.js programs into S5 programs; we demonstrate the scope of this reference interpreter by describing the modifications to programs necessary for execution. We outline how we envisage Security Annotations being used by developers to detect security vulnerabilities through case study within our interpreter.

A Client-Server Application. We implement a small chat application which takes as argument a confidential message a client wishes to transmit to a server[2]. The server and client negotiate a key exchange, and an encrypted copy of this message is sent to the server, which decrypts it. We omit authentication from this case study for simplicity of presentation. WebCrypto is not implemented in Node.js, so we construct a synchronous mock using the Node.js crypto module.

---

[2] The source code for this application is available alongside the reference interpreter.

Execution in S5. Library mocks are necessary to execute the case study in S5. S5 does not support asynchronous code, so we construct a synchronous mock of the networking API, net. An extension to asynchronous code is possible in principle based on an existing formalization of JavaScript promises [18]. Second, cryptographic operations are mocked as stub functions returning objects of the same underlying structure. Finally, S5 programs do not take input, so we declare process.argv to simulate this.

Completing the WebCrypto Shim. Listing 3 contains an annotated shim of a fragment of WebCrypto for use by developers. These method specifications follow the same structure as Listing 2. getRandomValues fills the supplied array with random values, so this array is annotated with CSRV. Despite the lack of a return, the annotation on this array persists because the annotation is attached directly to the object. generateKey constructs a key (or key pair) object for the supplied algorithm; postconditions of this method are differentiated by case analysis. deriveKey is used to compute a shared secret key from the other party's public key and the private key. The contract for decrypt is similar to encrypt; we do not enforce Ciphertext against data—or that the IV is randomly generated—to allow decryption of messages received across a network. importKey allows public keys received across a network to be formatted for use with other WebCrypto APIs. This API allows the upcasting of arbitrary data; however, without importKey, it would be impossible to use WebCrypto across a network.

A Security Property Violation. When constructing the IV, the developer ensures that it can be encoded directly as an ASCII string. Despite correctly generating an IV of the same size as the cipher block size (calling getRandomValues on a Uint8Array of size 16), they reduce entropy of the IV by zeroing the top bit of each element of this array. This causes the IV to contain only 112 bits of entropy, less than the block size: a potential security flaw which does not visibly affect runtime behavior. To detect such bugs, a developer includes our WebCrypto shim. The IV is initially generated by a WebCrypto API call and annotated with CSRV; however, the manipulation of the array drops the annotation (per [E-SetField] in Fig. 6). Since the iv property of the alg object is not annotated with CSRV, the call to encrypt fails, FailedSecurityCheck is thrown and this security flaw is reported to the developer. When the loss of entropy is removed, no error is thrown; the security pre- and postconditions enforced in the shim are respected.

6   Properties of Security Annotations

We discuss safety guarantees for S5 programs with Security Annotations (Sect. 6.1) and extend this to security guarantees (Sect. 6.2). Finally, we apply this to prove security of our case study (Sect. 6.3). Throughout this section, we assume all programs discussed terminate.

6.1   Safety Guarantees

We adopt a relatively modest notion of safety: first, a program is safe if it does not evaluate to an exception as a result of a function argument failing to meet the annotation guard. Second, the program should not coerce the annotation of a non-annotatable value, e.g., **null as** <CSRV>. This gives us the definition:

```
1   SecAnn <CSRV * Message * CryptKey>;
2   SecAnn <PrivKey * PubKey * SymKey> Extends <CryptKey>;
3   SecAnn <Plaintext * Ciphertext> Extends <Message>;
4
5   window.oldCrypto = window.crypto;
6   let wc = window.oldCrypto.subtle;
7   const grvShim = function(arr) {
8     window.oldCrypto.getRandomValues(arr);
9     arr as <CSRV>;
10  };
11  const gkShim = async function(alg, extractable, keyUsages) {
12    let key = await wc.generateKey(alg, extractable, keyUsages);
13    if (/RSA|ECD/.test(alg.name)) {
14      key.privateKey = key.privateKey as <PrivKey * CSRV>;
15      key.publicKey = key.publicKey as <PubKey * CSRV>;
16    } else if(/AES|HMAC/.test(alg.name)) {
17      key as <SymKey * CSRV>;
18    } else { throw FailedSecurityCheck; }
19    return key;
20  };
21  const dkShim = async function(alg :S ["public", <PubKey>],
22    masterKey : <PrivKey>, derivedKeyAlg, extractable, keyUsages) {
23    let key = await wc.deriveKey(alg, masterKey, derivedKeyAlg, extractable,
24      keyUsages);
25    return (key as <SymKey>);
26  };
27  const decShim = async function(alg, key, data) {
28    if (/AES/.test(alg.name)) {
29      (function(arg : <SymKey>) {})(key);
30    } else if (/RSA/.test(alg.name)) {
31      (function(arg : <PrivKey>) {})(key);
32    } else { throw FailedSecurityCheck; }
33    var res = await wc.decrypt(alg, key, data);
34    return ((cpAnn(data, res) drop <Ciphertext>) as <Plaintext>);
35  };
36  const ikShim = async function(type, key, alg, extractable, keyUsages) {
37    let pubKey = await wc.importKey(type, key, alg, extractable, keyUsages);
38    return (pubKey as <PubKey>);
39  };
40  const wcShim = { generateKey: {value: gkShim}, deriveKey: {value: dkShim},
41    encrypt: {value: encShim}, decrypt: {value: decShim},
42    importKey: {value: ikShim}};
43  defineProperty(window.crypto, "subtle", { value: wcShim});
44  defineProperty(window.crypto, "getRandomValues", {value: grvShim});
```

Listing 3: An annotated shim for a fragment of the WebCrypto API.

Definition 1 (Annotation Safety). An S5 program is *safe with respect to Security Annotations* (or, *annotation safe*) if the execution of the program does not result in either a FailedSecurityCheck or NotAnnotatable exception.

Although programs in S5 are deterministic, programs in JavaScript (or any meaningful language) are not: their execution depends on the DOM or user input. Suppose $\mathcal{P}$ is a program expecting input, we extend Definition 1 as follows:

Definition 2 (Annotation Safety for Programs with Input). $\mathcal{P}$, is *annotation safe* if no execution of the program results in either a FailedSecurityCheck or NotAnnotatable exception.

Consider a family of S5 programs, Π, which are deterministic and simulate input by declaring a global variable process.argv assigned to an object containing N fields. For each field, f_i suppose there is an accompanying value v_i. For each v_i, we fix a base type and range over all possible prevalues (and **undefined**, which simulates a lack of input). If v_i is a reference to an object, we range over all possible objects θ. The resulting family of programs represents the space of possible executions for $\mathcal{P}$. We can therefore reformulate Definition 2:

Lemma 3. *Let $\mathcal{P}$ be an S5 program with input and Π the family of deterministic programs p describing all possible inputs for $\mathcal{P}$. Then $\mathcal{P}$ is annotation safe if and only if every program $p \in \Pi$ is annotation safe.*

Proof. By construction, each execution of $\mathcal{P}$ is considered as a separate deterministic program P so the result is immediate. □

Since this family Π is very large, we formalize safety in terms of a subset of these programs. Let π be the set of all $p \in \Pi$ following exactly the same sequence of evaluation judgments. This set of S5 programs corresponds to a single control-flow path of $\mathcal{P}$: so if any p is annotation safe, so are all programs in π. Since the union of all (clearly disjoint) possible paths π is equal to the overall family of programs Π, we can obtain a simpler notion of safety for $\mathcal{P}$:

Theorem 4. *Let Π be the family of deterministic programs describing all possible inputs for $\mathcal{P}$. Consider all disjoint subsets $\pi \subseteq \Pi$ representing single control flow paths of $\mathcal{P}$, and for each, choose a single $p \in \pi$. Then $\mathcal{P}$ is annotation safe if and only if each p is annotation safe.*

Proof. Suppose first that $\mathcal{P}$ is annotation safe. Then by Lemma 3, we know every $P \in \Pi$ is annotation safe. Since each $\pi \subseteq \Pi$, each p must be annotation safe as required. For the other direction, suppose each p is annotation safe. Pick one such p, and the subset of Π to which it belongs, π. Let p' be some other program in π, and suppose that p' is not annotation safe. Then the execution of p' results in either a FailedSecurityCheck or NotAnnotable exception. This means that the final evaluation judgment applied in the evaluation of p' is either [E-APPFAIL], [E-ASW'], [E-DROPW'], [E-CPW'V] or [E-CPVW']. Since p and p' both belong to π, they follow the same sequence of evaluation judgments. But then p is not annotation safe, which is a contradiction. Thus each p in π is annotation safe, and extending this across all disjoint subsets π of Π, each program in Π must be annotation safe. Applying Lemma 3 again, we are done.   □

This result says that if any set π is not safe, then some control-flow path in $\mathcal{P}$ violates the Security Annotation specification of the program, indicating a possible security vulnerability. This description of safety requires us to find these subsets π to obtain a guarantee. In practice, this is equivalent to enumerating all control flow paths of a program over all types of input values and objects, which makes our mechanism ideally suited for combination with feedback-directed fuzzing or dynamic symbolic execution [17].

6.2   Security Guarantees

Let L be a library and L' an annotated shim of this library; any security guarantees are conditional on the correctness of L, e.g., that WebCrypto itself is a correct implementation of cryptographic primitives. Let P be an S5 program which calls L, and suppose the developer of P in-lines this annotated shim in a program $P' = L'; P$. We assume that P does not contain any expressions which manipulate Security Annotations. We can make the following (overapproximate) claim, which states that the whenever P' is annotation safe, it respects the security properties enforced by the Security Annotation specifications of the methods in L'.

Lemma 5. *Suppose P' is annotation safe. Then the Security Annotation specifications described in L' are respected.*

Proof. Suppose a Security Annotation specification in L' is not respected. Then some function precondition fails, so the judgment [E-APPFAIL] is evaluated, contradicting our assumption that P' is annotation safe. Since P does not involve the manipulation of Security Annotations, any annotations must be the postconditions of an API call in L'; hence these specifications are respected.   □

Analogously to Sect. 6.1, we extend this result to programs with input:

Theorem 6. *Let $\mathcal{P}$ be a program with input and suppose $\mathcal{P}' = L'; \mathcal{P}$ is annotation safe. Then the Security Annotation specifications described in L' are respected.*

Proof. This is immediate from the combination of Theorem 4 and Lemma 5.   □

6.3   Security Guarantees in Practice

We use Theorem 6 to describe concrete security guarantees for the case study outlined in Sect. 5.3, which are conditional on the correctness of WebCrypto. Recall that after fixing the security vulnerability involving the ASCII-encoded IV, when a message supplied as argument, the program executes without error;

if no message is provided the application simply reports this to the user and exits. Both control-flow paths of this program are annotation safe. Referring to the specifications described in our WebCrypto shim (Listing 3), there are two caveats to our claim; the first assumes the developer does not leak keying material and the second relates to the omission of authentication from the case study.

Theorem 7. *Suppose that: (i) neither the symmetric key nor either party's secret keys are leaked across the network, and (ii), an attacker impersonates neither party. Then encrypted messages sent by the client can only be read by the server.*

Proof. The application does not manipulate annotations; when executed with a non-annotated copy of the library the program is annotation safe. As described above, both control-flow paths of the program are annotation safe with our annotated library in-lined, we can directly apply Theorem 6. It remains to demonstrate the specification enforced by the annotation library. The encryption—via AES-CBC with a 128-bit key—is secure only when the symmetric key has been securely derived, and the IV is a block-sized CSRV (Listing 2). Our Web-Crypto specification enforces the CSRV portion of the contract directly: calling getRandomValues annotates the IV with CSRV (lines 7–9 of Listing 3), and this array is not subsequently modified, the annotation check on entry to encrypt passes.

Second, the symmetric key used for AES must be shared between the two parties secretly. The key is derived through an ECDH key exchange; both the server and client use generateKey (lines 11–20 of Listing 3) to compute a key pair. Public keys are exchanged, and validated it through importKey (lines 36–39). The client supplies their private key and the server's public key to deriveKey (lines 21–26). Neither key has been tampered with, so the client's key is annotated with PrivKey and the server's with PubKey. This satisfies the guard of deriveKey, and so the key for AES is computed, and annotated SymKey. The provenance of the secret key as derived from safe API calls can be confirmed, so the guard against the key in encrypt succeeds (line 10 of Listing 2). Therefore, only someone in possession of the private key corresponding to the server's public key can read the message supplied as data to this API.   □

7 Related Work

Checking Cryptographic API Usage. Mitchell et al. [19] introduce Security Annotations within a lambda calculus (discussed in Sect. 2.1); this paper extends this work to JavaScript. Recent work on cryptographic API use in Android applications shows that the majority of cryptographic bugs are due to misuse of APIs [16]; Egele et al. [8] show that such errors are common. Nadi et al. [20] survey usage of Java cryptographic APIs, and argue that the APIs are too low-level and require implicit understanding of the underlying cryptographic protocols. Krüger et al. [15] present *CrySL*, a domain specific language for the specification of correct usage of cryptographic APIs, focusing on the Java

Cryptography Architecture. Our approach of encoding pre- and postconditions via security annotations on values and objects embraces the dynamicity of JavaScript which is notoriously difficult to statically analyze.

JavaScript Analysis. While our approach is purely dynamic, various dialects allow for the static checking of JavaScript code [6,7,23,30]. The effective use of such static typing approaches would require modification of APIs and semantics, e.g., prohibiting byte array indexing of Key types. Design-by-contract systems for JavaScript [13] enforce program properties directly expressible within the language. Our work focuses on security properties which cannot be directly expressed in this manner. Previous work on cryptographic testing for JavaScript focuses on implementations of the underlying cryptographic protocols. This work runs parallel to our own: we assume the correctness of these implementations and check existing usage of these APIs. Taly et al. [29] describe an automatic analysis to ensure security-critical APIs correctly protect resources from untrusted code. Domain-specific languages [2,3,14] have been proposed to enable verification of bespoke implementations by cryptographic experts. Existing programs are not amenable to this approach, since these languages are small subsets of JavaScript without many of the common idioms and advantages of the language.

Type-Based Approaches for Security. Type systems for F#, such as F7 [1,4,5] and F* [28], allow for the description of security properties of terms via dependent types which are checked statically. Static security type systems [24] to enforce secure information flow offer strong guarantees but have proved impractical in the JavaScript setting. Work on JavaScript monitors for information flow [10,26] provide mechanisms for dynamic enforcement of this in JavaScript; work on information flow monitoring in the presence of libraries [11] extends the applicability of monitor-based approaches. We follow a similar dynamic tag-based approach as such approaches [10], however we adopt a fine-grained system allowing for declassification coupled with precondition checking through annotation guards on functions. COWL [12,27] is an information flow control system for web browsers preventing third-party library code from leaking sensitive information, achieved via the labeling of browser contexts.

Formalizing JavaScript. Various formalizations of JavaScript exist [9,21,22,25]. λ_{JS} [9] and its successor S5 [22] provide a small language modeling the key features of JavaScript and have been extended to provide models for static and dynamic analyses. S5 remains close to the minimal lambda calculus described by Mitchell et al. [19], which allowed for a natural translation of Security Annotations.

8   Conclusions and Future Work

In this paper we described a formal model for Security Annotations in JavaScript, a mechanism to help non-expert developers avoid introducing security-critical bugs. We introduced a runtime semantics for Security Annotations in a core of JavaScript and presented a reference implementation of this system. We specified a partial fragment of the WebCrypto API in terms of Security Annotations, and demonstrated how to use it to detect a potential security vulnerability. Finally, we described the security guarantees offered by Security Annotations.

In future work, we plan to further develop Security Annotations as a runtime analysis for JavaScript by implementing them as an extension for the full language via source code instrumentation. The semantics described in this paper and accompanying implementation serve as a reference to guide the correctness of Security Annotations in full JavaScript.

A   Syntax of S5

For convenience we provide the complete syntax of S5 from the work of Politz et al. [22] in Fig. 7.

$$
\begin{aligned}
r :=&\qquad\qquad\qquad\qquad\qquad\qquad\qquad\qquad\qquad\qquad\qquad\qquad\qquad\text{object references}\\
l :=&\qquad\qquad\qquad\qquad\qquad\qquad\qquad\qquad\qquad\qquad\qquad\qquad\qquad\qquad\qquad\text{locations}\\
v :=&\quad \texttt{null}\mid\texttt{undefined}\mid\texttt{str}\mid\texttt{num}\mid\texttt{true}\mid\texttt{false}\mid r\mid\texttt{func}(x,...)\{e\}\\
e :=&\quad v\mid x\mid l\mid x:=e\mid\texttt{op1}(e)\mid\texttt{op2}(e,e)\mid e(e,...)\mid e;e\mid\texttt{let}\,(x=e)\,e\mid\texttt{if}\,(e)\,\{e\}\,\texttt{else}\,\{e\}\\
\mid&\quad \texttt{label}:x\,e\mid\texttt{break}\,x\,e\mid\texttt{err}\,v\mid\texttt{try}\,e\,\texttt{catch}\,x\,e\mid\texttt{try}\,e\,\texttt{finally}\,e\mid\texttt{throw}\,e\mid\texttt{eval}(e,e)\\
\mid&\quad \{ae\,\texttt{str}:pe,...\}\quad\textit{object literals}\\
\mid&\quad e[\langle a\rangle]\mid e[\langle a\rangle=e]\quad\textit{object attributes}\\
\mid&\quad e[e\langle a\rangle]\mid e[e\langle a\rangle=e]\quad\textit{property attributes}\\
\mid&\quad \texttt{props}(e)\quad\textit{property names}\\
\mid&\quad e[e]^e\mid e[e=e]^e\mid e[\texttt{delete}\,e]\quad\textit{properties}\\
o :=&\quad \texttt{class}\mid\texttt{extensible}\mid\texttt{proto}\mid\texttt{code}\mid\texttt{primval}\\
a :=&\quad \texttt{writable}\mid\texttt{config}\mid\texttt{value}\mid\texttt{enum}\\
ae :=&\quad [\texttt{class}:e,\texttt{extensible}:e,\texttt{proto}:e,\texttt{code}:e,\texttt{primval}:e]\\
av :=&\quad [\texttt{class}:v,\texttt{extensible}:v,\texttt{proto}:v,\texttt{code}:v,\texttt{primval}:v]\\
pe :=&\quad [\texttt{config}:e,\texttt{enum}:e,\texttt{value}:e,\texttt{writable}:e]\mid[\texttt{config}:e,\texttt{enum}:e,\texttt{get}:e,\texttt{set}:e]\\
pv :=&\quad [\texttt{config}:v,\texttt{enum}:v,\texttt{value}:v,\texttt{writable}:v]\mid[\texttt{config}:v,\texttt{enum}:v,\texttt{get}:v,\texttt{set}:v]\\
p :=&\quad pv\mid[]\\
\texttt{op1} :=&\quad \texttt{string->num}\mid\texttt{log}\mid\texttt{prim->bool}\mid...\\
\texttt{op2} :=&\quad \texttt{string-append}\mid+\mid\div\mid|>|\mid...\\
\theta :=&\quad \{[av]\,\texttt{str}:pv,...\}\\
\sigma :=&\quad \cdot\mid\sigma,l:v\\
\Theta :=&\quad \cdot\mid\Theta,r:\theta
\end{aligned}
$$

$$
\begin{aligned}
E_{ae} :=&\quad [\texttt{class}:E',\texttt{extensible}:e,\texttt{proto}:e,\texttt{code}:e,\texttt{primval}:e]\mid[\texttt{class}:v,\texttt{extensible}:E',\texttt{proto}:e,\texttt{code}:e,\texttt{primval}:e]\\
\mid&\quad [\texttt{class}:v,\texttt{extensible}:v,\texttt{proto}:E',\texttt{code}:e,\texttt{primval}:e]\mid[\texttt{class}:v,\texttt{extensible}:v,\texttt{proto}:v,\texttt{code}:E',\texttt{primval}:e]\\
\mid&\quad [\texttt{class}:v,\texttt{extensible}:v,\texttt{proto}:v,\texttt{code}:v,\texttt{primval}:E']\\
E_{pe} :=&\quad [\texttt{config}:E',\texttt{enum}:e,\texttt{value}:e,\texttt{writable}:e]\mid[\texttt{config}:v,\texttt{enum}:E',\texttt{value}:e,\texttt{writable}:e]\\
\mid&\quad [\texttt{config}:v,\texttt{enum}:v,\texttt{value}:E',\texttt{writable}:e]\mid[\texttt{config}:v,\texttt{enum}:v,\texttt{value}:v,\texttt{writable}:E']\\
\mid&\quad \texttt{config}:E',\texttt{enum}:e,\texttt{get}:e,\texttt{set}:e]\mid[\texttt{config}:v,\texttt{enum}:E',\texttt{get}:e,\texttt{set}:e]\\
\mid&\quad [\texttt{config}:v,\texttt{enum}:v,\texttt{get}:E',\texttt{set}:e]\mid[\texttt{config}:v,\texttt{enum}:v,\texttt{get}:v,\texttt{set}:E']\\
E' :=&\quad \bullet\mid E':=e\mid v:=E'\mid\texttt{op1}(E')\mid\texttt{op2}(E',e)\mid\texttt{op2}(v,E')\mid E'(e,...)\mid v(v,...,E',e,...)\mid E';e\mid v;E'\mid\texttt{let}\,(x=E')\,e\\
\mid&\quad \texttt{if}\,(E')\,\{e\}\,\texttt{else}\,\{e\}\mid\texttt{throw}\,E'\mid\texttt{eval}(E',e)\mid\texttt{eval}(v,E')\mid\{E_{ae}\,\texttt{str}:pe,...\}\mid\{av\,\texttt{str}_1:pv,...,\texttt{str}_x:E_{pe},\texttt{str}_n:pe,...\}\\
\mid&\quad E'[\langle a\rangle]\mid E'[\langle a\rangle=e]\mid v[\langle a\rangle=E']\mid E'[e\langle a\rangle]\mid v[E'\langle a\rangle]\mid E'[e\langle a\rangle=e]\mid v[E'\langle a\rangle=e]\mid v[v\langle a\rangle=E']\mid\texttt{props}(E')\\
\mid&\quad E'[e]^e\mid v[E']^e\mid v[v]^{E'}\mid E'[\texttt{delete}\,e]\mid v[\texttt{delete}\,E']\\
E :=&\quad E'\mid\texttt{label}:x\,E\mid\texttt{break}\,x\,E\mid\texttt{try}\,E\,\texttt{catch}\,e\mid\texttt{try}\,E\,\texttt{finally}\,e\\
F :=&\quad E'\mid\texttt{label}:x\,F\mid\texttt{break}\,x\,F\qquad\textit{Exception Contexts}\\
G :=&\quad E'\mid\texttt{try}\,G\,\texttt{catch}\,e\qquad\textit{Local Jump Contexts}
\end{aligned}
$$

Fig. 7. The syntax of S5 [22].

References

1. Bengtson, J., Bhargavan, K., Fournet, C., Gordon, A.D., Maffeis, S.: Refinement types for secure implementations. ACM Trans. Prog. Lang. Syst. **33**(2), 8:1–8:45 (2011)
2. Bhargavan, K., Blanchet, B., Kobeissi, N.: Verified models and reference implementations for the TLS 1.3 standard candidate. In: IEEE Symposium on Security and Privacy (S&P) (2017)
3. Bhargavan, K., Delignat-Lavaud, A., Maffeis, S.: Defensive JavaScript – building and verifying secure web components. In: Aldini, A., Lopez, J., Martinelli, F. (eds.) FOSAD 2012-2013. LNCS, vol. 8604, pp. 88–123. Springer, Cham (2014). https://doi.org/10.1007/978-3-319-10082-1_4
4. Bhargavan, K., Fournet, C., Guts, N.: Typechecking higher-order security libraries. In: Ueda, K. (ed.) APLAS 2010. LNCS, vol. 6461, pp. 47–62. Springer, Heidelberg (2010). https://doi.org/10.1007/978-3-642-17164-2_5
5. Bhargavan, K., Fournet, C., Kohlweiss, M., Pironti, A., Strub, P.: Implementing TLS with verified cryptographic security. In: IEEE Symposium on Security and Privacy (S&P) (2013)
6. Chaudhuri, A., Vekris, P., Goldman, S., Roch, M., Levi, G.: Fast and precise type checking for JavaScript. Proc. ACM Prog. Lang. **1**(OOPSLA), 48:1–48:30 (2017)
7. Chugh, R., Herman, D., Jhala, R.: Dependent types for JavaScript. In: ACM SIGPLAN Conference on Object-Oriented Programming, Systems, Languages, and Applications (OOPSLA) (2012)
8. Egele, M., Brumley, D., Fratantonio, Y., Kruegel, C.: An empirical study of cryptographic misuse in android applications. In: ACM SIGSAC Conference on Computer and Communications Security (CCS) (2013)
9. Guha, A., Saftoiu, C., Krishnamurthi, S.: The essence of JavaScript. In: D'Hondt, T. (ed.) ECOOP 2010. LNCS, vol. 6183, pp. 126–150. Springer, Heidelberg (2010). https://doi.org/10.1007/978-3-642-14107-2_7
10. Hedin, D., Birgisson, A., Bello, L., Sabelfeld, A.: JSFlow: tracking information flow in JavaScript and its APIs. In: ACM Symposium on Applied Computing (2014)
11. Hedin, D., Sjösten, A., Piessens, F., Sabelfeld, A.: A principled approach to tracking information flow in the presence of libraries. In: Maffei, M., Ryan, M. (eds.) POST 2017. LNCS, vol. 10204, pp. 49–70. Springer, Heidelberg (2017). https://doi.org/10.1007/978-3-662-54455-6_3
12. Heule, S., Stefan, D., Yang, E.Z., Mitchell, J.C., Russo, A.: IFC inside: retrofitting languages with dynamic information flow control. In: Focardi, R., Myers, A. (eds.) POST 2015. LNCS, vol. 9036, pp. 11–31. Springer, Heidelberg (2015). https://doi.org/10.1007/978-3-662-46666-7_2
13. Keil, M., Thiemann, P.: TreatJS: higher-order contracts for JavaScripts. In: European Conference on Object-Oriented Programming (ECOOP) (2015)
14. Kobeissi, N., Bhargavan, K., Blanchet, B.: Automated verification for secure messaging protocols and their implementations: a symbolic and computational approach. In: IEEE European Symposium on Security and Privacy (EuroS&P) (2017)
15. Krüger, S., Späth, J., Ali, K., Bodden, E., Mezini, M.: CrySL: validating correct usage of cryptographic APIs. In: European Conference on Object-Oriented Programming (ECOOP) (2018)
16. Lazar, D., Chen, H., Wang, X., Zeldovich, N.: Why does cryptographic software fail?: a case study and open problems. In: Asia-Pacific Workshop on Systems (2014)

17. Loring, B., Mitchell, D., Kinder, J.: Sound regular expression semantics for dynamic symbolic execution of JavaScript. In: Proceedings of the ACM SIGPLAN Conference on Programming Language Design and Implementation (PLDI). ACM (2019)
18. Madsen, M., Lhoták, O., Tip, F.: A model for reasoning about JavaScript promises. Proc. ACM Prog. Lang. 1(OOPSLA), 861–8624 (2017)
19. Mitchell, D., van Binsbergen, L.T., Loring, B., Kinder, J.: Checking cryptographic API usage with composable annotations. In: ACM SIGPLAN Workshop on Partial Evaluation and Program Manipulation (PEPM) (2018)
20. Nadi, S., Krüger, S., Mezini, M., Bodden, E.: Jumping through hoops: why do Java developers struggle with cryptography APIs? In: International Conference on Software Engineering (ICSE) (2016)
21. Park, D., Stefănescu, A., Roşu, G.: KJS: a complete formal semantics of JavaScript. In: ACM SIGPLAN Conference on Programming Language Design and Implementation (PLDI) (2015)
22. Politz, J.G., Carroll, M.J., Lerner, B.S., Pombrio, J., Krishnamurthi, S.: A tested semantics for getters, setters, and eval in JavaScript. In: Symposium on Dynamic Languages (DLS) (2012)
23. Rastogi, A., Swamy, N., Fournet, C., Bierman, G.M., Vekris, P.: Safe & efficient gradual typing for TypeScript. In: ACM SIGPLAN-SIGACT Symposium on Principles of Programming Languages (POPL) (2015)
24. Sabelfeld, A., Myers, A.C.: Language-based information-flow security. IEEE J. Sel. Areas Commun. 21(1), 5–19 (2003)
25. Santos, J.F., Maksimovic, P., Naudziuniene, D., Wood, T., Gardner, P.: JaVerT: JavaScript verification toolchain. Proc. ACM Program. Lang. 2(POPL), 501–5033 (2018)
26. Santos, J.F., Rezk, T.: An information flow monitor-inlining compiler for securing a core of JavaScript. In: Cuppens-Boulahia, N., Cuppens, F., Jajodia, S., Abou El Kalam, A., Sans, T. (eds.) SEC 2014. IAICT, vol. 428, pp. 278–292. Springer, Heidelberg (2014). https://doi.org/10.1007/978-3-642-55415-5_23
27. Stefan, D., et al.: Protecting users by confining JavaScript with COWL. In: USENIX Symposium on Operating Systems Design and Implementation (OSDI) (2014)
28. Swamy, N., Chen, J., Fournet, C., Strub, P., Bhargavan, K., Yang, J.: Secure distributed programming with value-dependent types. In: ACM SIGPLAN International Conference on Functional Programming (ICFP) (2011)
29. Taly, A., Erlingsson, Ú., Mitchell, J.C., Miller, M.S., Nagra, J.: Automated analysis of security-critical JavaScript APIs. In: IEEE Symposium on Security and Privacy (S&P) (2011)
30. Vekris, P., Cosman, B., Jhala, R.: Refinement types for TypeScript. In: ACM SIGPLAN Conference on Programming Language Design and Implementation (PLDI) (2016)
31. Watson, M.: Web cryptography API. W3C recommendation, W3C, January 2017

Contingent Payments on a Public Ledger: Models and Reductions for Automated Verification

Sergiu Bursuc$^{(\boxtimes)}$ and Steve Kremer

Inria Nancy-Grand'Est & LORIA, Villers-lès-Nancy, France
sergiu.bursuc@inria.fr

Abstract. We study protocols that rely on a public ledger infrastructure, concentrating on protocols for zero-knowledge contingent payment, whose security properties combine diverse notions of fairness and privacy. We argue that rigorous models are required for capturing the ledger semantics, the protocol-ledger interaction, the cryptographic primitives and, ultimately, the security properties one would like to achieve.

Our focus is on a particular level of abstraction, where network messages are represented by a term algebra, protocol execution by state transition systems (e.g. multiset rewrite rules) and where the properties of interest can be analyzed with automated verification tools.We propose models for: (1) the rules guiding the ledger execution, taking the coin functionality of public ledgers such as Bitcoin as an example; (2) the security properties expected from ledger-based zero-knowledge contingent payment protocols; (3) two different security protocols that aim at achieving these properties relying on different ledger infrastructures; (4) reductions that allow simpler term algebras for homomorphic cryptographic schemes.

Altogether, these models allow us to derive a first automated verification for ledger-based zero-knowledge contingent payment using the Tamarin prover. Furthermore, our models help in clarifying certain underlying assumptions, security and efficiency tradeoffs that should be taken into account when deploying protocols on the blockchain.

1 Introduction

The blockchain and its associated public ledger promise a practical solution to a basic need for security protocols: a system that operates as stated, providing reliable outcome to all agents. Both deployed [1–4] and abstract [5,6] ledgers are ordered sequences of states - *state transition systems* respecting operational constraints. The goal of the underlying distributed protocols is to ensure that the ledger is indeed public, unique, alive and consistent. Protocols can then be based on transaction and smart contract semantics - i.e. rules that guide the state transition system - to implement functionality that would otherwise be inefficient or require trusted parties. Take *fair exchange*: two parties want to swap assets according to a contract that ensures fairness: any information or

© Springer Nature Switzerland AG 2019
K. Sako et al. (Eds.): ESORICS 2019, LNCS 11735, pp. 361–382, 2019.
https://doi.org/10.1007/978-3-030-29959-0_18

value transfer is reciprocated as planned [7]. The problem can be solved with optimistic assumptions, calling a trusted third party only when needed [8–10], or with digital (counter)cheques and transactions inside multi-party computations [11–13].

A public ledger provides an alternative solution to the problem, specified as a *zero-knowledge contingent payment* (ZKCP) for a seller and buyer. We suppose that the information of interest can be expressed as data (a *witness*) satisfying functional constraints (a desired *result*), e.g. a sudoku solution respects additive constraints, a prime factor decomposition satisfies multiplicative constraints, etc. ZKCP goals are: for the **Seller** - a delivered witness will be paid for; for the **Buyer** - a paid for witness will be delivered. Classically, these properties require trust and coordination with third parties. On public ledgers, reliable semantics and dedicated cryptographic protocols can minimize trust and interaction [14–18].

Challenges. Protocol actions occur at distinct levels: from local cryptographic objects, to network transactions, to ledger confirmation. Their respective semantics is useful in protocol design, where parties can agree on desired ledger actions beforehand, yet the concurrent environment opens up new challenges:

- *Multiple sessions, concurrent ledger access.* Asynchronicity leads to ambiguity about what it means to be paid. For example, a seller should ensure it will not be *paid* the same coin for two witnesses. If multiple sessions run in parallel, some with colluding parties, protocol messages may be mixed up and exploited. Valid transaction requests do not necessarily result in confirmed ledger transactions: if the adversary obtains private keys by exploiting the protocol, a race ensues between honest and adversarial messages claiming a coin. Protocols should ensure this does not happen - this is not usually an explicit goal.
- *Transaction finality.* In fact, it is commonly advised to wait for transactions to be finalized on the ledger to ensure payment. Yet, we show that ZKCP protocols (have to) provide a stronger property: as early as a transaction request is being sent over the network, one should ensure that the corresponding coin cannot be spent in any other way, because specific fields from the transaction may help the adversary in revealing secrets - so we cannot afford the transaction to fail.
- *Cryptographic interaction.* Ledger-based protocols produce complex cryptographic objects that engage ledger transitions at the same time as private data transfer, e.g. [15] relies on homomorphic encryption to produce a (secret) ECDSA signature that will perform a ledger transaction; this signature is committed in a zero-knowledge proof ensuring the corresponding ledger transition will furthermore reveal the witness. Such interaction between cryptography and the ledger extends the scope of crypto primitives to new protocols - dedicated, fine-grained security models are needed to evaluate them.
- *Security foundations.* Compounding all of above: ledger-based protocols are network cryptographic protocols executed in an adversarial environment. There is history of attacks and foundations for such protocols - see e.g. [19–23] for recent examples - showing the importance of rigorous security

specification and automated verification. Furthermore, we need generic models that allow a clear separation between security properties, ledger infrastructure and cryptographic protocols.

Our contributions address these challenges by formal models connecting the ledger, the ledger-based protocols, the cryptographic primitives and the desired security properties in a specification that can be used as input for automated verification tools. We use the Tamarin prover [24] for verification: it provides an expressive language to specify (cryptographic) state transition systems and to restrict their traces by logical formulas.

- *Public ledger.* We show that the model of the blockchain as a structured computational resource has a natural formal (or symbolic) counterpart combining multiset rewriting, term algebras and first order logic [24–26]. We identify minimal restrictions on multiset rewriting rules that make them function as a blockchain transition system, i.e. a smart contract. We also show how protocol rules can operate in order to exploit the ledger semantics. We specify the electronic coin functionality provided in e.g. Bitcoin [1] as an example (Sect. 3).
- *ZKCP on public ledgers.* We consider two ZKCP protocols [14,15] and perform their formal verification in a unified, generic model that captures their different features (Sects. 4 and 5). The specification tackles a strong attacker that can run multiple sessions, corrupt parties, control the network (in particular drop, reorder, replace the messages to the ledger) and exploit the cryptographic properties of messages. The formal security properties clearly circumscribe the expected ZKCP guarantees, both in their positive and in their negative aspects: e.g. a buyer will learn the witness or otherwise it can obtain a refund; a seller will obtain payment, unless there is a delivery delay to the ledger; etc. The security properties are parametric, so that different protocols can accordingly instantiate the notions of payment, time delay, witness extraction, etc.
- *Advanced cryptography.* The protocol we consider in Sect. 5 aims at a basic version of Bitcoin, with a minimal scripting language for signature verification; this calls for complex cryptography, intertwining homomorphic encryption, randomized signatures, Diffie-Hellman exponentiation and specialized zero-knowledge proofs. The corresponding formal specification as a message theory is out of the scope for any current automated verification tools. We provide a theoretical framework and a reduction result showing that it is sound to consider a simplified theory as input (Sect. 6). We start from a general theory where some of the function symbols are homomorphic: from $f(u, \overline{w})$ and v, one can derive $f(u * v, \overline{w})$, where $*$ is the product in an abelian group. In the reduced theory: (1) the homomorphic properties are restricted as follows: the adversary can derive $f(u * v, \overline{w})$ from $f(u, \overline{w})$ only if u is a product of messages created by honest parties; (2) the abelian group is degenerated: the adversary can derive the factors $u_1, \ldots, u_k$ of any product $u_1 * \ldots * u_k$, without being required to know any inverse.

2   Preliminaries: Computation Model

Term Algebra [27]. $\mathcal{F}$ denotes the set of function symbols and $\mathcal{F}^{(n)}$ those of arity n. The set of terms built from $\mathcal{F}$, a set of names and a set of variables is $\mathcal{T}$. Tuples of terms are denoted by an overline, e.g. $\overline{u} = (u_1, \ldots, u_n)$. We let $st(t)$ be the subterms of a term t, and $top(t)$ be its top symbol. $\mathcal{F}$ is endowed with a rewrite system: a set of rewrite rules $\mathcal{R}$, that we denote by $l \rightarrow r$, modulo a set of equations $\mathcal{E}$, that we denote by $l \approx r$. $\mathcal{R}$ or $\mathcal{E}$ can be empty. For a term t, $t{\downarrow}_{\mathcal{R}}$ is its normal form, obtained after applying all possible rewrite steps (modulo $\mathcal{E}$) from $\mathcal{R}$. Implicitly, terms are normalized and term equalities interpreted modulo $(\mathcal{R}, \mathcal{E})$.

Example 1. For the theory of randomized signatures, as instantiated e.g. by (EC)DSA [28], we let $\mathcal{F}_{\mathsf{sig}} = \{\mathsf{sign}, \mathsf{ver}, \mathsf{ok}, g\}$ and $\mathcal{R}_{\mathsf{sig}}$ be the signature verification rule: $\mathsf{ver}(\mathsf{sign}(x, y, z), x, g(y)) \rightarrow \mathsf{ok}$. Here $g(y)$ represents the public key corresponding to a secret key y, i.e. the group element that corresponds to raising a group generator g to a scalar power y. The third argument of sign takes the role of the randomness: $\mathsf{sign}(m, k, r_1)$ and $\mathsf{sign}(m, k, r_2)$ are two distinct signatures of m with key k.

The theory of an abelian group (AG), e.g. $\mathbb{Z}_q$, is modeled by the signature $\mathcal{F}_* = \{*, i\}$ and the set of equations $\mathsf{AG} = \{x * i(x) \approx 1, x * 1 \approx x\} \cup \mathsf{AC}$ where $\mathsf{AC} = \{x*y \approx y*x, (x*y)*z \approx x*(y*z)\}$ models associativity and commutativity.

Multiset Rewriting and State Transitions [24,26]. The signature is extended with fact symbols to represent adversarial knowledge, protocol state, freshness information, etc. A fact is represented by $F(t_1, \ldots, t_k)$, where F is a fact symbol and $t_1, \ldots, t_k$ are terms. There are the following special fact symbols: K - for attacker knowledge; Fr - for fresh data; In and Out - for protocol inputs and outputs. Other symbols may be added as required by the protocol, e.g. for representing the state. These symbols can be persistent (the corresponding facts cannot disappear), or linear (the corresponding facts are consumed by rules and protocol rules can update them). Persistent fact symbols are prefixed by !, e.g. !F. A multiset can contain multiple copies of the same linear fact.

A multiset rewriting (msr) rule is defined by $[L] {\dashv}[\, M \,{\mapsto}[N]$, where L, M, N are multisets of facts called respectively premises, actions and conclusions. We denote such a rule by $[L] \Rightarrow [N]$ when M is empty. To ease protocol specification, we extend the syntax of multiset rules with variable assignments and equality constraints, i.e. we can write rules of the form $[L] {\dashv} \Phi, M {\mapsto}[N]$ where L may contain expressions $x = t$ to define local variables and Φ is a set of equations of the form $u \approx v$. Equations are not directly supported in Tamarin, but can be easily encoded with restrictions as we show in Example 3. For two multisets of facts M_0, M_1 and rule $P = [L] {\dashv} \Phi, M {\mapsto}[N]$ we say that M_1 can be obtained from M_0 by applying the rule P, instantiated with θ if: (1) every equality in $\Phi\theta$ is true; (2) every fact in $L\theta$ is included in M_0 (counting multiplicities for linear facts); (3) M_1 is obtained from M_0 by removing linear facts included in $L\theta$ and adding all facts from $N\theta$.

A special set of *message deduction rules* defines how the attacker can derive new knowledge and make use of existing knowledge to interact with the protocol. Within this set, we distinguish *network deduction rules* and *intruder deduction rules*. Network deduction rules are fixed: they define outputs, inputs, public and fresh data.

$$[\mathsf{Out}(x)] \Rightarrow [\mathsf{K}(x)]; \quad [\mathsf{K}(x)] \Rightarrow [\mathsf{In}(x)]; \quad \Rightarrow [\mathsf{K}(y)]; \quad \Rightarrow [\mathsf{Fr}(z)]; \quad [\mathsf{Fr}(x)] \Rightarrow [\mathsf{K}(x)]$$

The semantics ensures that y and z above are instantiated to public, resp. fresh names.

Intruder deduction rules are of the form $[\mathsf{K}(u_1), \ldots, \mathsf{K}(u_k)] \Rightarrow [\mathsf{K}(v)]$ - defining operations on messages. These are typically $[\mathsf{K}(x_1), \ldots, \mathsf{K}(x_k)] \Rightarrow [\mathsf{K}(f(x_1, \ldots, x_k))]$ for all $f \in \mathcal{F}^{(k)}$. We also allow more general deduction rules, as in Example 2 and Fig. 4. Such rules can wlog replace rewrite rules $f(l_1, \ldots, l_k) \to r$ for symbols f with no other occurrence in the rewrite system and whose occurrence in protocol rules is not under a term context. An *intruder theory*, that we denote by $\mathcal{I}$, is thus given by a set of intruder deduction rules plus $(\mathcal{R}, \mathcal{E})$. For a set of terms $\{t_1, \ldots, t_n, t\}$ we let $\{t_1, \ldots, t_n\} \vdash t$ if $\mathsf{K}(t)$ can be obtained from $\mathsf{K}(t_1), \ldots, \mathsf{K}(t_n)$ using intruder deduction rules. *Protocol rules* model the execution of the protocol by honest parties. There are basic restrictions ensuring that protocol rules are a sound model of protocol executions [26]; we will follow them implicitly in our models and examples.

Example 2. Exponentiation in a Diffie-Hellman group can be represented by the rewrite rule $exp(g(x), y) \to g(x * y)$ together with the deduction rule $[\mathsf{K}(x_1), \mathsf{K}(x_2)] \Rightarrow [\mathsf{K}(exp(x_1, x_2))]$. Alternatively, the deduction rule $[\mathsf{K}(g(x)), \mathsf{K}(y)] \Rightarrow [\mathsf{K}(g(x * y))]$ allows to model the corresponding operation performed by the attacker (without requiring explicit application of exp). Similarly, a protocol rule can directly perform exponentiation without explicit use of the symbol exp, e.g. $[\mathsf{In}(g(x)), \mathsf{Fr}(y)] \Rightarrow [\mathsf{Out}(g(x * y))]$.

For a rule P, we let $facts(P)$, $in(P)$, $out(P)$, $lhs(P)$, $rhs(P)$, $act(P)$ be respectively the set of all facts, of input facts (e.g. $\mathsf{In}(u)$), of output facts (e.g. $\mathsf{Out}(u)$), of left-hand side facts (i.e. premises), of right-hand side facts (i.e. conclusions) and of action facts. For a set of facts $\mathbf{F}$, we let $msg(\mathbf{F})$ be the set of messages that are arguments of facts in $\mathbf{F}$. We let $io(P) = msg(in(P) \cup out(P))$.

Traces and Properties. A *trace* τ is a sequence of applications of $n \geq 1$ msr rules, interleaving applications of protocol, intruder and network deduction rules. For every $i \in \{1, \ldots, n\}$, we let P_i be the rule applied at step i and θ_i be the corresponding substitution. We define:

- $facts(\tau, i) = act(P_i)\theta_i\downarrow$ if P_i is a protocol or network deduction rule;
- $facts(\tau, i) = \{\mathsf{K}(v\theta_i\downarrow)\}$ if P_i is an intruder deduction rule with $rhs(P_i) = \{\mathsf{K}(v)\}$

For a set of rules Q, we denote by $traces(Q)$ the set of all valid traces that can be derived from elements in Q. Consider a set of timepoint variables, denoted by

$i, j, l, \ldots$, which will be interpreted over rational numbers. A *trace atom* is either $\bot$, or a term equality $t_1 \approx t_2$, or a timepoint ordering $i < j$, or a timepoint equality $i = j$, or an action fact $\mathbf{F}@i$ for a fact $\mathbf{F}$ and timepoint i. A *trace formula* is a first-order logic formula obtained from trace atoms by applying the usual quantification and logical connectives. Given a trace τ and trace formula ϕ, whose variables are all bound, the satisfaction relation $\tau \models \phi$, is defined recursively as expected, in particular $\tau \models \mathbf{F} @ i$ iff $\mathbf{F} \in facts(\tau, i)$.

For a set of rules Q and trace formulas Ψ, Φ, we let $Q \models \Phi$ iff $\forall \tau \in traces(Q)$. $\tau \models \Phi$ and $Q; \Psi \models \Phi$ iff $\forall \tau \in traces(Q)$. $\tau \models \Psi \Rightarrow \Phi$. For verification, $(Q; \Psi)$ will be a system specification and Φ a property to verify; Q defines local transition rules, while Ψ defines additional, global restrictions on the set of traces for the specified system.

Example 3. Consider the binary fact symbol Eq and the formula

$$\Psi_{\mathsf{eq}} : \forall x, y, i. \; \mathsf{Eq}(x, y) @ i \Rightarrow x \approx y.$$

An $\mathsf{Eq}(u, v)$ action in a rule allows then to test that $u \approx_{\mathcal{E}} v$ before proceeding. Take $P = [\mathsf{In}(u), \mathsf{In}(v), \mathsf{Fr}(s)] \!-\!\!\{ \mathsf{Eq}(u, v) \}\!\!\rightarrow\! [\mathsf{Out}(s)]$. Then $\mathsf{K}(a), \mathsf{K}(a), \mathsf{Eq}(a, a), \mathsf{K}(s)$ is a trace of P satisfying Ψ_{eq}, while $\mathsf{K}(a), \mathsf{K}(f(a)), \mathsf{Eq}(a, f(a)), \mathsf{K}(s)$ does not.

Consider the unary symbol Fresh and the restriction

$$\Psi_{\mathsf{fresh}} : \forall x, i, j. \; \mathsf{Fresh}(x) @ i \; \wedge \; \mathsf{Fresh}(x) @ j \Rightarrow i = j.$$

It ensures that every occurrence of $\mathsf{Fresh}(t)$ is with a different t. Assume we add $\mathsf{Fresh}(\langle u, v \rangle)$ as an action in P. Then, among $traces(P)$, $\ldots \mathsf{Eq}(a, a), \ldots, \mathsf{Eq}(a, a)$ does not satisfy Ψ_{fresh}, while $\ldots \mathsf{Eq}(a, a), \ldots, \mathsf{Eq}(b, b)$ does.

Example 4. Consider the set of rules Q_{keys}:

- $[\mathsf{Fr}(k)] \!-\!\!\{ !\mathsf{Key}(k) \}\!\!\rightarrow\! [!\mathsf{Pk}(g(k)), !\mathsf{Key}(k), \mathsf{Out}(g(k))]$
- $[!\mathsf{Key}(x)] \!-\!\!\{ \mathsf{Corrupt}(g(x)) \}\!\!\rightarrow\! [\mathsf{Out}(x)]$

It models a basic key infrastructure. The formula $\Phi : !\mathsf{Key}(x) @ i \Rightarrow \neg \exists j. \mathsf{K}(x) @ j$ says that keys are secret. Then $Q_{\mathsf{keys}} \not\models \forall x, i. \Phi$, since the second rule in Q_{keys} allows the attacker to corrupt keys. Now consider the protocol rule

$$Q_{\mathsf{sign}} : [\mathsf{Fr}(a), !\mathsf{Key}(x)] \!-\!\!\{ \mathsf{Honest}(g(x)), \mathsf{Sign}(x) \}\!\!\rightarrow\! [\mathsf{Out}(\mathsf{sign}(a, k, \rho_r))]$$

the formula $\Phi' : \mathsf{Sign}(x) @ j \Rightarrow \neg \exists j. \mathsf{K}(x) @ j$ - saying that keys used in Q_{sign} are secret - and the restriction: $\Psi_{\mathsf{hon}} : \forall x, i. \; \mathsf{Honest}(x) @ i \Rightarrow \neg \exists j. \mathsf{Corrupt}(x) @ j$. Then we have $Q_{\mathsf{keys}}, Q_{\mathsf{sign}}; \Psi_{\mathsf{hon}} \models \forall x, i. \Phi'$ because we have added the restrictions that keys in Q_{sign} are honest and that honest keys cannot be corrupted.

Public Data. Tamarin allows the use of variables that can be instantiated only with messages of a public sort. They are denoted by $\$x$, and can occur anywhere in a protocol msr rule. As in Example 4, we will use annotations of ρ for such data, e.g. ρ_r for a public nonce, ρ_{sn} for a serial number, etc.

Protocol State. Specifications rely on sequences of protocols rules $(P_0, \ldots, P_k)$, where each rule P_i should be executed before P_{i+1} and can pass on, via facts, state data to P_{i+1}. To avoid clutter, we use a symbol state_i to represent this transmission, and we allow P_{i+1} to reference any variables from P_i that should be formally passed via state facts. We denote by $\mathsf{state}_i \lceil x = u \rfloor$ the pattern matching of state variable x by a term u.

3   Public Ledgers: Facts, Rules, Coins

Coin Ledger. The protocols we consider are based on coin contracts of e.g. Bitcoin [1]: a *coin* is represented by an object $(\mathsf{sn}, g(k))$ on the ledger, where sn is a serial number, and $g(k)$ is the public key of the coin owner. Serial numbers are computed as the hash of the transaction that created the coin; for simplicity, we assume they are fresh public numbers. To spend a coin, i.e. transfer it to a new owner, the ledger expects a transaction request, attested by a signature from the current owner, containing the sn of the coin to be spent, the public key $g(k')$ of the new owner and (implicitly) the serial number sn' of the new coin. If the signature is valid, the coin $(\mathsf{sn}, g(k))$ is marked as spent, and a new coin $(\mathsf{sn}', g(k'))$ is created for the new owner. We call *basecoins* these coins.

We will also make use of *hashcoins*: *hashed timelock contracts* [29] used to establish trust relationships outside the ledger [30,31]. They perform a transaction by which one of the two parties, say A, obtains the preimage of a hash - which can e.g. be a key encrypting some data of interest - while the other party, say B, provides the hash preimage and obtains a basecoin in return. A performs a ledger transaction pledging one of A's coins into a hashcoin, providing the desired hash image and the public key of B. B can then claim the coin using a (signed) inverse of the image. A timeout mechanism ensures the coin can be returned to A if there was no action from B in due time. A hashcoin can be represented by a tuple $(\mathsf{sn}, g(k), h(x), g(k'))$ here $g(k)$ represents the coin creator, who can obtain it after timeout, $h(x)$ is the desired hash image, and $g(k')$ is the party that can claim sn by supplying x.

Formal Model. We consider two special sets of disjoint fact symbols: one for *ledger facts*, denoted by $\mathbf{F}_{\mathcal{L}}$, and one for *check facts*, denoted by $\mathbf{F}_{\mathcal{C}}$. Ledger facts will be used to represent the state of the ledger. For example, they can record who is the owner of an asset, what are the elements of a given transaction, etc. Ledger facts are assumed persistent because the ledger history cannot change. Check facts, on the other hand, will be used by protocols to restrict their executions with respect to the (current or past) states of the ledger. For example, they can be used to ensure that a coin, whose existence is recorded by a ledger fact, has not yet been spent.

Example 5. Let $\mathcal{F}_{\mathcal{L}}^{\mathsf{coin}} = \{!\mathsf{Coin}, !\mathsf{HCoin}, !\mathsf{Spend}, !\mathsf{Time}\}$ and $\mathcal{F}_{\mathcal{C}}^{\mathsf{coin}} = \{\mathsf{Unspent}\}$. The corresponding facts represent: $!\mathsf{Coin}(\mathsf{sn}, g(k)) @ i$ - a coin sn created at timepoint i belonging to the public key $g(k)$; $!\mathsf{HCoin}(\mathsf{sn}, \langle g(k_1), g(k_2), h(t) \rangle) @ i$ - a hashcoin sn that can be claimed for $g(k_2)$ by supplying t and a signature, or for $g(k_1)$ after timeout by supplying a signature; !Spend(sn, u, w, v) @ i - the transfer of a coin (sn, u) to a new owner v at timepoint i, relying on supporting data w: w is a signature when sn is a basecoin, plus possibly a hash preimage when sn is a hashcoin; !Time(sn) @ i marks the fact that the hashcoin sn was reclaimed after a timeout at timepoint i; Unspent(sn) @ i checks the ledger to ensure the coin sn is unspent at i.

The semantics of the ledger is defined by msr rules that can only be triggered by ledger facts and public inputs, and can only produce ledger facts and public outputs. Ledger restrictions ensure additional constraints for the states produced by the ledger. These rules and constraints define the ledger state transition system and make it available for external protocols, which may be executed by honest or adversarial parties.

Definition 1. *A msr rule P is a* ledger rule *if: (1) facts$(P) \subseteq in(P) \cup out(P) \cup$* $\mathbf{F}_\mathcal{L}$; *(2) rhs$(P) \subseteq act(P)$. P is* ledger-respecting *if $(act(P) \cup rhs(P)) \cap \mathbf{F}_\mathcal{L} = \emptyset$. A* ledger restriction *is a trace formula with facts in $\mathbf{F}_\mathcal{L} \cup \mathbf{F}_\mathcal{C}$.*

Properties of ledger rules in Definition 1 ensure that: (1) the ledger transition system depends only on ledger facts and public inputs; (2) all produced ledger facts are recorded as actions in the trace. In this paper we consider public ledgers, e.g. [1–4], so the ledger rules will also satisfy (3) $msg(rhs(P)) \subseteq msg(out(P))$. This is not an inherent restriction of the model, and partially public ledgers, e.g. [32], may be considered in the scope of Definition 1. Bearing in mind the properties (2) and (3) of our considered ledger rules, in order to simplify the presentation of our examples in the paper, we will avoid duplication, writing $[F_0] \!-\!\mid \Phi \mid\!\mapsto\! [F_1]$ instead of $[F_0] \!-\!\mid \Phi, F_1 \mid\!\mapsto\! [F_1, \mathsf{Out}(msg(F_1))]$ as expected. All protocol rules will be ledger-respecting as in Definition 1, so the only way to produce ledger facts is by passing through ledger rules; on the other hand, protocol rules can freely access ledger facts to check the state of the ledger, so we can have $lhs(P) \cap \mathbf{F}_\mathcal{L} \neq \emptyset$.

In Fig. 1, the rule $\mathsf{R}_{\mathsf{new}}$ abstracts the coin mining process; the other rules model formally the coin transactions as described above: spending coins to coins, to hashcoins, and back to coins. The rule $\mathsf{R}_{\mathsf{h2cr}}$ produces a ledger fact !Time(x_{sn}) to record that the corresponding coin was reclaimed after a timeout. The rules $\mathsf{S}_{\mathsf{c2h}}, \mathsf{S}_{\mathsf{h2c}}$ assume Hash and Inv to be defined by their context as a hash image of interest and a hash preimage.

Ledger restrictions define additional constraints that should be satisfied by the public ledger. If $facts(\Phi) \subseteq \mathbf{F}_\mathcal{L}$ then the restriction Φ is *inherent to the semantics of the ledger*, i.e. it is a check performed by the (distributed) trusted party that builds the ledger. On the other hand, if $\exists \mathbf{F} \in facts(\Phi) \cap \mathbf{F}_\mathcal{C}$, then Φ *restricts the execution of the protocols* with respect to the public ledger: a protocol rule P with a substitution θ such that $\mathbf{F}\theta \in act(P\theta)$ can perform a transition at timepoint i, only if $\mathbf{F}\theta$ @ i is consistent with $\Phi\theta$ and the previous ledger facts.

$\mathsf{R_{new}} : [\, !\mathsf{Pk}(x_{\mathsf{pk}}), \mathsf{In}(\langle s, x_{\mathsf{sn}}\rangle)] \multimap\!\{\, \mathsf{ver}(s, x_{\mathsf{sn}}, x_{\mathsf{pk}}) \approx \mathsf{ok} \,\}\!\!\rightarrow [\, !\mathsf{Coin}(x_{\mathsf{sn}}, x_{\mathsf{pk}})]$

$\mathsf{R_{c2c}} : [\, !\mathsf{Coin}(x_{\mathsf{sn}}, x_{\mathsf{pk}}), \mathsf{In}(u)] \multimap\!\{\, \varPhi_{\mathsf{c2c}}(x_{\mathsf{sn}}, x_{\mathsf{pk}}, u)\,\}\!\!\rightarrow [\, !\mathsf{Spend}(x_{\mathsf{sn}}, x_{\mathsf{pk}}, v), !\mathsf{Coin}(y_{\mathsf{sn}}, y_{\mathsf{pk}})]$

$\mathsf{R_{c2h}} : [\, !\mathsf{Coin}(x_{\mathsf{sn}}, x_{\mathsf{pk}}), \mathsf{In}(u)] \multimap\!\{\, \varPhi_{\mathsf{c2h}}(x_{\mathsf{sn}}, x_{\mathsf{pk}}, u)\,\}\!\!\rightarrow [\, !\mathsf{Spend}(x_{\mathsf{sn}}, x_{\mathsf{pk}}, s, y), !\mathsf{HCoin}(y_{\mathsf{sn}}, y)]$

$\mathsf{R_{h2c}} : [\, !\mathsf{HCoin}(x_{\mathsf{sn}}, y), \mathsf{In}(u)] \multimap\!\{\, \varPhi_{\mathsf{h2c}}(x_{\mathsf{sn}}, y, u)\,\}\!\!\rightarrow [\, !\mathsf{Spend}(x_{\mathsf{sn}}, y, s, y_{\mathsf{pk}}), !\mathsf{Coin}(z_{\mathsf{sn}}, y_{\mathsf{pk}})]$

$\mathsf{R_{h2cr}} : [\, !\mathsf{HCoin}(x_{\mathsf{sn}}, y), \mathsf{In}(u)] \multimap\!\{\, \varPhi_{\mathsf{h2cr}}(x_{\mathsf{sn}}, y, u)\,\}\!\!\rightarrow [\, \ldots, !\mathsf{Coin}(z_{\mathsf{sn}}, x_{\mathsf{pk}}), !\mathsf{Time}(x_{\mathsf{sn}})\,]$

where

$\mathsf{R_{c2c}} : u = \langle s, y_{\mathsf{sn}}, y_{\mathsf{pk}}\rangle; \varPhi_{\mathsf{c2c}} = \mathsf{ver}(s, \langle \mathsf{c2c}, x_{\mathsf{sn}}, y_{\mathsf{sn}}, y_{\mathsf{pk}}\rangle, x_{\mathsf{pk}}) \approx \mathsf{ok}; v = \langle s, y_{\mathsf{pk}}\rangle$

$\mathsf{R_{c2h}} : u = \langle s, y_{\mathsf{sn}}, y_{\mathsf{pk}}, y_h\rangle; \varPhi_{\mathsf{c2h}} = \mathsf{ver}(s, \langle \mathsf{c2h}, x_{\mathsf{sn}}, y_{\mathsf{pk}}, y_h\rangle, x_{\mathsf{pk}}) \approx \mathsf{ok}; y = \langle x_{\mathsf{pk}}, y_{\mathsf{pk}}, y_h\rangle$

$\mathsf{R_{h2c}} : y = \langle x_{\mathsf{pk}}, y_{\mathsf{pk}}, y_h\rangle; u = \langle s, y_{\mathsf{sn}}, y_w\rangle;$

$\quad \varPhi_{\mathsf{h2c}} = \mathsf{ver}(s, \langle \mathsf{h2c}, x_{\mathsf{sn}}, y_w\rangle, y_{\mathsf{pk}}) \approx \mathsf{ok} \wedge y_h \approx h(y_w) \qquad$ ***(similarly for $\mathsf{R_{h2cr}}$)***

Ledger-based protocol rules (typical examples)

$\mathsf{S_{c2c}} : [\, !\mathsf{Key}(x_{sk}), !\mathsf{Pk}(y_{\mathsf{pk}}), !\mathsf{Coin}(x_{\mathsf{sn}}, g(x_{sk})), x_s = \mathsf{sign}(\langle \mathsf{c2c}, x_{\mathsf{sn}}, \rho_{\mathsf{sn}}, y_{\mathsf{pk}}\rangle, x_{sk}, \rho_r)\,]$
$$\multimap\!\{\, \mathsf{Unspent}(x_{\mathsf{sn}})\,\}\!\!\rightarrow [\, \mathsf{Out}(\langle x_s, \rho_{\mathsf{sn}}, y_{\mathsf{pk}}\rangle)\,]$$

$\mathsf{S_{c2h}} : [\, !\mathsf{Key}(x_{sk}), !\mathsf{Pk}(y_{\mathsf{pk}}), !\mathsf{Coin}(x_{\mathsf{sn}}, g(x_{sk})), \mathsf{Hash}(y_h)\,]$
$$\multimap\!\{\, \mathsf{Unspent}(x_{\mathsf{sn}})\,\}\!\!\rightarrow [\, \mathsf{Out}(u_{\mathsf{c2h}})\,]$$

$\mathsf{S_{h2c}} : [\, !\mathsf{Key}(y_{sk}), !\mathsf{HCoin}(x_{\mathsf{sn}}, \langle x_{\mathsf{pk}}, g(y_{sk}), h(x_w)\rangle), \mathsf{Inv}(y_w)\,]$
$$\multimap\!\{\, \mathsf{Unspent}(x_{\mathsf{sn}}), \mathsf{Claim}(x_{\mathsf{sn}}, g(y_{sk}))\,\}\!\!\rightarrow [\, \mathsf{Out}(u_{\mathsf{h2c}})\,]$$

where $t_{\mathsf{c2h}} = \langle \mathsf{c2h}, x_{\mathsf{sn}}, y_{\mathsf{pk}}, y_h\rangle$; $u_{\mathsf{c2h}} = \langle \mathsf{sign}(t_{\mathsf{c2h}}, x_{sk}, \rho_r), \rho_{\mathsf{sn}}, y_{\mathsf{pk}}, y_h\rangle$

$\qquad\quad t_{\mathsf{h2c}} = \langle \mathsf{h2c}, x_{\mathsf{sn}}, x_w, \rho_{\mathsf{sn}}\rangle$; $u_{\mathsf{h2c}} = \langle \mathsf{sign}(t_{\mathsf{h2c}}, y_{sk}, \rho_r), \rho_{\mathsf{sn}}, y_w\rangle$

Fig. 1. *Ledger coin rules:* $\mathcal{L}_{\mathsf{base}} = \{\mathsf{R_{new}}, \mathsf{R_{c2c}}\};\ \mathcal{L}_{\mathsf{hash}} = \mathcal{L}_{\mathsf{base}} \uplus \{\mathsf{R_{c2h}}, \mathsf{R_{h2c}}, \mathsf{R_{h2cr}}\}$

Example 6. The following formulas define ledger restrictions for coins on $\mathcal{L}_{\mathsf{base}}, \mathcal{L}_{\mathsf{hash}}$

$$\varPsi_0 : \forall x, \overline{y}, \overline{z}, i, j.\ !\mathsf{Spend}(x, \overline{y})\ @\ i \wedge\ !\mathsf{Spend}(x, \overline{z})\ @\ j \Rightarrow i = j\ \wedge \overline{y} = \overline{z}$$

$$\varPsi_1 : \forall x, y, z, i, j.\ !F_1(x, y)\ @\ i \wedge\ !F_2(x, z)\ @\ j\ \Rightarrow i = j\ \wedge\ y = z$$
$$(\forall F_1, F_2 \in \{\mathsf{Coin}, \mathsf{HCoin}\})$$

$$\varPsi_2 : \forall x, \overline{y}, i, j.\ \mathsf{Unspent}(x)\ @\ i\ \wedge\ !\mathsf{Spend}(x, \overline{y})\ @\ j \Rightarrow i < j$$

They ensure that - no coin can be spent twice ($\varPsi_0$); - every fresh coin has a fresh serial number ($\varPsi_1$); - Unspent can hold at timepoint i only if the corresponding coin has not already been spent on the ledger ($\varPsi_2$). Note that $\varPsi_0, \varPsi_1$ are inherent ledger restrictions, while $\varPsi_2$ is a protocol ledger restriction. We let $\varPsi_{\mathsf{coin}} = \varPsi_0 \wedge \varPsi_1 \wedge \varPsi_2$.

4   Zero Knowledge Contingent Payments

We specify in a general framework the security guarantees that parties can expect from ZKCP protocols. We allow several parameters in definitions, that can be instantiated differently by specific protocols and ledgers - we illustrate it on $\mathcal{L}_{\mathsf{base}}$ and $\mathcal{L}_{\mathsf{hash}}$. We are interested in generic ZKCP protocols, where any functionality can be obtained by instantiating the protocol with a specific function f. Security is independent of the actual function f, so we consider a generic f in the following.

For intuition, consider first a protocol on $\mathcal{L}_{\mathsf{hash}}$ [14,16]. It assumes a zero-knowledge proof system showing that a ciphertext provided by a party contains a witness for a desired result, where the symmetric encryption key is the preimage of a given hash value. We represent such a proof by $zk(w, v, u)$ where w is the witness, v is the hash preimage used as symmetric key, and u is the secret key of the party constructing the proof (for brevity, we omit public data that may be part of the proof). The following rewrite rules represent symmetric encryption and zk proof verification:

$\mathsf{sdec}(\mathsf{senc}(x, y), y) \to x$ $\mathsf{ver}_{\mathsf{zk}}(\mathsf{zk}(x, y, z), \mathsf{senc}(x, y), f(x), h(y), g(z)) \to \mathsf{ok}.$

These define $\mathcal{I}_{\mathsf{hash}}$, where also $\forall f \in \mathcal{F}^{(k)}. [\mathsf{K}(x_1), \ldots, \mathsf{K}(x_k)] \Rightarrow [\mathsf{K}(f(x_1, \ldots, x_k))].$ Assume a seller with private key ks wants to sell w to a buyer with public key $g(kb)$.

Seller 1: generate a fresh key k; output $\mathsf{senc}(w, k), h(k), g(ks), zk(w, k, ks)$;

Buyer 1: receive above data from seller and, if the zk proof verifies, invoke $\mathsf{R}_{\mathsf{c2h}}$ on $\mathcal{L}_{\mathsf{hash}}$ to create a hashcoin for the given $h(k)$ and $g(ks)$:!HCoin$(\mathsf{sn}, \langle g(kb), g(ks), h(k)\rangle)$;

Seller 2: inspect $\mathcal{L}_{\mathsf{hash}}$ to see if the above coin was created; invoke $\mathsf{R}_{\mathsf{h2c}}$ with k and ks to claim the coin; this reveals k and thus reveals the witness;

Buyer 2: inspect $\mathcal{L}_{\mathsf{hash}}$ to see if $\mathsf{R}_{\mathsf{h2c}}$ was invoked for the created hashcoin; if yes, the ledger will also contain the key k that allows the decryption of the ciphertext received at step 1; if not, the rule $\mathsf{R}_{\mathsf{h2cr}}$ can be invoked after a time delay so that the coin is returned to the original owner.

Timeout. The fairness properties for the ZKCP protocols will be relative to the timely execution of certain operations. More precisely, if a certain action is not performed by a party in due time, then there is another action - grounded on the semantics of the ledger as in Example 7 or on cryptographic primitives as in Example 8 - that can be performed in order to compensate for the missing action.

Example 7 (Ledger timeout). Consider the rule $\mathsf{R}_{\mathsf{h2cr}}$ from Fig. 1 modeling the refund of a hashcoin after a timeout. The execution of this rule at timepoint i is accompanied on the ledger by the fact !Time(x_{sn}) @ i to record that this coin was spent due to a timeout. This allows to specify the possible effects of invoking $\mathsf{R}_{\mathsf{h2c}}$ on $\mathcal{L}_{\mathsf{hash}}$: either the transaction completes as expected, or there was a timeout, i.e. $\mathsf{R}_{\mathsf{h2cr}}$ was invoked. Consider the rule $\mathsf{S}_{\mathsf{h2c}}$ from Fig. 1; note the Claim action. Then $\mathcal{L}_{\mathsf{hash}}$ ensures the following property:

$$\forall x, y, z, z_1, z_2, i, j. \quad \begin{array}{c} \mathsf{Claim}(x, y) \ @\ i \ \wedge \\ !\mathsf{Spend}(x, z_1, z_2, z) \ @\ j \end{array} \Rightarrow \begin{array}{c} z = y \ \vee \\ !\mathsf{Time}(x) \ @\ j \end{array}$$

where $z = y$ happens in a normal execution, and !Time(x) @ j if the timeout occurs.

Example 8 (Cryptographic timeout [33,34]). Time commitment schemes allow to produce a commitment to a message that keeps it secret for a period of time. We represent a time commitment to u by $tcom(u)$ and consider the following rule $\mathsf{Q}_{\mathsf{tcom}}$: $[\mathsf{In}(tcom(x))]\!-\![!\mathsf{Time}(x)]\!\mapsto\![\mathsf{Out}(x)]$. We express that fresh committed data is either secret, or it was released after a timeout. Let P :

$[\mathsf{Fr}(s)] \dashv \mathsf{Tcom}(s) \vdash [\mathsf{Out}(tcom(s))]$. Then $\mathsf{Q}_{\mathsf{tcom}}, P \models \forall x, i, j.\ \mathsf{Tcom}(x) @ i\ \wedge$
$\mathsf{K}(x) @ j \Rightarrow \exists k.\ k < j \wedge !\mathsf{Time}(x) @ k$

$S_0 \colon [\ !\mathsf{Key}(x_{\mathsf{ks}}),\ !\mathsf{Witn}(x_{\mathsf{wtn}})\ ] \dashv \mathsf{Sell}(g(x_{\mathsf{ks}}), x_{\mathsf{wtn}}) \vdash [\ \mathsf{state}_0\ ]$

$S_1 \colon [\ \mathsf{state}_0, \mathsf{Fr}(k), x_{\mathsf{ew}} = senc(x_{\mathsf{wtn}}, k), x_\pi = zk(x_{\mathsf{wtn}}, k, x_{\mathsf{ks}})\ ] \Rightarrow [\ \mathsf{Out}((\langle x_\pi, x_{\mathsf{ew}}, h(k)\rangle), \mathsf{state}_1\ ]$

$S_2 \colon [\ \mathsf{state}_1, !\mathsf{HCoin}(x_{\mathsf{sn}}, \langle x_{\mathsf{pkb}}, g(x_{\mathsf{ks}}), h(k)\rangle)\ ] \dashv \mathsf{Unspent}(x_{\mathsf{sn}}), \mathsf{Claim}(g(x_{\mathsf{ks}}), x_{\mathsf{wtn}}, x_{\mathsf{sn}}, x_{\mathsf{sn}}) \vdash$
$\qquad\qquad [\ \mathsf{Out}((\langle \mathsf{sign}(\langle h2c, x_{\mathsf{sn}}, \rho_{\mathsf{sn}}, k\rangle, x_{\mathsf{ks}}), k, \rho_{\mathsf{sn}}\rangle)\ ]$

$B_0 \colon [\ !\mathsf{Res}(x_{\mathsf{res}}), !\mathsf{Key}(x_{\mathsf{kb}}), !\mathsf{Pk}(x_{\mathsf{pks}}), !\mathsf{Coin}(x_{\mathsf{sn}}, g(x_{\mathsf{kb}}))\ ] \Rightarrow [\ \mathsf{state}_0\ ]$

$B_1 \colon [\ \mathsf{state}_0, \mathsf{In}(\langle x_\pi, x_{\mathsf{ew}}, x_h\rangle)\ ] \dashv \mathsf{ver}_{\mathsf{zk}}(x_\pi, x_{\mathsf{ew}}, x_{\mathsf{res}}, x_h, x_{\mathsf{pks}}) \approx \mathsf{ok},$
$\quad \mathsf{Pay}(g(x_{\mathsf{kb}}), x_{\mathsf{res}}, \rho_{\mathsf{sn}}, \langle x_\pi, x_{\mathsf{ew}}, x_h\rangle) \vdash [\ \mathsf{Out}((\langle \mathsf{sign}(\langle c2h, x_{\mathsf{sn}}, \rho_{\mathsf{sn}}, x_{\mathsf{pks}}, x_h\rangle, x_{\mathsf{kb}}), \rho_{\mathsf{sn}}, x_{\mathsf{pks}}, x_h\rangle), \mathsf{state}_1\ ]$

$B_2^{\mathsf{go}} \colon [\ \mathsf{state}_1, !\mathsf{Spend}(\rho_{\mathsf{sn}}, z, \langle x_s, x_k\rangle, x_{\mathsf{pks}}), x_{\mathsf{wtn}} = sdec(x_{\mathsf{ew}}, x_k)\ ]$
$\qquad\qquad\qquad\qquad \dashv h(x_k) \approx x_h, f(x_{\mathsf{wtn}}) \approx x_{\mathsf{res}}, \mathsf{Witness}(x_{\mathsf{res}}) \vdash [\ ]$

$B_2^{\mathsf{ab}} \colon [\mathsf{state}_1, !\mathsf{HCoin}(x_{\mathsf{sn}}, \langle g(x_{\mathsf{kb}}), x_{\mathsf{pks}}, x_h\rangle)] \dashv \mathsf{Unspent}(x_{\mathsf{sn}}) \vdash [\mathsf{Out}((\langle \mathsf{sign}(\langle h2cr, x_{\mathsf{sn}}, \rho_{\mathsf{sn}}\rangle, x_{\mathsf{kb}}), \rho_{\mathsf{sn}}\rangle)]$

Fig. 2. Formal ZKCP on $\mathcal{L}_{\mathsf{hash}}$; $\mathsf{Seller} = (S_0, S_1, S_2)$; $\mathsf{Buyer} = (B_0, B_1, B_2^{\mathsf{go}}, B_2^{\mathsf{ab}})$

Definition 2. *Let Q be a set of (protocol and ledger) rules and Ψ be a set of restrictions. We say that (Q, Ψ) is a*

- *coin infrastructure if Q produces $!\mathsf{Spend}(u_{\mathsf{coin}}, \overline{u}, u_{\mathsf{pk}})$ ledger facts and $\Psi_{\mathsf{coin}} \subseteq \Psi$ (see Fig. 1 and Example 6);*
- *time infrastructure if Q produces $!\mathsf{Time}(u)$ actions (see Examples 7 and 8);*
- *key infrastructure if $Q_{\mathsf{keys}} \subseteq Q$ (see Example 4)*
- *function model if Q contains the rules Q_{func}:*

$$[\mathsf{Fr}(x_w)] \Rightarrow [!\mathsf{Witn}(x_w), \mathsf{Out}(f(x_w))]\ ;\ [\mathsf{Fr}(x_w)] \Rightarrow [!\mathsf{Res}(f(x_w)), \mathsf{Out}(x_w)]$$

If all of these are satisfied we say that (Q, Ψ) is a ZKCP-context.

The fact $!\mathsf{Witn}(x_w)$ from a function model is used by an honest seller to determine a witness, and the adversary (playing the role of the buyer) obtains a desired result $f(x_w)$. The fact $!\mathsf{Res}(f(x_w))$ is used by an honest buyer to determine a desired result, and the adversary (playing the role of the seller) obtains the corresponding witness x_w.

Definition 3. *A ZKCP Seller specification is given by a set of protocol rules that contains two special rules:*

$\quad$ **sell:** $[\ \ldots\ ] \dashv \mathsf{Sell}(t_{\mathsf{pk}}, t_{\mathsf{wtn}}) \vdash [\ \ldots\ ]$
$\quad$ **claim:** $[\ \ldots\ ] \dashv \mathsf{Claim}(t_{\mathsf{pk}}, t_{\mathsf{wtn}}, t_{\mathsf{time}}, t_{\mathsf{sn}}) \vdash [\ \ldots\ ]$

The *sell* rule models the start of a seller session, recording in $\mathsf{Sell}(t_{\mathsf{pk}}, t_{\mathsf{wtn}})$ the seller public key and the witness. The *claim* rule models the seller claiming a coin as payment, producing an action fact $\mathsf{Claim}(t_{\mathsf{pk}}, t_{\mathsf{wtn}}, t_{\mathsf{time}}, t_{\mathsf{sn}})$ where $t_{\mathsf{pk}}, t_{\mathsf{wtn}}$ are as above, t_{time} is timeout constrained data, and t_{sn} the claimed coin. In our case studies, t_{time} is either a sn as in Example 7 or a secret key share, cryptographically committed as in Example 8. See in Fig. 2 the formal Seller specification for the protocol above.

Definition 4. *Let (Q, Ψ) be a ZKCP-context and $\mathcal{S}$ be a ZKCP Seller specification. We say that these ensure* seller security *if $Q, \mathcal{S}; \Psi \models \Phi_S$, where Φ_S is defined in Fig. 3.*

Seller security: witness reveal vs payment: $\Phi_S := \Phi_0 \wedge \Phi_1 \wedge \Phi_2$

$\Phi_0 : \forall x_{\mathsf{pk}}, x_{\mathsf{wtn}}, i, j.\ \mathsf{Sell}(x_{\mathsf{pk}}, x_{\mathsf{wtn}}) \mathbin{@} i \wedge \mathsf{K}(x_{\mathsf{wtn}}) \mathbin{@} j \Rightarrow \exists k, y_{\mathsf{pk}}, x_t, x_{\mathsf{coin}}.\ \mathsf{Claim}(y_{\mathsf{pk}}, x_{\mathsf{wtn}}, x_t, x_{\mathsf{coin}}) \mathbin{@} k$

$\Phi_1 : \forall \bar{y}, \bar{z}, x.\ \mathsf{Claim}(\bar{y}, x) \mathbin{@} i \wedge \mathsf{Claim}(\bar{z}, x) \mathbin{@} j \Rightarrow i = j$

$\Phi_2 : \forall x_{\mathsf{pk}}, x_{\mathsf{wtn}}, x_t, x_{\mathsf{coin}}, i, j.\mathsf{Claim}(x_{\mathsf{pk}}, x_{\mathsf{wtn}}, x_t, x_{\mathsf{coin}}) \mathbin{@} i \wedge\ !\mathsf{Spend}(x_{\mathsf{coin}}, z, y, z_{\mathsf{pk}}) \mathbin{@} j$
$\Rightarrow z_{\mathsf{pk}} = x_{\mathsf{pk}} \vee \exists k.\ k \leq j \wedge\ !\mathsf{Time}(x_t) \mathbin{@} k$

Buyer security: pay gives witness or refund: $\Phi_B := [\ \forall i, j, x_{\mathsf{pk}}, x_{\mathsf{res}}, x_{\mathsf{coin}}, \bar{x}_{\mathsf{state}}.\ (\Phi_0 \wedge \Phi_1)\ ] \wedge \Phi_2$

$\Phi_0(\Psi_0) : \mathsf{Pay}(x_{\mathsf{pk}}, x_{\mathsf{res}}, x_{\mathsf{coin}}, \bar{x}_{\mathsf{state}}) \mathbin{@} i \wedge\ !\mathsf{Spend}(x_{\mathsf{coin}}, z, y, z_{\mathsf{pk}}) \mathbin{@} j \Rightarrow z_{\mathsf{pk}} = x_{\mathsf{pk}} \vee \Psi_0(y, \bar{x}_{\mathsf{state}})$

$\Phi_1(\Psi_1) : \mathsf{Pay}(x_{\mathsf{pk}}, x_{\mathsf{res}}, x_{\mathsf{coin}}, \bar{x}_{\mathsf{state}}) \mathbin{@} i \Rightarrow \Psi_1(x_{\mathsf{res}}, \bar{x}_{\mathsf{state}})$

$\Phi_2(\Psi_0, \Psi_1) : \forall x_{\mathsf{res}}, y, \bar{x}_{\mathsf{state}}.\ \Psi_0(y, \bar{x}_{\mathsf{state}}) \wedge \Psi_1(x_{\mathsf{res}}, \bar{x}_{\mathsf{state}}) \Rightarrow \exists x_w.\ x_{\mathsf{res}} = f(x_w)\ \wedge\ y, \bar{x}_{\mathsf{state}} \vdash x_w$

Fig. 3. Security properties for ZKCP on a ledger

Intuitively, the formula $\Phi_S = \Phi_0 \wedge \Phi_1 \wedge \Phi_2$ from Definition 4 ensures that:

- Φ_0: if the other party learns the witness, then (one of) the seller(s) for the corresponding witness is able to claim the payment of a coin into seller's account;
- Φ_1: the other party cannot lead the seller into accepting the same payment twice, e.g. for two different witnesses;
- Φ_2: the payment claimed by the seller will succeed as such on the ledger, unless the corresponding timeout event happened.

Note that, in Φ_0, the key y_{pk} into which payment is claimed is not necessarily equal to the key x_{pk} that engaged in selling the witness: the two keys can differ when there are two sellers for the same witness; then the adversary can learn the witness in one session without paying in the second one. Φ_1 requires care to ensure session specific payments; simply checking unspent conditions on the ledger is not sufficient in case of concurrent sessions. Φ_2 is important because the coin claimed by the seller is jointly constructed with the adversary, so we need to ensure that there is no other way to spend it. The following is proved automatically with Tamarin [35]:

Proposition 1. *For* Seller *of Fig. 2,* $Q_{\mathsf{keys}}, \mathcal{L}_{\mathsf{hash}}, \mathcal{I}_{\mathsf{hash}}, Q_{\mathsf{func}},$ Seller; $\Psi_{\mathsf{coins}} \models \Phi_S$.

ZKCP Buyer. As we can see in the $\mathcal{L}_{\mathsf{hash}}$-based protocol presented above, in order to ensure the witness delivery from a ZKCP protocol, the buyer should perform some verification actions on the data (e.g. zero-knowledge proofs) received during the protocol execution. We model these checks by a formula $\Psi_1(x, \bar{x}_{\mathsf{state}})$, where x represents the desired result for the function of interest, and $\bar{x}_{\mathsf{state}}$ represents protocol data that is relevant for buyer's verification actions. Ψ_1 and $\bar{x}_{\mathsf{state}}$ are protocol specific and they are parameters of our definition.

In addition to data received during the protocol execution, the buyer can also rely on data that is published on the ledger, and on the associated constraints that are ensured by the ledger semantics. We model these by $\Psi_0(y, \overline{x}_{\text{state}})$ where y represents the relevant ledger data. For example, in the $\mathcal{L}_{\text{hash}}$-based protocol, the semantics of the ledger ensures that the data y associated to the transaction that spends the hashcoin must contain the preimage of a hash recorded in $\overline{x}_{state}$, if the coin was spent by any party other than the buyer. A part of our security definition will require that Ψ_0 in conjunction with Ψ_1 does indeed reveal the witness. A second part of the definition will require that, if the buyer performed a payment transaction, then the buyer and the ledger will reach a state where Ψ_0 and Ψ_1 hold, or otherwise the buyer can obtain a refund.

Definition 5. *A ZKCP Buyer specification is given by a set of protocol rules that contains the special rule* **pay:** $[\ldots]\!\!-\!\![\ \mathsf{Pay}(t_{\text{pk}}, t_{\text{res}}, t_{\text{coin}}, \overline{u}_{\text{state}})\ ]\!\!\mapsto\![\ \ldots\ ]$.

The *pay* rule models the invocation of a payment transaction for a witness, where t_{pk} is the public key of the buyer, t_{res} is the desired result, t_{coin} is the target coin where the buyer makes the payment, and $\overline{u}_{\text{state}}$ is state information that is relevant for obtaining the witness. See Fig. 2 for the Buyer specification in the protocol described above.

Definition 6. *Let* (Q, Ψ) *be a ZKCP-context and* $\mathcal{B}$ *be a ZKCP Buyer specification. We say that these ensure* buyer security *if* $Q, \mathcal{B}; \Psi \models \Phi_B$, *where* Φ_B *is defined in Fig. 3.*

Intuitively, the formulas Φ_0, Φ_1, Φ_2 from Definition 6 ensures that:

- Φ_0: if the buyer has paid for a witness into a coin, then spending that coin on the ledger will either lead to a refund, i.e. $z_{\text{pk}} = x_{\text{pk}}$, or else the data y associated to the spending transaction together with buyer state data satisfy the constraint Ψ_0;
- Φ_1: before paying, the buyer performs checks entailing the constraint Ψ_1 for the desired result and the buyer state;
- Φ_2: Ψ_0 and Ψ_1 allow to derive a witness for the desired result, by combining transaction data y with data $\overline{x}_{\text{state}}$ gathered from the protocol execution.

Proposition 2. *For* Buyer *from Fig. 2 and* $Q = (Q_{\text{keys}}, \mathcal{L}_{\text{hash}}, \mathcal{I}_{\text{hash}}, Q_{\text{func}})$, *we have*

$$Q, \mathsf{Buyer}; \Psi_{\text{coins}} \models \Phi_B \begin{cases} \overline{x}_{\text{state}} : (x_\pi, x_{\text{ew}}, x_h, x_{\text{pks}}) \\ \Psi_0(y, \overline{x}_{\text{state}}) : \exists y_s, y_h.\ y \approx \langle y_s, y_h \rangle\ \wedge x_h \approx h(y_h) \\ \Psi_1(x_{\text{res}}, \overline{x}_{\text{state}}) : \mathsf{ver}_{\text{zk}}(x_\pi, x_{\text{ew}}, x_{\text{res}}, x_h, x_{\text{pks}}) \approx ok \end{cases}$$

We prove Φ_0 from Φ_B with Tamarin [35]. The properties Φ_1 and Φ_2 are simple local deduction properties that can be checked by hand (if the state of the buyer would be more complex, automated tools can also be used for that).

Observations: • the seller $(\mathcal{S})$ and buyer $(\mathcal{B})$ public keys are linked on the ledger, while this is not a necessary consequence of the security properties. $\mathcal{S}$ does not need to know the public key of $\mathcal{B}$ in advance, while $\mathcal{B}$ does need the public key of $\mathcal{S}$.
• private ledger keys of $\mathcal{S}$ and $\mathcal{B}$ do not have to be secret for security to hold:

our models allow corruption of any key by the adversary ($\mathcal{A}$). For $\mathcal{S}$, security follows from the fresh symmetric key created for each session and, for $\mathcal{B}$, from the trusted ledger. Note, however, that these keys allow $\mathcal{A}$ to spend the coins of their owner, but this is independent from the ZKCP protocol. In fact, a basic property of *any* ledger-based protocol should be that it does not reveal secret keys, i.e. $\forall x, i, j.$!Key(x) @ $i \land$ K(x) @ $j \Rightarrow \exists \ell.\ \ell < j \land$ Corrupt$(g(x))$ @ ℓ. We also prove this property in Tamarin for our models.
• $\mathcal{S}$ cannot reuse the same symmetric key and zero-knowledge proof in two different sessions, even if those sessions are for selling the same witness; • our intruder deduction rules assume a perfect zero-knowledge construction, in particular $\mathcal{A}$ cannot tweak the proof parameters in order to reveal the witness, as exploited by attacks of [16]. In the next section we show that intruder deduction rules can also model finer-grained properties of cryptographic constructions if required, in particular conditions when the witness may be revealed; • security for $\mathcal{S}$ depends on the timely delivery of transactions to the ledger, while this is not the case for $\mathcal{B}$, who could obtain both the witness and the money back if there was a time delay; • the proof x_π is not necessary for extracting the witness so it can be discarded after verification by $\mathcal{B}$; • our models consider a strong $\mathcal{A}$ and, as such, do not cover the case of weaker, multiple $\mathcal{A}$'s, e.g. for two different buyers that do not collude or do not control the network, but they can be extended to.

5   ZKCP Protocol on the Basecoin Ledger

Managing hashcoins - e.g. applying the hashing algorithm - sets tradeoffs for the agents that maintain the ledger; they may give priority to standard coins, i.e. preferring $\mathcal{L}_{\mathsf{base}}$ over $\mathcal{L}_{\mathsf{hash}}$. Another constraint that needs to be taken into account - by parties engaging in ZKCP - is the complexity of constructing and verifying the zero-knowledge proofs. In this section, we formalize and analyze the protocol of [15], which aims to implement the ZKCP functionality on $\mathcal{L}_{\mathsf{base}}$. Other works, e.g. [18], aim to minimize the zk burden by appealing to special contracts that will be executed only in case of dispute.

Cryptographic Primitives. For ZKCP on $\mathcal{L}_{\mathsf{base}}$, [15] adopts timed cryptographic commitments [33,34], as presented in Example 8, in order to emulate the ledger timeout. To link ledger transitions and data release, [15] exploits algebraic properties of the ECDSA signature used in Bitcoin: relying on homomorphic encryption, e.g. Paillier, an encrypted signature can be constructed from an encryption of the signing key, which can be constructed by adding shares of the signing key on top of an initial encrypted share [36–39]. A Diffie-Hellman group is used to establish a shared key. A special type of zk proof is also needed: a prover can encode the witness and convince the verifier that it can be extracted as soon as some committed structured data - for ZKCP: an ECDSA signature - is revealed. We rely on $\mathcal{I}_{\mathsf{base}}$ from Fig. 4 to model these crypto primitives. A term esign$(m, k, r_1, g(r_1 * r_2), pk(z))$ represents an encrypted partial signature of a message m, with signing key k, randomness share r_1, public randomness $g(r_1 * r_2)$, and encryption public key $pk(z)$. Combining it with the decryption key z and the complementary randomness share r_2, one can compute $\mathsf{sign}(m, k, r_1 * r_2)$. The rules for extract and $\mathsf{ver_{zk}}$ model the connection between a valid signature and witness extraction. Time commitments can be checked wrt the public part $g(x)$ of private data x.

$$\boxed{\begin{aligned}
&\mathsf{Hom_{\{g,enc\}}} : \; [\, \mathsf{K}(g(x)), \mathsf{K}(y) \,] \Rightarrow [\mathsf{K}(g(x * y))] \quad [\; \mathsf{K}(\mathsf{enc}(x, z)), \mathsf{K}(y) \,] \Rightarrow [\mathsf{K}(\mathsf{enc}(x * y, z))] \\
&\quad \mathsf{AG} : x * i(x) = 1, \; x * 1 = x, \; x * y = y * x, \; (x * y) * z = x * (y * z) \\
&\mathcal{R}_0 : \mathsf{homs}(\mathsf{enc}(k, y), m, r_1, r) \to \mathsf{esign}(m, k, r_1, r, y) \quad \mathsf{dec}(\mathsf{enc}(x, pk(y)), y) \to x \\
&\quad \mathsf{decs}(\mathsf{esign}(m, k, r_1, g(r_1 * r_2), pk(z)), r_2, z) \to \mathsf{sign}(m, k, r_1 * r_2) \\
&\quad \mathsf{ver}(\mathsf{sign}(x, y, z), x, g(y)) \to \mathsf{ok} \quad \mathsf{open}(\mathsf{com}(x, r), r) \to x \quad \mathsf{extract}(\mathsf{zk}(x, y, z), z) \to x \\
&\quad \mathsf{ver_{tc}}(\mathsf{tcom}(x), g(x)) \to \mathsf{ok} \quad \mathsf{ver_{zk}}(\mathsf{zk}(x, f(x), \mathsf{sign}(y, z, w)), f(x), y, g(z))) \to \mathsf{ok}
\end{aligned}}$$

Fig. 4. Intruder theory $\mathcal{I}_{\mathsf{base}}$; and $\forall f \in \mathcal{F}^{(k)}.[\mathsf{K}(x_1), \ldots, \mathsf{K}(x_k)] \Rightarrow [\mathsf{K}(f(x_1, \ldots, x_k))]$

Jointly Signing a Message. Assume two parties A_1 (holding k_1, r_1) and A_2 (holding k_2, r_2) want to create $\mathsf{sign}(t, k_1 * k_2, r_1 * r_2)$ for some agreed upon t. Then, say, A_1 can generate a fresh key pair $k, pk(k)$ and send $\mathsf{enc}(k_1, pk(k))$ to A_2. Relying on $\mathsf{Hom_{enc}}$, A_2 can obtain $\mathsf{enc}(k_1 * k_2, pk(k))$, which with $t, r_2, g(r_1 * r_2)$ as arguments to homs gives $\mathsf{esign}(t, k_1 * k_2, r_2, g(r_1 * r_2), pk(k))$. Sent back to A_1, the joint signature is derived by applying decs to this term and r_1, k. Note that A_1 gets the signature and can decide when to show it to A_2. On the other hand, both parties contribute to randomness in the signature; no party can force a particular value for the randomness. Both of these features will be needed to ensure the security properties for the ZKCP protocol:

(1) Based on DH key-exchange and commitments, compute a public key $pk_{12} = g(k_1 * k_2)$ such that the private key $k_1 * k_2$ is secret-shared between the seller ($\mathcal{S}$), who holds $k_1, g(k_2)$, and the buyer ($\mathcal{B}$), who holds $k_2, g(k_1)$. Similarly, secret-shared randomness $r_1 * r_2$ is computed: #Public : $pk_{12}, g(r_1 * r_2)$ Seller : k_1, r_1 Buyer : k_2, r_2#

(2) The key pk_{12} is used for an intermediate transfer from $\mathcal{B}$ to $\mathcal{S}$. The two agree on the transaction that transfers a coin from pk_{12} to $\mathcal{S}$: #Public : $t = \langle \mathsf{c2c}, \rho_{\mathsf{sn}}^1, \rho_{\mathsf{sn}}^2, g(\mathsf{ks}) \rangle$#, where $\rho_{\mathsf{sn}}^1, \rho_{\mathsf{sn}}^2$ are fresh public serial numbers and $g(\mathsf{ks})$ is the public key of $\mathcal{S}$. This transaction is not signed, so cannot yet lead to a transfer. Also, $\mathcal{B}$ has not yet transferred coins into pk_{12}.

(3) Based on crypto as shown above, $\mathcal{S}$ (with $\mathcal{B}$'s help) obtains $s = sign(t, k_1 * k_2, r_1 * r_2)$. $\mathcal{S}$ checks that s is valid by applying the signature verification algorithm. It then outputs the zero-knowledge proof $\pi = \mathsf{zk}(w, f(w), s)$ and a time commitment to $\mathcal{S}$'s share of the joint secret key: #Seller : s Public : $\pi, tcom(k_1)$#

(4) $\mathcal{B}$ verifies the proof and the time commitment, and transfers a coin to pk_{12}, leading to an update of the ledger: #Ledger : $!\mathsf{Coin}(\rho_{\mathsf{sn}}^1, pk_{12})$#

(5) The seller claims ρ_{sn}^1 by invoking $\mathsf{R_{c2c}}$ on the ledger, relying on the signature s obtained previously. The ledger will record a !Spend fact with the corresponding transaction data, including the signature:
$$\#\mathsf{Ledger} : !\mathsf{Spend}(\rho_{sn}^1, pk_{12}, s, g(ks))\#$$

(6) The buyer obtains s from the ledger and extracts the witness from the zk proof: $w = extract(\pi, s)$. If the seller aborted, no one can redeem the coin ρ_{sn}^1, until the time commitment reveals k_1, so the buyer can reconstruct $k_1 * k_2$ and redeem the coin. The formal specification is in Fig. 5, with details of joint signing omitted.

Proposition 3. *For* Seller *and* Buyer *from Fig. 5 and* $\mathsf{Q_{tcom}}$ *from Example 8,*

$$Q, \mathsf{Seller}; \Psi_{\mathsf{coins}} \models \Phi_S \quad Q, \mathsf{Buyer}; \Psi_{\mathsf{coins}} \models \Phi_B \quad Q = (\mathsf{Q_{keys}}, \mathsf{Q_{tcom}}, \mathcal{L}_{\mathsf{base}}, \mathcal{I}_{\mathsf{base}}, \mathsf{Q_{func}})$$
$$\textbf{where } \overline{x}_{\mathsf{state}} : \langle x_\pi, x_{\mathsf{tcom}}, x_{pk}^{12} \rangle, \Psi_0(y, \overline{x}_{\mathsf{state}}) : \exists z, x. \; x_\pi \approx \mathsf{zk}(z, x, x_s) \wedge y \approx x_s;$$
$$\Psi_1(x_{\mathsf{res}}, \overline{x}_{\mathsf{state}}) : \mathsf{ver}_{\mathsf{zk}}(x_\pi, x_{\mathsf{res}}, x_{\mathsf{tcom}}, x_{pk}^{12}) \approx \mathsf{ok}$$

Tamarin Verification: we prove Φ_S and Φ_0 for Φ_B automatically with Tamarin relying on the reduction that we present in the next section for termination within 1 min. We prove two helper lemmas along the way: (1) if the adversary knows a time commitment, then it either knows the committed message at an earlier time, or the commitment is constructed by an honest party; (2) fresh randoms and keys stay secret - unless opened by a time commitment. The Tamarin code is available online [35].

Observations: • as for $\mathcal{L}_{\mathsf{hash}}$, the $\mathcal{S}$ and $\mathcal{B}$ are linked on the ledger; the secret keys of any party can be corrupted, we prove however that the protocol does not itself reveal these keys; • the cryptographic constructions from [15] are a particular instance of $\mathcal{I}_{\mathsf{base}}$; it may admit more efficient instances, and our proofs could still be relied on for the security guarantees; • $\mathcal{I}_{\mathsf{base}}$ does not cover the full algebra of homomorphic encryption, where we have

---

$S_0: [\, !\mathsf{Key}(x_{ks}), !\mathsf{Witn}(x_{wtn}) \,] -\!\![\, \mathsf{Sell}(g(x_{ks}), x_{wtn}) \,]\!\!\mapsto [\, \mathsf{state}_0 \,]$

$S_1: [\, \mathsf{state}_0, \mathsf{Fr}(k_1), \mathsf{Fr}(r_1), \mathsf{Fr}(r) \,] \Rightarrow [\, \mathsf{Out}(\mathsf{com}(g(k_1), r)), \mathsf{Out}(g(r_1)), \mathsf{state}_1 \,]$

$S_2: [\, \mathsf{state}_1, \mathsf{In}(y_{k_2}), \mathsf{Fr}(k_e) \,] \Rightarrow [\, \mathsf{Out}(r), \mathsf{Out}(\mathsf{enc}(k_1, \mathsf{pk}(k_e))), \mathsf{state}_2 \,]$

$S_3: [\, \mathsf{state}_2 \lceil y_{k_2} = g(x_{k_2}) \rfloor, x_{pk}^{12} = g(x_{k_2} * k_1), c_k = \mathsf{tcom}(k_1), x_\pi = \mathsf{zk}(x_{wtn}, f(x_{wtn}), s) \,]$
　$(\mathsf{JointSign} \mapsto t = \langle \mathsf{c2c}, \rho_{sn}^1, \rho_{sn}^2, g(x_{ks}) \rangle, s = \mathsf{sign}(t, \dots) \,) \qquad\qquad \Rightarrow [\, \mathsf{Out}(\langle c_k, x_\pi \rangle), \mathsf{state}_3 \,]$

$S_4: [\, \mathsf{state}_3, !\mathsf{Coin}(\rho_{sn}^1, x_{pk}^{12}) \,] -\!\![\, \mathsf{Unspent}(\rho_{sn}^1), \mathsf{Claim}(g(x_{ks}), x_{wtn}, k_1, \rho_{sn}^1) \,]\!\!\mapsto [\, \mathsf{Out}(\langle s, \rho_{sn}^2, g(x_{ks}) \rangle) \,]$

$B_0: [\, !\mathsf{Res}(x_{res}), !\mathsf{Key}(x_{kb}), !\mathsf{Pk}(x_{pks}), !\mathsf{Coin}(x_{sn}^0, g(x_{kb})) \,] \Rightarrow [\, \mathsf{state}_0 \,]$

$B_1: [\, \mathsf{state}_0, \mathsf{In}(\langle x_{ck}, y_{r_1} \rangle), \mathsf{Fr}(k_2), \mathsf{Fr}(r_2) \,] \Rightarrow [\mathsf{Out}(\langle g(k_2), g(r_2) \rangle), \mathsf{state}_1 \,]$

$B_2: [\, \mathsf{state}_1 \lceil x_{ck} = \mathsf{com}(g(x_{k_1}), x_r), y_{r_1} = g(x_{r_1}) \rfloor, \mathsf{In}(x_r), x_{pk}^{12} = g(x_{k_1} * k_2), x_r^{12} = g(x_{r_1} * r_2) \,]$
　$(\mathsf{JointSign} \mapsto t = \langle \mathsf{c2c}, \rho_{sn}^1, \rho_{sn}^2, x_{pks} \rangle, s = \mathsf{sign}(t, \dots) \,) \qquad\qquad\qquad\qquad \Rightarrow [\mathsf{state}_2 \,]$

$B_3: [\, \mathsf{state}_2, \mathsf{In}(\langle x_{tcom}, x_\pi \rangle), \mathsf{Fr}(r) \,] -\!\![\, \mathsf{ver}_{\mathsf{zk}}(x_\pi, x_{res}, t, x_{pk}^{12}) \approx \mathsf{ok}, \mathsf{ver}_{\mathsf{tc}}(x_{tcom}, g(x_{k_1})) \approx \mathsf{ok},$
　$\mathsf{Pay}(g(x_{kb}), x_{res}, \rho_{sn}^1, \langle x_\pi, x_{tcom}, x_{pk}^{12} \rangle) \,]\!\!\mapsto$
　$\qquad\qquad\qquad\qquad [\, \mathsf{Out}(\langle \mathsf{sign}(\langle \mathsf{c2c}, x_{sn}^0, \rho_{sn}^1, x_{pk}^{12} \rangle, x_{kb}, r), \rho_{sn}^1, x_{pk}^{12} \rangle), \mathsf{state}_3 \,]$

$B_4^{\mathsf{go}}: [\, \mathsf{state}_3, !\mathsf{Spend}(\rho_{sn}^1, z, s, x_{pks}), x_{wtn} = extract(x_\pi, s) \,] -\!\![\, x_{res} \approx f(x_{wtn}), \mathsf{Witness}(x_{res}) \,]\!\!\mapsto [\,] $

$B_4^{\mathsf{ab}}: [\, \mathsf{state}_3, !\mathsf{Coin}(\rho_{sn}^1, g(x_k^{12})), \mathsf{In}(x_{k_1}), \mathsf{Fr}(r), x_k^{12} = x_{k_1} * k_2, x_s = \mathsf{sign}(\langle \rho_{sn}^1, \rho_{sn}^2, g(x_{kb}) \rangle, x_k^{12}, r) \,]$
　$\qquad\qquad -\!\![\, x_{tcom} \approx \mathsf{tcom}(x_{k_1}), \mathsf{Unspent}(\rho_{sn}^1) \,]\!\!\mapsto [\, \mathsf{Out}(\langle x_s, \rho_{sn}^1, g(x_{kb}) \rangle) \,]$

Fig. 5. ZKCP on $\mathcal{L}_{\mathsf{base}}$; Seller $= (S_0, \dots, S_4)$; Buyer $= (B_0, \dots, B_3, B_4^{\mathsf{go}}, B_4^{\mathsf{ab}})$

$[\mathsf{K}(\mathsf{enc}(x,z)),\mathsf{K}(\mathsf{enc}(y,z))\,]\Rightarrow[\mathsf{K}(\mathsf{enc}(x*y,z))]$. It is however sound when every ciphertext constructed by honest parties uses a fresh key, as in our case study; covering the full theory is a long-standing, still open, problem for protocol verification $\bullet$ the same shared key could be used for the exchange of several witnesses within the timeframe chosen for the time commitment; $\bullet$ contrary to $\mathcal{L}_{\mathsf{hash}}$, the zero-knowledge proof cannot be discarded by $\mathcal{B}$ after verification, since it is necessary for extracting the witness; $\bullet$ on $\mathcal{L}_{\mathsf{hash}}$, $\mathcal{B}$ sets the ledger timeout and $\mathcal{S}$ can accept to proceed; on $\mathcal{L}_{\mathsf{base}}$ it is the other way around with respect to crypto timeout.

6 Homomorphism and Abelian Group Reduction

We take a class of intruder theories that covers the one of Fig. 4; $\mathcal{F}$ contains a set of homomorphic functions $\mathcal{F}_{\mathsf{hom}}$. We reduce any $\mathcal{I}$ from this class to $\mathcal{I}_\Delta$ such that: $\mathcal{I}_\Delta$ is *simpler* than $\mathcal{I}$; $\mathcal{I}_\Delta$ is sound wrt $\mathcal{I}$. First, given any trace τ wrt $\mathcal{I}$, we show that there is $\mathcal{I}_\Delta$ generating τ and where: *(i)* the homomorphic properties are restricted by arguments from honest parties in τ; *(ii)* the abelian group is degenerated, allowing to obtain any factors from products. Second, we augment any set of rules $\mathcal{S}$ to $\mathcal{S}_\Delta$, which records as facts the homomorphic arguments of $\mathcal{S}$, and $\mathcal{I}_\Delta$ is generalized to cover any trace of $\mathcal{S}_\Delta$.

Definition 7. *A* base *for $\mathcal{F}$ is a function Δ with $dom(\Delta) = \mathcal{F}_{hom}$ and $\forall f \in \mathcal{F}_{hom}^{(n)}$. $\Delta(f) \subseteq \mathcal{T}^n$. We assume that Δ is closed modulo AC, i.e. $\Delta_f(u*v,\overline{w}) \Rightarrow \Delta_f(v*u,\overline{w})$ and similarly for associativity, and closed by: $\Delta_f(u*v,\overline{w}) \Rightarrow \Delta_f(u,\overline{w})$.*

We extend intruder deduction to rules of the form $[\Delta_f(\overline{x}),M] \Rightarrow [N]$, which have the same semantics as $[M] \Rightarrow [N]$ with the additional constraint that $\overline{x}\theta \in \Delta(f)$ holds for the substitution θ that instantiates the rule.

Definition 8. *We consider the class of intruder theories as defined below (left):*

Initial theory $\mathcal{I}$ (with Hom for all $f \in \mathcal{F}_{hom}$)	Reduced theory $\mathcal{I}_\Delta$ for base Δ
Hom : $[\,\mathsf{K}(f(x,\overline{z})),\mathsf{K}(y)\,] \Rightarrow [\mathsf{K}(f(x*y,\overline{z}))]$	Hom$_\Delta$: $[\,\Delta_f(x,\overline{z}),\mathsf{K}(y))\,] \Rightarrow [\mathsf{K}(f(x*y,\overline{z}))]$
AG : $x*i(x) = 1$, $x*1 = x$	AP : $[\,\mathsf{K}(x*y)\,] \Rightarrow [\mathsf{K}(x)]$
$x*y = y*x$, $(x*y)*z = x*(y*z)$	$x*y = y*x$, $(x*y)*z = x*(y*z)$
$\mathcal{R}_0 : \{l_1 \rightarrow r_1, \ldots, l_k \rightarrow r_k\}$	$\mathcal{R}_0 : \{l_1 \rightarrow r_1, \ldots, l_k \rightarrow r_k\}$

We assume that every $l \rightarrow r \in \mathcal{R}_0$ satisfies
H1: $top(l), top(r) \notin \mathcal{F}_{hom} \cup \{*, i\}$ **H2:** $\forall t \in st(r) \setminus st(l).\ top(t) \cap (\mathcal{F}_{hom} \cup \{*, i\}) = \emptyset$
Given such $\mathcal{I}$ and a base Δ, we define the reduced theory $\mathcal{I}_\Delta$ as above (right). $\mathcal{I}$, $\mathcal{I}_\Delta$ also contain the deduction rules $\forall f.[\mathsf{K}(x_1), \ldots, \mathsf{K}(x_k)] \Rightarrow [\mathsf{K}(f(x_1, \ldots, x_k))]$.

H1 and H2 help in proofs [40]; $\mathcal{R}_0$ from Fig. 4 respects them. Intuitively, we split the homomorphic argument of f in two parts, e.g. $f(u*v, \overline{w})$, where the factors of v are known by the adversary, while the factors of u are provided by honest parties (in $\mathcal{S}$). When the adversary applies Hom to such a term, to get e.g. $f(u*v*t, \overline{w})$, there is a *smaller* term $f(u, \overline{w})$ that can be used to obtain the same result, since the adversary knows $v*t$. The term u will be added by $\mathcal{S}_\Delta$ to $\Delta(f)$ so Hom$_\Delta$ can be applied on it.

Proposition 4. *For any S, M_0, M_1 s.t. M_1 can be derived from M_0 using rules in $S \cup \mathcal{I}$, there is Δ s.t. M_1 can be derived from M_0 using $S \cup \mathcal{I}_\Delta$; Δ can be iteratively constructed by a set S_Δ - augmenting each rule in S with a constant number of facts.*

Corollary 1. *For any S and formulas Ψ, Φ, we have $S_\Delta, \mathcal{I}_\Delta; \Psi \models \Phi \Rightarrow S, \mathcal{I}; \Psi \models \Phi$*

Scope. The reduction is sound for any set of protocol rules. However, since $\mathcal{I}_\Delta$ allows to freely decompose products, it gives too much power to the adversary (leading to false attacks) for certain classes of protocols, e.g. when a nonce r protects a secret s in $s * r$. The reduction is useful for proofs only when secret data is protected by (homomorphic) cryptographic constructions, e.g. exponentiation, encryption, etc.

7   Related and Future Work

Several works extend the scope of Tamarin to new cryptographic primitives [41–43] or infrastructure features [44,45]. Our models contribute to both of these directions. On the crypto side, an open question is to cover deductions like $\mathsf{enc}(u, k), \mathsf{enc}(v, k) \Rightarrow \mathsf{enc}(u * v, k)$, which would allow to model e.g. homomorphic tallying for voting [46]. Protocol verification modulo this theory is studied in [47], where abstractions different from ours are used for reducing the theory, but the case studies are limited to unification problems and relatively simple protocols.

Works complementary to ours aim to provide formal guarantees for code executed on the blockchain [48–50]. Our ledger models are, on one hand, grounded on such guarantees and, on the other hand, they allow to reason about the properties of higher-level protocols and applications. In future work, we can extend our models to cover more general smart contracts, hybrid ledgers and applications [18,32,51]. Current ZKCP protocols don't allow seller/buyer unlinkability, while the security properties leave scope for it. An open problem is ZKCP on ledgers with more privacy [52–54] and appropriate unlinkability notions.

Acknowledgment. The research leading to these results has received funding from the European Research Council (ERC) under the European Union's Horizon 2020 research and innovation program (grant agreements No. 645865-SPOOC).

References

1. Nakamoto, S.: Bitcoin: a peer-to-peer electronic cash system (2008). https://bitcoin.org/bitcoin.pdf
2. Wood, G.: Ethereum: a secure decentralised generalised transaction ledger (2014). https://gavwood.com/paper.pdf
3. Goodman, L.M.: Tezos - a self-amending crypto-ledger (2014). https://tezos.com/static/white_paper-2dc8c02267a8fb86bd67a108199441bf.pdf

4. Hanke, T., Movahedi, M., Williams, D.: DFINITY technology overview series, consensus system. CoRR, abs/1805.04548 (2018)
5. Garay, J., Kiayias, A., Leonardos, N.: The bitcoin backbone protocol: analysis and applications. In: Oswald, E., Fischlin, M. (eds.) EUROCRYPT 2015. LNCS, vol. 9057, pp. 281–310. Springer, Heidelberg (2015). https://doi.org/10.1007/978-3-662-46803-6_10
6. Pass, R., Seeman, L., Shelat, A.: Analysis of the blockchain protocol in asynchronous networks. In: Coron, J.-S., Nielsen, J.B. (eds.) EUROCRYPT 2017. LNCS, vol. 10211, pp. 643–673. Springer, Cham (2017). https://doi.org/10.1007/978-3-319-56614-6_22
7. Dashti, M.T., Mauw, S.: Fair exchange. In: Rosenberg, B. (ed.) Handbook of Financial Cryptography and Security, pp. 109–132. Chapman and Hall/CRC, Boca Raton (2010)
8. Asokan, N., Shoup, V., Waidner, M.: Optimistic fair exchange of digital signatures. In: Nyberg, K. (ed.) EUROCRYPT 1998. LNCS, vol. 1403, pp. 591–606. Springer, Heidelberg (1998). https://doi.org/10.1007/BFb0054156
9. Cachin, C., Camenisch, J.: Optimistic fair secure computation. In: Bellare, M. (ed.) CRYPTO 2000. LNCS, vol. 1880, pp. 93–111. Springer, Heidelberg (2000). https://doi.org/10.1007/3-540-44598-6_6
10. Micali, S.: Simple and fast optimistic protocols for fair electronic exchange. In: 22nd ACM Symposium on Principles of Distributed Computing (PODC 2003), pp. 12–19. ACM (2003)
11. Lindell, A.Y.: Legally-enforceable fairness in secure two-party computation. In: Malkin, T. (ed.) CT-RSA 2008. LNCS, vol. 4964, pp. 121–137. Springer, Heidelberg (2008). https://doi.org/10.1007/978-3-540-79263-5_8
12. Andrychowicz, M., Dziembowski, S., Malinowski, D., Mazurek, L.: Fair two-party computations via bitcoin deposits. In: Böhme, R., Brenner, M., Moore, T., Smith, M. (eds.) FC 2014. LNCS, vol. 8438, pp. 105–121. Springer, Heidelberg (2014). https://doi.org/10.1007/978-3-662-44774-1_8
13. Bentov, I., Kumaresan, R.: How to use bitcoin to design fair protocols. In: Garay, J.A., Gennaro, R. (eds.) CRYPTO 2014. LNCS, vol. 8617, pp. 421–439. Springer, Heidelberg (2014). https://doi.org/10.1007/978-3-662-44381-1_24
14. Bitcoin Wiki: Zero Knowledge Contingent Payment. https://en.bitcoin.it/wiki/Zero_Knowledge_Contingent_Payment
15. Banasik, W., Dziembowski, S., Malinowski, D.: Efficient zero-knowledge contingent payments in cryptocurrencies without scripts. In: Askoxylakis, I., Ioannidis, S., Katsikas, S., Meadows, C. (eds.) ESORICS 2016. LNCS, vol. 9879, pp. 261–280. Springer, Cham (2016). https://doi.org/10.1007/978-3-319-45741-3_14
16. Campanelli, M., Gennaro, R., Goldfeder, S., Nizzardo, L.: Zero-knowledge contingent payments revisited: attacks and payments for services. In: ACM SIGSAC Conference on Computer and Communications Security (CCS 2017), pp. 229–243. ACM (2017)
17. Goldfeder, S., Bonneau, J., Gennaro, R., Narayanan, A.: Escrow protocols for cryptocurrencies: how to buy physical goods using bitcoin. In: Kiayias, A. (ed.) FC 2017. LNCS, vol. 10322, pp. 321–339. Springer, Cham (2017). https://doi.org/10.1007/978-3-319-70972-7_18
18. Dziembowski, S., Eckey, L., Faust, S.: FairSwap: how to fairly exchange digital goods. In: ACM SIGSAC Conference on Computer and Communications Security (CCS 2018), pp. 967–984. ACM (2018)

19. Cohn-Gordon, K., Cremers, C.J.F., Garratt, L.: On post-compromise security. In: IEEE 29th Computer Security Foundations Symposium (CSF 2016), pp. 164–178. IEEE Computer Society (2016)
20. Cohn-Gordon, K., Cremers, C.J.F., Dowling, B., Garratt, L., Stebila, D.: A formal security analysis of the signal messaging protocol. In: IEEE European Symposium on Security and Privacy (EuroS&P 2017), pp. 451–466. IEEE Computer Society (2017)
21. Bhargavan, K., Blanchet, B., Kobeissi, N.: Verified models and reference implementations for the TLS 1.3 standard candidate. In: IEEE Symposium on Security and Privacy (SP 2017), pp. 483–502. IEEE Computer Society (2017)
22. Cremers, C., Horvat, M., Hoyland, J., Scott, S., van der Merwe, T.: A comprehensive symbolic analysis of TLS 1.3. In: ACM SIGSAC Conference on Computer and Communications Security (CCS 2017), pp. 1773–1788. ACM (2017)
23. Jacomme, C., Kremer, S.: An extensive formal analysis of multi-factor authentication protocols. In: 31st IEEE Computer Security Foundations Symposium (CSF 2018), pp. 1–15. IEEE Computer Society (2018)
24. Meier, S., Schmidt, B., Cremers, C., Basin, D.: The TAMARIN prover for the symbolic analysis of security protocols. In: Sharygina, N., Veith, H. (eds.) CAV 2013. LNCS, vol. 8044, pp. 696–701. Springer, Heidelberg (2013). https://doi.org/10.1007/978-3-642-39799-8_48
25. Cervesato, I., Durgin, N.A., Mitchell, J.C., Lincoln, P., Scedrov, A.: Relating strands and multiset rewriting for security protocol analysis. In: 13th IEEE Computer Security Foundations Workshop, CSFW 2000, Cambridge, England, UK, 3–5 July 2000, pp. 35–51. IEEE Computer Society (2000)
26. Schmidt, B., Meier, S., Cremers, C.J.F., Basin, D.A.: Automated analysis of Diffie-Hellman protocols and advanced security properties. In: 25th IEEE Computer Security Foundations Symposium (CSF 2012), pp. 78–94. IEEE Computer Society (2012)
27. Dershowitz, N., Jouannaud, J.-P.: Rewrite systems. In: van Leeuwen, J. (ed.) Handbook of Theoretical Computer Science, Volume B: Formal Models and Sematics (B), pp. 243–320. MIT Press, Cambridge (1990)
28. Vaudenay, S.: The security of DSA and ECDSA. In: Desmedt, Y.G. (ed.) PKC 2003. LNCS, vol. 2567, pp. 309–323. Springer, Heidelberg (2003). https://doi.org/10.1007/3-540-36288-6_23
29. Bitcoin Wiki: Hashed Timelock Contracts. https://en.bitcoin.it/wiki/Hashed_Timelock_Contracts
30. Bitcoin Wiki: Payment channels. https://en.bitcoin.it/wiki/Payment_channels
31. Bitcoin Wiki: Lightning Network. https://en.bitcoin.it/wiki/Lightning_Network
32. Hearn, M.: Corda: a distributed ledger (2016)
33. Rivest, R.L., Shamir, A., Wagner, D.A.: Time-lock puzzles and timed-release crypto. Technical report, MIT, Cambridge, MA, USA (1996)
34. Boneh, D., Naor, M.: Timed commitments. In: Bellare, M. (ed.) CRYPTO 2000. LNCS, vol. 1880, pp. 236–254. Springer, Heidelberg (2000). https://doi.org/10.1007/3-540-44598-6_15
35. Tamarin code for ZKCP protocol verification. https://www.dropbox.com/sh/ahzbbojm5z0e6a9/AAB6-Pz-RK3xwVznlaqaitfca?dl=0
36. Paillier, P.: Public-key cryptosystems based on composite degree residuosity classes. In: Stern, J. (ed.) EUROCRYPT 1999. LNCS, vol. 1592, pp. 223–238. Springer, Heidelberg (1999). https://doi.org/10.1007/3-540-48910-X_16

37. Lindell, Y.: Fast secure two-party ECDSA signing. In: Katz, J., Shacham, H. (eds.) CRYPTO 2017. LNCS, vol. 10402, pp. 613–644. Springer, Cham (2017). https://doi.org/10.1007/978-3-319-63715-0_21

38. Lindell, Y., Nof, A.: Fast secure multiparty ECDSA with practical distributed key generation and applications to cryptocurrency custody. In: ACM SIGSAC Conference on Computer and Communications Security (CCS 2018), pp. 1837–1854. ACM (2018)

39. Gennaro, R., Goldfeder, S.: Fast multiparty threshold ECDSA with fast trustless setup. In: ACM SIGSAC Conference on Computer and Communications Security (CCS 2018), pp. 1179–1194. ACM (2018)

40. Additional material: Tamarin code and long paper version. https://www.dropbox.com/sh/t74k3q4gxrmo0pw/AADvx0e8WDaZgyf0OQFlElICa?dl=0

41. Schmidt, B., Sasse, R., Cremers, C., Basin, D.A.: Automated verification of group key agreement protocols. In: IEEE Symposium on Security and Privacy (SP 2014), pp. 179–194 (2014)

42. Dreier, J., Hirschi, L., Radomirovic, S., Sasse, R.: Automated unbounded verification of stateful cryptographic protocols with exclusive OR. In: 31st IEEE Computer Security Foundations Symposium, CSF 2018, pp. 359–373. IEEE Computer Society (2018)

43. Dreier, J., Duménil, C., Kremer, S., Sasse, R.: Beyond subterm-convergent equational theories in automated verification of stateful protocols. In: Maffei, M., Ryan, M. (eds.) POST 2017. LNCS, vol. 10204, pp. 117–140. Springer, Heidelberg (2017). https://doi.org/10.1007/978-3-662-54455-6_6

44. Kremer, S., Künnemann, R.: Automated analysis of security protocols with global state. J. Comput. Secur. **24**(5), 583–616 (2016)

45. Backes, M., Dreier, J., Kremer, S., Künnemann, R.: A novel approach for reasoning about liveness in cryptographic protocols and its application to fair exchange. In: IEEE European Symposium on Security and Privacy (EuroS&P 2017), pp. 76–91. IEEE Computer Society (2017)

46. Baudron, O., Fouque, P.-A., Pointcheval, D., Stern, J., Poupard, G.: Practical multi-candidate election system. In: 20th Annual (ACM) Symposium on Principles of Distributed Computing (PODC 2001), pp. 274–283. ACM (2001)

47. Yang, F., Escobar, S., Meadows, C.A., Meseguer, J., Narendran, P.: Theories of homomorphic encryption, unification, and the finite variant property. In: Proceedings of the 16th International Symposium on Principles and Practice of Declarative Programming, Kent, Canterbury, United Kingdom, 8–10 September 2014, pp. 123–133 (2014)

48. Bartoletti, M., Zunino, R.: BitML: a calculus for bitcoin smart contracts. In: ACM SIGSAC Conference on Computer and Communications Security (CCS 2018), pp. 83–100 (2018)

49. Bhargavan, K., et al.: Formal verification of smart contracts. In: ACM Workshop on Programming Languages and Analysis for Security (PLAS@CCS 2016), pp. 91–96. ACM (2016)

50. Hildenbrandt, E., et al.: KEVM: a complete formal semantics of the ethereum virtual machine. In: 31st IEEE Computer Security Foundations Symposium (CSF 2018), pp. 204–217. IEEE Computer Society (2018)

51. Dziembowski, S., Faust, S., Hostáková, K.: General state channel networks. In: ACM SIGSAC Conference on Computer and Communications Security (CCS 2018), pp. 949–966. ACM (2018)

52. Ben-Sasson, E., et al.: Zerocash: decentralized anonymous payments from bitcoin. In: IEEE Symposium on Security and Privacy, SP 2014, pp. 459–474. IEEE Computer Society (2014)
53. Zyskind, G., Nathan, O., Pentland, A.: Enigma: decentralized computation platform with guaranteed privacy. CoRR, abs/1506.03471 (2015)
54. Malavolta, G., Moreno-Sanchez, P., Kate, A., Maffei, M., Ravi, S.: Concurrency and privacy with payment-channel networks. In: ACM SIGSAC Conference on Computer and Communications Security (CCS 2017), pp. 455–471. ACM (2017)

Symbolic Analysis of Terrorist Fraud Resistance

Alexandre Debant[1]([✉]), Stéphanie Delaune[1], and Cyrille Wiedling[2]

[1] Univ Rennes, CNRS, IRISA, Rennes, France
{alexandre.debant,stephanie.delaune}@irisa.fr
[2] DGA MI, Bruz, France
cwiedling@gmail.com

Abstract. Distance-bounding protocols aim at preventing several kinds of attacks, amongst which terrorist fraud, where a far away malicious prover colludes with an attacker to authenticate once, without giving him any advantage for future authentication. In this paper, we consider a symbolic setting and propose a formal definition of terrorist fraud, as well as two reduction results. When looking for an attack, we can first restrict ourselves to consider a particular (and quite simple) topology. Moreover, under some mild hypotheses, the far away malicious prover has a best strategy on which we can focus on when looking for an attack. These two reduction results make possible the analysis of terrorist fraud resistance using an existing verification tool. As an application, we analyse several distance-bounding protocols, as well as some contactless payment protocols using the ProVerif tool.

1 Introduction

Contactless devices deployed today in ticketing and building access-control applications are supposed to make our life easier but they also make possible new kinds of attacks, e.g. relay attacks. An attacker can use two transponders (two mobile phones could be sufficient) in order to relay over a large distance the information between e.g. a card and an access card reader. As a result, an unauthorised person will be able to enter a building using an access card located far away and possibly still in the pocket of his holder. With the deployment of contactless systems, ensuring "proximity authentication", through the use of secure protocols, is an important goal.

Relay attacks cannot be prevented by traditional cryptographic protocols. One possible defence is *distance bounding protocols*. The main goal of a distance bounding protocol consists of ensuring that a prover is within a close distance to a verifier by timing the round-trip delay of a cryptographic challenge-response exchange. Therefore the security of these protocols is based on the physical limits

This work has been partially supported by the European Research Council (ERC) under the European Union's Horizon 2020 research and innovation program (grant agreement No 714955-POPSTAR).

ⓒ Springer Nature Switzerland AG 2019
K. Sako et al. (Eds.): ESORICS 2019, LNCS 11735, pp. 383–403, 2019.
https://doi.org/10.1007/978-3-030-29959-0_19

of communication: transmission can not go faster than the speed of light. Since they have been introduced by Brands and Chaum in 1993 [8], many protocols have been designed and analysed against various threats. In general, distance bounding protocols shall resist to *distance fraud*: a malicious prover should not be able to successfully complete a session with an honest verifier who is far away (even with the help of some honest provers in the neighbourhood - so called *distance hijacking*). They should also resist to *mafia fraud* where typically an attacker abuses a far away prover to pass the protocol. In most cases, this is achieved by relaying messages between the prover and the verifier (the so-called *relay attack*). A more subtle notion is the notion of *terrorist fraud*. Here, a far away malicious prover colludes with an attacker who is close to the verifier to pass the protocol on his behalf. Such a scenario may occur if a legitimate worker want to enable a third party to access his office, located in a restricted area, when he is away. To prevent such behaviours, the protocol is said resistant to a terrorist fraud if this help is actually reusable meaning that the third party can use this extra information to impersonate the prover later on. The rationale is that a malicious prover will not accept to give such an advantage to his accomplice, and thus will not accept to collude with the attacker. This type of attack is very tricky and rather difficult to model and analyse since it requires to consider "terrorist" provers that are not fully dishonest in the sense that they are not willing for instance to reveal their credentials.

Formal symbolic modelling and analysing techniques have proved their usefulness for verifying security protocols, and nowadays several verification tools exist, e.g. ProVerif [5,6], Tamarin [26]. Since the seminal paper by Dolev-Yao in [16], a lot of progress has been done in the area of formal symbolic verification and it is now a common good practice to formally analyse a protocol using these techniques before their deployment. In this so-called Dolev-Yao model, messages are transmitted without introducing any delay preventing us to use this model to analyse protocols for which transmission delay plays an important role. To overcome this limitation, getting some inspiration from earlier works (e.g. [4,25,28]), some recent works have proposed to incorporate new features in existing symbolic models [11,13,14,23], making the analysis of distance bounding protocols possible relying on existing verification tools (e.g. ProVerif, Tamarin).

Our Contributions. In this paper, distance bounding protocols are modelled using the calculus we introduced in [14]. This calculus shares some similarities with the applied pi calculus [1,6], a well-established process algebra for modelling cryptographic protocols. Within this framework, we propose a formal definition of terrorist fraud. We will see that this notion is tricky and complex and require a quantification over all the topologies, but also another one to consider all the possible terrorist provers. Due to this, such a security property can not be analysed using techniques deployed in e.g. [13,14,23]. Our main contribution is to provide reduction results to reduce the number of topologies we have to consider during our analysis, and more importantly to reduce the possible behaviours of our terrorist prover. We will see that under some reasonable conditions, we are able to reduce the number of topologies to be considered to one (involving at most 4 participants), and the best strategy for the terrorist prover can also be fixed without missing any attack. Then, an interesting consequence of our results is that, following the approach used e.g. in [11,14], it becomes possible to rely on the automatic verification tool ProVerif (originally developed to analyse traditional security protocols) to analyse terrorist fraud in various distance bounding protocols. All the omitted proofs are available in the full version [15].

Related Works. Several attempts have been made in the computational model to formalise terrorist fraud, e.g. [2,17,18,30]. Avoine *et al.* [2] introduce a unified framework for clarifying the situation and make possible comparison between protocols. Since then, several formal definitions of terrorist fraud have been proposed [18,30], as well as protocols supposed to achieve this level of security, e.g. [3,9,22]. In contrast, the only definition we are aware of in the symbolic model is the one proposed by Chothia et al. in [11]. However, such a definition falls short when modelling behaviours of terrorist provers (see Sect. 3). Independently of our work, Mauw et al. proposed a definition more in line with the one we considered here [24]. However, their work falls short when it comes to the automation of security analysis (see Sect. 4.3).

2 Model for Distance Bounding Protocols

In this section, we introduce the process calculus we rely on to describe distance bounding protocols [14]. It shares some similarities with the applied pi calculus used e.g. by the ProVerif verification tool [6].

2.1 Messages

As usual in the symbolic setting, we model messages through a term algebra. We consider both equational theories and reduction relations to represent the properties of the cryptographic primitives.

Term Algebra. We consider two infinite and disjoint sets of *names*: $\mathcal{N}$ is the set of *basic names*, which are used to represent keys, nonces, whereas $\mathcal{A}$ is the set of *agent names*, *i.e.* names which represent the agents identities. We consider an infinite set Σ_0 of constant symbols that are used to represent values known by the attacker, as well as two infinite and disjoint sets of *variables*, denoted $\mathcal{X}$ and $\mathcal{W}$. Variables in $\mathcal{X}$ refer to unknown parts of messages expected by participants while variables in $\mathcal{W}$ are used to store messages learnt by the attacker.

We assume a signature Σ, *i.e.* a set of function symbols together with their arity. The elements of Σ are split into *constructor* and *destructor* symbols, *i.e.* $\Sigma = \Sigma_c \uplus \Sigma_d$. We denote $\Sigma^+ = \Sigma \cup \Sigma_0$, and $\Sigma_c^+ = \Sigma_c \cup \Sigma_0$. Given a signature $\mathcal{F}$, and a set of atomic data A, we denote by $\mathcal{T}(\mathcal{F}, \mathsf{A})$ the set of *terms* built from atomic data A by applying function symbols in $\mathcal{F}$. A *constructor term* is a term in $\mathcal{T}(\Sigma_c^+, \mathcal{N} \cup \mathcal{A} \cup \mathcal{X})$. We denote $vars(u)$ the set of variables that occur in a term u. A *message* is a constructor term u that is *ground*, *i.e.* such that $vars(u) = \emptyset$. The application of a substitution σ to a term u is written $u\sigma$. We denote $dom(\sigma)$ its *domain*, and $img(\sigma)$ its *image*. The positions of a term are defined as usual.

Example 1. We consider the signature $\Sigma_{ex} = \{kdf/3, shk/2, ok/0, eq/2, ans/3\}$. The symbol kdf models a key derivation function, shk is used to model a key shared between 2 agents. The symbols ok and eq are used to model equality tests, and ans is a function symbol that is used to model the answer provided by the prover. Another signature useful to model the exclusive-or operator is $\Sigma_{xor} = \{\oplus, 0\}$. Among all the symbols in $\Sigma_{ex} \cup \Sigma_{xor}$ only eq is a destructor.

Equational Theory. Following the approach developed in [6], constructor terms are subject to an *equational theory* allowing us to model the algebraic properties of the primitives. It consists of a finite set of equations of the form $u = v$ where $u, v \in \mathcal{T}(\Sigma_c, \mathcal{X})$, and induces an equivalence relation $=_E$ over constructor terms.[1]

Example 2. To reflect the algebraic properties of the exclusive-or operator, we may consider the equational theory E_{xor} generated by the following equations:
$$(x \oplus y) \oplus z = x \oplus (y \oplus z) \qquad x \oplus y = y \oplus x \qquad x \oplus 0 = x \qquad x \oplus x = 0.$$

Rewriting Rules. As in [6], we also give a meaning to destructor symbols. This is done through a set of rewrite rules of the form $g(t_1, \ldots, t_n) \to t$ where $g \in \Sigma_d$, and $t, t_1, \ldots, t_n \in \mathcal{T}(\Sigma_c, \mathcal{X})$. A term u can be *rewritten* in v if there is a position p in u, and a rewrite rule $g(t_1, \ldots, t_n) \to t$ such that $u|_p =_E g(t_1, \ldots, t_n)\theta$ for some substitution θ, and $v = u[t\theta]_p$ i.e. u in which the term at position p has been replaced by $t\theta$. Moreover, we assume that $t_1\theta, \ldots, t_n\theta$ as well as $t\theta$ are constructor terms. We only consider sets of rewrite rules that yield a *convergent* rewriting system (modulo E), and we denote $u\downarrow$ the *normal form* of a term u.

For modelling purposes, we split the signature Σ into two parts, Σ_{pub} and Σ_{priv}, and we denote $\Sigma_{pub}^+ = \Sigma_{pub} \cup \Sigma_0$. An attacker builds messages by applying public symbols to terms he knows and that are available through variables in $\mathcal{W}$. Formally, a computation done by the attacker is a *recipe*, *i.e.* a term in $\mathcal{T}(\Sigma_{pub}^+, \mathcal{W})$.

Example 3. Among symbols in $\Sigma_{ex} \cup \Sigma_{xor}$, only shk is in Σ_{priv}. The property of the symbol eq is reflected by the rule $eq(x, x) \to ok$. Note that $eq(u, v)$ reduces to a message if, and only if, $u =_E v$. A typical signature used to model security protocols is $\Sigma_{enc} = \{senc, sdec\}$. Depending on whether we want to model a decryption algorithm that may fail or not, we can either consider sdec as a destructor together with the rewrite rule $sdec(senc(x, y), y) \to x$, or consider both symbols as constructors, together with equation $sdec(senc(x, y), y) = x$. In the latter case, $sdec(c, k)$ will be considered as a "valid" message.

Given a set $\mathcal{U}$ of equations between terms, σ is a *unifier* for $\mathcal{U}$ if $u_1\sigma\downarrow =_E u_2\sigma\downarrow$ and both $u_1\sigma\downarrow$ and $u_2\sigma\downarrow$ are constructor terms for any $u_1 = u_2 \in \mathcal{U}$. We denote by $\mathsf{csu}(\mathcal{U})$ a set of unifiers for $\mathcal{U}$ which is also *complete*, i.e. such that for any σ unifier of $\mathcal{U}$, there exists $\theta \in \mathsf{csu}(\mathcal{U})$ such that $\sigma =_E \tau \circ \theta$ for some τ.

Example 4. Let $\mathcal{U} = \{x_0 = m_0, x_1 = k \oplus x_0; x_{ok} = eq(x_{rep}, ans(c, x_0, x_1))\}$ with $k = shk(p_0, v_0)$, and $m_0 = kdf(k, n_V, x_N)$. We have that $\mathsf{csu}(\mathcal{U}) = \{\theta\}$ where θ is the substitution: $x_0 \mapsto m_0; x_1 \mapsto k \oplus m_0; x_{rep} \mapsto ans(c, m_0, k \oplus m_0); x_{ok} \mapsto ok$.

---

[1] We only consider non-trivial theories, i.e. there exist u and v such that $u \neq_E v$.

2.2 Protocols

Protocols are modelled through processes that may receive and send messages.

Syntax. We consider the following grammar:

$$P, Q = 0 \mid \text{in}(x).P \mid \text{in}^{<t}(x).P \mid \text{let } x = v \text{ in } P \mid \text{new } n.P \mid \text{out}(u).P \mid \text{reset}.P$$

where $x \in \mathcal{X}$, $n \in \mathcal{N}$, $u \in \mathcal{T}(\Sigma_c^+, \mathcal{X} \uplus \mathcal{N} \uplus \mathcal{A})$, $v \in \mathcal{T}(\Sigma^+, \mathcal{X} \uplus \mathcal{N} \uplus \mathcal{A})$ and $t \in \mathbb{R}_+$.

We write $fv(P)$ (resp. $fn(P)$) for the set of *free* variables (resp. names) occurring in P, *i.e.* the set of variables (resp. names) that are not in the scope of an input or a let (resp. a new). In this work, we only consider 2-party protocols, and thus we consider *parameterised processes*, denoted $P(z_0, z_1)$, where z_0 and z_1 are variables from a special set $\mathcal{Z}$ (disjoint from $\mathcal{X}$ and $\mathcal{W}$). Intuitively, z_0 and z_1 will be instantiated by agent names: z_0 corresponds to the name of the agent that executes the process, and z_1 will be his interlocutor. A *role* $R = P(z_0, z_1)$ is a parameterised process such that $fn(R) = \emptyset$ and $fv(R) \subseteq \{z_0, z_1\}$. A *protocol* is given by two roles, denoted $V(z_0, z_1)$ and $P(z_0, z_1)$, and named respectively the *verifier role* and the *prover role*. Moreover, we will assume that the verifier role ends with a special construct $\text{end}(z_0, z_1)$ allowing us to see when he has completed his role and with whom. Formally, it simply means that, in the verifier role $V(z_0, z_1)$, the process 0 has been replaced by $\text{end}(z_0, z_1)$.

Example 5. As a running example and for illustrative purposes, we consider a strengthened version of the Hancke and Kuhn distance bounding protocol [20] (as briefly described in [29]). It relies on the use of a keyed public pseudo-random function (modelled as a free function symbol here) and the exclusive-or operator.

1. $V \rightarrow P$: N_V 3. $V \rightarrow P$: c_i
2. $P \rightarrow V$: N_P 4. $P \rightarrow V$: $\begin{cases} i^{\text{th}} \text{ bit of } \text{kdf}(k, N_V, N_P) \text{ if } c_i = 0 \\ i^{\text{th}} \text{ bit of } k \oplus \text{kdf}(k, N_V, N_P) \text{ if } c_i = 1 \end{cases}$

The protocol starts with both parties transmitting to each other their own nonce. Then, the verifier initiates the rapid phase during which the time measurement is performed. The verifier generates and sends a random bit c_i, and the prover has to reply immediately with the ith bit of $\text{kdf}(k, N_V, N_P)$ if $c_i = 0$ and the ith bit of $k \oplus \text{kdf}(k, N_V, N_P)$ otherwise. This rapid exchange is repeated a fixed number of times, and if enough correct answers are received within a sufficiently short time after the corresponding challenge c_i has been sent out, then the verifier is convinced that the prover is located in its vicinity. In our setting, this gives us:

$V(z_0, z_1) :=$
  $\text{new } n_V.\text{out}(n_V).\text{in}(x_N).$
  $\text{reset}.\text{new } c.\text{out}(c).\text{in}^{<2 \times t_0}(x_{\text{rep}}).$
  $\text{let } x_0 = \text{kdf}(\text{shk}(z_1, z_0), n_V, x_N) \text{ in}$
  $\text{let } x_1 = \text{shk}(z_1, z_0) \oplus x_0 \text{ in}$
  $\text{let } x_{ok} = \text{eq}(x_{\text{rep}}, \text{ans}(c, x_0, x_1)) \text{ in}$
  $\text{end}(z_0, z_1)$

$P(z_0, z_1) :=$
  $\text{new } n_P.\text{in}(y_N).\text{out}(n_P).$
  $\text{let } y_0 = \text{kdf}(\text{shk}(z_0, z_1), y_N, n_P) \text{ in}$
  $\text{let } y_1 = \text{shk}(z_0, z_1) \oplus y_0 \text{ in}$
  $\text{in}(y_c).$
  $\text{out}(\text{ans}(y_c, y_0, y_1)).0$

Symbolic analysis does not allow one to reason at the bit level, and thus, as done in e.g. [11,13,14,23], all the challenge bits c_i are collapsed into a single challenge/response exchange using a nonce. Furthermore, operations performed at the bit level are abstracted too. The response is therefore abstracted by an uninterpreted symbol of a function ans depending on both the challenge c and the two precomputed values y_0 and y_1.

Topology. The semantics of our processes depends on their location. This is formally defined through the notion of topology.

Definition 1. *A topology is a tuple* $\mathcal{T}_0 = (\mathcal{A}_0, \mathcal{M}_0, \mathsf{Loc}_0, v_0, p_0)$ *where:*

- $\mathcal{A}_0 \subseteq \mathcal{A}$ *is the finite set of agents composing the system;*
- $\mathcal{M}_0 \subseteq \mathcal{A}_0$ *is the subset of agents that are malicious;*
- $\mathsf{Loc}_0 : \mathcal{A}_0 \to \mathbb{R}^3$ *is a mapping defining the position of each agent in space.*
- p_0 *and* v_0 *are two agents in* $\mathcal{A}_0$ *that represent respectively the prover and the verifier w.r.t. which the analyse is performed.*

In our model, the distance between two agents is expressed by the time it takes for a message to travel from one to another. Therefore, we consider $\mathsf{Dist}_{\mathcal{T}_0} : \mathcal{A}_0 \times \mathcal{A}_0 \to \mathbb{R}$, based on Loc_0 that will provide the time a message takes to travel between two agents. It is defined as follows:

$$\mathsf{Dist}_{\mathcal{T}_0}(a, b) = \frac{\|\mathsf{Loc}_0(a) - \mathsf{Loc}_0(b)\|}{c_0} \text{ for any } a, b \in \mathcal{A}_0$$

with $\|\cdot\| : \mathbb{R}^3 \to \mathbb{R}$ the Euclidean norm and c_0 the transmission speed. We suppose, from now on, that c_0 is a constant for all agents, and thus an agent a can recover, at time t, any message emitted by any other agent b before $t - \mathsf{Dist}_{\mathcal{T}_0}(a, b)$.

Example 6. When analysing a distance bounding protocol, we have to consider a class of topologies. Typically, a mafia fraud is an attack in which at least three agents are involved: an honest verifier, an honest prover, and an attacker. Of course, in general more agents may be involved, and the set $\mathcal{C}_{\mathsf{MF}}$ of all the mafia fraud topologies is simply defined as follows: any topology $\mathcal{T} = (\mathcal{A}_0, \mathcal{M}_0, \mathsf{Loc}_0, v_0, p_0)$ such that $v_0, p_0 \in \mathcal{A}_0 \smallsetminus \mathcal{M}_0$.

Configuration. The semantics of our processes is given through a transition system defined over configurations. Given a topology $\mathcal{T}_0 = (\mathcal{A}_0, \mathcal{M}_0, \mathsf{Loc}_0, v_0, p_0)$, a *configuration* K over $\mathcal{T}_0$ is a tuple $(\mathcal{P}; \Phi; t)$, where:

- $\mathcal{P}$ is a multiset of *extended process* $\lfloor P \rfloor_a^{t_a}$ with $a \in \mathcal{A}_0$ and $t_a \in \mathbb{R}_+$;
- $\Phi = \{\mathsf{w}_1 \xrightarrow{a_1, t_1} u_1, \ldots, \mathsf{w}_n \xrightarrow{a_n, t_n} u_n\}$ is an extended frame, i.e. a substitution such that $\mathsf{w}_i \in \mathcal{W}$, $u_i \in \mathcal{T}(\Sigma_c^+, \mathcal{N} \uplus \mathcal{A})$, $a_i \in \mathcal{A}_0$ and $t_i \in \mathbb{R}_+$ for $1 \leq i \leq n$;
- $t \in \mathbb{R}_+$ is the global time of the system.

A *initial frame* is a frame such that $t_i = 0$ $(1 \leq i \leq n)$, and an *initial configuration* is a configuration such that $t = 0$. We write $\lfloor \Phi \rfloor_a^t$ for the restriction of Φ to the agent a at time t, *i.e.*:

$$\lfloor \Phi \rfloor_a^t = \left\{ \mathsf{w}_i \xrightarrow{a_i, t_i} u_i \mid (\mathsf{w}_i \xrightarrow{a_i, t_i} u_i) \in \Phi \text{ and } a_i = a \text{ and } t_i \leq t \right\}.$$

Example 7. Continuing Example 5, we consider $\mathcal{T}_0 = (\mathcal{A}_0, \mathcal{M}_0, \mathsf{Loc}_0, v_0, p_0)$ depicted below where $\mathcal{A}_0 = \{p_0, v_0, p\}$, and $\mathcal{M}_0 = \{p\}$.

The precise location of each agent is not relevant, only the distance between them matters. Here $\mathsf{Dist}_{\mathcal{T}_0}(p, v_0) < t_0$ whereas $\mathsf{Dist}_{\mathcal{T}_0}(p_0, v_0) \geq t_0$.

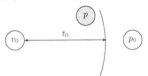

A possible initial configuration K_0 is given below:

$$\left(\lfloor P(p_0, v_0) \rfloor_{p_0}^0 \uplus \lfloor V(v_0, p_0) \rfloor_{v_0}^0 \; ; \{\mathsf{w}_1 \xrightarrow{p,0} \mathsf{shk}(p, v_0), \mathsf{w}_2 \xrightarrow{p,0} m_0, \mathsf{w}_3 \xrightarrow{p,0} m_1\}; 0 \right)$$

Here, p_0 and v_0 are honest agents playing respectively the prover's role and the verifier's role. The agent p is a malicious prover whose shared key with v_0 is given to the attacker through w_1. Here, we also assume that the attacker p also knows $m_0 = \mathsf{kdf}(\mathsf{shk}(p_0, v_0), n_V^0, n_P^0)$ and $m_1 = \mathsf{shk}(p_0, v_0) \oplus \mathsf{kdf}(\mathsf{shk}(p_0, v_0), n_V^0, n_P^0)$. These messages coming from an older session may have been given to him by p_0 to let the attacker exceptionally authenticate on his behalf. A more realistic configuration will include other instances of these two roles and will probably give more knowledge to the attacker.

Semantics. We now recall the semantics of our calculus as defined in [14].

TIM $(\mathcal{P}; \Phi; t) \longrightarrow_{\mathcal{T}_0} (\mathsf{Shift}(\mathcal{P}, \delta); \Phi; t + \delta)$ with $\delta \geq 0$

RST $(\lfloor \mathtt{reset}.P \rfloor_a^{t_a} \uplus \mathcal{P}; \Phi; t) \xrightarrow{a, \tau}_{\mathcal{T}_0} (\lfloor P \rfloor_a^0 \uplus \mathcal{P}; \Phi; t)$

OUT $(\lfloor \mathtt{out}(u).P \rfloor_a^{t_a}) \uplus \mathcal{P}; \Phi; t) \xrightarrow{a, \mathtt{out}(u)}_{\mathcal{T}_0} (\lfloor P \rfloor_a^{t_a} \uplus \mathcal{P}; \Phi \uplus \{\mathsf{w} \xrightarrow{a, t} u\}; t)$
with $\mathsf{w} \in \mathcal{W}$ fresh

LET $(\lfloor \mathtt{let}\ x = u\ \mathtt{in}\ P \rfloor_a^{t_a} \uplus \mathcal{P}; \Phi; t) \xrightarrow{a, \tau}_{\mathcal{T}_0} (\lfloor P\{x \mapsto u\downarrow\} \rfloor_a^{t_a} \uplus \mathcal{P}; \Phi; t)$
when $u\downarrow \in \mathcal{T}(\Sigma_c^+, \mathcal{N} \uplus \mathcal{A})$

NEW $(\lfloor \mathtt{new}\ n.P \rfloor_a^{t_a} \uplus \mathcal{P}; \Phi; t) \xrightarrow{a, \tau}_{\mathcal{T}_0} (\lfloor P\{n \mapsto n'\} \rfloor_a^{t_a} \uplus \mathcal{P}; \Phi; t)$
with $n' \in \mathcal{N}$ fresh

IN $(\lfloor \mathtt{in}^\star(x).P \rfloor_a^{t_a} \uplus \mathcal{P}; \Phi; t) \xrightarrow{a, \mathtt{in}^\star(u)}_{\mathcal{T}_0} (\lfloor P\{x \mapsto u\} \rfloor_a^{t_a} \uplus \mathcal{P}; \Phi; t)$

when there exist $b \in \mathcal{A}_0$ and $t_b \in \mathbb{R}_+$ such that $t_b \leq t - \mathsf{Dist}_{\mathcal{T}_0}(b, a)$ and:

- if $b \in \mathcal{A}_0 \setminus \mathcal{M}_0$ then $u \in img(\lfloor \Phi \rfloor_b^{t_b})$;
- if $b \in \mathcal{M}_0$ then $u = R\Phi\downarrow$ for some recipe R such that for all $\mathsf{w} \in vars(R)$ there exists $c \in \mathcal{A}_0$ such that $\mathsf{w} \in dom(\lfloor \Phi \rfloor_c^{t_b - \mathsf{Dist}_{\mathcal{T}_0}(c,b)})$.

Moreover, in case $\star$ is $< t_g$ for some t_g, we assume in addition that $t_a < t_g$.

The two first rules are specific to our timed model. The RST rule allows a process to reset its local clock, whereas the TIM rule allows time to elapse, meaning that all the clocks will be shifted by δ:

$$\mathsf{Shift}(\mathcal{P}, \delta) = \biguplus_{\lfloor P \rfloor_a^{t_a} \in \mathcal{P}} \mathsf{Shift}(\lfloor P \rfloor_a^{t_a}, \delta) \text{ and } \mathsf{Shift}(\lfloor P \rfloor_a^{t_a}, \delta) = \lfloor P \rfloor_a^{t_a + \delta}.$$

The remaining rules are quite standard. The OUT rule is used to output a message which is immediately added into the frame. The rule LET can be used to apply function symbols, e.g. let $x = \mathsf{dec}(y, k)$ in P applies decryption on top of y with the key k and store the resulting result in x (if this operation succeeds). Otherwise, the process is blocked. This construction is also useful to perform equality tests through the symbol eq as defined in Example 1 and used e.g. in Example 5. The NEW rule allows one to pick a fresh (i.e. previously unused) name. Finally, the IN rule is used to receive a message. One can note the additional side conditions which allows one to model timing constraints: all the messages needed to construct u have to be available to b (who sends u) at time $t_b \leq t - \mathsf{Dist}_{T_0}(b, a)$ to ensure that the message forged and sent by b will have enough time to travel and reach a.

Example 8. To illustrate our semantics, we give below a possible execution trace starting from the configuration K_0 given in Example 7. We have that:

$$K_0 \xrightarrow{(v_0,\tau).(v_0,\mathsf{out}(n_V))}_{T_0} \to_{T_0} \xrightarrow{(v_0,\mathsf{in}(n_I)).(v_0,\mathtt{reset}).(v_0,\tau).(v_0,\mathsf{out}(c))}_{T_0} (\mathcal{P}'; \Phi'; t')$$

$$\to_{T_0} \xrightarrow{(v_0,\mathsf{in}(m_{\mathsf{rep}})).(v_0,\tau).(v_0,\tau).(v_0,\tau)}_{T_0} (\lfloor \mathsf{P}(p_0, v_0) \rfloor_{p_0}^{t''} \uplus \lfloor \mathsf{end}(v_0, p_0) \rfloor_{v_0}^{t''-t'}; \Phi''; t'')$$

with $m_{\mathsf{rep}} = \mathsf{ans}(c, \mathsf{kdf}(\mathsf{shk}(p_0, v_0), n_V, n_I), \mathsf{shk}(p_0, v_0) \oplus \mathsf{kdf}(\mathsf{shk}(p_0, v_0), n_V, n_I))$, $t' \geq \mathsf{Dist}_{T_0}(v_0, p)$, $t'' \geq 3\mathsf{Dist}_{T_0}(v_0, p)$, $\Phi'' = \Phi' = \Phi_0 \uplus \{\mathsf{w}_4 \xrightarrow{v_0,0} n_V, \mathsf{w}_5 \xrightarrow{v_0,t'} c\}$.

Here, n_I is a name known to the attacker. Formally, we have that $n_I \in \Sigma_0$. During the first part of the execution (1st line), one instance of the TIM rule has been used. It is necessary to let the verifier receive n_I. Therefore, we have that $t' \geq \mathsf{Dist}_{T_0}(v_0, p)$. The attacker has learnt two messages that have been added into his initial frame Φ_0. Then, letting some time to elapse, the process located in v_0 is able to perform his input action. Indeed, the term m_{rep} can be forged by p using recipe $\mathsf{ans}(\mathsf{w}_5, R_0, R_1)$ where $R_0 = \mathsf{kdf}(\mathsf{w}_2 \oplus \mathsf{w}_3, \mathsf{w}_4, n_I)$ and $R_1 = \mathsf{w}_2 \oplus \mathsf{w}_3 \oplus R_0$. We may note that m_{rep} passes successfully all the tests, and v_0 ends his session thinking he is talking to p_0 (who is actually far away).

3   Modelling Mafia and Terrorist Frauds

Here, we aim at proposing a general definition of terrorist fraud in the symbolic setting. Due to its close relationship with the notion of mafia fraud, we first recall how mafia fraud is modelled following the definitions given in [14] before defining the more subtle notion of terrorist fraud.

We start by defining the notion of valid initial configurations which corresponds to the configurations that need to be studied when analysing a given protocol $\mathcal{P}$. Typically, such a configuration will contain instances of the roles of the protocol $\mathcal{P}$ under study.

Definition 2. *Let* $\mathcal{P}_{\mathsf{prox}}$ *be a protocol,* $\mathcal{T}_0 = (\mathcal{A}_0, \mathcal{M}_0, \mathsf{Loc}_0, v_0, p_0)$ *be a topology, and* Φ_0 *be an initial frame.* $K = (\mathcal{P}; \Phi; t)$ *is a valid initial configuration for* $\mathcal{P}_{\mathsf{prox}}$ *w.r.t.* $\mathcal{T}_0$ *and* Φ_0 *if* $t = 0$, $\Phi = \Phi_0$, *and for each* $\lfloor P' \rfloor_{a'}^{t'} \in \mathcal{P}$, *we have that* $t' = 0$, $a' \in \mathcal{A}_0$, *and either* $P' = \mathsf{V}(a', b')$ *or* $P' = \mathsf{P}(a', b')$ *for some* $b' \in \mathcal{A}_0$.

Now, depending on the type of frauds we consider, the set of topologies under study and the initial knowledge given to the attacker may vary.

3.1   Mafia Fraud

A *mafia fraud* is an attack in which generally three agents are involved: a verifier, an honest prover located outside the neighbourhood of the verifier, and an attacker. We consider here its general version which may involve an arbitrary number of participants and we reuse the definition given in [14]. The aim of the attacker is to convince the verifier that the honest prover is actually close to it. The set $\mathcal{C}_{\mathsf{MF}}$ representing all the mafia fraud topologies is given in Example 6.

Example 9. The topology depicted in Example 7 is a mafia fraud topology. Some other mafia fraud topologies that will be considered later on are depicted below:

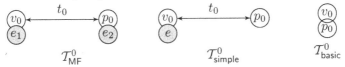

The initial knowledge Φ_0 we use for defining our initial configuration depends on the topology but it is reasonable to assume that this knowledge is uniform. Therefore, we assume that the initial knowledge of all the participants is given through a template $\mathcal{I}_0$, i.e. a set of terms in $\mathcal{T}(\Sigma_c^+, \{z_0, z_1\})$. Relying on $\mathcal{I}_0$, and considering a set $\mathcal{A}_0$ of agents, the initial knowledge of agent $a \in \mathcal{A}_0$ is given by:

$$\mathsf{Knows}_{\mathcal{I}_0}(a, \mathcal{A}_0) = \{u_0\{z_0 \mapsto a, z_1 \mapsto b\} \mid u_0 \in \mathcal{I}_0 \text{ and } b \in \mathcal{A}_0\}$$

Given $\mathcal{T} = (\mathcal{A}_0, \mathcal{M}_0, \mathsf{Loc}_0, v_0, p_0)$, we denote $\Phi_{\mathcal{I}_0}^{\mathcal{T}}$ the initial frame such that $\lfloor img(\Phi_{\mathcal{I}_0}^{\mathcal{T}}) \rfloor_a^0 = \mathsf{Knows}_{\mathcal{I}_0}(a, \mathcal{A}_0)$ when $a \in \mathcal{M}_0$, and $\lfloor img(\Phi_{\mathcal{I}_0}^{\mathcal{T}}) \rfloor_a^0 = \emptyset$ otherwise. Up to a renaming of the handles and some duplicates, $\Phi_{\mathcal{I}_0}^{\mathcal{T}}$ is uniquely defined.

Example 10. Continuing our running example, and considering the topology $\mathcal{T}_{\mathsf{MF}}^0 = (\mathcal{A}_{\mathsf{MF}}^0, \mathcal{M}_{\mathsf{MF}}^0, \mathsf{Loc}_{\mathsf{MF}}^0, v_0, p_0)$ (see Example 9), a typical template to derive the initial knowledge of the malicious agents is $\mathcal{I}_0 = \{\mathsf{shk}(z_0, z_1), \mathsf{shk}(z_1, z_0)\}$. Thus, considering the malicious agent e_i, the set $\mathsf{Knows}_{\mathcal{I}_0}(e_i, \mathcal{A}_{\mathsf{MF}}^0)$ will contain all the symmetric keys this malicious agent shares with other agents.

When analysing the protocol considering $\mathcal{T}_{\mathsf{MF}}^0$, we will consider an initial frame Φ_0 containing $\mathsf{shk}(a, b)$ for $(a, b) \in (\mathcal{A}_{\mathsf{MF}}^0 \times \mathcal{A}_{\mathsf{MF}}^0) \smallsetminus \{(v_0, p_0), (p_0, v_0)\}$.

Definition 3. *Let $\mathcal{P}_{\mathsf{prox}}$ be a protocol and $\mathcal{I}_0$ be a template. We say that $\mathcal{P}_{\mathsf{prox}}$ admits a mafia fraud w.r.t. t_0-proximity if there exist $\mathcal{T} \in \mathcal{C}_{\mathsf{MF}}$, and a valid initial configuration K for $\mathcal{P}_{\mathsf{prox}}$ w.r.t. $\mathcal{T}$ and $\Phi_{\mathcal{I}_0}^{\mathcal{T}}$ such that:*

$$K \rightarrow_{\mathcal{T}}^* (\lfloor \mathsf{end}(v_0, p_0) \rfloor_a^{t_a} \uplus \mathcal{P}; \Phi; t) \text{ with } \mathit{Dist}_{\mathcal{T}}(v_0, p_0) \geq t_0$$

where $\mathcal{T} = (\mathcal{A}_0, \mathcal{M}_0, \mathsf{Loc}_0, v_0, p_0)$.

3.2 Terrorist Fraud

Modelling terrorist fraud is tricky. We have to look for a semi-dishonest prover who colludes with the attacker with the aim of letting him authenticate exactly once. We will model this in two steps. First, we will consider all the possible behaviours for this semi-dishonest prover that will allow the attacker to authenticate at least once. Then, to be terrorist fraud resistant, we have to check that any of these behaviours will allow the attacker to re-authenticate later on.

In order to collude with the attacker, one possibility for the prover is to leak his credentials but it is in general not the only option. To define this notion, we consider a simple scenario where p_0 wants to authenticate to the far away verifier v_0 through the help of the attacker a located in the neighbourhood of v_0. This corresponds to the topology $\mathcal{T}_{\mathsf{simple}}^0$ given in Example 9.

Definition 4. *Let $\mathcal{P}_{\mathsf{prox}}$ be a protocol and $t_0 \in \mathbb{R}_+$. A semi-dishonest prover for $\mathcal{P}_{\mathsf{prox}}$ w.r.t. t_0 is a process P_{sd} together with an initial frame Φ_{sd} such that:*

$$(\{ \lfloor \mathsf{V}(v_0, p_0) \rfloor_{v_0}^0 ; \lfloor P_{\mathsf{sd}} \rfloor_{p_0}^0 \}; \emptyset; 0) \xrightarrow{\mathsf{tr}}_{\mathcal{T}_{\mathsf{simple}}^0} (\{ \lfloor \mathsf{end}(v_0, p_0) \rfloor_{v_0}^{t_v} ; \lfloor 0 \rfloor_{p_0}^{t_p} \}; \Phi; t)$$

for some t, t_v, t_p, and Φ such that Φ and Φ_{sd} coincide up to their timestamps.

Note that a semi-dishonest prover can be completely dishonest in the sense that he may leak all his credentials. However, such a semi-dishonest prover can not be honest, i.e. equal to the role of the prover as indicated by the protocol. Indeed, p_0 is located far away and has to authenticate. Thus, unless the protocol is very bad, the help of the attacker who is close to the verifier will be essential.

Example 11. Going back to our running example, some semi-dishonest provers with their frame are ($k = \mathsf{shk}(v_0, p_0)$, $m_0 = \mathsf{kdf}(k, n_V^0, n_P^0)$, and $m_1 = k \oplus m_0$):

1. $P_{\mathsf{sd}}^1 := \mathsf{out}(k)$ with $\Phi_{\mathsf{sd}}^1 = \{\mathsf{w}_1 \xrightarrow{v_0,0} n_V, \mathsf{w}_2 \xrightarrow{p_0,0} k, \mathsf{w}_3 \xrightarrow{v_0,0} c\}$;
2. $P_{\mathsf{sd}}^2 := \mathsf{new}\ n_P.\mathsf{in}(y_N).\mathsf{out}(n_P).\mathsf{let}\ y_0 = \mathsf{kdf}(k, y_N, n_P)$ in
$$\mathsf{let}\ y_1 = k \oplus y_0 \text{ in } \mathsf{out}(y_0).\mathsf{out}(y_1).$$
$$\mathsf{in}(y_c).\mathsf{out}(\mathsf{ans}(y_c, y_0, y_1))$$

with $\Phi_{\mathsf{sd}}^2 = \{\mathsf{w}_1 \xrightarrow{v_0,0} n_V, \mathsf{w}_2 \xrightarrow{p_0,0} n_P, \mathsf{w}_3 \xrightarrow{p_0,0} m_0, \mathsf{w}_4 \xrightarrow{p_0,0} m_1, \mathsf{w}_5 \xrightarrow{v_0,0} c,$
$$\mathsf{w}_6 \xrightarrow{p_0,0} \mathsf{ans}(c, m_0, m_1)\}.$$

The first one actually reveals all his credential to the attacker, and thus the attacker will be able to authenticate later on. The second one reveals less information to the attacker. This is still enough to authenticate once and we will see that this is actually also enough to authenticate later on (see Example 12).

We are now able to define our notion of terrorist fraud resistance. Intuitively, if the dishonest prover gives to his accomplice enough information to pass authentication once, then he will be able to authenticate again without his help.

Definition 5. *Let $\mathcal{P}_{\mathsf{prox}}$ be a protocol and $\mathcal{I}_0$ be a template. We say that $\mathcal{P}_{\mathsf{prox}}$ is terrorist fraud resistant w.r.t. t_0-proximity if for all semi-dishonest prover P_{sd} with frame Φ_{sd}, there exist $T \in \mathcal{C}_{\mathsf{MF}}$, a valid initial configuration K for $\mathcal{P}_{\mathsf{prox}}$ w.r.t. T and $\Phi_{\mathcal{I}_0}^T \cup \Phi_{\mathsf{sd}}$ such that:*

$$K \xrightarrow{\text{tr}}_T (\lfloor \mathsf{end}(v_0, p_0) \rfloor_{v_0}^{t'} \uplus \mathcal{P}; \Phi; t) \text{ with } \mathit{Dist}_T(v_0, p_0) \geq t_0$$

where $T = (\mathcal{A}_0, \mathcal{M}_0, \mathsf{Loc}_0, v_0, p_0)$.

Example 12. Going back to our running example, we have seen (see Example 8):

$$K_0 \xrightarrow{\text{tr}}_{T^0} (\lfloor \mathsf{end}(v_0, p_0) \rfloor_{v_0}^{t'} \uplus \mathcal{P}; \Phi; t).$$

This execution witnesses the fact that the dishonest prover P_{sd}^2 together with frame Φ_{sd}^2 gives enough information to the attacker to allow him to authenticate later on. This does not mean that the protocol is terrorist fraud resistant since we only consider one particular semi-dishonest prover. To be terrorist fraud resistant, the property has to hold for *any* semi-dishonest prover.

In our setting, we have the following relationship between mafia fraud and terrorist fraud resistance

Proposition 1. *Let $\mathcal{P}_{\mathsf{prox}}$ be a protocol and $\mathcal{I}_0$ be a template. If $\mathcal{P}_{\mathsf{prox}}$ admits a mafia fraud then $\mathcal{P}_{\mathsf{prox}}$ is terrorist fraud resistant (w.r.t. t_0-proximity).*

Indeed, whatever the distant semi-dishonest prover discloses (even no information at all), an attacker can still carry out the existing mafia fraud and re-authenticate, therefore impersonating the semi-dishonest prover again. In computational definitions, probability plays a role. In such a setting, a terrorist fraud exists when the semi-dishonest prover can help the attacker to maximise his attack success probability without giving him any advantage for future attacks. The fact that a mafia fraud already exists (with probability 1 in our setting) means that no help can improve the success probability for future attacks, and thus the protocol is terrorist fraud resistant. We may note that distance-bounding protocols designed to achieve terrorist fraud resistance aim also to resist against mafia fraud, thus in general achieving terrorist fraud resistance making the protocol vulnerable to a mafia fraud is not an interesting option.

3.3 Related Works

Up to our knowledge, the only existing definitions of terrorist fraud resistance in the symbolic setting are the one proposed by Chothia *et al.* in [11] and the recent one proposed by Mauw *et al.* in [24].

Chothia et al. Their notion of terrorist fraud is not modelled in two steps as we proposed. Instead, they consider a notion of terrorist prover. Such a process will perform operations on behalf of the attacker, e.g. encrypting and decrypting any values the attacker wishes, but it will never (at least directly) reveal his secrets. Their notion of terrorist prover is appealing but they do not explain how to write such a process. We think that writing such a process is not that easy.

Example 13. Consider a protocol relying on a hash function h and we assume that the terrorist prover holds a secret key k. A legitimate help that the terrorist prover may give to the attacker without leaking his secret key would consist in computing the hash value of a public data together with his secret key k. Therefore, the terrorist prover should contain the oracle: $\mathtt{in}(x).\mathtt{out}(\mathtt{h}(\langle k, x \rangle))$. In the same spirit, we could argue that $\mathtt{in}(x).\mathtt{out}(\mathtt{h}(\langle x, k \rangle))$ is also useful, and perhaps also $\mathtt{in}(x_1).\mathtt{in}(x_2).\mathtt{out}(\mathtt{h}(\langle x_1, \langle k, x_2 \rangle \rangle))$, etc. Iterating such a reasoning, we do not see how to write a finite terrorist prover that will provide all the valuable help his accomplice may need.

Moreover, when considering a protocol involving an operator with some algebraic properties, e.g. exclusive-or, it seems difficult (perhaps even impossible) to ensure that the terrorist prover will not reveal secrets indirectly).

Example 14. To illustrate this issue, we consider a specific primitive modelled using the equation $\mathtt{g}(\mathtt{f}_1(x, y), \mathtt{f}_2(x, y)) = y$. The functions $\mathtt{f}_1$ and $\mathtt{f}_2$ are two constructor symbols whereas $\mathtt{g}$ is a destructor symbol. Following the idea developed in [11], the terrorist prover should contain $\mathtt{in}(x).\mathtt{out}(\mathtt{f}_1(x, k))$ as well as $\mathtt{in}(x).\mathtt{out}(\mathtt{f}_2(\langle x, k \rangle))$. However, whereas it is legitimate to provide such an help to the attacker, it seems too strong to give him access to these oracles as soon as he will get $\mathtt{f}_1(m, k)$ and $\mathtt{f}_2(m_2, k)$ for some message m. This example clearly shows that, combining two legitimate helps, the attacker may retrieve some secrets. It is therefore not obvious to describe in a syntactic way the help the terrorist prover is willing to provide.

The main advantage of the definition of terrorist fraud proposed by [11] is probably the fact that it is more amenable to automation using existing verification tools. Indeed, even if the choice of terrorist prover mentioned in [11] is quite debatable, it is fixed, and can therefore be given in input to the verification tool.

Mauw et al. They consider a model based on multiset rewriting rules, and their definition of terrorist fraud is more in line with the one we proposed. In particular, their notion of "valid extensions" of a protocol seems to correspond to our notion of semi-dishonest prover. Then, their definition of terrorist fraud quantifies over all the possible "valid extensions" and this renders the automation of the security analysis difficult. Indeed, no existing verification tool is able to handle this quantification. In [24], they simply illustrate their technique on a toy distance bounding protocol. They provide a manual proof explaining how to get rid of this quantification for this particular toy protocol. Our work explains in a more systematic way how to get rid of this quantification, as well as the one regarding the topology. This is explained in Sect. 4.

4   Reduction Results

We first establish a result allowing us to focus on a particular topology. Then, we explain how we get rid of the quantification over semi-dishonest provers.

4.1   One Topology Is Enough

This reduction result regarding the topology is a direct consequence of the proof of the reduction result stated in [14] regarding mafia and distance hijacking frauds. The only new issue here is to take care of the initial frame which contains information from the semi-dishonest prover. This reduction results holds in a rather general setting. We simply assume that the protocol under study is executable.

Definition 6. *Given a template* $\mathcal{I}_0 = \{u_1, \ldots, u_k\}$, *a protocol* $\mathcal{P}$ *is* $\mathcal{I}_0$-*executable if for any term* u *(resp.* v) *occurring in an* out *or a* let *construction in* $\mathcal{P}$, *there exists a recipe* $R \in \mathcal{T}(\Sigma_{\text{pub}}^+, \{w_1, \ldots, w_k\} \uplus \mathcal{N} \uplus \mathcal{X})$ *such that* $u = R\sigma\!\downarrow$ *(resp.* $v\!\downarrow = R\sigma\!\downarrow$) *where* $\sigma = \{w_1 \mapsto u_1, \ldots, w_k \mapsto u_k\}$.

Example 15. Going back to our running example described in Example 5, we have that both roles are $\mathcal{I}_0$-executable considering $\mathcal{I}_0 = \{\mathsf{shk}(z_0, z_1), \mathsf{shk}(z_1, z_0)\}$.

We are now able to state our reduction result regarding terrorist fraud.

Theorem 1. *Let* $\mathcal{P}_{\text{prox}}$ *be an* $\mathcal{I}_0$-*executable protocol w.r.t. some template* $\mathcal{I}_0$. *We have that* $\mathcal{P}_{\text{prox}}$ *is terrorist fraud resistant w.r.t.* t_0-*proximity, if and only if, for all semi-dishonest prover* P_{sd} *with frame* Φ_{sd}, *there exists a valid initial configuration* K *for* $\mathcal{P}_{\text{prox}}$ *w.r.t.* $\mathcal{T}_{\text{MF}}^0$ *and* $\Phi_{\mathcal{I}_0}^{\mathcal{T}_{\text{MF}}^0} \cup \Phi_{\text{sd}}$ *such that:*

$$K \xrightarrow{\text{tr}}_{\mathcal{T}_{\text{MF}}^0} (\lfloor \mathsf{end}(v_0, p_0) \rfloor_{v_0}^{t'} \uplus \mathcal{P}; \Phi; t).$$

In other words, when analysing terrorist fraud, it is sufficient to consider one particular topology, namely $\mathcal{T}_{\text{MF}}^0$ (see Example 9). The key idea to establish the direct part of the theorem consists in showing that behaviours of agents other than p_0 and v_0 can be performed by processes executed by malicious agents, and can even be discarded relying on the fact that $\mathcal{P}_{\text{prox}}$ is $\mathcal{I}_0$-executable. Then, it remains to map any agent names different from p_0 and v_0 to e_1, and to show that the resulting trace remains executable.

4.2   One Semi-dishonest Prover Behaviour Is Enough

Our second reduction result allows us to focus on a particular semi-dishonest prover when performing our analysis. This results only holds under some hypotheses that are gathered below. We have to rely on the notion of being *quasi-free* for a symbol: $\mathsf{f} \in \Sigma_c$ is *quasi-free* if it occurs neither in the equations used to generate the relation $=_\mathsf{E}$ nor in the right-hand side of a rewriting rule.

Definition 7. *A distance bounding (DB) protocol is a protocol such that:*

(i) We have that $V(z_0, z_1) = \text{block}_V.\text{reset.new } c.\text{out}(c).\text{in}^{<2\times t_0}(x).\text{block}'_V$, *and* $P(z_0, z_1) = \text{block}_P.\text{in}(y_c).\text{out}(u).\text{block}'_P$ *where* block_X *and* block'_X *with* $X \in \{V, P\}$ *is a sequence of actions without reset and guarded input instructions. Moreover, we assume that* $\text{out}(c)$ *(resp.* $\text{in}(y_c)$*) corresponds to the* i_0^{th} *communication action of* $P(z_0, z_1)$ *(resp.* $V(z_0, z_1)$*) for some* i_0.

(ii) $(\lfloor V(v_0, p_0) \rfloor^0_{v_0} \uplus \lfloor P(p_0, v_0) \rfloor^0_{p_0} ; \emptyset; 0) \xrightarrow{\text{tr}}_{\mathcal{T}^0_{\text{basic}}} (\lfloor 0 \rfloor^0_{v_0} \uplus \lfloor 0 \rfloor^0_{p_0} ; \Phi; 0)$ *with*

$$\text{tr} = \begin{cases} (a_1, \text{out}(m_1)).(b_1, \text{in}(m_1)) \ldots (a_{i_0-1}, \text{out}(m_{i_0-1})).(b_{i_0-1}, \text{in}(m_{i_0-1})) \\ (v_0, \text{out}(m_{i_0})).(p_0, \text{in}(m_{i_0})).(p_0, \text{out}(m_{i_0+1})).(v_0, \text{in}^{<t}(m_{i_0+1})) \\ (a_{n-1}, \text{out}(m_{n-1})).(b_{n-1}, \text{in}(m_{n-1})) \ldots (a_n, \text{out}(m_n)).(b_n, \text{in}(m_n)) \end{cases}$$

up to τ *actions, and* $\{a_i, b_i\} = \{v_0, p_0\}$ *for any* $i \in \{1, \ldots, n\} \setminus \{i_0, i_0 + 1\}$.

(iii) Let $\mathcal{U} = \{x = u \mid \text{"let } x = u \text{ in" occurs in } V(v_0, p_0)\}$. *We assume that* $\text{csu}(\mathcal{U})$ *exists and is reduced to a singleton* $\{\theta_P\}$. *Moreover, we assume that* $(x_1, \ldots, x_k)\theta_P \downarrow \sigma = m_{i_1}, \ldots, m_{i_k}$ *where* $x_1, \ldots, x_k$ *are the variables occurring in input in the role* $V(v_0, p_0)$, $i_1, \ldots, i_k$ *are the indices among* $1, \ldots, n$ *corresponding to input performed by* v_0, *and* σ *is a bijective renaming from variables to names freshly generated by* $P(p_0, v_0)$ *when executing* tr.

(iv) We assume the existence of a context C *made of quasi-free public function symbols such that* $u = C[y_c, u_1, \ldots, u_p]$, *and* y_c *does not occur in* $u_1, \ldots, u_p$.

The two first conditions put some restrictions on the shape of the roles. In particular, we assume that if no attacker interferes, these two roles together will execute until the end. The third condition gives us the existence of a unique most general unifier (modulo E) and is actually satisfied by many term algebra of interest for protocol verification, e.g. the one described in Sect. 2.1. Actually, any rewriting system with only one rule per destructor will satisfy such an hypothesis. It may seem restrictive that in a normal execution messages that are exchanged have the shape indicated by θ_P but this requirement is in general always satisfied. Note that otherwise, it would mean that some terms sent by the prover are never entirely checked during the protocol execution, and thus are useless. Condition *(iv)* allows us to ensure that there exists a strategy for the semi-dishonest prover. This strategy will consist of sending the terms $u_1, \ldots, u_n$ in advance to his accomplice, and let him to compute (as indicated by C) the answer to the challenge from $u_1, \ldots, u_n$ and the challenge c' he will receive from the verifier. Actually, the best strategy will consist in considering C_P the smallest context (in terms of number of symbols) satisfying the requirements.

Example 16. Going back to our running example, all the conditions stated in Definition 7, are indeed satisfied. Assuming that names are not renamed when executing NEW, we obtain the following trace:

$$\text{tr} = \begin{cases} (v_0, \text{out}(n_V)).(p_0, \text{in}(n_V)).(p_0, \text{out}(n_P)).(v_0, \text{in}(n_P)) \\ (v_0, \text{out}(c)).(p_0, \text{in}(c)).(p_0, \text{out}(\text{ans}(c, m_0, m_1))).(v_0, \text{in}(\text{ans}(c, m_0, m_1))) \end{cases}$$

where $m_0 = \text{kdf}(\text{shk}(p_0, v_0), n_V, n_P)$ and $m_1 = \text{shk}(p_0, v_0) \oplus m_0$.

Regarding condition (iii), we have that θ_P as defined in Example 4 and $\sigma = \{x_N \mapsto n_P\}$ satisfy our requirement. Regarding condition *(iv)*, we have that $u_1 = y_0$, and $u_2 = y_1$, and thus $C_\mathcal{P}$ only contains the quasi-free symbol ans.

According to our definition, when analysing a protocol $\mathcal{P}_{\text{prox}}$ w.r.t. terrorist frauds you should consider all the possible semi-dishonest provers. However, for the class of distance bounding protocol we consider, we will show that we can restrict our attention to a particular dishonest prover that we define now.

Definition 8. *Let $\mathcal{P}_{\text{prox}}$ be a DB protocol as given in Definition 7. The* most general semi-dishonest prover *for $\mathcal{P}_{\text{prox}}$, denoted P^*, is the process:*

$$\big(\mathtt{block}_P.\mathtt{out}(u_1)\ldots\mathtt{out}(u_k).\mathtt{in}(y_c).\mathtt{out}(u).\mathtt{block}'_P\big)\{z_0 \mapsto p_0, z_1 \mapsto v_0\}$$

where $u_1, \ldots, u_p$ are the terms such that $u = C_\mathcal{P}[y_c, u_1, \ldots, u_p]$.
Its associated frame, denoted Φ^*, is the one obtained considering the normal execution and letting the attacker answer to the challenge relying on $C_\mathcal{P}$.

The most general semi-dishonest prover will help his accomplice by sending him (before the rapid phase starts) the material he needs to perform this phase alone. For this, the most general semi-dishonest prover will send messages corresponding to the maximal subterms of u that do not contain the challenge. This will be sufficient to answer to the challenge sent by the verifier, and we will see that this is actually the strategy that leaks the least information.

Example 17. Going back to our running example, P_{sd}^1 together with frame Φ_{sd}^1 as described in Example 11 corresponds to the most general semi-dishonest prover.

Note that the most general semi-dishonest prover P^* (as given in Definition 8) is a dishonest prover. This simply means that such a process when put together with $\lfloor \mathsf{V}(v_0, p_0) \rfloor_{v_0}^0$ can be fully executed considering the topology $\mathcal{T}_{\text{simple}}^0$. This is actually an easy consequence of our definition of DB protocol exploiting the fact that P^* and $\mathsf{P}(p_0, v_0)$ are rather similar. More interestingly, we can establish a strong relationship between the frame Φ^* (the one associated to P^*) and a frame Φ_{sd} associated to an arbitrary semi-dishonest prover P_{sd}.

Proposition 2. *Let $\mathcal{P}_{\text{prox}}$ be a DB protocol, and P^* be its most general semi-dishonest prover with Φ^* its associated frame. Let exec^* be the execution witnessing the fact that P^* together with Φ^* is a semi-dishonest prover, i.e.:*

$$\mathsf{exec}^* : (\{\, \lfloor \mathsf{V}(v_0, p_0) \rfloor_{v_0}^0 , \lfloor \mathsf{P}^* \rfloor_{p_0}^0 \}; \emptyset; 0) \xrightarrow{\mathsf{tr}^*}_{\mathcal{T}_{\text{simple}}^0} (\{\, \lfloor \mathsf{end}(v_0, p_0) \rfloor_{v_0}^{t_v^*} , \lfloor 0 \rfloor_{p_0}^{t_p^*} \}; \Phi^*; t^*).$$

Let P_{sd} be a semi-dishonest prover for $\mathcal{P}_{\text{prox}}$ together with its frame Φ_{sd}, and exec be the execution witnessing this fact, i.e.

$$\mathsf{exec} : (\{\, \lfloor \mathsf{V}(v_0, p_0) \rfloor_{v_0}^0 , \lfloor \mathsf{P}_{\text{sd}} \rfloor_{p_0}^0 \}; \emptyset; 0) \xrightarrow{\mathsf{tr}}_{\mathcal{T}_{\text{simple}}^0} (\{\, \lfloor \mathsf{end}(v_0, p_0) \rfloor_{v_0}^{t_v} , \lfloor 0 \rfloor_{p_0}^{t_p} \}; \Phi_{\text{sd}}; t).$$

We have that there exists a substitution $\sigma : \mathcal{N} \to \mathcal{T}(\Sigma_c^+, \mathcal{N} \cup \mathcal{A})$ from names freshly generated by P^* to constructor terms such that for any $\mathsf{out}(u)$ occurring in tr^*, there exists a recipe R such that $R\Phi_{\text{sd}}\!\downarrow =_\mathsf{E} u\sigma$.

Roughly, up to some substitution σ, we know that an arbitrary dishonest prover will disclose more information than the general one. Thus, to analyse terrorist fraud resistance, it is sufficient to consider the most general semi-dishonest prover. This actually corresponds to the best strategy for the terrorist prover.

Theorem 2. *Let $\mathcal{P}_{\mathsf{prox}}$ be a DB protocol and $\mathcal{I}_0$ be a template. Let Φ^* be the frame associated to the most general semi-dishonest prover of $\mathcal{P}_{\mathsf{prox}}$. We have that $\mathcal{P}_{\mathsf{prox}}$ is terrorist fraud resistant w.r.t. t_0-proximity if, and only if, there exists a topology $\mathcal{T} = (\mathcal{A}_0, \mathcal{M}_0, \mathsf{Loc}_0, v_0, p_0) \in \mathcal{C}_{\mathsf{MF}}$ and a valid initial configuration K_0 for $\mathcal{P}_{\mathsf{prox}}$ w.r.t. $\mathcal{T}$ and $\Phi^* \cup \Phi_{\mathcal{I}_0}^{\mathcal{T}}$ such that:*

$$K_0 \xrightarrow{\mathsf{tr}}_{\mathcal{T}} (\lfloor \mathsf{end}(v_0, p_0) \rfloor_{v_0}^{t'} \uplus \mathcal{P}; \Phi; t) \text{ with } \mathsf{Dist}_{\mathcal{T}}(v_0, p_0) \geq t_0.$$

We establish this result by showing that an execution trace tr starting with $\Phi^* \cup \Phi_{\mathcal{I}_0}^{\mathcal{T}}$ as an initial frame can be mimicked by an execution trace trσ starting with the initial frame $\Phi_{\mathsf{sd}} \cup \Phi_{\mathcal{I}_0}^{\mathcal{T}}$. In other words, P_{sd} is not better than P*: the information leaked by Φ_{sd} will also allow the accomplice to authenticate again.

4.3   Main Result

Applying Theorem 1 to reduce the topology, and then Theorem 2 to narrow down the number of semi-dishonest provers to consider, we get rid of the quantifications over semi-dishonest provers as well as the one regarding the topology. We now state our main reduction result.

Corollary 1. *Let $\mathcal{P}_{\mathsf{prox}}$ be a DB protocol and $\mathcal{I}_0$ be a template such that $\mathcal{P}$ is $\mathcal{I}_0$-executable. Let P* be the most general semi-dishonest prover for $\mathcal{P}$ together with its associated frame Φ^*. We have that $\mathcal{P}_{\mathsf{prox}}$ is terrorist fraud resistant w.r.t. t_0-proximity if, and only if, there exists a valid initial configuration K_0 for $\mathcal{P}_{\mathsf{prox}}$ w.r.t. $\mathcal{T}_{\mathsf{MF}}^0$ and $\Phi^* \cup \Phi_{\mathcal{I}_0}^{\mathcal{T}_{\mathsf{MF}}^0}$ such that:*

$$K_0 \xrightarrow{\mathsf{tr}}_{\mathcal{T}_{\mathsf{MF}}^{t_0}} (\lfloor \mathsf{end}(v_0, p_0) \rfloor_{v_0}^{t'} \uplus \mathcal{P}; \Phi; t).$$

We will see in the next section that our definition of DB protocol is quite general and covers most existing distance bounding protocols. However, some existing protocols, like Brands & Chaum [8] and MAD [10], do not qualify for our approach. The former does not satisfy our hypothesis *(iv)* whereas the latter starts with a commit on the challenge value, preventing it to be fresh (hypothesis *(i)* is not satisfied). Despite this, since these two protocols are subject to a terrorist fraud, we could simply exhibit the corresponding semi-dishonest prover and use our methodology to establish the existence a terrorist fraud.

A reduction result allowing one to get rid of the quantification over semi-dishonest provers is also suggested in [24]. The reduction result is not formally stated. Instead, the authors provide a manual proof of resistance to terrorist fraud for a specific DBToy protocol relying on the idea of least-disclosing message. Then, the authors claim that similar proofs can be done on all the case studies they have looked at. We would like to emphasise that even if our conditions (expressed in Definition 7) are not necessarily tight, the freshness of the challenge just as the rapid phase starts is necessary to ensure the completeness of our approach. Otherwise, a best strategy for the semi-dishonest prover could be to send out a message which contains the challenge. This condition is missing in [24] and therefore their approach is *not* complete even for protocols satisfying their least-disclosing message assumption.

Table 1. Results on our case studies (×: attack found, ✓: proved secure)

Protocols	MFR	TFR	Protocols	MFR	TFR
Basin's Toy Example [4]	✓	✓	Swiss-Knife [22]	✓	✓
Hancke and Kuhn [20]	✓	×	Modified Swiss-Knife [18]	✓	×
Modified Hancke and Kuhn [29]	✓	✓	Munilla *et al.* [27]	✓	×
TREAD-PKey V1 [3]	×	✓	SPADE [9]	×	✓
TREAD-PKey V1 Fixed [19]	✓	✓	SPADE Fixed [19]	✓	✓
TREAD-PKey V2 [3]	×	✓	SKI [7]	✓	✓
TREAD-PKey V2 Fixed [19]	✓	✓	PaySafe [12]	✓	×
TREAD-SKey [3]	✓	✓	NXP [21]	✓	×

5 Case Studies

Getting rid of the quantifications, we apply techniques already used in e.g. [12,14], to leverage the verification tool ProVerif to analyse terrorist fraud on distance bounding protocols.

5.1 Analysing Terrorist-Fraud Resistance Using Proverif

Based on the technique described in [14], we reuse the syntax of phases included in Proverif to model the guarded input of a Verifier. We will consider the same transformation, while adding an extra phase at the beginning (phase 0) to enrich the knowledge of the attacker with the frame provided together with the most-general semi-dishonest prover. Then, we consider a Verifier-Test modelled using three phases (1, 2 and 3) to see whether the adversary can re-authenticate itself by impersonating the Prover or not. As in [14], we also give to the adversary the possibility to play with all the agents present in the topology if they are close enough, since they can provide useful information.

Depending on Proverif outputs, we conclude on the terrorist-fraud security of the distance-bounding protocol. Either it is not possible to reach the end event of the Verifier-Test, or the tool returns a trace in which the event is reachable. In the first case, the attacker can not authenticate itself to the Verifier, even with the help provided by the Prover in phase 0, meaning that the protocol is vulnerable to a terrorist-fraud attack. In the second case, we first need to ensure that the trace provided by ProVerif is a valid trace in our model. If this is the case, then the adversary can authenticate itself to the Verifier again, without further help from the Prover, meaning that the protocol is terrorist-fraud resistant. Note that, even if in theory, our approach may not allow one to conclude (in case e.g. ProVerif does not terminate or simply say cannot be proved), we never encountered this situation when performing our case studies.

5.2 Our Results

We applied this methodology to different well-known distance-bounding protocols as long as they met the hypotheses needed by our approach, as mentioned in Sect. 4. As expected, numerous existing protocols qualify and the results are shown in Table 1. All our implementation files can be found in [15]. The tool concludes in less than a minute for most of the examples, except for two protocols: SPADE and SKI, where the extensive use of the xor operator may explain this noteworthy difference. To comply with the use of the symbolic approach, we needed to replace the actual bit-sized rapid exchanges by a single round of challenge-response using one fresh nonce, as presented in the examples throughout this paper. Moreover, due to Proverif limitations, we only considered, when needed, a weak version of the xor operator.

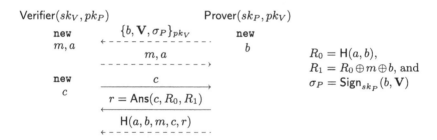

Fig. 1. Description of the SPADE (fixed) protocol

Our results confirm existing mafia frauds against the SPADE and the TREAD (PKey version) protocols [14,23]. Therefore we considered the fixed versions of these protocols mentioned in [19] and proved them mafia-fraud and terrorist-fraud resistant using our methodology. The fix, which consists in adding the Verifier identity in the first message sent by the Prover, is illustrated for the SPADE protocol in the Fig. 1 above.

We also extended our analysis to contactless payment protocols, e.g. Paysafe and NXP. While it was not surprising that they do not offer terrorist-fraud resistance, we consider that those protocols should claim if they want to support such a security property or not. Indeed, allowing terrorist fraud could be a feature of the card, permitting its user to agree for a one-time payment to a third-party while not being physically next to it, without risking any non-expected following payment, similarly to the current virtual credit card system.

5.3 Limitations

Even if our methodology is general enough to deal with a number of examples, we had to cope with some limitations. First, coming from the tool, Proverif, as mentioned earlier, we needed to weaken the xor operator. While our methodology could consider a different tool which deals better with such an operator, like Tamarin [26], it appears that Tamarin also behaves poorly depending on the considered protocols. Indeed, we faced up with non-termination issues when we tried to apply our methodology to the Brands and Chaum protocol within Tamarin. These termination issues are also visible in the case studies performed by Mauw *et al.* in [23] (using Tamarin) in which they often had to weaken the xor operator.

Second, as already discussed in Sect. 4.3, some limitations are due to the hypotheses we need on a distance-bounding protocols to conduct our formal development. We believe that we could relax our hypothesis regarding the freshness of the challenge up to a non-deductibility hypothesis to be able to apply our methodology to a protocol like MAD, but this is left to future work.

References

1. Abadi, M., Fournet, C.: Mobile values, new names, and secure communication. In: Proceedings of the 28th Symposium on Principles of Programming Languages (POPL'01), pp. 104–115. ACM Press (2001)
2. Avoine, G., Bingöl, M.A., Kardas, S., Lauradoux, C., Martin, B.: A framework for analyzing RFID distance bounding protocols. J. Comput. Secur. **19**(2), 289–317 (2011)
3. Avoine, G., et al.: A terrorist-fraud resistant and extractor-free anonymous distance-bounding protocol. In: Proceedings of the 12th ACM Asia Conference on Computer and Communications Security. ACM Press (2017)
4. Basin, D., Capkun, S., Schaller, P., Schmidt, B.: Formal reasoning about physical properties of security protocols. ACM Trans. Inf. Syst. Secur. (TISSEC) **14**(2), 16 (2011)
5. Blanchet, B.: An efficient cryptographic protocol verifier based on prolog rules. In: Proceedings of the 14th Computer Security Foundations Workshop (CSFW'01), pp. 82–96. IEEE Computer Society Press (2001)
6. Blanchet, B.: Modeling and verifying security protocols with the applied pi calculus and proverif. Found. Trends Priv. Secur. **1**(1–2), 1–135 (2016)
7. Boureanu, I., Mitrokotsa, A., Vaudenay, S.: Secure and lightweight distance-bounding. In: Avoine, G., Kara, O. (eds.) LightSec 2013. LNCS, vol. 8162, pp. 97–113. Springer, Heidelberg (2013). https://doi.org/10.1007/978-3-642-40392-7_8
8. Brands, S., Chaum, D.: Distance-bounding protocols. In: Helleseth, T. (ed.) EURO-CRYPT 1993. LNCS, vol. 765, pp. 344–359. Springer, Heidelberg (1994). https://doi.org/10.1007/3-540-48285-7_30
9. Bultel, X., Gambs, S., Gerault, D., Lafourcade, P., Onete, C., Robert, J.: A prover-anonymous and terrorist-fraud resistant distance-bounding protocol. In: Proceedings of the 9th ACM Conference on Security & Privacy in Wireless and Mobile Networks, (WISEC'16), pp. 121–133. ACM Press (2016)

10. Čapkun, S., Buttyán, L., Hubaux, J.-P.: Sector: secure tracking of node encounters in multi-hop wireless networks. In: Proceedings of the 1st ACM Workshop on Security of Ad Hoc and Sensor Networks, pp. 21–32. ACM (2003)

11. Chothia, T., de Ruiter, J., Smyth, B.: Modelling and analysis of a hierarchy of distance bounding attacks. In: Proceedings of the 27th USENIX Security Symposium, USENIX Security 2018 (2018)

12. Chothia, T., Garcia, F.D., de Ruiter, J., van den Breekel, J., Thompson, M.: Relay cost bounding for contactless EMV payments. In: Böhme, R., Okamoto, T. (eds.) FC 2015. LNCS, vol. 8975, pp. 189–206. Springer, Heidelberg (2015). https://doi.org/10.1007/978-3-662-47854-7_11

13. Debant, A., Delaune, S.: Symbolic verification of distance bounding protocols. In: Nielson, F., Sands, D. (eds.) POST 2019. LNCS, vol. 11426, pp. 149–174. Springer, Cham (2019). https://doi.org/10.1007/978-3-030-17138-4_7

14. Debant, A., Delaune, S., Wiedling, C.: A symbolic framework to analyse physical proximity in security protocols. In: Proceedings of the 38th IARCS Annual Conference on Foundations of Software Technology and Theoretical Computer Science, (FSTTCS'18), LIPIcs, vol. 122. Schloss Dagstuhl - Leibniz-Zentrum fuer Informatik (2018)

15. Debant, A., Delaune, S., Wiedling, C.: Symbolic Analysis of Terrorist Fraud Resistance. Research report, Univ Rennes, CNRS, IRISA, France, July 2019

16. Dolev, D., Yao, A.: On the security of public key protocols. IEEE Trans. Inf. Theory **29**(2), 198–208 (1983)

17. Dürholz, U., Fischlin, M., Kasper, M., Onete, C.: A formal approach to distance-bounding RFID protocols. In: Lai, X., Zhou, J., Li, H. (eds.) ISC 2011. LNCS, vol. 7001, pp. 47–62. Springer, Heidelberg (2011). https://doi.org/10.1007/978-3-642-24861-0_4

18. Fischlin, M., Onete, C.: Terrorism in distance bounding: modeling terrorist-fraud resistance. In: Jacobson, M., Locasto, M., Mohassel, P., Safavi-Naini, R. (eds.) ACNS 2013. LNCS, vol. 7954, pp. 414–431. Springer, Heidelberg (2013). https://doi.org/10.1007/978-3-642-38980-1_26

19. Gerault, D.: Security Analysis of Contactless Communication Protocols. Ph.D. thesis, Université Clermont Auvergne (2018)

20. Hancke, G.P., Kuhn, M.G.: An RFID distance bounding protocol. In Proceedings of the 1st International Conference on Security and Privacy for Emerging Areas in Communications Networks (SECURECOMM'05), pp. 67–73. IEEE (2005)

21. Janssens, P.: Proximity check for communication devices, 31 October 2017. US Patent 9,805,228

22. Kim, C.H., Avoine, G., Koeune, F., Standaert, F.-X., Pereira, O.: The swiss-knife RFID distance bounding protocol. In: Lee, P.J., Cheon, J.H. (eds.) ICISC 2008. LNCS, vol. 5461, pp. 98–115. Springer, Heidelberg (2009). https://doi.org/10.1007/978-3-642-00730-9_7

23. Mauw, S., Smith, Z., Toro-Pozo, J., Trujillo-Rasua, R.: Distance-bounding protocols: verification without time and location. In: Proceedings of the 39th IEEE Symposium on Security and Privacy (S&P'18), pp. 152–169 (2018)

24. Mauw, S., Smith, Z., Toro-Pozo, J., Trujillo-Rasua, R.: Post-collusion security and distance bounding. In: Proceedings of the 2019 ACM SIGSAC Conference on Computer and Communications Security. ACM (2019, to appear)

25. Meadows, C., Poovendran, R., Pavlovic, D., Chang, L., Syverson, P.: Distance bounding protocols: authentication logic analysis and collusion attacks. In: Pooven-dran, R., Roy, S., Wang, C. (eds.) Secure Localization and Time Synchronization for Wireless Sensor and Ad Hoc Networks, vol. 30, pp. 279–298. Springer, Boston (2007). https://doi.org/10.1007/978-0-387-46276-9_12

26. Meier, S., Schmidt, B., Cremers, C., Basin, D.: The TAMARIN prover for the symbolic analysis of security protocols. In: Sharygina, N., Veith, H. (eds.) CAV 2013. LNCS, vol. 8044, pp. 696–701. Springer, Heidelberg (2013). https://doi.org/10.1007/978-3-642-39799-8_48

27. Munilla, J., Peinado, A.: Distance bounding protocols for rfid enhanced by using void-challenges and analysis in noisy channels. Wirel. Commun. Mobile Comput. 8(9), 1227–1232 (2008)

28. Nigam, V., Talcott, C., Aires Urquiza, A.: Towards the automated verification of cyber-physical security protocols: bounding the number of timed intruders. In: Askoxylakis, I., Ioannidis, S., Katsikas, S., Meadows, C. (eds.) ESORICS 2016. LNCS, vol. 9879, pp. 450–470. Springer, Cham (2016). https://doi.org/10.1007/978-3-319-45741-3_23

29. Vaudenay, S.: On modeling terrorist frauds. In: Susilo, W., Reyhanitabar, R. (eds.) ProvSec 2013. LNCS, vol. 8209, pp. 1–20. Springer, Heidelberg (2013). https://doi.org/10.1007/978-3-642-41227-1_1

30. Vaudenay, S., Boureanu, I., Mitrokotsa, A. et al.: Practical & provably secure distance-bounding. In: Proceedings of the 16th Information Security Conference (ISC'13) (2013)

Secure Communication Channel Establishment: TLS 1.3 (over TCP Fast Open) vs. QUIC

Shan Chen[1(✉)], Samuel Jero[2], Matthew Jagielski[3], Alexandra Boldyreva[1], and Cristina Nita-Rotaru[3]

[1] Georgia Institute of Technology, Atlanta, Georgia
{shanchen,sasha}@gatech.edu
[2] Purdue University, West Lafayette, USA
sjero@sjero.net
[3] Northeastern University, Boston, USA
jagielski.m@husky.neu.edu, c.nitarotaru@neu.edu

Abstract. Secure channel establishment protocols such as TLS are some of the most important cryptographic protocols, enabling the encryption of Internet traffic. Reducing the latency (the number of interactions between parties) in such protocols has become an important design goal to improve user experience. The most important protocols addressing this goal are TLS 1.3 over TCP Fast Open (TFO), Google's QUIC over UDP, and QUIC[TLS] (a new design for QUIC that uses TLS 1.3 key exchange) over UDP. There have been a number of formal security analyses for TLS 1.3 and QUIC, but their security, when layered with their underlying transport protocols, cannot be easily compared. Our work is the first to thoroughly compare the security and availability properties of these protocols. Towards this goal, we develop novel security models that permit "layered" security analysis. In addition to the standard goals of server authentication and data privacy and integrity, we consider the goals of IP spoofing prevention, key exchange packet integrity, secure channel header integrity, and reset authentication, which capture a range of practical threats not usually taken into account by existing security models that focus mainly on the crypto cores of the protocols. Equipped with our new models we provide a detailed comparison of the above three protocols. We hope that our results will help protocol designers in their future protocol analyses and practitioners to better understand the advantages and limitations of novel secure channel establishment protocols.

Keywords: Applied cryptography · Provable security · TLS · QUIC · Secure channel · Availability · Network protocols

1 Introduction

MOTIVATION. Nowadays, more than half of all Internet traffic is encrypted according to a 2017 EFF report [20], with Google reporting that 93% of its traffic

© Springer Nature Switzerland AG 2019
K. Sako et al. (Eds.): ESORICS 2019, LNCS 11735, pp. 404–426, 2019.
https://doi.org/10.1007/978-3-030-29959-0_20

is encrypted as of January 2019 [1]. This widespread Internet traffic encryption is enabled by protocols that allow two parties (where one or both parties have a public key certificate) to establish a secure communication channel over the insecure Internet. Typically, the parties first authenticate all parties holding a public key certificate and agree on a session key—the key exchange phase. Then, this session key is used to encrypt the communication during the session—the secure channel phase. We will refer to such protocols as secure channel establishment protocols.

The main secure channel establishment protocol in use today is TLS. The session key establishment with TLS today involves 3 round-trip times (RTTs) of end-to-end communication, including the cost of establishing a TCP connection before the TLS connection. Further, this TCP cost is paid every time the two parties communicate with each other, even if the connection is interrupted and then immediately resumed. Given that most encrypted traffic is web traffic, this cost represents a significant performance bottleneck, a nuisance to users, and financial loss to companies. For instance, back in 2006 Amazon found that every 100 ms of latency cost them 1% in sales [34], while a typical RTT on a connection from New York to London is 70 ms [22].

Not surprisingly, many efforts in recent years have focused on reducing latency in secure channel establishment protocols. The focus has been on reducing the number of interactions (or RTTs) during session establishment and resumption without sacrificing much security. The most important protocols addressing this goal are TLS 1.3 [43] (the just-released successor to the current TLS 1.2 standard) and Google's QUIC [45].

With TLS 1.3, it is possible to reduce the number of RTTs (prior to sending encrypted data) during session resumption to 1, by utilizing a session ticket that was saved during a previous communication. The remaining 1-RTT during session resumption is due to the aforementioned TCP connection. However, one recent optimization for TCP, called TCP Fast Open (TFO) [10,42] extends TCP to allow for 0-RTT resumption connections, so that the client may begin data transmission immediately. The mechanism underlying this optimization is a cookie saved from previous communication, similar to the ticket used by TLS 1.3.

Like TLS 1.3, Google's QUIC uses weaker initial keys, under which data can be encrypted earlier, and a token saved from previous communication between the parties. But unlike TLS, QUIC operates over UDP rather than TCP. Instead of relying on TCP for reliability, flow control, and congestion control, QUIC implements its own data transmission functionality, integrating connection establishment with key exchange. These features allow QUIC to have 1-RTT full connections and 0-RTT resumption connections.

In addition to TLS 1.3 over TFO and QUIC over UDP, there is a new design for QUIC [23] (which we refer to as QUIC[TLS] [47] to indicate that it borrows the key exchange from TLS 1.3) over UDP. These 3 protocols win in terms of the number of interactions, but how does their security compare?

At first glance, the question is easy to answer. Recent works have done formal security analyses of TLS 1.3 [4–6, 11–15, 18, 28, 29, 33] and Google's QUIC [17, 35]. Most works confirm that (the cryptographic cores of) both protocols are provably secure under reasonable computational assumptions. Moreover, as shown in [18, 35], their 0-RTT data transmission designs cannot achieve the same strong security guaranteed by classical key exchange protocols with at least one RTT. In particular, the 0-RTT keys do not provide forward secrecy and the 0-RTT data suffers from replay attacks. Overall, it might seem that all three layered protocols mentioned above are equally secure.

However, a closer look reveals that the answer is not that simple. First, all aforementioned formal security analyses, except for [35] analyzing the IP spoofing (source validation) of QUIC, did not consider packet-level availability attacks. Therefore, it is not clear at the packet level what security can be achieved and what attacks can be prevented by these protocols. In other words, we have no formal understanding of what security can be obtained when layering protocols. We note that for protocols targeting low latency availability is essential, and since it can be assured to some degree by cryptographic means, a cryptographic analysis is very important. Also, TFO uses some cryptographic primitives, such as a cookie, to prevent IP spoofing, but, to the best of our knowledge, no formal analysis has been done. Furthermore, the security of QUIC[TLS] has not been formally analyzed (although some security aspects can be reduced to those of Google's QUIC and TLS 1.3).

OUR CONTRIBUTIONS. The goal of our work is to help public understanding of how security compares for the most latency-efficient secure channel establishment protocols on the market today. By including packet-level attacks in our analysis, our results also shed light on how the reliability, flow control, and congestion control of both approaches compare, in adversarial settings.

To compare security, we first need to define a general protocol syntax for secure channel establishment and fix a security model for it. We take *Quick Connections (QC)* protocol definition [35] as our starting point. To accommodate protocol syntaxes of TLS 1.3 and QUIC[TLS], we extend the QC protocol to a more general *Multi-Stage Authenticated and Confidential Channel Establishment (msACCE)* protocol, which allows more keys to be set during each session. The details are in Sect. 4.1.

Then, we extend the *Quick Authenticated and Confidential Channel Establishment (QACCE)* security model [35] to two msACCE security models— msACCE-std and msACCE-pauth—that are general enough for all layered secure channel establishment protocols mentioned above. The former model, msACCE-std, is fairly standard and is for core cryptographic security. The latter model, msACCE-pauth, is novel and is for packet-level security. For this packet-authentication model we extend the definition of IP-Spoofing Prevention from [35], and also define Key Exchange (KE) Header Integrity, KE Payload Integrity, Secure Channel (SC) Header Integrity, and Reset Authentication.

Equipped with our new models (see [9] and Sect. 4.2 for details), we study the security and availability functionalities provided by TFO+TLS 1.3,

UDP+QUIC, and UDP+QUIC[TLS]. We first confirm that all protocols provably satisfy the standard security notions of Server Authentication and Channel Security given that their building blocks are secure. The results mostly follow from prior works and we just have to argue that they still hold for our msACCE-std security model (which is an extension to previous models). Due to lack of space, we treat the above standard security notions and corresponding protocol security analyses in the full version [9], and here we focus on the novel packet-level security. We analyze the first 2 low latency protocols under our new model in Sect. 5 and refer to the full version [9] for the security analysis of UDP+QUIC[TLS]. Some of our theoretical findings capture practical availability attacks that the networking community has been slowly uncovering via manual investigation over the last 30 years [2, 7, 8, 21, 25–27, 30, 31, 36, 40, 41, 46, 48], such as TCP flow control manipulation, TCP acknowledgment injection, etc. Our findings also discover new weaknesses (e.g., those that allow manipulating the early key exchange packets without being detected by the communicating parties). Furthermore, our results prove security guarantees for certain goals (such as showing that TFO's cookie mechanism provably achieves the security goal of IP Spoofing Prevention and QUIC[TLS]'s stateless reset mechanism provably achieves the security goal of Reset Authentication). Table 1 in Sect. 5 summarizes our results.

2   Background

Network protocols are designed following a layered network stack model where each layer has its own functionality, defines an interface for use by higher layers, and relies only on the properties of lower layers. In this work, we are concerned with three layers: network, represented by the IP protocol; transport, represented by UDP and TCP with the Fast Open optimization (TFO); and application, represented by TLS or QUIC.

TCP Fast Open. TCP Fast Open (TFO) is an optimization which introduces a simple modification to the TCP connection establishment handshake to reduce the 1-RTT connection establishment latency of TCP and allow for 0-RTT handshakes. The mechanism through which 0-RTT is achieved is a cookie that is obtained by the client first time it communicates with a server and cached for later uses. This cookie is intended to prevent replay attacks while avoiding the need for servers to keep expensive state. It is generated by the server, authenticates client IP address, and has a limited lifetime. Generation and verification have low overhead. Cookies are sent in the TFO option field in SYN packets (see Fig. 1 for details).

TLS 1.3. The recently standardized TLS 1.3 [43] improves TLS 1.2. Most relevant, it enables 0-RTT handshakes at the TLS level. In a TLS 1.3 full connection (see Fig. 1, fourth message), the client begins by sending a ClientHello message containing a list of ciphersuites to use with key shares for each. The server responds with a ServerHello message containing the ciphersuite to use

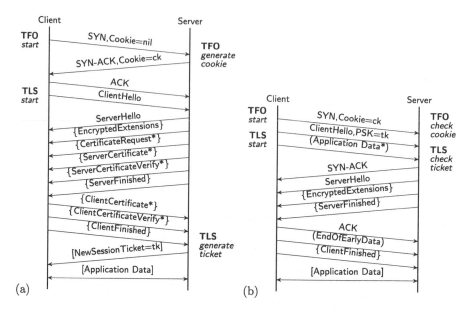

Fig. 1. TFO+TLS 1.3 (EC) DHE 2-RTT full handshake (a) and TFO+TLS 1.3 PSK-(EC) DHE 0-RTT resumption handshake(b). * indicates optional messages. () indicates messages protected using the 0-RTT keys derived from a pre-shared key. {} and [] indicate messages protected with initial and final keys.

and its key share. At this point, an initial encryption key is derived and all future messages are encrypted. The server also sends an EncryptedExtensions message containing any extension data, a CertificateRequest message if doing client authentication, a ServerCertificate message containing the server's certificate, a ServerCertificateVerify message containing a signature over the handshake with the private key corresponding to the server's certificate, and a ServerFinished message containing an HMAC of all messages in the handshake. The client receives these messages, verifies their contents, and responds with ClientCertificate and ClientCertificateVerify messages if doing client authentication before finishing with a ClientFinished message containing an HMAC of all messages in the handshake. At this point, a final encryption key is derived and used for encrypting all future messages. If the server supports 0-RTT connections, one final handshake message, the NewSessionTicket message, will be sent by the server to provide the client with an opaque session ticket to be used in a resumption session.

In later TLS 1.3 resumption connections to this server, the client uses the session ticket established in the prior full connection to do a 0-RTT connection. In this case, the client sends a ClientHello message indicating a pre-shared-key ciphersuite, a ciphersuite to use for the final key, and the cached session ticket. The client can then derive an encryption key and begin sending 0-RTT data. The server will verify the session ticket, use it to establish the same encryption key, and send a `ServerHello` message containing the ciphersuite to use and its final key share. At this point, an initial encryption key is derived and all future messages are encrypted. The server also sends an `EncryptedExtensions` message containing any extension data and a `ServerFinished` message containing an HMAC of all messages in the handshake. The client receives these messages, verifies their contents, and responds with an `EndOfEarlyData` message and a `ClientFinished` message containing an HMAC of all messages in the handshake. At this point, a final encryption key is derived and used for encrypting all future messages.

TLS 1.3 over TFO. Layering TLS 1.3 over TCP Fast Open enables true 0-RTT connections. In a full connection to a TFO+TLS 1.3 server, the client requests a TFO cookie in the TCP SYN and then does a full TLS 1.3 handshake once the TCP connection completes. This takes 3-RTTs (see Fig. 1), but provides a cached TFO cookie and cached TLS session ticket. In subsequent resumption connections to this server, the client can use the TFO cookie to establish a 0-RTT TCP connection and include the TLS 1.3 `ClientHello` message in the SYN packet. The TLS `ClientHello` message can use the cached TLS session ticket to perform a 0-RTT resumption handshake. Thus, the TCP and TLS 1.3 connections are established at the same time, as shown in Fig. 1.

QUIC over UDP. Quick UDP Internet Connections (QUIC) is a transport protocol developed by Google and implemented by Chrome and Google servers since 2013 [45]. QUIC provides a very similar set of services to TFO+TLS 1.3, however instead of modifying TCP to enable 0-RTT connection establishment, QUIC replaces TCP entirely, using UDP.

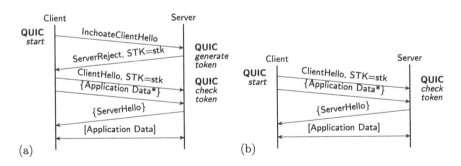

Fig. 2. QUIC 1-RTT full handshake (a) and UDP+QUIC 0-RTT resumption handshake (b). * indicates optional messages. {} and [] indicate messages protected with initial and final keys.

QUIC packets contain a public header and a set of frames that are encrypted and authenticated after initial connection setup. The header contains a set of public flags, a unique 64bit connection identifier referred to as `cid`, and a variable length packet number. All other protocol information is carried in control and stream (data) frames that are encrypted and authenticated.

To provide 0-RTT, QUIC caches information about the server that will enable the client to determine the encryption key to be used for each new connection. As shown in Fig. 2, the first time a client contacts a given server it sends an empty (Inchoate) `ClientHello` message. The server responds with a `ServerReject` message containing the server's certificate, an object called an `scfg`, (contains a variety of information about the server, including a Diffie-Hellman share from the server), supported encryption and signing algorithms, and flow control parameters. Along with the `scfg`, the server sends the client a source-address token or `stk`. The `stk` is used to prevent IP spoofing. It contains an encrypted version of the client's IP address and a timestamp.

With this cached information, a client can establish an encrypted connection with the server. It first ensures that the `scfg` is correctly signed by the server's certificate which is valid and then sends a `ClientHello` indicating the `scfg` its using, the `stk` value it has cached, a Diffie-Hellman share for the client, and a client nonce. After sending the `ClientHello`, the client can create an initial encryption key and send additional encrypted `Application Data` packets. In fact, to take advantage of the 0-RTT connection establishment it must do so. When the server receives the `ClientHello` message, it validates the `stk` and client nonce parameters and creates the same encryption key using the server share from the `scfg` and the client's share from the `ClientHello` message.

At this point, while both client and server have established the connection, setup encryption keys and all further communication between the parties is encrypted, the connection is not forward secure yet, meaning that compromising the server would compromise all previous communication because the server's Diffie-Hellman share is the same for all connections using the same `scfg`. To provide forward secrecy for all data after the first RTT, the server sends a `ServerHello` message after receiving the client's `ClientHello` which contains a newly generated Diffie-Hellman share. Once the client receives this message, client and server derive and begin using the new forward secure encryption key.

For the client that has connected to a server before, it can instead initiate a resumption connection. This consists of only the last two steps of a full connection, sending the `ClientHello` and `ServerHello` messages as shown in Fig. 2.

QUIC with TLS 1.3 Key Exchange over UDP. A new version of QUIC [23], which also supports 0-RTT, describes several improvements of the previous design. The most important change is replacing QUIC's key exchange with the one from TLS 1.3, as specified in the latest Internet draft [47]. We provide more details (e.g., about its new stateless reset feature) in the full version [9].

3   Preliminaries

Public Key Infrastructure. For simplicity, we assume the public keys used in our analysis are supported by a *public key infrastructure (PKI)* and do not consider certificates or certificate checks explicitly. In other words, we assume each public key is certified and bound to the corresponding party's identity.

PRF and AEAD. In the full version [9] we recall the security definitions of a *pseudorandom function (PRF) F* and a stateful *authenticated encryption with associated data (AEAD)* scheme sAEAD. Accordingly, there we provide the definitions for the corresponding advantages: $\mathbf{Adv}_F^{\mathsf{prf}}(A)$, $\mathbf{Adv}_{\mathsf{sAEAD}}^{\mathsf{aead}}(A)$. We also refer to [44] for the syntax and security definitions of a nonce-based AEAD scheme.

4 msACCE Protocol and Its Security

In this section, we define the syntax and two security models for *Multi-Stage Authenticated and Confidential Channel Establishment (msACCE)* protocols.

4.1 Protocol Syntax

Our msACCE protocol is an extension to the *Quick Connection (QC)* protocol proposed by Lychev *et al.* [35] and the *Multi-Stage Key Exchange (MSKE)* protocol proposed by Fischlin and Günther [17] (and further developed by [14,15,18,33]). Even though the authors of [35] claimed their QC protocol syntax to be general, TLS 1.3 does not fit it well because TLS 1.3 has two initial keys and one final key in 0-RTT resumption while QC captures only one initial key. On the other hand, the MSKE protocol and its extensions focus only on the key exchange phases.

Our msACCE protocol syntax inherits many parts of the QC protocol syntax but extends it to a multi-stage structure and additionally covers session resumptions (explicitly, unlike QC), session resets, and header-only packets exchanged in secure channel phases. The detailed protocol syntax is defined below.

A msACCE protocol is an interactive protocol between a client and a server. They establish keys in one or more stages and exchange messages encrypted and decrypted with these keys. Messages are exchanged via *packets*. A packet consists of source and destination IP addresses[1] $\mathsf{IP_s}, \mathsf{IP_d} \in \{0,1\}^{32} \cup \{0,1\}^{64}$, a header, and a payload. Each party P has a unique IP address IP_P.

The protocol is associated with the security parameter $\lambda \in \mathbb{N}_+$, a key generation algorithm Kg that takes as input 1^λ and outputs a public and secret key pair, a header space[2] (for transport and application layers) $\mathcal{H} \subseteq \{0,1\}^*$, a payload space $\mathcal{PD} \subseteq \{0,1\}^*$, header and payload spaces $\mathcal{H}_{\mathsf{rst}} \subseteq \mathcal{H}, \mathcal{PD}_{\mathsf{rst}} \subseteq \mathcal{PD}$ for reset packets (described later), a resumption state space $\mathcal{RS} \subseteq \{0,1\}^*$, a stateful AEAD scheme[3] sAEAD = (sG, sE, sD) (with a key space $\mathcal{K} = \{0,1\}^\lambda$, a message space $\mathcal{M} \subseteq \{0,1\}^*$, an associated data space $\mathcal{AD} \subseteq \{0,1\}^*$, and a

---

[1] For the network-layer protocols, we only consider the Internet Protocol and its IP address header fields because our model mainly focuses on the application and transport layers and additionally only captures the IP-spoofing attack.

[2] Some protocol header fields (e.g., port numbers, checksums, etc.) can be excluded if they are not the focus of the security analysis.

[3] To fit TLS 1.3's encryption scheme, unlike QACCE we model QUIC's encryption scheme as a more general stateful AEAD scheme rather than a nonce-based one.

state space $\mathcal{ST} \subseteq \{0, 1\}^*$), *disjoint*[4] message spaces $\mathcal{M}_{\mathsf{KE}}, \mathcal{M}_{\mathsf{SC}}, \mathcal{M}_{\mathsf{pRST}} \subseteq \mathcal{M}$ with $\mathcal{M}_{\mathsf{KE}}, \mathcal{M}_{\mathsf{SC}}$ for messages encrypted during key exchange and secure channel phases respectively and $\mathcal{M}_{\mathsf{pRST}}$ for pre-reset messages (described later) encrypted in a secure channel phase, a server configuration generation function scfg_gen described below.

The protocol's execution is associated with the universal notion of time divided into discrete periods $\tau_1, \tau_2, \ldots$. During its execution, both parties can keep states that are initialized to the empty string ε. In the beginning of each time period, the protocol may periodically update each server's configuration state scfg with scfg_gen (which takes as input 1^λ, a server secret key, and a time period, then outputs a server configuration state). Otherwise, scfg_gen is undefined and without loss of generality the protocol is executed within a single time period.

A *reset* packet enables a sender, who lost its session state due to some error condition (e.g., server reboots, denial-of-service attacks, etc.), to abruptly terminate a session with the receiver. A *pre-reset* message (e.g., a reset token in QUIC[TLS]) is sent to the receiver in a secure channel phase[5] before the sender loses its state in order to authenticate the sender's reset packet. Each session has *at most one* pre-reset message for each party. A *non-reset* packet is not a reset packet. A *header-only* packet has no payload.

We say a party *rejects* a packet if its processing the packet leads to an error (defined according to the protocol), and *accepts* it otherwise.

The protocol has two modes, *full* and *resumption*. Its corresponding executions are referred to as the full and resumption sessions. Each resumption session is associated with a *single* previous full session and we say the resumption session *resumes* its associated full session. In the beginning of a full or resumption session, each party takes as input a list of messages[6] $\mathcal{M}^{\mathsf{snd}} = (M_1, \ldots, M_l), M_i \in \mathcal{M}_{\mathsf{SC}}, l \in \mathbb{N}$ (where the total message length $|\mathcal{M}^{\mathsf{snd}}|$ is polynomial in λ and $\mathcal{M}^{\mathsf{snd}}$ can be empty) as well as the other party's IP address. In a full session, the server runs $\mathsf{Kg}(1^\lambda)$ to generate a public and secret key pair and sends its public key to the client as input. In a resumption session, each party additionally takes as input its own resumption state $rs \in \mathcal{RS}$ (set in the associated full session). In either case, the client sends the first packet to start the session.

A D-stage msACCE protocol consists of $D \in \mathbb{N}_+$ successive stages and each stage, e.g., the d-th ($d \in [D]$) stage, consists of one or two phases described as follows:

---

[4] Disjointness is a reasonable assumption as practical protocols (such as the 3 layered protocols that we consider) enforce different leading bits for different types of messages.

[5] A pre-reset message can also be carried within an *encrypted* key exchange packet. We consider it encrypted as a separate secure channel packet to get a clean packet-authentication security model described later.

[6] For simplicity, we consider transportation of *atomic* messages rather than a data *stream* that can be modeled as a stream-based channel [19] and later extended to capture multiplexing [37].

(1) *Key Exchange.* At the end of this phase each party sets its d-th stage key $k^d = (k_c^d, k_s^d)$. At most one of k_c^d and k_s^d can be $\perp$, i.e., unused.[7] If this is the final stage in a full session, each party can send additional messages[8] in $\mathcal{M}_{\mathsf{KE}}$ encrypted with k^d and by the end of this phase each party sets its own resumption state.

(2) *Secure Channel.* This phase is mandatory for the final stage but optional for other stages. In this phase, the parties can exchange messages from their input lists as well as pre-reset messages, encrypted and decrypted using the associated stateful AEAD scheme with k^d. The client uses k_c^d to encrypt and the server uses it to decrypt, whereas the server uses k_s^d to encrypt and the client uses it to decrypt. They may also send reset or header-only packets. At the end of this phase, each party outputs a list of received messages (which may be empty) $\mathcal{M}_i^{\mathsf{rcv}} = (M_1', \ldots, M_{l_i'}'), l_i' \in \mathbb{N}, M_i' \in \mathcal{M}_{\mathsf{SC}}$.

Each message exchanged between the parties must belong to some unique phase at some unique stage. One stage's second phase and the next stage's first phase may overlap, and the two phases in the final stage may also overlap. We call the final stage key the *session* key and the other stage keys the *interim* keys.

Correctness. Consider a client and a server running a D-stage msACCE protocol in either mode without sending any reset packet. Each party's input message list $\mathcal{M}^{\mathsf{snd}}$, in which the messages are sent among D stages according to any partitioning $\mathcal{M}^{\mathsf{snd}} = \mathcal{M}_1^{\mathsf{snd}}, \ldots, \mathcal{M}_D^{\mathsf{snd}}$, is equal to the other party's total output message list $\mathcal{M}^{\mathsf{rcv}} = \mathcal{M}_1^{\mathsf{rcv}}, \ldots, \mathcal{M}_D^{\mathsf{rcv}}$, in which the message order is preserved. Each party terminates its session upon receiving the other party's reset packet.

REMARK. With our more general protocol syntax, the ACCE [24] and QC [35] protocols can be classified into 1-stage and 2-stage msACCE protocols respectively.

4.2   Security Models

We propose two security models respectively for basic authenticated and confidential channel security and packet authentication. Our models do not consider the key exchange and secure channel phases independently, as was the case for some previous QUIC and TLS 1.3 security analyses [14,15,17,18,33], because QUIC's key exchange and secure channel phases are inherently inseparable and the TLS 1.3 full handshake does not fit into a composability framework, as discussed in [15,35]. We refer to the full version [9] for our basic model (which we call msACCE-std) that considers standard security goals such as server authentication and channel security (which captures data privacy and integrity) for msACCE protocols. Here we only present our novel msACCE packet-authentication (msACCE-pauth) model.

---

[7] This captures the case where a 0-RTT key only consists of a client encryption key while the server encryption key does not exist.

[8] This captures the post-handshake key exchange messages that are used for session resumption, post-handshake authentication, key update, etc.

MSACCE-PAUTH OVERVIEW. In this model, we consider security goals related to packet authentication beyond those captured by the basic model. Note that msACCE-std essentially focuses only on the packet fields in the application layer, while msACCE-pauth further covers transport-layer headers and IP addresses.

First, we consider IP spoofing prevention (a.k.a. source authentication) as with the QACCE model, but, as illustrated later, generalize one of the QACCE queries to additionally capture IP spoofing attacks in the full sessions. Then we define four novel packet-level security notions (elaborated later): *KE Header Integrity*, *KE Payload Integrity*, *SC Header Integrity*, and *Reset Authentication*, which enable a comprehensive and fine-grained security analysis of layered protocols.

In particular, KE Header and Payload Integrity respectively capture the header and payload integrity of key exchange packets. Such security issues have not been investigated before and, as we show later, lead to new availability attacks for both TFO+TLS 1.3 and UDP+QUIC. Furthermore, we employ SC Header Integrity to capture the header integrity of non-reset packets in secure channel phases. Note that, unlike the availability attacks shown in [35], successful attacks breaking our security notions are *harder or impossible to detect* by the client as they do not affect the client's session key establishment, so they are more harmful in this sense. Finally, our model captures malicious *undetectable* session resets in a secure channel phase with Reset Authentication.

MSACCE-PAUTH DEFINITIONS. Like previous models, we consider a very powerful adversary who can control communications between honest parties, can adaptively learn their stage keys, and can adaptively corrupt servers to learn their long-term keys and secret states. Our detailed security model is defined below.

Protocol Entities. The set of parties $\mathcal{P}$ consists of two disjoint type of parties: clients $\mathcal{C}$ and servers $\mathcal{S}$, i.e., $|\mathcal{P}| = |\mathcal{C}| + |\mathcal{S}|$.

Session Oracles. To capture multiple sequential and parallel protocol executions, each party $P \in \mathcal{P}$ is associated with a set of session oracles $\pi_P^1, \pi_P^2, \ldots$, where π_P^i models P executing a protocol instance in session $i \in \mathbb{N}_+$.

Matching Conversations. As part of the security model, *matching conversations* are used to model entity authentication, session key confirmation, and handshake integrity. A client (resp. server) oracle has a matching conversation with a server (resp. client) oracle if and only if both session oracles observe the same[9] *session identifier* sid defined according to the protocol specifications and security goals. Note that a msACCE protocol may have two different session identifiers in full and resumption modes, but for simplicity we use the same

---

[9] As discussed in [24], two session oracles having matching conversations with each other may not observe the same transcript due to the gap between one oracle sending a message and the other receiving it. We can use *symmetric* session identifiers to define matching conversations because our msACCE-std model focuses only on server authentication and we require session identifiers to exclude, if any, a client oracle's last key exchange message(s) sent immediately before it sets its session key.

notation sid. Compared to the general definition of matching conversations [3,24], sid is often defined as a *subset* of the whole communication transcript. For instance, QUIC's sid in QACCE [35] is defined as the second-round key exchange messages, i.e., ClientHello and ServerHello, while the first-round messages are excluded to allow for valid but different source-address tokens or signatures. Similarly, TLS 1.2's sid in ACCE [28] is defined as the first three key exchange messages, while the rest are excluded to allow for valid but different encrypted Finished messages.

Peers. We say a client oracle and a server oracle are each other's *peer* if they observe the same first-stage session identifier sid_1 (i.e., sid restricted to the first stage), which intuitively means that they set the first stage key with each other. Note that a client oracle may have more than one peers if sid_1 consists of only message(s) sent from the client oracle, which can be replayed to the same[10] server to establish multiple (identical) first-stage keys. Therefore, a session oracle's peer may not be its final unique communication partner. Instead, the real partner is the session oracle with which the oracle has a matching conversation.

Security Experiments. In the beginning of the experiments, run $\mathsf{Kg}(1^\lambda)$ for all servers to generate the public and secret key pairs and initialize the global states of all parties and the local states of all session oracles. In the beginning of each time period, run scfg_gen (if defined) for each server to update its configuration state scfg. We assume that both the server oracles and the adversary A are aware of the current time period. Let $N \in \mathbb{N}_+$ denote the maximum number of msACCE protocol instances for each party. The adversary A is given all public keys and the IP addresses associated with all parties and then interacts with the session oracles via the same Connect, Resume, Send, Reveal, Corrupt queries as in the msACCE-std model[11] (which respectively give the adversary abilities to start and resume a session, send key exchange messages and get responses, reveal session keys, and corrupt servers, referring to the full version [9] for more details), as well as the following:

- Connprivate(π_C^i, π_S^j, cmp), for $C \in \mathcal{C}$, $S \in \mathcal{S}$, $i, j \in [N]$, cmp $\in \{0, 1\}$.
  This query always returns $\bot$. If cmp $= 1$, π_C^i and π_S^j establish a *complete* full session privately without showing their communication to the adversary. If cmp $= 0$, π_C^i and π_S^j establish a *partial* full session privately such that the last packet sent from π_C^i right before π_S^j sets its first stage key is blocked.

  This query allows the adversary to establish a complete or partial full session between any client and server oracles without observing their communication. By taking an additional flag cmp as input, this query extends the QACCE Connprivate query [35] to model IP-spoofing attacks happening in both *full* and resumption sessions.

---

[10] In practice, 0-RTT replay attacks can be mounted to *different* servers with the same public-secret key pair. However, 0-RTT key exchange message(s) replayed to other servers with different public-secret key pairs will be rejected.

[11] Note that Encrypt and Decrypt queries are not needed because msACCE-pauth does not consider data privacy explicitly.

- Pack(π_P^i, ad, m), for $P \in \mathcal{P}, i \in [N], ad \in \mathcal{AD}, m \in \mathcal{M}_{SC} \cup \mathcal{M}_{pRST} \cup \{\texttt{prst}, \texttt{rst}\}$.

  This query returns $\perp$ if π_P^i is not in a secure channel phase. If $m \in \mathcal{M}_{SC} \cup \mathcal{M}_{pRST}$, it asks π_P^i to output the packet that it would send to its peer(s) for the specified associated data ad and message m according to the protocol, then returns this packet. If $m = \texttt{prst}$, π_P^i generates its pre-reset message (if any, hidden from the adversary), encrypts it with the specified associated data ad, and outputs the resulting packet, then this packet is returned. (Recall that each oracle has at most one pre-reset message, so at most one input message $m \in \mathcal{M}_{pRST} \cup \{\texttt{prst}\}$ is allowed to be queried.) If $m = \texttt{rst}$, this query asks π_P^i to output its reset packet (if any) and returns it.

  This query allows the adversary to specify any associated data and any message in a secure channel phase, then get the packet output by the specified session oracle. The adversary can also specify a session oracle to get the packet resulting from encrypting the session oracle's pre-reset message (which the adversary does not know) or get its reset packet.

- Deliver(π_P^i, pkt), for $P \in \mathcal{P}, i \in [N], pkt \in \{0,1\}^*$.

  This query returns $\perp$ if π_P^i is not in a secure channel phase. Otherwise, it delivers pkt to π_P^i and returns its response.

  This query allows the adversary to deliver any packet to a specified session oracle and get its response in a secure channel phase.

Advantage Measures. An adversary A against a msACCE protocol Π in msACCE-pauth has the following associated advantage measures.

- *IP-Spoofing Prevention.* We define $\mathbf{Adv}_\Pi^{\text{ipsp}}(A)$ as the probability that there exist a client oracle π_C^i and a server oracle π_S^j such that the following holds:
  1. π_S^j has set its first stage key right after a Send($\pi_S^j, (\text{IP}_C, \text{IP}_S, \cdot, \cdot)$) query;
  2. S was not corrupted before π_S^j set its first stage key;
  3. The only allowed queries concerning both C and S in the time period associated with π_S^j are:
     - Connprivate($\pi_C^x, \pi_S^y, \cdot$) for any $x, y \in [N]$, and
     - Send($\pi_S^y, (\text{IP}_C, \text{IP}_S, \cdot, \cdot)$) for any $y \in [N]$, where $(\text{IP}_C, \text{IP}_S, \cdot, \cdot)$ is the last packet received by π_S^y right before it sets its first stage key.

  The above captures the attacks in which the adversary fools a server into accepting a spurious connection request seemingly from an impersonated client, without observing any previous communication between the client and server in the same time period.

- *KE Header Integrity.* We define $\mathbf{Adv}_\Pi^{\text{int-keh}}(A)$ as the probability that there exist a client oracle π_C^i and a server oracle π_S^j such that the following holds:
  1. π_C^i has set its session key and has a matching conversation with π_S^j;
  2. S was not corrupted before π_C^i set its session key;
  3. No interim keys of π_C^i or its peer(s) were revealed;
  4. In a key exchange phase before π_C^i set its session key, π_C^i (resp. π_S^j) accepted a packet with a new header that was not output by π_S^j (resp. π_C^i).

The above captures the attacks in which the adversary modifies the protocol header of a key exchange packet of the communicating parties without affecting the client setting its session key. In the above definition, we assume that a client sets its session key *immediately* after sending its last key exchange packet(s) (if any). Then, a forged packet that leads to a successful attack cannot be any of these last packet(s), which have not yet been sent to the server. The same assumption is made for KE Payload Integrity defined below.

- *KE Payload Integrity.* We define $\mathbf{Adv}_{\Pi}^{\text{int-kep}}(A)$ as the probability that there exist a client oracle π_C^i and a server oracle π_S^j such that the same 1–3 conditions as in the above KE Header Integrity notion and the following holds:

  4. In a key exchange phase before π_C^i set its session key, π_C^i (resp. π_S^j) accepted a packet with a new payload that was not output by π_S^j (resp. π_C^i).

  The above captures the attacks in which the adversary modifies the payload of a key exchange packet of the communicating parties without affecting the client setting its session key.

- *SC Header Integrity.* We define $\mathbf{Adv}_{\Pi}^{\text{int-h}}(A)$ as the probability that A outputs (P, i, d) such that the following holds:

  1. If $P = S \in \mathcal{S}$, π_S^i has a matching conversation with a client oracle π_C^j; if $P = C \in \mathcal{C}$, denote S as π_C^i's target server;
  2. S was not corrupted before π_P^i set its last stage key; If *forward secrecy* is not required for the d-th stage keys, S was not corrupted in the same time period associated with π_P^i;
  3. No stage keys of π_P^i or its peer(s) were revealed.
  4. In the secure channel phase of the d-th stage, π_P^i accepted a non-reset packet with a new header that was not output by its peer(s) (via Pack queries), or π_P^i accepted a non-reset header-only packet.

  The above captures the attacks in which the adversary creates a valid non-reset secure channel packet by forging the protocol header. Note that in the above security notion an invalid header forgery is detected *immediately* after the malicious packet is received and processed, while the detection of invalid packet forgeries in a key exchange phase (e.g., for plaintext packets) can be *delayed* to the point when the client sets its session key, according to the definitions of KE Header and Payload Integrity.

- *Reset Authentication.* We define $\mathbf{Adv}_{\Pi}^{\text{rst-auth}}(A)$ as the probability that A outputs (P, i, d) such that the same 1~3 conditions as in the above SC Header Integrity notion hold and the following holds:

  4. In the secure channel of the d-th stage, π_P^i accepted a packet output by a Pack$(\cdot, \cdot, \texttt{prst})$ query to its peer $\pi_{P'}^j$. Later (in the d-th or a later stage), π_P^i accepted a reset packet but A made no Pack$(\pi_{P'}^j, \cdot, \texttt{rst})$ queries.

The above captures the attacks in which the adversary forges a valid reset packet. Note that such attacks are *undetectable* by the accepting party, as opposed to a network attacker that simply drops packets.

We say a msACCE protocol Π achieves a security notion in our msACCE security models if the associated advantage is negligible (in λ) or for any *probabilistic-polynomial-time (PPT)* A.

REMARK ABOUT MSACCE SECURITY MODEL COMPLETENESS AND LOW-LAYER INTEGRITY. Since the payload integrity in secure channels is captured by msACCE-std, together with msACCE-pauth our models *completely* capture the authentication (or integrity) of all packet fields in the transport and application layers. Furthermore, msACCE-pauth captures (network-layer) IP-Spoofing Prevention against weaker off-path attackers (i.e., those can only inject packets without observing the communication), but leaves other integrity attacks on low layers (e.g., network, link, and physical layers) uncovered. Such attacks may affect packet forwarding, node-to-node data transfer, or raw data transmission, which are outside the scope of our work.

5   Provable Security Analysis

We now analyze and compare the security of TFO+TLS 1.3 and UDP+QUIC, and refer to the full version [9] for the security analysis of UDP+QUIC[TLS]. The security results are summarized in Table 1. As mentioned in the Introduction, by [18] results, no protocol achieves forward secrecy for 0-RTT keys or protects against 0-RTT data replays (which contribute to the first two rows in the table). The third and fourth rows reflect security results in our basic msACCE-std model (see the full version [9] for detailed analyses), which are derived by adapting existing security results [16,18,33,35] to our model. We now move to the detailed msACCE-pauth security analyses and start with TFO+TLS 1.3.

Table 1. Security comparison

	TFO+TLS 1.3	UDP+QUIC	UDP+QUIC[TLS] [9]
0-RTT Key Forward Secrecy [18]	✗	✗	✗
0-RTT Data Anti-Replay [18]	✗	✗	✗
Server Authentication [9]	✓	✓	✓
Channel Security [9]	✓	✓	✓
IP-Spoofing Prevention	✓	✓	✓
KE Header Integrity	✗	✗	✗
KE Payload Integrity	✓	✗	✗
SC Header Integrity	✗	✓	✓
Reset Authentication	✗	✗	✓

5.1   TLS 1.3 over TFO

We refer to Appendix A.1 for TFO+TLS 1.3's protocol definition. Its session identifier sid_{TLS} is defined as all key exchange messages from ClientHello to ServerFinished, excluding TCP headers and IP addresses. The msACCE-pauth security analyses are shown as follows.

IP-Spoofing Prevention. This security of TFO+TLS 1.3 is provided by the TFO component through TCP sequence number randomization and TFO cookies. By modeling the cookie generation function, an AES-128 block cipher, as a PRF $F : \{0,1\}^n \times \{0,1\}^\lambda \to \{0,1\}^n$, we have the following theorem with the proof in the full version [9]:

Theorem 1. *For any PPT adversary A making at most q Send queries, there exists a PPT adversary B such that:*

$$\mathbf{Adv}^{\mathsf{ipsp}}_{TFO+TLS\ 1.3}(A) \leq |\mathcal{S}|\mathbf{Adv}^{\mathsf{prf}}_F(B) + \frac{q}{\min\{2^{|\mathsf{sqn}|}, 2^n\}} \ .$$

KE Header Integrity. TFO+TLS 1.3 does not achieve this security notion because TCP headers are never authenticated. We find a new practical attack below, where a PPT adversary A can always get $\mathbf{Adv}^{\mathsf{int\text{-}keh}}_{TFO+TLS\ 1.3}(A) = 1$:

TFO Cookie Removal. A can first make $\pi_C^{i'}$ complete a full handshake with $\pi_S^{j'}$ (via Connect, Send queries), then query $\mathsf{Resume}(\pi_C^i, \pi_S^j, i')$ $(i > i', j > j')$ to get the output packet $(\mathrm{IP}_C, \mathrm{IP}_S, H, pd)$, which is a SYN packet with a TFO cookie. A then modifies the opt field of H to get a new $H' \neq H$ that contains no cookie. The resulting SYN packet will be accepted by π_S^j, which will then respond with a SYN-ACK packet that does not contain a TFO cookie, indicating a fallback to the standard 3-way TCP. As a result, a 1-RTT handshake is needed to complete the connection and any 0-RTT data sent with SYN would be retransmitted. This eliminates the entire benefit of TFO without being detected, resulting in reduced performance and increased handshake latency. A similar attack is possible by removing the TFO cookie in a server's SYN-ACK packet.

Interestingly, clients are supposed to cache negative TFO responses and avoid sending TFO connections again for a lengthy period of time. This is because the most likely explanation for this behavior is that the server does not support TFO, but only standard TCP [10]. As a result, performing this attack for a single connection prevents TFO from being used with this server for a lengthy time period (i.e., days or weeks).

KE Payload Integrity. TFO+TLS 1.3 is secure in this regard simply because $\mathsf{sid}_{\mathrm{TLS}}$ consists of the payloads of all key exchange packets exchanged between the communicating parties before the client set its session key. That is, for any client oracle that has a matching conversation with any server oracle, by definition they observe the same $\mathsf{sid}_{\mathrm{TLS}}$ and hence no key exchange packet payload can be modified, i.e., $\mathbf{Adv}^{\mathsf{int\text{-}kep}}_{TFO+TLS\ 1.3}(A) = 0$ for any PPT adversary A.

SC Header Integrity. TFO+TLS 1.3 does not achieve this security again because of the unauthenticated TCP headers. A PPT adversary A can get $\mathbf{Adv}^{\mathsf{int\text{-}h}}_{TFO+TLS\ 1.3}(A) = 1$ by either modifying the TCP header of an encrypted packet (e.g., reducing the window value) or by forging a header-only packet (e.g., removing the payload of an encrypted packet and changing its ack value). Such packets are valid and will be accepted by the receiving session oracle.

The above fact exposes the adversary's ability to arbitrarily modify or even entirely forge the information in the TCP header, which is being relied on to provide reliable delivery, in-order delivery, flow control, and congestion control for the targeted flow. This leads to a whole host of availability attacks that the networking community has been slowly uncovering via manual investigation over the last 30 years [2, 7, 8, 21, 25–27, 30, 31, 36, 40, 41, 46, 48]. Some of the practical attacks are described in the full version [9].

Reset Authentication. TFO+TLS 1.3 is insecure in this sense because its reset packet, TCP Reset, is an unauthenticated header-only packet. This leads to a practical attack below, where a PPT adversary A always gets $\mathbf{Adv}^{\text{rst-auth}}_{\text{TFO+TLS 1.3}}(A) = 1$:

TCP Reset Attack. A can first make two session oracles complete a handshake using Connect, Send queries, then use Pack, Deliver queries to let them exchange secure channel packets. By observing these packet headers, A can easily forge a valid reset packet by setting its RST bit to 1 and the remaining header fields to reasonable values. This attack will cause TCP to tear down the connection immediately without waiting for all data to be delivered.

Note that even an off-path adversary who can only inject packets into the communication channel may be able to accomplish this attack. The injected TCP reset packet needs to be within the receive window for the client or server, but [48] demonstrated that a surprisingly small number of packets is needed to achieve this, thanks to the large receive windows typically used by implementations.

5.2 QUIC over UDP

We refer to Appendix A.2 for UDP+QUIC's protocol definition. Its session identifier sid_{QUIC} is defined as the ClientHello payload and ServerHello, excluding IP addresses. The msACCE-pauth security analyses are shown as follows.

IP-Spoofing Prevention. In [35], QUIC has been proven secure against IP spoofing based on the AEAD security. Their IP-spoofing security notion is the same as our IP-Spoofing Prevention notion for UDP+QUIC except that ours additionally captures attacks in full sessions. However, since source-address tokens are validated in both full and resumption sessions, their results can be trivially adapted to show that UDP+QUIC achieves IP-Spoofing Prevention.

KE Header and Payload Integrity. UDP+QUIC does not achieve these security notions because its first-round key exchange messages, i.e., InchoateClientHello and ServerReject, and any invalid ClientHello are not fully authenticated. Interestingly, a variety of existing attacks on QUIC's availability discovered in [35] are all examples of key exchange packet manipulations (e.g., the server config replay attack, connection ID manipulation attack, etc.), but these attacks cause connection failure and hence are easy to detect. However, successful attacks breaking KE Header or Payload Integrity will be harder (if not impossible) to detect.

For KE Header Integrity, we do not find any harmful attacks but theoretical attacks exist. For instance, a PPT adversary A can get $\mathbf{Adv}^{\text{int-keh}}_{\text{UDP+QUIC}}(A) = 1$ as follows. A can first query $\mathsf{Connect}(\pi^i_C, \pi^j_S)$ to get the output packet $(\text{IP}_C, \text{IP}_S, H, pd)$, then modify the $\mathtt{flag}$ and $\mathtt{sqn}$ fields of H to get a new header $H' \neq H$ that only changes $\mathtt{sqn}$'s length but not its value. The resulting packet will be accepted by π^j_S. This attack has no practical impact on UDP+QUIC but it successfully modifies the protocol header without being detected.

For KE Payload Integrity, we find a new practical attack described below where a PPT adversary A can get $\mathbf{Adv}^{\text{int-kep}}_{\text{UDP+QUIC}}(A) \approx 1$:

ServerReject Triggering. A can first let $\pi^{i'}_C$ complete a full handshake with $\pi^{j'}_S$ with $\mathsf{Connect}, \mathsf{Send}$ queries, then query $\mathsf{Resume}(\pi^i_C, \pi^j_S, i')$ $(i > i', j > j')$ to get the output $\mathtt{ClientHello}$ packet. A then modifies its payload by replacing the source-address token $\mathtt{stk}$ with a random value, which with high probability is invalid. Sending this modified packet to π^j_S will trigger a $\mathtt{ServerReject}$ packet containing a new valid $\mathtt{stk}$. This as a result downgrades the original 0-RTT resumption connection to a full 1-RTT connection, which causes increased latency and results in the retransmission of any 0-RTT data. Note that this attack is hard to detect because π^i_C may think its original $\mathtt{stk}'$ has expired (although this does not happen frequently).

SC Header Integrity. UDP+QUIC is secure in this regard because it does not allow header-only packets to be sent in the secure channel phases and the *entire* protocol header is taken as the associated data authenticated by the underlying AEAD scheme. Therefore, UDP+QUIC's SC Header Integrity can be reduced to its level-1 Channel Security. Formally, for any PPT adversary A there exists a PPT adversary B such that $\mathbf{Adv}^{\text{int-h}}_{\text{UDP+QUIC}}(A) \leq 2\mathbf{Adv}^{\text{cs-1}}_{\text{UDP+QUIC}}(B)$, where the constant 2 is due to advantage definition differences between creating a valid forgery and guessing a correct bit.

Reset Authentication. UDP+QUIC does not achieve this security notion because, similar to TCP Reset, its reset packet $\mathtt{PublicReset}$ is not authenticated either. In the following availability attack, a PPT adversary A can always get $\mathbf{Adv}^{\text{rst-auth}}_{\text{UDP+QUIC}}(A) = 1$:

PublicReset Attack. A can first make two session oracles complete a handshake using $\mathsf{Connect}, \mathsf{Send}$ queries, then use $\mathsf{Pack}, \mathsf{Deliver}$ queries to let them exchange secure channel packets. By observing these packet headers, A can easily forge a valid (plaintext) reset packet by setting its PUBLIC_FLAG_RESET bit to 1 and the remaining packet fields to reasonable values (which is easy because it simply contains the connection ID $\mathtt{cid}$, the sequence number of the rejected packet, and a nonce to prevent replay). This attack will cause similar effects as described in the TCP Reset attack. Note that this vulnerability is fixed in QUIC[TLS] (see the full version [9]).

6 Conclusion

Our work is the first to provide a thorough, formal, and fine-grained security comparison of the most efficient secure channel establishment protocols on the market today. By including packet-level attacks in our analysis, our results shed light on how the reliability, flow control, and congestion control of TFO+TLS 1.3, UDP+QUIC, and UDP+QUIC[TLS] compare besides their basic security, in adversarial settings.

We found that availability functionalities provided by transport-layer protocols like TCP can be easily compromised without packet-level authentication, which may undermine the performance of their supporting application-layer protocols. To protect against availability attacks, new protocols should better implement and authenticate their own transport functionalities like QUIC does. Besides, the key exchange packet integrity should also be scrutinized to avoid serious undetectable availability attacks.

Acknowledgments. We thank the anonymous reviewers for their comments. This paper is based upon work supported by the National Science Foundation under Grant No. 1422794.

A TFO+TLS 1.3 and UDP+QUIC Protocol Definitions

A.1 TFO+TLS 1.3 Protocol Definition

Referring to the msACCE protocol syntax, a TFO+TLS 1.3 2-RTT full handshake (see Fig. 1) is a 2-stage msACCE protocol in the full mode and a 0-RTT resumption handshake (see Fig. 1) is a 3-stage msACCE protocol in the resumption mode. Note that we focus only on the main components of the handshakes and omit more advanced features such as 0.5-RTT data, client authentication, and post-handshake messages (except `NewSessionTicket`). In a full handshake, the initial keys are set after sending or receiving `ServerHello` and the final keys (i.e., session keys) are set after sending or receiving `ClientFinished` (but only handshake messages up to `ServerFinished` are used for final key generation). In a 0-RTT resumption handshake, the parties set 0-RTT keys to encrypt or decrypt 0-RTT data, after sending or receiving `ClientHello`.

According to the TFO and TLS 1.3 specifications [10,43], the TFO+TLS 1.3 header contains the TCP header [39]. We ignore some uninteresting header fields such as port numbers and the checksum because modifying them only leads to redirected or dropped packets. Such adversarial capabilities are already considered in the msACCE security models. We thus define the header space $\mathcal{H}$ as containing the following fields: a 32-bit sequence number `sqn`, a 32-bit acknowledgment number `ack`, a 4-bit data offset `off`, a 6-bit reserved field `resvd`, a 6-bit control bits field `ctrl`, a 16-bit window `window`, a 16-bit urgent pointer `urgp`, a variable-length ($\leq$320-bit) padded options `opt`. For encrypted packets, $\mathcal{H}$ additionally contains the TLS 1.3 record header fields: an 8-bit type `type`, a 16-bit version `ver`, and a 16-bit length `len`. We further define reset packets as those with the RST bit (i.e., the 4-th bit of `ctrl`) set to 1. Note that scfg_gen is undefined.

TLS 1.3 enforces different content types for encrypted key exchange and secure channel messages. For simplicity, we define $\mathcal{M}_{KE}$ and $\mathcal{M}_{SC}$ as consisting of bit strings differing in their first bits. $\mathcal{M}_{pRST} = \varnothing$. We refer to the full version [9] for the remaining TFO details and to [6,18] for the detailed descriptions of TLS 1.3 handshake messages and key generations in earlier TLS 1.3 drafts as well as [43] for the latest updates.

A.2   UDP+QUIC Protocol Definition

Referring to the msACCE protocol syntax, an UDP+QUIC 1-RTT full handshake (see Fig. 2) is a 2-stage msACCE protocol in the full mode and a 0-RTT resumption handshake (see Fig. 2) is a 2-stage msACCE protocol in the resumption mode. The initial keys are set after sending or receiving `ClientHello` and the final keys (i.e., session keys) are set after sending or receiving `ServerHello`.

According to the UDP and QUIC specifications [32,38,45], the UDP+QUIC header contains the UDP header [38] and the QUIC header (described below). As with the TCP header, we ignore the port numbers and checksum in the UDP header. Similarly, we also ignore the UDP length field because it only affects the length of the QUIC header and payload. We thus can completely omit the UDP header and define the header space $\mathcal{H}$ as containing the following fields: an 8-bit public flag `flag`, a 64-bit connection ID `cid`, a variable-length ($\leq$48-bit) sequence number `sqn`, and other optional fields. We further define reset packets as those with the PUBLIC_FLAG_RESET bit (i.e., the 7-th bit of `flag`) set to 1. A reset packet header only contains `flag` and `cid`.

As with TLS 1.3, we define $\mathcal{M}_{KE}$ and $\mathcal{M}_{SC}$ as consisting of bit strings differing in their first bits. $\mathcal{M}_{pRST} = \varnothing$. We refer to [35] for the detailed descriptions of scfg_gen and QUIC handshake messages and key generations.

References

1. HTTPS encryption on the web - Google transparency report (2018). https://transparencyreport.google.com/https/overview
2. Abramov, R., Herzberg, A.: TCP ack storm DoS attacks. In: Camenisch, J., Fischer-Hübner, S., Murayama, Y., Portmann, A., Rieder, C. (eds.) SEC 2011. IAICT, vol. 354, pp. 29–40. Springer, Heidelberg (2011). https://doi.org/10.1007/978-3-642-21424-0_3
3. Bellare, M., Rogaway, P.: Entity authentication and key distribution. In: Stinson, D.R. (ed.) CRYPTO 1993. LNCS, vol. 773, pp. 232–249. Springer, Heidelberg (1994). https://doi.org/10.1007/3-540-48329-2_21
4. Bhargavan, K., Blanchet, B., Kobeissi, N.: Verified models and reference implementations for the TLS 1.3 standard candidate. In: Security and Privacy (SP), pp. 483–502. IEEE (2017)
5. Bhargavan, K., Fournet, C., Kohlweiss, M., Pironti, A., Strub, P.-Y., Zanella-Béguelin, S.: Proving the TLS handshake secure (as it is). In: Garay, J.A., Gennaro, R. (eds.) CRYPTO 2014. LNCS, vol. 8617, pp. 235–255. Springer, Heidelberg (2014). https://doi.org/10.1007/978-3-662-44381-1_14

6. Brendel, J., Fischlin, M., Günther, F.: Breakdown resilience of key exchange protocols and the cases of newhope and TLS 1.3. Cryptology ePrint Archive, Report 2017/1252 (2017)
7. Cao, Y., Qian, Z., Wang, Z., Dao, T., Krishnamurthy, S.V., Marvel, L.M.: Off-path TCP exploits: global rate limit considered dangerous. In: USENIX Security Symposium (2016)
8. Centre for the Protection of National Infrastructure: Security assessment of the transmission control protocol. Technical report CPNI Technical Note 3/2009, Centre for the Protection of National Infrastructure (2009)
9. Chen, S., Jero, S., Jagielski, M., Boldyreva, A., Nita-Rotaru, C.: Secure communication channel establishment: TLS 1.3 (over TCP Fast Open) vs. QUIC. Cryptology ePrint Archive, Report 2019/433 (2019). https://eprint.iacr.org/2019/433
10. Cheng, Y., Chu, J., Radhakrishnan, S., Jain, A.: TCP Fast Open. RFC 7413 (Experimental), December 2014
11. Cremers, C., Horvat, M., Scott, S., van der Merwe, T.: Automated analysis and verification of TLS 1.3: 0-RTT, resumption and delayed authentication. In: 2016 IEEE Symposium on Security and Privacy (SP), pp. 470–485 (2016). https://doi.org/10.1109/SP.2016.35
12. Cremers, C., Horvat, M., Hoyland, J., Scott, S., van der Merwe, T.: A comprehensive symbolic analysis of TLS 1.3. In: Proceedings of the 2017 ACM SIGSAC Conference on Computer and Communications Security, pp. 1773–1788. ACM (2017)
13. Delignat-Lavaud, A., et al.: Implementing and proving the TLS 1.3 record layer. In: 2017 IEEE Symposium on Security and Privacy, SP 2017, pp. 463–482. IEEE Computer Society (2017)
14. Dowling, B., Fischlin, M., Günther, F., Stebila, D.: A cryptographic analysis of the TLS 1.3 handshake protocol candidates. In: ACM SIGSAC Conference on Computer and Communications Security, CCS 2015, pp. 1197–1210. ACM, New York (2015)
15. Dowling, B., Fischlin, M., Günther, F., Stebila, D.: A cryptographic analysis of the TLS 1.3 draft-10 full and pre-shared key handshake protocol. Cryptology ePrint Archive, Report 2016/081 (2016). https://eprint.iacr.org/2016/081
16. Dowling, B.J.: Provable security of internet protocols. Ph.D. thesis, Queensland University of Technology (2017)
17. Fischlin, M., Günther, F.: Multi-stage key exchange and the case of Google's QUIC protocol. In: Proceedings of the 2014 ACM SIGSAC Conference on Computer and Communications Security, pp. 1193–1204. ACM (2014)
18. Fischlin, M., Günther, F.: Replay attacks on zero round-trip time: the case of the TLS 1.3 handshake candidates. In: 2017 IEEE European Symposium on Security and Privacy (EuroS&P), pp. 60–75. IEEE (2017)
19. Fischlin, M., Günther, F., Marson, G.A., Paterson, K.G.: Data is a stream: security of stream-based channels. In: Gennaro, R., Robshaw, M. (eds.) CRYPTO 2015. LNCS, vol. 9216, pp. 545–564. Springer, Heidelberg (2015). https://doi.org/10.1007/978-3-662-48000-7_27
20. Gebhart, G.: Tipping the scales on HTTPS: 2017 in review, December 2017. https://www.eff.org/deeplinks/2017/12/tipping-scales-https
21. Gilad, Y., Herzberg, A.: Off-path attacking the web. In: WOOT, pp. 41–52 (2012)
22. IP Latency Statistics — Verizon Enterprise Solutions: Verizon Enterprise Solutions (2018). http://www.verizonenterprise.com/about/network/latency/
23. Iyengar, J., Thomson, M.: QUIC: a UDP-based multiplexed and secure transport, January 2019. https://quicwg.org/base-drafts/draft-ietf-quic-transport.html

24. Jager, T., Kohlar, F., Schäge, S., Schwenk, J.: On the security of TLS-DHE in the standard model. In: Safavi-Naini, R., Canetti, R. (eds.) CRYPTO 2012. LNCS, vol. 7417, pp. 273–293. Springer, Heidelberg (2012). https://doi.org/10.1007/978-3-642-32009-5_17

25. Jero, S., Lee, H., Nita-Rotaru, C.: Leveraging state information for automated attack discovery in transport protocol implementations. In: IEEE/IFIP International Conference on Dependable Systems and Networks (2015)

26. Jero, S., Hoque, E., Choffnes, D., Mislove, A., Nita-Rotaru, C.: Automated attack discovery in TCP congestion control using a model-guided approach. In: Network and Distributed Systems Security Symposium (NDSS) (2018)

27. Joncheray, L.: A simple active attack against TCP. In: USENIX Security Symposium (1995)

28. Krawczyk, H., Paterson, K.G., Wee, H.: On the security of the TLS protocol: a systematic analysis. In: Canetti, R., Garay, J.A. (eds.) CRYPTO 2013. LNCS, vol. 8042, pp. 429–448. Springer, Heidelberg (2013). https://doi.org/10.1007/978-3-642-40041-4_24

29. Krawczyk, H., Wee, H.: The OPTLS protocol and TLS 1.3. In: 2016 IEEE European Symposium on Security and Privacy (EuroS&P), pp. 81–96. IEEE (2016)

30. Kumar, V.A., Jayalekshmy, P.S., Patra, G.K., Thangavelu, R.P.: On remote exploitation of TCP sender for low-rate flooding denial-of-service attack. IEEE Commun. Lett. **13**(1), 46–48 (2009)

31. Kuzmanovic, A., Knightly, E.: Low-rate TCP-targeted denial of service attacks and counter strategies. IEEE/ACM Trans. Netw. **14**(4), 683–696 (2006)

32. Langley, A., Chang, W.: QUIC crypto (2016). https://docs.google.com/document/d/1g5nIXAIkN_Y-7XJW5K45IblHd_L2f5LTaDUDwvZ5L6g/edit

33. Li, X., Xu, J., Zhang, Z., Feng, D., Hu, H.: Multiple handshakes security of TLS 1.3 candidates. In: 2016 IEEE Symposium on Security and Privacy (SP), pp. 486–505. IEEE (2016)

34. Linden, G.: Make data useful (2006). https://sites.google.com/site/glinden/Home/StanfordDataMining.2006-11-29.ppt

35. Lychev, R., Jero, S., Boldyreva, A., Nita-Rotaru, C.: How secure and quick is QUIC? Provable security and performance analyses. In: 2015 IEEE Symposium on Security and Privacy (SP), pp. 214–231. IEEE (2015)

36. Morris, R.: A weakness in the 4.2 BSD unix TCP/IP software. Technical report, AT&T Bell Leboratories (1985)

37. Patton, C., Shrimpton, T.: Partially specified channels: the TLS 1.3 record layer without elision. In: ACM SIGSAC Conference on Computer and Communications Security. ACM (2018)

38. Postel, J.: User datagram protocol. RFC 768 (Standard) (1980)

39. Postel, J.: Transmission control protocol. RFC 793 (Standard) (1981)

40. Qian, Z., Mao, Z.M.: Off-path TCP sequence number inference attack - how firewall middleboxes reduce security. In: IEEE Symposium on Security and Privacy, pp. 347–361 (2012)

41. Qian, Z., Mao, Z.M., Xie, Y.: Collaborative TCP sequence number inference attack: how to crack sequence number under a second. In: ACM Conference on Computer and Communications Security (2012)

42. Radhakrishnan, S., Cheng, Y., Chu, J., Jain, A., Raghavan, B.: TCP fast open. In: Proceedings of the Seventh COnference on emerging Networking EXperiments and Technologies, p. 21. ACM (2011)

43. Rescorla, E.: The Transport Layer Security (TLS) Protocol Version 1.3. RFC 8446, August 2018

44. Rogaway, P.: Authenticated-encryption with associated-data. In: Proceedings of the 9th ACM Conference on Computer and Communications Security, pp. 98–107. ACM (2002)
45. Roskind, J.: QUIC(quick UDP internet connections): multiplexed stream transport over UDP. Technical report, Google (2013)
46. Savage, S., Cardwell, N., Wetherall, D., Anderson, T.: TCP congestion control with a misbehaving receiver. ACM SIGCOMM Comput. Commun. Rev. **29**(5), 71–78 (1999)
47. Thomson, M., Turner, S.: Using transport layer security (TLS) to secure QUIC, January 2019. https://quicwg.org/base-drafts/draft-ietf-quic-tls.html
48. Watson, P.: Slipping in the window: TCP reset attacks. Technical report, CanSecWest (2004). http://bandwidthco.com/whitepapers/netforensics/tcpip/TCPResetAttacks.pdf

Attacks

Where to Look for *What You See Is What You Sign?* User Confusion in Transaction Security

Vincent Haupert[(⊠)] and Stephan Gabert

Friedrich-Alexander University Erlangen-Nürnberg, Erlangen, Germany
{vincent.haupert,stephan.gabert}@fau.de

Abstract. The *What You See Is What You Sign* (WYSIWYS) scheme is a popular transaction verification method in online banking which is designed to prevent fraud even if the transfer-issuing device is compromised. To evaluate its practical effectiveness, we asked 100 online banking customers to pay two invoices by credit transfer. The second transfer was attacked by secretly replacing the beneficiary's account number and displaying the fraudulent transaction details on the confirmation page that asks a customer for a one-time password as generated by their second factor device. The attacked authentication method was the same the participants also use in private with their principal bank. Our attack is highly effective and causes many participants to use the fraudulent details displayed onscreen for verification instead of the original invoice. On top of that, a majority did not verify their transactions at all. Participants with a technical background and experience with certain as well as multiple transaction authentication methods were seen to be less likely to fall victim to the attack.

1 Introduction

Conducting an online banking credit transfer leverages two-factor authentication (2FA) and includes two steps: issuing and confirming. First, the customer *issues* a transfer by logging in with her login credentials, filling in the beneficiary's account number, and the amount. Second, the *confirmation* step requires the payer to approve the transaction using a transaction authentication number (TAN), which is generated by means specific to the bank and as well as the customer's individual choice. As this process yields the TAN, it is referred to as the TAN method. In the confirmation phase, a customer also has to verify the transfer using the details that the TAN method displays, and must abort it if they do not match the desired details. This principle is referred to as "What You See Is What You Sign" (WYSIWYS) [16].

In the course of our research, we noted that many large German banks also display the transfer's details on their confirmation page. This behavior is not only misleading but also dangerous as it suggests that the transfer-issuing device is trustworthy. As a consequence, it encourages the customer to perform an insecure

© Springer Nature Switzerland AG 2019
K. Sako et al. (Eds.): ESORICS 2019, LNCS 11735, pp. 429–449, 2019.
https://doi.org/10.1007/978-3-030-29959-0_21

transaction verification that relies on the TAN device and the details displayed within the online banking website. To verify a transaction securely, however, the user needs to compare the transfer details—that the TAN device displays—with the source that is used to issue the transaction, e.g., an invoice.

The banks approach raises the question if online banking customers are aware that the transfer-issuing device must not be part of the transaction verification step. To that end, we implemented an attack that does not only at first secretly replace a transfer's beneficiary but second also displays the fraudulent details at the confirmation page that asks the user for a one-time password as generated by their TAN method. The latter step aimed at misguiding the user to compare the transaction details displayed by the TAN method with the fraudulent details injected into the online banking website.

We evaluate our attack with 100 online banking customers recruited from an IT company. Our results show that the attack is highly effective and in fact causes a participant to perform a faulty transaction verification. Our findings also suggest that the concept of a secondary verification during the confirmation step is flawed beyond repair: neither user education nor improved usability of a TAN method is going to solve the problem as long as the WYSIWYS scheme remains in place. We therefore emphasize the need for a new transaction security approach that guarantees confidentiality, authenticity and integrity as soon as the user enters the transfer details, eliminating the verification step altogether.

In summary, our contributions advance the state in online banking transaction security substantially and methodologically:

– We use a novel, highly practical and effective attack that does only target the transfer-issuing device while the TAN device remains of integrity.
– Our study is first to rely on *the same* TAN method the participants also use in private with their principal bank. This ensures that the participant is familiar with the TAN method she uses when the attack occurs. Previous work either taught the participants how to use the TAN methods [29] or incorporated participants without experience with the TAN method [11].
– We present a large sample size of 100 above-average tech-savvy participants. Also, the distribution of our participants' TAN methods roughly matches the general population [20].
– In contrast to the previous work, each participant is only attacked once. This avoids carry-over effects.
– To not affect the participants' behavior, they conducted the study autonomously and privately within a familiar environment.

The remainder of this paper is organized as follows: The next sections relate our study to previous works, describe the methodology of our study and the attack we performed. This is followed by the presentation of our participants and the results. After this, we discuss our findings before drawing our conclusion.

2   Related Work

We first outline the previous work concerned with user and transaction authentication before we relate it to our own study.

2.1   User Authentication

Krol et al. conducted a user study with 21 United Kingdom (UK) online banking customers, examining website logins, payment setups, and the login into smartphone apps [15]. They observed that the satisfaction of participants dropped while handling hardware tokens and in spite of using them over a period of eleven days, the participants could not automate the authentication process and were continually being disrupted from their primary task. Research also dealt with the usability of hardware tokens, e.g., YubiKey [22] and FIDO U2F [5].

Schechter et al. evaluated different website authentication measures that were designed to protect users from different site-forgery attacks [24]. They asked 67 bank customers to conduct common online banking tasks. For each task, the users had to re-login and were confronted with increasingly alarming clues that their connections were insecure. As all participants failed to correctly respond to absent HTTPS indicators, Schechter's study corroborated with prior studies, suggesting the ineffectiveness of HTTPS indicators.

2.2   Transaction Authentication

Zomai et al. investigated whether participants were able to detect attacked transactions by correctly verifying the transaction authentication messages sent via e-mail, simulating the smsTAN procedure [29]. 92 participants took part in their laboratory study using a simulated online banking system. Each of the participants had to execute ten transactions: eight transactions were legitimate and two contained an altered account number. While one transaction, at first, only altered one digit of the eight-digit account number, another transaction contained an account number with five digits changed. They concluded that the smsTAN method is prone to attacks that alter the beneficiary because their more realistic second attack succeeded in 21% of the cases.

Hartl and Schmuntzsch examined the perceptions of online banking users towards fraudulent attacks, including the altering of the destination account number and the transferred amount [11]. This was performed in a user-centered study, consisting of two experiments, each of which was conducted in a laboratory setting with 25 participants. Throughout the second experiment, they used the think-aloud method, i.e., asked the participants to express their thoughts loudly. Their first experiment found that the participants rate the usability of the chipTAN method below the smsTAN method. In the second experiment, each participant had to execute three transactions, where every single transaction was attacked in a different way. When the last attack secretly changed a transaction's beneficiary and the amount, they observed that 71% of the participants did not detect the fraud while using the smsTAN or the chipTAN method.

Comparison to Our Work. As summarized in Table 1, the studies of Zomai et al. and Hartl and Schmuntzsch are close to our own work as they also evaluate transaction authentication security while performing similar attacks, but our study has the following significant methodological advances:

Table 1. Our study compared to the related work in transaction security.

	Zomai et al.	Hartl et al.	Our Study
Publication	2008	2016	2019
Participants	53	25	100
Mean Duration	N/A	60 min	9,5 min
Methodology			
Study Form	Remote	Laboratory	Laboratory
Deception	○	N/A	●
Recruitment	University	University	IT Company
Supervised	○	●	○
Transactions	10	3	2
TAN Methods			
sms-/chip-/appTAN	●/○/○	●/●/○	●/●/●
Personal Method	○	○	●
Modus Operandi			
Amount	○	●	○
Altered Account Digits	5/8 (62,5%)	N/A	16/22 (72,7%)
Altered User Interface	○	○	●
Attacked Transactions	2	3	1
Victim Rate	21%	71%	82%

Personal TAN Method: Our attack only targeted the TAN method that the participants also use with their principal bank. Moreover, we investigated popular and widely applied transaction authentication methods, including smartphone-based procedures.

Primary Task: Our participants had an easily manageable and realistic task of paying two invoices. We only performed a single attack to avoid bias.

Unsupervised Execution: We did not supervise our participants but required them to execute the study's task autonomously in an environment that was familiar to them.

Attack: Our attack only tampered with the beneficiary's account number but left the amount unchanged. In addition, it also manipulated the details that the participants saw within the website during transaction confirmation.

3   Methodology

In the course of the study, the participants had to pay two different invoices by credit transfer using two different TAN methods. The second transaction always used the TAN method that the participants also used with their principal bank to legitimize transfers. This transaction was attacked by secretly replacing the original transaction account number with a fraudulent number and it tampered with certain aspects of the appearance of the online banking.

Based on the model of *Sparkasse*, a popular German bank, we built a browser-based online banking system that supports the most prevalent TAN methods for transaction confirmation [20]:

smsTAN: Sends the transaction confirmation containing the TAN code via short message service (SMS) to the customer's mobile phone.

chipTAN: Uses a dedicated device—the TAN generator—and the customer's bank card to generate the TAN and to display the transaction details on the integrated display. The TAN generator receives the transaction data from a flickering code shown on the confirmation page.

appTAN: A TAN method that works in a similar way to the smsTAN procedure but delivers the information over the Internet—e.g., via push notifications— to a smartphone app.

When the participants accessed the invoice to get the payment details, we registered every key press, mouse movement, touch or paste event. If more than five seconds passed since the last event, an invoice access was signaled to our server. To avoid security-priming, our call-for-participation e-mail pretended to conduct a study that was concerned with the usability of the mentioned TAN methods.

3.1   Hypotheses

Grounded in the previous work and in our pilot study with 17 participants, we hypothesized the following:

H1 Participants who relied on the invoice for verification in the first transaction use the altered details displayed by the website during the verification of the second transaction.

There is a relationship between falling victim and the participant's

H2 personal TAN method.
H3 online banking usage duration.
H4 familiarity with different TAN methods.
H5 technical background.

3.2   Study Environment

We conducted our study in cooperation with a department of a medium-sized IT company whose business area lays primarily within software development. The specific department had approximately 240 employees and is responsible for the development of the communication and security components of their products.

Ethical Guidelines. Prior to our study, we jointly reviewed our study proposal with the department's management, several data security and privacy officials, and the Works Council[1]. We agreed that participation is entirely voluntary and

---

[1] Neither our university nor the company had an institutional review board (IRB).

that we would not record any personally identifiable information. As a consequence, we collected ranges instead of distinct data points, e.g., for the age (cf. Table 2 for details).

At the end of our study, we jointly debriefed the entire department. Participants had a chance to make remarks and to ask questions as a part of an open dialogue. In case a participant detected the attack, i.e., did not fall victim, an individual debriefing took place immediately. Most participants were thankful and stated that the study was an eye-opener for them and that they would be more careful about such transactions from that point. Some people also asked for additional information regarding the security of their TAN method. To the best of our knowledge, our study did not leave any lingering negative effect that we wanted to completely avoid.

Recruitment. Each participant took part in our study voluntarily by responding to an e-mail that asked them to participate in our pretended usability study. To reduce the participants' effort and to allow for a familiar environment, we arranged our setup in isolated conference rooms near their workplace.

Participant Devices. All the participants had to operate Google Chrome on a computer running Windows 7—the company's default operating system—and an LG Nexus 5X smartphone running Android 8.1 to use the smsTAN and the appTAN method. The computer was connected to the company's default peripheral devices that all of the employees were familiar with. To ensure a high degree of familiarity for the chipTAN users, we served them with three different TAN generators, as offered by the most popular local banks.

3.3   Study Procedure

Briefing. In the beginning, we asked the participants to not interrupt us with any questions to enable a similar level of knowledge for everyone. Next, they filled in a basic data form that asked for their age, sex, and profession. After outlining the study's procedure, we exposed the study's primary task: performing two credit transfers using a different TAN method for each transfer. Furthermore, we introduced the basic handling of the smartphone and presented the TAN methods. Finally, we urged the participants to put themselves in the place of paying their invoices at home. Accordingly, we left the room to allow for an autonomous study execution. In the case of a technical issue, however, the participant had the possibility to interrupt the study at any time by clicking a dedicated interruption button that was embedded in the website of the study. It is noteworthy that we refrained from mentioning the study's claimed usability purpose once again. Instead, we focused on a neutral description of the study's procedure and task.

Questionnaire I. Prior to the transactions, the participants had to complete Questionnaire I. This step was mainly concerned with determining the personal

TAN method that participants used with their principal bank but it did ask for further information about their online banking background.

Transaction I. In this step, the participants had to perform a first transaction with a TAN method different from the one they use with their principal bank. This transaction was free from any tampering and had the intention to familiarize the participants with the process of performing a transaction within the study's website. As Questionnaire I also unveiled the experiences with other TAN methods, we used this information to assign a procedure that the participant was familiar with. If a participant did not specify any experience beyond her personal method, our study algorithm assigned a TAN method. Overall, the platform tried to balance the TAN methods used in Transaction I.

To issue the transaction, the participant had to fill in the payment details found on the invoice. After sending the transfer order to our server, the participant was forwarded to the transaction confirmation page to verify and confirm the transfer with the possibly unfamiliar TAN method. On this page, we also gave instructions on how to operate the TAN method, just like a real banking website.

Transaction II. Right after Transaction I, the participant had to perform the second transaction with her personal TAN method using a new invoice. Apart from this, Transaction II worked analogously. While sending the transfer order, however, our attack took place. This included replacing the beneficiary's account number in the background and showing the fraudulent transaction details on the confirmation page. We describe the details of our attack in Sect. 4.

If a participant aborted the transaction, she was counted as a non-victim. The same applied to participants who noticed the deviation without aborting the transaction right-away but instead chose to talk to us in person by interrupting the study. We considered a participant a victim if she did not abort the transaction and the post-study conversation did not challenge the validity of this outcome.

Questionnaire II. Although the closing questionnaire also asked for the participants' ease-of-use ratings of the operated TAN methods, it was primarily concerned with pinpointing whether and how they verified the transactions.

Debriefing. Once the overall study had been completed, we debriefed the entire department. Owing to the study environment, we refrained from debriefing the participants who did not abort Transaction II as this would have increased the risk of spreading the study's structure and real intentions. Nevertheless, we encouraged each participant to disclose any further remarks regarding their participation. This had the intention to spot participants who confirmed Transaction II even though they noted a deviation but considered it a bug on our platform. If a participant detected the fraud, the debriefing took place immediately. In this case, we repeated the necessary steps for secure transaction verification and encouraged the participant to continue to adhere to this process.

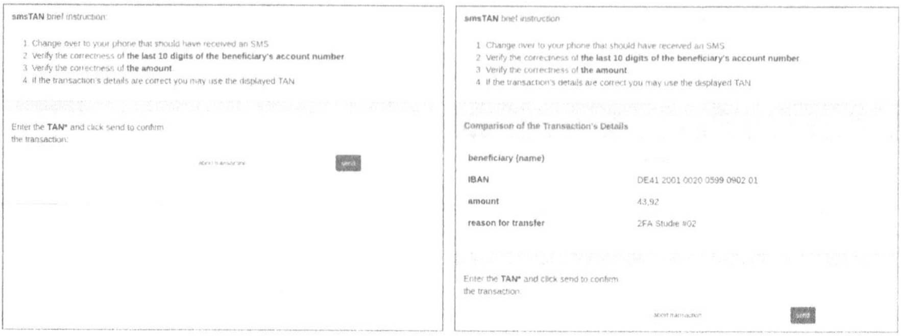

(a) Transaction I: not attacked.   (b) Transaction II: attacked.

Fig. 1. The different appearance of the confirmation page of Transaction I and II.

4 Attack Procedure

4.1 Threat Model

We assume that the user issues the transaction on one and confirms it on another device. In this scenario, she issues the transaction through her browser-based online banking and confirms it using a TAN method on a second device. In particular, the TAN method provides dynamic linking and displays the transaction's details for verification.

Our threat model considers the transaction-issuing computer as an untrustworthy device. In contrast to that, we assume that the transaction-confirming device possesses integrity. This enables an attacker to manipulate a transfer's details in the background without the user noticing. Furthermore, an adversary has full control over the information the user's online banking displays through her browser. The adversary, however, is not able to confirm the transaction autonomously. This implies that the user could detect and abort the transaction by correctly verifying the unaltered details displayed on the TAN device.

Our assumptions are valid, because they leverage a threat model that real-world malware already applied very successfully: in the United States alone, the ZeuS banking malware infected approximately 3.6 million computers during 2009 and 2010 [9]. In fact, malware like ZeuS made the described threat model the best practice and gave rise to 2FA with dynamic linking in online banking [10].

4.2 Course of Events

In our study, we used a man-in-the-browser attack implemented through a malicious browser add-on. When the participant clicked the send button to issue Transaction II, our attack started and performed the following actions:

Account Number Manipulation. Sending the data from Transaction II caused our attack to stop the original request. If the beneficiary's account number was a valid international banking account number (IBAN), the attack changed it to the adversary's account number and relayed the request to the server. The original account number that was contained in the invoice of Transaction II is vastly different from the one we used for our attack:

Original DE62 3702 0500 0000 1020 30
Forged   DE41 2001 0020 0599 0902 01

We assume that customers are usually aware of the amount they have to pay, which is why we decided to leave it unchanged. The payee's IBAN, however, is frequently unknown to the payer. Both the original and the forged IBAN belong to German banks, because credit transfers within the same nation are particularly hard to detect for fraud detection systems in the bank's backend [4].

Confirmation Page: Transfer Details. Next, the participant needed to provide a TAN on the transaction confirmation page, which was also subject to our attack. In contrast to the first transaction's unmodified confirmation page, the second transaction's tampered confirmation page did not only show the usage instructions of the TAN method and an input element to enter the TAN but also a highlighted text box that contained the details of the fraudulent transaction. The injected text instructed the participant to perform an insecure transaction verification: Instead of comparing the details shown on their TAN device to the invoice, the text demanded a comparison to the displayed details. A screenshot of the confirmation page for each transaction is given in Fig. 1.

5   Results

Overall, 82 out of 100 participants did neither abort Transaction II nor did they raise any concern about its integrity. In the following, we present our study population and test the hypotheses outlined in Sect. 3.1.

We used Fisher's exact test (FE) with mid-p correction to determine the independence of the victim variable to another binary variable. This non-parametric statistical significance test is used as an exact alternative to the chi-squared test as it also produces valid results if the sample sizes are small [18]. The mid-p approach accounts for the overly conservative outcome of the traditional Fisher's exact test [12]. In the case of an ordinal dependent variable, we used the Mann–Whitney U test (MWU), which is a nonparametric test as well. Both tests were always applied two-sided. To control the false discovery rate due to multiple hypothesis testing, we corrected the resulting p-values using the two-stage step-up method of Benjamini et al. [2]. The corrected p-values were subsequently compared to the established threshold for statistical significance, that is $\alpha = 0.05$. The null hypothesis was only rejected if $p < \alpha$.

5.1   Study Population

In total, we incorporated 100 participants for our evaluation. Owing to the corporate environment, our study acquired data on a diverse set of German

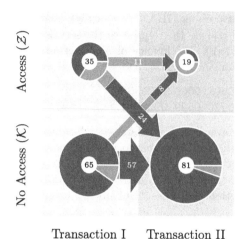

	Trans. I		Trans. II	
	$\mathcal{Z}$	$\mathcal{K}$	$\mathcal{Z}$	$\mathcal{K}$
V	23	59	5	77
¬V	12	6	14	4
$\sum$	35	65	19	81
	$\mathcal{Z}{\to}\mathcal{Z}$	$\mathcal{Z}{\to}\mathcal{K}$	$\mathcal{K}{\to}\mathcal{K}$	$\mathcal{K}{\to}\mathcal{Z}$
V	2	21	56	3
¬V	9	3	1	5
$\sum$	11	24	57	8

Access ($\mathcal{Z}$)   No Access ($\mathcal{K}$)

Transaction I   Transaction II   V: Victim ■   ¬V: Non-Victim ■

Fig. 2. Invoice access flows: Each circle represents the number of participants who did or did not access the invoice during the confirmation. The arrows show how their behavior in Transaction II corresponds to Transaction I.

employees of a medium-sized software company with different demographics and backgrounds. 65 of our participants were male and 35 female. Their age was widely distributed: on average, our participant was aged between 31–40, the oldest participant 61–70 and the youngest 19–25. We assume that most of them had a technical background as 74 participants stated that their job was associated with IT. Given the company's main business area and the department we conducted the study with, we assume that even the group of 26 non-IT participants had an above-average understanding of technology if not information security. With respect to online banking, the participants can be roughly divided into two equal groups that had either up to ten years (53) or even more than ten years (47) of experience with online banking. As a consequence, the average participant can be described as highly experienced. Ten participants even stated that they performed online banking transactions at work. Overall, the participants can be regarded as familiar with online banking. For additional information, refer to Table 2.

5.2   Transaction Verification (H1)

A crucial step for transaction security is the user's verification of the transaction details during confirmation: if any of the transaction's data displayed on the customer's TAN device does not match the invoice, she must abort the transaction; the customer must not use any data displayed on the transaction-initiating channel, as it may be compromised. To evaluate if our participants verified their transactions using the original invoice, we monitored all accesses to it. Please note that such an event only indicates that the participant consulted the invoice but not to which extent. It does, however, provide a strong indication that the participant verified either the invoiced amount, the account number or both.

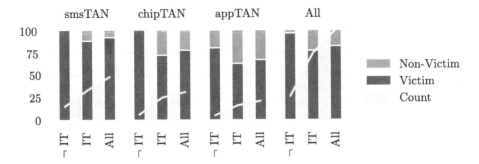

Fig. 3. Performances in Transaction II depending on a technical background and the TAN method.

The overall invoice accesses and the flow from Transaction I to II is given in Fig. 2. It shows that two-thirds ($N = 68$) acted consistently in both transactions with the majority ($N = 57$) neither accessing the invoice at the first nor the second; this insecure behavior results in a victim rate of 98.25% ($N = 56$). The group with the best performance accessed the invoice in both transactions ($N = 11$) yielding a victim rate of 18.18% ($N = 2$). The remainder ($N = 32$) checked the invoice in either of the transactions: Eight participants accessed the invoice only during the second transaction with a victim rate of 37.50% ($N = 3$).

The 24 participants who accessed the invoice only in the first, but not in the second transaction, were of special interest as we regard this behavior as an indicator for a successful attack (H1): 21 fell victim and three aborted the second transaction, yielding a victim rate of 87.50%. In Questionnaire II, only two of these victims mentioned that they omitted the transaction verification altogether while the remainder claimed that they checked the transactions' integrity. On the contrary, the three participants who detected the attack told us in the post-study conversation that they immediately aborted the transaction without checking the invoice again as the deviation was apparent. Testing H1 gave a statistically significant result ($p < 0.001$, $OR = 0.032$, FE, 2×2).

5.3   Personal TAN Methods (H2)

As visualized in Fig. 3, 92% of the 48 participants using smsTAN as their personal TAN method, 77% of the 31 using chipTAN, and 67% of the 21 using appTAN fell victim to our attack. This already suggests a dependance between the personal TAN method and falling victim (H2) and is supported by a statistically significant result ($p = 0.033$, FE, 2×3). Participants using the smsTAN method performed significantly worse ($p = 0.024$, $OR = 4.053$, FE, 2×2) while participants using the appTAN method performed significantly better ($p = 0.033$, $OR = 0.324$, FE, 2×2); only participants using chipTAN did not yield a statistically significant difference ($p = 0.221$, $OR = 0.650$, FE, 2×2).

At the end of the study, the participants also had to rate the ease-of-use of the TAN method applied in Transaction II (Likert scale, $L = [1; 5], 1 = $

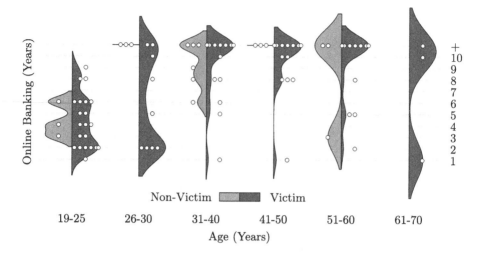

Fig. 4. Distribution of (non-)victims according to their age and banking experience.

strongly agree, 5 = strongly disagree). Overall, the vast majority agreed (32) or strongly agreed (65) that their personal TAN method is easy to use. Only three participants remained neutral and no-one disagreed that the ease-of-use of their TAN method is good. While looking at the distinct TAN methods, the smsTAN method was rated the best, followed by the appTAN and the chipTAN method. On average, victims tended to rate their personal TAN method better ($L = 1.31$) than non-victims ($L = 1.67$).

5.4 Experience (H3, H4, H5)

Online banking experience relies on different parameters. One assumption is that participants who have been using online banking for a longer time can be regarded more experienced and, hence, are less likely to fall victim to our attack (H3). As Fig. 4 already suggests, we did not find statistically significant support for this assumption ($p = 0.118$, $U = 887.500$, MWU). Still, the 15 participants with a maximum usage time of two years all fell victim to the attack. Additionally, this group is particularly young.

Another way to infer online banking experience is the number of TAN methods known to a participant (H4). In our test sample, 96.88% of the 32 participants who were only familiar with the method they used in Transaction II were victims. 68 participants at least knew yet another TAN method and had a victim rate of 75%. If a participant knew at least three or four TAN methods, the victim rate reached a minimum of 57.89% ($N = 19$) and 60% ($N = 5$), respectively. We conclude that a participant who was familiar with multiple TAN methods was significantly more likely to detect the fraud ($p = 0.002$, $U = 1085.5$, MWU).

We anticipated that participants in a technical profession would perform differently compared to participants with a non-technical job (H5). As Fig. 3

shows, the victim rate for the 74 participants with a technical background is lower (77.03%) than for the non-technical staff (96.15%, $N = 26$). In fact, only one of the non-technical participants detected the fraud. Testing this hypothesis yielded a statistically significant result ($p = 0.033$, $OR = 0.134$, FE, 2×2).

6 Discussion

The most prevalent reason why our participants did not detect the fraud was that they did not verify the transactions using the invoice. For the majority of the participants, such behavior was consistent in both transactions, i.e., they neither accessed the invoice in Transaction I nor in II.

Awareness. This suggests that online banking customers are not aware that transaction verification using the original invoice is an essential security task [7, 24, 28]. Our post-study conversations support this assumption: three participants explicitly mentioned that they personally never verify transaction details and that they only realized this due to our last questionnaire. One participant even raised the question of whether it was a threat to not verify these details.

Liability. Research suggests that this is due to online banking customers deeming it unlikely that they become victims of fraud themselves; still, if they would encounter fraud, they do not feel responsible for any negative outcomes [6, 23]. It is, however, the responsibility of the customer to verify the transaction correctly: failure to adhere is considered gross negligence by most banks and they will hold the customer liable [19].

Intuition. If a victim verified Transaction II, she often used the unauthentic data displayed on the confirmation site. From the perspective of the customer, this behavior is intuitive and plausible due to three reasons: First, the user immediately sees this site after issuing the transaction; hence, she will already grasp the displayed information unintentionally. Second, the user has to interact with this page in order to complete the transfer. The confirmation requires the customer to at least enter the TAN. In the case of the chipTAN method, she even needs to read the animated flicker code with her TAN generator. Third, the majority of banks does display the transfer details on the confirmation page. As a result, the customer is used to see this data there.

Technical Background. Participants with a technical background were significantly more likely to detect the attack than non-technical ones. This makes sense as individuals with a technical background have a better understanding of the associated technical processes. Hence, they also have a better ability to assess risks and make correct security decisions [21]. Female participants and our youngest group (ages 18–25) were more vulnerable. These findings are coherent with behavioral studies that evaluate phishing susceptibility [3,13,26]. Similar to Sheng et al., we do not regard the female sex as a determining factor for their higher victim rate but their lower affinity to technology [26].

Online Banking Experience. Knowing at least one TAN method beyond the personal one also had an overall positive effect on detecting the fraud in Transaction II. This is, however, not a result of a stressful experience during Transaction I due to the application of an unfamiliar transaction method: On average, the victims were quicker in the first transaction than the non-victims, which suggests that the victims, in general, perform essential security tasks with less care or omit them completely. When an online banking customer sets up a new method, she usually has to consult a manual and further information from the bank. We suppose that this helps in identifying the critical security steps and to actually adhere to them in practice.

TAN Method. Partially, the three TAN methods performed significantly different: users of the appTAN method performed best, smsTAN worst, and chipTAN is in between but has still a below-average victim rate. This trend is also very consistent when only looking at the victim rate of IT participants. To provide an explanation, we compare how each TAN method presents the transaction details to a customer and which actions she had to take to see the TAN.

- *Structured*: Only the smsTAN method does not display the transaction details in a structured form but rather provides all the details in a block of continuous text.
- *All at once*: Both sms- and appTAN display all the transaction details— IBAN, amount, and the TAN—at once. Due to technical limitations of the starburst display, the chipTAN method presents these details one after another.
- *Instant*: Right after issuing the transaction, the sms- and appTAN methods immediately deliver the verification data including the TAN. The chipTAN method requires substantially more time.
- *Interaction*: The smsTAN method does not require interaction to see the TAN and even allows for reading the full SMS message on the lock screen. The appTAN message also creates a notification on the lock screen but to see the actual TAN, one at least has to click on the notification message to open the app. To get the TAN via the chipTAN method, one is required to insert the bank card into the TAN generator, scan the flicker code and to successively accept the displayed amount and destination account number by pressing a button.

On average, the sms- and the appTAN method required the same time for confirmation and both receive similar ease-of-use ratings. Unsurprisingly, victims tended to require less time for confirmation. Therefore, we assume that the user's attention tends to be attracted if the TAN device displays the transaction details in a well-arranged form. This is in line with previous research that already showed that the font and the color have a significant effect on the user's attention [8].

Against this background, we suspect that the appTAN method's neater organization helps to quickly identify the important fields and therefore increases the likelihood that people verify the transaction. The opposite is true for the smsTAN method that prints all the details in a block of continuous text ending with the TAN. We speculate that this unstructured organization makes it more likely that the participant will go directly for the TAN. Correspondingly, all smsTAN users who we found to read the TAN using the notification text rather than opening the SMS app, fell for our attack. Even though the chipTAN method is rated worst in terms of ease-of-use, it still features a structured way of displaying the verification details, and has a below-average, but still a higher victim rate than the appTAN method. chipTAN's idea of forcing the user to separately verify the amount and the destination account number may seem plausible, but we suspect chipTAN's inability to display all the information at once to be a drawback. Additionally, consistent with the findings of Kiljan et al., we observed victims to execute the confirmation faster than non-victims [14] and consequently, the user might just click forward until reaching the TAN.

7   Limitations

Although we took great care during all steps of our research and even ran a pilot study to closely examine our design, implementation, execution, and evaluation, some study aspects still have limitations to a different extent.

Ecological Validity. The participants might have acted less securely than they would have done using their personal online banking account. Schechter et al. evaluated the security behavior of three groups when they logged into their online banking website [24]: members of Group 1 and 2 played a role and did not use their own accounts. In contrast to Group 1, Group 2 was security-primed; the members of Group 3 used their personal online banking credentials. When comparing Group 3 to the union of Group 1 and Group 2, they found that Group 3 acted significantly more secure. They conclude that role playing causes participants to perform study tasks less securely. The independent comparison of Group 1—which roughly compares to our study participants—to Group 3 did, however, not show a significant difference with respect to their security behavior.

We acknowledge that including an additional group using their personal bank account would have been beneficial for the ecological validity of our results. Using the participants' personal accounts, however, would insert a threat into the study design that would have been difficult to contain: in contrast to Schechter et al., not only would we have attacked the login process but also an actual transaction. Our joint risk-benefit assessment raised strong ethical concerns and ultimately rejected such a study protocol.

Anyway, our main interest was not *if* participants verify their transactions but rather *how* their security behavior changed from the untampered first to the attacked second transaction. Performing a transaction in a secure or insecure fashion is also a matter of habituation [1]: it only consists of a few steps and a user is either used to performing none, some or all of these steps. A limited realistic risk would not rule out such behavior.

Study Population. Our study population was recruited from an IT company. Therefore, it is not representative: most of the participants' profession was directly connected to IT and the majority was male. While we acknowledge that a more general population would foster the generalizability of the results, we consider the tech-savviness of our population a best case scenario: if even tech-savvy people are unable to verify transactions securely, this is likely also true for the general online banking users who lack this understanding.

Invoice Format. In this paper, we focused on our attack's efficacy. However, to explore the impact of the invoice format, 50 participants each used either the study's computer or a dedicated tablet to access the invoice. The respective victim rates of both groups were very near each other (84% and 80%) suggesting that the invoice format has no quantifiable effect on detecting the attack.

8   Conclusion

In spite of using the personal transaction authentication method, the majority of our study's participants failed to detect the real-time credit transfer manipulation which tampered with the destination account number. Even though our study indicates broad satisfaction with individual transaction authentication methods, people are not aware, neglect the core security tasks or are easily deceived: the majority of the victims did not verify the transaction's integrity using the original invoice. Still, if they were in the habit of verification, they could be tricked in performing a faulty transaction verification by asserting the transaction's integrity by using injected details within the browser session.

Against this background, we are glad that our findings led the German cooperative banks to stop displaying the transaction details on the confirmation page. Although the change was not yet implemented in July 2019, we hope that other banks will follow this example. Nevertheless, our results also suggest that this alone will not solve the problem as the attacker is in control of all displayed information. User education—even though it is a desirable goal—is not expected to introduce a substantial change, particularly not in the short term [25]. Our study also showed that technical individuals were more likely to detect the fraud but this information alone shows that the majority is still vulnerable.

Therefore, we might need to rethink the currently employed WYSIWYS scheme that relies on the secondary verification of the transaction details. Instead, authentication methods should guarantee integrity as soon as the user enters the details [17]. Leveraging the trusted execution environments (TEEs), which are already present in the majority of today's smartphones, is a promising approach for transaction security. Technically, TEEs like ARM's TrustZone can already provide secure in- and output today but they still lack the necessary operating system interfaces [27]. Nevertheless, their wide hardware-side availability might be a key factor for user acceptance and usable security, particularly including—but not limited to—transaction security.

Appendix

Table 2. Victim rate (O, %) and frequency (N) depending on participant demographics and their personal TAN method.

	SMS O	SMS N	Chip O	Chip N	App O	App N	All O	All N
Sex								
Male	90	30	75	20	60	15	78	65
Female	94	18	82	11	83	6	89	35
Age								
18–25	93	14	83	6	75	4	88	24
26–30	100	2	75	4	67	6	75	12
31–40	85	13	57	7	75	4	75	24
41–50	89	9	83	6	67	3	83	18
51–60	100	8	86	7	50	4	84	19
61–70	100	2	100	1			100	3
Profession								
Advisor	100	2					100	2
Executive	100	2	100	2			100	4
IT	88	33	72	25	62	16	77	74
Service	100	3	100	1	100	1	100	5
Other	100	8	100	3	75	4	93	15
Banking Experience in Years								
1	100	4					100	4
2	100	4	100	2	100	5	100	11
3	100	2	0	2			50	4
4	67	3	100	1			75	4
5	100	3	100	3			100	6
6	100	4	100	1	0	2	71	7
7								
8	80	5	100	2	100	3	90	10
9			50	2			50	2
10	100	2	100	3			100	5
+	90	21	71	14	58	12	77	47
Transactions per Month								
0	100	1					100	1
1	100	5	100	2	50	2	89	9
2	89	9	50	4	33	3	69	16
3	86	7	88	8	83	6	86	21
4	100	4	60	5	100	1	80	10
5	90	10	75	8	75	4	82	22
6	100	2			0	1	67	3
7	100	3	100	2			100	5
8	100	1			100	1	100	2
9								
10	67	3	100	1			75	4
11–15	100	2			100	1	100	3
+	100	1	100	1	50	2	75	4
Total	92	48	77	31	67	21	82	100

...

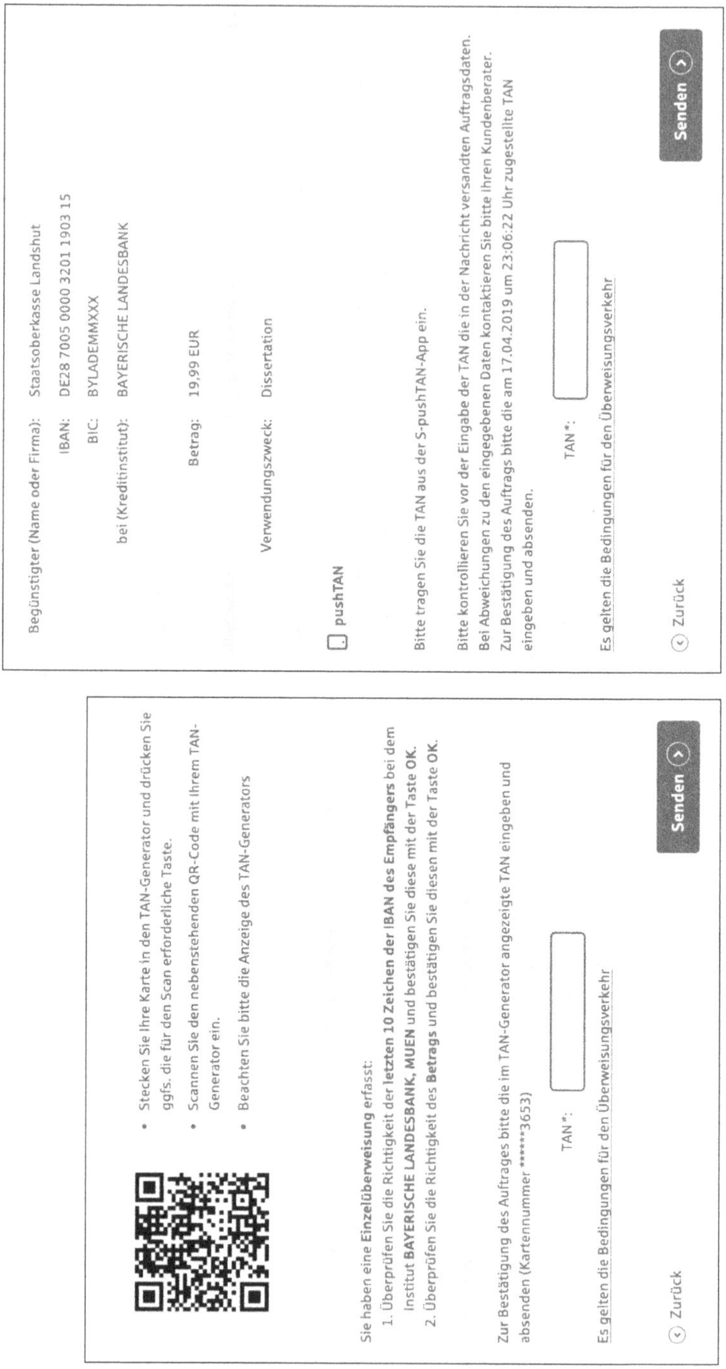

Begünstigter (Name oder Firma):   Staatsoberkasse Landshut

IBAN: DE28 7005 0000 3201 1903 15

BIC: BYLADEMMXXX

bei (Kreditinstitut):   BAYERISCHE LANDESBANK

Betrag: 19,99 EUR

Verwendungszweck: Dissertation

☐ pushTAN

Bitte tragen Sie die TAN aus der S-pushTAN-App ein.

Bitte kontrollieren Sie vor der Eingabe der TAN die in der Nachricht versandten Auftragsdaten. Bei Abweichungen zu den eingegebenen Daten kontaktieren Sie bitte Ihren Kundenberater. Zur Bestätigung des Auftrags bitte die am 17.04.2019 um 23:06:22 Uhr zugestellte TAN eingeben und absenden.

TAN*:

Es gelten die Bedingungen für den Überweisungsverkehr

⌄ Zurück

Senden ⌃

(b) appTAN: Confirmation page shows the full transaction details.

Stecken Sie Ihre Karte in den TAN-Generator und drücken Sie ggfs. die für den Scan erforderliche Taste.

Scannen Sie den nebenstehenden QR-Code mit Ihrem TAN-Generator ein.

Beachten Sie bitte die Anzeige des TAN-Generators

Sie haben eine Einzelüberweisung erfasst:

1. Überprüfen Sie die Richtigkeit der **letzten 10 Zeichen der IBAN des Empfängers** bei dem Institut **BAYERISCHE LANDESBANK, MUEN** und bestätigen Sie diese mit der Taste **OK**.

2. Überprüfen Sie die Richtigkeit des **Betrags** und bestätigen Sie diesen mit der Taste **OK**.

Zur Bestätigung des Auftrages bitte die im TAN-Generator angezeigte TAN eingeben und absenden (Kartennummer *****3653)

TAN*:

Es gelten die Bedingungen für den Überweisungsverkehr

⌄ Zurück

Senden ⌃

(a) chipTAN: Confirmation page shows no transaction details.

Fig. 5. Sparkasse Nürnberg (April 17, 2019): Whether the bank displays transaction details on the confirmation page even depends on the TAN method the customer uses with the bank. Our tests show that *Sparkasse* shows no details on confirm for the chipTAN method but displays the full transaction details if the sms- or appTAN method is used.

References

1. Anderson, B.B., Kirwan, C.B., Jenkins, J.L., Eargle, D., Howard, S., Vance, A.: How polymorphic warnings reduce habituation in the brain: insights from an fMRI study. In: Proceedings of the 33rd Annual ACM Conference on Human Factors in Computing Systems, CHI 2015, Seoul, Republic of Korea, 18–23 April 2015, pp. 2883–2892 (2015)

2. Benjamini, Y., Krieger, A.M., Yekutieli, D.: Adaptive linear step-up procedures that control the false discovery rate. Biometrika **93**(3), 491–507 (2006)

3. Blythe, M., Petrie, H., and Clark, J.A.: F for fake: four studies on how we fall for phish. In: Proceedings of the International Conference on Human Factors in Computing Systems, CHI 2011, Vancouver, BC, Canada, 7–12 May 2011, pp. 3469–3478 (2011)

4. Carminati, M., Baggio, A., Maggi, F., Spagnolini, U., Zanero, S.: FraudBuster: temporal analysis and detection of advanced financial frauds. In: Giuffrida, C., Bardin, S., Blanc, G. (eds.) DIMVA 2018. LNCS, vol. 10885, pp. 211–233. Springer, Cham (2018). https://doi.org/10.1007/978-3-319-93411-2_10

5. Das, S., Dingman, A., and Camp, L.J.: Why johnny doesn't use two factor: a two-phase usability study of the FIDO U2F Security Key. In: Financial Cryptography and Data Security - 22nd International Conference, FC 2018, Curaçao, 26 February– 2 March, 2018, Revised Selected Papers (2018)

6. Davinson, N., Sillence, E.: Using the health belief model to explore users' perceptions of 'being safe and secure' in the world of technology mediated financial transactions. Int. J. Hum. Comput. Stud. **72**(2), 154–168 (2014)

7. Dhamija, R., Tygar, J.D., and Hearst, M.A.: Why phishing works. In: Proceedings of the 2006 Conference on Human Factors in Computing Systems, CHI 2006, Montréal, Québec, Canada, 22–27 April 2006, pp. 581–590 (2006)

8. Egelman, S., Schechter, S.: The importance of being earnest [in security warnings]. In: Sadeghi, A.-R. (ed.) FC 2013. LNCS, vol. 7859, pp. 52–59. Springer, Heidelberg (2013). https://doi.org/10.1007/978-3-642-39884-1_5

9. Etaher, N., Weir, G.R.S., Alazab, M.: From ZeuS to Zitmo: trends in banking malware. In: 2015 IEEE TrustCom/BigDataSE/ISPA, Helsinki, Finland, 20–22 August 2015, vol. 1, pp. 1386–1391 (2015)

10. European Union Agency for Network and Information Security: Flash note: EU cyber security agency ENISA; "High Roller" online bank robberies reveal security gaps (2012). https://www.enisa.europa.eu/news/enisa-news/copy_of_eu-cyber-security-agency-enisa-201chigh-roller201d-online-bank-robberiesreveal-security-gaps. Accessed June 05 2018

11. Hartl, V.M.I.A., Schmuntzsch, U.: Fraud protection for online banking - a user-centered approach on detecting typical double-dealings due to social engineering and inobservance whilst operating with personal login credentials. In: Tryfonas, T. (ed.) HAS 2016. LNCS, vol. 9750, pp. 37–47. Springer, Cham (2016). https://doi.org/10.1007/978-3-319-39381-0_4

12. Hwang, J.T.G., Yang, M.-C.: An optimality theory for mid p-values In 2 x 2 contingency tables. Statistica Sinica **11**(3), 807–826 (2001)

13. Jagatic, T.N., Johnson, N.A., Jakobsson, M., Menczer, F.: Social phishing. Commun. ACM **50**(10), 94–100 (2007)

14. Kiljan, S., Vranken, H.P.E., van Eekelen, M.C.J.D.: What you enter is what you sign: input integrity in an online banking environment. In: 2014 Workshop on Socio-Technical Aspects in Security and Trust, STAST 2014, Vienna, Austria, 18 July 2014, pp. 40–47 (2014)
15. Krol, K., Philippou, E., Cristofaro, E.D., and Sasse, M.A.: "They brought in the horrible key ring thing!" Analysing the usability of two-factor authentication in UK online banking. In: Proceedings of the NDSS Workshop on Usable Security, USEC 2015, San Diego, California, USA, 8–11 February 2015 (2015)
16. Landrock, P., Pedersen, T.P.: WYSIWYS? - what you see is what you sign? Inf. Sec. Techn. Rep. **3**(2), 55–61 (1998)
17. Li, S., Sadeghi, A.-R., Heisrath, S., Schmitz, R., Ahmad, J.J.: hPIN/hTAN: a lightweight and low-cost E-banking solution against untrusted computers. In: Danezis, G. (ed.) FC 2011. LNCS, vol. 7035, pp. 235–249. Springer, Heidelberg (2012). https://doi.org/10.1007/978-3-642-27576-0_19
18. Lydersen, S., Fagerland, M.W., Laake, P.: Recommended tests for association in 2 x 2 tables. Stat. Med. **28**(7), 1159–1175 (2009)
19. Murdoch, S.J., et al.: Are payment card contracts unfair? (short paper). In: Grosssklags, J., Preneel, B. (eds.) FC 2016. LNCS, vol. 9603, pp. 600–608. Springer, Heidelberg (2017). https://doi.org/10.1007/978-3-662-54970-4_35
20. Norisbank GmbH: norisbank-Umfrage zum Thema Online-Banking, German (2016). https://www.norisbank.de/ueberuns/presseinformation-norisbank-umfrageonline-banking-ein-viertel-der-deutschen-nutzt-veraltetes-tan-verfahren.html. Accessed 20 May 2018
21. Onarlioglu, K., Yilmaz, U.O., Kirda, E., Balzarotti, D.: Insights into user behavior in dealing with internet attacks. In: 19th Annual Network and Distributed System Security Symposium, NDSS 2012, San Diego, California, USA, 5–8 February 2012 (2012)
22. Reynolds, J., Smith, T., Reese, K., Dickinson, L., Ruoti, S., Seamons, K.: A tale of two studies: the best and worst of YubiKey usability. In: 2018 IEEE Symposium on Security and Privacy, SP 2018, San Francisco, CA, USA, 20–22 May 2018, pp. 1090–1106 (2018)
23. Rosoff, H., Cui, J., and John, R.S.: Behavioral experiments exploring victims' response to cyber-based financial fraud and identity theft scenario simulations. In: Tenth Symposium on Usable Privacy and Security, SOUPS 2014, Menlo Park, CA, USA, 9–11 July 2014, pp. 175–186 (2014)
24. Schechter, S.E., Dhamija, R., Ozment, A., Fischer, I.: The emperor's new security indicators. In: 2007 IEEE Symposium on Security and Privacy (S&P 2007), Oakland, California, USA, 20–23 May 2007, pp. 51–65 (2007)
25. Schneier, B.: Stop trying to fix the user. IEEE Secur. Priv. **14**(5), 96 (2016)
26. Sheng, S., Holbrook, M.B., Kumaraguru, P., Cranor, L.F., Downs, J.S.: Who falls for phish?: a demographic analysis of phishing susceptibility and effectiveness of interventions. In: Proceedings of the 28th International Conference on Human Factors in Computing Systems, CHI 2010, Atlanta, Georgia, USA, 10–15 April 2010, pp. 373–382 (2010)
27. Sun, H., Sun, K., Wang, Y., Jing, J.: TrustOTP: transforming smartphones into secure one-time password tokens. In: Proceedings of the 22nd ACM SIGSAC Conference on Computer and Communications Security, Denver, CO, USA, 12–16 October 2015, pp. 976–988 (2015)

28. Watson, B., Zheng, J.: On the user awareness of mobile security recommendations. In: Proceedings of the 2017 ACM Southeast Regional Conference, Kennesaw, GA, USA, 13–15 April 2017, pp. 120–127 (2017)

29. Zomai, M.A., AlFayyadh, B., Jøsang, A., McCullagh, A.: An experimental investigation of the usability of transaction authorization in online bank security systems. In: Brankovic, L., Miller, M. (eds.) Sixth Australasian Information Security Conference, AISC 2008, Wollongong, NSW, Australia, January 2008. CRPIT, pp. 65–73. Australian Computer Society (2008)

On the Security and Applicability of Fragile Camera Fingerprints

Erwin Quiring[1(✉)], Matthias Kirchner[2(✉)], and Konrad Rieck[1(✉)]

[1] TU Braunschweig, Braunschweig, Germany
{e.quiring,k.rieck}@tu-bs.de
[2] Binghamton University, Binghamton, USA
kirchner@binghamton.edu

Abstract. Camera sensor noise is one of the most reliable device characteristics in digital image forensics, enabling the unique linkage of images to digital cameras. This so-called camera fingerprint gives rise to different applications, such as image forensics and authentication. However, if images are publicly available, an adversary can estimate the fingerprint from her victim and plant it into spurious images. The concept of fragile camera fingerprints addresses this attack by exploiting asymmetries in data access: While the camera owner will always have access to a full fingerprint from uncompressed images, the adversary has typically access to compressed images and thus only to a truncated fingerprint. The security of this defense, however, has not been systematically explored yet. This paper provides the first comprehensive analysis of fragile camera fingerprints under attack. A series of theoretical and practical tests demonstrate that fragile camera fingerprints allow a reliable device identification for common compression levels in an adversarial environment.

Keywords: Fragile camera fingerprint · PRNU · Authentication

1 Introduction

Minimal, inevitable manufacturing imperfections of digital camera sensors lead to the photo-response non-uniformity (PRNU) signal, a highly unique and reliably detectable camera device characteristic [8]. Similar to a robust digital watermark, the PRNU signal is unnoticeably present in any image taken by the same camera, but differs between images from different cameras. These properties make the PRNU a natural *camera fingerprint*. It has found widespread applications in forensics to attribute digital images to their source camera [8]. Recent works have also proposed to use the PRNU as a means to link mobile device authentication to inherent hardware characteristics of the mobile device [2,26].

In practice, however, these use cases face the problem of *fingerprint copy-attacks* [10,19]. If Alice shares images from her camera with the public, Mallory can estimate Alice's fingerprint, plant it into her images, and pretend that an arbitrary image was captured by Alice's camera. The so-called *triangle test* [13]

© Springer Nature Switzerland AG 2019
K. Sako et al. (Eds.): ESORICS 2019, LNCS 11735, pp. 450–470, 2019.
https://doi.org/10.1007/978-3-030-29959-0_22

detects such attacks *ex post*, but it potentially requires an exhaustive search over all public images shared by Alice. A proactive defense based on the notion of *fragile camera fingerprints* has recently been proposed by Quiring and Kirchner [23] for scenarios that warrant camera identification from high-quality (uncompressed) images. Here, the camera owner Alice can exploit an asymmetry in the quality of accessible data by only sharing JPEG-compressed images with the public while retaining her uncompressed images private. As a result, she will always be able to provide her full fingerprint from high-quality images when asked to do so. In contrast, Mallory's estimate of Alice's fingerprint from public JPEG images will only contain the part that is robust to lossy JPEG compression while lacking the fragile component. A test for the presence of the fragile fingerprint will then prevent Mallory from making an uncompressed image look like one of Alice's uncompressed images.

In forensics applications, fragile camera fingerprints are of particular relevance to the prevention of fingerprint-copy attacks in support of high-quality image forgeries, which may otherwise convey a false sense of trustworthiness [4]. Equally important, fragile fingerprints are currently the only scalable approach to establish mobile device authentication based on physical camera characteristics that mitigates fingerprint leakage from public images: conducting the triangle test [13] on every authentication attempt is computationally infeasible, and an alternative proposal for a targeted fingerprint-copy attack detector by Ba et al. [2] can be defeated by an adversary with two cameras.

The practical applicability of fragile camera fingerprints in these security-related scenarios crucially depends on their robustness against attacks. As Quiring and Kirchner's work [23] only provided preliminary results in this regard, this paper sets out to deliver a thorough and more comprehensive security analysis. Specifically, we examine the amount of information that Mallory can estimate, recover and exploit in a series of theoretical and empirical considerations. First, we analytically derive an upper bound on the correlation between Alice's and Mallory's fingerprint estimates with respect to the JPEG quality of publicly shared images Mallory has access to. Second, to test for dependencies beyond linear correlation, a kernel statistical test is used to assess whether Alice's fragile fingerprint is statistically independent of Mallory's fingerprint. Third, we demonstrate that practical attempts to recover quantized JPEG coefficients from potentially remaining dependencies do not increase Mallory's ability to mount successful attacks. Fourth, we test the resistance of fragile fingerprints against practical fingerprint-copy attacks. We finally illustrate that fragile fingerprints and the triangle test are a powerful combination in forensics applications.

The rest of this paper is organized as follows. Section 2 reviews the background of sensor noise forensics before Sect. 3 discusses fragile fingerprints and their possible applications. Section 4 provides a comprehensive analysis of Mallory's attack surface, while Sect. 5 reports on experiments around the applicability of fragile fingerprints. Section 6 concludes the paper.

2   Background

Before introducing fragile fingerprints, we give a short primer on camera identification, the possible fingerprint-copy attack, and the triangle test as defense. Throughout our work, the *notation* is as follows: vectors and matrices are set in boldface font. Operations on vectors and matrices are point-wise if not stated otherwise; the operator • denotes matrix multiplication.

2.1   Camera Identification from Sensor Noise Fingerprints

Due to sensor element manufacturing imperfections, each camera image does not only contain the original noise-free image content I^0, but also the PRNU K as a camera-specific, multiplicative noise factor. A common simplified model of the image capturing process assumes the final image I to take the form [8]

$$I = I^0 + I^0 K + \Gamma, \tag{1}$$

where Γ reflects a variety of other additive noise terms. Due to its multiplicative nature, the PRNU is not present in images with dark scene contents (i.e., $I^0 \approx 0$). Extensive experiments have demonstrated that the PRNU factor K represents a unique and robust camera fingerprint [14] that can be estimated from a number of images $I_1, \ldots, I_N$ taken with a given camera of interest. The standard approach utilizes a denoising filter $F(\cdot)$ and models noise residuals $W_k = I_k - F(I_k)$ as [8]

$$W_k = I_k K + \Theta_k. \tag{2}$$

Modeling noise Θ subsumes Γ and residues of the image content due to inherent imperfections of the denoising filter in separating image content from noise. Adopting an i.i.d. Gaussian noise assumption for Θ, the maximum likelihood (ML) estimator of K is [8]

$$\hat{K} = \left(\sum_{k=1}^{N} W_k I_k \right) \cdot \left(\sum_{k=1}^{N} (I_k)^2 \right)^{-1}. \tag{3}$$

A more simple estimator takes the pixel-wise average of the noise residuals [19]. A post-processing step is recommended to clean $\hat{K}$ from so-called non-unique artifacts, e.g., due to demosaicing or lens distortion correction [8,11,12]. Given a query image J of unknown provenance, camera identification then works by computing the residual $W_J = J - F(J)$, and evaluating its similarity to a camera fingerprint estimate against a set threshold τ,

$$\phi_{W_J, J\hat{K}} = \text{sim}(W_J, J\hat{K}) \gtrless \tau. \tag{4}$$

Suitable similarity measures for this task are normalized correlation or peak-to-correlation energy (PCE) [8,19].

2.2 Fingerprint-Copy Attack

Following the procedure described in Sect. 2.1, Mallory may obtain an estimate of Alice's camera fingerprint from a set of N_E publicly available images. Denoting this estimate $\hat{K}_E$, Mallory can then attempt to make an arbitrary image J look as if it was captured by Alice's camera. The multiplicative nature of PRNU suggests a *fingerprint copy attack* of the form [19]

$$J' = [J(1 + \alpha \hat{K}_E)], \tag{5}$$

with $\alpha > 0$ being the scalar fingerprint strength parameter. Attacks of this type have been demonstrated to be effective, in the sense that they can successfully mislead a camera identification algorithm in the form of Eq. (4). However, the attack's success generally depends on a good choice of α: too low values mean that the bogus image J' may not be assigned to Alice's camera; a too strong embedding will make the image appear suspicious [13,20]. In practical scenarios, Mallory may have to apply further processing to make her forgery more compelling, e.g., removing the genuine camera fingerprint [7,16], synthesizing demosaicing artifacts [17], and removing or adding traces of JPEG compression [25].

2.3 Triangle Test

Under realistic assumptions, it is impossible to prevent Mallory from forcing a high similarity score in Eq. (4) for arbitrary images from a foreign camera. Yet Alice can utilize that noise residuals computed with practical denoising filters will always contain remnants of image content to establish that image J' underwent a fingerprint-copy attack [13]. The key observation here is that the already existing similarity between a noise residual W_I from an image I taken with Alice's camera and the noise residual $W_{J'}$ due to a common PRNU term will be slightly increased by some shared residual image content, if I contributed to Mallory's fingerprint estimate $\hat{K}_E$. Alice can thus test which of her public images have been used by Mallory to mount the attack by evaluating whether the similarity of their noise residuals W_I with $W_{J'}$ is suspiciously large.

Because the additional correlation imposed by shared image content is generally rather weak and also varies with macroscopic image characteristics, Goljan et al. [13] propose a *triangle test* to calibrate the test statistic. Specifically, the test does not only consider the observed correlation $\nu_{W_I, W_{J'}}$ between residuals W_I and $W_{J'}$, but it also employs a correlation predictor to estimate the correlation $\tilde{\nu}_{W_I, W_{J'}}$ between W_I and $W_{J'}$ if image I had *not* participated in the computation of $\hat{K}_E$. This predictor takes the correlation between Alice's own fingerprint and both W_I and $W_{J'}$ into account—hence the name triangle test. Assuming a linear relationship between the observed and the predicted correlation, the proposed test then evaluates

$$\nu_{W_I, W_{J'}} - \theta \tilde{\nu}_{W_I, W_{J'}} - \mu \gtrless t \tag{6}$$

for a suitably chosen threshold t. The parameters θ and μ are estimated from a set of *safe* images, for which it can be guaranteed that they have not been used by Mallory. We refer to Goljan et al. [13] for a detailed exposition of the correlation predictor and the parameter estimators. The test statistic in Eq. (6) is expected to have zero mean when two noise residuals share only a common PRNU term. A larger difference indicates an additional shared term, possibly due to image I's involvement in the attack. Observe that Alice may have to test *all images* ever made public by her as part of a comprehensive defense. We finally point out that a number of fingerprint-copy attack variations have been proposed recently that are reportedly less likely to be exposed by the triangle test (e.g. [20]).

3   Fragile Camera Fingerprint

As a novel and proactive defense against fingerprint-copy attacks, Quiring and Kirchner [23] introduce the notion of fragile camera fingerprints that vanish under lossy JPEG compression. The idea is based on two mild assumptions: (1) Alice's device supports capturing images in uncompressed format, which is true nowadays for many devices operating under mobile platforms, such as iOS and Android; (2) Alice only shares JPEG images with the public, which is already today's quasi-standard for image online storage and sharing. When combined, these two assumptions allow Alice to effectively exploit an asymmetry in the quality of data access. With full access to her camera, Alice is always in the position to present a fingerprint estimate $\hat{K}$ from uncompressed images while Mallory is restricted to estimate $\hat{K}_E$ from JPEG-compressed images.

On a technical level, the concept of fragile camera fingerprints exploits the lossy nature of JPEG compression. JPEG maps each non-overlapping 8×8 pixel block in an image to 8×8 discrete cosine transform (DCT) coefficients. Each of the 64 coefficients quantifies the influence of a particular frequency subband and will be quantized based on an 8×8 quantization table with quantization factors for the 64 DCT subbands. Larger quantization factors mean that the DCT coefficients in the corresponding subband are more likely to be quantized to zero. Quantization factors generally increase with decreasing JPEG quality and grow towards the bottom right corner of the quantization table to suppress high-frequency image details more aggressively.

In consequence, Mallory's camera fingerprint estimate from JPEG-compressed images will be strongly distorted in the high-frequency DCT subbands due to larger quantization errors. If the quantization is too strong, Mallory's images will lack high-frequency content altogether and so will her fingerprint estimate. In other words, her estimate only comprises the fingerprint component that is robust to JPEG compression. A fingerprint estimate from uncompressed images is in turn distributed almost evenly over all subbands [23]. Hence, Alice has access to a *fragile camera fingerprint*, computed from the high-frequency subbands only.

To obtain the fragile part, it is instructive to define a mode-selective highpass filter $H_c(\cdot)$. Based on a binary multiplicative mask $\boldsymbol{H}_c = [h_{i,j}], 1 \leqslant i,j \leqslant 8$,

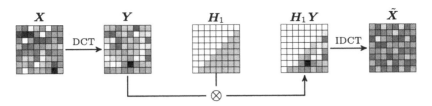

Fig. 1. Fragile fingerprint computation based on a subband-selective filter $H_1(\boldsymbol{X})$: Each pixel block $\boldsymbol{X}$ is mapped to its DCT representation $\boldsymbol{Y}$, element-wise multiplied by a binary mask $\boldsymbol{H}_1$, and transformed back to the spatial domain to give $\tilde{\boldsymbol{X}}$.

the filter retains a defined set of DCT subbands and sets all other subband coefficients to zero. Alice should choose $\boldsymbol{H}_c$ depending on the maximum JPEG quality of her published images. For a sufficiently conservative choice, she can assume that the retained subbands are available exclusively to her. Quiring and Kirchner [23] propose to parameterize $\boldsymbol{H}_c$ with a cut-off along the $(-c)$-th anti-diagonal of the DCT coefficient matrix,

$$h_{i,j} = [(i + j - 8 - c) > 0], \qquad (7)$$

where $[\cdot]$ denotes the Iverson bracket. Figure 1 summarizes the internal steps of $H_c(\cdot)$ for cut-off parameter $c = 1$, which retains all DCT subbands in the lower right triangle. Equipped with H_c, a refined similarity test of the form

$$\phi_{\boldsymbol{W_J}, \boldsymbol{J}\hat{\boldsymbol{K}}}(c) = \text{sim}\left(H_c(\boldsymbol{W_J}), H_c(\boldsymbol{J}\hat{\boldsymbol{K}})\right) \gtrless \tau. \qquad (8)$$

then establishes camera identification from fragile fingerprints, which is of particular relevance in the following two application scenarios.

Digital Image Forensics. Testing for the presence of camera fingerprints facilitates device identification and image manipulation detection in forensic applications [8]. Fragile camera fingerprints can benefit scenarios that warrant the analysis of high-quality images, for instance when uncompressed images ought to be presented as a source of particularly high trustworthiness. In this case, Alice can establish that a spurious image was not captured by her camera by having kept her uncompressed images private. She presents the fragile fingerprint when needed, potentially in combination with cryptographic safeguards [21] or in some form of zero-knowledge proof to further secure her fragile fingerprint from leakage.

Mobile Device Authentication. Camera fingerprints have been proposed as building blocks for augmenting mobile device authentication schemes with physical hardware characteristics [2,5,26]. Yet like with device signatures from other types of hardware sensors, the vulnerability to fingerprint-copy/spoofing attacks is of particular concern [1]. To the best of our knowledge, the concept of fragile fingerprints is the only existing approach that would address the problem in a proactive and scalable manner. Performing a triangle test upon every authentication attempt is computationally infeasible, let alone that Alice may object to the idea of sharing all her images with the service she wants to authenticate to.

Ba et al. [2] attempt to work around that issue in their authentication protocol by requiring the user to take two images of different visual codes during the identification phase. Similar to the triangle test, the reasoning is that two spoofed images will correlate implausibly strongly as they do not only share Alice's fingerprint but also the one from Mallory's camera. This measure can be easily circumvented by an attacker who uses two different devices to take the respective pictures however. In this way, Mallory prevents the additionally shared signal.

In summary, fragile camera fingerprints enable novel applications in image forensics and mobile device authentication. Their applicability, however, depends on the robustness against attacks. In the remainder of this work, we thus perform a comprehensive security analysis.

4   Security Analysis

A secure application of fragile camera fingerprints demands that Mallory cannot estimate the fragile fingerprint from JPEG-compressed images. We guide our analysis along the following three questions:

(Q1) Can we bound the quality of Mallory's fingerprint estimate $\hat{K}_E$?
(Q2) Can Mallory improve her fingerprint estimate by exploiting the quantized high-frequency or robust low-frequency information?
(Q3) Can Mallory perform a successful fingerprint-copy attack?

4.1   Datasets and Experimental Setup

Where empirical tests are warranted, we adopt the setup described by Quiring and Kirchner [23]. The dataset consists of images from the Dresden Image Database [9] (DDB) and the RAISE Image Database [6], cf. Table 1.

Table 1. Number of images per test set and camera.

Database	Camera model	Fingerprint estimate		Benchmark data	
		Camera 0	Camera 1	Camera 0	Camera 1
Dresden [9]	Nikon D70	25	25	175	188
	Nikon D70s	25	25	175	174
	Nikon D200	25	25	360	370
RAISE [6]	Nikon D7000	300	—	4648	—

In particular, we use 25 homogeneously lit flat field images of each DDB camera to obtain uncompressed fingerprint estimates. 1442 natural images serve as benchmark data. We present aggregated results over the six cameras in the following, as all gave similar results. The RAISE database only provides natural images. We randomly select 300 images for fingerprint computation, leaving us with 4648 images for a benchmark set that facilitates the study of attacks where Mallory has access to a large number of public images. Note that the usage of 300 natural images for fingerprint estimation can be attributed to the heterogenous content of natural images. In an authentication scenario, a user can be asked to take a much smaller number of suitable images (e.g. a white wall) without nuisance image content. If not stated otherwise, we use the standard Wavelet denoiser to obtain noise residuals [19] and the ML formulation in Eq. (3) to estimate fingerprints.

In order to also guide our evaluation at the practically used JPEG quality, we collected over 1.4 Million JPEG images from Twitter, Instagram, Imgur, Deviantart and Flickr. The average JPEG quality is 83.5 with a standard deviation of 9.2. This, for instance, fits to recommendations from Flickr, Wikimedia and the official Android documentation that recommend qualities less than 90.

4.2 (Q1) Analytical Quality of Fingerprint Estimation

Our first objective is to establish a bound on the quality of Mallory's fingerprint estimate from Alice's camera irrespective of a concrete image data set to reflect Mallory's chances of performing a successful fingerprint-copy attack. In particular, we adopt the notion of *quality of fingerprint estimation* by Goljan et al. [13]. We derive an analytical expression for the correlation between Alice's fingerprint from uncompressed images, $\hat{K}$, and Mallory's fingerprint from compressed images, $\hat{K}_E$,

$$\text{cor}(H_c(\hat{K}), H_c(\hat{K}_E)). \tag{9}$$

This quantity can be seen as a simplified version of the similarity measure in Eq. (8) for images taken under ideal conditions, e.g. homogeneously lit. As we focus on high-frequency subbands only, less image content disturbs the fingerprint calculation. Thus, $H_c(J\hat{K})$ resembles $H_c(\hat{K})$, as well $H_c(W_J) \approx H_c(\hat{K}_E)$.

We make three assumptions to simplify the calculation. First, Mallory computes her fingerprint from the same, but compressed, image set that Alice uses for her uncompressed estimate. This will yield a loose upper bound for cases where Mallory obtains a different JPEG-compressed image set that Alice has not used. Moreover, we apply a simple fingerprint estimator that takes the pixel-wise average of noise residuals. Finally, we assume a negligible correlation between individual DCT subbands and across images. The first and the second assumption imply that the fingerprint calculation can be modeled as pixel-wise averaging. Denote X_i the i-th uncompressed image from Alice's camera and $\tilde{X}_i$ its JPEG-compressed version to rewrite Eq. (9) as

$$\text{cor}(H_c(\hat{K}), H_c(\hat{K}_E)) = \text{cor}\left(\sum_i H_c(X_i), \sum_i H_c(\tilde{X}_i)\right). \tag{10}$$

Appendix A establishes that the *sample correlation coefficient* based on Eq. (10), $r(c)$, can be computed in the DCT domain directly. We write $\boldsymbol{Y}_i$ and $\tilde{\boldsymbol{Y}}_i$ for the DCT representations of $\boldsymbol{X}_i$ and $\tilde{\boldsymbol{X}}_i$, respectively, to obtain

$$r(c) \cong \mathrm{cor}\left(\textstyle\sum_i(\boldsymbol{H}_c\,\boldsymbol{Y}_i), \sum_i(\boldsymbol{H}_c\,\tilde{\boldsymbol{Y}}_i)\right). \tag{11}$$

The coefficient is parametrized by the cut-off c from Eq. (7). High-pass filter H_c is now made explicit through the DCT mask $\boldsymbol{H}_c$ (see Sect. 3), yielding a convenient formulation to compute the sample correlation coefficient between Alice's and Mallory's fingerprint directly in the DCT domain. This formulation thus allows us to use known statistical distribution models for DCT coefficients.

We continue to derive the *population correlation coefficient* by assuming a Laplacian distribution for the AC DCT coefficients [24]. Specifically, denote $Y_{i,s}$ the random variable representing the s-th subband of the i-the uncompressed image. Equivalently, denote $\tilde{Y}_{i,s}$ the respective quantized counterpart to reflect the effect of JPEG compression on $Y_{i,s}$. Appendix B establishes the general relation between the two random variables in terms of their covariance, which can be expressed solely on the basis of the distribution of the uncompressed variable $Y_{i,s}$. We highlight this by defining $\mathrm{Cov}^+(Y_{i,s}) = \mathrm{Cov}(Y_{i,s}, \tilde{Y}_{i,s})$. A similar derivation for the variance yields $\mathrm{Var}^+(Y_{i,s}) = \mathrm{Var}(\tilde{Y}_{i,s})$. Appendix B shows how aggregating these quantities over the various subbands $s \in S_c$ as specified by filter H_c of various images leads to the following formulation for the population correlation coefficient:

$$\rho(c) \cong \frac{\sum_i \sum_{s \in S_c} \mathrm{Cov}^+(Y_{i,s})}{\sqrt{\sum_i \sum_{s \in S_c} \mathrm{Var}(Y_{i,s})}\sqrt{\sum_i \sum_{s \in S_c} \mathrm{Var}^+(Y_{i,s})}}. \tag{12}$$

This equation is a first step towards an analytical understanding of the impact of JPEG-induced quantization on the ability to estimate fragile camera fingerprints. Specifically, it allows Alice to deduce the expected correlation of Mallory's fingerprint with her fingerprint based on general DCT distribution assumptions. Note that the derived correlation is computed under the assumption of a strong attacker: Mallory bases her fingerprint estimation on the same image set as Alice; her images only differ in that they are JPEG-compressed. Consequently, Eq. (12) can serve as upper bound for the more realistic scenario when Mallory has only access to a different image set. Alice, as camera owner, will always be able to create new images for her fingerprint. The next section demonstrates the validity of our analytical derivation under practical conditions for both scenarios.

4.3   (Q1) Empirical Quality of Fingerprint Estimation

We start with the quality of Mallory's fingerprint estimate when Alice and Mallory operate on the same image set, and then continue with different image sets.

Same Image Sets. In a first step, we compute the population correlation coefficient ρ from Eq. (12) on a set of 250 synthetic images. Each image follows a zero-mean Laplacian distribution with a randomly generated scale parameter. This allows us to examine ρ on idealized conditions. We compare ρ with its empirical counterpart, r, as given in Eq. (11). Figure 2a shows that the two derived quantities are consistent under varying JPEG compression levels.

In the next experiment, we use natural images from the Nikon D7000. We give Mallory access to $N_E = 250$ JPEG-compressed images, derived from the same set that Alice uses for her fingerprint. Varying the JPEG quality and cut-off parameter c, we compute ρ and r. The computation of ρ involved a standard maximum likelihood estimator to obtain the Laplace scale parameter for each DCT subband per image. For benchmark purposes, we also include the sample correlation coefficient ϕ_1 between Alice's and Mallory's fingerprint, both calculated with the ML formulation in Eq. (3). We repeat the experiments five times and report averaged results for ρ, r and ϕ_1 in Figs. 2b–c for $c \in \{1,2\}$. The curves resemble each other reasonably well, with r generally predicting a slightly higher fingerprint quality than ρ due to the implied independence assumptions in the latter. As c increases, ρ slowly approaches ϕ_1. This indicates that the analytically derived ρ is a good approximation of Mallory's fingerprint quality under idealized conditions particularly in high-frequency DCT subbands.

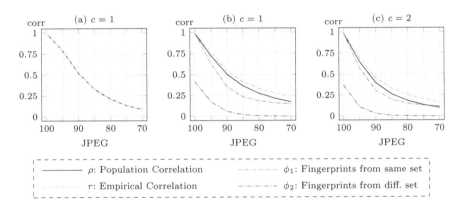

Fig. 2. Quality of fingerprint estimation. Results from (a) $N_E = 250$ synthetic images and (b)–(c) $N_E = 250$ natural Nikon D7000 images.

Different Image Sets. In a more realistic scenario, we assume Alice and Mallory to work on different image sets. Figures 2b and c thus include ϕ_2, the corresponding sample correlation coefficient between Alice's and Mallory's fingerprints as obtained with the ML estimator, averaged over five randomly compiled JPEG image sets of size $N_E = 250$ that Alice has not used for computing $\hat{K}$. Alice's camera-specific fingerprint from 300 images was kept constant throughout all repetitions. Not surprisingly, the population correlation coefficient ρ is a loose upper bound to the observed correlation ϕ_2 when Mallory operates on a different image set: ϕ_2 approaches zero quickly with increasing c and decreasing JPEG quality. Appendix C gives additional insights by reporting the correlations for a much larger number of JPEG images, N_E. Mallory's fingerprint quality increases only slowly with the number of available JPEG images. For a suitable combination of JPEG quality and cut-off parameter c, the correlation remains extremely small. As a result, less restrictive quality and cut-off parameters are possible compared to the contrived situation where Alice and Mallory access the same images.

Analysis Summary. Overall, strong guarantees for a scenario where Mallory has access to JPEG-compressed versions of the very images Alice used for her fingerprint are possible for JPEG qualities of 70 or smaller. In a more realistic scenario with different image sets, a secure operation is already possible with JPEG quality factors 90 or lower. For JPEG 85—the average quality factor on various image platforms (see Sect. 4.1)—Alice may choose $c \geqslant 3$ to ensure a reliable identification in an adversarial environment.

4.4   (Q2) Independence Test

The previous section has analyzed the correlation between Alice's and Mallory's high-frequency fingerprint estimates—deriving first bounds when Alice's fingerprint remains private. We continue with this analysis under the scenario of different image sets in the following sections.

Quiring and Kirchner have shown [23] that the high-frequency pixel part kept by H_c is uncorrelated to the complementary low-frequency part kept by $L_c = H_c$ XOR 1. Consequently, Mallory cannot exploit linear dependencies between her robust low-frequency fingerprint and Alice's fragile fingerprint. However, correlation does not cover all modes of dependence. In this section, we thus examine if Mallory can exploit non-linear dependencies and conduct a kernel statistical test of independence. In particular, we choose the Hilbert-Schmidt independence criterion[1] (HSIC)[15]. In simplified terms, this test maps the possibly non-linear dependencies to a linear space where independence is tested. The test is consistent in the sense that the level of *alpha* controls the type I error (detects dependence although independence is true) while the type II errors goes to zero for an increasing sample size [15].

We consider the following two scenarios. First, we test if Alice's high frequency fingerprint is independent to Mallory's high-frequency fingerprint from JPEG-compressed images:

$$\mathcal{H}_0 : H_c(\hat{\boldsymbol{K}}) \perp\!\!\!\perp H_c(\hat{\boldsymbol{K}}_E). \tag{13}$$

Equivalently, the second scenario tests if Alice's high frequency fingerprint is independent to Mallory's full fingerprint from JPEG-compressed images:

$$\mathcal{H}_0 : H_c(\hat{\boldsymbol{K}}) \perp\!\!\!\perp \hat{\boldsymbol{K}}_E. \tag{14}$$

---

[1]   We use a Gaussian kernel, an alpha value of 0.05, and split the images into 320×320 pixel blocks with varying offsets to keep the sample size manageable.

We grant Mallory access to $N_E = 150$ images of each DDB camera and $N_E = 1000$ RAISE images. We aggregate results over ten randomly compiled sets of size N_E.

For both scenarios, Fig. 3 depicts the observed $\mathcal{H}_0$ acceptance rates, i.e. the percentage of cases for which we cannot detect a measurable dependence between the two quantities under test. This rate increases with lower JPEG qualities or larger cut-off parameters c. In the first scenario, the test statistic suggests independence at a considerable rate for $c = 4$ and JPEG quality 90 for all cameras. Interestingly, the second scenario—where Alice's high frequency fingerprint is tested against Mallory's full fingerprint—is characterized by a lower rate of independence. A comparison of both scenarios thus suggests that remaining dependencies may result from the low-frequency part. This dependency would have to be non-linear, as the low- and high-frequency signal are not correlated to each other. As we show in the next section, it is unclear how Mallory can exploit these potentially remaining dependencies in practice, however.

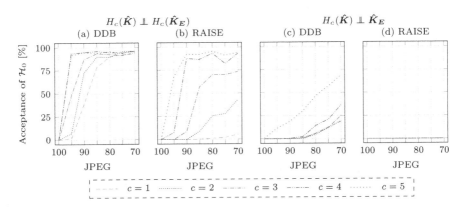

Fig. 3. Kernel statistical test of independence. Plots (a) and (b) depict the first scenario; Plots (c) and (d) the second scenario for both databases.

We surmise that the notably less conclusive results on the RAISE data are due to non-trivial remnants of image content in the noise residuals. In contrast to the Dresden database, Alice's fingerprint is here calculated from natural instead of homogeneously lit images, raising the bar for establishing independence considerably.

Analysis Summary. The chosen HSIC test establishes statistical independence for suitable JPEG and cut-off parameters, which gives a strong evidence that Mallory cannot exploit any dependence to recover Alice's fingerprint. Considering the high-frequency signals, Alice may choose $c \geqslant 3$ for quality factor 85.

4.5   (Q2) DCT Recovery

In the next experiment, we examine if Mallory can exploit remaining dependencies to recover DCT coefficients. Although a DCT coefficient that is quantized to zero does not reveal information about the fingerprint, non-zero coefficients may leak information at least with their sign. By averaging enough images, Mallory may thus obtain a coarse fingerprint estimate. We test below if Mallory can improve her fingerprint by recovering DCT coefficients that were quantized to zero.

We adapt the systematic approach by Li et al. [18], since it is in principle also applicable to the recovery of high-frequency DCT coefficients. The recovery is a linear optimization problem with the objective to minimize the spatial distance of neighboring pixels within and across the 8×8 pixel blocks from JPEG compression. The first constraint is that the recovered pixel values must correspond to their DCT coefficients. Second, DCT coefficients that should not be recovered are fixed. Finally, the pixel and DCT coefficients have to be within their dynamic range. The optimization problem can be summarized as

$$\min \sum_{l,l'} |\boldsymbol{X}(l) - \boldsymbol{X}(l')| \tag{15}$$

$$\text{s.t. } \boldsymbol{X} - \boldsymbol{D}^\top \bullet \boldsymbol{Y} \bullet \boldsymbol{D} = \boldsymbol{0}, \tag{16}$$

$$\boldsymbol{Y}(s) = \boldsymbol{Y}^*(s), \tag{17}$$

$$\boldsymbol{X}(l) \in [x_{\min}, x_{\max}], \ \boldsymbol{Y}(s) \in [y_{\min}, y_{\max}], \tag{18}$$

where l and l' are the indices of neighboring pixels in the spatial domain, $\boldsymbol{D}$ denotes the DCT transformation matrix, and s is the index of a DCT subband. The second constraint fixes with $\boldsymbol{Y}^*$ all DCT coefficients that are not part of the subbands retained by filter H_c or are non-zero in the subbands retained by H_c. As a result, we recover only zero-valued DCT coefficients that H_c retains. For each image, and for each 8×8 pixel block, we set up such an optimization problem and include its direct neighboring blocks.

Table 2. Contingency table of DCT recovery from 50 Nikon D70 images

		Fraction Predicted Sign					
		JPEG 100			JPEG 95		
		neg	zero	pos	neg	zero	pos
Fraction True Sign	neg	0.08	0.09	0.05	0.11	0.15	0.09
	zero	0.16	0.08	0.16	0.07	0.11	0.07
	pos	0.05	0.09	0.24	0.09	0.15	0.17

We report results for 50 images from a Nikon D70 over the JPEG qualities 100 and 95 as well as the cut-off frequency $c = 1$. The performance does not change considerably for smaller JPEG qualities or larger cut-off frequencies and thus are omitted. Table 2 depicts a contingency table that summarizes the frequency of correctly predicted signs. This is the case when the sign of the predicted DCT coefficient equals the sign from the corresponding original uncompressed image or both the predicted and uncompressed coefficient lie in the zero range $[-0.25, 0.25]$. Even for JPEG quality 100, the recovery cannot reliably predict the sign. The correct distinction drops further for a smaller JPEG quality and tends towards a random classifier. In each case, the correlation to Alice's fragile fingerprint decreases when Mallory uses the recovered images for her estimate. In contrast, the recovery of low-frequency subbands is successful with an average recovery rate of 70%. However, only the correlation to Alice's low-frequency fingerprint increases in our experiments.

Analysis Summary. The recovery of the correct sign is partly possible for low-frequency subbands, while the recovery of high-frequency subbands is already difficult for JPEG quality 100. Mallory can thus not improve her estimate of Alice's fragile fingerprint through a DCT recovery.

4.6   (Q3) Fingerprint-Copy Attack

We finally consider a realistic fingerprint-copy attack where Mallory plants her calculated fingerprint estimate $\hat{K}_E$ from Alice's camera into 100 randomly chosen uncompressed images taken by a different camera (see Sect. 2.2). Figure 4 depicts the average PCE values with respect to the embedding strength for varying JPEG qualities. We present results only for the Nikon D7000 from the RAISE database with $N_E = 4648$. This allows us to depict the effect when Mallory uses a large number of public images. We refer to Quiring and Kirchner [23] for results from the DDB, which are similar to the results reported here.

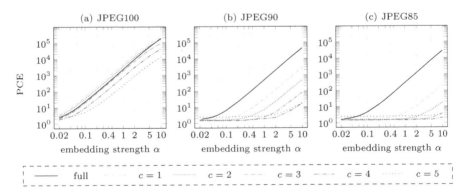

Fig. 4. Fingerprint-copy attack with fragile fingerprints. Average PCE values as a function of the embedding strength α with $N_E = 4648$ (Nikon D7000) for different JPEG qualities.

As expected, high-quality JPEG 100 images enable Mallory to perform a successful attack due to the negligible quantization (Fig. 4(a)). The situation is substantially different with stronger compression. For JPEG 90, only the full fingerprint gives high PCE values for small embedding strengths. Yet, larger cut-offs demand extremely strong embeddings to achieve high PCEs. For JPEG quality 85, no choice of α will produce Mallory's desired result with $c \geqslant 3$.

Analysis Summary. Fragile fingerprints allow a secure identification starting from JPEG 90 and lower. In accordance to our results from previous sections, no choice of α will allow an attack with $c \geqslant 3$ for quality factor 85.

5 Application Analysis

We finally examine the application of fragile sensor noise fingerprints. First, we verify that they are still discriminative enough to distinguish different cameras. Second, we compare them with the triangle test against fingerprint-copy attacks.

5.1 Camera Identification

In the following, we show that fragile fingerprints allow a reliable camera identification compared to traditional *full* camera fingerprints. We only consider uncompressed images here by the very nature of fragile fingerprints. The PCE is used as similarity measure for images of each camera (true positives) and all remaining natural images from the Dresden Image Database (true negatives). Figure 5a shows the ROC curves for different cut-off frequencies c—aggregated over 1442 images from the six DDB cameras. The full frequency range is included for comparison.

Although a fragile fingerprint with $c = 1$ employs only 28 DCT coefficients in each block, it achieves the same detection performance as the full fingerprint with 64 coefficients. An almost perfect detection is possible with $c \leqslant 4$ for the Dresden database. The results for the Nikon D7000 camera are comparable for $c \leqslant 3$. We contribute this smaller choice of c to a more perturbed fingerprint estimate of this camera—due to more image content in the respective noise residuals.

Analysis Summary. Fragile fingerprints allow a reliable camera identification. Together with our security analysis, for a common JPEG quality factor of 85, Alice can choose $c = 3$ to achieve both a reliable camera identification and attack resistance.

5.2 Comparison with Triangle Test

While the triangle test cannot be recommended for authentication, it is a reasonable defense in digital image forensics. Our final experiment highlights its powerful combination with fragile fingerprints in forensic applications against fingerprint-copy attacks. Our previous results underline that remaining fingerprint information after quantization are usable for large embedding strengths with too small cut-off parameters ($c \leqslant 2$). However, the triangle test shows its

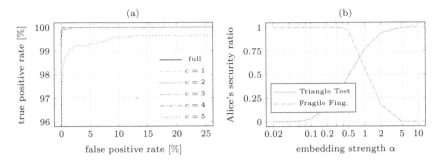

Fig. 5. Applications. Plot (a) shows the camera identification of uncompressed images. Plot (b) depicts the defense performance against fingerprint-copy attack using the triangle test and fragile fingerprints (JPEG quality 90, $c = 1$).

strengths exactly in these cases, as the additional residual image content from the forgery process emerges more clearly with a larger embedding strength [13].

In the following, we assume Mallory to have access to $N_E = 150$ public JPEG images with quality factor 90 from Alice's Nikon D200 camera. Mallory embeds her spoofed fingerprint into an uncompressed image from another camera while varying α as defined in the previous section. On the defender side, the linear parameters θ and μ of the test statistic are estimated from 200 images that Mallory has not used, cf. Eq. (6). We set the threshold t such that the false alarm probability is 10^{-3}. Finally, Alice reports her security ratio: the percentage of images that Mallory has used and that are correctly marked as those. We repeat the process over 100 randomly chosen uncompressed images where Mallory embeds her spoofed fingerprint. Figure 5b depicts the averaged security ratio.

For reference, we include the corresponding results with the fragile fingerprint approach. We focus on $c = 1$ and JPEG quality 90, where Mallory obtains considerably high PCE values with a fingerprint-copy attack (see Fig. 4(b)). In particular, we estimate the distribution of the PCE values from uncompressed images with a Gaussian kernel density estimator. The PCE threshold under which an image is not assumed as one from Alice's camera is set such that the false positive probability is 10^{-3}. Alice's security ratio expresses the percentage of Mallory's images that do not exceed the PCE threshold and thus are correctly identified as being not from Alice's camera.

Figure 5b emphasizes that both approaches are a powerful combination when Mallory has just access to JPEG images. At the point where Mallory starts to circumvent fragile fingerprints, the triangle test already detects more than 50% of images that are involved in Mallory's attack; usually enough to raise suspicion that Mallory has forged the image under investigation. In summary, Mallory faces the following dilemma: A too strong fingerprint strength is likely to be uncovered by the triangle test; with a too weak embedding, Mallory's forged image will not be identified as one of Alice's images. By using the triangle test in addition, Alice can even use smaller cut-off values for her fragile fingerprint.

6   Conclusion

This paper contributes to a thorough understanding of fragile camera fingerprints by providing a comprehensive security analysis. In multiple tests, we confirm that Mallory cannot estimate Alice's camera fingerprint from JPEG-compressed images with common compression levels. Our analysis thus motivates the usage of fragile fingerprints in various applications, such as authentication or digital image forensics. Finally, we note that the concept of fragile fingerprints effectively demonstrates how asymmetries in the quality of accessible data can be exploited. In the context of recent unification attempts between related research disciplines [3,22], this may foster novel strategies in adversarial machine learning or signal processing.

Acknowledgments. The authors gratefully acknowledge funding from Deutsche Forschungsgemeinschaft (DFG) under the project RI 2469/3-1, from the German Federal Ministry of Education and Research (BMBF) under the project FIDI (FKZ 16KIS0786K), and by the NSF grant 1464275. The first author also thanks the German Academic Exchange Service (DAAD) for financial support during his stay in Binghamton.

A   Sample Correlation Coefficient

The objective is to compute Pearson's sample correlation coefficient between two images u and v equivalently in the DCT domain. Without loss of generality, we focus on an 8×8 pixel block, so that the correlation is given as

$$r = \frac{n \sum u(l)v(l) - \sum u(l) \sum v(l)}{n \sqrt{\sum u(l)^2 - \left(\sum u(l)\right)^2} \sqrt{\sum v(l)^2 - \left(\sum v(l)\right)^2}} \tag{19}$$

where $u(l)$ and $v(l)$ are the pixel values. The total number of pixel values or DCT coefficients is given by n, thus for one block $n = 64$. To obtain the same correlation value just with the DCT representation U and V of both images, we use the following identities between spatial pixels and DCT coefficients:

$$n \sum u(l)v(l) = n \sum U(l)V(l) \tag{20}$$

$$\sum u(l) \sum v(l) = n^2 \, \bar{u} \, \bar{v} = n \, U(0)V(0) \tag{21}$$

$$n \sum u(l)^2 = n \sum U(l)^2 \tag{22}$$

$$\left(\sum u(l)\right)^2 = (n \, \bar{u})^2 = n \, U(0)^2. \tag{23}$$

Incorporating these identities in Eq. (19) and canceling n, we obtain the following correlation equation for one 8×8 pixel block:

$$r = \frac{\sum U(l)V(l) - U(0)V(0)}{\sqrt{\sum (U(l)^2) - U(0)^2}\sqrt{\sum (V(l)^2) - V(0)^2}} \tag{24}$$

The generalization over all image blocks yields the same result. If we now just focus on AC coefficients, the DC coefficient $U(0)$ and $V(0)$ become zero. As the AC coefficient's mean goes to zero, Eq. (24) corresponds to Eq. (19). In other words, we can directly feed the AC DCT coefficients into the standard Pearson correlation equation.

B   Population Correlation Coefficient

Given a quantizer and uniform step size q, we denote by U an uncompressed image as random variable and by V its quantized output, $V = \lfloor U/q + 0.5 \rfloor \cdot q$. The objective is to compute the population correlation coefficient between U and V:

$$\rho = \frac{\mathrm{Cov}(U,V)}{\sqrt{\mathrm{Var}(U)}\sqrt{\mathrm{Var}(V)}}. \tag{25}$$

The following general relations between the random variable U and output V can be established when U is assumed to have a symmetrical and zero-mean pdf $f_U(x)$ with characteristic function $\Phi_U(x)$ [27]:

$$\mathrm{Var}(V) = \mathrm{Var}(U) + \frac{q^2}{12} + \frac{q^2}{\pi^2} \sum_{k=1}^{\infty} \Phi_U\left(\frac{2\pi k}{q}\right) \cdot \frac{(-1)^k}{k^2}$$

$$+ \frac{2q}{\pi} \sum_{k=1}^{\infty} \Phi_U'\left(\frac{2\pi k}{q}\right) \frac{(-1)^{k+1}}{k} \tag{26}$$

$$\mathrm{Cov}(U,V) = \mathrm{Var}(U) + \frac{q}{\pi} \sum_{k=1}^{\infty} \Phi_U'\left(\frac{2\pi k}{q}\right) \frac{(-1)^{k+1}}{k} \tag{27}$$

For a zero-mean Laplacian distribution with parameter λ, the characteristic function is given as:

$$\Phi_U(x) = \frac{\lambda^2}{x^2 + \lambda^2}. \tag{28}$$

To highlight that the covariance and variance terms are only based on variable U, we write $\mathrm{Cov}(U,V) = \mathrm{Cov}^+(U)$ and $\mathrm{Var}(V) = \mathrm{Var}^+(U)$.

In the next step, to determine the fingerprint quality, we need to calculate the correlation after averaging the uncompressed images and their compressed counterparts, respectively:

$$\mathrm{cor}\left(\sum_i U_i, \sum_i V_i\right). \tag{29}$$

We start with the distribution on one subband and denote by $U_{i,s}$ and $V_{i,s}$ the s-th subband of the i-th image and its compressed version. The aggregation over various subbands follows from the linear property of the covariance and the assumption of uncorrelated DCT subbands:

$$\text{Cov}\left(\sum_s U_{i,s}, \sum_s V_{i,s}\right) = \sum_s \text{Cov}(U_{i,s}, V_{i,s}). \tag{30}$$

This is also possible for the variance of a sum of random variables. Finally, we assume the images to be uncorrelated to average the covariance over all images:

$$\text{Cov}\left(\sum_i U_i, \sum_i V_i\right) = \sum_i \sum_s \text{Cov}(U_{i,s}, V_{i,s}). \tag{31}$$

Taking all together, the population correlation coefficient is given as

$$\rho\left(\sum_i U_i, \sum_i V_i\right) = \frac{\sum_i \sum_s \text{Cov}^+(U_{i,s})}{\sqrt{\sum_i \sum_s \text{Var}(U_{i,s})}\sqrt{\sum_i \sum_s \text{Var}^+(U_{i,s})}}. \tag{32}$$

C   Empirical Quality of Fingerprint Estimation

For the different image set scenario, Table 3 shows the correlations for $N_E = 2000$ and $N_E = 4648$ JPEG images. $N_E = 4648$ is the maximum number of available images in our setup, so that its values are from a single instance of the experiment.

Table 3. Quality of fingerprint estimation (RAISE)

N_E	JPEG	c					
		Full	1	2	3	4	5
2000	100	0.6241	0.6070	0.5613	0.4867	0.3858	0.2654
	95	0.5484	0.3853	0.2694	0.1622	0.0824	0.0551
	90	0.4633	0.1588	0.0793	0.0375	0.0181	0.0185
	85	0.4030	0.0550	0.0178	0.0071	0.0031	0.0065
	80	0.3619	0.0195	0.0026	−0.0003	0.0002	0.0045
	75	0.3301	0.0070	−0.0029	−0.0024	0.0004	0.0023
	70	0.3093	0.0035	−0.0042	−0.0036	−0.0001	0.0017
4648	100	0.6526	0.6387	0.5968	0.5279	0.4330	0.3151
	95	0.5890	0.4654	0.3531	0.2269	0.1208	0.0808
	90	0.5054	0.2162	0.1130	0.0543	0.0264	0.0277
	85	0.4451	0.0757	0.0248	0.0099	0.0040	0.0094
	80	0.4045	0.0272	0.0033	−0.0008	−0.0005	0.0047
	75	0.3732	0.0100	−0.0044	−0.0035	0.0006	0.0033
	70	0.3535	0.0053	−0.0058	−0.0053	−0.0003	0.0022

References

1. Alaca, F., van Oorschot, P.C.: Device fingerprinting for augmenting web authentication: Classification and analysis of methods. In: Annual Conference on Computer Security Applications (ACSAC) (2016)
2. Ba, Z., Piao, S., Fu, X., Koutsonikolas, D., Mohaisen, A., Ren, K.: ABC: enabling smartphone authentication with built-in camera. In: Proceedings of Network and Distributed System Security Symposium (NDSS) (2018)
3. Barni, M., Pérez-González, F.: Coping with the enemy: advances in adversary-aware signal processing. In: IEEE International Conference on Acoustics, Speech, and Signal Processing (ICASSP) (2013)
4. Böhme, R., Freiling, F.C., Gloe, T., Kirchner, M.: Multimedia forensics is not computer forensics. In: Geradts, Z.J.M.H., Franke, K.Y., Veenman, C.J. (eds.) IWCF 2009. LNCS, vol. 5718, pp. 90–103. Springer, Heidelberg (2009). https://doi.org/10.1007/978-3-642-03521-0_9
5. Bojinov, H., Michalevsky, Y., Nakibly, G., Boneh, D.: Mobile device identification via sensor fingerprinting. CoRR abs/1408.1416 (2014)
6. Dang-Nguyen, D.T., Pasquini, C., Conotter, V., Boato, G.: RAISE: a raw images dataset for digital image forensics. In: 6th ACM Multimedia Systems Conference (2015)
7. Entrieri, J., Kirchner, M.: Patch-based desynchronization of digital camera sensor fingerprints. In: IS&T Electronic Imaging: Media Watermarking, Security, and Forensics (2016)
8. Fridrich, J.: Sensor defects in digital image forensic. In: Sencar, H., Memon, N. (eds.) Digital Image Forensics. There is More to a Picture than Meets the Eye, pp. 179–218. Springer, New York (2013). https://doi.org/10.1007/978-1-4614-0757-7_6
9. Gloe, T., Böhme, R.: The Dresden Image Database for benchmarking digital image forensics. J. Digit. Forensic Pract. 3(2–4), 150–159 (2010)
10. Gloe, T., Kirchner, M., Winkler, A., Böhme, R.: Can we trust digital image forensics? In: 15th International Conference on Multimedia (2007)
11. Gloe, T., Pfennig, S., Kirchner, M.: Unexpected artefacts in PRNU-based camera identification: a 'Dresden Image Database' case-study. In: ACM Multimedia and Security Workshop (2012)
12. Goljan, M., Fridrich, J.: Sensor-fingerprint based identification of images corrected for lens distortion. In: Memon, N., Alattar, A.M., Delp, E.J. (eds.) Media Watermarking, Security, and Forensics. Proceedings of SPIE, vol. 8303, p. 83030H (2012)
13. Goljan, M., Fridrich, J., Chen, M.: Defending against fingerprint-copy attack in sensor-based camera identification. IEEE Trans. Inf. Forensics Secur. (TIFS) 6(1), 227–236 (2011)
14. Goljan, M., Fridrich, J., Filler, T.: Large scale test of sensor fingerprint camera identification. In: Delp, E.J., Dittmann, J., Memon, N., Wong, P.W. (eds.) Media Forensics and Security. Proceedings of SPIE, vol. 7254, p. 72540I (2009)
15. Gretton, A., Fukumizu, K., Teo, C.H., Song, L., Schölkopf, B., Smola, A.J.: A kernel statistical test of independence. In: Advances in Neural Information Processing Systems (NIPS) (2008)
16. Karaküçük, A., Dirik, A.E.: Adaptive photo-response non-uniformity noise removal against image source attribution. Digit. Investig. 12, 66–76 (2015)
17. Kirchner, M., Böhme, R.: Synthesis of color filter array pattern in digital images. In: Delp, E.J., Dittmann, J., Memon, N., Wong, P.W. (eds.) Media Forensics and Security. Proceedings of SPIE, vol. 7254, p. 72540K (2009)

18. Li, S., Karrenbauer, A., Saupe, D., Kuo, C.C.J.: Recovering missing coefficients in DCT-transformed images. In: IEEE International Conference on Image Processing (ICIP) (2011)
19. Lukáš, J., Fridrich, J., Goljan, M.: Digital camera identification from sensor pattern noise. IEEE Trans. Inf. Forensics Secur. (TIFS) 1(2), 205–214 (2006)
20. Marra, F., Roli, F., Cozzolino, D., Sansone, C., Verdoliva, L.: Attacking the triangle test in sensor-based camera identification. In: IEEE International Conference on Image Processing (ICIP) (2014)
21. Mohanty, M., Zhang, M., Asghar, M.R., Russello, G.: e-PRNU: Encrypted domain PRNU-based camera attribution for preserving privacy. IEEE Trans. Dependable Secur. Comput. (TDSC) (2019)
22. Quiring, E., Arp, D., Rieck, K.: Forgotten siblings: unifying attacks on machine learning and digital watermarking. In: IEEE European Symposium on Security and Privacy (EuroS&P) (2018)
23. Quiring, E., Kirchner, M.: Fragile sensor fingerprint camera identification. In: IEEE International Workshop on Information Forensics and Security (WIFS) (2015)
24. Reininger, R.C., Gibson, J.D.: Distributions of the two-dimensional DCT coefficients for images. IEEE Trans. Commun. 31(6), 835–839 (1983)
25. Stamm, M.C., Liu, K.J.R.: Anti-forensics of digital image compression. IEEE Trans. Inf. Forensics Secur. (TIFS) 6(3), 1050–1065 (2011)
26. Valsesia, D., Coluccia, G., Bianchi, T., Magli, E.: User authentication via PRNU-based physical unclonable functions. IEEE Trans. Inf. Forensics Secur. (TIFS) 12(8), 1941–1956 (2017)
27. Widrow, B., Kollár, I.: Quantization Noise. Cambridge University Press, Cambridge (2008)

Attacking Speaker Recognition Systems with Phoneme Morphing

Henry Turner$^{(\boxtimes)}$, Giulio Lovisotto, and Ivan Martinovic

University of Oxford, Oxford, UK
{henry.turner,giulio.lovisotto,ivan.martinovic}@cs.ox.ac.uk

Abstract. As voice interfaces become more widely available they increasingly implement speaker recognition, to provide both personalized functionalities and security via authentication. In this paper, we present a method that transforms the voice of one person so that it resembles the voice of a victim, such that it can be used to deceive speaker recognition systems into believing an utterance was spoken by the victim. The transformation only requires short pieces of audio recordings from the source and victim voices, and does not require specific words to be spoken by the victim. We show that the attack can be improved by using a population of source voices and we provide a metric to identify promising source voices, from within such a population.

We evaluate our attack along a set of dimensions, including: varying quantity, quality and types of known victim audio, verification and identification systems, white- and black-box models and both over-the-wire and over-the-air access. We test the audio transformation on two different proprietary models: (i) the Azure Speaker Recognition API and (ii) the Siri voice activation of an Apple iPhone, showing that individuals can easily be impersonated by obtaining as little as one minute of their audio, even when such audio is recorded in noisy conditions. With attempts from only three source voices, our attack achieves success rates of over 40% in the weakest assumption scenario against the Azure Verification API and rates of over 80% in all scenarios against Siri.

Keywords: Voice conversion · Speaker · Authentication · Biometrics

1 Introduction

As voice interfaces become more popular, voice-based devices are now adding speaker recognition to their capabilities, so they can understand both *what* has been said (speech recognition) and *who* has said it (speaker recognition). Speaker recognition allows for customized functionality, as well as authentication, removing the burden of other less user-friendly authentication approaches (e.g., PINs or passwords). Nowadays, speaker recognition is available in commercial products such as Google Home [16] or Apple Siri [2]. Additionally, speaker recognition is increasingly been deployed for over the phone authentication by companies in the financial sector (e.g., HSBC [18], Lloyds Bank [25]).

© Springer Nature Switzerland AG 2019
K. Sako et al. (Eds.): ESORICS 2019, LNCS 11735, pp. 471–492, 2019.
https://doi.org/10.1007/978-3-030-29959-0_23

Recent studies have focused on analyzing the security of speech recognition systems [7,8,33,35,36], often with attacks which use adversarial machine learning techniques to craft malicious audio. These studies have shown that many voice assistants are vulnerable to these types of attacks, and that commands can inconspicuously be injected or hidden in other sounds, such as songs [35]. However, as speaker recognition becomes widely available and used for sensitive functions, additional investigations are needed to assess its security guarantees. When targeting a speaker recognition system, rather than inconspicuously inject voice commands, the adversary's goal is to unlock access to a voice-protected device by replaying audio that resembles the device owner's voice.

Previous work in this area focused on creating complex and expensive models for synthesizing audio or converting one's own voice into the voice of the victim [10,13,19,21,26,31]. Generally the training audio is collected in a well-isolated studio environment and the ultimate goal of the generated audio is to deceive a human listener. However, from an adversarial perspective, obtaining audio of spoken utterances could be suspicious or unfeasible for certain victims. The unavailability of long samples of victim audio brings two limitations in re-creating the victim's voice: (i) models based on parallel datasets for voice conversion can not be used and (ii) synthesizers or conversion methods based on deep models do not reach sufficient accuracy, as intra-user variability is not efficiently captured. A detailed analysis of related work is given in Sect. 2.

In this paper, we present a voice conversion attack that manipulates individual phonemes from a source voice into sounding like those of a target voice. This attack is not aimed at deceiving humans, but at deceiving speaker recognition systems. The transformation is based on morphing phoneme-related features in the Mel frequency cepstrum space [27], which is a representation of sound commonly used as feature inputs for voice recognition systems. Our transformation only requires knowledge of the number of phonemes in the target language and a piece of audio from the victim. We show that such an attack can be improved by using a population of candidate source voices (easily available online), as some voices are better transformed into others. We provide a method of identifying which source voices are likely to succeed in impersonating a target voice.

We evaluate the transformation on different speaker recognition systems. We use a white-box model to learn how to improve the voice conversion and we show that the attack can successfully fool black-box models in both *over-the-wire* and *over-the-air* access. We conduct our evaluation across a different set of assumptions for the adversary, including (i) amount of known audio and (ii) recording noise. We further show that our transformation can be used on verification systems unlocked with a *text-dependent* keyphrase, as well as *text-independent* voice identification systems.

The main contributions of this paper are the following:

- We propose a new voice conversion method based on the creation of a phoneme mapping function between a source and a target voice in MFCC space, which only requires knowledge of the language's number of phonemes.

- We analyze the effectiveness of the transformation across different assumptions regarding quantity and quality of training data, identification and verification use-cases. We show that only few authentication attempts can deceive the proprietary models of the Azure Speaker Recognition APIs.
- We further test the attack over-the-air on the Siri assistant of Apple iOS, achieving success rates of over 50% with only one authentication attempt in the worst case.

2   Related Work

Prior work in this area focused on two different domains. The first consists of attacks on speech recognition, where the aim is to inconspicuously inject malicious commands into voice assistants (e.g., "delete my contact list"). This is done both by generating new audio that is inaudible to the user or by modifying existing audio in a way that is non-perceivable by a human. The second domain consists of attacks on speaker recognition, where an adversary attempts to impersonate a victim's voice. Impersonation attacks are particularly threatening in verification (authentication) scenarios, where a system uses voice-based access control, but can also be dangerous in identification use-cases, where an adversary could fool the system about their identity. We cover both domains in this section.

2.1   Speech Recognition

For speech recognition, several works attempted to create inconspicuous ways to embed or hide speech commands which trigger specific actions on voice assistants. Vaidya et al. [33] introduced obfuscated voice commands, which are recognized and executed by voice systems but unintelligible to a human listener. This is done through repeated application of a Mel Frequency Cepstrum Coefficient (MFCC) based audio mangler, which applies and then inverts the MFCC transform. This work is extended in [7], showing that an attacker can perform this attack even in more realistic conditions, such as black-box models, and in the presence of background noise, while retaining the non-intelligibility of the commands for humans. Yuan et al. [35] demonstrate a technique which allows an adversary to embed speech commands into songs, which allows an attack to be conducted in front of a victim with greater ease. In [8] this is extended to allow any pre-chosen command to be embedded into a given audio sample, such that a human does not perceive the command. This allows a human to hear one utterance but the system to believe it is has heard something entirely different. A slightly different approach is taken in [36], where Zhang et al. demonstrate embedding commands entirely in (human-)inaudible frequency range, but which are still accepted by voice assistants.

Our Work. As opposed to speech recognition, we specifically focus on the security of speaker recognition systems. This means that our work is related to speech recognition, but does not overlap directly. An adversary could design a way to combine our method with a speech recognition attack to bypass impersonation while still achieving inconspicuous malicious transcription. Compared to speech recognition attacks, we **do not require** the audio to have non-intelligible or inaudible properties. Since the adversary wants to be able to interact with the voice-based system directly to perform some malicious activity, they require temporary unsupervised access to the device, and as such nothing is gained by the audio being imperceptible. We also retain the goal of **correct transcription**, so that keyphrases are still accepted by the system.

2.2   Speaker Recognition

The goal of attacks on speaker recognition systems is to impersonate users, that is to create audio that is incorrectly interpreted by the system as belonging to a specific user. Attacks against speaker recognition systems can be divided into four categories: (i) *impersonation*, (ii) *replay*, (iii) *speech synthesis* and (iv) *voice conversion* [14]. In *mimicry* attacks, human impersonators attempt to alter their own voice in order to mimic another person's voice [23]. Replay attacks involve replaying (with a loudspeaker) audio samples to the system, either in whole or by merging parts of other audio files together [24]. Speech synthesis aims to create a model for generating completely artificial speech. In [10] De Leon et al. proposed a technique based on a Hidden Markov Model (HMM), which adapts a background model in order to derive an audio synthesizer. The analysis show that such a synthesizer can impersonate users in the well known Gaussian Mixture Model (GMM) [3] 81% of the time.

The method presented in this paper falls in the voice conversion category, where the goal is to convert the perceived speaker identity of a given utterance. Many works have addressed the problem of voice conversion and recently the popularity of the Voice Conversion Challenge [32] gave way to a numerous set of works [13,19,21,26,31]. Approaches such as [26] use a probabilistic mapping of vocal tract models to convert between speakers, where as [21] use a GMM trained on aligned audio from victim and attacker, which can then be applied to the source audio.

Both speech synthesis and voice conversion approaches have been shown to achieve good results in re-creating a person's voice. However, these approaches are designed for non-adversarial scenarios, where large volumes of high-quality audio for each speaker are available to train models. Additionally, voice conversion approaches often require labelled *parallel* training data: both source and target speaker uttering the same known sentences, so that a model can be trained by mapping them on a one-to-one basis. Furthermore, these approaches are generally targeted at fooling human listeners, imposing many constraints on how realistic the voice sounds.

Our Work. We address the voice conversion problem from an adversarial perspective, which brings **limited availability of audio**: both in quantity and in quality (noise). Additionally, we focus on **fooling systems** rather than human listeners. Fooling a human listener would not provide an advantage to the adversary in our case (the system is unsupervised at the time of the attack).

Fig. 1. Threat model. The adversary initially records audio of the victim. This is used to create a transformation, which is applied to some source audio and replayed to the device (e.g., with a loudspeaker).

In our approach we learn a phoneme-specific transformation from a source voice to the victim voice, guaranteeing that each phoneme from the source can be transformed to a similarly-sounding phoneme for the victim. This allows the correct transcription to be retained for the speech recognition, while at the same time transforms the source voice so that it resembles the victim's voice. The method works with limited amounts of text-independent voice data, and even in the presence of noise, and only requires knowledge of the approximate number of phonemes in a language. The goal of our analysis is to evaluate the security of speaker recognition systems in realistic threat scenarios.

3   Threat Model

The phases of an attack are shown in Fig. 1. The adversary first records the victim speaking and then constructs a mapping function between another individual's voice and the victim's voice. They then use this function to transform the other individual's voice into the victim's and replays the transformed audio into the system, with the goal of impersonating the victim.

Background. Users interact with a speaker recognition system, either verification or identification. In the case of verification, the system requires users to utter a specific sentence, hereafter *keyphrase*, and uses such utterance to recognize users, in either authentication or identification use cases. As an example, a laptop could use speaker authentication with the "Hey Siri, it's me" keyphrase in order to be unlocked (rather than typing a password). The keyphrase could either be fixed or contain a challenge, such as asking to speak today's date or utter a set of numbers being shown on the screen at the time of authentication.

Capabilities. Adversaries can: (i) record audio of the victims talking, (ii) replay audio to the voice recognition system (e.g., with a loudspeaker).

Knowledge. Following from the capabilities, adversaries have some knowledge of the victims voice trait (from recording audio of them talking). Additionally, the adversary has a set of audio samples containing spoken words for a population of individuals. This can be achieved easily by utilizing free speech datasets such as VoxForge [34]. However, adversaries are limited along the following dimensions:

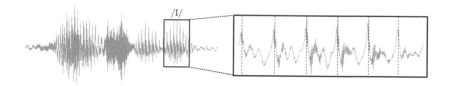

Fig. 2. Sound wave of the utterance "Hey Siri". Within the same phoneme (/ɪ/) a wave pattern repeats itself, depending on the fundamental frequency of voice [15].

1. *black-box model*: adversaries do not know what voice processing and recognition algorithms are in place, and thus cannot optimize their attack for a specific method.
2. *recorded utterances*: adversaries cannot record victims uttering the exact keyphrase required for authentication, nor its individual words (not all of them). This is straightforward when the keyphrase includes a challenge, but also reasonable when it does not. Keyphrases are typically designed so that they do not occur in normal day-to-day speech, to avoid unwanted authentications.
3. *audio quality*: adversaries may only be able to record audio in public settings. This means that the recorded audio would have poor quality, as it involves a combination of (i) background noise, (ii) recording from a distance, (iii) recorded audio being emitted by loudspeakers rather than victims themselves.
4. *audio duration*: adversaries can only record the victim for a limited amount of time before raising suspicion. Consequently, they might have a weak representation of victims vocal characteristics, increasing modelling difficulty.

Scenarios. Following from the considerations of the previous paragraphs, we define three different scenarios that represent realistic attack situations.

– *Conference*: the attacker is attending a conference where the victim is giving a talk, and records the victim speaking during their talk. The recorded audio is not of the victim directly, but is a recording of the room speakers connected to the victim's microphone.
– *Cafe*: the attacker is at the same cafe where the victim is enjoying a coffee while having a conversation with other people. The victim's audio is recorded from a distance and is subject to background noise.
– *Ideal*: the attacker obtains high quality audio of the victim from the internet and uses it for their attack. The audio is extracted from a source such as a podcast, or a video of the victim speaking.

All attackers finalize the attack by playing their generated audio to the device. If attackers want to avoid detection, depending on the scenario, they can wait for the device to be left unattended before replaying audio to the device. These adversaries guide our experimental design. We further discuss how we model them in Sect. 5.

4   Attack Method

Overview. We construct the attack using the concept of phonemes, which are the individually perceivable units of sound in spoken language. We show in Fig. 2 how phonemes appear in an audio wave of a spoken word: each phoneme is composed of a repeating wave pattern. The attack aims to transform each of these phoneme-related patterns so that they closely resemble the victim's. This is done by deriving a function which maps phonemes spoken by a known speaker into phonemes that resembles those spoken by the victim. The strength of using such an approach is that all knowledge requirements about the structure of the spoken language are removed. This way, an attacker can also afford to ignore the relationship between these phonemes and utterances (i.e., whether a particular phoneme occurs in an audio sample). In fact, no phoneme extraction is necessary, knowing the approximate number of phonemes for the language is sufficient (in spoken British English there are 44 phonemes [17]). We construct the mapping in the MFCC domain, as opposed to modifying the raw audio wave. We show that mapping the outputs of the MFCC extraction and reconstructing the audio wave afterwards is sufficient for the transformation to work.

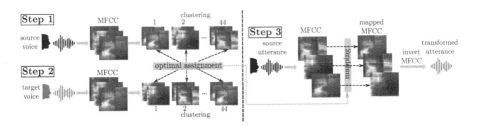

Fig. 3. Steps to craft transformed utterances. In the first and second step the adversary computes the optimal mapping between the source and the target phonemes, in the third step they use the mapping to transform a specific utterance from the source.

4.1   Formulation

Given two speakers S and T (*source* and *target*) and a set of known audio recordings produced by them s_i, t_j, the transformation works as follows. Initially, the audio recordings are transformed into the MFCC spectrum, for a single audio file a we obtain a set of samples (due to the windowing process) as follows:

$$\text{MFCC}(a) = \{m_0^{(a)}, \ldots, m_n^{(a)}\} \tag{1}$$

where the number of points n depends on the audio length. We extract MFCC features for all audio recordings a_i belonging to a speaker. Then we use K-means clustering, where K is the number of phonemes in the language, ($K = 44$ in our case) on all the samples (separately for T and S) to infer the clusters $C_k^{(S)}, C_k^{(T)}$, where each cluster represents a phoneme. With the clusters, we also obtain the cluster centroids $C_S = \{s_1, \ldots, s_K\}$ and $C_T = \{t_1, \ldots, t_K\}$.

Afterwards, we compute an optimal mapping between individual cluster centroids from the two sets C_S, C_T. We formulate the optimization as an assignment problem, which we solve with the Hungarian algorithm [22]. We use l_1 as the distance function between two centroids. The output of the mapping consists in a set of pairs (k, j) where $k, j \in \{1, \ldots, K\}$ and the pair (k, j) indicates that points belonging to cluster k for speaker S should be transformed into points belonging to cluster j for the speaker T to maximize the similarity.

We implement the above transformation using a linear shift in MFCC space. Given $m_i^{(a)} \in C_k^{(S)}$ and given the optimal mapping for cluster k, pair (k, j), we compute a transformed sample $o_i^{(a)}$ as follows:

$$o_i^{(a)} = m_i^{(a)} + t_j - s_k. \tag{2}$$

For an entire audio recording a, Eq. 2 is applied sequentially to each sample $m_i^{(a)}$ in MFCC(a), resulting in a set of transformed samples $\{o_0^{(a)}, \ldots, o_n^{(a)}\}$. Finally we invert the MFCC transformation using the method shown by Ellis [12], to give the transformed audio a^*:

$$a^* = \text{MFCC}^{-1}(\{o_0^{(a)}, \ldots, o_n^{(a)}\}) \tag{3}$$

4.2 Attack Execution

There are three steps to generate the attack audio, shown in Fig. 3. In the first step, adversaries compute the phoneme clustering for a source voice, which can be their own. In the second step, they obtain a recording of the target's voice and compute clustering for this data. Immediately afterwards, the adversary can compute the optimal phoneme mappings between the source and the target clusters. In the final step the adversary selects a source utterance, usually the keyphrase or a voice command used by the system, applies the transformation in Eq. 2 and creates a transformed utterance audio to be played to the system. The first step can always be computed *offline*, that is before the adversary selects a target, while the remaining steps depend on when the adversary is able to record the victim speaking and when they obtain physical access to the system.

Choice of Source Speaker. We found that the selection of source speaker greatly affects the quality of the transformation, meaning that certain voices can be more accurately mapped to certain targets. We therefore extend our attack to consider a population of individuals as sources, that the adversary can obtain by downloading online voice datasets, or recruiting a population of people to provide a set of potential source voices. This way, the adversary can compute mappings for each individual in the population, and later has several candidates to choose as the source utterance in the last phase of the attack (see Fig. 3). As it is reasonable for adversaries to limit the number of *failed attempts* (i.e., playing an attack utterance and being rejected or wrongly classified by the system), one strategy is to estimate the chance of successful impersonation based on the mapping output.

Following these considerations, given a mapping composed of a set of pairs $(k_1, j_1), \ldots, (k_K, j_K)$ we use the sum of the L_1 norm of paired cluster centroids as an indicator:

$$\epsilon = \sum_{i=1}^{K} ||s_{k_i} - t_{j_i}||_1 \tag{4}$$

Intuitively, the lower the distance (error, ϵ) between the mapped clusters, the more accurate the transformation becomes. Therefore, whenever the adversary carries out an attack they sort the possible source voices based on increasing ϵ and use them as sources in this order.

5   Experimental Design

In this section we describe our data collection method, then present how we model the adversaries of Sect. 3 and describe the target systems considered for the evaluation.

5.1   Data Collection

Collection Procedure. We collected audio data from 20 male native English speakers, recruited mainly through social media and mailing lists. Participants were mostly from southern England, and aged between 18 and 30. Recording sessions took place in an isolated room in a university building, taking approximately 30 min. Recordings were conducted using an AmazonBasics Portable USB Condenser Microphone, connected to a Windows laptop. Recordings used the inbuilt "Voice Recorder" software. Participants were instructed to keep the distance between themselves and the microphone between 5 and 15 cm. The data collection was approved by an ethical review board at our University, Reference: SSD/CUREC1A_CS_C1A_18_032. Participants were informed of the purpose of the study and informed consent was obtained from them prior to commencing any recording sessions. As voice is personally identifying information, we do not publicly share the voice dataset.

Transcripts. The participants were required to utter sentences from four different categories: (i) conference transcripts, (ii) conversation transcripts, (iii) commands and (iv) enrollment transcripts. Each utterance source is designed to re-create the scenarios mentioned in Sect. 3. The enrollment and commands transcripts are identical for every participant, while for conference and conversation, to increase the dissimilarity of spoken words, we randomly assign one out of five transcripts to each user[1]. Transcripts were split into utterances of roughly equal length, with an utterance typically containing a single sentence.

---

[1] Transcript summaries are available in Appendix A.

5.2 Adversary Modelling

Conference Attacker. This attacker only obtains audio samples coming from utterances from the conference transcripts. In order to recreate the "conference" effect (the recorded audio coming from distant loudspeakers), we apply the following processing to the original audio. First we apply the Freeverb [30] algorithm to generate reverberation in the audio (following *data augmentation* practices used in Kaldi [29]). To simulate recording from a distance, we apply a low-pass filter (with cutoff at 8KHz) to attenuate higher frequencies, and scale the amplitude of the signal to reduce the volume.

Cafe Attacker. This attacker only obtains audio samples coming from utterances from the conversation transcripts. In order to recreate the "cafe" effect (recording from a distance plus background chatter and noise), we apply the same processing used for Conference Attacker (with less reverberation). Additionally, we mix the audio file with common cafe background noise[2] (the overlaid noise segment is chosen randomly per sample).

Ideal Attacker. This attacker uses the clean recorded audio from the data collection, with no post-processing or noise applied to it. The Ideal Attacker represents a worst-case scenario where the adversary obtains good quality audio samples, and we use it as an indication of the empirical upper bound for the attacker's success rate.

Audio Duration. In order to evaluate the effect of different amounts of audio on the attack success, we model two different audio durations in our experiments: *all* and *one minute*. The *all* case represents the case where we use all audio collected for a given scenario (either conference or cafe). The audio quantity averages 317.7 s for the Conference Attacker and 330.5 s for the Cafe Attacker, including pre- and post- speech silence. Ideal Attacker uses all the audio available for that victim, giving an average of 648.2 s per victim. In the *one minute* case, we randomly sample utterances from the related transcripts until we reach a cumulative total of 60 s of audio, including silence parts. We choose to systematically analyze each combination of these, creating six different scenarios (three attackers, two audio lengths).

5.3 Target Systems

We evaluate our experiments against speaker recognition systems, both in the identification and verification use-case. We use three different systems for the evaluation: (i) Spear [20] (ii) Azure Speaker Recognition APIs[3] and (iii) Apple iOS Siri ("Hey Siri"). The Spear toolbox is a set of libraries used to train and evaluate speaker recognition models, which we download and train locally with the VoxForge [34] dataset. Meanwhile, Azure Speaker Recognition only offers

---

[2] https://youtube.com/watch?v=BOdLmxy06H0.
[3] https://azure.microsoft.com/en-us/services/cognitive-services/.

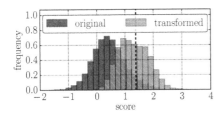

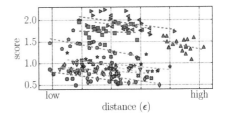

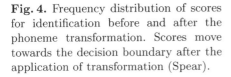

Fig. 4. Frequency distribution of scores for identification before and after the phoneme transformation. Scores move towards the decision boundary after the application of transformation (Spear).

Fig. 5. Similarity score between transformed audio and target user templates, computed by the classifier, as a function of distance between voices. Reduced distance leads to an increase in score (Spear).

online (subscription-based) API access. Microsoft reported that the verification API has performance "competitive with the best published number" and that the identification API has "high precision (above 90%) [which] is obtained at around a 5% rejection rate" [28][4]. Apple iOS Siri provides a real world test of the attack against a widely deployed system, which is used for accessing functions on iOS devices. Apple reports that the end-to-end performance of the system has an imposter acceptance rate of 3.2% [2] and an EER of 4.3% on the speaker recognition task alone (i.e not including keyphrase matching). In all cases, we treat the system as a black-box model: we never change nor adapt the method of Sect. 4.

6   Experimental Evaluation

In this section we first show some preliminary results on the Spear system, then show the results on the Azure Speaker API and finally on the Apple iPhone Siri.

6.1   Spear Toolkit

Setup. We use the Spear toolkit to train a GMM-based classifier, with 20 MFCC features plus their first and second derivatives as input features. Throughout our Spear experiments we use audio data obtained from the VoxForge [34] database. Specifically, we use data from users who define themselves as speaking "American English" and take the 63 users with the longest total amount of recorded audio. The users are then randomly split into three groups of 15 plus one of 18: (i) one group for training the background model, (ii) one for refining the model parameters (development set), (iii) one enrolled into the system (test set), and we use the larger (iv) fourth group as voice sources for the attack.

---

[4] We conducted our experiments against the Microsoft APIs in January 2019.

The classifier decides whether an input audio file belongs to certain enrolled user by computing a similarity score between the audio and the enrolled template for every user (identification), with larger scores being closer matches. We compute the EER on the development set by varying the score threshold for acceptance, we find EER to be 7% corresponding to a decision boundary threshold of 1.38. We use the learned threshold on the (unseen) test set to compute the system recognition rates, which leads to a false accept rate of 3.7% and a false reject rate of 0%. Since we are using Spear as a baseline system to quickly evaluate the attack, we only consider the Ideal attacker in this section.

Results. Figure 4 shows two frequency distributions of distance scores from the acceptance decision boundary (vertical dashed line, set at the EER). The original distribution corresponds to distances obtained by testing an impersonation attack with non-modified voice samples (zero-effort attack), all possible source-target pairs (15×18) are used for the visualization. The transformed distribution shows the distance scores for the same samples, but when applying the transformation of Sect. 4, no population is used in this case. Figure 4 shows that applying the transformation greatly increases the likelihood of the sample lying above the decision threshold and therefore being accepted.

Figure 5 shows how the mapping accuracy affects the success rate of the attack. The figure reports the distance from the decision boundary (score) of transformed samples, as a function of the error ϵ measuring the mapping (in)accuracy (see Sect. 4.2): lower error is correlated with higher matching score ($r = .48$). In Fig. 5, each marker identifies all the data points related to a particular source voice (i.e., for source voice i, each $i \rightarrow j$ transformation with j being a target voice). For each source, we fit a linear regression curve to highlight this trend and we can see that as the distance (error) ϵ increases, the score of transformed samples decreases. Figure 5 also shows how some victim voices are more vulnerable to being impersonated than others, with clusters of higher scoring points belonging to some victims. In the next section we build on these results to evaluate the attack against the Azure APIs.

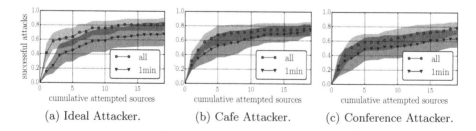

(a) Ideal Attacker.   (b) Cafe Attacker.   (c) Conference Attacker.

Fig. 6. Results of the different attackers on ASV, considering different amounts of audio. Shaded areas show results within one standard deviation, averaged over the four keyphrases.

6.2 Azure Speaker Verification

Setup. The idea behind this experiment is to see whether the attack can be successfully conducted against a commercially available API, with a proprietary model for speaker verification. The Azure Speaker Verification API (hereafter ASV) is text-dependent and has a set of keyphrases that can be used with it. We collected audio of five of these keyphrases, which we require each participant to speak four times. Each user is enrolled using four samples of a given phrase (ASV requires at least three samples). There are no parameters within ASV to modify its performance, and as such no way to adjust any thresholds associated with acceptance or rejection[5].

We generate attack samples for these keyphrases using each of our participants as a victim, and using all the remaining participants as source voices, for each of our scenarios in turn. As we have four repetitions of each keyphrase, the attacker performs four authentication attempts for one source before moving to the next source. We submit each of these attack samples to ASV and receive a reject/accept response. Across all scenarios we create and evaluate a total of 38,400 attack samples, which we use to evaluate the performance of our attack.

Table 1. Percentage of successful attacks using up to three source voices on ASV, computed for all scenarios and keyphrases.

Keyphrase	Ideal		Conference		Cafe	
	1 min	all	1 min	all	1 min	all
KP_1:"my voice is stronger than passwords"	26.3%	52.6%	47.4%	57.9%	42.1%	57.9%
KP_2:"my password is not your business"	68.4%	94.7%	84.2%	89.5%	89.5%	89.5%
KP_3:"apple juice tastes funny after toothpaste"	21.1%	42.1%	15.8%	31.6%	21.1%	42.1%
KP_4:"you can activate security system now"	63.2%	73.7%	31.6%	52.6%	47.4%	73.7%

Results. Table 1 shows the results of verification experiments, for each scenario and keyphrase. The values in Table 1 are the percentages of successful impersonation attacks, which are calculated in the following way: the adversary attempts impersonation with the first three sources in the ϵ-ranked list (see Sect. 4), if any of these are successful then we count this as a successful attack.

There is significant variability in the results between different keyphrases: KP_2 obtains the highest success rate on average (85%), while KP_3 performs the lowest (28%). This might be related to the mapping accuracy of the phonemes that form these utterances, which degrades when some phonemes are underrepresented (i.e., they occur in low number) in the known victim audio. For example, the phonemes [dʒ], [ʊ] and [θ] all occur in KP_3, and are the 7th, 4th and 3rd least common phonemes respectively [6], and therefore likely to be

---

[5] We had to remove one phrase, "Houston we have had a problem", as participants spoke the phrase as "Houston we have a problem", a popular misconception.

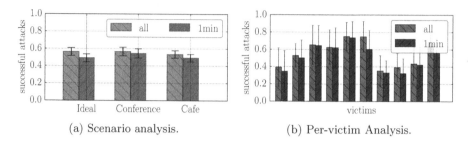

(a) Scenario analysis.   (b) Per-victim Analysis.

Fig. 7. Average successful impersonations on ASI. Results show that changes in audio quantity and quality only have small effects on success rate. Plots show the successful attacks for each scenario.

under represented. We see differing success rates across scenarios and amount of known audio, with the one minute audio scenario performing consistently worse (−16%) than the all audio scenario. Ideal Attacker performs the best, but even the noisy audio of Conference and Cafe Attacker achieves high success rates.

Figure 6 shows the cumulative successful attacks as the adversary attempts impersonation with each source voice in his dataset (sources are ranked by ϵ). Unexpectedly, Cafe and Conference attacker do not seem to greatly suffer from the additional audio noise in comparison to Ideal. This suggests that even noisy recordings of the victim audio might carry sufficient information about his vocal tracts and further confirms that most of the distinctiveness of one's voice comes from lower frequencies, which best survive noise during the recording. The plots additionally show how one minute of audio is also sufficient (though with a slight decrease in success rate when compared to all audio) to re-create one's voice. The curve slope indicates that the ranking of possible sources brings a greater percentage of successes in the beginning, where promising sources are tested first. We can see that at around three attempted sources (corresponding to 12 authentication attempts), the adversary can get up to 60% success rate depending on the scenario. Even if there are only marginal increments in the successful attacks after testing 15 sources, using a larger population of sources would increase overall attack effectiveness, as this increases the likelihood of having promising source voices, which can be mapped accurately to the victim.

6.3 Azure Speaker Identification

Setup. The Azure Speaker Identification API (hereafter ASI) is text-independent and requires a set of users to be enrolled, which are candidate users for who is speaking. In this case, enrollment requires a minimum of 30 s of audio per speaker, once silence is removed. To enroll users, we use audio specifically collected for this purpose, enrolling half of our participants in the system (see Appendix A for details). This gives us 10 potential victims, and 10 attackers, for a total of 100 source-victim pairs.

Table 2. Percentage of incorrect and *empty* responses for the experiment on ASI, for each attacker and audio duration. ASI returns *empty* when the provided audio does not match any of the enrolled users. We report Misclassified whenever the returned identity does not match the target victim.

	Ideal		Conference		Cafe	
	1 min	all	1 min	all	1 min	all
Misclassified	31.1%	27.6%	28.1%	26.4%	31.9%	29.2%
None	19.9%	16.0%	17.4%	16.9%	19.0%	17.3%

ASI accepts an audio sample as input and replies with the inferred identity from the list of the 10 enrolled users, or an *empty* reply when an audio sample does not match any of them. It is not possible to adjust any threshold for ASI, and as such there is no way of adjusting the threshold for when empty set is returned. We send all command utterances that have been transformed between a particular source and victim to ASI, but we concatenate audio files together into groups of four to obtain audio samples of approximately 8 seconds. This is because ASI is designed for longer audio samples, and without this concatenation the system returns none, as the samples are too short to make a decision. In total we submit 5,400 requests to ASI to conduct our experiments.

Results. Figure 7a shows the overall success rate for ASI for the three attackers and the two audio length combinations. In this use case each success corresponds to a submitted audio sample that is identified by the system as belonging to the victim. We see that the performance is broadly consistent across the scenarios, with a slight worsening of the recognition rates for the Cafe Attacker in particular (though not statistically significant, averaged over the 100 source-victim pairs) The performance slightly decreases in the one minute of audio case, but again with a minimal effect in the overall success.

Interestingly our results also reveal more information about ASI and its sensitivity. Table 2 shows that for all scenarios ASI was more likely to assign a speaker to an incorrect label than it was to return the empty user classification. This suggests that the decision boundaries across different users are not very conservative and that generally they can not deal well with outliers.

Figure 7b shows how the successful attacks distribute over different victims. The plot highlights that certain voices are more vulnerable to this type of attack than others: comparing the hardest to attack with the easiest to attack victim we get a difference of around 40% in the success rate. Similar uneven distributions of rates have been noticed before in previous work [1,11]. This suggests that some voices might be inherently harder to replicate, however, in our data, this might be due to a sample bias: some voices might significantly differ from our "average voice". A larger dataset would be required to investigate further whether this is the case.

6.4   Apple iPhone's Siri

Setup. In order to measure the capability of the attack of being conducted over-the-air, we test the samples against the voice activation functionality of the Apple's Siri digital assistant on an iPhone 6S, running iOS version 12.2. We use the collected voice recordings of each of our 20 participants to enrol them onto the device. For both enrolment and attacks, we use a Bose SoundLink Mini 2 speaker to replay the participants audio samples. The speaker is placed 6 cm away from the smartphone in an office environment. Initial enrolment requires the user to pronounce four different phrases, which we construct by combining the original recordings of the collected "Hey Siri" utterance with the remaining words of the enrollment utterance added by splicing together audio from other recordings of the same individual. Siri speaker recognition updates the user template after a successful access [2]. Therefore, after a successful attack we erase the user profile and repeat the enrollment process.

We test the system along the same dimensions as our previous experiments. When conducting the attack, we play a single transformed utterance of the keyphrase ("Hey Siri"), from each source voice, in the order suggested by our error function (nearest to furthest). If Siri activates, i.e., the voice is recognized as belonging to the legitimate user, we consider the attack successful and we do not present further samples. At the time of writing, Apple claimed Siri had an imposter accept rate of 3.2% [2].

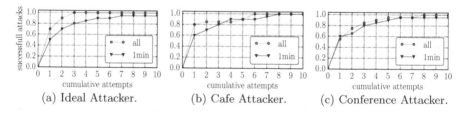

(a) Ideal Attacker.   (b) Cafe Attacker.   (c) Conference Attacker.

Fig. 8. Results for different attackers on Siri. Plots show ratio of successful impersonations as the adversary consecutively attempts the attack with different source voices.

Results. Figure 8 shows the percentage of victims successfully impersonated after a given number of attempts, for each attacker and the two known audio amounts. The results show that performance is consistent with previous experiments, in that the differing scenarios lead to slightly worse success rate, and that performance is also worse in the one minute audio case. Our results demonstrate that the Siri voice activation is easily fooled by our attack. For all scenario and amount of known audio combinations over 70% of victims can be attacked in three attempts or fewer. Excluding one individual in two of the one minute scenario-time combinations, who could not be impersonated, all other attacks were successfully conducted in 8 attempts or fewer. In our dataset an utterance of "Hey Siri" took approximately 2 seconds, meaning that in most cases 20 seconds would suffice to successfully carry the attack out.

7   Discussion

Implications. The attack presented in this paper shows that a minimal amount of voice from a victim can be sufficient for an adversary to impersonate that victim with a high success rate. The attack's only requirement is to obtain a recording of the victim talking. Sources such as social media, podcasts and recordings of public speaking events are all easily available sources of such audio. Consequently, the audio becomes even easier to gather for higher profile targets. The ease of collection of voice samples in adversarial scenarios brings an inherent security vulnerability of voice-based systems, as highlighted by our analysis. We point out this vulnerability in order to raise awareness of the limitations of such authentication mechanisms, so that they can be accounted for during the the the design of voice-based systems.

Our analysis highlights the weaknesses of voice-based authentication (and identification) in adversarial scenarios. This is not strictly due to the recognition algorithms themselves but rather to the availability and ease of collection of voice biometric samples. We point out this vulnerability in order to raise awareness to the limitations of such authentication mechanisms, so that these can be accounted for during the the design of voice-based systems.

Replay Detection. Similarly to other voice-based attacks, our method involves replaying audio to the system microphone via a speaker. This is necessary for all attacks on voice systems that use only over-the-air interaction, and do not require harder to obtain over-the-wire access. A set of works have addressed the detection of replay attacks on such systems [4,5,9,13,14,37]. Some detection techniques rely on a combination of better hardware (e.g., multiple microphones) or require additional interactions from the user. Often replay detection evolves into an arms race with the adversaries improving their audio sample to present the features required to bypass detection. This work is orthogonal to replay detection, which could be bypassed with enough investment from an attacker.

Rate-Limiting. Oftentimes in verification systems, the number of failed authentication attempts can be used to temporarily block the authentication or swap it with more secure alternatives. For example, in Apple FaceID the face recognition is disabled after five failed authentication attempts, at which point a PIN is required to unlock the phone. We find that even if the 5-attempts limit were the same for Siri, a high percentage of victims would still be attack-able (90% in the 1 min ideal scenario). Keeping the number of sequentially allowed failures low before locking the system becomes an immediate an effective way to prevent our and other population-based attacks.

8   Conclusions

In this paper, we describe a method to transform a source voice into a victim's voice to deceive speaker recognition systems. The transformation maps individual phonemes between the source and target voices and only requires knowledge of the number of language phonemes, a set of source voices (easily available online) and an audio sample of the victim speaking. Furthermore, we identify a metric for determining which voice among a group of voices is most likely to lead to a successful authentication.

We evaluate the attack under a set of scenarios that include different amounts and quality of victim audio and different systems. We test our attack on both the Azure Speaker Recognitions APIs and the Apple iOS Siri voice assistant. On Azure, for verification, we show that 12 authentication attempts are sufficient to successfully impersonate victims in 40% up to 68% of cases, using just one minute of victim audio for training, even in noisy recordings conditions. For identification, the method achieves much higher success rates reaching over 50% on average with a single attempt. We demonstrate that high success rates can be obtained even when testing the attack over-the-air on Siri: 80% of victims can be impersonated within three attempts, which correspond to only 8 s of audio in total.

Compared to previous work, these findings reveal that limited quantity and quality of audio have only limited impacts on the overall success of this attack. Given the increasing availability of potential victim's audio, our analysis highlights the vulnerability of using voice as a biometric for access control in adversarial settings, suggesting that such weakness should be included in the design phase of such systems.

Acknowledgements. This work was supported by a grant from Mastercard and the Engineering and Physical Sciences Research Council [grant numbers EP/N509711/1 and EP/P00881X/1].

A   Audio Collected

A.1   Commands

Command data was sourced as both utterances that could be presented to systems in existence, as well as commands used specifically by the Azure Speaker recognition system for verification. The utterances recorded were as follows:

1. Hey Siri (Repeated 4 times)
2. Ok Google (Repeated 4 times)
3. What is the weather like?
4. What time is it?
5. Who am I?
6. How tall is the shard?
7. My voice is stronger than passwords (Repeated 4 times)
8. My password is not your business (Repeated 4 times)
9. Apple juice tastes funny after toothpaste (Repeated 4 times)
10. Houston we have had a problem (Repeated 4 times)
11. You can activate security system now (Repeated 4 times)
12. My voice is my password (Repeated 4 times)

A.2   Conference

Conference talk transcripts were obtained from popular TED talks. The transcripts were shortened, so that they contained approximately the first 6 min of a given talk. The transcripts were then split into individual utterances, with each utterance being recorded as a separate audio file by the participant. Five different conference talk transcripts were used, which are the following:

1. Do schools kill creativity? by Sir Ken Robinson -
   www.ted.com/talks/ken_robinson_says_schools_kill_creativity/transcript
2. Your body language may shape who you are by Amy Cuddy -
   www.ted.com/talks/amy_cuddy_your_body_language_shapes_who_you_are/
   transcript
3. What makes a good life? by Robert Waldinger -
   www.ted.com/talks/robert_waldinger_what_makes_a_good_life_lessons_from_
   the_longest_study_on_happiness/transcript
4. How great leaders inspire action by Simon Sinek -
   www.ted.com/talks/simon_sinek_how_great_leaders_inspire_action/transcript
5. The power of vulnerability by Brené Brown -
   www.ted.com/talks/brene_brown_on_vulnerability/transcript

A.3   Cafe

Our conversation audio is derived from TED talks where two people are having a conversation. A single speakers audio was extracted from each transcript, and the transcript was shortened until it was approximately 6 min in length. Five different conversation transcripts were used, which were dervied from the following talks:

1. SpaceX's plan to fly you across the globe in 20 min - Gwynne Shotwell -
   https://www.ted.com/talks/gwynne_shotwell_spacex_s_plan_to_fly_you_
   across_the_globe_in_30_minutes/transcript
2. How Netflix changed entertainment - Reed Hastings -
   https://www.ted.com/talks/reed_hastings_how_netflix_changed_
   entertainment_and_where_it_s_headed/transcript
3. Mammoths resurrected, geoengineering and other thoughts from a futurist -
   Stewart Brand -
   https://www.ted.com/talks/stewart_brand_and_chris_anderson_mammoths_
   resurrected_geoengineering_and_other_thoughts_from_a_futurist/transcript
4. The future we're building and boring - Elon Musk - https://www.ted.com/
   talks/elon_musk_the_future_we_re_building_and_boring/transcript
5. What everyday citizens can do to claim power on the internet - Fadi Cehadé
   -
   https://www.ted.com/talks/fadi_chehade_what_everyday_citizens_can_do_
   to_claim_power_on_the_internet/transcript

A.4   Enrolment

Enrolment audio was used to enroll individual speakers with the Azure Speaker Recognition API for identification. Participants were asked to read the first 6 paragraphs of the speech given by UK Prime Minister David Cameron at the start of the London 2012 Olympics. The speech can be found on the UK government speeches website at the following URL: https://www.gov.uk/government/speeches/pms-speech-at-olympics-press-conference

References

1. Allix, K., Bissyandé, T.F., Klein, J., Le Traon, Y.: Are your training datasets yet relevant? In: Piessens, F., Caballero, J., Bielova, N. (eds.) ESSoS 2015. LNCS, vol. 8978, pp. 51–67. Springer, Cham (2015). https://doi.org/10.1007/978-3-319-15618-7_5
2. Apple Siri Team: Personalized Hey Siri - Apple (2018). https://machinelearning.apple.com/2018/04/16/personalized-hey-siri.html. Accessed 7 Jul 2019
3. Bimbot, F., et al.: A tutorial on text-independent speaker verification. EURASIP J. Adv. Signal Process. **2004**(4), 101962 (2004)
4. Blue, L., Abdullah, H., Vargas, L., Traynor, P.: 2MA: verifying voice commands via two microphone authentication. In: Proceedings of the 13th on Asia Conference on Computer and Communications Security, pp. 89–100. ACM (2018)
5. Blue, L., Vargas, L., Traynor, P.: Hello, is it me you're looking for?: differentiating between human and electronic speakers for voice interface security. In: Proceedings of the 11th Conference on Security & Privacy in Wireless and Mobile Networks, pp. 123–133. ACM (2018)
6. Blumeyer, D.: Relative frequencies of english phonemes (2012). https://cmloegcmluin.wordpress.com/2012/11/10/relative-frequencies-of-english-phonemes/. Accessed 27 Apr 2019
7. Carlini, N., et al.: Hidden voice commands. In: Proceedings of the 25th USENIX Security Symposium, pp. 513–530 (2016)
8. Carlini, N., Wagner, D.: Audio adversarial examples: targeted attacks on speech-to-text. In: IEEE Security and Privacy Workshops, pp. 1–7. IEEE (2018)
9. Chen, S., et al.: You can hear but you cannot steal: defending against voice impersonation attacks on smartphones. In: Proceedings of the 37th International Conference on Distributed Computing Systems, pp. 183–195. IEEE (2017)
10. De Leon, P.L., Pucher, M., Yamagishi, J., Hernaez, I., Saratxaga, I.: Evaluation of speaker verification security and detection of HMM-based synthetic speech. Transactions on Audio, Speech and Language Processing (2012)
11. Eberz, S., Rasmussen, K.B., Lenders, V., Martinovic, I.: Evaluating behavioral biometrics for continuous authentication. In: Proceedings of the 12th Asia Conference on Computer and Communications Security, pp. 386–399 (2017)
12. Ellis, D.P.W.: PLP and RASTA (and MFCC, and inversion) in Matlab (2005). http://www.ee.columbia.edu/~dpwe/resources/matlab/rastamat/. Accessed 8 Jul 2019
13. Ergünay, S.K., Khoury, E., Lazaridis, A., Marcel, S.: On the vulnerability of speaker verification to realistic voice spoofing. In: Proceedings of the 7th International Conference on Biometrics Theory, Applications and Systems, pp. 1–6. IEEE (2015)

14. Evans, N., Kinnunen, T., Yamagishi, J.: Spoofing and countermeasures for automatic speaker verification. In: Proceedings of the Annual Conference of the International Speech Communication Association pp. 925–929 (2013)
15. Fant, G.: Acoustic theory of speech production: with calculations based on X-ray studies of Russian articulations. No. 2, Walter de Gruyter (1970)
16. Google: Set up Voice Match on Google Home - Google Home Help (2018). https://support.google.com/googlehome/answer/7323910. Accessed 8 Jul 2019
17. Helland, T., Kaasa, R.: Dyslexia in english as a second language. Dyslexia 11(1), 41–60 (2005)
18. HSBC: Voice ID — HSBC UK (2018). https://www.hsbc.co.uk/1/2/voice-id. Accessed 8 Jul 2019
19. Hsu, C.C., Hwang, H.T., Wu, Y.C., Tsao, Y., Wang, H.M.: Voice conversion from non-parallel corpora using variational auto-encoder. In: Proceedings of the Signal and Information Processing Association Annual Summit and Conference, pp. 1–6. IEEE (2016)
20. Khoury, E., El Shafey, L., Marcel, S.: Spear: an open source toolbox for speaker recognition based on Bob. In: Proceedings of the International Conference on Acoustics, Speech and Signal Processing, pp. 1655–1659. IEEE (2014)
21. Kinnunen, T., Wu, Z.Z., Lee, K.A., Sedlak, F., Chng, E.S., Li, H.: Vulnerability of speaker verification systems against voice conversion spoofing attacks: the case of telephone speech. In: Proceedings of the International Conference on Acoustics, Speech and Signal Processing, pp. 4401–4404. IEEE (2012)
22. Kuhn, H.W.: The hungarian method for the assignment problem. Naval Res. Logistics Q. 2(1–2), 83–97 (1955)
23. Lau, Y.W., Tran, D., Wagner, M.: Testing voice mimicry with the YOHO speaker verification corpus. In: Proceedings of the 9th International Conference on Knowledge-Based Intelligent Information And Engineering Systems, vol. 3584, pp. 15–21 (2005)
24. Lindberg, J., Blomberg, M.: Vulnerability in speaker verification-a study of technical impostor techniques. In: Proceedings of the 6th European Conference on Speech Communication and Technology (1999)
25. Lloyds Bank: Voice ID — Lloyds Bank (2019). https://www.lloydsbank.com/contact-us/voice-id.asp. Accessed 8 Jul 2019
26. Matrouf, D., Bonastre, J.F., Fredouille, C.: Effect of speech transformation on impostor acceptance. In: Proceedings of the 31st International Conference on Acoustics Speech and Signal Processing, vol. 1. IEEE (2006)
27. Mermelstein, P.: Distance measures for speech recognition, psychological and instrumental. Pattern Recogn. Artif. Intell. 116, 374–388 (1976)
28. Microsoft ML Blog Team: Now available: Speaker & video apis from microsoft project oxford. https://blogs.technet.microsoft.com/machinelearning/2015/12/14/now-available-speaker-video-apis-from-microsoft-project-oxford/
29. Povey, D., et al.: The kaldi speech recognition toolkit. In: Proceedings of the 2011 Workshop on Automatic Speech Recognition and Understanding. IEEE (2011)
30. Smith, J.O.: Physical audio signal processing. https://ccrma.stanford.edu/~jos/pasp/Freeverb.html. Accessed 8 Jul 2019
31. Sun, L., Li, K., Wang, H., Kang, S., Meng, H.: Phonetic posteriorgrams for many-to-one voice conversion without parallel data training. In: Proceedings of the 2016 International Conference on Multimedia and Expo, pp. 1–6. IEEE (2016)
32. Toda, T., et al.: The voice conversion challenge 2016. In: Proceedings of the Annual Conference of the International Speech Communication Association (2016)

33. Vaidya, T., Zhang, Y., Sherr, M., Shields, C.: Cocaine noodles: exploiting the gap between human and machine speech recognition. In: Proceedings of the 9th USENIX Workshop on Offensive Technologies (2015)
34. Voxforge Dataset: Free speech... recognition. http://www.voxforge.org/. Accessed 8 Jul 2019
35. Yuan, X., et al.: Commandersong: a systematic approach for practical adversarial voice recognition. In: Proceedings of the 27th USENIX Security Symposium, pp. 49–64 (2018)
36. Zhang, G., Yan, C., Ji, X., Zhang, T., Zhang, T., Xu, W.: Dolphinattack: inaudible voice commands. In: Proceedings of the 24th SIGSAC Conference on Computer and Communications Security, pp. 103–117. ACM (2017)
37. Zhang, L., Tan, S., Yang, J., Chen, Y.: Voicelive: a phoneme localization based liveness detection for voice authentication on smartphones. In: Proceedings of the 23rd SIGSAC Conference on Computer and Communications Security, pp. 1080–1091. ACM (2016)

Practical Bayesian Poisoning Attacks on Challenge-Based Collaborative Intrusion Detection Networks

Weizhi Meng[1]([✉]), Wenjuan Li[1,2], Lijun Jiang[3], Kim-Kwang Raymond Choo[4], and Chunhua Su[5]

[1] Department of Applied Mathematics and Computer Science,
Technical University of Denmark, Lyngby, Denmark
weme@dtu.dk
[2] Department of Computer Science,
City University of Hong Kong, Kowloon Tong, Hong Kong
[3] Cyber Tree Research Center, Pokfulam, Hong Kong
[4] Department of Information Systems and Cyber Security,
The University of Texas at San Antonio, San Antonio, USA
[5] Division of Computer Science, University of Aizu, Aizuwakamatsu, Japan

Abstract. As adversarial techniques constantly evolve to circumvent existing security measures, an isolated, stand-alone intrusion detection system (IDS) is unlikely to be efficient or effective. Hence, there has been a trend towards developing collaborative intrusion detection networks (CIDNs), where IDS nodes collaborate and communicate with each other. Such a distributed ecosystem can achieve improved detection accuracy, particularly for detecting emerging threats in a timely fashion (before the threat becomes common knowledge). However, there are inherent limitations due to malicious insiders who can seek to compromise and poison the ecosystem. A potential mitigation strategy is to introduce a challenge-based trust mechanism, in order to identify and penalize misbehaving nodes by evaluating the satisfaction between challenges and responses. While this mechanism has been shown to be robust against common insider attacks, it may still be vulnerable to advanced insider attacks in a real-world deployment. Therefore, in this paper, we develop a collusion attack, hereafter referred to as *Bayesian Poisoning Attack*, which enables a malicious node to model received messages and to craft a malicious response to those messages whose aggregated appearance probability of normal requests is above the defined threshold. In the evaluation, we explore the attack performance under both simulated and real network environments. Experimental results demonstrate that the malicious nodes under our attack can successfully craft and send untruthful feedback while maintaining their trust values.

Keywords: Intrusion detection · Collaborative network ·
Insider threat · Bayesian Poisoning Attack ·
Challenge-based trust mechanism

© Springer Nature Switzerland AG 2019
K. Sako et al. (Eds.): ESORICS 2019, LNCS 11735, pp. 493–511, 2019.
https://doi.org/10.1007/978-3-030-29959-0_24

1 Introduction

Intrusion detection/prevention systems (IDSs/IPSs; collectively referred to as IDSs in this paper) are widely deployed in computing networks, with the purpose of identifying and isolating intrusion attempts [11,26]. Traditionally, an IDS can be classified as either *network-based (NIDS)* or *host-based (HIDS)* [29]. As the importance of cyber security is increasingly recognized by both organizations and governments, so does the sophistication of cyber attackers. For example, an isolated IDS in any organization would easily be bypassed by zero-day attacks, since they (IDS and the organization) are not able to learn from ongoing attack campaigns faced by their peers or other industry sectors, either in the same jurisdiction or any part of the world. Thus, this maximizes the impact of a cyber attack in the sense that the same exploit or vulnerability can affect tens to hundreds or thousands of IDSs and organizations. However, if we are able to learn from an ongoing attack that is faced by organization X in country Y, then the entire ecosystem would be better prepared against attackers making use of the same exploit or vulnerability.

This gives rise to collaborative intrusion detection networks (CIDNs), so that IDS nodes can collaborate and communicate with each other [5,35]. Due to its distributed architecture, insider attacks are a key threat to the ecosystem [3]. For example, in a *collusion attack*, two or more malicious nodes can collude to provide untruthful information of alarm ranking and reduce the effectiveness of alarm aggregation. Thus, we need to establish some form of robust trust mechanisms to safeguard CIDNs against insider attacks.

In the literature, challenge-based trust mechanisms (shortly *challenge mechanisms*) are a promising solution to defend CIDNs against insider attacks, by identifying malicious nodes through evaluating the satisfaction between challenges and responses [8]. More specifically, a *challenge* can contain a set of alarms asking for the severity level, and can be sent to evaluate the trustworthiness of the suspected/tested nodes. Under this mechanism, the testing node knows the severity of the alarms; thus, it can utilize the received responses to derive a trust value (e.g., satisfaction level) for the target node. Studies, such as those in [5–7], have demonstrated that the challenge-based trust mechanism can mitigate common insider attacks like collusion attacks and betrayal attacks.

However, challenge mechanisms reply on two assumptions, namely: (*assumption A1*) challenges are sent out in a way that makes it toilsome for anyone to distinguish the challenges from normal messages; and (*assumption A2*) malicious nodes always send feedback contrary to its truthful judgment. In practice, however, malicious nodes may act more dynamically and have a complex behavior [8]. For example, malicious nodes may act faithfully most of the times and only untruthfully on some occasions (e.g., targeting specific events or systems). Therefore, existing challenge mechanisms may not be able to mitigate advanced insider attacks. For instance, Li et al. [16] developed the *passive message fingerprint attack (PMFA)* to distinguish challenges from normal requests; thus, circumventing the challenge-based trust mechanism. However, this attack can be mitigated by controlling the timing of sending normal requests.

Motivation and Contributions. Given the potential of challenge mechanisms to protect CIDNs against a range of attacks, including common insider attacks, we posit the importance of enhancing the robustness of such mechanisms against advanced attacks that are practical in nature. Focused on this issue, in this work, we develop an advanced collusion attack, coined *Bayesian Poisoning Attack*. In this attack, a malicious node can model the received messages and successfully send a untruthful response to messages that have a higher probability of being a normal request; thus, circumventing *assumption A1* of the challenge-based trust mechanism. Specifically, building on *PMFA*, we develop the *Bayesian Poisoning Attack*, where two or more malicious nodes can collude to collect messages and give untruthful answers to a normal request, without adversely affecting their trust values. Hopefully, the findings of this work will simulate further interest in designing more robust challenge-based CIDNs to deal with advanced insider attacks, as well as other practical attacks. In the end, we also discuss some countermeasures to defend our attack.

In the next section, we will revisit challenge-based CIDNs, including briefly introducing their key building blocks. In Sect. 3, we analyze the assumptions used in the existing challenge mechanisms and describe our *Bayesian poisoning attack*. In Sect. 4, we describe our evaluation setup and explain our findings under both simulated and real CIDN environments. Specifically, we show that our attack can help a malicious entity identify an appropriate timing for giving untruthful feedback, and it is effective to compromise the challenge-based trust mechanism in practical deployment. Related literature is reviewed in Sect. 5, and the last section concludes our work.

2   Challenge-Based CIDNs

Intuitively, challenge-based CIDNs employ the challenge-based trust mechanisms to defend against insider attacks. Figure 1 depicts the high-level architecture of a common challenge-based CIDN and its key building blocks. This architecture can be applied to network structure, such as wireless sensor networks (WSNs) and Internet of Things (IoT).

Network Interactions. In the architecture, each IDS node can choose its partners or collaborators, based on its own policies and experience. These nodes can be associated if they have a collaborative relationship (e.g., vendor, and organizations/entities within the same system). Each node can maintain a list of their collaborated nodes, called *partner list* (or *acquaintance list*). Such list is customizable and stores information of other nodes (e.g., public keys and their current trust values). Before a node can join the network, it has to register with a trusted certificate authority (*CA*) and obtain its unique proof of identity (e.g., a key pair with a public key and a private key). As shown in Fig. 1(a), if node *C* wishes to join the network, it needs to send an application to a network node, say node *A*. Then, node *A* makes a decision and sends back an initial *partner list*, if node *C* is accepted.

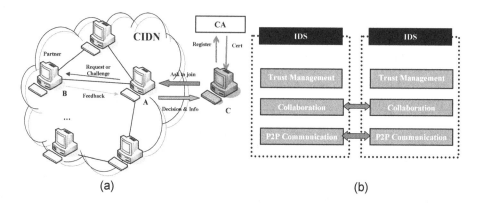

Fig. 1. (a) High-level architecture of a common challenge-based CIDN and (b) key building blocks.

CIDNs allow IDS nodes to exchange the necessary and required messages in-between to improve the performance. There are two major types of interactive messages, namely: challenges and normal requests.

- *Challenges.* A challenge contains a set of IDS alarms asking to label their severity. A testing node can send a challenge to other tested nodes and obtain the relevant feedback. As the testing node knows the severity of the sent alarms, it can use the received feedback to derive a trust value (e.g., satisfaction level) for the tested node.
- *Normal requests.* A normal request is sent by a node for alarm aggregation. Other IDS nodes should send back alarm ranking information as their feedback. Alarm aggregation is an important feature for CIDNs, which can help improve the detection performance, and it usually considers the feedback from trusted nodes.

Network Components. Figure 1(b) shows the key building blocks in a CIDN node, including *trust management component, collaboration component* and *P2P communication.*

- *Trust management component.* This component is responsible for evaluating the trustworthiness of other nodes. Under the challenge mechanism, the trustworthiness of other nodes is mainly computed by evaluating the received feedback. Each node can send out either normal requests or challenges for alert ranking (consultation). To protect challenges, it is worth noting that challenges should be sent out in a random manner and in a way that makes them difficult to be distinguished from a normal alarm ranking request.
- *Collaboration component.* This component is mainly responsible for assisting a node to evaluate the trustworthiness of other nodes by sending out *normal requests* and/or *challenges*, and upon receiving the relevant *feedback* to evaluate its truthfulness. As shown in Fig. 1, if node A sends a *request/challenge* to node B, then node B will send back the relevant feedback.

– *P2P communication.* This component is responsible for connecting with other IDS nodes and providing network organization, management and communication among IDS nodes.

Robustness. It has been shown that challenge-based trust mechanisms can enhance the CIDN's resilience in mitigating common insider attacks, such as Sybil, newcomer, betrayal and collusion attacks [5–8].

– *Sybil attack.* This attack occurs when a malicious node creates a large number of fake identities [2], with the aim of having an unfair influence on the alert aggregation. As shown in Fig. 1, an IDS node should register with a *CA* and obtain a unique proof identity; thus, mitigating such an attack. Clearly, if the *CA* is corrupted, then this attack will work. However, *CA* has a vested interest to ensure that they are not compromised or known to have laxed security practices, as this will affect their bottomline.
– *Newcomer (re-entry) attack.* This attack occurs when a malicious node registers as a new user, in order to erase its bad history. Challenge-based CIDNs begin by giving low initial trust values to all newcomers, so that the influence of new nodes on alarm aggregation is minimal. This is somewhat analogous to the credit history system, where one's creditworthiness is built over time (e.g., based on the factors like payment history and age of credit history).
– *Betrayal attack.* This attack occurs when a trusted node becomes malicious. To defeat such an attack, a high trust value should only be established after a lengthy interaction and consistently good behavior (again, similar to the credit history system), and only a few bad actions will ruin the trust value (in the context of the credit history system, bad activities like derogatory marks due to payment default, or hard credit inquiries). In particular, it employs a forgetting factor to give more credits to recent behaviors.
– *Collusion attack.* This attack happens when a group of malicious peers collude to provide false alarm rankings in order to compromise the network. Challenge-based trust mechanisms can uncover malicious peers via sending the challenges, where the trust values of malicious nodes can decrease rapidly if their untruthful feedback is detected.

3 Our Proposed Attack

In this section, we discuss the underlying assumptions (or threat model) made by challenge-based trust mechanisms, and describe our attack.

3.1 Threat Model and Assumption Analysis

As previously discussed, challenge-based mechanisms can be effective in defending against most common insider attacks, based on the following two assumptions.

– **A1.** Challenges are sent out in a random way, which is challenging to be distinguished from normal messages.
– **A2.** Malicious nodes always send feedback contrary to its true assessment (i.e., misreporting a malicious event as benign, and vice versa).

These two assumptions are key to protecting *challenges* and identifying malicious nodes. In particular, the first assumption implies two conditions: *a random manner* and *hard to distinguish*. These ensure that an IDS node cannot distinguish a challenge from normal requests. Thus, malicious nodes have a trivial possibility of identifying challenges, and have to respond to each message.

The second assumption implies a *maximal harm model*, where an adversary always chooses to report untruthful feedback with the intention to bring the most negative impact to the request sender [7]. As an example, whenever a malicious node receives a ranking request, it will reply with a 'no risk' for an alarm whose real risk level could be 'medium', because this feedback can maximize the impact at the sender side.

Are These Two Assumptions Realistic/Practical? These assumptions are reasonable in scenarios, where attackers (or *naive attackers*) choose a *maximal harm model*. In practical implementations, however, attackers can choose to go under the radar in order to avoid detection. For example, why would an attacker risk been identified as malicious by 'lying' all the times? Would it not make more sense to 'lie' only on events of importance (e.g., some sort of 'sleeper' node)? In other words, advanced attackers, including advanced persistent threat (APT) attackers, would likely behave normally/truthfully most of the time (referred to as 'advanced attack' where attackers can perform complex operations, unlike naive attacks in the *maximal harm model*, in this paper).

Thus, the existing challenge-based trust mechanisms that rely on the two assumptions will be insecure against such advanced attackers. This is the premise of our proposed attacks, to be described next.

3.2   Bayesian Poisoning Attacks

An example of an insider attack not captured in existing CIDN systems is the *passive message fingerprint attack (PMFA)* of Li et al. [16]. In such an attack, the attacker is able to distinguish normal requests from messages, based on the observation that a generic CIDN would send normal requests to trusted nodes at the same time in practice. In other words, if several nodes receive the same message (containing the same alarm set), then this message is very likely to be a normal request (and not a challenge).

However, this attack can be easily mitigated through controlling the timing of sending normal requests (i.e., sending the next request after getting a response from the last request). In this case, *PMFA* can be largely mitigated. In this work, we develop the *Bayesian Poisoning Attack*, in which malicious nodes can send untruthful feedback to those messages who have a high probability of being a normal request.

Main idea. The challenge mechanism can be compromised if malicious nodes can only send untruthful feedback to normal requests, but send truthful feedback to challenges. As a result, the key idea is to find an appropriate timing to deliver malicious feedback. Based on this key idea, our developed *Bayesian Poisoning Attack* aims to passively collect messages and send untruthful feedback in a

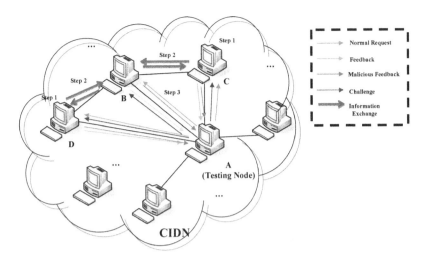

Fig. 2. Steps of Bayesian poisoning attacks on challenge-based CIDNs.

probability that is computed by the Bayesian inference model. That is, our attack can decide whether an incoming message has a high probability of being a normal request. Subsequently, suspicious nodes are able to send untruthful feedback only to normal requests, while providing truthful answers to other received messages.

Figure 2 provides an example to illustrate how such attack operates in practice. Suppose a testing node A delivers either requests or challenges to its partners. Under the mechanism, all tested nodes should provide feedback after receiving the messages. Assume nodes B, C and D to be suspicious/malicious, we explain our attack with detailed steps as follows.

- **Step 1.** At this stage, every suspicious node starts collecting and recording all received messages from the testing node. In this attack, we accept the first assumption that challenges are sent out in a random way, which is challenging to be distinguished from normal messages. Thus, malicious nodes have to passively collect data at this stage.
- **Step 2.** At this stage, suspicious nodes can collaborate with each other to exchange recorded messages. In practice, in order to rank alarms, normal requests have to be delivered to all trusted nodes. This opens a chance to distinguish normal request from messages [16]. Taking node B as an example, it can compare the recorded messages from nodes C and D. A message could be a normal request with a high probability, if a match is identified.
- **Step 3.** Based on the number of identified normal requests and the number of received messages, our attack builds a model and computes the probability of normal requests. By given a threshold, suspicious nodes can return untruthful feedback to the messages with a high probability of being a normal request. For other messages, malicious nodes can still return truthful answers.

Bayesian Inference Model. This is a statistical method of inference, by using the Bayes' rule to predict the probability for a hypothesis as additional evidence [33]. To compute the appearance probability of a normal request, suppose there are N messages received from the testing node, among which k messages are normal requests. Assume a Binomial distribution controls the probability of observing $n(N) = k$. The equation is shown below.

$$P(n(N) = k|p) = \binom{N}{k}p^k(1-p)^{N-k} \tag{1}$$

where $n(N)$ describes how many normal requests are received, and p describes how likely a message to be a normal request. Binomial distribution describes a distribution where there are two mutually exclusive outcomes to an event. It helps identify a sequence of n trials where each has the same probability of p. The ultimate goal of our model is to predict the possibility: $P(V_{N+1} = 1|n(N) = k)$; that is, measuring how likely the $(N + 1)^{th}$ message can be a normal request. According to the Bayesian theorem, we can have the following:

$$P(V_{N+1} = 1|n(N) = k) = \frac{P(V_{N+1} = 1, n(N) = k)}{P(n(N) = k)} \tag{2}$$

where $P(V_{N+1} = 1|n(N) = k)$ describes how likely the $(N + 1)^{th}$ message is a normal request, if we receive N messages which contain k normal requests. We further apply a marginal probability distribution[1] and can have the followings:

$$P(n(N) = k) = \int_0^1 P(n(N) = k|p)f(p) \cdot dp \tag{3}$$

$$P(V_{N+1} = 1, n(N) = k) = \int_0^1 P(n(N) = k|p)f(p)p \cdot dp \tag{4}$$

To estimate the prior information regarding $p \in [0, 1]$, it is reasonable to assume that it is decided by a uniform prior distribution $f(p) = 1$. According to Eqs. (2) to (4), we can obtain the following equation, which can describe the appearance possibility of a normal request, P_{req}, within a time period.

$$
\begin{aligned}
P_{req} = P(V_{N+1} = 1|n(N) = k) &= \frac{\int_0^1 P(n(N) = k|p)f(p)p \cdot dp}{\int_0^1 P(n(N) = k|p)f(p) \cdot dp} \\
&= \frac{k+1}{N+2}
\end{aligned}
\tag{5}
$$

Bayesian Modeling of Normal Request Distribution. In a real-world deployment, the number of challenges is often pre-defined whereas the number of normal requests is dynamic based on the network traffic. The challenge mechanism assumes that the challenges are randomly sent, but a real-world environment can only achieve pseudo-randomness. To emphasize the identification

---

[1] Marginal distribution describes the possibility of various values of the variables in the subset, without considering the values of the other variables.

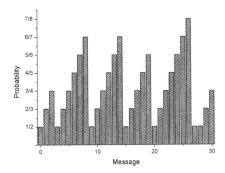

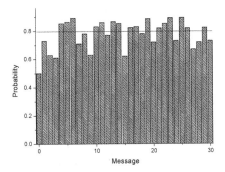

Fig. 3. An example of appearance probability of normal requests (P_{req}) for a node in one day.

Fig. 4. Aggregated appearance probability of normal requests after one month.

of a challenge, we restore P_{req} to $1/2$ when detecting a message is not a normal request. Subsequently, after collecting messages a period of time, it is feasible to model the appearance probability of normal requests based on Eq. (5). The aggregated appearance probability of normal requests for node I ($AP_{req}(I)$) and message j can be computed as below.

$$AP_{req}^{j}(I) = \frac{\sum_{1}^{DN} P_{req}^{j}}{DN} \qquad (6)$$

In the above equation, DN denotes the number of days.

Figure 3 shows an example of P_{req} for a node in one day, where a probability of $1/2$ means an identification of a message that is not a normal request. To model the appearance probability of normal requests, there is a need to monitor the data for a longer period of time. Thus, we continue collecting statistics of messages, and Fig. 4 depicts a Bayesian distribution of the normal request based on Eq. (6), after a month. It is shown that the appearance probability of normal requests varies with messages. For an attacker, it is critical to select a proper threshold, with the purpose of having a better chance to behave maliciously to normal requests. In this work, we select a threshold of 0.8 to strike a balance between the attack performance and the risk of being detected. For instance, given the threshold of 0.8, our attack allows one to send 16 untruthful feedback to corresponding messages, as shown in Fig. 4.

In summary, after selecting a threshold, suspicious nodes can decide whether to send malicious answers to those messages whose aggregated appearance probability of normal requests is above the threshold, and respond truthfully to other messages. This can circumvent the challenge-based trust mechanism; thus, malicious nodes can have a negative impact on the process of alarm aggregation while maintaining their reputation.

Table 1. Parameter settings in the experiment.

Parameters	Value	Description
ε_l	10/day	Low request frequency
ε_h	20/day	High request frequency
r	0.8	Trust threshold
λ	0.9	Forgetting factor
m	10	Lower limit of received feedback
d	0.3	Severity of punishment
T_s	0.5	Trust value for newcomers

4 Evaluation

We mainly perform two experiments in this section to investigate our attack performance with simulated settings and a real network, respectively.

- *Experiment-1.* We first evaluate our *Bayesian poisoning attack* in a simulated CIDN environment, in comparison with naive collusion attack and *PMFA*.
- *Experiment-2.* We then collaborate with an information center to exploit the impact of our attack in a practical CIDN, e.g., how the reputation of suspicious nodes changes and the influence on aggregating alarms.

4.1 CIDN Settings

A total of 25 nodes that are randomly distributed in the simulated CIDN environment with a 5 × 5 grid region. Snort [32] was deployed in each node as IDS component. A node can build a *partner list* by communicating with other nodes after a time period. To facilitate the comparison with previous work [6,7], we set the initial trust values of all nodes in the *partner list* as $T_s = 0.5$.

To measure the reputation of each partner node, a challenge can be delivered randomly with an average rate of ε. In this work, we adopted the same frequency levels: a low level of ε_l and a high level of ε_h. Intuitively, we should be confident about a highly trusted or untrusted node; thus, we can set a low request frequency for these nodes. By contrast, we should set a high request frequency to evaluate the nodes with a medium trust value around the threshold. To make a comparison with other competing approaches, we use the same settings as in [6,7,14]. Table 1 describes the parameter settings.

Node Expertise. Similar to previous work, we also adopted three levels of expertise to describe the detection capability of an IDS node, such as low (0.1), medium (0.5) and high (0.95). In particular, we can use the below beta function to measure the expertise of an IDS.

$$f(p'|\alpha, \beta) = \frac{1}{B(\alpha, \beta)} p'^{\alpha-1}(1 - p')^{\beta-1}$$

$$B(\alpha, \beta) = \int_0^1 t^{\alpha-1}(1 - t)^{\beta-1}dt \qquad (7)$$

In the above equation, $p'(\in [0,1])$ describes the possibility of an intrusion under the examination of an IDS. l means the expertise level, $d(\in [0,1])$ indicates the difficulty level, and $f(p'|\alpha, \beta)$ describes the possibility that under d, a node with l can identify an intrusion with p'. Intuitively, a bigger l reflects a better chance of correctly detecting an attack, whereas a bigger d indicates it is harder to identify an attack. The derivation of α and β can refer to the previous work [6].

$$\alpha = 1 + \frac{l(1-d)}{d(1-l)}r$$

$$\beta = 1 + \frac{l(1-d)}{d(1-l)}(1-r)$$

(8)

In the above equation, $r \in \{0,1\}$ describes the desirable detection outcomes. Generally, given a fixed d, the node with higher expertise can have better detection performance. For instance, if $d = 0$, then a node with $l = 1$ can identify an attack without errors.

Node Trust Evaluation. To measure the reputation of a node, a randomly generated challenge can be delivered to the tested node. Then we can calculate the satisfaction level based on the received feedback. In particular, the reputation of a node i according to node j can be computed as below [5]:

$$T_i^j = (w_s \frac{\sum_{k=0}^{n} F_k^{j,i} \lambda^{tk}}{\sum_{k=0}^{n} \lambda^{tk}} - T_s)(1-x)^{d'} + T_s,$$

(9)

where n counts the number of received feedback, and $F_k^{j,i} \in [0,1]$ describes the satisfaction level regarding the received feedback k. The *forgetting factor*, denoted as λ, emphasizes more weights on the recent feedback. w_s means a *significant weight* varying with the received feedback. If the number of received feedback is smaller than m, then $w_s = \frac{\sum_{k=0}^{n} \lambda^{tk}}{m}$; otherwise, $w_s = 1$. In addition, x describes how many 'do not know' answers are received within a time period, d' is used to punish 'do not know' answers.

Satisfaction Level. Let $e \in [0,1]$ denote an expected feedback, $r \in [0,1]$ denote an actual received feedback, and $F (\in [0,1])$ denote the satisfaction level. Then we can have the followings based on [6,7]:

$$F = 1 - (\frac{e-r}{max(c_1e, 1-e)})^{c_2} \quad e > r$$

(10)

$$F = 1 - (\frac{c_1(r-e)}{max(c_1e, 1-e)})^{c_2} \quad e \leq r$$

(11)

In the above equations, c_1 indicates the penalty degree for errors, and c_2 indicates the sensitivity degree. To make the comparison workable with pervious studies like [6], we adopted $c_1 = 1.5$ and $c_2 = 1$ in the simulation.

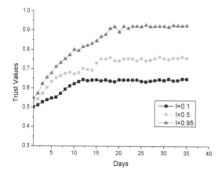
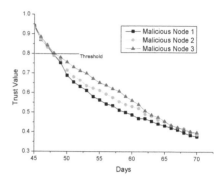

Fig. 5. Convergence of trust values of IDS nodes regarding three expertise levels.

Fig. 6. Trust values of malicious nodes under naive collusion attacks.

4.2 Experiment-1

In this experiment, we attempt to evaluate the initial performance of our attack, naive collusion attack and *PMFA* [16]. Note that naive collusion attack adopts a maximal harm model, as discussed earlier. Under this attack, malicious nodes can cooperate to always respond with untruthful alarm ranking. Figures 5 and 6 depict the convergence of trust values and the reputation of malicious nodes under this attack, respectively.

Figure 5 shows the convergence of trust values for nodes with three expert levels. The observations echoed those of [5,6]; that is, a node with higher expertise can obtain better reputation. For example, the nodes with an expertise of high can reach a trust value above 0.9. In our settings, the reputation of all nodes started to be converged after a period of 15–20 days.

To launch naive collusion attack, we then choose three expert nodes ($I = 0.95$) randomly, which could behave maliciously from Day 45. We denote these nodes as *malicious node 1*, *malicious node 2* and *malicious node 3*. Figure 6 presents the malicious nodes' reputation under this attack. It is observed that within 2–3 days, the reputation of malicious nodes could decrease very fast to below the threshold of 0.8. This is because naive-collusion nodes always behave maliciously, and it is easy to be detected. Subsequently, challenge-based CIDNs can operate well under the native collusion attack, by decreasing malicios nodes' trust values in a short time period.

Advanced Attacks. We further investigate the performance of our attack, as well as those of the *passive message fingerprint attack (PMFA)*. Similarly, we adopted the same three expert nodes of *malicious node 1*, *malicious node 2* and *malicious node 3*. We further remark that the CIDN controls the timing of sending the normal request (i.e., send next request after getting a response from the last request). Figures 7 and 8 show the malicious nodes' reputation and the average errors, respectively.

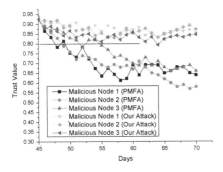

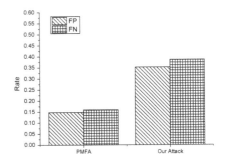

Fig. 7. Trust values of malicious nodes under our attack and PMFA.

Fig. 8. Average false rates in alarm aggregation under our attack and PMFA.

Figure 7 shows that the reputation of malicious nodes in *PMFA* could drop to below the threshold of 0.8 gradually, because *PMFA* can only ensure that at most one malicious node can identify the normal request, while the other colluding nodes could be identified by challenges. It is found that the trustworthiness of the malicious nodes under our attack decreased slightly but still remained above the threshold. This is because the nodes under our attack only responded untruthfully occasionally.

Figure 8 shows the average alarm aggregation errors between PFMA and our attack. The errors could include both *false negatives (FN)* and *false positions (FP)*. It is easily observed that the alarm aggregation errors are about 14%–16% and 35%–38% under *PMFA* and our attack, respectively. Our attack can make a larger impact on the alarm aggregation process.

Thus, our results demonstrate the feasibility of our attack, where suspicious nodes can have a better chance of behaving maliciously to most normal requests, while providing a truthful response to the remaining messages. In this case, our attack enables malicious nodes acting maliciously without losing their reputation, thus can still make an impact on alarm aggregation.

4.3   Experiment-2

We further collaborated with an information center (including over 1000 personnel) and validate our attack performance in a practical CIDN environment. The information center deploys a wired CIDN, which contains up to 55 nodes, where the incoming network traffic can reach 1305 packets on average. We adopted the same setting as shown in Table 1. Before the experiment, we implemented the challenge mechanism and waited for the trust values to become stable. During this period, each node collected messages and established a Bayesian distribution of normal requests. Similarly, we also selected three expert nodes randomly to be malicious. The main results are depicted in Figs. 9 and 10.

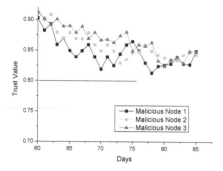

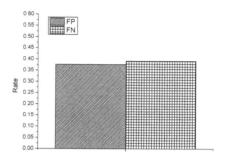

Fig. 9. Trust values of malicious nodes under our attack in a real CIDN.

Fig. 10. Average false rates in alarm aggregation under our attack in a real CIDN.

- Figure 9 depicts that the malicious nodes' reputation under our attack could remain above the threshold of 0.8; thus, these nodes can make a negative impact on the alarm aggregation.
- Figure 10 shows that the caused average alarm aggregation errors could be around 37%–39% in the center environment. This is because the suspicious nodes under our attack without detection could keep behaving untruthfully to make an influence on the alarm aggregation.

Thus, our results validate the viability of our attack in a practical CIDN environment, and reveal the limitations of existing challenge-based trust mechanisms against such a practical attack.

4.4   Discussion and Countermeasures

As noted above, existing challenge-based CIDNs need to be redesigned to take into consideration practical attacks such as the attack we reveal in this paper. In other words, sending challenges in a random manner may not be good enough to protect the robustness of challenge-based CIDNs. To defeat our proposed attack, we discuss some potential countermeasures as below.

- One possible solution is to insert a special alarm in a normal request to validate the response. Such special alarm should be inserted in a random position every time, in order to raise the cracking difficulty.
- It is a promising way to combine other types of trust into challenge-based CIDNs. For instance, we can examine the packets that are sent by malicious nodes (denote as packet-level trust), as these nodes are most likely to deliver malicious traffic during an attack [24].
- There is also a good idea to involve some validation mechanisms, which can help check whether the received feedback is malicious or not. Due to the popularity of blockchain technology, it can be considered to help build a trusted feedback-chain that can be validated by all peers.

4.5   Limitations

In this work, our main purpose is to exploit the robustness of challenge-based CIDNs by designing a practical insider attack - *Bayesian Poisoning Attack*. Due to the scope, there are some limitations and open challenges on this topic.

- *CIDN deployment.* Distributed/collaborative intrusion detection has been proposed for decades, while these systems are mainly deployed at a small-scale, i.e., security-sensitive organizations, and security companies. With the current threats being more sophisticated, there is a trend towards developing a more practical, effective and robust DIDS/CIDN in various organizations. Our work is an effort to stimulate more research in this direction.
- *Existing security mechanisms.* There are many other security mechanisms in practice, like OSINT-based curated security feeds/platforms, and security information and event management (SIEM) system that correlates events coming from multiple sensors. Because of our focus, we did not discuss the existing security mechanisms, but intuitively, DIDS/CIDN is an alternative to collaborate with existing security solutions.

In the current literature, distributed/collaborative intrusion detection has been applied to many disciplines. For example, Shekari *et al.* [30] focused on supervisory control and data acquisition (SCADA) and proposed a radio frequency-based distributed intrusion detection system (RFDIDS), which uses radio frequency (RF) emissions to monitor the power grid substation activities. Hence, our work advocates the need of enhancing intrusion detection by enabling collaboration among various detectors, but also figures out the open challenge on how to design a practical, effective and robust DIDS/CIDN.

5   Related Work

Intuitively, it is challenging for an isolated IDS to learn about the evolving, real-time threat landscape. Thus, there is a need for sharing of information and threats, for example via a distributed system. Examples of such systems include *Centralized/Hierarchical systems* (e.g., Emerald [28] and DIDS [31]), *Publish/subscribe systems* (e.g., COSSACK [27] and DOMINO [36]), and *P2P Querying-based systems* (e.g., Netbait [1] and PIER [10]). CIDN is yet another example, and the focus of this paper. Specifically, in a CIDN [35], an IDS node can achieve better accuracy by collecting and communicating relevant information from other IDS nodes (i.e., collating the alerts from other nodes and synthesizing a global and aggregated alarm). However, insider attack is a major threat for such collaborative networks, as shown by researchers such as Li *et al.* [12]. Specifically, Li *et al.* [12] proposed a system based on the emerging decentralized location and routing infrastructure, and assumed that all peers are trusted. This is clearly vulnerable to insider attacks, such as betrayal attacks where some nodes become malicious suddenly (e.g., due to compromise).

The need to establish appropriate and strong trust models to defend against insider attacks is well-studied. Duma *et al.* [3], for example, proposed a P2P-based overlay for intrusion detection (Overlay IDS) that mitigated such insider threats, by using a trust-aware engine for correlating alerts and an adaptive scheme for managing trust. Tuan [34] utilized the game theory to model and analyze the processes of reporting and exclusion in a P2P network. They identified that if a reputation system is not incentive compatible, then peers in the system will be less inclined to report a malicious peer.

While challenge-based trust mechanisms are an effective approach of building trust among CIDN nodes (i.e., trustworthiness of a node depends on the received answers to the challenges), they are not infallible. Fung et al. [5] proposed a HIDS collaboration framework, which enables each HIDS to evaluate the trustworthiness of others based on its own experience by means of a forgetting factor. The forgetting factor can give more emphasis on the recent experience of the peer. Then, they improved their trust management model by using a Dirichlet-based model to measure the level of trustworthiness among IDS nodes, according to their mutual experience [6]. This model has strong scalability properties and is sufficiently robust against common insider threats, as demonstrated by their evelution findings. As feedback aggregation is a key component in a challenge mechanism, they further applied a Bayesian approach to feedback aggregation to minimize the combined costs of missed detection and false alarm [7].

To further improve the detection accuracy of challenge-based CIDNs, Li *et al.* [13] explained that different IDS nodes may have different levels of sensitivity in detecting different types of intrusions. They also proposed a notion of *intrusion sensitivity* that measures the detection sensitivity of an IDS in detecting different kinds of intrusions. For example, if a signature-based IDS node has more signatures (or rules) in detecting DoS attacks, then it should be considered to be more powerful in detecting such attacks, in comparison to other nodes with relatively fewer signatures. This notion is helpful when making decisions based on the collected information from different nodes, as it can help detect intrusions and correlate IDS alerts through emphasizing the impact of an *expert IDS*. Li *et al.* [14] further proposed an *intrusion sensitivity-based trust management model* for automating the allocation of *intrusion sensitivity*, using machine learning techniques such as knowledge-based KNN classifier [22]. The use of *intrusion sensitivity* could also be beneficial for alarm aggregation and defending against pollution attacks [15]. Experimental results demonstrated that *intrusion sensitivity* can decrease the trust values of malicious nodes promptly. Other related studies on intrusion detection enhancement include those of [4,9,18–21,24,25]

Challenge-based CIDNs are robust against common insider attacks, whereas some advanced insider threats are still feasible. Li *et al.* [16] showed an advanced insider attack named *passive message fingerprint attack (PMFA)*, where multiple suspicious nodes could work together to identify normal requests from the received messages. They further introduced another attack called Special On-Off Attack *SOOA* [17], which could send truthful answers to partial messages while behaving maliciously to other messages. The random poisoning attack [23] is a special case of $SOOA$, in which malicious nodes can send a malicious response with a possibility of $1/2$. The main difference between the above studies and our work is that we use a Bayesian approach to identify normal requests with a high possibility, hence each malicious node can have their own possibility list.

6   Conclusion

With the purpose of enhancing the robustness of challenge-based CIDNs against a broader range of attacks, we posit the importance of designing advanced and practical attacks. In this paper, we developed a type of collusion attack, *Bayesian Poisoning Attack*, which enables a malicious node to establish an appearance probability of normal requests based on Bayesian inference. In our attack, malicious nodes can respond untruthfully to messages, which have a higher possibility to be a normal request. In the evaluation, we compare our attack with naive collusion attack and PMFA under both simulated and practical environment, and experimental results demonstrated the utility of our attack (i.e., malicious nodes can respond untruthfully, while maintaining their trust values and causing errors in the alarm aggregation). We also discuss some potential countermeasures (e.g., combining other trust types) to defeat such type of attack, which could be one of our future work. Our work attempts to stimulate more research in building robust and practical challenge-based CIDNs.

Acknowledgments. We would like to thank all anonymous reviewers for their helpful comments in improving the paper. Weizhi Meng was partially supported by H2020 SU-ICT-03-2018 CyberSec4Europe.

References

1. Chun, B., Lee, J., Weatherspoon, H., Chun, B.N.: Netbait: a Distributed Worm Detection Service. Technical Report IRB-TR-03-033, Intel Research Berkeley (2003)
2. Douceur, J.R.: The sybil attack. In: Druschel, P., Kaashoek, F., Rowstron, A. (eds.) IPTPS 2002. LNCS, vol. 2429, pp. 251–260. Springer, Heidelberg (2002). https://doi.org/10.1007/3-540-45748-8_24
3. Duma, C., Karresand, M., Shahmehri, N., Caronni, G.: A trust-aware, P2P-based overlay for intrusion detection. In: DEXA Workshop, pp. 692–697 (2006)
4. Friedberg, I., Skopik, F., Settanni, G., Fiedler, R.: Combating advanced persistent threats: from network event correlation to incident detection. Comput. Secur. **48**, 35–57 (2015)
5. Fung, C.J., Baysal, O., Zhang, J., Aib, I., Boutaba, R.: Trust management for host-based collaborative intrusion detection. In: De Turck, F., Kellerer, W., Kormentzas, G. (eds.) DSOM 2008. LNCS, vol. 5273, pp. 109–122. Springer, Heidelberg (2008). https://doi.org/10.1007/978-3-540-87353-2_9
6. Fung, C.J., Zhang. J., Aib, I., Boutaba, R.: Robust and scalable trust management for collaborative intrusion detection. In: Proceedings of the 11th IFIP/IEEE International Conference on Symposium on Integrated Network Management (IM), pp. 33–40 (2009)

7. Fung, C.J.; Zhu, Q., Boutaba, R., Basar, T.: Bayesian decision aggregation in collaborative intrusion detection networks. In: NOMS, pp. 349–356 (2010)

8. Fung, C.J., Boutaba, R.: Design and management of collaborative intrusion detection networks. In: Proceedings of the 2013 IFIP/IEEE International Symposium on Integrated Network Management (IM), pp. 955–961 (2013)

9. Gou, Z., Ahmadon, M.A.B., Yamaguchi, S., Gupta, B.B.: A petri net-based framework of intrusion detection systems. In: Proceedings of the 4th IEEE Global Conference on Consumer Electronics, pp. 579–583 (2015)

10. Huebsch, R., et al.: The architecture of PIER: an internet-scale query processor. In: Proceedings of the 2005 Conference on Innovative Data Systems Research (CIDR), pp. 28–43 (2005)

11. Kiennert, C., Ismail, Z., Debar, H., Leneutre, J.: A survey on game-theoretic approaches for intrusion detection and response optimization. ACM Comput. Surv. (CSUR) $51(5)$, 90 (2018)

12. Li, Z., Chen, Y., Beach, A.: Towards scalable and robust distributed intrusion alert fusion with good load balancing. In: Proceedings of the 2006 SIGCOMM Workshop on Large-Scale Attack Defense (LSAD), pp. 115–122 (2006)

13. Li, W., Meng, Y., Kwok, L.-F.: Enhancing trust evaluation using intrusion sensitivity in collaborative intrusion detection networks: feasibility and challenges. In: Proceedings of the 9th International Conference on Computational Intelligence and Security (CIS), pp. 518–522. IEEE (2013)

14. Li, W., Meng, W., Kwok, L.-F.: Design of intrusion sensitivity-based trust management model for collaborative intrusion detection networks. In: Zhou, J., Gal-Oz, N., Zhang, J., Gudes, E. (eds.) IFIPTM 2014. IAICT, vol. 430, pp. 61–76. Springer, Heidelberg (2014). https://doi.org/10.1007/978-3-662-43813-8_5

15. Li, W., Meng, W.: Enhancing collaborative intrusion detection networks using intrusion sensitivity in detecting pollution attacks. Inf. Comput. Secur. $24(3)$, 265–276 (2016)

16. Li, W., Meng, W., Kwok, L.-F., Ip, H.H.S.: PMFA: toward passive message fingerprint attacks on challenge-based collaborative intrusion detection networks. In: Proceedings of the 10th International Conference on Network and System Security (NSS), pp. 433–449 (2016)

17. Li, W., Meng, W., Kwok, L.F.: SOOA: exploring special on-off attacks on challenge-based collaborative intrusion detection networks. In: Proceedings of GPC, pp. 402–415 (2017)

18. Meng, Y., Kwok, L.F.: Enhancing false alarm reduction using voted ensemble selection in intrusion detection. Int. J. Comput. Intell. Syst. $6(4)$, 626–638 (2013)

19. Meng, Y., Li, W., Kwok, L.F.: Towards Adaptive character frequency-based exclusive signature matching scheme and its applications in distributed intrusion detection. Comput. Netw. $57(17)$, 3630–3640 (2013)

20. Meng, W., Li, W., Kwok, L.-F.: An evaluation of single character frequency-based exclusive signature matching in distinct IDS environments. In: Proceedings of the 17th International Conference on Information Security (ISC), pp. 465–476 (2014)

21. Meng, W., Li, W., Kwok, L.-F.: EFM: enhancing the performance of signature-based network intrusion detection systems using enhanced filter mechanism. Comput. Secur. 43, 189–204 (2014)

22. Meng, W., Li, W., Kwok, L.-F.: Design of intelligent KNN-based alarm filter using knowledge-based alert verification in intrusion detection. Secur. Commun. Netw. $8(18)$, 3883–3895 (2015)

23. Meng, W., Luo, X., Li, W., Li, Y.: Design and evaluation of advanced collusion attacks on collaborative intrusion detection networks in practice. In: Proceedings of the 15th IEEE International Conference on Trust, Security and Privacy in Computing and Communications (TrustCom), pp. 1061–1068 (2016)
24. Meng, W., Li, W., Kwok, L.-F.: Towards effective trust-based packet filtering in collaborative network environments. IEEE Trans. Netw. Serv. Manage. **14**(1), 233–245 (2017)
25. Mishra, A., Gupta, B.B., Joshi, R.C.: A comparative study of distributed denial of service attacks, intrusion tolerance and mitigation techniques. In: Proceedings of the 2011 European Intelligence and Security Informatics Conference, pp. 286–289 (2011)
26. Nisioti, A., Mylonas, A., Yoo, P.D., Katos, V.: From intrusion detection to attacker attribution: a comprehensive survey of unsupervised methods. IEEE Commun. Surv. Tutorials **20**(4), 3369–3388 (2018)
27. Papadopoulos, C., Lindell, R., Mehringer, J., Hussain, A., Govindan, R.: COS-SACK: coordinated suppression of simultaneous attacks. In: Proceedings of the 2003 DARPA Information Survivability Conference and Exposition (DISCEX), pp. 94–96 (2003)
28. Porras, P.A., Neumann, P.G.: Emerald: event monitoring enabling responses to anomalous live disturbances. In: Proceedings of the 20th National Information Systems Security Conference, pp. 353–365 (1997)
29. Scarfone, K., Mell, P.: Guide to Intrusion Detection and Prevention Systems (IDPS). NIST Special Publication 800-94 (2007)
30. Shekari, T., Bayens, C., Cohen, M., Graber, L., Beyah, R.: RFDIDS: radio frequency-based distributed intrusion detection system for the power grid. In: Proceedings of the 26th Annual Network and Distributed System Security Symposium (NDSS) (2019)
31. Snapp, S.R., et al.: DIDS (Distributed Intrusion Detection System) - motivation, architecture, and an early prototype. In: Proceedings of the 14th National Computer Security Conference, pp. 167–176 (1991)
32. Snort: An an open source network intrusion prevention and detection system (IDS/IPS). http://www.snort.org/
33. Sun, Y., Yu, W., Han, Z., Liu, K.: Information theoretic framework of trust modeling and evaluation for ad hoc networks. IEEE J. Sel. Areas Commun. **24**(2), 305–317 (2006)
34. Tuan, T.A.: A game-theoretic analysis of trust management in P2P systems. In: Proceedings of ICCE, pp. 130–134 (2006)
35. Wu, Y.-S., Foo, B., Mei, Y., Bagchi, S.: Collaborative Intrusion Detection System (CIDS): a framework for accurate and efficient IDS. In: Proceedings of the 2003 Annual Computer Security Applications Conference (ACSAC), pp. 234–244 (2003)
36. Yegneswaran, V., Barford, P., Jha, S.: Global intrusion detection in the DOMINO overlay system. In: Proceedings of the 2004 Network and Distributed System Security Symposium (NDSS), pp. 1–17 (2004)

A Framework for Evaluating Security in the Presence of Signal Injection Attacks

Ilias Giechaskiel$^{(\boxtimes)}$, Youqian Zhang, and Kasper B. Rasmussen

University of Oxford, Oxford, UK
{ilias.giechaskiel,youqian.zhang,kasper.rasmussen}@cs.ox.ac.uk

Abstract. Sensors are embedded in security-critical applications from medical devices to nuclear power plants, but their outputs can be spoofed through electromagnetic and other types of signals transmitted by attackers at a distance. To address the lack of a unifying framework for evaluating the effect of such transmissions, we introduce a system and threat model for signal injection attacks. We further define the concepts of existential, selective, and universal security, which address attacker goals from mere disruptions of the sensor readings to precise waveform injections. Moreover, we introduce an algorithm which allows circuit designers to concretely calculate the security level of real systems. Finally, we apply our definitions and algorithm in practice using measurements of injections against a smartphone microphone, and analyze the demodulation characteristics of commercial Analog-to-Digital Converters (ADCs). Overall, our work highlights the importance of evaluating the susceptibility of systems against signal injection attacks, and introduces both the terminology and the methodology to do so.

Keywords: Signal injection attacks · Non-linearities · Security metrics · Analog-to-Digital Converters · Electromagnetic interference

1 Introduction

In our daily routine we interact with dozens of sensors: from motion detection in home security systems and tire pressure monitors in cars, to accelerometers in smartphones and heart rate monitors in smartwatches. The integrity of these sensor outputs is crucial, as many security-critical decisions are taken in response to the sensor values. However, specially-crafted adversarial signals can be used to remotely induce waveforms into the outputs of sensors, thereby attacking pacemakers [9], temperature sensors [4], smartphone microphones [8], and car-braking mechanisms [18]. These attacks cause a system to report values which do not match the true sensor measurements, and trick it into performing dangerous actions such as raising false alarms, or even delivering defibrillation shocks.

The root cause of these vulnerabilities lies in the unintentional side-effects of the physical components of a system. For example, the wires connecting sensors

© Springer Nature Switzerland AG 2019
K. Sako et al. (Eds.): ESORICS 2019, LNCS 11735, pp. 512–532, 2019.
https://doi.org/10.1007/978-3-030-29959-0_25

to microcontrollers behave like low-power, low-gain antennas, and can thus pick up high-frequency electromagnetic radiations. Although these radiations are considered "noise" from an electrical point of view, hardware imperfections in the subsequent parts of the circuit can transform attacker injections into meaningful waveforms. Specifically, these radiations are digitized along with the true sensor outputs, which represent a physical property as an analog electrical quantity. This digitization process is conducted by Analog-to-Digital Converters (ADCs), which, when used outside of their intended range, can cause high-frequency signals to be interpreted as meaningful low-frequency signals.

Despite the potential that signal injection attacks have to break security guarantees, there is no unifying framework for evaluating the effect of such adversarial transmissions. Our work fills this gap through the following contributions:

1. We propose a system model which abstracts away from engineering concerns associated with remote transmissions, such as antenna design (Sect. 2).
2. We define security against adversarial signal injection attacks. Our definitions address effects ranging from mere disruptions of the sensor readings, to precise waveform injections of attacker-chosen values (Sect. 3).
3. We introduce an algorithm to calculate the security level of a system under our definitions and demonstrate it in practice by injecting "OK Google" commands into a smartphone (Sect. 4).
4. We investigate how vulnerable commercial ADCs are to malicious signal injection attacks by testing their demodulation properties (Sect. 5).
5. We discuss how our model can be used to inform circuit design choices, and how to interpret defense mechanisms and other types of signal injection attacks in its context (Sect. 6).

Overall, our work highlights the importance of testing systems against signal injection attacks, and proposes a methodology to test the security of real devices.

2   System and Adversary Model

Remote signal injection attacks pose new challenges from a threat-modeling perspective, since the electrical properties of systems suggest that adversaries cannot arbitrarily and precisely change any sensor reading. To create a threat model and define security in its context, we need to first abstract away from specific circuit designs and engineering concerns related to remote transmissions. To do so, we separate the behavior of a system into two different transfer functions. The first function describes circuit-specific behavior, including how adversarial signals enter the circuit (e.g., through PCB wires acting as antennas), while the second one is ADC-specific, and dictates how the signals which have made it into the circuit are digitized. We describe this model in greater detail in Sect. 2.1, taking a necessary detour into electrical engineering to show why our proposal makes for a good system model. We then explain some sources of measurement errors even in the absence of an adversary in Sect. 2.2 and finish by detailing the capabilities and limitations of the adversary in Sect. 2.3. Both sub-sections are crucial in motivating the security definitions of Sect. 3.

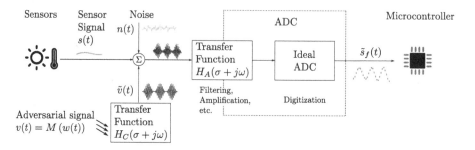

Fig. 1. System model: an adversarial signal $v(t)$ enters the circuit and is transformed via the transfer function H_C. It is digitized along with the sensor signal $s(t)$ and the noise $n(t)$ through an ADC-specific transfer function H_A. In successful attacks, the digitized signal will contain the demodulated version $w(t)$ of the attacker signal $v(t) = M(w(t))$, where M is the modulation function (e.g., amplitude modulation over a high-frequency carrier).

2.1   Circuit Model

Analog-to-Digital Converters (ADCs) are central in the digitization process of converting signals from the analog to the digital realm, and our circuit block diagram (Fig. 1) reflects that. In the absence of an adversary, the ADC digitizes the sensor signal $s(t)$ as well as the environmental noise $n(t)$, and transfers the digital bits to a microcontroller. We model the ADC in two parts: an "ideal" ADC which simply digitizes the signal, and a transfer function H_A. This transfer function describes the internal behavior of the ADC, which includes effects such as filtering and amplification. The digitized version of the signal $\tilde{s}_f(t)$ depends both on this transfer function, and the sampling frequency f of the ADC. An adversarial signal can enter the system (e.g., through the wires connecting the sensor to the ADC) and add to the sensor signal and the noise. This process can be described by a second, circuit-specific transfer function H_C, which transforms the adversarial signal $v(t)$ into $\tilde{v}(t)$. Note that components such as external filters and amplifiers in the signal path between the point of injection and the ADC can be included in either H_A or H_C. We include them in H_A when they also affect the sensor signal $s(t)$, but in H_C when they are specific to the coupling effect. H_C and H_A are discussed in detail below.

Circuit Transfer Function H_C. To capture the response of the circuit to external signal injections, we introduce a transfer function H_C. This transfer function explains why the adversarial waveforms must be modulated, and why it is helpful to try and reduce the number of remote experiments to perform. For electromagnetic interference (EMI) attacks, the wires connecting the sensor to the ADC pick up signals by acting as (unintentional) low-power and low-gain antennas, which are resonant at specific frequencies related to the inverse of the wire length [10]. Non-resonant frequencies are attenuated more, so for a successful attack the adversary must transmit signals at frequencies with relatively low attenuation. For short wires, these frequencies are in the GHz range [10], so the low-frequency waveform $w(t)$ that the adversary wants to inject into the output

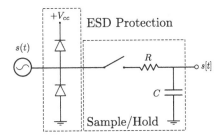

Fig. 2. The sample-and-hold mechanism of an ADC is an RC low-pass filter. Electrostatic Discharge (ESD) protection diodes can also introduce non-linearities.

of the ADC $\tilde{s}_f(t)$ may need to be modulated over a high-frequency carrier using a function M. We denote this modulated version of the signal by $v(t) = M(w(t))$.

H_C is also affected by passive and active components on the path to the ADC, and can also be influenced by inductive and capacitive coupling for small transmission distances, as it closely depends on the circuit components and their placement. Specifically, it is possible for 2 circuits with "the same components, circuit topology and placement area" to have different EMI behavior depending on the component placement on the board [11]. Despite the fact that it is hard to mathematically model and predict the behavior of circuits in response to different signal transmissions, H_C can still be determined empirically using frequency sweeps. It presents a useful abstraction, allowing us to separate the behavior of the ADC (which need only be determined once, for instance by the manufacturer) from circuit layout and transmission details.

Note, finally, that H_C can also account for distance factors between the adversary and the circuit under test: due to the Friis transmission formula [3], as distance doubles, EMI transmission power needs to quadruple. This effect can be captured by increasing the attenuation of H_C by 6 dB, while defense mechanisms such as shielding can be addressed similarly. This approach allows us to side-step engineering issues of remote transmissions and reduce the number of parameters used in the security definitions we propose in Sect. 3.

ADC Transfer Function H_A. Every system with sensors contains one or more ADCs, which may even be integrated into the sensor chip itself. ADCs are not perfect, but contain components which may cause a mismatch between the "true" value at the ADC input and the digitized output. In this section, we describe how these components affect the digitization process.

Although there are many types of ADCs, every ADC contains three basic components: a "sample- or track-and-hold circuit where the sampling takes place, the digital-to-analog converter and a level-comparison mechanism" [13]. The sample-and-hold component acts as a low-pass filter, and makes it harder for an adversary to inject signals modulated at high frequencies. However, the level-comparison mechanism is essentially an amplifier with non-linearities which induces DC offsets, and allows low-frequency intermodulation products to pass through. These ADC-specific transformations, modeled through H_A, unintentionally demodulate high-frequency signals which are not attenuated by H_C.

Sample-and-Hold Filter Characteristics. A sample-and-hold (S/H) mechanism is an RC circuit connected to the analog input, with the resistor and the capacitor connected in series (Fig. 2). The transfer function of the voltage across the capacitor is $H_{S/H}(j\omega) = \frac{1}{1+j\omega RC}$, and the magnitude of the gain is $G_{S/H} = \frac{1}{\sqrt{1+(\omega RC)^2}}$. As the angular frequency $\omega = 2\pi f$ increases, the gain is reduced: the S/H mechanism acts as a low-pass filter. The $-3\,\mathrm{dB}$ cutoff frequency is thus $f_{cut} = \frac{1}{2\pi RC}$, which is often higher than the ADC sampling rate (Sect. 5). Hence, "aliasing" occurs when signals beyond the Nyquist frequency are digitized by the ADC: high-frequency signals become indistinguishable from low-frequency signals which the ADC can sample accurately.

Amplifier Non-linearities. Every ADC contains amplifiers: a comparator, and possibly buffer and differential amplifiers. Many circuits also contain additional external amplifiers to make weak signals measurable. All these amplifiers have harmonic and intermodulation non-linear distortions [15], which an adversary can exploit. Harmonics are produced when an amplifier transforms an input v_{in} to an output $v_{out} = \sum_{n=1}^{\infty} a_n v_{in}^n$. In particular, if $v_{in} = \hat{v} \cdot \sin(\omega t)$, then:

$$v_{out} = \left(\frac{a_2 \hat{v}^2}{2} + \frac{3a_4 \hat{v}^4}{8} + \cdots \right) + (a_1 \hat{v} + \cdots)\sin(\omega t) - \left(\frac{a_2 \hat{v}^2}{2} + \cdots \right)\cos(2\omega t) + \cdots$$

This equation shows that "the frequency spectrum of the output contains a spectral component at the original (fundamental) frequency, [and] at multiples of the fundamental frequency (harmonic frequencies)" [15]. Moreover, the output includes a DC component, which depends only on the even-order non-linearities of the system. Besides harmonics, intermodulation products arise when the input signal is a sum of two sinusoids (for instance when the injected signal sums with the sensor signal): $v_{in} = \hat{v}_1 \cdot \sin(\omega_1 t) + \hat{v}_2 \cdot \sin(\omega_2 t)$. In that case, the output signal contains frequencies of the form $n\omega_1 \pm m\omega_2$ for integers $n, m \neq 0$. These non-linearities demodulate attacker waveforms, even when they are modulated on high-frequency carriers.

Diode Rectification. Figure 2 shows that the input to an ADC can contain reverse-biased diodes to ground and V_{cc} to protect the input from Electrostatic Discharge (ESD). When the input to the ADC is negative, or when it exceeds V_{cc}, the diodes clamp it, causing non-linear behavior. When the sensor signal $s(t)$ is positive, this behavior is also asymmetric, causing a DC shift [15], which compounds with the amplifier non-linearities.

Conclusion. All ADCs contain the same basic building blocks, modeled through H_A. Although the sample-and-hold mechanism should attenuate high-frequency signals beyond the maximum sampling rate of the ADC, non-linearities due to ESD diodes and amplifiers in the ADC cause DC offsets and the demodulation of signals through harmonics and intermodulation products. Section 5 exemplifies these effects through experiments with different types of ADCs.

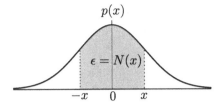

Fig. 3. Noise probability distribution $p(x)$. The shaded area represents the probability $\epsilon = N(x) = \Pr[|n(t)| \leq x]$.

2.2 Sampling Errors in the Absence of an Adversary

The digitization process through ADCs entails errors due to quantization and environmental noise. Quantization errors exist due to the inherent loss of accuracy in the sampling process. An ADC can only represent values within a range, say between V_{min} and V_{max} volts, with a finite binary representation of N bits, called the *resolution* of the ADC. In other words, every value between V_{min} and V_{max} is mapped to one of the 2^N values that can be represented using N bits. As a result, there is a *quantization error* between the true sensor analog value s and the digitized value $\tilde{s}$. The maximum value of this error is

$$Q = \frac{V_{max} - V_{min}}{2^{N+1}} \geq |s - \tilde{s}| \tag{1}$$

The second source of error comes from environmental noise, which may affect measurements. We assume that this noise, denoted by $n(t)$, is independent of the signal being measured, and that it comes from a zero-mean distribution, i.e., that the noise is *white*. The security definitions we introduce in Sect. 3 require an estimate of the level of noise in the system, so we introduce some relevant notation here. We assume that $n(t)$ follows a probability distribution function (PDF) $p(x)$, and define $N(x)$ as the probability that the noise is between $-x$ and x, as shown in Fig. 3, i.e.,

$$N(x) = \Pr\left[|n(t)| \leq x\right] = \int_{-x}^{x} p(u)du$$

Note that typically the noise is assumed to come from a normal distribution, but this assumption is not necessary in our models and definitions.

We are also interested in the inverse of this function, where given a probability $0 \leq \epsilon < 1$, we want to find $x \geq 0$ such that $N(x) = \epsilon$. For this x, the probability that the noise magnitude falls within $[-x, x]$ is ϵ, as also shown in Fig. 3. Because for some distributions there might be multiple x for which $N(x) = \epsilon$, we use the smallest such value:

$$N^{-1}(\epsilon) = \inf\{x \geq 0 : N(x) = \epsilon\} \tag{2}$$

Since $N(x)$ is an increasing function, so is $N^{-1}(\epsilon)$.

To account for repeated measurements, we introduce a short-hand for sampling errors, which we denote by $E_s(t)$. The sampling errors depend on the sensor input into the ADC $s(t)$, the sampling rate f, the discrete output of the ADC $\tilde{s}_f(t)$ as well as the conversion delay τ, representing the time the ADC takes for complete a conversion:

$$E_s(t) = \begin{cases} |\tilde{s}_f(t+\tau) - s(t)| & \text{if a conversion starts at } t \\ 0 & \text{otherwise} \end{cases} \tag{3}$$

2.3 Adversary Model

Our threat model and definitions can capture a range of attacker goals, from attackers who merely want to disrupt sensor outputs, to those who wish to inject precise waveforms into a system. We define these notions precisely in Sect. 3, but here we describe the attacker capabilities based on our model of Fig. 1. Specifically, in our model, the adversary can only alter the transmitted adversarial signal $v(t)$. He/she cannot directly influence the sensor signal $s(t)$, the (residual) noise $n(t)$, or the transfer functions H_A and H_C. The adversary knows H_A, H_C, and the distribution of the noise $n(t)$, although the true sensor signal $s(t)$ might be hidden from the adversary (see Sect. 3.2). The only constraint placed on the adversarial signal is that the attacker is only allowed to transmit signals $v(t)$ whose peak voltage level is bounded by some constant V_{PK}^{Adv}, i.e., $|v(t)| \leq V_{PK}^{Adv}$ for all t. We call this adversary a V_{PK}^{Adv}-*bound adversary*, and all security definitions are against such bounded adversaries.

We choose to restrict voltage rather than restricting power or distance, as it makes for a more powerful adversarial model. Our model gives the adversary access to any physical equipment necessary (such as powerful amplifiers and highly-directional antennas), while reducing the number of parameters needed for our security definitions of Sect. 3. Distance and power effects can be compensated directly through altering V_{PK}^{Adv}, or indirectly by integrating them into H_C, as discussed in Sect. 2.1.

3 Security Definitions

Using the model of Fig. 1, we can define security in the presence of signal injection attacks. The V_{PK}^{Adv}-bound adversary is allowed to transmit any waveform $v(t)$, provided that $|v(t)| \leq V_{PK}^{Adv}$ for all t: the adversary is only constrained by the voltage budget. Whether or not the adversary succeeds in injecting the target waveform $w(t)$ into the output of the system depends on the transfer functions H_C and H_A. For a given system described by H_A and H_C, there are three outcomes against an adversary whose only restriction is voltage:

1. The adversary can disturb the sensor readings, but cannot precisely control the measurement outputs, an attack we call *existential injection*. The lack of existential injections can be considered *universal security*.
2. The adversary can inject a target waveform $w(t)$ into the ADC outputs with high fidelity, performing a *selective injection*. If the adversary is unable to succeed, the system is *selectively secure* against $w(t)$.

Table 1. Correspondence between security properties of a sensor system, adversarial injection attacks, and the resulting ADC waveform errors (signals).

Security	Injection	ADC error $E_s(t)$
Universal	Existential	Bounded away from 0
Selective	Selective	Target waveform $w(t)$
Existential	Universal	Non-trivial waveforms $w(t)$

3. The adversary can *universally inject* any waveform $w(t)$. If there is any non-trivial waveform for which he/she fails, the system is *existentially secure*.

This section sets out to precisely define the above security notions by accounting for noise and quantization error (Eq. (1)). Our definitions capture the intuition that systems are secure when there are no adversarial transmissions, and are "monotonic" in voltage, i.e., systems are more vulnerable against adversaries with access to higher-powered transmitters. Our definitions are also monotonic in noise: in other words, in environments with low noise, even a small disturbance of the output is sufficient to break the security of a system. Section 3.1 evaluates whether an adversary can disturb the ADC output away from its correct value sufficiently. Section 3.2 then formalizes the notion of selective security against target waveforms $w(t)$. Finally, Sect. 3.3 introduces universal injections by defining what a non-trivial waveform is. The three types of signal injection attacks, the corresponding security properties, and the ensuing ADC errors (injected waveforms) are summarized in Table 1.[1]

3.1 Existential Injection, Universal Security

The most primitive type of signal injection attack is a simple disruption of the sensor readings. There are two axes in which this notion can be evaluated: adversarial voltage and probability of success (success is probabilistic, as noise is a random variable). For a fixed probability of success, we want to determine the smallest voltage level for which an attack is successful. For a fixed voltage level, we want to find the probability of a successful attack. Alternatively, if we fix both the voltage and the probability of success, we want to determine if a system is secure against disruptive signal injection attacks.

The definition for universal security is a formalization of the above intuition, calling a system secure when, even in the presence of injections (bounded by adversarial voltage), the true analog sensor value and the ADC digital output do not deviate by more than the quantization error and the noise, with sufficiently high probability. Mathematically:

---

[1] The terminology chosen was inspired by attacks against signature schemes, where how broken a system is depends on what types of messages an attacker can forge [7].

Definition 1 (Universal Security, Existential Injection). *For $0 \leq \epsilon < 1$, and $V_{PK}^{Adv} \geq 0$, we call a system **universally** (ϵ, V_{PK}^{Adv})-**secure** if*

$$Pr\left[E_s(t) \geq Q + N^{-1}\left(\frac{\epsilon + 1}{2}\right)\right] \leq \frac{\epsilon + 1}{2} \tag{4}$$

*for every adversarial waveform $v(t)$, with $|v(t)| \leq V_{PK}^{Adv}$ for all t. Q is the quantization error of the system, N^{-1} is the noise distribution inverse defined in Eq. (2), and E_s is the sampling error as defined by Eq. (3). The probability is taken over the duration of the attack, i.e., at each sampling point within the interval $t_{start} \leq t \leq t_{end}$. We call a successful attack an **existential injection**, and simply call a system universally ϵ-secure, when V_{PK}^{Adv} is implied.*

We first show that in the absence of injections, the system is universally ϵ-secure for all $0 \leq \epsilon < 1$. Indeed, let $x = N^{-1}\left(\frac{\epsilon + 1}{2}\right)$, so that $Pr\left[|n(t)| \leq x\right] = \frac{\epsilon + 1}{2}$. Then, in the absence of injections,

$$Pr\left[E_s(t) \geq Q + N^{-1}\left(\frac{\epsilon + 1}{2}\right)\right] = Pr\left[|n(t)| \geq x\right]$$

$$= 1 - \frac{\epsilon + 1}{2} = \frac{1 - \epsilon}{2} \leq \frac{\epsilon + 1}{2}$$

which holds for all $0 \leq \epsilon < 1$, as desired. This proof is precisely the reason for requiring a noise level and probability of at least 50% in the definition: the proof no longer works if $(1 + \epsilon)/2$ is replaced by just ϵ. In other words, mere noise would be classified as an attack by the modified definition.

Voltage. We now show that a higher adversarial voltage budget can only make a system more vulnerable. Indeed, if a system is universally (ϵ, V_1)-secure, then it is universally (ϵ, V_2)-secure for $V_2 \leq V_1$. For this, it suffices to prove the contrapositive, i.e., that if a system is not universally (ϵ, V_2)-secure, then it is not universally (ϵ, V_1)-secure. For the proof, let $v(t)$ be an adversarial waveform with $|v(t)| \leq V_2$ such that Eq. (4) does not hold, which exists by the assumption that the system is not universally (ϵ, V_2)-secure. Then, by the transitive property, $|v(t)| \leq V_1$, making $v(t)$ a valid counterexample for universal (ϵ, V_1) security.

Probability. The third property we show is probability monotonicity, allowing us to define a "critical threshold" for ϵ, above which a system is universally secure (for a fixed V_{PK}^{Adv}), and below which a system is not universally secure. Indeed, for fixed V_{PK}^{Adv}, if a system is universally (ϵ, V_{PK}^{Adv})-secure, then it is universally $(\epsilon + \delta, V_{PK}^{Adv})$-secure for $0 \leq \delta < 1 - \epsilon$, as

$$Pr\left[E_s(t) \geq Q + N^{-1}\left(\frac{\epsilon + \delta + 1}{2}\right)\right]$$

$$\leq Pr\left[E_s(t) \geq Q + N^{-1}\left(\frac{\epsilon + 1}{2}\right)\right] \leq \frac{\epsilon + 1}{2} \leq \frac{\epsilon + \delta + 1}{2}$$

because N^{-1} is increasing. The contrapositive is, of course, also true: if a system is not universally secure for a given ϵ, it is also not universally secure for $\epsilon - \delta$ with $0 \leq \delta \leq \epsilon$.

Thresholds. For a given security level ϵ, then, we can talk about the maximum (if any) V_{PK}^{Adv} such that a system is universally (ϵ, V_{PK}^{Adv})-secure, or conversely the minimum (if any) V_{PK}^{Adv} such that a system is not universally (ϵ, V_{PK}^{Adv})-secure. This is the **critical universal voltage level** V_c for the given ϵ. Moreover, for any V_{PK}^{Adv}, there is a unique **critical universal security threshold** ϵ_c such that the system is universally (ϵ, V_{PK}^{Adv})-secure for $\epsilon_c < \epsilon < 1$ and not universally (ϵ, V_{PK}^{Adv})-secure for $0 \le \epsilon < \epsilon_c$. By convention we take $\epsilon_c = 0$ if the system is secure for all ϵ, and $\epsilon_c = 1$ if there is no ϵ for which the system is secure. This critical threshold indicates the security level of a system: the lower ϵ_c is, the better a system is protected against signal injection attacks.

3.2   Selective Injection and Security

The second definition captures the notion of security against specific target waveforms $w(t)$: we wish to find the probability that a V_{PK}^{Adv}-bounded adversary can make $w(t)$ appear in the output of the ADC. Conversely, to define security in this context, we must make sure that the digitized signal $\tilde{s}_f(t)$ differs from the waveform $s(t) + w(t)$ with high probability, even if plenty of noise is allowed. There are two crucial points to notice about the waveform $w(t)$. First, $w(t)$ is not the raw signal $v(t)$ the adversary is transmitting, as this signal undergoes two transformations via H_C and H_A. Instead, $w(t)$ is the signal that the adversary wants the ADC to think that it is seeing, and is usually a demodulated version of $v(t)$ (see Fig. 1). Second, $w(t)$ does not necessarily cancel out or overpower $s(t)$, because that would require predictive modeling of the sensor signal $s(t)$. However, if the adversary can predict $s(t)$ (e.g., by monitoring the output of the ADC, or by using identical sensors), we can then ask about security against the waveform $w'(t) = w(t) - s(t)$ instead. Given this intuition, we can define selective security as follows:

Definition 2 (Selective Security, Selective Injection). *For $0 \le \epsilon < 1$, and $V_{PK}^{Adv} \ge 0$, a system is called **selectively** $(\epsilon, w(t), V_{PK}^{Adv})$-**secure** if*

$$Pr\left[E_{s+w}(t) \ge Q + N^{-1}\left(\frac{(1-\epsilon)+1}{2}\right)\right] > \frac{2-\epsilon}{2} \tag{5}$$

*for every adversarial waveform $v(t)$, with $|v(t)| \le V_{PK}^{Adv}$ for all t, where the probability is taken over the duration of the attack. Q is the quantization error of the system, N^{-1} is the noise distribution inverse defined in Eq. (2), and $E_{s+w}(t) = |\tilde{s}_f(t+\tau) - s(t) - w(t)|$ during sampling periods, and 0 otherwise. We call a successful attack a **selective injection**, and simply call a system selectively ϵ-secure, when V_{PK}^{Adv} and $w(t)$ are clear from context.*

This definition is monotonic in voltage and the probability of success, allowing us to talk about "the" probability of success for a given waveform:

Voltage. A similar argument shows that increasing V_{PK}^{Adv} can only make a secure system insecure, but not vice versa, i.e., that if a system is selectively $(\epsilon, w(t), V_1)$-secure, then it is selectively $(\epsilon, w(t), V_2)$-secure for $V_2 \le V_1$. We can thus define the **critical selective voltage level** V_c^w for a given ϵ and $w(t)$.

Probability. If a system is selectively ϵ-secure (against a target waveform and voltage budget), then it is selectively $(\epsilon + \delta)$-secure for $0 \leq \delta < 1 - \epsilon$, because

$$P = Pr\left[E_{s+w}(t) \geq Q + N^{-1}\left(\frac{1 - (\epsilon + \delta) + 1}{2}\right)\right]$$

$$\geq Pr\left[E_{s+w}(t) \geq Q + N^{-1}\left(\frac{1 - \epsilon + 1}{2}\right)\right]$$

$$> \frac{2 - \epsilon}{2} \geq \frac{2 - (\epsilon + \delta)}{2}$$

If the system is not selectively ϵ-secure, then it is not selectively $(\epsilon - \delta)$-secure.

Given the above, for a given waveform $w(t)$ and fixed V_{PK}^{Adv}, we can define a waveform-specific **critical selective security threshold** ϵ_c^w such that the system is vulnerable for all ϵ^w with $0 \leq \epsilon^w < \epsilon_c^w$ and secure for all ϵ^w with $\epsilon_c^w < \epsilon^w < 1$. By convention we take $\epsilon_c^w = 0$ if there is no ϵ for which the system is vulnerable, and $\epsilon_c^w = 1$ if there is no ϵ for which the system is secure.

Threshold Relationship. The critical universal threshold of a system ϵ_c is related to the critical selective threshold ϵ_c^0 against the zero waveform $w(t) = 0$ through the equation $\epsilon_c^0 = 1 - \epsilon_c$. Indeed, if a system is not universally ϵ-secure, then $P = Pr\left[E_s(t) \geq Q + N^{-1}\left(\frac{\epsilon+1}{2}\right)\right] > \frac{\epsilon+1}{2}$, so $\frac{2-(1-\epsilon)}{2} = \frac{\epsilon+1}{2} < P = Pr\left[E_{s+0}(t) \geq Q + N^{-1}\left(\frac{(1-(1-\epsilon))+1}{2}\right)\right]$, making the system selectively $(1 - \epsilon)$-secure for the zero waveform. Conversely, if a system is selectively $(1 - \epsilon)$-secure for the zero waveform, then it is not universally ϵ-secure. The fact that a low critical universal threshold results in a high critical selective threshold for the zero threshold is not surprising: it is easy for an adversary to inject a zero signal by simply not transmitting anything.

3.3 Universal Injection, Existential Security

The final notion of security is a weak one, which requires that the adversary cannot inject at least one "representable" waveform into the system, i.e., one which is within the ADC limits. We can express this more precisely as follows:

Definition 3 (Representable Waveform). *A waveform $w(t)$ is called **representable** if it is within the ADC voltage levels, and has a maximum frequency component bounded by the Nyquist frequency of the ADC. Mathematically, $V_{min} \leq w(t) \leq V_{max}$ and $f_{max} \leq f_s/2$.*

Using this, we can define security against at least one representable waveform:

Definition 4 (Existential Security, Universal Injection). *For $0 \leq \epsilon < 1$, and $V_{PK}^{Adv} \geq 0$, a system is called **existentially** (ϵ, V_{PK}^{Adv})-**secure** if there exists a representable waveform $w(t)$ for which the system is selectively $(\epsilon, w(t), V_{PK}^{Adv})$-secure. We call a system existentially ϵ-secure when V_{PK}^{Adv} is clear. If there is no such $w(t)$, we say that the adversary can perform any **universal injection**.*

Table 2. The adversary can easily disturb the smartphone output (existential injection), and inject human speech (universal injection). Selective injections of sines are less precise than exponentials of the same frequency.

Injection	Resulting signal	Crit. thres.
Existential	$w(t) \neq 0$	0.892
Selective	$w(t) = e^{\sin(2\pi f_m t)}$	0.747
Selective	$w(t) = \sin(2\pi f_m t)$	0.562
Universal	"OK Google" commands	≤ 0.562

As above, voltage and probability are monotonic in the opposite direction.

Voltage. If a system is existentially (ϵ, V_1)-secure, then it is (ϵ, V_2)-secure for $V_2 \leq V_1$. By assumption, there is a representable $w(t)$ such that the system is selectively $(\epsilon, w(t), V_1)$-secure. By the previous section, this system is $(\epsilon, w(t), V_2)$-secure, concluding the proof.

Probability. If a system is existentially (ϵ_1, V)-secure, then it is (ϵ_2, V)-secure for $\epsilon_1 \leq \epsilon_2$. By assumption, there is a representable $w(t)$ such that the system is selectively $(\epsilon_1, w(t), V)$-secure. By the previous section, the system is also $(\epsilon_2, w(t), V)$-secure, as desired.

Thresholds. Extending the definitions of the previous sections, for fixed ϵ we can define a **critical existential voltage level** V_c^{exist} below which a system is existentially ϵ-secure, and above which the system is existentially ϵ-insecure. Similarly, for a fixed adversarial voltage we can define the **critical existential security threshold** ϵ_c^{exist}, above which the system is existentially secure, and below which the system is insecure.

In some cases, security designers may wish to adjust the definitions to restrict target waveforms (and existential security counterexamples) even further. For instance, we might wish to check whether an adversary can inject all waveforms which are sufficiently bounded away from 0, periodic waveforms, or waveforms of a specific frequency. The proofs for voltage and probability monotonicity still hold, allowing us to talk about universal security against $\mathcal{S}$-representable waveforms: waveforms which are representable and also in a set $\mathcal{S}$.

4   Security Evaluation of a Smartphone Microphone

In this section, we illustrate how our security definitions can be used to determine the security level of a commercial, off-the-shelf smartphone microphone. We first introduce an algorithm to calculate the critical selective security threshold ϵ_c^w against a target waveform $w(t)$ in Sect. 4.1. We then use the algorithm to calculate the critical thresholds of a smartphone in Sect. 4.2. Finally, we comment on universal security in Sect. 4.3, where we show that we are able to inject complex "OK Google" commands. We summarize our results in Table 2.

4.1   Algorithm for Selective Security Thresholds

In this section, we introduce an algorithm to calculate the critical selective security threshold ϵ_c^w of a system against a target waveform $w(t)$, using a transmitted signal $v(t)$. The first step in calculating the security level is determining the noise distribution. To that end, we collect N measurements of the system output $\tilde{s}_f(t)$ during the injection and pick one as the *reference* signal. We then pick $1 \le k \le N-2$ of them to calculate the noise (*estimation* signals), while the remaining are used to verify our calculations (*validation* signals).

Our algorithm first removes any DC offset and re-scales the measurements so that the root-mean-square (RMS) voltages of the signals are the same. The repeated measurements are then phase-aligned, and we calculate the distance between the reference signal and the estimation signals. The average of this distance should be very close to 0, as the signals are generated in the same way. However, the standard deviation σ is non-zero, so we can model noise as following a zero-mean normal distribution $n(t) \sim N(0, \sigma^2)$. We can then find the critical threshold between the reference signal and any target *ideal* waveform $w(t)$ as follows: we first detrend, scale, and align the ideal signal to the reference waveform, as with the estimation signals. Then, we calculate the errors (distance) between the ideal and the reference signal. Finally, we perform a binary search for different values of ϵ, in order to find the largest ϵ for which Eq. (5) does not hold: this is the critical threshold ϵ_c^w. To calculate the inverse of the noise, we use the percentile point function $ppf(\epsilon)$, which is the inverse of the cumulative distribution function, and satisfies $N^{-1}(\epsilon) = ppf((1+\epsilon)/2)$. Note that since the critical universal threshold ϵ_c is related to the selective critical threshold of the zero waveform ϵ_c^0 through $\epsilon_c = 1 - \epsilon_c^0$ (Sect. 3.2), the same algorithm can be used to calculate the critical universal security threshold ϵ_c.

4.2   Existential and Selective Injections into a Smartphone

We demonstrate how our algorithm can be used in a realistic setup using a Motorola XT1541 Moto G3 smartphone. We inject amplitude-modulated $f_m = 1\,\text{kHz}$ signals using a Rohde & Schwarz SMC100A/B103 generator into the headphone jack of the phone, following direct power injection (DPI) methodology [6]. We collect $N = 10$ measurements of 2^{15} sample points per run using an "Audio Recorder" app, and record the data at a frequency of $f_s = 44.1\,\text{kHz}$ in a $[-1,1]$ dimensionless range (AAC encoding). We first AM-modulate f_m over $f_c = 200\,\text{MHz}$ using an output level of $V_{RMS}^{Adv} = V_{PK}^{Adv}/\sqrt{2} = 0.2\,\text{V}$. This injection is demodulated well by the smartphone and has a similarity (as indicated by the Pearson Correlation Coefficient) of over 0.98 compared to a pure 1 kHz tone. We call this example the "clean" waveform. The second injection, which we call the "distorted" waveform, uses $f_c = 25\,\text{MHz}$, $V_{RMS}^{Adv} = 0.9\,\text{V}$, and has a similarity of less than 0.55 to the ideal tone. Example measurements of these signals and "ideal" signals (see below) are shown in Fig. 4.

The algorithm first calculates the noise level using the reference signals. As expected, the error average is very close to 0 (usually less than 10^{-6}), while standard deviation σ is noticeable at around 0.0015. Taking the reference signals

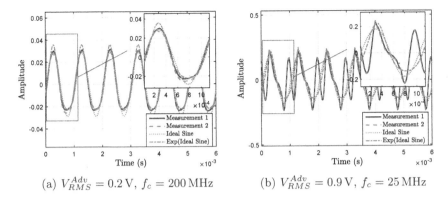

(a) $V_{RMS}^{Adv} = 0.2\,\mathrm{V}$, $f_c = 200\,\mathrm{MHz}$ (b) $V_{RMS}^{Adv} = 0.9\,\mathrm{V}$, $f_c = 25\,\mathrm{MHz}$

Fig. 4. Clean (a) and Distorted (b) waveforms injected into the smartphone, with ideal sine and exponential sine functions for comparison.

Table 3. Mean and std. deviation (μ, σ) of critical selective thresholds ϵ_c^w for different target signals $w(t)$. Injections using the clean waveform are always more successful than with the distorted waveform. Validation signals are injected with high fidelity, and are better modeled by an exponential rather than a pure sine.

Waveform	Validation	Ideal Sine	$e^{IdealSine}$	$w(t) \neq 0$
Clean	$(0.98, 0.03)$	$(0.56, 0.04)$	$(0.75, 0.06)$	$(0.89, 0.01)$
Distorted	$(0.95, 0.09)$	$(0.31, 0.05)$	$(0.34, 0.05)$	$(0.71, 0.04)$

as the target signal $w(t)$, the critical selective thresholds are close to 1. In other words, even if the injected waveforms do not correspond to "pure" signals, the adversary can inject them with high fidelity: the system is not selectively secure against them with high probability.

We also tried two signals as the signal $w(t)$ that the adversary is trying to inject: a pure 1 kHz sine wave, and an exponential of the same sine wave. The averages and standard deviations for the calculated thresholds over all combinations of k and reference signals are shown in Table 3. As we would expect, the thresholds for the distorted waveform are much lower than the values for the clean waveform: the signal is distorted, so it is hard to inject an ideal signal. We also find that the exponential function is a better fit for the signal we are seeing, and can better explain the harmonics. Table 3 also includes the critical universal injection threshold based on the two waveform injections. This threshold is much higher for both waveforms, as injections disturb the ADC output sufficiently, even when the demodulated signal is not ideal.

4.3 Universal Injections on a Smartphone

In this section, we demonstrate that the smartphone is vulnerable to the injection of arbitrary commands, which cause the smartphone to behave as if the user initiated an action. Using the same setup of direct power injection (Sect. 4.2), we

Table 4. The ADCs used in our experiments cover a range of different properties.

ADC	Manufacturer	Package	Type	Bits	Max f_s	f_{cut}
TLC549	Texas Instruments	DIP	SAR	8	40 kHz	2.7 MHz
ATmega328P	Atmel	Integrated	SAR	10	76.9 kHz	0.1–11.4 MHz
Artix7	Xilinx	Integrated	SAR	12	1 MHz	5.3 MHz
AD7276	Analog Devices	TSOT	SAR	12	3 MHz	66.3 MHz
AD7783	Analog Devices	TSSOP	$\Delta\Sigma$	24	19.79 Hz	[50,60 Hz]
AD7822	Analog Devices	DIP	Flash	8	2 MHz	128.4 MHz

first inject a modulated recording of "OK Google, turn on the flashlight" into the microphone port, checking both whether the voice command service was activated in response to "OK Google", and whether the desired action was executed. We repeat measurements 10 times, each time amplitude-modulating the command at a depth of $m = 100\%$ with $V_{RMS}^{Adv} = 0.6$ V on 26 carrier frequencies f_c: 25 MHz, 50 MHz, and 100–2400 MHz at a step of 100 MHz. The voice-activation feature ("OK Google") worked with 100% success rate (10/10 repetitions) for all frequencies, while the full command was successfully executed for 23 of the 26 frequencies we tested (all frequencies except $f_c \in \{1.3, 2.0, 2.4\text{GHz}\}$). Increasing the output level to $V_{RMS}^{Adv} = 0.9$ V, increased success rate to 25/26 frequencies. Only $f_c = 2.4$ GHz did not result in a full command injection, possibly because the Wi-Fi disconnected in the process.

We repeated the above injections, testing 5 further commands to (1) call a contact; (2) text a contact; (3) set a timer; (4) mute the volume; and (5) turn on airplane mode. The results remained identical, regardless of the actual command to be executed. As a result, all carrier frequencies which are not severely attenuated by H_C (e.g., when coupling to the user's headphones) are vulnerable to injections of complex waveforms such as human speech.

5   Commercial ADC Response H_A to Malicious Signals

As explained in Sect. 2, an adversary trying to inject signals remotely into a system typically needs to transmit modulated signals over high-frequency carriers. As H_C is unique to each circuit and needs to be re-calculated even for minor changes to its components and layout [5], the first step to determine the system vulnerability is to understand the behavior H_A of the ADC used.

To do so, we inject signals generated via a Rohde & Schwarz SMC100A/B103 signal generator directly into 6 ADCs and determine their demodulation characteristics. The ADCs come from 4 manufacturers in different packages and are controlled via different protocols. The maximum sampling rate f_s of the ADCs ranges from a few Hz to several MHz, while the resolution ranges from 8 to 24 bits. The ADC types include Delta-Sigma ($\Delta\Sigma$), half-flash, and successive approximation (SAR). Table 4 shows these properties along with the -3 dB cut-off frequency f_{cut}, calculated using the R, C parameters in the ADCs' datasheets.

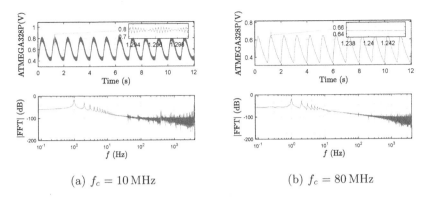

(a) $f_c = 10\,\mathrm{MHz}$ (b) $f_c = 80\,\mathrm{MHz}$

Fig. 5. Example ATmega328P output for power $P = 0\,\mathrm{dBm}$, signal frequency $f_m = 1\,\mathrm{Hz}$, and modulation depth $m = 50\%$. The signal exhibits the correct fundamental frequency, but also contains strong harmonics and a high-frequency component, which is attenuated as the carrier frequency f_c increases.

We inject sinusoidal signals of different frequencies f_m, which have been amplitude modulated (AM) on different carrier carrier frequencies f_c. In other words, we consider the intended signal to be $w(t) = \sin(2\pi f_m t)$, the sensor signal to be absent $(s(t) = 0)$, and evaluate how "close" $w(t)$ is to the ADC output $\tilde{s}_f(t)$. Due to space restrictions, we only describe typical results for each ADC.

ATmega328P. Figure 5 presents two example measurements of outputs of the ATmega328P, both in the time domain and in the frequency domain. The input to the ADC is a $f_m = 1\,\mathrm{Hz}$ signal modulated over different high-frequency carriers. As shown in the frequency domain (bottom of Fig. 5), the fundamental frequency f_m dominates all other frequencies, so the attacker is able to inject a signal of the intended frequency into the output of the ADC. However, the output at both carrier frequencies has strong harmonics at $2f_m, 3f_m, \ldots\,\mathrm{Hz}$, which indicates that the resulting signal is not pure. Moreover, there is a residual high-frequency component, which is attenuated as the carrier frequency f_c increases. Finally, there is a frequency-dependent DC offset caused, in part, by the ESD diodes, while the peak-to-peak amplitude of the measured signal decreases as the carrier frequency increases. This is due to the low-pass filtering behavior of the sample-and-hold mechanism, which also explains why we are only able to demodulate signals for carrier frequencies until approximately $150\,\mathrm{MHz}$.

TLC549. The TLC549 (Fig. 6a) also demodulates the injected signal, but still contains harmonics and a small high-frequency component.

AD7783. As the AD7783 (Fig. 6b) only has a sampling frequency of $f_s = 19.79\,\mathrm{Hz}$, aliasing occurs when the baseband signal exceeds the Nyquist frequency $f_s/2$. For example, when the baseband frequency is $f_m = 10\,\mathrm{Hz}$, the fundamental frequency dominating the measurements is of frequency $2f_m - f_s = 20 - 19.79 = 0.21\,\mathrm{Hz}$, with a high-frequency component of $f_s - f_m = 9.79\,\mathrm{Hz}$.

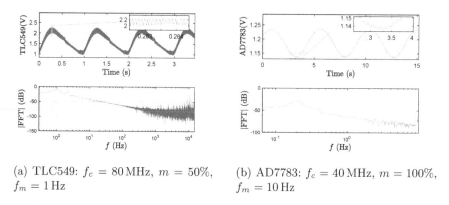

(a) TLC549: $f_c = 80\,\text{MHz}$, $m = 50\%$,   (b) AD7783: $f_c = 40\,\text{MHz}$, $m = 100\%$,
$f_m = 1\,\text{Hz}$ $f_m = 10\,\text{Hz}$

Fig. 6. Example TLC549 (a) and AD7783 (b) outputs for a transmission power of $P = 5\,\text{dBm}$. Both ADCs demodulate the injected signal, but present harmonics and some high-frequency components. The AD7783 signal is aliased.

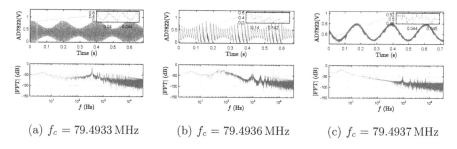

(a) $f_c = 79.4933\,\text{MHz}$ (b) $f_c = 79.4936\,\text{MHz}$ (c) $f_c = 79.4937\,\text{MHz}$

Fig. 7. Example AD7822 output for power $P = -5\,\text{dBm}$, signal frequency $f_m = 5\,\text{Hz}$, and depth $m = 50\%$. Signal demodulation requires a fine-tuned f_c.

AD7822, AD7276, Artix7. The three remaining ADCs contain strong high-frequency components which dominate the low-frequency signal. Their outputs appear to be AM-modulated, but at a carrier frequency which is below the ADC's Nyquist frequency. However, with manual tuning of the carrier frequency, it is possible to remove this high frequency component, causing the ADC to demodulate the input. This is shown for the Flash ADC AD7822 in Fig. 7, where we change the carrier frequency f_c in steps of 100 Hz.

Conclusion. The results of our experiments lead to the following observations:

1. **Generality** – All 6 ADCs tested are vulnerable to signal injections at multiple carrier frequencies, as they demodulate signals, matching the theoretical expectations of Sect. 2.1. As the ADCs are of all major types and with a range of different resolutions and sampling frequencies, the conclusions drawn should also be valid for other ADC chips.
2. **Low-Pass Filter** – Although all ADCs exhibited low-pass filtering characteristics, the maximum vulnerable carrier frequency for a given power level was multiple times the cut-off frequency of the RC circuit at the input of

the ADC. This extended the frequency range that an attacker could use for transmissions to attack the system.

3. **Power** – The adversary needs to select the power level of transmissions carefully: too much power in the input of the ADC can cause saturation and/or clipping of the measured signal. Too little power, on the other hand, results in output that looks like noise or a zero signal.

4. **Carrier Frequency** – Some ADCs were vulnerable at any carrier frequency that is not severely attenuated by the sample-and-hold mechanism. For others, high-frequency components dominated the intended baseband signal of frequency f_m in the ADC output for most frequencies. Even then, carefully-chosen carrier frequencies resulted in a demodulated ADC output.

6   Discussion

We now discuss how our work can inform design choices. To start, choosing the right ADC directly impacts the susceptibility to signal injection attacks. As shown in Sect. 5, some ADCs distort the demodulated output, and are thus more resilient to clean sinusoidal injections. Moreover, other ADCs require fine-grained control over the carrier frequency of injection. As the adversarial signal is transformed through the circuit-specific transfer function H_C, the adversary may not have such control, resulting in a more secure system.

Having chosen the appropriate ADC based on cost, performance, security, or other considerations, a designer needs to assess the impact of H_C. Prior work has shown that even small layout or component changes affect the EMI behavior of a circuit [5,11,21]. Since the ADC behavior can be independently determined through direct power injections, fewer experiments with remote transmissions are required to evaluate the full circuit behavior and how changes in the circuit's topology influence the system's security.

Our selective security definition and algorithm address how to determine the vulnerability of a system against specific waveforms. Universal security, on the other hand, allows us to directly compare the security of two systems for a fixed adversarial voltage budget through their critical universal security thresholds. Moreover, given a probability/threshold ϵ, we can calculate the critical universal voltage level, which is the maximum output level for which a system is still universally ϵ-secure.

Our smartphone case study showed that our framework can be used in practice with real systems, while our "OK Google" experiments demonstrated that less-than-perfect injections of adversarial waveforms can have the same effect as perfect injections. This is because there is a mismatch between the true noise level of a system and the worst-case noise level that the system expects. In other words, injections worked at all carrier frequencies, even when the demodulated output was noisy or distorted. This is a deliberate, permissive design decision, which allows the adversary to succeed with a range of different and noisy waveforms $w(t)$, despite small amplitudes and DC offsets.

Although not heavily discussed in this paper, our model and definitions are general enough to capture alternative signal injection techniques. For instance, electro-mechanical sensors have resonant frequencies which allow acoustic injection attacks [20,23]. H_C can account for such imperfections in the sensors themselves, attenuating injection frequencies which are not close to the resonant frequencies. Our system model also makes it easy to evaluate countermeasures and defense mechanisms in its context. For example, shielding increases the attenuation factor of H_C, thereby increasing the power requirements for the adversary (Sect. 2.1). Alternatively, a low-pass filter (LPF) before the ADC and/or amplifier changes H_A, and attenuates the high-frequency components which would induce non-linearities. Note, however, that even moving the pre-amplifier, LPF and ADC into the same IC package does not fully eliminate the vulnerability to signal injection attacks (Sect. 7) as the channel between the analog sensor and the ADC cannot be fundamentally authenticated.

7   Related Work

Ever since a 2013 paper by Kune et al. showed that electromagnetic (EM) signals can be used to cause medical devices to deliver defibrillation shocks [9], there has been a rise in EM, acoustic, and optical signal injection attacks against sensor and actuator systems [6]. Although some papers have focused on vulnerabilities caused by the ADC sampling process itself [1], others have focused on exploiting the control algorithms that make use of the digitized signal. For example, Shoukry et al. showed how to force the Anti-Lock Braking Systems (ABS) to model the real input signal as a disturbance [18]. Selvaraj et al. also used the magnetic field to perform attacks on actuators, but further explored the relationship between frequency and the average injected voltage into ADCs [17]. By contrast, our paper primarily focused on a formal mathematical framework to understand security in the context of signal injection attacks, but also investigated the demodulation properties of different ADCs.

Our work further highlighted how to use the introduced algorithm and definitions to investigate the security of a smartphone, complementing earlier work which had shown that AM-modulated electromagnetic transmissions can be picked up by hands-free headsets to trigger voice commands in smartphones [8]. Voice injection attacks can also be achieved by modulating signals on ultrasound frequencies [25], or by playing two tones at different ultrasound frequencies and exploiting non-linearities in components [16]. Acoustic transmissions at a device's resonant frequencies can also incapacitate [20] or precisely control [22] drones, with attackers who account for sampling rate drifts being able to control the outputs of accelerometers for longer periods of time [23]. Moreover, optical attacks can be used to spoof medical infusion pump measurements [12], and cause autonomous cars and unmanned aerial vehicles (UAVs) to drift or fail [2,14,24].

It should be noted that although the literature has primarily focused on signal injection attacks, some works have also proposed countermeasures. These defense mechanisms revolve around better sampling techniques, for example by adding unspoofable physical and computational delays [19], or by oversampling and selectively turning the sensors off using a secret sequence [26].

Overall, despite the extensive literature on signal injection attacks and defenses, the setup and effectiveness of different works is often reported in an inconsistent way, making their results hard to compare [6]. Our work, recognizing this gap, introduced a formal foundation to define and quantify security against signal injection attacks, working towards unifying the reporting methodology for competing works.

8   Conclusion

Sensors guide many of our choices, and we often blindly trust their values. However, it is possible to spoof their outputs through electromagnetic or other signal injection attacks. To address the lack of a unifying framework describing the susceptibility of devices to such attacks, we defined a system and adversary model for signal injections. Our model is the first to abstract away from specific environments and circuit designs and presents a strong adversary who is only limited by transmission power. It also makes it easy to discuss and evaluate countermeasures in its context and covers different types of signal injection attacks.

Within our model, we defined existential, selective, and universal security, capturing effects ranging from mere disruptions of the ADC outputs to precise injections of all waveforms. We showed that our definitions can be used to evaluate the security level of an off-the-shelf smartphone, and introduced an algorithm to calculate "critical" thresholds, which express how close an injected signal is to the ideal signal. Finally, we characterized the demodulation characteristics of commercial ADCs to malicious injections. In response to the emerging signal injection threat, our work paves the way towards a future where security can be quantified and compared through our methodology and security definitions.

References

1. Bolshev, A., Larsen, J., Krotofil, M., Wightman, R.: A rising tide: design exploits in industrial control systems. In: USENIX Workshop on Offensive Technologies (WOOT) (2016)
2. Davidson, D., Wu, H., Jellinek, R., Singh, V., Ristenpart, T.: Controlling UAVs with sensor input spoofing attacks. In: USENIX Workshop on Offensive Technologies (WOOT) (2016)
3. Friis, H.T.: A note on a simple transmission formula. Proc. IRE (JRPROC) **34**(5), 254–256 (1946)
4. Fu, K., Xu, W.: Risks of trusting the physics of sensors. Commun. ACM **61**(2), 20–23 (2018)
5. Gago, J., Balcells, J., González, D., Lamich, M., Mon, J., Santolaria, A.: EMI susceptibility model of signal conditioning circuits based on operational amplifiers. IEEE Trans. Electromagn. Compat. **49**(4), 849–859 (2007)
6. Giechaskiel, I., Rasmussen, K.B.: Taxonomy and challenges of out-of-band signal injection attacks and defenses. arXiv:1901.06935 (2019)
7. Goldwasser, S., Micali, S., Rivest, R.L.: A digital signature scheme secure against adaptive chosen-message attacks. SIAM J. Comput. **17**(2), 281–308 (1988)

8. Kasmi, C., Lopes-Esteves, J.: IEMI threats for information security: remote command injection on modern smartphones. IEEE Trans. Electromagn. Compat. **57**(6), 1752–1755 (2015)

9. Kune, D.F., et al.: Ghost talk: mitigating EMI signal injection attacks against analog sensors. In: IEEE Symposium on Security and Privacy (S&P) (2013)

10. Leone, M., Singer, H.L.: On the coupling of an external electromagnetic field to a printed circuit board trace. IEEE Trans. Electromagn. Compat. **41**(4), 418–424 (1999)

11. Lissner, A., Hoene, E., Stube, B., Guttowski, S.: Predicting the influence of placement of passive components on EMI behaviour. In: European Conference on Power Electronics and Applications (2007)

12. Park, Y.S., Son, Y., Shin, H., Kim, D., Kim, Y.: This ain't your dose: sensor spoofing attack on medical infusion pump. In: USENIX Workshop on Offensive Technologies (WOOT) (2016)

13. Pelgrom, M.J.M.: Analog-to-Digital Conversion, 3rd edn. Springer, Cham (2017). https://doi.org/10.1007/978-3-319-44971-5

14. Petit, J., Stottelaar, B., Feiri, M., Kargl, F.: Remote attacks on automated vehicles sensors: experiments on camera and LiDAR. Black Hat Europe (2015)

15. Redouté, J.M., Steyaert, M.: EMC of Analog Integrated Circuits, 1st edn. Springer, Dordrecht (2009). https://doi.org/10.1007/978-90-481-3230-0

16. Roy, N., Hassanieh, H., Roy Choudhury, R.: BackDoor: making microphones hear inaudible sounds. In: International Conference on Mobile Systems, Applications, and Services (MobiSys) (2017)

17. Selvaraj, J., Dayanikli, G.Y., Gaunkar, N.P., Ware, D., Gerdes, R.M., Mina, M.: Electromagnetic induction attacks against embedded systems. In: Asia Conference on Computer and Communications Security (ASIACCS) (2018)

18. Shoukry, Y., Martin, P., Tabuada, P., Srivastava, M.: Non-invasive spoofing attacks for anti-lock braking systems. In: Bertoni, G., Coron, J.-S. (eds.) CHES 2013. LNCS, vol. 8086, pp. 55–72. Springer, Heidelberg (2013). https://doi.org/10.1007/978-3-642-40349-1_4

19. Shoukry, Y., Martin, P.D., Yona, Y., Diggavi, S., Srivastava, M.B.: PyCRA: physical challenge-response authentication for active sensors under spoofing attacks. In: Conference on Computer and Communications Security (CCS) (2015)

20. Son, Y., et al.: Rocking drones with intentional sound noise on gyroscopic sensors. In: USENIX Security Symposium (2015)

21. Sutu, Y.H., Whalen, J.J.: Statistics for demodulation RFI in operational amplifiers. In: International Symposium on Electromagnetic Compatibility (EMC) (1983)

22. Trippel, T., Weisse, O., Xu, W., Honeyman, P., Fu, K.: WALNUT: waging doubt on the integrity of MEMS accelerometers with acoustic injection attacks. In: IEEE European Symposium on Security and Privacy (EuroS&P) (2017)

23. Tu, Y., Lin, Z., Lee, I., Hei, X.: Injected and delivered: fabricating implicit control over actuation systems by spoofing inertial sensors. In: USENIX Security Symposium (2018)

24. Yan, C., Xu, W., Liu, J.: Can you trust autonomous vehicles: contactless attacks against sensors of self-driving vehicle. DEFCON (2016)

25. Zhang, G., Yan, C., Ji, X., Zhang, T., Zhang, T., Xu, W.: DolphinAttack: inaudible voice commands. In: Conference on Computer and Communications Security (CCS) (2017)

26. Zhang, Y., Rasmussen, K.B.: Detection of electromagnetic interference attacks on sensor systems. In: IEEE Symposium on Security and Privacy (S&P) (2020)

Secure Protocols

Formalizing and Proving Privacy Properties of Voting Protocols Using Alpha-Beta Privacy

Sébastien Gondron[(✉)] and Sebastian Mödersheim

DTU Compute, Richard Petersens Plads, Building 324,
2800 Kongens Lyngby, Denmark
{spcg,samo}@dtu.dk

Abstract. Most common formulations of privacy-type properties for security protocols are specified as bisimilarity of processes in applied-π calculus. For instance, voting privacy is specified as the bisimilarity between two processes that differ only by a swap of two votes. Similar methods are applied to formalize receipt-freeness. We believe that there exists a gap between these technical encodings and an intuitive understanding of these properties.

We use (α, β)-privacy to formalize privacy goals in a different way, namely as a reachability problem. Every state consists of a pair of formulae: α expresses the publicly released information (like the result of the vote) and β expresses the additional information available to the intruder (like observed messages). Privacy holds in a state if every model of α can be extended to a model of β, i.e., the intruder cannot make any deductions beyond what was deliberately released; and privacy of a protocol holds if privacy holds in every reachable state.

This allows us to give formulations of voting privacy and receipt-freeness that are more declarative than the common bisimilarity based formulations, since we reason about models that are consistent with all observations like interaction with coerced (but potentially lying) voters. Also, we show a relation between the goals: receipt-freeness implies voting privacy.

Finally, the logical approach also allows for declarative manual proofs (as opposed to long machine-generated proofs) like reasoning about a permutation of votes and the intruder's knowledge about that permutation.

Keywords: Formal security models · Logic and verification · Privacy preserving systems · Voting protocols · Receipt-freeness · Security requirements · Security protocols

1 Introduction

Privacy is essential for freedom: to make a choice like a vote in a completely free way, i.e., determined only by one's own convictions, context, interests and

K. Sako et al. (Eds.): ESORICS 2019, LNCS 11735, pp. 535–555, 2019.
https://doi.org/10.1007/978-3-030-29959-0_26

expectations (rather than those of others), it is crucial that this choice cannot be observed by others. However, it is not sufficient to give people the possibility to make the choice in a private way: we also have to actually prevent them from *proving* what they have chosen. While one has the right to say what one has chosen (by the freedom of speech), we must also guarantee the possibility to *lie* about it, too. The reason is that otherwise we limit the privacy through a back-door, as there can arise pressure to prove what one has chosen, especially when bribery or abuse of power comes into play. This paper investigates the tension between privacy and coercion with the focus on voting privacy, however, this is also relevant in other areas like electronic medical prescriptions (preventing pressure from the pharmaceutical industry onto doctors).

Related to the understanding of privacy goals is the problem that a dem-agogue can easily raise doubts about the legitimacy of an election. Our best chance to defeat this are open source systems that scientists, and ideally also ordinary people, can understand and convince themselves to be correct. The less obscure, the harder it is to defame, and the easier to recognize criticisms as unfounded. One of the challenges for describing systems in both a formally precise and intuitive way is privacy goals and their subtle relation to coercion.

Most common formulations of privacy-type properties for security protocols are specified as bisimilarity of processes in applied-π calculus [1–4], and we regard this as a rather technical way to encode the properties: it is quite hard to intu-itively understand what such a bisimilarity goal actually entails and what not. While one can get insights from a failed proof when the goal is too strong, one cannot easily see when it is too weak (with respect to one's intuition).

This paper gives a model-theoretic way to formalize and reason about pri-vacy and receipt-freeness. We build on the framework of (α, β)-privacy [5], that defines privacy as a state-based safety property, where each state consists of two formulae α, the deliberately released high-level information like the result of an election, and β, the observations that the intruder could make. During transi-tions, the information in α and β can only increase (by adding new conjuncts to the formulae). The question is (for every reachable state), whether every model of α is compatible with the observations in β: if not, the intruder is able to rule out some models of α and thus has obtained more information about the system than we have deliberately released. In particular we use this to come as close as possible to the following intuitive definition of privacy goals:

(a) **Voting privacy:** the number of voters and the result of the election are published at the end of the election. The intruder should not find out more than that about voters and votes.
(b) **Receipt-freeness:** no voter has a way to prove how they voted. This can be indirectly expressed by saying: for everything that could have happened according to (a), the voter can make up a consistent "story".

Our contribution is a general methodology to modeling voting privacy and receipt-freeness with (α, β)-privacy that can be applied for a variety of pro-tocols. This in particular includes a proof methodology that allows for simple model-theoretic arguments, suitable for manual proofs and proof assistants like

Isabelle and Coq. We illustrated this practically at hand of the FOO'92 protocol as an example, showing in particular how the use of permutations in the reasoning can lead to elegant proofs. In the model we propose, α is the same for both voting secrecy and receipt-freeness; the difference lies in β, namely in the challenge for a coerced voter to make a consistent story. From this construction it immediately follows that receipt-freeness implies vote secrecy.

We do regard our models in (α, β)-privacy as a complementary view to existing approaches like [6]. We believe that their formalizations may be equivalent in some sense to ours (at least we found no examples where the notions would differ), and regardless, our models aim to provide a fresh perspective. This holds in particular as it allows for a different style of proofs that are in some sense easier to conduct. While we do not consider any questions of automation, a hope is that this may also broaden the scope of methods for automatically analyzing privacy-type goals.

2   Preliminaries

It is common in protocol verification to consider an algebraic model of messages, namely interpreting functions in the quotient algebra modulo a set of algebraic equations (i.e., two terms are different *unless* the algebraic equations deem them equal). Many approaches usually reason about only logical implications, i.e. derivations that follow in *every* interpretation. In contrast, we here reason about the different interpretations of formulae and hence have to make the interpretation of functions explicit. For this reason, we use *Herbrand logic* [7], a variant of first-order logic, that allows us just that.

2.1   Herbrand Logic

For brevity, we only highlight the differences to standard first-order logic, the precise definition that we use can be found in the original paper on (α, β)-privacy [5]. The main point is that in Herbrand logic fixes the universe in which to interpret all symbols. To that end, we consider always a signature $\Sigma = \Sigma_f \uplus \Sigma_i \uplus \Sigma_r$ that distinguishes three kinds of symbols: Σ_f the set of *uninterpreted function symbols*, Σ_i the set of *interpreted function symbols* and Σ_r the set of *relation symbols*. Let $\mathcal{T}_{\Sigma_f}$ be the set of (ground) terms that can be built using symbols in Σ_f, and let $\approx$ be a congruence relation on $\mathcal{T}_{\Sigma_f}$, then the *Herbrand universe* is the quotient algebra $\mathcal{A} = \mathcal{T}_{\Sigma_f} / \approx$. Note that the universe A of $\mathcal{A}$ thus consists of equivalence classes of terms, i.e., $A = \{ [\![t]\!]_\approx \mid t \in \mathcal{T}_{\Sigma_f} \}$ where $[\![t]\!]_\approx = \{ t' \mid t \in \mathcal{T}_{\Sigma_f} \wedge t \approx t' \}$. Algebra $\mathcal{A}$ also fixes the "interpretation" of all uninterpreted function symbols, namely $f^{\mathcal{A}}([\![t_1]\!]_\approx, \ldots, [\![t_n]\!]_\approx) = [\![f(t_1, \ldots, t_n)]\!]_\approx$.

The interpreted function symbols Σ_i and the relation symbols Σ_r behave as in standard first-order logic, namely as function and relation symbols on the universe. To highlight syntactically the distinction between uninterpreted and interpreted function symbols, we write $f(t_1, \ldots, t_n)$ if $f \in \Sigma_f$ and $f[t_1, \ldots, t_n]$ if $f \in \Sigma_i$. Given a signature Σ, a set of variables $\mathcal{V}$ distinct from Σ, and a congruence $\approx$, and thus fixing a universe A, we define an *interpretation* $\mathcal{I}$ (w.r.t. $\Sigma, \mathcal{V}$, and $\approx$) as a function such that $\mathcal{I}(x) \in A$ for every $x \in \mathcal{V}, \mathcal{I}(f) : A^n \to A$ for every $f \in \Sigma_i$ of arity n, and $\mathcal{I}(r) \subseteq A^n$ for every $r \in \Sigma_r$ of arity n. (The functions of Σ_f are determined by the quotient algebra). We define a model relation $\mathcal{I} \models \phi$ (formula ϕ holds under $\mathcal{I}$) as standard and use common notations like $\phi \models \psi$.

For the rest of the paper, we assume that Σ_f contains the constant 0 and the unary function s, and Σ_i contains the binary function $+$. This means that the universe contains the natural numbers $0, s(0), s(s(1)), \ldots$ which we often write as $0, 1, 2, \ldots$. We characterize $+$ by the following axiom that we also generally assume for the rest of this paper:

$$\alpha_{ax} = \forall x, y. \quad x + 0 = x \wedge x + s(y) = s(x + y) \tag{1}$$

Note that this characterization is only possible due to the expressive power of Herbrand logic (in standard First-Order Logic one cannot characterize the universe appropriately).

2.2   Encoding of Frames

We use, as it is standard in security protocol verification, a black-box algebraic model. We choose a subset $\Sigma_{op} \subseteq \Sigma_f$ of uninterpreted functions to be the *operators* available to the intruder. For instance we generally require $0, s \in \Sigma_{op}$, so the intruder can "generate" any natural number.[1] For representing the intruder knowledge, we use the concept of frames:

Definition 1 (Frame [5]). *A frame is written as $F = \{\!| m_1 \mapsto t_1, \ldots, m_l \mapsto t_l |\!\}$ where the m_i are distinguished constants and the t_i are terms that do not contain any m_i. We call $m_1, \ldots, m_l$ the domain and $t_1, \ldots, t_l$ the image of the frame. We write $F\{\!|t|\!\}$ for replacing in the term t every occurrence of m_i with t_i, i.e., F works like a substitution. F^D denotes the restriction of F to sub-domain D.*

The m_i can be regarded as *memory locations* of the intruder, representing that the intruder knows the messages t_i. The set of *recipes* is the least set that contains $m_1, \ldots, m_l$ and that is closed under all the cryptographic operators Σ_{op}.

In order to formalize frames in Herbrand logic, we introduce two new symbols: a unary predicate symbol *gen* that characterizes the set of recipes and a unary interpreted function symbol kn_F that encodes the frame F as a function from recipes to messages. The following axioms characterize these symbols.

---

[1] The fact that $+ \notin \Sigma_{op}$ does not limit the intruder: all natural arithmetic reasoning is part of the models relation already (thanks to α_{ax}).

Definition 2 ($\phi_{gen}(D)$ and $\phi_{frame}(F)$ [5])**.** *For a frame $F = \{|m_1 \mapsto t_1, \ldots,$ $m_l \mapsto t_l|\}$ with domain $D = \{m_1, \ldots, m_l\}$, a unary predicate gen and an interpreted unary function symbol kn_F, we define the Herbrand logic formulae:*
$$\phi_{gen}(D) \equiv \forall r.gen(r)$$
$$\iff \left(r \in D \vee \bigvee_{f^n \in \Sigma_{op}} \exists r_1, \ldots, r_n . r = f(r_1, \ldots, r_n) \wedge gen(r_1) \wedge \ldots \wedge gen(r_n)\right)$$
$$\phi_{frame}(F) \equiv kn_F[m_1] = t_1 \wedge \ldots \wedge kn_F[m_l] = t_l \wedge$$
$$\bigwedge_{f^n \in \Sigma_{op}} \forall r_1, \ldots, r_n : gen.\,kn_F[f(r_1, \ldots, r_n)] = f(kn_F[r_1], \ldots, kn_F[r_n])$$

The axiom $\phi_{gen}(F)$ defines the unary predicate *gen* to be the set of recipes from D and Σ_{op}. Here we write $f^n \in \Sigma_{op}$ to denote that f is an n-ary function symbol. We can use *gen* like a type and for instance write $\forall r : gen.\phi$ as shorthand for $\forall r.gen(r) \implies \phi$. The axiom $\phi_{frame}(F)$ characterizes that kn_F works like a substitution on recipes, mapping m_i to t_i.

Two frames F_1 and F_2 with the same domain are called *statically equivalent*, if on every pair of recipes, F_1 produces the same result iff F_2 does:

Definition 3 ($\phi_\sim(F_1, F_2)$ [5])**.** *Let F_1 and F_2 be frames with the same domain.*

$$\phi_\sim(F_1, F_2) \equiv \forall r, s : gen.\,kn_{F_1}[r] = kn_{F_1}[s] \iff kn_{F_2}[r] = kn_{F_2}[s]$$

2.3 Alpha-Beta Privacy

(α, β)-privacy is mainly based on the specification of two formulae α and β in Herbrand Logic for every reachable state. α is the intentionally released information, i.e. the "non-technical" information or the "payload". β represents all other observations that the intruder made, e.g. messages he has seen, also called the "technical" information. This distinction between payload and technical is at the core of (α, β)-privacy. We formalize it by a distinguished subset $\Sigma_0 \subset \Sigma$ of the alphabet, where Σ_0 contains only the non-technical information, such as votes and addition, while $\Sigma \setminus \Sigma_0$ includes cryptographic operators. The formula α is always over just Σ_0, while β can use the full Σ.

Definition 4 (Model-theoretical (α, β)-privacy [5]). *Consider a countable signature Σ and a payload alphabet $\Sigma_0 \subset \Sigma$, a formula α over Σ_0 and a formula β over Σ such that $fv(\alpha) = fv(\beta)$, both α and β are consistent and $\beta \models \alpha$. We say that (α, β)-privacy holds (model-theoretically) iff every Σ_0-model of α can be extended to a Σ-model of β. Here a Σ-interpretation $\mathcal{I}'$ is an extension of a Σ_0-interpretation $\mathcal{I}$ if they agree on all variables and all the interpreted function and relation symbols of Σ_0.*

For the rest of this paper, we consider as α only *combinatoric* formulae, which means Σ_0 is finite and contains only uninterpreted constants. Then α has only finitely many models (that assign constants of Σ_0 to the free variables of α).

While classical bi-similarity approaches are always about the distinguishability between two alternatives, in (α, β)-privacy every reachable state represents only one single situation that can occur, and it is the question how far the intruder can know what happened. The intruder knowledge is for this reason more complex: besides the concrete messages he knows, we also model that he may know something about the structure of messages, e.g. that a particular encrypted message in his knowledge contains the vote v_1, where v_1 is a free variable of α. We thus define the intruder knowledge by two frames *concr* and *struct* where *struct* may contain free variables of α, and *concr* is the same except that all variables are instantiated with what really happened, e.g. $v_1 = 1$. For simplicity let us use in Herbrand formulae also *concr* and *struct* as two interpreted functions (instead of kn_{concr} and kn_{struct}) and we call them the *concrete* and *structural knowledge*. We always use *gen* to refer to the recipes for both (since they must have the same domain).

The clou is that we require as part of β that *struct* and *concr* are statically equivalent. That means, if the intruder knows that two concrete constructible messages are unequal, then also their structure has to be unequal, and vice-versa. For instance, let $h \in \Sigma_p \setminus \Sigma_{op}$ and

$$struct = \{m_1 \mapsto h(v_1), m_2 \mapsto h(v_2)\} \text{ and } concr = \{m_1 \mapsto h(0), m_2 \mapsto h(1)\}.$$

Then every model of β has the property $v_1 \neq v_2$. Suppose $\alpha \equiv v_1, v_2 \in \{0, 1\}$, then (α, β)-privacy is violated, since for instance $v_1 = 0, v_2 = 0$ is a model of α, but cannot be extended to a model of β. If $\alpha \equiv v_1, v_2 \in \{0, 1\} \wedge v_1 + v_2 = 1$ however, then all models of α are compatible with β and privacy is preserved.

Definition 5 (Message-analysis problem (adapted from [5])). *Let α be combinatoric, and struct and concr be two frames with domain D. We say that β is a message-analysis problem if $\beta \equiv MsgAna(D, \alpha, struct, concr)$ with:*

$$MsgAna(D, \alpha, struct, concr)$$
$$\equiv \alpha \wedge \phi_{gen}(D) \wedge \phi_{frame}(struct) \wedge \phi_{frame}(concr) \wedge \phi_\sim(struct, concr)$$

Typically, we consider for every state one distinguished model θ of α, called the *reality*, and have $concr = \theta(struct)$.

3   Verifying Voting Privacy

An (α, β)-pair characterizes a single state of a transition system. To illustrate voting privacy and receipt-freeness we pick a few reachable states of the voting protocol FOO'92 and prove (or disprove) fulfillment of some properties. In fact, a manual proof for the entire infinite state-space is possible by appropriate generalization, but for the purpose of illustration, this would be overkill.

First, let us look at α and for simplicity consider a choice between 0 or 1 (all definitions can be easily extended to more complex voting choices). We use a sequence of variables $v_1, \ldots, v_N$ to model the votes. During each transition where an honest voter i sends a message that contains their vote v_i, we augment α by $v_i \in \{0, 1\}$, since the intruder does not know more than they will cast a valid vote. For dishonest voters, it is more complicated and actually depends on the protocol, since dishonest voters (or the intruder) may not follow the protocol and, e.g., replay a message of some honest voter (thus not necessarily knowing what vote they have cast). Anyway in this case one should augment α with $v_i = b$ for the concrete b that they have cast, since the intruder is allowed to know all dishonest votes. Finally, when the result is about to be published and suppose R of the votes v_i are 1, then we finally augment α with the information $\sum_{i=1}^{N} v_i = R$. Therefore, from this point on, the intruder is allowed to know the result, but before this point, it is already a violation if he can obtain a partial result (beyond the votes of the dishonest agents). For all examples in this paper we have

$$\alpha \equiv v_1 \in \{0,1\} \wedge \ldots \wedge v_N \in \{0,1\} \wedge \sum_{i=1}^{N} v_i = R \,, \tag{2}$$

i.e., N honest voters have cast their votes, and R of them are 1. In fact, we also use the same formula in examples for receipt-freeness since we want that the same amount of information is kept secret, just some honest voters are "under more pressure" from the intruder.

3.1   The FOO'92 Voting Protocol in Alpha-Beta Privacy

The FOO'92 protocol [8] has been formally studied with the Applied π-calculus [9]; for a full description we refer to that paper, and we only introduce relevant aspects on the fly. The final result of FOO'92 is the publication of a bulletin board of cryptographic messages containing all the votes. More precisely, each entry contains $sign(priv(A), commit(v_i, r_i))$ and r_i for some $i \in \{1, \ldots, N\}$. This is the signature with the private key of an administrator A and containing a cryptographic commitment of the vote with some (initially secret) random value r_i. Here we assume as part of Σ_{op} the following operators: $sign$ for signature, $verify$ for signature verification, and $retrieve$ for obtaining the message under the signature; this is characterized by the equations $retrieve(sign(priv(A), m)) \approx m$ and $verify(pub(A), sign(priv(A), m)) \approx yes$. Moreover we have $commit$, $vcommit$ and $open$ for commitments with the properties $open(commit(m, r), r) \approx m$ and $vcommit(r, commit(m, r)) \approx yes$.

Let us consider an intruder who just obtains this bulletin board. This is not unrealistic since the exchanges in the other phases are best protected by anonymous channels, anyway. It is crucial that the bulletin board lists its entries in some unpredictable order. To model that, we introduce an interpreted function $\pi[\cdot]$ that is a permutation on $\{1, \ldots, N\}$.[2] To conveniently make use of this function, we like to also access the votes v_i and the random values r_i (these are uninterpreted constants of $\Sigma \setminus \Sigma_0$) through a function and thus introduce two further interpreted functions $v[\cdot]$ and $r[\cdot]$ with the property $v_i = v[i]$ and $r_i = r[i]$ for each $1 \leq i \leq N$.

---

[2] i.e. $\forall i. \, 1 \leq i \leq N \implies 1 \leq \pi[i] \leq N \wedge \forall j. \, 1 \leq j \leq N \wedge \pi[i] = \pi[j] \implies i = j$.

We can then describe the structural knowledge of the intruder who initially knows all public keys and has seen the bulletin board by the following frame:

$$\begin{aligned}struct = \{\!| m_0 \mapsto pub(A), m_1 \mapsto pub(V_1), \ldots, m_n \mapsto pub(V_N), \\ m_{N+1} \mapsto sign(priv(A), commit(v[\pi[1]], r[\pi[1]])), \ldots, \\ m_{2N} \mapsto sign(priv(A), commit(v[\pi[N]], r[\pi[N]])), \\ m_{2N+1} \mapsto r[\pi[1]], \ldots, m_{3N} \mapsto r[\pi[N]] |\!\}\end{aligned}$$

To obtain the concrete knowledge frame, we need to replace the interpreted terms by their actual values. For π this means the actual permutation on the bulletin board; let us call it π_0. Mind π_0 is not a symbol of Σ but an actual permutation. Further let $\theta_0 \models \alpha$ be an interpretation of each v_i with $0, 1$ that is a model of α, i.e., the true vote of every voter. Note that both π_0 and θ_0 are arbitrary, so the proofs we give hold for every such choice. Then, the concrete knowledge is obtained by replacing $\pi[x]$ by $\pi_0(x)$, $v[x]$ by $\theta_0(v_x)$ and $r[x]$ by r_x. Now we can specify $concr$ as follows:

$$\begin{aligned}concr = \{\!| m_0 \mapsto pub(A), m_1 \mapsto pub(V_1), \ldots, m_n \mapsto pub(V_N), \\ m_{N+1} \mapsto sign(priv(A), commit(\theta_0(v_{\pi_0(1)}), r_{\pi_0(1)})), \ldots, \\ m_{2N} \mapsto sign(priv(A), commit(\theta_0(v_{\pi_0(N)}), r_{\pi_0(N)})), \\ m_{2N+1} \mapsto r_{\pi_0(1)}, \ldots, m_{3N} \mapsto r_{\pi_0(N)} |\!\}\end{aligned}$$

Thus the $concr$ frame replaces every occurrence of $v[\pi[i]]$ by $\theta_0(v_{\pi_0(i)})$ and every $r[\pi[i]]$ by $r_{\pi_0(i)}$. The point is that in the concrete messages that the intruder observes, everything is instantiated with respect to π_0 and θ_0, while the structural knowledge about these messages is with respect to $\pi[\cdot]$ and $v[\cdot]$, i.e., reflecting what the intruder knows that about the content of a message. E.g. $v[\pi[j]]$ reflects that the intruder knows that this is the vote of the voter who has entry number j on the bulletin board, but he may be unable to find out the true permutation π_0 and neither the votes directly as a function of the voters.

$$\beta \equiv \bigwedge_{i=1}^{N} \Big(v[i] = v_i \wedge r[i] = r_i \Big) \wedge \mathrm{MsgAna}(D, \alpha, struct, concr) \tag{3}$$

Let us call S the state with this β and the α of (2).

3.2 Voting Privacy Holds in S

To show that (α, β)-privacy holds in S, we need to show how an arbitrary model of α can be extended to a model of β. To that end, we consider an arbitrary model $\theta_I \models \alpha$, called an *intruder hypothesis*, i.e., that maps each v_i to $\{0, 1\}$ so that their sum is R. We show how θ_I can be extended to a model $\mathcal{I} \models \beta$. In other words, we show that β does not allow the intruder to logically rule out any hypothesis about the votes v_i. We do this construction for an arbitrary θ_I, thus, *every* model of α can be extended to a model of β.

Since $\mathcal{I}$ must be an extension of θ_I, we have $\mathcal{I}(v_i) = \theta_I(v_i)$ for all votes v_i. Further, we need to give an interpretation for all other symbols of Σ, in our example $gen(\cdot)$, $struct[\cdot]$, $concr[\cdot]$, $\pi[\cdot]$, $r[\cdot]$ and of course $v[\cdot]$. For the symbols gen, $struct$, and $concr$ there is not much choice so that they satisfy the formulae ϕ_{gen}, $\phi_{frame}(struct)$ and $\phi_{frame}(concr)$, and we give a canonical construction for them (i.e., the same construction applies for any message analysis problem). More interesting is to find an interpretation of the protocol specific functions $\pi[\cdot]$, $r[\cdot]$ and $v[\cdot]$, so that $\mathcal{I} \models \phi_\sim(struct, concr)$, i.e., satisfying the static equivalence of $struct$ and $concr$ modulo $\approx$. While this is generally difficult, we are sometimes in luck: in some cases (α, β)-privacy allows for a relatively easy proof by reasoning about permutations – i.e. how "human provers" would like to do it. Indeed, for the state S, we can find an interpretation for $\pi[\cdot]$ (and the other functions) such that $\mathcal{I}(struct) = \mathcal{I}(concr)$. In this case $\mathcal{I} \models \phi_\sim(struct, concr)$ follows trivially. Note that here we do not even need to reason about algebraic properties of the operators (i.e. the congruence relation $\approx$) to conduct the proof.

The proof idea for this is actually straightforward in this case. Remember that S entails "what really happened", i.e., a particular model $\theta_0 \models \alpha$ and a particular permutation π_0 that reflect the true outcome of the vote, and the true permutation under which the votes have been published. The idea is that any discrepancy between θ_I and θ_0 can be "balanced" by an appropriate interpretation of π. More precisely, the voting function is interpreted following the intruder hypothesis, i.e. $v[i]$ is $\theta_I(v_i)$ for all voters. Since both $\theta_0 \models \alpha$ and $\theta_I \models \alpha$, we have $\sum_{i=1}^N \theta_0(v_i) = \sum_{i=1}^N \theta_I(v_i) = R$. Since $v_1, \ldots, v_N \in \{0, 1\}$, the list $[\theta_I(v_1), \ldots, \theta_I(v_N)]$ is a permutation of $[\theta_0(v_1), \ldots, \theta_0(v_N)]$. Thus we can find a permutation $\psi \colon \{1, \ldots, N\} \to \{1, \ldots, N\}$ such that $\theta_I(v_i) = \theta_0(v_{\psi(i)})$ for all $i \in \{1, \ldots, N\}$. Intuitively, ψ is the discrepancy between θ_I and θ_0. Then let us define π_I as the intruder's hypothesis of $\pi \colon \pi_I = \psi^{-1} \circ \pi_0$. Finally, r is interpreted accordingly, as the commitment secrets permuted the same way that the votes, i.e. a value $r[i]$ is $r_{\psi(i)}$. Let us thus define (recall the Herbrand universe is $A = \{[\![t]\!]_\approx \mid t \in \mathcal{T}_{\Sigma_I}\}$):

Definition 6 (A model of the functions). *Let $\mathcal{I}$ map v to the function $\mathcal{I}(v) \colon A \to A$, r to the function $\mathcal{I}(r) \colon A \to A$ and π to the function $\mathcal{I}(\pi) \colon A \to A$:*

$$\mathcal{I}(v)([\![t]\!]_\approx) = [\![\theta_I(v_t)]\!]_\approx \quad \textit{if } t \in [\![\{1, \ldots, N\}]\!]_\approx \textit{ and } \mathcal{I}(v)([\![t]\!]_\approx) = [\![t]\!]_\approx \textit{ otherwise}$$
$$\mathcal{I}(r)([\![t]\!]_\approx) = [\![r_{\psi(t)}]\!]_\approx \quad \textit{if } t \in [\![\{1, \ldots, N\}]\!]_\approx \textit{ and } \mathcal{I}(r)([\![t]\!]_\approx) = [\![t]\!]_\approx \textit{ otherwise}$$
$$\mathcal{I}(\pi)([\![t]\!]_\approx) = [\![\pi_I(t)]\!]_\approx \quad \textit{if } t \in [\![\{1, \ldots, N\}]\!]_\approx \textit{ and } \mathcal{I}(\pi)([\![t]\!]_\approx) = [\![t]\!]_\approx \textit{ otherwise}$$

Example 1. Given three voters, i.e. $N = 3$ and the result of the vote is $R = 2$, the true result of the vote is $\theta_0 = \{v_1 \mapsto 1, v_2 \mapsto 1, v_3 \mapsto 0\}$ and the actual permutation is $\pi_0 = \left(\begin{smallmatrix} 1 & 2 & 3 \\ 1 & 3 & 2 \end{smallmatrix}\right)$, the bulletin board is then:

Bulletin board	j	1	2	3
	$v_{\pi_0(j)}$	1	0	1

Let us consider one possible intruder hypothesis, i.e. one model of α, $\theta_I = \{v_1 \mapsto 0, v_2 \mapsto 1, v_3 \mapsto 1\}$. It is then possible to isolate one permutation: $\psi = \left(\begin{smallmatrix} 1 & 2 & 3 \\ 3 & 1 & 2 \end{smallmatrix}\right)$. We can then build $\pi_I = \left(\begin{smallmatrix} 1 & 2 & 3 \\ 2 & 1 & 3 \end{smallmatrix}\right)$.

The construction of the remaining items is generic for all message analysis problems, namely *struct* and *concr* behave like substitutions and that *gen* is true exactly for the recipes:

Definition 7 (A model of *gen*, *struct* and *concr*). *Let D be the domain of the considered frames. Then we define*

$$\mathcal{I}(gen) = \{[\![t]\!]_\approx \mid t \in \mathcal{T}_{\Sigma_{op} \cup D}\}$$
$$\mathcal{I}(struct)([\![t]\!]_\approx) = \mathcal{I}(struct\{\!|t|\!\}) \text{ for all } t \in \mathcal{T}_{\Sigma_f}$$
$$\mathcal{I}(concr)([\![t]\!]_\approx) = \mathcal{I}(concr\{\!|t|\!\}) \text{ for all } t \in \mathcal{T}_{\Sigma_f}$$

This interpretation expresses that *gen* is exactly the set of recipes. For *struct* and *concr*, we define the meaning by first applying the actual frames $struct\{\!|\cdot|\!\}$ and $concr\{\!|\cdot|\!\}$ as substitutions to a given term t, i.e. replacing the labels $m_i \in D$ in t; afterwards, we apply $\mathcal{I}$ to the resulting term since $struct\{\!|t|\!\}$ in general contains variables and interpreted function symbols that need to be interpreted.

This interpretation is well-defined because it does not depend on the choice of the representative of the equivalence classes, e.g. if $s \approx t$ then $struct\{\!|s|\!\} \approx struct\{\!|t|\!\}$. It is immediate that $\mathcal{I}$ is a model of $\phi_{frame}(struct)$ and $\phi_{frame}(concr)$:

Lemma 1. $\mathcal{I} \models \phi_{frame}(struct)$ *and* $\mathcal{I} \models \phi_{frame}(concr)$.

It remains to show that $\mathcal{I} \models \phi_\sim(struct, concr)$. In general, such a proof of static equivalence of two frames can be difficult (especially by hand). However, in our case we have $\mathcal{I}(struct) = \mathcal{I}(concr)$ by construction—we have designed the interpretation of π so that this holds—and then static equivalence is immediate:

Lemma 2. *If* $\mathcal{I}(struct) = \mathcal{I}(concr)$ *then* $\mathcal{I} \models \phi_\sim(struct, concr)$.

Theorem 1. *Voting privacy holds in the state S.*

This FOO'92 example demonstrates the declarativity of the (α, β)-privacy approach, in particular that we are able to reason about permutations allows for a rather simple proof how "human provers" would like it: after a small insight (the discrepancy between θ_I and θ_0 can be balanced in the interpretation of π) then the rest all falls into place.

3.3   Voting Privacy Holds in S'

In many cases it is not as easy as before. For instance, in the FOO'92 protocol, we have a first phase where send a blind signature of their vote-commitment to an administrator and receive a signature from that administrator. Let us now consider a state S' where the intruder has seen also all theses blinded signatures (the formula α is again (2)):

$$struct = \{\!|m_0 \mapsto pub(A), m_1 \mapsto pub(V_1), \ldots, m_N \mapsto pub(V_N),$$
$$m_{N+1} \mapsto sign(priv(A), commit(v[\pi[1]], r[\pi[1]])), \ldots,$$
$$m_{2N} \mapsto sign(priv(A), commit(v[\pi[N]], r[\pi[N]])),$$
$$m_{2N+1} \mapsto r[\pi[1]], \ldots, m_{3N} \mapsto r[\pi[N]],$$
$$m_{3N+1} \mapsto sign(priv(V_1), blind(commit(v[1], r[1]), b_1)), \ldots,$$
$$m_{4N} \mapsto sign(priv(V_N), blind(commit(v[N], r[N]), b_N)),$$
$$m_{4N+1} \mapsto sign(priv(A), blind(commit(v[1], r[1]), b_1)), \ldots,$$
$$m_{5N} \mapsto sign(priv(A), blind(commit(v[N], r[N]), b_N))\!|\}$$

Here, we have augmented the frame from S by the $3N + i$ messages from the voters and the $4N + i$ replies from the administrator, and b_i is the corresponding blinding secret of voter V_i. We assume the following properties about $blind$: $unblind(x, blind(x, m)) \approx m$ and $sign(x, blind(y, m)) \approx blind(y, sign(x, m))$, so that each voter can unblind the reply message from the administrator. The concrete frame $concr$ is again obtained by replacing $\pi[x]$ by $\pi_0(x)$, $v[x]$ by $\theta_0(v_x)$ and $r[x]$ by r_x.

Note that the messages between voters and administrators are actually shown in the order of the voters rather than under a permutation. The reason is that such a permutation would not make the problem harder for the intruder, since the signatures of the voters already identify which message belongs to whom and the replies from the administrator could probably be linked due to timing.

Now the difficulty is that we cannot find an interpretation $\mathcal{I}$ such that $\mathcal{I}(struct) = \mathcal{I}(concr)$, because the messages at $3N + i$ are signed by the individual voters and are thus linked to the voters.[3] Instead, the point is here that, due to the blinding, the intruder cannot derive anything useful from these messages. Formally, we show for the same $\mathcal{I}$ as constructed for S (for given $\theta_I \models \alpha$), that the weaker property $\mathcal{I} \models \phi_\sim(struct, concr)$ still holds in S'. This therefore requires a full static equivalence proof modulo the properties of $\approx$ which is quite involved (cf. for instance [10]) and we give only a sketch in the appendix. This allows us to conclude:

Theorem 2. *Voting privacy holds in the state S'.*

4   Receipt-Freeness

We now assume that the intruder tries to influence one particular voter, let us call him Dan and identify him with the first voter V_1. We will later briefly discuss the case when the intruder tries to influence several voters. The question is whether Dan can *prove* to the intruder how he voted by a kind of "receipt". The protocol does not explicitly produce any such receipt, but revealing all messages that

---

[3] In fact, due to the $3N + i$ messages, in any model $\mathcal{I}$ where $\mathcal{I}(struct) = \mathcal{I}(concr)$ we necessarily also have $\theta_0 = \theta_I$, and thus there cannot be such a simple construction for every $\theta_I \models \alpha$.

Dan knows could allow the intruder to verify how Dan voted, i.e., that Dan is unable to lie about his vote. For instance, for FOO'92, we will now show, if the⟨ intruder has observed all the messages between voters and administrators (state S'), and if Dan reveals his blinding factor, then the intruder can indeed identify Dan's vote with certainty. If we consider however FOO'92 without the blinded signature messages (as in state S) and the intruder sees only the final bulletin board, Dan can claim any vote to be his—and the intruder has no chance to falsify that claim. Mind that does not hold in the state before the commitments are opened as we also discuss below.

4.1 Formalizing Receipt-Freeness

Consider a given state where we want to check whether the protocol is receipt-free with respect to the voter Dan. The intruder can ask Dan to reveal his *entire knowledge*, i.e., all the secrets Dan knows (his private key, his commitment value and his blinding factor) as well as messages that Dan has received from other parties, like the administrator. If Dan has any "receipt" (in the broadest sense of the word), then it is something that can be derived from this knowledge. The point is that Dan does not necessarily tell the truth, but can present any collection of messages that can be constructed from his knowledge. We call this *Dan's story*. Dan's story has to be consistent with whatever the intruder can check, e.g., Dan cannot lie about his private key, since the intruder knows his public key. We thus want to express that a state is receipt-free, if for every model $\theta_I \models \alpha$, Dan can come up with a consistent story (in particular consistent with θ_I). We do not even change the formula α, but only add an additional challenge to β: that the intruder obtains a story from Dan, i.e. what he claims to be his knowledge. We see receipt-freeness as preserving voting privacy even under this additional challenge. From that actually follows a relation between the goals: receipt freeness implies voting privacy.

We reason about Dan's knowledge similarly to the intruder's knowledge: we introduce the frames $concr_{Dan}$ and $struct_{Dan}$ whose domain $D_{Dan} = \{d_1, \ldots, d_l\}$ is disjoint from the domain D of the intruder knowledge: $D_{Dan} \cap D = \emptyset$. If we consider that the protocol itself is not a secret, the intruder "knows" $struct_{Dan}$, i.e., what the messages are supposed to be according to protocol, and Dan's story has to be consistent with this. The idea is that what Dan can lie about is $concr_{Dan}$. We let Dan choose any recipes $s_1, \ldots, s_l$ (with respect to D_{Dan}), one for each item in his knowledge and send $concr[s_1], \ldots, concr[s_l]$ as his story to the intruder. The augmented intruder knowledge has then domain $D \cup D_{Dan}$ where the $concr$'s are filled with Dan's story and the $struct$ is identical with $struct_{Dan}$, i.e., what it is supposed to be. This is captured by the formula ϕ_{lie}:

Definition 8 (ϕ_{lie}).

$\phi_{lie}(struct, concr, struct_{Dan}, concr_{Dan})$
$\equiv struct[d_1] = struct_{Dan}[d_1] \wedge \ldots \wedge struct[d_l] = struct_{Dan}[d_l]$
$\wedge \exists s_1, \ldots, s_l: gen_{D_{Dan}}.\big(concr[d_1] = concr_{Dan}[s_1] \wedge \ldots \wedge concr[d_l] = concr_{Dan}[s_l]\big)$

In fact, $\mathcal{I} \models \phi_{lie}(concr, struct)$ (w.r.t. the whole domain $D \cup D_{Dan}$) means that Dan's story is consistent with the protocol (i.e., the *struct* values) and $\mathcal{I}$'s interpretation of the free variables of α. Thus we define:

Definition 9 (Receipt-freeness problem). *We say that β is a receipt-freeness problem (with respect to a combinatoric α, the frames struct and concr with domain $D \cup D_{Dan}$, the frames $struct_{Dan}$ and $concr_{Dan}$ with domain D_{Dan}) if $\beta \equiv \mathrm{RcpFree}(D, D_{Dan}, \alpha, struct, concr, struct_{Dan}, concr_{Dan})$ where:*

$$RcpFree(D, D_{Dan}, \alpha, struct, concr, struct_{Dan}, concr_{Dan})$$
$$\equiv \phi_{gen_{D_{Dan}}}(D_{Dan}) \wedge \phi_{frame}(struct_{Dan}) \wedge \phi_{frame}(concr_{Dan})$$
$$\wedge MsgAna(D \cup D_{Dan}, \alpha, struct, concr) \wedge \phi_{lie}(struct, concr, struct_{Dan}, concr_{Dan})$$

We say receipt-freeness holds if the (α, β)-pair is consistent. We call $\beta' \equiv \mathrm{MsgAna}(D, \alpha, struct, concr)$ the message-analysis problem underlying β.

β is always consistent since there is at least one way to satisfy β: the truth (i.e. Dan selects $s_i = d_i$ for each $1 \leq i \leq l$). Note that the story of Dan may be the truth when this is compatible with the intruder hypothesis (e.g. when $\theta_I = \theta_0$) without breaking receipt-freeness. What matters is only that the intruder cannot rule out any model of α, including the truth when θ_I coincides with θ_0.

The consistent "story" is here represented by the axiom ϕ_{lie}. For every receipt-freeness problem, we also defined an underlying message-analysis problem that is just a restriction of the original receipt-freeness problem. Indeed, the message-analysis problem is part of the receipt-freeness problem and can be restricted over the domain D. In that sense, the next proposition relates the two privacy properties.

Proposition 1. $RcpFree(D, D_{Dan}, \alpha, struct, concr, struct_{Dan}, concr_{Dan}) \models$ $\mathrm{MsgAna}(D, \alpha, struct, concr)$.

It is then sufficient to prove receipt-freeness to prove plain voting privacy.

4.2   Receipt-Freeness in S

FOO'92 does not satisfy receipt-freeness as shown in [6], and even though our notion of receipt-freeness is defined differently, it agrees with their results. FOO'92 serves well anyway for illustration: in the final state S that we have considered before (where the intruder has seen only the final bulletin board), receipt-freeness *does* hold as we now show.

Example 2. Let us first continue with Example 1. In the intruder's hypothesis θ_I that we considered, the intruder supposes Dan (i.e. V_1) has voted 0, but he actually voted 1 (see θ_0). Dan can however point to a vote that is consistent with θ_I, namely the second entry on the bulletin board, and claim it to be his vote. While the intruder may have doubts about Dan's story, he just *cannot rule out* that Dan speaks the truth.

Let us first consider S, augment it to a receipt-freeness problem with respect to a voter Dan and show that receipt-freeness actually holds in this state. We first need to define what the knowledge of voter Dan is. The structural information is very similar to the intruder's information that consists of the published information (the bulletin board and the public keys); additionally Dan also knows his private key, his own vote, his own commitment value and his blinding factor. We did not include the blinded message as it can be reconstructed using the blinding factor.

$$struct_{Dan} = \{\!| d_0 \mapsto pub(A), d_1 \mapsto pub(V_1), \ldots, d_n \mapsto pub(V_N),$$
$$d_{N+1} \mapsto sign(priv(A), commit(v[\pi[1]], r[\pi[1]])), \ldots,$$
$$d_{2N} \mapsto sign(priv(A), commit(v[\pi[N]], r[\pi[N]])),$$
$$d_{2N+1} \mapsto r[\pi[1]], \ldots, d_{3N} \mapsto r[\pi[N]], d_{3N+1} \mapsto priv(Dan), d_{3N+2} \mapsto v[1],$$
$$d_{3N+3} \mapsto r[1], d_{3N+4} \mapsto b_1 |\!\}$$

The concrete frame is again obtained by replacing $\pi[x]$ by $\pi_0(x)$, $v[x]$ by $\theta_0(v_x)$ and $r[x]$ by r_x. The formula α is the same for receipt-freeness as for voting privacy, i.e., the intruder still is not supposed to find out anything more than the published result of the election (in particular not what Dan has voted). He has more information in β due to the story that Dan gives to the intruder as part of the receipt-freeness definition:

$$\beta_{\mathrm{RF}} \equiv \bigwedge_{i=1}^{N} v[i] = v_i \wedge r[i] = r_i$$

$$\wedge \; \mathrm{RcpFree}(D, D_{Dan}, \alpha, struct, concr, struct_{Dan}, concr_{Dan})$$

When it comes to crafting his story for the public values, Dan has no choice but to tell the truth. As the intruder knows Dan's public key, Dan also has to tell the truth for his private key. For his blinding factor, he may also use the truth as the intruder has not witnessed the exchange with the administrator. For d_{3N+2} (the actual vote) and d_{3N+3} (the commitment value), Dan needs to adapt his story to what the intruder "wants to hear", i.e. to a given θ_I (and π_I). Observe at this point the order of quantifications here: we want to show that every model $\theta_I \models \alpha$ can be extended to a model $\mathcal{I} \models \beta_{\mathrm{RF}}$ where β_{RF} entails an existential quantifier for Dan's story. So we have to show how, given θ_I, we can construct $\mathcal{I}$ and a value for the recipes of the story $s_1, \ldots, s_l$ that satisfies all conditions. We take exactly the same construction for $\mathcal{I}$ (depending on θ_I) that we used for state S, i.e., using the discrepancy ψ between the intruder hypothesis θ_I and the reality θ_0 (i.e., such that $\theta_0(v_{\psi(i)}) = \theta_I(v_i)$) for interpreting $\pi[\cdot]$, namely as the permutation $\pi_I = \psi^{-1} \cdot \pi_0$. It is sufficient to show that Dan can make his story consistent with this interpretation, namely by pointing to the vote $\psi(1)$ as being his own vote. Let $d_{N+\psi(1)}$ and $d_{2N+\psi(1)}$ be the indices in Dan's knowledge for the signed commitment and commitment values on the bulletin board at position $\psi(1)$. He can claim this entry by choosing:

$$s_{3N+2} = open(retrieve(d_{N+\psi(1)}), d_{2N+\psi(1)}) \text{ and } s_{3N+3} = d_{2N+\psi(1)}$$

For all other values s_i, Dan says the truth, i.e. $s_i = d_i$. With this we can conclude:

Theorem 3. (α, β_{RF})-*privacy holds, i.e., receipt-freeness holds in* S.

One may argue that the choice of s_{3N+2} and s_{3N+3} is hardly a *strategy* for Dan, since the choice is based on the permutation ψ (that neither Dan nor the intruder would know), but formally that is fine since the existential quantifier over the s_i only requires that there *is* a recipe that works, and thus our construction is just the simplest way to conduct the proof of receipt-freeness. Dan can choose any vote on the bulletin board that matches the intruder's expectation for Dan $\theta_I(v_1)$.

The aspect of strategy becomes more relevant if we consider the case that more than one voter is bribed by the intruder, because the intruder knows that some agent is lying if more than one points to the same vote. This becomes an issue when the intruder has bribed a significant part of the voters, which may be possible when a vote is held among a small consortium. If the bribed voters have no way to "coordinate" their story, the risk of a collision (that reveals the lie) comes into play. For instance, suppose there are 100 voters, and 40 voted yes. If the intruder has bribed 20 of them, there is a substantial chance that two or more of them point to the same vote if they cannot coordinate their story.

We observe that our definition of receipt-freeness is independent of what the intruder actually wants: we actually have formalized that agents vote however they want and we prove that they can get away with lying—however only with respect to models of α. If the intruder has bribed more voters than actually want to vote for the intruder's preferred choice, then the expected outcome is not a model of α (since the result is not compatible with all bribed people having voted the way the intruder wants). Both this and the previous issue (of coordination) are problems that arise when a significant part of the votership is bribed: they may be coerced into voting what the intruder wants out of fear not to get away with lying after all. These are the boundaries where a *possibilistic* approach like (α, β)-privacy makes sense and where probabilities and behavior models would be needed. We see it as a strong point for the declarativity of (α, β)-privacy that such subtle points become clearly visible from the formalization and discussion of examples.

4.3 Violation of Receipt-Freeness in FOO'92

To see the problems of FOO'92 with receipt-freeness, let us consider just the state after the third phase of the protocol. In this case, the bulletin board contains all the ballots (the signed commitments) but the commitment secrets have not yet been revealed. In this state receipt-freeness does not hold: Unopened commitments violate receipt freeness, since the creator of the commitment is in a unique position to prove authorship to the intruder (by revealing the commitment secret). Effectively, this allows the intruder to bribe agents for obtaining the commitment secrets, and this is captured by our notion of receipt freeness.

This is in particular relevant since voters could refuse to make the last step (the protocol cannot force them, since, by construction, one cannot see who the missing voters are).

While it is intuitively clear that receipt-freeness is violated in this intermediate step, let us prove that it is violated according to our formal definition. Consider the bulletin board without the commitments open, i.e. the same frame as in state S but removing the elements $m_{2N+1}, \ldots, m_{3N}$ (the commitment values). Since in this case also the result has not been published yet, we have here $\alpha = v_1, \ldots, v_N \in \{0, 1\}$, i.e. the intruder knows nothing more than there are N binary votes in the game.

The knowledge of the coerced voter Dan is the same as in the previous subsection, except for removing the entries $d_{2N+1}, \ldots d_{3N}$ which contain the $r[\pi[i]]$ that have not yet been published at this point, of course. The intruder again asks Dan to reveal his knowledge as before, which entails that Dan must claim some vote on the bulletin board to be his own and present a fitting commitment secret, namely $struct_{Dan}[d_{3N+3}] = r[1]$. Thus the only consistent story that Dan can give for this value is the truth: $s_{3N+3} = d_{3N+3}$. That in turn is only consistent with a given intruder hypothesis $\theta_I \models \alpha$ if $\theta_I(v_1) = \theta_0(v_1)$, i.e., it rules out any model that does not state Dan's vote correctly. Thus, at this point, Dan has *proved* to the intruder what he voted.

In fact, this demonstrates how our notion of receipt-freeness is connected to voting secrecy, namely whether the information given by Dan proves anything to the intruder, i.e., whether it allows him to rule out any model θ_I of α. Note that this is a very fine notion: receipt-freeness would be violated even in a state where Dan cannot precisely prove what he voted, but only giving the intruder enough information to rule out *some* model of α.

5   Related Work

This work is based on the framework of (α, β)-privacy [5], which is in turn based on Herbrand logic [7]. As a variant of First-Order Logic, using the ground terms of uninterpreted function symbols as a universe, Herbrand logic is very expressive, e.g. it can axiomatize natural number arithmetic. The main idea of (α, β)-privacy is to depart from the most popular approach of specifying privacy as bisimilarity of pairs of processes as in [1–4]. Instead, we define privacy as a reachability problem of states, where each state is characterized by (at least) two formulae, namely α giving the public high-level information (like a voting result), and β containing all observations that the intruder could make.

While [5] has already defined voting secrecy, this paper gives the first adaption of (α, β)-privacy to a real-world voting protocol, namely FOO'92 [8]. Another core contribution is the formalization of receipt-freeness, namely as a refinement of standard voting secrecy. Here, the high-level information α remains the same (i.e., the same information must be kept private), but the intruder gets extra observations as part of β through the interaction with a voter Dan. The most similar work is [6] where voting privacy, receipt-freeness and coercion-resistance have been expressed with observational equivalence (see also [11]).

The formalization of these properties rely on labeled bisimilarity of two processes, also proving a hierarchy between these goals. We believe that our formalization in (α, β)-privacy is more declarative and intuitive, due to its model-theoretic formulation. An interesting question for future work is how the two approaches compare, i.e., whether one can captures anything as an attack that the other does not. If they turned out to be equivalent in some sense instead, then this would indicate that the "right" concept has been hit.

Another question is automation. There are several fragments of bisimilarity for which automation is being developed. However some protocols, even the relatively simple FOO'92, are hard to analyze fully automatically: for instance, [6] is at the high-level a manual proof, reducing the problem to a static equivalence of two frames (which is then automated). Only in the recent paper [12] a fully automatic analysis of FOO'92 is given. Our focus on a declarative formalization rather than automation concerns allows often for very simple proofs, e.g. in FOO'92 in S, which basically amounts to finding a fitting interpretation for a permutation. This is exactly how one may want to prove such a property manually or in a proof assistant like Isabelle or Coq.

6   Conclusion

(α, β)-privacy was introduced as a simple and declarative way to specify privacy goals and reason about them. We present here the first major use-case using this framework. This use-case illustrates the refined voting privacy goal that we have defined in this work. Indeed, we showed how for any model θ of α, we could step by step construct a model $\mathcal{I}$ of β. On top of this privacy property, we defined a new property: receipt-freeness. We showed that receipt-freeness implies voting privacy. We illustrated these properties for a voting system, but both privacy and receipt-freeness are actually relevant to a variety of areas, for instance healthcare privacy [13]. Indeed, prescriptions by a medial doctor have similar requirements regarding privacy and even receipt-freeness: for instance, we want to prevent that a doctor could be coerced by a pharmaceutical company to prescribe specific medication, which is actually a receipt-freeness problem.

We are currently investigating coercion resistance as a stronger variant of receipt-freeness, where the intruder can initially determine values for the coerced voter to use. To counter such attacks, one needs protocols with a different setup than FOO'92, allowing re-voting. This also requires to formalize more details about the underlying transition system than we did in this work, including how the intruder can take a more active part in the protocol. In fact, it is part of ongoing work to provide languages, proof strategies and potentially automated tools for specifying and verifying transition systems with (α, β)-privacy. The idea is here that the formula β can be automatically derived from what happens (like message exchanges) and that only α needs to be specified by the modeler, namely indicating at which point which information is deliberately released.

A   Proofs

Lemma 1. $\mathcal{I} \models \phi_{frame}(struct)$ and $\mathcal{I} \models \phi_{frame}(concr)$.

Proof. Following Definition 7, $\mathcal{I}$ models the first conjunct of $\phi_{frame}(struct)$ and $\phi_{frame}(concr)$.

It remains to show that $\mathcal{I}$ models the last conjunct of $\phi_{frame}(struct)$ and $\phi_{frame}(concr)$. Let $f^n \in \Sigma_{op}$. Let $r_1, \ldots, r_n$ be n recipes in $\mathcal{T}_{\Sigma_{op} \cup D}$. Note that $\mathcal{I}(r_i) = [\![r_i]\!]_{\approx}$. It is sufficient to show that $\mathcal{I} \models struct[f(r_1, \ldots, r_n)]) = f(struct[r_1], \ldots, struct[r_n])$.

$$
\begin{aligned}
\mathcal{I}(struct[f(r_1, \ldots, r_n)]) &= \mathcal{I}(struct)(\mathcal{I}(f(r_1, \ldots, r_n))) \\
&= \mathcal{I}(struct)([\![f(r_1, \ldots, r_n)]\!]_{\approx}) \\
&= [\![struct\{\!|f(r_1, \ldots, r_n)|\!\}]\!]_{\approx} \text{ by Def. 7,} \\
&= [\![f(struct\{\!|r_1|\!\}, \ldots, struct\{\!|r_n|\!\})]\!]_{\approx}, \\
&= f([\![struct\{\!|r_1|\!\}]\!]_{\approx}, \ldots, [\![struct\{\!|r_n|\!\}]\!]_{\approx}), \\
&= f(\mathcal{I}(struct)([\![r_1]\!]_{\approx}), \ldots, \mathcal{I}(struct)([\![r_n]\!]_{\approx})), \text{ by Def. 7,} \\
&= f(\mathcal{I}(struct)(\mathcal{I}(r_1)), \ldots, \mathcal{I}(struct)(\mathcal{I}(r_n))) \\
&= f(\mathcal{I}(struct[r_1]), \ldots, \mathcal{I}(struct[r_n])) \\
&= \mathcal{I}(f(struct[r_1], \ldots, struct[r_n])).
\end{aligned}
$$

Therefore we proved that $\mathcal{I} \models \phi_{frame}(struct)$. By a similar reasoning, we prove that $\mathcal{I} \models \phi_{frame}(concr)$. Thus $\mathcal{I} \models \phi_{frame}(struct)$ and $\mathcal{I} \models \phi_{frame}(concr)$.

Lemma 2. If $\mathcal{I}(struct) = \mathcal{I}(concr)$ then $\mathcal{I} \models \phi_{\sim}(struct, concr)$.

Proof. Suppose $\mathcal{I}(struct) = \mathcal{I}(concr)$. Recall that $struct$ and $concr$ have the same domain D so $gen_{struct} = gen_{concr} = gen$. Let r and s be two recipes in $\mathcal{T}_{\Sigma_{op} \cup D}$. Suppose now that $\mathcal{I} \models struct[r] = struct[s]$.

$$
\begin{aligned}
\mathcal{I} \models struct[r] = struct[s] \text{ iff } &\mathcal{I}(struct)(\mathcal{I}(r)) = \mathcal{I}(struct)(\mathcal{I}(s)) \\
\text{iff } &\mathcal{I}(concr)(\mathcal{I}(r)) = \mathcal{I}(concr)(\mathcal{I}(s)) \\
\text{iff } &\mathcal{I} \models concr[r] = concr[s]
\end{aligned}
$$

Thus $\mathcal{I} \models \phi_{\sim}(struct, concr)$.

Theorem 1. Voting privacy holds in the state S.

Proof. First, let us prove that $\mathcal{I}(struct) = \mathcal{I}(concr)$. For the $struct$, we just have to look at the interpretation of $v[\pi[i]]$ and $r[\pi[i]]$ because all the other terms are uninterpreted symbols. For $i \in \{1, \ldots, N\}$,

$$
\begin{aligned}
\mathcal{I}(v[\pi[i]]) &= \mathcal{I}(v)(\mathcal{I}(\pi)([\![i]\!]_{\approx})) = \mathcal{I}(v)([\![\pi_I(i)]\!]_{\approx}) = \mathcal{I}(v)([\![(\psi^{-1} \circ \pi_0)(i)]\!]_{\approx}) \\
&= [\![\theta_I(v_{\psi^{-1}(\pi_0(i))})]\!]_{\approx} = [\![\theta_0(v_{\pi_0(i)})]\!]_{\approx} \\
\mathcal{I}(r[\pi[i]]) &= \mathcal{I}(r)(\mathcal{I}(\pi)([\![i]\!]_{\approx})) = \mathcal{I}(r)([\![\pi_I(i)]\!]_{\approx}) = \mathcal{I}(r)([\![(\psi^{-1} \circ \pi_0)(i)]\!]_{\approx}) \\
&= [\![r_{(\psi \circ \psi^{-1} \circ \pi_0)(i)}]\!]_{\approx} = [\![r_{\pi_0(i)}]\!]_{\approx}.
\end{aligned}
$$

Since for the *concr*, the messages are of the form $m_{N+i} \mapsto sign(priv(A), commit(\theta_0(v_{\pi_o(i)}), r_{\pi_0(i)})))$, we have $\mathcal{I}(struct) = \mathcal{I}(concr)$. Then we have shown that for every model $\theta_I \models \alpha$, i.e. any possible intruder's hypothesis, we can find a model $\mathcal{I}$ of β that agrees with θ_I, i.e. $\mathcal{I}(v[i]) = \theta_I(v_i)$ for all votes v_i.

Theorem 2. Voting privacy holds in the state S'.

Proof (Sketch). As a first step, let us extend the two frames by the messages that the intruder can deduce by decomposition steps:

$$struct = \{|\ldots, m'_{N+1} \mapsto commit(v[\pi[1]], r[\pi[1]]), \ldots,$$
$$m'_{2N} \mapsto commit(v[\pi[N]], r[\pi[N]]), m'_{2N+1} \mapsto v[\pi[1]], \ldots, m'_{3N} \mapsto v[\pi[N]],$$
$$m'_{3N+1} \mapsto blind(commit(v[1], r[1]), b_1), \ldots,$$
$$m'_{4N} \mapsto blind(commit(v[N], r[N]), b_N)|\}$$

No further subterms can be obtained by decomposition, and the checks that verifiers give us are analogous between $\mathcal{I}(struct)$ and $\mathcal{I}(concr)$.

Consider any two equivalent terms $s \approx t$ that do not contain destructors or verifiers. While $\approx$ allows to reorder signatures and blindings, it cannot remove or introduce any signature or blinding, i.e., if $sign(k, m)$ is a subterm of s, then there is a subterm $sign(k, m')$ of t (modulo $\approx$) for some term m'. Similar statements hold for *blind* and *commit*.

Suppose now two recipes r_1 and r_2 that only contain constructors (*sign*, *blind*, *commit*) and labels, and suppose $\mathcal{I}(struct[r_1]) = \mathcal{I}(struct[r_2])$. We show that then also $\mathcal{I}(concr[r_1]) = \mathcal{I}(concr[r_2])$. (The proof for the other direction is similar).

The proof is by induction over the maximum depth of r_1 and r_2 where $depth(m_i) = 0$ and $depth(f(t_1, \ldots, t_n)) = 1 + max_{i=1}^n(depth(t_i))$. For depth 0, i.e., two labels, it is trivial: for two distinct labels the result is the same only on plain votes (i.e. m'_{2N+i}), and here $\mathcal{I}(concr) = \mathcal{I}(struct)$.

Suppose now the statement holds for all r'_1, r'_2 up to depth $\mathfrak{N}$, we show that it also holds for all r_1 and r_2 up to depth $\mathfrak{N} + 1$. We proceed by case distinction (omitting symmetric cases).

1. r_1 is a label and r_2 is of depth $\mathfrak{N} + 1$ (otherwise it is already covered). Thus r_2 starts with a constructor, which we can distinguish:
   - $r_2 = sign(r', r'')$. Now $\mathcal{I}(struct[r'])$ is a term that the intruder uses as a signing key and that is a known term to him. Note that no message contains a signature with a signing key known to the intruder. It is thus actually impossible that $\mathcal{I}(struct(r_1)) = \mathcal{I}(struct(r_2))$, since signatures cannot disappear in constructor terms.
   - A similar proof shows that $r_2 = commit(r', r'')$ and $r_2 = blind(r', r'')$ is impossible.

2. Both r_1 and r_2 are composed, at least one, say r_1, is of depth $\mathfrak{N}+1$. Again let us consider the case that $r_1 = sign(r'_1, r''_2)$, the proof for *commit* and *blind* is similar.

Again, since signatures cannot disappear in constructor terms, $\mathcal{I}(struct[r_2])$ must contain a subterm $sign(k, m)$ with $k = \mathcal{I}(struct[r'_1])$. Since k is a term the intruder can construct, and he knows no key that has been used for signing in his knowledge, this signature was constructed by the intruder in r_2 as well. Thus $r_2 \approx sign(r'_2, r''_2)$ such that $\mathcal{I} \models struct[r'_1] = struct[r'_2] \wedge struct[r''_1] = struct[r''_2]$. Since r'_1, r'_2, r''_1, and r''_2 are all of size smaller or equal to $\mathfrak{N}$, so we can apply the induction hypothesis and conclude $\mathcal{I} \models concr[r'_1] = concr[r'_2] \wedge concr[r''_1] = concr[r''_2]$ and thus $\mathcal{I} \models concr[r_1] = concr[r_2]$.

Theorem 3. (α, β_{RF})-privacy holds, i.e., receipt-freeness holds in S.

Proof The idea once again here is to prove that for all $\theta_I \models \alpha$, $\mathcal{I}(struct) = \mathcal{I}(concr)$. We extend the proof of Theorem 1. *gen* is extended to the domain $D \cup D_{Dan}$. The frames *struct* and *concr* are also extended to the new domain as explained with the knowledge of Dan. We already described Dan's strategy for lying. By definition, $\mathcal{I}(v[1]) = [\![\theta_I(v_1)]\!]_\approx$ and $\mathcal{I}(r[1]) = [\![r_{\psi(1)}]\!]_\approx$

Since $\mathcal{I}(concr[d_{3N+2}]) = \mathcal{I}(concr_{Dan}[s_{3N+2}]) = [\![\theta_0(v_{\psi(1)})]\!]_\approx = [\![\theta_I(v_1)]\!]_\approx$ and $\mathcal{I}(concr[d_{3N+3}]) = \mathcal{I}(concr_{Dan}[s_{3N+3}]) = [\![r_{\psi(1)}]\!]_\approx$ by construction, we still have $\mathcal{I}(struct) = \mathcal{I}(concr)$. Thus, in the augmented state S, receipt-freeness holds.

References

1. Abadi, M., Blanchet, B., Fournet, C.: The applied pi calculus: mobile values, new names, and secure communication. J. ACM **65**(1), 1–41 (2017)
2. Blanchet, B., Abadi, M., Fournet, C.: Automated verification of selected equivalences for security protocols. In: Proceedings of the 20th IEEE Symposium on Logic in Computer Science (LICS 2005), pp. 331–340. IEEE (2005)
3. Cortier, V., Rusinowitch, M., Zalinescu, E.: Relating two standard notions of secrecy. Log. Methods Comput. Sci. **3**(3), 303–318 (2007)
4. Delaune, S., Ryan, M., Smyth, B.: Automatic verification of privacy properties in the applied pi calculus. In: Karabulut, Y., Mitchell, J., Herrmann, P., Jensen, C.D. (eds.) IFIPTM 2008. IFIPAICT, vol. 263, pp. 263–278. Springer, Boston (2008). https://doi.org/10.1007/978-0-387-09428-1_17
5. Mödersheim, S., Viganò, L.: Alpha-beta privacy. ACM Transactions on Privacy and Security. Preprint available as DTU Compute Technical report-2018-7 (2018). http://imm.dtu.dk/~samo/abpn.pdf
6. Delaune, S., Kremer, S., Ryan, M.: Verifying privacy-type properties of electronic voting protocols. J. Comput. Secur. **17**(4), 435–487 (2009)
7. Hinrichs, T., Genesereth, M.: Herbrand Logic. Technical report LG-2006-02, Stanford University, Stanford, CA, USA (2006)
8. Fujioka, A., Okamoto, T., Ohta, K.: A practical secret voting scheme for large scale elections. In: Seberry, J., Zheng, Y. (eds.) AUSCRYPT 1992. LNCS, vol. 718, pp. 244–251. Springer, Heidelberg (1993). https://doi.org/10.1007/3-540-57220-1_66

9. Kremer, S., Ryan, M.: Analysis of an electronic voting protocol in the applied pi calculus. In: Sagiv, M. (ed.) ESOP 2005. LNCS, vol. 3444, pp. 186–200. Springer, Heidelberg (2005). https://doi.org/10.1007/978-3-540-31987-0_14

10. Chadha, R., Cheval, V., Cioâcă, Ş., Kremer, S.: Automated verification of equivalence properties of cryptographic protocols. ACM Trans. Comput. Logic **17**(4), 108–127 (2016)

11. Arapinis, M., Liu, J., Ritter, E., Ryan, M.: Stateful applied pi calculus: observational equivalence and labelled bisimilarity. J. Log. Algebraic Methods Program. **89**, 95–149 (2017)

12. Blanchet, B., Smyth, B.: Automated reasoning for equivalences in the applied pi calculus with barriers. J. Comput. Secur. **26**(3), 367–422 (2018)

13. Dong, N., Jonker, H., Pang, J.: Formal analysis of privacy in an eHealth protocol. In: Foresti, S., Yung, M., Martinelli, F. (eds.) ESORICS 2012. LNCS, vol. 7459, pp. 325–342. Springer, Heidelberg (2012). https://doi.org/10.1007/978-3-642-33167-1_19

ProCSA: Protecting Privacy in Crowdsourced Spectrum Allocation

Max Curran, Xiao Liang$^{(\boxtimes)}$, Himanshu Gupta, Omkant Pandey,
and Samir R. Das

Stony Brook University, Stony Brook, USA
{mcurran,liang1,hgupta,omkant,samir}@cs.stonybrook.edu

Abstract. Sharing a spectrum is an emerging paradigm to increase spectrum utilization and thus address the unabated increase in mobile data consumption. The paradigm allows the "unused" spectrum bands of licensed primary users to be shared with secondary users, as long as the allocated spectrum to the secondary users does not cause any harmful interference to the primary users. However, such shared spectrum paradigms pose serious privacy risks to the participating entities, e.g., the secondary users may be sensitive about their locations and usage patterns. This paper presents a privacy-preserving protocol for the shared spectrum allocation problem in a crowdsourced architecture, wherein spectrum allocation to secondary users is done based on real-time sensing reports from geographically distributed and crowdsourced spectrum sensors. Such an architecture is highly desirable since it obviates the need to assume a propagation model, and facilitates estimation based on real-time propagation conditions and high granularity data via inexpensive means.

We design our protocol by leveraging the efficiency and generality of recently developed fast and secure two-party computation (S2PC) protocols. We show that this approach leads to practical solutions that outperform the state-of-the-art in terms of both efficiency as well as functionality. To achieve the desired computational efficiency, we optimize the spectrum allocation algorithm to select a small number of relevant reports based on certain parameters. This results in a faster RAM program for power allocation which, under suitable adjustments to underlying arithmetic operations, can be efficiently implemented using S2PC. We use the standard "ideal/real paradigm" to define the security of spectrum allocation and prove security of our protocol (in the semi-honest model). We also provide data from extensive simulations to demonstrate the accuracy, as well as computational and communication efficiency of our schemes.

1 Introduction

The RF spectrum is a natural resource in great demand due to the unabated increase in mobile (and hence, wireless) data consumption [5]. The research community has addressed this capacity crunch via development of *shared spectrum paradigms*, where the *unused* spectrum bands of a licensed primary user (PU)

© Springer Nature Switzerland AG 2019
K. Sako et al. (Eds.): ESORICS 2019, LNCS 11735, pp. 556–576, 2019.
https://doi.org/10.1007/978-3-030-29959-0_27

can be allocated to an unlicensed secondary user (SU) as long as SU's usage does not cause harmful (wireless) interference to the PU. In a commonly used architecture for such shared spectrum systems, a centralized spectrum manager (SM) allocates available spectrum to SUs upon request, based on PUs' parameters and signal attenuation (path-loss) characteristics. In the *crowdsourced sensing* model we follow, the path-loss values are estimated from real-time sensing reports of geographically distributed and crowdsourced spectrum sensors (SS). Crowdsourcing allows high granularity spectrum data collection via relatively inexpensive means, and most importantly, obviates the need to *assume* a signal propagation model. However, presence of many independent entities makes the shared spectrum system particularly prone to leakage of private information (e.g., location of radar transmitter) [11,25,31]. As the viability of crowdsourced paradigm may depend upon privacy assurance of the crowdsourcing users (i.e., SS devices), it is critical to develop secured spectrum allocation protocols that preserve privacy of all entities. The goal of our work is to develop an efficient privacy-preserving spectrum allocation scheme in the context of the aforementioned shared spectrum architecture.

1.1 Spectrum Allocation Model, Security Challenges, Related Work

Crowdsourced Shared Spectrum Architecture. Spectrum allocation in shared spectrum systems has been studied extensively (see [47] for a survey). In the centralized SM architecture, it is generally assumed that the SM has complete knowledge of the PU parameters. Many prior works assume a propagation model which allows spectrum allocation power to be computed via simple techniques (see [47] survey). However, in practice, since even the best-known propagation models [17,20,38] have unsatisfactory accuracy, spectrum allocation must be done overly conservatively for correctness. Crowdsourced sensing has the potential to eliminate this limitation.

In a crowdsourced architecture, for a spectrum allocation *query* from the SU, the spectrum manager (SM) first estimates appropriate signal path-loss values from known PUs' parameters and real-time sensing reports of crowdsourced spectrum sensors (SS), and then use the estimated path-loss values to allocate spectrum to the SU. Allocation based on real-time channel conditions is important for accurate power allocation, as the conditions affecting signal attenuation (e.g., air, rain, vehicular traffic) may change over time. However, spectrum allocation based on sensing reports can be challenging, due to need for accurate path-loss estimation techniques from relatively inexpensive sensors – but the challenge is mitigated with the availability of a large number of sensing reports via crowdsourced spectrum sensing [9,30]. The practicality of crowdsourced sensing architectures has been demonstrated in research projects [8,9,55] as well as commercial ventures such as Flightaware [3]. Malicious behavior of some SS nodes (faulty sensing reports) can be handled by appropriate fault-tolerance strategies [14].

Spectrum Allocation Algorithm. For a given SU query, the goal of the spectrum allocation algorithm is to allocate maximum possible power to the

SU such that its transmission at the allocated power would not interfere with PU's reception at any of its receivers. There are many
ways to model PU receivers, e.g., a coverage region around PU.
As in [29], we assume a finite
set of representative receivers
called PURs around a PU. Each
PUR is associated with an *initial threshold*, which is continually updated, to signify the
maximum additional interference it can tolerate from the
SUs. At a high-level, for a single SU request (see Sect. 3.1
for multiple SUs), the spectrum
allocation algorithm consists of
the following steps: (i) compute

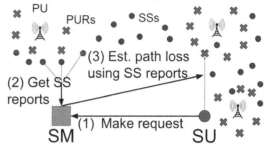

Fig. 1. Spectrum allocation in a shared spectrum
system

the path loss between the SU and each of the PURs, (ii) allocate spectrum
as below, (iii) update the PURs' thresholds. See Fig. 1. More formally, let us
denote the path loss function by $P(,)$; we discuss estimation of this function
in more detail in Sect. 3.1. If an SU S_i at location ℓ_i is allowed to transmit at
power t_i, then the signal power received at PUR R_j at location ℓ_j is given by
$p_{ij} = t_i \cdot P(\ell_i, \ell_j)$. To ensure that p_{ij} is less than each R_j's current threshold τ_j,
the maximum power that can be allocated to S_i is:

$$\min_{j} \frac{\tau_j}{P(\ell_i, \ell_j)}. \tag{1}$$

Once a certain transmit power t_i has been allocated to an SU S_i, the threshold
for a PUR at location ℓ_j is updated as:

$$\tau_j = \tau_j - t_i \times P(\ell_i, \ell_j). \tag{2}$$

Security Challenges. Despite the great potential of shared spectrum
paradigms in improving spectrum utilization efficiency, these systems suffer from
serious privacy and security risks – particularly, due to the presense of many
independent entities. The data collected by SM from SU/SS/PU entities contains sensitive information such as the locations, transmit power, sensing reports,
requested spectrum, etc. For example, a PU can be a military entity, an SU can
be telecom operator, or an SS can be a private user. It is critical to protect the
location, behavior and other information of such entities for personal privacy,
corporate secrecy, and/or national security interests. Furthermore, the viability
of crowdsourced paradigm may depend upon privacy assurance of the crowdsourcing users (i.e., SS devices).

   In order to ensure privacy of participating entities, it is essential that the SM
does not learn any information about them (including the allocated spectrum
power since it can reveal approximate location of the requesting SU). Furthermore, the scheme must not introduce too much latency, to maintain system's

prompt responsiveness to SU requests; moreover, a delayed response may render the spectrum availability information obsolete and thus useless. Such strong privacy and efficiency requirements introduce several technical difficulties that are hard to resolve using basic cryptography. Indeed, the spectrum allocation function, which includes estimation of the path-loss values (as described in Sect. 3.1) computed by the SM, has a rather complex algorithm. While this can be handled using fully homomorphic encryption (FHE) [22], current FHE schemes are far from practical. Another option is to consider general-purpose secure multiparty computation (MPC) protocols [23,51]. While MPC would be impractical if all sensor nodes are involved in the computation, it can be quite efficient for smaller computations involving two (or three) parties. This is the approach we take since, in the setting of secure spectrum allocation, two semi-trusted non-colluding parties are naturally available: the SM and a key server (KS). The non-trivial part is to express the computation (at the time of SU request) as a small circuit or RAM program.

Related Works. The privacy and security issues in shared spectrum systems have received serious attention in the research community only in the last decade (see [25] for a survey). Due to the aforementioned difficulties, existing works focus on simpler versions of spectrum allocation. In particular, many privacy-preserving works have focused on the database-centric architecture, where the spectrum allocation is done based on a spectrum database, often maintained and controlled by a third party (e.g., Google, Spectrum Bridge, RadioSoft, etc.). Here, the security solutions have focused on protecting SU's location privacy by either anonymizing its location/identity [35,46,54], private retrieval from the database [10,19], or differential privacy or data obfuscation techniques [21,31] (also used to protect PU privacy [11,42]). Most works in the crowdsourced spectrum management have focused on protecting privacy of SS nodes only, e.g., location leakage of spectrum sensors from their sensing reports. These include encryption approaches to conceal the sensing reports [26,28,36] or using intermediate nodes to hide location [27,28,37], which incurs significant computation and communication overheads. Other approaches consider distributed architectures [32] or architectures involving multiple service providers [48]. In summary, most works have focused on privacy of SUs/SSs only, and either use data obfuscation techniques or incur substantial overheads.

State-of-the-Art. The state-of-the-art as well as closest to our work is the P^2-SAS system [16] which works in a simplified model where (a) rather than using SSs' real-time sensing reports, the SM pre-computes a signal attenuation map based on an *assumed* propagation model such as Longley-Rice [44]; (b) SM does not compute the actual allocation value; instead, the SM only provides a binary yes/no answer indicating whether the SU can transmit at the requested power v. Roughly speaking, these simplifications allow P^2-SAS to express the computation as a *linear* function which can be computed over encrypted values using the Paillier cryptosystem [40]. Since SM is not fully trusted, P^2-SAS also introduces a key server (KS) who is responsible for generating relevant keys but does not see the encrypted data held by the SM. P^2-SAS yields a solution in the semi-honest model where parties follow the protocol instructions and do not collude (but may analyze the data in their possession). Despite its limitations, P²-SAS makes significant progress on this problem: it can serve yes/no answers to SU requests with 97–98% accuracy under seven seconds, with appropriate acceleration strategies including parallelization of many computational steps.

1.2 Our Contributions

In this work, we present the first general solution to the problem of privacy-preserving spectrum allocation in the crowdsourced spectrum sensing model wherein a centralized spectrum manager orchestrates spectrum allocation using sensing reports from crowdsourced spectrum sensors. Our overall contributions are as follows:

- We present a new architecture for the problem of privacy preserving spectrum allocation based on fast and general-purpose S2PC protocols [6,12,13,33,34]. Our protocol computes the power allocation based on the *current* sensing reports by the SS nodes. Since the conditions affecting signal attenuation (e.g., air, rain, vehicular traffic) may change, path-loss estimation based on real-time sensing reports is important for accurate power allocation. In contrast, the state-of-the-art system P²-SAS pre-computes a signal attenuation map over a grid based on an *assumed* propagation model, which then remains static and does not reflect the latest conditions. We remark that pre-computation of a attenuation map from sensing reports (i.e., without assuming a propagation model) in a *privacy-preserving* manner is also non-trivial.
- Our protocol is an order of magnitude faster that the state-of-the-art systems. More specifically, our protocol can compute the *actual* power allocation in 2–2.5 s on average whereas P²-SAS takes 7 s for a yes/no answer which must be iterated a few times to compute the actual allocation. See Table 1.
- As the spectrum allocation computation involving large number of sensing reports is computationally very expensive to be carried out over S2PC directly, we optimize the spectrum allocation algorithm to use only a small number of relevant sensing reports. We show experimentally that this optimization does not affect the quality of power allocation. Overall, this optimization results in a faster RAM program which can be efficiently implemented using fast S2PC protocols.
- To circumvent implementation issues in using available libraries for "S2PC for RAM program" (see Sect. 3.2), we build a custom solution that can be implemented in Ivory [43]. More specifically, we design a method for performing oblivious read/write operations, and use these routines with fast S2PC for (small) circuits to obtain a protocol that is proven secure in the semi-honest model under the standard ideal-world/real-world paradigm. We use additional optimizations such as moving arithmetic operations outside the S2PC framework whenever possible to extract further efficiency.
- The generality of our approach allows us to support *simultaneous allocation* queries in which several SUs simultaneously request for power allocation as

Table 1. Summary of results

Algorithm	Time	Error wrt. plaintext	Error wrt. optimal	Comm. cost
Two SMs	2 s	2.10^{-4} dB	1 dB (Log), 4 dB (L-R)	0.15 MB
SM-KS	2.5 s	2.10^{-4} dB	1 dB (Log), 4 dB (L-R)	5.35 MB
P^2-SAS [16]	7 s	–	2.72%	5 MB

opposed to just one. The knowledge of several SU requests at once allows the computation of power allocation for each one of them in a more fair and optimal manner. Ours is the first system to support such simultaneous allocation; it is not possible in P^2-SAS or other known solutions since they commonly rely on some form of homomorphic encryption, which severely limits the type of functions they can compute within the encryption.

Results Summary. Table 1 shows the average time and accuracy of our designed schemes to serve each SU request in a large area with 400 PUs and 40,000 SSs in two propagation models (used to generate the ground truth), viz., Log-distance (Log) and Longley-Rice (L-R). Table shows results for two of our schemes: Two SMs (two spectrum managers) and SM-KS (SM and a key server). To handle the SU request, we select 10 PUs and SSs appropriately using a grid of 100×100 over the area. See Sect. 4 for further details. As the P^2-SAS [16] work outputs only yes/no answers, the P^2-SAS entry below shows accuracy as percentage of false positives and negatives.

2 Defining Semi-honest Secure Spectrum Allocation

We define the functionality for spectrum allocation within the framework of secure multi-party computation. Informally, a MPC protocol is said to be *secure* if any information learned by an adversary can also be generated (or "simulated") by an ideal-world *simulator*. We assume familiarity with standard MPC framework (a formal treatment is given in our full version [4]). In the following, we define the ideal functionality for our spectrum allocation task. We focus on *semi-honest model with static corruption*, which means the set of corrupted parties is fixed before the execution of the protocol and all parts (including the corrupted ones) follow the protocol. We also assume authenticated communication channels between each pair of parties.

Ideal Functionality for Spectrum Allocation. The spectrum allocation functionality involves the following participants: the requesting SU S_i, PUs, PURs, SSs, and the two spectrum managers SM_0 and SM_1. We note that the roles of PUs, PURs, and SSs in the protocol are limited in that they only provide data for the computation but do not receive any output. For clarity of presentation, we will use PNs (acronym for Private Nodes) to represent all PURs, PUs and SSs. Also, even though PNs consist of many independent nodes, for ease of presentation, we will treat the entire set of PNs as one single party and use D

to denote the concatenation of their data. The above simplifications are merely for clarity of presentation and do not affect the generality of our results.

The spectrum allocation functionality f^{SA} is described as follows (details are given in Sect. 3.1):

- **Input:** The requesting SU S_i sends its location ℓ_i to f^{SA}. SM_0 and SM_1 input nothing to f^{SA}, but we use the symbol $\perp$ as a placeholder for them. All the PNs (i.e., all the PURs, PUs and SSs, as mentioned above) send their data D to f^{SA}.
- **Computation:** Upon receiving the above input $(\ell_i, \perp, \perp, D)$, f^{SA} does the following (as described in Sect. 3.1):
  - For $j \neq i$, compute the path loss $P(\ell_i, \ell_j)$ between the S_i and R_j
  - Calculate the proper transmit power t_i to S_i per Eq. (1)
  - Update the thresholds for each PUR location ℓ_j per Eq. (2)
- **Output:** $(t_i, \perp, \perp, \perp)$ are the outputs to participants (S_i, SM_0, SM_1, PNs) respectively.

We note that SM_0 and SM_1 neither send any input nor receive any output from f^{SA}. Even though the SMs are "dummy" within f^{SA} functionality, their existence is important to define and prove the security of our protocol.

Correctness and Security. For a protocol Π, we define its correctness and security w.r.t. f^{SA} in the following way.

Definition 1 (Correctness). *We say that Π correctly computes f^{SA} if the following holds except for negligible probability*

$$\mathsf{output}_\Pi(\ell_i, \perp, \perp, D) = f^{\mathsf{SA}}(\ell_i, \perp, \perp, D) \tag{3}$$

where the tuple $(\ell_i, \perp, \perp, D)$ denotes the input data from (S_i, SM_0, SM_1, PNs) and output_Π is the output function of protocol Π.

Definition 2 (Security). *We say that Π securely computes f^{SA} in a semi-honest model with static corruption if there exists a probabilistic polynomial-time algorithm $\mathcal{S}^\Pi$ such that for every $I \subseteq \{S_i, SM_0, SM_1, PNs\}$ that does not contain both SM_0 and SM_1,*

$$\{\mathcal{S}^\Pi(I, \mathsf{input}_I, f_I^{\mathsf{SA}}(\ell_i, \perp, \perp, D))\} \overset{c}{\equiv} \{\mathsf{view}_I^\Pi(\ell_i, \perp, \perp, D)\} \tag{4}$$

where the tuple $(\ell_i, \perp, \perp, D)$ denotes the input data from (S_i, SM_0, SM_1, PNs), input_I denotes the input of parties in set I and $\mathsf{view}_I^\Pi(\ell_i, \perp, \perp, D)$ is the views of parties in set I at Π's termination on input $(\ell_i, \perp, \perp, D)$.

We remark that, in our model, set I cannot simultaneously include both SM servers since they are non-colluding. The definitions are easy to modify to work with a single SM and a KS, or other equivalent setups.

3 Secure Spectrum Allocation

Our secured approach to spectrum allocation is based on on the S2PC technique, but we incorporate various optimizations to make the overall approach viable for our context. We start with describing the plaintext (unsecured) version of our spectrum allocation algorithm.

3.1 Plaintext Algorithm

For a new SU request, the `Plaintext` algorithm can be described as a sequence of the following steps (as per Sect. 1.1): (i) compute the path loss between the SU and each of the PURs, (ii) allocate spectrum as per Eq. (1), and (iii) update the thresholds of the PURs based on the allocation to the SU. We describe the first step in detail below; the other two steps are just straightforward assignment of values to appropriate variables. Later, we motivate and discuss selection of SSs and PUs to make the algorithm more computationally efficient, without much compromise in spectrum utilization.

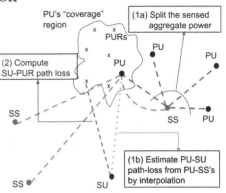

Fig. 2. Path loss estimation

Path Loss Estimation. As per Eq. (1), we need to compute the path loss between the requesting SU S_i and each of the PUs' receivers (i.e., PURs). For a given PUR R_{jk} of a PU P_j, we compute the path loss $P(S_i, R_{jk})$ between R_{jk} and S_i as follows. See Fig. 2.

1. First, we compute the path loss $P(S_i, P_j)$ between the SU S_i and PU P_j in two steps as follows:
   (a) Compute path loss $P(P_j, C_\ell)$ from PU P_j to each of the spectrum sensors C_ℓ. Since a spectrum sensor C_ℓ only senses the *aggregate* power received from all PUs, computing path loss from PU P_j to C_ℓ requires splitting the sensed power across the PUs (as described later).
   (b) Use interpolation to compute the path loss $P(S_i, P_j)$.
2. Then, we compute the desired path loss $P(S_i, R_{jk})$ from the above computed $P(S_i, P_j)$.

We now describe each of the above steps below.

(1a) Estimating $P(P_j, C_\ell)$ From Sensed Power at C_ℓ. As mentioned above, a spectrum sensor C_ℓ senses only the *aggregate* power received from all the PUs. Thus, we must first "split" the total received power of C_ℓ among the PUs; we do this splitting based on the weighted distance as follows. Let r_ℓ be the total power received at C_ℓ, and t_x be the transmit power of a PU P_x. Then, we estimate the power received r_{jl} at C_ℓ due to PU P_j as:

$$r_{jl} = \frac{t_j/d(C_\ell, P_j)^{\alpha_s}}{\sum_{P_x} t_x/d(C_\ell, P_x)^{\alpha_s}} \times r_\ell \tag{5}$$

Above, $d()$ is the distance function and α_s is an exponent parameter that is used to control the above splitting. Now, we can easily compute the path loss $P(P_j, C_\ell)$ as:

$$P(P_j, C_\ell) = r_{jl}/tj \qquad (6)$$

Note that the above estimation of $P(P_j, C_\ell)$ does not depend upon S_i, and then can be precomputed.

(1b) Interpolation to Compute $P(S_i, P_j)$. Once we have estimated the path loss between a PU P_j and every SS C_ℓ, we use interpolation to estimate the path loss from P_j to the current SU S_i under consideration. Prior works [9,52] have used Ordinary Kriging (OK), k-nearest neighbors (k-NN) classifier, or inverse distance weighted (IDW) approaches for such interpolation—with k-NN and OK performing similarly [52]. Here, for simplicity, we start with the IDW approach, and later refine it to using IDW over k nearest neighbors (making the overall scheme akin to a more sophisticated version of the traditional k-NN scheme [52]). Using IDW, we get (here, C_x is a SS node):

$$P(S_i, P_j) = \frac{\sum_{C_x} P(C_x, P_j)/d(S_i, C_x)^{\alpha_p}}{\sum_{C_x} 1/d(S_i, C_x)^{\alpha_p}} \qquad (7)$$

Above, α_p is an exponent parameter that is used to control the above interpolation.

(2) Compute Path Loss $P(S_i, R_{jk})$ from SU to PUR. We now use the estimated path loss between the SU S_i and a PU P_j to estimate the path loss between the SU S_i and the PU P_j's PURs. Each PUR R_{jk} is represented by its location. To estimate the desired path loss $P(S_i, R_{jk})$, we assume a uniform log-distance path loss model within the triangle of nodes P_j, S_i and R_{jk}. In particular, we use:

$$P(S_i, R_{jk}) = \frac{P(S_i, R_j)(d(S_i, R_{jk}))^{\alpha_p}}{(d(S_i, R_j))^{\alpha_p}} \qquad (8)$$

Selection of PUs and SSs for Computational Efficiency. Involving all the PUs and SSs in the above path loss estimation is quite inefficient, as the number of PUs and especially SSs can be very large. This computational efficiency is particularly critical in the secured S2PC implementation. Thus, to improve computational efficiency, we devise a strategy to select only a small number of PUs and SSs—that are most pertinent to the SU S_i requesting spectrum. Note that the PUs that are very far away from S_i are unlikely to be affected by the spectrum allocated to S_i, especially if there are sufficiently many PUs that are close enough to S_i. Similarly, only the SSs that are close to the selected PUs (and thus to the SU S_i) are going to be much useful in the above interpolation step. Note that in the interpolation step, the SSs are weighted by the inverse distance to S_i; thus, SSs that are far away from S_i will have minimal impact. Based on the above arguments, for the sake of computational efficiency, we thus select PUs and SSs that are "close" to the given SU S_i and use only these PUs and SSs in the above computations. In particular, given an SU S_i, we pick k_{ss}

nearest SSs, and k_{pu} nearest PUs; here, the distance to SSs is unweighted, but the distance to a PU is weighted by the average of the thresholds of its PURs. The k_{ss} and k_{pu} values may be chosen based on the density of PUs and SSs. Our simulation results (see Sect. 4) show that only a small number of close-by SS and PU nodes suffice to obtain sufficiently accurate path-loss, if the density of SS nodes is sufficiently high.

Grid Based Implementation. To implement the selection of SSs and PUs efficiently, we employ a grid-based heuristic wherein we divide the given area into cells using horizontal and vertical grid lines, and associate with each cell the list of PUs and SSs that should be selected if the requesting SU is at the cell's center. When a request of SU S_i comes, we determine the cell C in which the S_i lies, and use the PUs and SSs associated with C for path-loss estimation steps. It is important to note that this grid-based heuristic is not exact, i.e., it may not return the nearest set of SSs and weighted PUs as it approximates the position of a requesting SU S_i by the center of C, the cell in which S_i lies. However, our simulation results show that the grid-based approach is computationally efficient and sufficiently accurate for our purposes. Note that the set of PUs associated with some cell may need to be updated due to updates to the PUR thresholds after every spectrum allocation (recall that the distance to PUs are weighted by the average of their PUR thresholds); for efficiency, we only update the thresholds of the PURs of the selected PUs.

Handling Multiple SUs. The above describes the process to allocate spectrum to a single SU request. Multiple SU requests can be handled one at a time, except that in step (1a) above, we need to also account for the fact that a SS may sense power from SU transmissions. This can be handled easily by storing information about the active SUs with the containing cell, and incorporating it in the (1a) step. Multiple SU requests can also be handled *simultaneously*, to incorporate a given fairness constraint, by solving a system of linear equations (with one equation for each PUR) within our S2PC framework. Detailed implementation, optimization, and evaluation of supporting multiple SU requests is deferred to our future work.

3.2   Secured Algorithm Using Two SMs

In this section, we present the secured implementation of our plain algorithm between two spectrum managers. We first present the solution in the simpler setting where there are two semi-honest SMs, and then show how to replace the second SM with a key server. This allows us to focus on core issues related to security and efficiency first.

   At a high-level, this secured algorithm works by having all the PNs secret-share their data to the two SMs, who will then run S2PC protocols between two SMs for each stage of our plain algorithm. Most of our spectrum allocation algorithm involves only simple arithmetic operations which can be implemented efficiently in S2PC; the only parts that require special attention are the following:

in our grid-based interpolation, SMs need to read data from the selected PNs and update the threshold for PURs. These operations happen on the large data array secret-shared between the two SMs.

A direct S2PC implementation will be quite inefficient. One option is to use "S2PC for RAM program" [24,39]. However, the actual implementation using known libraries for efficient S2PC for RAM program [7,15,24,45,49,50,53] runs into several issues. While there are several available implementations that offer different features, these are maintained by individual researchers/teams and often incompatible with each other. Our spectrum allocation algorithm best operates as a RAM program often switching between arithmetic and boolean operations, and it becomes difficult to obtain a workable solution existing known implementations. Therefore, we design a novel oblivious read/write algorithms, which allow fast and secure access of the secret-shared data array. These algorithms can be easily incorporated into our secured protocol.

In the remainder of this subsection, we first give a formal description of our secured protocol, and then present our oblivious Read/Write algorithm in detail.

Protocol 1 (Secured Spectrum Allocation). *Our secured spectrum allocation protocol Π consists of the following stages (subprotocols):*

Π_{off}*: All the PNs secret-share their data D as $D_0 + D_1$ (using an additive secret sharing scheme), and send D_0 (resp. D_1) to SM_0 (resp. SM_1). These two SMs then run an S2PC protocol implementing the functionality f_{off}, which denotes all the steps in Sect. 3.1 before the request of any SU S_i arrives. Specifically, it includes step (1a) of* **Path Loss Estimation** *and the construction of the grid system used to choose proper subset of PUs and SSs for efficient computation. The result is stored in an array data structure A for later use. At the end of this stage, SM_0 and SM_1 get A_0 and A_1 respectively, which are secret shares of A (i.e. $A_0 + A_1 = A$). We remark that the task of this stage should be done off-line (before any request of SU arrives) to improve efficiency.*

Π_{slct}*: This is the selecting stage to get the subset J of indices of array A, which indicates the data needed for pass loss estimation. Π_{slct} asks S_i to secret-share its location $\ell_i = \ell_i^0 + \ell_i^1$ to SM_0 and SM_1. Then the two SMs run an S2PC protocol implementing the functionality $f_{\text{slct}} : (\ell_i^0, \ell_i^1) \rightarrow (J_0, J_1)$ described as follows. f_{slct} takes input (ℓ_i^0, ℓ_i^1) from SM_0 and SM_1 respectively. It first recovers $\ell_i = \ell_i^0 + \ell_i^1$ and then computes the indices as specified in* **Selection of PUs** *and SSs in Sect. 3.1, resulting in a set of indices J. Then the protocol secret shares $J = J_0 + J_1$ to SM_0 and SM_1 as the output of this stage.*

Π_{read}*: SM_0 and SM_1 use J_0 and J_1 respectively as input to read data from A, following our Secured Array-Entry Read algorithm (specified later). At the end of this sub-protocol, $A[j]$ will be secrete shared as $A_0''[j] + A_1''[j]$ for every $j \in J$. The output of this stage to SM_0 (resp. SM_1) is the sequence of secret shares $\{A_0''[j]\}_{j \in J}$ (resp. $\{A_1''[j]\}_{j \in J}$).*

Π_{alloc}*: SM_0 and SM_1 use $\{A_0''[j]\}_{j \in J}$ and $\{A_1''[j]\}_{j \in J}$ as input to calculate the allocated transit power t_i. t_i is then secret-shared to $t_i^0 + t_i^1$. SM_0 (resp. SM_1) gets t_i^0 (resp. t_i^1) as output. This sub-protocol again is implemented via 2PC.*

Π_{update}: SM_0 and SM_1 run an S2PC protocol implementing the computation of the new threshold τ_j as per Eq. (2). The results are again secret shared. SM_0 holds $\{\tau_j^0\}_{j \in J}$, and SM_1 holds $\{\tau_j^1\}_{j \in J}$ such that $\tau_j^0 + \tau_j^1 = \tau_j$ for all $j \in J$.

Π_{write}: SM_0 and SM_1 use $\{\tau_j^0\}_{j \in J}$ and $\{\tau_j^1\}_{j \in J}$ as input to update data in $\{A[j]\}_{j \in J}$. This sub-protocol is implemented as our Secured Array-Entry Write algorithm (specified later).

Π_{output}: SM_0 (resp. SM_1) sends t_i^0 (resp. t_i^1) as it received in Π_{alloc} to S_i. S_i recovers $t_i = t_i^0 + t_i^1$ as the final output of the main protocol Π. □

Secured Array-Entry Read. Consider an array $A[1..n]$. The secret sharing of array $A[1..n]$ entails that SM_0 and SM_1 store $A_0[1..n]$ and $A_1[1..n]$ respectively with $A_0[i]$ and $A_1[i]$ as two random numbers such that $A_0[i] + A_1[i] = A[i]$. Now, let's say we are given an index j (that has been "computed" in S2PC), and we wish to "load" the entry $A[j]$ into S2PC without either SM learning about either the index j or the entry $A[j]$ being accessed. We use the

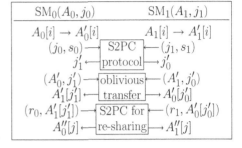

Fig. 3. Array-entry read operation

oblivious transfer (OT) technique [18,41] to implement our solution; the OT techniques allows two parties to exchange information securely. In particular, if one party has the array and the other party has the index of interest, then OT allows the first party to transfer $A[j]$ to another without either party knowing the other party's input parameter. In our context, the additional challenge is that neither the index j nor the array A is known to either of the parties; these values are shared across the two SMs. We address this challenge by random "shifting" of the indexes and array values at each SM, and engage in S2PC appropriately as described below. Our solution to access an entry $A[j]$ into S2PC securely involves the following steps:

We start with assuming that, from earlier stages in the execution of S2PC, the target index j is shared across the two SMs. Thus, at the beginning of this stage, SM_0 holds j_0 and A_0 as input while SM_1 holds j_1 and A_1 as input; here, j_0 and j_1 are the secret shares of our target index j, and A_0 and A_1 are secret shares of data array A.

1. First, each SM creates new arrays by shifting the indices and entries of the given arrays by fixed random values. More formally, SM_0 and SM_1 create arrays $A_0'[1..n]$ and $A_1'[1..n]$ as:

$$A_0'[i] = A_0[(i + s_0)\%n] + r_0, \quad A_1'[i] = A_1[(i + s_1)\%n] + r_1$$

where s_0 and r_0 (resp. s_1 and r_1) are random numbers chosen by SM_0 (resp. SM_1).

2. Now, S2PC protocol transfers appropriate indices to the SMs. In particular, SM_0 (resp. SM_1) holding j_0 and s_0 (resp. j_1 and s_1) as input run a S2PC protocol to implement the following functionality f: Upon receiving inputs from SM_0 and SM_1, f recovers $j = j_0 + j_1$ and sends $j_1' := (j + s_1)\%n$ (resp. $j_0' := (j + s_0)\%n$) to SM_0 (resp. SM_1) as the output.

3. Now, the SMs exchange array entries via OT. In particular, SM_0 fetches $A_1'[j_1']$ from SM_1, and SM_1 fetches $A_0'[j_0']$ from SM_0.

4. Then SM_0 (resp. SM_1) uses $A_1'[j_1']$ and r_0 (resp. $A_0'[j_0']$ and r_1) as input to run a S2PC protocol implementing the following functionality f: Upon receiving inputs from SM_0 and SM_1, f recovers $A[j]$ as

$$A[j] = A_0'[j_0'] + A_1'[j_1'] - r_0 - r_1$$

and then secret shares the $A[j]$ as $A_0''[j] + A_1''[j]$, and sends $A_0''[j]$ (resp. $A_1''[j]$) to SM_0 (resp. SM_1) as the final output.

Secured Array-Entry Write. Consider an array $A[1..n]$ again as above, where the SM_0 and SM_1 store the secret shares $A_0[1..n]$ and $A_1[1..n]$ respectively of the array. Now, given two private values (secret-shared across the SMs) j and d, we wish to update the array entry $A[j]$ by adding d to it. We achieve the above update of $A[j]$ to $A[j] + d$ in a secured manner by adding **zero** to the remaining entries $A[i]$ (for $i \neq j$). One simple (but inefficient) way to achieve the above is as follows.

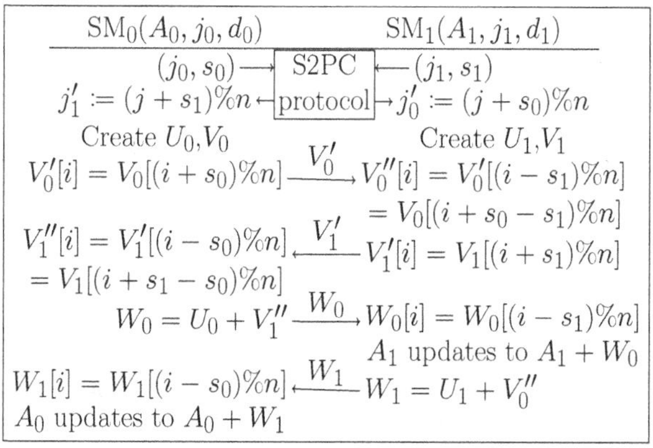

$$
\begin{array}{ll}
SM_0(A_0, j_0, d_0) & SM_1(A_1, j_1, d_1) \\
\hline
(j_0, s_0) \rightarrow \boxed{\text{S2PC}} \leftarrow (j_1, s_1) \\
j_1' := (j + s_1)\%n \leftarrow \text{protocol} \rightarrow j_0' := (j + s_0)\%n \\
\text{Create } U_0, V_0 & \text{Create } U_1, V_1 \\
V_0'[i] = V_0[(i + s_0)\%n] \xrightarrow{V_0'} V_0''[i] = V_0'[(i - s_1)\%n] \\
 & = V_0[(i + s_0 - s_1)\%n] \\
V_1''[i] = V_1'[(i - s_0)\%n] \xleftarrow{V_1'} V_1'[i] = V_1[(i + s_1)\%n] \\
= V_1[(i + s_1 - s_0)\%n] \\
W_0 = U_0 + V_1'' \xrightarrow{W_0} W_0[i] = W_0[(i - s_1)\%n] \\
 & A_1 \text{ updates to } A_1 + W_0 \\
W_1[i] = W_1[(i - s_0)\%n] \xleftarrow{W_1} W_1 = U_1 + V_0'' \\
A_0 \text{ updates to } A_0 + W_1 \\
\end{array}
$$

Fig. 4. Array-entry write operation

- At start, SM_0 (resp. SM_1) holds j_0 and d_0 (resp. j_1 and d_1) as input, where j_0 and j_1 are the secret shares of the target index j while d_0 and d_1 are the secret shares of value d to be added to $A[j]$.
- SM_0 creates an array $D_0[1..n]$ of random and private numbers.
- SM_0 holding D_0 and d_0 as input and SM_1 holding d_1 as input execute a S2PC protocol implementing the following functionality f: Upon receiving input from SMs, f computes the "complement" D_1 of D_0 such that $D_0[i] + D_1[i] = 0$ for $i \neq j$ and $D_0[j] + D_1[j] = d$. f sends D_1 to SM_1 as the output.
- Finally, each SM updates its array as: $A_0[i] = A_0[i] + D_0[i]$ and $A_1[i] = A_1[i] + D_1[i]$ for all i (including j).

The above approach however can be very inefficient due to a large number of operations ($O(n)$ additions) computed in S2PC. To circumvent this, we propose another approach that limits the number of arithmetic operations at S2PC to a small constant while pushing most of the arithmetic operations to the SMs. We achieve this by creating two arrays at each SM, shifting their indexes and exchanging them appropriately. We use the term *shifting* an array $B[1..n]$ by m to mean the operation $B[i] = B[(i + m)\%n]$. For $b \in \{0, 1\}$, our approach works as follows:

- *Input.* Same as in the above approach, SM_b holds A_b, j_b and d_b as input.
- *Creating j'_b.* Each SM_b samples a random number s_b. Then each SM_b on input (j_b, s_b) execute a S2PC protocol implementing the following functionality f: Upon receiving SMs' input, f recovers $j = j_0 + j_1$ and sends $j'_{1-b} := (j + s_{1-b})\%n$ to SM_b as the output.
- *Updating Arrays U_b and V_b.* Each SM_b creates two arrays U_b and V_b, such that $U_b[i] + V_b[i] = d_b$ for $i = j'_{1-b}$ and 0 otherwise. Here, the idea is that these arrays (after manipulation) will eventually be sent over to the other SM (i.e., SM_{1-b}) who will be able to shift these arrays by s_{1-b}, to get the share of d in the jth index.
- *Manipulation and Exchange of V_b.* Now, each SM_b shifts V_b further by s_b (its private random number) and sends it over to the other SM (i.e., SM_{1-b}). The SM_b on receiving V_{1-b} shifts it by $-s_b$. Thus, each SM_b has V_{1-b} which has been shifted by $s_b + s_{1-b} - s_b = s_{1-b}$.
- *Addition of Local Update Arrays, and Exchange.* Each SM_b now adds the locally available U_b and V_{1-b} (each has a shift of s_{1-b}) to get W_b. At this point, W_0 and W_1 are such that, if we ignore their shifts, their respective entries add up to zero and d. SMs exchange their W_0 and W_1.
- *Final Updating.* Each SM_b now has W_{1-b} (with a shift of j_{1-b}). The array W_{1-b} is finally shifted by $-s_b$ and added to A_b array.

Correctness and Security. The correctness of Protocol 1 is obvious. We give a sketch of its security proof in Appendix A; see [4] for the detailed proof.

3.3   Secure Allocation Using One SM and a Key Server

We now modify the secured algorithm from previous subsection to the case of a single SM and a key server. A key server (KS) is a semi-trusted entity in that it can use its persistent storage to only store the cryptographic keys and no other data. We can implement our secured approach over a single SM and a KS, with the following modification to the secret sharing mechanism.

An entity E with the data a_i that it wants to share (in our task, E could be a SS/PU/PUR node with its input) will ask KS for an AES key k_i. E secret shares a_i to $a_{i0} + a_{i1}$. It then sends a_{i0} and $AES_{k_i}(a_{i1})$ to SM, where $AES_{k_i}(a_{i1})$ is the AES-encrypted a_{i1} with key k_i. This finishes the secret sharing stage. After all the necessary data is shared in this way to SM, it can run our aforementioned protocol Π with KS playing the role of SM_1. More specifically, SM sends the

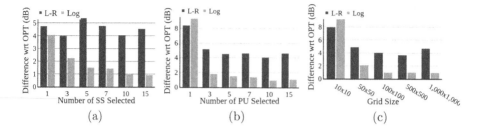

Fig. 5. Average difference in power allocated by Plaintext and Optimal schemes for varying number of (a) selected SSs, (b) selected PUs, and (c) grid size.

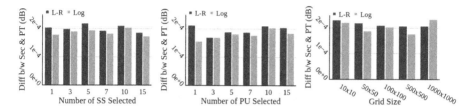

Fig. 6. Average difference in spectral power allocated by secured (i.e., 2-SMs or SM-KS) and Plaintext schemes for varying parameter values.

encrypted shares to KS, who has the corresponding AES keys for decryption. Now we are in the setting where two parties hold the secret shares of input for the spectrum allocation task. They can then run protocol Π as if KS is SM_1.

The above mechanism enables secured two-party computation using S2PC protocol without requiring S2PC to perform any cryptographic operations. Also, it can be used easily to implement the secure read and write operations as described in the previous subsection.

4   Simulation Results

In this section, we evaluate our developed techniques for secured spectrum allocation, by demonstrating its accuracy and computational efficiency.

S2PC Implementation. The core component of our designed algorithm is the use of S2PC protocol to securely compute certain arithmetic operations. To aid our implementation, we use a pre-existing S2PC library Ivory [43]. Ivory provides pre-built circuits for simple operations over integers; these circuits can be used to compute more complex functions using S2PC protocol. Limited by the Ivory library, we use a fixed-point representation for values in S2PC. In particular, we represent a real value v in terms of a standard int value x, such that $v = x \times 2^k$ where k is a (positive or negative) *constant* which determines the precision level of the fixed point value. We use 64 bits to represent real values.

Simulation Setup and Parameters. Similar to the settings in the most closely related work [16], we consider a geographic area of $10\,\text{km} \times 10\,\text{km}$, with 400 PUs

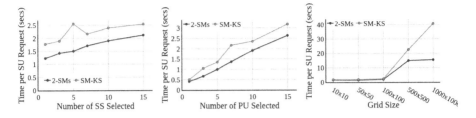

Fig. 7. Time taken by the secured algorithms for varying parameter values.

and 40000 SSs randomly distributed in the area; we use a large number of spectrum sensors to demonstrate the scalability of our approach in high-density crowdsourced settings. We use 5 PURs for each PU located at 100 m around the PU. In each of the plots below, we vary one of the parameter settings while keeping the other parameter settings to their default values. In particular, the default values for various parameter settings are as follows: number of selected PUs: 10, number of selected SSs: 10, grid of 100 × 100. We consider two signal propagation models, viz., log-distance (`Log`) and Longley-Rice (`L-R`) [44], to generate the "ground truth" data, i.e., the sensing reports at the SSs, based on the power and location of each PU. Log-distance (`Log`) model is a simple model, wherein the signal attenuation at a distance d is proportional to d^α where α is the path-loss exponent constant. In contrast, the Longley-Rice (`L-R`) is a complex model of wireless propagation, which takes multiple parameters, such as geolocation of transmitter (TX) and receiver (RX), their antenna configuration, terrain data, weather, and soil condition. In particular, we use the SPLAT! application [1] to generate path losses based on `L-R` model for desired pairs of points.

Accuracy of Plaintext (`PT`) Algorithm vs. Optimal (`OPT`). We start with evaluating the accuracy of our `PT` algorithm (Sect. 3.1) with respect to the optimal or "ground truth" (denoted by `OPT`) scheme which allocates maximum spectrum power possible based on the true path-loss values derived directly from the underlying propagation model. Recall that accuracy of `PT` algorithm is affected by three aspects of the algorithm: (i) path-loss estimation error, (ii) selection strategy, which selects only the nearest SSs and PUs, and the (iii) grid-based implementation which approximates a SU's location with the containing grid-cell's center and updates the PUR thresholds of only the PUs that are associated with the containing grid-cell. See Fig. 5, which plots the average spectrum difference (in dB) between the spectrum power allocated by the `PT` algorithm and the optimal `OPT`, for varying number of selected SSs and PUs and grid size, for Log-distance and Longley-Rice propagation models. For the Log-distance model, as mentioned in Sect. 3.1, the first and the third steps of our path-loss estimation process are provably 100% accurate if the chosen exponent is the same as that of the underlying model (as is the case in the simulations); thus, the path-loss estimation errors in the Log-distance model are solely due to the second (interpolation) step. In Fig. 5, we observe that for the Log-distance (`Log`) model, the difference between the `PT` and `OPT` schemes on average is minimal (1–2 dB) when the number of selected PUs and SSs is 10, and the grid size is at least as 100×100. For the Longley-Rice (L-R) model, the average error is about 4–5 dB for similar parameter values; this is largely expected, as the complex L-R model depends on various terrain-specific factors and thus is more difficult to estimate accurately compared to the Log model which depends solely on distance between points. In summary, a small number (10–15) of SSs and PUs are sufficient to minimize the error, and choosing a larger number of SSs or PUs is not helpful. Also, a 100×100 grid seems fine enough. This justifies our selection strategy and its grid-based implementation, and facilitates computational efficiency of our secured schemes as described below.

Accuracy of Secured vs. Plaintext Algorithms. We now present statistics for the accuracy of our secured schemes (Sect. 3.2), as compared to the Plaintext (PT) algorithm. Note that the two secured schemes, viz., using two SMs (2-SMs) or an SM plus a key server KS (SM-KS), allocate the same spectrum power and thus will have the same accuracy—as they differ only in their implementation. In Fig. 6, we plot the difference between the spectrum power allocated by our secured schemes and the Plaintext (PT) algorithm, for varying number of selected SSs or PUs or grid size, for Log-distance (Log) and Longley-Rice (L-R) propagation models. Here, the range of the values for number of SSs or PUs selected is partly dictated by the results in Fig. 5 which show that only a small number (10–15) of SSs of PUs are sufficient for minimizing the error of the Plaintext algorithm. Figure 6 shows that across all parameter values of interest the difference between the Secured and Plaintext is near zero dB.

Computation Time. Figure 7 plots computation time taken by the two secured schemes, viz., 2-SMs (using two SMs) and SM-KS (one SM and a key server) for varying grid size, # of selected SSs, and # of selected PUs selected. We use a virtual machine with 48GB ram and 6 virtual CPUs—with each vCPU implemented as a single hardware hyper-thread on a Intel Xeon E5 v3 (Haswell) platform [2]. We observe that the computation time taken by either scheme is of the order of 2–3 s, except for grids larger than 500×500 (due to higher grid-table sizes). However, as shown in prior results, a 100×100 grid is fine enough for delivering high accuracy.

Communication Overhead. The communication overhead of our secured schemes was observed to be minimal. In particular, for the optimal parameters of a grid of 100×100 and 10 selected SSs and PUs each, the secured schemes (2-SMs as well as SM-KS) incur a communication overhead of about 150 KB in computing the arithmetic and access operations. The SM-KS scheme incurs an additional communication overhead of 5.2 MB to transfer the grid array. Thus, the total communication overhead for the 2-SMs scheme is 150 KB, while that for the SM-KS scheme is 5.35 MB.

5   Conclusions and Future Work

In this work, we developed an efficient privacy-preserving spectrum allocation scheme in a crowdsourced sensing architecture of shared spectrum paradigms, and demonstrated its viability via extensive simulations. As in prior works [16], we assumed a semi-honest adversary model. Building efficient privacy-preserving spectrum allocation protocols under malicious adversary model is a challenging open problem, especially since there are no known general-purpose S2PC protocols that are efficient enough in the malicious-adversary setting. In addition, our future work is focussed on developing privacy-preserving protocols for other problems in the crowdsourced sensing architecture, e.g., localization of unauthorized access users (intruders), creating of spectrum occupancy maps.

A   Security Proof

Theorem 1 (Security of Protocol 1). *Protocol 1 is a secure multi-party computation implementation of the plaintext algorithm shown in Sect. 3.1 with respect to semi-honest adversaries which do not corrupt* SM_0 *and* SM_1 *at the same time.*

Proof (Sketch; see [4] for a detailed proof). We need to show a simulator for different combinations of views for all possible subset $I \subseteq \{S_i, SM_0, SM_1, PNs\}$ such that I does not contain SM_0 and SM_1 at the same time (Recall that we assume they do not collude). For Protocol 1, we claim that it will be sufficient if we can construct a simulator for each party separately (which is not necessarily true for general MPC protocols). This is because both S_i (except for its final output t_i) and PNs receive no message during the execution of Π. Simulators for them can be constructed in a "dummy" way by just outputting the input/output of S_i and PNs. So the essential part of Protocol 1 is actually a S2PC protocol between SM_0 and SM_1. And it is not hard to verify that once SM_0 and SM_1 are not corrupted at the same time, the simulator for a spectrum manager can be composed with the aforementioned "dummy" simulators of S_i and PNs arbitrarily, to get a whole simulator for any corrupted set I that goes through the security proof. Therefore, we only need to construct a simulator for SM_0 (SM_1's role is symmetric to that of SM_0).

Notice that for each of the 6 subprotocols described in Protocol 1, the input/output of SM_0 are secret shares of some data. Due to the security of the secret-sharing scheme, those shares is (purely) random. So if we substitute each subprotocols by invoking the corresponding simulator on a random string, we will get the final simulator for SM_0. A formal proof involves a sequence of hybrids where we substitute each subprotocol (with its simulator) in order and proves indistinguishability in a careful but standard way.

We remark that the existence of simulators for subprotocols Π_{off}, Π_{slct}, Π_{alloc} and Π_{update} is guaranteed by the S2PC protocols used to implement them. We still need to show simulators for Π_{read} and Π_{write}. The read algorithm (Fig. 3) involves two S2PC protocols and one oblivious transfer, where all the input/output are random secret shares. So a simulator can be constructed in a straightforward way. The write algorithm (Fig. 4) consists of a S2PC protocol followed by four message exchanges, which look random. So a simulator for it can also be easily constructed. This completes the proof for Theorem 1.   □

References

1. https://www.qsl.net/kd2bd/splat.html
2. https://cloud.google.com/compute/docs/cpu-platforms
3. FlightFeeder for Android, FlightAware. http://flightaware.com/adsb/android
4. Full version. https://www.cs.stonybrook.edu/~hgupta/procsa.pdf
5. Andrews, J., et al.: What will 5G be? IEEE JSAC **32**, 1065–1082 (2014)
6. Ben-David, A., Nisan, N., Pinkas, B.: FairplayMP: a system for secure multi-party computation. In: Proceedings of the 15th ACM Conference on Computer and Communications Security, pp. 257–266. ACM (2008)
7. Buescher, N., Weber, A., Katzenbeisser, S.: Towards practical RAM based secure computation. In: Lopez, J., Zhou, J., Soriano, M. (eds.) ESORICS 2018. LNCS, vol. 11099, pp. 416–437. Springer, Cham (2018). https://doi.org/10.1007/978-3-319-98989-1_21
8. Calvo-Palomino, R. Giustiniano, D., Lenders, V., Fakhreddine, A.: Crowdsourcing spectrum data decoding. In: IEEE INFOCOM 2017 - IEEE Conference on Computer Communications (2017)
9. Chakraborty, A., Rahman, M.S., Gupta, H., Das, S.R.: SpecSense: crowdsensing for efficient querying of spectrum occupancy. In IEEE INFOCOM 2017 - IEEE Conference on Computer Communications (2017)
10. Chor, B., Goldreich, O., Kushilevitz, E., Sudan, M.: Private information retrieval. In: Proceedings of 36th Annual Symposium on Foundations of Computer Science, pp. 41–50. IEEE (1995)
11. Clark, M.A., Psounis, K.: Trading utility for privacy in shared spectrum access systems. IEEE/ACM Trans. Netw. **26**, 259–273 (2017)
12. Damgård, I., Pastro, V., Smart, N., Zakarias, S.: Multiparty computation from somewhat homomorphic encryption. In: Safavi-Naini, R., Canetti, R. (eds.) CRYPTO 2012. LNCS, vol. 7417, pp. 643–662. Springer, Heidelberg (2012). https://doi.org/10.1007/978-3-642-32009-5_38
13. Demmler, D., Schneider, T., Zohner, M.: ABY-a framework for efficient mixed-protocol secure two-party computation. In: NDSS (2015)
14. Ding, G., Song, F., Wu, Q., Zou, Y., Zhang, L., Feng, S., Wang, J.: Robust spectrum sensing with crowd sensors. In: IEEE VTC (2014)
15. Doerner, J., Shelat, A.: Scaling ORAM for secure computation. In: Proceedings of the 2017 ACM SIGSAC Conference on Computer and Communications Security, pp. 523–535. ACM (2017)
16. Dou, Y., Zeng, K.C., Li, H., Yang, Y., Gao, B., Ren, K., Li, S.: P2-SAS: privacy-preserving centralized dynamic spectrum access system. IEEE J. Sel. Areas Commun. **35**(1), 173–187 (2017)
17. Drocella, E., Richards, J., Sole, R., Najmy, F., Lundy, A., McKenna, P.: 3.5 GHz exclusion zone analyses and methodology. Technical report (2015)
18. Even, S., Goldreich, O., Lempel, A.: A randomized protocol for signing contracts. Commun. ACM **28**(6), 637–647 (1985)
19. Fan, B., Andersen, D.G, Kaminsky, M., Mitzenmacher, M.D.: Cuckoo filter: practically better than bloom. In: Proceedings of the 10th ACM International on Conference on emerging Networking Experiments and Technologies, pp. 75–88. ACM (2014)
20. U. FCC: Longley-rice methodology for evaluating TV coverage and interference. OET Bulletin, 69 (2004)

21. Gao, Z., Zhu, H., Liu, Y., Li, M., Cao, Z.: Location privacy in database-driven cognitive radio networks: attacks and countermeasures. In: 2013 Proceedings of IEEE INFOCOM, pp. 2751–2759. IEEE (2013)
22. Gentry, C.: Fully homomorphic encryption using ideal lattices. In: Proceedings of the 41st Annual ACM Symposium on Theory of Computing, pp. 169–178. ACM (2009)
23. Goldreich, O., Micali, S., Wigderson, A.: How to play any mental game. In: Proceedings of the Nineteenth Annual ACM Symposium on Theory of Computing, pp. 218–229. ACM (1987)
24. Gordon, S.D., et al.: Secure two-party computation in sublinear (amortized) time. In: Proceedings of the 2012 ACM Conference on Computer and Communications Security, pp. 513–524. ACM (2012)
25. Grissa, M., Hamdaoui, B., Yavuza, A.A.: Location privacy in cognitive radio networks: a survey. IEEE Commun. Surv. Tutor. **19**, 1726–1760 (2017)
26. Grissa, M., Yavuz, A., Hamdaoui, B.: LPOS: location privacy for optimal sensing in cognitive radio networks. In: 2015 IEEE Global Communications Conference (GLOBECOM), pp. 1–6. IEEE (2015)
27. Grissa, M., Yavuz, A., Hamdaoui, B.: An efficient technique for protecting location privacy of cooperative spectrum sensing users. In: 2016 IEEE Conference on Computer Communications Workshops (INFOCOM WKSHPS), pp. 915–920. IEEE (2016)
28. Grissa, M., Yavuz, A.A., Hamdaoui, B.: Preserving the location privacy of secondary users in cooperative spectrum sensing. IEEE Trans. Inf. Forensics Secur. **12**(2), 418–431 (2017)
29. Hoang, A.T., Liang, Y., Islam, M.H.: Power control and channel allocation in cognitive radio networks with primary users' cooperation. IEEE Trans. Mob. Comput. **9**, 348–360 (2010)
30. Ishwar, P., Kumar, A., Ramchandran, K.: Distributed sampling for dense sensor networks: a "Bit-Conservation Principle". In: Zhao, F., Guibas, L. (eds.) IPSN 2003. LNCS, vol. 2634, pp. 17–31. Springer, Heidelberg (2003). https://doi.org/10.1007/3-540-36978-3_2
31. Jin, X., Zhang, R., Chen, Y., Li, T., Zhang, Y.: DPSense: differentially private crowdsourced spectrum sensing. In: Proceedings of the 2016 ACM SIGSAC Conference on Computer and Communications Security, pp. 296–307. ACM (2016)
32. Kasiri, B., Lambadaris, I., Yu, F.R., Tang, H.: Privacy-preserving distributed cooperative spectrum sensing in multi-channel cognitive radio MANETs. In: 2015 IEEE International Conference on Communications (ICC), pp. 7316–7321. IEEE (2015)
33. Kolesnikov, V., Schneider, T.: Improved garbled circuit: free XOR gates and applications. In: Aceto, L., Damgård, I., Goldberg, L.A., Halldórsson, M.M., Ingólfsdóttir, A., Walukiewicz, I. (eds.) ICALP 2008. LNCS, vol. 5126, pp. 486–498. Springer, Heidelberg (2008). https://doi.org/10.1007/978-3-540-70583-3_40
34. Kreuter, B., Shelat, A., Shen, C.-H.: Billion-gate secure computation with malicious adversaries. In: USENIX Security Symposium, vol. 12, pp. 285–300 (2012)
35. Li, H., Pei, Q., Zhang, W.: Location privacy-preserving channel allocation scheme in cognitive radio networks. Int. J. Distrib. Sens. Netw. **12**(7), 3794582 (2016)
36. Li, S., Zhu, H., Gao, Z., Guan, X., Xing, K., Shen, X.: Location privacy preservation in collaborative spectrum sensing. In: 2012 Proceedings of IEEE INFOCOM, pp. 729–737. IEEE (2012)

37. Mao, Y., Chen, T., Zhang, Y., Wang, T., Zhong, S.: Protecting location information in collaborative sensing of cognitive radio networks. In: Proceedings of the 18th ACM International Conference on Modeling, Analysis and Simulation of Wireless and Mobile Systems, pp. 219–226. ACM (2015)

38. Medeisis, A., Kajackas, A.: On the use of the universal Okumura-Hata propagation prediction model in rural areas. In: 2000 IEEE 51st Vehicular Technology Conference Proceedings, VTC 2000-Spring Tokyo, vol. 3, pp. 1815–1818. IEEE (2000)

39. Ostrovsky, R., Shoup, V.: Private information storage. In: STOC, vol. 97, pp. 294–303. Citeseer (1997)

40. Paillier, P.: Public-key cryptosystems based on composite degree residuosity classes. In: Stern, J. (ed.) EUROCRYPT 1999. LNCS, vol. 1592, pp. 223–238. Springer, Heidelberg (1999). https://doi.org/10.1007/3-540-48910-X_16

41. Rabin, M.O.: How to exchange secrets with oblivious transfer. IACR Cryptology ePrint Archive 2005, 187 (2005)

42. Rajkarnikar, N., Peha, J.M., Aguiar, A.: Location privacy from dummy devices in database-coordinated spectrum sharing. In: 2017 IEEE International Symposium on Dynamic Spectrum Access Networks (DySPAN), pp. 1–10. IEEE (2017)

43. Rindal, P.: Ivory (2018). https://github.com/ladnir/Ivory-Runtime

44. Seybold, J.: Introduction to RF Propagation. Wiley, New York (2005)

45. Stefanov, E., et al.: Path ORAM: an extremely simple oblivious ram protocol. In: Proceedings of the 2013 ACM SIGSAC conference on Computer and Communications Security, pp. 299–310. ACM (2013)

46. Sweeney, L.: k-anonymity: a model for protecting privacy. Int. J. Uncertain. Fuzziness Knowl. Based Syst. 10(05), 557–570 (2002)

47. Tragos, E.Z., Zeadally, S., Fragkiadakis, A.G., Siris, V.A.: Spectrum assignment in cognitive radio networks: a comprehensive survey. IEEE Commun. Surv. Tutor. 15(3), 1108–1135 (2013)

48. Wang, W., Zhang, Q.: Privacy-preserving collaborative spectrum sensing with multiple service providers. IEEE Trans. Wirel. Commun. 14(2), 1011–1019 (2015)

49. Wang, X., Chan, H., Shi, E.: Circuit ORAM: on tightness of the Goldreich-Ostrovsky lower bound. In: Proceedings of the 22nd ACM SIGSAC Conference on Computer and Communications Security, pp. 850–861. ACM (2015)

50. Wang, X.S., Huang, Y., Chan, T.H., Shelat, A., Shi, E.: SCORAM: oblivious ram for secure computation. In: Proceedings of the 2014 ACM SIGSAC Conference on Computer and Communications Security, pp. 191–202. ACM (2014)

51. Yao, A.C.-C.: How to generate and exchange secrets. In: 27th Annual Symposium on Foundations of Computer Science, pp. 162–167. IEEE (1986)

52. Ying, X., Kim, C.W., Roy, S.: Revisiting TV coverage estimation with measurement-based statistical interpolation (2015)

53. Zahur, S., et al.: Revisiting square-root ORAM: efficient random access in multiparty computation. In: 2016 IEEE Symposium on Security and Privacy (SP), pp. 218–234. IEEE (2016)

54. Zhang, L., Fang, C., Li, Y., Zhu, H., Dong, M.: Optimal strategies for defending location inference attack in database-driven CRNs. In: 2015 IEEE International Conference on Communications (ICC), pp. 7640–7645. IEEE (2015)

55. Zhang, T., Leng, N., Banerjee, S.: A vehicle-based measurement framework for enhancing whitespace spectrum databases. In: Proceedings of ACM Mobicom (2014)

Breaking Unlinkability of the ICAO 9303 Standard for e-Passports Using Bisimilarity

Ihor Filimonov, Ross Horne[(⊠)], Sjouke Mauw, and Zach Smith

Computer Science and Communications, University of Luxembourg,
Esch sur Alzette, Luxembourg
ross.horne@uni.lu

Abstract. We clear up confusion surrounding privacy claims about the ICAO 9303 standard for e-passports. The ICAO 9303 standard includes a Basic Access Control (BAC) protocol that should protect the user from being traced from one session to another. While it is well known that there are attacks on BAC, allowing an attacker to link multiple uses of the same passport, due to differences in implementation; there still remains confusion about whether there is an attack on unlinkability directly on the BAC protocol as specified in the ICAO 9303 standard. This paper clarifies the nature of the debate, and sources of potential confusion. We demonstrate that the original privacy claims made are flawed, by uncovering attacks on a strong formulation of unlinkability. We explain why the use of the bisimilarity equivalence technique is essential for uncovering our attacks. We also clarify what assumptions lead to proofs of formulations of unlinkability using weaker notions of equivalence. Furthermore, we propose a fix for BAC within the scope of the standard, and prove that it is correct, again using a state-of-the-art approach to bisimilarity.

1 Introduction

The Basic Access Control (BAC) mechanism for e-passports, which forms part of the ICAO 9303 standard [1], has been in operation since 2005. Since then, an improved access control mechanism, the Password Authenticated Connection Establishment (PACE) protocol [6], has been standardised in order to address known limitations with the security of BAC. However, the BAC protocol is still being implemented by a growing number of e-documents, not only e-passports. For example, many national identity cards are compliant with the BAC protocol in the ICAO 9303 standard. This means that, firstly, even a relatively minor attack on privacy is of concern to a large number of citizens internationally; and, secondly, the ICAO 9303 standard is being used in a wider range of contexts that do not necessarily have system security comparable to an airport, facilitating more sophisticated attacks.

For the above reasons, it is imperative that we clarify the existence of and nature of attacks on the privacy of BAC explained in this paper. The notion of privacy we are concerned with is a strong form of unlinkability, meaning that an e-passport that satisfies such a privacy property cannot be linked from one session to another, by a third party snooping in on wireless communications. Such a privacy issue is of concern to users carrying e-passports, who do not wish third parties to track their movements.

Unlinkability can be formulated in the following terms: an attacker cannot observe any difference between a scenario where each session with an e-passport reader is with

© Springer Nature Switzerland AG 2019
K. Sako et al. (Eds.): ESORICS 2019, LNCS 11735, pp. 577–594, 2019.
https://doi.org/10.1007/978-3-030-29959-0_28

a new e-passport and a scenario where the same e-passport may be involved in more than one session. Strong unlinkability assumes, in addition, that the attacker has the power to make some decisions, such as feeding a challenge into a remote reader rather than a reader in the vicinity of the e-passport. We will explain that it is critical that the additional power given to the attacker by *strong unlinkability* is modelled by using *bisimilarity* as the notion of equivalence.

To understand why strong unlinkability, expressed in terms of bisimilarity, is important, we must clarify the story in the literature up until this paper. The first paper [4] formally analysing unlinkability of e-passports, using symbolic techniques, formulated weak unlinkability as a property of traces, and strong unlinkability as an equivalence problem in terms of bisimilarity. That paper mainly concerns an attack particular to the implementation of the French e-passport, exploiting distinguishable error messages from which the attacker can infer whether authentication was partially successful.

The problem with the above mentioned paper [4] is that they also make claims about e-passports implementing the ICAO 9303 standard with a single error message for all types of authentication failure, such as the UK e-passport. They make the claim that the UK e-passport satisfies the strong form of unlinkability, expressed using bisimilarity. The primary contribution we make is to clarify that their claim is **false**. Taking exactly the same conditions—the way they define strong unlinkability and how they model the UK e-passport—we discover a counter proof for their claims, and provide a witness in terms of a modal logic formula describing an attack on strong unlinkability.

We survey related work [9–12, 19], contributing to the story behind symbolically analysing the unlinkability of BAC. With the exception of the original paper, the papers surveyed concern alternative definitions of unlinkability expressed in terms of trace equivalence rather than bisimilarity. This survey of trace-based approaches we use to emphasise the impact of using bisimilarity rather than trace equivalence when verifying unlinkability of protocols such as BAC. We also highlight other parameters impacting whether a model proves unlinkability or discovers an attack.

A secondary contribution is to propose a fix for the BAC protocol, within the scope of the ICAO 9303 standard [1]. We again showcase bisimilarity as a technique for analysing privacy properties, providing a proof that strong unlinkability holds by defining a bisimulation that is witness to our claims. Finally, we discuss implications of our analysis, for example, how our attack on strong unlinkability applies to a wide range of protocols, not limited only to PACE and a minimal example of an RFID protocol used as an illustrative example. We also touch on practical implications of our attack, which are distinct from existing practical attacks on unlinkability [5, 14].

Summary. In Sect. 2 we investigate and refine the analysis of the BAC protocol for e-passports implemented similarly to the UK e-passport, reporting on different models and results, and identifying the fundamental modelling problems surrounding unlinkability. In Sect. 3 we introduce the strong unlinkability problem for a simplified authentication protocol that we will use as an example throughout the paper, we also note a fix for the protocol (encrypting the error message). Section 4 recalls background material on a state-of-the-art presentation of bisimilarity facilitating our analysis. In Sect. 5, we show how bisimilarity can be used to discover attacks on strong unlinkability. Finally, in Sect. 6 we return to the original formulation of the UK version of the BAC protocol, demonstrating how our attack lifts to an attack on strong unlinkability, invalidating the original claim [4].

2   An Investigation into Unlinkability Claims About BAC

In this section, we briefly survey, clarify, and expand upon the body of work symbolically analysing the Basic Access Control (BAC) protocol. The purpose of BAC is to mutually authenticate an e-passport and reader (e.g., at passport control in an airport), and establish a short-term key used in proceeding communication (e.g., transmitting personal information about the owner).

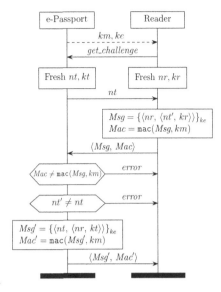

Fig. 1. BAC protocol for the UK e-passport

The BAC protocol is sketched informally in Fig. 1, where dashed lines ($\dashrightarrow$) indicate a message transmitted via an OCR session on a page of the e-passport, and solid lines are wireless communications between a chip and reader. The reader first sends a constant message *get_challenge* requesting a challenge—a nonce nt sent by the e-passport—which is used during the mutual authentication of the e-passport and reader. The standard specifies that an "operating system dependent error" [1] should be sent when authentication fails. Such a failure occurs when the e-passport receives an authentication request from the reader, and either the message authentication code (MAC) is wrong, or a nonce in the message does not match the challenge nt previously sent by the e-passport.

2.1   The Key Paper Defining Strong Unlinkability, but with a Flawed Claim

The primary contribution of this paper is to clarify that the first paper symbolically analysing the BAC protocol, as implemented by countries such as the UK (Fig. 1), contained a flawed claim. Arapinis *et al.* [4] define *weak unlinkability* as a property of traces, faithful to the ISO standard for unlinkability [2]. They then argue for a stronger property, called *strong unlinkability*, expressed using bisimilarity. Their work is accompanied with a trace that *correctly* demonstrates that the French BAC protocol violates both their definitions of unlinkability. Regarding the UK BAC protocol, they say:

> Checking the bisimulation by hand, we find that *SystemUK* $\approx_l$ *SystemUK'* holds: A repeating tag in the *SystemUK* process is matched by a new tag in the idealised *SystemUK'* version of the system.

Unfortunately, their statement above is false. In their work, *SystemUK* is a system specification in which the same e-passport can be used many times, and *SystemUK'* is an idealised specification in which each e-passport is used only once. The above statement *SystemUK* $\approx_l$ *SystemUK'* claims the system specification and idealised specification are indistinguishable to an attacker, expressed in terms of *labelled bisimilarity* [3]. Later, in

Sects. 5 and 6, we will demonstrate that there is a witness invalidating the bisimilarity claim above, and therefore there is an attack on strong unlinkability.

Although Arapinis *et al.* claim, in the quote above, to have proven strong unlinkability by hand, no proof exists. Confusion was partly down to an old bug[1] in ProVerif.

2.2 Alternative Models of Unlinkability Based on Trace Equivalence

There exist several examples of tool-supported analysis of weak unlinkability of the BAC protocol, using trace equivalence. The PhD thesis of Cheval [9] and work on disunification [11] is the basis of this line of work. The tool APTE [10] is the first such tool able to directly verify finite trace equivalence properties of protocols with if-then-else branches. To demonstrate the APTE tool, a survey is performed on a range of protocols. However, the verification of the UK BAC protocol does not terminate after 2 days, and the authors mark it "safe?".

The DEEPSEC [12] prover is a state-of-the-art tool for analysing *finite trace equivalence* for security protocols. Depending on how the UK BAC protocol is modelled it can, for two sessions, **both** find an attack [12], and claim that no attack exists. In our GitHub repository[2], we provide details on both modelling scenarios. In summary, an attack is discovered if the fixed scenario with two different e-passports is compared to a specification where all e-passports differ. In contrast, DEEPSEC discovers no attack whenever we consider that, in reality, for two sessions, we either have two identical e-passports or two different e-passports. Indeed the attack discovered using a fixed configuration is considered not to be practical (no trace can be executed to confirm the presence of the same e-passport twice, and the attack is longer than necessary).

Paper	Equivalence Type	Model Scope		Observable	Claim made	
		Finiteness	Config.	Constant Message	Attack Found?	Correct?
Arapinis *et al.* [4]	**Bisim.**	Unbounded	Arbitrary	**Yes**	No	flawed
APTE [10]	Trace	2 Sessions	Fixed	No	?	N/A
DEEPSEC [12]	Trace	2 Sessions	Fixed	No	Yes	OK
DEEPSEC (ours)	Trace	2 Sessions	**Arbitrary**	Yes	No	OK
Hirschi *et al.* [19]	**Trace**	Unbounded	Arbitrary	No	No	OK

Fig. 2. Comparison table of various analyses of the UK e-passport. Note all the above assume the number of internal communications is unobservable.

A summary of the above findings is presented in Fig. 2. We highlight only the most important differences between these models, mentioned previously, namely: bisimilarity vs. trace equivalence; and, unbounded vs. arbitrary bounded vs. fixed bounded. Another critical modelling parameter is the choice of observables, notably the constant *get_challenge* message in Fig. 1. This impacts whether **strong** unlinkability holds, by

---

[1] This information on an old bug in ProVerif is due to Stéphanie Delaune and Vincent Cheval.

[2] https://github.com/ZDSmith/bac-protocol-unlinkability.

allowing an attacker to count the number of reader sessions based on the number of observed *get_challenge* messages. This parameter does not affect **weak** unlinkability.

Note on terminology: We use the term *strong unlinkability* in exactly the sense it was originally communicated in CSF'10 [4]. A source of potential confusion is that a paper communicated in S&P'16 [19] presents a proof of what they claim to be strong unlinkability. That claim may be misleading, since they, in fact, significantly change the definition of strong unlinkability. The most important change they make is to use trace equivalence rather than bisimilarity. If we have a proof, with trace equivalence replacing bisimilarity in the definition of strong unlinkability, then *weak unlinkability* follows as a corollary (this fact follows by adapting Theorem 2 in the original paper [4], since the proof of Theorem 2 does not rely on finer properties of bisimilarity). Note also that they [19] change slightly, but significantly, the observables in the model of BAC. Their forthcoming journal version [20] acknowledges and discusses this terminology mismatch.

Sometimes changing definitions of terms is of little consequence; for example, differences between *secrecy* as a trace property and *secrecy* expressed in terms of bisimilarity are insignificant [15]. However, the thesis of our paper is that the same does not apply to privacy. Trace equivalence gives the attacker less power to resolve choices, and hence misses attacks, such as on the unlinkability of BAC. Related work also highlights the power of bisimilarity for discovering attacks in the context of the anonymity of the MUTE file sharing system [13], and in discussions comparing strong unlinkability, weak unlinkability and computational unlinkability games [8].

---

3   Minimal Variant of the BAC Authentication Protocol

The analysis of the full e-passport protocol involves some large messages, which can obscure the essential problems with the protocol. Therefore, initially, we make two simplifications to the analysis for pedagogical and methodological reasons:

1. We present a minimal mutual authentication protocol that features the same problems with strong unlinkability as the BAC protocol for e-passports.
2. We show our attack can be discovered systematically by using a slightly finer notion of bisimilarity better suited to symbolic analysis.

Both of the above initial simplifications to our analysis are lifted later, in Sect. 6. Our use of a minimal authentication protocol also highlights, as mentioned in the introduction, that the problems with strong unlinkability in this work affect a wider class of authentication protocols, where the same key is used in different sessions.

3.1   An Illustrative Minimal Protocol for Mutual Authentication

We now describe our cut-down mutual authentication protocol in Fig. 4, sufficient to explain problems with the full BAC protocol. Our protocol is similar to the Feldhoffer protocol [18], which was proposed as a minimal mutual authentication protocol for

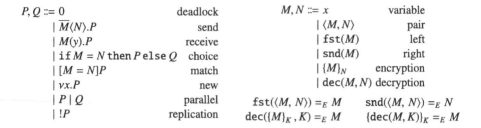

$$P, Q ::= 0 \qquad\qquad\qquad \text{deadlock}$$
$$| \; \overline{M}\langle N\rangle.P \qquad\qquad\quad \text{send}$$
$$| \; M(y).P \qquad\qquad\quad \text{receive}$$
$$| \; \text{if } M = N \text{ then } P \text{ else } Q \quad \text{choice}$$
$$| \; [M = N]P \qquad\qquad\; \text{match}$$
$$| \; vx.P \qquad\qquad\qquad \text{new}$$
$$| \; P \,|\, Q \qquad\qquad\qquad \text{parallel}$$
$$| \; !P \qquad\qquad\qquad\quad \text{replication}$$

$$M, N ::= x \qquad\qquad \text{variable}$$
$$| \; \langle M, N\rangle \qquad\quad \text{pair}$$
$$| \; \text{fst}(M) \qquad\quad \text{left}$$
$$| \; \text{snd}(M) \qquad\quad \text{right}$$
$$| \; \{M\}_N \qquad\quad \text{encryption}$$
$$| \; \text{dec}(M, N) \; \text{decryption}$$

$$\text{fst}(\langle M, N\rangle) =_E M \qquad \text{snd}(\langle M, N\rangle) =_E N$$
$$\text{dec}(\{M\}_K, K) =_E M \qquad \{\text{dec}(M, K)\}_K =_E M$$

Fig. 3. A syntax for applied π-calculus processes with a message theory.

RFID tags. A difference, compared to the Feldhoffer protocol, is that we include an error message which is used by the RFID tag to signal a failed authentication session to the reader. For minimality, we also simplify the response of the tag (the Feldhoffer protocol responds with $\{\langle n, m\rangle\}_k$ rather than simply m).

Like the ICAO 9303 standard BAC protocol for e-passports, our minimal protocol achieves a strong authentication property called *synchronisation* [16], which is easily checked using automated tools such as Scyther [16]. The key differences, compared to BAC, is that BAC also establishes a shared session key, and uses message authentication codes to improve message integrity.

We make use of the applied π-calculus for modelling processes. The syntax of processes is presented in Fig. 3, along with a message theory featuring pairs and symmetric encryption (encryption using a shared secret key).

3.2 Modelling Our Minimal Authentication Protocol in the Applied π-calculus

In the applied π-calculus, an honest reader in our minimal example in Fig. 4 can be modelled as follows.

$$Reader \triangleq c(k).vm.a(x).\overline{a}\langle\{m, x\}_k\rangle$$

Channel c is a private channel used to read a secret key (for e-passports, calculated using data read from a page using OCR). The reader receives a challenge x, generates a fresh name m (the counter-challenge) and transmits the nonce and challenge encrypted together using the session key, $\{\langle m, x\rangle\}_k$.

The tag is modelled in the applied π-calculus as follows.

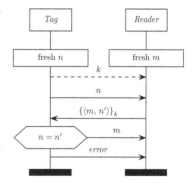

Fig. 4. A linkable authentication protocol.

$$Linkable \triangleq \overline{c}\langle k\rangle.vn.\overline{a}\langle n\rangle.a(y). \text{if } \text{snd}(\text{dec}(y, k)) = n \text{ then } \overline{a}\langle\text{fst}(\text{dec}(y, k))\rangle$$
$$\text{else } \overline{a}\langle error\rangle$$

The private channel c is used to transmit a private key unique to the tag (for e-passports modelling the act of presenting a page to an OCR reader). The tag generates and sends a fresh challenge n. The response to the challenge y is received. If the response contains the challenge, tested by $\mathtt{snd}(\mathtt{dec}(y,k)) = n$, then the counter-challenge $\mathtt{fst}(\mathtt{dec}(y,k))$ is sent. Otherwise, an error is sent. The error message signals to the reader that authentication has failed, resulting in the protocol not successfully completing.

Combining the above reader and tag, we can describe the system as follows.

$$Linkable\_System \triangleq vc.(!Reader \mid !vk.!Linkable)$$

Notice that channel c, used for sending and receiving the key of the tag, is bound, hence private. This suggests that an attacker does not have the power to intercept messages on this channel (modelling a session with an OCR reader). However, other communications take place on a public channel a which an attacker can snoop over, e.g., reading using an antenna in the vicinity, and writing using a fake tag.

In the above system specification, the replicated reader, written !*Reader*, indicates that any number of sessions of the reader can be initiated in parallel. The sub-process !*vk*.!*Linkable* indicates that any number of tags can be created in parallel, each with a unique key k identifying them; and, furthermore, each tag can enter any number of sessions using the same identity k, in parallel.

Unlinkability properties can be expressed using the above system specification and the idealised specification below:

$$Linkable\_Spec \triangleq vc.(!Reader \mid !vk.Linkable)$$

Notice the only difference between *Linkable_System* and *Linkable_Spec* is the absence of replication after the generation of the key. Thus, in *Linkable_Spec*, each new session is with a new tag, with a freshly generated key.

We formulate strong unlinkability as an equivalence problem by setting out to showing that *Linkable_System* and *Linkable_Spec* are equivalent from the perspective of an attacker. In principle, the idea is that if an attacker cannot tell the difference between a scenario where the same tag is allowed to be used in multiple sessions and the scenario where each tag is really used once, then you cannot link two uses of the same tag.

The important point in this paper is that strong unlinkability in fact **fails**. Indeed for our minimal authentication example we can prove the following inequality, where $\sim$ is a suitable notion of bisimilarity.

$$Linkable\_System \nsim Linkable\_Spec$$

The use of bisimilarity grants the attacker more power than trace equivalence, essentially allowing the attacker to resolve certain choices (in this case, to which reader the challenge is sent). We will explain such attacks in the remaining sections of this paper.

3.3 Fixing Protocols to Achieve Strong Unlinkability

Beyond finding new attacks and shorter attacks, bisimilarity can also be used to provide proofs of strong unlinkability when they exist. For many calculi, it is established that bisimilarity is asymptotically more efficient to check than trace equivalence, particularly in the limits [23] (for infinitely many sessions). Indeed, with expertise, finding a bisimulation in the limit is relatively easy here.

Consider the variant of our running example given in Fig. 5. Notice that the error message is encrypted, along with a nonce to ensure that the ciphertext is different on each execution. Note, we assume that a fresh ciphertext $\{r, error\}_k$ and a nonce m are indistinguishable. This prevents an attacker intercepting communications from distinguishing between a correct response and an error message.

To verify the fixed minimal authentication protocol, we consider the following specification, in which the else branch has been modified:

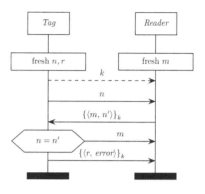

Fig. 5. Unlinkable authentication protocol.

$$Unlinkable \triangleq \overline{c}\langle k\rangle.vn.\overline{a}\langle n\rangle.a(y).\,\text{if}\,\text{snd}(\text{dec}(y,k)) = n\,\text{then}\,\overline{a}\langle\text{fst}(\text{dec}(y,k))\rangle$$
$$\text{else}\,vr.\overline{a}\langle\{\langle r, error\rangle\}_k\rangle$$

The fixed system and specification are thereby stated as follows.

$$Unlinkable\_System \triangleq vc.(!Reader \mid !vk.!Unlinkable)$$
$$Unlinkable\_Spec \triangleq vc.(!Reader \mid !vk.Unlinkable)$$

Indeed, we can prove $Unlinkable\_System \sim Unlinkable\_Spec$ holds, where $\sim$ is a suitable notion of bisimilarity. This establishes that strong unlinkability holds for our fixed basic authentication protocol. The same fix can be applied to BAC, which is a fix within the scope of the ICAO 9303 standard [1], since the standard does not exclude encrypting the error message in the BAC protocol.

4   Background on Bisimilarity for the Applied π-Calculus

We briefly recall a concise formulation of (strong) early bisimilarity for the applied π-calculus. Our presentation makes use of extended processes (in normal form), and a pure labelled transition system which simplifies the analysis of bisimilarity. Note the presentation we adopt here makes it relatively easy to quickly discover our attack.

Extended processes in normal form $vx.(\sigma \mid P)$ are subject to the restriction that the variables in dom(σ) are fresh for x, fv(P) and fv$(y\sigma)$, for all variables y (i.e., σ is idempotent, and substitutions are fully applied to P). We follow the convention that operational rules are defined directly on extended processes in normal forms. Note adopting normal forms removes the need for several additional conditions that must be imposed in other formulations of bisimilarity for the applied π-calculus [3].

We require a standard notion of static equivalence, which checks two processes are indistinguishable in terms of the messages output so far.

Definition 1 (static equivalence). *Extended processes in normal form $vx.(\sigma \mid P)$ and $vy.(\theta \mid Q)$ are statically equivalent whenever, for all pairs of messages M and N such that $(\text{fv}(M) \cup \text{fv}(N)) \cap (x \cup y) = \emptyset$, we have $M\sigma =_E N\sigma$ if and only if $M\theta =_E N\theta$.*

We require the following definitions for composing extended processes in parallel and with substitutions, defined whenever $z \notin \mathrm{fv}(B) \cup \mathrm{fv}(\rho)$ and $\mathrm{dom}(\sigma) \cap \mathrm{dom}(\theta) = \emptyset$.

$$\sigma \mid \theta \mid Q \triangleq \sigma \cdot \theta \mid Q \qquad\qquad (\sigma \mid P) \mid (\theta \mid Q) \triangleq \sigma \cdot \theta \mid (P \mid Q)$$

$$\rho \mid vz.A \triangleq vz.(\rho \mid A) \qquad B \mid vz.A \triangleq vz.(B \mid A) \qquad vz.A \mid B \triangleq vz.(A \mid B)$$

The above definitions are employed in our definition of (early) labelled transitions (Fig. 6), which are defined directly on extended processes in normal form. Labels on transitions are either: τ—an internal communication; $\overline{M}(z)$—an output on channel M binding the output message to variable z; or $M\,N$—an input on channel M receiving message N. (Notice if-then-else makes no additional τ-transitions in this presentation).

$$\frac{}{M(x).P \xrightarrow{M\,N} P\{^N/_x\}} \text{INP} \qquad \frac{x \notin \mathrm{fv}(M) \cup \mathrm{fv}(N) \cup \mathrm{fv}(P)}{\overline{M}\langle N\rangle.P \xrightarrow{\overline{M}(x)} \{^N/_x\} \mid P} \text{OUT} \qquad \frac{A \xrightarrow{\pi} B \quad x \notin \mathrm{n}(\pi)}{vx.A \xrightarrow{\pi} vx.B} \text{RES}$$

$$\frac{P \xrightarrow{\pi\sigma} A \quad \sigma \text{ fresh for } \mathrm{bn}(\pi)}{\sigma \mid P \xrightarrow{\pi} \sigma \mid A} \text{ALIAS} \qquad\qquad \frac{P \xrightarrow{\pi} A \quad \mathrm{bn}(\pi) \cap \mathrm{fv}(Q) = \emptyset}{P \mid Q \xrightarrow{\pi} A \mid Q} \text{PAR-L}$$

$$\frac{P \xrightarrow{\pi} A}{\text{if } M = M \text{ then } P \text{ else } Q \xrightarrow{\pi} A} \text{THEN} \qquad\qquad \frac{Q \xrightarrow{\pi} A \quad M \neq_E N}{\text{if } M = N \text{ then } P \text{ else } Q \xrightarrow{\pi} A} \text{ELSE}$$

$$\frac{P \xrightarrow{\pi} A}{[M = M]P \xrightarrow{\pi} A} \text{MAT} \qquad \frac{P \xrightarrow{\overline{M}(x)} vz.(\{^N/_x\} \mid P') \quad Q \xrightarrow{M\,N} Q' \quad (\{x\} \cup z) \cap \mathrm{fv}(Q) = \emptyset}{P \mid Q \xrightarrow{\tau} vz.(P' \mid Q')} \text{CLOSE-L}$$

$$\frac{P \xrightarrow{\pi} A}{!P \xrightarrow{\pi} A \mid !P} \text{REP-ACT} \qquad \frac{P \xrightarrow{\overline{M}(x)} vz.(\{^N/_x\} \mid Q) \quad P \xrightarrow{M\,N} R \quad z \cap \mathrm{fv}(P) = \emptyset}{!P \xrightarrow{\tau} vz.(Q \mid R \mid !P)} \text{REP-CLOSE}$$

Fig. 6. An *early* labelled transition system, plus symmetric rules for parallel composition and choice. The equational theory over message terms can be applied at any point. The set of free variables and α-conversion are as standard, where $vx.P$ and $M(x).P$ bind x in P. Define the bound names such that $\mathrm{bn}(\pi) = \{x\}$ only if $\pi = \overline{M}(x)$ and $\mathrm{bn}(\pi) = \emptyset$ otherwise. Define the names such that $\mathrm{n}(M\,N) = \mathrm{fv}(M) \cup \mathrm{fv}(N)$, $\mathrm{n}(M(x)) = \mathrm{fv}(M) \cup \{x\}$ and $\mathrm{n}(\tau) = \emptyset$.

The early labelled transition system and static equivalence together can be used to define the following (strong) version of early bisimilarity.

Definition 2 (early bisimilarity). *A symmetric relation between extended processes $\mathcal{R}$ is an early bisimulation only if, whenever $A \mathcal{R} B$ the following hold:*

- *A and B are statically equivalent.*
- *If $A \xrightarrow{\pi} A'$ there exists B' such that $B \xrightarrow{\pi} B'$ and $A' \mathcal{R} B'$.*

Processes P and Q are early bisimilar, written $P \sim Q$, whenever there exists an early bisimulation $\mathcal{R}$ such that $P \mathcal{R} Q$.

Notice initially we consider here a strong notion of bisimilarity, where the number of internal communications can be counted. This initially simplifies the analysis. To be precise, the strong semantics preserves a notion called *image finiteness*, which is lost in the weak setting and imposes additional technical challenges. However, later we show attacks discovered lift to the weak setting (by including more observables).

5   Finding Attacks on Privacy Using Bisimilarity

In order to refer to intermediate states, we can break down the sub-states of *Reader* and *Linkable*, from Sect. 3 as follows.

$$W_i \triangleq a(x).vm.\overline{a}\big\langle \{m, x\}_{k_i} \big\rangle \qquad U(n, y)_i \triangleq \text{if snd}(\text{dec}(y, k_i)) = n$$
$$Linkable_i \triangleq \overline{c}\langle k_i \rangle.vn.T(n)_i \qquad\qquad \text{then}\, \overline{a}\langle \text{fst}(\text{dec}(y, k_i)) \rangle$$
$$T(n)_i \triangleq \overline{a}\langle n \rangle.a(y).U(n, y)_i \qquad\qquad \text{else}\, \overline{a}\langle error \rangle$$

The real system, which allows multiple instances of the same tag, can perform the following two τ actions followed by an output action $\overline{a}(u)$. The idealised specification on the right below follows with the same actions as best it can. Note we abbreviate multiple transitions by writing sequences of actions on the label.

$$Linkable\_System \xrightarrow{\tau\,\tau\,\overline{a}(u)} Broken\_System' \qquad Linkable\_Spec \xrightarrow{\tau\,\tau\,\overline{a}(u)} Broken\_Spec'$$

The states reached above are of the following form.

$$Broken\_System' \triangleq vc, k_1, n_1, n_2.(\, \{^{n_1}/_u\} \mid W_1 \mid W_1 \mid !Reader \mid$$
$$a(y).U(n_1, y)_1 \mid T(n_2)_1 \mid !Linkable_1 \mid !vk.!Linkable\,)$$
$$Broken\_Spec' \triangleq vc, k_1, k_2, n_1, n_2.(\, \{^{n_1}/_u\} \mid W_1 \mid W_2 \mid !Reader \mid$$
$$a(y).U(n_1, y)_1 \mid T(n_2)_2 \mid !vk.Linkable\,)$$

At this point, we can swap the system for the specification (exploiting the symmetry of a bisimulation), and *Broken_Spec'* performs the sequence of actions below.

$$Broken\_Spec' \xrightarrow{a\,u\,\overline{a}(v)\,a\,v\,\overline{a}(w)} vc, k_1, k_2, n_1, n_2, m.(\, \left\{^{n_1, \{m, n_1\}_{k_2}, error}/_{u, v, w}\right\} \mid W_1 \mid 0 \mid !Reader$$
$$\mid 0 \mid T(n_2)_2 \mid !vk.Linkable\,)$$

If the system and specification were equivalent (which they are not), then the system *should* be able to perform the same actions to reach a state where the system appears to be identical to the idealised specification, from the perspective of the attacker. The longest *Broken_System'* can keep up this bisimulation game is as follows.

$$Broken\_System' \xrightarrow{a\,u\,\overline{a}(v)\,a\,v\,\overline{a}(w)} vc, k_1, n_1, n_2, m.(\, \left\{^{n_1, \{m, n_1\}_{k_1}, m}/_{u, v, w}\right\} \mid W_1 \mid 0 \mid !Reader$$
$$\mid 0 \mid T(n_2)_1 \mid !Linkable_1 \mid !vk.!Linkable\,)$$

The important step above is the first input action $a\,u$. This transition affects sub-process W_2 in *Broken_Spec'*, which evolves to $\overline{a}\big\langle \{m, n_1\}_{k_2} \big\rangle$, i.e. a reader ready to respond to challenge n_1 **by using key** k_2. In contrast, *Broken_System'* can only reach a state with sub-process $\overline{a}\langle\{m, n_1\}_{k_1}\rangle$ which is ready to respond to the same challenge n_1 **but using key** k_1 (note there are two equivalent ways the system can act at this point, since two readers with key k_1 are active—both options lead to the same outcome). Both the system and specification then proceed with the actions $\overline{a}(v)$, $a\,v$, then $\overline{a}(w)$, corresponding to intercepting the response of the reader v, relaying v to the tag, and obtaining the output w of the tag.

After the four transition steps described above, the real system satisfies the equation $w \neq error$. In contrast, for the idealised specification we have that $w = error$ holds. Performing this test represents an attacker intercepting the third output on channel a, named w above, and checking whether or not it is an error message. If the system does not produce an error following this strategy, then unlinkability is violated. This way, we can link the two sessions, since we have proof that they must involve the same tag. Notice test $w = error$ confirms *static equivalence* is violated.

6   Lifting Our Attack to the Setting of Labelled Bisimilarity for the ICAO 9303 Standard BAC Protocol

Previously, in Sects. 3 and 5, we emphasised that we discussed a slightly simpler protocol than BAC which exhibits the same problems with strong unlinkability. We also used a stronger notion of bisimilarity, allowing the attack to be discovered more easily. These decisions were made in order to present details of the attack more clearly.

We simplify the presentation of our attack by making the following methodological point. When we discover an attack under stronger assumptions, we can lift the attack to a setting with weaker assumptions, and then check the attack is still valid. In this section, we follow exactly this methodology—we describe how the attack lifts to the setting of BAC under a weak notion of bisimilarity, exactly as assumed in the original paper symbolically analysing BAC [4] (which, recall, made the opposite claims without providing proofs).

In order to conduct our analysis, we require a constructor representing message authentication codes. We extend the message language with function $\mathrm{mac}(M, N)$, with no new equations in the message theory. For readability, we employ the abbreviation $\mathrm{let}\, x = M \,\mathrm{in}\, P \triangleq P\{^M/_x\}$ in the following specifications of the UK e-passport and (generic) e-passport reader.

$$MainUK \triangleq \overline{c_k}\langle ke, km\rangle.d(x).[x = get\_challenge]vnt.\overline{c}\langle nt\rangle.d(y).$$
$$\mathrm{if}\,\mathrm{snd}(y) = \mathrm{mac}(\mathrm{fst}(y), km)\,\mathrm{then}$$
$$\mathrm{if}\,nt = \mathrm{fst}(\mathrm{snd}(\mathrm{dec}(\mathrm{fst}(y), ke)))\,\mathrm{then}$$
$$vkt.\mathrm{let}\,m = \{\langle nt, \langle \mathrm{fst}(\mathrm{dec}(\mathrm{fst}(y), ke)), kt\rangle\rangle\}_{ke}\,\mathrm{in}$$
$$\overline{c}\langle m, \mathrm{mac}(m, km)\rangle$$
$$\mathrm{else}\,\overline{c}\langle error\rangle$$
$$\mathrm{else}\,\overline{c}\langle error\rangle$$
$$Reader \triangleq c_k(x_k).\overline{c}\langle get\_challenge\rangle.d(nt).vnr.vkr.$$
$$\mathrm{let}\,m = \{\langle nr, \langle nt, kr\rangle\rangle\}_{\mathrm{fst}(x_k)}\,\mathrm{in}\,\overline{c}\langle m, \mathrm{mac}(\langle m, \mathrm{snd}(x_k)\rangle)\rangle$$

Similarly to our minimal authentication example, we can express the system and idealised specification, respectively, as follows.

$$SystemUK \triangleq vc_k.(!Reader \mid !vke.vkm.!MainUK)$$
$$SystemUK' \triangleq vc_k.(!Reader \mid !vke.vkm.MainUK)$$

We also employ labelled bisimilarity [3] which makes use of weak transitions, $A \overset{\pi}{\Longrightarrow} B$ which allow zero or more τ transitions to occur before and after the transition π, or zero transitions if $\pi = \tau$. Notice $B \overset{\pi}{\Longrightarrow} B'$ is the only difference compared to Def. 2.

Definition 3 (labelled bisimilarity). *A symmetric relation between extended processes $\mathcal{R}$ is a labelled bisimulation only if, whenever $A \mathcal{R} B$ the following hold:*

- *A and B are statically equivalent.*
- *If $A \overset{\pi}{\longrightarrow} A'$ there exists B' such that $B \overset{\pi}{\Longrightarrow} B'$ and $A' \mathcal{R} B'$.*

Labelled bisimilarity $\approx_l$ is the greatest labelled bisimulation.

Now, by following a similar strategy described in the previous section, we can prove that strong unlinkability fails, expressed as follows.

$$SystemUK \not\approx_l SystemUK'$$

A little more work is required, compared to the previous section, since we must count the number of *get_challenge* messages sent and received rather than number of τ transitions. However, we can go through essentially the same symbolic reasoning to discover a similar attack to the previous section. Rather than repeating the same analysis but on a larger specification, we instead present a shorter way to describe such attacks and informally describe how it can be exploited in a practical fashion.

6.1 Describing the Attack Using a Modal Logic Formula

We can concisely describe attacks on privacy using modal logic formulae. Attacks on labelled bisimilarity can be described using the modal logic *classical $\mathcal{FM}$* ($\mathcal{F}$ is for free inputs, $\mathcal{M}$ is for match [24]). A syntax for *classical $\mathcal{FM}$* is presented below.

$$\phi ::= M = N \qquad \text{equality} \qquad\qquad \text{abbreviations:}$$
$$\mid \phi \wedge \phi \qquad \text{conjunction} \qquad M \neq N \triangleq \neg(M = N)$$
$$\mid \langle \pi \rangle \phi \qquad \text{diamond} \qquad [\pi]\phi \triangleq \neg\langle\pi\rangle\neg\phi$$
$$\mid \neg\phi \qquad\quad \text{negation} \qquad \phi \vee \psi \triangleq \neg(\neg\phi \wedge \neg\psi)$$

The semantics of classical $\mathcal{FM}$ is presented below.

$$vx.(\sigma \mid P) \models M = N \text{ iff } M\sigma =_E N\sigma \text{ and } x \cap (\mathrm{fv}(M) \cup \mathrm{fv}(N)) = \emptyset$$
$$A \models \langle\pi\rangle\phi \qquad\qquad \text{iff there exists } B \text{ such that } A \overset{\pi}{\Longrightarrow} B \text{ and } B \models \phi.$$
$$A \models \phi_1 \wedge \phi_2 \qquad\qquad \text{iff } A \models \phi_1 \text{ and } A \models \phi_2.$$
$$A \models \neg\phi \qquad\qquad\quad \text{iff } A \models \phi \text{ does not hold.}$$

Using classical $\mathcal{FM}$, we can define a witness that two processes are not labelled bisimilar, as expressed using this soundness and completeness theorem. Note this is a more standard classical version of a theorem in related work [21].

Theorem 1 (soundness and completeness). *$P \approx_l Q$, whenever, for all formula ϕ, we have $P \models \phi$ if and only if $Q \models \phi$.*

From the contrapositive of the above theorem, whenever $P \not\approx_l Q$, there exists a formula ϕ such that $P \models \phi$ holds, but $Q \not\models \phi$.

In the case of the failure of strong unlinkability of the UK BAC protocol, we have the following classical $\mathcal{FM}$ formula, say ψ.

$$\langle d\, get\_challenge \rangle \langle \overline{c}(x) \rangle \langle \overline{c}(y) \rangle \langle \overline{c}(z) \rangle ($$
$$x = get\_challenge \wedge y = get\_challenge \wedge z \neq get\_challenge \wedge$$
$$[d\, z](\,\langle \overline{c}(u) \rangle \langle d\, u \rangle \langle \overline{c}(v) \rangle (u \neq get\_challenge \wedge v \neq get\_challenge \wedge v \neq error)$$
$$\vee\, [\overline{c}(w)](w = get\_challenge)\,))$$

For this formula we can verify *SystemUK* $\models \psi$ holds. Clearly, interpreting such a witness for non-bisimilarity requires considerable expertise. The first part of the formula, until input $[d\,z]$, starts an e-passport session and two reader sessions, and then sends the challenge, named z in the formula, from the e-passport. The later branches of the formula check whether or not the reader sessions are with the same e-passport or not. The critical step is $[d\,z]$, which ranges over all ways in which the challenge z can be fed back into the system as an input. In the bisimulation game, this corresponds to a swapping of perspective, where the idealised specification leads, rather than the system (as illustrated in the attack on the minimal authentication protocol in Sect. 5). In practical terms, this means that the attacker takes control over where the input $d\,z$ is performed.

Now consider *SystemUK'*. We show that *SystemUK'* $\not\models \psi$. Notice that the branch $[\overline{c}(w)](w = get\_challenge)$ covers the possibility that the input is fed in when a *get_challenge* message is expected, leaving no possible output actions other than those starting a fresh session. Notice also the possibility of an error occurring too early ($u = error$) is also accommodated. Importantly, regardless of how *SystemUK'* plays the first four actions, in the state reached, there exists an input $d\,u$ which fails to match any of the eventualities described by the formula.

Note there are many such distinguishing formulae, each describing subtly different attacks on strong unlinkability. We select this one, as it formally justifies the practical description of the attack in the next section.

6.2 Practical Steps to Implement a Discovered Attack

Here, we give an example of a practical attack that might be carried out in the real world, based on the attack on strong unlinkability given in the previous section. We assume the presence of a Dolev-Yao [17] adversary, who can block or redirect messages. Importantly, we assume that the adversary cannot interfere with the credentials on the e-passport, for example by snooping on an OCR session.

The aim of our attack will be to identify the e-passport who has most recently interacted with a specific reader device (which need not be under adversary control). For example, in an airport, the attacker may wish to identify people who have travelled through the "priority" lane, as they are more likely to be airline staff or other people of interest. The attack proceeds at follows:

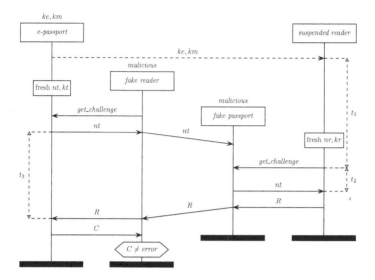

Fig. 7. Attack on UK e-passport: implementation involving fake reader and fake e-passport, informally. The critical moment is choosing where to feed nt. Assume $Msg = \{\langle nr, \langle nt, kr \rangle \rangle\}_{ke}$, $Msg' = \{\langle nt, \langle nr, kt \rangle \rangle\}_{ke}$, $R = \langle Msg, \text{mac}(Msg, km) \rangle$ and $C = \langle Msg', \text{mac}(Msg', km) \rangle$.

(1) An honest agent has their OCR details read by the targeted reader device.
(2) The adversary blocks any RF communication between the (now-scanned) e-passport and the reader. The agent presumes that the machine is faulty and moves on.
(3) The adversary brings a custom reader device close to an agent. This custom reader initiates the BAC protocol with the agent's e-passport.
  – The fake reader does not make use of, or attempt to read, any OCR data. It acts as if this phase has already been completed.
(4) The fake reader relays messages from the e-passport to the reader suspended in (2), for example by using a RF retransmitter located close to the reader.
  – The suspended reader still has OCR data stored from the earlier step.
(5) If the e-passport that the adversary is communicating with is indeed the e-passport that was scanned by the reader (as is depicted in Fig. 7), then the protocol will complete successfully, and the adversary will see an encrypted data packet.
  – If the e-passport does not match the previously scanned one, the adversary will see a constant error message.

The adversary never learns the keys of any e-passport in this case, but they do not need to - they need only distinguish whether or not the final message is a constant term or an encrypted packet.

In Fig. 7, we highlight three key timing constraints on this attack. The hard constraint, labelled t_2, is the maximum time a genuine e-pasport reader waits between issuing a request and receiving a response from an e-passport. We conducted experiments on open source e-passport readers and found that t_2 is bounded above by approximately 1.1 seconds. To perform this experiment we implemented a fake e-passport, to interact with an open source e-passport reader[3].

---

[3] https://github.com/tananaev/passport-reader.

The constraint t_3 represents how long an e-passport is willing to wait before receiving the next command after sending a challenge. It has no technical upper bound, as a tag remains active (and awaiting commands) for as long as it is powered. The flow of messages in Fig. 7 shows it is possible to arrange t_3, such that is is bounded above by a few seconds. Therefore, if the e-passport itself implements a timeout (which typically they do not) it would be easy to stay within that timeout bound.

A key practical concern in step (2) is the duration for which an e-passport reader will hold on to OCR details, indicated as t_1 in Fig. 7. This is dependent on the specific *firmware* implementation of the reader (the OCR reader and RF session with BAC combined). Certainly for open source readers for smart phones, this is not an obstacle. To avoid this attack, airport e-passport readers should require that an upper bound is enforced on t_1. It is also unknown if a reader discards stored OCR data after it believes it has finished executing the BAC protocol. This should be enforced, to ensure that the attack cannot be repeated (i.e. we can attempt to link only one passport with the last OCR scan).

An important point is that, if we interpret Fig. 7 simply as a trace of inputs and outputs then it is not an attack. To see why, observe that even if the suspended reader has different keys as expected in the idealised specification, then another (currently unused) reader can be employed to produce the same sequence of actions. The use of bisimilarity is essential.

7 Conclusions

Our primary contribution is to clear up confusion regarding the unlinkability of the BAC, when implemented with a single plaintext error message, as in the UK e-passport. We clarify that, contrary to claims previously made [4], there is a real attack on strong unlinkability. The attack can be discovered quickly from the strategy that causes the search for bisimulation to fail. While the attack is not as easy as the known attack on the French e-passport, the attack is practical, as clarified in Sect. 6.2.

Our secondary contribution is to clarify how different modelling assumptions may lead to different conclusions about the unlinkability of BAC. Our conclusion from this survey is that in a model faithful to the problem, there is no attack on the unlinkability of BAC that can be described as a simple trace. Our attacks on strong unlinkability make non-trivial use of bisimilarity; in practical terms this corresponds to the attacker making a decision about which reader receives a challenge. Thus we have:

- An attack, Sect. 6, correcting the original claim about strong unlinkability expressed in terms of **bisimilarity** [4].
- No attack expressible as a **trace**, a claim supported by our DEEPSEC code in Sect. 2, and by adapting [19].

Note that in both cases, we make the assumption that the initial configuration of the system is not fixed, as discussed in Sect. 2. Also, in both cases, internal communications, modelled by τ-transitions, are assumed to be unobservable and a *get_challenge* message is observable.

We also make significant methodological contributions. We discovered this attack by employing a state-of-the-art approach to bisimilarity checking, never before applied to a problem of this complexity. Our attack was discovered systematically, by the following methodology.

1. We search for a proof using a finer notion of bisimilarity called *open bisimilarity* [7,21,25,26], which lazily explores the state space.
2. When a distinguishing strategy is discovered using open bisimilarity, we determine whether it is an attack by constructing a distinguishing formula in an intermediate modal logic called intuitionistic $\mathcal{FM}$ [21,22].
3. Given our formula, we check whether the formula is still distinguishing under classical assumptions. This confirms there is also an attack on early bisimilarity.
4. We check the attack is also valid in the setting of labelled bisimilarity [3] (for which τ-transitions are silent), by checking where a lack of image finiteness allows additional processes to be created that may have an impact on the analysis.

While the above methodology discovers and confirms our attack systematically, undoubtedly employing the above methodology required mastery of state-of-the-art work on bisimilarity. Thus future work includes improving tool support.

Further perspectives on BAC and unlinkability. We note that the impact of our work extends beyond the BAC protocol. Attacks on strong unlinkability we discover can be adapted to a wide range of authentication protocols. We propose a general form for an authentication protocol that may fail strong unlinkability.

- The same keys are used between the e-document and multiple readers.
- A failed authentication session behaves observably differently from a successful authentication session.

Note observable differences between successful and failed sessions may be due to an error message, as in the French and UK implementations of the BAC protocol; but may also be due to the presence or absence of a valid message expected during authentication. Therefore our attack adapts also to a variant of BAC that signals a failed authentication session without any error message.

The latter point may be trickier to mitigate in practice. It may be possible to observe the presence or absence of a message exchanged after authentication is complete. In the ICAO 9303 standard, this phase is called the *secure messaging phase*. Such a practical extension of our attack is a concern perpendicular to the study of the BAC protocol in this work.

Another modelling dimension is the question of whether attacks such as those highlighted in this paper are down to inadequate definitions of unlinkability. A way to avoid our attacks by modifying the definition of unlinkability is to sequentialise entire sessions, such that exactly one reader starts and one passport starts, and **both** must have used up all their actions before proceeding with any action in a new session. This essentially models the situation where a round trip between an e-passport and remote reader becomes infeasible (e.g., due to stricter timeouts). The current work however focuses on clarifying established definitions of unlinkability.

Acknowledgements. We thank the following people for their time and knowledge during the investigation of these results: Vincent Cheval, Ugo Chirico, Stéphanie Delaune, Lucca Hirschi, and Steve Kremer.

References

1. Machine readable travel documents. part 11: Security mechanisms for MRTDs. Technical report Doc 9303. Seventh Edition, International Civil Aviation Organization (ICAO) (2015). https://www.icao.int/publications/Documents/9303_p11_cons_en.pdf
2. ISO 15408-2: Common criteria for information technology security evaluation. part 2: Security functional requirements. Technical report. CCMB-2017-04-002, ISO/IEC standard (2017). https://www.commoncriteriaportal.org/files/ccfiles/CCPART2V3.1R5.pdf
3. Abadi, M., Blanchet, B., Fournet, C.: The applied pi calculus: mobile values, new names, and secure communication. J. ACM **65**(1), 1:1–1:41 (2017)
4. Arapinis, M., Chothia, T., Ritter, E., Ryan, M.: Analysing unlinkability and anonymity using the applied pi calculus. In: 2010 23rd IEEE Computer Security Foundations Symposium (CSF), pp. 107–121. IEEE (2010)
5. Avoine, G., Beaujeant, A., Hernandez-Castro, J., Demay, L., Teuwen, P.: A survey of security and privacy issues in epassport protocols. ACM Comput. Surv. **48**(3), 47:1–47:37 (2016)
6. Bender, J., Fischlin, M., Kügler, D.: Security analysis of the PACE key-agreement protocol. In: Samarati, P., Yung, M., Martinelli, F., Ardagna, C.A. (eds.) ISC 2009. LNCS, vol. 5735, pp. 33–48. Springer, Heidelberg (2009). https://doi.org/10.1007/978-3-642-04474-8_3
7. Briais, S., Nestmann, U.: Open bisimulation, revisited. Theor. Comput. Sci. **386**(3), 236–271 (2007)
8. Brusó, M., Chatzikokolakis, K., Etalle, S., den Hartog, J.: Linking unlinkability. In: Palamidessi, C., Ryan, M.D. (eds.) TGC 2012. LNCS, vol. 8191, pp. 129–144. Springer, Heidelberg (2013). https://doi.org/10.1007/978-3-642-41157-1_9
9. Cheval, V.: Automatic verification of cryptographic protocols: privacy-type properties. PhD thesis, Laboratoire Spécification et Vérification, ENS Cachan (2012)
10. Cheval, V.: APTE: an algorithm for proving trace equivalence. In: Ábrahám, E., Havelund, K. (eds.) TACAS 2014. LNCS, vol. 8413, pp. 587–592. Springer, Heidelberg (2014). https://doi.org/10.1007/978-3-642-54862-8_50
11. Cheval, V., Comon-Lundh, H., Delaune, S.: A procedure for deciding symbolic equivalence between sets of constraint systems. Inf. Comput. **255**(Part 1), 94–125 (2017)
12. Cheval, V., Kremer, S., Rakotonirina, I.: DEEPSEC: Deciding equivalence properties in security protocols theory and practice. In: 2018 IEEE Symposium on Security and Privacy (S&P), pp. 529–546 (2018)
13. Chothia, T.: Analysing the MUTE anonymous file-sharing system using the pi-calculus. In: Najm, E., Pradat-Peyre, J.-F., Donzeau-Gouge, V.V. (eds.) FORTE 2006. LNCS, vol. 4229, pp. 115–130. Springer, Heidelberg (2006). https://doi.org/10.1007/11888116_9
14. Chothia, T., Smirnov, V.: A traceability attack against e-passports. In: Sion, R. (ed.) FC 2010. LNCS, vol. 6052, pp. 20–34. Springer, Heidelberg (2010). https://doi.org/10.1007/978-3-642-14577-3_5
15. Cortier, V., Rusinowitch, M., Zalinescu, E.: Relating two standard notions of secrecy. Log. Methods Comput. Sci. **3**(3), 1–29 (2007)
16. Cremers, C.J.F.: The scyther tool: verification, falsification, and analysis of security protocols. In: Gupta, A., Malik, S. (eds.) CAV 2008. LNCS, vol. 5123, pp. 414–418. Springer, Heidelberg (2008). https://doi.org/10.1007/978-3-540-70545-1_38
17. Dolev, D., Yao, A.: On the security of public-key protocols. IEEE Trans. Inf. Theory **2**(29), 198–208 (1983)

18. Feldhofer, M., Dominikus, S., Wolkerstorfer, J.: Strong authentication for RFID systems using the AES algorithm. In: Joye, M., Quisquater, J.-J. (eds.) CHES 2004. LNCS, vol. 3156, pp. 357–370. Springer, Heidelberg (2004). https://doi.org/10.1007/978-3-540-28632-5_26

19. Hirschi, L., Baelde, D., Delaune, S.: A method for verifying privacy-type properties: the unbounded case. In: 2016 IEEE Symposium on Security and Privacy (S&P), pp. 564–581. IEEE (2016)

20. Hirschi, L., Baelde, D., Delaune, S.: A method for unbounded verification of privacy-type properties. J. Comput. Secur. **27**(3), 277–342 (2019)

21. Horne, R.: A bisimilarity congruence for the applied π-calculus sufficiently coarse to verify privacy properties, (arXiv:1811.02536) (2018), https://arxiv.org/abs/1811.02536

22. Horne, R., Ahn, K.Y., Lin, S.W., Tiu, A.: Quasi-open bisimilarity with mismatch is intuitionistic. In: Dawar, A., Grädel, E. (eds.) Proceedings of 33rd Annual ACM/IEEE Symposium on Logic in Computer Science, Oxford, United Kingdom, 9–12 July 2018, pp. 26–35 (2018)

23. Kanellakis, P.C., Smolka, S.A.: CCS expressions, finite state processes, and three problems of equivalence. Inf. Comput. **86**(1), 43–68 (1990)

24. Milner, R., Parrow, J., Walker, D.: Modal logics for mobile processes. Theor. Comput. Sci. **114**(1), 149–171 (1993)

25. Sangiorgi, D.: A theory of bisimulation for the π-calculus. Acta Informatica **33**(1), 69–97 (1996)

26. Tiu, A., Dawson, J.: Automating open bisimulation checking for the spi calculus. In: 2010 23rd IEEE Computer Security Foundations Symposium. pp. 307–321. IEEE (2010)

Symmetric-Key Corruption Detection: When XOR-MACs Meet Combinatorial Group Testing

Kazuhiko Minematsu$^{(\boxtimes)}$ and Norifumi Kamiya

NEC Corporation, Kawasaki, Japan
k-minematsu@ah.jp.nec.com, kamiya@bc.jp.nec.com

Abstract. We study a class of MACs, which we call corruption detectable MAC, that is able to not only check the integrity of the whole message, but also detect a part of the message that is corrupted. It can be seen as an application of the classical Combinatorial Group Testing (CGT) to message authentication. However, previous work on this application has an inherent limitation in its communication cost. We present a novel approach to combine CGT and a class of linear MACs (XOR-MAC) that breaks this limit. Our proposal, XOR-GTM, has a significantly smaller communication cost than any of the previous corruption detectable MACs, while keeping the same corruption detection capability. Our numerical examples for storage application show a reduction of communication by a factor of around 15 to 70 compared with previous schemes. XOR-GTM is parallelizable and is as efficient as standard MACs. We prove that XOR-GTM is provably secure under the standard cryptographic assumptions.

Keywords: MAC · Corruption detection ·
Combinatorial Group Testing · XOR-MAC

1 Introduction

MAC and Corruption Detection. A Message Authentication Code (MAC) is a symmetric-key cryptographic function for ensuring the message authenticity. In a typical MAC protocol, the sender of a message M computes a fixed, short tag T as a function of a MAC: $T = \mathrm{MAC}(K, M)$ for the secret key K. On receiving the tuple (M', T') from the sender, which may be corrupted by the adversary, the receiver checks if the tuple is correct by performing the tag computation $\widehat{T} = \mathrm{MAC}(K, M')$ using the shared K and comparing T' and $\widehat{T}$.

The standard MAC functions, such as HMAC or CMAC, are quite efficient, and their securities have been extensively studied. However, the naïve application described above only tells us whether M' has been corrupted or not, and nothing about how M' is corrupted, i.e. the locations of the corruptions. Suppose a message can be divided into m parts, say the entries in a database or the sectors in a HDD. If we take a MAC tag for each part, the number of tags is m. This scheme gives us full information on the corrupted parts, however, does not scale as the amount of tag information grows linearly with m. We want to reduce the number of tags without losing the detection ability too much. This is a fundamental problem for many applications, such as storage integrity protection and low-power wireless communication. In particular, the size of a trusted storage for maintaining the integrity of a large, untrusted storage has been an important issue in the storage security research [36,37] and the commercial solutions such as Tripwire. In a broader sense, where a cryptographic hash function or a digital signature may be used as well as MACs, similar problems occur at verification of downloaded software, malware classification, and digital forensics etc. The underlying problem is how to minimize the number of tags keeping the sufficient ability to detect the corrupted parts. We call a MAC scheme for this purpose *a corruption detectable MAC*.

Combinatorial Group Testing and Its Applications. It is known that the corruption detectable MAC can be seen as an application of Combinatorial Group Testing (CGT) [22], a method invented by Dorfman in WWII [16] to effectively find blood samples infected by syphilis. It has been studied for long years, mainly from the viewpoint of theoretical computer science and applications to biology, such as DNA library screening [34]. CGT has been applied to many other areas, such as machine learning and data mining [32,44], signal processing [19], and sensor network [24] etc.

Suppose the sender wants to authenticate a message M consisting of m data items, where at most d items of M are assumed to be corrupted when M is sent to the receiver. What the sender can do is to take t MAC tags for certain subsequences of M for some $t \leq m$, corresponding to *group testing* in CGT. How tags are computed is completely specified by a $t \times m$ binary matrix $\mathbf{H}$, called a test matrix. The trivial scheme described earlier uses the identity matrix and thus is inefficient. However, it is known that if $\mathbf{H}$ has a property called d-disjunct[1], we can detect $d' \leq d$ corrupted items. It is known that d-disjunct matrix can be built with $O(d^2 \log m)$ rows, thus the use of d-disjunct matrix can significantly reduce the number of tags if d is much smaller than m.

Despite the simple and natural problem, corruption detectable MACs have received surprisingly less attention to date. To our knowledge, Crescenzo et al. [13,15] and Goodrich et al. [22] are the earliest work on this direction. Corruption-localizing hash function was proposed at ESORICS 2009 [14] and subsequently studied [9,12,14]. Minematsu [33] at ESORICS 2015 studied the computational aspects of corruption detectable MACs. An application of CGT to aggregate MAC [28] was studied by Hirose and Shikata [23].

Limitation of Previous Schemes. The most of previous corruption detectable MACs and the variants used existing d-disjunct matrices for their test matrices.

---

[1] The minimum condition is weaker (d-separable or $\bar{d}$-separable), however this does not guarantee an efficient detection.

We call it DirectGTM for the direct use of a disjunct matrix in a Group-Test-based MAC. Constructions of d-disjunct matrix have been extensively studied (see Sect. 3.2), however, finding one with optimally small number of rows for given m and d is still a hard combinatorial problem even for tiny d. Besides, if d is $O(\sqrt{m})$ it is impossible to build a non-trivial d-disjunct matrix. Consequently, the communication efficiency of DirectGTM is inherently bounded by the current knowledge of constructions of small-row disjunct matrix. The aforementioned work by Minematsu [33] (hereafter Min15) showed that the computation cost of DirectGTM can be effectively reduced to that of the single MAC function if we employ a MAC function similar to XOR-MAC [4] or PMAC [7]. However, the communication cost (i.e. the number of tags) is not reduced.

Beyond DirectGTM. We break the above limitation by presenting a new class of corruption detectable MACs. Our scheme has a structure very similar to Min15 for generation of tags, where a message subsequence specified by a row of test matrix (**H**) is processed by a hash-then-encrypt MAC function. However, the verification is different from Min15 in that we use the *decryption* of tags instead of the tags themselves. This seemingly tiny change will bring a ultimate difference from Min15, since it allows us to use any *linear combination* of (decrypted) tags for a verification of a new subsequence that is not specified by **H**! Surprisingly, this suggests that **H** is not necessarily d-disjunct, but only the *row span* of **H** over GF(2) is required to be d-disjunct. Therefore, the communication efficiency is determined not by the number of rows but the *rank* of d-disjunct matrix. We define the appropriate security notions for such a scheme, which we call XOR-GTM, and show XOR-GTM is provably secure using the standard symmetric-key primitives, such as a pseudorandom function (PRF) and a tweakable pseudorandom permutation (TPRP). Example 1 at Sect. 4.3 shows a toy example of our scheme and how it can reduce the communication cost.

Efficient Instantiations. Efficient instantiations of XOR-GTM are not easy. Despite the numerous studies on small-row d-disjunct matrices, their GF(2)-rank has rarely been studied. Even worse, as far as we studied, the state-of-the-art constructions tend to have a high rank, implying only a marginal gain from (ideal) DirectGTM. Instead, somewhat surprisingly, we find that some classes of near-square d-disjunct matrices, which are *almost useless* for CGT in general, are quite useful for us. The matrices we found are not new: one of them is a modified Hadamard matrix and the other is a point-line incidence matrix defined over finite geometry. Both are classical and have been extensively studied for decades. However, when we instantiate XOR-GTM with them (more precisely, the bases of the row vectors of these matrices are used as the test matrix), we could achieve what is impossible with *any* instantiation of DirectGTM including Min15. In more detail, by using Hadamard matrix, DirectGTM can detect $d = 2$ corruptions with $\log_2(m+1)+1$ tags, which is better than any DirectGTM scheme with 2-disjunct test matrix by a factor of 3 to 5. Moreover, with point-line incidence matrices, we can detect corruptions of $d = O(\sqrt{m})$ parts with $t = O(\sqrt{m})$ tags. This exhibits a very strong advantage over the existing schemes. In our numerical examples for storage application (Sect. 7), XOR-GTM needs fewer tags than the trivial scheme by a factor of roughly 15 to 70, while any instantiation of DirectGTM with a d-disjunct test matrix has almost no gain.

As well as Min15, XOR-GTM is parallelizable and incremental, in the sense of [3]. The computation of XOR-GTM is very efficient at it is essentially the same as taking a single MAC tag for the message. For our instantiations, the underlying matrices are highly structured, which is useful for efficient implementation. This gives another great advantage in comparison to the naïve use of a d-disjunct matrix since the small-row disjunct matrix is typically very complex.

Further Related Work. In the context of cryptography in general, CGT has been used for various related applications such as [1,8,11,40,45]. Although the interaction between CGT and cryptography has not received much attentions thus far, we believe it is very promising.

2 Preliminaries

2.1 Basic Notations

Let $\{0,1\}^\infty$ be the set of all binary strings, including the empty string ε. The bit length of $X \in \{0,1\}^\infty$ is denoted by $|X|$. Here, $|\varepsilon| = 0$. We define $\{0,1\}^* \overset{\text{def}}{=} \{0,1\}^\infty \setminus \{\varepsilon\}$. For a binary string X, its hamming weight is denoted by $\mathrm{Hw}(X)$. We define a set of m-tuples of non-empty strings as $\{0,1\}^{*m} \overset{\text{def}}{=} (\{0,1\}^*)^m$, and define $\{0,1\}^{*\leq m} \overset{\text{def}}{=} \bigcup_{i=1}^m \{0,1\}^{*i}$. We write $\{0,1\}^{\infty m} \overset{\text{def}}{=} (\{0,1\}^\infty)^m$ to denote the set of m-tuples of possibly empty strings. Here, (ε, v) and (v, ε) for $v \neq \varepsilon$ are distinct elements of $\{0,1\}^{\infty 2}$. A uniform sampling over a set $\mathcal{X}$ is written as $X \overset{\$}{\leftarrow} \mathcal{X}$. The base of logarithm is 2 unless otherwise written.

For a positive integer n, let[2] $[\![n]\!] = \{1,\ldots,n\}$ and $(\!|n|\!) = \{0,\ldots,n-1\}$. For a finite set $\mathcal{X}$, $2^{\mathcal{X}}$ denotes the power set, and let $\mathsf{cmp} : \mathcal{X} \times \mathcal{X} \to \{0,1\}$ be the comparison function, i.e. $\mathsf{cmp}(X,Y) = 0$ if $X = Y$ and $\mathsf{cmp}(X,Y) = 1$ if $X \neq Y$. For $M = (M[1],\ldots,M[m]) \in \{0,1\}^{*m}$ and $M' = (M'[1],\ldots,M'[m]) \in \{0,1\}^{*m}$, we define vector comparison $\mathsf{vdiff}(M,M')$ and index difference $\mathsf{diff}(M,M')$ as

$$\mathsf{vdiff}(M,M') = (\mathsf{cmp}(M[1],M'[1]),\ldots,\mathsf{cmp}(M[m],M'[m])),$$
$$\mathsf{diff}(M,M') = \{i \in [\![m]\!] : M[i] \neq M'[i]\}. \tag{1}$$

For $X = (X[1],\ldots,X[m]) \in \{0,1\}^m$, let $M \ominus X \in \{0,1\}^{*m'}$ be a vector obtained by subtracting $M[i]$s for all i s.t. $X[i] = 0$, where $m' = \mathrm{Hw}(X)$. For example, if $m = 4$ and $X = (1,0,1,0)$, $M \ominus X = (M[1], M[3])$.

Disjunct Matrix. Let $\mathbf{M}$ be an $n \times m$ binary matrix. We write $\mathbf{M}_{i,*}$ to denote the i-th row, and $\mathbf{M}_{*,j}$ to denote the j-th column, and $\mathbf{M}_{i,j}$ to denote the entry at i-th row and j-th column. For simplicity we may abbreviate $\mathbf{M}_{i,*}$ to $\mathbf{M}_i$. The rows and columns of $\mathbf{M}$ are interchangeably seen as sets, e.g., $\mathbf{M}_i = \{j \in [\![m]\!] : \mathbf{M}_{i,j} = 1\}$, and $a \in \mathbf{M}_i$ means $\mathbf{M}_{i,a} = 1$.

---

[2] It is customary to use $[n]$ but we want to avoid confusion, say with $M[i]$.

For $X, Y \in \{0,1\}^n$, $X \vee Y$ denotes the bitwise Boolean sum (logical OR) of X and Y. We say $\mathbf{M}$ is d-disjunct [17] if, for any $\mathcal{S} \subseteq [\![m]\!]$ and $|\mathcal{S}| \in [\![d]\!]$, $\mathbf{M}_{*,j} \not\subseteq \bigvee_{h \in \mathcal{S}} \mathbf{M}_{*,h}$ holds for any $j \notin \mathcal{S}$. That is, a sum of any distinct $i \leq d$ columns of $\mathbf{M}$ does not cover any other column. An $m \times m$ identity matrix is trivially m-disjunct. A d-disjunct matrix is also said to have *disjunctness* of d. The most important property of d-disjunct matrix is the number of rows for given d and m (See Sect. 3.2). For convention, a d-disjunct matrix is said to be "ideal" or "optimal" when it has the smallest number of rows for fixed d and m.

2.2   Cryptographic Functions

A keyed function with key space $\mathcal{K}$, domain $\mathcal{X}$, and range $\mathcal{Y}$ is a function $F : \mathcal{K} \times \mathcal{X} \rightarrow \mathcal{Y}$. We may write $F_K(X)$ for $F(K, X)$, and if $\mathcal{X} = \mathcal{M} \times [\![\ell]\!]$ for some positive integer ℓ, write $F_K^i(M)$ to denote $F_K(M, i)$ for $(M, i) \in \mathcal{X}$. A tweakable block cipher (TBC) [30] $E : \mathcal{K} \times \mathcal{T} \times \mathcal{X} \rightarrow \mathcal{X}$ is a keyed permutation over $\mathcal{X}$ with additional tweak input in $\mathcal{T}$, i.e., $E(K, T, *)$ for any $(K, T) \in \mathcal{K} \times \mathcal{T}$ is a permutation over $\mathcal{X}$. We may write $E_K^T(X)$ instead of $E(K, T, X)$ or $E_K(T, X)$. The decryption of X with tweak T is written as $E_K^{-1}(T, X)$ or $E_K^{T,-1}(X)$.

A uniform random function (URF) $\mathsf{R} : \mathcal{X} \rightarrow \mathcal{Y}$ is a keyed function with uniform key distribution over all functions from $\mathcal{X}$ to $\mathcal{Y}$. A uniform random permutation (URP) $\mathsf{P} : \mathcal{X}' \rightarrow \mathcal{X}$ is defined analogously. A tweakable uniform random permutation (TURP) with tweak space $\mathcal{T}$ and message space $\mathcal{X}$ is denoted by $\widetilde{\mathsf{P}} : \mathcal{T} \times \mathcal{X} \rightarrow \mathcal{X}$, which is a set of independent URPs indexed by $\mathcal{T}$. The decryption of $\widetilde{\mathsf{P}}$ is denoted by $\widetilde{\mathsf{P}}^{-1}$. Let $\mathcal{A}$ be an adversary who (possibly adaptively) queries to the oracle $\mathcal{O}$ and outputs a bit as a final decision. The advantage of $\mathcal{A}$ in distinguishing two oracles, $F : \mathcal{K} \times \mathcal{X} \rightarrow \mathcal{Y}$ and $F' : \mathcal{K}' \times \mathcal{X} \rightarrow \mathcal{Y}$, is defined as

$$\mathbf{Adv}_{F_K, F'_{K'}}^{\mathsf{ind}}(\mathcal{A}) \overset{\text{def}}{=} \left| \Pr[K \xleftarrow{\$} \mathcal{K} : \mathcal{A}^{F_K} \Rightarrow 1] - \Pr[K' \xleftarrow{\$} \mathcal{K}' : \mathcal{A}^{F'_{K'}} \Rightarrow 1] \right|,$$

where $\mathcal{A}^{F_K} \Rightarrow 1$ denotes the probability that $\mathcal{A}$'s final decision is 1 when the oracle is F_K. We define $\mathbf{Adv}_{F_K, \mathsf{R}}^{\mathsf{ind}}(\mathcal{A}) \overset{\text{def}}{=} \mathbf{Adv}_{F_K}^{\mathsf{prf}}(\mathcal{A})$ where $\mathsf{R} : \mathcal{X} \rightarrow \mathcal{Y}$ is a URF. It is called the PRF-advantage of F_K (for $\mathcal{A}$). We say F_K is a PRF when $\mathbf{Adv}_{F_K}^{\mathsf{prf}}(\mathcal{A})$ is sufficiently small for all practical adversaries [2]. For a TBC $E : \mathcal{K} \times \mathcal{T} \times \mathcal{X} \rightarrow \mathcal{X}$, we define the Tweakable PRP (TPRP) advantage as $\mathbf{Adv}_{E_K}^{\mathsf{tprp}}(\mathcal{A}) = \mathbf{Adv}_{E_K, \widetilde{\mathsf{P}}}^{\mathsf{ind}}(\mathcal{A})$ for $\mathcal{A}$ using chosen-plaintext (encryption) queries.

3   Previous Corruption Detectable MACs

3.1   DirectGTM

Given a $t \times m$ binary test matrix $\mathbf{H}$, the basic form of a corruption detectable MAC is described as follows. For message $M \in \{0,1\}^{*m}$, the sender first computes

$$T[i] = \mathsf{MAC}_K(M \ominus \mathbf{H}_i, i) \tag{2}$$

for all $i \in [\![t]\!]$, using a MAC function $\mathsf{MAC} : \mathcal{K} \times \{0,1\}^{* \leq m} \times [\![t]\!] \to \{0,1\}^n$. The output is the tag vector $T = (T[1], \ldots, T[t]) \in (\{0,1\}^n)^t$. The verifier receives (M', T'), which may be a corrupted version of (M, T), and computes $\widehat{T} = (\widehat{T}[1], \ldots, \widehat{T}[t])$, where $\widehat{T}[i] = \mathsf{MAC}_K(M' \ominus \mathbf{H}_i, i)$, and compares T' with $\widehat{T}$ to obtain $\mathsf{vdiff}(T', \widehat{T})$. Then, the verifier tries to detect the corrupted items, by subtracting $\mathbf{H}_i$ (as a set) from $[\![m]\!]$ for all $i \in [\![t]\!]$ such that $\mathsf{cmp}(T'[i], \widehat{T}[i]) = 0$. The remaining set indicates the indexes of the corrupted items. In the context of CGT, the above procedure is called *naïve decoding* [17]. The following is a well-known fact from the property of d-disjunct matrix.

Proposition 1. *Suppose* $\mathbf{H}$ *is d-disjunct and* $\mathsf{diff}(M, M') \leq d$ *and* $T' = T$. *Then, the naïve decoding correctly detects all the corrupted items if* $\mathsf{cmp}(T'[i], \widehat{T}[i]) = \mathsf{cmp}(M \ominus \mathbf{H}_i, M' \ominus \mathbf{H}_i)$ *for all* $i \in [\![t]\!]$.

Proposition 1 holds since any negative (uncorrupted) item is included in at least one test that does not contain any positive (corrupted) item. We call a corruption detectable MAC of the above form DirectGTM. While there are some differences, the previous corruption detectable MACs and the variants are classified as DirectGTM.

Min15 [33] studied the computational overhead of DirectGTM from the standard MAC. Min15 showed that one can reduce the computation cost almost as low as the standard MAC independent of the test matrix, by employing a deterministic MAC similar to XOR-MAC [4] or PMAC [39]. Nevertheless, Min15 is an instantiation of DirectGTM as it needs d-disjunct $\mathbf{H}$ to detect d corruptions.

3.2 Constructions of Disjunct Matrix

The construction of disjunct matrix has been extensively studied from the viewpoint of designs and codes. Classical examples are Macula [31] and Kautz and Singleton [29]. The Du-Hwang book [17] describes a number of known constructions. Eppstein et al. proposed Chinese Reminder Sieve (CRS) [20]. Thierry-Mieg proposed Shifted Transversal Design (STD) [43] for biological applications.

Let $t_{\min}(d, m)$ be the minimum number of rows for a d-disjunct matrix of m columns. It is known that $t_{\min}(d, m) = \Theta(d^2 \log m)$ [17]. The seminal work of Porat and Rothschild [38] showed an order-optimal and deterministic construction of d-disjunct matrix, however it needs a large (though polynomial) search for matrix generation. Besides, the optimality *including the constant* is not known. Only the case $d = 1$ has been solved: 1-disjunct matrix implies that no column is contained in another column. Such a matrix is called a completely separating system, and has about $\log m$ rows [17]. If we relax the condition to a weaker one (1-separability), the concrete construction of $\lceil \log m \rceil$ rows is easy as it is achieved by making all columns distinct. However, even for the case $d = 2$, the question of optimal construction remains open for decades.

Lower Bounds. A lower bound of $t_{\min}(d, m) \geq \min\left\{\binom{d+2}{2}, m\right\}$ was shown by Dýachkov and Rykov [18], attributed to Bassalygo. An improved bound was shown by Shangguan and Ge [41]:

$$t_{\min}(d, m) \geq \min\left\{\frac{d^2(15 + \sqrt{33})}{24}, m\right\}. \tag{3}$$

Moreover, there is a conjectured lower bound by Erdös et al. [21]:

$$t_{\min}(d, m) \geq \min\left\{(d+1)^2, m\right\}, \tag{4}$$

which was later shown to be correct for $d \leq 5$ (see [41]).

4 Our Proposal

4.1 Breaking the Barrier of DirectGTM

For the previous DirectGTMs, the choice of test matrix was independent of the choice of MAC_K, and a d-disjunct matrix or its variant was suggested to be used as $\mathbf{H}$. Thus, to reduce the communication cost of DirectGTM, we must find a small-row d-disjunct matrix. Unfortunately, this is a hard problem even for tiny d and even impossible when d is close to $\sqrt{m}$, as shown in the previous section. This limits the practical usefulness of DirectGTM.

We break this barrier by exploiting a certain linearity in the MAC computation. Suppose we have a Min15 scheme with t tests (tags). There is an intermediate vector $S = (S[1], \ldots, S[t])$, where $S[i]$ is a keyed hash value of a subsequence of M specified by $\mathbf{H}_i$, and an encryption of $S[i]$ yields the i-th tag $T[i]$. We observe that checking at $T[i]$ is equivalent to checking at $S[i]$, and even more, any linear combination of $S[i]$s will yield another test, i.e., a verification of a new subsequence of M.

For example, if $T[1]$ is a tag for $(M[1], M[2])$ and $T[2]$ is a tag for $(M[2], M[3])$, the verifier can use $S[1] \oplus S[2]$ as a test for $(M[1], M[3])$. This is done by computing $S[1]$ and $S[2]$ from the decryption of the received tags and seeing if $S[1] \oplus S[2]$ agrees with the value computed from M, denoted by $\widehat{S}[1] \oplus \widehat{S}[2]$. Hence, without explicitly sending a tag for $(M[1], M[3])$, we could perform three tests with two tags. In other words, when the authenticator takes MAC tags based on $\mathbf{H}$, the verifier can use (any sub-matrix of) the row span of $\mathbf{H}$ as a *virtual* test matrix. This can bring significantly richer information to the verifier without increasing the communication.

4.2 Syntax

We first define the syntax of the corruption detectable MAC. Let m, t, and n be positive integers. They are the fixed parameters, but it is easy to extend to the case of variable parameters. A corruption detectable MAC consists of four algorithms. The key generation $\mathsf{KG} : \mathbb{N} \to \mathcal{K}$ takes a security parameter $p \in \mathbb{N}$ and returns a key $K \in \mathcal{K}$. The key K is shared by the legitimate parties (authenticator and verifier).

The tagging function $\mathsf{Tag} : \mathcal{K} \times \mathcal{M} \to \mathcal{T}$ takes a message $M \in \mathcal{M}$ and a key $K \in \mathcal{K}$ to return a tag vector $T \in \mathcal{T}$, where $\mathcal{M} = \{0,1\}^{*m}$ and $\mathcal{T} = (\{0,1\}^n)^t$. We write as $M = (M[1], \ldots, M[m]) \in \mathcal{M}$ and $T = (T[1], \ldots, T[t]) \in \mathcal{T}$, where $M[i]$ is called a message item (or item for short), and $T[i]$ is called a tag string (or tag for short). The verification function $\mathsf{Ver} : \mathcal{K} \times \mathcal{M} \times \mathcal{T} \to \mathcal{D}$ with $\mathcal{D} = \{0,1\}$ is for verification: $\mathsf{Ver}_K(M', T') = 0$ denotes the tuple (M', T') is authenticated (no corruption), while $\mathsf{Ver}_K(M', T') = 1$ denotes the tuple is not authenticated, thus an authentication failure. Finally, the detection function $\mathsf{Det} : \mathcal{K} \times \mathcal{M} \times \mathcal{T} \to 2^{[\![m]\!]}$ takes key K and the possibly corrupted tuple (M', T') to return a candidate of the index set of corrupted message items $\mathcal{P} \in 2^{[\![m]\!]}$. For example, $\{1, 3\} \leftarrow \mathsf{Det}_K(M', T')$ means $M'[1]$ and $M'[3]$ are considered to be corrupted.

In addition, we define the string-wise verification function $\mathsf{SVer} : \mathcal{K} \times \mathcal{M} \times \mathcal{T} \to \mathcal{D}^t$ that takes K, M' and T' to return $B \in \mathcal{D}^t$. Here, $B = (B[1], \ldots, B[t]) = (0, \ldots, 0)$ corresponds to $\mathsf{Ver}_K(M', T') = 0$ and any $B \neq (0, \ldots, 0)$ means $\mathsf{Ver}_K(M', T') = 1$ with some additional information. Thus it potentially gives about t-bit information on verification failure. The precise meaning of $B[i]$ will depend on the scheme. While SVer may be of practical relevance, we use it to simplify our security analysis. This syntax will be used to define our security notions at Sect. 5.

4.3 XOR-GTM

We present our corruption detectable MAC, XOR-GTM. The name comes from the similarity to XOR-MAC [4], though, XOR-MAC is a plain stateful MAC, which takes a message and a nonce and creates an atomic tag.

Parameters. XOR-GTM is a deterministic MAC over $\mathcal{M} = \{0,1\}^{*m}$ for a fixed, positive integer m. It has two parameters, $t \times m$ binary test matrix $\mathbf{H}$ and its *extension rule* R. Here, R specifies the linear combinations of rows of $\mathbf{H}$, and is defined as $R = (R_1, \ldots, R_v)$, where $R_i \subseteq [\![t]\!]$, for some $v \geq t$. We define $\mathbf{H}^R$ as a $v \times m$ *extended test matrix* obtained by taking the linear combinations of rows of $\mathbf{H}$ specified by R, that is,

$$\mathbf{H}_i^R = \bigoplus_{j \in R_i} \mathbf{H}_j, \text{ for all } i \in [\![v]\!]. \tag{5}$$

For simplicity, we assume $R_i = \{i\}$ for $i \in [\![t]\!]$. Hence, $\mathbf{H}^R$ is a $v \times m$ matrix obtained by adding $v - t$ rows to $\mathbf{H}$. For $X = (X[1], \ldots, X[t]) \in (\{0,1\}^n)^t$, we define $X^R = (X^R[1], \ldots, X^R[v]) \in (\{0,1\}^n)^v$ as

$$X^R[i] = \bigoplus_{j \in R_i} X[j], \text{ for all } i \in [\![v]\!], \tag{6}$$

which is an expansion of X by R.

To avoid trivial attacks and apparently redundant tests, we require the following soundness conditions for $\mathbf{H}$ and R.

Definition 1. *A pair of $\mathbf{H}$ and R (or equivalently, $\mathbf{H}^R$) is said to be sound if all rows of $\mathbf{H}^R$ are distinct and there is an all-one row.*

For simplicity, we assume $\mathbf{H}_1$ is all-one whenever $\mathbf{H}$ is sound. The cryptographic components of XOR-GTM are PRF $F : \mathcal{K} \times [\![m]\!] \times \{0,1\}^* \to \{0,1\}^n$ and TBC $G : \mathcal{K}' \times [\![t]\!] \times \{0,1\}^n \to \{0,1\}^n$ for tweak space $[\![t]\!]$. The procedures of XOR-GTM are as follows.

Tag Computation. For message $M \in \{0,1\}^{*m}$, we define

$$\mathsf{XOR\text{-}GTM}[F_K].\mathrm{hash}(M) = (S[1], \ldots, S[t]), \text{ where } S[i] = \bigoplus_{j \in \mathbf{H}_i} F_K^j(M[j]). \quad (7)$$

The tag computation procedure $(\mathsf{XOR\text{-}GTM}[F_K, G_{K'}].\mathrm{tag}(M))$ first performs the above and compute

$$T[i] = G_{K'}^i(S[i])$$

for all $i \in [\![t]\!]$ and outputs $T = (T[1], \ldots, T[t])$, which is called a tag vector.

Verification and Corruption Detection. The verification of tuple (M', T') $(\mathsf{XOR\text{-}GTM}[F_K, G_{K'}].\mathrm{verify}(M', T'))$ first computes

$$\widehat{T} = \mathsf{XOR\text{-}GTM}[F_K, G_{K'}].\mathrm{tag}(M'), \quad (8)$$

and checks if $\widehat{T} = T'$. In fact, as we assumed $\mathbf{H}_1$ is all-one, checking the first components of $\widehat{T}$ and T' will suffice. If they do not match, the receiver tries to detect corruptions by the detection function $\mathsf{XOR\text{-}GTM}[F_K, G_{K'}].\mathrm{detect}(M', T')$. It computes $S' = (S'[1], \ldots, S'[t])$ for $S'[i] = G_{K'}^{i,-1}(T'[i])$, and also computes $\widehat{S} = \mathsf{XOR\text{-}GTM}[F_K].\mathrm{hash}(M')$. It expands $\widehat{S}$ and S' to $\widehat{S}^R$ and $(S')^R$ using (6). The detection function finally performs the naïve decoder with $\mathbf{H}^R$. That is, for all $i \in [\![v]\!]$ such that $\widehat{S}^R[i] = (S')^R[i]$, it removes all the elements of $\mathbf{H}_i^R$ (as a set) from $[\![m]\!]$, and outputs the remaining set as the indexes of the corrupted items. See Fig. 1 for the pseudocodes.

Relationship to Min15. When $v = t$, $\mathbf{H}^R = \mathbf{H}$ and $T^R = T$ hold, and the tagging, verification and detection functions are identical to those of Min15, except the fact that we explicitly require the invertibility of G while Min15 does not. The equivalence of verification holds because $T[i] = \widehat{T}[i]$ is equivalent to $G_{K'}^{i,-1}(T[i]) = G_{K'}^{i,-1}(\widehat{T}[i])$.

Example 1. Let $m = 4$, $t = 3$ and $v = 6$. We define $\mathbf{H}$ and $\mathbf{H}^R$ as follows. Here, $R = (\{1\}, \{2\}, \{3\}, \{1, 2\}, \{2, 3\}, \{1, 2, 3\})$.

$$\mathbf{H} = \begin{pmatrix} 1 & 1 & 0 & 0 \\ 0 & 1 & 1 & 0 \\ 0 & 0 & 1 & 1 \end{pmatrix}, \quad \mathbf{H}^R = \begin{pmatrix} 1 & 1 & 0 & 0 \\ 0 & 1 & 1 & 0 \\ 0 & 0 & 1 & 1 \\ 1 & 0 & 1 & 0 \\ 0 & 1 & 0 & 1 \\ 1 & 0 & 0 & 1 \end{pmatrix}. \quad (9)$$

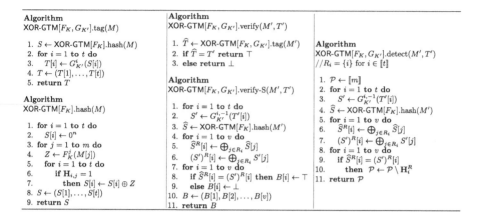

Algorithm XOR-GTM$[F_K, G_{K'}]$.tag(M)	Algorithm XOR-GTM$[F_K, G_{K'}]$.verify(M', T')	
1. $S \leftarrow$ XOR-GTM$[F_K]$.hash(M) 2. for $i = 1$ to t do 3. $T[i] \leftarrow G^i_{K'}(S[i])$ 4. $T \leftarrow (T[1], \ldots, T[t])$ 5. return T	1. $\widehat{T} \leftarrow$ XOR-GTM$[F_K, G_{K'}]$.tag(M') 2. if $\widehat{T} = T'$ return $\top$ 3. else return $\perp$	Algorithm XOR-GTM$[F_K, G_{K'}]$.detect(M', T') $//R_i = \{i\}$ for $i \in [\![t]\!]$
Algorithm XOR-GTM$[F_K]$.hash(M)	Algorithm XOR-GTM$[F_K, G_{K'}]$.verify-S(M', T')	1. $\mathcal{P} \leftarrow [\![m]\!]$ 2. for $i = 1$ to t do 3. $S' \leftarrow G^{i,-1}_{K'}(T'[i])$ 4. $\widehat{S} \leftarrow$ XOR-GTM$[F_K]$.hash(M') 5. for $i = 1$ to v do 6. $\widehat{S}^R[i] \leftarrow \bigoplus_{j \in R_i} \widehat{S}[j]$ 7. $(S')^R[i] \leftarrow \bigoplus_{j \in R_i} S'[j]$ 8. for $i = 1$ to v do 9. if $\widehat{S}^R[i] = (S')^R[i]$ 10. then $\mathcal{P} \leftarrow \mathcal{P} \setminus \mathbf{H}^R_i$ 11. return $\mathcal{P}$
1. for $i = 1$ to t do 2. $S[i] \leftarrow 0^n$ 3. for $j = 1$ to m do 4. $Z \leftarrow F^j_K(M[j])$ 5. for $i = 1$ to t do 6. if $\mathbf{H}_{i,j} = 1$ 7. then $S[i] \leftarrow S[i] \oplus Z$ 8. $S \leftarrow (S[1], \ldots, S[t])$ 9. return S	1. for $i = 1$ to t do 2. $S' \leftarrow G^{i,-1}_{K'}(T'[i])$ 3. $\widehat{S} \leftarrow$ XOR-GTM$[F_K]$.hash(M') 4. for $i = 1$ to v do 5. $\widehat{S}^R[i] \leftarrow \bigoplus_{j \in R_i} \widehat{S}[j]$ 6. $(S')^R[i] \leftarrow \bigoplus_{j \in R_i} S'[j]$ 7. for $i = 1$ to v do 8. if $\widehat{S}^R[i] = (S')^R[i]$ then $B[i] \leftarrow \top$ 9. else $B[i] \leftarrow \perp$ 10. $B \leftarrow (B[1], B[2], \ldots, B[v])$ 11. return B	

Fig. 1. XOR-GTM using $t \times m$ test matrix $\mathbf{H}$ and extension rule R with v elements.

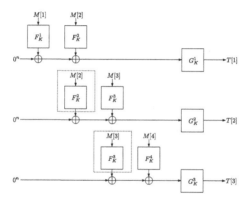

Fig. 2. XOR-GTM for $m = 4$ and $t = 3$ (we omit the first all-one row). The invocations of F in a dotted box can be avoided by caching.

For message $M \in \{0,1\}^{*3}$, XOR-GTM generates $T = (T[1], T[2], T[3])$ where

$$T[1] = G^1_{K'}(S[1]), \quad S[1] = F^1_K(M[1]) \oplus F^2_K(M[2]) \tag{10}$$

$$T[2] = G^2_{K'}(S[2]), \quad S[2] = F^2_K(M[2]) \oplus F^3_K(M[3])) \tag{11}$$

$$T[3] = G^3_{K'}(S[3]), \quad S[3] = F^3_K(M[3]) \oplus F^4_K(M[4])). \tag{12}$$

The linear combinations of hash values (S) specified by R are:

$$S[4] = S[1] \oplus S[2] = F^1_K(M[1]) \oplus F^3_K(M[3]) \tag{13}$$

$$S[5] = S[2] \oplus S[3] = F^2_K(M[2]) \oplus F^4_K(M[4]) \tag{14}$$

$$S[6] = S[1] \oplus S[2] \oplus S[3] = F^1_K(M[1]) \oplus F^4_K(M[4]). \tag{15}$$

Given (M', T'), the (basic) verification is done by comparing $T' = (T'[1], T'[2], T'[3])$ with $\widehat{T} = $ XOR-GTM$[F_K, G_{K'}](M')$. To detect the corruptions, we decrypt T' by $G_{K'}$ to obtain $S' = (S'[1], S'[2], S'[3])$ and compute $\widehat{S} = (\widehat{S}[1], \widehat{S}[2], \widehat{S}[3])$ from M', and expand S' and $\widehat{S}$ as (13), (14), (15) to obtain $(S')^R$ and $\widehat{S}^R$ (the computation of T is shown in Fig. 2).

In fact, $\mathbf{H}^R$ comes from Macula [31] with parameter $(n, k, d) = (4, 3, 2)$, hence is 2-disjunct. Thus, this example detects at most 2 corruptions among 4 items using 3 tags, which is impossible with DirectGTM as there is no 3×4 2-disjunct matrix from (4). We note that this example is just to understand the idea: $\mathbf{H}^R$ is not sound as it lacks all-one row (hence not secure), and adding an all-one row will make it useless.

Efficient Computation. Since $\mathbf{H}_i$ may intersect with other $\mathbf{H}_j$, a straightforward tag computation will bring lots of redundant F calls. However, the computation of T can be done by m calls of F_K and t calls of $G_{K'}$ as well as Min15. See Fig. 1. A nice thing is that this feature is independent of the contents of $\mathbf{H}$. Usually $m \gg t$ (as this is why we use CGT!), hence, XOR-GTM is roughly as efficient as the standard MACs applied to the whole message. See Sect. 7 for our preliminary implementation result.

5   Security Analysis

We show XOR-GTM is a secure MAC under the standard unforgeability notion [5,6], and more importantly, it is hard to forge the detection procedure, if F_K is a PRF and $G_{K'}$ is a tweakable PRP.

5.1   Security Notions

The first security notion is Tag Vector Unforgeability (TVUF), which is essentially the same as the standard unforgeability of deterministic MACs. The second is Tag String Unforgeability (TSUF), a stronger notion of unforgeability. The third is Decoder Unforgeability (DUF), which captures the hardness of fooling the naïve decoder to detect corruptions. To define them, we introduce several oracles. Following the syntax defined at Sect. 4.2, we consider a corruption detectable MAC MAC_K as a tuple $(\mathsf{KG}, \mathsf{Tag}, \mathsf{Ver}, \mathsf{SVer}, \mathsf{Det})$. We assume the key $K \in \mathcal{K}$ has been generated by $\mathsf{KG}(p)$ in advance, for a security parameter p.

Definition 2 *(Oracles). A tagging oracle $\mathcal{O}_T$ accepts M and returns $T = \mathsf{Tag}_K(M)$. The tag vector verification oracle $\mathcal{O}_V$, or simply the verification oracle, accepts $(M', T') \in \mathcal{M} \times \mathcal{T}$ and returns $\mathsf{Ver}_K(M', T')$. The tag string verification oracle $\mathcal{O}_{SV}$ accepts (M', T') and returns $\mathsf{SVer}_K(M', T')$. The detection oracle $\mathcal{O}_D$ accepts $(M', T') \in \{0,1\}^{*m} \times \mathcal{T}^t$ and returns $\mathsf{Det}_K(M', T')$.*

A query to $\mathcal{O}_T$ is called a tagging query and written as T-query. Queries to other oracles are called analogously.

Definition 3 *(TVUF). Let $\mathcal{A}_1$ be an adversary who (possibly adaptively) queries to $\mathcal{O}_T$ and $\mathcal{O}_V$. We say $\mathcal{A}_1$ forges if it receives 0 from $\mathcal{O}_V$ by querying (M', T') without making a tagging query M'. The advantage of $\mathcal{A}_1$ is defined as*

$$\mathbf{Adv}^{\mathsf{tvuf}}_{\mathsf{MAC}_K}(\mathcal{A}_1) \overset{def}{=} \Pr[\mathcal{A}_1^{\mathcal{O}_T,\mathcal{O}_V} \ forges]. \tag{16}$$

Definition 4 *(TSUF). Let $\mathcal{A}_2$ be an adversary who queries to $\mathcal{O}_T$ and $\mathcal{O}_{SV}$. We say $\mathcal{A}_2$ forges if it receives $B = (B[1], \ldots, B[t])$ from $\mathcal{O}_{SV}$ that indicates a non-trivial tag-string forgery. That is, for an SV-query (M', T') and the corresponding response B from $\mathcal{O}_{SV}$, there exists $i \in [\![t]\!]$ such that $B[i] = 0$ and $(M' \ominus \mathbf{H}_i, T'[i]) \neq (M \ominus \mathbf{H}_i, T[i])$ holds for any (M, T) obtained from a previous T-query and its response. The advantage of $\mathcal{A}_2$ is defined as*

$$\mathbf{Adv}^{\mathsf{tsuf}}_{\mathsf{MAC}_K}(\mathcal{A}_2) \overset{def}{=} \Pr[\mathcal{A}_2^{\mathcal{O}_T,\mathcal{O}_{SV}} \ forges]. \tag{17}$$

Definition 5 *(DUF). Let $\mathcal{A}_3$ be an adversary who queries to $\mathcal{O}_T$ and $\mathcal{O}_D$. We assume $\mathcal{A}_3$ is d-corrupting, i.e. any D-query (M', T') satisfies (1) $T' = T$ holds for a previous T-query (M, T), where M is called a target message, and (2) $1 \leq |\mathsf{diff}(M', M)| \leq d$. We say $\mathcal{A}_3$ forges if $\mathcal{O}_D$ fails, that is, it returns $\mathcal{P} \neq \mathsf{diff}(M', M)$. We define*

$$\mathbf{Adv}^{\mathsf{duf}(d)}_{\mathsf{MAC}_K}(\mathcal{A}_3) \overset{def}{=} \Pr[\mathcal{A}_3^{\mathcal{O}_T,\mathcal{O}_D} \ forges]. \tag{18}$$

The security against tag vector forgery is measured by TVUF advantage, and we say $\mathsf{MAC_K}$ is secure against tag vector forgery if $\mathbf{Adv}^{\mathsf{tvuf}}_{\mathsf{MAC_K}}(\mathcal{A}_1)$ is sufficiently small for all practical adversaries. The security against tag string forgery and decoder forgery are defined similarly.

These notions are the same as Min15, except TSUF which is slightly different.

Notes on DUF. Our DUF notion is to capture the hardness of fooling the decoder when an adversary corrupts a target message M to some M'. Naturally we expect such target is unique, however Definition 5 allows distinct multiple messages, say M_i and M_j, to be chosen as the target for a single attempt of corruption, iff they yield the same tag vectors. This is not a definitional problem, rather our preference of unifying queries into two types, either M (for tagging) or (M, T) (for verification or detection) for all three notions. In fact, we can modify the definition so that the target is always unique (say by querying a tuple (M, M') and the oracle computes $T' = T$ from M). Moreover, a non-trivial tag collision breaks our scheme as it tells some non-trivial information on the outputs of F_K, and we count it as one of bad events in our provable security analysis (see Sect. 5.2). Thus both definitions have no significant difference in practice. See Sect. A for other discussions on DUF.

5.2   Provable Security Bounds

XOR-GTM$[F_K, G_{K'}]$ is defined by the algorithms of Fig. 1 (where KG is trivially defined and omitted): $\mathsf{Tag}_{\mathbf{K}}$ = XOR-GTM$[F_K, G_{K'}]$.tag, and $\mathsf{Ver}_{\mathbf{K}}$ = XOR-GTM$[F_K, G_{K'}]$.verify, and $\mathsf{SVer}_{\mathbf{K}}$ = XOR-GTM$[F_K, G_{K'}]$.verify-S, and $\mathsf{Det}_{\mathbf{K}}$ = XOR-GTM$[F_K, G_{K'}]$.detect, where $\mathbf{K} = (K, K')$.

We show the security bounds of XOR-GTM$[F_K, G_{K'}]$ assuming $t \times m$ H and R (consisting of v elements) are sound and $\mathbf{H}^R$ is d-disjunct. For the proofs, due to the space limitation, we here provide a sketch for DUF. The proofs of TVUF and TSUF bounds are similar to those of Min15, and deferred to the full version as well as the full proof of DUF.

Theorem 1 *(TVUF security of XOR-GTM). For any $\mathcal{A}_1$ using q_t T-queries and q_v V-queries with time complexity τ, we have*

$$\mathbf{Adv}^{\mathsf{tvuf}}_{\mathsf{XOR\text{-}GTM}[F_K, G_{K'}]}(\mathcal{A}_1) \leq \mathbf{Adv}^{\mathsf{prf}}_{F_K}(\mathcal{A}_F) + \mathbf{Adv}^{\mathsf{tprp}}_{G_{K'}}(\mathcal{A}_G) + \frac{tq^2 + q_v}{2^n},$$

where $q = q_t + q_v$, for some $\mathcal{A}_F$ using mq queries and $\tau' = O(\tau)$ time, and $\mathcal{A}_G$ using tq queries and $\tau'' = O(\tau)$ time.

Theorem 2 *(TSUF security of XOR-GTM). For any $\mathcal{A}_2$ using q T-queries and q_v SV-queries with time complexity τ, we have*

$$\mathbf{Adv}^{\mathsf{tsuf}}_{\mathsf{XOR\text{-}GTM}[F_K, G_{K'}]}(\mathcal{A}_2) \leq \mathbf{Adv}^{\mathsf{prf}}_{F_K}(\mathcal{A}_F) + \mathbf{Adv}^{\mathsf{tprp}}_{G_{K'}}(\mathcal{A}_G) + \frac{tq^2 + tq_v}{2^n},$$

where $q = q_t + q_v$, for some $\mathcal{A}_F$ using mq queries and $\tau' = O(\tau)$ time, and $\mathcal{A}_G$ using tq queries and $\tau'' = O(\tau)$ time.

Theorem 3 *(DUF security of XOR-GTM). For any d-corrupting $\mathcal{A}_3$ using q_t T-queries and q_d D-queries with time complexity τ, we have*

$$\mathbf{Adv}^{\mathsf{duf}(d)}_{\mathsf{XOR\text{-}GTM}[F_K, G_{K'}]}(\mathcal{A}_3) \leq \mathbf{Adv}^{\mathsf{prf}}_{F_K}(\mathcal{A}_F) + \mathbf{Adv}^{\mathsf{prf}}_{G_{K'}}(\mathcal{A}_G) + \frac{vq^2 + vq_d}{2^n},$$

where $q = q_t + q_d$, for some $\mathcal{A}_F$ using $m(q + q_d)$ queries and $\tau' = O(\tau)$ time, and $\mathcal{A}_G$ using vq queries and $\tau'' = O(\tau)$ time.

These bounds show that XOR-GTM is provably secure if the number of queries is sufficiently smaller than $2^{n/2}$, which is quite common to the MAC modes of n-bit block ciphers, such as CMAC [25].

5.3   Proof Sketch of Theorem 3

We prove an information-theoretic bound for XOR-GTM$[\mathsf{R}_F, \widetilde{\mathsf{P}}_G]$ using URF R_F and TURP $\widetilde{\mathsf{P}}_G$. The derivation of a computational analogue is standard [2]. We consider a variant of DUF oracle, DUF' oracle denoted by $\mathcal{O}_{D'}$, which takes the same input as $\mathcal{O}_D$ but returns the raw decoder input. That is, when $\mathcal{O}_{D'}$

takes (M', T'), $M' = (M'[1], \ldots, M'[m])$ and $T' = (T'[1], \ldots, T'[t])$, it returns $\widehat{B} = (\widehat{B}[1], \ldots, \widehat{B}[v])$ with $\widehat{B}[i] = \mathsf{cmp}(S'[i], \widehat{S}[i])$ and

$$S'[i] = \widetilde{\mathsf{P}}_G^{i,-1}(T'[i]), \text{ for } i \in [\![t]\!], \tag{19}$$

$$S'[j] = \bigoplus_{k \in R_j} S'[k], \text{ for } j \in \{t+1, \ldots, v\}, \tag{20}$$

$$\widehat{S}[i] = \bigoplus_{j \in \mathbf{H}_i^R} \mathsf{R}_{F,j}(M'[j]). \tag{21}$$

A query to $\mathcal{O}_{D'}$ will be called a D'-query. Let $\mathcal{P}$ be the output of naïve decoder taking $\widehat{B}$. An adversary of DUF' game is said to win (forge) if $\mathcal{P} \neq \mathsf{diff}(M, M')$.

Since the naïve decoder is a public function of $\widehat{B}$, the adversary $\mathcal{A}'$ in DUF' game can always simulate the adversary $\mathcal{A}$ in the original DUF game, using the same numbers of T- and D/D'-queries as $\mathcal{A}$. Hence we have

$$\mathbf{Adv}^{\mathsf{duf}(d)}_{\mathsf{XOR\text{-}GTM}[\mathsf{R}_F, \widetilde{\mathsf{P}}_G]}(\mathcal{A}) \leq \mathbf{Adv}^{\mathsf{duf}(d)}_{\mathsf{XOR\text{-}GTM}[\mathsf{R}_F, \widetilde{\mathsf{P}}_G]}(\mathcal{A}'), \tag{22}$$

where the latter term denotes the advantage under DUF' game, which we want to bound. From the invertibility of $\widetilde{\mathsf{P}}_G$, the right hand side of the above can be bounded by TSUF advantage of another scheme $\mathsf{DirectGTM}[\mathsf{R}_F, \widetilde{\mathsf{P}}_G]$ that uses $v \times m$ test matrix $\mathbf{H}' = \mathbf{H}^R$ (where the tweak space of $\widetilde{\mathsf{P}}_G$ is augmented if needed) when the adversary simulates DUF game (in its SV-queries). Therefore, we have

$$\mathbf{Adv}^{\mathsf{duf}'(d)}_{\mathsf{XOR\text{-}GTM}[\mathsf{R}_F, \widetilde{\mathsf{P}}_G]}(\mathcal{A}) \leq \mathbf{Adv}^{\mathsf{tsuf}}_{\mathsf{DirectGTM}[\mathsf{R}_F, \widetilde{\mathsf{P}}_G]}(\mathcal{A}') \tag{23}$$

for some $\mathcal{A}'$ using q_t T-queries and q_d SV-queries. Combining Eq. (22) and Theorem 2 with Eq. (23), we complete the proof.

6 Instantiations of XOR-GTM

6.1 Finding Useful Matrices

For XOR-GTM, we need a d-disjunct matrix of a small rank instead of a small number of rows. However, the rank was rarely studied in the existing constructions of disjunct matrix. Moreover, the state-of-the-art constructions tend to have a high rank. For example, we investigated the rank of matrices from CRS [20] and STD [43] used by Min15. As far as we tried, the rank was around $0.95t$ to $0.90t$ for the matrices of t rows, hence only up to 10% reduction in communication. This phenomenon is more or less expected, as these matrices are designed to have a small number rows and not to have a small rank.

In the following, we show several low-rank d-disjunct matrix constructions which can be used as $\mathbf{H}^R$ in XOR-GTM. The corresponding $\mathbf{H}$ is obtained as a basis matrix (i.e. a matrix obtained by the basis of row vectors of $\mathbf{H}^R$), and R is determined accordingly. Interestingly, all matrices are near-square, thus not the choice for the common applications of CGT. However, they achieve a smaller communication cost than any instantiation of DirectGTM.

6.2   Hadamard Matrix

We found a class of square matrices derived from Sylvester-type Hadamard matrix that has the following properties: (1) it is $m \times m$ matrix with $m = 2^s - 1$ for a positive integer s and (2) the rank is at most $s + 1$ and (3) it is 2-disjunct for any $s \geq 1$. If we use this matrix as $\mathbf{H}^R$ for XOR-GTM, it allows us to reduce the number of tags of DirectGTM with optimal 2-disjunct matrix by a factor of around 3 to 5. The details will be in the full version.

6.3   Matrix from Finite Geometry

The example of Sect. 6.2 is scalable in terms of m, however, still d is fixed to 2. In the following, we show two matrix classes that are scalable both for m and d. They are based on finite geometry. See e.g. [26] for the technical terms that will appear in the following descriptions.

Table 1. Disjunct matrice from projective plane.

s	1	2	3	4	5	6	7	8	9	10	11	12	13
Rows	7	21	73	273	1057	4161	16513	65793	262657	1049601	4196353	16781313	67117057
Rank	4	10	28	82	244	730	2188	6562	19684	59050	177148	531442	1594324
Disjunctness	2	4	8	16	32	64	128	256	512	1024	2048	4096	8192
Bound	6	15	45	153	561	2145	8385	33153	131841	525825	2100225	8394753	33566721

Let s be a positive integer. Let $\mathbf{P}^{(s)}$ be a square matrix of $m = 2^{2s} + 2^s + 1$ rows, and is defined as a point-line incidence matrix for the two-dimensional finite projective plane over $\mathrm{GF}(2^s)$. To be more concrete, each row (column) of $\mathbf{P}^{(s)}$ represents $2^{2s} + 2^s + 1$ points (lines) over the projective plane. All points and lines on the projective plane are indexed, and $\mathbf{P}^{(s)}_{i,j}$ is 1 if i-th point is on the j-th line, and 0 otherwise. It is known that the $\mathrm{GF}(2)$ rank of $\mathbf{P}^{(s)}$ is $t = 3^s + 1$ [42]. Its disjunctness is proved as follows.

Proposition 2. $\mathbf{P}^{(s)}$ is 2^s-disjunct.

Proof. $\mathbf{P}^{(s)}$ has the following properties [26]:

(A) Each column (resp. row) has uniform weight $2^s + 1$;
(B) Any two columns (resp. rows) have exactly one 1-entry in common.

We observe that by (B), any two columns of $\mathbf{P}^{(s)}$ have exactly one intersection. It follows that any column has at most 2^s intersections with the union of any other 2^s columns, and thus it cannot be contained in that union since any column has weight $2^s + 1$ by (A). This proves the proposition.   □

An example of $\mathbf{P}^{(s)}$ is shown in Example 2. We call this instantiation XOR-GTM-PPI for the use of Projective-Plane-Incidence matrix. It uses t independent rows of $\mathbf{P}^{(s)}$ as $\mathbf{H}$ and defines R accordingly so that $\mathbf{H}^R = \mathbf{P}^{(s)}$. Therefore, XOR-GTM-PPI can detect $d = 2^s = O(\sqrt{m})$ corruptions using $t = 3^s + 1 = O(\sqrt{m})$ tags. This implies a significant improvement over DirectGTM, since t grows as $t = d^{\log 3} + 1 \approx d^{1.58}$ and $t_{\min}(d, m) = O(d^2 \log m)$. Table 1 shows the profiles of the disjunct matrices obtained by the projective plane.

Example 2. $\mathbf{P}^{(1)}$ is a 7×7 matrix of rank 4 and disjunctness 2 which is described as follows (note: it depends on the field polynomial).

$$\mathbf{P}^{(1)} = \begin{pmatrix} 0 & 1 & 1 & 0 & 1 & 0 & 0 \\ 0 & 0 & 1 & 1 & 0 & 1 & 0 \\ 0 & 0 & 0 & 1 & 1 & 0 & 1 \\ 1 & 0 & 0 & 0 & 1 & 1 & 0 \\ 0 & 1 & 0 & 0 & 0 & 1 & 1 \\ 1 & 0 & 1 & 0 & 0 & 0 & 1 \\ 1 & 1 & 0 & 1 & 0 & 0 & 0 \end{pmatrix}. \tag{24}$$

The first 4 rows are linearly independent, and they span the row space of $\mathbf{P}^{(1)}$.

More from Affine Plane. We found that matrices derived from Affine plane are also useful. Whereas the space of possible (m, d, t) realized by the projective-plane matrices is sparse and thus may not fit in the real-world use cases, a class of affine-plane matrices proposed by Kamiya [27] for LDPC code (a class of linear error-correcting codes) provides a greater flexibility in the possible space of (m, d, t). The details will be in the full version.

Table 2. Numerical examples for XOR-GTM-PPI. The last column (improvement factor) shows the inverse ratio of Tag size to that of Trivial scheme.

Target: 4.4 TB HDD	Total tag size	Corrupted data	Imp. factor
Trivial scheme	17.18 GB	No limit	1
DirectGTM	14.85 GB	135 MB	1.15
XOR-GTM-PPI ($s = 15$)	229.58 MB	135 MB	74.82
Target: 1.1 TB HDD	Total tag size	Corrupted data	Imp. factor
Trivial scheme	4.29 GB	No limit	1
DirectGTM	3.71 GB	68 MB	1.15
XOR-GTM-PPI ($s = 14$)	76.52 MB	68 MB	56.06
Target: 4.3 GB memory	Total tag size	Corrupted data	Imp. factor
Trivial scheme	16.79 MB	No limit	1
DirectGTM	14.50 MB	5 MB	1.15
XOR-GTM-PPI ($s = 10$)	0.94 MB	5 MB	17.86

7   Comparison of **XOR-GTM-PPI** with **DirectGTM**

We compare the commutation cost of XOR-GTM-PPI and DirectGTM. Figure 3 shows the ratio t/m for XOR-GTM-PPI and DirectGTM, where the latter is assumed to use an ideal d-disjunct matrix achieving the lower bound of (3). Note that t/m represents the relative communication ratio from the trivial scheme using m tags, whose ratio is 1 (lower is better). Note that the plots of DirectGTM may be unachievable. We also show the conjectured lower bound (4) which was constantly 1 in the figure. The ratio of XOR-GTM-PPI quickly approaches to zero. For example, for $s = 1$ it is about 0.57 and for $s = 10$ it is about 0.056. In contrast, the communication ratio of DirectGTM is 1 up to $d = 5$ (as (4) holds for $d \leq 5$) and is more than 0.8 even if s is large.

Numerical Examples for Storage Integrity Applications. Suppose we apply XOR-GTM-PPI to detect corruptions in the storages, such as HDDs or USB memories. Here, a data item represents the contents of a sector which is 4,096 bytes. When $s = 15$, the size of a storage (HDD) amounts to about 4.4 TB, and XOR-GTM-PPI needs about 230 MB for storing the tags and can detect up to 135 MB corruptions. The trivial scheme, which computes a tag for each sector, and DirectGTM using a disjunct matrix achieving (3) need about 17.2 GB and 14.8 GB for the tags respectively. In terms of the amounts of tags, the improvement factor from the trivial scheme is 74.82 for XOR-GTM-PPI, while only 1.15 for the DirectGTM. Table 2 shows more examples.

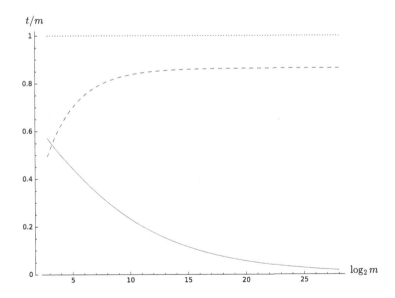

Fig. 3. Comparison of communication ratios. The red solid line: XOR-GTM-PPI. The blue dashed line: the lower bound of DirectGTM from (3). The black dotted line: the conjectured lower bound of DirectGTM from (4) (true for $d \leq 5$). (Color figure online)

Table 3. Preliminary implementation results of XOR-GTM-PPI showing cycles per input byte. Verification includes corruption detection. Environment: Ubuntu 16.04 on Intel Xeon E5-2699 (Broadwell) v4 at 2.2 GHz. Code written in C with gcc 5.4.0, using AESNI. Single PMAC runs at 5.2 cycles per byte for long inputs.

| Size of each | $s = 1$ | | $s = 2$ | | $s = 3$ | | $s = 4$ | | $s = 5$ | |
message item	tag	verf	tag	verf	tag	verf	tag	verf	tag	verf
1 KB	14.6	20.8	16.6	20.7	14.8	22.5	20.67	23.5	15.4	15.5
2 KB	14.5	18.2	14.5	18.2	10.8	17.6	15.0	15.1	16.8	16.9
4 KB	13.5	16.9	10.1	16.9	12.9	14.0	6.3	10.5	12.6	12.7
1 MB	5.2	8.5	5.2	5.2	5.2	5.2	5.2	5.2	5.2	5.2

Experimental Implementation. In a similar manner to Min15, we implemented XOR-GTM-PPI for tagging, verification and detection on a conventional server, using PMAC-AES for F and XEX-AES for G [39], for $s \in [\![5]\!]$. We have utilized the fact that the matrix $\mathbf{H}^R$ is circulant (see Example 2) for reducing memory. Since all the procedures need essentially $O(m\lceil x/128 \rceil)$ AES computations when $|M[i]| = x$ and simple linear operations, the computation cost is expected to be close to that of single PMAC-AES on entire M. In our implementations, we observed this when x is about 1 Mbyte. See Fig. 3 for our preliminary result. Improving the performance of implementation and an extension to larger s are future work.

8   Conclusions

We have shown a new approach to corruption detectable MAC. As well as previous work, our XOR-GTM is based on the theory of combinatorial group testing (CGT). However, using the linearity in the MAC computation, our scheme breaks the inherent communication limit of previous schemes using d-disjunct test matrices. Besides, the computational cost is quite small, roughly the same as taking a single MAC for the whole data items, thus essentially minimum. We formalize the security notions and prove the security of XOR-GTM, and provide several instantiations of test matrices. Numerical examples for storage application suggest significant improvement from any of previous scheme.

Acknowledgements. The authors would like to thank Hiroyasu Kubo, Nao Shibata, and Maki Shigeri for implementation, and anonymous reviewers of ESORICS 2019 and Eurocrypt 2019 for their insightful comments.

A   Discussions on Decoder Unforgeability

As well as previous work [22,33], we assume that only the message is corrupted for defining DUF, which is more restrictive than the standard attack model for

MACs. This is because when a tag is corrupted the verifier cannot decide whether both the data and tag are corrupted, or only the tag is corrupted. This is not a specific limitation of our scheme: it holds for the trivial scheme and Min15 as well. The avoidance of tag-only corruption is practical for some use cases. In a storage integrity protection system, MACs are applied to a large storage and the tags are usually stored in a small, trusted place (e.g. a secure hardware or an isolated server).

Meanwhile, it is also possible to extend our notions to capture the tag corruption (which corresponds to false positives in the test outcomes) or approximate detection. This will require us to extend the notion of disjunctness as studied in the context of CGT [10,34,35,43]. See also Sect. 3.5 of Min15.

References

1. Atallah, M.J., Frikken, K.B., Blanton, M., Cho, Y.: Private combinatorial group testing. In: AsiaCCS, pp. 312–320. ACM (2008)
2. Bellare, M., Desai, A., Jokipii, E., Rogaway, P.: A concrete security treatment of symmetric encryption. In: FOCS, pp. 394–403. IEEE Computer Society (1997)
3. Bellare, M., Goldreich, O., Goldwasser, S.: Incremental cryptography and application to virus protection. In: STOC, pp. 45–56. ACM (1995)
4. Bellare, M., Guérin, R., Rogaway, P.: XOR MACs: new methods for message authentication using finite pseudorandom functions. In: Coppersmith, D. (ed.) CRYPTO 1995. LNCS, vol. 963, pp. 15–28. Springer, Heidelberg (1995). https://doi.org/10.1007/3-540-44750-4_2
5. Bellare, M., Kilian, J., Rogaway, P.: The security of the cipher block chaining message authentication code. J. Comput. Syst. Sci. **61**(3), 362–399 (2000)
6. Black, J., Rogaway, P.: CBC MACs for arbitrary-length messages: the three-key constructions. In: Bellare, M. (ed.) CRYPTO 2000. LNCS, vol. 1880, pp. 197–215. Springer, Heidelberg (2000). https://doi.org/10.1007/3-540-44598-6_12
7. Black, J., Rogaway, P.: A block-cipher mode of operation for parallelizable message authentication. In: Knudsen, L.R. (ed.) EUROCRYPT 2002. LNCS, vol. 2332, pp. 384–397. Springer, Heidelberg (2002). https://doi.org/10.1007/3-540-46035-7_25
8. Boneh, D., Di Crescenzo, G., Ostrovsky, R., Persiano, G.: Public key encryption with keyword search. In: Cachin, C., Camenisch, J.L. (eds.) EUROCRYPT 2004. LNCS, vol. 3027, pp. 506–522. Springer, Heidelberg (2004). https://doi.org/10.1007/978-3-540-24676-3_30
9. De Bonis, A., Di Crescenzo, G.: Combinatorial group testing for corruption localizing hashing. In: Fu, B., Du, D.-Z. (eds.) COCOON 2011. LNCS, vol. 6842, pp. 579–591. Springer, Heidelberg (2011). https://doi.org/10.1007/978-3-642-22685-4_50
10. Cheraghchi, M.: Noise-resilient group testing: limitations and constructions. Discrete Appl. Math. **161**(1–2), 81–95 (2013)
11. Chor, B., Fiat, A., Naor, M.: Tracing traitors. In: Desmedt, Y.G. (ed.) CRYPTO 1994. LNCS, vol. 839, pp. 257–270. Springer, Heidelberg (1994). https://doi.org/10.1007/3-540-48658-5_25
12. Di Crescenzo, G., Arce, G.: Data forensics constructions from cryptographic hashing and coding. In: Shi, Y.Q., Kim, H.-J., Perez-Gonzalez, F. (eds.) IWDW 2011. LNCS, vol. 7128, pp. 494–509. Springer, Heidelberg (2012). https://doi.org/10.1007/978-3-642-32205-1_39

13. Crescenzo, G.D., Ge, R., Arce, G.R.: Design and analysis of DBMAC, an error localizing message authentication code. In: GLOBECOM, pp. 2224–2228. IEEE (2004)
14. Di Crescenzo, G., Jiang, S., Safavi-Naini, R.: Corruption-localizing hashing. In: Backes, M., Ning, P. (eds.) ESORICS 2009. LNCS, vol. 5789, pp. 489–504. Springer, Heidelberg (2009). https://doi.org/10.1007/978-3-642-04444-1_30
15. Crescenzo, G.D., Vakil, F.: Cryptographic hashing for virus localization. In: WORM, pp. 41–48. ACM Press (2006)
16. Dorfman, R.: The detection of defective members of large populations. Ann. Math. Stat. **14**(4), 436–440 (1943)
17. Du, D., Hwang, F.: Combinatorial Group Testing and Its Applications. Applied Mathematics. World Scientific, Singapore (2000)
18. Dýachkov, A.G., Rykov, V.V.: A survey of superimposed code theory. Probl. Control. Inf. Theory **12**(4), 229–242 (1983)
19. Emad, A., Milenkovic, O.: Poisson group testing: a probabilistic model for boolean compressed sensing. IEEE Trans. Signal Process. **63**(16), 4396–4410 (2015)
20. Eppstein, D., Goodrich, M.T., Hirschberg, D.S.: Improved combinatorial group testing algorithms for real-world problem sizes. SIAM J. Comput. **36**(5), 1360–1375 (2007)
21. Erdös, P., Frankl, P., Füredi, Z.: Families of finite sets in which no set is covered by the union of R others. Israel J. Math. **51**(1), 79–89 (1985)
22. Goodrich, M.T., Atallah, M.J., Tamassia, R.: Indexing information for data forensics. In: Ioannidis, J., Keromytis, A., Yung, M. (eds.) ACNS 2005. LNCS, vol. 3531, pp. 206–221. Springer, Heidelberg (2005). https://doi.org/10.1007/11496137_15
23. Hirose, S., Shikata, J.: Non-adaptive group-testing aggregate MAC scheme. In: Su, C., Kikuchi, H. (eds.) ISPEC 2018. LNCS, vol. 11125, pp. 357–372. Springer, Cham (2018). https://doi.org/10.1007/978-3-319-99807-7_22
24. Inan, H.A., Kairouz, P., Özgür, A.: Sparse group testing codes for low-energy massive random access. In: Allerton, pp. 658–665. IEEE (2017)
25. Iwata, T., Kurosawa, K.: OMAC: one-key CBC MAC. In: Johansson, T. (ed.) FSE 2003. LNCS, vol. 2887, pp. 129–153. Springer, Heidelberg (2003). https://doi.org/10.1007/978-3-540-39887-5_11
26. Assmus, E.F., Key, J.D.: Designs and Their Codes. Cambridge Tracts in Mathematics, vol. 103. Cambridge University Press, Cambridge (1992)
27. Kamiya, N.: High-rate quasi-cyclic low-density parity-check codes derived from finite affine planes. IEEE Trans. Inf. Theory **53**(4), 1444–1459 (2007)
28. Katz, J., Lindell, A.Y.: Aggregate message authentication codes. In: Malkin, T. (ed.) CT-RSA 2008. LNCS, vol. 4964, pp. 155–169. Springer, Heidelberg (2008). https://doi.org/10.1007/978-3-540-79263-5_10
29. Kautz, W.H., Singleton, R.C.: Nonrandom binary superimposed codes. IEEE Trans. Inf. Theory **10**(4), 363–377 (1964)
30. Liskov, M., Rivest, R.L., Wagner, D.: Tweakable block ciphers. In: Yung, M. (ed.) CRYPTO 2002. LNCS, vol. 2442, pp. 31–46. Springer, Heidelberg (2002). https://doi.org/10.1007/3-540-45708-9_3
31. Macula, A.J.: A simple construction of d-disjunct matrices with certain constant weights. Discrete Math. **162**(1–3), 311–312 (1996)
32. Macula, A.J., Popyack, L.J.: A group testing method for finding patterns in data. Discrete Appl. Math. **144**(1–2), 149–157 (2004)

33. Minematsu, K.: Efficient message authentication codes with combinatorial group testing. In: Pernul, G., Ryan, P.Y.A., Weippl, E. (eds.) ESORICS 2015. LNCS, vol. 9326, pp. 185–202. Springer, Cham (2015). https://doi.org/10.1007/978-3-319-24174-6_10

34. Ngo, H.Q., Du, D.Z.: A survey on combinatorial group testing algorithms with applications to DNA library screening. DIMACS Ser. Discret. Math. Theor. Comput. Sci. **55**, 171–182 (2000)

35. Ngo, H.Q., Porat, E., Rudra, A.: Efficiently decodable error-correcting list disjunct matrices and applications. In: Aceto, L., Henzinger, M., Sgall, J. (eds.) ICALP 2011. LNCS, vol. 6755, pp. 557–568. Springer, Heidelberg (2011). https://doi.org/10.1007/978-3-642-22006-7_47

36. Oprea, A., Reiter, M.K.: Space-efficient block storage integrity. In: NDSS. The Internet Society (2005)

37. Oprea, A., Reiter, M.K.: Integrity checking in cryptographic file systems with constant trusted storage. In: USENIX Security Symposium. USENIX Association (2007)

38. Porat, E., Rothschild, A.: Explicit nonadaptive combinatorial group testing schemes. IEEE Trans. Inf. Theory **57**(12), 7982–7989 (2011)

39. Rogaway, P.: Efficient instantiations of tweakable blockciphers and refinements to modes OCB and PMAC. In: Lee, P.J. (ed.) ASIACRYPT 2004. LNCS, vol. 3329, pp. 16–31. Springer, Heidelberg (2004). https://doi.org/10.1007/978-3-540-30539-2_2

40. Rudra, A.: CSE 709: compressed sensing and group testing, Part I (fall 2011 seminar) (2011)

41. Shangguan, C., Ge, G.: New bounds on the number of tests for disjunct matrices. IEEE Trans. Inf. Theory **62**(12), 7518–7521 (2016)

42. Smith, K.J.C.: Majority Decodable Codes Derived from Finite Geometries. Institute of Statistics Mimeo Series 561 (1967)

43. Thierry-Mieg, N.: A new pooling strategy for high-throughput screening: the shifted transversal design. BMC Bioinform. **7**, 28 (2006)

44. Ubaru, S., Mazumdar, A.: Multilabel classification with group testing and codes. In: ICML. Proceedings of Machine Learning Research, vol. 70, pp. 3492–3501. PMLR (2017)

45. Zaverucha, G.M., Stinson, D.R.: Group testing and batch verification. In: Kurosawa, K. (ed.) ICITS 2009. LNCS, vol. 5973, pp. 140–157. Springer, Heidelberg (2010). https://doi.org/10.1007/978-3-642-14496-7_12

Useful Tools

Finding Flaws from Password Authentication Code in Android Apps

Siqi Ma[1]([✉]), Elisa Bertino[2], Surya Nepal[1], Juanru Li[3], Diethelm Ostry[1], Robert H. Deng[4], and Sanjay Jha[5]

[1] CSIRO, Sydney, Australia
{siqi.ma,surya.nepal,diet.ostry}@csiro.au
[2] Purdue University, West Lafayette, USA
bertino@purdue.edu
[3] Shanghai Jiao Tong University, Shanghai, China
jarod@sjtu.edu.cn
[4] Singapore Management University, Singapore, Singapore
robertdeng@smu.edu.sg
[5] University of New South Wales, Sydney, Kensington, Australia
sanjay.jha@unsw.edu.au

Abstract. Password authentication is widely used to validate users' identities because it is convenient to use, easy for users to remember, and simple to implement. The password authentication protocol transmits passwords in plaintext, which makes the authentication vulnerable to eavesdropping and replay attacks, and several protocols have been proposed to protect against this. However, we find that secure password authentication protocols are often implemented incorrectly in Android applications (apps). To detect the implementation flaws in password authentication code, we propose GLACIATE, a fully automated tool combining machine learning and program analysis. Instead of creating detection templates/rules manually, GLACIATE automatically and accurately learns the common authentication flaws from a relatively small training dataset, and then identifies whether the authentication flaws exist in other apps. We collected 16,387 apps from Google Play for evaluation. GLACIATE successfully identified 4,105 of these with incorrect password authentication implementations. Examining these results, we observed that a significant proportion of them had multiple flaws in their authentication code. We further compared GLACIATE with the state-of-the-art techniques to assess its detection accuracy.

Keywords: Password authentication protocol ·
Mobile application security · Authentication protocol flaws ·
Vulnerability detection · Automated program analysis

1 Introduction

Although a variety of authentication protocols are proposed, most Android applications (apps for short) with online services are still using password to authenticate user's identity because it is simple and inexpensive to create, use and

© Springer Nature Switzerland AG 2019
K. Sako et al. (Eds.): ESORICS 2019, LNCS 11735, pp. 619–637, 2019.
https://doi.org/10.1007/978-3-030-29959-0_30

revoke [13]. To validate the identity in the password authentication protocol [18] (named as BPAP in this paper), a user sends a combination of username and password in plaintext to a server through a client app, and the server replies with an authentication-acknowledgement if the received password is valid.

While using BPAP over an insecure communication channel, the transmission and verification of password become vulnerable to many attacks, such as eavesdropping and replay attacks. In recent years, many cases of password leakage, even from those large corporations (e.g., Facebook and Yahoo), are reported. To regulate the use of password, some secure password authentication protocols (PAP) are proposed to help developers validate users' credential: (1) BPAP over Secure Socket Layer/Transport Layer Security (SSL/TLS) [4], which validates the identities of the client and the server by checking their certificates and hostname to set up a secure channel between them [12], and then the client sends the combination of username and password over the secure channel; and (2) nonce-based PAP [30], which utilizes the user's password as a secret key to compute a cryptographic function on a nonce value.

Unfortunately, we found that app developers tend to implement those secure password authentication protocols incorrectly even though the requirements for a secure password authentication are well-defined. A secure protocol with incorrect implementation makes the authentication process become vulnerable to attack. Suppose for example that in an app, a timestamp (Hour/Minute/Second) is generated for use in a password hash. An attacker could then launch replay attacks by using the hashed password at the same time every day.

To detect implementation flaws of PAP in Android apps, several approaches are proposed: MalloDroid [10] detects SSL implementation errors by checking network API calls and Internet permissions. SMV-Hunter [25] detects SSL vulnerabilities by launching MITM attacks, using generated inputs to simulate interactions between users and servers. Chen et al. [5] proposed an approach that targets the host head of HTTP implementations and launched a new attack "Host of Troubles" on those HTTP implementations, and analyzed their behaviour in handling the host headers. However, these approaches are highly implementation dependant (i.e., they rely on specific APIs and inputs that can only recognize certain protocols). To the best of our knowledge, there exist no approach that can analyze password authentication protocols in a more general scope (e.g., BPAP over SSL/TLS and nonce-based PAP). Moreover, most of the detected flaws are summarized in a manual and ad-hoc way, and thus the detection processes are neither automated nor general.

To address the limitations of previous approaches, i.e., implementation dependant and high manual-effort, we propose a novel approach to extend state-of-the-art insecure password authentication implementation detection. Our approach first uses a machine learning algorithm, agglomerative hierarchical clustering, to summarize detection rules in a fully automated way, and then utilizes a fine-grained program analysis to detect flaws in Android apps according to the generated rules. We implemented GLACIATE[1], an automated analysis tool

---

[1] GLACIATE: proGram anaLysis And maChIne leArning To dEtect.

to support end-to-end automatic detection of insecure password authentication implementations. Given only a small amount of training data, GLACIATE creates detection rules automatically. It generates enriched call graphs for the apps and groups similar enriched call graphs into different clusters, and mines the patterns of flaws in each cluster to obtain templates of insecure implementation. GLACIATE then uses a forward and backward program slicing to locate the code part of password authentication in an Android app, and compares it with the obtained templates to check whether the implementation is insecure.

To assess the effectiveness of GLACIATE, we compared GLACIATE with two state-of-the-art tools, MalloDroid [10] and SMV-Hunter [25]. We found that GLACIATE successfully identified 686 authentication flaws that are related to SSL/TLS, achieving precision, recall, and F1 metrics of 91.3%, 93.5%, and 92.4%, respectively. In the mean time, MalloDroid and SMV-Hunter only detected 201 and 572 flawed apps, respectively. Additionally, we downloaded 16,387 apps from Google Play and utilized GLACIATE for a large scale analysis. GLACIATE identified 5,667 apps that implemented password authentication protocols, and found that only 28% of them were implemented securely. Among the vulnerable apps detected, 65% suffered from authentication flaws related to SSL/TLS. While analyzing the transmitted passwords, 20% of them transmit passwords with insecure hash, or even in plaintext. Moreover, 15 apps violate all the requirements of establishing PAP.

Contributions: Overall, our contributions are as follows:

- We proposed a novel end-to-end approach to identify authentication flaws from the implementation code of secure password authentication protocols. By analyzing the authentication code of client apps, our approach locates all the authentication flaws accurately.
- We designed a fully automated detection tool, GLACIATE. With only limited training data, it uses both intra- and inter-procedural analyses to construct enriched call graphs which represent the call relationships and data dependencies in an app. GLACIATE then applies a clustering algorithm to construct rule templates automatically. GLACIATE subsequently uses program analysis to match an input app with those rule templates and so identify authentication flaws.
- We compared GLACIATE and state-of-the-art tools to assess its detection effectiveness. We also applied GLACIATE on a large dataset of Android apps to analyze the implementation code of secure password authentication protocols.

Organization: The rest of this paper is organized as follows. Section 2 provides background information on authentication protocols used in Android apps and their correct implementation. In Sect. 3, we give an overview of GLACIATE design and each component of GLACIATE in details. In Sect. 4, we evaluate the detection effectiveness of GLACIATE against our dataset and compare it with the accuracy of MalloDroid and SMV-Hunter. We discuss related work in Sect. 5 and Sect. 6 concludes the paper and outlines future work.

2   Common Violations of Password Authentication Protocols

In this section, we give an overview of the most commonly used secure password authentication protocols (SPAP) in Android. In Sect. 2.1, we describe security properties to establish secure password authentication protocols. and then we list four types of violations that are commonly existed in the password authentication implementation and describe how they can be exploited by attackers in Sect. 2.2.

2.1   Secure Password Authentication Protocol

The basic password authentication protocol (BPAP) is intended for users requiring authentication by a local computer or a remote server over a closed network, because BPAP is very simple, and only one message from the client to the server is required, without the need for any cryptographic operations. To establish a secure password authentication protocol (SPAP) over an opened network, the following authentication protocols are commonly used.

BPAP over SSL/TLS. A common mitigation of the BPAP vulnerabilities is using BPAP over SSL/TLS, where SSL/TLS is executed first to establish a secure communication channel between the client and the server and then the username and password are sent over the secure channel.

In SSL/TLS, the server is configured with a pair of public and private keys. The public key is certified by a Certification Authority (CA) which issues a public key certificate to the server. There are over 100 trusted CAs[2] to support Android apps. During the execution of the SSL/TLS protocol, it is crucial that the client correctly performs a number of verifications on the public key certificate received from the server. The verification steps are described as follows.

Step 1: Certificate Validation. The client verifies the server's certificate by performing three different checks [1,10]: (1) whether the certificate is signed by a trusted CA; (2) whether the certificate is self-signed; and (3) whether the certificate has expired.

Step 2: Hostname Verification. The client checks whether the hostname in the subjectAltname field of the certificate matches the host portion of the server's URL in order to make sure that the certificate indeed belongs to the server that the client is communicating with.

Nonce-Based Password Authentication Protocols. Another approach to counter password eavesdropping and replay attacks is the use of nonce-based password authentication protocols [14]. A nonce is a number used only once in the execution of a protocol. Depending on whether the nonce is a random number or a timestamp, nonce-based protocols can be classified into either challenge-response or timestamp-based password authentication protocols. In the former, the server sends a random number as a challenge to the client, and the client uses

---

[2] https://developer.android.com/training/articles/security-ssl.

the user's password as a secret key to compute a cryptographic function on the nonce (i.e., either by encryption of the nonce or a keyed hash of the nonce), and sends the result to the server. In the latter, the client uses the user's password as a secret key to compute a cryptographic function on a timestamp and sends the result to the server. Due to the use of a nonce, both protocols prevent replay attacks in the sense that any replayed protocol message can be detected as such by the server.

2.2 Authentication Flaws

A password authentication protocol is designed to meet specified security objectives, but its security can be undermined if the implementation is incorrect. We examine the authentication code in real-world apps and compare the implementations with the authentication primitives provided by the developer's guides[3]. Three types of authentication flaws listed below are discovered in Android apps.

Flaw 1: Insecure Password Transmission. Passwords are required to be encrypted and hashed by the client app before transmission. An app without encrypting passwords makes the authentication protocol become vulnerable to eavesdropping and replay attacks. Consider the situation of transmitting an encrypted password without being hashed, the password is easily to be leaked at the server-side.

Flaw 2: Insecure Server Connection. To establish a secure channel between apps and their servers, each app should follow two verification steps mentioned in Sect. 2.1 to validate a server. However, we observe that some apps incorrectly implement these two steps by simply accepting either all certificates or all hostnames.

Accepting all certificates represents that invalid certificates, including certificates signed by untrusted CAs, self-signed certificates, or expired certificates, are also acceptable. It makes an app become vulnerable to several attacks, such as MITM attacks, phishing attacks, and impersonation attacks. An attacker can use a forged certificate to connect with the app to steal users' usernames and passwords.

Only checking the certificate from a server is not enough. An app should also check if the hostname in the certificate matches that in the server's URL. A mismatch in hostname indicates that the server is using someone else's (probably valid) certificate in the SSL/TLS handshake. Any app with this flaw is potentially vulnerable to be connected to a malicious counterfeit server.

Flaw 3: Repeatable Timestamp. Timestamps must be used with great caution in any authentication protocol. For the timestamp-based password authentication protocol, a timestamp in the format of Minute/Second results in the protocol message being replayed every hour at the same minute and second without being detectable by the server. A prudent practice is to have the timestamp in the format of Year/Month/Day/Hour/Minute/Second. This ensures the

---

[3] Android Developers: https://developer.android.com/.

uniqueness of the timestamp and hence the protocol message in any foreseeable future.

Another potential authentication flaw is use of a repeatable challenge in the challenge-response password authentication protocol. However, without access to the source code of the authentication server, we are not aware of any efficient techniques to determine the randomness of the challenge generated by the server. Hence, we leave the analysis of this implementation flaw in Android apps as part of our future work.

3   GLACIATE

In this section, we describe how GLACIATE detects authentication flaws automatically (i.e. without manual predefined rules). Figure 1 illustrates the workflow of GLACIATE, which contains two phases, *Rules Creation* and *Flaws Detection*. We provide details of each phase below.

3.1   Rules Creation

The rules creation phase generates *rule templates* by processing labeled apps in three steps - flow sequence construction, learning cluster generation, and detection rules mining.

Flow Sequence Construction. GLACIATE extracts *enriched call graphs* by analyzing the Jimple code of each app and traverses each enriched call graph to construct *flow sequences*. Details to construct flow sequences are listed below.

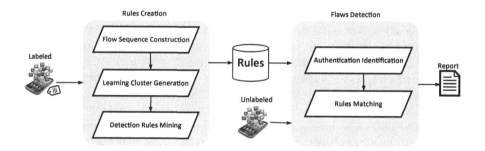

Fig. 1. Workflow of GLACIATE

Enriched Call Graphs Generation. GLACIATE applies Soot [27] to translate low-level Android bytecode into its intermediate representation (IR) (i.e., Jimple code in this paper) and generates enriched call graphs. Each node in an enriched call graph represents either a local function or an external method[4],

---

[4] A local method is a method designed by developers, and an external method is a system or library call.

which can be represented by a 4-tuple: (*ClassName*, *ReturnType*, *MethodName*, *ParameterTypes[]*). An edge connecting two nodes has three types: *Call Edge*, *Control Flow Edge* and *Data flow Edge* that represent a method invocation, flow of control and flow of data, respectively. The enriched call graph is generated in the following steps:

1. GLACIATE first performs an intra-procedural analysis [3] to extract method calls in each method and control flow relationships among those calls. At the end of this process, for every method, we have a graph that captures the control flow relationships among method calls made in the method.
2. Next, for each graph constructed in Step 1, GLACIATE examines the declared arguments and variables to extract data dependencies. According to each data dependency, a data flow edge is created between two nodes, and the data flow edge is labeled with the corresponding argument/variable through which the data dependency occurs.
3. Finally, we combine the graphs extracted in Steps 1 and 2, across all methods by adding edges corresponding to method invocations.

Each enriched call graph may have redundant methods. GLACIATE performs *local distortions* [21] to alter the graph topology (i.e., remove redundant methods), without changing the code's functionality. To remove redundant functions, GLACIATE first splits an enriched call graph into smaller pieces based on the local method <init>. It then removes the <init> method which has only one connected local method.

Flow Sequence Conversion. A flow sequence consists of a sequence of *vectors*, each of which has four elements $(S_{from}, S_{to}, V_{in}, V_{out})$, indicating that method S_{from} is the caller of method S_{to}, values V_{in} are input parameters of method S_{to}, and values V_{out} are returned parameters of method S_{to}. Note that V_{in} and V_{out} can be null to specify a method without any input parameters or return values.

Given an enriched call graph, GLACIATE extracts the corresponding flow sequences in three steps:

1. Following call edges, GLACIATE collects method invocations from the enriched call graph and constructs pairs in the form of (S_{from}, S_{to}).
2. Following data flow edges, GLACIATE inserts input values V_{in} and returned values V_{out} of each callee into the corresponding pair to construct a vector $(S_{from}, S_{to}, V_{in}, V_{out})$.
3. Following control flow edges, GLACIATE extracts the sequence of vectors. Note that we generate a flow sequence for each condition while processing the decision making statements (e.g., if-else, switch, break).

Learning Cluster Generation. GLACIATE computes the similarity between each enriched call graph and the other enriched call graphs, and groups the similar enriched call graphs to produce *learning clusters*. Details are shown as below.

Similarity Computation. Based on the app labels, GLACIATE first classifies enriched call graphs into five groups (Secure Group, Group 1, Group 2, Group 3, and Group 4), which correspond to secure authentication, authentication with flaw 1, authentication with flaw 2, authentication with flaw 3, and authentication with flaw 4, respectively.

Within each group, GLACIATE compares enriched call graphs mutually, and computes similarity scores by applying pairwise comparison [2]. Two enriched call graphs are deemed to be similar only if their flow sequences are similar. To check for this similarity, GLACIATE proceeds in the following steps:

1. GLACIATE constructs a pairwise comparison matrix to find the highest similarity score between two enriched call graphs. The flow sequences FS of an enriched call graph ECG_i are listed on top row of the pairwise comparison matrix, and the flow sequences FS' of another enriched call graph ECG_j are listed on the left hand column of the pairwise comparison matrix.
2. GLACIATE compares flow sequences of two enriched call graphs by extracting the longest common substring (LCS) [23] and fills the corresponding blank matrix cell with the LCS length L of two flow sequences.
3. From each column, GLACIATE extracts the cell with the highest value L^{max}. The column and row of each cell should be unique.
   If two cells from the same row are picked, GLACIATE then selects the next highest value L^{next} in each column and computes $L^{max} + L^{next}$ interlaced. GLACIATE chooses the pair (L^{max}, L^{next}) with the highest sum value.
4. Finally, GLACIATE computes the similarity score as $S_{Sim}(ECG_i, ECG_j) = \sum L^{max}$.

Group Clustering. Given the similarity scores, GLACIATE performs *agglomerative hierarchical clustering* [15], which works by measuring pairwise distances between data points and grouping the data points one by one on the basis of selecting nearest neighbours. GLACIATE uses the $ECGs$ as a set of data points and then applies the following steps to cluster them. We use the reciprocal of the similarity score as the distance between two $ECGs$.

1. Given the ECGs, GLACIATE first labels each ECG as a single cluster $C(ECG)$.
2. For two enriched call graphs ECG_1 and ECG_2, GLACIATE uses the reciprocal of the similarity score to denote the distance between them as $dist(1, 2)$.
3. Next, GLACIATE finds the closest pair of clusters $C(ECG)_m$ and $C(ECG)_n$ from those single clusters, according to $dist(m, n) = dist_{min}(i, j)$, where the minimum is over all pairs of clusters in the current clustering.
4. GLACIATE merges clusters $C(ECG)_m$ and $C(ECG)_n$ to form a new cluster, and repeats from Step 2 until all the data points are merged into a single cluster.
5. GLACIATE finally picks a distance threshold T_{dist} to cut the single cluster into several different clusters, each of which is a learning cluster, used to generate rule templates.

Table 1. Indicator instructions

Secure protocols	Instruction #	Indicator instructions
BPAP	1	java.net.PasswordAuthentication char[] getPassword
	2	java.net.Authenticator java.net.PasswordAuthentication requestPasswordAuthentication
SSL	3	javax.net.ssl.SSLSocketFactory java.net.Socket createSocket
	4	javax.net.ssl.SSLContext javax.net.ssl.SSLConext getInstance
	5	javax.net.ssl.SSLSession java.security.cert.Certificate[] getLocalCertificates
	6	javax.net.ssl.TrustManagerFactory javax.net.ssl.TrustManagerFactory getInstance
	7	java.Security.cert.X509Certificate void verify
	8	java.security.cert.X509Certificate: void checkValidity
	9	javax.net.ssl.HostnameVerifier boolean verify
Timestamp	10	java.lang.System long currentTimeMillis

3.2   Detection Rules Mining

GLACIATE learns a *rule template* from each learning cluster. A rule template consists of a set of *indicator instructions*, which specifies methods that are invoked by all enriched call graphs, and a *rule sequence*, which specifies a subsequence of vectors that is executed by all enriched call graphs.

To create a rule template from a learning cluster, GLACIATE executes an iterative pattern mining which captures higher-order features from flow sequences. A vector in a flow sequence, corresponding to a method invocation and a data flow, can be treated as a feature. We apply an algorithm to mine *closed unique iterative patterns* [22], which can capture all frequent iterative patterns without any loss of information. In each learning cluster, GLACIATE compares enriched call graphs and proceeds in the following steps:

1. GLACIATE observes the frequent vectors appeared in all enriched call graphs and creates a set of indicator instructions. We manually selected nine indicator instructions from the document provided by Android[5], which are listed in Table 1.

---

[5] Android Doc: https://developer.android.com/training/articles/security-ssl#java.

2. Starting from a frequent vector, GLACIATE creates a rule sequence. GLACIATE searches for the following vector that appears in every enriched call graph, and if found, includes it in the rule sequence. The rule sequence is created successfully only if its length is longer than a threshold min_{rule}. Step (2) is executed recursively until the rule sequence is closed (i.e., does not grow).
3. For each rule sequence, GLACIATE finally replaces all concrete identifier values (i.e., variables) with placeholders.

3.3 Flaws Detection

GLACIATE detects authentication flaws by selecting the most suitable template in two steps as follows. These two steps are iterated until no further vulnerable code segments are detected.

Authentication Identification. To detect whether there is any implemented password authentication protocols, GLACIATE checks for matches with the sets of indicator instructions. It compares flow sequences with each set of indicator instructions and computes how many indicator instructions in the set match. However, "noise" or unrelated vectors are present among the indicator instructions. The "noise" can correspond to unrelated method invocations, such as toString(), <init>, etc. In view of this, we decide that a flow sequence matches a set of indicator instructions if at least 80% of the indicator instructions are matched.

Rules Matching. There are likely to be multiple rule templates which match an enriched call graph. Instead of analyzing all the flow sequences of an enriched call graph, GLACIATE applies program slicing [28] to compare flow sequences with the corresponding matched rule templates one by one and in the following three steps.

1. GLACIATE first identifies where the indicator instructions are located.
2. Beginning with each indicator instruction, GLACIATE compares the vectors in the flow sequence FS with the vectors in the rule sequence RS by performing forward program slicing. If sequences in FS can be matched with sequences in RS, this enriched call graph will be labeled the same as RS, that is, secure, flaw 1, flaw 2, flaw 3, or flaw 4. Noting that FS may include some redundant vectors (i.e., redundant method invocations), FS and RS are matched if RS is a subsequence of FS.
3. GLACIATE proceeds to the next detection template which matched, and executes Step (2) until all matched rule templates have been analyzed.

4 Evaluation

In this section, we report the results of two experiments. The first experiment assesses the performance of GLACIATE and compares it with MalloDroid [10] and

`SMV-Hunter` [25], state-of-the-art tools for identifying flaws in the implementation of SSL/TLS validation in Android apps. `MalloDroid` is a semi-automated detection tool, which requires manually-defined templates. `SMV-Hunter` is an automatic detection tool that requires the manually generated inputs are accurate enough to trigger vulnerabilities accurately. Differently, `GLACIATE` is designed to detect violations in authentication code automatically, and as far as we are aware, there are no other tools that can learn rules and detect authentication flaws in this way. The second experiment demonstrates how `GLACIATE` automatically analyze a large collection of Android apps to gain further insights on the prevalence of authentication implementation flaws in these apps.

4.1 Assessment of `GLACIATE`

Dataset. We randomly collected 1,200 free apps from Google Play. In order to ensure that our dataset has a wide coverage and does not have a bias towards any particular type of app, we included apps from six categories: *Communication, Dating, Finance, Health & Fitness, Shopping,* and *Social Networking,* and 200 apps from each category.

Due to the lack of an open source labeled dataset of apps with identified authentication flaws, we created our own. As most implementations of password authentication protocols follow the same structure, we believed that the structures are generalizable enough for our purpose.

For creating this ground-truth dataset, we asked a team of annotators (1 PhD student and 2 postdoctoral research fellows), all with more than 7 years of programming experience in Java, to check whether implementations of password authentication protocols in apps followed the rules that we created. We first required team members to label apps independently. Then all members went through the labels together and discussed any apps that were labeled differently. The team had to come to an agreement before an app could be included in the dataset. To evaluate whether the agreement was good enough, we computed the Fleiss's Kappa score [11]. The kappa score of the agreement is 0.901, which means there was almost perfect agreement. Ultimately this procedure found a total of 1,205 implementations of password authentication protocols in 742 Android apps (since some apps implement multiple protocols), and 1,087 authentication flaws were identified in 695 apps (Flaw 1: 284, Flaw 2: 736, Flaw 3: 67).

Experiment Design. We used 10-fold cross validation [17] to evaluate the effectiveness of `GLACIATE`. Furthermore, we compare `GLACIATE` with `MalloDroid` [10] and `SMV-Hunter` [25]. While detecting authentication flaws, we set $T_{dist} = 1.3$ to ensure that enriched call graphs in each cluster would be highly similar to each other, and $min_{rule} = 2$.

To assess the performance of `GLACIATE`, we generated an evaluation matrix of the precision, recall, and F1 metrics. Precision is for measuring how accurate our tool performs, recall reflects how many vulnerabilities are actually detected, and F1 is used to balance precision and recall.

Performance. For comparison, we applied the `MalloDroid`, `SMV-Hunter` and `GLACIATE` to the entire dataset. Since `MalloDroid` and `SMV-Hunter` only detect SSL/TLS-related flaws (i.e., flaw 2 in this paper), we limited `GLACIATE` to detect flaw 2 (736 flaws in total) in this test. From the results we computed the precision, recall and F1 over the entire dataset for each tool.

Table 2. Detection result: `GLACIATE`, `MalloDroid`, and `SMV-Hunter`

Flaw	GLACIATE		MalloDroid		SMV-Hunter	
	Detected	Correct	Detected	Correct	Detected	Correct
Flaw 2	751	686	214	201	627	572
Precision	91.3%		93.9%		91.2%	
Recall	93.5%		27.3%		77.7%	
F1	92.4%		42.3%		83.9%	

Table 2 shows the assessment results. `GLACIATE` correctly detects 686 out of 736 flaws, with precision, recall, and F1 values of 91.3%, 93.5%, and 92.4%, respectively. On the other hand, `MalloDroid` can only detect 201 flaws, achieving a recall of only 27.3%. `SMV-Hunter` successfully detects 572 SSL/TLS-related flaws with precision, recall and F1 values of 91.2%, 77.7%, and 83.9%. Though `MalloDroid` has fewer false positives, as evident from the marginally higher precision (i.e., 93.9% against 91.3%), `GLACIATE` detects about 2.4 times more flaw 2 than `MalloDroid`. Compared with `SMV-Hunter`, `GLACIATE` detects 20.2% more flaws and has a 1.2% better precision. This means that `GLACIATE` generates proportionally fewer false positives than `SMV-Hunter`.

TrustManagers are responsible for managing the trust material that is used for deciding whether the received public key certificates should be accepted. Besides the vulnerable TrustManagers detected by `MalloDroid`, `GLACIATE` also finds three new types of vulnerable TrustManagers, namely BlindTrustManager, InsecureTrustManager and AllTrustingTrustManager. Apps with these vulnerable TrustManagers suffer from flaw 2.

`GLACIATE`: **Further Analysis of Performance.** In comparing the detection performance of `GLACIATE` and `MalloDroid`, we find that `MalloDroid` fails to correctly analyze apps that implement authentications across different classes, which means `MalloDroid` is unable to analyze method invocation relationships and cannot extract inter-component communications in apps. Furthermore, comparing the results for `GLACIATE` and `SMV-Hunter`, `SMV-Hunter` relies on user inputs to trigger the recognition of authentication flaws. However, it is a challenging to generate accurate inputs to trigger the procedures.

`GLACIATE` did fail to analyze some apps. Since `GLACIATE` is built on top of Soot, each app has to be decompiled using Soot. In total, Soot was unable to decompile 184 apps, failing in "Soot.PackManager". This method runs the

ThreadPoolExecutor multiple times, and the executor Runnable is unable to handle those threads separately. These fail-to-decompile apps can be reconsidered when Soot is next upgraded[6].

4.2 GLACIATE: Large Scale Analysis of Password Authentication

For this analysis, we downloaded 16,387 free apps at random from Google Play and used our ground truth to build our detection model for further analysis. We first checked whether our collected apps implemented any password authentication protocols. In total, 13,747 apps were successfully analyzed, and 5,667 (41%) of them implemented BPAP. Further analyses were performed on those 5,667 apps. Apps failed to be analyzed by GLACIATE are unable to be decompiled by Soot.

Table 3. Secure password authentication protocols in Android apps

# of apps	Secure password authentication protocols
3,353	Only BPAP over SSL/TLS
804	Only timestamp-based password authentication
385	Both BPAP over SSL/TLS and timestamp-based password authentication

Based on the detection report generated by GLACIATE (see Table 3), we find that 4,542 apps establish secure password authentication protocol by using at least one protection protocol. Among the apps with at least one protection protocol, we observe that 3,738 implemented BPAP over SSL/TLS, which indicates that SSL/TLS is the most common protection mechanism in practice. We also identify 385 apps with both protections, i.e., BPAP over SSL/TLS and timestamp-based password authentication protocols. By further analyzing those apps with multiple password authentication protocols, we find that some apps implement multiple login schemes (e.g., Facebook login, Wechat login, Tencent login), and their developers import external authentication libraries directly to implement those login schemes. The library providers offer a variety of password authentication protocols[7].

The password authentication protocol is suppose to be securely implemented. To our surprise, A large portion of apps have flaws discussed in Sect. 2 in their authentication code (shown in Table 4). Only 1,562 apps in our dataset implemented secure password authentication protocols. GLACIATE reports that passwords in 1,125 apps are not been well-protected. For these apps with Flaw 1, we

---

[6] The exception, "ERROR heros.solver.CountingThreadPoolExecutor - Worker thread execution failed: Dex file overflow", was posted in March, 2018. Soot might solve this problem in its next version.

[7] BPAP with SSL/TLS is nevertheless most used.

Table 4. Authentication flaws in Android apps

# of apps	Authentication flaws
1,125	Insecure Password Transmission (Flaw 1)
2,684	Insecure Server Connection (Flaw 2)
250	Repeatable Timestamp (Flaw 3)
1,562	No flaw

observe that some of them use MD5 hash functions with a constant salt, which is easy for attackers to find collision. However, most passwords are transmitted in plaintext over an insecure HTTP channel. As SSL/TLS is the most common mechanism used to protect BPAP, SSL/TLS-related flaw is also the most common one, i.e., flaw 2 (i.e., Insecure Server Connection). We also investigate whether apps have multiple flaws. In what follows we discuss further insights gained from this analysis.

Flaw 2: Insecure Server Connection. This is the most common implementation flaw presented in 2,684 apps; that is, nearly 47% of the apps with password authentication meet this authentication flaw. This result indicates that developers are security conscious and understand that secure communication (e.g., SSL/TLS) should be used for transmitting passwords. However, they seem to be unaware of the importance of validating certificates and hostnames of the server, and the consequences of accepting invalid certificates and mismatched servers, or they decide not to validate certificates and hostnames with the aim of improving the app's run-time performance.

Certificate Validation. In total, GLACIATE identifies 2,417 apps suffers the flaws of accepting invalid certificates. A certificate validation includes two aspects: signature validation and a certificate expiration check. The authentication code is insecure unless both checks are executed. Based on the trusted CAs provided by Android[8], we classify invalid certificates into certificates signed by invalid CAs, self-signed certificates, and expired certificates. Table 5 lists the number of apps with these types of certificate flaws. Those certificate validations are incomplete in that 1,298 apps only verify whether certificates are signed by valid CA but neglect to check whether they are self-signed or expired, and 185 apps only verify two of the necessary checks of certificate validity. Almost 35% of the apps with flaw 2 do not have any certificate validation at all.

Hostname Verification. 2,059 of apps with flaw 2 accept all hostnames. Comparing this result with the result of certificate checking, a smaller number of apps suffer from this, since more aspects are required to be checked when validating certificates, i.e., expiry date and signature.

---

[8] The list of trusted CAs can be found in https://www.digicert.com/blog/official-list-trusted-root-certificates-android/.

Table 5. Apps with incomplete certificate validation

# of apps	Certificate validations performed
1,298	Only implement one check, whether the certificates are signed by an invalid CA
54	Only implement two checks, whether the certificates are self-signed or signed by an invalid CA
131	Only implement two checks, whether the certificates are expired or signed by an invalid CA
934	None of the above (e.g., they do not implement any certificate verification)

Flaw 3: Repeatable Timestamp. Most apps with timestamp-based password authentication are securely implemented, but nevertheless 250 out of 804 apps used a repeatable timestamp.

Multiple Flaws. We also collected information about apps which were found to have multiple violations. For the apps that used both protection mechanisms, `GLACIATE` identified 37 apps suffering from two types of authentication flaws. Authentication code in 29 apps accept all certificates and generate repeatable timestamps. 8 of them implement the authentication protocol as accepting all host names and generating repeatable timestamps. Additionally, `GLACIATE` detected 15 apps that violates all the authentication requirements, that is, accepting all certificates and all hostnames, and use repeatable timestamps. These results suggest that the capability of analyzing multiple password authentication protocols in the same app is essential for a complete identification of vulnerabilities.

5   Related Work

In the following, we first discuss detection techniques that are rule-based and attack-based. We then discuss fully-automated approaches that use machine learning algorithms.

5.1   Rule-Based Techniques

Most existing techniques detect vulnerabilities by using pre-defined rules/templates [9,10,24,29]. `CRYPTOLINT` [9] detects cryptographic misuses in Android apps. According to the manually predefined cryptographic rules, `CRYPTOLINT` computes a super control flow graph for each app and uses program slicing to identify the violations. `MalloDroid` [10] is a detection tool for checking whether the SSL/TLS code in Android apps are potentially vulnerable to MITM attacks. By checking the network API calls and Internet permissions, `MalloDroid` determine whether the code has vulnerabilities, including accepting all certificates, accepting all hostnames, trusting many CAs, and using mixed-mode/no SSL. However, because it only analyzes the network API calls, `MalloDroid` is unable to identify all the potential flaws due to its inability to extract the inter-component communications. Instead of performing code analysis, `HVLearn` [24] is a black-box learning approach that infers certificate templates from the certificates with certain common names by using an automata learning algorithm. It further detects those invalid certificates that cannot be matched with certificate templates. However, this approach can only be applied to the certificates with specific common names.

Besides these static analysis techniques, some dynamic approaches have been proposed without analyzing the code [6,26]. `Spinner` [26] is a tool that uses a dynamic black-box detection approach to check certificate pinning vulnerabilities which may hide improper hostname verification and enable MITM attacks. Without requiring access to the code, `Spinner` generates traffic that includes a certificate signed by the same CA, but with a different hostname. It then checks whether the connection fails. A vulnerability is detected if the connection is established and encrypted data is transmitted. However, some unnecessary input will be generated while applying a fully automated approach.

To address the limitations of dynamic analysis, some approaches use a hybrid analysis (i.e., static and dynamic analysis) [16,25]. `SMV-Hunter` [25] simulates user interactions and launches MITM attacks to detect SSL vulnerabilities. However, its detection performance relies on how well user inputs were created, and some vulnerabilities cannot be identified since they are not triggered by the MITM attacks.

Compared to these techniques, `GLACIATE` is a fully automated tool that does not require any manual effort. Instead of summarizing detection rules manually, we use machine learning to learn those rules automatically.

5.2 Attack-Based Techniques

Instead of using any rules/templates, some approaches launch attacks to locate vulnerabilities [5,7,8,31]. `AUTHScope` [31] targets the vulnerabilities at the server side. Since it is difficult to extract the source code running on the remote servers, `AUTHScope` sends various network requests to the server and applies differential traffic analysis to identify when the server does not provide proper token verification. Instead of launching one attack, six different attack scenarios are launched by `AndroSSL` [7], which provides an environment for developers to test their apps against connection security flaws. The environment has an actual server that accepts authentication requests and static and dynamic URLs without verifying the hostnames and certificates.

5.3 Machine Learning Techniques

Manual effort involving is tedious, inefficient, and expensive. To address this drawback, machine learning is proposed to construct a fully automated detection approach.

VulDeePecker [20] and SySeVr [19] detect vulnerabilities by using deep learning, which can replace human expert effort while learning. By extracting library/API function calls, VulDeePecker generates training vectors to represent the invocations of these function calls. It then trains a BLSTM neural network model with the training vectors. To improve the detection accuracy, SySeVr collects more features, including function calls, array usage, pointer usage, and arithmetic expressions for training. Although VulDeePecker and SySeVr can detect many types of vulnerabilities without any manual effort, one important requirement for the training dataset is that each code segment may include only one vulnerability.

The above detection approaches that use machine learning algorithms have the desirable property of working automatically and we investigated their application to our problem. We extracted control flow graphs and used different machine learning algorithms (i.e., CNN, decision tree, naive Bayes, SVM, and logistic regression) to build detection models. However the detection results were found to be poor.

6 Conclusion

In this paper, we proposed a novel end-to-end approach for the automatic detection of flaws in the implementation of authentication in mobile apps. The detection tool, GLACIATE, analyzes whether the secure password authentication protocols are correctly implemented in apps. GLACIATE first uses clustering and pattern mining techniques to learn rules automatically from a small training dataset, followed by a program analysis technique which uses these rules to detect flaws. GLACIATE automates the whole process so that it only needs few manual efforts to build a small labeled dataset and achieves a better detection accuracy. We assessed the detection accuracy of GLACIATE on a dataset of 16,387 real world Android apps. GLACIATE identifies 5,667 apps with secure password authentication protocols, but only 28% of them implemented the protocols correctly. We intend to make GLACIATE available as an open source tool that can contribute to the development of secure Android apps.

Acknowledgments. This work was partially supported by the Key Program of National Natural Science Foundation of China (Grant No. U1636217), the General Program of National Natural Science Foundation of China (Grant No. 61872237), the National Key Research and Development Program of China (Grant No. 2016YFB0801200).

References

1. Alghamdi, K., Alqazzaz, A., Liu, A., Ming, H.: IoTVerif: an automated tool to verify SSL/TLS certificate validation in Android MQTT client applications. In: Proceedings of the Eighth ACM Conference on Data and Application Security and Privacy, pp. 95–102. ACM (2018)

2. Barzilai, J.: Deriving weights from pairwise comparison matrices. J. Oper. Res. Soc. **48**(12), 1226–1232 (1997)
3. Burke, M., Cytron, R.: Interprocedural dependence analysis and parallelization, vol. 21. ACM (1986)
4. Canvel, B., Hiltgen, A., Vaudenay, S., Vuagnoux, M.: Password interception in a SSL/TLS channel. In: Boneh, D. (ed.) CRYPTO 2003. LNCS, vol. 2729, pp. 583–599. Springer, Heidelberg (2003). https://doi.org/10.1007/978-3-540-45146-4_34
5. Chen, J., Jiang, J., Duan, H., Weaver, N., Wan, T., Paxon, V.: Host of troubles: multiple host ambiguities in http implementations. In: Proceedings of the 2016 ACM Conference on Computer and Communications Security (CCS), pp. 1516–1527. ACM (2016)
6. Chen, J., et al.: IoTFuzzer: discovering memory corruptions in IoT through app-based fuzzing. In: Proceedings of the 21st Annual Network and Distributed System Security Symposium (NDSS). Citeseer (2018)
7. Gagnon, F., Ferland, M.-A., Fortier, M.-A., Desloges, S., Ouellet, J., Boileau, C.: AndroSSL: a platform to test Android applications connection security. In: Garcia-Alfaro, J., Kranakis, E., Bonfante, G. (eds.) FPS 2015. LNCS, vol. 9482, pp. 294–302. Springer, Cham (2016). https://doi.org/10.1007/978-3-319-30303-1_20
8. D'Orazio, C.J., Choo, K.K.R.: A technique to circumvent SSL/TLS validations on iOS devices. J. Future Gener. Comput. Syst. **74**, 366–374 (2017)
9. Egele, M., Brumley, D., Fratantonio, Y., Kruegel, C.: An empirical study of cryptographic misuse in Android applications. In: Proceedings of the 2013 ACM Conference on Computer and Communications Security (CCS), pp. 73–84. ACM (2013)
10. Fahl, S., Harbach, M., Muders, T., Baumgärtner, L., Freisleben, B., Smith, M.: Why Eve and Mallory love Android: an analysis of Android SSL (in) security. In: Proceedings of the 2012 ACM Conference on Computer and Communications Security (CCS), pp. 50–61. ACM (2012)
11. Fleiss, J.L., Levin, B., Paik, M.C.: Statistical Methods for Rates and Proportions. Wiley, New York (2013)
12. Hubbard, J., Weimer, K., Chen, Y.: A study of SSL proxy attacks on Android and iOS mobile applications. In: Proceedings of IEEE 11th Consumer Communications and Networking Conference (CCNC), pp. 86–91. IEEE (2014)
13. Liu, J., Ma, J., Zhou, W., Xiang, Y., Huang, X.: Dissemination of authenticated tree-structured data with privacy protection and fine-grained control in outsourced databases. In: Lopez, J., Zhou, J., Soriano, M. (eds.) ESORICS 2018. LNCS, vol. 11099, pp. 167–186. Springer, Cham (2018). https://doi.org/10.1007/978-3-319-98989-1_9
14. Juels, A., Triandopoulos, N., Van Dijk, M.E., Rivest, R.: Methods and apparatus for silent alarm channels using one-time passcode authentication tokens. US Patent 9,515,989 (2016)
15. Karypis, G., Han, E.H., Kumar, V.: Chameleon: hierarchical clustering using dynamic modeling. J. Comput. **32**(8), 68–75 (1999)
16. Koch, W., Chaabane, A., Egele, M., Robertson, W., Kirda, E.: Semi-automated discovery of server-based information oversharing vulnerabilities in Android applications. In: Proceedings of the 26th ACM International Symposium on Software Testing and Analysis (ISSTA), pp. 147–157. ACM (2017)
17. Kohavi, R., et al.: A study of cross-validation and bootstrap for accuracy estimation and model selection. In: IJCAI, Montreal, Canada, vol. 14, pp. 1137–1145 (1995)
18. Lamport, L.: Password authentication with insecure communication. J. Commun. ACM **24**(11), 770–772 (1981)

19. Li, Z., et al.: SySeVr: a framework for using deep learning to detect software vulnerabilities. arXiv preprint arXiv:1807.06756 (2018)
20. Li, Z., et al.: VulDeePecker: a deep learning-based system for vulnerability detection. arXiv preprint arXiv:1801.01681 (2018)
21. Linkola, S., et al.: A feature-based call graph distance measure for program similarity analysis (2016)
22. Lo, D., Cheng, H., Han, J., Khoo, S.C., Sun, C.: Classification of software behaviors for failure detection: a discriminative pattern mining approach. In: Proceedings of the 15th ACM International Conference on Knowledge Discovery and Data Mining (KDD), pp. 557–566. ACM (2009)
23. Ma, S., Thung, F., Lo, D., Sun, C., Deng, R.H.: VuRLE: automatic vulnerability detection and repair by learning from examples. In: Foley, S.N., Gollmann, D., Snekkenes, E. (eds.) ESORICS 2017. LNCS, vol. 10493, pp. 229–246. Springer, Cham (2017). https://doi.org/10.1007/978-3-319-66399-9_13
24. Sivakorn, S., Argyros, G., Pei, K., Keromytis, A.D., Jana, S.: HVLearn: automated black-box analysis of hostname verification in SSL/TLS implementations. In: Proceedings of 2017 IEEE Symposium on Security and Privacy (SP), pp. 521–538. IEEE (2017)
25. Sounthiraraj, D., Sahs, J., Greenwood, G., Lin, Z., Khan, L.: SMV-hunter: large scale, automated detection of SSL/TLS man-in-the-middle vulnerabilities in Android apps. In: Proceedings of the 21st Annual Network and Distributed System Security Symposium (NDSS). Citeseer (2014)
26. Stone, C.M., Chothia, T., Garcia, F.D.: Spinner: semi-automatic detection of pinning without hostname verification. In: Proceedings of the 33rd ACM Annual Computer Security Applications Conference (ACSAC), pp. 176–188. ACM (2017)
27. Vallée-Rai, R. Co, P., Gagnon, E., Hendren, L., Lam, P., Sundaresan, V.: Soot: a Java bytecode optimization framework. In: CASCON First Decade High Impact Papers, pp. 214–224. IBM Corp. (2010)
28. Weiser, M.: Program slicing. In: Proceedings of the 5th International Conference on Software Engineering (ICSE), pp. 439–449. IEEE Press (1981)
29. Xiong, B., Xiang, G., Du, T., He, J.S., Ji, S.: Static taint analysis method for intent injection vulnerability in Android applications. In: Wen, S., Wu, W., Castiglione, A. (eds.) CSS 2017. LNCS, vol. 10581, pp. 16–31. Springer, Cham (2017). https://doi.org/10.1007/978-3-319-69471-9_2
30. Yang, C.C., Yang, H.W., Wang, R.C.: Cryptanalysis of security enhancement for the timestamp-based password authentication scheme using smart cards. IEEE Trans. Consum. Electron. **50**(2), 578–579 (2004)
31. Zuo, C., Zhao, Q., Lin, Z.: AUTHScope: towards automatic discovery of vulnerable authorizations in online services. In: Proceedings of the 2017 ACM Conference on Computer and Communications Security (CCS), pp. 799–813. ACM (2017)

Identifying Privilege Separation Vulnerabilities in IoT Firmware with Symbolic Execution

Yao Yao[1,2], Wei Zhou[2], Yan Jia[1,2], Lipeng Zhu[1,2], Peng Liu[3],
and Yuqing Zhang[1,2(✉)]

[1] School of Cyber Engineering, Xidian University, Shaanxi, China
[2] National Computer Network Intrusion Protection Center,
University of Chinese Academy of Sciences, Beijing, China
zhangyq@nipc.org.cn
[3] College of Information Sciences and Technology, Pennsylvania State University,
State College, PA, USA

Abstract. With the rapid proliferation of IoT devices, we have witnessed increasing security breaches targeting IoT devices. To address this, considerable attention has been drawn to the vulnerability discovery of IoT firmware. However, in contrast to the traditional firmware bugs/vulnerabilities (e.g. memory corruption), the privilege separation model in IoT firmware has not yet been systematically investigated. In this paper, we conducted an in-depth security analysis of the privilege separation model of IoT firmware and identified a previously unknown vulnerability called *privilege separation* vulnerability. By combining loading information extraction, library function recognition and symbolic execution, we developed `Gerbil`, a firmware-analysis-specific extension of the `Angr` framework for analyzing binaries to effectively identify privilege separation vulnerabilities in IoT firmware. So far, we have evaluated `Gerbil` on 106 real-world IoT firmware images (100 of which are bare-metal and RTOS-based device firmware. Gerbil have successfully detected privilege separation vulnerabilities in 69 of them. We have also verified and exploited the privilege separation vulnerabilities in several popular smart devices including Xiaomi smart gateway, Changdi smart oven and TP-Link smart WiFi plug. Our research demonstrates that an attacker can leverage the privilege separation vulnerability to launch a border spectrum of attacks such as malicious firmware replacement and denial of service.

Keywords: Internet of Things · Firmware analysis ·
Privilege separation

1 Introduction

According to latest report [6], the IoT device has eclipsed the mobile phone as the most common connected device by 2018, which means we have been living

ⓒ Springer Nature Switzerland AG 2019
K. Sako et al. (Eds.): ESORICS 2019, LNCS 11735, pp. 638–657, 2019.
https://doi.org/10.1007/978-3-030-29959-0_31

in a world surrounding by IoT devices. Through interacting with IoT cloud, mobile app, and other entities, IoT devices allow users to monitor and control their living spaces from anywhere at any time. When the user is at home, he can directly send a command to the devices to control it through his mobile app. If he is not in the same LAN with the IoT devices, he still can monitor and control the devices via the IoT cloud. The cloud will forward the command to the devices. Meanwhile, we observe that some operations are performed only when the IoT device is interacting with the IoT cloud, while some other operations are performed only when the device is physically touched (e.g., pushing a button) by a human user. Hence, whether an operation is legitimate (i.e., legal) depends on whom the IoT device is interacting with. One goal of the attacker could be maliciously "confusing" the firmware running on the device in such a way that illegal operations get performed. For example, if a user wants to rebind a smart cleaning robot to another account, the user has to physically press a button on the robot to reset it into the initial state. However, if the rebind operation could accidentally be carried out through commands sent by mobile app or cloud, this would give an opportunity for attackers to bind the device with the attacker's account without physical access.

To understand why an operation triggered by physically pushing a button could be accidentally carried out through commands sent by a mobile app or cloud, we have conducted in-depth root cause analysis and found that the main root cause is as follows. (a) We found that when an operation triggered by physically pushing a button is being performed on an IoT device, one set of functions in the firmware binaries will be executed. We denote this set as set A. (b) We found that when a command sent by a mobile app, cloud or other entities is being executed on the IoT device, other sets of functions will be executed. According to sender entity of the command, we denote the set as set B, C and so on. (c) We found that when the intersection of set A and set B or C is not empty, the attacker could be provided with the above-mentioned attacking opportunity. Since the IoT devices are interacting with various entities such as mobile apps, IoT cloud, gateway, etc., if any two sets are overlapped, it may cause potential risks. The root cause we found is essentially a *privilege separation* vulnerability.

Although researchers have made great efforts in IoT security, we found they still focus on the classic security issues in IoT research such as privacy leak [9,24], authentication bypass [14,18] and memory corruption flaws [2]. To our knowledge, few studies have been systematically conducted on privilege separation vulnerabilities involved in IoT firmware. Furthermore, state-of-the-art dynamic and static firmware analysis approaches [7,20,23,25] have limited ability to analyze the lightweight IoT firmware (i.e., RTOS-based or bare-metal firmware) in large-scale, let alone identify logic privilege separation vulnerabilities due to following challenges. To begin with, converting a lightweight firmware image into an object that can be statically or dynamically analyzed is an open problem [18]. It is not clearly known how to identify the necessary loading information, e.g., load base address architecture and segmentation information, due to the unknown executable and linkable format of the lightweight firmware, which puts a barrier to take advantage of current binary code analysis tools (e.g., IDA Pro [15] and Angr [19]). Also, existing solutions for dynamical analysis of IoT firmware are far from mature. They are usually designed only for a Linux-based operating system [23], or must be tightly coupled with real hardware environment [25]. However, a large number of real-world IoT devices run RTOSs or bare-metal systems. How to test a variety of lightweight firmware images without real devices remains challenging. Furthermore, even if symbolically executing only a path of IoT firmware, it might also get stuck with path explosion caused by the infinite loops or complex calculation functions such as AES encryption.

To systematically detect the privilege separation vulnerabilities in a variety of IoT firmware, we first collected and analyzed the popular IoT binary formats, and implemented a tool to automatically extract the loading information from IoT firmware. Since symbolically executing entire binary IoT firmware without full-system emulation is not feasible, we developed an assistant tool to slice the part of IoT firmware where most likely exist privilege separation vulnerabilities and slice this portion of code for the symbolic execution. Next, we designed and implemented a path exploration scheme on the top of symbolic execution. It can skip complex library functions via library function recognition to mitigate path explosion and is also able to restore indirect call to explore deeper paths. Finally, we combined the above approaches together as a novel dynamic analysis framework called Gerbil for detecting privilege separation vulnerabilities in large-scale IoT firmware. According to Gerbil output, we successfully identify privilege separation vulnerabilities in 60 real-world IoT firmware. Through further verification, we found the most of them can be exploited.

In summary, our contributions are as follows:

1. We performed the first in-depth analysis of the privilege separation vulnerability associated with IoT firmware to fill gaps in previous research.
2. We developed an extension of the Angr framework for IoT firmware analysis including loading information extraction, library function recognition and indirect control flow recovery.
3. We designed and implemented a path exploration scheme on the top of symbolic execution to explore more paths, mitigate the path explosion and output more meaning path constrains at same time.
4. We successfully discovered privilege separation vulnerabilities in 69 out of 106 real-world IoT firmware images and evaluated the hazards of the privilege separation vulnerability with several real smart devices.

We are releasing Gerbil as an open-source tool in Github repo[1] in the hope that it will be used for further IoT firmware analysis research.

2   Background

In this section, we first introduce the general privilege separation model involved in real-world IoT firmware. Then, we demonstrate the potential

---

[1] https://github.com/daumbrella/Gerbil.

privilege separation vulnerability behind this model. Note that to clarify the remainder of the presentation, we highlight the key terminologies in bold.

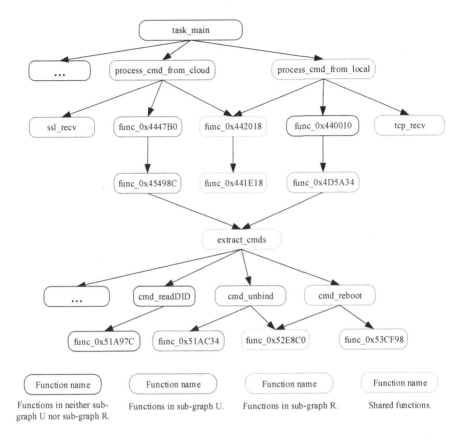

Fig. 1. A part of call graph of an IoT firmware image. (Color figure online)

2.1 Privilege Separation Model Involved in IoT Firmware

IoT devices are designed to interact with human beings via mobile app, cloud or physical access (e.g., pushing a button), to perform a variety of operations. Thus, the main logic of IoT firmware is to perform specific operations corresponding to different commands sent by its interactive entities (e.g., the mobile app, the IoT cloud, and the gateway). To be specific, after receiving messages from various interactive entities, the device deciphers and parses the messages and performs the specific tasks corresponding to the commands extracted from the messages.

Figure 1 shows the call graph of the major functions of *task_main* (generated by disassembling the firmware) which is responsible for processing all receiving network data. Some library functions have been renamed according to their original semantic. Section 3.2 details how we recognize library functions. Each node denotes a function and each edge represents the calling relationship between two functions. To finally finish the tasks corresponding to a specific command in the interactive message, a sequence of functions will be invoked. Thus, the collection of functions in the execution path from receiving a message to executing a specific command can be considered as an individual call **sub-graph** of the whole call graph in IoT firmware. For instance, as shown in Fig. 1, to perform a remote "unbind" command received from *ssl_recv* function, the sub-graph U, which is indicated in red will be invoked, while the sub-graph R, which is used to handle a local "reboot" command from *tcp_recv* function is indicated in blue. The functions shared by multiple sub-graph U and R are in green. We refer to a function shared by two or more call sub-graphs as **shared function**.

There are two kinds of key function in a call sub-graph. The **caller function** represents the highest node (i.e, start point) of a call sub-graph. For example, function *process_cmd_from_cloud* function and *process_cmd_from_local* in Fig. 1 are the caller functions of sub-graph U and R respectively. We refer to the caller function used to process commands from local interactive entities such as a mobile app and a gateway as a local caller function. The caller function used to process commands from a remote interactive entity (i.e., the IoT cloud) is a remote caller function. The caller function used to process commands corresponding to physical access is a physical caller function. The **command function** represents the nearest node to the last shared functions in a call sub-graph, which is always the first function used to perform a specific command (e.g., *cmd_reboot* and the *cmd_unbind* in sub-graph U and R in Fig. 1). Similar to caller function, generally the three most common kinds of command functions in IoT firmware are local, remote and physical.

In addition, commands sent by different interactive entities usually serve different purposes. For example, remote commands sent by the cloud are usually responsible for device management services such as unbinding the device with an owner and updating the firmware, while the device control commands (e.g., turn on/off the device) are usually sent by a mobile app locally. To this end, the developer should implement a strict **privilege separation model** to divides a firmware into parts and grant each part with different privileges to finish specific tasks through letting the IoT device perform certain operations.

2.2   Privilege Separation Vulnerability

Ideally, if an IoT firmware image strictly implements the privilege separation model, its call graph should have the following property: the two sub-graphs of any two different caller functions should not have any common nodes unless the common nodes have identical set of descendant (callee) nodes in the two sub-graphs. For instance, the shared function *func_0x442018* only calls shared function *func_0x441E18* function in sub-graph U or R. However, due to time-to-market pressure and the limited storage space of IoT devices, we found that developers usually implement some **over-privileged shared functions** which can be reached from different caller functions but can also call different command functions in real-world IoT firmware. Due to the over-privileged shared function,

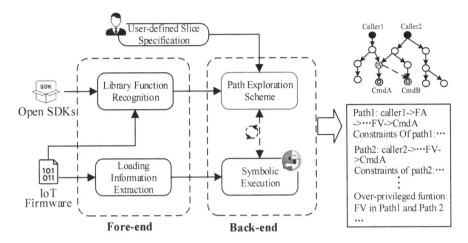

Fig. 2. Gerbil overview.

there will be an execution path from the caller function of one sub-graph to the command function which belongs to another sub-graph with different caller function. We call such an unexpected execution path as a privilege separation vulnerability.

As an example, the *extract_cmds* function in Fig. 1 can be reached from caller function *process_cmd_from_cloud* in sub-graph U, but it can also be reached from *process_cmd_from_local* in sub-graph R. Thus, *extract_cmds* function is an over-privileged shared function. Consequently, an unexpected execution path from the *process_cmd_from_local* function to the *func_unbind* function can be triggered. In this case, a local attacker has a chance to send a remote "unbind" command to the device to unbind user's device unconsciously. Other severe consequences can happen when IoT firmware opens up other unexpected execution paths. We discuss further attack effects through exploiting privilege separation vulnerability with real-world IoT firmware in Sect. 4.4.

3 Gerbil Framework Design and Implementation

In this section, we detail the design and implementation of core components of Gerbil as shown in Fig. 2. Gerbil is a firmware-analysis-specific extension of Angr [19], which is a python framework for analyzing binaries. Angr combines both static and dynamic symbolic analysis; accordingly, the fore-end modules of Gerbil are used to extract loading information and restore library function semantic of IoT firmware. In the back-end, we propose a novel path exploration scheme on top of the symbolic execution engine of Angr to mitigate the path explosion and explore more promising paths for IoT firmware. Furthermore, to effectively identify privilege separation vulnerabilities, the user-defined slice specification could help the analyst to slice the firmware which parts is most likely to contain privilege separation vulnerabilities for symbolic execution.

3.1 Loading Information Extraction

Before analyzing firmware, the analysis tools have to know the basic loading information, including architecture, base address, entry point, segmentation information, etc. For Unix-based (e.g., Linux) firmware they usually adopt the common standard executable and linkable format (ELF). Thus, their loading information can be easily extracted from the ELF header of the firmware. However, many lightweight firmware images (i.e., bare-metal and RTOS-based firmware) do not have a common fixed binary format and it is generally unknown for state-of-the-art binary analysis tools to properly initialize the loading environment of these firmware.

```
 0          1          2          3          0          1          2          3
| -+-+-+-+-+-+-+-+-+-+-+-+-+-+-+-+-+-+-+-+-+-+-+-+-+-+-+-+-+-+-+-+|
| Magic = 'MRVL'                    | SDK version                  |
| -+-+-+-+-+-+-+-+-+-+-+-+-+-+-+-+-+-+-+-+-+-+-+-+-+-+-+-+-+-+-+-+|
| Creation time                     | Number of segments           |
| -+-+-+-+-+-+-+-+-+-+-+-+-+-+-+-+-+-+-+-+-+-+-+-+-+-+-+-+-+-+-+-+|
| ELF version                       | Segment_i type=0x2           |
| -+-+-+-+-+-+-+-+-+-+-+-+-+-+-+-+-+-+-+-+-+-+-+-+-+-+-+-+-+-+-+-+|
| Segment_i Offset                  | Segment_i  Size              |
| -+-+-+-+-+-+-+-+-+-+-+-+-+-+-+-+-+-+-+-+-+-+-+-+-+-+-+-+-+-+-+-+|
| Segment_i Load_address            | Segment_i CRC32-checksum      |
| -+-+-+-+-+-+-+-+-+-+-+-+-+-+-+-+-+-+-+-+-+-+-+-+-+-+-+-+-+-+-+-+|
|                          Segment Data                          |
| -+-+-+-+-+-+-+-+-+-+-+-+-+-+-+-+-+-+-+-+-+-+-+-+-+-+-+-+-+-+-+-+|
```

Listing 1. Binary Format of Marvell MW300/302 MCU (Byte Width)

We found that the lightweight firmware running on the same series of microcontrollers (MCU) adopts a similar binary format, which can be easily found in the corresponding public MCU datasheet. In addition, identifying the MCU model of IoT firmware is also effortless, because it is common practice that developers hard-code the corresponding MCU model in the firmware. For instance, we find "MRVL" and "MW300" string in XiaoMi plug firmware, which indicates it runs on Marvell MW300 MCU. As an example, we show the binary format of the firmware which runs on Marvell MW300/302 MCU in Listing 1. As indicated by each field of the binary format, we can easily extract the corresponding loading information such as load address and segmentation information.

Therefore, we maintained an up-to-date binary format database of popular IoT MCUs[2]. Then we implemented a Python script to automatically search the strings referring to the MCU model in the IoT firmware. If its MCU model matches one MCU record in the database, the script extracts the loading information according to the corresponding binary format. Otherwise, we will try to find the binary format of this unknown MCU model and add it to our database.

In addition, some functions use absolutely-addressed memory accesses to call the function pointers stored sequentially in device memory. In most cases, such

---

[2] https://www.postscapes.com/iot-chips-modules/.

memory pointers are hard-coded in the data segment of firmware and loaded to the memory during booting. Thus, after identifying the data segment of firmware, we also copy it to the memory map used beforehand by the symbolic execution.

3.2 Library Function Recognition

Typically, to protect the intellectual property of the company, IoT manufacturers have stripped the symbols and most of debug strings. However, to reduce the time to market and to be compatible with the central IoT cloud interfaces, manufacturers usually implement the same system and communication libraries and even common peripheral functions (e.g., FreeRTOS, lwIP and WiFi interfaces) in all their firmware. Since these library functions usually take charge of the core functionality of IoT devices, restoring the original function context of libraries can greatly minimize the manual work involved in the firmware analysis, particularly, for security analysis. For example, if we can follow the data and control flow of specific encryption functions and we are able to locate the cryptographic keys or the derived key for data encryption and decryption.

To address this challenge, we implemented a function matching algorithm used by FLIRT [17] to recognize the library functions of IoT firmware. To be specific, we collected widely used IoT libraries from official GitHub repos of popular MCU manufacturers and IoT platform providers. Then we compiled them to conduct a library function comparison with the tested firmware. If a matching was found, we directly got its semantic and are able to restore it during static and dynamic analysis.

3.3 Path Exploration Scheme

The original symbolic execution engine of Angr has some drawbacks for exploring paths of IoT firmware, including overlooking indirect call and path explosion. In the following, we detail how to solve them in practice. The overview of our path exploration scheme is shown in Fig. 3.

Adding High-Level Constraints. The original path constraints generated by Angr are directly based on the byte value of registers and memory, which is obscure for analyst and inconvenient for further manual analysis. Thus, we add library function context to the symbolic execution path constraints to provide more useful and meaning information for analyst. Specifically, if current jump address is a library function address (line 4 in Fig. 3) we add library function name and parameters corresponding to the current register values of *SimState* (which is used to synchronize execution context during symbolic execution including register value, memory data, symbol variable constraints, etc.) as high-level constraints to current path constraints.

Skipping Selected Library Function. Library functions are usually irrelevant to application-specific logic and most logic vulnerabilities such as our identified privilege separation vulnerability are associated with application scenarios. Thus, to mitigate the well-known path explosion problem, Gerbil is able

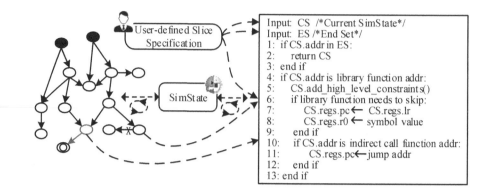

Fig. 3. Path exploration scheme (Color figure online).

to exclude the complicated library functions selected by the analyst from symbolic execution and assign a new symbol value as the return value for skipped functions. Lines 6–9 in Fig. 3 clearly demonstrate this process.

Indirect Call Restoration. Through manual analysis, we found there are two kinds of typical indirect call (i.e., callback and message queue) that cannot be identified by Angr, but have been frequently used in IoT firmware.

A callback, also known as a "call-after" function, is any executable code that is passed as an argument to other functions that are expected to call execute the argument under a certain conditions. For instance, as shown in Fig. 4a, the *local/remote_process* function passes a callback function pointer *tcp/udp_calback* to *tcp/udp_register* function to parse a network packet. When the *tcp/udp_register* function receives a network packet, it will automatically call the callback function. Thus, we consider the function which registers a callback function to have a call relationship with this callback function.

Message queues are frequently used to send data between functions, which also implies a indirect call relationship. For example, *handle_msg* function waits for the data from message queue through *recv_msg_from_queue* function and *data_process* function writes processed data to this queue as shown in Fig. 4b. Therefore, the functions which send and receive the data from the same message queue have an indirect call relationship.

To add the above indirect call paths to the original execution path, we first record the address of all functions which have an indirect call relationship with other functions. Then during symbolic execution, we check whether the current jump address of the Angr *SimState* matches these addresses as shown in line 10 in Fig. 3. If a match is found, we replace the jump address with the indirect function address in line 11. For instance, when a symbolic execution engine complete the right red circle function in Fig. 3 which has an indirect call relationship with the left one, it will not stop exploring this path but continue to execute the left red function.

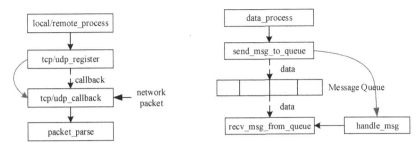

(a) Indirect Call via a Callback Function   (b) Indirect Call via a Message Queue

Fig. 4. Two typical modes of indirect call in IoT firmware

3.4 User-Defined Slice Specification

Since Gerbil is not a full system emulation, we have to let analysts set the start and end points of symbolic execution. In this work, we carry out symbolic execution on the parts of the firmware may occur privilege separation vulnerabilities. As we mentioned in Sect. 2.2, the privilege separation vulnerability is caused by over-privileged shared functions involved in the paths from caller functions to command functions. Thus, we need to set caller functions as start points and command functions as end points. However, it is difficult to recognize the call and command functions through manual analysis. We provide an assistant tool, *User-defined Slice Specification*, based on the call graph to help analysts locate the caller and command functions. To provide a more complete call graph beforehand, we first improve the control flow graph generation tool CFGFast[3] used by Angr. To be specific, we restore the indirect control flows as we did in path exploration scheme implementation. In addition, we also found the function prologues used by CFGFast to identify the start point of functions were incomplete, so we also added the missing function prologues for it.

Command Function. Although identifying all interactive commands by manual analysis is impossible, it is simple to find several specific commands. For example, we can easily find some strings such as "unbind" and "reset" which refer to the names of specific commands in the firmware, then further identify which functions use these strings. These functions are the command functions in most cases. Next, we search the nearest shared parent node of any two command functions, which is most likely to deal with other commands in the call graph. Then we can use these functions to find more command functions. For instance, as shown in Fig. 1, the *cmd_reboot* and the *cmd_unbind* functions use "unbind" and "reset" strings respectively. Their nearest common parent node is *extact_cmds* and it is also used to call other command functions like *cmd_readDID*. Therefore, we only ask the analyst to input at least two command functions and our tool is able to list most command functions in the firmware.

---

[3] https://docs.angr.io/built-in-analyses/cfg.

Caller Function. In comparison to caller functions, it is much easier to find functions which are used for receiving the network data at first, because IoT firmware usually uses common library functions such as *ssl_recv* and *tcp_recv* to receive network data. Therefore, instead of inputting all the caller function address, we only ask analyst to input the name of these library functions. After determining receiving network data functions and commands functions, we can find all the paths between them. Then we can list all the highest nodes in every path, which are the caller functions as mentioned in Sect. 2.1.

Note that in case we miss or choose the wrong caller or command functions, we also provide an interface for analysts to override the output of caller and command function sets.

3.5 Result Generation

After determining the caller and command function collection, we first input the caller functions as the start point collection and command functions as the end point collection to the symbolic execution engine. Then the symbolic execution engine explores all possible paths based on the path exploration scheme and outputs possible routes from the caller functions to command functions and corresponding path constraints. Finally, we mark all the functions (except for command functions) which can be reached from more than one caller function as over-privileged shared functions according to our definition in Sect. 2.2. For example, where the right side of Fig. 3 shows the output of Gerbil, the function FV can be passed from different caller functions in path 1 and path 2, which is an over-privileged function.

4   Evaluation

We first evaluate the performance of components of Gerbil and how their capabilities of them benefit IoT firmware analysis. Then we show the result of using Gerbil to identify privilege separation vulnerabilities with real-world IoT firmware. Finally, we elaborate three cases to show how to verify and exploit privilege separation vulnerabilities based on the Gerbil output results (i.e., identified over-privileged shared functions).

Gerbil comprises over 1,000 lines Python in total. More specifically, the loading information extraction module has 93 lines, the library function recognition module (excluding FLIRT library functions) has 288 lines, the path exploration scheme implement has 460 lines (excluding Angr SDK functions), the assistant tool used to identify caller and command function collection for used-define policy has 110 lines and the result generation module has 70 lines. We run Gerbil on a machine running GNU/Linux Ubuntu 16.04 LTS with a dual-core 3.6 GHz CPU and 16 GB memory.

4.1 Lightweight Firmware Collection

To protect intellectual property (IP), most IoT device manufacturers do not make their firmware public especially for the devices running RTOS or bare-metal systems. Thus, to test how Gerbil deals with diverse lightweight IoT firmware used in real-world, we first leveraged the *phantom* devices introduced by research [22] to download and collect a total of 173 firmware images used by different kinds of IoT devices (e.g., gateways, cameras, air conditioners, etc.) from cloud service of five popular IoT device vendors including Alibaba, JD, XiaoMi, TP-Link, and iRobot. In this paper, we focus on the ARM-based and MIPS microcontrollers which are most widely used in IoT device, thus the firmware run on other architecture like Xtensa cannot support by most analysis tools such as Angr are out of our evaluation. Note that the design of Gerbil is applicable to other architectures as well. We also leave the encrypted firmware out of our scope. Finally, we evaluated Gerbil on the rest 106 IoT firmware including 100 lightweight firmware images and 6 linux-based firmware images.

4.2 Performance Analysis of Gerbil

Loading Information Extraction. Except for six Linux-based firmware which can be automatically loaded by Angr, we successfully identified the different kinds of binary format of all tested lightweight firmware as shown in Table 1. Then, we extracted all the loading information used by symbolic execution with 100% accuracy. We have shared our collection of all binary formats of lightweight firmware at GitHub repo[4].

Table 1. Accuracy of the loading information extraction

MCU model	MW300	RTL8711B	RTL8159A	RTL8159A	HF-MC101	STM32F4
# Firmware	43	26	15	11	3	2
Accuracy rate	100%	100%	100%	100%	100%	100%

#: the number of

Library Function Recognition. The IoT library database we collected mostly from two sources. One is *MCU-related SDKs* on the official GitHub repos of popular MCU manufacturers (e.g., Marvell and STMicroelectronics) which are usually implemented in the firmware running on corresponding MCUs, including RTOS and common cryptographic functions and peripheral interfaces. The another is *platform-related* SDKs implemented by device vendors to support devices communicating with popular IoT platform such as Joylink, Alink, MIJIA, and AWS IoT. Our database contains over 20,000 library functions including 2,893 functions of platform-related SDKs and 17,538 functions in MCU-related SDKs.

---

[4] https://github.com/daumbrella/LoadLightweightFirmware.

To measure the performance of our library function recognition, we calculated the ratio of recognized library functions to total functions as shown in Table 2. The lower rate is mainly due to our insufficient database rather than technical reasons. For example, we did not gather the MCU-related SDKs running on RTL8711B, RTL8159A and STM32F4XX MCUs. In addition, the platform-related SDKs used by tested firmware running on STM32F4XX are previous versions of those we collected. The technical limitations of our library function recognition are discussed in Sect. 5.1

Table 2. The recognition ratio of library function recognition

MCU model	Platform	# Firmware	$ Function number	Recognition ratio
MW300/302	MiJia	36	2084	21.81%
	Joylink	1	1748	23.05%
	Alink	2	1707	26.36%
	AWS IoT	4	2246	26.97%
HF-MC3000	Alink	3	4957	30.57%
	Joylink	8	4191	23.59%
HF-MC101	Joylink	3	2648	78.97%
RTL8711B	Joylink	8	4169	2.72%
	Alink	18	4156	2.74%
RTL8159A	Alink	14	4330	2.76%
	MiJia	1	3358	3.25%
STM32F4XX	Alink	2	2247	1.29%

#: the number of $: the average of

Control Flow Graph Restoration. To identify caller and command functions in IoT firmware, we first improve the CFG generation tool used by Angr as we described in Sect. 3.4. Figure 5a and b show a visualized comparison between the number of call graph nodes and edges generated by Gerbil and original Angr with all tested firmware. We can clearly see that Gerbil's restoration of control graphs of most tested firmware was significantly improved compared to original Angr.

4.3   Identifying the Privilege Separation Vulnerability

Gerbil run the 106 test firmware within ten minutes in average (including only symbolic execution time). Since firmware which runs on devices fabricated by the same vendor usually adopts the same privilege separation model, the results of Gerbil's output are categorized according to device vendor as shown in Table 3. The results show that Gerbil identified 69 firmware images have one or more over-privileged shared functions (i.e, privilege separation vulnerabilities). After manual verification, we found that most privilege separation vulnerabilities can

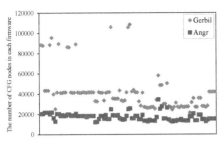

(a) Comparison of the Number of CFG Nodes Generated by Angr and Gerbil

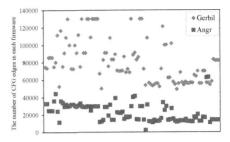

(b) Comparison of the Number of CFG Edges Generated by Angr and Gerbil

Fig. 5. Comparison of CFG restoration between Angr and Gerbil

be exploited. In general, there are two or three caller functions of one firmware corresponding to the three different interactive entities (local mobile app, remote IoT cloud and physical user access). However, the Alibaba devices only support remote commands, which means there is only one caller function in their firmware. Thus, their devices are immune to privilege separation vulnerabilities.

Table 3. Detection results of tested firmware

Detection results	XiaoMi	Alibaba	JD	TP-Link	iRobot
# firmware	37	39	20	6	4
# vulnerable firmware	37	0	14	4	4
# caller functions in each firmware	3	1	2	2 or 3	2
$ command functions in each firmware	36.5	31.3	26.2	21.3	13

#: the number of $: the average of

4.4   Impact Analysis of Privilege Separation Vulnerabilities Exploitation

In this subsection, we use three vulnerable firmware, including the TP-Link smart WiFi plug, Xiaomi Smart Gateway and JD smart oven with model Changdi CRWF321ML, to demonstrate how to exploit our identified privilege separation vulnerabilities and several attack effects.

TP-Link Smart WiFi Plug. We found one over-privileged shared function can be reached by remote and local caller functions in the firmware of the TP-Link smart WiFi plug and 52 command functions can be invoked by this over-privileged shared function. Thus, we can send remote device control commands locally. Next, we use an example of how to achieve an illegal device occupation attack by taking advantage of this over-privileged function.

According to the user manual, we know only one legitimate user is allowed to bind a TP-Link smart home device at a time. To this end, the TP-Link cloud assigns a unique device ID (i.e, *deviceId*) to one device and binds it with one user account. If other users request to bind the same device again, the cloud will refuse this request unless the device has already been unbound by the original user. In addition, we found the command function *set_device_id* is normally used by the IoT cloud to assign *deviceId* to the device. However, leveraging our identified over-privileged function, this command can also be performed locally. Therefore, a local attacker can send a *set_device_id* command to change the *deviceIdA* of a unsold device to the *deviceIdB* which has been bound with his account. When consumers buy this device, they cannot bind it to their accounts, because the deviceIdB is already bound to the attacker's account. Worse still, the device cannot be unbound, because the victim does not have the attacker's account. Thus, the attacker can illegally occupy this device forever.

Xiaomi Smart Gateway. Similar to the TP-Link smart plug, the XiaoMi smart gateway firmware has one over-privileged function shared by local and remote caller function. Furthermore, all command functions can be directly called by this function. Therefore, all remote commands can be sent by a local interactive entity. In addition to abusing the commands which used to complete simple tasks like setting the device ID in above example, we show how to distribute malicious firmware to the device through a complicated *OTA_update* command function.

Normally, when new version firmware is available in a cloud, the cloud will send the download URL to the corresponding device. Then the device downloads the firmware from the URL. Due to over-privileged shared functions, we can also trigger this command locally. However, simply invoking the *OTA_update* command function cannot successfully complete the whole process of updating firmware. The *OTA_update* function will further call a sequence of functions to download, parse and verify the firmware. If one function cannot be completely finished, the whole process will be fail.

To ensure the completion of all necessary functions, we can use Gerbil again to identify the path constraints. Through manual analysis, we know if firmware has been successfully updated, the device will reply with a finalization message. Thus, we input the command function as the start point and functions which send the finalization message as end point to the Gerbil. According to path constraints of Gerbil, we can construct a firmware contrived to meet all the constraints. For example, we found the device uses the MD5 message-digest algorithm to verify the firmware, so we can calculate the MD5 value matching our manipulated firmware.

JD Smart Oven with Model Changdi CRWF321ML. There are three over-privileged shared functions in Changdi smart oven firmware. One of them can be reached from all three caller functions and invoke most command functions. We identify 22 command functions called by this shared function including setting worktime and temperature etc. In contrast to vulnerabilities that can be successfully exploited, We show some commands cannot be abused by over-privileged function and explain the reason in this case.

Command function *unbind* and *reset* can only be invoked when user physically pushing the corresponding button on the oven in normal use. Due to the over-privileged shared function, these functions can also be called by local caller function. However, we found these two command functions are not successfully completed if we invoke them from a local or remote caller function. After manual reverse-engineering, we found the button peripheral value will be checked after these two command functions invoked. Since the value of peripheral register can only be changed through physically touching (e.g., pressing or releasing the button), the oven cannot perform these two commands sent by mobile app or cloud.

5   Discussion

In this section, we discuss the how to prevent privilege separation vulnerabilities. At the same time, we also discuss the limitations of Gerbil and how to mitigate them in our plan for future work.

5.1   Mitigation

Above all, developers should deploy a strict privilege separation model in IoT firmware. To be specific, operations carried out by the device should be clearly divided into several mutually independent sets based on interactive entity, e.g., cloud-set and local-set. Therefore, depending on which set a command belongs to, each caller function should be granted appropriate privileges. More importantly, the control flow and data flow from the cloud caller function, local caller function and physical caller function should be strictly separated. In addition, if the developer has to use a shared function to handle commands from different interactive entities, they should require an additional verification of the identity of the caller function in the shared function.

As an alternative, the manufacturer can eliminate local interface to IoT devices, as with Alibaba's devices. In other words, every command must be routed to the cloud and IoT devices only accept commands from the cloud. In this case, even if the user is at home, the commands must go through the cloud, resulting in a longer latency. However, we argue that latency is not a critical metric in the smart home scenario, and sacrificing some performance for security is worthwhile. In addition, smart devices should enhance authentication of interactive entities. In the interaction scenarios, the lack of local authentication makes the privilege separation vulnerability easier to exploit.

5.2   Limitation

First, the function recognition method used by Gerbil is based on the FLIRT algorithm. However, FLIRT cannot handle the problem of signature conflicts. Thus, if multiple functions generate the same code signature, only one of them can be selected for identification. In order to solve the conflict problem, we plan to integrate other function recognition methods such as the control flow based method [16] and function semantic based method [12].

Second, using Gerbil to perform symbolic execution requires human intervention. In this work, we have developed an assistant tool to help analyst easily slice the portion of firmware which is most likely to have privilege separation vulnerabilities for symbolic execution. However, Gerbil cannot perform symbolic execution on entire binary firmware images if analysts want to use Gerbil to identify other kinds of vulnerabilities, they have to rely on manual analysis for the slice specification. We will integrate other technology like taint track optimize the Gerbil to minimize manual work.

Third, not all privilege separation vulnerabilities can be successfully exploited and need to be further verified. Since it is hard to find the entire execution path for successfully and completely performing one command in firmware, we use command function which is the first individual function to perform a specific command as the end point for symbolic execution to identify privilege separation vulnerabilities. In most cases, if the command functions are invoked, they will automatically call all necessary program related to finishing the tasks indicated by the corresponding command. However, for some commands associated with complicated processes like updating the firmware, command function will carry out some further additional checks to the parameters, as we mentioned in Sect. 4.4. Thus, the analyst has to invoke target command functions to verify whether the corresponding commands have actually carried out or not. If not, the analyst need to do further manual analysis or reuse Gerbil to figure it out.

6   Related Work

We review related research on IoT security from two aspect: privilege management and firmware analysis.

Privilege Management. Fernandes et al. [8] revealed that over 55% of SmartApps in Samsung's store are over-privileged because the privilege management of capabilities implemented in the programming frameworks are too coarse-grained. On the other hand, many IoT platforms support trigger-action services such as IFTTT. Fernandes et al. [10] also found that the OAuth tokens for the IFTTT services are over-privileged, which can be misused by attacker to invoke API calls that are outside the capabilities of the trigger-action service itself. Some corresponding mitigation [11,13,21] also has been proposed. Our work focuses on the privilege separation model of involved in IoT firmware implementation, instead of the privilege management problem in IoT cloud services

Firmware Analysis. Several approaches are proposed for detecting the vulnerabilities in IoT firmware, including static analysis [4], dynamic analysis [1,3,25], and fuzzing [5,23]. Costin et al. [4] carried out a large-scale analysis of IoT firmware by coarse-grained comparison of files and modules. Chen et al. [1] proposed and implemented a robust software-based full system emulation, FIRMADYNE, based on kernel instrumentation. However, their approaches only work for Linux-based embedded firmware, whereas a large number of real-world IoT devices run RTOS or bare-metal systems and have limit ability to find logic vulnerabilities. Avatar [25] enables dynamic program analysis for embedded firmware by access to the physical hardware, either through a debugging interface, or by installing a custom proxy in the target environment. However, such hardware requirements are usually unrealistic for real-world devices (e.g., in the presence of locked hardware), and not suitable for testing large-scale firmware.

For combining static and dynamic analysis, and closest to our work, Firmalice [18], an IoT binary analysis framework, utilizes symbolic execution on the part of firmware binary to identify the authentication vulnerabilities. Compared to Firmalice, Gerbil greatly enhances the capabilities for symbolic execution to deal with unknown lightweight IoT firmware. For example, Gerbil can restore the library function semantic information in IoT firmware thus it can output function-level path constraints and skip complicated library functions to mitigate path exploration.

7   Conclusion

In this paper, we approached the vulnerability analysis of IoT firmware from a new angle -the privilege separation model- and identified privilege separation vulnerability caused by over-privileged shared function abuse. Then, we presented Gerbil, a firmware-analysis-specific extension of Angr to detect privilege separation vulnerabilities in IoT firmware with little manual analysis. The high-level idea is to identify over-privileged shared functions based on path constraints of symbolic execution. With the help of Gerbil, we show that privilege separation vulnerabilities widely exist in real-world IoT firmware. We also demonstrated how to verify and exploit privilege separation vulnerabilities with real-world devices. Besides, our evaluation shows that all components of the Gerbil can efficiently help IoT firmware analysis. Finally, we proposed several defensive design suggestions to prevent the generation of privilege separation vulnerabilities in the first place and our plan for Gerbil's future improvement.

Acknowledgments. We would like to thank the anonymous reviewers for their helpful feedback. Wei Zhou and Yuqing Zhang were support by National Key R&D Program China (2016YFB0800700), National Natural Science Foundation of China (No. U1836210, No. 61572460) and in part by CSC scholarship. Peng Liu was supported by NSF CNS-1505664 and NSF CNS-1814679. Note that any opinions, findings, and conclusions or recommendations expressed in this material are those of the authors and do not necessarily reflect the views of any funding agencies.

References

1. Chen, D.D., Woo, M., Brumley, D., Egele, M.: Towards automated dynamic analysis for linux-based embedded firmware. In: NDSS, pp. 1–16 (2016)
2. Chen, J., Diao, W., Zhao, Q., Zuo, C.: IoTFuzzer: discovering memory corruptions in IoT through app-based fuzzing. In: 25th Annual Network and Distributed System Security Symposium, NDSS 2018, San Diego, California, USA (2018)

3. Choi, Y.H., Park, M.W., Eom, J.H., Chung, T.M.: Dynamic binary analyzer for scanning vulnerabilities with taint analysis. Multimedia Tools Appl. **74**(7), 2301–2320 (2015)
4. Costin, A., Zaddach, J., Francillon, A., Balzarotti, D.: A large-scale analysis of the security of embedded firmwares. In: 23rd USENIX Security Symposium (USENIX Security 2014), pp. 95–110 (2014)
5. Costin, A., Zarras, A., Francillon, A.: Automated dynamic firmware analysis at scale: a case study on embedded web interfaces. In: Proceedings of the 11th ACM on Asia Conference on Computer and Communications Security, pp. 437–448. ACM (2016)
6. Ericson: The Ericsson Mobility Report (2019). https://www.ericsson.com/en/mobility-report
7. Feng, Q., Zhou, R., Xu, C., Cheng, Y., Testa, B., Yin, H.: Scalable graph-based bug search for firmware images. In: Proceedings of the 2016 ACM SIGSAC Conference on Computer and Communications Security, pp. 480–491. ACM (2016)
8. Fernandes, E., Jung, J., Prakash, A.: Security analysis of emerging smart home applications. In: 2016 IEEE symposium on security and privacy (SP), pp. 636–654. IEEE (2016)
9. Fernandes, E., Paupore, J., Rahmati, A., Simionato, D., Conti, M., Prakash, A.: FlowFence: practical data protection for emerging IoT application frameworks. In: Proceedings of Usenix Security Symposium, pp. 531–548 (2016)
10. Fernandes, E., Rahmati, A., Jung, J., Prakash, A.: Decentralized action integrity for trigger-action IoT platforms. In: Proceedings of Network and Distributed Systems Symposium (NDSS), pp. 18–21 (2018)
11. He, W., et al.: Rethinking access control and authentication for the home Internet of Things (IoT). In: 27th USENIX Security Symposium (USENIX Security 2018), pp. 255–272 (2018)
12. Jacobson, E.R., Rosenblum, N.E., Miller, B.P.: Labeling library functions in stripped binaries. In: Proceedings of the 10th ACM SIGPLAN-SIGSOFT Workshop on Program Analysis for Software Tools, pp. 1–8. ACM (2011)
13. Jia, Y.J., et al.: ContexIoT: towards providing contextual integrity to appified IoT platforms. In: NDSS (2017)
14. Jiang, Y., Xie, W., Tang, Y.: Detecting authentication-bypass flaws in a large scale of IoT embedded web servers. In: Proceedings of the 8th International Conference on Communication and Network Security, pp. 56–63. ACM (2018)
15. Pro, I.: Fast library identification and recognition technology (2019). https://www.hex-rays.com/products/ida/tech/flirt/in_depth.shtml
16. Qiu, J., Su, X., Ma, P.: Using reduced execution flow graph to identify library functions in binary code. IEEE Trans. Softw. Eng. **42**(2), 187–202 (2016)
17. Rays, H.: Fast library identification and recognition technology (2015). https://www.hex-rays.com/products/ida/tech/flirt/in_depth.shtml
18. Shoshitaishvili, Y., Wang, R., Hauser, C., Kruegel, C., Vigna, G.: Firmalice-automatic detection of authentication bypass vulnerabilities in binary firmware. In: NDSS (2015)
19. Shoshitaishvili, Y., et al.: SoK: (State of) the art of war: offensive techniques in binary analysis. In: IEEE Symposium on Security and Privacy (2016)
20. Stephens, N., et al.: Driller: augmenting fuzzing through selective symbolic execution. In: NDSS, pp. 1–16, no. 2016 in 16 (2016)
21. Tian, Y., et al.: Smartauth: user-centered authorization for the Internet of Things. In: 26th USENIX Security Symposium (USENIX Security 2017), pp. 361–378 (2017)

22. Wei, Z., et al.: Discovering and understanding the security hazards in the inter-actions between IoT devices, mobile apps, and clouds on smart home platforms. In: 28th USENIX Security Symposium (USENIX Security 2019). USENIX Association, Santa Clara (2019). https://www.usenix.org/conference/usenixsecurity19/presentation/zhou

23. Yaowen, Z., Ali, D., Heng, Y., Chengyu, S., Hongsong, Z., Limin, S.: FIRM-AFL: high-throughput greybox fuzzing of IoT firmware via augmented process emulation. In: 28th USENIX Security Symposium (USENIX Security 2019). USENIX Association, Santa Clara (2019). https://www.usenix.org/conference/usenixsecurity19/presentation/zheng

24. Yu, H., Lim, J., Kim, K., Lee, S.B.: Pinto: enabling video privacy for commodity IoT cameras. In: CCS, pp. 1089–1101. ACM (2018)

25. Zaddach, J., Bruno, L., Francillon, A., Balzarotti, D., et al.: AVATAR: a framework to support dynamic security analysis of embedded systems' firmwares. In: 21st Annual Network and Distributed System Security Symposium, NDSS, pp. 1–16 (2014)

iCAT: An Interactive Customizable Anonymization Tool

Momen Oqaily[1]($\boxtimes$), Yosr Jarraya[2]($\boxtimes$), Mengyuan Zhang[2]($\boxtimes$),
Lingyu Wang[1]($\boxtimes$), Makan Pourzandi[2]($\boxtimes$), and Mourad Debbabi[1]($\boxtimes$)

[1] Concordia Institute for Information Systems Engineering,
Concordia University, Montreal, QC, Canada
{m_oqaily,wang,debbabi}@encs.concordia.ca
[2] Ericsson Security Research, Ericsson Canada, Montreal, QC, Canada
{yosr.jarraya,mengyuan.zhang,makan.pourzandi}@ericsson.com

Abstract. Today's data owners usually resort to data anonymization tools to ease their privacy and confidentiality concerns. However, those tools are typically ready-made and inflexible, leaving a gap both between the data owner and data users' requirements, and between those requirements and a tool's anonymization capabilities. In this paper, we propose an interactive customizable anonymization tool, namely *iCAT*, to bridge the aforementioned gaps. To this end, we first define the novel concept of *anonymization space* to model all combinations of per-attribute anonymization primitives based on their levels of privacy and utility. Second, we leverage NLP and ontology modeling to provide an automated way to translate data owners and data users' textual requirements into appropriate anonymization primitives. Finally, we implement *iCAT* and evaluate its efficiency and effectiveness with both real and synthetic network data, and we assess the usability through a user-based study involving participants from industry and research laboratories. Our experiments show an effectiveness of about 96.5% for data owners and 92.6% for data users.

1 Introduction

Nowadays, network data has become a highly valuable resource for different stakeholders as its analysis can serve many use-cases. However, data owners are generally reluctant to share their data due to the risk of information disclosure and potentially staggering financial fines imposed by privacy regulations such as the European General Data Protection Regulation (GDPR) [19]. This reluctance is worsened with the increase in the number of the publicly announced data breach and misuse incidents[1,2]. To this end, data anonymization is a well-known solution for easing data owners' concerns. However, the effectiveness of sharing

---

[1] https://www.wsj.com/articles/google-exposed-user-data-feared-repercussions-of-disclosing-to-public-1539017194.

[2] https://www.techworld.com/security/uks-most-infamous-data-breaches-3604586/.

© Springer Nature Switzerland AG 2019
K. Sako et al. (Eds.): ESORICS 2019, LNCS 11735, pp. 658–680, 2019.
https://doi.org/10.1007/978-3-030-29959-0_32

anonymized data critically depends on data owners to make the right choice of anonymization approach, and to apply the approach properly to achieve the right trade-off between utility and privacy. However, this can be a difficult task since most data owners likely lack a systematic understanding of the search space (i.e., all possible anonymization approaches). To make things worse, most existing anonymization tools only provide very limited choices, and manually translating privacy/utility requirements into the tools' anonymization capabilities is usually tedious and error-prone, as demonstrated in the following.

Motivating Example. Figure 1 depicts how three data users translate their different analysis needs into utility requirements (left), while the data owner translates his/her levels of trust for those users into different privacy requirements (right). Four existing anonymization tools (top-center) are applied to the four data attributes (middle-center) to show the limitations (bottom-center).

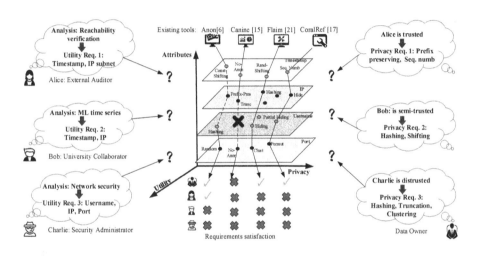

Fig. 1. The motivating example

- The existing anonymization approach assumes that each data user (e.g. Alice) can easily understand what is needed for his/her analysis (e.g., verifying network reachability) and translate that need into concrete utility requirements (e.g., the timestamps and the subnet relationship of IPs need to be preserved). This might not be the case in practice (as confirmed by our user-based experiments in Sect. 5), which could lead to many iterations between the data owner and the data user before finding the right answer.
- It is also expected that the data owner can easily understand his/her level of trust for each data user and translate it into concrete privacy requirements (e.g., Alice can only be given prefix-preserving and sequentially numbered data), and he/she is willing to understand each user's utility requirement (since the user is not involved in selecting the tool), and reconcile them with

his/her privacy requirements. However, real-world data owners are usually not so considerate and might simply go with whatever provided by some handy anonymization tools.

- As shown in the middle of Fig. 1, existing tools generally only implement a small set of anonymization primitives suitable for a subset of the data attributes. Theoretically, the data owner can resort to a collection of such tools to cover all attributes. However, practically, this could be a difficult task since most tools do not offer the needed customization, e.g., which attributes to anonymize and to what privacy/utility levels, and the selected tools may not be compatible with each other and such incompatibility can potentially result in erroneous or inconsistent results.

In this paper, we propose an *interactive customizable anonymization tool*, namely *iCAT*, to address the aforementioned challenges. Intuitively, *iCAT* is designed to cover the entire "space" shown in the middle of Fig. 1 (instead of a few points covered by each existing tool), and to help both the data owner and data users by automating their requirements translation. Specifically, we first propose the novel concept of *anonymization space*, which models all possible combinations of existing anonymization primitives (which are applicable to the given data attributes) as a lattice based on their relationships in terms of privacy and utility. Second, as an application of the anonymization space concept, the privacy and utility requirements are jointly enforced through a simple access control mechanism. Third, we develop an ontology-driven Natural Language Processing (NLP) approach to automatically translate the textual requirements from both parties into combinations of anonymization primitives inside the anonymization space. Therefore, our main contributions are threefold:

1. To the best of our knowledge, our notion of anonymization space is the first systematic model of existing anonymization primitives that characterizes their capabilities in terms of privacy and utility, as well as their relationships. This model provides data owners with clearer understanding of possible anonymization choices, and it also, for the first time, allows the data users to be actively involved in the decision process.
2. To realize the potential of anonymization space, we design and implement an automated tool, *iCAT*, by leveraging existing anonymization primitives and a popular NLP engine [16]. In contrast to most of the existing anonymization tools, *iCAT* provides more flexibility (by allowing access to the entire anonymization space) and better usability (by automating requirements translation). The interactive nature of *iCAT* also implies the potential of a new paradigm for providing data anonymization as a service.
3. We evaluate the effectiveness and efficiency of *iCAT* using both synthetic and real data, and assess its usability through a user-based study involving participants from both industry and academia. Our results demonstrate the effectiveness and efficiency of our solution.

The remainder of this paper is organized as follows. Section 2 defines our anonymization space model and describes the privacy/utility access control.

In Sect. 3, we describe the requirements translation process using NLP and ontology modeling. Section 4 details the implementation. Section 5 gives experimental results. Section 6 provides more discussions. Section 7 reviews related works and Sect. 8 concludes this paper.

2   Anonymization Space

In this section, we first define our threat model, then we review existing anonymization primitives and finally we define the *anonymization space* model and privacy/utility access control mechanism.

2.1   Threat Model

We define the parties involved in the data anonymization process and their trust relationships as the following:

- The data owner, who has useful datasets that can be used for different purposes, is interested in protecting the privacy of his/her data to avoid any data misuse. The data owner has different trust levels of the data users, which will determine the amount of information that he/she is willing to outsource.
- The data users, who have different use-cases of the data (e.g., auditing, research purposes, etc.), are interested in having the maximum data utility, in order to achieve valid results. The data users trust the data owners and are willing to share their use-cases with them.

   In scope threats: We assume that both data owner and user will follow the procedure to express their requirements, while the latter is interested in obtaining output with higher utility if the tool provides him/her such an opportunity.

   Out of scope threats: Our tool is not designed to mitigate any weakness or vulnerability of the underlying anonymization primitives (e.g., frequency analysis, data injection attacks, or data linkage attacks). Whereas, those primitives are used as a black box in our data anonymization module and can be replaced by other, better primitives when available. Moreover, we consider the failure in requirement translation by the NLP engine out of the scope.

2.2   Anonymization Primitives

There exist many data anonymization primitives in the literature even though most existing tools only support a limited number of those primitives (a detailed review of related work is provided in Sect. 7). To facilitate further discussions, Table 1 provides a list of common anonymization primitives, examples of plain data, and the corresponding anonymized data obtained using the primitives [3].

---

[3] This list is not meant to be exhaustive, and our model and methodology can be extended to include other anonymization primitives.

2.3   Lattices-Based Anonymization Space

Following our motivating example shown in Fig. 1, suppose the data owner is dissatisfied with those existing anonymization tools. Instead, he/she would like to apply the anonymization primitives given in Table 1. Obviously, he/she would find himself/herself facing a plethora of choices as follows:

Table 1. Anonymization primitives

Primitive	Plain data example	Corresponding anonymized data
Prefix-preserving	IP1:**12.8.3**.4; IP2:**12.8.3**.5	IP1:**51.22.7**.33; IP1:**51.22.7**.19
Truncation	IP1:12.8.**3.4**; IP2:12.8.**3.5**	IP1:12.8.**X.X**; IP2:12.8.**X.X**
Const. substitution	Version:2.0.1	Version: VERSION
Const. shifting	Time1: **2019**-03-31; Time2: **2019**-03-30	Time1: **2022**-03-31; Time2: **2022**-03-30
Random shifting	Time1: **2019**-03-31; Time2: **2019**-03-30	Time1: **2003**-03-31; Time2: **2015**-03-30
Sequ. numbering	Time1: 2019-03-31; Time2: 2019-03-30	Time1: T1; Time2: T2
Partial hiding	Time1: 2019-**03-31**; Time2: 2019-**03-30**	Time1: 2019-**X-X**; Time2: 2019-**X-X**
Hashing	ID:40018833	ID: H3%s2*D9
Clustering	Port1:**225**; Port2: **277**	Port1:**200**; Port2: **277**
Permutation	Port1:**225**; Port2: **277**	Port1:**277**; Port2: **225**
Randomization	Port1: **225**; Port2: **277**	Port1:**423**; Port2: **29**

- First, each data attribute may be anonymized using a different collection of the anonymization primitives (e.g., IPs may work with prefix preserving, truncation, hashing, etc., while IDs with clustering, hashing, etc., and both can be either completely hidden or plainly given with no anonymization).
- Second, different anonymization primitives applied to an attribute may yield different levels of, and sometimes incomparable, privacy and utility (e.g., for IPs, hashing provides more privacy/less utility than prefix preserving, whereas they are both incomparable to truncation or randomization).
- Finally, the data owner and data users' requirements typically involve multiple attributes, as demonstrated in Fig. 1, and sometime in a complex fashion, e.g., the data owner might say "I can only give you the data with the IPs hashed, or with the IDs clustered, but not both", while a data user asks "I know I may not get the data with the IPs truncated and the IDs hashed, but what would be my next best option?"

The above discussions clearly demonstrate a need for a systematic way to represent and organize all the possible choices of anonymization primitives that can be applied to a given dataset. For this purpose, we propose a novel concept, namely *anonymization space*, by considering each data attribute as a *dimension*, and each combination of anonymization primitives that can cover all the attributes as a *point* inside the anonymization space. Considering the fact that anonymization primitives are not always comparable in terms of privacy/utility, and inspired by the Denning's Axioms [4,20], we consider the collection of anonymization primitives applicable to each attribute to form a lattice based on their relationships in terms of privacy and utility, and the product of all those lattices (which is also a lattice by lattice theory [5]) represents the anonymization space. The following more formally defines those concepts.

Definition 1 *(**Anonymization Space**). Given* $\mathbb{A} = \langle a_1, a_2, \ldots, a_n \rangle$ *as a sequence of attributes to be anonymized, and given* $F_i = \{f_1, f_2, \ldots, f_m\}$ $(1 \leq i \leq n)$ *as the set of anonymization primitives that are applicable to* a_i, *we define*

- *the attribute lattice* $\mathcal{L}_i (1 \leq i \leq n)$ *as a lattice* $\langle F_i, \prec \rangle$ *where for any* $f_1, f_2 \in F_i$, *we have* $f_1 \prec f_2$ *iff* f_1 *provides better utility and more stringent privacy than* f_2 *when both are applied to* a_i, *and*
- *the anonymization space corresponding to* $\mathbb{A}$ *as* $\prod_{i=1}^{n} \mathcal{L}_i$.

Example 1. Figure 2A (top) shows some examples of anonymization primitives and Fig. 2B shows their applicability (using their indices) to six attributes. Figure 2C shows the six attribute lattices. Due to space limitations, we omit the anonymization space (which would have a size of 20, 736).

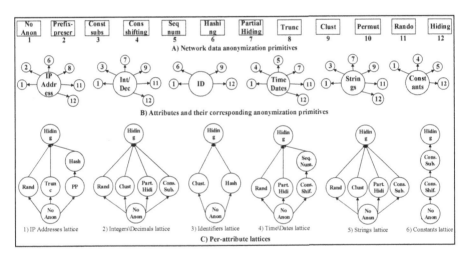

Fig. 2. *An example anonymization space* (**A**) Examples of anonymization primitives with their indices, (**B**) Examples of data attributes and their applicable anonymization primitives and (**C**) The attribute lattices.

By providing a clearer picture of the anonymization primitives and their relationships, the anonymization space concept may have many use cases. For our purpose, we show how the concept can be used to jointly enforce the privacy and utility requirements through a simple access control mechanism (inspired by the Bell–LaPadula (BLP) model [3]), while allowing the data user to be actively involved in the anonymization process. Specifically, if we consider each point (which is a collection of anonymization primitives) in the anonymization space as a privacy/utility *level*, then the data owner's privacy requirement can be mapped to such a level (this mapping will be automated in Sect. 3), and everything above this level will also satisfy the privacy requirement since by definition it will yield more privacy, namely the *privacy-up* rule. Conversely, a data user's requirement can also be mapped to a level below which any level would also satisfy the utility requirement, namely the *utility-down* rule. This is more formally stated in Definition 2.

Definition 2 *(Privacy/Utility Access Control). Given the data attributes* $\mathbb{A}$, *the corresponding anonymization space* $\mathbb{AS} = \prod_{i=1}^{n} \mathcal{L}_i$, *and the privacy requirement* $L_p \in \mathbb{AS}$ *and utility requirement* $L_u \in \mathbb{AS}$ *(specified by the data owner and data user, respectively), any* $L \in \mathbb{AS}$ *will satisfy both requirements iff* $L_p \prec L$ *(privacy up) and* $L \prec L_u$ *(utility down) are both true.*

Example 2. Figure 3 shows an example of anonymization space corresponding to the IP and ID attributes. The data owner requires **Ha** (hashing) for IPs and **NA** (no anonymization) for IDs. By the privacy-up rule, all levels inside the upper shaded area will also satisfy privacy requirements. The following discusses two data users' utility requirements.

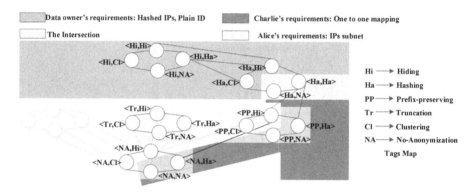

Fig. 3. An example of *anonymization space* for attributes IP and ID, and the privacy/utility access control for Alice and Charlie

1. Charlie requires to preserve the one-to-one mapping for both IPs and IDs. Following the utility-down rule, the dark gray area highlights all the levels that satisfy Charlie's utility requirements. Also, the area with crossing lines includes all levels that satisfy both the privacy and utility requirements, i.e., $\langle$**Ha, Ha**$\rangle$ and $\langle$**Ha, Na**$\rangle$.
2. Alice requires to preserve the IP subnets. The light gray area highlights all the levels that satisfy Alice's utility requirement. Since there is no intersection between the upper shaded area and the light gray area, no level can satisfy both the privacy-up and utility-down rules, which means no anonymization primitive can satisfy both the privacy and utility requirements for Alice. However, the anonymization space makes it easy to choose an alternative level that will satisfy the privacy requirement while providing the best possible utility to Alice, e.g., $\langle$**Ha, Na**$\rangle$.

3   Requirements Translation

To ease the burden on both data owners and data users, *iCAT* accepts requirements expressed in a natural language (English in our case) and translate them into anonymization primitives. In this section, we first discuss requirements translation using NLP and ontology modeling, and then explain ambiguity resolution.

Requirements Processing Using NLP. The first step in translating the data owner and data user's requirements into combinations of anonymization primitives in the anonymization space is to understand them linguistically. For this purpose, *iCAT* leverages the Stanford Parser CoreNLP [16], which provides a set of natural language processing tools. Initially, the CoreNLP parser separates the English requirements into different sentences. Since CoreNLP can mark up the structure of sentences in terms of phrases and syntactic dependencies and indicate which noun phrases refer to the same entities, we can obtain the sentence representing each requirement. After that, the Part-Of-Speech Tagger (POS Tagger) tool from CoreNLP is leveraged to filter and prepare the requirements for the ontology modeling step (c.f. Sect. 3). The POS tagger returns the sentences' words as a pair consisting of tokens and their part of speech tags (the linguistic type of the words, i.e., noun, verb, adjective, etc.). After that, unrelated words (i.e., pronouns, symbols, adverbs, etc.) are filtered out from each requirement, which will speed up the requirements translation.

Example 3. Figure 4 shows how a data owner's requirement "Data stored based on time occurrence" is processed to obtain the attribute data type *timestamp* and the associated anonymization primitive *shifting*.

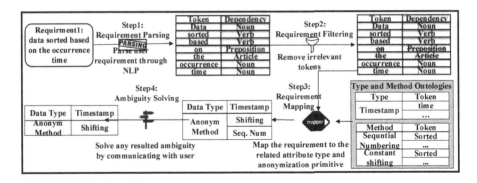

Fig. 4. Example showing the requirement translation process

Ontology Modeling. We use ontology modeling to define the relationship between requirements and data attributes/anonymization primitives as follows. *Ontology Learning.* We first define the concepts for data owner and user as: **(i)** anony-methods; **(ii)** method-func; **(iii)** attribute-types; **(iv)** attribute-synon.

Based on our definitions, the instances of the anony-methods are the existing anonymization primitives and the method-func instances are manually created based on the functionality and unique properties that each anonymization primitive can achieve. Moreover, the instances of the attribute-type concept are the given attributes types and the attribute-synon instances are manually created based on the use/synonymous of each attribute type. After that, we find the relationships between those concepts' instances by defining relations between the anony-methods and the method-func concepts. Also, by defining relations between the attribute-types and the attribute-synon instances. For example, Fig. 5 shows the type-ontologies related to the time-stamp attribute type and the method-ontology related to the constant shifting anonymization primitive. After that, we store the resulted ontologies into two separate tables, namely the type-ontology and the method-ontology.

Requirements Mapping. We apply the learned ontologies to the processed and filtered requirements from the NLP in order to find the data attributes and the anonymization primitives corresponding to the user's requirements. This is done by matching every tokenized word in the processed requirement with the type and the method ontologies tables shown in Fig. 4 as follows.

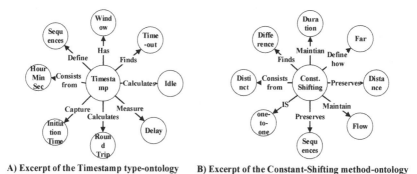

A) Excerpt of the Timestamp type-ontology   B) Excerpt of the Constant-Shifting method-ontology

Fig. 5. Ontologies of timestamp and constant shifting.

1. For each tokenized word in each annotated requirement, the tokenized word is matched first with the type ontology and then with the method ontology.
2. If the tokenized words are mapped to only one record from the type ontology table and one record from the method ontology table, then the requirement is translated properly, and the mapper will pass to the second requirement.
3. If none of the tokenized words match any record in both type and method ontologies tables, the word is dropped from the sentence annotations table.
4. If the user tokenized words fail to map to any record from the type and/or method ontologies or if the tokenized words have multiple matching, then the mapper will return an error message to the user reporting this issue and forward this conflict to the ambiguity solving process as discussed next.

Ambiguity Resolution. Ambiguity can occur for several reasons. We discuss how *iCAT* handles it as follows.

- The sentences entered by the user are mistakenly parsed at requirement parsing step (because of typos or NLP failures), which is not due to *iCAT*.
- The same requirements can be translated into different anonymization methods. For example, consider the following requirement; *Req-1: each IP address must be mapped to one IP address.* Both IP hashing and prefix-preserving can satisfy this requirement. In this case, the ambiguity solver of *iCAT* will display a small multi-choice menu to the user, such that this ambiguity can be resolved interactively.
- The same requirement can be expressed in different ways; For example, *the sequence of events is mandatory* versus *the order of logged records must be preserved.* This issue is discussed in Sect. 6.
- The data user's requirement is mapped to anonymization primitives that do not satisfy the data owner's requirement. In this case, *iCAT* suggests alternative anonymization primitives that offer the closest utility level to what is specified by the data owner.

4   Implementation

Figure 6 illustrates the flowchart (left) and main architecture (right) of *iCAT*, as detailed below.

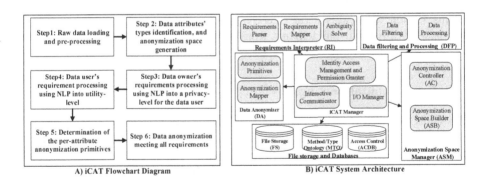

A) iCAT Flowchart Diagram   B) iCAT System Architecture

Fig. 6. Flowchart of *iCAT*.

iCAT **Flowchart.** As shown in Fig. 6A, raw data is loaded into *iCAT* and pre-processed by the data owner where he can filter the attributes and clean the records if necessary (**step 1**). Then, the data attribute types are identified and used to build the anonymization space lattice and generate the privacy/utility access control model (**step 2**). Third, the data owner interacts with *iCAT* to input his privacy requirements (in natural languages) for a data user (**step 3**).

These requirements are parsed and mapped to a privacy-level in the anonymization space. After that, the data user inputs the utility requirements which are also parsed and mapped to a utility-level in the anonymization space (**step 4**). Based on the privacy and utility levels, *iCAT* identifies the right combination of anonymization primitives (**step 5**). Finally, the data is anonymized and returned to the data user (**step 6**).

iCAT **Architecture.** We provide a brief description of the main architecture of *iCAT*, as shown in Fig. 6B, while leaving more details to the Appendix due to space limitations. All the modules of *iCAT* are implemented in Java. The Data Loading and Processing (DLP) module is used to load the data, and enables filtering and cleansing operations. These operations allow performing statistical disclosure control for balancing privacy risks and data utility. The Requirements Interpreter (RI) module translates the data owner's and data user's requirements into data attributes types and anonymization primitives. The *iCAT* Manager module associates the data user identity with the privacy-level specified by the data owner and interacts with the data owner or data user. The I/O Manager module is responsible for configuring the data source and the loading the actual data. The Anonymization Space Manager module is for generating the anonymization space and implementing the access control mechanism. Finally, the Data Anonymizer module is for anonymizing the data and it is designed in a modular way to easily accommodate new anonymization primitives.

5   Experiments

In this section, we evaluate the effectiveness and usability of *iCAT* through a user-based study with participants from both industry and academia working on data analysis. Also, we evaluate the efficiency of *iCAT* using real data.

5.1   Experimental Settings

Datasets Selection. We used four datasets in our experiments as shown in Table 2. The first is the Google cluster dataset [10], i.e., traces from requests processed by Google cluster management system. The second is cloud logs collected from different OpenStack Neutron services. The third dataset is a database dump of the OpenStack Nova service. The fourth dataset is the BHP-OBS machine learning dataset [23]. We select the aforementioned datasets for the following reasons: (**i**) The privacy constraints and requirements are already known for datasets from the industrial collaborator; (**ii**) The public datasets are widely used in research labs and the structure and usability of the data (as implementations exist to validate) could be easily identified by the researcher participants.

Participants. We have two types of participants, i.e., data owner participants and data user participants. To solicit participants, we have placed an advertisement on the university campus and also sent it to our industrial collaborators. The on-campus flyer requires that: (**i**) participants should be able to pose clear

Table 2. Different datasets used in evaluating *iCAT* and their statistics

Datasets	Format	# of records	# of attributes	# of requirements
DS1: Google cluster	CSV	2,000	9	56
DS2: OpenStack Neutron	log	2,000	18	62
DS3: OpenStack Nova	DB	2,000	22	44
DS4: BHPOBS ML	text	1,027	22	43

requirements (e.g., how to use the data and what properties need to be preserved). (**ii**) participants should be able to evaluate the usefulness and usability of the data after the experiments. The request sent to research collaborators indicates that: (**i**) participants should be able to write their institutional privacy constraints and requirements that govern data sharing; (**ii**) participants should be able to verify whether the final anonymized output of the data meets those requirements/constraints. As a result, we have recruited nine researchers from different research labs, and 14 participants from four industrial organizations. Table 3 summarizes the participants' experience level in percentage, where we categorize them based on their educational level and industrial experience.

Table 3. Distribution of participants over the user experience levels

Category	Research		Industry	
Expertise level	M.Sc.	Ph.D.	Junior	Senior
Participants percentage	30.4%	8.6%	43.4%	17.6%
Overall percentage	39%		71%	

Procedures. We divided our experiments into four main data anonymization operations based on the used datasets and asked the participants to select one of them corresponding to their domain. After that, the participants had to input their requirements and interact with *iCAT* until the anonymization operation finishes. Finally, we asked the participants to fill a post-experiment questionnaire to report the correctness of data usefulness and the privacy constraints. Note that, we recorded the requirements entered by the participants to evaluate the effectiveness of *iCAT* as it will be explained next.

5.2   Effectiveness

The main goal of this experiment is to evaluate the quality of the requirements translation. Since this is a multi-class problem, we evaluate the effectiveness of our system as the percentage of the requirements that were correctly translated by *iCAT*. To this end, we manually investigated the recorded user's requirements and categorized the failures as follows: (**i**) the privacy leakage/utility loss caused

by both data owners/users through mistakenly choosing anonymized methods.
(ii) the failures caused by *iCAT* misrecognizing either the data owners or the
data user's requirements. Fig. 7A and B demonstrate the effectiveness of the
translation process from both data owner and user sides. Figure 7C shows a
detailed analysis of the failed requirements.

Results. The overall effectiveness of translating data owners' requirements is
relatively high as shown in Fig. 7A; the lowest percentage of correctly translated
results is 87.5%. This is justified as the ambiguity solver implemented by *iCAT*
reduces the error rate through interactive communication with the users, where
they can directly intervene in the case of uncertain requirements. On the other
hand, the two main reasons of translation's failures are: **(i)** the correctness of
the ontology modeling; **(ii)** NLP fails to translate when the user's input contains
typos. The percentage of failures for both Ontology and NLP are presented in
Fig. 7A in white and gray patterns. By comparing through the dataset, we also
observe that the number of attributes affects the success rate of the requirements translation in the opposite manner. Hence, users need to express their
requirements more precisely to differentiate between different attributes.

Similarly to the previous experiment, the ambiguity solver contributes to
the high accuracy in the translation of data users' requirements as shown in
Fig. 7B. Besides the aforementioned two main reasons, we observed that data
user participants often fail to understand the mapping between anonymization
primitives suggested by *iCAT*'s ambiguity solver and their utility requirements.
This lesson has led us to add a pop-up message showing an example of each
primitive in order to guide the user and avoid selecting the wrong suggestion.

Figure 7C shows our analysis results about the failed requirements. We can
only observe privacy loss from data owners' side due to a miss in the ontology
modeling, which has been fixed afterward. Utility loss could be caused at both
data owners and data users' sides due to an incorrect translation of data owners'
requirements and the misinterpreting of the anonymization methods by data
users. Some no-translation requirements are due to typos in the input requirements. We will discuss those issues and how to address them in the following
section.

5.3   Usability

The usability of *iCAT* is evaluated based on two questionnaires. The first follows
the standardized usability questionnaires [2] and consists of 19 questions. It
provides the evaluation of the users' satisfaction towards the services provided by
the tool (e.g., whether this tool converges the views and bridges the gaps between
data owners and users). The second surveys the sensitivity of the attributes and
the trust-level in different actors used to propose privacy/utility access control
mechanism for different attributes anonymization.

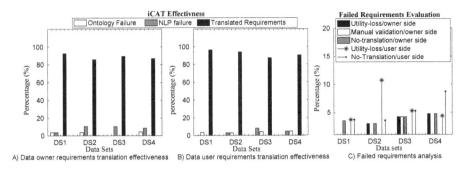

Fig. 7. The effectiveness of requirements translation

Results. Table 4 shows a summary of our main evaluation criteria and the average rating out of seven. The results show that the data users are extremely positive by the fact that they are part of the anonymization process through expressing their requirements. On the other hand, the data owner participants from industry clearly show interests in this tool because they can have different anonymization levels of the same input data instead of the encrypt/hide policy which they currently use. Data users also report that the tool requires some privacy expertise, especially when it comes to deal with the ambiguity solver. As mentioned before, to this issue, we have revised our design by adding concrete examples for the anonymization primitives to make them easier to understand.

Table 4. Usability results based on questionnaire designed following [2]

Category	Question	Score/7
Ease of use, interactivity and user friendly	It was simple to use *iCAT*	6.3
	I can effectively complete my work using *iCAT*	5.2
	I am able to complete my work quickly using *iCAT*	4.8
	I am able to efficiently complete my work using *iCAT*	5.45
	I feel comfortable using *iCAT*	5.7
	It was easy to learn to use *iCAT*	4.2
	I believe I became productive quickly using this system	6.4
	The interface of this system is pleasant	6.5
	Like using the interface of this system	6.6
Errors detecting, reporting and recovery	*iCAT* gives error messages to fix problems	5.7
	I recover easily/quickly when I make a mistake	5.8
iCAT does not need support/background to use	It is easy to find the information I needed	4.4
	The information provided for *iCAT* is easy to understand	3.5
	The information is effective in completing the tasks	3.6
	The information organization on *iCAT* screens is clear	5.7
This system has all the functions and capabilities I expect it to have Comment		6.1
The information provided with this system is clear (e.g., online help and other documentation)		NA
The overall satisfaction	I am satisfied with how easy it is to use *iCAT*	5.3
	I am satisfied with this system	6.2

The second questionnaire is an online form and the results of this questionnaire are shown in the table of Fig. 8. We applied the marginal distribution and drew the trend of each attribute and actor as shown in Figs. 8A and B. In general, we can observe that the attributes and actors are associated with different sensitivity levels. The attribute *Time, ID, Constant* and *Numbers* have similar data sharing strategy; internal actors could have low privacy and high utility results, while competitors would be only provided with high privacy and low utility data. The main reason is those attributes are not as sensitive as personally identifiable information, but still can leak information that can be used to stage security attacks. Attribute *IP* and *Numbers* (salary in our survey) are considered to be sensitive attributes for all level actors who prefer to apply at least level 2 anonymization on them. This can be due to sharing policies or cultural background which makes them less willing to share the information carried by those attributes. Figure 8B confirms the trust levels of the actors through the levels of anonymization methods they are mostly assigned. Internal auditors are mostly granted with level 1 anonymization only, while competitors could only get level 6 anonymization results. External auditors and researchers (generally under NDA) share similar trusted levels. This shows the participants share

Attribute	Actor	Level1	Level2	Level3	Level4	Level5	Level6
Time	I	95%				5%	
	E	45%	38%	6%	6%		5%
	R	25%	50%	10%	5%		10%
	C	5%			5%	20%	70%
ID	I	80%	5%	5%			10%
	E	5%		70%		20%	5%
	R	50%	5%	5%	10%	20%	10%
	C	10%				25%	65%
String	I	55%	5%	40%			
	E			70%	15%	15%	
	R	25%		60%	5%	10%	
	C			20%	25%	55%	
IP	I	75%	20%		5%		
	E		35%	15%	20%	20%	5%
	R		40%		40%	10%	10%
	C					25%	75%
Constant	I	40%	40%	20%			
	E		55%	20%	10%	5%	10%
	R	45%	10%	30%	5%	10%	
	C	25%	5%			15%	55%
Number	I	60%	30%			5%	5%
	E	25%	50%	5%			20%
	R	5%	50%	5%	20%		20%
	C		5%			45%	55%

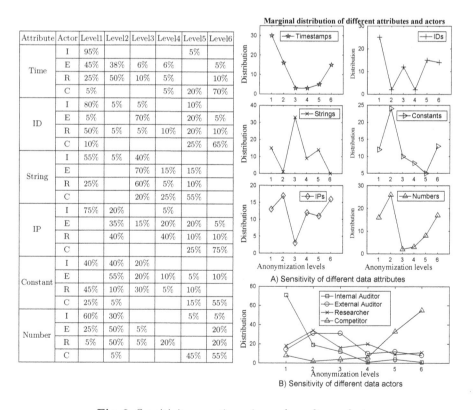

A) Sensitivity of different data attributes

B) Sensitivity of different data actors

Fig. 8. Sensitivity questionnaire and results analysis

similar visions related to the internal auditor and competitors and consider the external auditors and researchers harmless.

5.4   Efficiency

In order to evaluate the overhead from different modules of *iCAT*, we measure the time, memory and CPU consumption.

Results. Figure 9 shows the time, memory and CPU consumption of the data anonymization process according to the four datasets. We measure the aforementioned resource consumption according to four different events: **(i)** E1: Data loading and pre-processing; **(ii)** E2: Anonymization space and access control matrix generation; **(iii)** E3: Ontology mapping; **(iv)** E4: NLP translation. We also evaluate the resource consumption of anonymization. The first three results in Fig. 9 are the overhead at the data owner side and the last two results are for the data user. From data owner side, beside the onetime effort to load the data, other operations have negligible consumptions. The overhead resulted from the last two events at the data user side is related to the use of NLP server and the anonymization primitives' implementation, which are both out of our control.

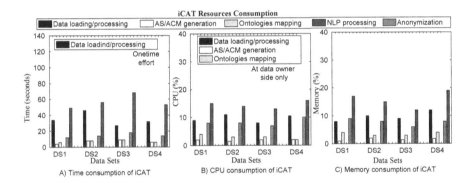

Fig. 9. The resources consumption of *iCAT*

6   Discussions

Compositional Analysis. A well-known issue in anonymization is that releasing multiple views of the same data may breach privacy since an adversary can combine them. However, by the definition of our anonymization space lattice, whatever levels inside its 'privacy-up' region can be safely released, because all those views contain strictly less information than the specified privacy level (in fact, those views may be derived from the latter) so combining them lends the adversary no advantage. If, however, the data user is mistakenly assigned different privacy levels at different time, then he/she can potentially combine those views to gain more information. However, the anonymization space lattice makes it easy for the data owner to see exactly what he/she will gain (i.e., the GLB of those levels) and take appropriate actions.

Business-Case. Nowadays data is becoming the most valuable asset and the determiner of success in many aspects. We believe $iCAT$ can be used to provide "data anonymization as a service" in which the data owner sets the desired privacy level for each (type of) data user, without worrying about their utility requirements. Afterward, the data users can query the tool in an interactive manner without any intervention from the data owner. The data owner can be sure that the privacy is preserved, whereas the data users can obtain as many anonymized views of the data as needed for different analyses.

Privacy Analysis. $iCAT$ does not propose any new anonymization primitive, but relies on the correctness of existing solutions. The privacy/utility level of $iCAT$ output will be exactly the same as that of the anonymization primitives being used. However, it is possible that $iCAT$ may mistakenly translate the data owner requirements and map them to unsafe levels. Therefore, in our design, the data owner-side requirement translation is only intended as a suggestion, which requires further validation by the data owner.

Tricking iCAT. As the data user and owner requirements are enforced independently by iCAT, the data user cannot influence iCAT to use a primitive that breaches the data owner's requirements. This is enforced as follows: *(i)* during requirements translation, the ontologies for the data owner and user, respectively, are stored and used separately; *(ii)* iCAT, by design, does not allow the data owner to publish the dataset until a privacy level is assigned to each data attribute (either by processing requirements through NLP or manually).

Data Linkage. We emphasize that such a limitation, de-anonymizing a given dataset using publicly available data, is not due to iCAT as we mentioned earlier in our threat model (Sect. 2.1). Nonetheless, using iCAT, the data owner will have the flexibility to assign a privacy level for each data attribute and for each data user. As a result, the data owner can always specify a higher privacy level that is more resistant to linkage attacks (e.g., randomization) for less trusted users or more sensitive attributes.

Ontologies Learning. As we mentioned in our experiments, we have reported requirements translation failures due to missing ontologies matching. We believe a major opportunity here is to add a feedback module that learns the new ontologies from both data owners and data users' responses. We consider this feedback module as future work.

7   Related Work

This section reviews existing works and their limitations.

Cryptography-Based Anonymization Tools. Most of the existing tools in this category use cryptography-based anonymization primitives, such as prefix-preserving, hashing and permutation. Existing tools in this category are used

Table 5. Comparing existing network data anonymization tools. The symbol ✓ indicates that the proposal offers the corresponding feature.

Tool Name	Anonymized fields					Anonymization primitive					
	NF fields	IP	Port	Header	Payload	Pref-Pres	Hiding	Permutation	Truncation	Hashing	Shifitng
AnonToo [8]	✓	✓				✓	✓	✓		✓	
CANINE [15]	✓	✓	✓			✓	✓	✓	✓		✓
CoralReef [17]	✓	✓	✓			✓	✓		✓		
Flaim [21]	✓	✓	✓			✓	✓	✓		✓	✓
IPsumdump [6]		✓	✓			✓					
NFDump [12]	✓					✓					
SCRUB [24]		✓	✓	✓		✓	✓				✓
TCPanon [9]				✓		✓					
tcpdpriv [11]		✓	✓	✓	✓	✓	✓	✓			
TCPmkpub [18]		✓	✓	✓	✓	✓		✓			
TCPurify [7]		✓		✓		✓	✓	✓			

to anonymize the network traces and mainly anonymize the TCP header. Some of those tools support live interfaces anonymization. Table 5 compares those tools according to the anonymized fields (e.g., IP, header, port, etc.) and the anonymization primitives they use. As shown in the table, unlike *iCAT*, none of those tools can support all the attributes or anonymization primitives (let alone the flexibility for customization).

Replacement-Based Anonymization Tools. The existing tools in this category deal mainly with log files and anonymize data by replacing the sensitive attributes (e.g., passwords, IPs, paths) in the log with some values predefined by the user in the so-called rule-file or generated using deterministic cryptography algorithms. The rule file contains patterns used by the tool to perform pattern matching and the conversion state of the anonymization can be stored in a look-up table. Table 6 compares between these tools in terms of anonymized fields, anonymization primitives used and how the mapping is achieved. This category of anonymization provides a higher utility output, compared to the first category, because it preserves some property of the original data (e.g., equality, format, order, etc.). However, this also leaves the door open for de-anonymization attacks, known as semantic attacks (e.g., frequency analysis, injection and shared text matching attacks). Moreover, those tools are generally not user-friendly and require knowledge about conducting tool-based search patterns and managing the conversion state of the anonymized data.

Table 6. Comparing different features of existing replacement anonymization tools. The symbol ✓ indicates that the proposal offers the corresponding feature.

Tool	Anonymized fields						Anonymization primitive					Mapping	
Name	Number	Path	ID	String	IP	Timestamp	Hiding	Substitution	Randomization	Hashing	Shifting	Look-up table	Algorthim
Camouflage [13]	✓		✓	✓	✓	✓	✓	✓	✓	✓		✓	✓
Loganon [22]	✓		✓	✓	✓	✓		✓				✓	
Log-anon [22]			✓	✓	✓			✓				✓	
Flaim [21]			✓	✓	✓	✓		✓	✓	✓	✓		✓
NLM [14]		✓	✓	✓	✓		✓		✓				✓
bsmpseu [1]	✓	✓	✓	✓	✓	✓		✓	✓		✓		✓

8   Conclusion

We presented in this paper *iCAT*, a novel anonymization tool that brings customization and interactivity to the data anonymization process to bridge the existing gap between the data owners and the data users. Our tool leveraged existing anonymization primitives in a systematic fashion based on the novel concept of anonymization space. It also improved the usability by providing users with the means to express their requirements using natural languages and found for them the best-fit combination of anonymization primitives inside the anonymization space using our ontology-driven NLP approach. Finally, *iCAT* proposed a new privacy/utility access control model that allow involving the data user in the anonymization process without compromising the data owner's privacy requirements. The main limitations of our work and the corresponding future directions are as follows. First, we have mainly focused on the relational model in this paper and we believe our tool can be extended to handle other data models. Second, currently the ontology modeling is done offline, and implementing a feedback module that allow for ontologies learning from users' requirements can further improve the performance and minimize the use of the ambiguity solver. Third, we have focused on network data, and extending our model to cover more applications is left as future work.

Acknowledgment. The authors thank the anonymous reviewers for their valuable comments. This work is partially supported by the Natural Sciences and Engineering Research Council of Canada and Ericsson Canada under CRD Grant N01823 and by PROMPT Quebec.

Appendix

The following details each module of *iCAT* as shown in Fig. 6B.

(A) Data Loading and Processing (DLP). This module is used to load the data, and enables filtering and cleansing operations. This module consists of following sub-modules:

Data Processing: This sub-module enables performing data pre-processing and adjustment operations. It can also automatically detect all data attributes and their types, which are needed by the Anonymization Space Manager to build the anonymization space lattice.

Data Filtering: This sub-module deploys several algorithms that can be automatically and manually used to filter and remove records from data (e.g., column deletion, row deletion, searched deletion and frequency deletion).

(B) Requirements Interpreter (RI). This module translates the data owner's and data user's requirements into data attributes types and anonymization primitives. It consists of the following three sub-modules:

Requirements Parser: It takes the English statement and transforms them into a set of requirements using the Stanford CoreNLP. Then, it processes and filters those requirements using the POS tool.

Requirements Mapper: This sub-module takes the parsed requirements and communicates with the Method-Ontology and the Type-Ontology databases in order to map each requirement into the related attribute type and then the corresponding anonymization primitives.

Ambiguity Solver: This sub-module is mainly responsible of communicating with the user (i.e. data owner or data user) through the Interactive Communicator (IC) sub-module in order to solve any ambiguity that occurs at the Requirement Mapper sub-module.

(C) iCAT Manager.

Identity Access Management and Permission Granter (IPG): This module associates the data user identity with the privacy-level specified by the data owner, which is needed to determine the anonymization sub-space assigned to him based on privacy-up principle.

Interactive Communicator: This sub-module is mainly responsible for interacting with the data owner or data user and handles the communications between them and the RI module.

I/O Manager: This module is responsible for configuring the data source from where the data is fetched (e.g. from a file system or a database) and the loading of the actual data to be anonymized.

(D) Anonymization Space Manager. This module is mainly responsible of generating the anonymization space and implementing the access control mechanism over the anonymization space for the data user. This module consists of the following sub-modules:

Anonymization Space Builder (ASB): This sub-module automatically builds the entire anonymization space, which consists of all available combination of anonymization primitives for each data attribute based on its type. Building the anonymization space lattice is detailed in Sect. 2.3. The resulting anonymization-space lattice will be stored in the Access Control database.

Anonymization Controller: This module implements the access control mechanism over the anonymization space for the data user. It receives the utility-level from the data user and perform an intersection/masking operation between the privacy level and utility level in order to determine the allowed combinations of anonymization primitives. It also ensures that the Data Anonymizer only accesses the allowed anonymization primitives for the user.

(E) Data Anonymizer. This module is mainly responsible for anonymizing the data with the respect to the trust-level assigned to the users. It is designed in a building-blocks manner such that if there exist new or more efficient anonymization primitives they can be easily integrated into *iCAT*. This module holds the following sub-modules:

Anonymization Primitives: This sub-module holds the implementation of all existing anonymization algorithms corresponding to the 12 anonymization primitives discussed in Sect. 2.

Anonymization Mapper: This sub-module is responsible of creating a mapping file that maps the plain-text data into their anonymized values for later recognition purposes (e.g., if hashing is used to anonymize IP addresses, a file contains the original IP addresses and their hashes are created).

References

1. Rieck, K.: Pseudonymizer for solaris audit trails (2018). http://www.mlsec.org/bsmpseu/bsmpseu.1
2. Assila, A., Ezzedine, H., et al.: Standardized usability questionnaires: features and quality focus. Electron. J. Comput. Sci. Inf. Technol. eJCIST **6**(1), 15–31 (2016)
3. Bell, E.D., La Padula, J.L.: Secure computer system: unified exposition and multics interpretation (1976)
4. Denning, D.E.: A lattice model of secure information flow. Commun. ACM **19**(5), 236–243 (1976)
5. Donnellan, T.: Lattice Theory. Pergamon Press, Oxford (1968)
6. Kohler, E.: Ipsumdump tool (2015). https://read.seas.harvard.edu/~kohler/ipsumdump/
7. Blanton, E.: Tcpurify tool (2019). https://web.archive.org/web/20140203210616/irg.cs.ohiou.edu/~eblanton/tcpurify/
8. Foukarakis, M., Antoniades, D., Antonatos, S., Markatos, E.P.: Flexible and high-performance anonymization of NetFlow records using anontool. In: Third International Conference on Security and Privacy in Communications Networks and the Workshops, SecureComm 2007, pp. 33–38. IEEE (2007)
9. Gringoli, F.: TCPanon tool (2019). http://netweb.ing.unibs.it/~ntw/tools/tcpanon/
10. Google: Traces from requests processed by Google cluster management system (2019). https://github.com/google/cluster-data
11. Greg Minshall of Ipsilon Networks: Tcpdpriv (2005). http://ita.ee.lbl.gov/html/contrib/tcpdpriv.html
12. Haag, P.: Nfdump (2010). World Wide Web. http://nfdump.sourceforge.net
13. IMPREVA: Camouflage data masking (2018). https://www.imperva.com/products/data-security/data-masking/
14. Kayaalp, M., Sagan, P., Browne, A.C., McDonald, C.J.: NLM-scrubber (2018). https://scrubber.nlm.nih.gov/files/
15. Li, Y., Slagell, A., Luo, K., Yurcik, W.: CANINE: a combined conversion and anonymization tool for processing netflows for security. In: International Conference on Telecommunication Systems Modeling and Analysis, vol. 21 (2005)
16. Manning, C., Surdeanu, M., Bauer, J., Finkel, J., Bethard, S., McClosky, D.: The Stanford CoreNLP natural language processing toolkit. In: Proceedings of 52nd Annual Meeting of the Association for Computational Linguistics: System Demonstrations, pp. 55–60 (2014)
17. Moore, D., Keys, K., Koga, R., Lagache, E., Claffy, K.C.: The CoralReef software suite as a tool for system and network administrators. In: Proceedings of the 15th USENIX Conference on System Administration, pp. 133–144. USENIX Association (2001)
18. Pang, R., Allman, M., Paxson, V., Lee, J.: The devil and packet trace anonymization. ACM SIGCOMM Comput. Commun. Rev. **36**(1), 29–38 (2006)

19. Rules for the protection of personal data inside and outside the EU. Gdpr (2018). https://ec.europa.eu/info/law/law-topic/data-protection_en
20. Sandhu, R.S.: Lattice-based access control models. Computer **26**(11), 9–19 (1993)
21. Slagell, A.J., Lakkaraju, K., Luo, K.: FLAIM: a multi-level anonymization framework for computer and network logs. LISA **6**, 3–8 (2006)
22. Sys4 Consults: A generic log anonymizer (2018). https://github.com/sys4/loganon
23. UCIMLR: Burst Header Packet flooding attack on Optical Burst Switching Network Data Set (2019). https://archive.ics.uci.edu/ml/datasets/
24. Yurcik, W., Woolam, C., Hellings, G., Khan, L., Thuraisingham, B.: SCRUB-tcpdump: a multi-level packet anonymizer demonstrating privacy/analysis trade-offs. In: 2007 Third International Conference on Security and Privacy in Communications Networks and the Workshops-SecureComm 2007, pp. 49–56. IEEE (2007)

Monitoring the GDPR

Emma Arfelt[1]([☒]), David Basin[2], and Søren Debois[1]

[1] IT University of Copenhagen, Copenhagen, Denmark
{ekoc,debois}@itu.dk
[2] ETH Zurich, Zurich, Switzerland
basin@inf.ethz.ch

Abstract. The General Data Protection Regulation (GDPR) has substantially strengthened the requirements for data processing systems, requiring *audits at scale*. We show how and to what extent these audits can be automated. We contribute an analysis of which parts of the GDPR can be monitored, a formalisation of these parts in metric first-order temporal logic, and an application of the MONPOLY system to automatically audit these parts. We validate our ideas on a case study using log data from industry, detecting actual violations. Altogether, we demonstrate both in theory and practice how to automate GDPR compliance checking.

Keywords: Data protection · GDPR · Compliance checking · Monitoring

1 Introduction

Problem. The EU's General Data Protection Regulation (GDPR) [24], which came into force in May 2018, is one of the most important changes and strengthening of privacy regulations in decades. The GDPR constitutes a legal data protection regime imposed on organisations processing personally identifiable information about EU citizens. The regulation is as comprehensive as it is severe: failure to comply with the technical and organisational requirements it imposes may result in fines up to the larger of 20 million Euro or 4% of the organisation's worldwide annual turnover.

The GDPR requires extremely fine-grained control over an organisation's data processing activities. For example, *every single use* of a data subject's personally identifiable data must have a *documented* legal basis. Data that is no longer necessary or conforms to that basis must promptly be deleted. Moreover, data subjects have certain rights concerning access to their data and imposing restrictions on processing activities regarding them. To be compliant, organisations must not only meet these requirements, but *document* this in a way that supports audits.

This work supported in part by Innovation Fund Denmark project EcoKnow (7050-00034A). This paper does not constitute legal advice.

The GDPR raises numerous technical challenges for data protection researchers. Our focus in this paper is on tool-supported compliance checking: *how and to what extent can organisations automatically demonstrate compliance,* especially given that the GDPR's requirements apply to all data processing activities?

This raises sub-questions including:

1. What does the GDPR specifically require of systems?
2. What observations must we make of systems to verify compliance with these requirements?
3. To what extent can we automate compliance checking?

Approach Taken.   For (1), we perform an in-depth analysis of the GDPR, identifying all articles that pose specific requirements on systems; see Figs. 2, 3 and 4.

For (2), we identify among these articles those actions involving data processing, data subjects' rights, granting or revoking consent, or claiming a legal basis for processing. To automate audits, we will require that these actions are logged. We encounter two challenges here. First, GDPR relevant actions like "process data" or "revoke consent" are unlikely to directly appear as events in actual logs. We shall show that it is possible to *transform* logs so that this information is explicitly represented, enabling automated audits. Second, we shall see that automated audits cannot entirely replace human audits. For example, the GDPR requires that "information about processing is communicated to the data subject." While we can log information on the transmission of a message, we cannot in general check that the message's *contents* complies with the GDPR. Our work provides a complementary approach to auditing: Human auditors must verify by inspection and sampling that messages and documents have the proper contents. Machines can in turn be used to verify that such messages, documents, and processing activities happen when required. That is, human auditors are needed for intelligence and understanding whereas machines serve to verify compliance at scale.

For (3), we express the requirements in the articles identified in (1) as metric first-order temporal logic (MFOTL) formulae [6] over the actions identified in (2). MFOTL is a natural choice. The GDPR speaks about events, their associated data, and their temporal relationships (both qualitative and quantitative); this calls for a metric first-order temporal logic. Moreover, MFOTL is supported by the MONPOLY tool, which implements a monitoring algorithm efficient enough for practical use [5,7].

As a simple example, consider GDPR Article 15(1), governing the *Right to Access*, which requires that any data subject has the right to demand from the controller access to all personal data concerning him that is processed by the controller. A simplified form of this article expressed in MFOTL might be:

ds_access_request (*dsid*) IMPLIES EVENTUALLY[0,30d] grant_access(*dsid*) .

Here the universally quantified variable *dsid* ranges over distinct data subjects, and the interval [0, 30d] expresses that the controller must respond within 30 days.

MONPOLY can be used *on-line* to monitor system events as they occur to find violations of this formula in real time. Alternatively, it can be used *off-line* to support a compliance audit, given the logged events. In either case, MONPOLY will either declare "No violations", or "Violation of rule r found at time-point t" for each violation found. In this way, we obtain an automated audit tool.

Contributions. The answers to our research questions lead to a methodology for monitoring data protection requirements, in particular for auditing a system's compliance with the GDPR.

1. We identify GDPR clauses that can be verified by observing logged actions.
2. We encode in MFOTL key clauses of the GDPR, namely Articles 5(1c,1e), 6(1), 7(3), 13(1), 15(1), 17(1–2), 18(1–2), and 21(1).
3. We carry out a case study on an industry log and show how to extract GDPR-specific actions, and use MONPOLY to find violations.

Altogether, we show that our MFOTL formalisation enables the algorithmic verification of essential parts of the GDPR. We note that the articles we verify are among the ones subject to the highest administrative fines, hence verifying compliance and non-compliance for these is particularly important.

Related work. Our paper is the first that provides running, automatic, compliance verification for the GDPR. Alternative approaches have been proposed based on design mechanisms or static analysis. In system design work, researchers have investigated augmenting existing formalisms with the concepts needed for reasoning about or enforcing the GDPR, e.g., adding relations between data and users, or relations between processing activities and consent or legal basis [1,2]. On the analysis side, [10,11] proposes variations of taint analysis to track the dispersal of personally identifiable information in GDPR-sensitive programs. Moreover, [3] proposes a mechanism to statically audit GDPR compliance that avoids directly analysing source code, extracting instead audit-relevant information from requirements specifications. A similar idea is presented in [19], which combines an ontology of GDPR concepts [20] with established methods for analysing business processes for regulatory compliance [12,13].

Outside of work specifically targeting the GDPR, several proposals have been made to use the "purpose of processing" as a factor in access control decisions [9,17,18,21,26]. In particular, the use of information-flow analysis (viz. taint analysis above) to support access control decisions was investigated in [15]. Closer to the present work, [22] investigated comparing business process models with information access logs to infer the legitimacy of processing for the purposes of access control. This idea might be used to refine the logged action representing a "legal basis" in the present paper from simply a claim that such a basis exists to support for this claim by appeal to the underlying business process (see also [3]).

Both MFOTL and MONPOLY have been previously applied to privacy policies. In [4], examples of data protection rules were formulated in MFOTL. More recently, [14] investigated automatically rewriting data-flow programs to conform to privacy policies specified in MFOTL. The question arises whether the MFOTL formulae identified in the present paper can be directly used as inputs to that rewriting process. In general, the question of monitoring compliance for business processes has received considerable interest [16]; the log we consider in Sect. 6 is essentially the log of a business process execution.

Overview. In Sect. 2, we recall MFOTL's syntax and semantics and the MON-POLY tool. Then, in Sect. 3, we analyse the GDPR and clarify which articles can neither be formalised nor monitored. We proceed to formalise in Sect. 4 the remainder of the GDPR in MFOTL. In Sect. 5, we show how to use these formulae for run-time monitoring with MONPOLY. In Sect. 6, we apply our formalisation to an industry log and we draw conclusions in Sect. 7.

2   Background on MonPoly and MFOTL

We use Metric First-order Temporal Logic (MFOTL) [6] to formalise GDPR requirements, and we use the MONPOLY [5,7] monitoring tool to decide whether a log conforms to a given MFOTL formula.

Metric First-order Temporal Logic (MFOTL) combines the two key properties needed to capture GDPR data protection policies: (1) the ability to relate individuals via first-order predicates, primarily data subjects, data classes, and data references, and (2) the ability to speak about events and data changing over time. Below, we briefly recall MFOTL; for a comprehensive reference, see [6].

A *signature* S is a tuple (C, R, ι), where C is a finite set of constant symbols, R is a finite set of predicate symbols disjoint from C, and the function $\iota :$ $R \to \mathbb{N}$ associates each predicate symbol $r \in R$ with an arity $\iota(r) \in \mathbb{N}$. To illustrate, the signature for the previously presented formula regarding access defines two predicate symbols: ds_access_request($dsid$) and grant_access($dsid$). Let $S = (C, R, \iota)$ be a signature and V a countably infinite set of variables, assuming $V \cap (C \cup R) = \emptyset$. The *syntax of formulae* over the signature S is given by the grammar in Fig. 1. We present only a fragment of MFOTL, omitting equality, ordering, and the **PREVIOUS** operators, which we shall not need.

A *structure* $\mathcal{D}$ over the signature S comprises a domain $|\mathcal{D}| \neq \emptyset$ and interpretations $c^{\mathcal{D}} \in |\mathcal{D}|$ and $r^{\mathcal{D}} \subseteq |\mathcal{D}|^{\iota(r)}$, for each $c \in C$ and $r \in R$. A *temporal structure* over S is a pair $(\bar{\mathcal{D}}, \bar{\tau})$, where $\bar{\mathcal{D}} = (\mathcal{D}_0, \mathcal{D}_1, \dots)$ is a sequence of structures over S and $\bar{\tau} = (\tau_0, \tau_1, \dots)$ is a sequence of natural numbers, such that (1) $\bar{\tau}$ is non-decreasing and has no constant suffix ("time always eventually advances"); (2) $\bar{\mathcal{D}}$ has constant domains, that is, $|\mathcal{D}_i| = |\mathcal{D}_{i+1}|$, for all $i \geq 0$; and (3) each constant symbol $c \in C$ has a rigid interpretation, that is, $c^{\mathcal{D}_i} = c^{\mathcal{D}_{i+1}}$, for all $i \geq 0$. We denote c's interpretation by $c^{\bar{\mathcal{D}}}$. There can be successive time points with equal timestamps, and the relations $r^{\mathcal{D}_0}, r^{\mathcal{D}_1}, \dots$ in a temporal structure

Meta-variables:

$t_1, t_2, \ldots$ range over $V \cup C$ r
x over R
V over values
I over intervals over $\mathbb{N}$.

Syntax:

$$\phi ::= r(t_1, \ldots, t_{\iota(r)})$$
$$| \ \mathsf{NOT} \ \phi$$
$$| \ \phi \ \mathsf{OR} \ \phi$$
$$| \ \mathsf{EXISTS} \ x. \ \phi$$
$$| \ \phi \ \mathsf{SINCE}[I] \ \phi$$
$$| \ \phi \ \mathsf{UNTIL}[I] \ \phi$$

Semantics:

$(\bar{\mathcal{D}}, \bar{\tau}, v, i) \models r(t_1, \ldots, t_{\iota(r)})$	iff	$(v(t_1), \ldots, v(t_{\iota(r)})) \in r^{\mathcal{D}_i}$
$(\bar{\mathcal{D}}, \bar{\tau}, v, i) \models \mathsf{NOT} \ \phi$	iff	$(\bar{\mathcal{D}}, \bar{\tau}, v, i) \not\models \phi$
$(\bar{\mathcal{D}}, \bar{\tau}, v, i) \models \phi \ \mathsf{OR} \ \phi$	iff	$(\bar{\mathcal{D}}, \bar{\tau}, v, i) \models \phi$ or $(\bar{\mathcal{D}}, \bar{\tau}, v, i) \models \psi$
$(\bar{\mathcal{D}}, \bar{\tau}, v, i) \models \mathsf{EXISTS} \ x. \ \phi$	iff	$(\bar{\mathcal{D}}, \bar{\tau}, v[x/d], i) \models \phi,$ for some $d \in |\bar{\mathcal{D}}|$
$(\bar{\mathcal{D}}, \bar{\tau}, v, i) \models \phi \ \mathsf{SINCE}[I] \ \psi$	iff	for some $j \leq i, \ \tau_i - \tau_j \in I, (\bar{\mathcal{D}}, \bar{\tau}, v, j) \models \psi,$
		and $(\bar{\mathcal{D}}, \bar{\tau}, v, k) \models \phi,$ for all $k \in [j+1, i+1)$
$(\bar{\mathcal{D}}, \bar{\tau}, v, i) \models \phi \ \mathsf{UNTIL}[I] \ \psi$	iff	for some $j \geq i, \ \tau_j - \tau_i \in I, \ (\bar{\mathcal{D}}, \bar{\tau}, v, j) \models \psi,$
		and $(\bar{\mathcal{D}}, \bar{\tau}, v, k) \models \phi,$ for all $k \in [i, j)$

Fig. 1. MFOTL syntax and semantics

$(\bar{\mathcal{D}}, \bar{\tau})$ corresponding to a predicate symbol $r \in R$ may *change* over time. In contrast, the interpretation of the constant symbols $c \in C$ and the domain of the $\mathcal{D}_i$s do not change over time.

A *valuation* is a mapping $v : V \to |\bar{\mathcal{D}}|$. We abuse notation by applying a valuation v also to constant symbols $c \in C$, with $v(c) = c^{\bar{\mathcal{D}}}$. For a valuation v, a variable x, and $d \in |\bar{\mathcal{D}}|$, $v[x/d]$ is the valuation mapping x to d and leaving other variables' valuation unchanged. The *semantics* of MFOTL, $(\bar{\mathcal{D}}, \bar{\tau}, v, i) \models \phi$, is given in Fig. 1, where $(\bar{\mathcal{D}}, \bar{\tau})$ is a temporal structure over the signature S, with $\bar{\mathcal{D}} = (\mathcal{D}_0, \mathcal{D}_1, \ldots), \bar{\tau} = (\tau_0, \tau_1, \ldots), v$ a valuation, $i \in \mathbb{N}$, and ϕ a formula over S.

Terminology and notation We use the following standard syntactic sugar:

$$\mathsf{ONCE}[I] \ \phi := \top \ \mathsf{SINCE}[I] \ \phi$$
$$\mathsf{EVENTUALLY}[I] \ \phi := \top \ \mathsf{UNTIL}[I] \ \phi$$
$$\mathsf{ALWAYS}[I] \ \phi := \mathsf{NOT} \ \mathsf{EVENTUALLY}[I] \ \mathsf{NOT} \ \phi$$

We sometimes omit the interval I, understanding it to be $[0, \infty)$.

Article(s)	Description
1–4	General provisions
6(2–4)	Member state restrictions on lawful processing
23	General member state restrictions
51–62	Supervisory authority
63–76	European data protection board
77–84	Remedies and penalties
92–99	Delegated acts and implementing acts

Fig. 2. Articles unrelated to the compliance of an individual organisation.

MONPOLY [7] is a monitoring tool for deciding whether a log satisfies a formula in metric first-order temporal logic. Operationally, MONPOLY accepts as inputs a signature, an MFOTL formula, and a log, and outputs the list of entries in the log that violate the formula [7]. The log must consist of a sequence of time-stamped system events ordered ascending by time. Technically, MONPOLY accepts a formula φ with free variables $\bar{x}$ and checks ALWAYS FORALL $\bar{x}.\varphi$. That is, it checks that FORALL $\bar{x}.\varphi$ holds at every time point. As MONPOLY must report the time points at which this formula is *violated*, in practice, MONPOLY searches for and reports time points where the negated formula $\neg\varphi$ is satisfied.

3   Limits to GDPR Monitoring

The GDPR [24] comprises 99 articles imposing specific rights and obligations on entities processing the personally identifiable information of "data subjects." In this section, we briefly categorise those articles that are not amendable for formalisation or are not suitable for automated compliance checking.

Articles Unrelated to Compliance. As with any legal document, part of the GDPR is devoted to the legal framework surrounding the regulation: how EU member states should integrate the regulation into their local laws, the legislation's territorial scope, etc. These articles have no bearing on the question whether a particular organisation is in compliance, and as such, these are not relevant for mechanised compliance checking. We list these articles in Fig. 2.

Articles Unrelated to System Behaviour. The GDPR also imposes requirements unrelated to data processing or data subjects, regulating instead the form and functioning of the data processing organisation itself [25]. For instance, such an organisation must have a mechanism for notifying its local supervisory authority in case of a data breach, it must appoint a data protection officer, and it must be able to document that its systems comply with best IT-security practices. While these are clearly rules that an organisation can follow or break, such actions do not happen at scale.

Altogether, this class of articles, listed in Fig. 3, makes no requirements on observable system actions, and so are irrelevant for compliance monitoring.

Articles	Brief explanation
24–29	Organisational requirements
31	Cooperation with supervisory authority
32	Security of the system
33–34	Notification upon data breach
35–39	DPIA and DPO
40–43	Codes of conduct and certificates
44–50	Transfers to third countries
85–91	Specific processing situations

Fig. 3. GDPR articles unrelated to system actions.

Art.	Desc.	Art.	Desc.
5(1) a-b,d,f; (2)	Principles of processing	14	Indirect collection
7(1–2,4)	Conditions for consent	16	Right to rectification
8	Child's consent	19	Requirement to notify
10	Processing of criminal records	20	Right to data portability
11	Processing w/o identification	22	Profiling
12	Transparency wrt. rights	30	Records of processing
13(3–4)	Information upon collection		

Fig. 4. GDPR articles which do not directly relate system actions or regulate content

Articles Requiring Interpretation. Many GDPR articles do not directly describe system actions, but regulate the contents of communications, e.g., Article 13(1) on information that controllers must provide, or Article 5(1d) requiring processed data to be accurate and up to date. We list the articles that do not directly relate to system actions (and not otherwise subject to auditing at scale) in Fig. 4.

We shall see in Sect. 4.2 that even when we cannot verify that communicated contents satisfy the GDPR, we can at least monitor that communication *took place*.

4   Formalisable Articles

We can formalise and monitor articles where controllers, processors, or data subjects are required to take specific, observable actions in response to other specific, observable actions.

Recall that formalisation in MFOTL comprises two things: (1) a signature, specifying the actions and data we must be able to observe, and (2) a formula over that signature, specifying how those actions and data should evolve over time. We present below a signature of relevant actions, and a set of formulae over that signature formalising articles of the GDPR.

The elements of this signature are given as typed predicates. The procedure to formalise a requirement of the GDPR is as follows. First, identify both actions

688   E. Arfelt et al.

Predicate	Action
ds_deletion_request(*data, dataid, dsid*)	Data subject requests deletion
ds_access_request(*dsid*)	Data subject requests access
ds_consent(*dsid, data*)	Data subject gives consent
ds_restrict(*data, dataid, dsid*)	Data subject restricts processing of specific data
ds_repeal(*data, dataid, dsid*)	Data subject lift their restriction on specific data
ds_object(*dsid, data*)	Data subject objects to processing based on Art. 6 (1e-f)
legal_grounds(*dsid, data*)	Organisation claims legal basis
ds_revoke(*dsid, data*)	Data subject revokes consent
delete(*data, dataid, dsid*)	Controller deletes specified data
grant_access(*dsid*)	Controller grants access to specified data subject
share_with(*processorid, dataid*)	Controller shares data with a particular processor
inform(*dsid*)	Controller informs data subject about collection of data
notify_proc(*processorid, dataid*)	Controller notifies a processor of deletion
use(*data, dataid, dsid*)	Controller processes data of specified data subject
collect(*data, dataid, dsid*)	Controller collects data of specified data subject

Fig. 5. MFOTL signature for the GDPR formalisation

that trigger a requirement, e.g., *a data subject revokes his consent*, and those that are the required response, e.g., *the data controller ends processing*. Second, model these actions as predicates in an MFOTL signature. Finally, express the required causality as an MFOTL formula. In this section, we formalise GDPR Articles 5(1c), 5(1e), 6(1), 7(3), 13(1), 15(1), 17(1–2), 18(1–2), and 21(1). The corresponding signature and rules are given in Figs. 5 and 6 respectively. Note that MONPOLY imposes some syntactic restrictions; thus to run some of the rules with MonPoly, we must negate them by hand. These are marked with '*' in Fig. 6.

We proceed by illustrating this analysis for the representative cases of Article 6(1) and 7(3) and we conclude by discussing outliers.

4.1   The Common Case: Articles 6(1) and 7(3)

Article 6 is at the GDPR's core: it defines what is required for lawful processing.

Processing shall be lawful only if and to the extent that at least one of the following applies:
(a) the data subject has given consent to the processing of his or her personal data for one or more specific purposes;

(b) *processing is necessary for the performance of a contract to which the data subject is party or in order to take steps at the request of the data subject prior to entering into a contract; [...]*

To formalise this requirement, we must be able to observe both the processing of data and the establishment of legal grounds for that processing. While we cannot verify that a claim of legal grounds will hold up in court, we can, however, verify whether there exists a *claim* of legal grounds at all. A legal ground is for a specific class of data and a specific data subject. Thus we must be able to observe from our system an action legal_ground, represented as

$$\text{legal\_ground}(dsid, \, data),$$

which is a predicate we add to our signature. The first argument to legal_ground represents a class of data (e.g. "ADDRESS" or "TELEPHONE NUMBER"), and the second is an identifier for a data subject. Note that MONPOLY supports types, but for reasons of space we omitted this from Sect. 2 and our account here.

As the GDPR has special rules for consent-based processing (as we demonstrate later), it is convenient to single-out consent from other legal bases mentioned in Article 6(1). For this, we need the predicate

$$\text{ds\_consent}(dsid, \, data).$$

When data is eventually used, we must know both which class of data is being processed and which data subject that data concerns. We shall see later (for erasure requirements) that we need a reference to the actual data as opposed to just its class (i.e. "+1 451 451-0000" or "DATABASE ROW 2769" as opposed to "TELEPHONE NUMBER"):

$$\text{use}(data, \, dataid, \, dsid).$$

This predicate takes a data class, an identifier for the actual data processed, and an identifier for the data subject.

The GDPR in general conflates the *use of data* with *collecting data* into the single term *processing of data*. To formalise some articles, we will however need this distinction, so we add the following predicate to our signature:

$$\text{collect}(data, \, dataid, \, dsid).$$

We now formalise that a data controller must have either consent from data subjects or another legal basis to process any data [[24], Article 6, sec. 1]. Otherwise the processing of data is prohibited. We formalise this requirement as our first MFOTL formula:

use(*data, dataid, dsid*) IMPLIES
  ONCE (ds_consent(*dsid, data*) OR legal_ground(*dsid, data*)).

Recall that we consider MFOTL formulae to be implicitly forall-quantified over their free variables. Hence, the above formula states that for any class of data *data*, any concrete reference *dataid* to such data, and any data subject *dsid*, then: If at any point in time we observe processing of any data *dataid* of class *data* for *dsid*, then, there must be a point in the past where we observed either consent from that *dsid* for processing *data*, or other legal grounds.

As a second, more subtle, example, consider Article 7(3), "Conditions for consent." It states that a data subject can revoke his consent at any time:

> *The data subject shall have the right to withdraw his or her consent at any time. [...]*

Absent other legal grounds, subsequent processing would then be illegal (viz. Article 6). To model this, we add to our signature a predicate representing a revocation of consent:

$$\text{ds\_revoke}(dsid, data),$$

and the formula:

use(*data, dataid, dsid*) IMPLIES (ONCE legal_grounds(*dsid, data*))
   OR (NOT ds_revoke(*dsid, data*) SINCE ds_consent(*dsid, data*)).

That is, if at some time point t we process data, then either we have legal grounds (in which case the revocation does not affect the right to process the data) or before that point t, consent was obtained and at no point between t and the given consent do we have a revocation. Note that this formula also finds violations in situations where Article 6 is violated.

4.2 Articles Requiring Content Interpretation

As discussed in Section 3, we can monitor whether a required action is taken, and leave to a human auditor the question of whether the content complies with requirements prescribed by the GDPR. Articles 13, 15, 17(1), 18, and 21, describing the rights of the data subjects, has such conditions. These rights might frequently be exercised, and thus it is impractical to rely solely on human audits to determine if the company has responded as required. A human auditor could decide if the company's strategy for responding is compliant, whereas monitoring can help ensure, at scale, that the company responds when appropriate.

As an example, consider Article 17(1) "Right to erasure." This article defines under what circumstances a data controller or processor must delete data:

> *The data subject shall have the right to obtain from the controller the erasure of personal data concerning him or her without undue delay and the controller shall have the obligation to erase personal data without undue delay where one of the following grounds applies: [...]*

We refrain from further specifying the data subject's ground for deletion, referencing them all under the single action "deletion requested" (ds_deletion_request).

We similarly omit explicitly modelling the exceptions mentioned in 17(3). It requires further human interpretation to determine the legality of a data subject's claim, and whether the controller is obligated to delete the data.

At this point, we must distinguish between classes of data and individual data items. There are two reasons: (1) the data subject may request some but not all data in a class to be erased, e.g., a data subject may request that an airline removes as an emergency contact his ex-wife but not his father. (2) To properly verify compliance, we need a formula that identifies and specifies the removal of every single data item processed for this data subject. Altogether, the action for the deletion request is

$$\mathsf{ds\_deletion\_request}(\mathit{data},\ \mathit{dataid},\ \mathit{dsid}).$$

Upon receiving such a request, the data controller must then respond and delete the data. This action must also be observable:

$$\mathsf{delete}(\mathit{data},\ \mathit{dataid},\ \mathit{dsid}).$$

The deletion in Article 17(1) is subsequently required to happen *without undue delay*, which in Recital 59(3) is limited to "at most one month." It is now straightforward to model this rule:

$$\mathsf{ds\_deletion\_request}\ (\mathit{data},\ \mathit{dataid},\ \mathit{dsid})$$
$$\mathsf{IMPLIES\ EVENTUALLY[0,30d]\ delete}(\mathit{data},\ \mathit{dataid},\ \mathit{dsid}).$$

That is, if at some time point t we are required to delete some particular data then within 30 days after t, we must observe this data being deleted. Moreover, it should be impossible to subsequently *process* deleted data:

$$\mathsf{use}(\mathit{data},\ \mathit{dataid},\ \mathit{dsid})\ \mathsf{IMPLIES}$$
$$\mathsf{NOT\ ONCE\ ds\_deletion\_request}(\mathit{data},\ \mathit{dataid},\ \mathit{dsid}).$$

4.3 Articles Not Monitorable

We conclude this section by considering Articles 5(1c,1e), "Data minimisation" and "Storage limitation." These articles require that:

> *Personal data shall be: [...]*
> (c) *adequate, relevant and limited to what is necessary in relation to the purposes for which they are processed ('data minimisation'); [...]*
> (e) *kept [...] for no longer than is necessary for the purposes for which the personal data are processed; [...] ('storage limitation');*

That is, we can never collect or store data that we will not subsequently use for a legitimate purpose (1c). Moreover, not only must we delete that data once it has outlived its purpose, with some exceptions, perpetual storage is prohibited outright (1e).

Storage Limitation. Recall that when we write EVENTUALLY ϕ, we implicitly intend the interval $[0, \infty)$, and thus formalising (1e) is straightforward:

collect (*data,dataid,dsid*) IMPLIES EVENTUALLY delete(*data, dataid, dsid*).

However, this formula is not finitely falsifiable and hence it cannot be monitored. Because it uses the unbounded EVENTUALLY modality, it is a *liveness* property, requiring something to eventually happen, without stipulating exactly when.

Data minimisation Here is an attempt to specify Article (1c):

collect (*data,dataid,dsid*) IMPLIES EVENTUALLY use(*data, dataid, dsid*).

By the semantics of MFOTL, this formula requires that the collected data must find use *in every run* of the system. This interpretation is likely too strong. As an example, when customers book long-haul flights, they may provide an emergency contact. However, the airline will only use this contact should an accident occur, so in the majority of cases, this data will be collected, not used, and then deleted.[1] Moreover, this requirement is also not monitorable because it is not finitely falsifiable, and requires some relaxation to be formulated precisely.

We formulate both data minimisation and storage limitation and include them in the Fig. 6. However, as described above, neither are monitorable.

5   Run-Time Monitoring

We now turn to the question: Does our formalisation of GDPR requirements lend itself to run-time monitoring? We show how to take logs of running systems and use a tool to *verify automatically* that these logs conform to the given formulae.

5.1   Methodology

Having established that the formulae of Fig. 6, or equivalent formulations thereof, are accepted as inputs to MONPOLY, we turn to the question of how to obtain a log containing the actions described in Fig. 5. System logs conventionally contain information about which events happened and when they occurred [7]. For example, the event that a data subject asks for access or that data was shared with other processors, and the date and time this occurs.

It is not conventional (at least prior to the GDPR) to log whether an organisation has a legal ground for data processing (and *which* legal ground) or obtained consent from a data subject. However, entries in a system log often *reflect* GDPR actions such as establishing a legal basis. For instance, if a customer clicked "purchase" in a web-shop, this establishes a legal basis for using the customer's postal

---

[1] In fact, in 2017, no commercial airline passengers died from plane crashes [23], and thus presumably emergency contact data was unnecessary.

Article	MFOTL Formula
5(1)(c) Data minimisation	collect (*data*, *dataid*, *dsid*) IMPLIES EVENTUALLY use(*data*, *dataid*, *dsid*)
5(1)(e) Storage limitation	collect (*data*, *dataid*, *dsid*) IMPLIES EVENTUALLY delete(*data*, *dataid*, *dsid*)
6(1) Lawful processing	use(*data*, *dataid*, *dsid*) IMPLIES ONCE (ds_consent(*dsid*, *data*) OR legal_grounds (*dsid*, *data*))
7(3) Consent	use(*data*, *dataid*, *dsid*) IMPLIES (ONCE legal_grounds (*dsid*, *data*)) OR (NOT ds_revoke(*dsid*, *data*) SINCE ds_consent(*dsid*, *data*))
13(1) Info. on collection	collect (*data*, *dataid*, *dsid*) IMPLIES NEXT inform(*dsid*) OR ONCE inform(*dsid*)
15(1) Right to access	ds_access_request (*dsid*) IMPLIES EVENTUALLY[0,30d] grant_access(*dsid*)
17(1) Right to erasure	ds_deletion_request (*data*, *dataid*, *dsid*) IMPLIES EVENTUALLY[0,30d] delete(*data*, *dataid*, *dsid*)
17(1) Right to erasure	use(*data*, *dataid*, *dsid*) IMPLIES NOT ONCE delete(*data*, *dataid*, *dsid*)
17(2) Right to erasure*	ds_deletion_request (*data*, *dataid*, *dsid*) AND ONCE share_with (processorid , *dataid*) AND NOT EVENTUALLY[0,30d] notify_proc(procid , *dataid*)
18(1-2) Right to restriction of processing*	use(*data*, *dataid*, *dsid*) AND (NOT ds_repeal (*data*, *dataid*, *dsid*) SINCE ds_restrict (*data*, *dataid*, *dsid*))
21(1) Right to object	use(*data*, *dataid*, *dsid*) IMPLIES (NOT ds_object (*dsid*, *data*) SINCE legal_grounds(*dsid*, *data*))

Fig. 6. MFOTL formulae expressing GDPR requirements

address for shipping. In general, we can infer GDPR actions from log entries by having domain experts apply their knowledge of the system to log entries.

Altogether, we propose the following methodology for partially verifying a system's compliance with the GDPR using run-time monitoring:

1. Identify available logs.
2. Identify the types of records in each log and relate each type to GDPR actions (Fig. 5). In general, this may require input from a domain expert and a systems expert, and possibly also a GDPR expert. Write a script or a program to transform automatically logs entries to GDPR actions.
3. Run MONPOLY on the transformed log, using the rules of Fig. 6.

Dreyer log entry title	GDPR action and description
Application received	ds_consent(*"APPL"*, i)
	When submitting his application, an applicant must also provide explicit consent for subsequent processing.
Complete	delete(*"APPL"*, i) / delete(*"ACCOUNT"*, i)
	The application has been approved and fully payed out. There are no remaining purposes for storing collected data.
Approve	legal_grounds(i, *"ACCOUNT"*)
	When an application is approved, we have legal grounds for storing and using the account number of the applicant.
Retract application	ds_deletion_request(*"APPL"*, i, i)
	If the applicant retracts the application, we no longer have legitimate purposes for storage or processing. We model this by requiring application data to be deleted.
Notify (rejected)	delete(*"APPL"*, i, i)
	Once we have notified the applicant that his application has been rejected, we delete the application.
Review (and others)	use(*"APPL"*, i, i)
	Along with various other actions, the application is reviewed processing the data inside it.
Round ends (and others)	(no action)
	Remaining records do not process data and thus are not relevant for monitoring.

Fig. 7. Mapping of Dreyer log entries to GDPR actions. The i refers to the application instance id available in the log.

Obviously, this methodology depends on being able to find or infer GDPR relevant actions in the logs. We shall see in the next section how such inference is possible from an otherwise unhelpful looking real-world log.

6   Case Study

We now apply the above methodology to a concrete, real-life industry log previously published in [8], which described the context of this log as follows:

The Dreyer Foundation awards grants to [...] activities [...] promoting the development of the lawyer and architect professions [...]. Roughly, an application is processed as follows. Applications are accepted in rounds. In each round, first, a caseworker pre-screens applications, weeding out obvious rejects. The remaining applications are independently reviewed by 2–4 reviewers, at least one of which must be an architect or a lawyer, depending on the type of application. Once all reviews are in, the Foundation's board decides on which applications to accept at a board meeting. Successful applications then have a running payout, until the grant period expires and an end-report is produced.

```
  78 63;20140108 0955;Appl. received  @1389171305 ds_consent("63", "APPL")
 520 63;20140127 1802;Pass screening  @1390842175 use("APPL", "63", "63")
1483 63;20140313 1027;Lawyer review   @1394702823 use("APPL", "63", "63")
1505 63;20140313 1322;Review          @1394713322 use("APPL", "63", "63")
1565 63;20140316 2336;Review          @1395009396 use("APPL", "63", "63")
1861 63;20140323 2212;Arch. review    @1395609120 use("APPL", "63", "63")
2130 63;20140327 0917;Record decision @1395908246 use("APPL", "63", "63")
2135 63;20140327 0918;Board meeting
2691 63;20140409 0300;Round ends
3071 63;20140415 1450;Round approved
3308 63;20140416 1036;Notify 1        @1397637397 use("APPL", "63", "63")
3544 63;20140416 1925;Round approved
3779 63;20140416 1925;Approve         @1397669105 legal_grounds("63", "ACCOUNT")
4679 63;20140521 1141;Notify 2        @1400665291 use("APPL", "63", "63")
5378 63;20140626 1402;Payout 1        @1403784135 use("ACCOUNT", "63", "63")
5423 63;20140626 2054;Payment done    @1403808852 use("ACCOUNT", "63", "63")
11224 63;20150503 2328;Final report    @1430689888 use("ACCOUNT", "63", "63")
                                                   use("APPL", "63", "63")
11235 63;20150503 2352;Complete        @1430689922 delete("APPL", "63", "63")
                                                   delete("ACCOUNT", "63", "63")
```

Fig. 8. Excerpt of Dreyer log (left) and corresponding transformed log (right).

Step 1: Define the log

The log itself is from an adaptive case-management system supporting this work; it documents the processing steps taken. The log contains 12,151 events concerning 587 individual applications processed in the period December 2013–June 2015. We present an excerpt of the log in Fig. 8. In the interest of presentation, we have removed and shortened the individual fields within each line of the log, re-ordered the remaining fields, and translated some log-entries to English. Note that the excerpt is non-contiguous, with actual line numbers in the log for each line given on the left. The excerpt describes a successful application, going through initial submission (78), screening (520), reviews (1483–1861), board meeting and eventual approval (2130–3779), payout (5378–5423), and finally inclusion in the end report of the round (11224–11235). Along the way, the applicant is notified about the application's state (3308, 4679).

Step 2: Transform the log

Most importantly we must extract from this log the actions listed in Fig. 5 using domain knowledge of the meaning of the system actions underlying the log entries. We give the full list of Dreyer log actions, their semantics, and the corresponding GDPR actions in Fig. 7. We encourage the reader to carefully consider the "Description" column, which explains exactly how domain knowledge justifies the connection between a log entry and a GDPR action.

The opening "Appl(ication) received" entry signifies the applicant filling in and submitting an electronic application form. This form includes a tick box indicating consent to subsequent processing for the purpose of considering the application; the application cannot be submitted without ticking this box. Thus, we can associate with this log entry the ds_consent action for the application data.

The Dreyer log gives us little information about exactly what data is processed. But we know that the application in its entirety is necessarily processed in reviews and decision making, and that the (subsequently supplied) account number of a successful applicant is used in payout steps. We note that by the purpose limitation, there is no legal ground to request an account number for payouts until a grant is awarded.

The data subject is not directly represented in the log; however, the log contains (first field) a number uniquely identifying the application. As each application conveniently has exactly one applicant, we conflate the application id and the data-subject. Altogether, we interpret the first line (78) in Fig. 8 as the GDPR action ds_consent("APPL", 0063), that is, consent from the data subject identified by 0063 to the processing of his application data.

Once we have established the mapping table in Fig. 7, it is straightforward to automatically transform an input log into a MONPOLY-compatible log of GDPR actions. We have constructed such an automatic transformation; the result of applying it to our log excerpt is also shown in Fig. 8. The lines of the original and transformed log are aligned vertically, e.g., line 5378 of the input (left) yields the transformed line @1403808852 use(...) (right).

Altogether, this demonstrates that we *can* extract GDPR-relevant actions from a realistic industry log. Our coverage, however, is only partial: the mapping of Dreyer log entries does not contain the actions necessary to monitor, e.g., the right to access (Article 15(1)) or erasure of previously shared data (Article 17(2)).

Step 3: Verify compliance with monitoring
We can now provide the transformed log and the formulae capturing the GDPR rules from Fig. 6 as inputs to MONPOLY. We discover the following violations:

- 8 violations of lawful processing (Article 6(1)). Of these, 7 arise because an account number was submitted *before* the application was approved, thus processing that data without legal grounds. The remaining violation arose because in a single instance, money was paid out even though the application in question was never recorded as approved (or rejected) in the log. Hence payment information was used without legal grounds.
- 8 violations of the Right to Erasure (Article 17(1)), part (i). These 8 were all retracted shortly after being submitted; however, they were never deleted.
- 1 violation of the Right to Erasure (Article 17(1)), part (ii). In this instance, the last payment of a successful application was acknowledged and recorded in the log only *after* the entire application was recorded as completed.

These violations range from seemingly inconsequential mistakes (*a payment being recorded late*) to a definite violation (*not having a process for deleting no-longer necessary data*). We note that by the letter of the GDPR, there were no false positives: inconsequential mistakes are still violations.

This log pre-dates the GDPR: When it was produced, the Dreyer foundation was not obligated to be GDPR compliant.

Summary
Altogether, we have demonstrated that our proposed method of using MON-POLY *can* in fact find instances of GDPR non-compliance in a real-life industry log. Moreover, with the GDPR formulae (see Fig. 6) already in place, the only significant work required to check the log is to map the log's contents to GDPR actions; that is, working out Fig. 7. This work required domain knowledge (e.g., you only need the account number once the application is approved) *in combination* with an understanding of the GDPR (e.g., you need a legal ground to store the account number). Once the mapping is established, it is trivial to write a small program to automatically produce the transformed log suitable for MONPOLY. Subsequent processing by MONPOLY is then automatic: the log in question is processed nearly instantaneously.

7   Conclusion

Our analysis has shown that monitoring can be used to automate compliance checking for significant parts of the GDPR. We explained why some parts of the GDPR elude monitoring and require other auditing measures or other forms of verification. We also identified and tackled challenges in extracting relevant actions for monitoring from real-world logs. Finally, we showed the value of this in a case study where we found violations ranging from apparently inconsequential to almost certainly non-compliant.

We see this work as a beginning: providing automated support for compliance checking for the GDPR and similar privacy regulations. As future work, we would like to apply our ideas to larger case studies, to both help organisations improve their handling of data and to verify their compliance. A research question here concerns how best to instrument systems with logging functionality to produce adequate logs at the right level of detail. Another question concerns distinguishing between personally identifiable information and other kinds of information, as we now only verify that the controller took the required actions. Progress here could, for example, allow us to extend our approach to monitor articles that impose requirements on content.

References

1. Antignac, T., Scandariato, R., Schneider, G.: A privacy-aware conceptual model for handling personal data. In: Margaria, T., Steffen, B. (eds.) ISoLA 2016. LNCS, vol. 9952, pp. 942–957. Springer, Cham (2016). https://doi.org/10.1007/978-3-319-47166-2_65
2. Antignac, T., Scandariato, R., Schneider, G.: Privacy compliance via model transformations. In: 2018 IEEE European Symposium on Security and Privacy Workshops (EuroS&PW), pp. 120–126. IEEE (2018)
3. Basin, D., Debois, S., Hildebrandt, T.: On purpose and by necessity: compliance under the GDPR. In: Proceedings of the 22nd International Conference on Financial Cryptography and Data Security (FC 2018), Lecture Notes in Computer Science, Nieuwpoort, Curaçao, February 2018. Springer. Accepted for publication

4. Basin, D., Harvan, M., Klaedtke, F., Zalinescu, E.: Monitoring data usage in distributed systems. IEEE Trans. Softw. Eng. **39**(10), 1403–1426 (2013)

5. Basin, D., Harvan, M., Klaedtke, F., Zălinescu, E.: MONPOLY: monitoring usage-control policies. In: Khurshid, S., Sen, K. (eds.) RV 2011. LNCS, vol. 7186, pp. 360–364. Springer, Heidelberg (2012). https://doi.org/10.1007/978-3-642-29860-8_27

6. Basin, D., Klaedtke, F., Müller, S.:. Monitoring security policies with metric first-order temporal logic. In: Proceedings of the 15th ACM Symposium on Access Control Models and Technologies, pp. 23–34. ACM (2010)

7. Basin, D., Klaedtke, F., Zalinescu, E.: The monpoly monitoring tool. In: RV-CuBES 2017 An International Workshop on Competitions, Usability, Benchmarks, Evaluation, and Standardisation for Runtime Verification Tools, vol. 3 of Kalpa Publications in Computing, pp. 19–28. EasyChair (2017)

8. Debois, S., Slaats, T.: The analysis of a real life declarative process. In: IEEE Symposium Series on Computational Intelligence, SSCI 2015, Cape Town, South Africa, 7–10 December 2015, pp. 1374–1382. IEEE (2015)

9. Kabir, M.E., Wang, H., Bertino, E.: A conditional purpose-based access control model with dynamic roles. Expert Syst. Appl. **38**(3), 1482–1489 (2011)

10. Ferrara, P., Olivieri, L., Spoto, F.: Tailoring taint analysis to GDPR. In: Medina, M., Mitrakas, A., Rannenberg, K., Schweighofer, E., Tsouroulas, N. (eds.) APF 2018. LNCS, vol. 11079, pp. 63–76. Springer, Cham (2018). https://doi.org/10.1007/978-3-030-02547-2_4

11. Ferrara, P., Spoto, F.: Static analysis for GDPR compliance. In: Proceedings of the Second Italian Conference on Cyber Security, Milan, Italy, 6th - 9th February 2018, vol. 2058 of CEUR Workshop Proceedings. CEUR-WS.org (2018)

12. Governatori, G.: Business process compliance: an abstract normative framework. Inf. Technol. **55**(6), 231–238 (2013)

13. Governatori, G., Sadiq, S.: The journey to business process compliance. Handbook of Research on Business Process Modeling, pp. 426–454. IGI Global, Pennsylvania (2009)

14. Guerriero, M., Tamburri, D.A., Nitto, E.D.: Defining, enforcing and checking privacy policies in data-intensive applications. In: Proceedings of the 13th International Conference on Software Engineering for Adaptive and Self-Managing Systems, SEAMS 2018, pp. 172–182, New York, NY, USA, ACM. event-place: Gothenburg, Sweden (2018)

15. Kumar, N.V.N., Shyamasundar, R.K.: Realizing purpose-based privacy policies succinctly via information-flow labels. In: 2014 IEEE Fourth International Conference on Big Data and Cloud Computing, pp. 753–760, December 2014

16. Thao Ly, L., Maggi, F.M., Montali, M., Aalst, W.M.P., van der Rinderle-Ma, S.: Compliance monitoring in business processes: functionalities application and tool-support. Inf. Syst. **54**, 209–234 (2015)

17. Masoumzadeh, A., Joshi, J.B.D.: PuRBAC: purpose-aware role-based access control. In: Meersman, R., Tari, Z. (eds.) OTM 2008. LNCS, vol. 5332, pp. 1104–1121. Springer, Heidelberg (2008). https://doi.org/10.1007/978-3-540-88873-4_12

18. Ni, Q., et al.: Privacy-aware role-based access control. ACM Trans. Inf. Syst. Secur. **13**(3), 24:1–24:31 (2010)

19. Palmirani, M., Governatori, G.: Modelling legal knowledge for GDPR compliance checking. Front. Artif. Intell. Appl. **313**, 101–110 (2018)

20. Palmirani, M., Martoni, M., Rossi, A., Bartolini, C., Robaldo, L.: Legal ontology for modelling GDPR concepts and norms. In: Legal Knowledge and Information Systems: JURIX 2018: The Thirty-first Annual Conference, vol. 313, p. 91. IOS Press (2018)

21. Peng, H., Gu, J., Ye, X.: Dynamic purpose-based access control. In: 2008 IEEE International Symposium on Parallel and Distributed Processing with Applications, pp. 695–700, December 2008

22. Petković, M., Prandi, D., Zannone, N.: Purpose control: did you process the data for the intended purpose? In: Jonker, W., Petković, M. (eds.) SDM 2011. LNCS, vol. 6933, pp. 145–168. Springer, Heidelberg (2011). https://doi.org/10.1007/978-3-642-23556-6_10

23. Shepardson, D.: 2017 safest year on record for commercial passenger air travel (2018). https://reut.rs/2CvBTEH

24. European Union. Regulation (eu) 2016/679 of the european parliament and of the council of 27 April 2016 on the protection of natural persons with regard to the processing of personal data and on the free movement of such data, and repealing directive 95/46/ec (general data protection regulation) (2016)

25. Voigt, P., von dem Bussche, A.: The EU General Data Protection Regulation (GDPR). Springer, Cham (2017). https://doi.org/10.1007/978-3-319-57959-7

26. Yang, N., Barringer, H., Zhang, N.: A purpose-based access control model. In: Third International Symposium on Information Assurance and Security, pp. 143–148, August 2007

Blockchain and Smart Contracts

Incentives for Harvesting Attack in Proof of Work Mining Pools

Yevhen Zolotavkin$^{(\boxtimes)}$ and Veronika Kuchta

Monash University, Clayton, Australia
{yevhen.zolotavkin,veronika.kuchta}@monash.edu

Abstract. PoW consensus largely depends on mining that mostly happens in the pools where Pay Per Share (PPS) and Pay Per Last N Shares (PPLNS) are the most common reward schemes that are offered to the affiliated miners by pool managers. In this paper, we demonstrate that in the system consisting of PPS and PPLNS pools, manager who governs the both pools may have incentive for a new type of "pool harvesting" attack that is harmful for honest miners. In order to profit from the attack on PPLNS pool manager declares that a non-existent miner A joins that pool. She then collects the portion of reward that corresponds to the mining power of the proclaimed miner A. We demonstrate that for the mining community, such unfavorable outcome is worsened by the manager incentives to misrepresent (or not report) the true power of PPS pools, which complicates unified estimation of the level of decentralization in blockchain.

1 Introduction

Being one of the massively adopted products of blockchain technology major cryptocurrencies have been seen as the next advanced instrument for digital transactions capable to comfortably assist ever growing global population in their day to day needs. Since the very inception they enormously benefited from permanent attention within research community which resulted in a number of solid publications addressing different aspects of their use [8, 15, 22]. Proof of Work (PoW) consensus in many ways pioneered the domain bringing to the academic test grounds vital debates about incentives to participate in the blockchain and support its functionality [16].

Many of the challenges of PoW cryptocurrencies can be explained through the phenomenon of pooled mining. In the pools, miners produce partial solutions, shares, requiring significantly less computations in comparison to the full solutions resulting in new blocks. This allows miners to submit shares with the frequency that is proportional to their personal mining power, and, thus demonstrating to the pool manager their constant involvement into mining process. In the event of discovering full solution, manager re-distributes the reward among miners depending on the reward principle in the pool. On one hand this is demanded by the miners who wish to reduce variance in receiving reward.

© Springer Nature Switzerland AG 2019
K. Sako et al. (Eds.): ESORICS 2019, LNCS 11735, pp. 703–725, 2019.
https://doi.org/10.1007/978-3-030-29959-0_34

For providing pool infrastructure manager usually charges pool mining fee from the miners. Regrettably, such convenience results in a compromise with decentralization and independent governance [10].

It has been shown that dependency on the pools resulted in multiple attacks and vulnerabilities including *double spending* [17–19,22], *block withholding* [4,7,12,27], *selfish mining* [13,26], and it's generalization [23] among other attacks [10,21,31]. In spite of the previous efforts to underpin issues related to PoW mining and solve them, it should be noted that incentives arising from intertemporal utilities for different pool participants have long been ignored [14]. Here we provide arguments on why such aspect should be taken into consideration.

Time preference is an essential component of financial analysis reflecting present-time investing opportunities associated with holding funds, and, conversely the lack of opportunities in case of guaranty of monetary compensation in the future. In spite of the century-long history of incorporating time discounting models into financial tools such as bank deposits and bonds, the services that bring them into the domain of cryptocurrencies are relatively new [6,9,28]. It can not, however, be ignored that corresponding changes are quickly adopted by the customers and gaining popularity due to multiple reasons including fast-paced development of cryptocurrency derivatives and marginal trades segments of the market [5]. As a result of the wider adaptation of time discounting models, infrastructures dependent on projections of cryptocurrency inflow will indisputably employ them. Being one of such proxies PoW mining pools represent an interesting object for detailed research focused on incentives to deviate from mining protocols designed without considering time discounting. Unfortunately, such deviation may result in attacks which severely distort ability to support functionality of blockchain and, therefore, should be addressed by the community.

In this paper, our attention is on the system of two mining pools with different reward principles governed by the same manager. We demonstrate that collective participation in mining process can be exploited by the malicious manager in the environment of compensation mechanisms where reward is proportionally distributed among pool miners in one of the pools. Under honest operation, accepting new miners in the pool that shares reward may cause a temporal reduction in compensations of other permanent members. This fact is tolerated (and in many cases is welcomed) by the steady miners in anticipation of boosted productivity of the pool in the near future. Here, we question on how such timetolerance can be exploited by a dishonest pool manager seeking to benefit from interest-earning on the compensations that she deliberately delays.

Mining conglomerates offering miners a choice between two or more reward approaches are broadly represented across majority of popular PoW cryptocurrencies [2,27]. In such structures, Pay Per Share (PPS) and Pay Per Last N Shares (PPLNS) are the most popular remuneration schemes in use which principles, however, differ significantly. Being one of the oldest reward schemes, PPS provides instant compensation for every submitted share. For the miners, this comes at the price of charging higher mining fee (usually around 2%) due to the requirement for financial stability for the manager during the periods of bad luck when expected number of submitted shares does not result in finding a full solution.

On the other hand, PPLNS charges lower fee (near 1%) while sharing the rewards among the most recent N shares only at the moments when full block solutions are found in the pool. This principle of mining reward is illustrated on Fig. 1 with a window size of $N = 20$ shares. For simplicity's sake we assume existence of 2 miners A and B with mining powers of 40% and 60%, respectively. In the event of finding a full solution, both miners receive payments that are proportional to the number their submitted shares within the most recent reward window. For example, the latest payment on this scheme is proportionally distributed among A and B according to their contributions, i.e. miner A receives $\frac{8}{20}$ of total reward, while miner B receives $\frac{12}{20}$ of total reward.

Unfortunately, in the majority of PPLNS pools managers are the sole authority performing allocation of the reward to the miners. As we demonstrate further, this imperfection is to be blamed for the new *pool harvesting* attack.

We proceed as follows. In Sect. (2) we employ time discounting and the theory of expected utility (EUT) to model incentives of the manager. We develop sufficient condition for the profitability of *pool harvesting* attack, propose a new method to implement attack on practice, and prove that the method provides non-negative incentive at any moment during attack. In Sect. (3) address aspects related to attack simulation and detection of malicious manipulations by honest miners in PPLNS pool. Finally, in Sect. (4) we discuss our results, experimental limitations, possible effect on the community, and directions for further research.

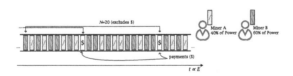

Fig. 1. PPLNS pool with two miners

2   Pool Harvesting Attack

We start by providing a high level idea of the attack (see Fig. 2) followed by the formal representation of the model and the method. In order to increase her personal utility, malicious manager M who is in charge of PPS pool and PPLNS pool declares that a non-existent miner A with mining power p_A joins PPLNS pool at time t_0. Despite the fact that other honest miners in PPLNS may monitor performance of A and demand that full solutions are submitted by that miner, fractional rewards can be collected by A prior to that. Such form of compensation is favorable for M due to: *(i)* the properties of time discounting, and *(ii)* ability to select which blocks (possibly yielding lower rewards) will be submitted to PPLNS pool.

We will demonstrate that early fractional compensations received from PPLNS pool indeed outweigh reward for the full solution. In the case of attack, manager receives fractions $F_A(t)$ of every block reward obtained by PPLNS pool. These fractions are proportional to the declared power p_A and are non-decreasing in time. Since the manager does not need to report to the honest miners about the shares received from miner A, they are unable to verify such claim immediately. However, in the long run manager needs to hide her malicious behavior which requires simulation of mining process by miner A who delivers blocks to the PPLNS pool (see Fig. 2).

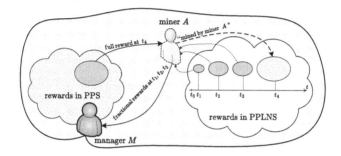

Fig. 2. Generalized scheme of pool harvesting attack.

Assuming that all the honest miners uninterruptedly work in PPLNS pool, over period of time $[t_0, t]$ they are able to test the validity of the claim made by miner A as follows: by conducting One Poisson Mean Test (OPMT), they compare the declared power p_A with the actual number of blocks λ submitted by miner A during that time period [30]. Further in the text, we will call this requirement *detection constraint*. In order to satisfy such detection constraint the manager needs to submit to PPLNS pool some of the blocks mined in the other pool with PPS reward system. These blocks are declared in PPLNS pool as the blocks that were mined by miner A.

2.1   Preliminaries

Starting from moment t_0, we register events of mining new blocks in the system consisting of PPS and PPLNS pools controlled by the manager M. We presume that the system is closed meaning that neither new miners join these pools nor any of the miners who are already affiliated with one of the pools ever leaves it. Mining power of the pools are P_1 and P_2 for PPS and PPLNS pools, respectively. We will further define three mutually exclusive sets of natural numbers that form the set of all events $\mathbb{S}$: *(1)* set $\mathbb{L}$ of events in PPS pool that are not manipulated; *(2)* set $\mathbb{M}$ of event in PPLNS pool that are not manipulated; *(3)* set $\mathbb{A}$ of event that originate in PPS pool and can be introduced into PPLNS pool during the attack (see Table 1). The following relations hold:

$$\mathbb{S} = \mathbb{A} \cup \mathbb{L} \cup \mathbb{M}; \quad \mathbb{A} \cap \mathbb{L} = \varnothing; \quad \mathbb{A} \cap \mathbb{M} = \varnothing; \quad \mathbb{L} \cap \mathbb{M} = \varnothing.$$

We define "no attack" scenario as such where all the events in PPS and PPLNS pools can be indexed using $\mathbb{A} \cup \mathbb{L}$ and $\mathbb{M}$, respectively. In contrast, "attack" scenario is such where manager M declares events in PPS pool using indices from $\mathbb{L}$ and events in PPLNS pool using indices from $\mathbb{A} \cup \mathbb{M}$. The case when $\mathbb{A} \neq \varnothing$ is of particular interest and further in the paper we assume that such quality is preserved.

Every block that is mined in the system is indexed in one of the sets $\mathbb{A}$, $\mathbb{L}$, $\mathbb{M}$ only once. A pair of similarly indexed attributes describe each block. For instance, block B_i, $i \in \mathbb{L}$ is attributed with $\{t_i, R_i\}$ meaning that it is mined at time t_i and yields reward R_i. We will use definition of "time of termination" $t_{\mathcal{T}}$ in order to specify all the events $\mathbb{S}^{t_{\mathcal{T}}}$ in the system that happen prior to $t_{\mathcal{T}}$.

Table 1. Notations for the Model

Notation	Description
$\mathbb{M}$	Set of non-manipulated blocks in PPLNS pool
$\mathbb{L}$	Set of non-manipulated blocks in PPS pool
$\mathbb{A}$	Set of the manipulated blocks from PPS pool
$\mathbb{S}$	Set of all blocks in the system of two pools controlled by manager M
W_M	Wealth of non-malicious manager
W_{M^*}	Wealth of (malicious) manager during Harvesting attack
t	time in the system of two pools
t_0	moment of the start of the attack
$t_{\mathcal{T}}$	time of termination of mining
$f(\cdot)$	time-discounting function
P_1	mining power of PPS pool
P_2	mining power of PPLNS pool
p_A	mining power of non-existent miner A whose presence is declared in PPLNS by pool manager
E_B	mining energy needed to mine a block
E_N	mining energy to Produce N shares forming reward window in PPLNS pool
$\tilde{R}$	Standard block reward excluding transaction fees
R	total block reward distributed according to $\mathcal{N}(\mu_R, \sigma_R)$
ϕ_1	Mining fee in PPS pool
ϕ_2	Mining fee in PPLNS pool

The following hold: *(i)* $\forall i \, (t_{i+1} \geq t_i \geq t_0)$; *(ii)* $\forall i \, \left(R_i \geq \tilde{R} \right)$, where $\tilde{R}$ is the standard block reward excluding transaction fees (for example, in BitCoin network such reward is worth 12.5 BTC). We note that the discrete random variables t_i and R_i are mutually independent.

Every reward R_j for the block B_j ($j \in \mathbb{M}$ in case of "no attack", $j \in \{\mathbb{M} \cup \mathbb{A}\}$ in case of "attack") should be distributed at time t_j among the miners of PPLNS pool according to the PPLNS reward mechanism.

2.2   Model for Manager Incentives

Here we discuss attack incentives by comparing utilities for honest and malicious managers that we obtain using Expected Utility Theory (EUT) which is an essential component of economical and statistical models supporting decision-making processes [24].

We begin with the discussion of wealth acquired during the time $\left[t_0, t_T \right]$ by non-malicious and malicious managers, denoted $W_M \left(t_T \right)$ and $W_{M^*} \left(t_T \right)$, respectively. These values will be used further to compare utilities $U \left(W_M \left(t_T \right) \right)$ and $U \left(W_{M^*} \left(t_T \right) \right)$. In particular, we question sufficient conditions for the case where expected utility denoted $E[U(\cdot)]$ of malicious manager in an 'attack' scenario is greater than expected utility of honest manager in a 'no attack' scenario.

Sufficient Condition for the Profitability of "attack" Scenario. We resort to EUT to demonstrate the following result (for the proof see Appendix (A)).

Theorem 1. *Let M^* denote a malicious manager of PPS and PPLNS pools. If $W_{M^*}(t_T) > W_M(t_T)$ then the manager is incentivized to perform a harvesting attack over her pools.*

Hence, our further task is to define wealth $W_M(t_T)$ and $W_{M^*}(t_T)$ and discuss conditions providing

$$W_{M^*}(t_T) > W_M(t_T). \tag{1}$$

Wealth of the Manager Under "no attack" Scenario. Wealth $W_M \left(t_T \right)$ is received as a result of compensations associated with events $\mathbb{L}^{t_T} \cup \mathbb{A}^{t_T}$ and $\mathbb{M}^{t_T}$ that are registered in PPS and PPLNS pools, respectively. The corresponding components of wealth will be denoted $W_M^1 \left(t_T \right)$ for PPS pool and $W_M^2 \left(t_T \right)$ for PPLNS pool. Let us analyze the wealth that the manager acquires from PPS pool during $\left[t_0, t_T \right]$. During this time, manager collects rewards $\{R_i\}$, $i \in \left\{ \mathbb{L}^{t_T} \cup \mathbb{A}^{t_T} \right\}$ that should be discounted using time discounting function $f(\cdot)$. This will sum up to the component $\sum_{i \in \{ \mathbb{L}^{t_T} \cup \mathbb{A}^{t_T} \}} R_i f \left(t_i - t_0 \right)$. The manager is obliged to compensate mining activity to the miners of PPS pool. In contrast to the mining block B_i which is an event that is discrete in time, compensation of the mining shares can be represented as a continuous process. This is explained by the small amount of computations that are required to obtain a share, and, hence, high frequency of their submissions. During time $\Delta t \to 0$ pool miners spends energy $P_1\Delta t$. This effort constitutes $\frac{P_1\Delta t}{E_B}$ of the total effort to mine a block, which in expectation requires energy E_B. Any such contribution at time t is immediately compensated with $(1-\phi_1)\tilde{R}\frac{P_1\Delta t}{E_B}$ which is discounted with $f(t-t_0)$, where ϕ_1 is the mining fee withheld by the manager. Total wealth effect associated with compensation paid by the manager M to the miners is $-(1-\phi_1)\frac{\tilde{R}}{E_B}\int_{t_0}^{t_T} P_1 f(t-t_0)\mathrm{d}t$. Hence, the total wealth of M collected from PPS pool is:

$$W_M^1(t_T) = \sum_{i\in\{\mathbb{L}^{t_T}\cup\mathbb{A}^{t_T}\}} R_i f(t_i - t_0) - (1-\phi_1)\frac{\tilde{R}}{E_B}\int_{t_0}^{t_T} P_1 f(t-t_0)\mathrm{d}t. \quad (2)$$

Let us discuss the wealth collected by the manager from PPLNS pool. The only possible income of the honest manger is created by withholding mining fee ϕ_2 from the set $\{R_j\}$, $j \in \mathbb{M}^{t_T}$ of rewards received by PPLNS pool. Therefore, total wealth from PPLNS pool is

$$W_M^2(t_T) = \phi_2 \sum_{j\in\mathbb{M}^{t_T}} R_j f(t_j - t_0). \quad (3)$$

For the manager M, the total wealth acquired from PPS and PPLNS pools is defined as:

$$W_M(t_T) = W_M^1(t_T) + W_M^2(t_T)$$
$$= \sum_{i\in\{\mathbb{L}^{t_T}\cup\mathbb{A}^{t_T}\}} R_i f(t_i - t_0) - (1-\phi_1)\frac{\tilde{R}}{E_B}\int_{t_0}^{t_T} P_1 f(t-t_0)\mathrm{d}t$$
$$+ \phi_2 \sum_{j\in\mathbb{M}^{t_T}} R_j f(t_j - t_0). \quad (4)$$

Wealth of the Manager Under "attack" Scenario. In pool harvesting attack that happens during $[t_0, t_T]$, manager M declares that events $\mathbb{L}^{t_T}$ occur in PPS pool while events $\mathbb{M}^{t_T} \cup \mathbb{A}^{t_T}$ occur in PPLNS pool. The total wealth $W_{M^*}(t_T)$ is therefore composed out of the "declared" wealth $W_{\hat{M}}(t_T)$ of the manager and wealth $W_A(t_T)$ of miner A.

Declared Wealth of Manager $= W_{\hat{M}}(t_T)$. This wealth is acquired from the rewards $\{R_i\}$, $i \in \mathbb{L}^{t_T}$ and from rewards $\{R_j\}$, $j \in \{\mathbb{M}^{t_T}\cup\mathbb{A}^{t_T}\}$. Corresponding components of wealth from PPS and PPLNS pools will be denoted as $W_{\hat{M}}^1(t_T)$ and $W_{\hat{M}}^2(t_T)$, respectively. Wealth $W_{\hat{M}}^1(t_T)$ is defined as:

$$W_{\hat{M}}^1(t_T) = \sum_{i\in\mathbb{L}^{t_T}} R_i f(t_i - t_0) - (1-\phi_1)\frac{\tilde{R}}{E_B}\int_{t_0}^{t_T} P_1 f(t-t_0)\mathrm{d}t. \quad (5)$$

Wealth $W_{\hat{M}}^2$ obtained as a result of collecting mining fee ϕ_2 in PPLNS pool is defined as:

$$W_{\hat{M}}^2(t_T) = \phi_2 \sum_{j \in \{\mathbb{M}^{t_T} \cup \mathbb{A}^{t_T}\}} R_j f(t_j - t_0). \tag{6}$$

Total declared wealth of manager M is $W_{\hat{M}}(t_T) = W_{\hat{M}}^1(t_T) + W_{\hat{M}}^2(t_T)$. Replacing $W_{\hat{M}}^1, W_{\hat{M}}^2$ by (5), (6) yields

$$W_{\hat{M}}(t_T) = \sum_{i \in \mathbb{L}^{t_T}} R_i f(t_i - t_0) - (1 - \phi_1)\frac{\tilde{R}}{E_B} \int_{t_0}^{t_T} P_1 f(t - t_0) dt + \phi_2 \sum_{j \in \{\mathbb{M}^{t_T} \cup \mathbb{A}^{t_T}\}} R_j f(t_j - t_0).$$

Wealth of miner $A = W_A(t_T)$. Let us calculate the wealth $W_A(t_T)$ of miner A in PPLNS pool. The compensation paid to the miner A is determined by the effort that she contributed to the mining in the most recent reward window N. Further, instead of discrete number of shares N we will measure that window as equivalent of energy E_N that is required to mine N shares. At any moment in time $t_j, j \in \{\mathbb{M}^{t_T} \cup \mathbb{A}^{t_T}\}$ the miner is ought to be compensated according to the fraction $F_A(t_j)$ of her mining contribution within E_N.

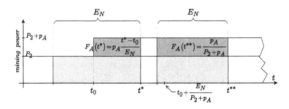

Fig. 3. Mining power diagram for PPLNS pool and corresponding reward fraction for miner A.

We assume steady mining where none of the miners changes her pool. Starting from the moment t_0 contribution of miner A increases linearly in t_j until it reaches value $\frac{p_A}{P_2 + p_A}$ at $t = t_0 + \frac{E_N}{P_2 + p_A}$, and, remains further constant (see Fig. 3):

$$F_A(t_j) = \begin{cases} \frac{(t_j - t_0)p_A}{E_N}, & \text{if } t_j \le t_0 + \frac{E_N}{P_2 + p_A}; \\ \frac{p_A}{P_2 + p_A}, & \text{else.} \end{cases} \tag{7}$$

For example, from Fig. 3 it can be observed that $t_0 < t^* < t_0 + \frac{E_N}{P_2 + p_A} < t^{**}$ meaning that $0 < F_A(t^*) < F_A(t^{**})$. Indeed, by the moment t^*, the amount of energy that has been spent on mining in PPLNS pool by miner A equals to $p_A(t^* - t_0)$ which determines the ratio of her contribution inside PPLNS reward window of size E_N as $p_A \frac{t^* - t_0}{E_N}$. On the other hand, by the moment t^{**} that sliding window contains only mining contributions produced during $\left[t^{**} - \frac{E_N}{P_2 + p_A}, t^{**}\right]$.

Hence, energy consumed by A inside that window equals to $\frac{p_A E_N}{P_2 + p_A}$ and her ratio is $\frac{p_A}{P_2 + p_A}$.

Total wealth of miner A over the whole period of mining is

$$W_A(t_T) = (1 - \phi_2) \sum_{j \in \{M^{t_T} \cup A^{t_T}\}} R_j F_A(t_j) f(t_j - t_0).$$

Finally, the total wealth of the malicious manager is expressed as:

$$W_{M^*}(t_T) = W_{\tilde{M}}(t_T) + W_A(t_T) = \sum_{i \in L^{t_T}} R_i f(t_i - t_0) - (1 - \phi_1) \frac{\tilde{R}}{E_B} \int_{t_0}^{t_T} P_1 f(t - t_0) dt$$

$$+ \phi_2 \cdot \sum_{j \in \{M^{t_T} \cup A^{t_T}\}} R_j f(t_j - t_0) + (1 - \phi_2) \cdot \sum_{j \in \{M^{t_T} \cup A^{t_T}\}} R_j F_A(t_j) f(t_j - t_0).$$

$$(8)$$

Re-defined Sufficient Condition for Attack. The condition in (1) is equivalent to $W_{M^*}(t_T) - W_M(t_T) > 0$. We substitute $W_{M^*}(t_T)$ and $W_M(t_T)$ by their definitions in (8) and (4), respectively and obtain:

$$W_{M^*}(t_T) - W_M(t_T) = (1 - \phi_2)\left(\sum_{j \in \{M^{t_T} \cup A^{t_T}\}} R_j F_A(t_j) f(t_j - t_0) - \sum_{k \in A^{t_T}} R_k f(t_k - t_0) \right) > 0.$$

This inequality can be reduced to

$$\sum_{j \in M^{t_T}} R_j F_A(t_j) f(t_j - t_0) + \sum_{j \in A^{t_T}} R_j F_A(t_j) f(t_j - t_0) - \sum_{k \in A^{t_T}} R_k f(t_k - t_0) > 0,$$

which is guaranteed if and only if the following condition is satisfied:

$$\sum_{j \in M^{t_T}} R_j F_A(t_j) f(t_j - t_0) > \sum_{k \in A^{t_T}} R_k \left(1 - F_A(t_k) \right) f(t_k - t_0). \tag{9}$$

It is remarkable that, for example, such sufficient condition is independent from mining fees ϕ_1, ϕ_2 in PPS and PPLNS pools, respectively.

Honest Miners in PPLNS Pool. We show that the achieved condition (9) will have significant implications for the utility of mining for honest miners in PPLNS pool. Assuming that these miners use the same function $f(t - t_0)$ to discount their future earnings, we add the discounted rewards of honest miners in PPS pool $\sum_{j \in M^{t_T}} R_j f(t_j - t_0)$ to the left-and-right-hand sides of the inequality in (9), multiply it by $(1 - \phi_2)$, and obtain the following condition:

$$(1 - \phi_2) \sum_{j \in M^{t_T}} R_j f(t_j - t_0) > (1 - \phi_2) \sum_{i \in \{M^{t_T} \cup A^{t_T}\}} R_i \left(1 - F_A(t_i) \right) f(t_i - t_0). \tag{10}$$

Left-hand side of (10) expresses wealth $W_H(t_T)$ of the honest miner in "no attack" scenario while the right-hand side represents the wealth $W_{H^*}(t_T)$ of honest miners during pool harvesting attack. It can be observed that in the first instance miners share the whole reward R_j in each of the events in $\mathbb{M}^{t_T}$. In the second instance, due to the presence of miner A in the pool, honest miners receive fractional reward $R_i\left(1 - F_A(t_i)\right)$ while the set of events $\mathbb{M}^{t_T} \cup \mathbb{A}^{t_T}$ is larger. As a result of (10), $E\left[U\left(W_H(t_T)\right)\right] > E\left[U\left(W_{H^*}(t_T)\right)\right]$ meaning that attack is harmful for honest miners in PPLNS pool.

Method of Attack. Further we will discuss a heuristic method for attack which guarantees condition (9) and (in many cases) satisfies the detection constraint.

Definition 1. (Net Charge vs. Net Delivery). *The left-hand-side of* (9) *describes a wealth component* **"net charge"** *that miner A charges from honest miners in PPLNS pool:*

$$\mathcal{C}_L\left(\mathbb{M}^t\right) := \sum_{j \in \mathbb{M}^{t_T}} R_j F_A(t_j) f(t_j - t_0). \tag{11}$$

The right-hand-side of (9) *describes a component* **"net delivery"** *that miner A delivers to the honest miners in PPLNS pool:*

$$\mathcal{C}_R\left(\mathbb{A}^t\right) := \sum_{k \in \mathbb{A}^{t_T}} R_k\left(1 - F_A(t_k)\right) f(t_k - t_0). \tag{12}$$

The following method determines a set $\mathbb{A}^t$ consisting of manipulated blocks from PPS pool at moment $t \in [t_0, t_T]$:

1. at time t_0 declare non-existent miner A with power p_A in PPLNS pool;
2. monitor for the next event in the system at moment t:
    (a) *if* $t \leq t_T$ proceed to (3);
    (b) *else* terminate;
3. modify one of the sets:
    (a) *if* event x in PPS pool, add x to $\mathbb{A}^{t-}$ iff $\mathcal{C}_L\left(\mathbb{M}^t\right) > \mathcal{C}_R\left(\mathbb{A}^{t-} \cup x\right)$[1];
    (b) *if* event y in PPLNS pool, add y to $\mathbb{M}^t$;
    (c) *else*, add x to $\mathbb{L}^t$;
4. go to (2).

From (9) it should, however, be noticed that incentive to attack is present at the moments for events in the sets $\mathbb{A}$ and $\mathbb{M}$ only. Let us further extend our discussion by considering continuous domain for t in (9). As a result, we will take into account continuous nature of functions $F_A(t)$ and $f(t - t_0)$. This is summarized in the next theorem and addressed in the experimental section (for the proof see Appendix (A)).

---

[1] Moment t_- is defined as $t_- = \lim_{\Delta t \to 0} (t - \Delta t)$.

Theorem 2. *At any continuous time $t \leq t_\mathcal{T}$ proposed method for attack guarantees validity of condition*

$$\sum_{j \in \mathbb{M}^t} R_j F_A(t_j) f(t - t_0) > \sum_{k \in \mathbb{A}^t} R_k \Big(1 - F_A(t)\Big) f(t - t_0)$$

under exponential discounting function $f(t - t_0) = e^{-k(t - t_0)}$.

As a result of Theorem (2) malicious manager M who follows the attack method always has an incentive for attack.

2.3 Manager Incentives to Operate PPS Pool

Productivity of PPS pool does not affect the way its miners are rewarded. Hence, manager is not obliged to report about the true power and productivity (number of the blocks found) in PPS pool. Without such information, any theorizing about blockchain decentralization is incomplete. For example, significant proportion of the blocks on BitCoin blockchain are anonymized meaning that they are either produced by solo miners, or in the pools with reward system(s) where productivity does not affect the payoff of the miners [11,27].

If, however, manager reports about productivity of PPS pool, it is important to model her incentives based on the data she provides. We assume that decision to run a pool should be rational and manager must profit from it. The lack of such incentive may indicate that manager benefits from unlawful sources including pool harvesting attack. Here we demonstrate that incentives to run PPS pool depend on several parameters including power of the pool, mining fee ϕ_1 and statistical distribution of R. Further, we examine special condition of pool harvesting attack. For this result we use relation that exists between EUT and Mean Variance (MV) analysis (for the proof see Appendix (B)).

Lemma 1. *Under exponential discounting, manager reveals set $\mathbb{L}$ only if condition*

$$\left(\frac{\mu_R}{(1 - \phi_1)\tilde{R}} - 1\right)\big|\mathbb{L}^{t_\mathcal{T}}\big| > \big|\mathbb{A}^{t_\mathcal{T}}\big| \tag{13}$$

is satisfied.

In case when this condition is not satisfied manager is unable to reveal the true data about the set $\mathbb{L}$ of non-manipulated blocks because economical incentives to run such pool in an honest way are absent. This will further complicate evaluations of the level of decentralization in the blockchain.

3   Experimental Evaluation

We ponder on whether the attacker who follows the method remains undetected by honest miners in PPLNS pool. To answer this question, we conduct experiment and discuss details such as the range of input parameters, generation of

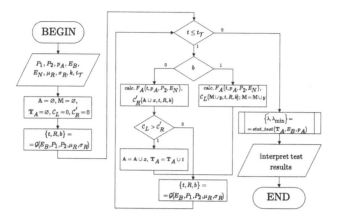

Fig. 4. Detailed diagram of the experiment.

random variables that characterize mining outcomes, and statistical tests which represent detection constraint (see Fig. 4). In order to keep attack undetected, miner A should produce full solutions at the rate which is determined by energy required to mine a block and her mining power, i.e. $\{E_B, p_A\}$. The actual rate of block submissions can be derived from the time array $\mathbf{T}_A$ which is obtained by recording the moments of submission of full solutions from PPS to PPLNS pool (Fig. 4). On the diagram, we denote $C'_R(\mathbb{A}^t)$ a challenge value which is not approved yet. Each event is characterized by time, reward and origin which are denoted using triplet $\{t, R, b\}$ where b is a binary value indicating either PPS (0) or PPLNS (1) pool. The triplet is generated using random generator $\mathcal{G}(\cdot)$ on inputs E_B, P_1, P_2 governing time and origin of the next event, and inputs μ_R, σ_R denoting mean and standard deviation of normal distribution $\mathcal{N}(\mu_R, \sigma_R)$ which determines random monetary value of the block reward. Parameter k determines intensity of time discounting for the function $f(t - t_0) = e^{-k(t-t_0)}$ which affects values of C_L and C'_R. Such exponential function is popular for the studies conducted in behavioral economics and game theory [1].

3.1 Wealth and Utility of the Attacker

With the aim to better understand differences between the wealth functions for the honest and malicious managers we refer to Fig. 5. These results were obtained for the condition $E_B = 1$. With total mining power of the whole blockchain network equal 1 we presume that on average, a block is mined at every single unit of time. For example, the full timespan of mining simulation depicted on Fig. 5a can represent a system of PPS and PPLNS pools on BitCoin network where wealth is compared during the period of nearly 417 days. Because of the obligation to compensate shares for PPS miners on a regular basis, the both functions may experience periods of negative wealth growth which are explained by bad luck in finding full block solutions. It can be observed that the both functions $W_M(t)$

and $W_{M^*}(t)$ are asymptotically converging in the second half of the experiment to the value of $W_c \approx 158.4$. This is due to time discounting that is incorporated in the wealth function. Irrespective of the behavior of $W_M(t)$ of honest manager the method of attack guarantees that $W_{M^*}(t)$ of malicious manager is always above it (see Theorem (2)). However, in order to remain undetected by the honest miners in PPLNS pool, the attacker needs to sacrifice her wealth which happens every time when an event is added to $\mathbb{A}^t$ at time t (see Fig. 5b). It can be observed that near such moments wealth $W_M(t)$ is growing faster than $W_{M^*}(t)$, and as a result, the gap between the graphs shrinks.

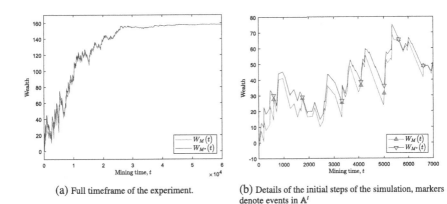

(a) Full timeframe of the experiment.

(b) Details of the initial steps of the simulation, markers denote events in $\mathbb{A}^t$

Fig. 5. Wealth of honest and malicious managers during the experiment, $P_1 = 6 \times 10^{-3}$, $P_2 = 10^{-2}$, $\phi_1 = 0.02$, $\phi_2 = 0.01$, $k = 10^{-4}$, $p_A = 1.2 \times 10^{-3}$, $E_B = 1$, $E_N = 2 \times E_B$.

Utility Function. There is a wide selection of functions that may be used to express utility of the manager [24]. We resort to quadratic utility $U(W) = W - bW^2$ due to its simplicity. Because $U'(W) = 1 - 2bW$ maximal utility is reached at $W = \frac{1}{2b}$. The parameters of the utility should be selected in a way that it is non-decreasing on wealth $W \in [0, W_{\max}]$, which requires that $b \in \left[0, \frac{1}{2W_{\max}}\right]$. For the lowest value $b = 0$, utility is equal to wealth, $U(W) = W$, and represents risk-neutral manager. On the other hand, due to the convergence of the wealth (see Fig. 5a), the upper limit of b converges to a small value that is always greater than zero. This can be used to represent risk-averse manager who has concave utility function. On Fig. 6 we display differences between the utilities, $\Delta U(t) = U\left(W_{M^*}(t)\right) - U\left(W_M(t)\right)$ of malicious and honest managers, respectively. Case $b = 0$ Fig. 6a reflects difference between the wealth. The results for a higher $b = \frac{1}{2 \times 1.05 \times W_c}$, are provided on Fig. 6b. For the both illustrations on Fig. 6 $\Delta U(t) \approx 0$ for $t_z > 5 \times 10^4$, but incentive to attack is significant for the early stage of mining. Parameter k may have several interpretations including those related to investment decisions, where it expresses the opportunities to earn interest that are lost due to postponing payments in time [1]. For example, rate $k = 10^{-4}$ implies discount $e^{-0.0001}$ for a reward deferred for a unit of time in our experiment. Due to the difference in block mining rate in our simulated environment and real settings, such discount may be assumed happening every 10 minutes in BitCoin network. This further requires opportunity to invest BitCoin with an interest surpassing 54% for a month – the rate which rarely happens on practice even in a very speculative economic environment. On the other hand, $k = 10^{-6}$ in our experiment is equivalent to a moderate rate of 5.4% for a year – the financial opportunity that can be easily found among many cryptocurrency brokers who practice margin lending [5,6,9].

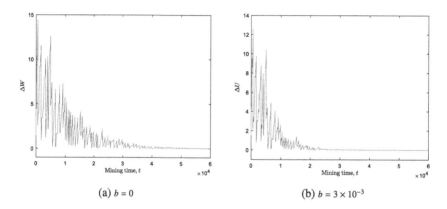

(a) $b = 0$ (b) $b = 3 \times 10^{-3}$

Fig. 6. Difference between utilities of malicious and honest managers, computed using wealth from Fig. 5.

3.2 Test Results and Their Interpretation

We studied how efficiently the malicious manager can hide the fact of attack under different intensity of time discounting, k, and different degree of involvement in the attack, p_A/P_1. For the details about detection constraint see [20].

Organization of Simulation. The experiments were organized in two pairs with 10^2 trials in each experiment. The first experiment in each pair was accomplished with $k = 10^{-4}$ and the second with $k = 10^{-6}$. Attack involvement was set to 20% for the first and 90% for the second pair resulting in $p_A = 1.2 \times 10^{-3}$ and $p_A = 5.4 \times 10^{-3}$, respectively (see Figs. 7 and 8). For each of the trials, the mining in PPS and PPLNS pools and actions of the malicious manager were simulated according to the diagram on Fig. 4 with the following values: expected energy to find a block $E_B = 1$, contribution considered for compensation by PPLNS window $E_N = 2 \times E_B$, total power of PPS and PPLNS pools equal to $P_1 = 6 \times 10^{-3}$, $P_2 = 10^{-2}$, respectively; standard reward for the block (excluding transaction fees) $\tilde{R} = 12.5$, distribution of the total reward (including fees) $R := \mathcal{N}(\mu_R = 13.7, \sigma_R = 0.4)$. Without loss of generality, we set $t_0 = 0$. Array $\mathbf{T}_A$ was analyzed to calculate the number of events $\lambda(t)$ for time intervals $[t_0, t]$, $t \leq t_T$.

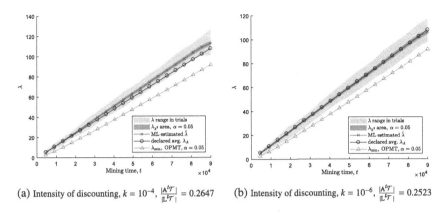

(a) Intensity of discounting, $k = 10^{-4}$, $\frac{|A^l\mathcal{T}|}{|L^l\mathcal{T}|} = 0.2647$ (b) Intensity of discounting, $k = 10^{-6}$, $\frac{|A^l\mathcal{T}|}{|L^l\mathcal{T}|} = 0.2523$

Fig. 7. Test results for pool harvesting attack, $p_A = 1.2 \times 10^{-3}$

Visualized Data. The expected number of events produced by the miner on $[t_0, t]$ is $\lambda_A(t) = p_A \frac{t-t_0}{E_B}$ which changes linearly in time. We use λ_A to calculate $\lambda_{\min}$ in OPMT with $\alpha = 0.05$ [30]. Because of the fact that the both λ_A and $\lambda_{\min}$ depend on p_A and time only, they are identical for Figs. 7a and b and for Figs. 8a and b. On the other hand, value of k affects decisions of malicious manager M and, consequently, defines values λ from each of the 10^2 trials, for every moment in time. We depict range for λ, estimate its mean $\hat{\lambda}$, and corresponding confidence intervals λ_{χ^2} for $\alpha = 0.05$.

Results of the Tests. It can be seen that OPMT is passed in all the trials of the both experiments depicted on Fig. 7 as the ranges for λ are placed notably above the $\lambda_{\min}$. For the experimental results on Fig. 8, however, there are moments when OPMT is not passed in all trials. At the initial stages of the attack on Fig. 8a H_0 can be rejected for some of the trials, while on Fig. 8b H_0 can be rejected for some trials at any moment. For the χ^2-Goodness of fit test, λ_A is within confidence interval at any moment for Fig. 7b only which means that these are the sole experimental settings where expected performance is matched. Results from Fig. 7a demonstrate that the declared λ_A is outperformed in most cases. Mixed data about that test can be obtained from Fig. 8a where λ_A is above and below the confidence interval at different attack moments. Finally, we witness under-performance of $\hat{\lambda}$ (including the confidence interval area) compared to the required λ_A on the whole duration of the attack in the last experiment (Fig. 8b).

Summary of the Experiments. With higher value of k wealth of malicious manager faster outweighs the wealth of honest manager which, in turn, allows the attacker to create more submissions to PPLNS pool. This increases chances to pass the tests because λ in trials is increasing. On the other hand, the main challenge of higher involvement into attack is due to higher expectations for the performance of the miner A, λ_A. Since PPS pool is the only source of the blocks that is available for manipulation, it is more difficult to guarantee such

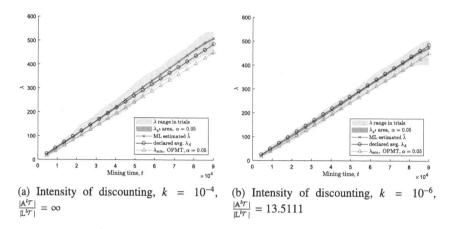

(a) Intensity of discounting, $k = 10^{-4}$, $\frac{|A^t\tau|}{|L^t\tau|} = \infty$

(b) Intensity of discounting, $k = 10^{-6}$, $\frac{|A^t\tau|}{|L^t\tau|} = 13.5111$

Fig. 8. Test results for pool harvesting attack, $p_A = 5.4 \times 10^{-3}$

exceptional statistical property due to the aspect of luck that is associated with mining.

Lastly, if the attack remains hidden from the honest miners in PPLNS pool, manager may either reveal or hide the origin of the blocks in $\mathbb{L}$. Her decision is governed by the condition (13). For instance, for $\phi_1 = 0.02$ we obtain value $\frac{\mu_R}{(1-\phi_1)\tilde{R}} - 1 \approx 0.1216$ which remains the same for all the experiments and should be compared with $\frac{|A^t\tau|}{|L^t\tau|}$ in order to understand the decision of the manager. As a result of this ratio being higher than 0.1216 across our simulations, manager will not disclose the origin of the blocks in any of the experiments (Figs. 7 and 8).

4   Discussion

In this paper, we investigated a new type of incentive for malicious behavior for a manager who governs PPS and PPLNS mining pools. It arises due to preference in receiving monetary compensations earlier in time. The attack requires introducing a non-existent miner A to PPLNS pool whose actions are totally controlled by the manager. The miner will then demand from the pool a reward proportional to the mining power p_A declared by her (see Fig. 2).

Three main questions that we analyze in regards to the attack are:
(*i*) what is the technique that guarantees its profitability to the malicious manager?
(*ii*) how successful is such technique in hiding the statistical evidence of the attack?
(*iii*) how the attack may hamper blockchain decentralization and related studies?

We deploy EUT to compare incentives of the honest and malicious managers by representing their utilities as functions of the wealth acquired from governing

PPS and PPLNS pools. Sufficient condition for the incentive to attack is presented in (1) and developed further in (9) for the framework with three exclusive subsets $\mathbb{A}$, $\mathbb{L}$ and $\mathbb{M}$ (see Table 1). We next reason on whether such sufficient condition can be satisfied at any given moment starting from t_0 if the manager utilizes the proposed method for attack under exponential time discounting (see Theorem (2)). The manager makes the decision on whether to attack or not at moment t_0 when the events in the system of the two pools are not known to her yet. In order to support such decision we run computer simulation demonstrating that the utility of the attacker can be substantially higher than the utility of a honest manager at the beginning of attack (Fig. 5). We presume that disruptions of mining process of different kinds can happen in the real settings in future where chances of interruption increase over time. This aspect requires additional investigation while going beyond our model of incentives in this paper [3, 29]. We, however, speculate that higher profitability of attack in the near future horizon emphasizes practicality of the proposed method when compared to the approaches with linear wealth accumulation in time. On the other hand, the method does not necessary maximize the utility of attacker over the set of possible events. The attack incentives diminish in the distant future while, nevertheless, remaining positive (see Theorem (2)).

The heuristic nature of the proposed method, however, does not guarantee concealing of the statistical evidence in all the attack cases. In order to verify manager's ability to hide the attack we conducted several series of experiments with different intensities of time discounting and different values of declared mining power p_A. As a result of simulation (diagram presented on Fig. 4) we collected the array $\mathbf{T}_A$ of block submission moments. Honest miners in PPLNS pool expect from miner A producing full block solutions which are distributed in time according to Poisson distribution with parameter $\lambda_A \sim p_A$. The test hypotheses that compare data in $\mathbf{T}_A$ with declared parameter λ_A were verified by us in One Poisson Mean Test (OPMT) and χ^2-Goodness of fit test [30]. We conclude that the harvesting attacks under lower k and higher p_A are more likely to be detected by honest miners. This makes the proposed statistical tests a useful mean to safeguard miners in PPLNS pools from severe malicious manipulations. On the other hand, less severe attacks with lower p_A and under higher intensity of time discounting k were not detected during the experiment. This fact leaves a room for further research including development of multivariate statistical test that allow to work with hypotheses combining occurrence of events with the reward value R.

Correct estimation for the degree of decentralization in PoW cryptocurrencies requires information on how mining power is governed by independent managers. In some reward systems like, for instance, PPLNS such information is inevitably revealed due to the specifics of reward process occurring only upon discovery of a new block. Due to such openness, in most cases, blocks mined in PPLNS pools appear identified on blockchain explorer [11]. Thus, power of the pool can be estimated based on the number of blocks mined in a unit of time. In contrast to that, other reward system like, for example, PPS compensate miners on a regular basis which is independent from pool productivity. Information about power of such pools may either be provided by their managers, or restored from the testimonies about personal power of the miners affiliated with the pools. With the latter source being inherently unreliable we ponder at the manager incentives to report blocks under pool harvesting attack. For the necessary condition (13) to reveal pool productivity (set $\mathbb{L}$) developed in Lemma (1) we assume that such pool should be profitable for the manager. If, for instance, revealed $\mathbb{L}$ does not show incentive to run such PPS pool in a honest manner, mining community may distrust such manager. In order to avoid damage to her reputation she may either not associate the both PPS and PPLNS with her, or not reveal $\mathbb{L}$ (for example, on blockchain explorer the source of such anonymous blocks appears as "unknown"). Each of these manager decisions will distort the comprehension of distribution of mining power in the network. For example, during our experiment, we confirmed mismatch with necessary condition for the profitability of PPS pool. Consequently, pool harvesting attack with such settings can be considered as a disorienting factor for studies of blockchain decentralization.

Block reward $R := \mathcal{N}(\mu_R, \sigma_R)$ and the size of PPLNS compensation window E_N play important role in understanding pool harvesting attack and should be studied in the future. For example, our intuitive reasoning is that for higher E_N detection will become an easier task because of a slower rising fraction F_A. According to the method, slower growth in profitability of attack will cause longer delays in submitting blocks which may be detected by OPMT.

A number of assumptions was made for the paper. First, we consider that miners in PPLNS pool submit shares to the manager but are unable to verify submissions of the others, which allows claiming of reward fraction by miner A without the need to regularly submit shares. This may, for instance, contradict with sharechain realization of PPLNS that is practiced in some mining pools [25]. However, due to stricter requirements to time-synchronization (demanding lower network latency) for the submitted shares, broader developments for such pools are constrained on practice. Second, information about authorship for each block (produced in the pool) is available on the web-portal of PPLNS pool. Hence, miners are able to analyze mining productivity of each identity registered with the pool. In the pools that do not reveal this information statistical test for compliance of miner A is impossible, which significantly simplifies the task of attacker. Third, we presume that honest miners do not leave PPS and PPLNS pools and new miners do not join them which represents a closed system. Modeling of attack incentives, as well as conducting corresponding statistical tests for an open system would require a set of additional assumptions that go beyond our scope, but will be considered in the future research. Fourth, we do not analyze consequences for unsuccessful harvesting attack that is detected by honest miners in PPLNS. As a result, we do not inquire possible reaction of honest miners to the unfavorable changes in pool settings. In the presence of alternative pools this topic, however, may be of interest for game-theoretical research.

A   Theorems

Theorem 1. *Let M^* denote a malicious manager of PPS and PPLNS pools. If $W_{M^*}(t_T) > W_M(t_T)$ then the manager is incentivized to perform a harvesting attack over her pools.*

Proof. Because of the requirement $U'(W) > 0$ we state that under $W_{M^*}(t_T) > W_M(t_T)$ we have $U(W_{M^*}(t_T)) > U(W_M(t_T))$. Finally, we state that

$$E\left[U\left(W_{M^*}(t)\right)\right] > E\left[U\left(W_M(t)\right)\right].$$

$\square$

Theorem 2. *At any continuous time $t \le t_T$ proposed method for attack guarantees validity of condition*

$$\sum_{j \in \mathbb{M}^t} R_j F_A(t_j) f(t - t_0) > \sum_{k \in \mathbb{A}^t} R_k \left(1 - F_A(t)\right) f(t - t_0)$$

under exponential discounting function $f(t - t_0) = e^{-k(t-t_0)}$.

Proof. The proposed method of attack always guarantees validity of (9). We perform the proof of this theorem using induction proof technique. Let us denote the last event that happened in $\mathbb{A} \cup \mathbb{M}$ prior t as t_e. We then express the questioned inequality as

$$\sum_{j \in \mathbb{M}^t} R_j F_A(t) f(t - t_e + t_e - t_0) > \sum_{k \in \mathbb{A}^t} R_k \left(1 - F_A(t)\right) f(t - t_e + t_e - t_0).$$
(14)

Since $F_A(t)$ is non-decreasing it is sufficient to demonstrate that

$$\sum_{j \in \mathbb{M}^t} R_j F_A(t_e) f(t - t_e + t_e - t_0) > \sum_{k \in \mathbb{A}^t} R_k \left(1 - F_A(t_e)\right) f(t - t_e + t_e - t_0).$$
(15)

Claim: There exists a homomorphic function which satisfies the following relation:

$$f(t - t_e + t_e - t_0) = f(t - t_e) \odot f(t_e - t_0),$$

where $\odot$ denotes a homomorphic operation. This claim is true if we chose $f(t - t_0) = e^{-k(t-t_0)}$ and $\odot$ be a multiplicative operation. Then the condition in (16) is equivalent to

$$f(t_e - t_0) \odot \sum_{j \in \mathbb{M}^t} R_j F_A(t_e) f(t - t_e) > f(t_e - t_0) \odot \sum_{k \in \mathbb{A}^t} R_k \left(1 - F_A(t_e)\right) f(t - t_e). \quad (16)$$

Canceling out $f(t_e - t_0)$ yields $\sum\limits_{j \in \mathbb{M}^t} R_j F_A(t_e) f(t - t_e) > \sum\limits_{k \in \mathbb{A}^t} R_k \left(1 - F_A(t_e)\right)$

$f(t - t_e)$.

$\square$

B   Lemma

Lemma 1. *Under exponential discounting, manager reveals set $\mathbb{L}$ only if condition*

$$\left(\frac{\mu_R}{(1-\phi_1)\tilde{R}} - 1\right)\left|\mathbb{L}^{t_{\mathcal{T}}}\right| > \left|\mathbb{A}^{t_{\mathcal{T}}}\right| \tag{13}$$

is satisfied.

Proof. In the system of PPS and PPLNS pools, manager makes a binary decision $\mathcal{B} \in \{0,1\}$ that maximizes $E\left[U\left(\mathcal{B} \cdot W_M^1(t_{\mathcal{T}}) + W_M^2(t_{\mathcal{T}})\right)\right]$. First, $\mathcal{B} = 1$ only if $E\left[W_M^1(t_{\mathcal{T}})\right] > 0$. In acc. to M-V analysis $E\left[U\left(W_M^1(t_{\mathcal{T}}) + W_M^2(t_{\mathcal{T}})\right)\right] \geq E\left[W_M^2(t_{\mathcal{T}})\right]$ requires that either :

$$E\left[W_M^1(t_{\mathcal{T}}) + W_M^2(t_{\mathcal{T}})\right] \geq E\left[W_M^2(t_{\mathcal{T}})\right] \text{ OR } var\left(W_M^1(t_{\mathcal{T}}) + W_M^2(t_{\mathcal{T}})\right) \leq var\left(W_M^2(t_{\mathcal{T}})\right).$$

Further, we consider the first cond. since the second inequality is impossible to satisfy. Because $W_M^1(t_{\mathcal{T}})$ and $W_M^2(t_{\mathcal{T}})$ are independent, we demand $E\left[W_M^1(t_{\mathcal{T}})\right] > 0$. Let us substitute[2] expression for $W_M^1(t_{\mathcal{T}})$ from Eq. (5):

$$E\left[W_M^1(t_{\mathcal{T}})\right] = E\left[\sum_{i\in\mathbf{PPS}} R_i f(t_i - t_0) - (1-\phi_1)\frac{\tilde{R}P_1^*}{E_B}\int_{t_0}^{t_{\mathcal{T}}} f(t - t_0)\mathrm{d}t\right] > 0 \Rightarrow$$

$$\Rightarrow E\left[\sum_{i\in\mathbf{PPS}} R_i f(t_i - t_0)\right] > (1-\phi_1)\frac{\tilde{R}P_1^*}{E_B}\int_{t_0}^{t_{\mathcal{T}}} f(t - t_0)\mathrm{d}t. \tag{17}$$

with the right-hand side of this inequality being constant. In the left-hand side of (17) we observe that

$$E\left[\sum_{i\in\mathbf{PPS}} R_i f(t_i - t_0)\right] = \sum_{i\in\mathbf{PPS}} E\left[R_i f(t_i - t_0)\right] = \mu_R \sum_{i\in\mathbf{PPS}} E\left[e^{-k(t_i - t_0)}\right] \tag{18}$$

because variables R_i and t_i, $i \in \mathbf{PPS}$, are mutually independent and $E[R_i] = \mu_R$. We introduce $\{z_j\} := \{t_{i_j} - t_{i_j-1}\}$, $2 \leq j \leq n$. We further notice that

$$\sum_{i\in\mathbf{PPS}} E\left[e^{-k(t_i - t_0)}\right] = \sum_{j=2}^{n} E\left[\prod_{l=2}^{j} e^{-kz_l}\right]. \tag{19}$$

---

[2] We use notations P_1^* and $\mathbf{PPS}$, $|\mathbf{PPS}| = n$ to designate the power and the set of events in PPS pool that are declared by the manager.

According to PoW mining principle, variable z is i.i.d and, hence, Eq. (19) yields

$$\sum_{j=2}^{n} E\left[\prod_{l=2}^{j} e^{-kz_l}\right] = \sum_{j=2}^{n}\prod_{l=2}^{j} E\left[e^{-kz(l-1)}\right] = \frac{1-\left(E\left[e^{-kz}\right]\right)^{n}}{1-E\left[e^{-kz}\right]} E\left[e^{-kz}\right], \quad (20)$$

where the last equation on the right side of the Eq. (20) follows from geometric series $\left(\sum_{i=1}^{n} q^i = \frac{1-q^n}{1-q}q \text{ if we set } q = e^{-kz} < 1\right)$. Random variable z can be described by it's density function $d(z) = \lambda_m e^{-\lambda_m z}$. Then

$$E\left[e^{-kz}\right] = \int_{0}^{\infty} f(z)d(z)d(z) = \lambda_m \int_{0}^{\infty} e^{-z\left(k+\lambda_m\right)} dz = \frac{\lambda_m}{k+\lambda_m}. \quad (21)$$

Now, using result from (19)–(21), the last expression in Eq. (18) is:

$$\mu_R \sum_{i\in \mathbf{PPS}} E\left[e^{-k(t_i-t_0)}\right] = \mu_R \frac{1-\left(\frac{\lambda_m}{k+\lambda_m}\right)^{n}}{1-\frac{\lambda_m}{k+\lambda_m}}\frac{\lambda_m}{k+\lambda_m} = \mu_R\frac{\lambda_m}{k}\left(1-\left(\frac{\lambda_m}{k+\lambda_m}\right)^{n}\right). \quad (22)$$

For the right-hand side of (17) and the exponential time-discounting $f(t-t_0) = e^{-k(t-t_0)}$ we have

$$\left(1-\phi_1\right)\frac{\tilde{R}P_1^*}{E_B}\int_{t_0}^{t_T} f(t-t_0)dt = \left(1-\phi_1\right)\frac{\tilde{R}P_1^*}{kE_B}\left(1-e^{-k\left(t_T-t_0\right)}\right). \quad (23)$$

Without loss of generality we note that $\lambda_m = \frac{n}{t_T-t_0}$. As a result, we rewrite Eq. (17) as

$$\mu_R\frac{\lambda_m}{k}\left(1-\left(\frac{\lambda_m}{k+\lambda_m}\right)^{n}\right) \overset{?}{>} \left(1-\phi_1\right)\frac{\tilde{R}P_1^*}{kE_B}\left(1-e^{-k\frac{n}{\lambda_m}}\right). \quad (24)$$

Let us compare components $1-\left(\frac{\lambda_m}{k+\lambda_m}\right)^{n}$ and $1-e^{-k\frac{n}{\lambda_m}}$ in the expressions for the left-and-right-hand sides of Eq. (24), respectively. We apply Taylor expansion to the function e^{k/λ_m} and derive that $e^{\frac{k}{\lambda_m}} > 1 + \frac{k}{\lambda_m}$, meaning that

$$1-\left(\frac{\lambda_m}{k+\lambda_m}\right)^{n} < 1-e^{-k\frac{n}{\lambda_m}}, \quad (25)$$

which dictates the following necessary condition:

$$\mu_R\frac{\lambda_m}{k} > \left(1-\phi_1\right)\frac{\tilde{R}P_1^*}{kE_B}. \quad (26)$$

Alternatively, replacing $\lambda_m = \frac{n}{t_T - t_0}$ we obtain necessary condition for (17):

$$\frac{nE_B}{(t_T - t_0)P_1^*} > (1 - \phi_1)\frac{\tilde{R}}{\mu_R}. \tag{27}$$

In the left side of (27), numerator represents expected amount of energy that is required to produce set of events **PPS**. Denominator expresses the actual energy that is spent in PPS pool by its miners. An obvious observation from the right-hand side of (27) is that inequality can be easier satisfied for larger mining fee ϕ_1 and higher transaction fees (which define μ_R) in BitCoin network.

In case of pool harvesting attack manager can only report $\mathbf{PPS} = \mathbb{L}^{t_T}$ events versus $\mathbb{L}^{t_T} \cup \mathbb{A}^{t_T}$ that can be reported by honest manager. We assume that miners of PPS pool communicate with each other and collectively estimate the total power of PPS pool as $P_1^* = E_B\frac{\left|\mathbb{L}^{t_T}\right| + \left|\mathbb{A}^{t_T}\right|}{t_T - t_0}$. Substituting this into (27) produces

$$\left(\frac{\mu_R}{(1 - \phi_1)\tilde{R}} - 1\right)\left|\mathbb{L}^{t_T}\right| > \left|\mathbb{A}^{t_T}\right|. \qquad \square$$

References

1. Angner, E.: A Course in Behavioral Economics. Palgrave Macmillan, New York (2012)
2. Antpool: Statistics (2019). https://www.antpool.com/poolStats.htm
3. Arnold, F., Hermanns, H., Pulungan, R., Stoelinga, M.: Time-dependent analysis of attacks. In: Abadi, M., Kremer, S. (eds.) POST 2014. LNCS, vol. 8414, pp. 285–305. Springer, Heidelberg (2014). https://doi.org/10.1007/978-3-642-54792-8_16
4. Bag, S., Ruj, S., Sakurai, K.: Bitcoin block withholding attack: analysis and mitigation. IEEE Trans. Inf. Forensics Secur. **12**(8), 1967–1978 (2017)
5. BITMEX: Trading on BitMEX (2019). https://www.bitmex.com/app/tradingOverview
6. BlockFi: Earn a 6.2% Annual Yield on Your Crypto (2019). https://blockfi.com/crypto-interestaccount/
7. Chatterjee, K., Goharshady, A.K., Ibsen-Jensen, R., Velner, Y.: Ergodic mean-payoff games for the analysis of attacks in crypto-currencies. In: 29th International Conference on Concurrency Theory (CONCUR 2018), pp. 11:1–11:17. Schloss Dagstuhl. Leibniz-Zentrum fuer Informatik (2018)
8. Chávez, J.J.G., Silva Rodrigues, C.K. da: Automatic hopping among pools and distributed applications in the Bitcoin network. In: 2016 XXI Symposium on Signal Processing, Images and Artificial Vision (STSIVA), pp. 1–7 (2016)
9. Coinlend: Automated Margin Lending: A Possibility for Passive Income with Cryptocurrencies. Press Release (2018)
10. Courtois, N.T., Emirdag, P., and Wang, Z.: On detection of Bitcoin mining redirection attacks. In: ICISSP 2015 - Proceedings, pp. 98–105. SciTePress (2015)
11. Explorer, B.: Block Explorer (2019). https://www.blockchain.com/explorer
12. Eyal, I.: The miner's dilemma. In: 2015 IEEE Symposium on Security and Privacy, pp. 89–103 (2015)

13. Eyal, I., Sirer, E.G.: Majority is not enough: Bitcoin mining is vulnerable. Commun. ACM **61**(7), 95–102 (2018)
14. Fisch, B., Pass, R., Shelat, A.: Socially optimal mining pools. In: Devanur, N.R., Lu, P. (eds.) WINE 2017. LNCS, vol. 10660, pp. 205–218. Springer, Cham (2017). https://doi.org/10.1007/978-3-319-71924-5_15
15. Garay, J., Kiayias, A., Leonardos, N.: The Bitcoin backbone protocol with chains of variable difficulty. In: Katz, J., Shacham, H. (eds.) CRYPTO 2017. LNCS, vol. 10401, pp. 291–323. Springer, Cham (2017). https://doi.org/10.1007/978-3-319-63688-7_10
16. Gervais, A., Karame, G.O., WüNust, K., Glykantzis, V., Ritzdorf, H., Capkun, S.: On the security and performance of proof of work blockchains. In: Proceedings of the 2016 ACM SIGSAC Conference, CCS '16, pp. 3–16. ACM (2016)
17. Karame, G.O., Androulaki, E., Capkun, S.: Double-spending fast payments in Bitcoin. In: ACM CCS 2012 - Proceedings, pp. 906–917. ACM (2012)
18. Karame, G.O., Androulaki, E., Roeschlin, M., Gervais, A., Čapkun, S.: Misbehavior in Bitcoin: a study of double-spending and accountability. ACM Trans. Inf. Syst. Secur. **18**(1), 2:1–2:32 (2015)
19. Kroll, J.A., Davey, I.C., Felten, E.W.: The economics of Bitcoin mining, or Bitcoin in the presence of adversaries. In: Proceedings of WEIS, p. 11 (2013)
20. Kuchta, V., Zolotavkin, Y.: Detection constraint for Harvesting Attack in Proof of Work mining pools (2019). https://doi.org/10.26180/5d2464e40a00d
21. Liu, H., Ruan, N., Du, R., Jia, W.: On the strategy and behavior of Bitcoin mining with N-attackers. In: ASIACCS 2018, Proceedings, pp. 357–368. ACM (2018)
22. Nakamoto, S.: Bitcoin: a peer-to-peer electronic cash system (2008)
23. Nayak, K., Kumar, S., Miller, A., Shi, E.: Stubborn mining: generalizing selfish mining and combining with an eclipse attack. In: 2016 IEEE European Symposium on Security and Privacy (EuroS P), pp. 305–320 (2016)
24. von Neumann, J., Morgenstern, O., Kuhn, H., Rubinstein, A.: Theory of Games and Economic Behavior: 60th Anniversary, Commemorative edn. Princeton University Press (2007)
25. P2Pool: P2Pool Bitcoin Mining Pool Global Statistics (2018). http://p2pool.org/stats/index.php. Accessed 19 March 2018
26. Qin, R., Yuan, Y., Wang, S., Wang, F.: Economic issues in Bitcoin mining and blockchain research. In: 2018 IEEE Intelligent Vehicles Symposium (IV), pp. 268–273 (2018)
27. Rosenfeld, M.: Analysis of Bitcoin Pooled Mining Reward Systems. arXiv preprint arXiv:1112.4980 (2011)
28. Smith, A.: An Inquiry Into the Nature and Causes of the Wealth of Nations. Simon & Brown, New York (2011)
29. Smith, D.: Reliability, Maintainability and Risk: Practical Methods for Engineers including Reliability Centred Maintenance and Safety-Related Systems. Elsevier Science, New York (2011)
30. Weerahandi, S.: Exact Statistical Methods for Data Analysis. Springer, New York (2003)
31. Zolotavkin, Y., García, J., Rudolph, C.: Incentive compatibility of pay per last n shares in Bitcoin mining pools. In: Rass, S., An, B., Kiekintveld, C., Fang, F., Schauer, S. (eds.) Decision and Game Theory for Security, vol. 10575, pp. 21–39. Springer, Cham (2017). https://doi.org/10.1007/978-3-319-68711-7_2

A Lattice-Based Linkable Ring Signature Supporting Stealth Addresses

Zhen Liu[1]([✉]), Khoa Nguyen[2], Guomin Yang[3], Huaxiong Wang[2], and Duncan S. Wong[4]

[1] Shanghai Jiao Tong University, Shanghai, China
liuzhen@sjtu.edu.cn
[2] School of Physical and Mathematical Sciences,
Nanyang Technological University, Jurong East, Singapore
{khoantt,HXWang}@ntu.edu.sg
[3] University of Wollongong, Wollongong, Australia
gyang@uow.edu.au
[4] CryptoBLK and Abelian Foundation, Kowloon, China
duncanwong@cryptoblk.io

Abstract. First proposed in CryptoNote, a collection of popular privacy-centric cryptocurrencies have employed Linkable Ring Signature and a corresponding Key Derivation Mechanism (KeyDerM) for keeping the payer and payee of a transaction anonymous and unlinkable. The KeyDerM is used for generating a fresh signing key and the corresponding public key, referred to as a stealth address, for the transaction payee. The stealth address will then be used in the linkable ring signature next time when the payee spends the coin. However, in all existing works, including Monero, the privacy model only considers the two cryptographic primitives separately. In addition, to be applied to cryptocurrencies, the security and privacy models for Linkable Ring Signature should capture the situation that the public key ring of a signature may contain keys created by an adversary (referred to as adversarially-chosen-key attack), since in cryptocurrencies, it is normal for a user (adversary) to create self-paying transactions so that some maliciously created public keys can get into the system without being detected .

In this paper, we propose a new cryptographic primitive, referred to as Linkable Ring Signature Scheme with Stealth Addresses (SALRS), which comprehensively and strictly captures the security and privacy requirements of hiding the payer and payee of a transaction in cryptocurrencies, especially the adversarially-chosen-key attacks. We also propose a lattice-based SALRS construction and prove its security and privacy in the random oracle model. In other words, our construction provides

The work was supported by the National Natural Science Foundation of China (No. 61672339), the National Cryptography Development Fund (No. MMJJ20170111), the Gopalakrishnan - NTU Presidential Postdoctoral Fellowship 2018, the National Research Foundation, Prime Minister's Office, Singapore under its Strategic Capability Research Centres Funding Initiative, the Singapore Ministry of Education under Research Grant MOE2016-T2-2-014(S), and the Abelian Foundation.

© Springer Nature Switzerland AG 2019
K. Sako et al. (Eds.): ESORICS 2019, LNCS 11735, pp. 726–746, 2019.
https://doi.org/10.1007/978-3-030-29959-0_35

strong confidence on security and privacy in twofolds, i.e., being proved under strong models which capture the practical scenarios of cryptocurrencies, and being potentially quantum-resistant. The efficiency analysis also shows that our lattice-based SALRS scheme is practical for real implementations.

Keywords: Lattice-Based · Linkable ring signature · Stealth Address · Cryptocurrency · Privacy

1   Introduction

Conventional cryptocurrencies such as Bitcoin or Ethereum support the pseudonym level of anonymity, namely, the wallet addresses and the real identities are delinked while transactions are linked. For privacy coins, such as Monero or Zcash, one of the objectives in terms of anonymity is to keep both the payer and payee of a transaction anonymous and unlinkable.

For example, in CryptoNote [25], Linkable Ring Signature (LRS) [20] and Key Derivation Mechanism [25] (KeyDerM) are employed. When a payer, say Alice, wants to pay Bob (the payee) through a transaction, Alice uses KeyDerM to generate a derived public key DPK from Bob's master public key MPK, and uses DPK as Bob's address in the transaction. As MPK never appears, transactions involving Bob as the receiver cannot be identified. KeyDerM is also referred to as the Stealth Address (SA) [27] mechanism. When Bob wants to spend his coins on the derived public key DPK, i.e. acting as the payer of a transaction TX, he generates a linkable ring signature σ on the transaction TX (as the message) under a set (referred to as a 'ring') of derived public keys R such that DPK $\in R$. Anyone can verify σ without being able to find out the actual signer is corresponding to DPK. The linkability is used for detecting any double-spending attempt, namely if two signatures are generated by Bob corresponding to DPK, they will be detected as linked as the coin corresponding to DPK is supposed to be used only once.

LRS and SA have attracted much attention recently in the community, for example, [5,8,9,11,21,22,26,28], and in cryptocurrencies, for example, Monero [24], which uses LRS and CryptoNote's KeyDerM as its underlying building blocks, and has a market capitalization valued at more than 1 billion USD [10]. However, as shown in Table 1, all the existing works [1–3,14–16,19,20,29–31] either only consider LRS or SA in the setting of standard signature schemes [11,21] rather than both of these primitives. Even in CrypotNote [25] and Monero [24], LRS and SA are both considered, but still separately rather than being analyzed under a unified security model, despite that LRS and SA are used in a tightly-coupled fashion in both CryptoNote and Monero. In particular, the signing keys and public keys used in LRS are generated by the SA mechanism. It is *not known* whether the security and privacy properties still hold when keys used by LRS are generated by the SA mechanism, while the SA mechanism does not generate keys independently.

The linkability of LRS requires that if two signatures are generated under the same key pair, these signatures can be linked publicly. Another feature of LRS, referred to as non-slanderability, requires that an adversary cannot frame a user by creating a signature that is linked to a signature of the user. Anonymity requires that for a signature with respect to ring R, no one can identify the real signer's public key out of R. When considering these security and privacy requirements of LRS, we investigate under the assumption that each key pair is generated independently. However, this is no longer the fact when LRS is used in CryptoNote or Monero as keys are generated using the SA mechanism. For SA, the master-public-key-unlinkability [21] property requires that given a derived public key and the corresponding (standard) signatures, an adversary cannot tell the master public key, from which the derived public key is generated, out of a set of known master public keys. Another requirement called derived-public-key-unlinkability [21] captures that given two derived public keys and corresponding (standard) signatures, an adversary cannot tell whether the two derived public keys are from the same master public key.

As Linkable Ring Signature and Stealth Address are used in practical scenarios, i.e., cryptocurrencies, *another concern is whether the security and privacy models, under which they are analyzed, capture the scenarios well*. In particular, in cryptocurrencies, an attacker may create some public keys maliciously and issue transactions using these public keys as payee's addresses. As long as these malicious created keys are well-formed, they will get into the blockchain as the normal ones and a user may include these malicious created keys in their rings to sign their transactions. As a result, to be practical, the security and privacy models must consider the attacks in such a scenario, which referred to as *adversarially-chosen-key attacks*. However, as shown in Table 1, the existing linkability models either do not consider the adversarially-chosen-key attacks or consider them but do not capture the application scenarios of cryptocurrencies.

1.1 Our Results

To address the above concerns, in this paper, we propose a new cryptographic primitive, named Linkable Ring Signature Scheme with Stealth Addresses (SALRS), which *comprehensively and strictly* captures the security and privacy requirements of hiding the payer and payee of a transaction in cryptocurrencies. Particularly, all the security models (namely strong unforgeability, signer-linkability, and signer-non-slanderability) and privacy models (namely signer-anonymity, master-public-key-unlinkability, and derived-public-key-unlinkability) are defined under SALRS, rather than under Linkable Ring Signature or Stealth Address separately. Also, all the models strictly capture the practical requirements of cryptocurrencies, especially the adversarially-chosen-key attacks.

We also propose a lattice-based SALRS construction and prove its security and privacy in the random oracle model. In other words, our construction provides strong confidence on security and privacy in twofolds: being proved under strong models which capture the practical scenarios of cryptocurrencies,

Table 1. Comparison with existing LRS and SA schemes

	Consider LRS and SA together	Capture adversarially chosen-key attacks in linkability model	Potentially quantum resistant
[1, 29, 30]	×, only LRS	×, have flaws[a]	×
[2, 3, 8, 19, 20, 26, 31]	×, only LRS	×	×
[14–16]	×, only LRS[b]	√[b]	×
[24, 25]	×, LRS and SA separately	×	×
[32]	×, only LRS[c]	×	√
[5, 9, 28]	×, only LRS	×	√
[22]	×, only LRS	×, have flaws [a]	√
[11, 21]	×, only SA	NA	×
this work	√	√	√

[a]The linkability models of [1, 22, 29, 30] have flaws, as an adversary can trivially succeed, by outputting two signatures which are obtained by querying the signing oracle on two different public keys.

[b][14–16] proposed Traceable Ring Signature, which is similar to Linkable Ring Signature. The linkability model in [14–16] captures the adversarially-chosen-key attacks, but requires that all the signatures use the same ring.

[c]In [32], a key derivation mechanism for generating one-time public keys for the payees is proposed, but the derived public keys' anonymity (unlinkability to the payee's long-term key) is not considered.

and being potentially quantum-resistant. The efficiency analysis also shows that our lattice-based SALRS scheme is practical for real implementations. Table 1 shows a comparison between our results in this work and the existing works on Linkable Ring Signature and Stealth Address. It is worth noting that although lattice-based Linkable Ring Signature schemes [5, 22, 28, 32] have been proposed recently, to the best of our knowledge, no lattice-based Stealth Address scheme has been introduced so far. Also, although some lattice-based ring signature schemes [13, 18] can achieve logarithmic signature size in terms of the number of signers in the ring, these schemes are mainly of theoretical interest since they will produce much larger signatures for a normal ring size in real scenarios. In other words, our construction is the first practical and potentially quantum-resistant solution that hides the payers and payees of transactions in cryptocurrencies.

1.2   Outline

In Sect. 2 we propose and formalize the primitive Linkable Ring Signature Scheme with Stealth Addresses (SALRS), including the algorithm definitions and the security and privacy models. In Sect. 3 we propose a lattice-based SALRS construction, and prove its security and privacy in Sect. 4. The paper is concluded in Sect. 5.

2   Definitions of SALRS

In this section, we first define the SALRS system, which captures the cryptographic functionalities that a cryptocurrency needs to hide the payers and payees of the transactions. Then we formalize the security and privacy models that strictly capture the practical scenarios in cryptocurrencies.

2.1   Algorithm Definition

A Linkable Ring Signature Scheme with Stealth Addresses (SALRS) consists of the following algorithms:

- Setup(λ) $\rightarrow$ PP. This is a probabilistic algorithm. On input a security parameter λ, the algorithm outputs system public parameters PP.
  The system public parameters PP *are common parameters used by all participants in the system, for example, the message space* $\mathcal{M}$*, the hash functions, etc.* In the following, λ and PP are implicit input parameters to every algorithm.
- MasterKeyGen() $\rightarrow$ (MPK, MSK). This is a probabilistic algorithm. The algorithm outputs a (master public key, master secret key) pair (MPK, MSK).
  Each user runs MasterKeyGen *algorithm to generate his (master public key, master secret key) pair.*
- DerivedPublicKeyGen(MPK) $\rightarrow$ DPK. This is a probabilistic algorithm. On input a master public key MPK, the algorithm outputs a derived public key DPK.
  Anyone can run this algorithm to generate a fresh derived public key from a master public key.
- DerivedPublicKeyOwnerCheck(DPK, MPK, MSK) $\rightarrow$ 1/0. This is a deterministic algorithm. On input a derived public key DPK and a (master public key, master secret key) pair (MPK, MSK), the algorithm outputs a bit $b \in \{0, 1\}$, with $b = 1$ meaning that DPK is a valid derived public key generated from MPK and $b = 0$ otherwise.
  The owner of a master public key can use this algorithm to check whether a public key is derived from his master public key. In a cryptocurrency, a payee can use this algorithm to check whether he is the intended receiver of a coin on the public key.
- DerivedPublicKeyPublicCheck(DPK) $\rightarrow$ 1/0. This is a deterministic algorithm. On input a derived public key DPK, the algorithm outputs a bit $b \in \{0, 1\}$, with $b = 1$ meaning that DPK is a well-formed derived public key and $b = 0$ otherwise.
  Anyone can use this algorithm to check whether a derived public key is well-formed. In a cryptocurrency, a payer can use this algorithm to check whether the derived public keys owned by others are well-formed so that he can use them as ring numbers for his ring signature generation.

- $\mathsf{Sign}(M, R, \mathsf{DPK}, (\mathsf{MPK}, \mathsf{MSK})) \to \sigma$. On input a message M, a ring of well-formed derived public keys $R = (\mathsf{DPK}_1, \ldots, \mathsf{DPK}_r)^1$, a derived public key $\mathsf{DPK} \in R$, and the master key pair $(\mathsf{MPK}, \mathsf{MSK})$ for DPK, the algorithm outputs a signature σ on the message M with respect to the ring R.
  The derived public keys $\mathsf{DPK}_1, \ldots, \mathsf{DPK}_r$ may be generated from different master public keys.
- $\mathsf{Verify}(M, R, \sigma) \to 1/0$. This is a deterministic algorithm. On input a message M, a ring of well-formed derived public keys R, and a purported signature σ on the message M with respect to the ring R, the algorithm outputs a bit $b \in \{0, 1\}$, with $b = 1$ meaning valid and $b = 0$ otherwise.
- $\mathsf{Link}(M_0, R_0, \sigma_0, M_1, R_1, \sigma_1) \to 1/0$. This is a deterministic algorithm. On input two valid signatures (M_0, R_0, σ_0), (M_1, R_1, σ_1), the algorithm outputs a bit $b \in \{0, 1\}$, with $b = 1$ meaning linked and $b = 0$ meaning unlinked.

Correctness. The scheme must satisfy the following correctness property: Let $\mathsf{PP} \leftarrow \mathsf{Setup}(\lambda)$,

- for any $(\mathsf{MPK}, \mathsf{MSK}) \leftarrow \mathsf{MasterKeyGen}()$, $\mathsf{DPK} \leftarrow \mathsf{DerivedPublicKeyGen}(\mathsf{MPK})$, it holds that $\mathsf{DerivedPublicKeyOwnerCheck}(\mathsf{DPK}, \mathsf{MPK}, \mathsf{MSK}) = 1$ and $\mathsf{DerivedPublicKeyPublicCheck}(\mathsf{DPK}) = 1$.
- for any message $M \in \mathcal{M}$, any ring of well-formed derived public keys R, and any $\mathsf{DPK}_s \in R$ such that $\mathsf{DerivedPublicKeyOwnerCheck}(\mathsf{DPK}_s, \mathsf{MPK}, \mathsf{MSK}) = 1$ for some master key $(\mathsf{MPK}, \mathsf{MSK})$, it holds that $\mathsf{Verify}(M, R, \mathsf{Sign}(M, R, \mathsf{DPK}_s, \mathsf{MPK}, \mathsf{MSK})) = 1$.
- for any messages $M_0, M_1 \in \mathcal{M}$, any well-formed derived public key rings R_0, R_1, and any $\mathsf{DPK}_{s_0} \in R_0, \mathsf{DPK}_{s_1} \in R_1$ such that $\mathsf{DerivedPublicKeyOwnerCheck}(\mathsf{DPK}_{s_i}, \mathsf{MPK}_i, \mathsf{MSK}_i) = 1$ for some master key $(\mathsf{MPK}_i, \mathsf{MSK}_i)$ $(i = 0, 1)$, let $\sigma_i \leftarrow \mathsf{Sign}(M_i, R_i, \mathsf{DPK}_{s_i}, \mathsf{MPK}_i, \mathsf{MSK}_i)$ $(i = 0, 1)$. It holds that $\mathsf{Link}(M_0, R_0, \sigma_0, M_1, R_1, \sigma_1) = 1$ if $\mathsf{DPK}_{s_0} = \mathsf{DPK}_{s_1}$, and $\Pr[\mathsf{Link}(M_0, R_0, \sigma_0, M_1, R_1, \sigma_1) = 0] \geq 1 - negl(\lambda)$ if $\mathsf{DPK}_{s_0} \neq \mathsf{DPK}_{s_1}$, where $negl$ is a negligible function.

Remark: Note that it is open on whether the Sign algorithm is probabilistic or deterministic, which may depend on the concrete constructions.

2.2 Security and Privacy Models of SALRS

Below we define the security and privacy for SALRS. The security includes unforgeability, signer-linkability, and signer-non-slanderability, while the privacy includes signer-anonymity, master-public-key-unlinkability and derived-public-key-unlinkability. Unforgeability captures that only the user knowing the secret key for some public key in a ring can generate a valid signature with respect

---

[1] Below, we regard the public key ring as an ordered set, namely, it consists of a set of public keys, and when it is used in Sign and Verify algorithms, the public keys are ordered and each one has an index.

to the ring. Signer-linkability captures that with respect to *one* derived public key, if the key owner generates two or multiple valid signatures, these signatures will be detected to be linked, and this captures the security requirement of preventing double-spending in cryptocurrencies. Signer-non-slanderability captures that no one can frame other users by creating a signature that is linked to a signature of the target user. Signer-anonymity captures that given a valid signature with respect to a ring of derived public keys, no one can identify the signer's derived public key out of the ring. Master-public-key-unlinkability captures that given a derived public key and the corresponding signatures, no one can tell which master public key, out of a set of known master public keys, is the one from which it was derived. Derived-public-key-unlinkability captures that given two derived public keys and the corresponding signatures, no one can tell whether they are derived from the same master public key. Signer-anonymity captures the privacy-protection requirement in cryptocurrency of hiding the payer, while master-public-key-unlinkability and derived-public-key-unlinkability captures the privacy-protection requirements of hiding the payee and cutting the link between the payees of different transactions, respectively.

With these security and privacy models, SALRS captures the security and privacy-protection requirements of cryptocurrencies in the most practical setting. Especially, the rings are allowed to contain the derived public keys that an adversary generated from his own master public keys. This reflects the situations in practice that, an attacker may generate some derived public keys from his own master public keys, and issue transactions among these keys, attempting to launch some attacks, such as double-spending, or to compromise other users' security and/or privacy. On the other side, we show that signer-linkability and signer-non-slanderability together implies unforgeability, and master-public-key-unlinkability implies derived-public-key-unlinkability. Thus, for a SALRS construction, we only needs to focus on its signer-linkability, signer-non-slanderability, signer-anonymity, and master-public-key-unlinkability.

Definition 1 (Strong Unforgeability). *A SALRS scheme is strongly unforgeable if for any probabilistic polynomial time (PPT) adversary $\mathcal{A}$ and for any polynomial $n(\cdot)$, the advantage of $\mathcal{A}$ in the following game* $\mathsf{Game}_{\mathsf{euf}}$*, denoted by $Adv_{\mathcal{A}}^{euf}$, is negligible.*

1. **Setup.** PP ← Setup$(\lambda; \omega)$ *is run, where ω is the randomness used in* Setup$()$. *PP and ω are given to $\mathcal{A}$.*
   $\{(\mathsf{MPK}_i, \mathsf{MSK}_i) \leftarrow \mathsf{MasterKeyGen}()\}_{i=1}^{n(\lambda)}$ *are run and* $\{\mathsf{MPK}_i\}_{i=1}^{n(\lambda)}$ *are given to $\mathcal{A}$.*
   An empty set $L_{dpk} = \emptyset$ is initialized, which will be used to store the valid derived public keys derived from the target master public keys. Note that L_{dpk} captures the scenarios that the valid derived public keys are stored on the blockchain and are publicly accessible.
   Note that giving to $\mathcal{A}$ the randomness ω, which is used by the Setup algorithm, implies the setup is public. This is to capture that the security does not rely on a trusted setup which may incur concerns on the existing of trapdoors.

2. **Probing Phase.** $\mathcal{A}$ *can adaptively query the following oracles:*
   - *Derived Public Key Adding Oracle* ODPKAdd$(\cdot,\cdot)$:
     On input a derived public key DPK *and a master public key* MPK$_i$, *this oracle returns* $b \leftarrow$ DerivedPublicKeyOwnerCheck(DPK, MPK$_i$, MSK$_i$) *to* $\mathcal{A}$. *If* $b = 1$, *set* $L_{dpk} = L_{dpk} \cup \{DPK\}$.
     This captures that $\mathcal{A}$ can try and test whether the derived public keys generated by him are accepted by the owner of the corresponding master public key.
   - *Signing Oracle* OSign$(\cdot,\cdot,\cdot)$:
     On input a message $M \in \mathcal{M}$, *a ring of well-formed derived public keys* R, *and a derived public key* DPK $\in R \cap L_{dpk}$, *this oracle returns* $\sigma \leftarrow$ Sign$(M, R, DPK, MPK_i$, MSK$_i)$ *to* $\mathcal{A}$, *where* (MPK$_i$, MSK$_i$) *is the master key pair for* DPK.
     Note that it only requires that the derived public key DPK is in L_{dpk}, i.e., the attacking targets for which the master secret keys are unknown to the adversary, without requiring $R \subseteq L_{dpk}$. This captures that $\mathcal{A}$ can obtain the signatures for messages, derived public key ring, and derived public key of its choice, where **the ring may contain deprived public keys which are created by the adversary even from the master public keys which are also created by the adversary (referred to as** adversarially-chosen-key attack**)**.
3. **Output Phase.** $\mathcal{A}$ *outputs a message* $M^* \in \mathcal{M}$, *a ring of well-formed derived public keys* R^*, *and a signature* σ^*.

Let $S_{so} = \{(M, R, DPK, \sigma)\}$ *be the query-answer tuples for* OSign$(\cdot,\cdot,\cdot)$. $\mathcal{A}$ *succeeds if (1)* Verify$(M^*, R^*, \sigma^*) = 1$, *and (2)* $R^* \subseteq L_{dpk}$, *and (3)* $(M^*, R^*, ?, \sigma^*) \notin S_{so}$, *where '?' means wildcard, i.e.* (M^*, R^*, σ^*) *is not a (message, derived public key ring, signature) tuple obtained by querying* OSign$(\cdot,\cdot,\cdot)$. *The advantage of* $\mathcal{A}$ *is* $Adv_{\mathcal{A}}^{euf} = \Pr[\mathcal{A}\ succeeds]$.

Remark: In the above model, as the adversarially-chosen-key attacks are considered, i.e., the adversary is allowed to specify the derived public key ring to contain well-formed derived public keys generated from the master public keys created by himself, it is not necessary to provide an oracle of corrupting the master secret keys in $\{$MSK$\}_{i=1}^{n(\lambda)}$. The situations for the following models are similar.

Definition 2 (Signer-linkability). *A SALRS scheme is signer-linkable if for any PPT adversary* $\mathcal{A}$, *the advantage of* $\mathcal{A}$ *in the following game* Game$_{snlink}$, *denoted by* $Adv_{\mathcal{A}}^{snlink}$, *is negligible.*

1. **Setup.** PP $\leftarrow$ Setup$(\lambda; \omega)$ *is run, where* ω *is the randomness used in* Setup$()$. PP *and* ω *are given to* $\mathcal{A}$.
2. **Output Phase.** $\mathcal{A}$ *outputs* $k(\geq 2)$ *(message, ring of well-formed derived public keys, signature) tuples* $(M_i^*, R_i^*, \sigma_i^*)$ $(i = 1, \ldots, k)$.

$\mathcal{A}$ succeeds if (1) $\mathsf{Verify}(M_i^*, R_i^*, \sigma_i^*) = 1$ $(i = 1, 2, \ldots, k)$, and (2) $\mathsf{Link}(M_i^*, R_i^*, \sigma_i^*, M_j^*, R_j^*, \sigma_j^*) = 0$ $\forall i, j \in [1, k]$ s.t. $i \neq j$, and (3) $|\cup_{i=1}^{k} R_i^*| < k$. The advantage of $\mathcal{A}$ is $Adv_{\mathcal{A}}^{snlink} = \Pr[\mathcal{A}$ succeeds$]$.

Remark: Note that the adversary's target is to attack the linkability property of the system, rather than attacking other users, thus we do not need to consider the target master public keys or derived public keys. Also, as the adversary is allowed to create the master public keys and derived public keys of its choice, we do not need to consider the signing oracles, corruption oracles, etc.

Definition 3 (Signer-non-slanderability). *A SALRS scheme is signer-non-slanderable if for any PPT adversary $\mathcal{A}$ and for any polynomial $n(\cdot)$, the advantage of $\mathcal{A}$ in the following game* $\mathsf{Game_{snnsl}}$, *denoted by $Adv_{\mathcal{A}}^{snnsl}$, is negligible.*

1. **Setup.** *Same as that of* $\mathsf{Game_{euf}}$ *in Def. 1.*
2. **Probing Phase.** *Same as that of* $\mathsf{Game_{euf}}$ *in Def. 1.*
3. **Output Phase.** $\mathcal{A}$ *outputs two (message, ring of well-formed derived public keys, signature) tuples* $(\hat{M}, \hat{R}, \hat{\sigma})$ *and* (M^*, R^*, σ^*).

Let $S_{so} = \{(M, R, \mathsf{DPK}, \sigma)\}$ *be the query-answer tuples for* $\mathsf{OSign}(\cdot, \cdot, \cdot)$. $\mathcal{A}$ *succeeds if (1)* $\mathsf{Verify}(M^*, R^*, \sigma^*) = 1$, *and (2)* $(\hat{M}, \hat{R}, \hat{\mathsf{DPK}}, \hat{\sigma}) \in S_{so}$ *for some* $\hat{\mathsf{DPK}} \in \hat{R} \cap L_{dpk}$, *and (3)* $(M^*, R^*, \hat{\mathsf{DPK}}, \sigma^*) \notin S_{so}$, *and (4)* $\mathsf{Link}(M^*, R^*, \sigma*, \hat{M}, \hat{R}, \hat{\sigma}) = 1$. *The advantage of* $\mathcal{A}$ *is* $Adv_{\mathcal{A}}^{snnsl} = \Pr[\mathcal{A}$ *succeeds*$]$.

Definition 4 (Signer-Anonymity). *A SALRS scheme is signer-anonymous if for any PPT adversary $\mathcal{A}$ and for any polynomial $n(\cdot)$, the advantage of $\mathcal{A}$ in the following game* $\mathsf{Game_{snano}}$, *denoted by $Adv_{\mathcal{A}}^{snano}$, is negligible.*

1. **Setup.** *Same as that of* $\mathsf{Game_{euf}}$ *in Def. 1.*
2. **Probing Phase 1.** *Same as the* Probing Phase *of* $\mathsf{Game_{euf}}$ *in Def. 1.*
3. **Challenge Phase.** $\mathcal{A}$ *outputs a message M^*, a ring of well-formed derived public keys R^*, and two distinct indices $1 \leq i_0, i_1 \leq n(\lambda)$, such that*
   (1) $\mathsf{DPK}_{i_0}, \mathsf{DPK}_{i_1} \in R^* \cap L_{dpk}$, *and*
   (2) none of $\mathsf{OSign}(\cdot, \cdot, \mathsf{DPK}_{i_0})$, $\mathsf{OSign}(\cdot, \cdot, \mathsf{DPK}_{i_1})$ *was queried. A random bit $b \in \{0, 1\}$ is chosen, and $\mathcal{A}$ is given the signature $\sigma \leftarrow \mathsf{Sign}(M^*, R^*, \mathsf{DPK}_{i_b}, \mathsf{MPK}, \mathsf{MSK})$, where $(\mathsf{MPK}, \mathsf{MSK})$ is the master key pair for DPK_{i_b}.*
4. **Probing Phase 2.** *Same as the* **Probing Phase 1**, *but with the restriction that none of* $\mathsf{OSign}(\cdot, \cdot, \mathsf{DPK}_{i_0})$, $\mathsf{OSign}(\cdot, \cdot, \mathsf{DPK}_{i_1})$ *is queried.*
5. **Output Phase.** $\mathcal{A}$ *outputs a bit b' as its guess to b.*

The advantage of $\mathcal{A}$ is $Adv_{\mathcal{A}}^{snano} = |\Pr[b' = b] - \frac{1}{2}|$.

Definition 5 (Master-Public-Key-Unlinkability). *A SALRS scheme is Master Public-Key-Unlinkable if for any PPT adversary $\mathcal{A}$ and for any polynomial $n(\cdot)$, the advantage of $\mathcal{A}$ in the following game* $\mathsf{Game_{mpkunl}}$, *denoted by $Adv_{\mathcal{A}}^{mpkunl}$, is negligible.*

1. **Setup.** *Same as that of* $\mathsf{Game}_{\mathsf{euf}}$ *in Def. 1.*
2. **Probing Phase 1.** *Same as the* Probing Phase *of* $\mathsf{Game}_{\mathsf{euf}}$ *in Def. 1.*
3. **Challenge.** $\mathcal{A}$ *outputs two distinct indices* $1 \leq i_0, i_1 \leq n(\lambda)$. *A random bit* $b \in \{0,1\}$ *is chosen, and* $\mathsf{DPK}^* \leftarrow \mathsf{DerivedPublicKeyGen}(\mathsf{MPK}_{i_b})$ *is given to* $\mathcal{A}$. *Set* $L_{dpk} = L_{dpk} \cup \{\mathsf{DPK}^*\}$.
4. **Probing Phase 2.** *Same as* **Phase 1**, *except that* $\mathsf{ODPKAdd}(\mathsf{DPK}^*, \mathsf{MPK}_{i_j})$ *(for* $j \in \{0,1\}$*) cannot be queried.*
5. **Guess.** $\mathcal{A}$ *outputs a bit* $b' \in \{0,1\}$ *as its guess to* b.

The advantage of $\mathcal{A}$ *is* $Adv_{\mathcal{A}}^{mpkunl} = |\Pr[b' = b] - \frac{1}{2}|$.

Remark: Note that $\mathsf{OSign}(\cdot, \cdot, \mathsf{DPK}^*)$ can be queried. This captures that neither the derived public key or the signatures leak the corresponding master public key.

Definition 6 (Derived-Public-Key-Unlinkability). *A SALRS scheme is Derived Public-Key-Unlinkable if for any PPT adversary* $\mathcal{A}$ *and for any polynomial* $n(\cdot)$, *the advantage of* $\mathcal{A}$ *in the following game* $\mathsf{Game}_{\mathsf{dpkunl}}$, *denoted by* $Adv_{\mathcal{A}}^{dpkunl}$, *is negligible.*

1. **Setup.** *Same as that of* $\mathsf{Game}_{\mathsf{euf}}$ *in Def. 1.*
2. **Probing Phase 1.** *Same as the* Probing Phase *of* $\mathsf{Game}_{\mathsf{euf}}$ *in Def. 1.*
3. **Challenge.** $\mathcal{A}$ *outputs two distinct indices* $1 \leq i_0, i_1 \leq n(\lambda)$.
   A random bit $c \in \{0,1\}$ *is chosen.*
   Compute $\mathsf{DPK}_0^* \leftarrow \mathsf{DerivedPublicKeyGen}(\mathsf{MPK}_{i_c})$.
   A random bit $b \in \{0,1\}$ *is chosen.*
   If $b = 0$, *compute* $\mathsf{DPK}_1^* \leftarrow \mathsf{DerivedPublicKeyGen}(\mathsf{MPK}_{i_c})$,
   otherwise, compute $\mathsf{DPK}_1^* \leftarrow \mathsf{DerivedPublicKeyGen}(\mathsf{MPK}_{i_{1-c}})$.
   $(\mathsf{DPK}_0^*, \mathsf{DPK}_1^*)$ *are given to* $\mathcal{A}$. *Set* $L_{dpk} = L_{dpk} \cup \{\mathsf{DPK}_0^*, \mathsf{DPK}_1^*\}$.
4. **Probing Phase 2.** *Same as* **Probing Phase 1**, *except that* $\mathsf{ODPKAdd}(\mathsf{DPK}_j^*, \mathsf{MPK}_{i_k})$ *(for* $j, k \in \{0,1\}$*) can be queried on at most one* $j \in \{0,1\}$.
5. **Guess.** $\mathcal{A}$ *outputs a bit* $b' \in \{0,1\}$ *as its guess to* b, *i.e., guess whether* DPK_0^* *and* DPK_1^* *are from the same master public key.*

The advantage of $\mathcal{A}$ *is* $Adv_{\mathcal{A}}^{dpkunl} = |\Pr[b' = b] - \frac{1}{2}|$.

Remark: Note that $\mathsf{OSign}(\cdot, \cdot, \mathsf{DPK}_j^*)$ (for $j = 0, 1$) can be queried, and this captures that neither the derived public keys or the corresponding signatures leak whether they are from the same master public key.

As the above models captures the security and privacy requirements that the practice imposes on SALRS, the following two theorems show that *for a SALRS scheme, we only need to consider its signer-linkability, signer-non-slanderability, signer-anonymity, and master-public-key-unlinkability.*

Theorem 1. *If a SALRS scheme is signer-linkable and siner-non-slanderable, then it is strongly unforgeable.*

Proof. The proof resembles that for a similar conclusion in the setting of Traceable Ring Signature in [16]. We give the proof in Appendix A.

Theorem 2. *If a SALRS scheme is master-public-key-unlinkable, then it is derived-public-key-unlinkable.*

Proof. Observe $\mathsf{Game_{mpkunl}}$ and $\mathsf{Game_{dpkunl}}$, it is easy to see that, if there exists an adversary $\mathcal{A}$ that wins $\mathsf{Game_{dpkunl}}$ with non-negligible advantage, we can construct an algorithm $\mathcal{B}$ that interacts with $\mathcal{A}$ for game $\mathsf{Game_{dpkunl}}$, and makes use of $\mathcal{A}$'s output to win $\mathsf{Game_{mpkunl}}$ with non-negligible advantage. We defer the proof details to the full version.

3   Our Construction

In this section, we first present some preliminaries in Sect. 3.1, including the concept of key-privacy in Key-Encapsulation Mechanism (KEM), which we will use as a building block for our SALRS construction, and some background of lattice. Then we propose a lattice-based SALRS construction in Sect. 3.2 and give the concrete parameters and building blocks in Sect. 3.3.

3.1   Preliminaries

3.1.1 Key-Privacy in KEM
Our construction will use KEM as a building block, but requires the underlying KEM to have an additional property, referred to as key-privacy, which asks that an adversary in possession of a ciphertext not be able to tell which specific public key, out of a set of known public keys, is the one under which the ciphertext was created, meaning the receiver is anonymous from the point of view of the adversary. It is worth mentioning that Bellare et al. [6] considered a similar concept on the setting of Public Key Encryption (PKE). Below we extend the usual KEM and formalize the concept of KEM with key-privacy.

Syntax. To capture the practice better, we augment the usual formalization of KEM to cover the cases that users may share some fixed "global" information.

A *key-encapsulation mechanism* (KEM) scheme is a tuple of probabilistic polynomial-time algorithms (Setup, KeyGen, Encaps, Decaps) such that:

- Setup(λ) → GP. On input a security parameter λ, the algorithm outputs system global parameters GP.
  The system global parameters GP *are common parameters used by all participants in the system, which may be just the security parameter* λ, *or include some additional information, for example, the key space, the ciphertext space, the hash functions, etc. As we will consider the key-privacy, here we require that* GP *include the key space* $\mathcal{K}$ *and ciphertext space* $\mathcal{C}$.
- KeyGen(GP) → (PK, SK). This is a probabilistic algorithm. On input GP, the algorithm outputs a (public key, secret key) pair (PK, SK).

– Encaps(GP, PK) → (C, κ). This is a probabilistic algorithm. On input GP and a public key PK, the algorithm outputs a ciphertext $C \in \mathcal{C}$ and a key $\kappa \in \mathcal{K}$.
– Decaps(GP, C, PK, SK) → $\kappa/\bot$. This is a deterministic algorithm. On input GP, a ciphertext $C \in \mathcal{C}$, and a (public key, secret key) pair (PK, SK), the algorithm outputs a key $\kappa \in \mathcal{K}$ or a special symbol $\bot$ to indicate rejection.

Correctness. It is required that with all but negligible probability over GP ← Setup(1^λ), (PK, SK) ← KeyGen(GP), and the random coins of Encaps, if Encaps(GP, PK) outputs (C, κ), then Decaps(GP, C, PK, SK) outputs κ.

Security and Key-Privacy. Below we formalize the security and key-privacy models.

Definition 7 (CCA-Security of KEM). *A KEM scheme is CCA-secure if for any PPT adversary $\mathcal{A}$, the advantage of $\mathcal{A}$ in the following game* Game$_{ccasec}$, *denoted by $Adv_{\mathcal{A}}^{ccasec}$, is negligible.*

1. **Setup.** GP ← Setup($\lambda; \omega$) *is run, where ω is the randomness used in* Setup(). GP *and ω are given to $\mathcal{A}$.* (PK, SK) ← KeyGen(GP) *is run and* PK *is given to $\mathcal{A}$.*
   Note that giving to $\mathcal{A}$ the randomness ω, which is used by the Setup algorithm, implies the setup is public. This is to capture that the security does not rely on a trusted setup which may incur the concerns on the existing of trapdoors.
2. **Challenge Phase.** (C^*, κ) ← Encaps(GP, PK) *is run. A random bit b is chosen. If $b = 0$, set $\kappa^* := \kappa$, otherwise choose a uniformly random $\kappa^* \xleftarrow{R} \mathcal{K}$. $\mathcal{A}$ is given (C^*, κ^*).*
3. **Probing Phase.** *$\mathcal{A}$ can adaptively query an oracle* ODecaps($\cdot$), *which takes a ciphertext $C \in \mathcal{C}$ and returns κ ←* Decaps(GP, C, PK, SK) *to $\mathcal{A}$, with the restriction that $\mathcal{A}$ cannot query* ODecaps($\cdot$) *on the challenge C^*.*
4. **Output Phase.** *$\mathcal{A}$ outputs a bit b'.*

The advantage of $\mathcal{A}$ is $Adv_{\mathcal{A}}^{ccasec} = |\Pr[b' = b] - \frac{1}{2}|$.

Definition 8 (CCA-Key-Indistinguishability of KEM). *A KEM scheme is CCA-key-indistinguishable if for any PPT adversary $\mathcal{A}$, the advantage of $\mathcal{A}$ in the following game* Game$_{ccaki}$, *denoted by $Adv_{\mathcal{A}}^{ccaki}$, is negligible.*

1. **Setup.** *Same as that of* Game$_{ccasec}$.
2. **Challenge Phase.** (C, κ^*) ← Encaps(GP, PK) *is run. A random bit b is chosen. If $b = 0$, set $C^* := C$, otherwise choose a uniformly random $C^* \xleftarrow{R} \mathcal{C}$. $\mathcal{A}$ is given (C^*, κ^*).*
3. **Probing Phase.** *Same as that of* Game$_{ccasec}$.
4. **Output Phase.** *$\mathcal{A}$ outputs a bit b'.*

The advantage of $\mathcal{A}$ is $Adv_{\mathcal{A}}^{ccaki} = |\Pr[b' = b] - \frac{1}{2}|$.

3.1.2 Lattice Background

Rings, Norms and Invertible Ring Elements. Let q be an even (resp. odd) positive integer, and denote by $\mathbb{Z}_q$ the integers modulo q, which will be represented in the range $(-\frac{q}{2}, \frac{q}{2}]$ (resp. $[-\frac{q-1}{2}, \frac{q-1}{2}]$). Let n be an positive integer, and let R and R_q be the rings $\mathbb{Z}[X]/(X^n+1)$ and $\mathbb{Z}_q[X]/(X^n+1)$, respectively. For $w = a_0 + a_1 X + \ldots + a_{n-1} X^{n-1} \in R$, define the l_∞, l_1 and l_2 norms of w as follows:

$$\|w\|_\infty = \max_i |a_i|, \qquad \|w\|_1 = \sum_i |a_i|, \qquad \|w\|_2 = \sqrt{|a_0|^2 + \ldots + |a_{n-1}|^2}.$$

Similarly, for $\mathbf{w} = (w_1, \ldots, w_k) \in R^k$, define:

$$\|\mathbf{w}\|_\infty = \max_i \|w_i\|_\infty, \qquad \|\mathbf{w}\|_1 = \sum_i \|w_i\|_1, \qquad \|\mathbf{w}\|_2 = \sqrt{\|w_1\|_2^2 + \ldots + \|w_k\|_2^2}.$$

Let S_η denote the set of all elements $w \in R$ such that $\|w\|_\infty \leq \eta$. As shown in [23], for prime $q > 2^{20}$ such that $q = 17 \bmod 32$, and for $\eta < \frac{1}{\sqrt{8}} \cdot q^{1/8}$, all non-zero elements of S_η are invertible in R_q.

Let $\mathbf{B}_\theta$ denote the set of all elements in R_q such that have θ coefficients that are either -1 or 1 and the rest are 0. Again, for prime $q > 2^{20}$ such that $q = 17 \bmod 32$, all elements of $\mathbf{B}_\theta$ are invertible and the difference of any two distinct elements from $\mathbf{B}_\theta$ is also invertible in R_q.

(Inhomogeneous) Module-SIS. The Inhomogeneous Module-SIS problem with parameters (n, q, k, ℓ, β) consists in finding $\mathbf{x} \in R^{k+\ell}$ such that $\|\mathbf{x}\|_2 \leq \beta$ and $[\mathbf{A} \mid \mathbf{I}] \cdot \mathbf{x} = \mathbf{t}$, for uniformly random $\mathbf{A} \in R_q^{k \times \ell}$, $\mathbf{t} \in R_q^k$ and $k \times k$ identity matrix $\mathbf{I}$. The problem can be adapted straightforwardly into its infinity-norm version, where $\mathbf{x}$ must satisfy $\|\mathbf{x}\|_\infty \leq \beta$. The homogeneous version is defined with $\mathbf{t} = \mathbf{0}$ and $\mathbf{x} \neq \mathbf{0}$.

Module-LWE. The Module-LWE problem with parameters (n, q, k, ℓ, η) is as follows. Let $\mathbf{A} \in R_q^{k \times \ell}$ be a uniformly random matrix. Let $\mathbf{b} = \mathbf{As} + \mathbf{e} \in R_q^k$, where $\mathbf{s} \in S_\eta^\ell$, $\mathbf{e} \in S_\eta^k$ have entries chosen according to some distribution over S_η (e.g., the uniform distribution or a Gaussian distribution). The search variant of Module-LWE asks to recover $\mathbf{s}$ given $(\mathbf{A}, \mathbf{b})$. The decision variant (decision-Module-LWE) asks to distinguish $(\mathbf{A}, \mathbf{b})$ from a uniformly random pair over $R_q^{k \times \ell} \times R_q^k$. In this paper, similar to [5], we use a transformed version of the decision-Module-LWE problem, which is to distinguish $(\mathbf{A}, \mathbf{As})$ from $(\mathbf{A}, \mathbf{r})$ where $\mathbf{A} \leftarrow R_q^{k \times l}$, $\mathbf{s} \leftarrow S_\eta^l$ and $\mathbf{r} \leftarrow R_q^k$.

As shown in [17], the Module-SIS and Module-LWE problems enjoy worst-case to average-case reductions from hard problems in module lattices. Concrete parameters of these problems that provide high post-quantum security against the best known attacks are given in Dilithium [12] and Kyber [7].

3.2 Construction

– Setup(1^λ) → PP. On input a security parameter λ, the algorithm sets the parameters $n, q, k, l, m, \eta, \gamma, \theta$ as specified in Sect. 3.3 below. Let Π_{kem} be a lattice-based KEM scheme which is CCA-secure and CCA-key indistinguishable, and let $\mathcal{C}_{kem}$ and $\mathcal{K}_{kem}$ denote Π_{kem}'s ciphertext space and key space, respectively. Let $H_\mathsf{A} : \{0,1\}^* \mapsto R_q^{k \times l}$, ExpandV : $\mathcal{K}_{kem} \mapsto S_\eta^l$, $H_\theta : \{0,1\}^* \mapsto \mathbf{B}_\theta$, and $H_m : R_q^k \mapsto R_q^{m \times l}$ be functions that will be viewed as random oracles in the analyses. The algorithm does:
  1. Choose a random string $cstr \in \{0,1\}^*$, and set $\mathbf{A} := H_\mathsf{A}(cstr)$.
  2. Run $\mathsf{GP}_{kem} \leftarrow \Pi_{kem}.\mathsf{Setup}(1^\lambda; \omega)$, where ω is the randomness used in $\Pi_{kem}.\mathsf{Setup}()$.
  3. Output the public parameters

$$\mathsf{PP} = \big(n, q, k, l, m, \eta, \gamma, \theta, (H_\mathsf{A}, cstr, \mathbf{A}), (\Pi_{kem}, \omega, \mathsf{GP}_{kem}),$$
$$\mathsf{ExpandV}, H_\theta, H_m\big).$$

Note that including $(H_\mathsf{A}, cstr)$ and ω in PP is to ensure that no one knows any trapdoor for matrix $\mathbf{A}$ and GP_{kem} respectively.

In the following, PP are implicit input parameters to every algorithm.

– MasterKeyGen() → (MPK, MSK). On input the implicit inputs, namely, the public parameters PP, the algorithm does:
  1. Run $(\mathsf{PK}_{kem}, \mathsf{SK}_{kem}) \leftarrow \Pi_{kem}.\mathsf{KeyGen}(\mathsf{GP}_{kem})$.
  2. Choose a uniformly random $\mathbf{s} \xleftarrow{R} S_\eta^l$, and set $\mathbf{t} \leftarrow \mathbf{A}\mathbf{s}$.
  3. Output master public key MPK and master secret key MSK

$$\mathsf{MPK} := \big(\mathsf{PK}_{kem}, \mathbf{t}\big), \quad \mathsf{MSK} := \big(\mathsf{SK}_{kem}, \mathbf{s}\big).$$

– DerivedPublicKeyGen(MPK) → DPK. On input a master public key $\mathsf{MPK} = (\mathsf{PK}_{kem}, \mathbf{t})$, the algorithm does:
  1. Run $(C, \kappa) \leftarrow \Pi_{kem}.\mathsf{Encaps}(\mathsf{PK}_{kem})$.
  2. Set $\mathbf{s}' := \mathsf{ExpandV}(\kappa) \in S_\eta^l$, $\mathbf{t}' \leftarrow \mathbf{A}\mathbf{s}'$, and set $\hat{\mathbf{t}} \leftarrow \mathbf{t} + \mathbf{t}'$.
  3. Output a derived public key $\mathsf{DPK} := (C, \hat{\mathbf{t}})$.
– DerivedPublicKeyOwnerCheck(DPK, MPK, MSK) → 1/0. On input a derived public key DPK and a (master public key, master secret key) pair (MPK, MSK) with $\mathsf{MPK} = (\mathsf{PK}_{kem}, \mathbf{t})$, and $\mathsf{MSK} = (\mathsf{SK}_{kem}, \mathbf{s})$, the algorithm does:
  1. Check whether $\mathsf{DPK} \in \mathcal{C}_{kem} \times R_q^k$ holds. If it does not hold, return 0, otherwise, parse DPK to $\mathsf{DPK} := (C, \hat{\mathbf{t}}) \in \mathcal{C}_{kem} \times R_q^k$.
  2. Run $\kappa \leftarrow \Pi_{kem}.\mathsf{Decaps}(C, \mathsf{PK}_{kem}, \mathsf{SK}_{kem})$.
  3. Set $\mathbf{s}' := \mathsf{ExpandV}(\kappa)$ and $\mathbf{t}' \leftarrow \mathbf{A}\mathbf{s}'$.
  4. If $\hat{\mathbf{t}} \overset{?}{=} \mathbf{t} + \mathbf{t}'$ holds, return 1, otherwise return 0.
– DerivedPublicKeyPublicCheck(DPK) → 1/0. On input a derived public key DPK, the algorithm checks whether $\mathsf{DPK} \in \mathcal{C}_{kem} \times R_q^k$ holds. If it holds, return 1, otherwise return 0.

- Sign$(M, R, \mathsf{DPK}, (\mathsf{MPK}, \mathsf{MSK})) \to \sigma$. On input a message M, a ring of well-formed derived public keys $R = (\mathsf{DPK}_1, \ldots, \mathsf{DPK}_r)$, a derived public key $\mathsf{DPK} \in R$, and the master key pair $(\mathsf{MPK}, \mathsf{MSK})$ for DPK where $\mathsf{MPK} = (\mathsf{PK}_{kem}, \mathbf{t})$ and $\mathsf{MSK} = (\mathsf{SK}_{kem}, \mathbf{s})$, the algorithm does:
    1. For $i = 1$ to r, parse $\mathsf{DPK}_i := (C_i, \hat{\mathbf{t}}_i) \in \mathcal{C}_{kem} \times R_q^k$ and set $\mathbf{H}_i := H_m(\hat{\mathbf{t}}_i)$.
    2. Let $\bar{i}$ be the index of DPK in R, i.e. $\mathsf{DPK} = \mathsf{DPK}_{\bar{i}} = (C_{\bar{i}}, \hat{\mathbf{t}}_{\bar{i}})$.
        Run $\kappa \leftarrow \Pi_{kem}.\mathsf{Decaps}(C_{\bar{i}}, \mathsf{PK}_{kem}, \mathsf{SK}_{kem})$. Set $\mathbf{s}'_{\bar{i}} := \mathsf{ExpandV}(\kappa)$ and $\hat{\mathbf{s}}_{\bar{i}} \leftarrow \mathbf{s} + \mathbf{s}'_{\bar{i}}$. Note that it holds that $\hat{\mathbf{t}}_{\bar{i}} = \mathbf{A}\hat{\mathbf{s}}_{\bar{i}}$.
    3. Set $\mathbf{I} \leftarrow \mathbf{H}_{\bar{i}}\hat{\mathbf{s}}_{\bar{i}}$.
    4. Choose a uniformly random $\mathbf{y} \xleftarrow{R} S_\gamma^l$.
    5. Set $\mathbf{w}_{\bar{i}} \leftarrow \mathbf{A}\mathbf{y}$, $\mathbf{v}_{\bar{i}} \leftarrow \mathbf{H}_{\bar{i}}\mathbf{y}$.
    6. For $i = \bar{i} + 1, \ldots, r, 1, \ldots, \bar{i} - 1$, do
        (a) Set $c_i \leftarrow H_\theta(M, R, \mathbf{w}_{i-1}, \mathbf{v}_{i-1}, \mathbf{I})$.[2]
        (b) Choose a uniformly random $\mathbf{z}_i \leftarrow S_{\gamma-2\theta\eta}^l$.
        (c) Set $\mathbf{w}_i \leftarrow \mathbf{A}\mathbf{z}_i - c_i\hat{\mathbf{t}}_i$, $\mathbf{v}_i \leftarrow \mathbf{H}_i\mathbf{z}_i - c_i\mathbf{I}$.
    7. Set $c_{\bar{i}} \leftarrow H_\theta(M, R, \mathbf{w}_{\bar{i}-1}, \mathbf{v}_{\bar{i}-1}, \mathbf{I})$.
    8. Set $\mathbf{z}_{\bar{i}} \leftarrow \mathbf{y} + c_{\bar{i}}\hat{\mathbf{s}}_{\bar{i}}$.
    9. If $\mathbf{z}_{\bar{i}} \in S_{\gamma-2\theta\eta}^l$, output $\sigma := (c_1, \{\mathbf{z}_i\}_{i=1}^r, \mathbf{I}) \in \mathbf{B}_\theta \times (S_{\gamma-2\theta\eta}^l)^r \times R_q^m$, otherwise go to Step 4.
- Verify$(M, R, \sigma) \to 1/0$. On input a message M, a ring of well-formed derived public keys $R = (\mathsf{DPK}_1, \ldots, \mathsf{DPK}_r)$, and a signature $\sigma = (c_1, \{\mathbf{z}_i\}_{i=1}^r, \mathbf{I})$, the algorithm does:
    1. If $(c_1 \notin \mathbf{B}_\theta) \vee (\exists i \in \{1, \ldots, r\} \text{ s.t. } \mathbf{z}_i \notin S_{\gamma-2\theta\eta}^l)$, then return 0.
    2. For $i = 1, 2, \ldots, r$, do
        (a) Parse DPK_i to $\mathsf{DPK}_i := (C_i, \hat{\mathbf{t}}_i) \in \mathcal{C}_{kem} \times R_q^k$ and set $\mathbf{H}_i := H_m(\hat{\mathbf{t}}_i)$.
        (b) Set $\mathbf{w}_i \leftarrow \mathbf{A}\mathbf{z}_i - c_i\hat{\mathbf{t}}_i$, $\mathbf{v}_i \leftarrow \mathbf{H}_i\mathbf{z}_i - c_i\mathbf{I}$.
        (c) Set $c_{i+1} \leftarrow H_\theta(M, R, \mathbf{w}_i, \mathbf{v}_i, \mathbf{I})$.
    3. If $c_{r+1} \overset{?}{=} c_1$ holds, return 1, otherwise return 0.
- Link$(M_0, R_0, \sigma_0, M_1, R_1, \sigma_1) \to 1/0$. On input two valid (message, derived public key ring, signature) tuples (M_0, R_0, σ_0), (M_1, R_1, σ_1) where $\sigma_0 = (c_1^{(0)}, \{\mathbf{z}_i^{(0)}\}_{i=1}^{r_0}, \mathbf{I}^{(0)})$, $\sigma_1 = (c_1^{(1)}, \{\mathbf{z}_i^{(1)}\}_{i=1}^{r_1}, \mathbf{I}^{(1)})$, if $\mathbf{I}^{(0)} \overset{?}{=} \mathbf{I}^{(1)}$ holds, the algorithm returns 1, otherwise returns 0.

3.3 Correctness and Concrete Parameters

This section analyzes the correctness of the proposed lattice-based SALRS scheme, specifies the parameters achieving 128 bits of security and evaluates the efficiency of the scheme.

Correctness. We first note that, the validity and well-formedness of a derived public key DPK, as verified by algorithms DerivedPublicKeyOwnerCheck and DerivedPublicKeyPublicCheck respectively, follows directly from the construction of DPK, the correctness of the underlying KEM scheme Π_{kem} and the fact that $\hat{\mathbf{t}} = \mathbf{t} + \mathbf{A}\mathbf{s}' = \mathbf{t} + \mathbf{t}' \in R_q^k$. Next, for an honestly generated signature

---

[2] Note that 1 is regarded as $r + 1$, i.e., $c_1 \leftarrow H_\theta(M, R, \mathbf{w}_r, \mathbf{v}_r, \mathbf{I})$.

$\sigma = (c_1, \{\mathbf{z}_i\}_{i=1}^r, \mathbf{I})$, it holds that $c_1 \in \mathbf{B}_\theta$ and $\mathbf{z}_i \in S_{\gamma-2\theta\eta}^l$ for all $i \in \{1, \ldots, r\}$. Furthermore, by construction, the value c_{r+1} computed at Step 2 of algorithm Verify satisfies $c_{r+1} = c_1$. Therefore, σ is accepted by Verify.

We next analyze the correctness of algorithm Link. Let $\sigma_0 = (c_1^{(0)}, \{\mathbf{z}_i^{(0)}\}_{i=1}^{r_0}, \mathbf{I}^{(0)})$ and $\sigma_1 = (c_1^{(1)}, \{\mathbf{z}_i^{(1)}\}_{i=1}^{r_1}, \mathbf{I}^{(1)})$ be generated by $\mathsf{Sign}(M_0, R_0, \mathsf{DPK}_0, (\mathsf{MPK}_0, \mathsf{MSK}_0))$ and $\mathsf{Sign}(M_1, R_1, \mathsf{DPK}_1, (\mathsf{MPK}_1, \mathsf{MSK}_1))$, respectively. For $i = 0, 1$, let $\mathsf{DPK}_i = (C_i, \hat{\mathbf{t}}_i)$ and note that $\mathbf{I}^{(i)} = H_m(\hat{\mathbf{t}}_i)\hat{\mathbf{s}}_i$, where $\hat{\mathbf{s}}_i = \mathbf{s}_i + \mathbf{s}_i'$ and $\mathbf{s}_i, \mathbf{s}_i'$ are generated as specified by the scheme. Note that, if $\mathsf{DPK}_0 = \mathsf{DPK}_1$, then we have $\hat{\mathbf{s}}_0 = \hat{\mathbf{s}}_1$ and thus, $\mathbf{I}^{(0)} = \mathbf{I}^{(1)}$. In this case, algorithm Link outputs 1.

In the case $\mathsf{DPK}_0 \neq \mathsf{DPK}_1$, we will demonstrate that, with overwhelming probability, algorithm Link outputs 0. Indeed, if $\hat{\mathbf{t}}_0 \neq \hat{\mathbf{t}}_1$, then $H_m(\hat{\mathbf{t}}_0), H_m(\hat{\mathbf{t}}_1)$ are uniformly random and distinct, $\hat{\mathbf{s}}_0$ and $\hat{\mathbf{s}}_1$ are also distinct. Hence, the probability that $\mathbf{I}^{(0)} = H_m(\hat{\mathbf{t}}_0)\hat{\mathbf{s}}_0 = H_m(\hat{\mathbf{t}}_1)\hat{\mathbf{s}}_1 = \mathbf{I}^{(1)}$ is negligible (this is true if small elements of R_q are invertible). Now, suppose that $\hat{\mathbf{t}}_0 = \hat{\mathbf{t}}_1$ and $C_0 \neq C_1$. Then, unless one accidentally finds a collision where $\hat{\mathbf{s}}_0 \neq \hat{\mathbf{s}}_1$ and $\mathbf{A}\hat{\mathbf{s}}_0 = \mathbf{A}\hat{\mathbf{s}}_1$ (which happens only with negligible probability), we must have $\hat{\mathbf{s}}_0 = \hat{\mathbf{s}}_1$. The latter may occur in two scenarios:

- $\mathbf{s}_0 \neq \mathbf{s}_1$ and $\mathbf{s}_0' \neq \mathbf{s}_1'$, but $\mathbf{s}_0 + \mathbf{s}_0' = \mathbf{s}_1 + \mathbf{s}_1'$. Due to the randomness of the generations of $\mathbf{s}_0, \mathbf{s}_1, \mathbf{s}_0', \mathbf{s}_1'$, this scenario only happens with negligible probability.
- $\mathbf{s}_0 = \mathbf{s}_1$ and $\mathbf{s}_0' = \mathbf{s}_1'$. Note that, if $\mathbf{s}_0, \mathbf{s}_1$ are obtained by two different executions of algorithm MasterKeyGen, then $\mathbf{s}_0 = \mathbf{s}_1$ only happens with negligible probability. Furthermore, two different executions of algorithm DerivePublicKeyGen with $C_0 \neq C_1$ should produce distinct $\mathbf{s}_0', \mathbf{s}_1'$ with overwhelming probability.

The above analysis shows that the given SALRS scheme is correct with overwhelming probability.

Lattice-Based Instantiation of the KEM Scheme Π_{kem}. We employ Kyber [7] to instantiate Π_{kem}, by setting GP_{kem} contains only the parameters $(n, k, q, \eta, d_u, d_v, d_t)$ and the hash function. Note that, the ciphertext in the CPA version of Kyber is pseudorandom based on the Decision Module-LWE (D-MLWE) assumption, and it hides not only the plaintext but also the public key. The CCA version of Kyber thus can be easily shown to satisfy not only CCA-security but also CCA-key-indistinguishability. For concreteness, we will use the Kyber variant Kyber768, which features public key size 1184 bytes and ciphertext size 1088 bytes.

Signing Trials. At Step 9 of the signing algorithm, if $\mathbf{z}_{\bar{i}} = \mathbf{y} + c_{\bar{i}}\hat{\mathbf{s}}_{\bar{i}} \notin S_{\gamma-2\theta\eta}^l$, then the signer has to go back to Step 4. Let us compute the probability of such restarting for uniformly random $\mathbf{y} \xleftarrow{R} S_\gamma^l$, $c_{\bar{i}} \in \mathbf{B}_\theta$ and $\hat{\mathbf{s}}_{\bar{i}} = \mathbf{s} + \mathbf{s}_{\bar{i}}' \in S_{2\eta}^l$. First, we have $\mathbf{x} := c_{\bar{i}}\hat{\mathbf{s}}_{\bar{i}} \in S_{2\theta\eta}^l$. For each entry $y_j \xleftarrow{R} [-\gamma, \gamma]$ of $\mathbf{y}$, and each entry $x_j \in [-2\theta\eta, 2\theta\eta]$ of $\mathbf{x}$, the probability that $y_j + x_j$ falls into the "safe zone"

$[-(\gamma - 2\theta\eta), \gamma - 2\theta\eta]$ is exactly the ratio between the cardinalities of the range $[-(\gamma - 2\theta\eta), \gamma - 2\theta\eta]$ and the range $[-\gamma, \gamma]$. Therefore, we have:

$$\Pr[\mathbf{z}_{\bar{i}} \in S^l_{\gamma-2\theta\eta}] = \frac{|S^l_{\gamma-2\theta\eta}|}{|S^l_\gamma|} = \left(1 - \frac{2\theta\eta}{\gamma + 1/2}\right) \approx e^{-2nl\theta\eta/\gamma},$$

where we use the fact that parameter γ is set to be large compared to $1/2$. As a result, the probability of restarting is approximately close to $1 - e^{-2nl\theta\eta/\gamma}$. In particular, if we set parameters $n, l, \theta, \eta, \gamma$ so that $2nl\theta\eta/\gamma < \log_e(3)$ (see below), then, on average, the signer has to run Step 4-Step 9 of the signing algorithm less than 3 times.

Concrete Parameters and Efficiency. To set parameters that yield a scheme with at least 128 bits of security, we rely on the parameters and analyses of Dilithium [12], Kyber [7,23] and [4]. In particular, modulus q is set so that every element of R_q with infinity norm less than $\frac{1}{\sqrt{8}} \cdot 2^{35/8}$ is invertible, and parameters $n, l, \theta, \eta, \gamma$ are set so that the number of signing trials is less than 3 on average. Similar to [12], we can use SHAKE-256 to implement the functions H_A, ExpandV, and H_m, and use the SampleInBall algorithm in [12, Fig. 2] to implement H_θ. Table 2 shows the concrete parameters and efficiency of the proposed lattice-based SALRS.

Table 2. Concrete parameters and efficiency of the proposed lattice-based SALRS.

Parameter	Value
Dimension n	256
Modulus q	Prime $q \approx 2^{35}$ and $q = 17 \bmod 32$
Module SIS/LWE parameters (k, l, m)	$(3, 5, 1)$
Bounds $(\theta, \eta, \gamma, \gamma - 2\theta\eta)$	$(60, 3, 699453, 699093)$
Master public key (MPK) size	4.44 KB
Master secret key (MSK) size	2.97 KB
Derived public key (DPK) size	4.34 KB
Signature size ($r = 8$)	27.4 KB
Signature size ($r = 16$)	53.6 KB
Signature size ($r = 32$)	106.1 KB
Signature size ($r = 64$)	211.1 KB

4   Proofs of Security and Privacy

Theorem 3. *The SALRS scheme is signer-linkable in the random oracle model.*

Proof. We prove that the SALRS scheme is signer-linkable under the Module-SIS (MSIS) assumption. Due to space limitation, we defer the proof details to the full version.

Theorem 4. *The SALRS scheme is signer-anonymous in the random oracle model.*

Proof. We prove that the SALRS scheme has signer-anonymity under the Decision Module-LWE (D-MLWE) assumption. Due to space limitation, we defer the proof details to the full version.

Theorem 5. *The SALRS scheme is signer-non-slanderable in the random oracle model.*

Proof. We prove that the SALRS scheme is signer-non-slanderable under the Module-SIS (MSIS) and Decision Module-LWE (D-MLWE) assumptions. Due to space limitation, we defer the proof details to the full version.

Theorem 6. *The SALRS scheme is master-public-key-unlinkable in the random oracle model.*

Proof. Suppose the underlying KEM scheme is CCA secure and CCA Key Indistinguishable, we prove that the SALRS scheme is master-public-key-unlinkable under the Decision Module-LWE (D-MLWE) assumption. Due to space limitation, we defer the proof details to the full version.

5   Conclusion

In this paper, we proposed a new cryptographic primitive, referred to as Linkable Ring Signature Scheme with Stealth Addresses (SALRS), which comprehensively and strictly captures the security and privacy requirements of hiding the payer and payee of the transactions in cryptocurrencies. We also proposed a lattice-based SALRS construction and proved its security and privacy in the random oracle model. As a result, our construction provides strong confidence on security and privacy in twofolds, being proved under strong models which capture the practical scenarios of cryptocurrencies, and being potentially quantum-resistant. The efficiency analysis also shows that our lattice-based SALRS scheme is practical for real implementations.

A   A Proof of Theorem 1

Proof (Sketch). Due to page limitation, below we give the proof sketch and defer the proof details to the full version.

Suppose there exists an adversary $\mathcal{A}$ that breaks the strong unforgeability, i.e. succeeds in $\mathsf{Game}_{\mathsf{euf}}$ with non-negligible advantage. We can construct an algorithm $\mathcal{B}$ that either succeeds $\mathsf{Game}_{\mathsf{snlink}}$ with non-negligible advantage or succeeds $\mathsf{Game}_{\mathsf{snnsl}}$ with non-negligible advantage.

$\mathcal{B}$ is offered two challengers $\mathcal{C}_0$ and $\mathcal{C}_1$, which will interact with $\mathcal{B}$ for $\mathsf{Game}_{\mathsf{snlink}}$ and $\mathsf{Game}_{\mathsf{snnsl}}$ respectively. On the other side, $\mathcal{B}$ interacts with $\mathcal{A}$ for $\mathsf{Game}_{\mathsf{euf}}$, making use of $\mathcal{C}_0$ or $\mathcal{C}_1$ behind, while it is indistinguishable from the view of $\mathcal{A}$.

At the **Output Phase** of $\mathsf{Game}_{\mathsf{euf}}$, $\mathcal{A}$ outputs a (message, derived public key ring, signature) tuple (M^*, R^*, σ^*), such that (1) $\mathsf{Verify}(M^*, R^*, \sigma^*) = 1$, and (2) $R^* \subseteq L_{dpk}$, and (3) (M^*, R^*, σ^*) is not returned by $\mathsf{OSign}(\cdot, \cdot, \cdot)$.

Wlog., let $R^* = (\mathsf{DPK}_1^*, \ldots, \mathsf{DPK}_k^*)$, $\mathcal{B}$ can obtain k (message, derived public key ring, signature) tuples $\{(M_i, R^*, \sigma_i)\}_{i=1}^k$ by making use of $\mathcal{C}_0$ or $\mathcal{C}_1$, such that (1) $\mathsf{Verify}(M_i, R^*, \sigma_i) = 1$ $(i = 1, 2, \ldots, k)$, and (2) $\mathsf{Link}(M_i, R^*, \sigma_i, M_j, R_j^*, \sigma_j) = 0 \; \forall i, j \in [1, k] \; s.t. \; i \neq j$, where σ_i corresponds to DPK_i^*. Consider these $k + 1$ signatures, we have that either the following **Case I** or the **Case II** happens:

- **Case I**: $\mathsf{Link}(M^*, R^*, \sigma^*, M_j, R^*, \sigma_j) = 0 \; \forall j \in \{1, \ldots, k\}$,
- **Case II**: $\exists \hat{i} \in \{1, \ldots, k\} \; s.t. \; \mathsf{Link}(M^*, R^*, \sigma^*, M_{\hat{i}}, R^*, \sigma_{\hat{i}}) = 1$.

If **Case I** happens, these $k+1$ signatures can be used to win $\mathsf{Game}_{\mathsf{snlink}}$, otherwise, the two signatures (M^*, R^*, σ^*), $(M_{\hat{i}}, R^*, \sigma_{\hat{i}})$ can be used to win $\mathsf{Game}_{\mathsf{snnsl}}$.

References

1. Au, M.H., Chow, S.S.M., Susilo, W., Tsang, P.P.: Short linkable ring signatures revisited. EuroPKI **2006**, 101–115 (2006). https://doi.org/10.1007/11774716_9
2. Au, M.H., Liu, J.K., Susilo, W., Yuen, T.H.: Constant-size id-based linkable and revocable-iff-linked ring signature. INDOCRYPT **2006**, 364–378 (2006). https://doi.org/10.1007/11941378_26
3. Au, M.H., Liu, J.K., Susilo, W., Yuen, T.H.: Secure id-based linkable and revocable-iff-linked ring signature with constant-size construction. Theor. Comput. Sci. **469**, 1–14 (2013). https://doi.org/10.1016/j.tcs.2012.10.031
4. Baum, C., Damgård, I., Lyubashevsky, V., Oechsner, S., Peikert, C.: More efficient commitments from structured lattice assumptions. SCN **2018**, 368–385 (2018). https://doi.org/10.1007/978-3-319-98113-0_20
5. Baum, C., Lin, H., Oechsner, S.: Towards practical lattice-based one-time linkable ring signatures. ICICS **2018**, 303–322 (2018). https://doi.org/10.1007/978-3-030-01950-1_18
6. Bellare, M., Boldyreva, A., Desai, A., Pointcheval, D.: Key-privacy in public-key encryption. In: Boyd, C. (ed.) ASIACRYPT 2001. LNCS, vol. 2248, pp. 566–582. Springer, Heidelberg (2001). https://doi.org/10.1007/3-540-45682-1_33
7. Bos, J.W., et al.: CRYSTALS - kyber: a CCA-secure module-lattice-based KEM. In: EuroS&P 2018. pp. 353–367 (2018). DOI: https://doi.org/10.1109/EuroSP.2018.00032
8. Boyen, X., Haines, T.: Forward-secure linkable ring signatures from bilinear maps. Cryptography **2**(4), 35 (2018). https://doi.org/10.3390/cryptography2040035
9. Branco, P., Mateus, P.: A code-based linkable ring signature scheme. ProvSec **2018**, 203–219 (2018). https://doi.org/10.1007/978-3-030-01446-9_12
10. CoinMarketCap: Top 100 cryptocurrencies by market capitalization. https://coinmarketcap.com. Accessed 27 Apr 2019
11. Courtois, N.T., Mercer, R.: Stealth address and key management techniques in blockchain systems. ICISSP **2017**, 559–566 (2017). https://doi.org/10.5220/0006270005590566
12. Ducas, L., et al.: Crystals-dilithium: a lattice-based digital signature scheme. IACR Trans. Cryptogr. Hardw. Embed. Syst. **2018**(1), 238–268 (2018). https://doi.org/10.13154/tches.v2018.i1.238-268

13. Esgin, M.F., Steinfeld, R., Sakzad, A., Liu, J.K., Liu, D.: Short lattice-based one-out-of-many proofs and applications to ring signatures. IACR Cryptol. ePrint Arch. **2018**, 773 (2018)

14. Fujisaki, E.: Sub-linear size traceable ring signatures without random oracles. CT-RSA **2011**, 393–415 (2011). https://doi.org/10.1007/978-3-642-19074-2_25

15. Fujisaki, E.: Sub-linear size traceable ring signatures without random oracles. IEICE Trans. **95-A**(1), 151–166 (2012). https://doi.org/10.1587/transfun.E95.A.151

16. Fujisaki, E., Suzuki, K.: Traceable ring signature. PKC **2007**, 181–200 (2007). https://doi.org/10.1007/978-3-540-71677-8_13

17. Langlois, A., Stehle, D.: Worst-case to average-case reductions for module lattices. Des. Codes Crypt. **75**(3), 565–599 (2015). https://doi.org/10.1007/s10623-014-9938-4

18. Libert, B., Ling, S., Nguyen, K., Wang, H.: Zero-knowledge arguments for lattice-based accumulators: logarithmic-size ring signatures and group signatures without trapdoors. In: EUROCRYPT 2016 Part II. pp. 1–31 (2016). DOI: https://doi.org/10.1007/978-3-662-49896-5_1

19. Liu, J.K., Au, M.H., Susilo, W., Zhou, J.: Linkable ring signature with unconditional anonymity. IEEE Trans. Knowl. Data Eng. **26**(1), 157–165 (2014). https://doi.org/10.1109/TKDE.2013.17

20. Liu, J.K., Wei, V.K., Wong, D.S.: Linkable spontaneous anonymous group signature for ad hoc groups (extended abstract). ACISP **2004**, 325–335 (2004). https://doi.org/10.1007/978-3-540-27800-9_28

21. Liu, Z., Yang, G., Wong, D.S., Nguyen, K., Wang, H.: Key-insulated and privacy-preserving signature scheme with publicly derived public key. EuroS&P 2019, to appear https://eprint.iacr.org/2018/956

22. Lu, X., Au, M.H., Zhang, Z.: Raptor: a practical lattice-based (linkable) ring signature. IACR Cryptol. ePrint Archive **2018**, 857 (2018). https://eprint.iacr.org/2018/857

23. Lyubashevsky, V., Seiler, G.: Short, invertible elements in partially splitting cyclotomic rings and applications to lattice-based zero-knowledge proofs. In: EUROCRYPT 2018 Part I. pp. 204–224 (2018). DOI: 10.1007/978-3-319-78381-9_8

24. Noether, S., Mackenzie, A.: Ring confidential transactions. Ledger **1**, 1–18 (2016)

25. van Saberhagen, N.: Cryptonote v 2.0 (2013). https://cryptonote.org/whitepaper.pdf

26. Sun, S., Au, M.H., Liu, J.K., Yuen, T.H.: Ringct 2.0: A compact accumulator-based (linkable ring signature) protocol for blockchain cryptocurrency monero. In: ESORICS 2017 Part II. pp. 456–474 (2017). DOI: https://doi.org/10.1007/978-3-319-66399-9_25

27. Todd, P.: Stealth addresses. https://lists.linuxfoundation.org/pipermail/bitcoin-dev/2014-January/004020.html

28. Torres, W.A.A., et al.: Post-quantum one-time linkable ring signature and application to ring confidential transactions in blockchain (lattice ringct v1.0). In: ACISP 2018. pp. 558–576 (2018). DOI: https://doi.org/10.1007/978-3-319-93638-3_32

29. Tsang, P.P., Wei, V.K.: Short linkable ring signatures for e-voting, e-cash and attestation. ISPEC **2005**, 48–60 (2005). https://doi.org/10.1007/978-3-540-31979-5_5

30. Tsang, P.P., Wei, V.K., Chan, T.K., Au, M.H., Liu, J.K., Wong, D.S.: Separable linkable threshold ring signatures. INDOCRYPT **2004**, 384–398 (2004). https://doi.org/10.1007/978-3-540-30556-9_30

31. Yuen, T.H., Liu, J.K., Au, M.H., Susilo, W., Zhou, J.: Efficient linkable and/or threshold ring signature without random oracles. Comput. J. **56**(4), 407–421 (2013). https://doi.org/10.1093/comjnl/bxs115
32. Zhang, H., Zhang, F., Tian, H., Au, M.H.: Anonymous post-quantum cryptocash. IACR Cryptol. ePrint Archive **2017**, 716 (2017). http://eprint.iacr.org/2017/716

Annotary: A Concolic Execution System for Developing Secure Smart Contracts

Konrad Weiss$^{(\boxtimes)}$ and Julian Schütte

Fraunhofer AISEC, Garching near Munich, Germany
{konrad.weiss,julian.schuette}@aisec.fraunhofer.de
https://www.aisec.fraunhofer.de

Abstract. Ethereum smart contracts are executable programs, deployed on a peer-to-peer network and executed in a consensus-based fashion. Their bytecode is public, immutable and once deployed to the blockchain, cannot be patched anymore. As smart contracts may hold Ether worth of several million dollars, they are attractive targets for attackers and indeed some contracts have successfully been exploited in the recent past, resulting in tremendous financial losses. The correctness of smart contracts is thus of utmost importance. While first approaches on formal verification exist, they demand users to be well-versed in formal methods which are alien to many developers and are only able to analyze individual contracts, without considering their execution environment, i.e., calls to external contracts, sequences of transaction, and values from the actual blockchain storage. In this paper, we present Annotary, a concolic execution framework to analyze smart contracts for vulnerabilities, supported by annotations which developers write directly in the Solidity source code. In contrast to existing work, Annotary supports analysis of inter-transactional, inter-contract control flows and combines symbolic execution of EVM bytecode with a resolution of concrete values from the public Ethereum blockchain. While the analysis of Annotary tends to weight precision higher than soundness, we analyze inter-transactional call chains to eliminate false positives from unreachable states that traditional symbolic execution would not be able to handle. We present the annotation and analysis concepts of Annotary, explain its implementation on top of the Laser symbolic virtual machine, and demonstrate its usage as a plugin for the Sublime Text editor.

Keywords: Smart contracts · EVM · Ethereum · Concolic execution · Program analysis

1 Introduction

Smart contracts are small programs, executed by all verifying nodes of a blockchain as part of a consensus protocol. The idea of smart contracts is to distribute not only data but also computation to a set of potentially untrusted

© Springer Nature Switzerland AG 2019
K. Sako et al. (Eds.): ESORICS 2019, LNCS 11735, pp. 747–766, 2019.
https://doi.org/10.1007/978-3-030-29959-0_36

peers, in order to create distributed applications ("DApps") that are not governed by a single party and operate correctly and reliably, as long as the majority of the blockchain network sticks to the protocol. In that sense, smart contracts implement the core business logic of DApps and are responsible for moving digital currency from one account (i.e., user) to another.

Ethereum, the most popular public implementation of the concept of smart contracts, is a permissionless public blockchain that uses the above concepts to create a digital currency called Ether, as well as a general-purpose distributed computing engine with a quasi-Turing complete execution model. [12]. Ether is publicly tradable similar to Bitcoin but also serves as the payment method for code execution of smart contracts in the Ethereum Virtual Machine (**EVM**), typically written in the programming language Solidity [13] and compiled into the EVM bytecode format which is then deployed to the peer-to-peer network.

In some applications, the amount of Ether controlled by a smart contract is enormous. From a security perspective, smart contract code can thus be regarded similar to code of smart card applets: the code implements simple functionality in a well-defined and constrained environment and is thus easy to verify, but errors in that code are not tolerable as extremely high values are at stake. At the same time, once deployed to the public, it is almost impossible to roll out security patches. Blockchains and DApps are created in a rapidly evolving industry where time-to-market is crucial, and smart contract developers rarely have a background in writing highly critical code or experience with formal verification methods. Various severe incidents have happened in the past, where vulnerabilities in smart contracts allowed to lock in or withdraw significant amounts of Ether from popular DApps. To name only a few, this includes the PoWH-Coin bug, the first Parity bug (153,037 ETH stolen) [3], the second Parity bug (513,774.16 ETH frozen) [5], and the DAO hack (3.6 mio. ETH stolen) [1] which finally lead to a hard fork of the Ethereum blockchain. These incidents suggest that writing secure smart contracts is challenging and effectively supporting developers in avoiding vulnerabilities is a necessity. Rigid formal verification methods have been proposed in the past [2] but later dismissed, as they put too high demands on developers who are no experts in this field. Simple static analysis approaches, on the other hand, help to avoid simple programming errors but are far from being precise enough to discover subtle flaws – especially those manifesting in the interaction between multiple contracts.

In this paper, we introduce *Annotary*, a concolic execution tool that supports Solidity developers in writing error-free smart contracts. In contrast to other tools which focus on searching predefined vulnerability patterns, we take a developer-centric perspective and allow developers to express their expectations in the form of annotations directly in the Solidity code. *Annotary* then conducts a concolic execution analysis of the compiled EVM bytecode against these annotations and informs the developer about potential violations – currently in the form of a plugin for the Sublime editor. We advance the state of the art in EVM analysis by including interactions between contracts and along chains of transactions in the analysis and make the following contributions.

1. extend concolic analysis of EVM bytecode to properly span contract interactions and sequences of transactions.
2. a backward-compatible extension of the Solidity language by annotations which allows developers to state verifiable properties
3. a proof-of-concept implementation of *Annotary*, including a Sublime Text plugin

2   Background

Although at a syntactical level, Solidity resembles C or JavaScript, its execution model has some peculiarities that require further discussion. Furthermore, we will provide some background on Mythril, a vulnerability scanning tool for Ethereum smart contracts, that we significantly extended in the process of developing *Annotary*.

2.1   Solidity and Smart Contracts

Solidity is a high-level language for implementing smart contracts and targets the Ethereum Virtual Machine (EVM) platform. It is statically typed, supports multiple inheritance, libraries, complex user-defined types, contracts as members, overloading and overwriting, abstraction and interfaces, as well as encapsulation through visibility modifiers. Solidity's contract-orientation appears similar to object-oriented languages, using the `contract` keyword instead of `class`. However, in contrast, to truly object-oriented languages, such type definitions do not end up in the actual bytecode which consequently only includes instantiations of contracts and their respective functions [13]. A special contract-creation transaction is used to invoke the "constructor" and as a result, the contract is instantiated and assigned a public address which only holds the code that can be called by transactions. It is also important to note that contracts created from the same code basis do not share any data or (static) functions.

Listing 1.1 illustrates some typical concepts of the Solidity language, including inheritance and two different ways to declare constructors. The constructor in ❷ is declared by naming the function equal to its contract (analog to languages like Java), while ❸ uses the newer `constructor` keyword (analog to JavaScript, albeit Solidity merely treats `constructor` as a function modifier), which became mandatory in version 5.0 [7] of Solidity to avoid vulnerabilities related to simply misspelling function names. The example also shows two patterns which are common in smart contracts: first, the constructor keeps track of the owner who originally deployed the contract by assigning the associated 20-byte address ❶ passed to the constructor to the `owner` field. This allows the contract to later distinguish between calls that are made by its original owner or by anyone else. Second, the contracts defines a nameless *default function* ❹ that is called when callers invoke the contract without referring to a specific function. In this case, the `require`-statement will roll back the transaction if the sender attempts to send any Ether (`msg.value`) to a non-existing function. To address a specific function in a transaction, it must include the function identifier, which is computed as the first four most significant bytes of the keccak256 hash of the function signature.

```
1  contract A {
2     address owner;
3     function A(){ owner = msg.sender; ❶ } ❷
4  }
5  contract B is A{
6     uint variable;
7     function constructor(){ variable = 1;} ❸
8     function setVar(uint var1){ ... }
9     function() payable { require(msg.value == 0);} ❹
10 }
```

Listing 1.1. Solidity smart contract example

Entities and Interactions. Ethereum is a distributed system building a single-ton computer with accounts as entities and transactions referring to accounts as the smallest units of computation. Accounts are identified by a 160-bit address, have a balance of Ether, a transaction counter, and two possibly empty fields: the associated bytecode and storage state. **Wallets** are contracts with empty byte-code and their 160-bit address is the hash of their public key. The holder of the private key signs transactions proving its origin to be the Wallet. Transactions to these accounts can only transfer Ether. Accounts with associated bytecode are **contract accounts** and receive their address in a deterministic process when a contract creation transaction is sent to the network. The construction-bytecode is run, and the resulting state of the contract is some possibly non-empty storage state and the runtime-bytecode.

Transactions are signed data packets that represent a message to an account by specifying its address in the **to**-field or a contract-creation transaction if the content is 0. **Messages** can be the result of a transaction or of subsequent deter-ministic calls between contracts when bytecode is executed. They are unsigned blocks of data sent from one account to another still associated with the verified initial sender of the transaction. If an account with non-empty bytecode receives a message, an instance of the EVM is started with the target account's bytecode and the message data as input. Returned data is passed to the calling EVM context or returned as transaction result.

2.2   EVM and Bytecode

EVM has a simple stack-based architecture with a word size of 256 bit that allows to directly map keccak-256 hashes to addresses. A predefined finite resource called **gas** must be assigned to each transaction and serves as the unit for compu-tational effort that is consumed by each EVM instruction. It thus helps to prevent Denial-of-Service (DoS) attacks by stopping the execution when it is depleted, making the EVM a *quasi*-Turing-complete machine that has a Turing-complete instruction set but can only execute a limited number of statements [24].

The simplicity of the EVM bytecode with its 70 main instructions made the EVM a popular target for formal verification projects [10,15,22]. During execution the EVM maintains three main types of memory that are also relevant for the analysis by *Annotary*:

The **world state** σ is a mapping from 160-bit addresses a to account states and is kept in a Merkle Patricia tree that represents the result of executing all transactions saved on the Ethereum blockchain. A mapped account state $\sigma[a]$ contains the **balance** $\sigma[a]_b$ in Wei, the smallest sub-unit of Ether (10^{18} Wei = 1 Ether), the **storage** $\sigma[a]_s$ as mapping from 256-bit integer values to 256-bit integer values $\sigma[a]_s : 2^{256} \rightarrow 2^{256}$, and the immutable **runtime bytecode** $\sigma[a]_c$ of an account that is executed in the case of message receipt.

The **execution environment** I contains data that is fixed during message processing, including the address of the current message recipient I_a whose code is executed, and the sender of the message I_s. I_o is the account associated with the original transaction and may differ from I_s for inter-contract messages. I_d contains the input data for the current execution, such as function parameters. I_v contains the value of Ether in Wei transfered from the sender I_s to the recipient I_a. I_b contains the runtime bytecode of I_a that is executed and I_H stores the header of the block that the current transaction will be mined in.

The **machine state** μ contains the variable and volatile part of the computation held only during message processing. These include the volatile operand LIFO stack μ_s with 256-bit words and a byte-addressable heap memory μ_m used for more complicated computation or larger chunks of data. It further holds the program counter μ_{pc} and the output byte-array μ_o of the execution. Changes of the execution are not persisted if not send or returned to a different account or stored in $\sigma[a]$.

2.3 Mythril and the Laser-SVM

Mythril [20] is an open-source security analysis tool for Ethereum smart contracts and serves as the foundation for *Annotary*.[1]

It uses LASER-SVM, an internal symbolic virtual machine, to explore smart contract bytecode in a depth-first search fashion over the control flow graph (CFG). For this, it operates on a representation of σ, I and μ. Values that are unknown during execution are represented as symbolic variables, and the explored execution paths are transformed into *path conditions*, i.e., constraint systems over the symbolic variables along the respective execution path. Mythril runs vulnerability detection modules that inspect the explored executions states for known vulnerability patterns and attempts to compute concrete input values leading to the execution of the vulnerability by solving the respective constraint system using the Z3 SMT solver [19]. As the EVM uses 256-bit operands for computation, Mythril uses a bit-vector algebra at a fixed size of 256 bits to

---

[1] As Mythril is under active development, this paper refers to the commit hash github.com/ConsenSys/mythril-classic/commit/b5afa9ff1aa2b5dc8863d29aa9e0a24 b34eb4747 of the project.

model arithmetic operations and boolean algebra. While Mythril and especially its LASER-SVM provide a good basis of concolic/symbolic execution for EVM bytecode, Mythril's goal is not to allow analysis of specifiable properties. Mythril lacks the following capabilities which *Annotary* aims to provide:

- The ability to let developers specify invariants and assertions in the contract and the ability to verify them *before* the potentially vulnerable contract is irrevocably deployed.
- A model of EVM instructions and execution semantics for inter-contract- and inter-transactional control flows.
- Reachability analysis of transaction sequences to reduce false positives.
- Symbolic execution of contract constructors with parameters.

3   Annotation Driven Concolic Analysis

Rather than exploitation, *Annotary* aims at secure development while expanding the analysis scope to inter-contract and inter-transactional analyses. We begin this section by outlining the overall system and then detailing the main aspects of the analysis. Figure 1 shows how *Annotary's* editor plugin passes source and configuration files to the analysis component and receives found annotation violations for visualization.

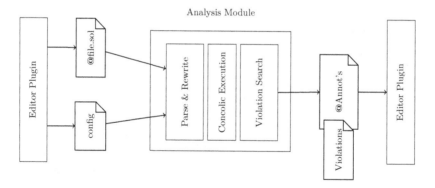

Fig. 1. *Annotary's* architecture with Solidity files undergoing analysis and violations reported to the editor plugin.

3.1   Annotations

Annotary specifies a set of annotations which developers can use to express invariants and restrictions directly in the Solidity source code. These annotations will then be translated into constraints or injected as asserts and analyzed to become part of the constraint system for an execution path. As annotations may include expressions, as well as references to Solidity functions and members, they require a separate compilation pass in addition to compilation of the actual source code. This is done by the annotation processor which takes annotations as input and translates them into EVM instructions by rewriting the original contract code. The purpose of the so added instructions is only to create additional constraints. To not alter the semantics such as state or control flow of the actual contract the execution of inserted code is isolated from the rest. When the symbolic execution reaches a state that violates any constraint derived from an annotation, the contract is considered to violate the developer's expectations, and the violation is reported to the developer. *Annotary* implements three types of annotations:

1. **Inline checks:** The annotation `"@check("BoolExpr")"` and its negation `"@never("BoolExpr")"` specify properties inside a contract function that are checks whether or not the specified condition holds. The condition can hold any boolean expression valid in solidity including calls to other functions and contracts.
2. **Contract invariants:** The annotation `"@invariant("BoolExpr")"` defines a contract wide condition that has to hold whenever a transaction persists its state.
3. **Set restrictions:** restricts writing to a member variable from outside of explicitly allowed functions. A state at a `SSTORE` instruction is reported a violation if the `SSTORE` writes to the protected variable and the function is not explicitly allowed to. Users can specify these restrictions with the following annotation:
   `"@set_restricted("["var="{[ContractName "."] MemberName[","]} ";"]}`
   `↪ ["func="]{"constructor"|FunctionName|FunctionSignature}")"`

3.2 Modeling Transaction Execution

Depending on the type of data, *Annotary* uses different strategies to treat memory locations either as concrete or as symbolic values. Concrete values will be initialized according to the EVM's actual behavior, i.e., storage on contract creation will be initialized by 0. Symbolic values refer to variables of the SMT constraint system which refer to specific memory locations. For instance, we write $\sigma[I_a]_s[key] \to BitVecRef(storage[key], 256)$ to denote the allocation of a variable key in storage. In general, when writing data to some memory location, *Annotary* supports both concrete and symbolic values and propagates data of the respective type to the memory location. When data is read from a previously unused location, however, it depends on the data type whether *Annotary* will treat it as symbolic or concrete.

Call data is modeled symbolically to represent all possible user interactions with the contract. **Memory** is treated concretely and reinitialized with the default value 0 for constructor and transaction execution. The **creation code** itself is known, but the appended initialization parameters are unknown at analysis time and thus handled symbolically. Reads after the end of the known instructions default to return symbolic variables.

Storage is set to the concrete type when the constructor is executed. On this first transaction, the content of storage is known and defaults to returning 0 when reading from unwritten locations.

Then, storage is reset to be empty and treated symbolically henceforth to represent the most generic state space and account for all unknown transactions that might have happened between construction and invocation of the smart contract.

3.3   Inter-contract Analysis

Annotary can correctly handle dependencies between contracts, including those which manifest only at Solidity but not at bytecode level.

Contract Inheritance: is the only relation that is not directly visible in byte-code and requires *Annotary* to pre- and post-processes Solidity code. It uses the C3-linearization of the inheritance hierarchy to identify transaction implementations defined by a parent contract that are callable once the child contract is deployed. Asserts referencing member variables of a child contract cannot be directly injected into the transaction function of the parent contract, as the member variable is not in the parent's scope. To solve this, *Annotary* generates a proxy function with the same signature in the child contract that delegates the call through the super keyword and injects the assert.

Nested Contract Creation: Contracts can create other contracts by piggy-backing the necessary constructor bytecode in their runtime bytecode. *Annotary* spawns a new symbolic execution with the creation bytecode extracted from the current transaction execution.

Inter-Contract Interactions: happen when the analyzed contract performs a message call or executes foreign contract code on their storage. Symbolically executing these interactions allows to resolve potentially returned values and to understand changes on the analyzed contracts state. *Annotary* implements symbolic execution for several EVM instructions for inter-contract interaction, lacking by Mythril, including CREATE, STATICCALL, RETURNDATACOPY, RETURNDATASIZE, and EXTCODECOPY. All instructions that trigger inter-contract interactions are executed with the appropriate concrete or symbolic persisting data type:

CALLCODE and DELEGATECALL execute external contract code referenced by the address of the external contract in the context of the current contract and can, therefore, change the contracts persistent storage. If address and code can be resolved, symbolic execution can account for these calls effects. If they cannot be resolved, storage has to be reset to be empty and symbolic, and the variables in the constraints are renamed to avoid collisions.

CALL and STATICCALL are executed with empty symbolic storage for the first interaction and with the initialized symbolic storage on further interactions.

CREATE deploys a new contract and executes the contract creation with empty concrete storage that is used for further interactions with the contract in the same transaction. In other transactions executions storage will be considered empty and symbolic.

3.4   Inter-transactional Analysis

Annotary implements inter-transactional reachability analysis to eliminate false positive violations that are not reachable considering the possible set of contract transactions.

Extracting   Transaction   Traces.   *Annotary*   uses   transaction   traces $\tau = \{\Delta, \Phi\}$ for inter-transactional analysis, information of a contract execution that persists after the execution is finished:

- Δ is a mapping of symbolic state variables k in $\sigma[I_a]$, e.g., storage slots or balance, of the currently analyzed contract to SMT bit vector expressions δ, representing the change that a transaction performs on the state.
- The trace constraints Φ are a set of conditions that have to hold such that the transaction represented by τ can be executed on the contract. Φ is a subset of the path constraints. Path constraints with no reference to the previous state, e.g., only to input data, are not included in Φ and do not lower the accuracy of reachability analysis.

Traces should represent state changing transactions that can appear amid a transaction sequence. The global states at the persisting instructions STOP and RETURN, are taken into consideration, while states at SELFDESTRUCT cannot be followed by further transactions and are therefore ignored. States with unchanged persisted values, e.g., in storage and balance, are filtered out due to irrelevance for the sequence and states with unsatisfiable path constraints due to inapplicability. Δ and Φ are extracted from global states that represent the unmodified contract execution, reducing constraints by all that are not relevant in an inter-transactional analysis.

Annotary differentiates between constructor transaction traces (τ_c) and message transaction traces (τ_m) and brings states that may violate an annotation into a transaction trace representation (τ_v) to allow reachability analysis.

Chain Transaction Traces. *Annotary* combines traces through expression substitution to explore the possible persisted states of a contract instead of iterative concolic execution. $\tau_{12} := \tau_1 \circ \tau_2$ represents the symbolic trace left onto the contract state when τ_1 is executed before τ_2. Definition 1 shows how traces are combined. The changes to the contract state Δ_1 that trace τ_1 applied exist at the beginning of trace τ_2. Therefore the changes Δ_1 have to be applied to the expressions used in Δ_2 and Φ_2.

$$\tau_1 := \{\Delta_1, \Phi_1\} \qquad \tau_2 := \{\Delta_2, \Phi_2\}$$

$$\tau_{12} := \{\Delta_{12} := \Delta_1 \circ_\Delta \Delta_2, \ \Phi_{12} := \Phi_1 \cup (\Delta_1 \circ_\Phi \Phi_2)\} \tag{1}$$

$\circ_\Phi$ in Definition 2 and $\circ_\Delta$ in Definition 3 are necessary operations to apply the storage changes Δ_1 to τ_2. Φ is a list and Δ is a mapping of expressions. The pairs (k', δ') in the mapping Δ can be used together with the SMT-solvers substitute function to replace appearance of a value k' in an expression e with δ'.

$$\Delta \circ_\Phi \Phi := [substitute(\Delta, \phi) : \phi \in \Phi] \tag{2}$$

$$\Delta_1 \circ_\Delta \Delta_2 := [(k, substitute(\Delta_1, \delta)) : (k, \delta) \in \Delta_2] \tag{3}$$

We further define two properties for traces, spanning one or more transactions: A trace τ is **valid** if its constraints are satisfiable. An invalid trace means that the constraints are not satisfiable and thus this sequence of instructions and calls among transactions is not executable at runtime. In the following, we denote satisfiability of a trace as $\mathsf{sat}(\tau)$. A trace can further be **state independent** if its constraints do not contain any symbolic variables k referencing the previous contract state. State independence means that execution of that trace does not depend on the prior execution of any other contracts and is denoted by $\mathsf{svar}(\tau) = \emptyset$.

Confidence Levels. By combining the properties of validity and state independence, *Annotary* expresses the confidence with which found violations will exist at runtime. *Annotary* supports the following confidence levels, from most to least confident:

1. **Single transaction violation**: For the intra-transactionally verified violating trace τ_v, $\mathsf{sat}(\tau_v) \wedge \mathsf{svar}(\tau_v) = \emptyset$ holds. In this case, the transaction violates the annotation.
2. **Chained transaction violation**: For a valid and state independent trace τ_{m*v} of optionaly many applications[2] of transactions from τ_m and finally τ_v (i.e., $\mathsf{sat}(\tau_{m*v}) \wedge \mathsf{svar}(\tau_{m*v}) = \emptyset$ holds). In this case, the annotation is violated, independent from which contract state the call is made.
3. **Constructed violation**: A sequence of traces starting from the constructor was found that can trigger the annotation violation and is $\mathsf{sat}(\tau_{cm*v}) \wedge \mathsf{svar}(\tau_{cm*v}) = \emptyset$. The attacker requires to be the contract creator or find a contract in the required state.
4. **Unconfirmed violation**: The chaining depth d was reached and there is at least one $\tau_{m^d v}$ that is $\mathsf{sat}(\tau_{m^d v}) \wedge \mathsf{svar}(\tau_{m^d v}) \neq \emptyset$.
5. **Violation avoiding context**: A point in the analysis was reached where the possibilities of chaining transactions to reach the violating state was exhausted. This means that although $\mathsf{sat}(\tau_v) \wedge \mathsf{svar}(\tau_v) \neq \emptyset$ it is also such that $\exists c \in \mathbb{N} : c <= d : (\nexists \tau_{m^c v} \in T : \mathsf{sat}(\tau_{m^c v})) \wedge \forall e \in \mathbb{N} : e <= c : \nexists \tau_{m^e v} \in T : \mathsf{sat}(\tau_{m^e v}) \wedge \mathsf{svar}(m^e v) = \emptyset$.
6. **Unsatisfiable violation**: The violating transaction τ_v is not satisfiable. This means $!\mathsf{sat}(execution\_constraints_{\tau_v})$.

---

[2] Shorthand notation: $\tau_a \circ \tau_b := \tau_{ab}$, application of d arbitrary set members $\tau_{m^d} := \tau_{m_1} \circ ... \circ \tau_{m_d}$.

Chaining Strategy. To check the validity of a found violation two high level strategies can be used to explore transaction traces:

Forward: Starting from the set of constructor and transaction traces $T_c \cup T_m$, the current trace chains are applied to $T_v \cup T_m$, and the new trace chain is checked for satisfiability. If the chain is satisfiable, the violation is confirmed.

Backward: Starting from the violating traces $\tau_v \in T_v$, the set of contract traces $T_c \cup T_m$ are applied to the set of remaining transaction chains. If an explored trace chain is valid and state independent, the violation is confirmed. If the form of the sequence is τ_{cm^*v} the exploration attempts to find a more threatening sequence τ_{m^*v}. *Annotary* uses this strategy depicted in Fig. 2 as it allows to differentiate between violations with confidence level **unconfirmed violation** and **violation avoiding context**. The size of initial traces is smaller if $|T_c \cup T_m| > |Tv|$. Trace chaining scales better if $|T_c \cup T_m| < |T_v \cup T_m| \iff |T_c| < |T_v|$.

Fig. 2. Backward strategy finding state independent sequence for both violations.

4   Implementing Annotary

This section elaborates on the implementation of the *Annotary*, i.e., a Sublime Text plugin and the inter-contract concolic analysis on top Mythrils Laser-SVM.

4.1   Preprocessing of Solidity Contracts

In a first preprocessing step, *Annotary* parses Solidity source files and extracts the annotations stating the conditions that will be analyzed. The input files are then parsed with the solidity compiler `solc` to gain the construction (bin) and runtime binaries (bin-runtime) of the contracts, the source code mappings (srcmap), that link the symbolically executed instructions to the code segments they were compiled from, the contracts application binary interface (ABI), which describes the transactions that can be executed and the expected input parameters, and finally the contract's abstract syntax tree (AST) to identify transaction endpoints, retrieve inheritance structures, functions and member variables.

   Annotary adds a *rewriting* pass to the compilation process that converts `@check` and `@invariant` annotations into corresponding sets of `assert` statements, as in Appendix A.2. Furthermore, *Annotary* modifies the LASER-SVM to isolate the execution of rewritten code from affecting the rest of the symbolic execution. We extended the LASER-SVM by a state processor that keeps track of instructions, result of the rewrite pass, excluding the resulting states from the set of unmodified contract states.

4.2   Concolic Execution

Annotary builds upon the LASER-SVM to extend inter-contract and adds inter-transactional analysis. We now guide the reader through the most significant building blocks that *Annotary* adds to LASER-SVM.

Symbolic Handling of Inter-contract Calls. *Annotary* extends LASER-SVM by adding handlers for instructions that were not supported, in order to close the semantic gap between LASER-SVM and EVM. The CREATE instruction is implemented by executing a contract creation transaction with the nested contract code extracted from the current contract. The prior transaction execution is resumed with the newly created contract in σ. Support for the STATICCALL instruction is added, analog to the CALL instruction with msg.value set to 0, as no funds are transferred, and a flag that prevents SSTORE-instruction in nested calls to write persistent storage. RETURNDATASIZE and RETURNDATACOPY are implemented by extracting size and data from the global state and copying them to stack and memory, respectively. If *Annotary* successfully resolves the concrete address that is given to EXTCODECOPY, the retrieved external code is copied to memory and treated concretely.

Pre-, and Post-processing and Filtering of States. *Annotary* modifies how the LASER-SVM processes instructions in its worklist to handle instructions differently that have been added to the unmodified contract code.

For instance, the ASSERT_FAIL instruction, would immediately terminate the execution when a given condition is not fulfilled. If that instruction has been inserted into the bytecode as a consequence of an @check annotation, however, we need a different semantic, as we want to detect the violation of the annotation, but not necessarily terminate the symbolic execution at that state. We thus extend LASER-SVM by *state labels* that mark individual states in the explored symbolic state space as *Violating* and/or *Ignore* to indicate that this state was the result of code modification to identify violations and shall be saved and/or isolated from the set of states representing the execution of the unmodified code.

4.3   Violation Identification and Classification

After the concolic execution, *Annotary* has access to the state space of the unmodified contract and a set of states violating the @check or @invariant annotations. We can map these directly to warnings that will be displayed to the developer at the corresponding line of code. The @set_restricted annotation limits write operations to a member variable to a set of valid functions and thus needs to search for violating states at SSTORE instructions. The writing function is identified over the instruction association to code and the saved path constraint that stems from the selected function identifier. The written Solidity member is identified through the storage index according to the computed outline in storage, which requires *Annotary* to keep track of relevant keccak256 results, depicted in Appendix A.3. *Annotary* searches through the state space for a path that starts at a violating location and ends in a state at a STOP or RETURN that would effectively persist the violating transaction to storage.

Chaining Transactions. *Annotary* chains transactions by merging selected states from the symbolic state space of one transaction into the state space of the previous transaction. The selection includes only relevant states, i.e. only those which have inter-transactional effects (e.g., write to storage).

When creating execution traces of transaction sequences, *Annotary* maintains meta-data that is assigned to the sequence and presents users more qualified information such as the *transaction depth* and the sequence of *contract functions*, as well as data to optimize the trace chaining operation, such as the set of *symbolic state variables* that references prior contract states and the set of *transaction variables*. Both sets allow to keep track of variables that have to be substituted or renamed when combining transactions and allows for an efficient implementation using the Z3 expression substitution functionality. However, chaining transactions will lead to an explosion of possible chains and thus explored states, limiting the depth of transaction sequences that can be analyzed. We illustrate this effect with real-world contracts in Sect. 5.

Annotary analyzes transactions preceeding a violating trace for two purposes. A valid chain confirms the inter-transactional validity of the violation and the resulting confidence level gives a more nuanced judgment of the violation. Algorithm 1.4 in Subsect. A.3 shows how the sequence of preceeding transactions with the highest confidence level that leads to a given violation is found. When the violating transaction sequence contains no symbolic state variables in the constraint expressions, a state independent chain of length one is found, it is assigned the confidence level *single transaction violation*. At every iteration step, all traces in $\tau_c \cup \tau_m$ are applied to the violating sequences of depth $n - 1$, which in the beginning is only the violating trace. Traces are only applied to a sequence if they overwrite a symbolic state variable and the set of constraints are checked for satisfiability before they are added to the set of violating sequences of length n. If a transaction sequence ends in a constructor trace τ_c, the chain is saved with the confidence level *Constructed violation* but the search for a more severe violating sequence is continued. If the trace is from the set τ_m and chained trace is state independent, the search is terminated with a sequence of confidence *Chained transaction violation*. If the set of new sequences is empty because all trace applications resulted in sequences with unsatisfiable constraints, the initial violation gets the confidence level *Violation avoiding context*. If the maximal depth is reached the violating trace is of confidence level *Unconfirmed violation*. After all violations are categorized, the annotation's violation confidence level is set to the highest level of the found sequences. Finally, all annotations with their violations are returned in JSON-format to the Sublime Text plugin.

4.4   Annotary Plugin

The *Annotary* plugin bridges the gap to concolic execution from within the Sublime Text editor. Annotations are written inside of Solidity files, and a context menu allows to run the search for violations. Annotations and violating code pieces are visualized inside of the documents, e.g., in Fig. 3 in Subsect. A.1. Hovering over them shows the confidence level, the violating transactions, and informative description. A config allows disabling trace chaining, set the depth of chained traces and followed jumps during concolic execution.

5   Discussion

We evaluated *Annotary* with respect to its effectiveness and efficiency. First, we assessed how *Annotary* performs with vulnerable contracts and if it would detect all vulnerabilities as expected. We thus created a sample set of 11 **small** contracts with known programming mistakes that have led to severe vulnerabilities in the past and added annotations that would have made *Annotary* detect the flaw. Among others, this set includes the following mistakes: one of the Parity bugs [5] allowed execution of an initialization function because of the unset member variable `initialized`. By adding an `@invariant(initialized==true)` annotation, *Annotary* was able to spot this vulnerability. This mistake is especially hard to spot for humans if non-obvious call paths over library functions allow the execution of the initialization function [3] or if typos such as `state =+ 1` (which evaluates to `state = 1`) instead of `state += 1` are present. A further included mistake is to erroneously expose functions that allow writing to some member variable by incorrectly setting (or omitting) one of Solidity's four visibility modifiers for functions. *Annotary* catches this error, if the member variable is annotated with `@set_restricted`. Another, especially subtle mistake is writing to uninitialized structs. Structs can be persisted in either memory or storage and if declared in "C style" and not marked otherwise, default to storage. If fields of a struct are written without prior initialization, the write operation will overwrite the first storage slots, which can lead to disastrous consequences. Consider this snippet, which overwrites the owner address by calling `doSth()`.

```
1   contract test {
2     struct MyStruct { uint myField; }
3     address owner;   // Keeps track of privileged owner
4
5     function doSth() {
6       MyStruct s;
7       s.myField = uint(msg.sender);   // Overwrites owner
8   } }
```

Annotary detects this vulnerability, if *owner* is annotated with `@set_restricted` (cf. Figure 3), even taking delegated calls into account. *Annotary* detects all programming mistakes in the "small" sample set. Table 2 lists the mistakes and used annotation types.

In a second step, we were interested in the performance of *Annotary* with real-world contracts and created a second sample set of 24 **large** contracts with the highest balance of Ether and available source code in the public Ethereum network. These contracts were not annotated and are not known to contain vulnerabilities, it is therefore not possible to create data underpinning the soundness and completeness of *Annotary*. Nevertheless, we evaluated the coverage of the symbolic execution, the runtime, and scalability with respect to the depth of chained execution traces to give an impression on *Annotary's* runtime. As can be seen from Table 1, the coverage of the "large" sample set is 80%, while the coverage of the **small** set is 88%. The average runtime for the "small" set is 4 seconds, which we consider well-suited for IDE integration, especially when considering that no performance optimizations have been done so far. For the real-world contracts from the "large" sets, the average runtime is with 700 s significantly higher due to larger code sizes. Columns **d<n>** in Table 1 illustrate how increasing the depth of the analyzed call chains adds significant runtime overhead. A feasible mode of operation might thus be to configure the depth of analysis in the IDE to be lower and to run a full analysis in a CI server.

Table 1. Average runtime of *Annotary's* analysis of the "small" and "large" sample

Type	Sample size	Coverage[%]	Sym. Exe.[s]	d1[s]	d2[s]	d3[s]	d4[s]	d5[s]	d6[s]
Small	11	88	1.3	0.07	0.13	0.34	0.82	1.9	4.1
Large	24	80	54.2	12.9	17.8	606	-	-	-

6 Related Work

Symbolic execution approaches with the pioneer Oyente [18] by Luu et al., the extension Osiris [23] by Torres et al., and Mythril [20] by Bernhard Mueller et al. use the results of symbolic execution and SMT-solving to find known vulnerabilities in an intra-transactional context. MAIAN [21] by Nikolic et al. extends this approach to an inter-transactional context and finds vulnerability patterns defined over multiple transactions. *Annotary* builds upon Mythril's LASER-SVM and extends it to support inter-contract analysis. Our work further differs from the aforementioned tools in that it supports inter-transactional executions chains. To the best of our knowledge, Teether [17] by Krupp and Rossow is the only publication that also considers transaction traces. However, Teether does not allow customizable checking of properties but rather searches already deployed contract for a single vulnerability pattern. Our contribution is thus the first customizable development framework for smart contract developers, supporting inter-contract and inter-transactional analyses. Further work related to our is Zeus [16] by Kalra et al., which translates Solidity into LLVM and performs model checking against policies. Vandal [11] by Brent et al. converts EVM bytecode to abstract semantic logic relations and analyzes logic constraints over them. Formal verification in the form of Why3 [14] was already integrated into the Solidity online IDE Remix, requiring developers to create semi-assisted proofs, but the support was later removed [6]. Other attempts include the formalization of contracts and EVM in F* [10] by Bargavan et al. and in the formal verification framework Lem [4], that do not precisely capture inter-contract analysis and do not support inter-transactional analysis. Ahrendt et al. propose to translate Solidity into Java to make use of KeY, a well-approved theorem proving framework for Java programs [9]. Hildenbrandt et al. introduced the KEVM [15], an executable formal specification of the EVM in the $\mathbb{K}$ framework which provides inter-contract and inter-transactional provability of claims by formulating all-path reachability statements. All these approaches require users to formulate desired properties in a formal language understood by the verifier, e.g., $\mathbb{K}$'s XML-style language or Why3's WhyML.

7   Conclusions

The field of secure development of smart contracts is still in its infancy and some of its challenges are fundamentally different from traditional software development due to the distributed computation model and the immutability of code. We contribute *Annotary* to this field, an approach that strikes a balance between rigid but hard-to-use formal methods and static source code analyzers which have no knowledge of intent, thus producing too many false positives. Our three main conclusions from this work are that first, annotations are a feasible way for developers to express their expectations and check their contracts for correctness in a language and environment they are comfortable with. Earlier work on integrating formal verification methods into Solidity has been dismissed for that reason, while the SMT-checking based approach that also *Annotary* adopts seems to be well received by the community (cf. [8,20]). Second, inter-contract and inter-transactional analysis are required to make sound statements about the security of a contract. Analysis of a single contract captures only a fraction of an actual Ethereum transaction and will not be able to create sound statements about safety and security guarantees. Third, the use of concrete values helps to increase precision and at the same time limit the complexity of the analysis. In contrast to traditional programs, where the specific execution environment is not known at the time of analysis, we can resolve concrete addresses referring to the Ethereum network and retrieve actual values from there.

The different confidence levels of *Annotary* allow for a more nuanced interpretation of findings by the developer, as opposed to traditional source code analyzers which rank all findings equally relevant. As part of our prototype evaluation, we have shown how *Annotary* detects common programming pitfalls and is able to detect cross-transaction vulnerabilities. The runtime analysis suggests its applicability in an IDE for smaller contracts and acceptable runtimes for larger contracts when integrated into continuous integration (CI) processes.

Acknowledgements. This work was partially funded by the Bavarian Ministry of Economics as part of the initiative Bayern Digital as well as the Fraunhofer Cluster of Excellence "Cognitive Internet Technologies".

A   Appendix

A.1   Annotary IDE Plugin

```
31  contract Wallet {
32      address owner;
33      @set restricted(var=owner; constructor, delegate.changeOwner(address))
34
35      function Wallet(address _owner, address wallet_lib) {
36          new WalletLibrary(_owner).delegatecall(
37              bytes4(sha3("initWallet(address)")), _owner);
38      }
39
40
41      function withdraw(uint amount) returns (bool success) {
42          return new WalletLibrary(owner).delegatecall(
43              bytes4(sha3("withdraw(uint)")), amount);
44      }
45
46      // fallback function gets called if no other function matches call
47      function () payable {
48          new WalletLibrary(owner).delegatecall(msg.data);
49      }
50  }
```

Fig. 3. Annotary marks violated annotations and violating code.

A.2   Code Rewritings

Inline Checks at annotation position: @check(condition) $\longrightarrow$ assert(condition);

Asserting Invariants - at empty block end: $\emptyset \longrightarrow$ assert(condition);.
- before empty return statement: return; $\longrightarrow$ assert(condition); return;.
- before return with value: return (exp1, ...); $\longrightarrow$ var (v_<nonce1>,...)
= (exp1, ...; assert(condition); return (v_<nonce1>, ...);.

Proxy Asserts to inherited Functions that - do not return values: $\emptyset \longrightarrow$ function
$\hookrightarrow$ f_name(param1, ...)... { super.f_name(param1, ...); assert(condition);}
- do return values: $\emptyset \longrightarrow$ function f_name(param1, ...)...{
var (v_<nonce1>,...)= super.f_name(param1, ...);
assert(condition); return (v_<nonce1>, ...); }

A.3   Algorithms

```
1  if o1 in keccakMap or o2 in keccakMap:
2      keccakMap[simplify(o1 + o2)] = get(keccakMap,
           ↪ o1) + get(keccakMap, o2)
```

Listing 1.2. Code added to the ADD-instruction to keep track of expression involved in index and mapping key computations.

```
1  for word in input:
2    if word in keccakMap:     word = keccakMap[word]
3    if result in keccakMap:     keccakMap[result] =
        ↪ Concat(keccakMap[result], word)
4    else:     keccakMap[result] = word
```

Listing 1.3. Code added to the SHA3-instruction to keep track of expression involved in index and mapping key computations.

```
1   check_severity(v, T_c, T_m, max_d, pref_ind):
2     T, τ_cv := T_c ∪ T_m, ⊥
3     if v.status == VSINGLE:
4       return v, VSINGLE
5     VS := Queue(v)
6     for d in {1..max_d}:                ◁ run until max depth
7       VS_new := Queue(v)
8       while VS != ∅:
9         vs := VS.pop()
10        for τ ∈ T
11          if τ_cv! =⊥ ∧τ ∈ T_c:
12            continue                    ◁ skip construction traces
13          if τ.storage.keys ∩ v.storage_vars != ∅:
14            vt = τ ∘ vs    ◁ apply trace
15            if vt ==⊥:
16              continue                  ◁ Chain not satisfiable
17            if τ ∈ T_c:
18              zeroize_storage_vars(vt)
19              if not satisfiable(vt.constraints)
20                continue ◁ zeroize and check const. trace
21            if sym_storage_vars(vt.constraint) == ∅:
22              if not pref_ind ∧ τ ∈ T_c:
23                τ_cv := vt, VCHAIN ◁ save found const. trace
24              else:
25                return vt, VCHAIN ◁ found violating chain
26            else:
27              VS_new.push(vt)    ◁ save open state
28        if VS_new == ∅:             ◁ trace chain space
             ↪ exhausted
29          if τ_cv != ⊥:
30            return τ_cv
31          else:
32            return ⊥, HOLDS
33        else:
34          VS := VS_new
35     if τ_cv != ⊥:                 ◁ max depth reached
36       return τ_cv
37     else:
38       return VS.pop(), VDEPTH
```

Listing 1.4. Algorithm to determine the severity level in a violating trace by analyzing the inter-transaction reachability.

Table 2. Uncovered implementation mistakes in "small" sample with annotation types.

Mistake	Uncovering annotation type
Over-/Underflow	@invariant
Struct cast to storage	@set_restricted
Misspelled constructor name	@set_restricted
Missing visibility modifier	@invariant & @set_restricted
Memory layout missmatch with delgation	@set_restricted & @check
Unmatched call forwarded to delegate	@set_restricted
Unset state (instanciated)	@invariant
Unchecked send return	@check
Arithmetic mistace (=+)	@check
Trick transaction origin	@invariant
Unreachable state/code	@invariant

References

1. Analysis of the dao exploit. http://hackingdistributed.com/2016/06/18/analysis-of-the-dao-exploit/. Accessed on 18 Nov 2018
2. Formal verification for solidity contracts - ethereum community forum. https://forum.ethereum.org/discussion/3779/formal-verification-for-solidity-contracts. Accessed on 18 Nov 2018
3. An in-depth look at the parity multisig bug. http://hackingdistributed.com/2017/07/22/deep-dive-parity-bug/. Accessed on 18 Nov 2018
4. pirapira/eth-isabelle: A lem formalization of evm and some isabelle/hol proofs. https://github.com/pirapira/eth-isabelle. Accessed on 25 Nov 2018
5. A postmortem on the parity multi-sig library self-destruct. https://www.parity.io/a-postmortem-on-the-parity-multi-sig-library-self-destruct/. Accessed on 18 Nov 2018
6. Remove why3 output - issue #543 - ethereum/remix-ide. https://github.com/ethereum/remix-ide/issues/543. Accessed on 25 Nov 2018
7. Solidity v0.5.0 breaking changes - solidity 0.5.1 documentation. https://solidity.readthedocs.io/en/develop/050-breaking-changes.html. Accessed on 20 Nov 2018
8. Smt checker poc 1 (2017), https://github.com/ethereum/solidity/projects/8
9. Ahrendt, W., et al.: Verification of smart contract business logic exploiting a java source code verifier. Fundamentals of Software Engineering (FSEN) (2019). https://git.io/fx6cn
10. Karthikeyan, B., et al.: Formal verification of smart contracts. In: Proceedings of the 2016 ACM Workshop on Programming Languages and Analysis for Security - PLAS 2016 (2016). DOI: https://doi.org/10.1145/2993600.2993611
11. Brent, L., et al.: Vandal: a scalable security analysis framework for smart contracts. arXiv preprint arXiv:1809.03981 (2018)
12. Buterin, V., et al.: Ethereum white paper (2014). https://github.com/ethereum/wiki/wiki/White-Paper (2013)
13. Ethereum: Solidity - solidity 0.4.24 documentation. https://solidity.readthedocs.io/en/v0.4.24/. Accessed on 20 Nov 2018

14. Filliâtre, J.-C., Paskevich, A.: Why3 — where programs meet provers. In: Felleisen, M., Gardner, P. (eds.) ESOP 2013. LNCS, vol. 7792, pp. 125–128. Springer, Heidelberg (2013). https://doi.org/10.1007/978-3-642-37036-6_8

15. Hildenbrandt, E., et al.: Kevm: a complete formal semantics of the ethereum virtual machine. In: 2018 IEEE 31st Computer Security Foundations Symposium (CSF). pp. 204–217. July 2018. DOI: https://doi.org/10.1109/CSF.2018.00022

16. Kalra, S., Goel, S., Dhawan, M., Sharma, S.: ZEUS: Analyzing Safety of Smart Contracts (2018). 10.14722/ndss.2018.23082

17. Krupp, J., Rossow, C.: teether: Gnawing at ethereum to automatically exploit smart contracts. In: 27th USENIX Security Symposium (USENIX Security 18). pp. 1317–1333 (2018)

18. Luu, L., Chu, D.H., Olickel, H., Saxena, P., Hobor, A.: Making smart contracts smarter. In: Proceedings of the 2016 ACM SIGSAC Conference on Computer and Communications Security. pp. 254–269. CCS 2016, ACM, New York, NY, USA (2016). https://doi.org/10.1145/2976749.2978309, http://doi.acm.org/10.1145/2976749.2978309

19. de Moura, L., Bjørner, N.: Z3: an efficient SMT solver. In: Ramakrishnan, C.R., Rehof, J. (eds.) TACAS 2008. LNCS, vol. 4963, pp. 337–340. Springer, Heidelberg (2008). https://doi.org/10.1007/978-3-540-78800-3_24

20. Mueller, B.: Smashing ethereum smart contracts for fun and real profit. HITB SECCONF Amsterdam (2018)

21. Nikolić, I., Kolluri, A., Sergey, I., Saxena, P., Hobor, A.: Finding the greedy, prodigal, and suicidal contracts at scale. In: Proceedings of the 34th Annual Computer Security Applications Conference. pp. 653–663. ACSAC 2018, ACM, New York, NY, USA (2018). DOI: https://doi.org/10.1145/3274694.3274743,http://doi.acm.org/10.1145/3274694.3274743

22. Park, D., Zhang, Y., Saxena, M., Daian, P., Roşu, G.: A formal verification tool for Ethereum VM bytecode. In: Proceedings of the 2018 26th ACM Joint Meeting on European Software Engineering Conference and Symposium on the Foundations of Software Engineering - ESEC/FSE 2018 (2018). https://doi.org/10.1145/3236024.3264591

23. Torres, C.F., Schütte, J., State, R.: Osiris: Hunting for integer bugs in ethereum smart contracts. In: Proceedings of the 34th Annual Computer Security Applications Conference, ACSAC 2018, pp. 664–676. ACM, New York (2018). https://doi.org/10.1145/3274694.3274737, http://doi.acm.org/10.1145/3274694.3274737

24. Wood, G.: Ethereum: a secure decentralised generalised transaction ledger. ethereum project yellow paper 151 (2014)

PDFS: Practical Data Feed Service
for Smart Contracts

Juan Guarnizo$^{(\boxtimes)}$ and Pawel Szalachowski$^{(\boxtimes)}$

Singapore University of Technology and Design, Singapore, Singapore
juan_guarnizo@mymail.sutd.edu.sg, pawel@sutd.edu.sg

Abstract. Smart contracts allow untrusting parties to arrange agreements encoded as code deployed on a blockchain platform. To release their potential, it is necessary to connect the contracts with the outside world, such that they can understand and use information from other infrastructures. However, there are many challenges associated with realizing such a system, and despite the existence of many proposals, no solution is secure, provides easily-parsable data, introduces small overheads, and is easy to deploy.

In this paper, we propose Practical Data Feed Service (PDFS), a system that combines the advantages of the previous schemes and introduces new functionalities. PDFS extends content providers by including new features for data transparency and consistency validations. This combination provides multiple benefits like content which is easy to parse and efficient authenticity verification without breaking natural trust chains. PDFS keeps content providers auditable and mitigates their malicious activities (like data modification or censorship) and allows them to create a new business model. We show how PDFS is integrated with content providers, report on a PDFS implementation and present results from conducted experimental evaluations.

Keywords: Blockchain · Smart contract · Data feed

1 Introduction

The concept of smart contracts was introduced by Szabo [13,26,27]. They allow mutually untrusting parties to arrange and execute agreements without involving any third trusted party. These agreements are expressed in a programming language, hence can encode any processing logic possible to express in the used language in a precise and unambiguous way. The concept has been unexplored for decades; however, with the rise of Bitcoin [23], distributed consensus, and blockchain platforms in general, smart contracts can finally be implemented in a practical way. Smart contracts deployed solely on a blockchain platform have some fundamental limitations. One problem is that a smart contract can only use resources available on the blockchain. This issue limits them from using external data provided by other infrastructures, like HTTP(S) data feeds. Ideally, smart contracts could process data provided by other infrastructures and

© Springer Nature Switzerland AG 2019
K. Sako et al. (Eds.): ESORICS 2019, LNCS 11735, pp. 767–789, 2019.
https://doi.org/10.1007/978-3-030-29959-0_37

use that to encode processing logic. Unfortunately, there are many challenges associated with that.

One such challenge is the authenticity of data feeds. Data provided to a smart contract should be authentic, so that the smart contract can verify its origin and execute accordingly. Unfortunately, the widely deployed Transport Layer Security (TLS) protocol [24] is inoperable in such a setting. Secure web servers that deploy it (i.e., running HTTP over TLS – HTTPS), cannot provide data authenticity to third parties like smart contracts. First approaches to make this data accessible to smart contracts were centralized oracles [6,9,18,31]. This introduced new trusted third parties which fetch HTTPS websites, parse them, and provide the data to smart contracts (which finally process it). These solutions present strong trust assumptions (i.e., a new trusted party). To relax it, a concept of oracles based on trust computing was proposed [31]. These oracles work similarly, however, the code run by them is executed with the Intel's Software Guard Extensions (SGX) [15] framework, which allows proving attestation of the code executed by the oracles. A disadvantage of this approach is to position Intel as a centralized trusted entity, and SGX as a trusted technology. In contrast to these approaches, TLS-N [25] enhances the TLS protocol by providing non-repudiation. TLS-N authenticates TLS records sent to clients during client-server TLS sessions. TLS-N requires TLS stack modifications and provides hard-to-process data feeds, but it does not introduce any new trusted entities.

In this paper, we propose PDFS, a practical data feed service for smart contracts that aims to fill the gap between oracle solutions and transport-layer authentication. Our architecture allows content providers to link their web entities with their blockchain entities. This design provides many benefits like security, efficiency, and possible new features. In PDFS, data is authenticated over blockchain but without breaking TLS trust chains or modifying TLS stacks. Moreover, content providers can specify data formats they would like to use freely; thus data can be easily-parsable and tailored for smart contracts. Besides that, PDFS provides content providers with a payment framework, but it does not allow content providers to misbehave by equivocating or censoring queries.

2   Background

2.1   Blockchain and Smart Contracts

Bitcoin [23] introduced the concept of open and decentralized consensus which, in combination with an append-only data structure, leaded to the existence of cryptocurrency without trusted parties. This combination and its variants are usually referred to as a blockchain. Bitcoin has inspired other systems (e.g., Litecoin [4] and Namecoin [5]). Interesting and promising platforms leverage blockchain to implement smart contracts. These systems rely on the append-only property provided by blockchain platforms that allow realizing smart contracts by a replicated execution (i.e., all participants execute the same code for the same inputs, thus maintaining the same state). Those platforms introduce high-level languages that allow to specify agreements by any parties and execute these agreements on top of the blockchain.

The most prominent smart contract platform is Ethereum [30]. It follows the replicated execution model, and it provides smart contract oriented high-level languages. In Ethereum, anyone can specify a smart contract (i.e., an object with a set of methods and an associated state) and deploy it on the blockchain (each smart contract gets a unique blockchain address). From this point, anyone can interact with the contract by sending transactions to its address and calling its method(s). Smart contracts can implement almost arbitrary logic, including monetary transfers, thus making this technology appealing to financial related services and other businesses.

2.2 Transport Layer Security

The Transport Layer Security (TLS) protocol [24] is one of the most widely deployed security protocols on the Internet. The protocol is designed for the client-server architecture. TLS aims to provide data confidentiality and integrity and authentication of protocol participants, but it was not designed to provide non-repudiation. Therefore, a communicating party (i.e., a client or a server) cannot prove to any third party that a given content was produced during the TLS connection. The TLS is prominently deployed for securing web traffic (i.e., HTTPS).

Authentication in TLS is based on the X.509 public-key infrastructure (PKI) [14]. Every entity that wishes to get its identity authenticated has to obtain a digital certificate asserting the identity and its public key. Certificates are issued by trusted entities called certification authorities, which are obligated to verify the identity of a requester and issue a certificate correspondingly. During a TLS connection establishment, a server presents its certificate to the client which verifies the certificate and the server's identity and then uses the corresponding public key to continue an agreement of a shared secret key. This key is used for protecting the subsequent communication.

2.3 Tamper-Evident Data Structure

A Tamper-evident Data Structure (henceforth as TDS) is a data structure that allows building log systems where an untrusted logger records clients' entries in an append-only log. The logger must be able to prove to auditors that: *(a)* every logged entry is still present in the log, and *(b)* one snapshot of the log is consistent with any its previous version.

Many early proposals aimed to achieve similar properties, mainly in the context of building a digital notary [11,19,20]. However, the semantics of TDS and multiple efficient constructions to achieve it were proposed by Crosby and Wallach [16]. In their system TDS is based on a Merkle tree [22] (also called a hash tree). A Merkle tree is a binary tree where leaf nodes are labeled with the hash of entries and non-leaf nodes are labeled with the hash of the concatenated labels of its child nodes. Therefore, the *root* of the tree is an aggregated integrity information about all its leaves.

In the Crosby-Wallach construction, the log structure is a Merkle hash tree with submitted entries as the leaves. The log is append-only, i.e., the entries are sorted in chronological order of their submission, and no leaf can be retrospectively removed or modified. The log supports the following history-related operations (we give examples of these operations in Sect. 4.3):

Addition of an entry. Whenever a new entry is added to a log, a new leaf is added to the tree, and the tree is re-computed (entries can be added in batches, so that the tree need not re-compute for every single entry). Adding new data entries requires re-computing $O(log\ n)$ nodes, where n is the number of log entries.

Membership Proof Generation for an entry produces a *membership proof* that proves that it is part of the log. The membership proof of an entry is the minimal set of tree nodes (i.e., hashes) required to reconstruct the root. In the described construction, a membership proof requires $O(log\ n)$ nodes.

Membership Verification for a given entry verifies whether the entry is part of the given log snapshot. It takes an entry, a membership proof, and a root value as input and verifies whether the entry matches the proof and whether the proof terminates at the given root (i.e., the computed path has the root at the end). The operation returns True if the verification is successful and False otherwise. It is efficient since it only requires $O(log\ n)$ hash operations.

Consistency Proof Generation for two different snapshots of the log, a newer and an older, provides a short proof (i.e., $O(log\ n)$ nodes) that the newer snapshot is an extension of the older one, i.e., the newer snapshot was produced by only appending entries to the older snapshot.

Consistency Verification takes as an input a consistency proof between two snapshots and verifies whether the consistency proof is correct, i.e., whether indeed the new version of the log was obtained by appending new entries. The verification procedure is also efficient (i.e., logarithmic in time and space) with respect to the log's size.

3   Architecture Overview

3.1   System Model

There are the following parties in a PDFS system:

Content Providers are entities that provide content. For a simple and intuitive description, we assume that the content is provided through the secure web (HTTPS); however, such a setting is not mandatory, and content providers do not have to run web services. Domain names identify content providers, and their content is accessed through URL addresses. Each content provider has a valid TLS certificate. In essence, content providers are not different from today's websites.

Contract Parties are mutually untrusting parties that would like to arrange a smart-contract-based agreement which requires data from a content provider.

Contract parties have to agree on who can act as the content provider for their *relying contract*. Therefore, content providers are trusted only locally by parties that want to trust them. We assume that the protocol parties have access to a blockchain platform with smart contracts enabled (e.g., Ethereum).

We assume an adversary whose goal is to produce fake data on behalf of a content provider. The adversary can eavesdrop, modify, and inject any protocol messages. She can also interact freely with protocol parties and the blockchain platform. We assume that the adversary cannot compromise underlying cryptographic primitives and protocols (i.e., TLS), and cannot violate properties of the deployed blockchain platform. Moreover, we assume that the adversary cannot compromise content providers' secret keys (i.e., the one used to interact with the blockchain, also known as wallet private key) and cannot obtain a malicious certificate for a content provider (i.e., cannot compromise the TLS PKI). However, we discuss such strong adversaries in Sect. 5.

We also assume a content provider trying to misbehave by launching an equivocation attack [28] or by censoring queries for its content. In the former case, the content provider should not be able to modify or delete any published content retrospectively. For the latter case, censorship is especially important in the context of the smart contract, as a content provider could influence a contract execution by censoring some required content. Thus for this attack, censorship attempts should be at least visible.

3.2 Desired Properties and Design Space

Below we list the desired properties of a data feeds service for smart contracts.

Easily parsable data feeds: data feeds should be easily parsable by smart contracts which use them. Besides practical implications like a more straightforward code base, this property improves the cost-effectiveness of smart contracts deployment, as smart contract platforms usually *charge* contract executions per number of operations.

Authenticity of data feeds: the high evidence that data feeds are authentic (i.e., were produced by a content provider trusted by contract parties) should be provided. Ideally, authenticity verification should follow a direct and natural trust chain (i.e., contract parties trusting example.com can specify in their contract that the contract can rely only on data provided by example.com).

Easy to adopt and deploy: all protocol parties (including content providers) should be able to start using the data feed system without major changes like requiring new infrastructure or non-backward compatible changes to lower-layer protocols. Ideally, the system should be implementable and deployable in today's setting with existing protocols and infrastructures.

Non-equivocation: Data feeds should be unable to modify or delete content retrospectively once data are committed and published. It enforces a content provider to verify and guarantees the correctness of data before performing publications. Preferably, providers should implement data structures that are append-only for their publications database.

3.3   High-Level Overview

Design decisions behind PDFS try to achieve all stated properties above. First of all, in our system non-repudiation is provided directly by content providers. This is similar to the approaches that modify the TLS protocol; however, the authentication is not conducted at the TLS layer. Instead, we introduce a layer of indirection that allows authenticating content on the blockchain.

In our design, content providers link their TLS identities with their blockchain identities and the locations of special smart contracts used for authenticating and verifying their content. Such a design provides multiple benefits. Firstly, it enables verifying blockchain identities, directly through the existing TLS PKI. Secondly, it allows relying contracts to validate the authenticity of data as simple as calling another smart contract's method (without involving any in-contract expensive public-key operations). Lastly, integrating content providers

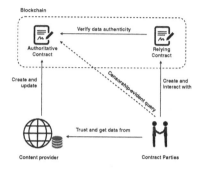

Fig. 1. High-level overview of PDFS.

with blockchain enables new features like keeping the providers accountable, proving their unavailability or providing a payment framework that can incentivize them to initiate the service. A high-level overview of our system is shown in Fig. 1, and in this section, we describe its steps and the main components.

The first step in our protocol is to create a *authoritative contract* by a content provider who wishes to participate in PDFS. The main aim of authoritative contracts is to enable other contracts to verify the authenticity of the content produced by content providers. Authoritative contracts provide additional functionalities by ensuring that content providers do not misbehave: (a) by retrospectively tampering with their data, or (b) by censoring queries sent to them.

Every authoritative contract provides an API that allows: *(a)* its owner (i.e., the content provider) to update it, *(b)* other contracts to verify that the content provider indeed produced given data, *(c)* contract parties to make *censorship-evident queries* to the content provider for the specific content (this option is used when the content provider seems unavailable or is censoring some queries).

In the second step, the content providers create a signed *manifest* that contains the following elements: *(a)* a location (i.e., a blockchain address) and interface structure of its authoritative contract, *(b)* metadata specifying details of provided content. The manifest is signed, and the manifest's signature is computed using the private key corresponding to the public key from the content provider's TLS certificate. Such a setting follows the natural trust chain; therefore, it allows contract parties to verify the authenticity of manifests directly, using the TLS PKI, and without breaking existing trust chains.

The content provider creates a TDS that will store data entries that the content provider wants to serve. The first entry of this data structure is the manifest. Although PDFS data may be published using HTTPS services, those services focus on data privacy and integrity. We define that the manifest must be signed and added into the TDS to extend security properties including non-repudiation and non-equivocation to it.

For every update, the content provider adds new data entries to its TDS, re-computes the data structure, and sends the new root and its corresponding consistency proof to the authoritative contract (they do not store any actual content, but only TDS roots — the short authentication information about the content.) The authoritative contract validates the sent information enforcing the append-only property (i.e., it makes sure that the content provider is appending data only – not modifying nor removing any entries). The data entries with their corresponding membership proofs are published at a pre-defined URL location, so that everyone can locate and access it.

Contract parties that would like to deploy a *relying contract* (i.e., a smart contract which depends on a data feed from an external website) have to find and agree on a content provider (this process is realized out of band). When contract parties find the content provider they would like to use, they locate and verify its manifest and authoritative contract, and associate the location of the authoritative contract as an oracle in their relying contract.

Whenever one contract party would like to call a method that uses content provider's data, it accesses the required data entry and its membership proof from the content provider and then calls this method with this pair (and a fee for content provider) as the arguments. Now, the method needs to verify whether the content provider indeed produced the data entry and to do so, the relying contract only requires to call the authoritative contract's membership verification method. When the data entry is verified, the relying contract's method can continue with its processing logic.

4   Details

In this section, we describe components of the PDFS architecture and explain its different steps from a content provider establishing its PDFS service until contract parties using the provider's data to make a transaction within their smart contract. We also discuss how the content provider maintains the service. As shown in Fig. 2, a PDFS service consists of an authoritative contract, a web service whose entries are kept within a TDS, and a manifest. We provide details of these components and their functionality in this section.

4.1   Service Initialization

In the first step, the content provider initializes a PDFS service by deploying an authoritative contract in the blockchain. This contract is designed to inter-act with the content provider's back-end service, relying contracts, and contract parties. Initially, the authoritative contract has empty storage; however, it will store root hashes of the deployed TDS. These root hashes will enable the contract to check on demand the consistency between two TDS snapshots (i.e., ensuring that the content provider updates its TDS correctly) and to conduct a membership verification (i.e., verifying for relying parties that an entry is part of the content provider's TDS). Further details of authoritative contracts are discussed in Sect. 4.2. Once it is deployed, the content provider gets an address of the authoritative contract instance.

Then, the content provider creates a manifest. The manifest is a file that describes details of the PDFS service. It is necessary for contract parties, since based on the manifest, they can create a workable relying contract. The manifest has to be authentic. Therefore, the content provider signs it. As TLS certificates issued by CA are widely trusted parties on the Internet, the content provider can sign the manifest using the private key corresponding to its TLS certificate for supporting HTTPS web traffic. Such a design choice has multiple

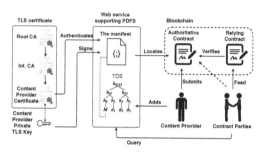

Fig. 2. Details of the PDFS architecture and parties interactions.

benefits. Firstly, it simplifies the signature creation and verification process since contract parties can obtain the required certificate by visiting the content provider's website. Secondly, the manifest is authenticated following an already existing trust chain. When the manifest is signed, it is added as the first element to the content provider's TDS. We define and describe the fields that a manifest contains:

URL corresponds to the URL address used by the content provider to publish data, and it indicates where contract parties can access data entries.

Authoritative Contract Address is the address in the blockchain associated with the deployed authoritative contract. Contract parties preload their relying contract with the value of this field (to allow them calling procedures or functions on the authoritative contract instance).

Authoritative Contract Interface is an abstract structural descriptor of the authoritative contract. It includes definitions of functions, access method, and parameters. Likewise the authoritative contract address, data contained in this field has to be embedded in the relying contracts as an object interface. This field is platform dependent (e.g., the ABI in Ethereum).

Data Structure describes the encoding or structure of data entries that the content provider stores in its TDS. Typically, content providers use widely adopted data encodings, such as JSON or XML. Thus, the content provider presents here which values and data types are expected to be found within every data entry. This field is necessary for contract parties to understand the semantics of data entries and to create their relying contracts able to parse data entries and implement their processing logic correctly.

Signature is a field that authenticates all values contained in the manifest. As described above, the signature is computed using the private key associated with the content provider's TLS certificate.

If the TLS certificate expires, the PDFS service is not affected for relying contracts already deployed. It is because contract parties use the certificate to verify the manifest signature before they create relying contracts. Furthermore, neither the authoritative contract nor relying contracts perform any signature verification later. Also, the content provider does not require to terminate the PDFS service if the TLS certificate is reissued using the same private-public key pair that was used in the manifest creation.

4.2 Authoritative Contract

The authoritative contract is a central point in the PDFS architecture. It interacts with the content provider back-end, relying contracts, and contract parties. Its primary goal is to ensure that the content provider indeed published a specific data entry. A detailed pseudo-code of the authoritative contract is shown in Algorithm 1. An authoritative contract consists of the functions that allow:

- The content provider to store root hashes once the consistency is verified. This procedure is executed by calling the UPDATE function (details about the consistency verification in Sect. 4.3). The UPDATE function can be executed only by the content provider. For efficient storage management and time delays or race conditions avoidance, the authoritative contract only stores an array of the last K root hash values committed (K is defined by the content provider).
- Relying contracts to make trustworthy transactions based on data entries whose origin and integrity are verified by calling the MEMBERSHIP function. This function checks whether a data entry and its membership proof is valid comparing to stored roots.
- Contract parties to make censorship-evident queries using the QUERY function and get responses by calling the GET_RESPONSE function. These queries and responses are sent over the blockchain, therefore they are publicly visible.

Functionalities offered to contract parties are designed to require payments for their executions. It allows content providers to adopt a new business model receiving payments for providing data over a PDFS service.[1]

---

[1] Fees for executing PDFS functions are different from fees for executing transactions on the blockchain (e.g., Ethereum gas cost).

Algorithm 1. Authoritative Contract Pseudo-Code.

FEE_{mem}: the cost for membership verification,

FEE_{query}: the cost for making a censorship-evident query,

locked: boolean value that indicates whether the authoritative contract can be updated,

roots: a map of roots hashes; it uses a timestamp as the key,

time: a value that indicates the last updating time,

queries: a map of censorship-evidence query made; it uses a number as the key,

responses: a map of responses for queries made; the key is associated to existing identifiers in the queries map,

counter: an incremental number used as the identifier for the queries made,

NOW(): the current block timestamp,

HASH(): a cryptographic hash function.

```
 1: procedure INIT
 2:     roots ← ∅
 3:     time ← 0
 4:     locked ← False
 5: end procedure
 6: procedure UPDATE(root, proof_cons)
 7:     assert(sender = owner)
 8:     assert(locked = False)
 9:     if CONSISTENCY(root, proof_cons) then
10:         time ← NOW()
11:         roots[time] ← root
12:     end if
13: end procedure
14: procedure LOCK
15:     assert(sender = owner)
16:     locked ← True
17: end procedure
18: procedure CONSISTENCY(root, proof_cons)
19:     if time = 0 then
20:         return true
21:     end if
22:     (root_new, root_old) ← MTH(proof_cons, ∅)
23:     return (root_new = root & root_old = roots[time])
24: end procedure
```

```
25: procedure MEMBERSHIP(data, proof_mem, fee)
26:     assert(fee = FEE_mem)
27:     leaf ← HASH(data)
28:     (root_mem, _) ← MTH(proof_mem, leaf)
29:     return root_mem ∈ roots
30: end procedure
31: procedure MTH(proof, leaf)
32:     i ← 0
33:     hash_x ← hash_y ← leaf
34:     if leaf = ∅ then
35:         i ← 1
36:         hash_x ← hash_y ← proof_(0).hash
37:     end if
38:     for i < LEN(proof) do
39:         if proof_(i).side = RIGHT then
40:             hash_x ← HASH(hash_x||proof_(i).hash)
41:         else
42:             hash_x ← HASH(proof_(i).hash||hash_x)
43:             hash_y ← HASH(proof_(i).hash||hash_y)
44:         end if
45:         i ← i + 1
46:     end for
47:     return (hash_x, hash_y)
48: end procedure

49: // Censorship Evidence functions
50: procedure QUERY(filter, fee)
51:     assert(fee = FEE_query)
52:     counter ← counter + 1
53:     queries[counter] ← filter
54:     return counter
55: end procedure
56: procedure STORE_RESPONSE(id, data)
57:     assert(sender = owner)
58:     assert(id ≤ counter)
59:     responses[id] ← data
60: end procedure
61: procedure GET_RESPONSE(id)
62:     assert(id ≤ counter)
63:     return responses[id]
64: end procedure
```

4.3   Data Update

Adding new data entries to the TDS requires re-computing the root. To run PDFS service properly, it also requires synchronization of changes between the content provider back-end (maintaining the TDS) and the authoritative contract which has to be updated to enable the membership verification of any newly added entry. To synchronize, the content provider submits the new root hash value along with a corresponding proof for the consistency verification. This verification uses the provided proof to re-calculate two hash values. and then, it compares those calculated hashes checking whether they are equal to the new root value to store and the last one stored in the authoritative contract accordingly. This guarantees that the new TDS is an extension of the last one committed confirming that no previous data entry has been altered or removed. If there is an error, the authoritative contract ignores the submitted data and

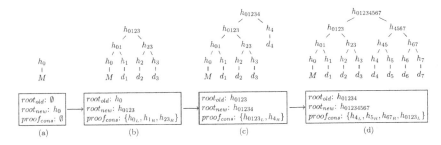

Fig. 3. An example of maintaining a TDS. It is a representation of information provided for the consistency verification when a new snapshot of the TDS is updated to the authoritative contract. Each element of the $proof_{cons}$ indicates the hash value and the corresponding side (h_{x_L} refers left position and h_{x_R} refers right position).

remains in the current state. Once the new root is accepted by the authoritative contract, the content provider can make the updated TDS accessible over HTTPS.

In Fig. 3, we show an example of how a TDS evolves when data entries are added, and what values are sent for submitting roots to the authoritative contract. In case (a), the new root is directly stored with no previous validation as it is the first one, and there is no consistency to evaluate. In case (b), the new root is submitted along with the following consistency proof ($proof_{cons}$). The authoritative contract uses the provided data to evaluate the TDS consistency. In this case, the consistency verification is easy to deduce since the previous root (h_0) is contained in the provided proof. Similarly in the case (c), the previous root (h_{123}) is contained in the $proof_{cons}$ array.

However, the case (c) shows a particular situation due to the TDS is unbalanced. It changes how the consistency verification works for the next root submission, the case (d). For it, the consistency proof provided is: $proof_{cons} = \{h_{4_L}, h_{5_R}, h_{67_R}, h_{123_L}\}$. Because of the unbalanced TDS, the consistency verification re-calculates both roots, the previous one (h_{1234}) and the new one ($h_{1234567}$) by using the same provided proof. To calculate the previous root, the consistency verification only needs the contained elements $\{h_{4_L}, h_{123_L}\}$. Furthermore, the complete array is used to re-calculate the new root. Therefore, the procedure can confirm the consistency of the new TDS.

4.4   Relying Contracts

A relying contract is a smart contract which is created by contract parties and needs content providers data to validate conditions and perform transactions. Before it is created, contracts parties agree on a content provider they trust which provides a PDFS service. After validating its manifest signature, contract parties extract the information contained in the manifest and use it to prepare and deploy a relying contract. In that way, the relying contract will interact with the correct authoritative contract and be able to: *(a)* execute the membership verification procedure, *(b)* get the response for a censorship-evident query, and *(c)* parse data entries and execute a processing logic depending on data entry fields. We provide a pseudo-code example of a relying contract in Algorithm 2.

When needed, contract parties request a specific data entry to the content provider, which responses a data entry along with its respective membership proof. Considering case (c) in Fig. 3, let us assume the content provider is queried for the data entry d_2, so its response will contain the asked data entry d_2 along with a membership proof $proof_{mem} = \{h_{3_R}, h_{01_L}, h_{4_R}\}$. Once that data is submitted to the relying contract, it will execute the membership verification intreating with the authoritative contract. As we see in this example, the provided proof and the data entry's hash value lead to re-calculate the root h_{1234} which is stored in the authoritative contract and it confirms data authenticity. If any value is modified, either the data or the proof, the membership verification re-calculates a different hash value which does not correspond to any stored root, so the verification fails.

Algorithm 2. Relying Contract Template.

```
    cc: authoritative contract object interface.    12: procedure IF_CENSORSHIP(id)
                                                     13:     data ← cc.GET_RESPONSE(id)
 1: procedure INIT(addr)                             14:     if data ≠ ∅ then
 2:     cc ← AUTHORITATIVE_CONTRACT(addr)            15:         ... Decode data input
 3: end procedure                                    16:         ... Decide and make transaction
 4: procedure SUBMIT_DATA(data, proof_mem, fee_mem)  17:     end if
 5:     v ← False                                    18: end procedure
 6:     v ← cc.MEMBERSHIP(data, proof_mem, fee_mem)
 7:     if v = True then                             19: interface AUTHORITATIVE_CONTRACT:
 8:         ... Decode data input                    20:     procedure MEMBERSHIP(data, proof, fee)
 9:         ... Decide and make transaction          21:     procedure GET_RESPONSE(id)
10:     end if                                       22:     ... Any additional procedure defined
11: end procedure
```

4.5   Censorship Evidence

Censorship is an especially challenging threat since a content provider censoring queries can influence executions of agreements based on smart contracts, and censorship is difficult to prove. However, PDFS extends the authoritative and the relying contract with functions to allow *censorship-evident queries*. So contract parties can query a content provider over the blockchain whenever they cannot obtain data directly through conventional channels (e.g., like HTTPS). All interactions, contract parties' query and content provider's response, are recorded as transactions in the blockchain. Therefore, they are visible for anyone, and any censorship attempt is publicly observable. We discuss censorship attacks further in Sect. 5.2.

4.6   PDFS Service Termination

Content providers might need to terminate a PDFS service due to operational management or security reasons. To do so, they can execute the LOCK function which disallows any future update attempt of the authoritative contract. Locking authoritative contracts does not introduce collateral damage to already-deployed relying contracts. A locked authoritative contract can be used for membership verifications as long as the corresponding root value is stored. In particular, the locking function might be useful in the case of a security breach (like a stolen blockchain private key), to prevent an adversary from submitting malicious root values (we discuss details in Sect. 5.1).

5   Security Discussion

In this section, we discuss different attacks and their implications over PDFS. However, this discussion is extended in Sect. A in the appendix which also addresses issues and disagreements that one might argue against our proposed solution.

5.1   PKI and Key Compromise

An adversary able to compromise the TLS PKI can create a malicious manifest and an authoritative contract, and can impersonate the content provider by creating arbitrary content. Interestingly, even if successful, such an adversary cannot undermine the security of the relying contracts already deployed since these contracts use the *correct* authoritative contract instance for data verification. Moreover, by deploying a new (malicious) authoritative contract, the adversary needs to deploy it over the blockchain, which makes the attack visible and detectable.

A more severe attack is a compromise of the private key used for the interactions between the content provider and the blockchain platform. In such a case, the adversary can add to the existing TDS malicious entries, re-compute the structure, and update the authoritative contract with a new root. Then, these malicious entries can be used by relying smart contracts for processing. However, even in that case the attack is visible since the authoritative contract is updated publicly, on the blockchain. Thus, the content provider will notice it and terminate its service (see Sect. 4.6).

5.2   Malicious Content Provider

PDFS prevents and mitigates some attacks conducted by a malicious content provider. The design of authoritative contracts in PDFS does not allow the content provider (or an adversary with the content provider's blockchain key) to retrospectively modify or remove content. The authoritative contract enforces the consistency of the TDS for every update (see Fig. 3). This property is also crucial for thwarting equivocation attacks [28]. A manifest file identifies the authoritative contract that guarantees that the content provider cannot equivocate as long as the blockchain platform is secure (see Sect. A.2 in the appendix).

The content provider can create multiple manifest files and authoritative contract, however, (a) it does not influence already deployed contracts, (b) is not necessarily a malicious activity, and (c) is visible over the blockchain; thus, it can be monitored.

PDFS provides non-equivocation by ensuring that content providers' database is append-only. However, it does not prevent a content provider from adding two semantically conflicting entries to their databases (e.g., two different results for a same football game). Conflicting entries can be harmful to relying contracts as they may lead to completely different execution paths. Since PDFS does not allow content providers to "overwrite" their entries, we suggest that such conflicts should be handled by relying contracts themselves. More precisely, using agreement protocols like implementing *grace periods* or submitting data from *multiple content providers* before making final decisions, such that any conflicting entry submitted can reverse contracts agreements.

A subtler attack is a content provider censoring queries. That risk is especially important, when a malicious content provider ignores contract parties' queries, pretending unavailability or displaying incorrect data that cannot be successfully verified by relying contracts. In such a case, PDFS allows contract parties to query the content provider over the blockchain for a required query (see Sect. 4.5). The content provider is obligated to response due to the query and content provider's response are publicly visible.

6   Realization in Practice

In this section, we demonstrate that PDFS fulfills the desired properties explained in Sect. 3.2. We fully implemented a proof of concept which involved both parties of a PDFS architecture (the content provider and contract parties). Although we tested PDFS under a generic scenario (see Sect. B.1 in the appendix), PDFS can be integrated into any context where smart contracts need to make decisions based on external data. Our solution allows content providers, regardless of the content and data type, to become a trustworthy data feed for smart contracts.

6.1   Implementation

To approach our implementation of PDFS, we developed a web service for the content provider using Go v1.10.1 as the programming language. It is a RESTFul API which offers data entries encoded in JSON format. This application is configured to support HTTPS, and we deployed a private PKI infrastructure and TLS certificates using OpenSSL v1.1. For contract parties, we implemented a client in Python v3.6.5 which is able to request data entries to the created web service. Smart contracts, the authoritative and the relying contract are coded in Solidity v0.4.21 and deployed in an Ethereum blockchain. To allow reproducibility of our experiments and evaluations, we publish our implementation at https://gitlab.com/juan794/pdfs.

6.2 Evaluation

In this section, we discuss results obtained from a series of experiments we performed. To evaluate PDFS, we used a computer which has 16 GB of RAM and a CPU Intel Core i7 7700H. We performed measurements regarding the execution cost which is expressed in Ethereum gas units, and then, converted to US dollars.

We analyzed the cost growth according to the number of data entries in the TDS. As shown in Fig. 4, we observe that the cost for the consistency and membership verification grows on a logarithmic scale as expected since we deployed a TDS using binary Merkle trees. In the case of the JSON parsing, the cost is constant and does not change with the TDS size. We also disaggregate total costs to investigate the details for executing PDFS procedures (see details in Table 1). In the case of having a data feed with more than 1 million (2^{20}) data entries, we observe that the consistency verification has a gas cost of 86,642 on average, where only 4% of this cost is related to the hash calculations. The remaining percentage corresponds to miscellaneous code, including storage and control statements, such as *asserts*. Moreover, we also measured the cost of executing a membership verification, and we observe that it has an average gas cost of 204,242. However, as JSON parsing is not natively supported in Ethereum, 55% of the total cost is spent on performing this task. On the other hand, the *gas* consumptions are 813,111 and 4,355,638 respectively for the authoritative contract and the relying contract deployment.

Next, we show in Fig. 4 what would be the maximum cost considering the two prices involved. For our measures, we assumed a price of 5 Gwei per gas unit and a price of US$105.05 per ether; those are maximum conversion rates presented at the writing time. As a result, the consistency verification costs around US $0.048 in a PDFS service that contains more than 1 million data entries. This means a cost of US $1.7x10^{-7} per data entry. On the other hand, the membership verification of one data entry in a TDS of that size (2^{20}) costs around US $0.11. We recall that it is including the JSON parsing which is a costly task on smart contracts. Therefore, we show that PDFS is costly viable to create and deploy a trustworthy data feed for a smart contract. The cost can decrease if Ethereum starts supporting JSON parsing natively or if content providers use a more efficient data entry encoding.

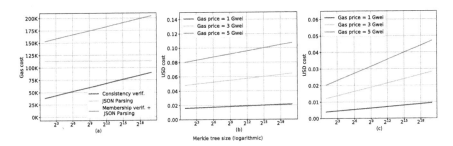

Fig. 4. Ethereum gas consumption and price variation analysis converted to US dollars. (a) Gas cost of PDFS operations (b) membership verification cost (c) consistency verification cost.

Table 1. Cost analysis for membership and consistency verification considering multiple sizes of the TDS.

TDS size	2^1	2^5	2^{10}	2^{15}	2^{20}
Membership verification cost					
JSON Parsing	113,349 (74%)	113,325 (69%)	113,293 (63%)	113,273 (59%)	113,298 (55%)
Hash calculation	447 (1%)	1,107 (1%)	1,933 (2%)	2,757 (2%)	3,583 (3%)
Miscellaneous	39,253 (25%)	49,369 (30%)	61,905 (35%)	74,633 (39%)	87,361 (42%)
Total	153,049	163,801	177,131	190,663	204,242
Consistency verification cost					
Hash calculation	149 (1%)	809 (2%)	1,634 (3%)	2,294 (3%)	3,284 (4%)
Miscellaneous	38,419 (99%)	48,551 (98%)	60,961 (97%)	71,158 (97%)	86,358 (96%)
Total	38,568	49,360	62,595	73,452	89,642

In Table 2, we show the *gas* consumption comparing PDFS against signature verification algorithms, such as ECRecover [2] (native in Ethereum), TLS-N implementation of secp256r1 [10] and RSA [7]. We observe that the

Table 2. Ethereum gas consumption of PDFS compared to signature verifications.

PDFS	secp256r1	RSA	ECRecover
87,361	1,854,634	596,287	38,887

Ethereum native function for signature verification is cheaper than PDFS. On the other hand, PDFS is significantly cheaper that implementations coded on Solidity programming language. Although those alternatives allow contract parties to verify integrity and provenance, they do not provide accountability or non-equivocation properties from content providers.

Lastly, we investigated the cost of censorship-evident queries and responses (see Sect. 4.5). As storing data in Ethereum smart contracts is expensive [30], we implemented this functionality with-

Table 3. The gas cost of the query and response operations.

Oper.	50 B	150 B	500 B	1 KB	2 KB	5 KB
Query	25,597	32,399	56,337	90,483	158,644	363,282
Resp.	25,804	32,606	56,544	90,690	158,851	363,489

out involving smart contract storage. Instead, queries and responses are published as blockchain transactions (as calls to the corresponding functions), but without storing them in authoritative contracts. That improves the cost efficiency greatly while providing the same functionality i.e., queries and responses can be read (as they are part of the blockchain) and responses are authentic (as they are sent within blockchain transactions signed by content providers). The gas cost of these operations depending on a size of a query and response are shown in Table 3. As presented, the cost grows linearly with query/response's size, but queries and responses of the same size have roughly the same cost.

7 Related Work

TLSNotary [9] is a service that introduces a third-party auditor which attests TLS session data exchanged between a client and a server. To provide this functionality, the protocol requires changes to the TLS protocol like an introduction of a dedicated client-auditor protocol. TLSNotary has many drawbacks. For instance, it is only compatible with TLS 1.0 and 1.1, while TLS 1.2 is widely deployed and recommended as default [8]. TLSNotary is specified with obsolete cryptography algorithms, and it supports only cipher suites with the RSA algorithm for a secret key establishment. As TLS records are being authenticated, the output obtained from TLSNotary is hard to parse and process by smart contracts. Although, the protocol has many disadvantages, it got adopted by other solutions, like Oraclize [6], which integrates multiple data feed systems. However, as combined with TLSNotary, it introduced a trusted third-party that holds secret keys used for auditing TLS sessions.

An alternative approach proposed is to use prediction markets for providing data feeds, such as [1] and [3]. In such systems, users try to predict real-world events by betting or voting for them. Usually, these systems are implemented on top of blockchain platforms, hence they could be easily integrated with smart contracts. Unfortunately, they have many drawbacks as in the case of disputes there is no responsible party (i.e., responsibility is distributed). Moreover, data feeds depend on human inputs which can be biased, slow, or incomplete.

Town Crier (TC) [31] takes a different approach to instantiate data feeds for smart contracts. TC deploys trusted computing (i.e., the Intel SGX technology [15]) to allow special applications to interact with HTTPS-enabled websites. In order to provide authentic data feeds, such an application, is executed within an SGX enclave. Thus, it is possible to conduct a remote attestation that the correct code was executed. The application establishes a secure TLS connection with a website and parses its content, which then can be used as an input to smart contracts. In contrast to TLSNotary, TC can provide easy-to-parse data and is flexible since there can be many applications. With the assumption that the contract parties have verified an attestation of the used enclave, TC allows relying contracts to avoid expensive public-key verifications by making assertions between enclaves and their blockchain identities (this is a similar concept as in PDFS). However, TC has some significant limitations. First of all, it positions Intel as a trusted party required to execute a remote attestation. Secondly, its security relies on the security of the SGX framework (undermined by recent severe attacks [29]) and the security of its attestation infrastructure, which is especially undesired as the SGX attestation infrastructure is a weakest-link-security system (i.e., one leaked attestation private key allows an adversary to attest any application). TC has inspired other systems, like ChainLink [18], which aims to decentralize TC applications by forming a network of them (to detect and deal with possible inconsistencies). Unfortunately, this design does not solve the main drawbacks of TC.

TLS-N [25] is a more generic approach to provide non-repudiation to the TLS protocol. In order to realize it, TLS-N modifies the TLS stack such that TLS records sent by a server are authenticated (in batches). Therefore, TLS-N clients can present received TLS-N records to third parties which can verify it, just trusting the server (without any other third trusted parties). The main drawbacks of TLS-N are in its deployability. It requires significant changes to the TLS protocol and as learnt from the previous deployments the TLS standardization and adoption processes are very slow. Because of the TLS-N's layer of authentication, TLS records are being authenticated which is inconvenient and expensive to process by smart contracts. Furthermore, the TLS layer is uncontrollable by web developers, and thus, most of their applications would need to be rewritten for TLS-N. Besides that, TLS-N relying contracts have to conduct an authentication verification which is a costly operation.

In Table 4 we compare PDFS with the competing schemes. As shown, PDFS makes data feeds authentic and easy to parse without major changes. It is easy to implement, and it does not require modifications beyond adding new functionalities in the content provider web service.

Table 4. Comparison to most related works.

	No third trusted party	Easy content parsing	Required changes on
TLSNotary [9]	—	—	TLS Protocol
TLS-N [25]	✓	—	TLS Protocol
Town Crier [31]	—	✓	—
PDFS	✓	✓	App

It is an advantages compared to the solutions which require changes on the TLS protocol for operating. Additionally, PDFS does not require an additional trusted party besides the content provider itself.

Moreover, we believe that the adoption of PDFS is much more likely than the adoption of competing schemes. In contrast to transport-layer authentication systems, PDFS requires changes only on the application layer. It also does not require trusted hardware or relies on ubiquitous TLS certificates following natural for HTTPS trust relationships. Last but not least, content providers are motivated by economic incentives as PDFS allows them to be paid for authenticating content which usually they publish for free.

8 Conclusions

In this paper, we proposed PDFS, a practical system that provides authenticated data feeds for smart contracts. In contrast to the previous work, PDFS seamlessly integrates content providers with the blockchain platform. This combination provides multiple benefits like efficient and easy data verification without any new trusted parties, and new interesting features that the previous platforms do not provide. Thanks to the deployed tamper-evident data structure (TDS) that is monitored by a smart contract, content providers cannot equivocate. To mitigate censorship, our scheme provides a blockchain based API for querying content providers. Besides that, native to blockchain platforms monetary transfers allow content providers to explore new business models, where relying contracts would pay a fee for the content verification. Last but not least, PDFS can be easily deployed today in the application layer without any modifications to underlying protocols.

We plan to investigate PDFS and its components in other applications. One particularly interesting example is a non-equivocation scheme for lightweight clients. Due to placing validation logic in smart contracts, it should be more efficient than, for instance, Catena [28], where clients have to collect and validate all related transactions by themselves. We believe PDFS could achieve the same property with much shorter proofs.

Acknowledgment. This research was supported by ST Electronics and National Research Foundation (NRF), Prime Minister's Office Singapore, under Corporate Laboratory @ University Scheme (Programme Title: STEE Infosec - SUTD Corporate Laboratory).

A   Extended Security Discussion

A.1   Data Authentication

Our first claim is that *an adversary cannot create a content on behalf of a content provider*. To achieve that, the adversary need to either: *(a)* tamper authenticated proofs generated by the content providers, or *(b)* update the authoritative contract on behalf of the content provider, or *(c)* forge the manifest binding the authoritative contract and identity of the content provider. All these attacks are out of scope our adversary model.

The first attack is infeasible due to the security of the tamper-evident data structured used [16]. More specifically, generating a membership proof for a non-element of the data structure is equivalent to breaking a deployed hash function. Therefore, the adversary to create such a proof for a malicious element has to extend the data structure by adding the element and updating the authoritative contract by a new root. However, in this attack, the adversary cannot update the authoritative contract as it enforces the update procedure (see Sect. 4.3). The update procedure allows only the contract's owner to update it. Therefore, without the content provider's blockchain key, the adversary cannot update the legitimate authoritative contract and prove on the malicious content.

For the last attack, the manifest's digital signature is verified using the TLS PKI. Thus, without the ability to (a) use a TLS private key of the content provider, or (b) obtain a digital certificate of the content provider, the adversary cannot create a malicious manifest on behalf of the content provider. These attacks are out of the scope of our adversary model, but we discuss them and their implications in the next section.

A.2   51%-Blockchain Attack

In this section we discuss how adversaries able to undermine the blockchain properties (although they are outside our adversary model) can impact PDFS. In particular, we focus on the 51%-attack [23] where an adversary possesses more than 50% of the total mining power of the blockchain network, which would allow her to rewrite the blockchain history. Such an adversary, could attack availability of PDFS (and any other blockchain application) by reverting or denying arbitrary transactions (or even authoritative contract creations).

An interesting scenario is an adversary colluding with a content provider. Besides availability attacks, the adversary could allow the content provider to equivocate by creating two conflicting TDS versions. One version would be maintained on the "main" blockchain, while the second one would exist only on the "malicious" blockchain mined by the adversary. Such an attack violates the desired property of keeping content providers consistent, and enables attacks similar as double-spending attacks [21].

Another interesting scenario is an adversary colluding with one of the contract parties to attack another contract party. Such an adversary cannot forge data entries or an outcome of the membership verification. However, it is a common practice that smart contracts define a timeout for inaction, after which deposits of the contract parties are sent back to them. In that case, the adversary could reverse a genuine transaction of the victim, causing the timeout from which the colluding party would benefit.

A.3   General Discussion

By analyzing the implications and costs of adopting it, we present PDFS as a viable alternative for smart contracts to receive authenticated data from content providers. In this paper, we focus on design a system with desired properties explained in Sect. 3.2. However, we are aware of issues and disagreements that one might argue against our proposed solution.

Firstly, one might claim that signature verification solutions would requires less effort for contract providers, and further, it provides properties of authenticity and provenance of data. Nevetherless, as observed in Sect. 6.2, PDFS is cheaper regarding *gas* cost and extends security properties to include accountability and non-equivocation for content providers. On the other hand, a naive solution would be to publish data hashes itself in a smart contract, however, that would be prohibitively expensive due to smart contract storage fees.

Secondly, we aimed a design for smart contracts data feed that avoids the complexity of alternative solutions and related works. We consider that modifying a protocol extensively used or including special hardware and network specifications makes a solution highly difficult to deploy; such as modifying the TLS protocol or including oracles using SGX. By contrast, PDFS offers as a simpler alternative that only requires changes on the application layer for content providers and contract-to-contract communication for contract parties. We consider it makes PDFS more practical and easy to adopt, even without taking the new business model that a content providers might get by providing data in a PDFS service.

Lastly, our current approach keeps the common trust chain with only includes contract parties who want to stablish an agreements and a content provider who is an autoritative entity who defines trustworthy data, also known as *the truth*.

Although the content provider may be able to misbahave, PDFS is not able to detect such actions due to data content is not analyzed, but that issue also affects the related works. However, it can be solved by including agreement protocols. For instance, the relying contract might revoke any agreement if two conflicting data are submitted within a time gap.

B   Case Study and Implementation Details

B.1   Case Study

In our proof of concept, we considered a scenario where contract parties decide to settle gambling agreement creating and deploying a smart contract which uses trusted data from a content provider who adopts PDFS in its service.

Content Provider. Following specifications in Sect. 4 and templates provided in Sect. B.2, our implementation of the content provider is a web service which offers data of football matches in JSON format. We configured it to support HTTPS, and we obtained a free dataset from https://www.football-data.org/. We implemented the TDS using Keccak-256 [12] as a cryptographic hash function. We chose Keccak as it is a state-of-the-art hash function (the current standard SHA-3 [17] is an instance of Keccak) and it allows us to reduce the cost of membership and consistency verifications due to its native support in the Ethereum platform.

Contract parties. It is an HTTP client application able to interact with the content provider and a relying contract. It is capable to get and validate the authenticity of the manifest, and it is able to submit data obtained from the content provider to the relying contract which executes the membership verification, interacting with the authoritative contract, and proceeds to parse the JSON data. In this case, we use a JSON parser coded in Solidity since it is not supported natively in Ethereum platform.

B.2   Implementations

In this section, we show examples of how JSON data look like in our implementation and experiments. The JSON examples are related to the case study explained in Sect. B.1.

```
{
"signed":{
  "url":"https://example.com/
  soccer",
  "sc_address":"0x539c94cb89E127
  ...",
  "sc_interface":
    "[{"constant":true,
      "inputs":[{"name":"json",
                 "type":"string
  "}],
        "name":"parseJSONdata",
        "outputs":[{"name":"",
                    "type":"bool
  "}],
      ...}]",
  "data_structure":
    "{id:string, local:string,
      visitor:string, localGoals:
int,
      visitorGoals:int}"
},
"signature":"63
  cc6a76fd07252ff4af4c..."
}
```

```
{
"content":{
  "id":"341576",
  "date":"2018-07-15T18:00:00Z"
  "local":"France",
  "visitor":"Croatia",
  "localGoals":4,
  "visitorGoals":2
},
"proofs":[
  {"side":0, "hash":"5e41f..."},
  {"side":1, "hash":"01950..."},
  ... more items]
}
```

Listing 1.2. A PDFS data entry example. It consist of the data content itself and its membership proof which is an array of elements containing a hash value and a side (0 indicates left side and 1 indicates right one).

Listing 1.1. A manifest example.

References

1. Augur. http://docs.augur.net/. Accessed 22 Jan 2019
2. Ethereum json rpc - eth sign. https://github.com/ethereum/wiki/wiki/JSON-RPC. Accessed 22 Jan 2019
3. Gnosis. https://gnosis.pm/resources/default/pdf/gnosis-whitepaper-DEC2017.pdf. Accessed 22 Jan 2019
4. Litecoin. https://litecoin.com. Accessed 22 Jan 2019
5. Namecoin. https://namecoin.org/. Accessed 22 Jan 2019
6. Oraclize. http://www.oraclize.it. Accessed 22 Jan 2019
7. Solrsaverify. https://github.com/adriamb/SolRsaVerify. Accessed 22 Jan 2019
8. Ssl pulse. https://www.ssllabs.com/ssl-pulse. Accessed 22 Jan 2019
9. Tlsnotary. https://tlsnotary.org/TLSNotary.pdf. Accessed 22 Jan 2019
10. tlsnutils. https://github.com/tls-n/tlsnutils. Accessed 22 Jan 2019
11. Bayer, D., Haber, S., Stornetta, W.S.: Improving the efficiency and reliability of digital time-stamping. Sequences II. Springer, New York (1993). https://doi.org/10.1007/978-1-4613-9323-8_24
12. Bertoni, G., Daemen, J., Peeters, M., Van Assche, G.: Keccak sponge function family main document. Submission to NIST (Round 2) **3**(30), 320–337 (2009)
13. Bhargavan, K., et al.: Formal verification of smart contracts: short paper, pp. 91–96 (2016)
14. Cooper, D., Santesson, S., Farrell, S., Boeyen, S., Housley, R., Polk, W.: Internet x. 509 public key infrastructure certificate and certificate revocation list (CRL) profile. Technical report (2008)
15. Costan, V., Devadas, S.: Intel SGX explained. IACR Cryptol. ePrint Archive **2016**(086), 1–118 (2016)

16. Crosby, S.A., Wallach, D.S.: Efficient data structures for tamper-evident logging. In: USENIX Security Symposium, pp. 317–334 (2009)
17. Dworkin, M.J.: Sha-3 standard: Permutation-based hash and extendable-output functions. Technical report (2015)
18. Ellis, S., Juels, A., Nazarov, S.: Chainlink a decentralized oracle network. Retrieved 11 March 2018 (2017)
19. Goodrich, M.T.: Efficient verification of web-content searching through authenticated web crawlers. Proc. VLDB Endow. 5(10), 920–931 (2012)
20. Haber, S., Stornetta, W.S.: How to time-stamp a digital document. In: Menezes, A.J., Vanstone, S.A. (eds.) CRYPTO 1990. LNCS, vol. 537, pp. 437–455. Springer, Heidelberg (1991). https://doi.org/10.1007/3-540-38424-3_32
21. Karame, G.O., Androulaki, E., Roeschlin, M., Gervais, A., Čapkun, S.: Misbehavior in bitcoin: a study of double-spending and accountability. ACM Trans. Inf. Syst. Secur. (TISSEC) 18(1), 2 (2015)
22. Merkle, R.C.: A certified digital signature. In: Brassard, G. (ed.) CRYPTO 1989. LNCS, vol. 435, pp. 218–238. Springer, New York (1990). https://doi.org/10.1007/0-387-34805-0_21
23. Nakamoto, S.: Bitcoin: A peer-to-peer electronic cash system (2008)
24. Rescorla, E.: The transport layer security (TLS) protocol version 1.3. Technical report (2018)
25. Ritzdorf, H., Wüst, K., Gervais, A., Felley, G., et al.: TLS-N: non-repudiation over TLS enabling ubiquitous content signing. In: Network and Distributed System Security Symposium (NDSS) (2018)
26. Szabo, N.: Smart contracts: building blocks for digital markets. EXTROPY: The Journal of Transhumanist Thought, (16) 18 (1996)
27. Szabo, N.: Formalizing and securing relationships on public networks. First Monday 2(9), (1997)
28. Tomescu, A., Devadas, S.: Catena: Efficient non-equivocation via bitcoin. In: 2017 IEEE Symposium on Security and Privacy (SP), pp. 393–409. IEEE (2017)
29. Van Bulck, J., et al.: Foreshadow: extracting the keys to the intel SGX kingdom with transient out-of-order execution. In: USENIX Security Symposium, pp. 991–1008 (2018)
30. Wood, G., et al.: Ethereum: a secure decentralised generalised transaction ledger. Ethereum Proj. Yellow Paper 151, 1–32 (2014)
31. Zhang, F., Cecchetti, E., Croman, K., Juels, A., Shi, E.: Town crier: an authenticated data feed for smart contracts. In: Proceedings of the 2016 ACM SIGSAC Conference on Computer and Communications Security, pp. 270–282. ACM (2016)

Towards a Marketplace for Secure Outsourced Computations

Hung Dang[1]([✉]), Dat Le Tien[2], and Ee-Chien Chang[1]

[1] National University of Singapore, Singapore, Singapore
{hungdang,changec}@comp.nus.edu.sg
[2] University of Oslo, Oslo, Norway
dattl@ifi.uio.no

Abstract. This paper presents Kosto – a framework that provisions a *marketplace for secure outsourced computations*, wherein the pool of computing resources aggregates that which are offered by a large cohort of independent compute nodes. Kosto protects the *confidentiality* of clients' inputs and the *integrity* of the outsourced computations using trusted hardware's enclave execution (e.g., Intel SGX). Furthermore, Kosto mediates *exchanges* between the clients' payments and the compute nodes' work in servicing the clients' requests without relying on a trusted third party. Empirical evaluation on the prototype implementation of Kosto shows that performance overhead incurred by enclave execution is as small as 3% for computation-intensive operations, and 1.5× for I/O-intensive operations.

1 Introduction

Recent years have witnessed an emergence of online marketplaces that offer alternatives to traditional vendor-specific service providers. Examples include Airbnb [1] in lodging, Uber [13] in transportation. In such marketplaces, the shared pool of resources is neither owned, provisioned nor controlled by a single party. Instead, it aggregates that which are offered by a large cohort of independent individuals. Designing a marketplace for secure outsourced computations, however, faces various technical challenges.

The first technical challenge is in protecting the *confidentiality* of the clients' data and the *integrity* of the outsourced computations, for the resource providers (or *compute nodes*) may be untrustworthy. Solutions to protect the confidentiality and integrity of outsourced computations have been studied in the literature [25–27,46]. For examples, homomorphic encryption [26,46] and secure multi-party computation [27] are designed to protect data confidentiality, while verification by replications [2,11] and verifiable computation [25] aim to protect computation integrity. Nevertheless, these approaches either incur high overheads, or support only a limited range of applications. These limitations hinder their adoption in practical systems.

H. Dang and D. Le Tien—Lead authors are alphabetically ordered.

© Springer Nature Switzerland AG 2019
K. Sako et al. (Eds.): ESORICS 2019, LNCS 11735, pp. 790–808, 2019.
https://doi.org/10.1007/978-3-030-29959-0_38

Another technical challenge is in mediating *exchanges* between clients' payments and compute nodes' work in servicing the clients' requests without relying on a trusted third party. One approach is to commits a remuneration for a task into an escrow which shall autonomously release the payment to the compute node upon successful task completion. This approach, however, does not generalize. For micro tasks that yield small remunerations, the transaction fee (i.e., the cost to conduct the payment transaction) becomes an overhead. On the other hand, compute nodes may inadvertently abort macro or complex tasks midway, exerting computational work but could not claim the reward. We believe that an ideal solution to mediate fair exchanges between clients' payments and compute nodes' work would require trusted metering of the compute nodes' work and a self-enforcing, autonomous agent (e.g., smart contract) responsible for settling payments based on the aforementioned metering.

In this paper, we present a framework that enables a marketplace for secure outsourced computations, which we name Kosto. Under our framework, the shared pool of computing resources is contributed to by a cohort of independent *compute nodes*. *Clients* in Kosto can request computational services from the compute nodes, while enjoying confidentiality protection on their data and integrity assurance on their outsourced computations. This is achieved by the use of Trusted Execution Environments (TEEs). In particular, each compute node in Kosto is capable of provisioning a TEE such as Intel SGX *enclave* for outsourced computations. The enclave prevents other processes, the operating system and even the owner of the compute node from tampering with the execution of the code loaded inside the enclave or observing its state. A compute node services a client' request by executing the outsourced computation inside an enclave that is attested to be correctly instantiated. The attestation allows secrets to be provisioned to the enclave only after it is instantiated.

Kosto mediates exchange of the clients' payment and compute nodes' work via a hybrid architecture that combines TEE-based metering with blockchain micro payment channel [10,37]. Our framework incorporates in each enclave an accounting logic that meters the compute node's work. Such metering is then translated to a *payment promise* with which the compute node can settle the payment escrow and claim the corresponding reward. This approach facilitates the exchange between the client and the compute node without incurring excessive transaction fee or involving a trusted third party.

Our experiments reveal that the overhead incurred by enclave execution and the trusted metering is as small as 3% for computation-intensive operations, and $1.5\times$ for I/O-intensive operations. We expect these overheads can be further reduced by incorporating optimizations that enhance the efficiency of enclave execution [36,44,47], thereby allowing Kosto to attain better efficiency.

In summary, this paper makes the following contributions.

- We propose a framework, called Kosto, which facilitates a marketplace for secure outsourced computations. Under our framework, both confidentiality of clients' inputs and integrity of the outsourced computations are protected through the use of TEEs. In addition, Kosto mediates fair exchanges between

clients' payments for the execution of the outsourced computations and compute nodes' work in servicing the clients' requests via a hybrid architecture that combines TEE-based metering with blockchain micro payment channel.
- We implement a prototype of Kosto and evaluate the overhead incurred by enclave execution and the TEE-based metering. The experiments shows that performance overhead incurred by enclave execution and trusted metering is as small as 3% for computation-intensive operations, and 1.5× for I/O-intensive operations.

2   Preliminaries

Intel SGX. Intel SGX [33] is a set of CPU extensions capable of providing hardware-protected TEE (or *enclave*). Each enclave is associated with a protected address space. The processor blocks any non-enclave code's attempt to access the enclave memory. Memory pages are encrypted using the processor's key prior to leaving the enclave. Intel SGX provides attestation mechanisms allowing an attesting enclave to demonstrate to a validator that it has been correctly instantiated [15], and to establish a secure, authenticated connection via which they can securely communicate sensitive data.

Ethereum Smart Contract. Ethereum enables *smart contract* which is an "autonomous agent" associated with a predefined executable code. Incentive and security mechanisms of the Ethereum ecosystem encourage miners to execute the contract's code faithfully [18]. A smart contract could be used to implement an *escrow* that enforces a payment from a payer to a payee once the payee has delivered some service to the payer, while keeping the payment inaccessible to the payee before such condition is met. The transaction fee to settle the escrow does not depend on the monetary value that the escrow holds. Consequently, should the payment value is too small (i.e., micro transaction), the transaction fee becomes a significant overhead.

Payment Channel. Payment channel enables two parties to transact a large number of micro payments without incurring high transaction fee or overloading the blockchain with excessive number of transactions [10, 37]. A channel is established after a deposit is made on the blockchain (on-chain). A payer makes a micro payment to the payee by issuing a digitally signed and hash-locked transfer, called *payment promise*, and sending it off-chain to the payee. The payee can use such payment promise to close the channel and claim the payment she has been promised so far at any time. The value of the payment promises should not exceed the on-chain deposit, otherwise it cannot be fully collateralized.

3   The Problem

3.1   System Model

We study a marketplace for secure outsourced general-purposed computations. Unlike vendor-specific cloud services, the pool of computing resources in such a marketplace aggregates that which are offered by a large cohort of independent *compute nodes* (discussed below). More specifically, we consider a system model that comprises the following three main parties: *clients, compute nodes* and *brokers*.

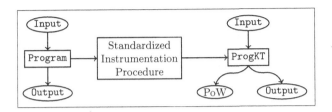

Fig. 1. The standardized instrumentation procedure that converts `Program` into `ProgKT`. PoW reflects the compute node's work in executing `Program` on `Input`.

– **Clients** are the system's end users. A client would like to execute a program `Program` on an input `Input`, obtaining an computation outcome `Output`. The program `Program` can be written by the client, or an open-source software provided by a third party. In either case, the client outsources such computational task to a *compute node* (which we shall define in the following). The clients are not expected to maintain constant connection with the compute node over the course of the outsourced computation. While the clients can discover the compute nodes and initiate the outsourced computation on their own, this approach is unlikely to scale. Instead, we propose to delegate such tasks to a *broker*.

– **Compute nodes** are machines equipped with commodity trusted processors (e.g., Intel SGX processors) capable of provisioning TEEs (or enclaves). A compute node services a client request by running its code in an enclave, and generating an attestation that proves the correctness of the code execution (and thus the result). In return, the compute node receives remuneration v proportional to computational work it has asserted in executing the outsourced task.

– **Brokers** facilitate node discovery and load balancing, and assist the clients in attesting correct instantiation of the enclaves housing the outsourced computations on the compute nodes. Brokers may charge clients and/or compute nodes certain commission fee in return to their services. To eliminate broker monopoly and single-point-of-failure, we allow multiple brokers to co-exist, thus enabling better brokering service for both clients and compute nodes.

Hereafter, we denote by $\mathcal{P}$ a client, by $\mathcal{C}$ a compute node, and by $\mathcal{B}$ a broker. The program to be executed on the compute node incorporates logic that meters the compute node's work in a fine-grained and tamper-proof fashion. For simplicity, let us assume that such logic is defined in the system configuration, and agreed upon by all clients and compute nodes. We further assume that there exists a standardized instrumentation procedure that converts the client's program Program into a program ProgKT that adheres to the metering logic requirements. Figure 1 illustrates an overview of the instrumentation, and the relation between ProgKT and Program.

3.2   System Goals

We now formalize the security guarantees that a marketplace for outsourced computations should offer. The guarantees motivate and justify our design choices.

– *Correct and attested execution* requires that the output Output obtained by the client correctly reflects the faithful execution of Program on Input.
– *Data confidentiality* requires that Input, and secret states of Program from a client remain encrypted outside the enclave memory, and thus are not known to any other party, including the compute node (e.g., its OS and its owner). The key to decrypt them resides only inside the enclave.
– *Fair exchange* requires that the work a compute node exhausts in executing the outsourced task is accurately metered and remunerated in fine granularity. At the same time, it dictates that a compute node gets the full reward for the outsourced computation if and only if a client gets a correct result of such computation.

Besides the security guarantees, for practical usability reason, we also wish to *limit the required interaction between client and compute node* and *optimize assignment of clients' request to compute nodes*. The former unburdens clients from constantly maintaining a connection with their assigned compute nodes prior to and during execution of the outsourced computations, while the latter maximizes the resource utilization in the marketplace.

3.3   Threat Model

Trust Assumptions. We study a threat model in which the parties (namely $\mathcal{C}, \mathcal{B}$ and $\mathcal{P}$) are mutually distrustful. We assume that a standardized instrumentation procedure that converts the client's program Program into a program ProgKT that meters the compute node's work in a fine-grained and tamper-proof fashion (Fig. 1) can be formally verified and therefore is trusted. We further assume that commodity trusted processors provisioning TEEs on the compute nodes, in particular Intel SGX processors, are implemented correctly and their protection mechanisms are not compromised. Finally, we make an assumption that the Ethereum blockchain is decentralised and trusted (i.e., it is publicly accessible, and its underlying consensus and smart contract execution mechanisms are intact).

Adversary. We consider a party who deliberately deviates from a prescribed protocol an *adversary*. The adversarial goal is to violate the system guarantees described earlier in Sect. 3.2, namely confidentiality of client's data, integrity of the outsourced computations, and the fair exchange between $\mathcal{P}$'s payment and $\mathcal{C}$'s work in servicing the former's request.

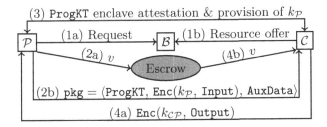

Fig. 2. Kosto overview. k_{CP} is derived from a secret chosen by C and k_P.

We assume the adversary is computationally bounded, and that the cryptographic primitives employed in the system (e.g., encryption scheme or hash function) are secure. Adversarial clients and brokers can deviate arbitrarily from the prescribed protocol, but they can neither control the compute node's operating system (OS) nor its enclaves' execution. An adversarial compute node can control its operating system, schedule its processes, reorder and tamper with its network messages. Nonetheless, it cannot tamper with the enclaves' execution, nor observe theirs internal state.

We do not consider side-channel attacks against the hardware and the enclave execution [45,48]. Besides, denial of service attack wherein an adversary denies service to honest clients, or blocks honest compute nodes from the system are beyond scope. Consequently, we require some compute nodes to behave correctly so as to guarantee the system's availability. As mentioned earlier, since the clients can serve as their own broker, handling compute node discovery and connecting to the compute nodes directly, there will always be honest self-serving brokers in the system, which eliminates the broker's single-point-of-failure problem.

4 Kosto Design

4.1 Workflow

P and C can post their requests and available resource offers to a broker B of their choice, perhaps based on B's reputation or quality of service. B then evaluates among all requests and offers it has received a suitable assignments of requests to compute nodes. Alternatively, the clients and the compute nodes can directly discover and connect to each other. In such case, they play an additional role of self-serving broker.

Let v be the remuneration that P pays to C in exchange for executing `Program` on `Input` and delivering the result `Output`. Kosto requires `Program` to be instrumented into `ProgKT` which incorporates trustworthy metering of the compute node's work. To guarantee payment to C upon its completion of the computational task, Kosto requires P to maintain a deposit worth at least v on an on-chain escrow. P sends $\texttt{pkg} = \langle \texttt{ProgKT}, \texttt{Enc}(k_P, \texttt{Input}), \texttt{AuxData}\rangle$ to C, wherein $\texttt{Enc}()$ is a symantically secure symmetric-key encryption scheme [29], and `AuxData` contains auxiliary data needed for the execution. $\mathcal{C}$ instantiates the `ProgKT` enclave, and attests to $\mathcal{P}$ that the enclave has been instantiated correctly. Upon successful attestation, a secret key $k_{\mathcal{P}}$ is provisioned to the `ProgKT` enclave, allowing it to process and compute on `Input`. Finally, the output `Output` of the computation is sent to $\mathcal{P}$. `Output` is encrypted in such a way that its decryption by $\mathcal{P}$ ensures full payment of v to $\mathcal{C}$. Figure 2 depicts the workflow in Kosto.

4.2   Enclave Execution

Kosto relies on Intel SGX [33] to offer attested execution and data confidentiality to the outsourced computations. The outsourced program `Program` should be SGX-compliant (i.e., it inherently supports SGX enclave execution). Techniques that enable enclave executions for unmodified legacy applications, such as Haven [16] and Panoply [41] are orthogonal to Kosto.

A compute node services the client's request by first instantiating the `ProgKT` enclave, and generating an attestation proving that the enclave has been instantiated correctly. The attestation mechanism allows $\mathcal{P}$ to establish a secure, authenticated connection to the enclave, via which the secret key $k_{\mathcal{P}}$ is communicated. The compute node then invokes the enclave execution on `Input` to collect the output `Output`. In addition to `Output`, the enclave also returns a "proof of work" indicating a computational effort that $\mathcal{C}$ has asserted thus far, which $\mathcal{C}$ can use to claim the remuneration. We elaborate on this in Sect. 4.3.

4.3   Fair Exchange

Kosto splits the reward v of the outsourced computation into two portions, namely $v_c = \alpha v$ and $v_d = (1 - \alpha)v$, where α is a parameter set by the client $\mathcal{P}$, and agreed upon by $\mathcal{C}$. The first portion (i.e., v_c) remunerates $\mathcal{C}$ for its work on a fine-grained basis, while the second portion (i.e., v_d) rewards the delivery of the result. The configuration of the parameter α, and by its extension, the remuneration policy, is beyond Kosto's scope.

$\mathcal{C}$ is entitled to v_c upon the completion of the outsourced computation. In case the computation is inadvertently aborted midway, $\mathcal{C}$ is still remunerated with a fraction of v_c according to its progress prior to the suspension. The remaining portion of v, namely v_d, is only payable to $\mathcal{C}$ when the computation output is delivered to $\mathcal{P}$. This discourages $\mathcal{C}$ from denying $\mathcal{P}$ of the result. Additional mechanism that disincentivises result withholding (e.g., requiring $\mathcal{C}$ to make a security deposit which is forfeited should they repeatedly abort the computation [17,30]) can also be incorporated into Kosto.

TEE-Based Metering. To enable an fair exchange described above, Kosto has to meter the compute node's work in a fine-grained and tamper-proof fashion. We follow Zhang et al. [49] in implementing a reliable metering logic inside the enclave. More specifically, Kosto requires the client's program `Program` to be instrumented into a wrapper program `ProgKT` (see Fig. 1). The wrapper program reserves the logic of the original program (i.e., it executes `Program`'s logic on

Input), while keeping a counter of the number of instructions that has been executed. This is then used as a measurement of the compute node's work.

ProgKT maintains the instruction counter in a reserved register which is inaccessiable to any other process. To prevent a malicious Program from manipulating the instruction counter, Kosto does not support Program that is multi-threaded or contains writeable code pages [5,49]. When the ProgKT enclave halts or exits, it returns a "proof of work" (i.e., the number of instruction executed) based on which Kosto settles the payment of v_c (or a fraction of it). We note that if the compute node (i.e., its OS) intentionally kills the enclave process, ProgKT does not return such proof of work, which eliminates a remuneration-draining attack where a malicious compute node deliberately interrupts the enclave execution before it finishes, so as to drain v_c without an intention of completing the outsourced computation.

We remark that the restriction of single-threaded Program is not necessary a severe limitation, for threading in SGX enclave is much different compared to that of legacy software [3]. In particular, one cannot create or destroy an SGX thread on the fly, and an SGX thread is mapped directly to a logical processor. Consequently, a typical SGX-compliant program (i.e., a program that inherently supports SGX-enclave execution) is often single-threaded.

On the Choice of Instruction Counting. One may argue that instructions are not the most accurate metric for CPU effort. Alternative metrics include CPU time and CPU cycles. Nevertheless, these metrics are subject to manipulation by the malicious OS. Even if they were not manipulated, they are incremented even when an enclave is swapped out [49]. Consequently, we believe that instruction counting is the most appropriate method for securely measuring the compute node's effort using available tools in SGX.

Micro Payments with Off-Chain Payment Channel. One naive approach to settle the proof of work is for $\mathcal{C}$ to send it to $\mathcal{P}$, who then responds with a transaction paying a corresponding amount of reward to $\mathcal{C}$. This approach, however, does not payment for $\mathcal{C}$ in case $\mathcal{P}$ neglects her outsourced computation. Another approach is to have $\mathcal{P}$ commit a number of equally-valued micro transactions, each of which contains a fraction of v_c, to a payment escrow on the blockchain, and to structure the proof such that it can be used to autonomously claim a subset or all of those micro transactions. Nonetheless, settling a large number of micro transactions on the blockchain incurs high overhead.

Kosto sidesteps this challenge by leveraging payment channel [10], allowing two parties to transact a large number of micro payments without incurring high transaction fee or overloading the blockchain with transactions. It is assumed that a payer and a payee maintain a payment channel (discussed in Sect. 2), and each micro payment is represented by a payment promise to be communicated off-chain (i.e., off the blockchain) between the payer and the payee. To settle the payments, the payee posted the latest payment promise (accompanied by settling-data such promise requires, if any) to the blockchain, thereby closing the channel. However, establishing a new channel for each pair of client and

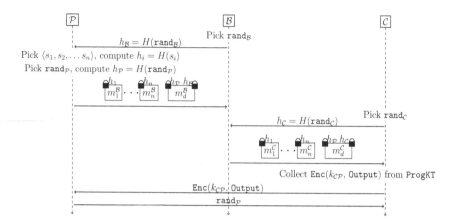

Fig. 3. An overview of the fair exchange in Kosto. $m_i^{\mathcal{B}}$ and $m_i^{\mathcal{C}}$ are hash-locked by h_i, $m_d^{\mathcal{B}}$ by $h_{\mathcal{P}}$ and $h_{\mathcal{B}}$, $m_d^{\mathcal{C}}$ by $h_{\mathcal{P}}$ and $h_{\mathcal{C}}$, and $k_{\mathcal{CP}} = k_{\mathcal{P}} \oplus \mathbf{rand}_{\mathcal{C}}$.

compute node is inefficient. Kosto, instead, makes use of multi-hop channels[1] to better utilize the channel capacity, requiring fewer channels to be established.

To this end, Kosto assumes that each client $\mathcal{P}$ maintains a payment channel with the broker $\mathcal{B}$ that, in turn, maintains a channel with each compute node $\mathcal{C}$. The payment from $\mathcal{P}$ to $\mathcal{C}$ does not require a direct channel; rather, it could be securely routed via $\mathcal{B}$, in a sense that once $\mathcal{C}$ collects a payment from $\mathcal{B}$, the latter is guaranteed of a corresponding payment from $\mathcal{P}$[2]. We assume that each payment channel has sufficiently large capacity (i.e., its on-chain deposit) to accommodate the payment of various outsourced computations during its lifetime.

Figure 3 summarizes the fair exchange of the reward v and the outsourced computation of ProgKT. v is split over $n+1$ micro payments, n of which summing up to v_c, while the last one is worth v_d. The protocol does not require any communication between $\mathcal{P}$ and $\mathcal{C}$ *prior to* or *during* the computation, nor an on-chain channel between them. It, however, requires an off-chain communication between $\mathcal{P}$ and $\mathcal{C}$ in the final step to decrypt the output.

Payment of v_c. Without loss of generality, let us assume that the payment of v_c is divided into n equally-valued payment promises, which are routed via $\mathcal{B}$. That is, $\mathcal{P}$ generates n payment promises to $\mathcal{B}$, and $\mathcal{B}$ generates the corresponding n payments promises to $\mathcal{C}$ with the same value and claiming condition.

To generate the n payment promises $\langle m_1^{\mathcal{B}}, m_2^{\mathcal{B}}, \ldots m_n^{\mathcal{B}} \rangle$ to $\mathcal{B}$, $\mathcal{P}$ first picks n random strings $\langle s_1, s_2, \ldots s_n \rangle$, and computes their hashes $\langle h_1, h_2, \ldots h_n \rangle$ (i.e., $h_i = H(s_i)$). A digest h_i is used to lock a promise $m_i^{\mathcal{B}}$, such that $\mathcal{B}$ can only use $m_i^{\mathcal{B}}$ to close the channel if it is aware of $\mathbf{s}_i$ such that $H(\mathbf{s}_i) = h_i$. The payment

---

[1] While we discuss unidirectional channels, Kosto supports bidirectional channels.

[2] While $\mathcal{B}$ could charge a service fee for the routing, for simplicity, we assume $\mathcal{B}$ offers such routing free of charge. Extending Kosto to support such service fee is trivial.

promise $m_i^{\mathcal{B}}$ is worth $[\texttt{debt}_{\mathcal{P}} + (i \times v_c)/n]$ wherein $\texttt{debt}_{\mathcal{P}}$ is the accumulated amount of unsettled payment for $\mathcal{P}$'s previous requests. Finally, $\mathcal{P}$ encrypts the random strings $\langle s_1, s_2, \dots s_n \rangle$ with $k_{\mathcal{P}}$, and attaches them as well as the payment promises to $\texttt{AuxData}$.

Similarly, $\mathcal{B}$ generates the corresponding promises $\langle m_1^{\mathcal{C}}, m_2^{\mathcal{C}}, \dots m_n^{\mathcal{C}} \rangle$ to $\mathcal{C}$. Each promise $m_i^{\mathcal{C}}$ is locked by h_i (i.e., the same hash-lock as $m_i^{\mathcal{B}}$), and worth $[\texttt{cred}_{\mathcal{C}} + (i \times v_c)/n]$ wherein $\texttt{cred}_{\mathcal{C}}$ is the accumulated unsettled credit that $\mathcal{C}$ is entitled to claim for its previous services. $\mathcal{B}$ includes these promises into the $\texttt{AuxData}$ before forwarding $\texttt{pkg}$ to $\mathcal{C}$.

Payment of v_d Upon Output Delivery. To ensure that the remaining portion of v, namely v_d, can only be collected upon the delivery of the output to $\mathcal{P}$, ProgKT encrypts the output using a key $k_{\mathcal{CP}}$ derived from $k_{\mathcal{P}}$ and a secret $\texttt{rand}_{\mathcal{C}}$ chosen and committed to by $\mathcal{C}$. At the same time, the full payment of v is encumbered until the disclosure of $\texttt{rand}_{\mathcal{C}}$.

As shown in Fig. 3, besides the n payment promises above, $\mathcal{P}$ generates another payment promise $m_d^{\mathcal{B}}$ to $\mathcal{B}$ that is worth $[\texttt{debt}_{\mathcal{P}} + v]$ and is hash-locked by two digests $h_{\mathcal{B}}$ and $h_{\mathcal{P}}$. Similarly, $\mathcal{B}$ also generate one more payment promise $m_d^{\mathcal{C}}$ to $\mathcal{C}$ that is worth $[\texttt{cred}_{\mathcal{C}} + v]$, and hash-locked by $h_{\mathcal{P}}$ and $h_{\mathcal{C}}$. The three hash-locks $h_{\mathcal{P}}$, $h_{\mathcal{B}}$ and $h_{\mathcal{C}}$ can be settled by three independent settling-data $\texttt{rand}_{\mathcal{P}}$, $\texttt{rand}_{\mathcal{B}}$ and $\texttt{rand}_{\mathcal{C}}$ chosen independently at random by the three parties $\mathcal{P}, \mathcal{B}$ and $\mathcal{C}$, respectively.

Dynamic Runtime Checks. The fair exchange requires the wrapper enclave ProgKT to perform some dynamic checks at runtime prior to executing Program's logic. More specifically, besides Input and AuxData, ProgKT also consumes the hash-lock $h_{\mathcal{C}}$ and $\texttt{rand}_{\mathcal{C}}$. It first verifies the validity of the settling-data $\langle s_1, s_2, \dots s_n \rangle$ (i.e., $h_i = H(s_i) \forall \langle h_i, s_i \rangle \in \texttt{AuxData}$). Next, it checks if $h_{\mathcal{C}} = H(\texttt{rand}_{\mathcal{C}})$. Only when the verification passes does it execute Program on Input, obtaining Output. It then encrypts Output with $k_{\mathcal{CP}} = k_{\mathcal{P}} \oplus \texttt{rand}_{\mathcal{C}}$, producing an encrypted output $\texttt{Enc}(k_{\mathcal{CP}}, \texttt{Output})$. Finally, the enclave returns the appropriate settling-data s_i based on the instruction counter and the encrypted output (if it successfully completes the computation) to $\mathcal{C}$.

Payment Settlement. The settling-data s_i renders the promise $m_i^{\mathcal{C}}$ claimable, enabling $\mathcal{C}$ to collect (a portion of) v_c according to its work. In order to collect a payment from a promise, one posts the corresponding settling-data to the blockchain, thereby making it publicly available.

To obtain the settling-data necessary to claim $m_d^{\mathcal{C}}$ (i.e., the full reward v), $\mathcal{C}$ has to send the encrypted output to $\mathcal{P}$, who then responds with $\texttt{rand}_{\mathcal{P}}$. If $\mathcal{C}$ chooses to settle the payment thereby closes the channel between $\mathcal{C}$ and $\mathcal{B}$, it has to post both $\texttt{rand}_{\mathcal{P}}$ and $\texttt{rand}_{\mathcal{C}}$ on the blockchain. Since all data posted to the blockchain are publicly available, $\mathcal{P}$ can now collect $\texttt{rand}_{\mathcal{C}}$ to compute $k_{\mathcal{CP}}$ and obtain Output, while $\mathcal{B}$ can collect $\texttt{rand}_{\mathcal{P}}$ to claim $m_d^{\mathcal{B}}$. Alternatively, should $\mathcal{C}$ wish to maintain the channel, it back-propagates the settling-data to $\mathcal{B}$ and $\mathcal{P}$ so that they can update $\texttt{cred}_{\mathcal{C}}$, $\texttt{debt}_{\mathcal{P}}$, and $\mathcal{P}$ can decrypt the encrypted output. In a situation where $\mathcal{P}$'s response is invalid (i.e., its digest produced by the standard hash function $H(\cdot)$ does not match $h_{\mathcal{P}}$), $\mathcal{C}$ can check this invalidity locally and use it as a evidence to accuse $\mathcal{P}$ of conducting mischief. In such situation, fair exchange requirement is still guaranteed (i.e., $\mathcal{C}$ does not claim v_d from $\mathcal{B}$, who in turn does not claim v_d from $\mathcal{P}$ and $\mathcal{P}$ cannot decrypt $\texttt{Enc}(k_{\mathcal{CP}}, \texttt{Output})$ to obtain $\texttt{Output}$).

4.4 Delegated Attestation

Kosto relieves $\mathcal{P}$ from conducting a remote attestation with $\mathcal{C}$ at the beginning of every request execution by implementing a *delegated attestation* scheme. The scheme requires each broker $\mathcal{B}$ to run an attestation manager enclave AM, and each compute node $\mathcal{C}$ to run a key handler enclave KH. The execution of AM and KH are protected by Intel SGX.

Without loss of generality, the delegated attestation builds a chain of trust that comprises three links. The first and second links are established via remote attestations between $\mathcal{P}$ as a validator and AM as an attesting enclave, and AM as a validator and KH as an attesting enclave. The final link entails ProgKT enclave to prove its correctness to KH via local attestation. Chaining all three links together, $\mathcal{P}$ gains confidence that the ProgKT enclave has been properly instantiated on the compute node $\mathcal{C}$ using the correct code, without contacting $\mathcal{C}$ or the IAS.

Each attestation manager enclave has its own (unique) public-private key pair $(\texttt{pk}_{\texttt{AM}}, \texttt{sk}_{\texttt{AM}})$ that are generated uniformly at random during the enclave instantiation. Upon successfully instantiating AM, $\mathcal{B}$ requests the trusted processor for its remote attestation $\pi_{\texttt{AM}} = \langle M_{\texttt{AM}}, \texttt{pk}_{\texttt{AM}} \rangle_{\sigma_{TEE}}$, where $M_{\texttt{AM}}$ is the enclave's measurement, and σ_{TEE} is a group signature signed by the processor's private key. The certificate $\pi_{\texttt{AM}}$ attests for the correctness of the AM enclave and its public key. Nonetheless, the only party that can verify $\pi_{\texttt{AM}}$ is the IAS acting as group manager [15]. Kosto converts $\pi_{\texttt{AM}}$ into a *publicly verifiable* certificate by having $\mathcal{B}$ obtain and store the IAS response $\texttt{Cert}_{\texttt{AM}} = \langle \pi_{\texttt{AM}}, \texttt{validity} \rangle_{\sigma_{IAS}}$ where σ_{IAS} is the IAS's publicly verifiable signature on $\pi_{\texttt{AM}}$ and the $\texttt{validity}$ flag. By examining $\texttt{Cert}_{\texttt{AM}}$, any party can verify the correctness of and establish a secure connection to the AM enclave.

Likewise, every compute node $\mathcal{C}$ runs a key handler enclave KH. $\mathcal{C}$ obtains (from the IAS) and stores a publicly verifiable certificate $\texttt{Cert}_{\texttt{KH}} = \langle \pi_{KH}, \texttt{valid} \rangle_{\sigma_{IAS}}$, where π_{KH} is KH's remote attestation containing its measurement M_{KH} and its unique public key $\texttt{pk}_{\texttt{KH}}$. By examining $\texttt{Cert}_{\texttt{KH}}$, any party can be assured of the correctness of KH and communicate securely with it.

Delegated Attestation Protocol. Fig. 4 depicts the workflow of Kosto's delegated attestation. After instrumenting Program into ProgKT and verifying the correctness of the instrumentation, $\mathcal{P}$ initiates the delegated attestation by obtaining $\texttt{Cert}_{\texttt{AM}}$ from $\mathcal{B}$ and verifies its validity. It then establishes a secure and authenticated channel with AM using $\texttt{pk}_{\texttt{AM}}$. $\mathcal{P}$ then sends $\texttt{pkg} = \langle \texttt{ProgKT}, \texttt{Enc}(k_{\mathcal{P}}, \texttt{Input}), \texttt{AuxData} \rangle$ to $\mathcal{B}$, and $k_{\mathcal{P}}$ to AM via the secure channel. Once $\mathcal{B}$ finds a compute node $\mathcal{C}$ that is willing to match $\mathcal{P}$'s request, AM obtains $\texttt{Cert}_{\texttt{KH}}$ from $\mathcal{C}$, verifies its validity, and establishes a secure and authenticated connection with $\mathcal{C}$'s KH to communicate $k_{\mathcal{P}}$. $\mathcal{B}$ then sends $\texttt{pkg}$ to $\mathcal{C}$.

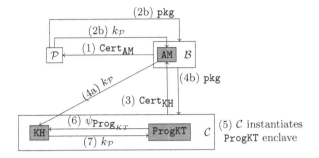

Fig. 4. An overview of the delegated attestation scheme.

The compute node instantiates an enclave to execute ProgKT, and performs a *local attestation* with KH to prove its correctness. Upon successfully attestation, KH sends the key k_P to the ProgKT enclave. Once the ProgKT enclave completes the computation, it returns the encrypted output, which is then sent to P (perhaps being routed through B).

This mechanism only invokes IAS to obtain attestation certificates for AM and KH, instead of constantly involving IAS in every task execution. Further, it allows P to post a request (along with the payment) and then go offline until the time she wishes to collect the output, as opposed to remaining online till her request is picked up by some computation node.

5 Security Arguments

5.1 Attested Execution and Data Confidentiality

Kosto's relies on Intel SGX [33] to offer attested execution and data confidentiality to outsourced computations. In particular, SGX enables isolated execution [43] ensuring that code loaded and running inside the enclaves cannot be tampered with by any other processes including the operating system or hypervisor. This, in combination with attestation capabilities, allows Kosto to offer attested execution in which the computation correctness is guaranteed. Moreover, data (i.e., input, output) and secret states of the enclave execution always remain encrypted outside of the enclave memory, thus their confidentiality are guaranteed. Furthermore, SGX memory encryption engine is capable of protecting data integrity and preventing memory replay attacks [28, 32].

Nonetheless, SGX's attested execution does not inherently offer protections against side-channel leakages [24, 40, 48]. The access pattern incurred by data (or code page) moving between the enclave and the non-enclave environment (e.g., page fault) could leak sensitive information about the code or data being processed within the enclave. Such side-channel leakage could be mitigated by ensuring that the enclave execution is *data oblivious*; i.e., the access pattern no longer depends on the input data [21]. While Kosto does not explicitly eliminate side-channel leakage, it could benefit from a vast amount of research on defenses against side-channel leakages [20,21,31,40,42], which we shall incorporate into Kosto in future work.

5.2 Fair Exchange

TEE-Based Metering. To enable an fair exchange between client's payment and compute node's computation, Kosto necessitates dynamic runtime checks incorporated within the enclave that houses the outsourced computation. We implement this by providing a compiler that instruments any SGX-compliant program Program into a wrapper program ProgKT. We believe that these additional steps and the overall instrumentation are simple enough to lend themselves to formal verification and vetting by Program writer, or by the client.

As we mentioned earlier, the original Program should not contain writable code pages, for they would allow the program to rewrite itself at runtime and thus evade the instrumentation. This could be enforced by requiring the code page to have either *write* or *executable* permission exclusively (i.e., it cannot have both permission at the same time). This practice has also been recommended by Intel to the enclave writers [5].

In addition, Kosto requires Program to be single-threaded. While the instruction counter is maintained in a reserved register which is inaccessible to any other processes (Sect. 4.3), it remains accessible by different threads of Program, should it be multi-threaded. Thus, a malicious program that has multiple threads could manipulate the instruction counter value by carefully crafting the interactions of its threads.

Payment of v_c. Kosto builds on payment channel [10] to enable efficient micro payments and relies on the security of the Ethereum blockchain to ensure payment escrow is faithfully executed. To optimize for efficiency and avoid overloading the blockchain, Kosto securely routes payment from $\mathcal{P}$ to $\mathcal{C}$ via the broker $\mathcal{B}$. A careful design of hash-lock payment promises, wherein promise from $\mathcal{P}$ to $\mathcal{B}$, and that of $\mathcal{B}$ to $\mathcal{C}$ could be settled using the same settling-data, guarantees that $\mathcal{B}$ can always claim from $\mathcal{P}$ which he pays to $\mathcal{C}$ on behalf of $\mathcal{P}$.

Ensuring Output Delivery. At the end of the computation, ProgKT enclave encrypts the Output using key $k_{\mathcal{CP}} = k_{\mathcal{P}} \oplus \text{rand}_{\mathcal{C}}$. Since $m_d^{\mathcal{C}}$ is partially locked by $\text{rand}_{\mathcal{C}}$, the decryption of the output and the settling of $m_d^{\mathcal{C}}$ are bound together. In particular, in order to claim $m_d^{\mathcal{C}}$, $\mathcal{C}$ has to post $\text{rand}_{\mathcal{C}}$ to the blockchain, making it publicly available. This enables $\mathcal{P}$ to compute $k_{\mathcal{CP}}$ and obtain Output. Should $\mathcal{P}$ deny $\mathcal{C}$ of $\text{rand}_{\mathcal{P}}$ after receiving the encrypted output, the latter does not reveal $\text{rand}_{\mathcal{C}}$, causing the output to remain encrypted. On the other hand, should $\mathcal{C}$ wish to deny $\mathcal{P}$ of the output, it would have to forfeit v_d. In sum, it is either the case that $\mathcal{P}$ obtains the output *and* $\mathcal{C}$ is entitled to claim $m_d^{\mathcal{C}}$, or both of them are denied of the exchange's outcome (i.e., Output for $\mathcal{P}$ and v_d for $\mathcal{C}$).

5.3 Delegated Attestation

Kosto's delegated attestation relies on AM and KH enclaves to attest correct instantiation of ProgKT enclave. Therefore, their correct instantiations are of utter importance. Fortunately, these enclave are fixed (as opposed to the ProgKT enclave that houses client-defined program), and thus are easy to vet and verify.

Kosto's delegated attestation requires minimal involvement of $\mathcal{P}$ (i.e., examine the publicly verifiable certificates $Cert_{AM} = \langle \pi_{AM}, validity \rangle_{\sigma_{IAS}}$). By checking that π_{AM} indeed contains the expected measurement $\mathcal{M}_{AM}$, that its validity flag indicates valid, and that the certificate has been properly certified (using Intel's published public key [9]), $\mathcal{P}$ can ascertain the correct instantiation of AM. Moreover, using the public key pk_{AM} included in π_{AM}, $\mathcal{P}$ can establish a secure and authenticated channel to AM via which the secret key $k_{\mathcal{P}}$ is communicated. Likewise, AM can verify the correct instantiation of KH and securely communicate $k_{\mathcal{P}}$ to the latter in the exact same manner. The security of the local attestation and communication between KH and ProgKT enclave follows directly from Intel SGX's specifications [15]. Therefore, provided that cryptographic primitives in use are secure, and SGX hardware protection mechanisms are not subverted, Kosto's delegated attestation is secure.

6 Evaluation

6.1 Experimental Setup

All experiments are conducted on a system that is equipped with Intel i7-6820HQ 2.70 GHz CPU, 16 GB RAM, 2TB hard drive, and running Ubuntu 16.04 Xenial Xerus. We evaluate the overhead of Kosto's enclave execution using a number of computational tasks including five benchmarks (i.e., mcf, deepsjeng, leela, exchang2, and xz) selected from SPEC CPU2017 [12], and two standard cryptographic operations (i.e., SHA256 and AES Encryption). The enclave trusted codebases are implemented using Intel SGX SDK [4]. To quantify the cost of task matching in Kosto, we measure the runtime of the Mucha-Sankowski algorithm [34] that we implemented in C. All experiments are repeated over 10 runs, and the average results are reported.

6.2 Cost of Enclave Execution

Overhead in Execution Time. We evaluate the five SPEC CPU2017 benchmarks in three different execution modes, namely *baseline*, *SGX-compliant* and *Kosto-compliant*. The baseline mode compiles the benchmarks as-is and runs them in untrusted execution environment. SGX-compliant mode requires porting the benchmarks to support SGX-enclave execution. This entails replacing standard system calls and libraries in the original code with SGX-compliant ones supported in the SGX SDK [4]. Finally, the Kosto-compliant mode further instruments SGX-compliant code with dynamic runtime checks and TEE-based metering discussed in previous section.

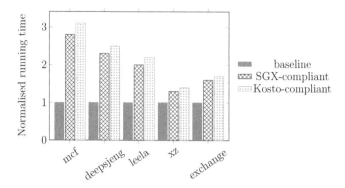

Fig. 5. Kosto's enclave execution overhead. The running time of each benchmark is normalized against its own baseline mode's.

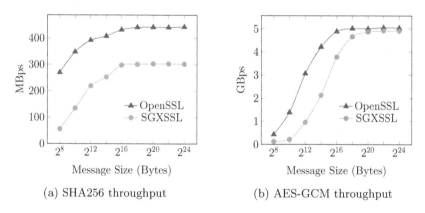

(a) SHA256 throughput   (b) AES-GCM throughput

Fig. 6. Throughput of enclave and non-enclave based cryptographic operations.

Figure 5 compares the running time of the five benchmarks in three modes, with the running time of each benchmark normalized against its own baseline. We observe that the SGX-compliant mode incurs from 1.5× to 3.7× overhead over the baseline. This overhead is mostly due to enclave's control switching. The instrumentations introduced in Kosto-compliant mode incur an extra 8%–14% overhead relative to the SGX-compliant mode.

Various techniques have been proposed for minimizing the overhead of enclave execution, typically by reducing the control switching between the enclave code and the untrusted application that services OS-provided functions [36,44,47]. We leave the incorporation of such optimization into Kosto for future work.

Overhead in Throughput. Next, we measure the overhead in throughput incurred by enclave execution on computation-intensive works. This set of experiments measure performances of SHA256 and AES-GCM encryption operations under *OpenSSL* [7] and Intel *SGXSSL* [6] implementations against exponentially increasing input size (ranging from 256 B to 4 MB). OpenSSL implementation runs in an untrusted non-enclave memory, whereas SGXSSL ports OpenSSL to support SGX enclave execution.

Figure 6a shows a significant gap between the throughput of SGXSSL and OpenSSL implementations of SHA256 when a message size is small (e.g., OpenSSL's throughput is upto 5× for 1 KB message). Nonetheless, such a gap reduces as the message size increases (e.g., as small as 1.5× for 4 MB message). A similar trend is observed in throughput of AES-GCM encryption (the decryption throughput is similar), with the throughput overhead incurred by enclave execution reduces from 6.3× for 1 KB message to 3% for 4 MB message. We attribute this throughput gap to the I/O cost and context switching that enclave execution incurs. Fortunately, this overhead is amortized as the input size increases.

7 Related Works

Decentralised Outsourced Computation. Golem [2] explores a marketplace for outsourced computation. Unlike Kosto, it does not feature the attested execution environment. Consequently, Golem needs to redundantly execute the same task on multiple compute nodes in order to verify the execution correctness. Concurrent to our work, AirTNT [14] proposes the use of enclave execution for outsourced computations, and devises a protocol that allows fair exchange between the client and the compute nodes. Such protocol necessitates a separate payment channel for every pair of client and compute node, and requires constant communication between the two parties over the course of the outsourced computation (i.e., highly interactive). Kosto, in contrast, alleviates the client and the compute nodes from these inconveniences.

Reliable Resource Accounting. Early approaches to resource accounting in the context of outsourced computations rely on nested virtualization and TPMs, or place a trusted resource observer underneath the service provider's software [19,39]. Alternatively, REM [49] instruments the client's program with dynamic runtime checks that maintain an instruction counter to self account its computational effort. The correctness and integrity of these runtime checks are enforced by the trusted hardware. Kosto adopts REM's approach in metering the compute nodes' work.

SGX-Based Systems. Trusted hardware, in particular Intel SGX processors, have been used to enhance security in various application domains, including data analytics [21,24,38], machine learning [35] and outsourced storage [20,23]. In addition, SGX has also been utilized to scale the blockchain [8,22]. To our knowledge, Kosto is the first solution to provision a full-fledged marketplace for secure outsourced computations using Intel SGX.

8 Conclusion

We have presented Kosto – a framework enabling a marketplace for secure outsourced computations. Kosto protects confidentiality of clients' input, integrity of the computations, and ensures fair exchange between the clients and the compute nodes. Our experiments show that Kosto is suitable for computation-intensive operations, incurring an overhead as low as 3% over untrustworthy non-enclave execution. I/O-intensive operations are also supported, albeit as a higher overhead (e.g., 1.5×). We leave an incorporation of enclave execution optimizations and defenses against side-channel leakages to future work.

Acknowledgement. This research has been supported by the National Research Foundation, Prime Minister's Office, Singapore under its Strategic Capability Research Centres Funding Initiative. We thank the anonymous reviewers their helpful feedback and insightful suggestions. Opinions and findings expressed in this work are those of the authors and do not necessarily reflect the views of any of the sponsors.

References

1. Airbnb. https://www.airbnb.com
2. Golem. https://golem.network/
3. Intel SGX notes. https://intelsgx.blogspot.com/2016/06/great-notice-about-basics-of-sgx.html
4. Intel SGX SDK for Linux. https://github.com/01org/linux-sgx
5. Intel Software Guard Extensions Enclave Writer's Guide. https://software.intel.com/sites/default/files/managed/ae/48/Software-Guard-Extensions-Enclave-Writers-Guide.pdf
6. Intel Software Guard Extensions SSL. https://github.com/intel/intel-sgx-ssl
7. OpenSSL Cryptography and SSL/TLS Toolkit. https://www.openssl.org/
8. Proof of elapsed time. https://sawtooth.hyperledger.org
9. Public key for Intel attestation service. https://software.intel.com/en-us/sgx/resource-library
10. Raiden network. http://raiden.network
11. SETI@home. https://setiathome.berkeley.edu/
12. SPEC CPU2017 Benchmarks. https://www.spec.org/cpu2017/Docs/overview.html
13. Uber. https://www.uber.com
14. Al-Bassam, M., Sonnino, A., Król, M., Psaras, I.: Airtnt: fair exchange payment for outsourced secure enclave computations. arXiv preprint arXiv:1805.06411 (2018)
15. Anati, I., Gueron, S., Johnson, S., Scarlata, V.: Innovative technology for CPU based attestation and sealing. In: HASP (2013)
16. Baumann, A., Peinado, M., Hunt, G.: Shielding applications from an untrusted cloud with haven. In: OSDI (2014)
17. Bentov, I., Kumaresan, R., Miller, A.: Instantaneous decentralized poker. In: Takagi, T., Peyrin, T. (eds.) ASIACRYPT 2017. LNCS, vol. 10625, pp. 410–440. Springer, Cham (2017). https://doi.org/10.1007/978-3-319-70697-9_15
18. Buterin, V.: Ethereum: a next-generation smart contract and decentralized application platform (2014). https://github.com/ethereum/wiki/wiki/White-Paper
19. Chen, C., Maniatis, P., Perrig, A., Vasudevan, A., Sekar, V.: Towards verifiable resource accounting for outsourced computation. In: ACM SIGPLAN Notices (2013)
20. Dang, H., Chang, E.C.: Privacy-preserving data deduplication on trusted processors. In: IEEE CLOUD (2017)

21. Dang, H., Dinh, T.T.A., Chang, E.C., Ooi, B.C.: Privacy-preserving computation with trusted computing via scramble-then-compute. In: PETs (2017)
22. Dang, H., Dinh, T.T.A., Loghin, D., Chang, E.C., Lin, Q., Ooi, B.C.: Towards scaling blockchain systems via sharding. In: SIGMOD (2019)
23. Dang, H., Purwanto, E., Chang, E.C.: Proofs of data residency: checking whether your cloud files have been relocated. In: AsiaCCS (2017)
24. Dinh, T.T.A., Saxena, P., Chang, E.C., Ooi, B.C., Zhang, C.: M2R: enabling stronger privacy in MapReduce computation. In: USENIX Security (2015)
25. Gennaro, R., Gentry, C., Parno, B.: Non-interactive verifiable computing: outsourcing computation to untrusted workers. In: Rabin, T. (ed.) CRYPTO 2010. LNCS, vol. 6223, pp. 465–482. Springer, Heidelberg (2010). https://doi.org/10.1007/978-3-642-14623-7_25
26. Gentry, C., et al.: Fully homomorphic encryption using ideal lattices. In: STOC (2009)
27. Goldreich, O.: Secure multi-party computation. Manuscript, Preliminary version (1998)
28. Gueron, S.: A memory encryption engine suitable for general purpose processors. IACR Cryptology ePrint Archive (2016)
29. Katz, J., Lindell, Y.: Introduction to Modern Cryptography. CRC Press, Boca Raton (2014)
30. Kumaresan, R., Bentov, I.: Amortizing secure computation with penalties. In: CCS (2016)
31. Liu, C., Wang, X.S., Nayak, K., Huang, Y., Shi, E.: ObliVM: a programming framework for secure computation. In: IEEE S&P (2015)
32. Matetic, S., et al.: ROTE: rollback protection for trusted execution. In: USENIX Security (2017)
33. McKeen, F., et al.: Innovative instructions and software model for isolated execution. In: HASP, Article no. 10 (2013)
34. Mucha, M., Sankowski, P.: Maximum matchings via Gaussian elimination. In: FOCS (2004)
35. Ohrimenko, O., et al.: Oblivious multi-party machine learning on trusted processors. In: USENIX Security (2016)
36. Orenbach, M., Lifshits, P., Minkin, M., Silberstein, M.: Eleos: ExitLess OS services for SGX enclaves. In: EuroSys (2017)
37. Poon, J., Dryja, T.: The Bitcoin lightning network: scalable off-chain instant payments (2016)
38. Schuster, F., et al.: VC3: trustworthy data analytics in the cloud using SGX. In: IEEE S&P (2015)
39. Sekar, V., Maniatis, P.: Verifiable resource accounting for cloud computing services. In: WSCC (2011)
40. Shinde, S., Chua, Z.L., Narayanan, V., Saxena, P.: Preventing page faults from telling your secrets. In: AsiaCCS (2016)
41. Shinde, S., Le Tien, D., Tople, S., Saxena, P.: Panoply: low-TCB Linux applications with SGX enclaves. In: NDSS (2017)
42. Stefanov, E., et al.: Path ORAM: an extremely simple oblivious RAM protocol. In: CCS (2013)
43. Subramanyan, P., Sinha, R., Lebedev, I., Devadas, S., Seshia, S.A.: A formal foundation for secure remote execution of enclaves. In: CCS (2017)
44. Taassori, M., Shafiee, A., Balasubramonian, R.: VAULT: reducing paging overheads in SGX with efficient integrity verification structures. In: ASPLOS (2018)

45. Van Bulck, J., et al.: Foreshadow: extracting the keys to the Intel SGX Kingdom with transient out-of-order execution. In: USENIX Security (2018)
46. van Dijk, M., Gentry, C., Halevi, S., Vaikuntanathan, V.: Fully homomorphic encryption over the integers. In: Gilbert, H. (ed.) EUROCRYPT 2010. LNCS, vol. 6110, pp. 24–43. Springer, Heidelberg (2010). https://doi.org/10.1007/978-3-642-13190-5_2
47. Weisse, O., Bertacco, V., Austin, T.: Regaining lost cycles with HotCalls: a fast interface for SGX secure enclaves. In: ISCA (2017)
48. Xu, Y., Cui, W., Peinado, M.: Controlled-channel attacks: deterministic side channels for untrusted operating systems. In: IEEE S&P (2015)
49. Zhang, F., Eyal, I., Escriva, R., Juels, A., Van Renesse, R.: REM: resource-efficient mining for blockchains. In: USENIX Security (2017)

Author Index